MIDDLE EAST CONTEMPORARY SURVEY

Volume X: 1986

MIDDLE EAST CONTEMPORARY SURVEY

Published for the Shiloah Institute
of the Moshe Dayan Center
for Middle Eastern and African Studies
at Tel Aviv University

Other volumes in this series:

Volume I, 1976-77
Volume II, 1977-78
Volume III, 1978-79
Volume IV, 1979-80
Volume V, 1980-81
Volume VI, 1981-82
Volume VII, 1982-83
Volume VIII, 1983-84
Volume IX, 1984-85

MIDDLE EAST CONTEMPORARY SURVEY

Volume X

1986

ITAMAR RABINOVICH, HAIM SHAKED
Editors

Barbara Newson, Executive Editor

Routledge
Taylor & Francis Group
LONDON AND NEW YORK

First published 1988 by Westview Press, Inc.

Published 2018 by Routledge
52 Vanderbilt Avenue, New York, NY 10017
2 Park Square, Milton Park, Abingdon, Oxon OX14 4RN

Routledge is an imprint of the Taylor & Francis Group, an informa business

Library of Congress Catalog Card Number: 78-648245
ISBN 13: 978-0-367-00324-1 (hbk)
ISBN 13: 978-0-367-15311-3 (pbk)

About the Book and Editors

Established in 1977, the *Middle East Contemporary Survey* (*MECS*), a unique annual record of political developments in the Middle East, is acknowledged as the standard reference work on events and trends in the region. Designed to be a continuing, up-to-date reference for scholars, researchers and analysts, policymakers, students, and journalists, it examines in considerable detail the rapidly changing Middle Eastern scene in all its complexity.

In each volume, the material is arranged in two parts. The first contains a series of essays on broad regional issues and on the overall relations of the region with other parts of the world. The second consists of country-by-country surveys of all the Arab states, as well as Turkey, Israel, and Iran. The accent in the second part is on elucidating the inner dynamics of each country's polity and society.

In a work of this kind, the events of the past year inevitably dictate the major themes of each volume. The topics discussed in Volume X, which covers the year 1986, include:

- The breakdown of the Husayn-'Arafat Agreement;
- Iranian successes on land against Iraq in the Gulf War;
- The rebellion of a police force in Cairo;
- The implementation of the rotation agreement in Israeli politics.

While surveying and analyzing these and other developments, this volume also explains why they did not amount and lead to substantive change in the patterns of Middle Eastern politics.

Maps, tables and a detailed index accompany the text.

Itamar Rabinovich is Professor of Middle Eastern and African History and Head of the Dayan Center at Tel Aviv University. **Haim Shaked** is Professor of Middle Eastern and African History and Senior Research Fellow at the Dayan Center. They are coeditors of *The Middle East and the United States: Perceptions and Policies.*

Preface

The Middle East Contemporary Survey (MECS) is an annual record and analysis of political, economic, military and international developments in the Middle East. The present volume is the tenth in a series which provides scholars, diplomats, students and informed laymen with a continuing, up-to-date reference work recording the rapidly changing events in an exceptionally complex part of the world. Every attempt has again been made to use the widest range of source material and maintain the highest possible academic standards.

Most of the essays in this volume have been researched and written by the members of the Shiloah Institute of the Dayan Center for Middle Eastern and African Studies at Tel Aviv University. Other contributions have been made by distinguished academics and experts from abroad.

The material in this volume is arranged in two parts. The first comprises a series of essays which study developments relating to internal and external issues, both regionally and internationally. Subjects explored in detail include Israeli-Arab and inter-Arab relations, as well as the international dimensions of the contending forces in the region. The second part comprises a country-by-country survey of each of the Middle Eastern entities, excluding the three North African states of Tunisia, Algeria and Morocco.

The period surveyed in this volume, unless otherwise indicated, is from January to December 1986. In order to avoid excessive repetition while at the same time achieving a comprehensive survey of the affairs of each country individually, extensive cross-references have been used.

In this volume, as in the previous one, the sections on economic affairs and the armed forces which, in previous volumes, were appended to each country survey, have been discontinued. This is due to the appearance, in recent years, of other surveys which are fully devoted to these two themes, and therefore provide much more data on them.

I.R. & H.S.

Acknowledgments

As editors we are grateful to a large number of contributors who have made this volume possible. First and foremost we recognize the work of the staff of the Dayan Center and its Shiloah Institute for Middle Eastern and African Studies at Tel Aviv University, whose individual contributions are acknowledged separately.

In the process of preparing this volume we were given much help by Alec Israel. Barbara Newson's role as executive editor has been indispensable. The exacting work of indexing has been carried out by Ronald Watson.

At the Dayan Center, Edna Liftman and Amira Margalith, assistants to the Head of the Center, were responsible for the complicated coordination of the production of the volume, and fulfilled a variety of other executive tasks with accuracy, skill and unflagging care. Others at the Center who must be singled out for special thanks are Lydia Gareh, Margaret Mahlab and Eleonora Segal, and the Dayan Documentation System team. Ruth Beit-Or prepared the maps for publication and David Levinson proofread large parts of the volume.

Finally, we would like to express our sincere thanks to Frederick A. Praeger, Barbara Ellington, and the staff of Westview Press for their help in the production and distribution of this volume of *MECS*. The first seven volumes of *MECS* were published by Holmes & Meier. The contribution made by Max Holmes and by Colin Legum to the launching of this project and to setting its standards remain invaluable and much appreciated.

I.R. & H.S.

Table of Contents

List of Maps

Transliteration

The Arabic language has been transliterated as follows:

b	for	ب	q	for	ق
d	for	ض، د	r	for	ر
dh	for	ذ	s	for	ص، س
f	for	ف	sh	for	ش
gh	for	غ	t	for	ط، ت
h	for	ه، ح	th	for	ث
j	for	ج	w (or u)	for	و
k	for	ك	y (or i)	for	ي
kh	for	خ	z	for	ظ، ز
l	for	ل	’	for	ا، ء
m	for	م	‘	for	ع
n	for	ن			

In addition, the following should be noted:

Long vowels are not marked for distinction from short ones. Thus ناظر = *nazir*, but also نظير = *nazir*.

The *hamza* is used only in the middle of a word.

The *shadda* is rendered by doubling the consonant containing it.

The *ta marbuta* is not shown, except in construct phrases. Thus *madina, madinat Nasr.*

The definite article is always shown as “al-”, regardless of the kind of letter following it.

Exceptions to the above are names of Lebanese and North African personalities who have adopted a French spelling for their names.

List of Initials and Acronyms

AAU	Arab-African Union
ALF	Arab Liberation Front
Aramco	Arabian-American Oil Company (now Saudi-nationalized company)
AUB	American University in Beirut
AWACS	airborne warning and control system (radar)
b/d	barrels per day
BP	British Petroleum
CD	Chamber of Deputies (Lebanon)
CENTCOM	US Central Command
CIA	Central Intelligence Agency (US)
CP	Citizen's Party (Turkey)
CPSU	Communist Party of the Soviet Union
DECA	Defense and Economic Agreement (Turkey and US)
Dev-Yol	*Devrimci Yol* — "Revolutionary Path" (Turkey)
DİSK	*Devrimci İşçi Sendikaları Konfederasyonu* (Revolutionary Trade Union Confederation, Turkey
DLP	Democratic Left Party (Turkey)
DMI	Dar al-Maal al-Islami (Islamic Finance House)
DP	Democrat Party (Turkey)
DTU	Dar Tadine al-Umma (finance company)
DUP	Democratic Unionist Party (Sudan)
EEC	European Economic Community
EOKA	*Ethniki Organosis Kyprio̊n Aganisto̊n* (National Organization of Cypriot Combatants)
FBI	Federal Bureau of Investigation (US)
FDP	Free Democratic Party (Turkey)
FLN	*Front de la Libération Nationale* (Algeria)
FRG	Federal Republic of Germany
GCC	Gulf Cooperation Council
GDP	gross domestic product
GDR	German Democratic Republic
GNP	gross national product
GPC	General People's Congress (Libya, YAR)
GPCom	General People's Committee (Libya)
GPO	Government Press Office (Israel)
GSS	General Secret Services (Israel)
GUNT	*Gouvernement d'Union Nationale de Transition* (Chad)
HH	His Highness
IAF	Israel Air Force
ICO	Islamic Conference Organization
ICP	Iraqi Communist Party
IDB	Islamic Development Bank
IDF	Israel Defense Forces
ILO	International Labor Organization
IMA	Iranian Medical Association
IMF	International Monetary Fund
int ed	international edition
IRGC	Iranian Revolutionary Guard Corps

IRP	Islamic Republican Party
JP	Justice Party (Turkey)
KCP	Kurdish Communist Party
KD	Kuwaiti dinars
KDP	Kurdish Democratic Party
KOTC	Kuwait Oil Tanker Company
LCP	Lebanese Communist Party
LF	Lebanese Forces
ME	Middle East(ern)
MERIP	Middle East Research and Information Project
MIDEAST-FOR	Middle East Air Force (US Navy)
MK	Member of Knesset (Israel)
MP	Motherland Party (Turkey)
MWL	Muslim World League
NATO	North Atlantic Treaty Organization
NC	National Command (Iraq)
nd	no date
NDP	National Democratic Party (Egypt, Turkey)
NIF	National Islamic Front
NLP	National Liberal Party (Lebanon)
np	no publisher
NPUG	National Progressive Unionist Grouping (Egypt)
NPF	National Progressive Front (Syria)
NRP	National Religious Party (Israel
NSC	National Security Council (US)
NSP	National Salvation Party (Turkey)
OAPEC	Organization of Arab Petroleum Exporting Countries
OAU	Organization of African Unity
OPEC	Organization of Petroleum Exporting Countries
PCP	Palestinian Communist Party
PDFLP	Popular Democratic Front for the Liberation of Palestine
PDRY	People's Democratic Republic of Yemen
Petromin	General Petroleum and Mineral Organization (Saudi Arabia)
PFLP	Popular Front for the Liberation of Palestine
PFLP-GC	Popular Front for the Liberation of Palestine — General Command
PLA	Palestine Liberation Army
PLF	Palestine Liberation Front
PLO	Palestine Liberation Organization
PNC	Palestine National Council
PNSF	Palestinian National Salvation Front
Polisario	Front for the Liberation of Al-Saqiyya al-Hamra and Rio de Oro
PPNF	Patriotic and Progressive National Front (Iraq)
PPP	People's Progressive Party (Sudan)
PPSF	Palestine Popular Struggle Front
PSP	Progressive Socialist Party
PUK	Patriotic Union of Kurdistan
RC	Regional Command (Iraq)
RCC	Revolutionary Command Council (Iraq)
RG	Revolutionary Guards
RPG	rocket-propelled grenade
RPP	Republican People's Party (Turkey)

SAC	Sudan African Congress
SADR	Saharan Arab Democratic Republic
SAIRI	Supreme Assembly of the Islamic Revolution in Iraq
SALT	Strategic Arms Limitation Talks
SAMA	Saudi Arabian Monetary Agency
SANU	Sudanese African National Union
SAVAK	State Intelligence and Security Organization (Iran)
SCP	Syrian Communist Party
SDI	Strategic Defense Initiative
SDPP	Social Democratic Populist Party
SEB	Supreme Education Board (Turkey)
SEEs	State Economic Enterprises (Turkey)
SFP	Sudan Federal Party
SIPRI	Stockholm Internal Peace Research Institute
SISC	Supreme Islamic Shi'i Council
SLA	South Lebanese Army
SNP	Sudan National Party
SPLA	Sudanese People's Liberation Army
SPLM	Sudanese People's Liberation Movement
SSNP	Syrian Social Nationalist Party
SSPA	Southern Sudanese Political Association
TMC	Transitional Military Council (Sudan)
TPP	True Path Party (Turkey)
TRNC	Turkish Republic of Northern Cyprus
Türk-İş	*Türkiye İşçi Sendikaları Konfederasyonu* (Trade Union Confederation of Turkey)
TWA	Trans-World Airlines
UAE	United Arab Emirates
UAEDh	UAE dirham
UK	United Kingdom
UN	United Nations
UNESCO	UN Educational, Scientific, and Cultural Organization
UNICEF	UN (International) Children's (Emergency) Fund
UNIDO	UN Industrial Development Organization
UNIFIL	UN Interim Force In Lebanon
UNSC	UN Security Council
UP	Umma Party (Sudan)
WAMY	World Assembly of Muslim Youth
WP	Welfare Party (Turkey)
YAR	Yemeni Arab Republic
YSP	Yemeni Socialist Party

List of Sources

Newspapers, Periodicals, Irregular and Single Publications

Name *(Place, Frequency of Publication)*	*Abbreviation*	*Notes*
L'Action (Tunis, daily)		Organ of the Socialist *Dustur* Party
Aerospace Daily (Washington, DC, daily)		
Al-Afaq (Cyprus, weekly)		
Africa (London, monthly)		
Africa Confidential (London, fortnightly)	*AC*	
Africa Now (London, monthly)		
Africa Research Bulletin (Exeter, England, monthly)	*ARB*	
Africa-Asia (Paris, fortnightly)		English-language edition of *Afrique-Asie*
Al-Ahali (Cairo, weekly)		Organ of the Nationalist Progressive Unionist Grouping
Al-Ahram (Cairo, daily)		
Al-Ahram International (London, daily)		
Al-Ahram al-Iktisadi (Cairo, weekly)		Published by *al-Ahram*, deals mainly with economic issues
Al-Ahrar (Cairo, weekly)		Organ of the Liberal Socialist Party
Al-Akhbar (Cairo, daily)		
Akhbar al-'Alam al-Islami (Mecca, weekly)		Published by the Muslim World League
Akhbar al-Khalij (Manama, daily)		
Akhbar al-Usbu' (Amman, weekly)		
Akhbar al-Yawm (Cairo, weekly)		Weekly edition of *al-Akhbar*
Akhir Sa'a (Cairo, weekly)		
Al-'Alam (London, weekly)		
Al-'Alam (Rabat, daily)		Organ of the *Istiqlal* Party
'Al-Hamishmar (Tel Aviv, daily)		Organ of the United Workers' Party *(Mapam)*
Alif Ba (Baghdad, weekly)		
Al-'Amal (Beirut, daily)		Organ of the Lebanese Phalanges

American-Arab Affairs (Washington, quarterly)		
American Metal Market (New York, daily)		
Al-Anba' (Kuwait, daily)		Pro-establishment but critical of specific government policies and of US attitudes toward the Middle East
Al-Anwar (Beirut, daily)		Rightist
Arab Press Service (Nicosia, weekly)	*APS*	
Arab News (London, daily)		Published by Saudi Research and Marketing Company
Arab Studies Quarterly (Belmont, MA, quarterly)		Published by the Association of Arab-American University graduates
Arab Times (Kuwait, daily)		
Arabia, The Islamic World Review (London, weekly)		Published by the Islamic Press Agency
Al-'Awda (East Jerusalem, fortnightly)		
Al-Ayyam (Khartoum, daily)		
Baltimore Sun (Baltimore, daily)		
Al-Ba'th (Damascus, daily)		Organ of the Syrian Ba'th Party
Al-Bayadir al-Siyasi (East Jerusalem, bi-weekly)		Sympathetic to al-Fath
Al-Bayan (Dubai, daily)		
Al-Bayraq (Beirut, daily)		
Al-Bilad (Jidda, daily)		
Boston Globe (Boston, daily)		
Briefing (Ankara, weekly)		
Chicago Tribune (Chicago, daily)		
Christian Science Monitor (Boston, daily)	*CSM*	
Commentary (New York, monthly)		Journal of significant thought and opinion on contemporary issues; published by the American Jewish Committee
Counterpoint (Darlinghurst, NSW, monthly)		Published by Business Press International
Country Reports (London, quarterly)	*CR*	Published by Economist Publications Ltd. Formerly *Quarterly Economic Review* (until No 2 1986)
Current Digest of the Soviet Press (Chicago, weekly)	*CDSP*	Translation from the Soviet Press. Published by the American Association for the Advancement of Slavic Studies, University of Illinois at Chicago Circle, Chicago

Current Turkish Thought (Istanbul, quarterly)		Published by Redhouse Yayinevi
Daily Telegraph (London, daily)	*DT*	
Davar (Tel Aviv, daily)		Organ of the Israeli Trade Union Federation (Histadrut)
Defense News (Springfield, VA, weekly)		
Defense Week (Washington, DC, weekly)		
Democratic Palestine (Cyprus, monthly)		English-language organ of the PFLP
Department of State Bulletin (Washington, DC, weekly)	*DSB*	
Al-Difa' al-'Arabi (Beirut, monthly)		Deals mainly with military affairs
Al-Dustur (Amman, daily)		
Al-Dustur (London, weekly)		Pro-Iraqi. Originally a Beirut weekly reflecting the Iraqi Ba'th views. Closed down by the Syrians (December 1976). Published in Paris until July 1977 and then in London
The Economist (London, weekly)		
Emirates News (Abu Dhabi, daily)		
Facts on File (New York, weekly)		
Al-Fajr (East Jerusalem, daily)		Sympathetic to the PLO
Al-Fajr (East Jerusalem, weekly)		English- and Hebrew-language weekly editions of *al-Fajr*
Al-Fajr al-Jadid (Tripoli, daily)		
Le Figaro (Paris, daily)		
Filastin al-Thawra (Nicosia, weekly)		Organ of the PLO. Ceased publication during the war in Lebanon. Resumed publication in Nicosia in October 1982
The Financial Times (London, daily)	*FT*	
Foreign Affairs (New York, quarterly)		
Foreign Report (London, weekly)	*FR*	Published by *The Economist*
Fourteenth October (Aden, daily)		Organ of the Yemeni Socialist Party (YSP)
Glasgow Herald (Glasgow, daily)		
Grassroots (Cape Town, monthly)		Newsletter for Black communities of the Western Cape
The Guardian (London, daily)		
Guardian Weekly (Manchester, weekly)		

The Guiding Star (Khartoum, monthly)		
Gulf Daily News (Bahrain, daily)		
Günaydın (Istanbul, daily)		
Günes (Istanbul, daily)		Independent. Supported by several businessmen. Began publication in February 1982
Al-Guraba (London, monthly)		
Ha'aretz (Tel Aviv, daily)		
Al-Hadaf (Damascus, weekly)		Organ of the PFLP. Transferred from Beirut after the war in Lebanon
Al-Hadaf (Kuwait, weekly)		
Hadashot (Tel Aviv, daily)		Began publication in March 1984
Al-Halij (Abu Dhabi, daily)		
Hatzofeh (Tel Aviv, daily)		Organ of the National Religious Party (*Mafdal*; NRP)
Al-Hawadith (London, weekly)		A Beirut weekly, reflecting pro-Phalangist tendencies. Published in London since November 1978
Hürriyet (Istanbul, daily)		
Al-Hurriyya (Nicosia, weekly)		Organ of the PDFLP. Ceased publication during the war in Lebanon. Resumed publication in Nicosia in February 1983
IJA Research Reports (London, 20 per year)		Published by the Institute of Jewish Affairs
Impact International (London, twice monthly)		
Insight (Washington, bi-monthly)		
International Defense Industries (weekly)	*IDI*	Published in the US by DMS
International Financial Statistics (Washington, monthly)	*IFS*	Published by the International Monetary Fund (IMF)
International Herald Tribune (Paris and Zurich, daily)	*IHT*	
Iran Press Digest (Tehran, weekly)	*IPD*	English-language summary of Iranian Press
Iran Times (London, weekly)	*IT*	
Al-'Iraq (Baghdad, daily)		
Israel Statistical Abstract (Jerusalem, annually)		Published by the Central Bureau of Statistics
Al-Ittihad (Abu Dhabi, daily)		
Al-Ittihad al-Usbu'i (Abu Dhabi, weekly)		

Izvestiia (Moscow, daily)		Organ of the Government of the USSR
Al-Jamahiriyya (Valletta, daily)		Pro-Libyan
The Jamahiriya Mail (Valletta, daily)	*JM*	Published by the Libyan Information Services
Jane's Defence Weekly (London, weekly)		
Al-Jazira (Riyadh, daily)		
The Jerusalem Post (Jerusalem, daily)	*JP*	
Jeune Afrique (Paris, weekly)	*JA*	Reflects views of Tunisian expatriates
Jewish Journal of Sociology (London, twice annually)		
Jordan Times (Amman, daily)	*JT*	
Journal of Palestine Studies (Washington, quarterly)		Published by the Institute of Palestine Studies and Kuwait University
Al-Jumhuriyya (Baghdad, daily)		
Al-Jumhuriyya (Beirut, daily)		
Al-Jumhuriyya (Cairo, daily)		
Jumhuriyye Islami (Tehran, daily)	*JI*	Organ of the Islamic Republican Party
Kayhan (Tehran, daily)		
Kayhan al-'Arabi (Tehran, daily)		
Kayhan Hava'i (Tehran, weekly)	*KH*	
Khaleej Times (Dubai, daily)		
Al-Khalij (Sharja, daily)		
Al-Kifah al-'Arabi (Beirut, weekly)		
Krasnaia Zvezda (Moscow, daily)		
Kull al-'Arab (Paris, weekly)		
Der Kurier (Vienna, daily)		
Libération (Paris, daily)		
Al-Liwa' (Amman, weekly)		
Los Angeles Times (Los Angeles, daily)	*LAT*	
Ma'ariv (Tel Aviv, daily)		
Al-Madina (Jidda, daily)		
Al-Majalis (London, weekly)		

Al-Majalla (London, weekly)		Published by Saudi Research and Marketing (UK) Ltd
Majallat al-Azhar (Cairo, monthly)		
Al-Masa (Cairo, weekly)		
Al-Masar (London, weekly)		Opposing the Iraqi regime
Al-Masir (Beirut, bi-weekly)		Magazine of the "Rectification Movement" of 'Atallah 'Atallah
Le Matin (Paris, daily)		
Le Matin du Sahara (Rabat, daily)		Semi-official
Al-Mawqif al-'Arabi (Beirut, weekly)		
Al-Mawqif al-'Arabi (Cairo, monthly)		
Mayo (Cairo, weekly)		
Memo (Cyprus, bi-weekly)		
MERIP Reports (Washington, DC, monthly)		
The Middle East (London, monthly)	*ME*	
Middle East Economic Digest (London, weekly)	*MEED*	
Middle East Economic Survey (Nicosia, weekly)	*MEES*	Published by the Middle East Research and Publishing Center, Beirut
Middle East Executive Reports (Washington, monthly)	*MEER*	
Middle East Insight (Washington, bi-monthly)		
Middle East International (London, monthly)	*MEI*	
Middle East Journal (Washington, quarterly)	*MEJ*	Published by the Middle East Institute
Middle East Review (New Brunswick, NJ, quarterly)		
Middle East Times (Nicosia, weekly)		
Mideast Markets (London, fortnightly)	*MM*	Published by *FT* Business Information Ltd
Mideast Report (New York, bi-weekly)		
Al-Mithaq al-Watani (Rabat, daily)		
Moment (Boston, MA, ten per year)		
Monday Morning (Beirut, weekly)		Right of Center
Le Monde (Paris, daily)		
Monitin (Tel Aviv, monthly)		

Monthly Petroleum Statistics Reports (Washington, monthly)		Published by the US Department of Energy
Al-Moudjahid (Algiers, daily)		French-language journal of the *Front de Libération Nationale* (FLN)
Al-Mujtama (Kuwait, weekly)		Organ of the Social Reform Associations. Sympathetic to Muslim Brotherhood views
Al-Mukhtar al-Islami (Cairo, monthly)		
Al-Musawwar (Cairo, weekly)		
Muslim World League Journal (Mecca, monthly)	*MWL Journal*	Published by MWL Press and Publications Department
Al-Mustaqbal (Paris, weekly)		Pro-Saudi
Al-Nahar (Beirut, daily)		Rightist
Al-Nahar al-'Arabi wal-Duwali (Paris and Zurich, weekly)	*NAD*	Weekly international edition of *al-Nahar*
Al-Nahar Arab Report and Memo (Beirut and Zurich, weekly)		English-language political and economic report of *al-Nahar*
Al-Nashra (Nicosia, weekly)		Deals with opposition movements in various Arab countries
National Interest (Washington, DC, quarterly)		
Near East Report (Washington, weekly)		
New African (London, monthly)		
Newark Star-Ledger (Newark, New Jersey, daily)		
New Leader (New York, bi-weekly)		News and opinion
Newspot (Ankara, weekly)		Turkish digest, published by Directorate-General of Press and Information
New Statesman (London, weekly)		
Newsweek (New York, weekly)		
New Times (Moscow, weekly)		English-language editon of *Novoe Vremia*
New York Post (New York, daily)	*NYP*	
The New York Review of Books (New York, fortnightly)		
The New York Times (New York, daily)	*NYT*	
Nidal al-Sha'b (Beirut, weekly)		
Le Nouvel Observateur (Paris, weekly		
Al-Nur (Cairo, weekly)		
The Observer (London, weekly)		
October		

(Cairo, weekly)		
L'Opinion (Paris, weekly)		
Orbis (Philadelphia, quarterly)		Published by Foreign Policy Research Institute
Orient (Hamburg, quarterly)		
L'Orient le Jour (Beirut, daily)		
El Pais (Madrid, daily)		
Pasdar-e Eslam (Qum, monthly)		Publication of the Revolutionary Guards
Petroleum Economist (London, monthly)	*PE*	
Petroleum Times (Maidstone, Kent, fortnightly)		
Petroleum Times Price Report (Maidstone, Kent, fortnightly)		
Peuples Méditerranéens (Paris, quarterly)		
Philadelphia Inquirer (Philadelphia, daily)		
Le Point (Paris, weekly)		
Pravda (Moscow, daily)		Organ of the Central Committee of the CPSU
Problems of Communism (Washington, DC, bi-monthly)		
Pulse (Ankara, daily)		English-language summary of Turkish Press
Al-Qabas (Kuwait, daily)		Kuwaiti nationalist; sympathetic to the Palestinian cause
Al-Qabas International (London, daily)		
Quarterly Economic Review (London, quarterly)	*QER*	Published by *The Economist* Intelligence Unit. At No 2 1986, Ceased publication under this title to become *Country Report (CR)*
Al-Quds (East Jerusalem, daily)		Known for favorable views toward Jordan
Al-Quwat al-Musallaha (Khartoum, weekly)		
Al-Ra'y (Amman, daily)		
Al-Ra'y al-'Amm (Kuwait, daily)		Kuwaiti nationalist; conservative
La Revue du Liban et de l'Orient Arabe (Beirut, weekly)		
Risalat al-'Iraq (Monthly)		Organ of the Iraqi Communist Party. Began publication in 1981. Place of publication not indicated
Al-Riyad (Riyadh, daily)		
Ruz al-Yusuf (Cairo, weekly)		

Al-Sabah (Tunis, daily)	
Al-Safir (Beirut, daily)	Reflects Libyan views
Al-Sahafa (Khartoum, daily)	
Sawt al-Bilad (Cyprus, weekly)	
Sawt al-Iraq (London, monthly)	Published by the Iraqi Islamic opposition
Sawt al-Sha'b (Amman, daily)	Started publication in early 1983
Al-Sayyad (Beirut, weekly)	
Al-Sha'b (Algiers, daily)	
Al-Sha'b (Cairo, weekly)	Organ of the Socialist Labor Party
Al-Sha'b (East Jerusalem, daily)	Sympathetic to the PLO
Al-Sharq (Beirut, daily)	Pro-Syrian
Al-Sharq al-Awsat (London, Jidda and Riyadh, daily)	
Al-Sharq al-Jadid (London, monthly)	
Al-Shira' (Beirut, weekly)	
Al-Siyasal (Khartoum, daily)	Reflects the views of the *Umma* Party
Al-Siyasa (Kuwait, daily)	Moderate; pro-Government
Der Spiegel (Hamburg, weekly)	
La Stampa (Milan, daily)	
Der Stern (Hamburg, weekly)	
Strategic Review (Waltham, MA, quarterly)	Published by the US Strategic Institute
Al-Sudani (Khartoum, daily)	
Sudanow (Khartoum, monthly)	Published by the Ministry of Culture and Information
Sudan Times (Khartoum, daily)	
Sunday Telegraph (London, weekly)	
Survival (London, bi-monthly)	Published by the International Institute for Strategic Studies
Svenska Dagbladet (Stockholm, daily)	
Al-Tadamun (London, monthly)	
Al-Tadamun al-Islami (Mecca, monthly)	
Al-Tali'a al-'Arabiyya	Pro-Iraqi

(Paris, weekly)		
Al-Tawhid (Tehran, bi-monthly)		
Tercüman (Istanbul, daily)		Conservative
Al-Thaqafa al-Jadida (Iraq, monthly)		Clandestine magazine published by the Iraqi Communist Party (ICP)
Al-Thawra (Baghdad, daily)		Organ of the Iraqi Ba'th Party
Al-Thawra (Damascus, daily)		
Al-Thawra (San'a, daily)		Semi-official
Al-Thawra al-Islamiyya (London and Washington, monthly)		Organ of the Islamic Revolutionary Movement in the Arabian Peninsula
Time (New York, weekly)		
The Times (London, daily)		
The Times of India (Delhi, daily and weekly)		
Tishrin (Damascus, daily)		
'Ukaz (Jidda, daily)		
'Uman (Muscat, twice a week)		Published by the Ministry of Information
Al-Urdunn al-Dimuqrati (Nicosia)		Organ of the Committee for the Defense of Democratic Freedoms in Jordan
Al-Usbu' al-'Arabi (Beirut, weekly)		
US News and World Report (Washington, DC, weekly)		
La Vanguardia (Barcelona, daily)		
Al-Wafd (Cairo, weekly)		Organ of the New *Wafd* Party
Al-Wahda (Cairo, monthly)		
The Wall Street Journal (New York, daily)	*WSJ*	
The Washington Post (Washington, daily)	*WP*	
The Washington Quarterly (Washington, quarterly)		
The Washington Report on Middle East Affairs (Washington, weekly)		
The Washington Times (Washington, daily)		
Al-Watan (Kuwait, daily)		Critical of Kuwait's Government; pro-Syrian
Al-Watan al-'Arabi (Paris, weekly)		Pro-Iraqi
Al-Yamama (Riyadh, weekly)		

Al-Yarmuk (Baghdad, weekly)	Military magazine, ussued by the Iraqi Defense Ministry
Al-Yawm (Amman, daily)	
Al-Yawm al-Sab'i (Paris, weekly)	Affiliated to the PLO. Started publication in 1984
Yedi'ot Aharonot (Tel Aviv, daily)	
Al-Zahf al-Akhdar (Tripoli, weekly)	Ideological weekly of the Revolutionary Committees; appears in both Arabic and English editions

News Agencies

Full Name	*Abbreviation*
Agence France Presse (Paris)	AFP
Algérie Presse Service (Algiers)	APS
Anatolia (Ankara)	
Associated Press (New York)	AP
Associazione Nazionale Stampa Associata (Rome)	ANSA
Deutsche Presse Agentur (Bonn)	DPA
Emirates News Agency (Abu Dhabi)	ENA
Gulf News Agency (Manama)	GNA
International Islamic News Agency (Jidda)	IINA
Iraqi News Agency (Baghdad)	INA
Islamic Revolution News Agency (Tehran)	IRNA
Jamahiriyya Arab News Agency (Tripoli)	JANA
Jewish Telegraphic Agency (New York)	JTA
Jordanian News Agency (PETRA; Amman)	JNA
Kuwaiti News Agency (Kuwait)	KUNA
Maghreb Arabe Presse (Rabat)	MAP
Middle East News Agency (Cairo)	MENA
Novinska Agencija Tanjug (Belgrade)	Tanjug
Pan-African News Agency (Dakar)	PANA
Qatari News Agency (Doha)	QNA
Reuters (London)	
Saudi Press Agency (Riyadh)	SPA
Sudanese News Agency (Khartoum)	SUNA
Syrian Arab News Agency (Damascus)	SANA
Telegrafnoe Agentstvo Sovetskovo Soiuza (Moscow)	Tass
Tunis Afrique Presse (Tunis)	TAP
United Press International (New York)	UPI
Wikalat al-Anba al-Filastiniyya (Palestinian News Agency; Damascus)	WAFA

Radio and Television Stations, and Monitoring Services

(Radio stations known by the location of their principal transmitter are not listed — their names being self-explanatory)

Name	*Abbreviation*	*Notes*
Associated Broadcasting TV	ABC TV	
British Broadcasting Corporation	BBC	
British Broadcasting Corporation, Summary of World Broadcasting: the ME and Africa	SWB	Monitoring reports published in English translation
Cable News Network	CNN	Atlanta, Georgia
Daily Report: Middle East and Africa	DR	Monitoring reports published in English translation by the US Foreign Broadcasting Information Service
Daily Report: Soviet Union	DR:SU	
Israel Defense Forces Radio	R.IDF	
Joint Publication Research Services: Near East and North Africa, Soviet Union, Sub-Saharan Africa, West Europe	JPRS	English-language translation from foreign Press. Occasionally includes monitoring reports as well
Lebanese Broadcasting Corporation		Lebanese Forces TV
R. Free Voice of Iran		Clandestine station apparently broadcasting from Iraq, reflecting views of expatriate Gen Gholam 'Ali Oveysi
R. Ihdin of Free and Unified Lebanon		Operated by Faranjiyya's faction
R. Liberty		Part of Radio Free Europe/ R. Liberty, a US Government-sponsored part of the international communication agency
R. SPLA		Voice of the Sudanese Revolutionary Armed Struggle
United States Information Agency	USIA	Washington
Voice of Free Lebanon		Military station of the Lebanese Phalanges
Voice of the Great Arab Homeland	R. Tripoli, VoGAH	Libyan transmitter to Arab audiences outside Libya, previously known as Voice of the Arab Homeland (VoAH)
Voice of the Homeland		Muslim leftist radio in West Beirut
Voice of Hope	VoH	Maj Sa'd Haddad's militia station broadcasting from Marj 'Ayyun in South Lebanon
Voice of Israel	VoI	Israeli national radio
Voice of Lebanon	VoL	Radio station operated by the Lebanese Phalanges
Voice of the Masses	R. Baghdad, VoM	A series of special programs in Arabic, Kurdish and Farsi; broadcast over R. Baghdad for a few hours each day
Voice of the Mountain		Radio station of the PSP, operating from the Shuf mountains
Voice of the National Alliance for the Liberation of Syria		Syrian opposition radio station, based in Baghdad
Voice of Palestine (Algiers)	VoP (Algiers)	PLO daily program over R. Algiers

Voice of Palestine (Baghdad)	VoP (Baghdad)	PLO main radio station transferred from Beirut after the war in Lebanon. Began transmitting in November 1982
Voice of Palestine (San'a)	VoP (San'a)	PLO daily program over R. San'a
Wireless File	WF	Published by the USIA Library, Washington

Note: Radio and news agency material not otherwise attributed is available in Hebrew translation at the Dayan Center archives.

Notes on Contributors

AMI AYALON, PhD (Princeton University, 1980). Senior Research Fellow at the Dayan Center. Senior Lecturer, Department of Middle Eastern and African History, Tel Aviv University. Author of *Language and Change in the Arab Middle East* (1987) and numerous articles on modern Middle Eastern political and cultural history. Editor of *Regime and Opposition in Egypt under Sadat* (1983, in Hebrew).

OFRA BENGIO, MA (Tel Aviv University, 1986). Junior Research Fellow at the Dayan Center. Fields of specialization: history and politics of Iraq. Contributed chapters to the *Middle East Record*, and articles.

URIEL DANN, PhD (Jerusalem, 1966), DPhil (Oxon, 1980). Professor of History at Tel Aviv University and Senior Research Fellow at the Dayan Center. Published *Iraq under Qassem; Studies in the History of Transjordan, 1920–49: The Making of a State; Hanover and England, 1740–1760; "The Numbered Days" of King Hussein: Jordan 1955–1967* (forthcoming); and articles. Editor of *The Great Powers in the Middle East, 1919–1939.*

SHAI FELDMAN, PhD (University of California, Berkeley, 1980). Senior Research Associate at the Jaffee Center for Strategic Studies, Tel Aviv University since 1977. Fields of specialization: nuclear armament, American-Israeli relations, and Israeli strategic issues. Author of *Israeli Nuclear Deterrence: A Strategy for the 1980s* (1982) and coauthor of *Deception, Consensus and War: Israel in Lebanon* (1984).

ROBERT O. FREEDMAN, PhD (Columbia University), is the Dean of the Peggy Meyerhoff Pearlstone School of Graduate Studies and Professor of Political Science at the Baltimore Hebrew College. Author of *Economic Warfare in the Communist Bloc: A Study of Soviet Economic Pressure against Yugoslavia, Albania and Communist China* (1970) and *Soviet Policy toward the Middle East since 1970* (1975, 1978, 1982). Editor of *World Politics and the Arab-Israeli Conflict* (1979), *Israel in the Begin Era* (1982), *The Middle East since Camp David* (1984), and *Soviet Jewry in the Decisive Decade 1971–80* (1984).

MORDECHAI GAZIT, MA (Hebrew University). Senior Research Fellow at the Dayan Center and the Leonard Davis Institute for International Relations, Hebrew University. Formerly Director-General, Office of the Prime Minister of Israel (1973–75); Director-General, Israel Ministry for Foreign Affairs (1972–73); Ambassador to France (1975–79); Minister, Embassy of Israel, Washington, DC (1960–65); Fellow, Center for International Affairs, Harvard University (1980–81).

GAD G. GILBAR, PhD (University of London, 1974). Associate Professor in the Department of Middle Eastern History, Haifa University. Associate Editor of the

Journal of Asian and African Studies. Fields of specialization: economic and social history of the Middle East. Published articles and edited books: *Ottoman Palestine 1800–1914: Studies in Economic and Social History* (1987); coeditor of *Studies in Islamic Society* (1984)

DORE GOLD, PhD (Columbia University, 1984). Senior Research Associate at the Jaffee Center for Strategic Studies, Tel Aviv University. Fields of specialization: Saudi Arabia and the Gulf states, US strategic interests in the Gulf region and the Middle East.

JACOB GOLDBERG, PhD (Harvard University, 1978). Senior Research Fellow at the Dayan Center. Chairman of the Editorial Board of the Dayan Center Occasional Papers Series. Fields of specialization: the modern and contemporary history of the Arab world with particular reference to Saudi Arabia. Publications: *The Foreign Policy of Saudi Arabia: The Formative Years, 1902–1918*; coeditor of *The Superpower Competition in the Middle East.*

JOSEPH KOSTINER, PhD (London School of Economics and Political Science, University of London, 1982). Research Fellow at the Dayan Center; Lecturer in the Department of Middle Eastern and African History at Tel Aviv University. Fields of specialization: history and current affairs of the Arabian Peninsula states. Published several papers on this subject. Author of *The Struggle for South Yemen* (1984).

MARTIN KRAMER, PhD (Princeton University, 1982). Associate Director and Senior Research Fellow at the Dayan Center. Fields of specialization: Islamic and pan-Islamic activism. Author of *Islam Assembled: The Advent of the Muslim Congress* (1986), and published articles on the modern history of the Middle East; editor of: *Protest and Revolution in Shi'i Islam* (1985 in Hebrew); *Shi'ism, Resistance and Revolution* (1987).

BRUCE MADDY-WEITZMAN, PhD (Tel Aviv University, 1988). Junior Research Fellow at the Dayan Center. Fields of specialization: contemporary Middle East history, inter-Arab relations, and the Arab-Israeli conflict. Published papers on Arab politics, and the Iraqi-Iranian conflict. Title of thesis: "The Crystallization of an Arab State System: Inter-Arab Politics, 1945–1954."

DAVID MENASHRI, PhD (Tel Aviv University, 1982). Senior Research Fellow at the Dayan Center and Lecturer in the Department of Middle Eastern and African History, Tel Aviv University. Field of specialization: the history and politics of Iran. Author of: *Iran: The Islamic Revolution and Beyond* (in press); *Iran in Revolution* (1988, in Hebrew). Published papers on Iranian politics and contributed chapters to *Middle East Record.*

YOSEF OLMERT, PhD (London School of Economics and Political Science, University of London, 1984). Research Fellow at the Dayan Center. Lecturer in the Department of Middle Eastern and African History at Tel Aviv University. Fields of specialization: political and ideological history of Syria and Lebanon. Published papers on various aspects of political development in Syria and Lebanon.

UZI RABI, BA (Tel Aviv University, 1986). Researcher at the Dayan Center and Instructor in the Preparatory Program, Tel Aviv University. Fields of specialization: Persian Gulf states and Palestinian armed operations.

ITAMAR RABINOVICH, PhD (University of California, Los Angeles, 1971). Professor, Department of Middle Eastern and African History, Tel Aviv University; Head of the Dayan Center and the Shiloah Institute. The incumbent of the Yona and Dina Ettinger Chair in Contemporary History of the Middle East. Fields of specialization: the modern and contemporary history of the Arab world with particular reference to Syria, Lebanon and inter-Arab affairs. Publications: *Syria under the Ba'th 1963–66: the Army Party Symbiosis; The Lebanese Civil War: A Documented History* (in Hebrew); and *The War for Lebanon 1970–83*; coeditor of *From June to October: The ME between 1967–73; The Middle East and the United States: Perceptions and Policies; Israel in the ME 1948-82*; and *Ethnicity, Pluralism and the State in the Middle East.*

ELIE REKHESS, PhD (Tel Aviv University, 1987). Senior Research Fellow at the Dayan Center. Fields of specialization: the Israeli Arabs and the Arabs on the West Bank and Gaza Strip. Published papers and studies on the Arab intelligentsia in Israel and on the West Bank; political trends and socioeconomic changes within the Arab population in Israel, the West Bank and Gaza, and on the Communist movement in Israel and the Arab world.

YEHUDIT RONEN, BA (Tel Aviv University, 1977). Junior Research Fellow at the Dayan Center. Fields of specialization: Sudan and Libya. She has contributed to previous volumes of *MECS* as well as to a number of edited volumes on the Middle East.

HAIM SHAKED, PhD (School of Oriental and African Studies, University of London, 1969). Professor, Department of Middle Eastern and African History, Tel Aviv University. Head of the Shiloah (now Dayan) Center (1973–80); Dean of the Faculty of Humanities, Tel Aviv University (1975–80). Fields of specialization: modern and contemporary history of the ME. Author of *The Life of the Sudanese Mahdi*, and coeditor of *From June to October: The Middle East between 1967–73* and *The Middle East and the United States: Perceptions and Policies.* Editor in Chief of *Mideast File.* Chairman, Editorial Board of the Dayan Center Monograph Series.

BENJAMIN SHWADRAN, MA, PhD (Clark University, 1945). Taught Middle Eastern Studies in the New York School for Social Research; Professor of Middle Eastern Studies and Director of Middle East Institute, Dropsie University, Philadelphia; taught in Hofstra University, New York. Professor of Modern Middle East History at Tel Aviv University since 1973. Formerly editor of *Middle Eastern Affairs* and of the Council for Middle Eastern Affairs Press. Among his publications are *Middle East Oil and the Great Powers* (three editions); *Jordan, a State of Tension;*

The Power Struggle in Iraq; General Index Middle Eastern Affairs; Neft Hamizrah Hatikhon: Berakha Veiyum; Middle East Oil: Issues and Problems.

ASHER SUSSER, PhD (Tel Aviv University, 1986). Senior Research Associate at the Dayan Center. Fields of specialization: history and politics of Jordan and the Palestinians. Author of *Between Jordan and Palestine: A Political Biography of Wasfi al-Tall* (in Hebrew), papers on Jordanian history and politics, and contributed chapters to the *Middle East Record.*

JOSHUA TEITELBAUM, BA (University of California, Los Angeles, 1980). Research Assistant at the Dayan Center and Instructor in the Overseas Students Program, Tel Aviv University. Fields of specialization: Palestinian history and politics, modern Islamic movements, Israeli Druze, and the history of the Arabian Peninsula. Completing MA thesis on "The *Hajj* and the Establishment of the Saudi State, 1924–1939," at Tel Aviv University.

WALTER F. WEIKER, PhD (Princeton University, 1962). Professor of Political Science at Rutgers University in Newark, New Jersey. Author of *The Turkish Revolution 1960–61* (Washington: The Brookings Institution, 1963), *Political Tutelage and Democracy in Turkey* (Leiden: E.J. Brill, 1973), *The Modernization of Turkey* (New York: Holmes & Meier, 1981), as well as numerous articles on modern Turkey.

YAEL YISHAI, PhD (Hebrew University, 1976). Professor of Political Science, University of Haifa. Author of *Israel: The Peaceful Belligerent 1967–1979* (with A. Sella); *Land or Peace: Whither Israel* (1987); *Interest Groups in Israeli Politics* (1981). Has published numerous articles on Israeli domestic politics.

PART ONE: CURRENT ISSUES

THE MIDDLE EAST IN PERSPECTIVE

The Middle East in 1986

ITAMAR RABINOVICH

Last year, when he wrote the introductory essay to *Middle East Contemporary Survey* IX, Gabriel Ben-Dor defined 1985 as a year of "incremental change" in the Middle East. A year earlier he had characterized ME politics as "the politics of fragmentation," and in 1983 he had viewed it as "the politics of uncertainty." This terminology indicates that, like several other students of current Middle Eastern affairs, Professor Ben-Dor has been hard put to identify a pattern or "an organizing principle" with which to impose at least a semblance of order on the confused reality of the Middle East during the early 1980s.

In earlier periods, if a dominant pattern or theme was not readily discernible, it was a major event — the Iranian Revolution, Egyptian-Israeli peace, or the war in Lebanon — around which much of the year's political chronology seemed to evolve. But in the early 1980s the Middle Eastern political scene seemed to have been shaped by several divergent and apparently unrelated processes and developments — the lingering war between Iran and Iraq, the stalemated Arab-Israeli peace process, the decline of the Arab oil economy, the Soviet-American competition (ever present, but ever changing), the disintegration of the system of inter-Arab relations, the domestic difficulties faced by several Middle Eastern regimes.

This configuration did not change in 1986. It was another year when much happened but little was altered in the general scheme of things in the Middle East.

America's policies and position in the Middle East were affected most significantly by developments that occurred in the final months of the year. In October, it was discovered that the Reagan Administration had misled its allies and the American media through a "disinformation campaign" directed at Libya, and that, more important, it had been negotiating with the Islamic Republic of Iran over hostages, going so far as to provide it directly and indirectly with arms. This was disconcerting to Washington's conservative Arab allies; but the ensuing scandal's more important ramifications lay in the enfeeblement of an Administration with two years in office ahead of it. President Reagan's failure in the November congressional elections and the more serious challenge presented by Mikhail Gorbachev's Soviet Union further reinforced this trend.

Earlier in the year the Administration's main efforts in the Middle East were invested in attempting to revive the Arab-Israeli peace process through Israeli-Jordanian negotiations, and in launching a campaign against terrorism. This culminated in the 14 April aerial raid on Libya, whose Government was perceived and presented as the main source of inspiration and support for anti-American terrorism. But in the latter part of 1986 the campaign abated as the Administration displayed a hesitant position toward Syria and subsequently was embarrassed by the disclosures of October.

These developments, the failure to formulate a satisfactory policy to deal with the new phase in the war between Iran and Iraq, and the strain in several bilateral relationships with Middle Eastern allies cast a shadow over Washington's position in the region but did not erode its primacy. The US was still the senior superpower in the Middle East, defending a position that the Soviet Union was seeking to diminish.

For the Soviet Union, 1986 in the Middle East began with a series of problems and threats. Domestic upheaval jeopardized its ascendancy in the People's Democratic Republic of Yemen. The escalating tension between the US and Libya presented a familiar dilemma. In case of an actual armed conflict, the Soviet Union would either have to intervene or be humiliated. As it happened, Moscow's passive attitude in April was embarrassing. This raised the more serious threat of an American-Syrian clash. However, Moscow was not presented with another dilemma, partly because Washington realized that the USSR's commitment to Syria was far more serious than its commitment to Libya.

The silver lining for the Soviets in the Middle East during these months came in February when King Husayn abrogated the agreement he had signed with the Palestine Liberation Organization (PLO) a year earlier. In Soviet eyes, this marked an American failure to orchestrate the revival of the Arab-Israeli peace process and to appear as the one superpower that could effectively conduct the process and shape the regional politics of the Middle East.

The Soviet Union's effort to change its own posture and image as a power identified with one side in the Arab-Israeli conflict and not having any contact with the other proceeded very slowly. In August, the first official diplomatic contacts with Israel since 1967 took place in Helsinki but were kept at the consular level.

In the regional politics of the Middle East it was the lingering war between Iran and Iraq that remained the most salient factor. A military decision could not be imposed and a political accommodation was still not feasible, but the balance tilted further toward Iran. In political terms, the fact that the Reagan Administration had been willing to deal with Iran and supply it with arms clearly had current and future significance. It indicated that the US continued to view Iran as the main prize in the Gulf struggle. In military terms, the capture of the Faw Peninsula, further attacks on Basra and the opening of yet another front in the Kurdish area in the North raised the specter of a decisive military victory with far-reaching ramifications.

The Gulf war and the support extended by Syria and Libya to Iran and by most of the other Arab states to Iraq remained the single most divisive issue in inter-Arab relations. King Husayn's efforts to use his improved relations with Syria's Hafiz al-Asad in order to draw the latter away from Iran and to effect a Syrian-Iraqi *rapprochement* proved futile. Husayn's efforts were calculated as the first phase of an attempt to restore at least a measure of unity to Arab ranks. The most glaring evidence of Arab disunity had been the failure of all efforts since September 1982 to convene an Arab summit conference. A summit *manqué* was convened in 1985 in Casablanca; the desire to improve on it and to convene a full-fledged summit in 1986 was not realized. Also unsuccessful were the efforts to normalize Egypt's relations with the rest of the Arab world. Some progress was made, but Egypt's position *vis-à-vis* the divided Arab system remained awkward.

The persistent divisiveness against the already familiar backdrop of declining oil power and oil revenues, Iran's menacing posture, Israel's continuing control of Arab territories and the inability to solve the Lebanese crisis nourished the sense of weakness and the malaise felt by many Arabs and expressed by their writers.

As previously mentioned, the main effort to revive the Arab-Israeli peace process was seriously undermined in February 1986 when King Husayn abrogated the 11 February 1985 agreement between Jordan and the PLO. What had begun in late 1984 as a combined venture by the US, Israel, Jordan and Egypt, was premised on the PLO's weakness and dependence on Jordan following the events of 1982–83 and on Shimon Peres' Premiership. The venture sought to revive the peace process through Jordanian-Israeli negotiations, with Palestinian participation and PLO endorsement. By October 1985 it had become evident that the venture was stalled. In February 1986, Husayn concluded that the PLO had taken advantage of him to bolster its position *vis-à-vis* Syria and abrogated the agreement. In a long speech delivered on 24 February, he explained his action and settled his scores with Yasir 'Arafat and the PLO. He said, among other things, that:

> On 6 February, Yasir 'Arafat had a meeting with our Prime Minister at his residence. The meeting was attended by the head of the Royal Court and by 'Abd al-Razzaq al-Yahya and Hani al-Hasan from the Palestinian side. 'Arafat informed the Prime Minister that despite the positive development of the American position, recognition of the legitimate rights of the Palestinian people did not encompass the right to self-determination to which, the PLO insisted, the US ought to give its prior approval.
>
> On 7 February, Yasir 'Arafat left Amman still insisting on his position and on the reason why the PLO was unable to accept Resolution 242. Hinging on this agreement, of course, was an immediate opening of an American-Palestinian dialogue on the basis of which we would have continued our efforts to convene an international peace conference to which the PLO would be invited to participate as a representative of the Palestinian people.
>
> Thus came to an end another chapter in the search for peace. Another extremely important and significant round of Jordanian-Palestinian action was terminated — after a full year of serious and persistent effort to transform the PLO role, referred to in the Arab peace plan, into a significant reality that would go beyond a mere statement of positions. It would have led to a presence and participation by the PLO in an international conference at the invitation of the United Nations Secretary-General, to represent its people and speak on their behalf with their adversary under the eyes of the world, side by side with the other parties concerned and the five permanent members of the Security Council.
>
> Yes, brothers and sisters: we have gone through a grueling year of intensive effort and faced a host of obstacles, in many instances exceeding the limits of our endurance. But we succeeded in achieving what had been felt to be impossible. We opened up avenues that had been considered closed to us and to our Arab and Palestinian brothers. We were able to carry the Fez Resolution to a point just preceding the international peace conference, for which it called. Buoyed on the one hand by progress achieved in providing a real opportunity for peace, and pained on the other by impediments when we were so close to the finishing line, we have felt it imperative to give a full public account of the

> situation and once again turn the matter over to the Palestinian forums in the occupied territories and the diaspora as well as Arab capitals and organizations.

'Arafat, for his part, despite pressure from his radical partners, refused to reciprocate by abrogating the agreement. Nor was the effort to bring about a Jordanian-Israeli agreement totally abandoned.

More fruitful was the US attempt to improve the Israeli-Egyptian relationship. A fundamental improvement was not feasible, but a partial improvement through an agreement on arbitration in the Taba dispute and the return of an Egyptian Ambassador to Tel Aviv was within reach. Israel and Egypt failed to reach such an agreement through bilateral contacts, and US intervention and mediation were required to effect it.

The violent dimension of the Arab-Israeli conflict manifested itself on several fronts: (a) in Shi'i and Palestinian conflict with Israeli and South Lebanese Army (SLA) forces; (b) in the Israeli-Palestinian conflict which manifested itself primarily in the West Bank and Gaza; (c) in terrorist activity; and (d) in the Syrian-Israeli conflict. In 1986, talk and fear of a Syrian-Israeli war reached a peak. Ironically, both sides acted on the basis of growing misperceptions. Many Israelis attributed to the Syrian doctrine of "strategic parity" an offensive edge and anticipated a full-blown or limited Syrian attack. In the same vein, Asad's speeches of late February and early March 1986, in which he explained that "strategic parity" was a long term goal, were perceived ominously in Israel where emphasis was placed on Asad's assertion on 27 February that "12 million Syrian citizens are capable of regaining the Golan...If the Israelis work to put the Golan within their borders, we will work to put the Golan in the middle of Syria."

In Syria, the frequent claims by Israeli leaders and spokesmen that Syria was preparing an attack were seen as political preparations for an attack. These fears were inflamed in the spring by the American raid on Libya. As Asad's efforts to dissociate himself from "international terrorism" clearly indicated, he was worried, in the aftermath of the raid on Libya, about the possibility of an attack by the US or both. In this respect the Syrian attempt to blow up an El Al plane in London remains an intriguing enigma. In any event, by the end of 1986, Syria appeared weak and isolated and the fear of a Syrian-Israeli war was largely dissipated.

An examination of domestic developments in Middle Eastern states in 1986 yields a generally gloomy picture.

Thus Ami Ayalon writes in this volume:

> During 1986 the Egyptian Government faced increasing socio-economic and political pressures that presented a serious challenge and at times jeopardized the stability of the State. By and large, however, the regime continued to control the political game, and the political institutions functioned effectively even in the face of mounting difficulties. Under the shadow of the oil crisis and diminishing resources, the Government's exchanges with its critics grew sharper. The regime had to contend with attacks in the opposition Press, strikes and demonstrations by students and workers, threats by underground groups of Muslim radicals, and, for the first time, an open revolt by units of the security forces in Cairo.
>
> This last incident, in February, was the most remarkable event of the year in

Egypt. It showed up, if only briefly, the curious phenomenon of a regime surviving in relative stability despite highly adverse material conditions. Faced with an unusually dangerous threat, the country's leadership responded with equally unusual severity by deploying large army units in the capital and imposing a curfew until the rebellion was quelled. Although the uprising was exceptionally violent and costly, it was also typical in its causes and consequences: the severe material and spiritual distress that erupted in desperate protest; the firm hand of the army-backed Government in suppressing it; and the eventual spectacle, by now all too familiar, of hundreds of men in iron cages on collective trial. By spring, the crisis was over and life in Egypt returned to its often tense routine as both the Government and the people braced themselves for future crises and possible confrontations.

Syria's domestic difficulties in 1986 can be viewed in two different ways. One would be a detailed examination of the regime's problems and their origins. It would point to four main areas: (1) The lingering uncertainty about the President's health and the unresolved question of his eventual succession. In this respect Rif'at Asad's continued stay in Europe was the single most important manifestation of an otherwise barely perceptible conflict. (2) The economic crisis which affected the system as a whole and the citizens individually and resulted in malaise, criticism and acrimonious debate in the regime's upper echelons. (3) Renewal of anti-regime terrorist attacks, apparently by radical Islamic elements. (4) A series of foreign policy failures which affected the domestic position of a regime whose legitimacy has traditionally depended to a considerable degree on its external successes.

But these developments can also be seen in a more general way as manifestations of the regime's failure to cope with the ambitious scheme it had undertaken several years earlier. Asad personally and the system he had built could not cope simultaneously with the tasks of maintaining power, developing Syria, guaranteeing a high standard of living for a large number of Syrians, maintaining strategic parity with Israel, managing Lebanon, seeking regional influence and dealing with the two superpowers. By the end of 1986 it was clear that some of the regime's most important policies had to be reassessed.

It was hardly surprising that the Iraqi-Iranian war had negative effects on the political systems of the protagonists; 1986 bore witness both to the cumulative effects of seven years of fighting and to the specific consequences of the year's events.

Saddam Husayn's regime was taxed by the political costs of its military setbacks. The Iraqi leader had to respond to criticism and pressure and his regime became less centralized and personalized. Senior military commanders were mentioned by name and quoted in the Iraqi media. The Ministers of Foreign Affairs and Information and the Director of Internal Security became regular participants in General Staff meetings. And in an effort to placate the larger public, the pace of economic liberalization was expedited and criticism of a "non-political" nature was allowed in the Iraqi Press.

In Iran a similar dynamic was at work based on the interplay between the conduct of the war, the economic situation and the factional conflict within the regime. For Iran, 1986 was a year of military success on the ground — but the dramatic breakthrough did not occur, losses were heavy and Iraq's superiority in the air exacted a heavy toll. The direct and indirect economic cost of the war remained very high and generated disaffection and criticism. There were manifestations of opposition to Ayatollah Ruhollah Khomeyni's regime but, on the whole, it remained sterile and insignificant. The important friction occurred within the regime's ranks and revolved around three issues:

(1) The struggle for Khomeyni's succession. His disciples realized that the designated successor, Ayatollah Husayn 'Ali Montazeri, was not really qualified for the task.
(2) A factional conflict for power between such figures as President 'Ali Khameneh'i and the Speaker of the *Majlis*, Ayatollah 'Ali Akbar Hashemi Rafsanjani, who were posturing for the post-Khomeyni era.
(3) The dissatisfaction displayed by radicals within the regime who did not belong to its "mainstream" or "establishment."

In 1986, more than 11 years after the outbreak of the Lebanese civil war, more than four years after Amin Jumayyil's election to the Presidency, and more than two and a half years after Syria's victory over its rivals in the Lebeanese arena, the Lebanese crisis seemed no nearer to resolution.

In December 1985, Syria tried to break the deadlock by persuading the leaders of the three principal militias in Lebanon — Nabih Barri of the Shi'i *Amal*, Walid Junblat, the leader of the Druze, and Elie Hobeika of the Maronite Lebanese Forces — to sign the "Damascus Accord." The agreement included a list of Maronite Christian concessions that were to lead to a new national consensus and greater institutionalization of Syria's influence. But the agreement collapsed within a month when the concessions made by Hobeika were used by his Maronite rivals to topple him. It was very significant that after a decade of hegemony in Lebanon, Syria's position there was still very tenuous and the authors of its policy were capable of such a gross error of judgment.

Indeed, Syria faced increasingly severe challenges in Lebanon in 1986 — the PLO's gradual return and entrenchment; the PLO's cooperation with *Hizballah* against Syria's mainstay, *Amal*; and Iran's growing influence.

In the absence of normal Lebanese political life most meaningful political activity took place within Lebanon's major communities. As has been mentioned, yet another coup took place within the Lebanese Forces when Samir Ja'ja' deposed Hobeika. The latter went to Damascus to plot his comeback, but his main effort was aborted in June. This was accomplished primarily by the Christian brigades of the Lebanese Army and was indicative of the cardinal role these units and the Army's commander, Michel 'Awun, had come to play in Christian-Maronite politics. It was not long before he was mentioned as a leading candidate for the Presidency in 1988.

In the Shi'i community the position of *al-Amal* and its leader, Barri, was eroded by several developments: internal opposition, criticism and assault by Iran and *Hizballah*, the onus of dealing with Israel and the SLA in the South, and the inability to cope with the PLO in southwest Beirut as well as in the Sidon-Tyre area.

The decline of oil revenues has already been mentioned above as an important factor shaping regional politics in the Middle East. Its repercussions on the economy and politics of such states as Egypt and Syria have also been noted. However, the conservative oil producing states of the Arabian Peninsula cushioned the domestic political effects of declining revenues by spending part of their huge financial reserves and by cutting projects devoid of direct political ramifications. Like the previous year, 1986 was for the conservative oil producers a time of political weakness and defensiveness — caused as much by the Iranian threat as by the retreat of the oil economy. But they did not go through serious domestic crises.

Israeli politics were governed by the question of the "rotation" of power agreement. The Government formed in September 1984 in the aftermath of the indecisive July elections was predicated on a unique power-sharing arrangement. The Labor Party's leader, Shimon Peres, was to be Prime Minister for just over two years and then exchange positions with Yitzhak Shamir, the Likud's leader, who became Foreign Minister. For two years the question of whether the rotation would actually take place hovered over Israeli politics. In October 1986, it did take place, but the uncertainty regarding the future of the National Unity Government persisted.

Before and after the rotation the stability of the Israeli Government was intimately linked to the issue of negotiations with Jordan over the West Bank and the Palestinian question. It was generally assumed in Israel and elsewhere that Peres believed in and sought a settlement with Jordan, but Shamir and his party were opposed to it. There was speculation that an impressive tentative agreement with King Husayn would be the one issue over which Peres was willing to break his arrangement with Shamir and call for new elections. For Husayn, this should have served as an inducement to take a bold initiative. But, as we have noted, the breakthrough that had not occurred in 1985 failed also to occur in 1986. The National Unity Government was considered a success during its first two years. It was credited with ending Israel's massive involvement in Lebanon, rehabilitating the country's economy, and calming the heated political atmosphere. But inherent in the power-sharing arrangement and in the undecided vote that underlay it was the inability to carry both Israel and its reluctant external partner through the threshold of negotiations.

THE MIDDLE EAST AND WORLD AFFAIRS

The United States and the Middle East in 1986

SHAI FELDMAN

The year began with an intense American effort to move the Middle East peace process forward, and ended with disappointment, despair, and inaction. It started with a quest for immediate results to be achieved through Israeli-Jordanian-Palestinian negotiations; it ended with escapism covered with much talk about a long-term effort to improve the quality of life in the West Bank and to alter the conflict's "atmospherics." All this in the hope of producing a social, political, and economic environment more conducive to future negotiations. When the year began, Washington's efforts to win support for its anti-terrorism policy were gaining ground; as the year ended, the credibility of this policy was shattered by the Iran arms fiasco. In early 1986, the region perceived the US as committed to the forces opposing Iranian Fundamentalism; it ended with great confusion in the minds of America's regional allies regarding Washington's priorities in the Middle East. Early in the year, President Ronald Reagan enjoyed a high standing and much leverage in the American political system; but as the year closed, it was diminished by Irangate-related questioning of his personal capacities, as well as by his party's earlier poor performance in the November elections, and particularly by its loss of control over the Senate. The year began as a high point in US-Israeli relations; as it ended, the cumulative effect of the Pollard spy case and Israel's involvement in the Iran arms affair had taken their toll: Israel's closest supporters in Washington were particularly hurt.

THE PEACE PROCESS

Very early in 1986, the US had been engaged in a serious effort to see whether Israeli-Jordanian-Palestinian negotiations could be launched. The investigation began after King Husayn's visit to Washington in May 1985, and had gained momentum by the end of the year. During his visit, the King acknowledged his willingness to enter into direct negotiations with Israel for the first time. Based on his talks with the leadership of the Palestine Liberation Organization (PLO) and his February 1985 accord with Yasir 'Arafat, Husayn also indicated that the PLO was willing to enter such negotiations based on United Nations Security Council Resolutions 242 and 338.[1]

Husayn's statements moved an Administration which for the previous two years had been reluctant to engage itself actively in efforts to resolve the Arab-Israeli dispute. By mid-1983, Reagan's September 1982 Middle East initiative had been rejected by both Israel and Jordan. Thus, clear partners for Middle East peace negotiations seemed non-existent.[2] Meanwhile, the US became another victim of the quagmire which was Lebanon. Syria refused to follow the script written for it in Washington and would not withdraw its forces from Lebanon; and contrary to America's expectations, Saudi Arabia would not, or could not, exert its pressure on

Syria to execute such a withdrawal.[3] Also, Egypt refused to return its Ambassador to Israel despite the May 1983 Israel-Lebanon accord and despite what Secretary of State George Shultz regarded as a personal commitment to do so given him by President Husni Mubarak.

This series of disappointments led key members of the Reagan Administration to conclude that there was little to be gained by trying to push the Middle East peace process forward.[4] American inaction was further influenced by the absence of perceived urgency: a new Arab-Israeli war did not seem imminent as no Arab state or combination of states seemed able or willing to challenge Israel militarily. As Israel was still mired in Lebanon, with its Army's morale undermined and its people demonstrating cumulative fatigue, an Israeli-initiated war also did not seem likely. Moreover, from the American point of view, the international oil picture had much improved by 1983–84, with surpluses promising to prevent any disruptions in supply. By 1983 the Iraqi-Iranian war had entered its fourth year, and it was argued that if a war at the heart of the oil region had not seriously affected supplies, there was little reason to worry that another Arab-Israeli war would have that effect. As of late 1984, the Reagan Administration preferred to allow Israel's new Government of National Unity to put its economic house in order, and to complete its withdrawal from Lebanon, before engaging it in a taxing peace process.[5] The combined effect of these developments resulted in a passive American approach to Middle East peace.

More than any other factor, the reduced importance of Middle East oil accounted for the diminished importance of the Middle East on America's national agenda. While the region competed with US-Soviet relations for top priority when President Carter took office, after 1981 Washington attached far more importance to its domestic economic policies, to attempts to strengthen its armed forces, and to containing revolutionaries in Central America, as well as to efforts in the war against global terrorism.[6] As Reagan's second term began, his Administration also invested much effort in attempts to reach arms-control agreements with the Soviets.[7] The Middle East thus slid to sixth place on the agenda, and considerably more importance was attached to the first five items than to the sixth.[8]

Relative positions on the national agenda determine the willingness of the President and the Secretary of State to invest time, intellectual effort, and political ammunition on each issue and problem. Thus, the lower priority given to the Middle East, coupled with the assessment that the region's political environment would make any effort to resolve the dispute extremely difficult and costly, caused Washington to refrain from such efforts until conditions improved.

In the Administration's view, Husayn's May 1985 visit justified at least a reassessment of its prior premises. For the first time, an Arab leader appeared to be willing to negotiate Israeli-Jordanian-Palestinian peace, based on Resolutions 242 and 338. The King nevertheless presented three preconditions: that negotiations be conducted in the framework of an international conference; that all five permanent members of the Security Council be invited to cosponsor the conference; and that the conference be preceded by a meeting between an American delegation and a joint Palestinian-Jordanian delegation.[9]

These conditions notwithstanding, the Administration decided that Husayn's positive statement of intent justified a more serious investigation of the possibility of producing Jordan as a partner for direct negotiations. Thus, in the months following

Husayn's visit, there were frequent visits to the Middle East by American diplomats, including Assistant Secretary of State Richard Murphy, and endless discussions between America's Ambassadors in Israel and Jordan and the leaders of both countries. These visits and discussions focused on two issues: first, Palestinian representation: the production of Palestinians who might be acceptable for membership in a Palestinian-Jordanian delegation; and second, direct negotiations: ensuring that the American-Jordanian-Palestinian meeting, and the subsequent international conference, would indeed lead to direct Israeli-Jordanian-Palestinian talks.[10] The issue of Soviet participation in such a conference was never discussed seriously, as the US expressed a series of preconditions which stood little chance of being met.

As 1985 came to a close, America's efforts focused increasingly on the issue of Palestinian representation in the proposed international conference, as interest in a pre-conference American-Jordanian-Palestinian meeting diminished.[11] In this framework, the Administration attempted simultaneously to help Husayn gain the PLO's approval of Palestinians who might be acceptable to Israel as their nation's representatives;[12] and to make the PLO itself a legitimate partner for future negotiations.[13] In its efforts to gain both objectives, the Administration made a number of concessions: first, it altered one of its preconditions for negotiations with the PLO, substituting its long-standing demand that it recognize Israel's right to exist with a more modest demand that it express its willingness to negotiate with Israel;[14] second, it hinted that if the PLO were to accept Resolutions 242 and 338, declare an end to terrorism, and express its willingness to negotiate with Israel, the US would not object to inviting the PLO to the proposed international conference;[15] finally, although the US continued to reject the PLO's demand that it recognize the Palestinians' right to self-determination, it now provided the contingent that if the PLO were to meet America's preconditions and come to the conference, the US would not regard the making of such a demand as illegitimate.[16] Within the framework of these efforts, State Department spokesman Charles Redman said on 10 February 1986: "The Palestinian problem is more than a refugee question." Redman indicated that the US did not believe that Resolutions 242 and 338 provided a complete response to the Palestinian problem: "There should be no confusion between Resolution 242 and the legitimate rights of the Palestinian people. They deal with different issues and are in fact complementary."[17]

At the same time, Assistant Secretary of State Murphy continued to shuttle between Israel's Prime Minister Shimon Peres and Jordan's King Husayn, attempting to reach an agreement on modalities for the proposed conference. Murphy's task was to ensure conference procedures that would allow the conduct of direct negotiations.[18]

In his speech of 22 February 1986, Husayn analyzed his failure to gain 'Arafat's support for negotiations and announced the suspension of his efforts to coordinate a policy jointly with the PLO. Unwilling or unable to proceed without the PLO's support, Husayn removed himself — at least for the duration of 1986 — as a viable Arab partner for negotiations. His speech brought the brief period of American activism in the Middle East peace process to an end. Subsequent to the speech, the US reverted to its pre-May 1985 low profile in Arab Israeli peacemaking.[19]

Preferring to avoid being seen as having entirely abandoned its interest in Middle East peace, the Administration returned to a previous theme: the need to improve the quality of life in the West Bank and the Gaza Strip. The purpose was to alter the distribution of power in the West Bank between the PLO and the King's supporters, in the latter's favor and in the hope that this would allow Husayn sufficient backing for direct negotiations in the future.[20] But even on this more limited front, America's conduct was merely tentative. Unable or unwilling to commit the resources required for Husayn's $150m West Bank Development Plan, the US seemed increasingly disengaged.[21] During his July trip to the Middle East, Vice-President George Bush inquired whether some progress in the peace process could be made. Murphy traveled to the area again in early September, but both efforts seemed largely like pro-forma demonstrations that the US remained interested in Middle East peace.[22] Attempts by public figures, such as Senator Charles Mathias, following his March trip to the Middle East, as well as by then Prime Minister Peres, during a September trip to Washington, to persuade the Administration to reengage itself in the peace process, left it unmoved.[23] Instead, the Administration preferred to revert to its mid-1985 passive approach.[24]

By year's end, US-Jordanian relations suffered new strains: against the background of the Administration's continuous refusal to supply Husayn with sophisticated weapons, end-November news about the sale of American arms to Iran, to be used against Jordan's Iraqi allies, left Amman bewildered and frustrated about Washington's priorities in the Middle East.

And yet, one development in the peace process carried unexpected side benefits for the US in 1986: considerable improvement in its ties with Morocco. This occurred after two years of coolness in Washington's relations with Rabat, resulting from the Morocco-Libya "treaty of union" announced in August 1984. Following the late August meeting between King Hasan II and Prime Minister Peres, Mu'ammar Qadhdhafi canceled the "union" with Morocco. In the immediate aftermath of the meeting, the King did not respond to signals sent by Vice-President Bush, indicating his desire to visit Morocco.[25] But the combined effect of the Hasan-Peres summit, and the subsequent cancellation of the Morocco-Libya treaty, was to enable the Administration to provide Rabat with $150m in aid. Washington's assistance had been threatened by the continued anger of Congress over the 1984 treaty. Subsequently, improved US-Morocco ties also resulted in expanded lending to Morocco through the International Monetary Fund.[26]

The improvement in US-Morocco relations took place despite a simultaneous improvement in Washington's ties with Algeria. The latter resulted from President Chedli Benjedid's decision to cultivate friendlier relations with the US.

UNITED STATES-LIBYAN RELATIONS

Efforts to contain and deter international terrorism comprised a second focus of America's Middle East policy in 1986. During the year, much of the Administration's attitude and behavior toward Libya and Syria resulted from the two countries' conduct or support of terrorism. The first half of the year saw the peak in American efforts to establish a tough and effective anti-terrorism policy; as the year closed, much of the policy's credibility lay in ruins.

The military involvement in Lebanon between late 1982 and early 1984 had resulted in greater American sensitivity to the implications of international terrorism. A debate as to the best means of addressing the problem developed in 1984, with Shultz advocating the adoption of strong preemptive and preventive measures. Bush and Secretary of Defense Caspar Weinberger called for the exercise of great caution, with the latter declaring a long list of preconditions for America's use of force.[27] During the 1984 presidential election campaign, Reagan seemed indecisive regarding which course to follow.[28]

The intensified direct experience with terrorism, arising from America's presence in Lebanon, created a strong predisposition to deal seriously with the problem. Washington's further observation, in late 1985, of the extent to which its strategic objectives in the region could be derailed by terrorist actions, contributed to a greater willingness to act. In the late fall, the hijacking of the *Achille Lauro* — an Italian pleasure ship docked off the port of Alexandria — and the on-board murder of an American citizen, Leon Klinghoffer, contributed to the halting of efforts to launch an Israeli-Jordanian-Palestinian peace process. The murderous terrorist attacks on the airports of Rome and Vienna had the same effect. Thus, by early 1986, the realities of international terrorism had created a political environment more conducive to the tough policies urged by Shultz.

These developments coincided with the Administration's particularly negative predisposition toward the Qadhdhafi regime. Soon after Reagan's inauguration in early 1981, his Secretary of State, Alexander Haig, sought to establish a new record of constancy and credibility in the Middle East. Libya appeared to provide an ideal testing ground: Qadhdhafi's behavior as well as his association with the Soviet Union caused him to be intensely disliked in the US. This meant that anti-Libyan action was not likely to result in excessive domestic criticism; and the limited extent of Moscow's commitment to Qadhdhafi meant that tough measures might be adopted without risking a confrontation with the Soviets. Libya was also relatively weak, hence a costly Libyan response also seemed unlikely. Finally, Qadhdhafi appeared to be relatively isolated in the Arab world, which diminished the possibility that actions against him might result in a negative all-Arab response.

In May 1981, the US closed its embassy in Tripoli, and in August of that year, in response to Libyan involvement in efforts to overthrow the Numayri regime in Sudan, the Administration moved an aircraft carrier to the northern outskirts of the Gulf of Sidra. An air battle took place, and two Libyan fighter aircraft were downed.[29] In December 1981-January 1982, Reagan claimed that Qadhdhafi had dispatched assassination squads to the US; the claim was never confirmed by substantive evidence.[30] In early August 1983, in response to Libya's military involvement in Chad, the Administration repositioned US navy units in proximity to the Libyan coast.[31] Two Libyan MiG-23s, having flown too close to the aircraft carrier *Eisenhower*, were chased off by navy fighters.[32] Thus Libya became a demonstration ground for America's willingness to back up its Middle East policy with the use of force.

Washington's propensity to confront Qadhdhafi, coupled with the Administration's belief that Libya had orchestrated the December 1985 terrorist attacks in the airports of Rome and Vienna, made a tough American response almost inevitable. On 7 January 1986, by Presidential Executive Order, the US banned virtually all economic activity with Libya.[33] The sanctions forced all US firms, including those engaged in the production of oil, to cease all transactions with and operations in Libya, and to leave the country.[34] Then, in late March, Sixth Fleet units moved southward into the Gulf of Sidra, formally challenging what the US considered an unacceptable claim by

Libya that its territorial waters included a 160 km-wide zone. On 24 March, Libya's air-defense units launched a number of long-range SA-5 missiles, as well as one SA-2 missile, against US fighters flying over the northern edges of the Gulf, and Libyan missile boats were dispatched in the direction of America's naval units. The US responded by bombing the SA-5 missile batteries and radar installations at the Ghurdabliya air base, and by sinking one Libyan missile boat and damaging another.[35]

The first US-Libyan military confrontation of 1986 did not result in enhanced American deterrence of Qadhdhafi-inspired terrorism. On the contrary, the US soon found itself compelled to address new evidence of such terrorism, this time aimed directly at American targets. On 4 April 1986, a bomb exploded in a West Berlin discotheque, "La Belle," a regular meeting place of American soldiers in the city. An American serviceman and a Turkish woman were killed, and 230 people, 79 of them Americans, were injured. US intelligence soon retrieved and deciphered messages sent from Tripoli to Libya's People's Bureau in East Berlin, ordering the attack. Once again, Qadhdhafi had tipped the scales within the Reagan Administration in favor of those advocating the use of force.[36]

Thus, on 10 April, Reagan was reported to have authorized military retaliation against Libya.[37] Not much room was left for surprise as the American media discussed possible targets for attack in great detail. On 14 April, the complex "Operation El Dorado Canyon" was implemented, involving 150 aircraft. Libyan airfields in Tripoli and Benghazi, the Sidi Bilal radar installations, and Qadhdhafi's headquarters in the *Bab al-'Aziziyya* barracks, were the targets of the combined US navy and air force attack.[38] The extent of America's displeasure with Qadhdhafi was reflected in the two public-opinion polls conducted after the operation: in contrast to their post-Vietnam reservations about the use of force, 71–76 per cent of the respondents expressed their approval of the attack.[39]

"Operation El Dorado Canyon" was the peak of America's anti-terrorism policy. Indeed, the attack established the policy's credibility: during the following months, Qadhdhafi would avoid being linked to acts of international terrorism. Indeed, the success of the operation allowed the Reagan Administration to apply its policy to a second target of its anti-terrorism policy: namely, Syria.

The above developments were accompanied by intense US diplomatic activity in Europe throughout the first half of 1986 to encourage its allies to adopt similar measures of their own *vis-à-vis* Libya and Syria. By midyear, these efforts had reached their peak: Britain's reaction to evidence of Syrian-orchestrated terrorism (see below), and supportive statements issued in other European capitals, indicated that Washington had at least been successful in creating wide opposition to terrorism. America's North Atlantic Treaty Organization (NATO) allies finally seemed persuaded that an uncompromising approach should be adopted toward such supporters of terrorism as Libya, Syria, and Iran. Moreover, Washington's conduct could now also be counted as successful in affecting the behavior of Libya and Syria: Libyan support of terrorism declined dramatically during the second half of 1986, and Syria made considerable efforts, at least at the declaratory level, to disassociate itself from international terrorism.

But these successes were only temporary. A series of events soon brought about a dramatic deterioration of America's anti-terrorism policy. The first negative development occurred in early October, when *The Washington Post* revealed that news reports circulated two months earlier, to the effect that Qadhdhafi was about to launch a new wave of terrorism, were the product of a "disinformation" campaign orchestrated by the National Security Council headed by John Poindexter. The purpose of the campaign had been to unnerve Qadhdhafi by having him believe that the US was about to launch a preemptive strike aginst him. This was reportedly done in the hope of enhancing the prospects of a coup against him.[40] The American news media, having discovered that they had been made a tool of the Administration's schemes, raised an uproar, and one result was the resignation of State Department spokesman Bernard Kalb. More important, the credibility of Washington's anti-terrorism policy was eroded: America's NATO allies could no longer be sure that information provided by the US regarding Libya's terrorist activities were not falsehoods distributed solely for the purpose of gaining their support.

Then, in late October, it was leaked that for over a year the Administration had been engaged in an arms-for-hostages trade with the Khomeyni regime. Within that framework, hundreds of *TOW* anti-tank missiles, as well as some *HAWK* anti-aircraft missiles, were delivered by Israel to Iran in late 1985. During 1986, additional anti-tank and anti-aircraft missiles, as well as spare parts for other weapons systems, were sent by the US to Iran.[41] Washington's newly revealed behavior, contradicting its stated general policy as well as the specific arms embargo it had imposed against Iran, shattered the credibility of its anti-terrorism policy. The political storm that developed in Washington underscored the policy's bankruptcy.[42] By the year's end, America's approach to combating terrorism had of necessity become increasingly defensive and apologetic.

Grave setbacks to its anti-terrorism effort notwithstanding, the US continued to exert continuous pressure on Qadhdhafi. In early December, Secretary of Defense Caspar Weinberger held extensive talks with the French Prime Minister Jacques Chirac and Defense Minister André Giraud, to coordinate attempts to beat back Libyan forces that had been occupying areas in northern Chad since 1983.[43] On 16 December, Reagan determined, under the terms of the Foreign Assistance Act, that "an unforeseen emergency situation exists" in northern Chad, requiring the delivery of up to $15m in military assistance to that country.[44] A few days later, US cargo planes were already airlifting weapons to the Chad armed forces in the north.[45] America's military assistance would contribute to Libya's defeat in Chad in 1987.

UNITED STATES-ISRAELI RELATIONS

A number of issues caused considerable strains in US-Israeli relations during 1986. Yet these strains did not significantly damage the general intimacy that characterized relations between the two countries, particularly since late 1983.

One source of difficulty was the Pollard affair. Following the arrest in November 1985 of Jonathan Jay Pollard, a young employee of US Naval Intelligence caught spying for Israel, the two Governments conducted extensive talks to defuse the situation. Having apologized for what they characterized as a "rogue operation," Israel's leaders announced the abolition of the intelligence unit responsible for the unauthorized operation. They also promised to return the documents stolen and to make the Israeli officials involved available for questioning. After these commitments were made, the terms of their implementation became the subject of prolonged negotiation and considerable tension between Washington and Jerusalem.

While Reagan and Shultz attempted to limit the damage caused by the affair, the agencies in charge of investigating and prosecuting such affairs, the Federal Bureau of Investigation and the US Attorney's Office, worked hard to convict Pollard and his wife, Ann Henderson Pollard. Their efforts, which included the use of documents returned by Israel in the framework of the post-arrest understanding, resulted in cooperation from Pollard. However, the information he provided exacerbated the tension: the American authorities described Israel's "candor" as less than total, and accused Jerusalem of trying to conceal key participants in the affair and of failing to return most of the stolen documents. Discussion of these points became an important part of US-Israeli relations throughout 1986.[46]

A second source of strain was Israel's development of the *Lavi* fighter jet. While Israel's production of a state-of-the-art combat aircraft continued to enjoy support in Congress, key elements of the Administration opposed the project for various reasons. Within the Department of State and the Department of Defense, officials were worried that the enormous costs entailed would leave insufficient funds for Israel's other defense requirements. They were further concerned that such deficits would compel Israel to request ever greater sums from the US, and that given the mood prevailing on Capitol Hill, Congress would respond affirmatively at the expense of other foreign aid programs, thereby jeopardizing America's policy in other key regions of the world. Secretary of State Shultz seemed to oppose the program on economic grounds; the budget deficits likely to be caused by excessive costs were bound to threaten the economic recovery program which Israel adopted in late 1985 and early 1986.[47] Secretary of Defense Weinberger based his opposition on both of the aforementioned grounds, but was probably also critical of financing the development and production of a foreign competitor to the products of America's aircraft industries.[48]

By 1986, the US-Israeli debate on the *Lavi* focused on comparing the costs of producing the Israeli plane with the costs of purchasing an American alternative. Meanwhile, an increasing number of Israelis, including ranking officers of the Israel Defense Forces, had become extremely critical of the project, and their reservations were used by the Pentagon in its arguments against the *Lavi*. Deputy Under-Secretary of Defense Dov Zackheim, who had conducted a number of studies of the *Lavi*'s expected cost, argued that the plane was far too expensive for Israel. An extremely unpleasant discussion took place between Weinberger and Defense Minister Rabin, during the latter's visit to Weinberger's office in early May 1986. There were also heated debates on the subject between Rabin and visiting delegations headed by Zackheim in early June 1986.[49] The *Lavi* debate continued on and off throughout the year.

Added to the Pollard and the *Lavi* issues were others that involved the transfer of sensitive technologies. In a number of instances in 1986, Israel was accused by the Justice Department and US customs officials of having violated American restrictions on technology transfers. Israel was said to have illegally purchased technologies for the production of cluster bombs and tank guns.[50] Israelis were also reportedly caught attempting to break into a high-tech company in Illinois.[51] Most of the accusations proved to be without foundation, but the media reports received considerable attention and damaged Israel's reputation in the US.

By the end of the year, with the revelation of the Iran arms deal, a new source of strain emerged: Israel's involvement in the affair. In this case Israel had merely responded to an appeal made by Reagan's National Security Council (NSC). But questions about the precise nature of Israel's involvement, and the extent to which Israelis encouraged their American counterparts to overcome their hesitations, were to remain open. More important, in cooperating with the relevant NSC officials, Israel had become a cosponsor of policies pursued against the wishes of its closest friends in the Administration, notably Shultz. Israel had also helped to circumvent the spirit, if not the letter, of laws passed by Congress, a critically important source of support. Such conduct could not but leave some of Israel's closest supporters in America puzzled.

And yet, despite these sources of strain, the US and Israel drew closer together in 1986. Economic and military aid was provided at the highest level ever of $3 bn. Israel eventually accecpted a $120m cut from this sum, but that was due to the automatic reductions imposed by the Gramm-Rudman deficit-reduction amendment, and had nothing to do with America's attitude toward Israel. During 1986, the US also provided Israel with $750m in additional emergency economic aid, and legislated another $3 bn aid package to be provided during fiscal year 1987. The US continued to be involved in efforts to ensure Israel's economic recovery: the joint US-Israel economic team, formed in 1985, met twice during 1986 to review the progress made.

Strategic cooperation between the two countries, which had reached to unprecedented dimensions since late 1983, remained extensive in 1986, despite a slight, temporary post-Pollard coolness at the beginning of the year. By the second half of 1986, such cooperation seemed to have reached new levels: the Administration and Congress gave both declaratory and legal expressions of their willingness to allow Israel many of the privileges provided to America's NATO allies and to declare Israel a major non-NATO ally.[52] Arrangements allowing reciprocal no-cost leasing of weapons and cooperation in the research and development of conventional weapons — particularly in the realm of anti-tactical-missile systems — were all legislated in the fall of 1986. On 6 May, an agreement outlining the framework of Israel's participation in the Strategic Defense Initiative (SDI) was signed by Weinberger and Rabin, and, on 5 November, the first major contract within that framework was signed by the US Department of Defense and the Israeli Defense Ministry.[53] On 30 July, the US and Israel concluded the framework for the construction of a Voice of America transmitter in Israel.[54] The 1987 Department of Defense budget, legislated in 1986, included for the first time a $64m appropriation for the construction in Israel of storage depots for the pre-positioning of ammunition.[55]

These developments amounted to the institutionalization of US-Israeli strategic cooperation, which was encouraged by Shultz, who said privately "that he felt so strongly about Israel's strategic importance" that he wanted to "build institutional arrangements so that... if there is a [future] Secretary of State who is not positive about Israel, he will not be able to overcome the bureaucratic relationship between Israel and the US that we have established."[56]

Moreover, the configuration of forces in the US seemed to promise Washington's continued positive predisposition toward Israel: the November 1986 elections resulted in an even more friendly Congress.[57] Positive sentiments continued to be expressed by the general public: a midyear *Washington Post*-ABC News poll found Americans more sympathetic to Israel than to the Arab nations by 62 per cent to 13 per cent.[58]

UNITED STATES-EGYPTIAN RELATIONS

Considerable tension characterized America's relations with Egypt in early 1986, following the October 1985 *Achille Lauro* affair. Egypt's decision to allow safe exit to the responsible Palestinian terrorists and to their leader, Abu al-'Abbas, was severely and extensively criticized. President Mubarak claimed that the release had occurred without his "knowledge and authorization," but there was information to the contrary. Concurrently, Egypt took strong exception to the interception by US navy fighters of the Egypt Air plane carrying the escaping terrorists. Although these events took place in late 1985, they affected the atmosphere of US-Egyptian relations in early 1986.

During the middle of the year, the US facilitated Egyptian and Israeli efforts to reach an agreement on the terms of arbitrating their dispute over Taba, a small strip of land south of Eilat. Ownership of this microterritory had not been settled prior to Israel's complete withdrawal from Sinai and had remained unresolved ever since. With and without America's mediation, Egyptian and Israeli officials had attempted since mid-1982 to agree on the modalities for arbitrating the dispute. Much of the discussion focused on formulating the questions the arbitrators were to be asked. When Vice President Bush visited Egypt and Israel in late July and early August, he and his staff attempted to resolve the procedural obstacles. However, their hope that an agreement on the terms of arbitration would be signed in the Vice President's presence did not come to fruition. More progress was achieved by Assistant Secretary Murphy during his early September visit to Cairo. Indeed, his talks facilitated the agreement that was later reached.[59]

Cairo's subsequent nomination of an Ambassador to Tel Aviv somewhat eased US-Egyptian tensions. Washington had been urging the normalization of Egyptian-Israeli relations since mid-1983. Egypt's compliance suppressed questions that had been previously raised in some Washington quarters, and particularly in Congress, regarding Cairo's commitment to peace. It paved the way for closer US relations with Egypt by reducing fears that the latter's strengthening might pose a future threat to Israel. America's ties with Egypt and Israel again became less mutually exclusive.

During the second half of 1986, much of the discourse between Washington and Cairo focused on the former's effort to ease the burden of Egypt's debt to the US. The Reagan Administration, fearing that the deterioration of Egypt's economy would result in a rise of Fundamentalism and the destabilization of the pro-Western regime, attached much importance to the effort. Egypt's yearly repayments were extremely high, due to the high fixed interest rates charged on the loans it took to finance its arms purchases. The rates were twice as high as those current in 1986. One way of easing Egypt's burden would have been to refinance its loans through the commercial banking system at the prevailing rates. However, due to Egypt's poor financial standing, commercial banks would not refinance its loans without a US guarantee of the loans. In turn, such a guarantee would have required a special congressional appropriation, which was unfeasible given the budgetary crunch in Washington throughout 1986. An alternative entertained by the Administration was to enable Egypt to repay its debt at the ongoing commercial rate, and to require that it pay the difference between the commercial rate and the original rates at the time of the loan's maturity.[60] Mubarak found that the plan would mean being presented with a prohibitively high bill in 10–15 years' time, and rejected it. At the end of 1986, Washington was still searching for ways to resolve the problem.

As the year came to a close, new strains in US-Egyptian relations developed. Allied with Iraq and concerned about the possible regional ramifications of any evidence of Iranian fundamentalist success, Cairo was shocked by the news about the sale of American arms to Khomeyni's regime. Such tension merely added to the long list of previous difficulties in US-Egypt relations. These difficulties evolved from Egypt's conduct in the *Achille Lauro* affair; from America's inability to meet Egypt's expectations in the economic spheres; and from Washington's continuing frustration over aspects of its strategic cooperation with Egypt, especially with the latter's reluctance — because it feared the domestic consequences — to provide the US with permanent facilities along the Red Sea. But these problems did not affect Washington's basically close ties with Cairo. Thus, in 1986, Congress passed legislation leading to the Administration's declaration, early in 1987, that Egypt was a major non-NATO ally.[61] This declaration not only institutionalized Egypt's elevated political standing in Washington, it also created new possibilities for future strategic cooperation.

THE UNITED STATES AND SYRIA

As noted earlier, much of US-Syrian relations were dominated in 1986 by the issue of Syria's involvement in, and support of, international terrorism. Nothing exemplifies this better than Reagan's late-April statement, following his use of force against Libya, that the US would also employ military measures against Syria should it have clear evidence linking it with terrorism against Americans.[62]

The Administration has maintained an open account with the Damascus regime since 1983. In America's eyes, President Hafiz al-Asad supported the Shi'ite Fundamentalists who launched the October 1983 attack on the Marines' barracks in Beirut, killing 241 US servicemen. Syria later refused to withdraw its forces from Lebanon, thus undermining the US-mediated May 1983 Israel-Lebanon accord. On 2 April 1986, a bomb exploded on a Trans-World Airlines flight from Athens. Four persons were killed in the operation executed by the Abu Nidal group headquartered in Damascus.[63] On 18 April 1986, Scotland Yard arrested Nizar Hindawi, a Palestinian who a day earlier had placed a bomb in the suitcase of his Irish girl friend, Ann Murphy, whom he had instructed to board an El Al plane for Tel Aviv at Heathrow Airport. Hindawi was arrested when he left a safehouse provided by the Syrian embassy in London. Reagan's statement was largely a reaction to Syria's reported attempt to blow up the El Al plane.

Yet America's approach toward Syria's involvement in international terrorism was based on a number of contradictory considerations. First, establishing a credible anti-terrorism policy required that the measures adopted against Libya be applied to other states involved in terrorism in order to avoid the appearance of being inconsistent. Second, the fact that Syria was a much more potent regional power meant that its ability to resist American measures was much greater. Syria's likely responses to these measures also meant that the costs of applying force would be much greater. Indeed, the unwillingness of Congress to withstand the costs of standing up to Syria were demonstrated during America's 1982–84 involvement in Lebanon. Third, Syria's potential role in the Middle East peace process, either positive or negative, required that ramifications on the process be taken into account when considering any anti-Syrian action. Fourth, Syria's denials of its role in international terror, unlike Qadhdhafi's explicit admissions, meant greater difficulties in mobilizing domestic support for anti-Syrian measures.

Hence, despite Reagan's April statement and much incoming information about Syria's role in a number of terrorist incidents, in late May Shultz was still saying that he did not want to "prejudge" the Damascus regime. He also refused to say how the US would respond once all the facts were known:

> These are investigations. There are several being conducted by different European governments and we are cooperating with the investigations. When the investigations are complete, we will, of course, be very interested to know what the results are. We don't want to prejudge the results. We want to go about this properly. However, we have the same attitude toward terrorism from whatever source it comes and we have tried to make this plain.[64]

The constraints on US action that arose from Syria's other roles in the Middle East were felt in mid-1986. Following increased tension in South Lebanon when Syria attempted to stabilize and entrench its military presence there, the US mediated between Jerusalem and Damascus to prevent escalation. Technically, the mediation included talks by US Ambassadors in Damascus and Tel Aviv with government officials in Israel and Syria, and at least one trip to Damascus by Assistant Secretary Murphy.[65] In mid-July, the Administration went so far as to contemplate a visit to Damascus by Bush. Such a visit was urged by King Husayn, reportedly in the hope that it would lead to reduced Syrian resistance to the Middle East peace process.[66] The visit did not take place, but the fact that it was seriously considered so soon after Reagan had threatened the use of military forces against Syria was indicative of Washington's dilemma.

The extent to which America's conflicting considerations, and developments in the international arena, forced constant changes in its attitude toward Asad's regime, was soon to be demonstrated. On 24 October, when a British court found Nizar Hindawi guilty and said Syria was directly responsible for the attempt to bomb the El Al airliner, the US followed Britain's example and broke off diplomatic relations with Syria, recalling Ambassador William L. Eagleton Jr from Damascus. Shultz now said that the available evidence showed "clearly and unambiguously...that the Government of Syria takes part in terrorism...When a country does that it isolates itself from the international community...I can promise you we are prepared to take [further] action. We want it to be action that works."[67]

Indeed, by mid-November, the Administration imposed a number of political and economic sanctions against Syria. This followed an earlier trip to Europe by the head of the State Department's anti-terrorism unit, Ambassador L. Paul Bremer, in an attempt to mobilize the NATO allies' support for such moves.[68] Like Britain, the US found little European support for joint steps, with Greece, Spain, Italy, and France particularly reluctant to antagonize Damascus.[69] But on 14 November, the Administration decided to go ahead and reduce the size of its embassy staff in Damascus; to bar high-level visits between US and Syrian officials; to further restrict its exports to Damascus, forbidding any export credits to Syria; and to terminate the air transport agreement between the two countries, forbidding the sale of tickets in the US for travel on Syrian Arab Airlines.[70] On 4 December, the State Department spokesman announced that the US would no longer issue visas on Syrian government service passports. These steps were taken following revelations that Syria had granted such passports to individuals who were subsequently found to have been involved in terrorist activities in Europe.[71]

THE PERSIAN GULF

America's approach to the Persian Gulf is traditionally affected by its ongoing interests in the area: ensuring free access to the oil producers and preventing the expansion of the military presence and political influence of the Soviets in the region. Following Khomeyni's revolution and the Iraqi-Iranian war, more specific objectives were added: the prevention of an escalation of the war and of a surge of Fundamentalism in the Gulf region at large. An early termination of the fighting and the prevention of an Iranian military victory thus became of prime interest to the US. Washington declared a position of neutrality in the Gulf war; pledged to pursue all possible means to end it honorably; embargoed the export of arms to both Iran and Iraq; and promised to stem the flow of arms to Iran from other countries as well.[72]

During the year under review, America's conduct in the Gulf region was affected by its alarm regarding Iran's military advances in the war and evidence of increased Soviet political presence in the Gulf states. An example of the latter was the Omani announcement in October 1985 concerning the planned establishment of diplomatic relations with the Soviet Union, soon to be followed by a similar move by the United Arab Emirates.[73]

In January 1986, the Iranian Navy detained and boarded the American cargo ship *President Taylor* for inspection. The ship was reportedly outside the Persian Gulf when the interception occurred. The Administration's reaction was relatively mild: while the White House announced "serious concern" about the incident, the State Department stated that there were circumstances under which inspection of neutral ships by a belligerent party was legitimate.[74]

In February, Iran achieved a major breakthrough in the war when it invaded Faw Island at the southern tip of the Shatt-al-'Arab, cutting off the commercial port of Basra — Iraq's second largest city — from the Persian Gulf. The battle of Faw reflected Iran's ability to throw large numbers of highly motivated soldiers into the war, and to exploit the marsh areas where Iraq found it difficult to fully utilize its tank-dominant land forces, superior air power, and advanced chemical capability.

Alarmed by these developments, the Administration sent Bush to the area, with the purpose of recommitting America to its regional allies' defense. Visiting Saudi Arabia, Bush stated: "The greatest danger now is that the war will spread beyond its current boundaries... that there might be an attempt to close the Straits of Hormuz or that Iran might break through Iraqi lines and attack neighboring countries, something it has threatened to do...The US is fundamentally, irrevocably committed to maintaining the free flow of oil through the Gulf." Bush further said that the earlier decision to deploy the Sixth Fleet in the Gulf of Sidra, and the resulting clashes with Qadhdhafi, demonstrated America's resolve to keep the navigation lanes open.[75]

America's options for dealing with threats in the Gulf were limited, however, by both regional and domestic constraints. While the Gulf states, including Saudi Arabia, continued to oppose a greater US military presence on their soil, Congress restricted the further sale of sophisticated arms to Saudi Arabia.[76] Only a month after the Vice President's visit to Riyadh, both Houses of Congress rejected a $354m missile sale to the Saudis.[77] In early June, the Senate approved by the narrowest possible margin a more limited $265m missile sale to Riyadh.[78]

Congressional opposition to the sale of arms to Iraq was so strong that the Administration refrained completely from proposing it. Instead, it limited itself to supplying Iraq with battlefield intelligence, particularly satellite data vital to its conduct of the war. In October and November, the head of the Central Intelligence Agency (CIA), William J. Casey, reportedly met with Iraqi intelligence officials to coordinate the intelligence exchange.[79]

By mid-November, Washington's Gulf policy had suffered an enormous blow with the revelations regarding its orchestration of the sale of arms to Iran. The sale contradicted everything the US seemed to be signaling to the Gulf region. A top Administration official admitted the problem immediately: "The Arabs and everyone else are demanding to know what our policy is... on sending arms to Iran... We've been so holier-than-thou on... not aiding Iran's war effort that we're going to have a tough time for a while explaining what happened."[80] Indeed, Iraq's Ambassador to Washington was quick to express his shock concerning the discrepancy between America's declared policy and actual conduct, as revealed in the arms affair. Thus, 1986 ended with US policy in the region raising "serious concern in Iraq and among its Arab allies, such as Egypt, Jordan, Saudi Arabia, Kuwait, and the rest of the Gulf states."[81]

UNITED STATES-SUDANESE RELATIONS

The considerable strains that developed in America's relations with Sudan in 1985 continued in early 1986. The US reacted to the severe famine in the Horn of Africa in 1985 by providing $500m of emergency aid to the countries of the Horn, including Sudan. During that year, Sudan was the largest African recipient of US aid: $450m of economic and military aid and famine relief.[82] However, following the April 1985 revolution that ended the rule of Ja'far al-Numayri, US-Sudanese relations deteriorated. The new regime strengthened ties with Libya and adopted a cool approach toward the US and Egypt, both associated with Numayri's rule. It also put on trial government officials who had participated in the US-orchestrated exodus of Jews from Ethiopia to Israel via Sudan.

Washington reacted to these events by cutting off all military assistance to Khartoum.[83] Nevertheless, the US continued to provide Sudan with economic aid; and it did this despite the fact that Sudan had lagged behind more than a year on repayments of its American debt.[84]

Relations with Sudan continued to deteriorate in early 1986: in March, an employee of the US embassy in Khartoum was shot; and in April, thousands of Sudanese demonstrated against the US following the attack on Libya. Washington reacted by evacuating some 300 Americans from Khartoum.[85] Paradoxically, other events in April actually laid the basis for improved US-Sudanese ties: the 1–2 April elections to the Sudanese Assembly resulted in the election as Prime Minister of *Umma* leader al-Sadiq al-Mahdi.[86] By October, Mahdi had traveled to Washington for talks with Reagan; and by year's end, Sudan had taken steps to distance itself from Libya. As a result, US financial aid to Sudan was restored, and US diplomats returned to Khartoum.[87]

SUMMARY

While America's relations with Sudan and Morocco improved during 1986, this was not the case with respect to Washington's ties with other regimes in the Middle East. The US-sponsored peace process appeared to be permanently stalled, following the failure of all efforts to convene a peace conference. The Administration's unwillingness to increase its involvement in the process, because of the risks and uncertainties entailed, left both King Husayn and then-Prime Minister Peres disappointed. Jordan continued to be dismayed by the refusal of Congress to allow the supply of sophisticated arms to Amman, while US relations with Israel suffered from the Pollard affair, the debate over the *Lavi*, and Irangate. Early in the year, Washington showed its disappointment over Egypt's refusal to return its Ambassador to Israel; later in the year, Cairo demonstrated increasing signs of dismay over the sale of American arms to Iran and over Washington's failure to help alleviate Egypt's economic difficulties. America's ties with Syria and Libya, while far from friendly when the year began, became increasingly confrontational — sometimes violently so — as the year proceeded.

And yet America's overall standing in the Middle East remained surprisingly unaffected by its difficulties and disappointments in 1986. One possible reason for this was the enduring effect of previous American gains in the region, the result of wise conduct in the 1970s. The gains resulted from America's willingness to employ a wide variety of foreign policy tools and to compete with the Soviet Union, rather than merely oppose its designs. Consequently, most Middle East states have come to depend on Washington's commitment to their defense, and/or willingness to provide them with economic and/or military aid. Moreover, although America's interests in the Middle East remained numerous and varied, thus guaranteeing inevitable contradictions, Washington demonstrated an impressive capacity for maneuver in the face of such contradictions. Consequently, it continued to enjoy close ties with Egypt, Israel, Saudi Arabia, Jordan, the Gulf states, and Morocco, as well as improved relations with Iraq and Sudan, while the Soviet Union's strongholds in the region remained restricted to Libya, Syria, and Yemen. Measuring its achievements by the extent to which Soviet influence in the region remained contained, the US could still see 1986 as a successful year for its diplomacy in the Middle East.

NOTES

For the place and frequency of publications cited here, and for the full name of the publication, news agency, radio station or monitoring service where an abbreviation is used, please see "List of Sources." Only in the case of more than one publication bearing the same name is the place of publication noted here.

1. "Reagan Says Conditions Right to Pursue Mideast Peace," transcript of Reagan and Husayn departure remarks, and questions and answers, official text, USIA, 30 May 1987; "US Voiced 'Difficulties' on Proposals by Hussein," *IHT*, 31 May 1985; "Shultz Says Palestinians Accept UN Resolutions," transcript of Shultz news conference, official text, USIA, 31 May 1985.
2. Oswald Johnston, "President's Middle East Plan Falters," *LAT*, 20 February 1983.
3. Xu Shan-Nan, "The Reagan Administration's Middle East Policy," *Survival*, May-June

1984; Robert G. Neumann, "Is the US Middle East Initiative Alive?" *Washington Quarterly*, Winter 1984.
4. Martin Indyk, "Ignoring the Real 'Jordan Option'," *The National Interest*, Fall 1985.
5. Wolf Blitzer, "With No Strings Attached," *JP*, 14 December 1984.
6. Charles W. Kegley, Jr and Eugene R. Wittkopf, "The Reagan Administration's World View," *Orbis*, Spring 1982; Samuel F. Wells, Jr, "A Question of Priorities: A Comparison of the Carter and Reagan Defense Programs," *Orbis*, Fall 1983.
7. Zbigniew Brzezinski, "The US-Soviet Relationship: Paradoxes and Prospects," *Strategic Review*, Spring 1987.
8. Shai Feldman, *US-Israeli Relations: The Reagan Administration's Second Term* (Tel Aviv University: The Jaffee Center for Strategic Studies, Memorandum No 14, March 1985).
9. "US Voices 'Difficulties' on Proposals by Hussein," *IHT*, 31 May 1985.
10. Bernard Gwertzman, "US Maneuvering Between Israelis, Arabs," *IHT*, 25 July 1985; Michael H. Armacost, "The US and the Middle East: A Partnership for the Future," address before the National Association of Arab-Americans on 4 May 1985. *DSB*, July 1985.
11. Don Oberdorfer, "US is Said to be More Favorable to International Mideast Conference," *IHT*, 20 December 1985.
12. Wolf Blitzer, "Murphy to Start Another ME Tour Soon," *JP*, 29 January 1986.
13. Wolf Blitzer, "Shultz: We Bent over Backwards for the PLO," *JP*, 5 March 1986.
14. Rony Shaked *et al*, "The US: Peres Knew of the Commitments made to Husayn," *Yedi'ot Aharonot*, 23 February 1986.
15. Oded Granot *et al*, "The American Administration 'Softening' its Statement on Inviting the PLO to an International Conference," *Ma'ariv*, 23 February 1986; Rony Shaked *et al*, "The US: Peres Knew of the Commitments made to Husayn." *Yedi'ot Aharonot*, 23 February 1986; Akiva Eldar, "Shamir will protest to the US on its Change of Position Regarding PLO Participation in the Conference," *Ha'aretz*, 24 February 1986; "Stuck on Dead Center in Mideast," *US News and World Report*, 10 March 1986.
16. Zvi Bar'el, "The US Agrees that the Palestinians' Self-Determination will be Legitimate," *Ha'aretz*, 11 February 1986.
17. "The US: The Palestinians Have Just Rights," *Yedi'ot Aharonot*, 11 February 1986; *Mideast Observer*, 15 February 1986.
18. Oded Granot and Shefi Gabai, "Murphy Will Try to Gain Husayn's Willingness to Enter into Negotiations with Israel," *Ma'ariv*, 28 January 1986.
19. *US News and World Report*, op cit.
20. William Beecher, "Stalemated on Mideast," *Boston Globe*, 5 September 1986.
21. Nicholas Horrock, "Bush Finds Mideast Peace Linked to US Aid," *Chicago Tribune*, 3 August 1986.
22. Gerald Boyd, "Bush Is in Jordan on a Peace Effort," *NYT*, 31 July 1986; William Beecher, "Stalemated on Mideast," *Boston Globe*, 5 September 1986.
23. Charles Mathias, "Mideast: The American Influence is Eroding," *WP*, 2 April 1986; John M. Goshko, "US and Israel Pledge to Pursue Peace in Mideast," *WP*, 16 September 1986.
24. See "Pathetic Little Package: A Nonpolicy for the Mideast Peace Process," *Newsweek*, 24 March 1986; James McCartney, "A Mideast Accord at Dead End," *Philadelphia Inquirer*, 10 June 1986; William Beecher, "Stalemated on Mideast," *Boston Globe*, 5 September 1986.
25. David Hoffman, "Bush's Hopes for Morocco Visit Dashed." *WP*, 29 July 1986; Gerald M. Boyd, "Bush Abandons Plans to Visit Morocco during Mideast Trip," *NYT*, 29 July 1986.
26. "'When Adversaries Meet," *Time*, 4 August 1986; John T. Haldane, "Back on the Road to Morocco?" *The Washington Report on Middle East Affairs*, 8 September 1986.
27. "Debating the Military Option," *Newsweek*, 10 December 1984.
28. Leslie H. Gelb, "Reagan's Foreign Policy: Shifting Aim," *NYT*, 26 October 1984.
29. "US Responded to 'Unprovoked Attack' by Libyan Planes," Weinberger press conference on Libyan incident, official text, USIA, 20 August 1981.
30. Philip Taubman, "Reagan Denies Overreaction by US to Report of Libyan Assassin Team," *NYT*, 18 December 1981; "Why Reagan Moved Against Libya's Qadhdhafi," *US News and World Report*, 21 December 1981; William Chapman, "FBI Chief Unhappy over Publicity about Libyan Death Squad," *WP*, 4 January 1982.

31. Rafi Man, "Two American Aircraft Carriers to Begin Maneuvers opposite Libyan Coast," *Ma'ariv*, 2 August 1983.
32. "US F-14s Chase Libyan Jets over Mediterranean," *IHT*, 4 August 1984.
33. "Transcript of President Reagan's News Conference," *WP*, 1 August 1986. In the press conference, Reagan stated: "The Rome and Vienna murders are only the latest in a series of brutal terrorist acts committed with Qadhdhafi's backing. Qadhdhafi and other Libyan officials have publicly admitted that the Libyan Government has abetted and supported the notorious Abu Nidal terrorist group which was directly responsible for the Rome and Vienna attacks."
34. "Economic Sanctions to Combat International Terrorism," *DSB*, October 1986, pp 27–31.
35. "US Fighters Strike Missile Site in Libya, Hit Two Vessels in Gulf," *IHT*, 25 March 1986; Wolf Blitzer, "US Naval Planes Sink Libyan Boat, Destroy Base," *JP*, 25 March 1986; Amir Oren, "Three in a Boat," *Davar*, 28 March 1986; Oded Granot, "US Expects Libyan Response to Destruction of Radar and Sinking of Missile Boat," *Ma'ariv*, 25 March 1986.
36. "Reagan Calls for Prosecution against Perpetrators of West Berlin Bombing," White House briefing, USIA, 5 April 1986.
37. Amir Oren, "President Reagan Approved Pentagon Plan for Controlled Retaliation Focused on Libya," *Davar*, 11 April 1986.
38. *Time*, 28 April 1986.
39. Barry Sussman, "76% of Americans Polled Back Bombing of Libya," *WP*, 30 April 1986.
40. Bernard Weinraub, "Reagan Confirms Secret Plan to Unnerve Gadhafi," *IHT*, 10 October 1986; Lou Cannon, "Disinformation Plan Damaged Credibility, White House Admits," *IHT*, 6 October 1986.
41. For details of the Iran arms deal, see *The Tower Commission Report*, (New York: *New York Times* and Bantam Books, 1987). For a concise summary of the arms affair, see "Arms and Hostages: Two Years of Secret Deals," *NYT*, 25 December 1986.
42. "The US and Iran," *Time*, 17 November 1986; Bernard Gwertzman, "Iran Affair Puts US on Defensive," *IHT*, 10 November 1986.
43. *Middle East Insider*, 8 December 1986.
44. David K. Shipler, "US Sending Chad $15m in Arms," *NYT*, 19 December 1986.
45. James Brooke, "US Weapons Begin to Reach Chad," *NYT*, 23 December 1986.
46. Joe Pichirallo and Don Oberdorfer, "US Presses Israel on Spy Case," *WP*, 31 May 1986; Warren Strobel, "Pollard Pleads Guilty to Espionage," *The Washington Times*, 5 June 1986.
47. "US Opposition Mounting," R. Jerusalem in Hebrew, 1 June 1986 — DR, 2 June 1986.
48. Oded Granot, "Weinberger: Better for Israel to Stop the *Lavi* Project and Absorb Criticism than to Continue to Waste Enormous Fund. US Freezes Approval of Contracts and Agreements for the Production of the *Lavi*," *Ma'ariv*, 23 May 1986.
49. "Rabin, Shamir Leave for Visits to the Americas," R. Jerusalem in English, 2 May 1986 — DR, 2 May 1986.
50. *Yedi'ot Aharonot*, 6 August 1986.
51. Richard L. Berke, "Company's Dispute with Israel Prompts Inquiry Over Secrets," *NYT*, 20 August 1986.
52. "Israel to Be Put on Par with NATO: Bush Set to Reveal Better Arms Terms," *JP*, 30 July 1986. The US officially named Israel as a major non-NATO ally in February 1987. See "Israel Named Major Non-NAT0 Ally," *Near East Report*, 16 February 1987.
53. Warren Strobel, "Israeli Participation in SDI Expected to Help Both Sides," *The Washington Times*, 30 May 1986; "US, Israel Agreement on SDI Research," *JP*, 6 November 1986.
54. Zvi Zarhia and Eitan Rabin, "Agreement on Construction of Voice of America Transmitter Initialled," *Ha'aretz*, 31 July 1986; see also Shmuel Meir, "Voice of America in the Arava," *Ha'aretz*, 13 August 1986.
55. Zvi Bar'el, "Oman Competing with Israel in Military Cooperation with US" *Ha'aretz*, 11 August 1986.
56. Charles R. Babcock, "US-Israeli Ties Stronger than Ever," *WP*, 5 August 1986.
57. Wolf Blitzer, "Capitol Hill is Even More Friendly Now," *JP*, 7 November 1986.
58. Charles R. Babcock, "US-Israeli Ties Stronger than Ever," *WP*, 5 August 1986.

59. *Yedi'ot Aharonot*, 3 August 1986; "US Offers Proposals On Dispute Over Taba," *IHT*, 9 September 1986.
60. "US Offers Proposals to Ease Egyptian Debt," *JP*, 25 December 1986; "US Working Out Deal to Bail Egypt out of Its Massive Military Sales Debt," *Defense Week*, 1 December 1986.
61. "Israel Named Major Non-NATO Ally," *Near East Report*, 16 February 1987.
62. Amir Oren, "The US Will Employ Military Means against Syria and Iran if It Is Proved that They Are Linked to Terrorism," *Davar*, 25 April 1986.
63. "Terror Suspect Rode Jet Before Blast, Police Say," *IHT*, 4 April 1986.
64. Bill Kritzberg, "US Opposes 'prejudging' Syrian Role in Bombings," *The Washington Times*, 22 May 1986.
65. David B. Ottaway, "US Serving as Mediator Between Israel and Syria," *WP*, 13 June 1986.
66. Gerald M. Boyd, "Bush May Visit Syria to Spur Peace Talks," *NYT*, 16 July 1986.
67. David B. Ottaway and John B. Goshko, "Shultz Says El Al Bombing Attempt Proves Syrian Role in Terrorism," *IHT*, 3 November 1986.
68. Bernard Weinraub, "US Mulls Sanctions against Syria," *NYT*, 28 October 1986; Wolf Blitzer, "US Weighs More Moves against Syria," *JP*, 28 October 1986.
69. "US Pressing for Europe Sanctions against Syria," *JP*, 30 October 1986.
70. Wolf Blitzer, "US Imposes Sanctions against Damascus," *JP*, 16 November 1986; John M. Goshko, "US Adds Sanctions against Syria," *WP*, 15 November 1986.
71. Amnon Dankner, "US to Stop Issuing Entry Visas on Syrian Service Passports," *Davar*, 5 December 1986.
72. Nizar Hamdoon, "For US Impartiality in the Gulf War," *IHT*, 19 November 1986.
73. Bill Kritzberg, "Oman's Fresh Ties with Soviets Underscore its Strategic Weight," *The Washington Times*, 7 November 1986; Robert E. Hunter, "US Influence Is Eroding in Persian Gulf," *Defense News*, 17 February 1986.
74. Oded Granot, "US Investigating Detention of its Ship by Iran," *Ma'ariv*, 14 January 1986.
75. Charles P. Wallace, "Bush Assures Saudis on Oil Traffic in Gulf," *LAT*, 8 April 1986.
76. James A. Russell, "US Lays Groundwork in the Persian Gulf," *Defense Week*, 22 September 1986.
77. David B. Ottaway, "Saudi Lobby Losing Strength," *WP*, 10 May 1986.
78. William E. Smith, "Plight of the Moderates," *Time*, 16 June 1986.
79. Bob Woodward, "CIA Is Said to Provide Satellite Data to Iraq," *IHT*, 16 December 1986.
80. Bernard Gwertzman, "Iran Affair Puts US on Defensive," *IHT*, 10 November 1986.
81. Nizar Hamdoon, "For US Impartiality in the Gulf War," *IHT*, 19 November 1986.
82. Sheila Rule, "In Sudan, Tide Turns Against the US," *NYT*, 29 April 1986.
83. SUNA English service, 30 March 1986 — SWB, 1 April 1986.
84. SUNA, 1 April 1986 — SWB, 3 April 1986.
85. Sheila Rule, ibid.
86. Gus Constantine, "Sudan Quickly Drifts out of Western Orbit," *The Washington Times*, 28 April 1986.
87. Patrick Tyler, "Sudan-US Relations Return to Normal," *IHT*, 8 December 1986.

The Soviet Union and the Middle East in 1986

ROBERT O. FREEDMAN

Nineteen eighty-six was a mixed year for the Soviet Union in the Middle East. It began with a number of crises facing the new Soviet leader, Mikhail Gorbachev, including a power struggle in the People's Democratic Republic of Yemen (PDRY), that led to the decimation of its Communist leadership, and an ongoing conflict between the US and Libya over Libyan support for international terrorism. As the year went on, however, the USSR's position improved, partly because the US-mediated peace process floundered after the split between Jordan's King Husayn and the Palestine Liberation Organization (PLO) leader Yasir 'Arafat, and partly because of the Iran-Contra scandal which was a major blow to the US position in the Middle East.

The year began with Gorbachev facing a number of problems. The first was a serious crisis between the US and Libya; the Reagan Administration blamed Libyan leader Mu'ammar al-Qadhdhafi for a series of terrorist acts, including attacks at the Rome and Vienna airports in December 1985 that killed 19 people (16 in Rome and three in Vienna). Exacerbating the problem for Moscow was the fact that just before the airport attacks, Moscow had sent SAM-5 missiles to Libya, and this appeared to encourage Qadhdhafi, who justified the attacks as part of the "holy struggle" of the Palestinians, and threatened to "declare war in the Middle East and in the Mediterranean zone" and "follow and harass Americans in their own streets, if there was American or Israeli retaliation for the airport attacks."[1] The dilemma posed to Moscow by this situation was that if a confrontation took place, Moscow would have to decide whether to back Libya and thereby risk a confrontation with the US. For Gorbachev, a month before the 27th Congress of the Communist Party of the Soviet Union (CPSU), this posed a very difficult choice. On the one hand, he was seeking to introduce a program of economic and political reform and a foreign policy aimed at easing world tension wherever possible. As part of this policy, Moscow was seeking major arms control agreements with the US as well as an overall improvement in bilateral US-Soviet relations. Clearly, a major confrontation over Libya would risk undermining Gorbachev's policy. However, not supporting Libya also had its risks. In 1982, when Israel invaded Lebanon, the USSR, led by Leonid Brezhnev, limited itself essentially to proforma protests to Israel during the invasion, and to the US when it deployed Marines in Beirut. In 1983, when the US and Syria came into open conflict over Lebanon, Moscow, then led by Yuri Andropov, also maintained a low profile. In both cases, Moscow lost credibility in the Arab world for not resisting the US actions. Thus the USSR again risked losing credibility among Arabs if it did not take action in a conflict between the US and Libya.

As the January crisis proceeded, Gorbachev chose to maintain a low profile. Following a proforma condemnation of US policy by the Soviet Afro-Asian People's

Solidarity Organization,[2] the Foreign Ministry spokesman, Vladimir Lomeiko, replying to a question at a press conference on 6 January on how the USSR would react to a US-Libyan confrontation, stressed that Soviet actions were aimed at preventing conflicts, not at constructing "scenarios of its actions for their escalation."[3] Meanwhile tension appeared to ease somewhat when Libya's Secretary for Foreign Affairs, 'Ali 'Abd al-Salam al-Turayki, condemned the airport attacks and denied Libyan involvement in them,[4] and President Reagan on 7 January decided to limit the US response to alleged Libyan involvement in the attacks to economic sanctions.[5] These measures included the freezing of all Libyan assets in the US and a ban on trade between the two countries, and were aimed at ending the participation of US oil firms in the Libyan economy.[6] Perhaps believing that the imposition of economic sanctions meant that the US would not use military force against Libya, Moscow sharpened its tone; an *Izvestiia* editorial on 8 January 1986, after citing a Libyan Foreign Ministry statement condemning terrorism, warned:

> The state of the international situation in the Mediterranean region is by no means a matter of indifference for the Soviet Union. And it is not just that the relations which exist between the USSR and Libya are of a close and lasting nature and are based on long-standing traditions and on the manifestation of profound liking and mutual respect between the Soviet and Libyan peoples. Our country's course toward this region is also determined by the fact that the USSR, as a Mediterranean power, has a vital interest in the preservation of peace in the Mediterranean basin. Our country proceeds from the conviction that in this particular region, just as anywhere on earth, all problems and all situations that are fraught with conflict must be overcome solely by peaceful means and solely by political means.
>
> The situation can still be controlled and still allows one to stop before the danger mark is passed. There is still time to curtail the military preparations, to renounce plans for inflicting strikes against Libya, and to rebuff Israel which is itching for adventures... The question is simply whether Washington will manage to make a definitive decision from positions of restraint, conscious of all its responsibility for the morrow.[7]

As the USSR was counseling restraint, and asserting that Libya opposed terrorism, it could only have been embarrassed by the remarks of Salim Huwaydi, Libyan Cultural Attaché to the USSR, who said at a Moscow press conference that Libya supported the attacks at the Rome and Vienna airports because they were "actions of a partisan war, committed by revolutionaries."[8] While claiming "we are not for terrorism, we are resolutely against it," Huwaydi stated "we are in support of the acts perpetrated in Rome and Vienna because we support the people's struggle...."

Meanwhile, as the January crisis unfolded, Moscow made limited military moves in the Mediterranean. It stationed a submarine tender in Tripoli harbor and established a picket line of ships north of the Gulf of Sidra, long an area of contention between Libya and the US, which does not recognize Libya's claims to sovereignty over the Gulf and which shot down two Libyan planes there in 1981.[9] At the minimum, these ships could provide advance warning to Libya in case of a US attack; Moscow may have also felt that the presence of a Soviet vessel in Tripoli harbor would deter such an attack. In any case, the January crisis ended without any US military action against

Libya, and Moscow could only have been happy about that. Nonetheless, there were a number of people in the US, including Secretary of State George Shultz, who were advocating tougher measures toward Libya, and some American columnists were beginning to wonder if Reagan, because of his unwillingness to use force, was becoming another Jimmy Carter.[10] Perhaps emboldened by the lack of US military action, Qadhdhafi on 15 January publicly pledged to train and equip Arab guerrillas for "terrorist and suicide" missions.[11] But Moscow could only have been concerned that a Libyan-American military confrontation remained a real possibility.

In mid-January, however, Soviet attention was diverted from the Libyan crisis to the PDRY where an internecine leadership clash threatened the existence of the pro-Soviet Party that ruled the country. For many years Moscow had endeavored to create a set of Marxist institutions for this backward State, which it hoped would become a model of Soviet-style Socialism. The crisis, however, was to reveal the thinness of the Marxist patina. Essentially, it involved a power struggle between PDRY President 'Ali Nasir Muhammad and the man he had deposed in February 1980, 'Abd al-Fattah Isma'il.[12] For reasons that are not yet fully clear, someone in the Soviet leadership permitted Isma'il, then in exile in the USSR, to return to Aden in March 1985, just as Gorbachev was taking power. Following major disagreements at the PDRY Party Congress in October 1985, when Muhammad saw his position weakened (Muhammad was in favor of improved ties with the PDRY's Arab neighbors, and of increasing private initiative, especially in agriculture),[13] the PDRY President evidently decided to eliminate Isma'il once and for all by taking steps to murder him and his supporters at a cabinet meeting on January 1986. While Isma'il was killed, along with 'Ali Antar, Vice-Chairman of the Government Presidium, Salih Muslih Qasim, the PDRY Defense Minister, and 'Ali Fadi, Chairman of the Party Control Commission, the fighting between factions loyal to Isma'il and Muhammad spread throughout the PDRY and Soviet advisers and dependents were hastily evacuated. Ultimately, a pro-Soviet official, the Prime Minister, Haydar al-'Attas, who was touring India at the time of the crisis, was installed by the USSR as President; and Soviet warnings against outside intervention and its own involvement in the fighting tipped the balance against Muhammad, who was forced into exile.[14] Nonetheless, while Moscow was able to regain control of the situation, the crisis had several negative consequences for the USSR. First, with at least 4,000 members of the Yemeni Communist Party killed,[15] and a very pronounced degree of tribalism evident in the Muhammad-Isma'il conflict, the Marxist structure of the PDRY, which Moscow was seeking to establish as a model for other Arab states, suffered a major blow. Second, the vaunted security infrastructure that Moscow provided the PDRY proved faulty as both the USSR and East Germany seemed to have been taken by surprise by the January events. (This was evident in Moscow's confused reporting at the start of the crisis.)[16] Finally, the ouster of 'Ali Nasir Muhammad, who had sought to improve the PDRY's relations with its conservative Arab neighbors, and his replacement by more hard-line elements served to slow Soviet efforts to improve relations with the conservative Arab states of the Gulf.

That the last factor was of considerable concern to Moscow was evident in its reporting of post-crisis meetings between Soviet and PDRY officials. Thus, when Moscow's Number Two leader, Yegor Ligachev, met the PDRY delegation to the 27th CPSU Congress, headed by 'Ali Salim al-Bayd, the new First Secretary of the

PDRY Communist Party in early March, *Pravda* emphasized that Moscow had reminded the PDRY leadership of the necessity "of continuing a peace-loving foreign policy and strengthening good neighbor relations with the countries of the region."[17] Similarly, when the new PDRY Prime Minister, Yasin Numan, visited Moscow in early June, *Pravda* emphasized his efforts "to develop and strengthen relations with Arab states and with neighboring countries of the region."[18] Finally, one month later, when Soviet Middle East trouble-shooter Karen Brutents, who had been promoted to deputy head of the International Department of the CPSU's Central Committee, visited Aden, *Pravda* cited the PDRY leaders as declaring their "steadfast desire to maintain and develop good relations with all countries of the region, including bordering states."[19] Moscow had cause for its concern. Only a few months before the crisis in the PDRY, Oman and the United Arab Emirates, both of which had been targeted for PDRY-supported guerrilla attacks in the past, established diplomatic relations with the Soviet Union,[20] and both states were now worried about the possibility of a more radical regime in Aden resuming its pressure. Such a development, particularly when Moscow had repeatedly pledged its support for the new PDRY regime, would most likely chill relations between the USSR and the two Gulf states. To be sure, in his first interview with Western reporters, the new PDRY President, al-'Attas, stated: "We will make our best efforts to consolidate our relations with our brothers in North Yemen, Saudi Arabia and the six states of the Gulf Cooperation Council."[21] Nonetheless, North Yemen, to which 'Ali Nasir Muhammad had fled, signaled its wariness about developments in the PDRY when, during a visit by Vice President George Bush in April, the North Yemeni President, 'Ali Abdallah Salih, told Bush his Government was eager to improve relations with the US.[22] The US position had already been strengthened as a result of a US company, Hunt Oil, finding oil in the impoverished country; and Bush, who was warmly applauded by crowds lining the streets (despite a US military confrontation with Libya two weeks earlier), promised Salih a $5m increase in economic aid and passed on an invitation from President Reagan for him to visit Washington.[23]

Although Moscow had ensured that a pro-Soviet regime would retain control in a country of great geopolitical importance to it (the PDRY serves as the base for Soviet reconnaissance flights over the Indian Ocean, provides the main facilities for resupply and repair of the Soviet Indian Ocean fleet, and has the most extensive port accessible to the Soviet Navy between Camranh Bay and the Black Sea),[24] the foreign-policy consequences of events in the PDRY presented potential problems for Moscow. While one could expect that reconstruction would be the main priority of the new PDRY regime in the immediate future, its neighbors were clearly suspicious of its future foreign policy and this very suspicion contained problems for Moscow.

While the January 1986 Libyan-American and PDRY crises posed problems for the Soviet Union, Moscow was to benefit from a subsequent Middle Eastern development, which took place on the eve of the CPSU Congress. On 19 February, about a month after meeting with US Assistant Secretary of State Richard Murphy in London, and following two weeks of negotiations with PLO leader Yasir 'Arafat in late January and early February, King Husayn of Jordan publicly broke with 'Arafat and thus ended their year-long joint peace effort. In a major speech giving his view of what had happened, Husayn first noted that he had obtained a major concession from the US by getting it to agree to have the PLO invited to an international peace conference on the Middle East, along with the Soviet Union and other permanent members of the Security Council, if the PLO clearly stated "on the public record that it had accepted [UN Security Council] Resolutions 242 and 338, is prepared to negotiate peace with Israel and has renounced terrorism."[25] The next day, State Department spokesman Charles E. Redman confirmed the accuracy of Husayn's remarks — a development that caused both surprise and consternation in Israel.[26] 'Arafat, however, according to Husayn, wanted the US to go further by publicly agreeing to the legitimate rights of the Palestinian people, including their right to self-determination within the context of a confederation between Jordan and Palestine. Husayn then reportedly told 'Arafat that "the subject of self-determination within the context of a confederation was a matter for the Jordanians and Palestinians and that no other party had anything to do with it," and intimated that such a response from the PLO indicated that the organization might be "dealing with us on a basis of lack of confidence."[27] Husayn was probably correct, given PLO suspicions that the King would try to dominate any Palestinian-Jordanian confederation. Husayn concluded his speech by stating that he was "unable to continue to coordinate politically with the PLO leadership until such time as their word becomes their bond, characterized by commitment, credibility and constancy."[28]

The split between Husayn and 'Arafat was welcome to Moscow for several reasons. In the first place it appeared to put a final stop to the US attempt to organize talks between a joint PLO-Jordanian delegation and Israel (a possibility that had concerned Moscow following the Husayn-'Arafat agreement of February 1985), although 'Arafat, despite considerable pressure from within al-Fath,[29] was not to confirm the formal break with Husayn until the Palestine National Council meeting of April 1987. Second, with the Jordanian option now apparently closed to 'Arafat, Moscow may well have felt that the PLO leader would move to reunify his organization and move closer to the pro-Soviet Palestine Democratic Alliance of George Habash's Popular Front for the Liberation of Palestine, Na'if Hawatima's Democratic Front for the Liberation of Palestine and the Palestine Communist Party, if not yet to the Syrian-controlled elements of the PLO. Indeed, with relations betwen the PLO and Husayn already chilling in the latter part of 1985, 'Arafat evidently decided to mend his fences with the Soviet Union and sent Faruq Qaddumi to Moscow in early January 1986, where he met with Soviet Foreign Minister Eduard Shevardnadze. However, *Pravda*'s description of the talks as having taken place in a "businesslike atmosphere" indicated considerable disagreement between the two sides, although they both called for Palestinian unity on an "anti-imperialist basis" and for an international conference on the Middle East with the participation "of all interested sides, including the PLO."[30] Three months later, Soviet Middle East specialist Vladimir Polyakov held meetings in Damascus with the Syrians and with Habash and Hawatima in another Soviet effort to encourage Palestinian unity.[31]

While on balance the break between Husayn and 'Arafat was a positive development for Moscow, the Soviets were still concerned that Husayn, despite the US Congress's opposition to selling him arms until he made peace with Israel, might make a separate deal with Israel (and, presumably be rewarded with arms afterwards, much as Egypt had been), something that was regularly rumored in the Press.[32] Husayn's subsequent closure of PLO offices in Jordan, his arrest of Jordanian Communists, and his effort to forge an alternative Palestinian leadership on the West Bank (with Israel's tacit cooperation) were all factors that appeared to incline him in this direction. Indeed, three days after his public break with 'Arafat, Husayn noted that while he would respect a decision by Palestinians to preserve the PLO as their "sole legitimate representative," he would also welcome another "apparatus" to express their wishes.[33] Nonetheless, the murder of the pro-Jordanian Mayor of Nablus, Zafir al-Masri, on 2 March 1986, illustrated Husayn's difficulties in creating an alternative Palestinian leadership on the West Bank. On balance, therefore, Gorbachev clearly gained from the split between Husayn and 'Arafat, and the Soviet leader could therefore enter the 27th Party Congress of the CPSU relieved that the American-orchestrated peace process appeared at a dead end.

At the Congress itself it seemed as if Gorbachev had almost completely lost interest in the Middle East. The main emphasis of his speech was on internal reform, and his foreign policy emphases were on Soviet-American, Soviet-European, and Soviet-Asian relations, in that order. He referred to the Middle East only as one of a number of "hotbeds of war,"[34] a clear contrast with Brezhnev's speeches at previous Party Congresses, where the ME received a great deal of attention and certain Arab countries, such as Syria, were singled out for praise. Gorbachev did, however, indicate a desire to withdraw Soviet troops from Afghanistan, and stated that it was in the USSR's interest to have good and peaceful relations with all the states that bordered it. While Gorbachev's statements may have been considered as gestures to China, they may also have been directed at Iran. Soviet-Iranian relations had been strained from the time of Ayatollah Ruhollah Khomeyni's takeover in 1979; Iran had strongly criticized Moscow's occupation of Afghanistan, and had aided the guerrilla forces there.

If Gorbachev had hoped that the break between Husayn and 'Arafat would mean a period of reduced concern for the USSR in the Middle East, the region soon reasserted its claim for the Soviet leader's attention. On 4 March, the official Libyan news agency JANA reported a call by the Libyan Parliament (the General People's Congress) for the formation of suicide squads "to wreck US-Zionist interests everywhere."[35] Two weeks later, the US announced it was planning to cross Qadhdhafi's so-called "line of death" at the top of the Gulf of Sidra in what was called a "freedom of navigation exercise."[36] On 25 March, a military confrontation, which the USSR most probably expected,[37] took place (it should be noted that Moscow, like the US, does not recognize Libyan claims to the Gulf of Sidra). Libyan SAM-5 missiles were fired from their base at Surt (Sidra) at American planes participating in the naval maneuvers in the Gulf.[38] The US responded by attacking the SAM-5 base and also hitting three Libyan patrol boats, two of which were destroyed. While the military action was a minor one (especially when compared with the US strike at Tripoli three weeks later), the USSR was nonetheless faced with the problem of how to respond, particularly since Soviet advisers had presumably been at the SAM-5 base that had been attacked.[39]

The initial Soviet response was given by Vladimir Lomeiko, the same Soviet Foreign Ministry spokesman who had publicly responded to the US-Libyan confrontation in January. Lomeiko was quoted as saying at a press conference that "the Soviet Union has provided moral and political support to the Libyan people and will take all measures it considers appropriate within the framework of existing treaties."[40] Given the fact that the USSR and Libya had no mutual defense treaty, or even a Treaty of Friendship and Cooperation such as Moscow had with Syria, Iraq and South Yemen, Lomeiko's remarks made it clear that Moscow would not come to Libya's aid. Lomeiko also refused to answer a question about possible Soviet casualties in the US air strike. A Tass statement was also low-key, noting only that "the piratical action against Libya sharply aggravates the already explosive situation in the region and could also have serious consequences beyond its borders"; that "the Soviet people express their solidarity with the Libyan people"; and that the Soviet Union "has been and remains on the side of Libya in its just struggle for freedom and independence. It condemns the aggressive US actions in the most resolute manner and demands that they be stopped."[41] Gorbachev himself, speaking at a dinner in honor of visiting Algerian President Chedli Benjedid, also condemned the US action as "a challenge to the world public"[42] and used the opportunity to call for the simultaneous withdrawal of the US and Soviet fleets from the Mediterranean — a proposal quickly rejected by the US[43] — and for a general conference on the Mediterranean, with adjoining states and the US and USSR participating.

While the USSR was low-key in its response to the US-Libyan military confrontation, Qadhdhafi was not. Speaking at a rally in Tripoli on 28 March, he warned that if the confrontation continued, Libya would strike at military bases in any country aiding the US Sixth Fleet, thus transforming the US-Libyan conflict into a Libyan-NATO confrontation.[44] Two weeks later, Qadhdhafi claimed that the USSR and Libya had an agreement to cooperate in times of conflicts, and noted that while he did not expect the USSR to aid Libya militarily if hostilities were limited to the Mediterranean, "if the war spreads widely, then naturally the Soviet Union will not stand by with its hands tied during a war involving a superpower."[45]

As this situation developed, the Soviet leadership could not have been pleased either with Qadhdhafi's efforts to expand the US-Libyan conflict into a Libyan-NATO confrontation, or by his efforts to enmesh the USSR in the conflict, something Radio Tripoli again tried to do on 12 April when it asserted that Libya might call on the USSR for assistance against growing pressure from the US.[46] With another summit with the US on the horizon (Shultz and Shevardnadze were due to meet in mid-May to prepare the groundwork for the summit),[47] Gorbachev certainly had no desire to be drawn into a conflict over Libya. A Soviet delegation headed by Konstantin Katushev, which left Tripoli on 14 April, may have delivered a message of caution from Gorbachev (in addition to investigating why the SAM-5s fired at the US planes were so ineffective).[48] Significantly, Soviet ships had been pulled out of Tripoli harbor in early April, possibly in anticipation of another US strike.[49]

Alleged Libyan aid to terrorists, who in early April bombed a West Berlin discotheque frequented by US soldiers, precipitated another US attack on Libya, which in turn presented another unpleasant choice for Moscow. The US air strike, which took place on 15 April, was far more extensive than the one in March. Targets attacked included a PLO training base, military barracks, and the military section of the International Airport in Tripoli, along with military barracks in Benghazi and the military portion of Benghazi Airport.[50] Moscow's response to this attack, while somewhat sharper than its response in March, remained primarily symbolic. Thus, in addition to denouncing the US at the United Nations, the USSR canceled the scheduled mid-May meeting of Shultz and Shevardnadze, although spokesman Lomeiko stated at a news conference that if the US stopped showing "contempt for international law and morality" it might be possible to set a new date for the meeting.[51] However, despite the new chill in Soviet-American relations, Moscow did not cancel the agreement resuming Moscow-Washington flights by Aeroflot and Pan American, and the first flight took place on schedule on 29 April.[52] Nor did Moscow cancel technical talks for the upgrading of the US-Soviet hotline, which took place a week after the 15 April attack.[53]

If the Soviet response to the raid was essentially symbolic, its rhetoric was more heated. Thus, a Soviet government statement on 16 April branded the attack "barbaric" and "piratical" and said that the USSR demanded an immediate end to it — "otherwise, the Soviet Union will be forced to draw more far-reaching conclusions."[54] Gorbachev followed up the government statement with a message to Qadhdhafi that was printed on page one of *Pravda* on 17 April.[55] In it the Soviet leader, after first noting Soviet efforts to "stave off the threatening development of events surrounding Libya," which included "repeated serious warnings" to the US, and expressing his solidarity with Qadhdhafi and the Libyan people, promised to "continue to fulfill the commitments it has made with respect to the further strengthening of Libya's defense capability." Gorbachev's reply did not promise any protection for Qadhdhafi against the US, and may well have disappointed the Libyan leader whose radio, in the aftermath of the US attack, had called on "the Socialist community, led by the USSR," to "shoulder its international responsibilities in an actual war waged by NATO against a small, neutral people."[56] Perhaps in an effort to obtain further Soviet support, Libya's Number Two leader, 'Abd al-Salam Jallud, told a press conference on 18 April that Libya was considering offering the Soviet Union military bases on its territory.[57] Moscow did not respond publicly to the Libyan gesture, although in claiming that five US planes had been shot down (instead of the one which the US admitted had been lost),[58] Moscow may have been trying to upgrade the reputation of its weaponry which had been called into question by Libya's ineffective response to the attacks of 25 March and 15 April.

In the aftermath of the two American raids, Moscow confronted a mixed balance sheet. On the one hand, the US raids were unpopular in Western Europe. Only British Prime Minister Margaret Thatcher had allowed US planes to use bases for the raid; France had refused to give the US permission to overfly its territory. Popular opinion in both Britain and West Germany opposed the attacks. US relations with France, Germany and Italy were clearly strained over what Reagan perceived as a lack of allied support for his anti-terrorist policy,[59] and although the NATO alliance increasingly imposed economic and diplomatic sanctions against Libya as country after country publicly linked Libya with terrorism,[60] strains remained, and Gorbachev may have seen this as a possible weakening of the NATO alliance. In the Arab world, however, Libya called in vain for assistance. Its pleas for a *jihad* and economic sanctions against the US went unanswered (there were public demonstrations only in Tunisia and Sudan), and the Arab League proved unable even to convene a summit meeting to deal with the American attack.[61] This development indicated just how much of a *persona non grata* Qadhdhafi had become to his fellow Arabs, and demonstrated that Moscow would be unable to exploit the attack to promote the kind of "anti-imperialist" Arab unity it had wanted for so long.

The lack of a substantive Soviet response to the American attacks reportedly strained Soviet-Libyan ties[62] and raised questions of Soviet credibility in the Arab world, although Libya was not linked to the USSR by a formal treaty. The problem for Moscow was that the US had used Libyan involvement in terrorism as a pretext for attacking it, and when another Arab country, Syria, much closer to Moscow than Libya, became heavily involved in a terrorist incident involving an El Al flight from Heathrow, there was the risk of either another American — or an Israeli-American — retaliatory strike. Indeed, following the second attack on Libya, Reagan said that if there was "irrefutable evidence" linking Syria or Iran to terrorism, the US should attack them.[63]

Even before the Heathrow incident on 17 April, which involved a plan to blow up an El Al plane, Syrian-Israeli relations had become very tense; by May, there were a number of press reports that war would break out between the two countries.[64] Contributing to the heightened tension were the Syrian decision to construct a series of artillery and tank emplacements near Israel's security zone in South Lebanon, and Israel's forcing down of a Libyan pane which contained high-ranking Syrian Ba'th Party officials (instead of the PLO terrorists Israel was seeking). The most serious incident, however, was the attempted bombing of the El Al plane by Nizar Hindawi, who was soon found to have close links with the Syrian embassy in London.

As tension rose, Moscow, which had been accused by the US both before and after the 15 April attack on Libya of not doing enough to stop terrorists infiltrating into Western Europe from East Berlin,[65] took action.

On 16 April, the day after the US attack on Libya, State Department spokesman Bernard Kalb had complained:

> On March 27, we advised Soviet officials here [in Washington] and in Berlin that we had evidence indicating Libya was planning actions against US interests and citizens in Berlin. We urged the Soviets and East Germans to restrain the Libyans. Had they done so, this entire cycle of events could have been avoided.[66]

One month after Kalb's complaint, the East German Government, almost certainly acting under Soviet prodding, gave assurances to the US that it would not permit any embassy operating in East Berlin to be used as a base for terrorist attacks.[67] Gorbachev himself sought to distance Moscow from terrorism — and to dissuade both Syria and Libya from employing it as state policy — during Moscow visits by 'Abd al-Salam Jallud of Libya and 'Abd al-Halim Khaddam, one of Syria's Vice Presidents and its former Foreign Minister, at the end of May.

According to Moscow Television, Gorbachev, while condemning the American attacks, warned Jallud:

> The US's moral-political defeat does not rule out further adventures, and that is why vigilance, firmness, and a high level of defense capability by states that might become the target of an Imperialist attack, a sense of principle and *consistency in condemning those pretexts that the Imperialists use in this regard, especially terrorism in any of its forms, are required.*[68] [Author's emphasis.]

Moscow's failure to agree to a Treaty of Friendship and Cooperation with Libya during the Jallud visit — something the Libyans continued to want badly — may also be seen as a cautionary factor.

As far as the Khaddam visit was concerned, it appeared as if the Syrian leader was repeating the Libyan ploy of claiming that the USSR had an obligation to protect it, by portraying Syria as a country that stood at the forefront of the battle against an American-Israeli alliance, which, according to Khaddam, "threatens not only Syria and the Arabs, but also the security of all progressive forces in the world, including the Soviet Union."[69] For their part, the Soviets were more cautious. President Andrei Gromyko, in his dinner speech welcoming Khaddam, merely expressed "effective solidarity" with Syria and Libya and pointedly noted: "In the the USSR, there is the conviction that if the Arabs succeed in ensuring unity in their ranks, it would be an effective weapon in resisting their enemies' intrigues."[70] This was a not-so-subtle commentary on the fact that Syria, because of its role in dividing the PLO and its aid for Iran in the Iraqi-Iranian war, was a major cause of disunity in the Arab world. Gromyko did, however, promise continued support for Syria, including the "strengthening of its defense capability." Nonetheless, perhaps because he was not sure how far Syria could depend on Soviet support, President Hafiz al-Asad made a number of tactical moves to strengthen his country's position following the terrorist incident in London. Thus, he hinted at a reconciliation with Iraq and a turning away from Iran (a ploy, it turned out, which seemed primarily aimed at getting Iran to resume shipments of cut-rate oil). He also publicly denounced terrorism, including the attacks at the Rome and Vienna airports, and declared that Syria was willing to cooperate in combating terrorism.[71] Unfortunately for Asad, however, the Italian Interior Minister on 24 June undermined the new Syrian anti-terrorist posture by claiming that he had "concrete evidence" that Syria was one of the sources of international terrorism.[72] Two days later, there was another abortive attack on an El Al plane, this time in Madrid, and again Syria was implicated as one of the suspects, Nassar Hasan Ali, was shown to be a member of the pro-Syrian Abu Musa Palestinian guerrilla organization and to be traveling on a false Syrian passport.[73] While Syria publicly condemned the attack, and Asad sought to deflect US and Israeli pressure by promising to continue his efforts to free American hostages in Lebanon,[74] Syrian-Israeli tension rose. The diplomatic situation further worsened for Syria — and for the USSR — on 14 July when British authorities directly implicated Syria in the abortive bombing of the Israeli airline in London in April.[75]

Under these circumstances, with a US-Syrian or Israeli-Syrian confrontation now a real possibility, Moscow moved to exercise some creative diplomacy in an apparent attempt to prevent a confrontation. It suddenly announced its willingness to hold public consular talks with Israel. This diplomatic ploy, Moscow may well have felt, would deter an Israeli attack on Syria, lest it harm a possible improvement in Soviet-Israeli relations, which in turn held out the possibility of an increase in the number of Soviet Jews being allowed to leave the USSR. Secondly, it agreed to reschedule the Shultz-Shevardnadze meeting, which had been postponed because of the US attack on Libya in April. Once again, such a move would presumably deter a US attack on Syria, Moscow's close ally, because the Reagan Administration had been pressing for another summit meeting with the USSR. At the same time, Moscow again began to call for an international conference on the Middle East, but one arranged by a preparatory meeting of the permanent members of the Security Council — a proposal that was rapidly endorsed by both Egypt and Jordan.

There were, however, a number of other factors that may have prompted Moscow into its 4 August announcements of both diplomatic moves. First, there were serious domestic problems confronting Gorbachev: the nuclear disaster at Chernobyl towards the end of April; the precipitous drop in world oil prices in the middle of 1986 (more than 60 per cent of Soviet hard currency earnings come from oil and natural gas sales);[76] Gorbachev's efforts to restructure the Soviet economy; and the major economic difficulties facing the USSR. All these factors moved the Soviet leader toward an arms control agreement that would prevent another expensive spiraling of the arms race and might lead to increased trade with the US.[77] For this reason Gorbachev sought a second summit with Reagan; and, given Moscow's tendency to overestimate Jewish influence in the US, the new Soviet leader may well have felt that the gesture toward Israel would help pave the way for the summit. Also, at the end of July, the Middle Eastern diplomatic situation took a sudden turn for the worse for Moscow as Israeli Prime Minister Shimon Peres and King Hasan of Morocco held a surprise summit in Morocco — a development hailed by the US as "a historic opportunity to further the cause of peace in the Middle East."[78] (The last surprise summit, Moscow may well have recalled, occurred during Anwar al-Sadat's visit to Jerusalem in November 1977, which led to the Camp David Accords less than a year later.) While no agreement was reached at the summit, a joint communiqué was issued which described the talks as "exploratory" and emphasized the Arab Fez Plan as the basis for an agreement.[79] Moscow had to be concerned, particularly since the summit coincided with a visit to the Middle East by Vice President Bush, one of several visits he made to the region in 1986. While Syria broke diplomatic relations with Morocco, no other Arab state took similar action, although Hasan did agree to resign as President of the Arab League because of the criticism he received from a number of Arab countries and the PLO.[80] An additional problem for Moscow caused by the summit was Hasan's decision to cancel his 1984 Federation Agreement with Libya because of Libyan criticism of his meeting with Peres as an "act of treason."[81] Moscow had hoped Qadhdhafi's links with Morocco would pull that country away from the US, but such a possibility seemed aborted after the dissolution of the agreement.

In sum, therefore, it would appear that Moscow, concerned both about the possibility of an unwanted war between Israel and Syria (or an American attack on Syria), and by the surprise Hasan-Peres summit, and preoccupied with domestic problems, once again decided to send a major signal to Israel by agreeing to public talks at the consular level.[82] The talks were the highest level formal bilateral negotiations between the two states since Moscow broke diplomatic ties with Israel in 1967; and the public nature of the discussions, which Moscow had agreed upon at Israeli urging,[83] served Israel's needs by striking a major blow at Arab efforts to isolate and delegitimize Israel, despite Soviet efforts to play down the significance of the meetings in its propaganda in the Arab world.[84] Nonetheless, the talks, which took place in Helsinki on 18 August, did not immediately produce the results either side said it wanted, although the symbolic significance of the meetings was probably much more important than their content. While the Soviets wished to send a team of officials to make an inventory of Soviet property (primarily owned by the Russian Orthodox Church) in Israel, the Israeli delegation, under heavy domestic pressure from such individuals as Moshe Arens and Anatoly Shcharansky (a prominent refusenik whom Moscow had released in February), raised the issue of Soviet Jewry at the talks, and the meeting ended after 90 minutes.[85] Nonetheless, the very fact that the talks had been held, that one month later Israeli Prime Minister Peres and Soviet

Foreign Minister Shevardnadze held detailed (and apparently cordial) negotiations at the UN,[86] and that there were subsequent meetings between the Soviet and Israeli Ambassadors to the US, indicated that the Soviet Union was keeping alive its contacts with Israel.

If the Helsinki meeting did not produce immediate results for Israel, a meeting between Prime Minister Peres and Egyptian President Husni Mubarak in Alexandria three weeks later proved considerably more successful. Despite a terrorist attack on the main synagogue in Istanbul, which killed 21 worshippers and may have been timed to disrupt the talks,[87] an agreement was reached to send the dispute over the Taba border area to arbitration; Mubarak agreed to return the Egyptian Ambassador to Israel (the Ambassador had been recalled following the 1982 Sabra and Shatila massacres); and the two countries agreed to set up a committee to prepare the ground for an international conference on the Middle East.[88] The summit ended a long chill in Israeli-Egyptian relations. And the fact that, following the summit, the small Arab League State of Djibouti restored diplomatic relations with Egypt,[89] constituted a blow to Moscow, which had long sought to isolate Egypt in the Arab world because of its participation in the Camp David Accords.[90] While Moscow remained interested in the convening of an international conference on the Middle East, it took strong exception, as *Pravda* noted on 14 September, to the agreement by Peres and Mubarak to create a committee "to determine who will attend the conference and what its prerogatives will be."[91] This was particularly irksome to Moscow because, in August, Egyptian Foreign Minister Butrus Butrus-Ghali had endorsed the Soviet plan for a preparatory conference committee comprising the permanent members of the Security Council.[92]

Nonetheless, despite its displeasure with Egypt, Moscow had been seeking to improve relations with it since 1981, when Sadat was assassinated. A group of senior Soviet government officials spent a week in Cairo in March, meeting with Mubarak on 24 March. The leader of the Soviet delegation, Pavel Gilashvili, Deputy Chairman of the Presidium of the USSR Supreme Soviet, was quoted as saying that the USSR was looking for new avenues of cooperation with Egypt and that Mubarak had "injected great optimism into bilateral cooperation and friendship between Egypt and the Soviet Union."[93] A *Pravda* article by Vladimir Belyakov in late April, while discussing Egypt's serious internal problems including the Security Forces' uprising of late February, noted the possibilities for future improvements in Soviet-Egyptian relations.[94] A concrete step was taken in early December when, after 12 days of talks with Egyptian officials, Victor Demenstev, head of the Soviet State Bank, stated that the USSR was willing to provide Egypt with additional time to repay its military debts.[95] (An agreement was to be reached on the debt issue in 1987.) The Demenstev visit was of particular value to Mubarak because two weeks later the US also offered Egypt a plan of military debt relief.[96]

On the negative side of Soviet-Egyptian relations in 1986 was Egypt's continuing close military and economic relationship with the US (despite Egypt's inability to obtain increased American economic aid), which was highlighted by the joint military exercise "Sea Wind" conducted in the Mediterranean near Libya, although north of the Gulf of Sidra, at the end of August.[97] Moscow, which had praised Egypt's unwillingness to undertake a joint attack with the US against Libya in April,[98] showed concern that the August exercises might have the same goal.[99] A second problem in

Egyptian-Soviet relations emerged in mid-December when an Egyptian Communist plot against Mubarak was revealed, and 44 members of the illegal party were arrested.[100]

If there was a slow but steady improvement in Soviet-Egyptian relations, the same can be said for Moscow's ties with Egypt's southern neighbor, Sudan. Following the ouster of Ja'far al-Numayri in April 1985, Sudan began to distance itself from both the US and Egypt, and drew closer to the USSR and Libya.[101] The process continued in 1986, as the newly elected Sudanese Prime Minister, al-Sadiq al-Mahdi, paid an official visit to Moscow. Burdened by an overwhelming debt and by an Ethiopian-assisted rebellion in Sudan's southern province which was adding to the country's economic woes, al-Mahdi clearly hoped that Moscow would pressure its Ethiopian ally to reduce its support of the Sudanese rebels.[102] If that was al-Mahdi's hope, it was not realized, and the joint communiqué described the talks as having taken place in a "spirit of friendship and mutual understanding,"[103] a sign of considerable disagreement. Nonetheless, al-Mahdi put a positive face on the visit and was quoted by Tass as stating that his visit was only an "opening page" in Soviet-Sudanese relations and that contacts would be continued because "the Soviet leadership had demonstrated a constructive approach to the restoration of Soviet-Sudanese relations and had showed the readiness to develop them on the basis of equality."[104]

As Soviet-Sudanese relations improved, Sudanese ties with its main economic benefactor, the US, continued to be severely strained. The US, unhappy at what it saw as the growing Libyan influence in Sudan, evacuated three-quarters of its embassy staff following the shooting of an embassy communications worker in the aftermath of the US bombing of Libya in April.[105] While most of the evacuated Americans had returned by the end of the year, reportedly because Sudan had expelled the Libyans associated with terrorism about whom the US had complained,[106] US-Sudanese relations remained strained. And this could only benefit Moscow, given its zero-sum game view of its Middle Eastern competition with the US.

While Moscow's primary attention in the Middle East in 1986 was concentrated in the western section of the region, the Iraqi-Iranian war continued to pose problems for Soviet policy because it diverted the attention of the Arab world from the Arab-Israeli conflict, isolated Moscow's major clients, Syria and Libya, who backed Iran in the war, and also contributed to the strengthening of the US position in the Gulf. Gorbachev sought to deal with this situation by seeking to improve ties with Iran, after a long period of Soviet-Iranian tension. Nonetheless, just as the Khomeyni regime was later shown to have exploited US efforts to improve ties during what became known as the Iran-Contra scandal,[107] so too did it appear to manipulate similar efforts by Moscow. Thus, in early February 1986, the USSR First Deputy Foreign Minister, Georgii Kornienko, visited Tehran, becoming the highest ranking Soviet official to visit the Iranian capital since the ouster of the Shah. When Kornienko obtained an agreement from Tehran to resume Aeroflot flights to Iran, and Iran's Foreign Minister accepted an invitation to visit Moscow, Gorbachev may well have felt he was making headway in improving the Soviet position in that country.[108] Indeed, following Kornienko's visit, the Speaker of the Iranian Parliament, 'Ali Akbar Hashemi Rafsanjani, was quoted at a news conference as saying that Soviet-Iranian relations were improving and Kornienko's visit "will have a great effect on our relations with the Soviet Union and the Eastern world. One can be optimistic in fields such as technical military, economic, and possibly political relations."[109] Less than a week after Kornienko's visit, however, Iran embarked on a major offensive in its war against Iraq and seized valuable terrain around the city of Faw.[110] It might well have occurred to Moscow that Tehran had exploited the Kornienko visit and the impression of an improvement in Soviet-Iranian relations to deter the USSR from increasing its aid to Iraq during the Iranian offensive, lest Moscow lose the increased influence in Iran it had (apparently) just obtained. If Moscow did not see the significance of the Iranian ploy in February, Iran was to repeat the maneuver later in the year. In June, Iran announced its agreement to the first meeting in six years of the Standing Commission on Iranian-Soviet Economic Cooperation,[111] and in August there were visits to Moscow by the Iranian Deputy Foreign Minister for Economic and International Affairs, and the Iranian Petroleum Minister (the latter stated that Iran was planning to resume natural gas sales to Moscow, something that Moscow had long sought, and also stated: "We can cooperate with the Soviet Union as part of our defense strategy").[112] Then, in December, Moscow agreed to return the technicians it had pulled out of Iran in 1985,[113] during a Tehran visit by Konstantin Katushev, Chairman of the Soviet Committee for Foreign Economic Relations.

Iran again appeared to exploit the improvement of ties with Moscow by launching a major attack on Iraq at the beginning of January 1987, less than two weeks after Katushev's departure. Yet the attacks on Iraq were not the only Iranian actions troubling Moscow. In September, Iran stopped two Soviet freighters in the Gulf, the *Pyotr Yemtsov* and the *Tutov*, and searched them before allowing them to continue — actions that drew a protest from the Soviet Foreign Ministry.[114] A second major irritant for Moscow, besides Iran's continued prosecution of the Gulf war and its unwillingness to accept Iraqi offers to settle it, was its aid to the Afghan guerrillas. While Moscow changed leaders in Afghanistan in 1986, replacing Babrak Karmal with Muhammad Najibullah, announced the withdrawal of six Soviet regiments in October and its readiness to withdraw the rest of its troops if external aid to the guerrillas ceased, and on 1 January 1987, offered a cease-fire and a general amnesty,[115] Iran did not appear to be impressed, and continued its aid to the Afghan insurgents.[116] By far the most serious issue of all, however, in Soviet-Iranian relations in 1986 was the revelation in early November that the US had been secretly selling arms to Iran. On the surface, the scandal was a major boon for the USSR. The Reagan Administration lost credibility both in the US and Western Europe, because its arms-for-hostages deal undermined the anti-terrorist policy Reagan had long been pursuing. Secondly, the Arab states of the Gulf, which had depended to a considerable degree on the US for protection against Iran, were seriously discomfited by the revelation that the US had been secretly courting Iran with the weapons that enabled it to wage its war against Iraq more effectively. Finally, not only did the Gulf Arabs lose confidence in the US, but to a considerable degree so too did Egypt and Jordan, nations on which the US depended for support in its Middle East peace efforts. On the other hand, however, the fact that the US was again shipping arms to Iran held out the possibility of a reconciliation between the two — something that Moscow had long feared and sought to prevent by improving its own position in Tehran.[117] As the crisis unfolded, Soviet propaganda tried to exploit it by claiming that the US arms deal was both a device for prolonging the war (from which, Moscow asserted, the US benefited) and for interfering in Iran's internal affairs.

As 1986 drew to a close, Moscow could look back on a mixed year as far as its Middle Eastern position was concerned. On the negative side, Syria, its closest ally, while not involved in a war with Israel or subject to an attack by the US, was bogged down in Lebanon and suffering diplomatic sanctions by the US and a number of West European countries.[118] Libya, an important client which had suffered two American military attacks because of its support of terrorism, remained isolated in the Arab world and had its position in Chad collapse because of its mishandling of the insurgency it had supported there.[119] Finally, not only had Moscow been unable to end the Gulf war, but it also found itself manipulated by the Iranians. On the plus side for Moscow was the split between Husayn and 'Arafat, which appeared to put a stop to the American-orchestrated peace process, and the Iran-Contra debacle, which struck a major blow to US credibility in the entire Middle East.

NOTES

For the place and frequency of publications cited here, and for the full name of the publication, news agency, radio station or monitoring service where an abbreviation is used, please see "List of Sources." Only in the case of more than one publication bearing the same name is the place of publication noted here.

1. For analyses of Qadhdhafi's speech, see the report by James M. Dorsey, *WP*, 2 January, and the Knight Rider News Service Report, *Baltimore Sun*, 2 January 1986.
2. *Izvestiia*, 5 January 1986.
3. Tass, in English, 6 January — DR, 7 January 1986.
4. *WP*, 4 January 1986.
5. Reagan announced the sanctions at a news conference. See *NYT*, 8 January 1986.
6. *WP*, 8 January 1986.
7. Translated in DR, 8 January 1986.
8. *WP*, 15 January, 1986.
9. *NYT*, 14 January; *WP*, 15 January 1986.
10. See, for example, *CSM*, 29 January; *NYT*, 15 January; and *WSJ*, 16 January 1986.
11. *WP*, 16 January 1986.
12. For solid analyses of the crisis see Mark N. Katz, "Civil Conflict in South Yemen," *Middle East Review*, Fall 1986, pp 7–13, and David Pollock, "Moscow and Aden: Coping with a Coup," *Problems of Communism*, May-June 1986, pp 50–70.
13. Moscow was later to criticize Muhammad for favoring private enterprise. See Vitaly Naumkin, "South Yemen after the January Tragedy," *New Times*, No 48, 1986, pp 28–29.
14. *Pravda*, on 31 January 1986, denied reports of Soviet intervention.
15. The new PDRY Government reported in early December 1986, that 4,230 members of the party had been killed and that there had been $115m in property damage. (AP report, *NYT*, 7 December 1986.)
16. As late as 24 January 1986, Pavel Demchenko, writing in *Pravda*, reflected considerable confusion in describing the events in the PDRY.
17. *Pravda*, 4 March 1986 (translated in *CDSP*, Vol 38, No 10, p 10).
18. *Pravda*, 5 June 1986 (*CDSP*, Vol 38, No 23, p 13).
19. *Pravda*, 23 July 1986 (*CDSP*, Vol 38, No 29, p 16).
20. Cf Robert O. Freedman, "Moscow and the Middle East in 1985," *MECS* 1984–85.
21. *NYT*, 1 February 1986.
22. *WP*, 2 April 1986.
23. Ibid.
24. For a description of the Soviet military presence in the PDRY, see *WP*, 22 January 1986.
25. For the text of Husayn's speech, see DR, 20 February 1986.
26. *WP*, 21 February 1986.

27. DR, 20 February 1986, p F-14.
28. Ibid, p F-16.
29. *NYT*, 8 March 1986.
30. *Pravda*, 8 January (*CDSP*, Vol 38, No 1, p 20).
31. *JP*, 3 April 1986.
32. *WP*, 25 January 1986.
33. *NYT*, 23 February 1986.
34. *Pravda*, 25 February 1986.
35. *WP*, 5 March 1986.
36. *WP*, 21 March 1986.
37. An article in *Krasnaia Zvezda*, 22 March 1986, virtually predicted a US attack.
38. *WP*, 26 March 1986.
39. As to whether the Soviets were warned in advance, White House Press Secretary Larry Speakes said only that the USSR had been briefed "at the onset of the freedom of navigation exercises." (*NYT*, 25 March 1986.) According to a report in the *NYT* on 14 April 1986, Soviet advisers had deliberately avoided the fighting by staying in underground bunkers.
40. *WP*, 26 March 1986.
41. *Pravda*, 26 March 1986 (*CDSP*, Vol 38, No 12, p 28).
42. Tass report 26 March — DR:SU, 27 March 1986.
43. *WP*, 27 March 1986.
44. *NYT*, 29 March 1986.
45. *NYT*, 10 April 1986.
46. *NYT*, 13 April 1986.
47. *CSM*, 9 April 1986.
48. *WP*, 17 April 1986.
49. *WP*, 15 April 1987.
50. *NYT*, 18 April 1986.
51. *NYT*, 17 April 1986.
52. *NYT*, 29 April 1986. Aeroflot service to the US had been terminated by Reagan because of the imposition of martial law in Poland in 1981.
53. *WP*, 27 April 1986.
54. *Pravda*, 16 April 1986 (*CDSP*, Vol 38, No 15, pp 2–3).
55. *Pravda*, 17 April 1986 (*CDSP*, Vol 38, No 15, p 4).
56. *Baltimore Sun*, 17 April 1986.
57. *WP*, 19 April 1986.
58. *WP*, 23 April 1986. One should not rule out the possibility that had Qadhdhafi been killed in the US attack, a Libyan leader willing to grant Moscow bases and to be more circumspect in his foreign policy behavior might have succeeded him — a net benefit to the USSR.
59. For an analysis of the allied reaction, see *NYT*, 25 April 1987.
60. *NYT*, 13 May 1986.
61. *WP*, 3 May 1986.
62. *NYT*, 6 May 1986.
63. *NYT*, 24 April 1986.
64. *WP*, 15 May; *CSM*, 19 May; *NYT*, 19 May 1986. For a Soviet view, see *Pravda*, 15 May 1986.
65. *NYT*, 12 April 1986.
66. *WP*, 17 April 1986.
67. *WP*, 17 May 1986.
68. Moscow TV, in Russian, 27 May — DR:SU, 28 May 1986.
69. Moscow International Service in Arabic, 28 May — DR:SU, 29 May 1986.
    Syria had used this ploy in 1983 as well, during its prolonged confrontation with the US in Lebanon (see Robert O. Freedman, "Moscow and the Middle East in 1983," *MECS* 1982–83).
70. Moscow International Service in Russian, 28 May — DR:SU, 29 May 1986.
71. *JP*, 29 May 1986.
72. *NYT*, 25 June 1986.

73. *WP*, 28 June 1986.
74. *NYT*, 1 July 1986.
75. *WP*, 15 July 1986.
76. By April 1986 the price of oil had fallen to $12.40 a barrel, less than half of what it had been in January. Cf *NYT*, 9 April, 31 March 1986, and Allan Kroncher, "Oil Prices and the Soviet Economy," *Radio Liberty Research Report* No 298/86, 7 August 1986.
77. On 23 March 1986, the American Committee on East-West Accord had called for a relaxation of the trade restrictions imposed on the USSR (*NYT*, 24 March 1986).
78. *WP*, 23 July 1986.
79. The text of the communiqué is found in *NYT*, 25 July 1986. For the negative Soviet reaction to the summit, see *Izvestiia*, 26 July 1986, which condemned Israeli efforts to drive a wedge between the Arab countries.
80. For an analysis of the King's actions, see *WP*, 5 August 1986.
81. *WP*, 30 August 1986.
82. For a description of the events leading up to the talks, see *JP*, 5 August 1986.
83. Moscow, in raising the idea of the talks in the early spring, had insisted that they be private (interview with Israeli consular official, New York City, 29 August 1986). It would appear that the Soviet concern with the possibility of an Israeli-Syrian war induced Gorbachev to agree to public talks.
84. Cf *Izvestiia*, 13 August and *NYT*, 18 August 1986.
85. For the Soviet view of the talks, see the Tass report, in English, 19 August 1986 (DR:SU, 20 August 1986). For the Israeli view, see Helsinki Domestic Service, in Finnish, 18 August 1986 (DR, 19 August 1986 and R. IDF, 18 August — DR, 19 August 1986). One result of Shcharansky's coming to Israel was to raise the political stature of the Soviet Jewry movement, which now had such important politicians as Moshe Arens on its side. Hitherto, the main Knesset activists were fringe politicians, such as *Tehiya's* Geula Cohen.
86. See the report by Bernard Gwertzman, *NYT*, 23 September 1986. In his UN speech, Shevardnadze noted that Israel owed its existence "to, among others, the Soviet Union," and also reiterated Moscow's call for a preparatory committee "set up within the framework of the Security Council" to do the necessary work for convening an international conference on the Middle East. Moscow's report of the meeting is found in *Pravda*, 23 September 1986.
87. *CSM*, 9 September 1986.
88. *WP*, 13 September 1986. The joint communiqué was published in the *NYT*, 13 September 1986.
89. *JP*, *NYT*, 1 October 1986.
90. For a Soviet view of the meeting, see *Pravda*, 14 September 1986.
91. Ibid.
92. *JP*, 12 August 1986.
93. AP report, 24 March 1986, cited in *Radio Liberty Research Report* No 144/86, 28 March 1986.
94. *Pravda*, 28 April 1986.
95. *JP*, 9 December 1986.
96. *WP*, 24 December 1986. The US proposal would allow Egypt to postpone paying as much as $3 bn in interest until the year 2009.
97. For a description of the joint exercise, see *WP*, 24 August 1986.
98. The alleged attack plan is discussed in *WP*, 2 April 1986. For the Soviet praise of Egypt's rejection of it, see *Pravda*, 1 April 1986.
99. *Izvestiia*, 27 August 1986. Moscow was especially sensitive at this time because the US was in the midst of a major (if somewhat confused) disinformation campaign against Libya. (See *CSM*, 31 October 1986.)
100. *NYT*, 17 December 1986.
101. See Robert O. Freedman, "Moscow and the Middle East in 1985," *MECS* 1984–85.
102. For a background report on Soviet-Sudanese relations at this time, see Daniel Abele, *Radio Liberty Research Report* No 395/86, 20 October 1986.
103. *Pravda*, 18 August 1986.
104. Tass, 16 August 1986.
105. *WP*, 6 July 1986.

106. *WP*, 2 December 1986.
107. See *The Tower Commission Report* (New York: *NYT*, 1987), especially pp 36–39.
108. *WP*, 5 February 1986.
109. *NYT*, 10 February 1986.
110. AP report, *NYT*, 11 February 1986. For a Soviet view deploring the Iranian attack and urging a speedy end to the war, see *Pravda*, 14 February 1986.
111. For a survey of Soviet-Iranian interactions in 1986, see Bohdan Nahaylo, *Radio Liberty Research Report* No 47/87, 3 February 1987.
112. *JP*, 19 August 1986. See also the report in *WSJ*, 26 August 1986. Clearly, Iran also had its own interest in resuming natural gas sales, not least of which was the desire for hard currency to prosecute the war.
113. *WP*, 13 December 1986.
114. *WP*, 5 September 1986.
115. For an overview of Gorbachev's efforts to end the Afghan war in 1986, see Bohdan Nahaylo, *Radio Liberty Research Report* No 16/87, 11 January 1987.
116. *Izvestiia*, 2 December 1986, for a strong Soviet critique of "flagrant interference" by Iran in Afghanistan's internal affairs. The article claimed more than 60 attacks into Afghanistan by Iranian air and ground forces.
117. For a background analysis of Soviet policy toward Khomeyni's Iran, see Robert O. Freedman, "Soviet Policy toward the Persian Gulf from the Outbreak of the Iran-Iraq War to the Death of Konstantin Chernenko," in William J. Olson (ed), *US Strategic Interests in the Gulf Region*, (Carlisle, Pennsylvania: US Army War College, 1986), pp 43–80.
118. For the Soviet reaction to this unwelcome development, see *Pravda* editorial on 7 December 1986.
119. For Moscow's view of this development, see "Chad: Renewed Fighting," *New Times*, No 52, 1986, pp 12–13.

ARAB-ISRAELI RELATIONS

The Middle East Peace Process in 1986

MORDECHAI GAZIT

In 1985 the US continued its efforts to bring about negotiations on the unresolved portions of the Arab-Israel dispute. These efforts assumed a hectic pace at the start of 1986. At the end of January it almost seemed that a breakthrough was imminent and that an international conference, where serious bargaining would take place, was in the offing. However, in February 1986 the rupture occurred between King Husayn of Jordan and Yasir 'Arafat, Chairman of the Palestine Liberation Organization (PLO). This made it plain once more that procedural devices like the Amman Accord of February 1985 between Jordan and the PLO, even if they did result in a spurt of diplomatic activity, were bound to fail sooner or later as long as they were not accompanied by some real changes in the substantive positions of the parties.

Indeed, already at the end of 1985 it was more than doubtful whether the optimistic assertions of Israeli Prime Minister Shimon Peres and US Secretary of State George Shultz would be confirmed. Their assumption was that King Husayn was prepared to negotiate without receiving a promise as to what the outcome would be (see *Middle East Contemporary Survey* [*MECS*], 1984–85, p 60). With this state of affairs in 1985, it seemed unlikely that 1986 would be a better year for the peace efforts, yet it was not altogether a barren one. Three occurrences deserve mention: the well-publicized meeting of the Prime Minister of Israel and King Hasan of Morocco at Ifrane (22–23 July 1986); the Alexandria Summit (11–12 September 1986), when President Husni Mubarak of Egypt and Prime Minister Peres signaled the opening of the much-delayed Taba arbitration talks agreement and proclaimed 1987 a year of negotiations for peace; and Jordan's intensified involvement on the West Bank and the Gaza Strip, a development openly welcomed by Israel.

The US Assistant Secretary of State for Near Eastern and South Asian Affairs, Ambassador Richard Murphy, paid fewer visits to the region in 1986. The reduced pace, however, was not to be regretted if it meant that US diplomats had come to realize that it was pointless to go the rounds of Middle Eastern capitals in quest of a settlement based on territorial compromise. By then it had become obvious that it was unrealistic to think that any Israeli government, even one not paralyzed by a coalition of Labor and Likud, could negotiate an agreement on the exchange of territory for peace. It was not likely either that Jordan and the Palestinians were ready to consider a settlement on the basis of less than total withdrawal.

It must be taken for granted that US diplomats were perspicacious enough not to concentrate their efforts on this unobtainable goal. Thus when they did exert themselves, albeit at the slower pace imposed by the unfavorable conditions, they did so to avert total diplomatic disengagement. According to a new school of thought on conflict resolution, a complete cessation of all diplomatic efforts would have been positively harmful. This school held that diplomatic effort should not be relinquished merely because negotiations between parties did not materialize. Negotiations should not be expected too quickly; they would result from a patiently nurtured process. Harold Saunders, a former US Assistant Secretary of State for Near Eastern and South Asian Affairs (1978–81), had probably been the foremost exponent of this new diplomatic school of thought. Undeterred by the widening gap between the Arab and Israeli positions, he rejected the traditional line of thought that the US should not offer mediation until the parties were ready to negotiate. He favored almost continuous US diplomatic involvement. He affirmed that this was possible by departing from the narrower, traditional framework of diplomacy in favor of a "peace process" encompassing "a political process to set the stage for bringing governments closer to resolving problems between them...a continuing series of complex interactions between the parties and not just a game of chess where one would make a move and the other will react and so on sequentially."[1]

Others seemed to adopt Saunders' thinking. Ambassador Murphy referred on many occasions to "incremental progress" and "undramatic progress," stressing that he "did not predict any sudden breakthrough in the near future,"[2] when he described the US effort in recent years. One White House spokesman referred to the Hasan-Peres meeting as "part of a continuum of the evolving situation in the Arab-Israeli peace process."[3] Husayn and Mubarak were willing partners in the process, and Peres was ready to cooperate with both Americans and Arabs to advance it. After Peres' meeting with President Reagan in September 1986, the White House Press Secretary approvingly quoted the Israeli Prime Minister: "The peace process is part of peace itself. You can't distinguish between them."[4] Peres remained a firm believer in diplomacy always on the move, kindling hopes that sooner or later some real progress would occur. Without an ongoing peace process, despondency could set in and the region would be that much more likely to slide towards war. Diplomatic perpetual motion — even when there was no movement — had the advantage of keeping channels of communication open. Direct or indirect, open lines to the other side could reduce tensions and perhaps help find a crack in the wall of suspicion (see section on Israel in this chapter).

This new "process approach" was not, however, universally applauded. Former US Secretary of State Henry Kissinger warned: "In the Middle East, in my view, when you start something like a peace process, you have to succeed; you're held responsible for achieving your objectives. That is why I'm not in favor of processes unless you know what you want."[5] Kissinger's objections to the "process approach" made sense as long as US diplomacy was thought to be operating exclusively in pursuit of the unattainable territory-for-peace swap. An exchange of this kind and the instruments for its execution — an international conference, preceded perhaps by a preparatory committee with all the parties concerned participating — would certainly necessitate a tremendous outlay of US diplomatic energy with no prospect at all of success. One writer, Richard N. Haas, elaborated this point.[6] He pondered the advantages of the US being active diplomatically so as to "garner some credit round the world," even if there was a near certainty of failure. Weighing the pros and cons, however, he noted that these tactics would have undesirable effects both on Israelis and Arabs. Israelis who favor annexation of the occupied territories would be emboldened to take such steps to increase Israeli settlement on the West Bank. With increasing frustration the Arabs would observe the energetic comings and goings of US diplomats who failed to deliver the territories according to plan as they were supposed to do. Haas concluded that the US had little to gain from actively championing the territory-for-peace formula. Like Kissinger before him, however, Haas did not specify whether he would also object to American mediation if it set its sights lower, aimed at nothing more than the resolution of procedural questions. This was in fact all that US diplomacy had been trying to do since 1985.

In the natural course of events, however, the question of procedure would one day be settled successfully. This would lead to meetings where substance would be discussed with little certainty of reaching agreement. US diplomats were perfectly well aware of this, but it was no reason not to go on being available to the parties. If Jordan and Egypt continued to insist on a comprehensive settlement to be negotiated at an international conference and Israel did not even demur, for fear of losing Jordan as a partner in peacemaking, how could the US refuse to play its part? The US also kept up a modicum of diplomatic activity because it wanted to prevent anyone else, whether it be the Soviet Union or even the Europeans, from trying to fill the void that would be created if the US absented itself from the scene.

There was no change in 1986 in the basic positions of the key players in the region; Israel, Jordan, the Palestinians, Egypt and Syria.

In Israel, Yitzhak Shamir took over the Premiership from Peres in October. The accepted opinion was that with the Likud at the helm, the Israeli attitude would harden. However, with the National Unity Government committed to agreed policies, it could be argued that changes of personalities might affect style but not substance. Though reduced to the rank of Acting Prime Minister and Foreign Minister, Peres would insist on influencing major policy decisions. Furthermore, the peace process was "a continuum over a long period of time," as the US White House spokesman had affirmed. This was the most persuasive argument as to why it made little difference whether Peres or Shamir headed the Government. In a situation like this, Shamir could be counted on to be cooperative to the extent that none of his beliefs or principles were at stake.

Throughout 1986, Jordan remained immovably determined not to act as a surrogate either for the Palestinians or the PLO. It rejected 'Arafat as an *interlocuteur valable*, and would not claim that it wished to or was able to represent the Palestinians. Jordan maintained that the Palestinians themselves must decide which organization would speak for them. In adopting this position, Jordan remained faithful to the Rabat Conference decision of 1974, and also carried it to its logical conclusion. King Husayn explained to the Americans that it was out of the question for him to be the one to accept the final partition of Palestine between Israel and the Arabs, for this would "require telling two million Palestinian exiles that they [would] never be able to go back to their homes, which [were] now in Israel."[7] By using the phrase, "the final partition of Palestine," Husayn implied that at least three essential decisions were involved which not he, but the Palestinians would have to take. One was the acceptance of Israel as a permanent neighbor, the second was the question of exactly where the border would be drawn between Israel and the Jordanian-Palestinian Confederation, and finally the most difficult question, that of the Arab part of Jerusalem.

For the Palestinians, 1986 was another year of frustration and suffering. The PLO remained deeply divided. Although the break with King Husayn was brought about by 'Arafat's unyielding position on Palestinian self-determination, this did not make him any more acceptable to his opponents, especially those under Syrian patronage. For these pro-Syrian factions, the Amman Agreement was still an anathema. They suspected the agreement was a device to start negotiations in which the US would be the prime mover. So it was not enough that 'Arafat had suspended it; they demanded that it be abrogated. Although the talks would have been held within the framework of an international conference with Soviet representation, the pro-Syrian factions were convinced that the interests of the Palestinians would be sacrificed and that the outcome of the negotiations would serve US, Israeli and Jordanian interests only.

It was inevitable that a rift would develop between Husayn and 'Arafat when the latter refused to accept UN Security Council (UNSC) Resolution No 242 unconditionally. 'Arafat insisted on a prior US assurance of support for Palestinian self-determination. The Jordanians argued that self-determination was an internal Jordanian-Palestinian issue that would be settled between Jordan and the PLO as soon as the West Bank and the Gaza Strip were returned to the Arabs. It did not concern third parties. 'Arafat, however, could not be dissuaded from pressing the self-determination issue, not even in the context of the procedural talks that were being pursued. For Husayn this meant that he and 'Arafat would have to part. He knew for a fact that the Americans would not acknowledge the Palestinian right to self-determination, since this would signify a major policy change, involving a reversal of their undertaking to Israel going back to 1975.

'Arafat interpreted Jordan's insistence on his unconditionally accepting UNSC Resolution No 242 as a demand that he delegate full powers to Jordan. This he refused to do because it meant returning to the position in the pre-Rabat period, when the PLO was not recognized by the Arab countries as the exclusive representative of the Palestinians. Behind the disagreement between 'Arafat and Husayn there loomed the potentially explosive question even if not of immediate relevance: how were 'Arafat and his supporters interpreting the self-determination-cum-confederation-with-Jordan provision in the Amman Agreement? 'Arafat's demand for US assurance on self-determination meant that even the more moderate part of the PLO envisaged something quite different from what Husayn had in mind, something they hoped to get by means of US involvement.

Without Egypt there would have been no peace process, and it is noteworthy that Egypt's role was positive on the whole, despite the constraints in its US foreign policy. The first problem that had to be settled was the Taba arbitration agreement. Egypt was partly to blame that the talks were progressing so slowly until it became necessary for the US to close the remaining gaps. Still there was no doubt that Mubarak was anxious to meet Peres and secure an agreement. When the meeting finally did take place, Mubarak stressed that it was devoted almost entirely to the Palestinian question. The discussions did not, of course, bring the problem any closer to a solution. Mubarak, the realist, could hardly have expected that the result would be otherwise. His efforts to patch up the differences between Husayn and 'Arafat and his own contacts with the King had made him well acquainted with the formidable obstacles on the Arab side. He publicly affirmed that it was unreasonable to ask Israel alone to make efforts to solve the Palestinian question, while "we [the Arabs] defeat all moves toward peace."[8]

For Mubarak to be told by Peres that Israel would not object to an international conference was accepted as a triumph for Egyptian diplomacy. Mubarak had no problem with Israel's insistence that this conference should be no more than an "umbrella" under which the parties could negotiate freely. Thus Egypt and Israel appeared quite close to each other regarding the role of the conference.

It could be said that Syria's attitude towards the peace process in 1986 was at best the same as in 1985. President Hafiz al-Asad's speeches, his talk about energetically pursuing the goal of achieving strategic parity with Israel, and Syria's complicity in acts of international terrorism pointed to the conclusion that there was no prospect of Syria's becoming a partner in the 1986 peace process.

The *rapprochement* between Jordan and Syria began when Husayn was cooperating with 'Arafat. After the Husayn-'Arafat break in 1986, this relationship was relieved of 'Arafat's divisive presence. One probable reason why Husayn wanted to improve relations with Asad was because he hoped thereby to persuade Syria to lessen its opposition to Jordan's peace policy. Talcott Seelye, a former US Ambassador to Syria (1978–81), wrote that according to Syrian officials, Asad did not exert himself to frustrate Husayn's policy because he was convinced that anyway the peace initiative was not getting anywhere.[9]

As 1986 ended, no new elements were discernible in the positions of the parties capable of generating momentum towards peace. Still, Jordan's growing involvement on the West Bank in the second half of 1986 constituted a positive development. Ambassador Murphy indicated to a US Congressional Committee that it meant that Jordan was taking action to improve the quality of life for the Palestinians on the West Bank and in Gaza. It furthermore implied that Israel and Jordan agreed that Palestinian residents in these areas "must have greater control over their livelihood, civic life and future prospects."[10]

JORDAN

The tough problem facing Husayn after his break with 'Arafat in February 1986 was how to continue the peace process without a Palestinian partner. His frequently repeated affirmation that Jordan would not serve as a surrogate for the Palestinians genuinely reflected his position.[11] There were many reasons why this was so, and the 1974 Rabat Resolution was only one of them. The Palestinian population on the East Bank numbering over one million was a constant reminder that any move concerning the West Bank with its 850,000 Palestinian inhabitants was a very sensitive matter for Jordan. Although the East Bank Palestinians were on the whole well integrated into Jordan, it could not be taken for granted that they would support Husayn if he departed from the agreed Arab positions. One researcher pointed out that many of the roughly 250,000 Palestinians in the shantytowns and camps of Amman were "already disaffected and influenced by a more militant Palestinian nationalism" and could provoke serious trouble.[12]

In these circumstances, the mere fact that Husayn continued to be a partner in the peace process was in itself significant. In his speech to the Jordanian Parliament in November 1986, the King described Jordan's policy as "two-track." The first track aimed at convening the international conference for the Middle East with the PLO as one of the participants. The second aimed at "developing ways and means to support the steadfastness of the Palestinian people in their occupied Palestinian land."[13] While there appeared to be little new in these two goals, actually the second goal, in particular, went much further than the previous West Bank policies that had been carried out by Jordan since 1967. What was now contemplated was embodied in a Jordanian Five-Year Development Plan for both banks of the Jordan river. The amount of money proposed for the West Bank and Gaza was $1 bn, i.e., $200m annually.[14] Jordan hoped to obtain most of the money from foreign sources, but increased its own annual contribution from $34m to $64m.[15]

The two policies were complementary. By infusing more money into the West Bank, Jordan would give the Palestinians there an economic boost that the Israeli occupation authorities could not give them. Thus they could await the much talked-of international conference in somewhat improved conditions. Still many questions remained unanswered. A particularly difficult one was that of PLO participation in the international conference since 'Arafat was now excluded from participating in any negotiations. Who would represent the PLO? In all its statements Jordan affirmed that its new policy did not signify a political change.[16] Jordan also insisted that it had not embarked on the reinvigorated West Bank policy to compel the Palestinians to choose a new leadership.[17] Nevertheless, their policy could eventually bring about this result. How much time it would take for this to happen was another matter. By the end of 1986 the emergence of new leadership and the convening of an international conference seemed equally far away.

The Jordanian Information Minister frankly admitted that since 1967 Jordan had dealt with West Bank issues in a somewhat desultory fashion.[18] The Five-Year Plan and other measures were intended to change this. US urgings directed at the occupying power, Israel, to improve the quality of life of the West Bank Palestinians, could not fail to encourage Jordan as well to do much more than before. Israel could not do it alone whether for economic or for political reasons in the knowledge that the inhabitants would be suspicious of its motives.

Jordan was apprehensive of large-scale immigration of Palestinians from the West Bank. If this happened, they stressed, "Jordanian national security [would be] at stake."[19] They frequently referred to the mass Palestinian exodus in 1948 and again in 1967. To forestall another such exodus was clearly one of Jordan's motives for devising the new plan.

When Husayn visited Washington in June, he reportedly told US Congressmen that he had made up his mind to be more active in the West Bank; the Palestinians would realize that Jordan was no longer neglecting them. Actually, the decision to launch this policy antedated the visit. Marwan Dudin, the Jordanian Minister for the Occupied Territories, had begun to brief West Bank mayors and other Palestinian personalities about the plan a month before[20] and the whole move had been coordinated with Egypt. Husayn and Mubarak agreed to cooperate in settling the West Bank and Gaza issues in "unified steps." They concluded that it was pointless to try to solve the Gaza problem while ignoring the West Bank and vice versa.[21] A few weeks later Mubarak went one step further declaring: "The old system under which Gaza was our [Egypt's] trust territory and the West Bank Jordan's is no more." Egypt and Jordan wanted to achieve "a Palestinian entity that would be associated with Jordan." This was not a unilateral Egyptian position; it had become a Jordanian-Egyptian one.[22]

Jordan was equally forthright. The Jordanian Crown Prince, Hasan, in one of his first statements about the Five-Year Development Plan, affirmed that it was meant for both Banks.[23] It was no surprise, therefore, when the Gaza Strip was referred to in the official text of the plan a month later.[24] Soon after, on 3 August, Minister Dudin met with the former Mayor of Gaza, Rashshad al-Shawa, to inform him of details about the projects for the Gaza Strip.[25] Egypt's effacing itself and Jordan's readiness to assume increased responsibility for Gaza were politically significant aspects of the Five-Year Plan, which constituted an assertion of an augmented Jordanian role in both occupied territories west of the Jordan river. Nor was this all; Jordanian Prime Minister Rifa'i announced in September that Jordan was granting Jordanian passports valid for three years to Gazans living in Jordan. The number of persons who could benefit from this was far from negligible: over 60,000 passports would be issued.[26]

While this was happening Israel was pondering the problem of the densely-populated Gaza Strip. Since Egypt had broken off the autonomy talks in 1981, Israel had been left with no practical alternative way to cope with this problem in a manner commensurate with its interests. In the summer of 1986 Israel was still hoping to persuade Egypt to assume a more active role in Gaza. Egypt, however, was already looking to relieve itself of this burden (see section on Egypt in this chapter, below).

Jordan's new policies for the West Bank and Gaza seemed to be going ahead satisfactorily during the second half of 1986. By the end of September, Arab mayors had replaced Israeli officers in the three largest West Bank towns: Ramallah, al-Bira and Hebron.[27] At about the same time, a Jordanian commercial bank was permitted to resume operations after being closed for 19 years.[28] These two steps were intended to facilitate the implementation of the Development Plan. The question was whether enough money would be available to make a significant impact. These small steps with Israel's tacit agreement were perhaps the only immediate practical alternative, because the efforts of Jordan and Israel to reach agreeement on the procedural question of what kind of international conference could be convened were not producing the desired results. Most of the progress had already been made earlier in the year through Ambassador Murphy's mediation. The important questions that remained unresolved, including the crucial one of whether the plenary of the conference should be convened in case of deadlock and by whom, continued to defy solution. The road to the conference remained blocked.

EGYPT

In 1986, as in the immediately preceding years, Egyptian policy towards Israel was greatly influenced by the as yet unresolved parts of the Arab-Israel conflict. Egypt adhered to the peace agreement with Israel, and reaffirmed its fidelity to it, calling it a "strategic option."[29] Yet, for most of 1986, Egypt systematically postponed improving bilateral relations with Israel until the issues that it kept invoking as impediments to improvement, for example, Taba and Lebanon, were seen to be moving towards a resolution. Egypt took this stand despite Mubarak's declared interest in meeting with Peres before Shamir became Prime Minister in October. The Egyptian President believed that Peres was more flexible than Shamir and an agreement could be reached with him.[30] Yet Mubarak nearly missed the Israeli changeover deadline. Had it not been for Peres' insistence on holding the meeting, it would probably not have taken place in time.[31] Then when it did take place, not without prodding from Murphy, no tangible improvement in relations resulted. One Egyptian Minister accurately pointed out that in the nine years since Sadat's visit to Jerusalem, only the matters in dispute between Egypt and Israel (i.e., Sinai) had been settled. This Minister warned that relations between the two countries would not improve as long as the Palestinian question remained unsettled. He also deplored "the erosion, mutual indifference and disappearance of enthusiasm" in the relationship.[32]

Throughout the year, Egyptian diplomacy labored in vain to heal the rift between Husayn and 'Arafat. The suspension, though not abrogation, of the Amman Accord by the PLO hampered Egyptian efforts.[33] Despite this difficulty, Mubarak continued to call 'Arafat the best leader for the Palestinians, though he was certainly aware of Husayn's radically different opinion. Mubarak stated his conviction that the Palestinians would not be able to agree on any other person and opposed every attempt to change Palestinian leadership.[34] His favorable attitude toward 'Arafat did not blind him, however, to the hard facts of intra-Palestinian relations and the problem they engendered.[35]

At the summit meeting in Alexandria, Peres committed Israel to taking part in an international conference and agreed to a preparatory committee to precede it. Mubarak and other high-ranking Egyptian officials interpreted this Israeli undertaking as an achievement of their diplomacy. They said this was a concession made by Israel for the first time.[36] This claim was not exactly accurate as Israel had in fact accepted the idea of an international "forum" or "umbrella" a year earlier (see *MECS* 1984–85, p 74). If the Alexandria summit revealed any new element in the Israeli position, it was perhaps in respect to Israel's position regarding the preparatory committee; Israel's position had previously been less explicit. In deference to Jordan and the PLO, Egypt regarded the international conference as indispensable to the next stage of the peace process. However, Israel's firm insistence on direct negotiations led Mubarak to accommodate Peres and agree that the conference would be a mere "umbrella" to make bilateral meetings possible.[37]

The preparatory committee was seen as only a prelude to the international conference. Its composition would not differ much from that of the conference itself. Egypt's Foreign Minister Ismet 'Abd al-Majid specifically excluded the possibility that the conference could be limited to Egypt, Jordan and Israel. In fact, he stipulated that its nucleus must be the permanent members of the UNSC. In October, Egypt moreover proposed that the UNSC adopt a procedural resolution (i.e., one that cannot be vetoed) to empower the five permanent members to meet and begin to contact the parties to the dispute.[38] If Egypt did not actually move to implement this idea, it was because of US reservations.

Mubarak knew it would take some time for the international conference to materialize. First the preparatory committee would have to decide on such issues as venue, date and procedure.[39] The important question, however, was that of Palestinian representation. For the Egyptians it was axiomatic that the Palestinians would have to participate in all deliberations dealing with their future. Accordingly, throughout 1986 Egyptian diplomacy sought to find a formula to enable the Palestinians to be represented, looking to the Amman Accord to provide the answer.[40] In an address to the Egyptian Parliament, Mubarak referred to "the rights of the Palestinians to self-determination," but he qualified this by adding, "within the framework they chose when their representatives signed the Jordanian-Palestinian [Amman] Accord in February 1985." He also spoke of "the relationship that would emerge between Jordan and the Palestinian entity" after the recovery of the West Bank and Gaza.[41] Mubarak's repeated reference to the Amman Accord and his choice of the term "entity" in preference to "State" must certainly have caused concern to many in the PLO.

SYRIA

Syrian opposition to the peace process remained as determined as ever in 1986. Syrian President Hafiz al-Asad suspected that the US as the prime mover of the peace process was seeking to promote "a partial peace," which he perceived as one in which Syria's interests would be completely ignored and which would be entirely in Israel's favor. According to Asad, the US had no Middle Eastern policy of its own and was only serving "Israel-Zionist objectives."[42]

It is quite true that there were many valid reasons not directly related to Syria for the failure of the peace process to make any progress. However, Syria for its part prevented any real progress by its support of extremist PLO factions and international terrorism, and by its insistence on the narrowest interpretation of the 1982 Fez Resolution. Because of the Ifrane meeting (see section on Israel in this chapter), Syria broke off relations with Morocco even before Peres left Moroccan soil. It condemned the Ifran meeting as "a violation of the Arab League Charter and of the Arab Summit conference resolutions,"[43] thereby giving these documents the most rigorous interpretation.

It should be noted that Syria's attitude towards Husayn's participation in the peace process was more flexible. Meetings with the Jordanian King and his Prime Minister helped to convince the Syrians that Husayn was *grosso modo* abiding by the Fez injunctions. Syrian Vice President 'Abd al-Halim Khaddam could point to these facts: Asad and Husayn had agreed that there would be no direct negotiations with Israel; partial and unilateral solutions would be rejected; and they would settle for nothing else but a comprehensive settlement, in accordance with Arab Summit resolutions.[44]

Asad's views on peace as expressed in the year under review had not changed from those he had affirmed on occasion in previous years: total Israeli withdrawal; recognition of the rights of the Palestinians, including the right to determine freely their own fate; and to establish an independent state under PLO leadership. He reaffirmed that the framework needed to achieve these objectives was an international conference under UN auspices with the US, the Soviet Union and other countries attending.[45]

A former US Ambassador to Syria, Talcott Seelye, studied Asad's views on peace. He stated that even if Israel accepted all Syrian demands, there would not be peace in the normally accepted sense of the concept. Since Asad would not agree to diplomatic or other relations with Israel, there would be a state of nonbelligerency that would constitute peace only in the narrowest, legal sense. Even this, however, was nowhere in sight. When Asad said that he favored peace, he meant no more than the principle or formality of peace, explained Seelye. In fact, Seelye believed that "there would be no [comprehensive] peace in our time."[46] This was in all likelihood a correct assessment which followed inter alia from the "Greater Syria" concept that prevailed in Ba'thist Syria.[47] Fed by memories of the glory of the Ummayyad State, there continued to be hopes for an enlarged Syria to include Lebanon, Jordan, Israel and part of Iraq. This precluded the idea of a peace settlement which would require Syrian commitment to honor the post-settlement status quo.

At a press conference King Hasan of Morocco related two incidents which are relevant in this context. According to him, Khaddam declared in an open session of the Islamic Conference that the dream of the great Ummayyad State was universal in Syria. Furthermore, President Asad had strongly affirmed to a small Moroccan delegation that Syria had been cut up into pieces, stating, "The real Syria is Greater Syria."[48]

Syria not only opposed the peace process but continued in 1986 to build up its military strength. The declared goal was to reach strategic parity with Israel. From its inception in 1982, this concept was understood to cover not only the strictly military factor but all the economic, social, cultural, etc., elements which, when combined together, constituted Syria's total potential.[49] A theme that recurred in many Syrian statements was that strategic balance, far from leading to war, could prevent it. Its absence had not only prevented peace but had caused war.[50] The Syrian leaders were careful not to claim that the gap with Israel would be closed soon. More time was needed since it was not easy to catch up with a country that was "an enormous US base."[51]

It was reasonable to infer from these statements that Syria would be unlikely to start a full-scale war as long as it feared a crushing defeat. It was, however, equally reasonable not to exclude totally a limited military move designed to precipitate a diplomatic process from which Syria could hope to benefit. The Israelis certainly did not think that this eventuality could be altogether discounted. In periods of prolonged and rising tension between Syria and Israel such as occurred in the spring of the year, Syrian moves were difficult to evaluate. The strong evidence that implicated Syria in terrorist attacks in London and Madrid also raised the question as to how certain it was that Syria was not considering embarking on a course involving still higher risks.

ISRAEL

Once the Israeli Inner Cabinet made its decision (13 January) concerning arbitration on Taba and other disputed points along the Israeli-Egyptian border, Prime Minister Peres announced that he would proceed immediately to negotiate with Jordan and the Palestinians.[52] With Taba at least temporarily out of the way, Peres could devote more time to the larger and more important question of the Palestinians. He soon became deeply immersed in this matter during urgent meetings held with Ambassador Murphy in the Netherlands and England, meetings widely reported and commented on in the media. Although some progress towards settling procedural problems connected with the convening of an international conference was indeed made, it was hardly enough to enable substantive talks to start in a month or so, as Murphy had hoped.[53] The unresolved problems were the crucial ones: who would represent the Palestinians? Would Syria come to a conference if its authority were strictly limited? Would the Soviet Union and China meet the US-Israeli precondition for their participation and agree to set up diplomatic relations with Israel? Although Husayn had appealed to the Soviet Union to renew diplomatic ties with Israel and China was showing interest in the peace process, no immediate results were expected.[54]

Peres was not without hope about negotiations. As Murphy's efforts reached their peak, Peres stated in a public speech in London that he was convinced that if Husayn did not start to negotiate with Israel, the King might one day soon find that the territories had been given self-administration by Israel without Jordan's participation.[55]

Yitzhak Shamir, Israeli Vice Premier and Foreign Minister, did not directly oppose Peres' efforts at first, but he was not altogether supportive either. Both of them rejected an international conference that could impose a settlement on the parties. However, unlike Peres, Shamir showed no inclination to search actively for formulas that would make a noncoercive international setting acceptable to Israel and the Arabs. Only much later in the year Shamir clarified his stand which, in essence, was altogether opposed to any international conference. Peres, without being enamored of the idea of an international forum, accepted it so as to accommodate Husayn.[56] Husayn reciprocated. He was ready to discuss issues of mutual concern ahead of the territorial one. The most important was improvement of the quality of life of the Palestinians on the West Bank and Gaza Strip. Progress in the previous year had been limited. The first important step was taken in January 1986, in Nablus, where it finally proved possible to appoint a Palestinian mayor again when Jordan indicated to the candidate, Zafir al-Masri, that it did not object to his becoming mayor.[57]

Israel saw the failure of the talks between Husayn and 'Arafat as primarily concerning these two leaders. Peres continued to believe that talks with Jordan would eventually be possible, but the question remained of what to do in the interim. Israel proposed that the residents in the territories should be offered a greater say in running their own affairs, even while the existing Israeli civil and military administration remained in place. Peres said that "[Israel was] giving the residents the option of a devolution of powers from our administration to theirs."[58] To render this offer attractive, he stressed that it was not Israel's intention to force anything on the residents. It was for them to decide entirely on their own whether or not they wanted to avail themselves of the option Israel was giving them. If they took up the option, they need not fear that Israel would misconstrue this to be a substitute for a negotiated settlement. Their assuming administrative responsibilities would merely be a temporary measure. Israel stressed the point that it would energetically continue efforts to reach agreement with Jordan. The proposed devolution of powers would be coordinated with Jordan, if possible, since the inhabitants were Jordanian nationals, linked with Jordan in many ways. Still Israel did not expect any official blessing from Jordan.[59] Clearly Jordan preferred discretion. Israel for its part was outspoken. Peres stated openly that Israel would permit Jordan to increase its activities on the West Bank in order to improve its standing with the local population.[60] This devolution policy would not replace the broader "Jordanian option," which envisioned Jordan as a major partner in the final settlement.[61] Devolution was based on the expectation that Jordan would cooperate tacitly, that the inhabitants would see the advantages for themselves in what was offered them, and that Israeli security would not be threatened.[62]

One of Israel's prominent Arabists, Professor Emanuel Sivan, welcomed this proposal. He said that if it was meant seriously and gave the residents in the territories a real measure of self-government, it was "the only realistic potential brake on the ongoing process of annexation [by Israel]." He recalled that since Peres took office as Prime Minister in October 1984, the number of Jews in the territories, though not the number of settlements, had increased substantially. Development of the infrastructure and integration of the territories into Israel and its economy had also proceeded rapidly. In fact, the territories had become one vast market for Israeli produce.[63]

Devolution was not the only Israeli attempt to make headway. Immediately after Husayn announced that he had broken with 'Arafat, Israel's Defense Minister Rabin called upon the Palestinian leaders in the territories to join King Husayn in peace negotiations with Israel.[64] His call remained unanswered.

For a while it looked as if the Palestinians on the West Bank and in Gaza would resist all inducements to cooperate with the Israeli authorities beyond the already existing level. The assassination of the mayor of Nablus on 2 March 1986 raised doubt as to whether or not Israel could find candidates to head the municipalities in the three other large West Bank towns. For a while thereafter, all that Israel could do was to reaffirm its determination to keep the devolution option open despite such violent acts and hope that in time enough Palestinians would become amenable to the Israeli offers. Rabin and other Israeli leaders thought that at least a year or two would have to pass before "Jordan and the moderate Palestinians" would agree to negotiate.[65] As Rabin saw it, Husayn would enter into negotiations entailing real concessions on his part only when he judged his position sufficiently strengthened on the West Bank and in Gaza. Until this happened Husayn could not afford to commit himself to direct talks, which the PLO and Syria so flatly opposed. Husayn would be deterred from coming forward to negotiate until he knew what he would receive in terms of territory.[66]

In the meantime, the Israelis were encouraged by the developments. They described their relations with Jordan as amounting to "de facto peace."[67] They hinted that contacts existed between the two countries and that "very interesting things [had] taken place."[68] Peres considered Husayn "remarkably sincere" and "a serious leader."[69] He referred to several "understandings" — as distinct from agreements — reached with Jordan.

The so-called demographic problem continued to plague Israeli leaders, namely, the fear that the number of Arabs in Israel proper, combined with those in the occupied territories, would threaten the Jewish character of the State. If Israel annexed the territories, the Arabs would constitute close to 35% of the population and Israel would in fact become a binational State. Of 110,000 children born each year in Israel and the territories, 60,000 were Arab children and only 50,000 were Jewish children.[70]

The Gaza Strip in particular caused much concern. In the tiny territory of 350 sq km the population was 560,000 Palestinians. Within 20 years the number would probably double. Water resources were already depleted. Thus when the Labor Party formulated its platform on what territory should be retained by Israel for security reasons, it did not include the Gaza Strip.[71] There were reports throughout the year that Israel was trying to persuade Egypt to cooperate in introducing self-administration in the Strip. Egypt refused (see above, section on Egypt in this chapter). Jordan was more interested (see above, section on Jordan in this chapter), but its interest had limited practical meaning as long as its position remained unchanged regarding negotiation with Israel.

The deposed Mayor of Gaza, Rashshad al-Shawa, incontestably Gaza's outstanding personality, held talks with Peres and Mubarak about Gaza's future.[72] Mubarak raised the issue with Husayn. Not much progress was marked in these talks. The Arabs would not agree to Israel's suggestion to discuss arrangements concerning

Gaza. They held to their position that the Gaza issue could not be separated from all the other unresolved Arab-Israel problems. They would not accept autonomy even if it were offered under Arab (i.e., Egyptian) sovereignty, unless ultimate Palestinian independence was guaranteed beforehand.

The closing down of the PLO offices and the other measures taken by the Jordanian Government in July 1986 were welcomed by Israel as a step likely to improve the chances of peace. Peres saw it as a sign of "progress in the peace process" and as an indication that Jordan wished to strengthen its standing in Judea and Samaria.[73] These assessments were not far off the mark. The Jordanian Government appeared to have been freed of many constraints. Decisions could now be taken at a quicker pace, and there was less need to keep these decisions quiet. The part of Jordan's Five-Year Plan dealing with the West Bank and Gaza was given priority by Jordanian leaders. Before July was over, the Plan was ready.[74] Jordan openly admitted that it had asked West Bank personalities to agree to become the mayors of towns. Soon there were Arab mayors again in the three largest towns.[75]

In August, Israel reached agreement with Jordan over the old issue of the reopening of Arab banks. The agreement resulted from direct talks in London between representatives of both sides, with US involvement. The first bank opened on 3 November 1986.[76]

It was not certain by the end of 1986 whether or not Jordan would be able to raise as much as the $150-200m a year for the West Bank and Gaza, needed to implement the Five-Year Plan. It was apparent however, that the Jordanians were doing their best to obtain international aid. The size of the US program in the territories, carried out by private American voluntary agencies, had been expanding since late 1983, when US Secretary of State George Shultz directed that the effort be stepped up. In 1986 the US committed approximately $14.5m to the program. Besides helping the Jordanian Government, by making $5.5m available directly to it, the US was upgrading its own development efforts in the territories. This was, however, all the help that the US was likely to be able to give.[77]

How much financial aid would be available was important but perhaps not crucial. Equally significant from Israel's point of view was the question of whether or not Jordan's increased activity was making an impact on the territories. Rabin, responsible for the territories in his capacity as Defense Minister, said that it was. Jordan's policy, now almost identical with Israel's, would encourage a new Palestinian leadership to emerge. This augured well for the prospects of an Israeli-Jordanian agreement in the not too distant future. As on several earlier occasions, Rabin again estimated that this goal could be achieved in one to three years.[78] There were also less sanguine views. One Israeli journalist, reporting on the West Bank, noted the achievements but thought that the Israeli authorities had already done all they could within the confines of the existing policy. It was unlikely that the Government would transfer more powers to the Arabs in view of the opposition from the Israeli settlers, already apprehensive of a "creeping Arab annexation."[79] The Israeli Arabist Sivan believed that the dependence of the territories on Israel had created economic pressure groups in Israel who were ready to defend the existing situation as vital for their economic survival. They would not countenance a new economic policy.[80]

The Israeli authorities on the West Bank were under no illusion about the sentiments of the majority of the inhabitants. Their mood was truculent and the Israeli and

Jordanian policies could not change that. A study conducted in early summer 1986 by the Israeli authorities on the Gaza Strip concluded that the PLO would score a decisive victory if municipal elections were held then.[81] Four months later the head of the civilian administration acknowledged that the sympathy of the Palestinians still lay with the PLO.[82]

Israel's stand on Palestinian national demands remained unchanged. Peres and Shamir were equally opposed to the PLO, to 'Arafat and to Palestinian self-determination leading to an independent state. At the Labor party conference in April 1986, Peres declared that Israel was telling the Palestinians, "We recognize you as a people."[83] This declaration was made in the presence of Butrus Butrus-Ghali, the Egyptian Minister of State for Foreign Affairs, who appreciated it very much, although it meant little in actual practice. The next day Peres explained that Israel would not agree to Palestinian independence. It would favor a solution which would secure Palestinian rights in a Jordanian setting. Israel should be wary of supporting the notion of Palestinian self-determination so as not to alienate Husayn. To recognize the existence of a people, as Israel had done at Camp David, was one thing, to recognize a state was quite another.[84]

The meeting between King Hasan of Morocco and Prime Minister Peres in July received worldwide publicity. Peres met the King at his Ifrane palace three times, and they issued a joint communiqué.[85] Peres described the meeting as "a historic event in the Middle East peace process," and as "a move that is likely to transfer the dialogue on peace from the context of Israel and its neighbours to the broader context of relations between the Arab world and the Jewish world."[86] Peres hoped for broader significance because Hasan who was head of the Islamic Conference, chairman of its Jerusalem Committee and chairman of the Arab Summit conference (a position he resigned immediately after the meeting with Peres) would thus have greater influence than if he were only a king.

As far back as the 1960s, rumors were heard from time to time about secret relations between Morocco and Israel. More recently it became known that Rabin had visited Morocco in 1976 when he was Prime Minister. A year later, in September 1977, Foreign Minister Moshe Dayan of Israel met Sadat's special envoy, Hasan al-Tuhamy, in Morocco. There was a difference nevertheless this time — the Ifrane meeting was not kept secret. It was also unique because it was the first meeting since the Sadat visit to Jerusalem in 1977 between leaders from two countries that did not recognize each other formally. The resemblance between the meetings in Jerusalem and Ifran was, however, in reality not all that close. The Moroccan King made this point repeatedly. He affirmed that Sadat went to Jerusalem "to liberate his land [Sinai] that was occupied."[87] He, Hasan, did not have similar problems to discuss with Israel. He could not negotiate or reach agreement over issues that concerned other Arabs. By virtue of his being the chairman of the Arab Summit, no one could deny him the authority to meet an Israeli leader, explain the all-Arab position to him, i.e., the Fez Plan, and listen to that leader's observations. Hasan never intended to exceed this authority. The Fez Plan did not specifically ban contacts with Israel for such carefully circumscribed purposes, nor had any Arab League decision ever ruled differently.

For the Israelis, Hasan's insistence that no Arab taboo existed on meetings with Israel was the biggest gain from the Ifrane meeting. An Arab King had refused to bow to Arab rejectionist taboos and "had broken the barrier of embarrassment."[88]

Mubarak was no longer isolated, Egyptian leaders were no longer the only Arab leaders to meet Israelis openly. Peres also mentioned another positive aspect: Israel's substantive positions were much less of a problem to Hasan than the question of how to put them into writing. There was, so he said, "more common ground from a pragmatic standpoint than from that of formulation."[89] This affirmation, however, was speedily contradicted by King Hasan himself in his speech to the Moroccan people immediately after Peres left. The King said that the differences in positions had not narrowed at all. In line with the Fez Plan, he had expected Peres to express readiness to recognize the PLO and agree to Israeli withdrawal from all the occupied territories, but Peres had rejected these demands.[90] Thus the difficulty stemmed from differences in substantive positions, and could hardly be surmounted by formulation.

Peres bestowed on Hasan the title of "man of peace." Not every Arab leader would have thought that there was any sense in discussing the Fez Plan with the Israelis. Another Arab leader might have been deterred by the stigma attached to a meeting with an Israeli leader. The question remained, however, of why Hasan had agreed to meet with Peres although he knew beforehand that Israel would be likely to reject the Fez Plan. Replying to this question put to him by a reporter, Hasan explained that he wanted to prevent bloodshed. The next war between Israel and the Arabs would inflict terrible losses on both victor and vanquished because of advanced military technology. Another reason was his (Hasan's) desire to test Israel's readiness to make crucial concessions. If Israel failed this test, he wanted the whole world to know it. All in all, he was convinced that because he had exposed Israeli intransigence the outcome of the meeting was harmful to Israel's interests and favorable for Morocco and the Arabs. One reason left unsaid was probably the expectation that the meeting would enhance the King's prestige and strengthen his relations with the US and Europe, earning Morocco much-needed financial means to bolster up its shaky economy.[91]

Israel hoped that the meeting would encourage other Arab leaders to follow in Hasan's footsteps. For Peres personally, the meeting helped to establish him as an Israeli leader the Arabs could deal with. Peres rejected the Fez Plan, but he did hand Hasan documents in which he outlined Israel's intentions in the peace process. These were:

1. that Israel would not impose its sovereignty on the territories during the peace efforts;
2. an expression of readiness to meet "authentic" Palestinian leaders as soon as possible in order to search for a solution to the Palestinian problem in all its aspects;
3. Israel agreed to a peace conference with the Arab countries and the Palestinians, a conference that would be given an "international accompaniment as approved by all concerned."[92]

Perhaps one of the most significant aspects of the Ifrane meeting was the relatively restrained objections made by the Arab countries, with the exception of Syria who broke off diplomatic relations with Morocco.[93]

Soon after his return from Ifrane on 3 August 1986, Peres met with 25 Palestinian mayors and other personalities from the territories, in keeping with the promise he had made to King Hasan. He considered them genuine representatives of the inhabitants. He referred to them as "authentic Palestinians," meaning essentially non-PLO Palestinians able and willing to represent Palestinian interests. Israel affirmed that the political views of the Palestinian representatives did not have to please Israel, and that everyone would be entitled to his opinions and be free to express them. Only people who supported terror and violence would be disqualified. At this meeting Peres explained again, as he and his collegues had often done before, that Israel could only invite them to consider ways for developing the territories, but the decision whether to accept or not was entirely theirs.[94] There was no other similar meeting before Shamir took over three months later.

The Alexandria summit between Mubarak and Peres was a success. The joint communiqué stated that it marked "a new era" in bilateral relations and in the quest for peace.[95] At least equally significant was the Egyptian Foreign Minister's statement in an interview with a Hebrew newspaper that there was a feeling that a close relationship had been forged between the two leaders.[96] They declared 1987 a year of negotiations for peace, a declaration similar to the one which Peres had already proposed to King Hasan. Egypt and Israel also committed themselves to cooperate in their efforts to solve the Palestinian problem. In addition, as recorded above (see section on Egypt in this chapter), they agreed about the usefulness of convoking an international conference and a prior preparatory committee. Israel, however, was not at all in favor of a preparatory committee of the kind advocated by Soviet Secretary-General Mikhail Gorbachev and French President François Mitterrand at the Moscow meeting in July 1986,[97] the idea being a preliminary meeting of the five permanent members of the UNSC. This was precisely the sort of international interference that Israel took exception to. The meeting Israel had in mind was one consisting of representatives of Egypt, Israel and Jordan, where the permanent members of the UNSC would be backseat observers.[98] Peres did not reject the preparatory committee idea out of hand simply because he hoped it might hold some attraction for Jordan. Perhaps Jordan would come to talks where the purpose was procedural and the composition of the delegates was of a lower diplomatic level. If these talks bore fruit, then Jordan would be less averse to negotiations with Israel, even if the international conference setting was not identical with its initial proposal. Peres and his advisers called this stage-by-stage negotiations.[99]

The complete scenario envisioned four stages: secret talks over a period of two to three months; proximity talks with Jordan through a mediator; the convening of a preparatory committee; and, finally, the international conference.[100]

Ever since Peres announced in late 1985 that Israel was ready to participate in an international conference, he was forced to explain over and over again the conditions under which it would do so. He stressed:

(a) It was Jordan and not Israel that insisted on the international setting. Israel was merely accommodating Jordan in order to make the negotiations possible.

(b) Israel would take part in a conference whose aim it would be to create a propitious atmosphere, so that parties which had never met could come together for the first time. Israel would not come to a conference that had coercive power.

(c) The international forum would be no more than a venue for the parties to negotiate with each other directly.

(d) The international participation acceptable to Israel would be limited to countries having diplomatic relations with it. In the case of the Soviet Union, Israel furthermore expected the Soviet Union to permit its Jewish citizens to emigrate.[101]

The US gave full backing to the Israeli conditions, including the ones that dealt with the Soviet Union. For Shultz, direct negotiation was the essence of the peace process. While the idea of an international forum was not altogether excluded, its role would be only to serve "as a context for direct negotiations under the right circumstances."[102] There appeared to be little difference between his and Peres' positions. Nevertheless, when Peres went to Washington in the wake of the Alexandria summit, rumors spread that Shultz was concerned because the main outcome of that high-level meeting seemed to be Mubarak's statement that he and Peres had agreed to an international conference with Soviet participation. It was reported that in the face of Shultz's reservations, Peres played down his earlier endorsement of the conference.[103]

As already mentioned, Shamir remained reserved about even the weakened version of the conference, but in the year under review he did not reject it completely. He probably wanted to avoid a break with Peres. When he presented his Government to the Knesset after taking over from Peres, he merely said that no international conference could serve as a substitute for direct talks.[104] When Shamir elaborated on this some days later, he explained that since the matter had not taken a precise form, he saw no reason to take a final stand. All the same, the role he envisaged for it was that of an international gathering which would give effect to agreements negotiated directly between the parties. He was convinced that the Arabs and the Soviets would never agree to a forum that was merely an ornamental accessory.[105] Rabin's approach to the issue was wholly pragmatic. He believed there was no chance of holding a conference under the conditions acceptable to Israel, but that nevertheless the discussion about holding it at all had kept the peace process alive. No one could blame Israel for not trying.[106]

At the conclusion of Peres' Premiership, a former US Ambassador to Israel, Samuel Lewis, bestowed accolades on Peres for his "intense whirlwind diplomacy...marked by creativity...[and] a genuine commitment to find some accommodation with Jordan and the Palestinians."[107] Peres professed his belief in maintaining the diplomatic initiative rather than reacting to the initiatives of others.[108] The very continuation of the peace process was a contribution to peace. He thought that Husayn and Mubarak were using a new language when talking about Israel and that his relations with Mubarak had developed satisfactorily. Israel's image abroad had also appreciably improved.[109]

Shamir deserved his reputation as a hard-line Likud (Herut Party) politician. One Pulitzer Prize-winning correspondent wrote, however, that Shamir, perhaps facing his "last hurrah in political life," seemed eager to make a mark on the Middle East peace process.[110] A member of Shamir's party observed, however, that Shamir "saw little point in repeating Mr Peres' futile attempt to attract King Husayn to the negotiating table." He would attempt instead to develop better cooperation with local Palestinian leaders and lay the foundation for Palestinian autonomy on the West Bank."[111]

Doubtless Peres, too, would have preferred the autonomy option if he had found an Arab partner with whom to discuss it. Peres knew that a settlement which did not entail territorial compromise stood a better chance of being accepted by his Likud partners, and he did not abandon the search for a solution of this nature. In Alexandria, he discussed with Mubarak the concept of a Jordanian-Palestinian confederation as a basis for solving the Palestinian problem.[112] Soon afterward a

Labor Party Knesset Member raised the same idea with the King of Morocco.[113] It is of interest that no objections by Shamir to the idea is recorded. Perhaps this was so because former Premier Menahem Begin, Shamir's guide and mentor, once mentioned the possibility of a confederation between Israel and Jordan.[114] It is clear, however, that what Begin had in mind then was something completely different from what was intended by Peres and the Labor Party. Like Begin, Shamir and the Likud were totally opposed to any territorial concessions or changes on the West Bank in favor of Jordan and the Palestinians. Labor, on the other hand, was ready to make considerable territorial concessions on the West Bank, if Israel's security problems there were satisfactorily provided for. The territories conceded would constitute the West Bank part of the Jordanian-Palestinian Confederation.

Since Peres had referred to the confederation idea in somewhat abstract terms, Shamir saw no reason to object. However, both he and Peres must have realized that this would no longer be the case if and when the day came that the Arabs asked for a more concrete and detailed exposition of the Israeli views. The essential differences between the Labor and Likud positions could then no longer be glossed over.

NOTES

For the place and frequency of publications cited here, and for the full name of the publication, news agency, radio station or monitoring service where an abbreviation is used, please see "List of Sources." Only in the case of more than one publication bearing the same name is the place of publication noted here.

1. Interview with Harold Saunders, *American-Arab Affairs*, Winter 1985–86, No 15. Also in Saunders' book, *The Other Walls, The Politics of the Arab-Israeli Peace Process* (Washington D.C.: American Enterprise Institute for Public Policy Research, 1985), pp 105–41.
2. See, e.g., Murphy's prepared statement to the Senate Foreign Relations Committee, 17 April 1986.
3. WF, 24 July 1986, statement by White House deputy press secretary.
4. WF, full transcript, 17 September 1986.
5. Syndicated *LAT* article, printed in the *JP*, 25 May 1986.
6. Richard N. Haas, in *Commentary*, August 1986.
7. See Note 1.
8. News conference, 11 September 1986 — SWB, 13 September 1986.
9. Talcott W. Seelye in *American-Arab Affairs*, No 17, Summer 1986.
10. Testimony before the House Foreign Affairs Subcommittee on Europe and the Middle East, 8 October, WF, 8 October 1986.
11. E.g., TV interview with Evans and Novak, CNN, 22-23 February 1986. Published in *American-Arab Affairs*, Spring 1986, No 16.
12. Aaron D. Miller, "Jordan and the Arab-Israeli Conflict: The Hashemite Predicament," *Orbis*, Vol 29, No 4, Winter 1986.
13. Jordan TV, 1 November — DR, 3 November 1986.
14. *The Economist Intelligence Report*, No 4, 1986, "Jordan," p 10.
15. AP as quoted in *JP*, 12 December 1986.
16. See, e.g., Prime Minister Rifa'i interview on R. Monte Carlo, 2 October — DR, 3 October 1986.
17. See, e.g., Prime Minister Rifa'i interview with *al-Majalla*, 23–29 July — DR, 30 July 1986.
18. JNA, 21 July — DR, 22 July 1986.
19. *WSJ*; WF, 18 July 1986.
20. *Ha'aretz*, 12 June 1986, and R. Amman, 12 May — DR, 13 May 1986.

21. MENA, 31 May — DR, 2 June 1986.
22. MENA, 3 July — DR, 9 July 1986.
23. *JT*, 29 June — 1 July 1986.
24. *JT*, 31 July — 1 August — DR, 5 August 1986.
25. *JT*, 3 August — DR, 5 August 1986.
26. Rifa'i interview with *JT*, 17 September — DR, 17 September 1986, and statement by the Under Secretary of the Interior Ministry to *Akhbar al-Usbu'*, 2 October — DR, 3 October 1986.
27. *'Al-Hamishmar*, 30 September 1986.
28. *JP*, 2 September 1986; *Sawt al-Sha'b*, 22 September — DR, 22 September 1986; *JT*, 17 September — DR, 17 September 1986.
29. Butrus Butrus-Ghali, Egyptian Minister of State for Foreign Affairs, interview with *al-Anba*, Kuwait, 3 August — DR, 6 August 1986.
30. Mubarak interview with *Le Matin*, Paris — DR, 15 May 1986.
31. Mustafa Khalil, National Democratic Party deputy chairman, interview with *al-Ahram*, 24 September — DR, 25 September 1987.
32. Butrus-Ghali, interview with *Yedi'ot Aharonot*, 20 November 1986, also in a talk with Israeli Minister Moshe Shahal, R. Cairo, 25 November — DR, 26 November 1986.
33. Mubarak interview with *al-Ra'y al-'Amm*, 8 October — DR, 10 October 1986.
34. Mubarak interview with *Le Figaro*, 15 October — DR, 16 October 1986.
35. See Note 34.
36. Mubarak in statement to correspondents, R. Cairo, 29 September — DR, 30 September 1986; 'Abd al Majid interview in *al-Hawadith*, 10 October — DR, 11 October 1986.
37. E.g., Mubarak talking to journalists: (a) R. Cairo, 21 September — DR, 22 September 1986; (b) R. Cairo, 13 October — DR, 14 October 1986.
38. R. Monte Carlo, 18 September — DR, 19 September, and 8 October — DR, 10 October 1986.
39. See Note 33.
40. Mubarak news conference, R. Cairo, 2 December — DR, 3 December 1986.
41. Address to both Houses, R. Cairo, 12 November — DR, 14 November 1986.
42. Interview with *WP*, 18 May — DR, 19 May 1986.
43. Syrian official source, R. Damascus, 22 July — DR, 22 July 1986.
44. Interview with *al-Mustaqbal*, 17 May — DR, 19 May 1986.
45. Interview with *Libération*, Syrian TV, 18 February — DR, 19 February 1986.
46. Talcott W. Seelye, "The Syrian Perspective on the Peace Process," *American-Arab Affairs*, No 17, Summer 1986.
47. Yehoshua Porath (Hebrew University) in interview with *Yedi'ot Aharonot*, 19 March 1986; also Seelye, loc cit.
48. R. Rabat, 7 August — SWB, 9 August 1986.
49. Address by Asad, R. Damascus, 8 March — DR, 10 March 1986.
50. Asad interview with *WP*, Syrian TV, 18 May — SWB, 20 May 1986; Khaddam interview with R. Vienna, 10 July — DR, 11 July and his interview with *al-Sharq al-Awsat*, 12 July — DR, 15 July 1986.
51. Asad interview with *WP*, see Note 50; Talas, Syrian Defense Minister, interview with *Der Spiegel*, 22 September — DR, 23 September 1986.
52. VoI, 15 January — DR, 15 January 1986.
53. Peres interview with Israel TV, 24 January — DR, 27 January 1986.
54. Peres interview with *Hadashot*, 24 January — DR, 27 January 1986.
55. Speech at the Royal Institute of International Affairs, as reported in *Ma'ariv*, 23 January — DR, 24 January 1986.
56. Address at the Van Leer Institute, Jerusalem, 16 January as reported in *JP*, 21 January — DR, 22 January 1986.
57. See, e.g., Tahir al-Masri's interview with *al-Majalla*, 6–12 August — DR, 12 August 1986.
58. Excerpts from the Knesset protocol, 12 February, Government Press Office (GPO) text, 12 February 1986.
59. Interview with Israel TV, 13 February — DR, 14 February 1986.
60. Interview with CNN, reported by *Ha'aretz*, 1 April 1986.

61. VoI, 13 February — DR, 13 February 1986.
62. Rabin in a lecture at Haifa University, reported in *Ha'aretz*, 13 March 1986.
63. Hebrew University Professor Emmanuel Sivan, interview with *JP*, 16 February 1986.
64. As reported in *al-Quds*, 26 February — DR, 28 February 1986, and GPO text, 19 February 1986.
65. Rabin addressing reporters, 31 March — DR, 1 April 1986. Peres expressed a similar view: "If the [Husayn-'Arafat] rift continues, it will be possible to conduct separate talks. [But] this will take time — let there be no misunderstanding on this matter." Interview with *Hatzofeh*, 23 April — DR, 24 April 1986.
66. Interview with *Bamahane*, 16 April — DR, 18 April 1986; also interview on R. IDF, 5 October — DR, 7 October 1986.
67. Shamir in a TV interview reported by AFP 28 April — DR, 28 April 1986.
68. Peres, interview on Israel TV, 27 April — DR, 28 April 1986.
69. Interview with *Hadashot*, 13 May — DR, 14 May 1986.
70. Peres interview on VoI, 14 May, GPO text, 14 May 1986.
71. Peres interview with *JP*, April 23 1986.
72. Shawa interview with *JP*, 27 June — DR, 30 June 1986; *NYT* article, 23 May 1986.
73. For the reactions of Peres, Shamir and Rabin, see R. IDF, *Hadashot*, and VoI — DR, 8 July 1986, and R. IDF, 10 July — DR, 15 July 1986.
74. See, e.g., al-Rifa'i's interview with *al-Mustaqbal*, R. Amman, 29 July — DR, 31 July 1986; *JP*, July 30 1986. For full text see *JT*, 31 July-1 August — DR, 5 August 1986.
75. Foreign Minister Tahir al-Masri's interview with *al-Majalla*, 6–12 August — DR, 12 August 1986. The mayors assumed their duties on 29 September 1986.
76. VoI, 2 October — SWB, 3 October 1986; *JP*, 4 November — DR, 4 November 1986.
77. Murphy's testimony before the US House of Representatives Foreign Affairs Subcommittee on the Middle East, 14 August, USIS official text, 14 August 1986; also Murphy before the same Subcommittee, 8 October, WF, 8 October 1986.
78. Interviews with (a) R. IDF, 5 October — DR, 7 October 1986, and (b) *JP*, 30 September — DR, 6 October 1986.
79. Danny Rubinstein, *Davar*, 21 January 1987.
80. Professor Emmanuel Sivan, addressing a symposium on Israel's problems in the territories, as reported in *JP*, 23 December 1986.
81. *JP*, 12 June — DR, 12 June 1986.
82. JTA, 19 November 1986. A poll conducted in the territories in the late summer and published on 8 September 1986 found that over 93% considered the PLO as the sole and legitimate representative; 78% wanted a Palestinian state in the whole of Palestine (i.e., in lieu of Israel); 71% preferred 'Arafat to Husayn.
83. VoI, 8 April — DR, 9 April 1986. (The DR text renders the Hebrew word *am* [people] inaccurately as nation, for which the Hebrew word is *Umma*.)
84. BBC, 2 August 1986; *Ma'ariv* and *Ha'aretz*, 1 August 1986.
85. R. IDF, 24 July — DR, 24 July 1986; also Israel GPO Press Bulletin, 24 July 1986.
86. R. IDF, 24 July — DR, 24 July 1986, and Peres' Knesset statement, VoI, 28 July — DR, 29 July 1986.
87. Address to the Nation, R. Rabat, 23 July — DR, 24 July 1986.
88. Peres' Knesset address, VoI, 28 July — DR, 29 July 1986.
89. See Note 34. In his Knesset speech (see Note 37) Peres said, "The present gap is mainly a gap between different formulations."
90. See Note 36.
91. News conference, 7 August — DR, 8 August 1986; *WSJ*, 25 July 1986.
92. See Note 37.
93. For Arab media reaction, see *Foreign Media Analysis*, 8 August 1986.
94. SWB, 5 August 1986; *The Guardian*, 5 August 1986.
95. DR, 14 September 1986.
96. 'Abd al-Majid interview with *Ma'ariv*, 19 September — DR, 24 September 1986.
97. *Le Monde*, 11 July 1986.
98. Reported by *Yedi'ot Aharonot*, 18 September — DR, 18 September 1986.
99. *Ma'ariv*, 18 September, Israel GPO text of same date.

100. See Note 48.
101. See, e.g., Peres' statement after meeting with President Reagan, USIS official text, 15 September 1986; Knesset address, 7 October — DR, 7 October 1986.
102. Press conference, USIS official text, 15 September 1986.
103. *CSM* and *IHT* (*NYT* Service) both of 17 September 1986.
104. VoI, 20 October — DR, 20 October 1986.
105. Interview with *JP*, 24 October — DR, 27 October 1986; also interview with *Ma'ariv*, 2 December — DR, 3 December 1986.
106. Rabin interview on VoI, 17 September — DR, 3 December 1986.
107. Article in the *NYT*, 12 October 1986.
108. Interview with *Bamahane*, 7 May — DR, 12 May 1986.
109. In his interview with *JP*, 23 April 1986, he said, "Look how Mubarak talks about us, how Husayn talks about us"; also, interview with *Ma'ariv*, 3 October — DR, 6 October 1986; also interview on Israel TV, 27 November — DR, 2 December 1986; also interview with VoI, 23 September — DR, 23 September 1987.
110. Thomas L. Friedman, article in *NYT*, 21 October 1986.
111. Ehud Olmert, article in *NYT*, 21 October 1986.
112. *JP*, 26 September — DR, 29 September 1986.
113. VoI, 25 September — SWB, 27 September 1986.
114. VoI, 30 September, as reported in *JP*, 1 October 1986.

Armed Operations

UZI RABI and JOSHUA TEITELBAUM

During the period under review armed operations continued in all arenas: in Lebanon, in Israel, in the Israeli-administered territories, and internationally. Armed operations in South Lebanon against Israel Defense Forces (IDF) and South Lebanese Army (SLA) targets increased. Operations were carried out primarily by Shi'i groups as well as Palestinian and local left-wing organizations. Responsibility for most of the attacks was claimed by the Lebanese National Resistance Front (*Jabhat al-Muqawama al-Wataniyya al-Lubnaniyya*), an umbrella framework including Shi'is and others fighting the Israeli presence in South Lebanon. Unconvincingly, Palestine Liberation Organization (PLO) leaders claimed responsibility for the majority of the attacks, emphasizing that they were carried out by the Palestinian National Lebanese Joint Forces.[1] Notable targets for Shi'i operations in Lebanon in 1986, as previously, were official representatives and ordinary citizens of Western countries and Lebanese Jews. Five Lebanese Jews held hostage during the year were reportedly executed in Beirut. The "Oppressed of the Earth," a faction of the extremist Shi'i organization, *Hizballah*, took credit for the executions. According to the communiqué issued by the group, the executions took place in response to IDF reprisals against Shi'i villages in South Lebanon.[2] Others were taken as hostages as a means to apply pressure on Israel to free Shi'i detainees and evacuate the security zone.

The PLO extended its penetration in South Lebanon, mainly in Sidon and Tyre, with the aim of regaining its power base. The Organization exploited existing rivalries between the various groups in Lebanon, and it collaborated with *Hizballah* and left-wing elements. This enabled PLO constituent organizations to infiltrate the security zone to attack SLA and IDF targets. Since attempts to infiltrate into Israel proper by land or by sea were unsuccessful, the various factions operating against Israel increased their use of Katyusha rockets from within and north of the security zone; the number of Katyusha attacks doubled, from 31 in 1985 to 62 in 1986.[3] Israel retaliated on several occasions by bombing the training camps and headquarters of various Palestinian and Shi'i organizations. It continued its seemingly effective policy of maintaining the security zone, but at a high cost.

In addition to all-out attacks by the PLO against SLA military positions, IDF and SLA patrols were harassed and had to contend with roadside charges, light arms fire and rocket-propelled grenades (RPGs). Two IDF soldiers were captured by *Hizballah* in the security zone on 17 February 1986.

During the year there was a significant decrease in Palestinian operations in Israel proper and the Administered Territories. Senior Israeli officials cited the closing down of PLO offices in Amman, which began in April 1986 and made it more difficult for local *fida'iyyun* to obtain arms and explosives, as a central factor in the decrease of operations.[4] Another reason was the success of the Israeli security forces in capturing *fida'i* squads. The Israeli evacuation of Lebanon in February 1985 gave Israel more manpower to strengthen its presence and efficiency in the Administered Territories.[5]

These two factors led to a change in the pattern of *fida'i* activity. While a decline in the use of grenades, petrol bombs and explosives was discerned, there was a rise in the number of small squads using knives against Israeli targets. The number of stabbings increased from 17 in 1985 to 26 in 1986.[6] Most of the stabbings occurred in East Jerusalem and the Gaza Strip, against Israelis who were walking or driving alone. A general sense of insecurity affected Israeli visitors to the territories. On several occasions, Jewish vigilantes in Jerusalem retaliated against Arabs.

These squads were probably locally organized, and thus presented a serious problem for Israeli security forces. Their small size and the apparent lack of any connection to a familiar Palestinian organization made even more difficult the task of detection and intelligence. In an interview with the daily *al-Qabas*, Salah Khalaf ("Abu Iyad"), a Fath Central Committee member, asserted that the attacks were not initiated by the PLO and could thus be considered an important development in the armed struggle.[7]

Fida'i activity of a different nature was carried out by Palestinian prisoners who were released in the exchange of prisoners that took place in May 1985 (see appendix to chapter on armed operations, in *Middle East Contemporary Survey* [*MECS*] 1984-85). These operatives were organized while they were still imprisoned, according to Israeli security officials.[8] After they were released, some returned to *fida'i* activity and were again arrested. Some were deported from Israel. Among the most significant attacks made by such groups were the murders of an Israeli woman and a British tourist in Jerusalem. Collaboration between Israeli Arabs and those of the Administered Territories became more evident during the year. According to IDF sources *fida'iyyun* in the Administered Territories relied to some extent upon weaponry supplied by Israeli Arabs.[9] This might correlate with the arsenals discovered in several Israeli Arab villages. Moreover, Israeli Arabs have functioned in several cases as middlemen in recruiting people for *fida'i* organizations.

In 1986, operations against Israeli targets by the PLO mainstream were limited to the territory controlled by Israel rather than to the international arena. This was in keeping with the "Cairo Declaration" issued by PLO Executive Committee Chairman, Yasir 'Arafat, in November 1985 (see chapter on the PLO, *MECS* 1984–85). After having paid a heavy political price for its involvement in the Larnaca and *Achille Lauro* affairs (for details of the above incidents, see chapter on armed operations in *MECS* 1984–1985), the PLO mainstream sought to limit political damage by operating mainly in Israeli-controlled areas. Moreover, the Fath leadership might have reasoned that such activity could be interpreted as legitimate military activity against an occupying force by at least part of world opinion.

The PLO and its constituent organizations also made efforts to counter rising Jordanian influence in the West Bank by operating against targets considered to be pro-Israeli and pro-Jordanian. It is worthwhile mentioning in this regard the assassination of the mayor of Nablus, Zafir al-Masri, in March 1986, credit for which was claimed by the Popular Front for the Liberation of Palestine (PFLP), and other attempts against mayors nominated with Jordanian approval.

A further objective of the PLO mainstream was to regain its radical hard-line image and reestablish its position *vis-à-vis* the rejectionist factions. These factions, which had refused to join the conciliation efforts to reunite the PLO (see chapter on PLO), had accused ‘Arafat of deserting the armed struggle and accepting “American capitulatory solutions.”[10]

‘Arafat, however, in an interview with the Egyptian weekly *October*, said that although there were disagreements between the various factions, “we are all unanimous as to the need to escalate the activity in the occupied territories and on that basis we have to meet.”[11]

In the international arena, there was a decrease in operations against Jewish and Israeli targets. However, the casual brutality of the previous year's operations continued to be dominant and was reflected in the Istanbul massacre and the attempts to blow up El Al planes in London and Madrid (see below).

As in previous years, the rejectionist groups were responsible for most of the international Palestinian armed operations. However, Palestinian guerrilla groups appeared to be developing new methods of collaboration. In various attacks, there was reason to suspect cooperation among organizations, as for instance in the Hindawi affair (see below). Moreover, collaboration was reported to have taken place between radical Palestinians and extremist Shi‘i organizations and may also have occurred in the Istanbul massacre (see below).[12] This collaboration may reflect Shi‘i readiness to attack Israeli and Jewish as well as Western targets abroad. It also may point to the Shi‘i organization's lack of a logistical infrastrucure in Europe and its need to rely on more established partners.

The connection in these activities between Arab radical states and *fida'i* organizations has been unequivocally proven. Evidence of Syrian support for such activity emerged during the Hindawi investigation. It seems that the states that sponsored the operations, notably Syria, Iran and Libya, preferred to use proxies. These activities exemplify a new brand of operation that leaves no fingerprints and whose sponsors remain anonymous.

Major local and international incidents are discussed below; details of other incidents may be found in the chronology of events.

THE LIBYAN JET INTERCEPTION

On 4 February 1986 four Israeli aircraft intercepted a Libyan executive jet 70 miles northeast of Larnaca Airport. The passengers had left a conference of guerrilla organizations in Tripoli, Libya, and were on their way to Damascus.[13] After the plane was forced to land, the passengers were ordered to disembark and identify themselves. Four hours later they were permitted to reboard for take off to Damascus.

Although Israel had information that led it to believe that the jet was carrying two major Palestinian *fida'i* leaders, George Habash of the PFLP and Ahmad Jibril of the Popular Front for the Liberation of Palestine-General Command (PFLP-GC), the only people on board were Syrian and Lebanese officials and a three-member crew.[14]

The jet interception placed Israel in a minor diplomatic imbroglio. It felt it had to legally justify the interception of a civilian airliner, particularly since it had been among the nations that had strongly denounced such acts.

Extremist organizations and radical Arab states, including Libya and Syria, threatened to retaliate against Israel's civilian aircraft. The Syrian Chief of Staff, Gen Hikmat al-Shihabi, promised a response that Israel would not forget: “Syria,” he said, “would choose the method, time and place.”[15]

Israel took the precaution of rerouting its civilian air traffic out of range of Libyan fighter aircraft.

THE CAIRO ATTACK

On 19 March 1986 several unidentified men armed with automatic weapons attacked four Israelis who were on their way home after working at the Israeli Pavilion at the Cairo International Industrial Fair. One woman died and the other three victims were wounded.[16] In a statement to news agencies in Cairo, the "Egyptian Revolution Organization" (*Munazzamat al-Thawra al-Misriyya*) claimed responsibility for the attack.[17] The attackers used two vehicles: one was used to cut off the Israeli car, while weapons were fired from the second.[18]

Egypt condemned the attack and launched an extensive inquiry. Egyptian security officials believed the attack was linked to the visit to the fair by the Israeli Tourism Minister, Avraham Sharir, which was concluded 30 minutes before the shooting.[19]

The "Egyptian Revolution" had also taken responsibility for two previous operations against Israeli targets in Egypt: the shooting and injuring of an Israeli diplomat in March 1984, and the assassination of another in August 1985.[20]

The Egyptian Revolution is dedicated to fighting against the Israeli presence in Egypt bringing about the aboliton of the Camp David Accords, and returning Egypt and Israel to a state of war.

Operations claimed by the Egyptian Revolution have been attributed to Abu Nidal's group. The most prominent of these were the August 1985 assassination of an Israeli diplomat and the highjacking of an Egyptian aircraft to Malta in November 1985. In an interview, Abu Nidal claimed responsibility for these operations. Moreover, he claimed that they were carried out by local Egyptian cells supported and run by his organization.[21]

Nevertheless, it is difficult to determine whether there is in fact a link between Abu Nidal's group and the Egyptian Revolution. However, it dovetails with Abu Nidal's connections with Libya, which actively seeks to undermine the Mubarak regime. Libya, which was alleged to have sponsored the Egyptian Revolution, welcomed the attack, calling it "a heroic operation."[22]

THE HINDAWI AFFAIR

On 17 April 1986 an attempt was made at London's Heathrow Airport to blow up an El Al jumbo jet. The attempt was foiled after the 375 passengers had passed through the airport's own security system and before they boarded the plane for Tel Aviv. An El Al security officer detained one of the passengers, a young Irish woman, who was discovered to have in her bag a bomb weighing approximately 1.5 kg. It was timed to explode several hours after takeoff.[23]

The next day Scotland Yard arrested a Jordanian, Nizar Hindawi, who carried a Syrian diplomatic passport. During the interrogation Hindawi confessed and accused Syrian Intelligence of being responsible for the abortive attempt. It also became clear that the woman who had been apprehended was Hindawi's girlfriend; she had not known that she was carrying a bomb. After the preliminary investigation, Britain asked Syria to strip three of its representatives in Britain of their diplomatic immunity so that they could be questioned about the affair. When Syria declined the request, the three were asked to leave the country.[24]

During Hindawi's trial, the prosecution revealed that Hindawi had met with the head of Syrian Air Force Intelligence in Damascus, Gen Muhammad al-Khuli, from whom he received £12,000 to blow up an El Al airliner in midair. According to the prosecution, there was solid evidence indicating that Hindawi had cooperated with a Syrian government agent while representing a group named the "Jordanian Revolutionary Movement for National Salvation." The prosecution also revealed the complicity of the Syrian Ambassador, Dr Lutf 'Ali Haydar, who had been personally involved months before the attempted bombing in recruiting Hindawi for Syrian Intelligence.[25] According to the police report the sabotage attempt was planned by Lt Col Haytham Sa'id, Deputy Chief of Syrian Air Force Intelligence. It is possible the group was acting on Syria's behalf in a reprisal operation against Israel for the interception of the Libyan jet on 4 February 1986 (see above). It is also conceivable that Syria, as a quid pro quo, promised the group Syrian support in its struggle against the Jordanian regime.[26]

Hindawi's conviction resulted in the immediate severance of Britain's diplomatic relations with Syria.

It should be noted that two sabotage acts which took place in West Germany prior to this abortive attempt also bore the hallmarks of direct Syrian involvement. On 29 March 1986, a bomb exploded in the offices of the German-Arab Friendship Society, injuring 11 people. On 5 April 1986, a bomb exploded in the "La Belle" discothèque in West Berlin which is frequented by US military personnel. Two people died and 230 were injured.[27]

Several days later two men were arrested in connection with both bombings. One of them was Ahmad Hazi Hindawi, Nizar's brother. During their interrogation the two suspects admitted responsibility for the bombing at the German-Arab Friendship Society offices.

According to the West German police, the suspects claimed they were equipped with bomb devices by the Syrian embassy in East Berlin; and Ahmad Hindawi admitted that the approval for the London operation was given to his brother Nizar in Damascus.[28]

The US used the "La Belle" bombing as a pretext to bomb Libyan targets. Senior officials in the US Administration claimed that the "La Belle" sabotage bore signs of Libyan involvement. It is worth mentioning in this regard that the US considered the terrorist attacks at Vienna and Rome airports in December 1985 — carried out by Abu Nidal's group — sufficient justification for a military operation against Libya. Abu Nidal's group had won Libya's enthusiastic support. It seems quite obvious that the American retaliation was designed mainly to punish Libya for sponsoring terrorism and to deter other countries from doing the same.[29]

Following the Hindawi brothers' arrest other members of the group were detained in Italy. Among them were 'Awni Hindawi, believed to be their cousin, and three other Jordanian citizens. The arrests led to the discovery that the Hindawis maintained ties with Abu-Nidal's group and two other pro-Syrian Palestinian groups. One of the latter was that of Abu Musa (the Fath figure who led a revolt in 1983 against 'Arafat); the other was the PFLP-GC, led by Ahmad Jibril. Both openly operate headquarters in Damascus. The Hindawi brothers were trained in Abu Nidal's training camp near Damascus.[30]

The possible links among these pro-Syrian Palestinian groups may indicate the emergence of a new pattern of collaboration between terrorist organizations believed to come under the umbrella of terrorism-sponsoring countries such as Syria, Libya and Iran.

Further evidence of Syria's complicity in terrorist acts emerged when there was an attempt to bomb an El Al airliner on 26 June in Madrid. The culprit, who admitted that he was a member of Abu Musa's Fath faction, had a Syrian passport and was believed to have been briefed in Damascus. That organization, however, denied any involvement in the incident. The explosive used in the attempted bombing was identical to that used at the West Berlin discothèque.[31]

THE ISTANBUL MASSACRE

On 6 September, two men armed with automatic weapons and hand grenades attacked the newly refurbished Neveh-Shalom Synagogue in Istanbul during Sabbath services, killing 22 worshippers and wounding three others.

The gunmen gained entrance to the building by posing as press photographers, claiming they wanted to film the synagogue's reopening. Once inside, the gunmen barred the gates and began to throw hand grenades. According to one survivor, the gunmen poured gasoline on the dead bodies and then set them on fire.[32]

The attack also resulted in the death of the two gunmen. It was difficult to determine whether they were accidentally killed by their own grenades, or if it was a suicide operation. It is possible that the grenades had specially rigged short fuses for immediate detonation (rather than the standard three-to-five second delay), and were thus meant to cause their death. It is not known whether they were aware of the special fuses.[33]

Five organizations claimed responsibility for the Istanbul massacre. In Beirut, claims were made on behalf of two Muslim Shi'i fundamentalist organizations — the Islamic Resistance, a name used by *Hizballah*, and the Islamic Jihad, said to be an offshoot of the former. *Hizballah*, however, repudiated the claim made on its behalf a day later. Three previously unknown groups also claimed responsibility for the attack.[34]

Israeli military attributed the Istanbul massacre to Abu Nidal's group because of the methods used.

An examination of Abu Nidal's previous operations reveals a readily identifiable modus operandi. Generally speaking, Abu Nidal favors attacks against synagogues; he is believed to have been responsible for those carried out in Vienna, Paris and Brussels. Nor is it uncommon for Abu Nidal to use fictitious groups to claim responsibility in order to veil his operations. The previously unknown "Palestinian Revenge Organization," which claimed credit for the Istanbul massacre, might have been a cover for Abu Nidal.[35]

Furthermore, Abu Nidal has carried out attacks in more than one place simultaneously, as at the Rome and Vienna airports on 27 December 1985. The Istanbul killings were carried out at approximately the same time as an operation in Pakistan,[36] in which an American airliner was seized by four armed hijackers shortly after landing in Karachi from Bombay. Twenty-one people were killed, most of them after the gunmen started firing in response to a rescue attempt by Pakistani security forces.[37] All four gunmen were arrested. Under interrogation, one of the hijackers identified an Istanbul attacker from a photograph. According to the hijacker, he and the Istanbul gunmen had been trained by Abu Nidal in a Syrian training camp in Lebanon.[38]

The apparently careful preparation and almost casual brutality of these attacks seemed to indicate that one or both were carried out by Abu Nidal's group. Nonetheless, the possibility that these operations involved other terrorist groups collaborating with Abu Nidal would also have to be considered.

There are two other possibilities involving a new pattern of inter-organizational cooperation. One suggests a new alliance between Palestinian guerrillas and Marxist groups operating out of Lebanon; the other indicates collaboration between Shi'i fundamentalist groups and Palestinian guerrillas.[39]

Despite the assumed complicity of Abu Nidal's group in the massacre, a careful study might cast doubt on the assumption that any single terrorist group could have carried out the massacre without state-sponsored logistical support.

The weapons the terrorists left behind offered an important clue to the sponsors' identity. Polish-made machine guns and Soviet-made hand grenades were found at the scene. These weapons were of the same type as those found after the attempted bombing of an American officers' club in Ankara in April 1985.[40] The arrests of two Libyans in connection with that attempt gave rise to the suspicion that Libya had been involved in the Istanbul massacre. Turkish Intelligence has long kept Libya's diplomats under careful surveillance. It had also been quietly monitoring the weapons and false passports that Libya routinely sent to Turkey in embassy pouches and mail.[41] Turkish security forces suspected that the weapons used in the massacre had been smuggled into Turkey in diplomatic pouches by the Libyan embassy as well as the Syrian and Iranian embassies.[42]

Another clue to the identity of the massacre's sponsors emerged during the investigation by Turkish police of the July 1985 terrorist attack in Ankara, in which Ziyad al-Sati, a Jordanian diplomat, was murdered. In November 1986 the Turkish authorities charged six Palestinians with al-Sati's murder. The six admitted to being members of Abu Nidal's group and provided police with information that led directly to the Syrian embassy and to the arrest of two other men: 'Adnan 'Amri and 'Ali Kent.[43] The former, a translator at the Jordanian embassy, also claimed to be a member of Abu Nidal's group. He confessed to having worked for Syrian Intelligence. According to his confession, Syria had ordered Abu Nidal's group to carry out al-Sati's murder. 'Ali Kent, a Turk of Iranian origin, who identified himself as the chief administrator and liaison officer for the pro-Iranian Islamic Jihad, confessed to staging several clandestine operations in Turkey while working closely with Syria. Both testimonies seemed to indicate that these two groups were collaborating in Turkey under the patronage of terror-sponsoring Arab states, particularly Syria.[44] This pattern might apply to the Istanbul massacre also. It should be noted that the Turkish authorities quietly expelled a Syrian and two Iranian diplomats suspected of involvement in the murder of al-Sati. Though it was never publicly stated, there is reason to believe that those diplomats were also suspected by Turkish officials of complicity in the Istanbul massacre.[45] If Turkey had publicly accused Syria, Libya and Iran of involvement in the massacre, the consequences for the Turkish Government could have been painful. Thus it was to Turkey's advantage to blame the elusive Abu Nidal.

THE WESTERN WALL ATTACK

On 15 October 1986, at the Dung Gate near the Western Wall in the Old City of Jerusalem, three hand grenades were thrown at infantry brigade recruits and their relatives as they boarded buses after a swearing-in ceremony. One person was killed and 69 — civilians and soldiers — were wounded.[46] Responsibility for the attack was claimed by the PLO. In the statement given to news agencies in Cairo, an official PLO spokesman asserted that the attack reflected 'Arafat's attempt to escalate military actions against Israel. A day later Israel retaliated by bombing Palestinian positions in Lebanon.[47]

Israeli security forces captured three local youths who admitted responsibility for the attack. They claimed to belong to a group named the "Legions of Islamic Jihad in Palestine."[48] It seems that this group has no connection with the Shi'i organization, Islamic Jihad, which operates in Lebanon.

In the course of the interrogation it became clear that the attackers had acted as a cell organized under the patronage of 'Arafat's Fath. The link between al-Fath and the attackers had already been established at the al-Husayn Mosque in Amman in April 1985 by a man who identified himself as a member of the "Islamic Jihad arm of al-Fath." In December 1985, the attackers underwent training in a Fath training camp in Jordan. They were supplied with arms for the operation planned for several months later.[49]

The overall assistance given to the attackers emphasized the vital role al-Fath offices in Jordan had in planning terrorist acts until they were closed in July 1986.

The Western Wall attack illustrated the increasing collaboration between al-Fath and the Islamic Fundamentalists that had emerged among the Arabs in the territories. It seemed that al-Fath had taken advantage of this trend and had begun to make a greater appeal to Islamic sentiments in the recruiting of its operatives.[50]

The PLO attack apparently had several objectives. The first was to emphasize in the strongest terms to the Jordanians that the PLO was the sole representative of the Palestinian people. It aimed to show that Jordan's activities to strengthen its position in the territories were ineffective[51] (see essays on the PLO, and the West Bank and the Gaza Strip). Another objective was to issue a blunt warning to the mayors appointed by the Civil Administration not to cooperate with the Israelis.[52] Indeed, this would serve to substantiate the statement of the Israeli Defense Minister, Yitzhak Rabin, that Israel had received information about guerrilla attacks being planned in response to the nominations.[53]

CHRONOLOGY OF EVENTS[54]

ARMED OPERATIONS IN LEBANON

Date	*Place*	*Description*
1 January 1986	Rashaf	One SLA soldier wounded by RPG fire directed at an SLA installation.
16 January	Near Bint Jubayl	A soldier of the IDF slightly wounded by a roadside charge.
17 January		One SLA soldier slightly wounded by a roadside charge in the security zone.

Date	*Place*	*Description*
25 January	Near Lusa (north-east of Kilya)	One SLA soldier wounded by roadside charge.
2 February	Near 'Aynata	One SLA soldier killed while inspecting a booby-trapped Katyusha rocket.
11 February	Near Markaba	One SLA soldier wounded by small-arms fire.
12 February	East of al-Tiri Junction	Three SLA soliders wounded by roadside charge.
13 February	Al-Huqban (south of Tibnin)	One SLA soldier wounded when a Katyusha rocket was fired at his post.
14 February	Near the village of Bura	One SLA soldier wounded by small-arms fire.
17 February	Near Bayt Yahun	A three vehicle convoy was attacked by small-arms fire. Two IDF soldiers were kidnapped and two local drivers killed. During the search initiated by the IDF, two of its soldiers were killed as well as 18 armed men. The Islamic Resistance claimed credit for the kidnapping.
22 February	Northeast of 'Aramta	Four SLA soldiers wounded in a clash with armed man; two armed men also wounded.
26 February	Near Jabal Basil	One IDF soldier killed and four wounded in an ambush.
1 March	North of Shtula	One IDF soldier wounded in a clash with armed men.
6 March	Southeast of Bint Jubayl	One IDF soldier killed by roadside charge.
9 March	Northwest of Jabal-Basil	One IDF soldier killed and five wounded in a clash with armed men.
27 March	Qiryat Shemona	Seven Israeli civilians were wounded by Katyusha rocket fire. Three armed men were intercepted by the IDF on their way to Manara. The three were meant to seize hostages and negotiate the release of imprisoned terrorists.
4 April	Sidon	Two armed men killed and 15 wounded when Israel Air Force (IAF) planes attacked Palestinian installations.
30 April	Wadi Summaq	Three IDF soldiers wounded in a clash with armed men.
13 May	Metula	Three Israeli civilians wounded by Katyusha rocket fire.
21 May	Northwest of Yuhmur	One IDF soldier wounded in a clash with armed men. Two armed men were killed in a clash with IDF soldiers outside the security zone.
25 May	Near the village of Rumman	One SLA soldier killed in an ambush.

Date	*Place*	*Description*
22 June	Near Tel Lubya	Two IDF soldiers wounded by roadside charge.
27 June	East of Tuba	One IDF soldier slightly wounded by roadside charge.
2 July	Near Sujud	Two SLA soldiers were slightly wounded when Katyusha rockets were fired at their post.
	Bint Jubayl	One IDF soldier and a local resident wounded by small-arms fire.
5 July	The village of Falus (east of Sidon)	Two SLA soldiers were wounded when light artillery was fired at SLA forces; another two were wounded by Katyusha rocket fire in the above location.
10 July	Sidon	Nine armed men killed and 12 wounded when IAF planes attacked Palestinian installations. Two IDF soldiers killed and eleven wounded in a clash with armed men trying to infiltrate by sea. All four armed men were killed.
13 July	Northwest of Taybe	Three IDF soldiers wounded by a roadside charge.
15 July		A merchant ship was intercepted by the Israel Navy northwest of Beirut. Five al-Fath members were found on board.
19 July	Al-Huqban	Two SLA soldiers were slightly wounded when their post was attacked by Katyusha rocket fire.
31 July	Near Majdal Shams	One IDF soldier killed in a clash with armed men.
7 August		One SLA soldier killed and another wounded in a clash with armed men north of the security zone.
	Near al-Huqban	Two SLA soldiers wounded when their vehicle hit a mine.
10 August	Sujud	One SLA soldier killed and another wounded when Katyusha rockets were fired at an SLA post.
	‘Ayn al-Hilwa	Four armed men were killed and five wounded when IAF planes raided Palestinian installations.
11 August	West of Ba‘albak	Seven armed men were killed and two wounded when IAF planes raided Palestinian installations.
24 August	Near Jizzin	One SLA soldier killed and two wounded in a clash with armed men.
25 August	Tel-Lubya	Three armed men were killed by an SLA ambush. One SLA soldier was slightly wounded.

Date	*Place*	*Description*
30 August		Israel Navy intercepted a Syrian merchant ship on its way to Khalde port. An arsenal was discovered on board.
4 September	The village of Zibqin	One IDF soldier killed during an IDF raid.
5 September	Bayt Yahun	One SLA soldier wounded by small-arms fire.
7 September	Near 'Ayshiyya	Two armed men were killed when an explosive charge exploded prematurely.
10 September	South of Sidon	Two armed men killed and ten wounded when IAF planes attacked a Palestinian naval base.
11 September	Al-Huqban	Two SLA soldiers killed and four wounded when armed men attacked an SLA post. One SLA soldier wounded by Katyusha rocket aimed at SLA post.
14 September	Southeast of Jizzin	Three SLA soldiers killed and four wounded when armed men attacked an SLA post. Three others wounded by roadside charge while evacuation took place.
16 September	Al-Huqban	Two IDF soldiers slightly wounded when Katyusha rockets were fired at an SLA post.
17 September	Near al-Qutrani	One SLA soldier was killed and two were wounded when an SLA vehicle was ambushed by armed men. At the same time, Katyusha rockets were fired at SLA posts in the region and one SLA solider was wounded.
18 September	'Ayshiyya area	Four SLA soldiers killed and three wounded when armed men attacked two SLA posts.
20 September	Al-Huqban	Three IDF soldiers wounded by Katyusha rocket fire aimed at their post.
25 September	Sidon	Three armed men killed when IAF planes attacked Palestinian installations.
28 September	Talusa	One SLA soldier wounded in a clash with armed men.
4 October	North of Beaufort	One SLA soldier wounded when his vehicle hit a mine.
6 October	Northeast of Tripoli	One armed man wounded when IAF planes attacked Palestinian installations.
14 October	Northwest of Hasbaya	Two SLA soldiers wounded when their vehicle hit a mine.
16 October	Sidon	Four armed men killed and ten wounded in IAF air raid on Palestinian installations. In the course of the attack an IAF plane was hit and abandoned by its two crew members over the village of Tanburit. The pilot was slightly wounded and managed to escape, while the navigator was taken captive by *al-Amal.*

Date	*Place*	*Description*
20 October	Near Jabal Ghazlan	One IDF soldier wounded by small-arms fire.
28 October	North of the village of Falus	One SLA soldier wounded by small-arms fire aimed at an SLA installation.
4 November	West of the village of 'Ayshiyya	Four IDF soldiers wounded by mortar fire aimed at IDF post.
12 November	North of Hasbaya	Two armed men killed in a clash with IDF soldiers.
16 November	'Ayn al-Hilwa	One armed man killed and three wounded when IAF planes attacked Palestinian installations.
17 November	Sidon	Two armed men wounded when IAF planes attacked Palestinian installations.
19 November	Near the village of Sujud	One SLA soldier wounded by small-arms fire.
	Near al-Shumriyya	Three IDF soldiers wounded in mortar shelling aimed at IDF post.
20 November	Hamra (northeast of Ra's Bayada)	Five United Nations Interim Force in Lebanon (UNIFIL) soldiers and three local residents killed when a car bomb exploded near a UNIFIL roadblock.
27 November	'Ayn al-Hilwa	Six armed men were killed and five wounded when IAF planes attacked Palestinian installations.
2 December	North of 'Aramta	Three SLA soldiers slightly wounded when their vehicle hit a mine.
	Al-Surayri and Lusa	Four SLA soldiers were killed and five wounded when two SLA posts were attacked by armed men.
3 December	Near the village of Maydun	Two SLA soldiers were slightly wounded in a clash with armed men. Two armed men were killed.
5 December	North of Mis al-Jabal	Two IDF soldiers were slightly wounded when their tank hit a mine.
6 December	Bayt Yahun	Three SLA soldiers were slightly wounded in mortar shelling aimed at their post.
11 December	North of Tripoli	Seven armed men killed and ten wounded in IAF raid on Palestinian installations.
24 December	The village of Maydun	Seventeen armed men wounded when IAF planes attaked Palestinian installations.
25 December		A Cypriot ship was intercepted by the Israeli Navy and its crew and passengers were brought to Israel for interrogation. The passengers were identified as al-Fath members with instructions to carry out an attack against Israel.
31 December	Beirut	Three Lebanese Jews executed by the "Oppressed of the Earth."

ISRAEL, WEST BANK AND GAZA, AND INTERNATIONAL

Date	*Place*	*Description*
2 January	Lod	An Israeli taxidriver was shot dead in his taxi.
3 January	Ramat Gan	One Israeli wounded by a bomb planted in Ramat Gan.
11 January	Nablus	One Israeli border guard was killed and another wounded by gunfire attack. The PFLP and Abu Musa's organization claimed credit for the attack.
21 January	Afula	One Israeli wounded by an explosive charge.
27 January	Ramat Hasharon	Israeli woman driver was stabbed and wounded by a hitchhiker.
27 January	Jerusalem	Israeli driver stabbed and wounded.
29 January	Jordan valley	Two IDF soldiers killed and two wounded by light-arms fire aimed at an IDF patrol southeast of Mehula.
4 February	Ramat Gan	Three Israelis wounded by a bomb planted at a bus stop.
14 February	Benei B'raq	Three Israelis wounded when a bomb exploded in a city bus.
16 February	Tulkarm	An Israeli bus driver was slightly wounded when his bus came under light-arms fire.
17 February	Hadera	One Israeli was wounded by a bomb planted under a bus.
18 February	Gaza	Five IDF soldiers were slightly wounded when a grenade was thrown at their patrol.
25 February	Abu Tur	An armed man was killed while preparing an explosive charge.
2 March	Nablus	The mayor of Nablus was assassinated. The PFLP and Abu Nidal's group claimed credit.
3 March	Gaza	One Israeli stabbed and wounded at local market.
6 March	Beer Sheva	Israeli taxidriver was stabbed and wounded.
7 March	Jerusalem	A tourist was shot and wounded in the Old City.
8 March	Jerusalem	An IDF soldier was stabbed and wounded in the Old City.
	Jerusalem	An Israeli Arab was shot and slightly wounded in the Old City.
15 March	Jerusalem	An Israeli Arab was shot and slightly wounded in the Old City.
19 March	Cairo	An Israeli woman was killed and three others were wounded by several gunmen at the Cairo International Industrial Fair (for details see above).
23 March	Bir al-Maksur	An IDF soldier was stabbed and wounded after taking a ride with two Israeli Arabs.

Date	*Place*	*Description*
31 March	Jabaliya refugee camp (near Gaza)	One *Fida'i* was shot dead during an attempt to attack an IDF vehicle with an incendiary bomb.
8 April	Jerusalem	Ten passengers were wounded when an incendiary bomb was thrown at an Israeli bus.
11 April	Jordan valley	One *Fida'i* was killed and another wounded in a clash with an IDF patrol. The two who entered through Jordan belonged to the PFLP.
12 April	Dir Abu Mash'al (Ramallah region)	One Israeli civilian was killed and two others were wounded when an incendiary bomb was thrown at an Israeli bus.
13 April	Jerusalem	An Israeli woman was shot dead in her office in the Old City.
16 April	Jerusalem	A tourist was shot and wounded in the Old City.
17 April	London	An abortive attempt was made at London's Heathrow Airport to blow up an El Al jumbo jet (see above).
25 April	Hebron	An Israeli resident of Qiryat Arba' was stabbed and wounded.
27 April	Jerusalem	A tourist was shot dead in the Old City.
3 May	Gaza	An Israeli Arab was stabbed and wounded in the local market.
10 May	Jenin	An Israeli was stabbed and wounded while shopping.
25 May	Kfar Saba	An Israeli civilian was wounded by an explosive charge.
5 June	Nablus	An Israeli civilian was shot and slightly wounded.
	Jerusalem	Two Israeli civilians were wounded when a bomb exploded in a supermarket.
6 June	Hebron	An Israeli resident of Qiryat Arba' was stabbed and slightly wounded.
26 June	Tzur Natan	An Israeli tractor driver was slightly wounded when his vehicle hit an explosive charge.
26 June	Madrid	An abortive attempt was made at Madrid Airport to blow up an El Al airliner. The culprit admitted that he was a member of the pro-Syrian Abu Musa group.
29 June	Jerusalem	An Israeli was wounded when a grenade was thrown at an Israeli bus.
30 June	Tel Aviv	Five Israeli civilians were wounded by an explosive charge planted in a bus.
12 July	Jenin	One local resident was wounded when an incendiary bomb was thrown at a bus.

Date	*Place*	*Description*
13 July	Tel Aviv	One Israeli civilian was wounded by an explosive charge.
16 July	Halhul	One Israeli civilian was wounded when two incendiary bombs were thrown at a bus.
24 July	Jericho	Seven Israelis were wounded when a group of travelers were attacked with hand grenades. Five local residents were also wounded. The Popular Democratic Front for the Liberation of Palestine and "Force 17" of the al-Fath claimed responsibility.
7 August	Gaza	Three local policemen were wounded by an explosive charge.
10 August	Efrat Junction (West Bank)	Three IDF soldiers were slightly wounded by an explosive charge planted at a bus stop.
16 August	Jerusalem	An Israeli civilian was slightly wounded when two incendiary bombs were thrown at his vehicle.
19 August	Khan Yunis	A local policeman was stabbed and wounded.
21 August	Wadi Kelt (near Ramallah)	Two Israeli hikers were stabbed and wounded.
24 August	Nablus	An Israeli civilian was wounded by an incendiary bomb thrown at his vehicle.
29 August	Balata refugee camp	An Israeli civil guard was assaulted by two local residents.
4 September	Gaza Strip	Two IDF border guards were wounded by an explosive charge.
	Gaza	An IDF soldier was wounded by an explosive charge.
6 September	Istanbul	Twenty-two Jews were killed and three wounded by two armed men in a synagogue (for details, see above).
14 September	Hebron	An IDF soldier was stabbed and wounded by a woman. In the course of the assault she was shot dead.
26 September	Ramallah	A Jordanian officer who served as director of health services on the West Bank was stabbed and wounded.
27 September	Gaza	An Israeli civilian was stabbed and killed at the local market.
28 September	Nablus	An IDF soldier was assaulted and wounded.
1 October	Ramallah	The deputy director of the Ramallah hospital and Jordan's chief medical representative on the West Bank was stabbed and killed.
7 October	Gaza	An Israeli taxidriver was stabbed and killed while servicing his car.

Date	*Place*	*Description*
10 October	Hebron	An Israeli civilian was stabbed and wounded.
15 October	Jerusalem	One Israeli civilian was killed and 69 civilians and soldiers were wounded when hand grenades were thrown at infantry brigade recruits and their relatives after a military swearing-in ceremony (for details see above).
4 November	Khan Yunis	Two IDF soldiers were wounded in a grenade attack. The PLO took credit.
12 November	Gaza	An Israeli civilian was stabbed and wounded while shopping in the local market.
15 November	Jerusalem	An Israeli civilian was stabbed to death while walking in the Old City. The three attackers were arrested. Following this event a wave of anti-Arab riots erupted, lasting about a week.
12 December	Jerusalem	An Israeli civilian was stabbed and wounded in the Old City.
14 December	Jenin	The head of the educational department in the Civil Administration of the West Bank was stabbed and wounded.
18 December	Ramallah	An IDF soldier was wounded by a local teenager who attacked him with an axe.
31 December	Jerusalem	Three Israeli civilians were slightly wounded when two incendiary bombs were thrown at their bus.

NOTES

For the place and frequency of publications cited here, and for the full name of the publication, news agency, radio station or monitoring service where an abbreviation is used, please see "List of Sources."

1. See, for example, VoP (Baghdad), 13 June — DR, 17 June 1986.
2. *Ma'ariv*, 31 December 1986.
3. *Ha'aretz*, 21 January 1987.
4. *JP*, 3 September 1986.
5. R. IDF, 18 November — SWB, 20 November 1986.
6. *Ha'aretz*, 21 January 1987.
7. *Al-Qabas*, 17 April 1986.
8. *Ma'ariv*, 25 June 1986.
9. *Davar*, 4 May 1986.
10. *Ha'aretz*, 20 October 1986.
11. Ibid.
12. See Judith Miller in *NYT*, 4 January 1987.
13. The conference held in Libya in January 1986 included 22 radical Palestinian, Muslim, Communist and Arab groups under the umbrella of the "Pan-Arab Leadership of Arab Revolutionary Forces".
14. *Ma'ariv*, 5 February 1986.
15. *The Guardian*, 27 October 1986.
16. MENA, 19 March — DR, 20 March 1986.

17. Voice of Free Lebanon, 19 March — DR, 20 March 1986.
18. R. Cairo, 20 March — DR, 20 March 1986.
19. *Al-Watan al-'Arabi*, 28 March; *Ma'ariv*, 20 March 1986.
20. *Ha'aretz*, 21 March 1986.
21. Cited in *Ma'ariv*, 21 March 1986.
22. *Ma'ariv*, 23 March 1986.
23. VoI, 17 April—DR, 17 April; *FT*, 7 October 1986.
24. *FT*, 7 October 1986.
25. *The Guardian*, 27 October; *Yedi'ot Aharonot*, 26 October 1986.
26. *The Guardian*, 31 May 1986.
27. *NYT*, 22 April; *JP*, 23 April 1986.
28. *Ha'aretz*, 24 October 1986.
29. *NYT*, 31 May; 30 June 1986.
30. *IHT*, 15 September 1986.
31. *FR*, 3 July 1986.
32. *Newsweek*, 15 September; *JP*, 7 September 1986.
33. *NYT*, 4 January 1987.
34. *IHT*, 8 September; *JP*, 8 September 1986.
35. *JP*, 7 September 1986.
36. Ibid.
37. *NYT*, 6 September 1986.
38. *NYT*, 4 January 1987.
39. *FR*, 11 September; *Ha'aretz*, 13 November 1986.
40. *Newsweek*, 15 September 1986.
41. *NYT*, 4 January 1987.
42. *JP*, 9 September 1986.
43. *JP*, 19 November 1986; *NYT*, 4 January, 1987.
44. Ibid.
45. Ibid.
46. *IHT*, 16 October 1986.
47. *Newsweek*, 27 October 1986.
48. *Ha'aretz*, 20 October; *Ma'ariv*, 23 October 1986.
49. *Ha'aretz*, 6 February 1987.
50. *Ma'ariv*, 21 October 1986.
51. *Ha'aretz*, 20 October 1986.
52. *Nidal al-Sha'b*, 25 October 1986.
53. *IHT*, 16 October 1986.
54. The chronology was compiled with the assistance of the Jaffee Center for Strategic Studies, Tel Aviv University.

INTRA-REGIONAL AND MUSLIM AFFAIRS

Inter-Arab Relations

BRUCE MADDY-WEITZMAN

The broad lines of division within the Arab world which had been laid down at the end of the 1970s and the beginning of the 1980s remained unchanged during 1986. The Iraqi-Iranian war continued to be the most trenchantly divisive of all inter-Arab issues, with Syria and Libya, and to a much lesser extent Algeria and the People's Democratic Republic of Yemen (PDRY) bucking the views of the large majority of Arab states by openly siding with non-Arab Iran against Iraq. In a continuation of the trend of previous years, the Arab-Israeli conflict/peace process and the question of Egypt's place in the Arab world — the other two central inter-Arab issues — were of lower salience. Noteworthy were the intensive efforts of Jordan's King Husayn, backed by Saudi Arabia and Kuwait, during the first half of 1986 to move Syria away from its long-standing backing of Iran and toward a *rapprochement*, or at least a thaw, with Iraq. Were this to be achieved, went the thinking, the first full-scale Arab summit in four years could be held to fashion an all-Arab consensus on the Gulf war, the Arab-Israeli conflict, and perhaps even the nature of Egyptian-Arab relations. Thus, the decade-long process of inter-Arab fragmentation could be reversed, and perhaps the escalation of the war as well. As it happened, the effort to budge Syria failed, almost at the last moment, and no summit was convened. Although mediation efforts did not totally cease, the majority of Arab states were again reduced to watchful, and nervous, waiting as the Iranians renewed their offensive toward Basra at the end of the year.

Regarding Egypt, the war had already provided the necessary opening for Egypt's return — by degrees — to a position of centrality in the Arab world, first and foremost via its massive assistance in all forms to Iraq. Iran's gains on the battlefield during 1986 further strengthened the widespread Arab appreciation of Egypt's value, both actual and potential, as a counterweight to Iranian ambitions. On the whole, the ostracism of Egypt was a thing of the past as Cairo conducted political, economic and cultural relations with nearly every Arab country without renouncing its peace with Israel. This was further demonstrated at the end of January 1987, when Husni Mubarak was an honored and active participant in the fifth summit conference of the Islamic Conference Organization (ICO), held in Kuwait. His presence, despite the absence of official diplomatic ties between the two countries, was a poignant illustration of how much had changed in the Arab world since the late 1970s.

Whereas inter-Arab alignments remained largely in place, two widely divergent events and Arab reactions to them illustrated the degree to which Arab politics have been altered over the years. One was the American bombing raid on Libya on 15 April, the first direct military action by a global power against an Arab state since the 1956 Suez war. (The US had bombed Syrian positions in Lebanon in 1983, but had avoided attacking Syria proper.) Although Arab condemnations of the raid were almost unanimous, Libya's efforts to convene an emergency summit to formulate a joint Arab response were unsuccessful. Given Libya's near pariah status, this did not come as a surprise. Still, in historical terms, the contrast between the benefits reaped by Jamal 'Abd al-Nasir in the Arab world in 1956 and the tepid Arab response to Mu'ammar al-Qadhdhafi's calls for action in 1986 was, for all of the obvious differences between the two sets of events, inescapable. The second event was the surprise summit meeting in Ifrane, Morocco, between Israel's Prime Minister Shimon Peres and Morocco's King Hasan II on 22-23 July. Their basically exploratory talks had no discernible impact on the Arab-Israeli peace process. Yet the fact that a meeting was even held in the light of day between an Arab King (and chairman of the Arab Summit Conference) and an Israeli Prime Minister was a milestone in the history of Arab-Israeli relations. As such, the Arab reaction was instructive; whereas Hasan's initiative inevitably evoked memories of Anwar al-Sadat in 1977, the large degree of Arab restraint in this case stood in striking contrast (again despite the obvious differences between the two sets of events) to the militant condemnations of nine years earlier. Taken together, these two sets of events demonstrated the substantial, even profound, alterations in some of the fundamental "rules of the game" in Arab politics which had taken place over the previous decade.[1]

Subregional issues generated, on the whole, more dynamism than all-Arab concerns. In the Nile Valley-East Africa region, a newly-elected government in Sudan, facing massive internal problems, maneuvered gingerly between Egypt and Libya. Despite public Egyptian equanimity, however, the formerly cozy Egyptian-Sudanese relationship of Numayri's day belonged to the past, exemplified by the uncertain state of the various Nile Valley integration agreements. On the other hand, the newly forged Libyan-Sudanese relationship was not without considerable strains either. The southern part of the Arabian Peninsula seemed even more insular than usual, thanks to the bloody power struggle in the PDRY, in January 1986, and the subsequent concern of the new ruling group there to consolidate its power (see chapters on the two Yemens). In the Gulf, apart from the Iraqi-Iranian war, Bahrain and Qatar nearly came to blows over a disputed island, necessitating Saudi mediation (see chapter on the Gulf states). Finally, in the Maghrib, the breakup of the Moroccan-Libyan union in August 1986 — in the wake of the Hasan-Peres meeting — ended their two-year old anomalous alliance and thus the division of the Maghrib into two distinct groups. Whether or not this would affect Morocco's efforts to consolidate its hold in the Western Sahara remained to be seen.

EFFORTS TO HEAL THE RIFTS

The emergency (rump) Arab summit, held in Casablanca on 5–8 August 1985, had established two committees to "purify the Arab atmosphere" and to heal, or at least soften, inter-Arab divisions which had hardened during the previous year (see *Middle East Contemporary Survey* [*MECS*] 1984–85, pp 109–18. Little success was achieved during the rest of 1985 in easing relations between Syria and Iraq which, along with the Egyptian-Syrian relationship, was the most significant of all inter-Arab rifts. Neither was any progress noticeable in reconciling Iraq and Libya or the Palestine Liberation Organization (PLO) and Libya. However, the committee composed of Saudi Arabian, Tunisian and Arab League representatives had provided the formal framework for a Syrian-Jordanian thaw during the last half of 1985, after a nearly six-year freeze. This reconciliation process, based on at least a tactical confluence of interests between Damascus and Amman, was formalized by King Husayn's visit to Damascus at the very end of 1985 and continued during the first part of 1986. Apart from both the bilateral aspects and the Arab-Israeli Palestinian issues (for details, see below), the thaw raised the hopes of King Husayn, the Saudis and Kuwaitis that Syria might be willing to moderate its opposition to the Arab majority on vital inter-Arab issues, especially regarding the Gulf war.[2] These hopes were reinforced by signs that the Syrian-Iranian relationship was becoming frayed: as of December 1985, Iran had ceased its oil deliveries to Syria, originally contracted under the terms of the 1982 agreement in which Syria closed down the Iraqi oil pipeline traversing Syria to the Mediterranean. The cessation of Iranian deliveries may have been partly a result of difficulties stemming from war damage to Iran's Kharg Island oil terminal. However, the Iranians were also irritated by Syria's failure to repay its outstanding debts ($1–2 bn). Additional sources of tension were Iran's backing for the *Hizballah* Shi'ite faction in Lebanon (see chapter on Lebanon) and Iran's displeasure with the Syrian-Jordanian *rapprochement*. Concurrently, Iran's seizure of Iraq's Faw port and oil terminal during the second week of February 1986 placed Syria in an extremely uncomfortable position, for it both (a) seemed to belie Syrian assurances to its Arab critics that Iran was not interested in the acquisition of any Arab territory, and (b) brought the threat of war closer to the Gulf states, something which Damascus had consistently claimed to have been instrumental in preventing (see section on the war, below). Thus, for King Husayn, the Saudis and the Kuwaitis, renewed mediation efforts seemed both more urgent and more likely to bear fruit during the first months of 1986. Accordingly, Jordan's Prime Minister Zayd al-Rifa'i visited Damascus on 9 February; Saudi Arabia's Foreign Minister, Sa'ud al-Faysal, journeyed to Damascus on 21 February and King Husayn traveled to Baghdad on 4 March. According to Kuwait's Foreign Minister, the Algerians were also playing a positive role.[3]

Iraqi leaders were ready, even eager, to cooperate with these efforts, as long as it was Syria that would be required to alter its policies. While "the past was very bitter," Saddam Husayn told an interviewer, one should "not be bogged down [by it]. When Syria becomes ready to take one step, we will take a step, and when they become ready to establish normal relations with us... we will be ready." However, he continued, if Syria waited till the war's end before doing so, the Iraqi public would then "begin to recall Syrian behavior, making the process more difficult."[4]

Paradoxically, perhaps, the level of invective between Damascus and Baghdad rose during this period, centering on mutual allegations of subversive acts in each other's territory. On 5 February, Iraq's Director-General of Security, 'Ali Hasan al-Majid, revealed details of the activities of a Syrian-trained team of Iranian agents — apprehended two months earlier — which had been responsible for a number of sabotage actions in Baghdad. Moreover, he said, Syrian Intelligence had also charged one of the group with collecting information on Iraq's oil pipeline to Saudi Arabia.[5] One month later, Syria charged Iraq with responsibility for the explosion of a booby-trapped refrigerator truck near Damascus' northern entrance, the latest in "the Saddam agent regime's... tragic series of national and pan-Arab crimes"; according to People's Assembly Speaker Mahmud al-Zu'abi, these crimes had resulted in the death of hundreds of innocent civilians. Moreover, the Syrians hastened to declare before their Arab critics that the explosion constituted "a treacherous stab in the back of all sincere efforts aimed at clearing the Arab atmosphere."[6] Within weeks, Damascus belatedly charged Baghdad with an even more serious crime, the blowing up on 16 April of several public transportation vehicles, killing 144 civilians and injuring 149.[7]

THE LIBYAN-AMERICAN CONFRONTATION AND THE ARAB SUMMIT

In late April, the inter-Arab agenda became even more crowded and the efforts to reconcile inter-Arab differences more complicated. A brief account of the buildup of the Libya-US crisis will put these developments into perspective.

Their steadily escalating confrontation during the first four months of 1986 was particularly uncomfortable for the majority of Arab states. On the one hand, their disgust with Qadhdafi's regime and their generally pro-American orientation dictated a hands-off attitude. On the other hand, both the minimum requirements of Arab solidarity and, in many cases, a genuine unhappiness with the prospect of a superpower taking military action against *any* Arab state compelled action on Libya's behalf. Consequently, the Arab League Council discussed the crisis no less than four times — three in emergency sessions.

The first League Council meeting, on 4 January, condemned American warnings of possible retaliation against Libya following the bloody attacks by the Abu Nidal group at the Rome and Vienna airports (see *MECS* 1984–85, essay on armed operations).[8] Only Syria, Libya and Tunisia were represented at the session by their Foreign Ministers; nearly all the rest delegated their permanent representatives to the Arab League, indicating that the matter was not yet a particularly grave one for most Arab states.[9]

As American pressure on Libya increased, so did Arab concern. In the wake of US-declared economic sanctions against Libya on 7–8 January, Tripoli pressed for another emergency council meeting. After three postponements — the last in order to wait for the reaction of the European Economic Community (EEC) to America's call to participate in the sanctions[10] — the Council met on 30 January. This time, the number of Arab Foreign Ministers attending increased to eight.[11] The Libyans would have liked the meeting to have taken far-reaching economic counter-measures, including a counter-boycott of US petroleum companies, financial institutions and banks participating in the US-imposed sanctions. For demonstrative purposes, they also initially suggested that the Arab states liquidate existing investments in the US, refrain from making future ones, compensate Libya for assets frozen by Washington and help Libya find markets for its oil, or even increase their oil production and market it on behalf of Libya (like Saudi Arabia does for Iraq).[12] However, these proposals had no chance of being adopted, and the Libyans themselves did not press the matter. As it happened, the Council limited itself to:

1. condemnations of the US threats;
2. an unspecified warning to foreign companies against possible repercussions in the event of their compliance with US sanctions;
3. a commitment to provide Libya, if necessary, with technical expertise for its oil industry;
4. a vague reference to preventing any harm to the production and marketing of Libyan oil; and
5. a request to the United Nations Security Council to investigate American threats.[13]

Underneath this outward show of solidarity was considerable displeasure with Libya's oppositionist stance on nearly every other issue of consequence facing the Arab world. Inevitably, it was the Iraqi delegate to the session who voiced the sharpest criticism. Libya's demand for Arab support against external aggression, under the terms of the Arab League Charter and the Joint Defense Pact of 1950, should, he declared, be conditional on Libya's applying the same standards toward the Iraqi-Iranian war.[14] The Iraqis would reiterate this theme repeatedly during the coming months.

The regularly scheduled Arab League Council meeting in Tunis on 25–27 March took place in the shadow of the American-Libyan clashes in the Gulf of Sidra (24–25 March). Most Arab countries and some Arab media reacted vehemently to the clashes; however, Egypt, Saudi Arabia, Jordan and Iraq were all far more restrained. Nonetheless, a show of unanimity was made in the League Council, where the US was roundly condemned for its "blatant violation" of Libya's sovereignty and territorial integrity, and called on to cease all military operations against Libya. However, inter-Arab divisions over the Gulf war continued to intrude. The League Council's by now customary expression of "all-out solidarity" with Iraq and deep concern over "the Iranian threat to the security, sovereignty and territorial integrity of the Arab Gulf states" drew Syrian and Libyan reservations. The League should be careful, warned Syria's Foreign Minister, Faruq al-Shar', not to adopt resolutions that would only help bring about the war's expansion into the Gulf — something which, thanks primarily to Syria, had not occurred until now. As for the widely held view that Iran's Arab allies were in violation of the Joint Defense Pact, al-Shar' turned the argument on its head: it was Iraq, he declared, which was in violation of the pact, since it had consulted no other Arab parties before launching the war.[15]

The intertwining of the Libya-US and Iran-Iraq issues, with all the resulting Arab discord and paralysis, reached its climax in the aftermath of the US bombings on 15 April. This time, the Arab states were unanimous in condemning the US action. Libya immediately called for an emergency Arab summit to discuss only the attack. Its call for a single-issue summit was supported by Syria and the PDRY (Algeria and the new Government in Sudan wavered in their support).[16] Iran and Syria immediately joined with Libya in calling on Arab and Islamic countries to sever diplomatic, economic and military relations with the US.[17] (For more on the Syrian-Libyan-Iranian grouping, see section on the Iraqi-Iranian war, below.)

By contrast, the leading Arab countries of the majority camp (Iraq, Kuwait, Morocco, Jordan, the United Arab Emirates [UAE] and, more cautiously, Saudi Arabia) felt that the crisis atmosphere presented them with an opportunity to advance their own program. A summit, in their view, was indeed vital. However, it was absolutely necessary that it should address the gamut of issues facing the Arab world, and not only the American attack on Libya.[18] Thus, Morocco's King Hasan — acting in his capacity as chairman of the Arab Summit Conference — took the initiative and formally summoned Arab leaders to an emergency summit in Fez.[19] Shortly thereafter, the official dates of a preparatory Foreign Ministers' meeting were fixed for 29–30 April, to be followed on 3 May by the summit itself.[20]

Hasan's summit call bore a resemblance to his actions of the previous summer when he convened the emergency Casablanca summit. In both cases, he was attempting to break the inter-Arab stalemate before having obtained prior consensus for his actions.

As at Casablanca, his activist strategy failed to achieve a breakthrough. Libya, backed by Syria, continued to insist on a single-issue summit, and Libya's Number Two man, Staff-Maj 'Abd al-Salam al-Jallud, accused those favoring a wider agenda of "attempting to exploit the upcoming Arab summit to force [Libya] into making concessions."[21] In order to further emphasize their position, the Libyans suggested, again with Syrian backing, a new venue for the summit — the Libyan town of Sabha (Qadhdhafi's birthplace).[22]

Not surprisingly, the preparatory Foreign Ministers' meeting failed to resolve the agenda and venue disagreements. While the Arab majority suggested that the agenda include consideration of "aggression against the Arab world in general" (and thus cover the conflicts with Israel, Iran and even Somalia's dispute with Ethiopia), the Libyans and Syrians stood firm. A single-issue summit, they declared, was appropriate for emergency situations, while a multi-issue summit demanded careful preparation and should best be left for a regularly scheduled gathering.[23]

Consequently, the Foreign Ministers' conference announced on 1 May that further study and preparation were needed before a summit could be convened; their next meeting, they declared, would be held at some point soon in Morocco, following consultations to be spearheaded by Arab League Secretary-General Chedli Klibi.[24]

The Libyans termed the failure to convene a summit "terrible."[25] The Moroccans, for their part, were angry with both their union partner in Tripoli and its Syrian ally. The next Foreign Ministers' meeting (scheduled for around 15 June), declared Foreign Minister 'Abd al-Latif Filali, would take place regardless of whether Syria and Libya attended. "It is time," he stated, "that decisions in the Arab League be taken without achieving unanimity."[26] As it happened, this meeting was postponed.

THE FAILURE OF IRAQI-SYRIAN RECONCILIATION ATTEMPTS

For most Arab leaders, the disagreements over the terms of reference of an emergency Arab summit reinforced their feelings that an Iraqi-Syrian reconciliation was a *sine qua non* for achieving even a semblance of joint action *vis à vis* the gamut of issues facing the Arab world. Thus, the month of May witnessed a flurry of high-level diplomatic comings and goings designed to bring this about. These efforts were spearheaded by King Husayn. Husayn first discussed the matter with Hafiz al-Asad during the latter's visit to Amman on 5 May; then he journeyed twice to Baghdad, on 15 and 26 May, for talks with Saddam Husayn; following the first visit to Baghdad, King Husayn proceeded immediately to Damascus to meet with Asad — after the second, Jordan's Prime Minister Zayd al-Rifa'i conveyed the results to Asad in Athens, where he was on an official visit. The following day (28 May), Iraq's Foreign Minister, Tariq 'Aziz, flew to Kuwait and Saudi Arabia for consultations with leaders there. The result of these exchanges was the scheduling of talks between the Iraqi and Syrian Foreign Ministers, to take place on 13 June at a point along their common border. Jordanian expectations were considerable: in an interview conducted only three days prior to the scheduled meeting, King Husayn declared that the aim of the meeting was to explore the possibilities of a broad reconciliation. "We have our fingers crossed," he stated, ["that the meeting will] pave the way for a successful Arab summit."[27] At almost the last moment, however, the Syrians canceled the meeting. What had happened?

One element in Syria's willingness to at least consider the reconciliation process had undoubtedly been economic: the country's economy was in dire need of help (see chapter on Syria). Thus, Damascus found it prudent to at least give the appearance of being amenable to the mediation efforts: this would allow it to both put pressure on Iran to be more forthcoming in its assistance and to possibly extract promises of greater Arab aid (either as a substitute for, or in addition to, that of Iran). The Iranians understood the Syrian signal and responded forthwith: on 7 June, Iran made its first oil delivery to Syria in months, while on that same day Iran's Acting Foreign Minister, Muhammad 'Ali Besharati, flew to Damascus for clarifications of Syrian intentions. According to the Iranians, Asad reassured him that the ties between Tehran and Damascus were "strategic,"[28] i.e., that a dramatic Syrian shift away from Iran was not in the offing. One month later (after the Iraqi-Syrian meeting had been canceled), a high-level Syrian economic delegation to Tehran won an Iranian agreement to ease the pressure for debt repayment and to sell Syria 2.5 m tons of oil between October 1986 and March 1987 at concessionary prices.[29] From the Arab side, the Saudis denied reports that they agreed to guarantee a $1 bn loan to Syria in exchange for Syria's reconciliation with Iraq (and PLO leader Yasir 'Arafat), or that they had even offered to repay part of Syria's debts to Iran.[30] Nonetheless, a Western source quoted Jordanian officials as insisting that the Saudis had given Asad $2 bn in cash in spite of the breakdown in the reconciliation efforts.[31] Explaining Syria's behavior solely in terms of economic extortion, however, underplays the political-strategic factors at work. Regionally and globally, Syria was on the defensive: at odds with most of the Arab world over the Gulf war, its support of the Sh'ite *Amal* militia in its fight against 'Arafat's loyalists in Beirut's Palestinian refugee camps, and the question of Egypt's return to the Arab fold. Moreover, Syrian leaders were genuinely concerned about the possibility of an American and/or Israeli attack, in the wake of the US bombing of Libya and the widespread reports of Syrian involvement in both successful and foiled terror operations. Displaying flexibility toward Arab mediation entreaties was a part of Syria's efforts to avoid finding itself totally isolated in the event of an armed conflict. In this regard, Asad reportedly sought King Husayn's agreement, during their talks in May, to the stationing of Syrian anti-aircraft missiles batteries on Jordanian soil (see section on Jordanian-Syrian relations, below).

As for the content of any Syrian-Iraqi reconciliation, the Syrians operated on two levels. The first was both strategic and ideological: the Syrian-Iraqi "Charter for Joint National Action" of 1978, they insisted, should be reactivated, and serve as the basis for their future relations (for the agreement and its collapse, see *MECS* 1978–79, pp 236–40; for Syria's expression of this stand during the autumn of 1985, see *MECS* 1984–85, pp 116–17). Undoubtedly, there were ideological points to score by advocating the unity of the two Ba'th regimes. Far more important, however, was the strategic dimension. Syrian leaders explained repeatedly that implementing the unity agreements would result in a profound shift in the regional strategic balance. The Iranians would, *ipso facto*, no longer desire to continue fighting.[32] As for Arab-Israeli relations — the real issue for Syria — the balance of power would be fundamentally altered.[33] That this was the thrust of Syrian thinking was evidenced by an unusually frank admission by Syria's Defense Minister, Mustafa Talas, that Syria could dare to begin a war against Israel only if both Iraq and Jordan were aligned with it. This could only be achieved, he continued, after Saddam Husayn had been deposed.[34] Strictly speaking, this was probably correct; in any case, it belied any notion of Syrian benevolence toward the existing regime in Iraq, or that Syria held exaggerated hopes for its unity proposal.[35]

Simultaneously, the Syrians sought to focus on more narrow, bilateral issues, to test whether the Iraqis were willing to uncouple the specifics of Syrian-Iraqi relations from the issue of Syria's stand on the Gulf war. One matter under discussion was the possible reopening of the Iraqi oil pipeline traversing Syria to the ports of Baniyas and Tripoli (in Lebanon), which Damascus had shut down, in coordination with Iran, in 1982 (see *MECS* 1981–82, p 233). Another was the possible reopening of their common border, which had been effectively closed with the pipeline. The Syrians were also suggesting an agreement to curtail the activities of opposition groups operating in each other's territory.[36] Ironically, it was the Syrians who may well have been more in need of the pipeline's reopening (given the transit fees they would collect and their need for light Iraqi crude for their own oil refineries), at least so long as the Iranians failed to renew their own deliveries. One Middle Eastern source estimated that the Iranian oil connection was worth $100m more per annum than the Iraqi one.[37] The Iraqis, for their part, made a point of belittling the economic value of the pipeline's reopening, thanks to the prevailing world surplus of oil and the efficacy of its own substitute pipelines — via Turkey and Saudi Arabia — developed over the previous years.[38] Nonetheless, its reopening would undoubtedly have been welcomed in Baghdad, as it would provide it with (a) greater export capacity (despite the existing oil glut); (b) added security through the diversification of its oil exporting capability; and (c) perhaps even leverage in other areas of the relationship with Syria.

Belittling the pipeline's significance was part of Iraq's extremely skeptical public posture toward the reconciliation attempts. Iraqi leaders scornfully dismissed the idea of instantly changing their hostile relations into ones of unity.[39] (This was consistent with the general trend in the Arab world over the previous 15 years to reject "instant" unity packages in favor of a more gradual development of closer relations.) Unlike the Syrians, the Iraqis did not temporarily cease, or even lower, the anti-Syrian tone in their media,[40] lambasting (a) the Syrian-Iranian alliance "at a time when Iran is implementing...a colonialist policy to occupy Iraq and the Arab Gulf," and was being prevented from doing so only by Iraq's "steadfastness," not by Syria's supposed "pan-Arab stand and diplomatic abilities";[41] (b) Syria's "grand plot" in Lebanon against "the Lebanese and Palestinian people";[42] and (c) its alleged desire for a military confrontation with Israel or the US as a way out of its political and economic difficulties.[43] Apart from genuine Iraqi doubts as to whether Syria would make the concession they really wanted (distancing itself from Iran), Iraqi leaders were undoubtedly interested in playing up Syrian perfidies in the eyes of the other Arab countries in order to lay the blame at Syria's doorstep for any failure in the mediation efforts.

With their Arab allies/mediators again in mind, the Iraqis took care not to place procedural obstacles in the way of the process; they conceded, albeit relectantly, to Syria's demand that the meeting between their two Foreign Ministers be held in private, without the presence of third parties. (Iraq preferred the presence of a "fraternal" mediator, stated Tariq 'Aziz, because it ensured an "accurate account" of the meeting.[44] What he didn't say, but certainly knew, was that the the third party's views, whether he was a Jordanian or a Saudi, were likely to be closer to Iraq's than Syria's.) Apparently, the Syrians were willing to make an exception to this rule only if the meeting were at a summit level, with King Husayn being the logical host. (Asad could then directly confront Saddam Husayn with their 1978 unity agreements from which the latter had pulled back.)[45] The Iraqis preferred a lower-level meeting prior to any summit — thus the scheduled 13 June meeting between their Foreign Ministers.

When the moment of truth came, the Iraqis made it clear that they were unwilling to uncouple their demands for Syria's cessation of its alliance with Iran from the more narrow bilateral issues at hand. Nor were they willing to consider seriously Syria's insistence on referring to the 1978 agreements as the basis for their discussions. The Syrians, for their part, were not ready to break their ties with Iran, particularly since the Iranians were now more forthcoming in the oil/debt sphere, and perhaps even with regard to exercising more control over their sympathizers in Lebanon. Thus, faced with the prospect of being held up before the Arab world as the party responsible for the failure of the reconciliation process, the Syrians preferred to cancel the Foreign Ministers' meeting altogether.[46]

Although the Jordanians and Saudis were keenly disappointed with Syria's stance, they generally refrained from open criticism.[47] Both King Husayn and Saudi Crown Prince 'Abdallah periodically continued their mediation efforts, with Husayn making trips to Damascus and Baghdad in late July, and Baghdad again on 28 October, and 'Abdallah calling on the Syrians and Iraqis during the later part of October. However, no progress was registered and Syrian-Iraqi relations remained bitterly hostile.

THE IFRANE SUMMIT

For years, Morocco's King Hasan, Jordan's King Husayn, the Saudis and others had been frustrated by the Arab majority's inability to shape decisively a collective Arab policy, and had periodically suggested changing the Arab League's decision-making mechanism from one based on consensus to majority rule (see *MECS* 1981–82, pp 227–79; 1983–84, p 127). Hasan's convening of the Casablanca summit in August 1985 had been one attempt to present the Syrian-led opposition grouping with the *fait accompli* of a unified Arab majority stance on major Arab issues. His lack of success had not deterred him from further initiatives — witness his efforts to convene a summit during April 1986. Now, with inter-Arab affairs more deadlocked than ever following the breakdown in the Iraqi-Syrian reconciliation efforts, he acted again, and even more singularly. On 22–23 July, he hosted Israel's Prime Minister Peres in his summer residence in Ifrane. (For details, see essay on the peace process and chapter on Israel.) Ideally, for Hasan, the meeting would result in the convening of an Arab summit at which existing inter-Arab differences would dissipate and a new consensus would be forged.[48]

For some years already, Hasan had been carving out a special position toward Israel, based on both his understanding of Arab priorities and his vision of Semitic brotherhood, the latter stemming from a somewhat idyllic view of historical Jewish-Arab relations in Morocco (for previous steps by Hasan in this regard, see *MECS* 1983–84, p 124; 1984–85, p 134). In March-April 1986, Hasan caused a further stir by suggesting that the "broadest possible Arab summit" should delegate an Arab Head of State to open "exploratory talks with the highest Israeli authorities"; his job would be to present them with the decision of the 1982 Fez Summit (known as the "Arab Peace Plan") and thus force Israel to talk seriously.[49] In the continued absence of a summit, Hasan chose to assign the role to himself, while taking care to emphasize that the legitimacy of his action derived from his chairmanship of the seven-member committee established by the Fez Summit to explain its resolutions to the outside world. It was only on the basis of these resolutions, he stressed, that he had agreed to hold discussions with Peres.[50]

Throughout his televised address to the Moroccan nation in which he reported on the meeting, Hasan reiterated that his actions were consistent with, and on behalf of, the supreme principle of Arab solidarity. Nonetheless, in rebutting his Arab critics, he also stressed the singular character of Morocco *vis-à-vis* the bulk of the Arab world. While Morocco was an integral part (*juz' la yatajaz'a*) of the Arab homeland, the "courageous" Moroccan people would never have been able to "abandon" their land for 20 years to Israeli occupation; by contrast, the people of the Arab Mashriq (East) were "languid" (*khamilun*); they therefore could not give Morocco any "lessons in patriotism."[51]

Arab reaction to the Ifrane Summit was along well-established lines. Alone among the Arab states, Egypt welcomed it wholeheartedly, and received shortly afterwards a Moroccan envoy who reported to Mubarak and Foreign Minister 'Abd al-Majid on the outcome of the meeting.[52] From the majority Arab camp, Jordan and Saudi Arabia both denied any prior knowledge of the visit and criticized its "unilateral" nature in guarded terms, preferring to take a wait-and-see posture;[53] the Iraqis condemned it, calling Hasan's conduct "strange" and "deviant", but said it was the "logical outcome" of Syria's and Libya's "treasonous acts" over the years, which had severely weakened the Arab nation.[54] Much harsher and sustained criticism came from Syria, Libya, Algeria, Iran and the Palestinian organizations. Syria immediately broke off diplomatic relations for the second time in three years. (For the impact on Libyan-Moroccan relations, see section on Maghrib affairs, below.) Befitting his "neutral" status, Arab League Secretary-General Klibi refrained from criticizing Hasan, emphasized Israel's failure to respond positively to the Fez Plan, and called on Arab countries "to put aside [their] disputes" and convene an Arab summit, in order to strengthen "joint Arab action" on the Palestine question.[55] Two days later, Hasan relinquished his post as chairman of the Arab Summit Conference — a position he had invested with considerable content over the previous half-decade (the president of the immediately preceding summit is officially charged with organizing the next summit gathering). He did so "most bitterly... unwillingly and with pain," in order not to provide his opponents with an excuse for opposing or boycotting a summit.[56]

As it happened, the emergency summit idea never got off the ground and Hasan's initiative produced no immediate results during the rest of 1986. Still, the very fact of the Ifrane meeting and the varied Arab responses to it indicated both the distance which parts of the Arab world had traveled over the years regarding Israel, and the depth of existing inter-Arab divisions.

The lack of a summit continued to disturb the majority of Arab leaders for the remainder of the year. The regular Arab League Council session in September-October 1986 appointed a "formulation committee" to define the principles of "joint Arab action." Reportedly, they were to be based on a pan-Arab action charter prepared by Klibi: points of emphasis included insulating pan-Arab action from bilateral differences, adhering to the designated date and level of represenation set for its meetings, and paying the countries' shares of the Arab League budget on schedule.[57]

To complete this section, a brief summary of the most important "cross-bloc" bilateral relationship is necessary.

JORDANIAN-SYRIAN RELATIONS

The thaw in Jordanian-Syrian relations which was consummated in the last half of 1985 had been based on a tactical confluence of interests in several areas, including their positions regarding Yasir 'Arafat, the Arab-Israeli conflict/peace process and their respective places in the Arab world (for details, see *MECS* 1984–85, pp 117–18). In 1986, the channels for dialogue remained open. No less than six top-level meetings took place during the year — three between King Husayn and Hafiz al-Asad, and three between Asad and Jordan's Prime Minister, Zayd al-Rifa'i. This did not translate, however, into a real identity of views on regional issues — the Iraqi-Iranian war, the question of Egypt's return to the Arab fold and the ultimate nature of an Arab-Israeli peace settlement. Neither did they crystallize any joint strategy *vis-à-vis* Yasir 'Arafat's leadership of the PLO.[58] (It was their common opposition to his leadership, albeit for different reasons, which had contributed to the original thaw during the fall of 1985.) The absence of a joint communiqué following any of the Husayn-Asad meetings was a concrete indication of these fundamental divergences.

By contrast, the improvement of bilateral relations continued apace, although it must be emphasized that their economic ties had always been somewhat insulated from the highly charged political atmosphere of the previous six years. Highlights of this improvement during 1986 included the simplification of border procedures, an agreement on combating drug smuggling, the establishment of a joint free trade zone and the selling of Jordanian electricity to Syria.[59]

Apart from King Husayn's failed efforts to pry Syria away from Iran, much of his dialogue with Asad centered on Arab-Israeli issues, particularly during the heightened Syrian-Israeli tension during the spring of 1986. Numerous reports in the Arab media spoke of Asad's request to station Syrian anti-aircraft missiles in northern Jordan in expectation of a possible Israeli military thrust from that direction against Syria (a move which would bypass the Golan heights front).[60] There is no evidence that Husayn acceded to the request, although it is possible that he agreed to give the Syrian Air Force freedom to maneuver in Jordanian airspace in the event of an Israeli attack.[61] In the aftermath of the crisis, he reportedly stated frankly to Asad that Israeli military superiority was, for the time being, a given.[62]

Throughout the year, neither side pretended that it saw eye-to-eye with the other on regional issues. While the Jordanians were generally circumspect, and even emphasized that the existence of differences was a healthy phenomenon,[63] the Syrians insisted that the Jordanians had moved closer to Syria by rejecting "partial and unilateral resolutions" of the Arab-Israeli conflict and in agreeing to abide by Arab summit resolutions.[64] (For the joint statement to this effect, see *MECS* 1986–85, p 118.) By the end of the year the prospects for a Jordanian mediation between Syria and Iraq and for either war or negotiations with Israel were less strong than they had been six months earlier. Thus, the importance for each side of the Jordanian-Syrian relationship possessed less urgency, for the moment, than before. Moreover, there were renewed, if small, signs of stress: Turkey's formal charging of a Syrian diplomat with involvement in the assassination of a Jordanian diplomat a year earlier (Syria denied the charge);[65] a critical statement by Jordanian opposition figures issued over Radio Damascus;[66] and the complete silence in the Jordanian Parliament when King Husayn mentioned his continued reconciliation efforts with Asad.[67] Moreover, during the same speech, Husayn made a general condemnation of all forms of terror.[68]

Coming as it did after Britain's severing of relations with Syria following the Nizar Hindawi trial (see chapter on Syria), Husayn's statement, although disapproving of Britain's action, was a veiled criticism of Syrian behavior, something which Damascus could not have taken kindly to.

THE IRAQI-IRANIAN WAR AS AN INTER-ARAB ISSUE

THE GULF STATES

Apart from its all-Arab dimension, the Iraqi-Iranian war continued to be of the greatest and most immediate concern to the Arab littorals along the Gulf. Since the war's onset, their proximity had dictated a policy of delicate maneuvering between the two combatants in order to avoid overtly antagonizing either side and to keep the war zone itself from spreading in their direction. However, this never translated into a pure even-handed policy. Geography, ideology and prudence all dictated a degree of tilting toward Iraq, manifested in particular by generous levels of economic aid. The backing of the Gulf Cooperation Council (GCC) for Iraq jelled further, but again by degrees, once it became clear that it was Iran that posed the most immediate threat to the regional status quo. Even so, however, their identification with Iraq was not complete. In 1986, these dynamics were more pronounced, thanks to the war's intensification on all fronts (see essay on the war). Conversely, Iran's warnings, and even threats to the GCC states, and especially to Kuwait and Saudi Arabia, increased as well. Heightened GCC anxieties also further strengthened their appreciation of Egypt as a counterweight — both potential and actual — to Iran (see section on Egypt and the Arab world, below).

Ironically, the previous year had ended on an encouraging note for the Iranians: the GCC's Summit Conference in November 1985 had adopted a resolution on the war that was more even-handed than previous ones (see *MECS* 1984–85, pp 122–23). The Iranians had hoped it was a harbinger of things to come; however, this was not to be.[69] The war's escalation, beginning with Iran's seizure of Faw in February 1986, resulted in a steady exchange of condemnations, warnings, accusations and denials between Iran and the GCC states. Tehran denied that the war's escalation posed a threat to the Gulf states; what mattered was their conduct.[70] Iranian leaders expressed repeatedly their displeasure with the GCC states, particularly Saudi Arabia and Kuwait, for their tilt towards Iraq. In the area of oil, this included support for Iraqi violations of the Organization of Petroleum Exporting Countries (OPEC) resolutions setting production quotas, Saudi Arabia's transporting of Iraqi oil through a Saudi pipeline, and Riyadh's sale of neutral zone oil on Iraq's behalf.[71] Concerning military matters, the list of allegations was long: the transshipment of Iraqi war material through GCC ports;[72] the treatment of Iraqi war wounded in Kuwaiti hospitals;[73] the collection of intelligence information for Iraq via a Kuwaiti naval base;[74] the use of Kuwait's territories and airspace by Iraqi forces, particularly Bubiyan Island (the Iranians had long been as eager to prevent Iraq from using Bubiyan as Iraq had been to do so);[75] and assistance — including information supplied by Saudi AWACS aircraft — for long-range Iraqi air attacks against Iranian oil facilities at the southern end of the Persian Gulf near the Straits of Hormuz.[76] Until now, declared a Radio Tehran commentary, Iran had been remarkably tolerant. In fact, "perhaps in no war in the world can one find a country like Iran which has been so patient with the supporters and backers of its enemy."[77] However, this "Islamic forbearance and patience" had reached its limit; if the GCC states continued to extend help to Iraq, Iran would henceforth "consider them responsible for Iraq's aggressions."[78]

One concrete indication of Iran's displeasure was a series of large demonstrations in Tehran in front of the Kuwaiti and Saudi embassies, protesting against their pro-Iraqi policies. They proved, said an Iranian official, that "people's sentiments can only be controlled to a certain extent."[79] Another apparent response was an attack on 25 November by the Iranian Air Force against an Abu Dhabi offshore oil platform. The Iranians insisted that the Iraqis were the guilty party, in line with Iraq's alleged continuing efforts to destabilize the region.[80] Tehran even offered to assist in repairing the damage. However, a Western report identifying Iranian war planes as the culprits seems more credible.[81] As for the widespread feeling in the Arab world that only Iraq stood between Iran and the GCC states,[82] the Speaker of Iran's Parliament, 'Ali Akbar Hashemi-Rafsanjani, turned the argument on its head. Iran "would not harm our neighbors in the event of victory." The real danger, he continued, was that the "Iraqi nation," once liberated, was likely to lay the blame for the losses incurred by the war's continuation at Kuwait's doorstep, and act accordingly.[83]

The response of the Gulf states was multifaceted. They repeatedly denied Iranian allegations of active military involvement on Iraq's side;[84] they also issued their own protests against Iranian military actions (these included attacks on GCC oil tankers, alleged harassment of Kuwaiti naval vessels and the aforementioned bombing of Abu Dhabi's oil platform — although in the latter case Iran was not referred to by name).[85] GCC ministerial and summit resolutions, and separate declarations by Saudi Arabia, pledged to help defend their members, particularly Kuwait, from any Iranian aggression;[86] to back this up, combined GCC units ("Peninsula Shield" — see chapter on the Gulf states) were apparently moved forward, at one point, from their Saudi bases to Kuwait.[87] GCC statements also continued to praise Iraq's positive response to international efforts to negotiate an end to the war, and called on Iran to do the same;[88] this point was particularly emphasized by Kuwait's Deputy Prime Minister and Foreign Minister, Shaykh Sabah, at the Non-Aligned Summit in Harare, Zimbabwe, at the beginning of September.[89]

Nonetheless, the GCC states never lost sight of the fact that the Iranians had to be placated as well. "Nobody," said an Omani Foreign Ministry official, "can deny...that we...are Iran's neighbors and must live as neighbors."[90] Thus, for example, the 26–27 August GCC Ministerial Council meeting reiterated the November 1985 summit's endorsement of a settlement which would "safeguard the legitimate rights" of both Iraq and Iran.[91]

Saudi leaders, in particular, continued to conduct a delicate, if tense, dialogue with their Iranian counterparts. This had begun the previous year, with exchange visits by their respective Foreign Ministers.[92] In 1986, at least three Iranian officials visited Saudi Arabia.[93] No progress was evident in bridging their fundamental differences on the Gulf war (although Rafsanjani claimed at one point that Saudi Arabia had privately told Iran that it had halted its aid to Iraq).[94] The Saudis were also angry about Rafsanjani's supposed incitement of Iranian students to attack Kuwaiti and Saudi embassies;[95] as in previous years, another source of tension was the behavior of Iranian pilgrims in Saudi Arabia (see essay on Islamic affairs). At the same time, Riyadh's granting of permission to no fewer than 150,0000 Iranians to come on pilgrimage was a tangible indication that the Saudis felt it prudent to cultivate the Iranians. That the two countries possessed at least some mutual interests was demonstrated at the end of 1986 when Riyadh brought its oil pricing and production policies more into line with Tehran's (partly at Iraq's expense! — see essay on Middle East oil). Saudi prudence was also highlighted by the revelations of Saudi financier 'Adnan Khashoggi's role in Iranian arms purchases. Despite official Saudi denials of involvement, it was the sharpest demonstration yet of Riyadh's acutely felt need to hedge its bets in the Iraqi-Iranian conflict (for details of the affair, see chapters on Iran and Saudi Arabia, and essay on the US and the Middle East). Concurrently, the Saudis were reported to have shipped large amounts of refined petroleum products to Iran (this, too, was denied by Riyadh).[96] Whether or not the Iranians curbed, in return, their support for oppositionist Shi'ite elements in Saudi Arabia and the Gulf principalities — something the Saudis had reportedly demanded[97] — could not be ascertained. The Iraqis, for their part, refrained from commenting on Riyadh's overtures to Tehran, although Saddam Husayn undoubtedly raised the matter in his two-hour meeting with King Fahd (occasioned by Saddam's performance of the "minor pilgrimage" on 27–28 December 1986).[98] In general, Iraqi leaders were more forthcoming in praising Saudi Arabia and Kuwait for their assistance than they had been in previous years.[99] While there was indeed a further jelling of support for Iraq by the GCC states, Baghdad's more unreserved praise also reflected its own increasing dependence on them in the face of Iran's unrelenting pursuit of victory.

SYRIA AND ITS ALLIES

The Syrian-Iranian-Libyan "oppositionist" alliance, while shaky at times, remained intact during 1986, thanks to the three countries' overriding anti-Iraqi, anti-Israeli and anti-American orientations. Their Foreign Ministers held two tripartite sessions during the year, the fourth and fifth such gatherings in the last two years. The first, held in Tehran on 14--5 April, just as the Americans were bombing Libya, resulted in a call to all Arab and Islamic countries "to break off their political and economic relations with the US," while also declaring their countries' "revulsion" with (unnamed) Arab countries that were pro-American. The Foreign Ministers also repeated earlier condemnations of Iraq for initiating the "iniquitous war" against Iran. At the same time, their joint communiqué stressed — no doubt at Syria's insistence — Iran's lack of terrritorial ambitions in Iraq and its interests in "good neighborly relations and Islamic fraternity both with [the] Iraqi people and other Arab countries."[100] The second meeting, on 24–25 August in Damascus, apparently concentrated on coordinating positions in preparation for the upcoming Non-Aligned Foreign Ministers' and Summit Conferences in New Delhi and Harare, respectively.[101]

Of the three sets of bilateral relationships, the Syrian-Iranian one, really the linchpin of their respective regional policies, underwent more stress — particularly during the first six months of 1986 (see above) — than at any other time since their anti-Iraqi political-economic agreements of 1982. On the ideological level, Iran's advances on the war front were problematic for Syria in that they further exposed Damascus to widespread Arab charges of betraying Arab principles by supporting non-Arab Iran against Iraq. In coping with these charges, Syrian officials stoutly reiterated their claims to be moderating Iranian behavior *vis-à-vis* the Gulf states,[102] and, while defending Iran's military actions as the result of being in a state of war, declared that they would withdraw their support if Iran began showing expansionist inclinations.[103] (Most Arab leaders did not give Syria any credit for its proclaimed efforts.)[104]

The failure of Iraqi-Syrian reconciliation efforts and Iran's agreement to a new (albeit short-term) oil deal with Syria (see above) eased tensions considerably; subsequent diplomatic contacts were highlighted by the visit of Syria's Vice President 'Abd al-Halim Khaddam and Foreign Minister Faruq al-Shar' to Tehran on 22–23 August, and Iran's Foreign Minister 'Ali Akbar Velayati to Damascus on 29 November.

Apart from the political-economic tensions connected with Syrian-Iraqi reconciliation efforts, Iranian-Syrian differences surfaced periodically over Lebanon-related matters: the actions of *Hizballah*, the Palestinian-*Amal* struggles, and the holding of foreign hostages (see chapter on Lebanon). Still, despite these and other points of friction,[105] the strategic needs of both countries dictated the continuation of the Iranian-Shi'ite Muslim/Syrian-Ba'thist alliance.

The Syrian-Libyan relationship continued to be deemed beneficial by both sides as well. Syrian pilots were apparently present in Libya; they were variously reported as helping the Libyan Air Force confront the US challenge, and involved in putting down an anti-Qadhdhafi revolt within the Libyan Army.[106] Syrian military experts were also reportedly involved in manning Libya's advanced Soviet anti-missile batteries.[107] In the other direction, a Western report, quoting "highly-placed Western intelligence sources," stated that Qadhdhafi was supplying a lethal nerve gas warhead for Syria's Soviet-built *Scud*-B missiles aimed at Israel.[108] The relationship was highlighted by Hafiz al-Asad's visit to Qadhdhafi on 24–25 August. Their joint press statement issued at the close of their meeting stressed that "aggression against either [of their countries was] aggression against both of them;" and condemned the joint US-Egyptian military maneuvers then under way. It also lambasted the recently held Hasan-Peres meeting[109] (for the effect on Morocco's relations with Libya and Syria, see section on Maghrib affairs, below). Reports conflicted on whether Qadhdhafi responded favorably to Asad's request for economic help.[110] The two sides also apparently agreed to apply pressure on Algeria not to be too accommodating to Yasir 'Arafat in its attempt to heal internal PLO rifts (see essay on the PLO). Subsequent Algerian-Syrian contacts failed to resolve these differences; consequently, no tripartite Algerian-Libyan-Syrian summit — an idea mooted in all three countries following the Peres-Hasan and Peres-Mubarak meetings — was convened.[111] At the end of the year, Lebanon became an issue of contention between Libya and Syria (just as it had been between Iran and Syria), particularly Qadhdhafi's support for Palestinian groups fighting against the Syrian-backed *Amal* Shi'ite militia (for details on this and on Libyan and Iranian mediation efforts, see chapter on Lebanon).

As for Libyan-Iranian relations, each country continued to back the other in their respective conflicts with the US and Iraq.[112] The formal highpoint during 1986 was the visit to Libya by Iran's Foreign Minister Velayati and Minister of the Revolutionary Guards, Mohsen Rafiqdust, on 28–30 April. The bulk of the joint statement issued at the close of the visit was devoted to condemnations of the American bombing of Libya, couched in the by-now customary style of Islamic revolutionary fervor. (For an earlier manifestation of this style, see *MECS* 1983–84, p 152, Note 84.) As for the Gulf war, Libya reaffirmed its view that it had been imposed on Iran by the "fascist regime in Iraq," while Iran "denied any expansionist ambitions in...Iraq or elsewhere."[113] However, their respective stands on the war were not identical. At the beginning of 1987, Qadhdhafi proposed the creation of an "Islamic force" from Nigeria, Indonesia and Algeria to separate the warring sides.[114] One week later, in the face of hostile press reaction in Iran, Qadhdhafi angrily withdrew the suggestion and charged that a "fifth column" had infiltrated the ranks of the Iranian revolution. It was these forces, he declared, that had conducted the arms deals with the US and Israel (then being revealed in Washington).[115]

EGYPT AND THE ARAB WORLD

Egyptian-Arab relations presented a largely static picture in 1986. In part, this was a function of previous Egyptian gains. The preceding years had witnessed the progressive breakdown of most of the anti-Egyptian sanctions imposed in 1978–79 in the wake of Egypt's agreements with Israel (see chapters on inter-Arab relations in *MECS*, Volumes III–IX). Egypt's network of political, economic and cultural ties, whether formal or informal, now encompassed nearly all of the other Arab states; periodic contacts were even held with Syria and Libya, the only remaining staunch opponents to Egypt's full return to the Arab fold. On the negative side of the ledger, Egypt remained suspended from the Arab League, and only one league member, Djibouti — perhaps the most nominal of all — renewed full diplomatic relations with Cairo. (Sudan, Oman and Somalia had never broken off relations; Jordan restored full ties in September 1984.) Most of the others, although desiring to do so, continued to hold back, either waiting for someone else to take the initiative or for the issue to be resolved at an Arab summit. Saudi Arabia, for example, thought that Iraq was the most appropriate candidate, given Egypt's vital support for it in its war with Iran and given that Iraq had been the driving force behind the original anti-Egyptian sanctions.[116] The Iraqis, for their part, kept a low profile, favoring the summit avenue as the best way to restore Egypt to the Arab fold. Consequently, the absence of a summit precluded the issue from coming to a head.

Husni Mubarak's public posture toward Egypt's possible reinstatement was one of diffidence:

> The return to the Arab world does not occupy me very much. I maintain good bilateral relations with the majority of Arab states. It is no problem for me at all. As to a return to the Arab League, I do not think about it at all.[117]

Moreover, he told another interviewer, Egypt would not attend any Arab summit "where anyone [would try] to defame Egyptian dignity." He himself would not host a summit because, although "there are Arab countries that would like to come to Cairo...pressure is being exerted on them by those who lead terrorism in the Arab world [Syria and Libya]."[118]

Nonetheless, Egyptian officials were not totally indifferent to the matter of Egypt's return. According to a Saudi newspaper (quoting a "reliable source" in the Egyptian Foreign Ministry), Egyptian diplomats were dispatched to five (unnamed) Arab capitals during June 1986 bearing a draft proposal for the creation of an "Arab Cooperation Council." Cairo was said to have emphasized that the Council was not designed to compete with the Arab League, but rather to help it to unify Arab ranks and forge an all-Arab consensus on vital issues. In fact, such a body was likely to either serve as a pressure group on the League or emasculate it further. Three of the five Arab leaders were said to have agreed in principle to the proposal, while two pleaded for more time to consult with other Arab parties.[119] As it happened, nothing further was heard of the idea.

In lieu of any progress *vis-à-vis* the Arab League, the ICO continued to serve as a convenient "back door" for Egypt's formal reintegration into regional, multilateral affairs. The lifting of Egypt's suspension from the ICO in January 1984 had been an important milestone in the restoration of Egypt's regional standing (see *MECS* 1983–84, pp 127–30). In January 1986, Egypt actively participated for the second time in an ICO Foreign Ministers' conference in Fez, despite the objections of Libya and Syria (see essay on Islamic affairs). More importantly, at the end of the year, Kuwait's Emir, Shaykh Jabir al-Ahmad al-Sabah, personally invited Mubarak to attend the January 1987 ICO Summit Conference in his country. Mubarak's presence at the summit was a triumph, perhaps the most striking sign yet of the importance which much of the Arab world, and particularly the GCC states, attached to Egypt's involvement in regional affairs.

At the root of this desire, of course was the specter of the Gulf war's expansion in their direction and, in the worst case, an Iranian victory. Periodically, the question was raised as to what Egypt's response would be in the event of an expansion of the war. In a report not confirmed elsewhere, a Kuwaiti newspaper stated that Egyptian-GCC talks dealing with possible military coordination had been under way for some months.[120] Mubarak himself alluded only to the need for such coordination, and in general was quite guarded over possible Egyptian intervention in the event of an Iranian attack on one of the Gulf states. Egyptian intervention, he told interviewers, was conditional on a number of factors: requests from the states themselves; prior military coordination, "in order for [Egypt] to become acquainted with the capabilities, needs and plans of these states"; and the approval of Egypt's "constitutional institutions."[121] In any event, he emphasized, Egypt would not shirk its obligations under the Arab League's Joint Defense Pact of 1950; and nor should the other Arab states.[122]

While Egypt's support for the GCC states remained in the realm of speculation, its military contribution to Iraq's war effort was profound (see below). That the GCC countries valued Egypt's help to Iraq was indicated by the reported agreement of two unnamed GCC states (most likely Saudi Arabia and Kuwait) to finance Iraq's purchase of $500m of Egyptian-manufactured (or co-produced) weapons, including aircraft, missiles and artillery.[123]

As for the other "all-Arab" set of issues — those dealing with Arab-Israeli affairs, and Egypt's promotion of a joint Jordanian-Palestinian negotiating stance as a necessary condition for the convening of an international peace conference produced no results. Egypt's failure was certainly not due to a lack of effort. Mubarak held consultations with King Husayn on six occasions during 1986 (making a total of 18 meetings in just over two years — undoubtedly an inter-Arab record). Egyptian officials also continued to have frequent contacts with Yasir 'Arafat and his supporters. Nonetheless, they could not overcome a fundamental problem — the lack of agreement between Husayn and 'Arafat, epitomized by Husayn's breaking off his dialogue with 'Arafat in February 1986 (see chapter on Jordan, and essays on the PLO, and the peace process). In general, Egyptian officials avoided blaming either side for the breakdown and urged them to continue seeking an agreement with the help of Egypt's good offices.[124] Occasionally, however, Egyptian frustration did surface — but more with 'Arafat than with Husayn. "We are forced to say," Mubark told an interviewer, "that our Palestinian brothers cannot reach agreement on anything themselves. If the Palestinians can agree on only one word, [then] this will be something good."[125] At the same time, the editor of a Cairo weekly, expressing the view of the Egyptian leadership, declared that 'Arafat would be making a "grave historical error" if he were to cancel or freeze his agreement with Husayn.[126] In another sign of Egypt's annoyance with 'Arafat, Musa Sabri, editor of the Cairo daily *al-Akhbar*, wrote favorably about Abu Za'im, the Fath official who was mounting a Jordanian-backed challenge to 'Arafat's preeminence.[127]

On the other hand, the Jordanians and Egyptians did not see eye-to-eye on the peace process either. Jordan undoubtedly would have preferred to see Egypt give it more unqualified backing in its conflict with the PLO.[128] Along with nearly all of the other Arab states, Jordan distanced itself from Mubarak's summit meeting with Israel's Prime Minister Peres in mid-September.[129] The Jordanian Press was particularly critical,[130] and this "somewhat pained" Mubarak.[131] Following Egypt's inability to win Jordan's agreement to participate in a preparatory conference[132] — an idea raised at the Alexandria Summit (see essay on the peace process) — Mubarak renewed his efforts to convene a full conference, something which the Jordanians broadly approved of.

To complete this account, a survey of some of Egypt's bilateral relations and the broader issues surrounding them is now necessary.

EGYPT AND JORDAN

The deepening of the more purely bilateral aspects of Egyptian-Jordanian relations continued apace during 1986. The Egyptian-Jordanian Joint Higher Committee, first established in the fall of 1984 following the renewal of full diplomatic ties, met for the fourth and fifth time during the year, under the chairmanship of their respective Prime Ministers: once in Amman on 28–30 April, and once in Cairo on 25–26 October. In April, the two delegations followed up on previous agreements in such areas as economy, trade, transport, agriculture, information, tourism, education, internal security and manpower. Also added to the common agenda were discussions on industry, and health and medicine. The October session ended with three new agreements being signed — on oil exploration, extradition and an anti-narcotics drive.[133] Numerous ministerial visits to each other's capitals during the year dealt with these issues in more detail, and added to the atmosphere of steady progress.

Particularly noteworthy, both on the practical and symbolic levels, was the expansion of their land-sea link (Sinai-Nuwayba-'Aqaba). By the beginning of February 1986, between 300–350,000 people were reported to have used the route during the previous year, along with 13,000 cars and 1,000 trucks.[134] Egypt's completion in 1986 of a new road from the Suez Canal to Nuwayba across central Sinai shortened the traveling distance by 150 km, promising to further increase the route's popularity.

The dialogue in military-related affairs also continued. Jordan's Chief of Staff and Deputy Chief of Staff visited Egypt on separate occasions in January and April. Egyptian naval units called at 'Aqaba in February. Egypt's Defense Minister and

Commander in Chief of the Armed Forces, 'Abd al-Halim Abu Ghazala, led a military delegation to Jordan in mid-July. According to Abu Ghazala, the two countries concluded cooperation agreements in the areas of joint training, military industrialization, the exchange of military expertise and medical services. Joint military committees were to be established to put the agreements into effect.[135] Subsequently, an Arab source reported that Egypt, Jordan and France were holding consultations on the possible joint production of weapons, military equipment and ammunition.[136]

EGYPT AND IRAQ

Egypt's military and economic support for Iraq since 1981 had served as the most important vehicle for asserting Cairo's centrality in Arab affairs. In 1986, Egyptians continued to compose the largest single contingent of foreign workers in Iraq, although their numbers did begin to decline (see chapter on Iraq). Militarily, Egyptian help was vital in a number of areas. Most directly, Egypt reportedly conducted a three-day emergency airlift of weapons to Iraq during the Iranian offensive of Faw in February.[137] Iraq's Minister of Defense, Gen 'Adnan Khayralla, heading a military delegation to Egypt on 12–13 August, made further requests for arms. He also reportedly asked for Egyptian military experts to advise Iraq on aviation, long-range artillery, naval operations and air defense.[138] Periodic reports in the Western media and from Iran spoke of Egyptian experts participating in the fighting,[139] which Egyptian leaders took pains to deny: the Iraqis, Mubarak told an interviewer, had merely "sought the help of retired Egyptian military personnel who had...gone to work in Iraq." In any case, he continued, Iraq did not need Egyptian military experts.[140]

Throughout, Cairo emphasized that its support for Iraq was based on its adherence to pan-Arab principles, embodied in the Joint Defense Pact, and came with no strings attached (i.e., Egypt was not demanding that Iraq restore full diplomatic ties).[141] Nonetheless, Egyptian and Iraqi positions on the Gulf war were not identical. Initially, Egypt's Minister of State for Foreign Affairs Butrus Butrus-Ghali reminded an interviewer that Egypt had taken a "neutral position" on the war. It was only when Iraq called for peaceful negotiations based on the return to the territorial status quo ante — established by the 1975 Algiers Agreement — that Egypt tilted more decisively toward Iraq.[142] By contrast, the Iraqis never specifically referred to the Algiers Agreement, understandably so since Saddam Husayn had unilaterally canceled it on the eve of the war. However, Baghdad was in no position in 1986 to take issue with Egypt on this point. (For more narrow bilateral matters, see chapters on Egypt and Iraq.)

THE EGYPT-SUDAN-LIBYA TRIANGLE

Ironically, the most problematic areas for Egyptian foreign policy continued to be those involving its closest neighbors. The unceasing flux in Sudan — especially since the overthrow of Ja'far Numayri in April 1985 — was a source of ongoing concern for Egypt, particularly since Libya was sparing no effort to expand its influence there. Apart from Sudan, Egyptian-Libyan relations continued on their stormy course.

Regarding the latter, the main sore spot derived from the Libyan-American confrontation. Libyan leaders and the Libyan media were unswerving in their charges of Egyptian "collusion" with the US military actions.[143] This did not prevent Qadhdhafi from dispatching a message to Mubarak, via a Libyan military official, on 19 April — in the wake of the American attack — requesting large quantities of weapons. The appeal was rejected.[144] Another round of Libyan condemnations was engendered during the summer by joint American-Egyptian naval maneuvers along Egypt's north-west coast.[145] Concurrently, Libya's official news agency (JANA) charged that American officers were now commanding a number of Egyptian armed forces departments.[146]

For its part, Egypt trod a fine line between disgust with Qadhdhafi's actions and concern over too close an identification with the US. In the beginning of 1986, as the American-Libyan dispute took on crisis proportions, Cairo made a point of opposing American sanctions against Libya.[147] As the confrontation escalated in late March, Egypt took pains to present an even-handed appearance, calling on both sides to exercise restraint.[148] Moreover, while condemning Qadhdhafi's threats against Egypt,[149] Egypt also revealed, via *al-Ahram* editor Ibrahim Nafa', that it had rejected three American overtures to participate in a military strike against Libya.[150] In the aftermath of the American bombing, the most complete summary of Egypt's position was made by Minister of State for Foreign Affairs Butrus-Ghali. The US action, he told an interviewer, "runs counter to international law and the UN Charter." On the other hand, "one of the reasons for that action was [Libyan] terrorism"; Libya's policy of "destabilization in the Arab world, in Africa and in the world at large" was something that Egypt and all the Arab countries condemned.[151] At the same time, Egypt's Prime Minister, Dr 'Ali Lutfi, stated that Egypt had offered Libya an "integrated medical team" to deal with the casualties of the bombing, but Libya had turned down the offer.[152]

Throughout 1986, Qadhdhafi continued to pursue the two-track policy toward Sudan that he had adopted following Numayri's overthrow, with the overall objective of prying Sudan away from Egypt's orbit. The first track was on the governmental level: the cessation of support for the rebellion in the South, and apparently even active participation in the Sudanese Government's military effort there;[153] mediation between Sudan and Ethiopia; and the extension of vital economic aid. In a concrete sign of their deepening ties, numerous high-level visits were exchanged during the year: most notable were those of Sudan's Prime Minister, Defense Minister and Foreign Minister on 13–14 March;[154] Sudan's Defense Minister on 20–21 April, in which he expressed his solidarity with Libya following the American attack;[155] Sudan's newly elected Prime Minister, Sadiq al-Mahdi, on 9–10 August, and finally, Qadhdhafi's visit to Khartoum on 9–13 September.

Qadhdhafi's visit highlighted the underlying theme of Libya's foreign policy in general, and the second track of its policy toward Sudan, in particular. The only proper course of action, declared Qadhdhafi in interviews and speeches during his visit, was an "immediate union" between Syria and Libya; anything else would be "a waste of time...[and whoever opposed such a union] must be identified, exposed and fought, because [he] is the enemy of [the Arab] nation, its future and its aspiration."[156] For some time already, Qadhdhafi had assigned the task of teaching his Green Book revolutionary ideology and combating its opponents to Sudanese Revolutionary Committees, financed and directed by the expanded Libyan People's Bureau office in Khartoum.

The Sudanese reaction to Qadhdhafi's advocacy of unity was cautious; the idea was welcomed in general terms, but the issue was submitted neither to the Sudanese Parliament nor to a plebiscite, as had been suggested by various officials.[157] What they did agree on was what Libya's Ambassador to Sudan called a "practical example" for the proposed unity project — the establishment of a common zone in the Kufrah-Darfur border region in which each country's residents could enjoy free movement and all the rights of citizens of the other country.[158]

Apart from the integration aspects, Sudan's Darfur region held military value for Libya as a staging ground adjoining Chad. Libya had established a military presence there in 1985, "under pretext of food relief," and subsequently extended its activities.[159] Sudanese leaders were uncomfortable with their presence (reported to number 1,000 men) and periodically declared that they had in fact been withdrawn.[160] However, by year's end, they were still in place.

All of this provoked a response of watchful waiting in Cairo. The official line, expressed by the Secretary-General of Egypt's ruling National Democratic Party, Dr Hilmi al-Hadidi was that Egypt welcomed the improvement of relations between any two Arab countries as long as it caused no damage to other bilateral relations; the Sudanese people, he continued, could be trusted to protect their own interests in that regard.[161] Nonetheless, Libya's progress in Sudan and Egypt's own difficulties with the post-Numayri situation left Egyptian officials uneasy. As in 1985, the future of the Egyptian-Sudanese 1982 Nile Valley Integration Agreement continued to be uncertain. On 30 March, the official Sudanese News Agency announced that plans for political integration had been scrapped and that the Sudanese Cabinet had decided to refer the entire matter to the soon-to-be-elected Constitutional Assembly; the Cabinet was also said to have withdrawn its support for the Joint Nile Valley Parliament and other integration-related institutions.[162] Official reaction in Egypt was low-key, especially since the decision was not formally communicated to Cairo.[163] While Cairo officials denied the existence of any crisis in Sudanese-Egyptian relations, *al-Ahram* gave free rein to underlying Egyptian displeasure: cooperation ties, the paper stated, were "optional, not compulsory"; nonetheless, the manner and timing of the Sudanese decision — "when...the door was wide open for dialogue" — was incompatible with the "special relationship between the two parts of the Nile."[164] On 2 April, Sudan's Foreign Minister backtracked somewhat, calling the Sudanese Cabinet actions "recommendations," not "resolutions."[165] In subsequent visits to Egypt, various Sudanese officials spoke more favorably about the integration question. Sudan was "very enthusiastic" about integration, declared Sudan's State Council chairman Ahmad al-Mirghani. The Government was simply awaiting the completion of a committee report on all aspects of the process.[166]

Another sticking point in the relationship was Egypt's continued refusal to extradite Numayri; this was apparently one of the reasons behind the failure of the newly-elected (in April) Prime Minister, Sadiq al-Mahdi, to visit Cairo during the remainder of 1986. In the meantime, Egypt's strategy in Sudan mirrored Libya's: it continued to funnel military and economic aid to Khartoum, took an interest in improving Sudanese-Ethiopian ties and maintained ties with various political and non-governmental groupings.

MAGHRIB AFFAIRS

Intra-Maghrib alignments underwent one major change in 1986: the breakup of the two-year-old Moroccan-Libyan Arab-African Union (AAU; "federation" is actually a more accurate translation of *ittihad* but most references have always referred to their "union"). Concurrently, the region witnessed a renewed warming of Algerian-Libyan relations. Whether these two developments would result in a resumption of Libya's active support for the Polisario movement in its struggle with Morocco for the control of the Western Sahara remained to be seen. (The Algerians hoped that it would.)[167] The Western Sahara issue itself continued to be the overriding obstacle to improved Moroccan-Algerian relations,[168] although each side continued to ensure that the dispute did not escalate into active military conflict.[169]

In spite of Libya's shift in orientation, this did not mean that Morocco was now ranged against the four other Maghrib states. Tunisia and Mauritania, Algeria's partners in the 1983 Friendship and Concord Treaty, continued to maintain good relations with Rabat. Mauritania, as the weakest of all Maghrib states, sought to improve its ties with Libya as well, in order to insulate itself from regional disputes and therefore devote its attention to pressing internal affairs. On the other hand, Tunisia's relations with Libya, ruptured during the summer and fall of 1985 (see *MECS* 1984–85, pp 132–34), remained unsettled. Thus at the close of 1986, intra-Maghrib alignments presented a varying picture, as opposed to the previous 18 months when the region appeared to be divided into two distinct camps. Generally speaking, however, Libya's shift brought intra-Maghrib divisions more into line with the broader inter-Arab and regional fault lines. Libya's primary regional allies, Syria and Iran (not to mention Algeria), actively supported the Polisario with funds, weapons and training,[170] while Morocco was ranged against them on every major inter-Arab issue.

THE WESTERN SAHARA ISSUE

Militarily, Morocco continued to maintain the upper hand over the Polisario, thanks largely to its ever-expanding system of defensive walls. The fifth was completed during 1986, the sixth during the first part of 1987; together, they severely limited both the Polisario's ability to penetrate the Western Sahara via Mauritania and its access to the Atlantic seacoast.[171] Politically, the dispute remained at an impasse. Two rounds of indirect negotiations between Morocco and the Polisario representatives were held in New York on 9–14 April and 5–9 May under the auspices of the UN Secretary-General Javier Pérez de Cuellar and the Organization of African Unity (OAU) President, Abdou Diouf of Senegal. However, they produced no breakthrough in fixing the date and conditions for holding a referendum among the Saharan inhabitants to determine their future — something mandated by OAU and UN resolutions and officially favored by both parties.[172] Predictably, Algeria and the Polisario blamed Morocco for the lack of progress, and vice versa.[173]

Further afield, Morocco's diplomatic struggle against the Polisario's Government-in-Exile, the Saharan Arab Democratic Republic (SADR), was mixed. On the negative side, SADR continued to hold full membership in the OAU (Morocco had withdrawn from the OAU in November 1984 when SADR was seated, although Rabat remained in contact with the organization, via the OAU president). An additional setback at the end of 1985 was the extension of diplomatic recognition to

SADR by India.[174] Morocco managed to prevent further erosion of its diplomatic position in two other multilateral forums: it successfully lobbied against SADR's participation at an Arab-African ministerial dialogue in Damascus on 16 January,[175] and against SADR's admission to the Non-Aligned Movement at its September summit conference in Harare.[176] Bilaterally, relations with Egypt were ruffled by the Polisario issue on two different occasions: the first, in the fall of 1985, when Egypt voted in favor of Algeria's pro-Polisario resolution at the UN (for details, see *MECS* 1984–85, pp 131–32), apparently as a return gesture for Algeria's warming of ties; the second was the participation of a Polisario delegation at two conferences of OAU information ministers held in Cairo during the fall of 1985 and in the summer of 1986.[177] However, the Egyptians also took pains to reassure Morocco that they supported Morocco's "territorial unity" and did not recognize SADR.[178] Still, one sign that all was not well between them was the Moroccan media's criticism of Mubarak's September 1986 meeting with Shimon Peres and the resulting expressions of anger by Egypt.[179] Tunisia's endorsement in October 1986, for the second year in succession, of the Algerian position on the Western Sahara (direct Polisario-Moroccan talks and the right of the Saharan people to self-determination)[180] was not pleasing to Rabat either. However, Morocco preferred not to take issue with Tunisia, and their ties remained generally friendly.

Throughout the year, all of the Maghrib countries continued to refer to the need to build the "Greater Arab Maghrib." On 27–28 April, national party delegations from Tunisia (Socialist Destour), Morocco (*Istiqlal* and the Socialist Union of Popular Forces), and Algeria (*Front de la Libération Nationale*) met for the third time since 1983, in Tangier, to commemorate their original 1958 Tangier gathering and to "lay the pillars of unity between the peoples of the Great Arab Maghrib." This entailed pledges to continue efforts to establish a "Maghrib Advisory Council" whose participants would stem from their various legislative bodies; a permanent political committee, which would include three members from each of the four parties and convene at least twice a year; and the popularization of the Maghrib unity concept among various non-governmental institutions and organizations.[181] The conference's declaration on the Western Sahara issue was conspicuously vague in intent. (For the dispute over differing versions of their previous joint statement on the matter, see *MECS* 1983–83, p 142).

Two months later, King Hasan suggested a somewhat different notion: a "consultative institution" involving Morocco, Algeria and Tunisia, which would each choose their own representatives as they saw fit (in order for Hasan to include representatives from other Moroccan parties and factions).[182] Nothing further was heard of these ideas, nor was Tunisia any more successful than it had been during the previous year in attempting to convene an all-Maghrib summit (including Libya and Mauritania, as well).[183] Thus, although Maghrib leaders and officials continued to view the GCC as a model for their own region,[184] Moroccan-Algerian differences prevented the adoption of even initial steps at imitation.

THE MOROCCAN-LIBYAN BREAKUP

A number of meetings of joint committees, commissions and subcommissions of the Libyan-Moroccan AAU were held in early 1986.[185] King Hasan continued to speak positively about Mu'ammar al-Qadhdhafi ("a courteous...very pleasant [and] attentive man").[186] He also denied that the postponement of his scheduled visit to Libya had anything to do with differences between them.[187] Nonetheless, their alliance progressively unraveled in the spring and summer months, as a result of a course of events which brought their fundamental differences (on the Arab-Israeli conflict, the Iraqi-Iranian war, relations with the West and with Egypt, and Chad) into the open. The first major hitch stemmed from the American bombing of Libya. Although Hasan cabled his "sincere condolences" and "complete solidarity" to Qadhdhafi,[188] Morocco's inaction and the two countries' subsequent disagreement over the convening of an emergency Arab summit (see above) illustrated the limitations of their alliance. Nonetheless, Libya refrained, on the whole, from criticizing Morocco's failure to stand by it, an indication that Qadhdhafi still believed that the AAU shell was worth preserving.[189]

Matters came to a head, however, in late July, when Hasan met with Peres. Here too, Qadhdhafi showed, if only briefly, a reluctance to attack Hasan.[190] However, once confronted with the irrefutable fact of the meeting, Libya immediately characterized it as "treason," and a "blatant violation" of the AAU agreement.[191] At the same time, Qadhdhafi still refused to cancel the agreement itself — something reportedly urged on him by Syria[192] — maintaining that it belonged to the Libyan and Moroccan peoples, and not just the rulers.[193]

Hasan, by contrast, did not see the value in maintaining the AAU's existence any further. Thus, in response to the joint Qadhdhafi-Asad condemnation of the Ifrane meeting as a "treasonous action" and "a deviation from the pan-Arab commitment and Arab consensus,"[194] Hasan announced Morocco's "reluctant" abrogation of the treaty. The AAU, he explained, had been "unique" in that it had pursued social and economic union while ignoring ideological differences and preserving each country's sovereignty. Morocco had been patient with Libya — even if Qadhdhafi now refused to meet either with Moroccan envoys or with Hasan himself. However, the Qadhdhafi-Asad joint communiqué had gone too far. Unlike a speech to a mass audience, Hasan explained, in which "obscene words" might be uttered because of various "psychological factors," a joint communiqué was by its very nature formulated with great precision and thus had far more meaning. Therefore, Hasan declared, one could only conclude that the AAU was now held to be meaningless by Libya. As for Libya's efforts to denounce Hasan but still adhere to the union, one

> cannot be fooled by this joke...every Moroccan, in flesh and blood, is part of Hasan II...Therefore I can never disassociate my honor from your honor.

Finally, in an effort not to appear as an opponent of the principle of unity, Hasan expressed the belief that the AAU framework, although abrogated, would "remain a ...positive example to whoever is seeking union between two states."[195]

In response, Libya reiterated its belief in the union's continued validity (just as it had done in previous, similar situations with Tunisia, Algeria and the Federation of Arab Republics; see *MECS* 1982–83, p 217, and 1983–84, p 154, Note 125). Hasan's action, said Qadhdhafi, was "null and void, constitutionally and democratically." Libya, he declared, had already taken steps to bring the dispute before the International Court of Justice at The Hague — as stipulated by the original agreement founding the AAU — to determine responsibility for the discrediting of the "will" of the Libyan and Moroccan peoples.[196] Doing so, retorted Hasan's top political adviser, Ahmad Reda Gudeira, would be a waste of time.[197]

In evaluating Hasan's abrogation decision, it appears that he concluded that Morocco had already derived the maximum amount of benefit possible from the AAU, and that its continuation was neither necessary nor worth the trouble. For three years, Libya had refrained from extending military aid to the Polisario, something which Hasan admitted had been the prime motivating factor behind his desire for the union.[198] During those three years, Morocco had been able to gain the upper hand, militarily, in the Western Sahara and thus consolidate its hold considerably. Given both this strengthened position and Libya's preoccupation with other matters (the confrontation with the US, the weakening of the Libyan economy because of the drop in oil prices, and its increasingly problematic involvement in Chad — all of which made Qadhdhafi's grip on the reins of power less certain than before), Hasan must have calculated that Qadhdhafi's ability to cause him trouble, either in the Western Sahara or domestically, was severely limited.[199] Thus, Libya's insult to Moroccan honor became an appropriate occasion for Hasan to formally distance himself from the Libyan leader.

ALGERIAN-LIBYAN RELATIONS

The budding *rapprochement* between Libya and Algeria, apparent from the beginning of the year, could not have pleased Hasan either, although he steadfastly denied having any "complex" or "apprehension" about the matter.[200] The fall of 1985 had been a particularly tense time between Algiers and Tripoli, with Algeria standing squarely behind Tunisia during its crisis with Libya. However, both Algiers and Tripoli quickly demonstrated an interest in repairing ties which had been strained since the 1984 Moroccan-Libyan AAU agreement (see *MECS* 1984–85, pp 133–34 and 145, Note 191). The first major step came on 28 January, when Qadhdhafi flew to the Algerian town of 'Ain Amenes, approximately 50 km from the Libyan-Algerian border, to meet with Algeria's President, Chedli Benjedid. Although their meeting produced no joint communiqué and their respective news reports on the meeting's content differed substantially,[201] the meeting did nevertheless lay the groundwork for the steady improvement of bilateral ties during the ensuing months. For Libya, lining up support in the face of the American challenge was the most important policy consideration; for Algeria, it was a chance to attempt to mediate Libya's dispute with its Tunisian ally,[202] and perhaps to begin to pry Libya away from Morocco. In addition, their similar positions regarding OPEC oil pricing and production provided an important common denominator (see chapter on Middle East oil).

High-level visits continued throughout the year, including three by Libya's Staff-Maj Jallud (on 10–11 February, 22 June and 26 October), one by Algeria's Prime Minister 'Abd al-Hamid Brahimi (on 21–23 March) and a return visit by Benjedid to Tripoli (on 3–4 December). A number of bilateral cooperation agreements were concluded as well. The Libyans, who tended to describe these developments as steps on the road to unity,[203] would have undoubtedly liked something more in the way of a formal unity agreement,[204] as well as a more complete identification with Libya's oppositionist stand in Arab affairs (for example, Algeria kept separate its improved ties with Egypt, which first occurred during 1985, from its improved relationship with Libya). The Algerians, for their part, were content to stress their importance to the building of the Arab Maghrib.[205] Nonetheless, both sides could be satisfied with the warming of their bilateral ties. (For more details, see chapter on Libya.)

ALGERIAN-TUNISIAN RELATIONS

For Algeria, the ideal model for the Arab Maghrib was its relationship with Tunisia. Numerous joint meetings and ministerial-level visits during 1986 dealt with deepening cooperation in numerous fields: economic, commercial, social, cultural and information. Military ties deepened as well, a continuation from the previous year in the wake of Libya's threats to Tunisia.[206] Repeatedly, both countries emphasized that their 1983 Friendship and Concord Treaty, which had established "firm cooperation...built on mutual respect, good neighborliness and non-interference in internal affairs," was the ideal model for building the Arab Maghrib and should thus be embraced by all five Maghrib countries.[207] As a symbol of their common Maghrib heritage and destiny, the two countries marked with high-level visits and great fanfare the anniversary of the 8 February 1958 French bombing of Sakiet Sidi Youssef, a Tunisian-Algerian border village ("a day of resistance and solidarity...in which the blood of the devoted Tunisian and Algerian martyrs flowed together.")[208]

LIBYAN-TUNISIAN RELATIONS

By contrast, Libyan-Tunisian relations remained tense, although some progress was registered by the end of the year in dealing with the issues stemming from the expulsion of thousands of Tunisian workers in 1985. A number of meetings were held between their representatives: at the Arab League's office in Paris, as a result of Algerian mediation, during January 1986;[209] and in Geneva, under the auspices of the International Labor Organization (ILO), during August and November. According to Tunisia's Foreign Minister Hedi Mabrouk, they resulted in the release of some of the frozen assets belonging to expelled Tunisian workers (LD1.5m out of almost LD9m), and a Libyan commitment to compensate the Tunisians in a manner endorsed by the ILO.[210] Libya was also reported to have paid off a portion of its debts owed to Tunisian government-owned corporations.[211]

One of the results of their still-troubled relations was Tunisia's refusal to declare its solidarity with Libya *vis-à-vis* the US.[212] From their end, the Libyans accused Tunisia of allowing the Americans to use Tunisian airspace and territory to carry out the attack (Tunisia denied the charge).[213] Tunisian-Libyan differences on the American bombing — Tunisia's lack of solidarity with Libya, and Libya's anger — had an impact on the Tunisian domestic arena; and anti-American, anti-Government demonstrations in Tunisia were instigated by Tunisian opposition politicians, a number of whom were arrested for their activities.[214] According to a Kuwaiti newspaper, Tunisia ordered home Libya's representative at the Arab League headquarters in Tunis for his active involvement in organizing the demonstrations.[215]

CONCLUSION

At the close of 1986, events in Lebanon, long a cockpit and microcosm of inter-Arab divisions, again intruded on the collective Arab consciousness. The tightening of the siege of Palestinian refugee camps by Syrian-backed *Amal* units and concurrent fighting between Palestinian and *Amal* forces around Sidon (see chapter on Lebanon) impelled the convening — at the PLO's request — of two emergency Arab League

Ministerial Council sessions in Tunis (on 8–9 and 22 December). Frustration with Syria's position and actions was widespread; however, the Council's call for an end to the "armed attacks" against the Palestinian camps and the lifting of the siege did not mention Syria, or even *Amal*, by name.[216] The 22 December Council session also formed an eight-member committee — composed of the Foreign Ministers of Algeria, Jordan, the UAE, Tunisia, Kuwait, Mauritania, the Yemeni Arab Republic and Secretary-General Klibi — to mediate an end to the fighting.[217] Its lack of immediate progress symbolized, perhaps, the continued overall inter-Arab stalemate during 1986. Moreover, it demonstrated again that Syria still stood astride the central inter-Arab lines of division — ranged against Egypt on the Arab-Israeli conflict and Egypt's place in the Arab world; against Iraq on the Gulf war, and Fertile Crescent and Ba'thi primacy; and against Yasir 'Arafat, in Lebanon and over the future character and course of Palestinian Nationalism.

More generally, the combination of (a) existing inter-Arab divisions, (b) the general perception that the sharp drop in oil prices over the preceding years had reduced collective Arab leverage, and (c) the military and political achievements of non-Arab parties — Iran, Israel and the US — at Arab expense had resulted by the end of 1986 in increasingly profound feelings of frustration and weakness throughout the Arab world. King Husayn expressed this poignantly in a speech to graduates of the Command and Staff College in Amman on 13 December. America's justification of its arms shipments and dialogue with Iran, he told his audience, was Iran's strategic importance. "We Arabs," Husayn continued:

> Must ask ourselves: why doesn't the US Administration consider Iraq...the Gulf states...[in fact] all the Arab states... strategically important? The answer is as simple and strong as the question. It is the divisions which produce accusations and the fragmentation which produces contempt; it is the conflicting stands and regional isolationism which have undermined the structure and have created vacuums attracting foreign forces which are lying in wait.

Husayn's solution was an immediate Arab summit, in order

> to achieve Arab solidarity and joint Arab action to face the outside challenges threatening the Arab system and to solve Arab problems nourishing Arab divisions.[218]

However, it was not yet on the horizon.

NOTES

For the place and frequency of publications cited here, and for the full name of the publication, news agency, radio station or monitoring service where an abbreviation is used, please see "List of Sources." Only in the case of more than one publication bearing the same name is the place of publication noted here.

1. Gabriel Ben-Dor, *State and Conflict in the Middle East* (New York: Praeger, 1983); Fouad Ajami, "The End of Pan-Arabism," *Foreign Affairs*, Winter 1978–79; Daniel Dishon and Bruce Maddy-Weitzman, "Inter-Arab Relations" in *MECS* 1981–82, pp 265–67, and Maddy-Weitzman, "Inter-Arab Relations" in *MECS* 1984–85, p 134.

2. Husayn was reported to have pushed for an Iraqi-Syrian thaw during his meeting in Damascus. (*'Ukaz*, 2 January 1986.)
3. KUNA, 23 March — DR, 24 March 1986. Concurrent with the latest Iranian advances and new round of inter-Arab mediation efforts, the Arab League's seven-member committee on the Iraqi-Iranian war (first formed in March 1984), meeting in Baghdad on 12 February, called for an urgent meeting of the UN Security Council to pressure Iran into accepting an end to the fighting. (INA, 13 February — SWB, 15 February 1986.)
4. Saddam Husayn's interview in *al-Qabas*, 5 February, reported by INA, 5 February — DR, 6 February 1986.
5. *Alif Ba'*, 5 February 1987.
6. Damascus TV, 18 March — SWB, 20 March; message from Syria's Foreign Minister Faruq al-Shar' to Arab League Secretary-General Chedli Klibi, R. Damascus, 20 March — DR, 24 March 1986.
7. SANA, 7 May — DR, 8 May 1986. Initially, Syria had blamed Israel for the explosions. Iraq, for its part, denied all connection with the incident. (INA, 8 May — DR, 9 May 1986.)
8. The attacks themselves were condemned by the Council as well. The Council also resolved to try to persuade Spain to refrain from establishing diplomatic relations with Israel, and to make further efforts to prevent Black African states from doing so as well (this in the wake of the Ivory Coast's renewal of formal ties with Israel). (KUNA, 5 January — DR, 6 January 1986.)
9. MENA, 4 January 1986.
10. Arab League Secretary-General Chedli Klibi visited a number of European capitals during the latter part of January to urge restraint; as it happened, the EEC decided not to follow Washington's lead in imposing sanctions.
11. Among the Foreign Ministers attending were those of Morocco and Saudi Arabia, two of the leading states in the Arab majority grouping. Concurrently, Morocco's King Hasan, Qadhdhafi's partner in the 18-month-old AAU, made a special effort to moderate American hostility toward Libya. (Hasan's message to President Reagan, R. Rabat, 25 January — DR, 27 January 1986.)
12. JANA, 24 January — DR, 24 January; AFP, 30 January — DR, 31 January 1986.
13. TAP, 31 January — DR, 31 January 1986.
14. R. Baghdad VoM, 31 January — DR, 4 February 1986. At one point, Iraq's Foreign Minister, Tariq 'Aziz, even called for an urgent discussion of Syria's and Libya's continued membership in the Arab League. Failure to do so, he warned, would lead to the League's dissolution and a restructuring of regional relations (something he appeared to favor). (*Al-Thawra*, Baghdad, 7 March, quoted by INA, 7 March — DR, 10 March 1986.)
15. It is not clear whether Algeria and the PDRY also expressed informal reservations with the resolution. (KUNA, 26 March — SWB, 28 March; R. Damascus, 27 March; MAP, 28 March — DR, 31 March 1986.)
16. QNA, 13 April; R. Amman, 16 April — DR, 16 April 1986.
17. The call was made at a joint meeting of Syrian, Iranian and Libyan Foreign Ministers. (R. Damascus, 16 April — DR, 16 April 1986.)
18. KUNA, 16 April — DR, 16 April; KUNA, 17 April; *al-Thawra*, Baghdad, reported by INA, 18 April — DR, 21 April; R. Monte Carlo, 18 April; ENA, 19 April, reported by GNA, 19 April — DR, 20 April 1986.
19. KUNA, 24 April — DR, 24 April 1986.
20. R. Abu Dhabi, 27 April — DR, 28 April 1986.
21. QNA, 28 April — DR, 29 April 1986.
22. SANA, 29 April — DR, 30 April 1986.
23. KUNA, 29 April — DR, 30 April; *al-Nahar Arab Report and Memo*, 9 May 1986.
24. R. Riyadh, 1 May — DR, 2 May 1986.
25. R. Tripoli, 2 May — DR, 2 May 1986. For an Algerian newspaper's commentary on the "shameful Arab silence" in the wake of the US attack on Libya, see *al-Sha'b*, Algiers, 3 May, quoted by APS, 3 May — DR, 5 May 1986.
26. *Al-Nahar Arab Report and Memo*, 9 May 1986.
27. *WP*, 11 June 1986.
28. IRNA, 7 June — SWB, 8 June 1986.

29. IRNA, 19 July — SWB, 22 July 1986.
30. R. Riyadh, 15 June — DR, 16 June; SPA, 18 June — DR, 20 June 1986.
31. *WSJ*, 1 July 1986. Although some aid may have been granted, to both ease Syria's straits and encourage it to remain open to additional mediation attempts, the figure of $2 bn seems highly exaggerated, particularly since no reconciliation was achieved. Arab aid (mostly Saudi) to Syria had fallen from $1.8 bn mandated by the 1978–79 Baghdad Conferences, to $800m per annum.
32. Hafiz al-Asad's interview with a Jordanian press delegation, reported by KUNA, 30 September — DR, 1 October 1986.
33. The Syrians may well have been seeking a more immediate Iraqi commitment as well. Prior to the cancellation of the Syrian-Iraqi Foreign Ministers' meeting, a Jordanian newspaper, citing a Saudi source, reported that the expected Syrian-Iraqi *détente* would include an Iraqi pledge of support to Syria in confronting an Israeli plan to strike at Syrian forces in Lebanon. (*Al-Ra'y*, 6 June — DR, 6 June 1986.)
34. Interview in *Der Spiegel*, 22 September — DR, 23 September 1986.
35. For a Syrian newspaper's similar declaration that Saddam's fall would make possible Syrian-Iraqi unification under Asad's leadership, see *Tishrin*, 18 March 1986.
36. *Al-Sayyad*, 7 June; *al-Siyasa*, 14 June; *al-Khalij*, 25 June — DR, 27 June 1986.
37. *Al-Nahar Arab Report and Memo*, 23 May 1986.
38. *Al-Thawra*, Baghdad, 28 April 1986.
39. Interview with Tariq 'Aziz, *al-Hawadith*, 25 April 1986.
40. *Al-Siyasa*, 2 June — DR, 4 June; R. Monte Carlo, 13 June 1986.
41. *Al-Hawadith*, 25 April 1986. Iraq's Foreign Minister Tariq 'Aziz asked scornfully whether Syria's alliance with Iran grew only out of its desire to prevent the war's expansion; if so, what would Syria say if an important Arab country allied itself to Israel "in order to convince it not to expand its occupation of Palestine and the Golan?" (*Al-Thawra*, Baghdad, 10 March, reported by INA, 10 March — DR, 11 March 1986.)
42. R. Baghdad, VoM, 28 May — DR, 29 May 1986.
43. *Al-Thawra*, Baghdad, 14 May 1986. R. Baghdad also continued to broadcast the programs of Syrian opposition groups (e.g. Voice of the National Alliance for the Liberation of Syria, 31 May — DR, 2 June, SWB, 2 June 1986).
44. Interview with Tariq 'Aziz, *Le Figaro*, 7–13 June — DR, 16 June 1986.
45. *Al-Siyasa*, 27 May — DR, 29 May; *WSJ*, 2 June 1986.
46. *Al-Majalla*, 18–24 June — DR, 24 June 1986. According to Syria's Vice President, 'Abd al-Khalim Khaddam, the meeting was canceled because the Iraqis had reneged on previous commitments, conveyed via King Husayn, that it would take place on the basis of the "special relations" between them — in other words, the 1978 Charter which Syria was seeking to reactivate. In any case, he emphasized, the root of the Syrian-Iraqi dispute preceded the Iraqi-Iranian war and Syria's support for the Iranian revolution. (Interview with Khaddam, *al-Majalla*, 25 June-1 July — DR, 1 July 1986.) However, Syria's Defense Minister Talas subsequently confirmed that the cancelation was due to Iraq's insistence that Syria end its political and military backing of Iran. (*Der Spiegel*, 22 September — DR, 23 September 1986.)
47. On one occasion, Jordan's Foreign Minister Tahir al-Masri did express veiled criticism of Syria for canceling the meeting which, he said, was so vital for overcoming the collective Arab paralysis (*al-Majalla*, 6-12 August — DR, 12 August); on the other hand, Jordan's Prime Minister Zayd al-Rifa'i strenuously denied that Syria was the cause of the failure to convene an Arab summit (*al-Majalla*, 23 July 1986).
48. Hasan's address to the Moroccan nation, R. Rabat, 23 July — DR, 24 July 1986. In a letter explaining his move to Arab leaders, Hasan called it a "collective rescue operation" — the reference is to both the "tragedy" of the Palestinians and the unprecedented state of Arab disarray. (R. Rabat, 4 August — SWB, 6 August 1986.)
49. *Arab Times*, 24 March — DR, 26 March 1986; *Le Nouvel Observateur*, 4–10 April — DR, 22 April 1986.
50. Hasan's press conference, R. Rabat, 7 August — DR, 8 August 1986.
51. *Al-Mithaq al-Watani*, 25 July 1986.
52. MENA, 10 August — DR, 11 August 1986.

53. R. Amman, 22 July — DR, 22 July; SPA, R. Monte Carlo, 22 July — DR, 23 July; *Sawt al-Sha'b*, 24 July — DR, 24 July 1986.
54. *Al Thawra* and *al-Jumhuriyya*, Baghdad, 23 July — quoted by INA, 23 July — DR, 23 July 1986.
55. TAP, 26 July — SWB, 28 July 1986.
56. MAP, 27 July — DR, 28 July; Hasan's press conference, R. Rabat, 7 August — DR, 8 August 1986.
57. QNA, 19 October — DR, 20 October 1986.
58. Given that their common animosity toward 'Arafat could scarcely mask their opposing positions on the ultimate resolution of the Palestinian issue, it was hardly surprising that their reported discussions of possible alternatives to Yasir 'Arafat as PLO chief (*NAD*, 17 May 1986) did not lead to operative measures.
59. R. Monte Carlo, 14 January — DR, 15 January 1986; some 600,000 Syrians were said to be benefiting from Jordanian electricity. (*Al-Tali'a al-'Arabiyya*, 18 August 1986.)
60. *Al-Qabas*, 6 May; *al-Tadamun*, 17–23 May 1986.
61. *Ma'ariv*, 6 May 1986.
62. *Al-Qabas*, int ed, 4 August 1986.
63. *Al-Ra'y*, 7 May; interview with Foreign Minister Tahir al-Masri, *al-Usbu' al-'Arabi*, 4 August 1986.
64. Interview with Syria's Vice President, 'Abd al-Khalim Khaddam, *al-Mustaqbal*, 17 May — DR, 19 May 1986.
65. R. Bayrak, 21 November — SWB, 22 November; R. Beirut, 25 November 1986.
66. R. Damascus, 5 November — DR, 6 November 1986.
67. Commentary by Oded Zaray, *Ha'aretz*, 2 November 1986.
68. Amman TV, 1 November — DR, 3 November 1986.
69. For an Iranian expression of this hope and subsequent disappointment, see R. Tehran commentary, 2 July — SWB, 4 July 1986.
70. Interview with Rafasanjani, R. Tehran, 20 March — SWB, 22 March 1986.
71. Rafsanjani's Friday sermon at Tehran University, R. Tehran in Arabic, 28 February — SWB, 3 March 1986.
72. *FT*, 22 February 1986.
73. For the denial of such a Radio Tehran report, see *al-Qabas*, 3 March 1986.
74. R. Tehran in Arabic, 8 April — SWB, 10 April 1986.
75. Deputy Foreign Minister 'Ali Muhammad Besharati's press conference in Damascus, R. Monte Carlo, 23 February; R. Tehran, 1 November — SWB, 5 November 1986.
76. Interview with Rafsanjani, R. Tehran 13 August — SWB, 15 August; R. Tehran in Arabic, 3 September, quoted by SPA, 3 September — SWB, 5 September; Iranian govenment statement, R. Tehran 27 November — SWB, 29 November 1986.
77. R. Tehran commentary, 2 July — SWB, 4 July 1986.
78. R. Tehran in Arabic, 22 March — SWB, 25 March; interview with Rafsanjani in *Pasdar-e Eslam*, reported by R. Tehran, 27 July — SWB, 29 July 1986.
79. IRNA, 12 March — DR, 14 March 1986.
80. For an enumeration of these activities, especially directed against Kuwait, see R. Tehran in English, 13 November — SWB, 15 November; IRNA, 30 November — SWB, 3 December 1986.
81. *FT*, 5 December 1986.
82. In the words of the GCC's Secretary-General, 'Abdallah Bishara, Iraq's collapse would be "a nightmare," for it would destroy the regional balance of power and territorial status quo. (*Al-Hawadith*, 31 October — DR, 3 November 1986).
83. R. Tehran, 20 March — SWB, 22 March 1986.
84. KUNA, 23 February — SWB, 25 February; SPA, 3 September — SWB, 5 September; *al-Ra'y al-'Amm*, 11 November; Kuwaiti Foreign Ministry spokesman, reported by KUNA, 2 December — SWB, 4 December 1986.
85. KUNA, 23 February, 18 September — SWB, 25 February, 18 September; *al-Ittihad*, Abu Dhabi, 3 December — SWB, 6 December 1986.
86. Riyadh TV, 3 March — SWB, 5 March; *NYT*, 17 March; speech by Saudi Crown Prince 'Abdallah, *al-Tadamun*, 29 March-4 April; SPA, 3 August — SWB, 7 August; SPA, 27

August — DR, 28 August; Riyadh TV, 5 November — SWB, 6 November 1986.

87. Riyadh TV and SPA, 3 March — SWB, 5 March; *al-Thawra*, Baghdad, 11 March 1986.
88. E.g. Riyadh TV, 5 November — SWB, 6 November 1986.
89. KUNA, 3 September — DR, 5 September 1986.
90. Interview with Minister of State for Foreign Affairs, Yusuf Ibn 'Alawi, *al-Tadamun*, 22–28 November — DR, 9 December 1986.
91. SPA, 27 August — DR, 28 August 1986.
92. According to Saudi Arabia's Crown Prince 'Abdallah, these visits had produced no positive results. (*Al-Tadamun*, 29 March–4 April 1986.)
93. R. Tehran, 25 February; R. Riyadh, 23 March; R. Tehran, 27 July — SWB, 29 July 1986.
94. R. Tehran, 5 December — SWB, 6 December 1986.
95. R. Riyadh, 6 November — DR, 6 November 1986.
96. *IHT*, 24 November; SPA, 24 November — DR, 24 November 1986.
97. *Jeune Afrique*, 8 January 1986.
98. R. Baghdad, SPA, 28 December — SWB, 30 December 1986.
99. Interview with Saddam Husayn, *al-Qabas*, 5 February; interview with Foreign Minister Tariq 'Aziz, *al-Watan al-Arabi*, 2 May, reported by INA, 3 May — DR, 5 May; Saddam Husayn's Revolution Anniversary speech, R. Baghdad, VoM, 16 July — DR, 17 July 1986.
100. R. Tehran, 15 April; IRNA, 16 April — SWB, 17 April 1986.
101. R. Damascus, 25 August — DR, 26 August 1986.
102. At one point, during mid-May, this apparently included strong Syrian remonstrations against Iranian attacks on oil tankers and installations in the Gulf. (*Al-Bayan*, 15 May — DR, 16 May; *al-Qabas*, 28 May 1986.)
103. Asad's interview with *al-Qabas* (nd), quoted by R. Damascus, 24 January — SWB, 27 January 1986.
104. One partial exception to this was GCC Secretary-Genral 'Abdallah Bishara. He told an interviewer: "We in the GCC are aware of Syria's role and of its dialogue with Iran and the Iranian authorities, but we do wish the Arab states would all adopt a common Arab stand that would lead to an end to this war." (*Al-Hawadith*, 31 October — DR, 3 November 1986.)
105. E.g. Syria's issuing of a commemorative stamp which included Iran's Khuzistan province within the domain of the Arab world (*al-Siyasa*, 27 April 1986); and Iran's reported hosting of a delegation of the anti-regime, Syrian Muslim Brotherhood organization. (*Arab Times*, 14 May — DR, 16 May 1986).
106. NAD, 12 May; *NYP*, 24 April, quoted by R. Monte Carlo, 24 April 1986.
107. *Al-Ittihad*, Abu Dhabi, 26 August — DR, 28 August 1986.
108. *Sunday Telegraph*, 23 November — DR, 25 November 1986.
109. Press statement issued in Damascus and Tripoli, R. Damascus, 26 August — DR, 26 August 1986.
110. *Al-Watan al-'Arabi*, 5 September; *NAD*, 15 September 1986. The former, a pro-Iraqi publication, spoke of an agreement to ship Libyan weapons to Iran via Syria's Latakia port in return for Libyan payment to Iran for its oil deliveries to Syria. The latter stated that Qadhdhafi turned down Asad's aid requests.
111. *Al-Ittihad*, Abu Dhabi, 26 August — DR, 28 August; *al-Safir*, 27 September; *al-Bayan*, 29 September — DR, 1 October 1986.
112. Iraq continued to accuse Libya of supplying Iran with the surface-to-surface missiles being fired at Baghdad and officers to supervise their usage. (*Al-Yawm al-Sabi'*, 2 November 1986; see also *MECS* 1984–85, p 120.)
113. Joint statement issued in Tripoli and Tehran, JANA, 1 May — SWB, 3 May 1986.
114. *Al-Watan*, quoted by KUNA, 25 January — SWB, 26 January 1987.
115. Tripoli TV, 2 February — SWB, 4 February 1987.
116. Interview with Prince Turki Ibn 'Abd al-'Aziz, *al-Musawwar*, 14 February — DR, 20 February 1986.
117. Interview with Mubarak, *Der Spiegel*, 3 February — DR, 6 February 1986.
118. MENA, 22 April — DR, 23 April; *al-Ra'y al-'Amm*, 9 October, quoted by MENA, 8 October — DR, 10 October 1986.
119. *Al-Sharq al-Awsat*, 20 July 1986.

120. *Al-Ra'y al-'Amm*, 20 October 1986.
121. *Al-Ra'y al-'Amm*, 9 October, quoted by MENA, 8 October — DR, 10 October; *al-Watan al-'Arabi*, 10–16 October — DR, 14 October 1986.
122. MENA, 30 November — SWB, 2 December 1986.
123. *APS* (nd) — *IDI*, 8 September 1986.
124. In the words of Foreign Minister Ismat 'Abd al-Majid: "We must look more to the future than [the] past; we must not pass judgment on anyone — that is not part of our current role." (MENA, 22 February — DR, 24 February 1986.)
125. *Al-Watan al-'Arabi*, 10–16 October — DR, 14 October 1986.
126. *Al-Musawwar*, 12 September 1986.
127. *Al-Akhbar*, 18 April 1986.
128. For an indication to this effect, see *al-Usbu' al-'Arabi*, 31 March 1986.
129. Jordan's Prime Minister, Zayd al-Rifa'i, told reporters that he had been "very briefly informed of the results" of the talks. (*JT*, 17 September — DR, 17 September 1986.) For a lone declaration of support by an Arab newspaper for "the historical achievement" of Egyptian diplomacy at Alexandria, see *al-Siyasa*, 14 September 1986.
130. *Al-Ra'y*, 13, 14 September — DR, 15 September 1986. Jordanian press criticism of the summit led to an acrimonious exchange between two Egyptian and Jordanian newspapers over whether Arab parties were themselves to blame for the stalled peace process. (*Al-Akhbar*, 16 September, and *al-Ra'y*, 19 September 1986.)
131. *Al-Watan al-'Arabi*, 10-16 October — DR, 14 October 1986.
132. Interview with Jordan's Information Minister, Muhammad al-Khatib, *al-Tadamun*, 27 September-3 October — DR, 7 October 1986.
133. MENA, 29 April, R. Amman, 30 April — DR, 30 April, 1 May; MENA, 26 October — DR, 27 October 1986. For a more detailed survey of the agreements made up until April 1986, see *Sawt al-Sha'b*, 28 April 1986.
134. *Sawt al-Sha'b*, 10 February; *al-Ra'y*, 15 February 1986.
135. MENA, 15 July — DR, 16 July 1986.
136. *Al-Mustaqbal*, 9 August — DR, 11 August 1986.
137. *Al-Ra'y al-'Amm*, 16 February, reported by SANA, 16 February; *al-Ittihad*, Abu Dhabi, 17 February — DR, 19 February 1986.
138. *Al-Ra'y al-'Amm*, *al-Ahram*, 14 August 1986.
139. *CSM*, 22 January; R. Tehran, 22 May — SWB, 24 May 1986.
140. *Al Sayyad*, 3 April, quoted by MENA, 2 April — DR, 2 April 1986.
141. Ibid; *al-Majalla*, 21–27 May — JPRS, 23 June 1986.
142. Interview with Butrus-Ghali, *al-Musawwar*, 17 October 1986.
143. R. Tripoli, VoGAH, 3 April — SWB, 5 April; JANA, 28 April — DR, 28 April; on 16 May, R. Tripoli announced the uncovering of an Egyptian "espionage and sabotage" network which it said had assisted in the US bombings. (R. Tripoli, 16 May — DR, 29 May 1986.)
144. For a questioning of Qadhdhafi's real motives, and an enumeration of both the reasons behind Egypt's rejection of the request as well as Egypt's own counterdemands, see *al-Ahram*, 26 April, reported by MENA, 25 April — SWB, 28 April 1986.
145. JANA, 18 July, 20 August — SWB, 21 July, 20 August 1986.
146. JANA, VoGAH, 15 August — SWB, 18 August 1986.
147. Interview with Foreign Minister 'Abd al-Majid, *al-Ittihad*, Abu Dhabi, 2 February — DR, 4 February 1986.
148. For Egyptian pro-government newspaper editorials condeming the US "provocations" and "aggression" against Libya, see *al-Jumhuriyya* and *al-Ahram*, Cairo, 28 March, quoted by MENA, 28 March — DR, 28 March 1986.
149. On 28 March, Qadhdhafi declared that he would hold Egypt responsible for the consequences of its military (especially naval) cooperation with the US (Tripoli TV, 28 March — DR, 31 March 1986.)
150. *Al-Ahram*, 31 March 1986.
151. *El Pais*, 29 April — DR, 5 May; on occasion, Egyptian commentators included Syria as well in their condemnations of state-sponsored terrorism (e.g. R. Cairo commentary, 26 October — SWB, 29 October 1986).
152. MENA, 29 April — DR, 30 April 1986.

153. *WP*, 28 March 1986.
154. For the statement issued at the end of the visit, in which Sudan backed Libya's claim on the Gulf of Sidra, see JANA, 14 March — DR, 17 March 1986.
155. Interview with Defense Minister, Maj-Gen 'Uthman Abdallah, VoGAH, 20 April — SWB, 22 April 1986.
156. Tripoli TV, 11, 12 September — DR, SWB, 15 September 1986.
157. SUNA, 9, 25 April — DR, 10, 28 April; R. Tripoli, 10 April — SWB, 12 April 1986.
158. SUNA, 10 April — DR, 10 April 1986.
159. *Sudan Times*, 10 August, quoted by AFP, 11 August — DR, 12 August 1986.
160. Press conference by Prime Minister Sadiq al-Mahdi, SUNA, 21 August — SWB, 23 August; interview with Army Commander in Chief Fawzi Ahmad al-Fadil, *al-Sudani*, 29 September, quoted by AP, 30 September — DR, 30 September 1986.
161. *Al-Sharq al-Awsat*, 8 December 1986.
162. SUNA, 30 March — DR, 1 April 1986.
163. Statements by Mubarak's senior political adviser 'Usama al-Baz, and Foreign Minister 'Abd al-Majid, MENA, 31 March, 1 April — DR, 31 March, 2 April.
164. *Al-Ahram*, int ed, 4 April — DR, 8 April 1986.
165. MENA, 2 April — SWB, 4 April; SUNA reported that Mubarak had displayed "understanding" for the Cabinet's action. (SUNA, 3 April — DR, 8 April 1986.)
166. MENA, 6 July — SWB, 8 July 1986.
167. *APS* (nd), quoted by *Le Monde*, 2 September 1986.
168. In an interview, Hasan gave details of his submission to Algeria in 1984, prior to his agreement with Libya and in response to Algeria's suggestion, of a draft constitution for a Moroccan-Algerian federation. Such a federation, he had hoped, would have taken care of organizing the Western Sahara referendum. However, he stated, Algeria was only interested in gaining recognition for the Polisario (apparently as the dominant force in a Saharan entity to be federated to Morocco). (*Le Nouvel Observateur*, 28 March–3 April — DR, 8 April 1986; see also *MECS* 1983–84, pp 142 and 155, Note 141.)
169. One Arab publication reported prior to the breakup that Libya had already resumed aiding the Polisario. (*Al-Sayyad*, 6 June 1986.)
170. On one occasion, the Moroccans claimed to have killed an Iranian military instructor serving with the Polisario. (MAP, 1 February, quoted by Reuters, 1 February — *JP*, 2 February 1986.)
171. For an admission that the walls had caused the Polisario problems and a claim that they had been overcome, see interview with SADR President Muhammad 'Abd al-'Aziz, *al-Moudjahid*, 27 February — DR, 7 March 1986.
172. APS, 14 May — SWB, 17 May 1986.
173. APS, 18 July — SWB, 21 July; *L'Opinion*, 11 May, quoted by MAP, 11 May — DR, 12 May 1986.
174. King Hasan described India's action as "a trauma...like lightning in a calm sky." (MAP, 8 March — DR, 13 March 1986.)
175. For Morocco's threat to withdaw from the Arab League if the Polisario participated, see MENA, 8 January — DR, 10 January 1986.
176. For an expression of Morocco's satisfaction with the Harare gathering, see statement by Foreign Minister 'Abd al-Latif Filali, MAP, 9 September — SWB, 11 September 1986.
177. Interview with Filali, *al-Ahram*, 21 January 1986.
178. Interview with Foreign Minister 'Abd al-Majid, *Le Matin du Sahara* (nd), quoted by MAP, 25 January — DR, 3 February; interview with Prime Minister 'Ali Lutfi, *al-'Alam*, Rabat, quoted by MENA, 13 August — DR, 14 August 1986.
179. *Al-Akhbar*, 16 September; Mubarak's interview in *al-Watan al-'Arabi*, 10–16 October — DR, 14 October 1986.
180. Excerpt from minutes of high-level Algerian-Tunisian talks, issued at the close of Tunisian Prime Minister Rachid Sfar's visit to Algiers, R. Algiers, 5 October — DR, 7 October 1986.
181. For the texts of their "joint communiqué" and "political communiqué," see R. Algiers, 28 February — DR, 1 May 1986.
182. R. Rabat, 27 June — SWB, 30 June 1986.
183. MAP, 10 February — SWB, 12 February 1986.

184. See Hasan's interview in *Arab Times*, 24 March — DR, 26 March 1986.
185. Tripoli TV, 8 January — SWB, 14 January; MAP, 5 February — DR, 6 February; R. Rabat, 24 March — DR, 25 March 1986.
186. *Le Nouvel Observateur*, 4–10 April — DR, 27 April 1986.
187. MAP, 8 March — DR, 13 March 1986.
188. R. Rabat, 15 April — DR, 16 April 1986.
189. For a carefully worded, guarded exception to Libya's policy of silence, see *al-Jamahiriyya* (nd), quoted by JANA, 3 May — SWB, 6 May 1986.
190. JANA, 22 July — DR, 22 July 1986.
191. JANA, 26, 27 July — DR, 28 July 1986.
192. *Ma'ariv*, 18 August 1986.
193. Qadhdhafi's Revolution Anniversary speech, VoGAH, 31 August — SWB, 2 September 1986.
194. Press statement issued in Damascus and Tripoli, R. Damascus, 26 August — DR, 26 August 1986.
195. Hasan's address to the nation, and cable to Qadhdhafi declaring the abrogation. (R. Rabat, 29 August — DR, 2 September 1986.)
196. Qadhdhafi's Revolution Anniversary speech, VoGAH, 31 August — SWB, 2 September 1986.
197. AP, 3 September — *JP*, 4 September 1986.
198. "I had two guns trained on me [Algeria and Libya]. I had to neutralize one of them." *Le Nouvel Observateur*, 4-10 April — DR, 22 April 1986.
199. In any case the Moroccan security services were on full alert. On 31 August, Rabat announced the arrest of "a group of professionals of international terrorism" consisting of two Tunisians, a Palestinian and a Lebanese of Palestinian origin. (*Le Monde*, 2 September 1986.)
200. MAP, 8 March — DR, 13 March 1986.
201. The Algerian report, for example, stressed the two sides' adherence to Algeria's position on the Western Sahara and the Polisario, while the Libyan one treated the issue in general terms. By contrast, Libya's report emphasized Algeria's solidarity with Libya in the face of US "provocations," while Algeria's made no mention of the US-Libya crisis. (R. Algiers, Tripoli TV, 28 January — SWB, 30 January; *Jeune Afrique*, 12 February 1986.
202. *Al-Jazira*, 25 March 1986.
203. E.g., R. Tripoli, VoGAH, 9 December — SWB, 12 December 1986.
204. For a report of one Libyan proposal for a Syrian-Libyan-Algerian union, see *al-Watan*, 26 February 1986.
205. R. Algiers, 6 December — SWB, 9 December 1986.
206. For a report on their military consultations, emphasizing increased cooperation between their two navies, see R. Tunis, 22 October — DR, 24 October 1986.
207. Excerpts from the minutes of Algerian-Tunisian talks, issued at the close of Tunisia's Prime Minister, Rachid Sfar's visit to Algiers. (R. Algiers, 5 October — DR, 7 October 1986.)
208. *L'Action*, 9 February — DR, 21 February; R. Tunis, 10 February — SWB, 12 February 1987.
209. *Al-Sabah*, 13 January, quoted by KUNA, 13 January — DR, 13 January 1986.
210. *Le Matin du Sahara*, 14 October — DR, 24 October 1986.
211. *Al-Jazira*, 25 September; an earlier report (*al-Qabas*, 23 April) stated that Libya had agreed to pay off \$1.5m owed to Tunisia's national airline.
212. R. Tunis, 30 April — DR, 30 April 1986.
213. *The Guardian*, 25 April 1986.
214. KUNA, 17 April; *al-Watan*, 22 April, quoted by KUNA, 22 April — DR, 22 April 1986.
215. *Al-Qabas*, 23 April 1986.
216. KUNA, 9 December — DR, 10 December 1986.
217. KUNA, 23 December — DR, 23 December 1986.
218. R. Amman, 13 December — DR, 15 December 1986.

The Export of Islam

MARTIN KRAMER

Almost from Islam's inception, rivals staked incompatible claims to speak in the name of the true faith. This contest continued into modern times, and has been exacerbated by the rise of a radical Islam formulated in response to the challenge of the West. Some of these versions of Islam were identified with regimes; others, with populist or clandestine movements. Yet each of these contestants subscribed to the same conviction: that the Islam which it propounded had universal validity. Iran openly spoke of "exporting" its message of Islamic revolution, and so appropriated the term. But many other regimes and movements did the same, by a wide variety of means. The governments of Saudi Arabia, Egypt, and Libya actively exported their state-supported interpretations of Islam abroad. Independent fundamentalist movements, Sunni and Shi'i, did the same. Even the great powers gave encouragement to versions of Islam they deemed compatible with their interests. In 1986, these many rivals continued an intensive cross-exchange of ideas. When persuasion failed, some were not averse to the use of coercion. The competition in the marketplace of Islamic ideas had grown fierce; above all, the export of Islam remained a battle for uncommitted minds.

THE IMPASSE IN MUSLIM DIPLOMACY

The Jidda-based Islamic Conference Organization (ICO), the instrument of Muslim consensus-building, remained paralyzed by the apparent indifference of many of its 46 member States to the fate of the beleaguered organization. (On the development of the ICO's crisis, see *Middle East Contemporary Survey* [*MECS*], 1981–82, pp 283–84; 298–301; 1982–83, pp 235–37; 1983–84, pp 158–65; 1984–85, pp 146–48.) The ICO had failed to reconcile two warring member States, Iran and Iraq, and had yet to engineer a Muslim agreement on the question of Israel's legitimacy and the Soviet occupation of Afghanistan. The deliberations of the ICO's annual conferences of Foreign Ministers and the triennial Islamic summit conferences only drew more attention to these failings. ICO Secretary-General Sharifuddin Pirzada, who took up his office in December 1984, was not always willing to suffer his disappointments in silence, but necessity dictated that he blunt his criticism and seek to mend differences behind closed doors.

FOREIGN MINISTERS IN FEZ AND AFTERMATH

The ICO's 16th annual conference of Foreign Ministers met in Fez, Morocco, from 6–10 January 1986. Despite its swollen agenda of 91 items, the gathering did not move the Muslim consensus past the point where it stood following the previous meeting in San'a a year earlier. Once again, Iran, Libya, and Syria challenged Egypt's resumed membership in the ICO, on the grounds that relations with Israel were utterly incompatible with membership. (On Egypt's controversial status in the ICO, see *MECS* 1983–84, pp 127–30, 160–62). "How can a government that claims to be Arab and Muslim reach an accord with the Zionist enemy, which is hostile to Arabism and Islam?" asked Syrian Foreign Minister Faruq al-Shar'.[1] Egyptian Foreign Minister 'Ismat 'Abd al-Majid responded by noting that Egypt's hands, unlike those of Syria, were not stained with Palestinian blood — a reference to the Syrian-directed expulsion of the PLO from Tripoli in Lebanon.[2] In the end, the rejectionist challenge failed, and no changes were made to the detriment of Egypt.[3] A final resolution of the conference kept up the pretense of moral outrage, by calling upon all ICO member States to sever direct and indirect relations with Israel.[4] In response, Egypt's 'Abd al-Majid expressed his Government's formal reservations over a resolution which Egypt considered an infringement of its sovereignty.[5] By this time it seemed quite clear that the majority of member States did not really regard relations with Israel as sufficient grounds for exclusion from the ICO, however abhorrent such relations might be. The issue surfaced again in July 1986, when Morocco's King Hasan openly received Israeli Prime Minister Shimon Peres in Morocco. Hasan came under severe criticism in the wider Arab world, and was compelled to resign his presidency of the Arab League (see chapter on inter-Arab affairs). But Pirzada was probably truthful in affirming that there was no concurrent move to have Morocco expelled from the ICO.[6] For if Egypt's greater sin did not disqualify it from membership, how could Morocco be held to account for a lesser infraction?

The conference did make an unexpected demonstration of solidarity on Libya's behalf. The meeting coincided with US threats and sanctions against Libya, in retaliation for Libya's alleged role in the terrorist attacks at the Rome and Vienna airports (see chapter on armed operations). In two carefully worded statements, the conference condemned the US political and economic measures taken against Libya.[7] But at the same time, Iraqi Foreign Minister Tariq 'Aziz took the opportunity to openly reprimand Libya for continuing to "threaten neighboring Islamic countries," and urged Libya to "learn its lesson" from the threat it now faced.[8] The Libyan delegate reportedly sought a stiffer resolution calling for a Muslim counter-boycott of the US, but he could not muster the support.[9] In any event, words of Muslim support did not exercise any deterrent effect upon the US.

The complete absence of any reference to the Gulf war in the final resolutions came as the principal surprise of the conference. No one expected a breakthrough toward a cease-fire, but observers expected that the conference would reiterate past ICO resolutions.[10] Indeed, six member States proposed that the ICO issue a neutral "appeal" to both sides, in the hope of revitalizing the ICO's "good offices" committee. Iraq supported the proposal, but felt the appeal should be issued only to Iran, since Iraq already accepted ICO mediation; Iran opposed the appeal, on the grounds that it did not expressly label Iraq the aggressor.[11] The matter came up for discussion during a marathon seven-hour session, during which Iran and Iraq presented their grievances at length. But the last-minute decision of Pakistan, one of the proposal's sponsors, to rescind its sponsorship of the appeal, led to procedural mayhem from which the conference never extracted itself. This was the first time since the outbreak of the war that an ICO deliberation of this magnitude failed to include a reference to the Gulf war in its resolutions and recommendations.[12] Iraq openly counted this as defeat; Iran regarded it as a victory.[13] Pirzada was anxious to put the episode in the best light: it was wrong to deem the entire conference a failure simply because no agreeable formula could be reached on the war.[14] But the "good offices" committee remained moribund,[15] and there were even ICO member States which favored its dissolution.[16] The committee, led by Gambian President Dawda Jawara, apparently realized the uselessness of attempting mediation before both parties exhausted themselves. This plainly did not happen in 1986, as Iran launched offensive after offensive (see essay on Iraqi-Iranian war). The committee did not convene again until November 1986, when it met in Jidda in anticipation of the Islamic summit conference scheduled for Kuwait in January 1987. (The diplomacy preceding that summit will be considered in *MECS* 1987.)

On the question of Palestine, the Fez conference reiterated past resolutions. Shortly after the close of the conference, an Arab-Jewish clash on the grounds around the Dome of the Rock and al-Aqsa Mosque in Jerusalem led the Chairman of the Palestine Liberation Organization (PLO), Yasir 'Arafat, to request an emergency meeting of the ICO's Jerusalem Committee. The gathering, which met from 21–22 January 1986 under the presidency of King Hasan, passed numerous resolutions calling for intensified information efforts against the "Judaizing" of Muslim holy places.[17] 'Arafat emphasized in his speech to the meeting that Muslim shrines were not the only threatened holy places; Israel had also made "criminal attempts to violate the Christian shrines in that city."[18] No one in the Muslim world was better placed than Morocco's Hasan to raise the issue of Jerusalem in the Christian world. In August 1985, Hasan hosted a visit by Pope John Paul II, who addressed 80,000 Muslim youths in Casablanca. In the Vatican's eyes, Hasan was a prime candidate to represent Islam in any future Christian-Muslim dialogue; hence, 'Arafat's eagerness to work through the Jerusalem Committee in appealing to Christian conscience.[19] But Syria was not at all eager, for it regarded both Hasan and 'Arafat as arch compromisers of the struggle against Israel. Damascus thus continued its boycott of the Jerusalem Committee originally begun in May 1984 (see *MECS* 1983–84, p 164).

On the question of Afghanistan, Pirzada proceeded with great caution, pinning his hopes on the professed desire of Soviet leader Mikhail Gorbachev to see Soviet forces out of Afghanistan. At Fez, an Afghan delegation led by resistance leader Ahmad Gaylani announced that it was seeking full ICO membership for the Peshawar-based coalition of the seven groups bearing the brunt of the guerrilla fighting.[20] These would occupy the seat vacated following the ICO's January 1980 suspension of Afghanistan's membership in the organization.[21] But the attempt drew insufficient support, for Pirzada sought first to determine the sincerity of Gorbachev's interest in disengagement. This culminated in Pirzada's November 1986 visit to the Soviet Union, where he met with Gorbachev and Soviet Foreign Minister Eduard Shevardnadze. The Soviets withdrew six regiments from Afghanistan on the eve of Pirzada's visit, a move meant to indicate goodwill, but without military import.

Pirzada came away from his Moscow visit with "very positive impressions. Our positions are still not congruent, but one can see a desire in the new [Soviet] leadership to reach for the goodwill and friendship of the Muslim world. The desire is there, but what I feel is that perhaps the system is not yet ready with the necessary policy formulations." The Soviets told Pirzada that they wanted to disengage quickly from Afghanistan, but only if the survival of the Soviet-backed regime could be guaranteed — a solution Pirzada said "obviously will not work."[22] Through Pirzada's visit, both the Soviets and the ICO's Secretary-General sought to take each other's measure, but there was no actual movement toward a solution to the Afghan war during 1986. (Similar expectations fueled by Gorbachev also produced a positive Muslim response to another Soviet initiative, a conference gathering "Muslims for Peace"; see below.)

While it proved impossible to expand the Muslim consensus on political issues, the ICO did expand its membership by admitting Nigeria as a full member at the Fez meeting. Nigeria is a secular State, in which Muslims constitute the majority, but Christians and believers in traditional religions form large minorities. Until the Fez conference, Nigeria enjoyed only observer status in the ICO. At Fez, the Nigerian Government submitted its application for ICO membership without public debate in the country, prompting heated argument in Nigeria once word got out. Christian leaders saw the decision as a threat to Nigeria's official secularism, since it somehow implied that Nigeria was a Muslim State. The Nigerian Government of Maj-Gen Ibrahim Babangida (a Muslim) responded to the criticism by appointing a 26-man panel led by the Minister of Interior (a Christian) to "determine the implications" of Nigeria's full membership in the ICO.[23] The panel's report, submitted on 20 March 1986, resolved in favor of Nigeria's remaining in the ICO.[24] But Christians remained anxious. "We have now suddenly found our necks stuck in the yoke of the spiritual bondage of the ICO," declared the Anglican Bishop of Kaduna. "This is the beginning of our end as a nation."[25] The controversy had more to do with the fragile state of Muslim-Christian relations in Nigeria than with the real obligations of ICO membership. The ICO's purpose was political rather than religious; its membership already included other secular and multi-confessional States, such as Turkey and Lebanon.

ECONOMICS OF MUSLIM SOLIDARITY

A political consensus on the major crises affecting the Muslim world thus eluded the ICO in 1986, and its conference resolutions and Pirzada's statements went largely ignored in the wider world. Even worse, much of the organization's own membership demonstrated an indifference to its operation. This was understandable in the case of member States which invariably found themselves in the minority in ICO forums. Iranian Prime Minister Mir Husayn Musavi might be expected to declare that "the ICO is in its most ineffective form at present. In other words, there is no emphasis on principles and values."[26] But the malaise spread much further, as Pirzada discovered soon after taking office. He found the ICO Secretariat in desperate financial straits because of the failure of member States to fulfill their obligations. The ICO could not even meet its own payroll and running expenses, and Pirzada warned member States that this would thwart the ICO's efforts to combat Israel, get Soviet troops out of Afghanistan, and end the Iraqi-Iranian war.[27] One of the three ICO Assistant Secretaries-General made this admission: "Not all Muslim countries have fulfilled their financial commitments. It is obvious that the ICO needs funds to organize its activities effectively. Due to the lack of sufficient funds, many of the ICO's projects have not been fully operationalized."[28] An unnamed source close to the ICO went still further, asserting that Saudi Arabia was the only member State that met its financial obligations regularly.[29]

By late 1986, the cumulative deficit reportedly came to $17m. Pirzada declared that financial support "is the one area where response from some countries is not very encouraging... There are some countries, about ten, who are very regular in paying their annual contributions and another eight who also pay, but after a little effort."[30] Pirzada would later claim that his unusual appeal during 1986 met with a "good response," resulting in a "record payment" of 60 per cent of the contributions owed by member States.[31] Similar difficulties affected the institutions affiliated with the ICO. The International Islamic News Agency (IINA), first established in 1972, tottered on the verge of collapse. By the end of 1986, the IINA owed $2.3m, as a result of mismanagement and misuse of funds by the agency's executives. At the end of 1986, only seven member States had fully paid their assessed contributions for 1985; another 15 had made partial payment; and 24 had paid nothing at all.[32] A $700m plan for scientific cooperation between ICO member States also went nowhere, because of the ICO's inability to raise the $25m for a feasibility study.[33] This was the first time ICO officials had gone public with money complaints. The failure to meet obligations suggested that the ICO did not occupy a high place in the priorities of most member States, and that these were content to see the ICO lead a shoestring existence as a platform for political rhetoric. At the same time, ICO officials complained that member States harmed the effectiveness of the Secretariat and affiliated institutions by not applying a "rational recruitment policy" in sending representatives to serve at the Jidda headquarters.[34] This implied that postings to the ICO were regarded by some governments as simple sinecures.

It was in economics rather than politics that the ICO could point to a consistent record of achievement. The Jidda-based Islamic Development Bank (IDB), which began its activities in October 1975, had accomplished much in the course of its first decade. IDB financing in member States was applied to loans, equity investment, leasing, technical assistance, and foreign trade operations. The IDB's subscribed capital as of September 1985 stood at SDR1,952m. The largest subscribers were Saudi Arabia, SDR506m; Libya, SDR315m; Kuwait, SDR252m; United Arab Emirates, SDR195m; and Turkey, SDR160m. During the IDB's first decade of operation, it approved 523 projects valued at SDR4,813m. To handle this volume of business, the IDB's staff grew from 30 to 449 during the same period.[35] Only ICO member States had the right to the IDB membership and financing, and the IDB arguably buttressed the whole edifice of Muslim solidarity.

But there was a rub. Most of this financing did little to encourage trade among members, since the economies of Muslim States were geared to the production and consumption by the industrialized West. The trade volume of Muslim States among one another constituted only about 10 per cent of their total foreign trade.[36] To reduce the scale of this dependence, the ICO convened a conference of its standing Committee for Economic and Commercial Cooperation. Ministers of Finance and Agriculture met in Istanbul from 14–16 March 1986, in order to put together a plan for encouraging trade ties among ICO member States.[37] After much deliberation, the Standing Committee proposed the creation of a $300m fund to provide long-term commercial financing for mutual trade in "non-traditional" goods. Half the money would come from the IDB, and half from participating States.[38] Turkish Prime Minister Turgut Özal affirmed his Government's belief that "every concrete step toward economic cooperation will pave the way to defusing political tensions and enhancing our ties of friendship and brotherhood."[39] In future, he said, the Standing Committee's meetings would discuss transportation, communications, and energy.[40]

It was the old dream of a Muslim commonwealth, a vision thwarted in every modern generation by the economic realities of dependence. Its realization was arguably more remote than an end to the Gulf war, the restored independence of Afghanistan, or the liberation of Jerusalem.

When Pirzada viewed the ICO, he saw the full half of the glass. "How do you evaluate the functioning of an international organization like the ICO? One has to appreciate the fact that the ICO is not, or at least not yet, a supranational authority and therefore what it does or achieves is to be seen in the light of the fact that it is an association of sovereign States with their own limitations and particularisms. Yet it is a matter of great importance that these States have been coming together from time to time and at least exchanging their particular views and providing a statement of common position over a wide range of issues and problems affecting the Muslim world." With time, the sense of common interest would grow.[41] But Muslim critics were impatient, warning that "the organization has been unable to make any serious contribution to the solution or alleviation of the problems facing the Muslim States." The ICO, in this view, was all too likely to follow the road of the Arab League into oblivion.[42] The unresolved question was whether the ICO's progress would overtake the crisis of a divided Islam, before that crisis overwhelmed the ICO itself.

SAUDI SERVANTS OF ISLAM

Saudi Arabia's insistent claim to speak for all Islam stood in direct conflict with the simultaneous claims of Muslim rivals such as Iran and Libya. The struggle among these claimants led the Saudis to seize every opportunity to demonstrate their solicitude for Islam. Perhaps the most notable gesture of the year was made by Saudi King Fahd Ibn 'Abd al-'Aziz. The preferred honorific of Saudi kings had long been "His Majesty." By Fahd's own decision, this was dropped; he now preferred the title of "Servant of the Two Sacred Shrines" of Mecca and Madina (*khadim al-haramayn al-sharifayn*). "I have wanted to replace this phrase 'His Majesty' by something I adore and am honored to carry and that is 'Servant of the Two Sacred Shrines'," Fahd announced, and the Saudi Information Minister decreed that Fahd "should be addressed as such in written and spoken forms."[43] This preference for an explicitly Islamic titulature, with its subtle evocation of the caliphate, expressed both the breadth of the Saudi claim and a certain sense of insecurity about the traditional formulations of Saudi legitimacy.

Saudi Arabia continued to press its case for worldwide Muslim recognition in a variety of ways. The most important of these remained the Mecca-based Muslim World League (MWL; *Rabitat al-'Alam al-Islami*), the most ambitious of the Muslim missionary organizations, under the directorship of Secretary-General Dr 'Abdallah 'Umar al-Nasif. (On the MWL, see *MECS* 1981–82, pp 295–97; 1982–83, pp 246–47; 1983–84, pp 165–66; 1984–85, p 149.) The MWL's calendar consisted of numerous conferences which crowded the travel itineraries of its chief officers. Over the years, the MWL had created an extensive Muslim conference circuit, which served to strengthen Saudi ties with like-minded Muslim activists around the world. These friendships were cemented by Saudi support of Muslim associations and mosques abroad, administered for the most part by the MWL.

So extensive were the activities of the MWL that its old headquarters could no longer contain it. Throughout 1986, work progressed on new headquarters in Mecca:

a five-story building including offices, conference halls, a mosque, and a library. The complex cost SR90m. Future plans for the site called for building a new home for the MWL's training center for *imams* and missionaries, with dormitories for the students. The headquarters were scheduled for completion in May 1987.[44] With its move, the MWL would enjoy surroundings befitting an organization represented by 30 offices and 1,000 missionaries worldwide. According to Nasif, the MWL annually spent SR14m on these missionaries, and spent another SR5.6m in aid to various Muslim organizations throughout the world.[45] During the year, Nasif traveled extensively, disbursing financial support in his ever-widening wake. A former geology professor, Nasif cut the figure of a young and able technocrat who did not feign theological expertise and who wore Western suits while traveling in Europe and the Americas. With Nasif's management style and a sleek new headquarters, the MWL entered an era in which the medium mattered nearly as much as the message in spreading the word to the faithful.

The mission carried much more weight than in the bygone days of the 1970s, when the MWL had divided much of the field with Egypt. It now faced stiff competition from Iran and Libya, and had to use ever more advanced means of communication in order to be heard above the cacophony of Islamic preaching by others. But the MWL's activism rested upon the assumption that most Muslims could be convinced that Saudi Islam represented normative Islam, provided the Saudis could portray themselves effectively as guardians of Islam's holy cities and preeminent patrons of Islam everywhere.

This meant a high profile wherever Muslims were besieged. The Saudis could offer little military support to threatened Muslims, but they could demonstrate the alternative solidarity of the checkbook. For example, in Israel, the West Bank, and the Gaza Strip, the MWL was represented by the Mufti of Jerusalem, Shaykh Sa'd al-Din al-'Alami.[46] Through him and others, the MWL financed much of the restoration of the Hasan Bey Mosque between Tel Aviv and Jaffa, and provided maintenance support for other mosques, including al-Aqsa in Jerusalem.[47] It also financed the creation of the first Islamic studies college in Israel.[48] Israeli authorities reportedly turned a blind eye to this outside funding because the PLO was not involved[49] — this, despite the MWL's longstanding relationship with Yasir 'Arafat, who often attended the annual meeting of the MWL's governing constituent council, and who did so again in 1986.[50] There were countless other examples of the MWL's philanthropic involvement in places where Muslims were in the minority or under threat. This solicitude was celebrated during the sixth international conference of the World Assembly of Muslim Youth (WAMY), which met in Riyadh from 22–27 January 1986, and which devoted itself wholly to the plight of Muslim minorities. Established in 1972, WAMY organized conferences, published books and tracts, and ran six permanent youth camps — in Northern Cyprus, Bangladesh, Malaysia, Morocco, Saudi Arabia, and Brazil.[51]

In yet another demonstration of Muslim solidarity, Saudi Arabia sponsored a special committee to aid Afghan refugees in Pakistan. During its first two years, this committee, headed by the Governor of Riyadh, Prince Salman Ibn 'Abd al-'Aziz, spent 539m Pakistani rupees on foodstuffs, tents, blankets, and clothes for the refugees. By Saudi estimate, this constituted half of the total international and regional aid that flowed to the refugees. The committee's representatives in Pakistan, operating through the Saudi Red Crescent, also ran clinics, orphanages, homes for the disabled, and workshops.[52] This aid complemented Saudi support for the Afghan armed struggle (see *MECS* 1984–85, p 150). There were also some Arab Muslim volunteers in Afghan resistance ranks, who appeared to be mostly Saudis or Saudi-sponsored.[53]

Another form of solicitude for besieged Muslims consisted of special awards for prominent foreign Muslims who lent credibility to Saudi claims. The annual Faysal International Prize for Service to Islam, carrying a cash award of SR350,000, represented the most prestigious distinction of this kind. In 1986 the prize was divided between two recipients.[54] Ahmad Deedat, head of the Islamic Propagation Center in Durban, South Africa, hailed originally from Gujarat, and specialized in publicly debating Christian missionaries. He even challenged Pope John Paul II to a public debate in St Peter's Square — a challenge the Pope preferred not to answer.[55] Deedat instead debated lesser representatives of the rival faith, sometimes before as many as 7,000 listeners in London's Royal Albert Hall.[56] He shared the award with Roger Garaudy, a leading French intellectual of the Left who had converted to Islam a few years earlier, and then took up the political cause of Islam with a convert's zeal.

International Islamic banking represented another area in which Saudi entrepreneurs played a leading role. The underlying assumption of all Islamic banking was that no conflict existed between the principles of Islam and personal enrichment, provided such enrichment did not violate explicit provisions of Islamic law. The most important provision was Islam's banning of usurious lending, understood as the lending of any sum at a fixed rate of interest. Islamic banks employed a variety of circuitous techniques to satisfy this legal requirement. The market leader in international Islamic banking (aside from the ICO's own governmental IDB; see above), was the Dar al-Maal al-Islami (DMI), formed as a trust in 1981 under the laws of the Bahamas and operating in Geneva under Swiss law as a management company. DMI organized ventures in banking, insurance, and investment, through 22 subsidiaries in 12 countries. Its net assets at the end of fiscal year 1985 stood at $280m. The moving spirit behind DMI was Saudi Prince Muhammad al-Faysal Al Sa'ud. In his view, Islamic banking had "passed the stage of gaining expertise and [is] now capable of handling all economic problems and finding Islamic solutions for them."[57] His own DMI had cleaned house after its former chief executive, Ibrahim Kamil, had lost some $28m in the trading of precious metals. (On the DMI's development and difficulties, see *MECS* 1982–83, p 247; 1983–84, p 166; 1984–85, p 150.) In 1986, Kamil (who had already left his post as chief executive) resigned from the DMI's 18-member Board of Supervisors, although he still held an 8 per cent interest in the company. The Sudanese leader of the *Umma* Party (and later in the year Prime Minister) Sadiq al-Mahdi, also asked that his term as a board member not be renewed, apparently because of criticism in Sudan that the DMI was more interested in profit than in the welfare of the communities it claimed to serve.[58] But the DMI continued to claim that it operated wholly in accord with Islamic law, and that competitors "may not really be Islamic."[59]

Ibrahim Kamil meanwhile reappeared as the founder of the Geneva-based Dar Tadine al-Umma (DTU). This enterprise proposed to mine "Islamic gold dinars" and "Islamic silver dirhams" from the neighborhood of disused mines in Tanzania. As one analyst commented, "this sort of investment might well be worth speculation in the form of risk capital from wealthy investors. But it certainly does not look like the sort of thing a devout Muslim should plough his life savings into for the sake of his widow and children."[60] The DTU had to go to great lengths to establish that speculative trade in precious metals was even permissible in Islam.[61]

By now it was apparent that international Islamic banking had no more social conscience than any other kind of international banking. Its aim was to make profits for depositors and investors while adhering to the letter of Islamic law. And since Islamic banks had to create depositor confidence, they generally shunned investment in long-term development projects, preferring the security of trade financing. In this respect, Islamic banks helped fuel current consumption rather than long-term development. Finally, there was the question of just how "Islamic" the banks really were. Each bank retained one or more salaried "experts" whose task was to assure the bank's compliance with Islamic law. Muslim critics of the banks claimed that these persons issued debatable rulings that stretched the limits of the law, and that they could not do otherwise, since they were paid functionaries of the very banks they regulated. One possible solution mentioned in this debate was an independent, international supervisory board of Muslim scholars.[62] Without such regulation, international Islamic banking provided a rather wide arena for dubious banking practices.

EGYPT'S SUPPORTING ROLE

Egypt's role in propagating the message of a moderate Islam remained a modest one. With the Egyptian Government embattled at home by a burgeoning Fundamentalism, the diffusion abroad of Egypt's state-oriented version of Islam did not rank high on the list of priorities submitted by the regime to its clerics. Indeed, it seemed that much of the burden had been shifted to Saudi Arabia, which commanded more substantial resources.

But the Shaykh al-Azhar, Jadd al-Haqq 'Ali Jadd al-Haqq, did see himself as the first among believers, and in late 1985 and 1986 he embarked on several tours of other countries, including Brunei, Malaysia, Thailand, Singapore, Bangladesh, and Pakistan. During these trips, he sought to defend Egypt's policy from an Islamic point of view, and to attack Egypt's opponents from an Islamic angle. When asked in Bangladesh about the Egyptian-Israeli relationship, he declared that it was in accord with Islam, since a Muslim ruler could conclude a truce with a non-Muslim enemy; by the Egyptian-Israeli accords, Egypt received territory while Israel got no more than a piece of paper.[63]

On the other hand, by severely criticizing Khomeyni, the Shaykh al-Azhar entered into a headlong controversy with critics of the Egyptian regime. Jadd al-Haqq openly declared that the phenomenon of "Khomeynism" was remote from true Islam, and contradicted the Islamic principle of "no coercion in religion."[64] In taking this position, the Shaykh al-Azhar pitted his authority against Khomeyni's. But even in Egypt there were those who found Jadd al-Haqq wanting in the comparison. One critic pointed out that Khomeyni ruled by the will of the people while the Shaykh al-Azhar was an appointee. Khomeyni rid Iran of the Shah, cut off Israel's oil, and thwarted the superpowers. But what had the Shaykh al-Azhar done? "What did he do when the *Shari'a* law was abolished? Or when the Islamic *waqfs* were nationalized? Or when religious men were whipped?... Why didn't he protest, or speak out? Indeed what does he do in al-Azhar now?"[65] This kind of debate reflected the deeper rivalry between Egypt and Iran, as each sought to end its political isolation by maneuvering in the Arab expanse that separated them. In this contest, the Shaykh al-Azhar became the pivotal man in articulating Egypt's notion of a pluralistic Islam, daring to say about Iran what Saudi clerics only mumbled to themselves. But Jadd al-Haqq was not wholly compliant. In addition to his outspoken criticism of the Soviet presence in Afghanistan, he did not hesitate to denounce Israel for its alleged designs upon Muslim holy places in Jerusalem.[66] The challenge facing al-Azhar and its Shaykh was to preserve their traditional standing in Islam, to serve the regime, and to retain some credibility with radicals at a moment of growing radicalism. It remained to be seen whether these divergent goals could be achieved at one and the same time.

IRAN: TRIUMPH OF MODERATION?

From its inception, the Islamic Republic of Iran professed a commitment to a policy of encouraging Islamic movements abroad by a variety of means. Sometimes it employed campaigns of propaganda, at other times operations of armed subversion. Iran's prolonged war with Iraq made it necessary to moderate that policy in some parts of the Muslim world, where Iran feared that too aggressive an Iranian posture might work to Iraq's advantage. In the Gulf, Iran shelved plans for promoting Islamic revolution, lest the Gulf regimes recoil into the embrace of Iraq. But in more remote Lebanon, Iran invested great resources in supporting a movement bent upon establishing an Islamic Republic of Lebanon. (For the development of Iran's pan-Islamic policy, see *MECS* 1981–82, pp 288–92; 1982–83, pp 238–43; 1983–84, pp 167–74; 1984–85, pp 151–60.)[67]

As 1986 drew to a close, confusion clouded the issue of Iranian policy intentions, as a result of revelations about US-Iranian negotiations for the release of American hostages held by Iranian-backed Shi'is in Lebanon. (For other assessments of these negotiations, see chapter on Iran and essay on the US and the Middle East.) In the wake of the revelations, the US Administration maintained that the initial purpose of these contacts was not to strike an arms-for-hostages deal, but to reach out to Iranian "moderates." Was there a moderate camp in Iran, prepared to forgo an aggressive policy of exporting revolution to Lebanon and elsewhere in return for improved relations with the US? Or was the Iranian response to American overtures a calculated, short-term tactic, sanctioned by Imam Khomeyni, with the aim of gaining sorely needed hardware in a straightforward exchange for the release of American hostages?

Such questions had no unequivocal answers. Iranian Prime Minister Mir Husayn Musavi, addressing queries regarding Iran's alleged policy of exporting revolution, struck this note:

> What they call the export of revolution is in fact an effort to defend Islam everywhere. At present there are 40 foreign radio stations active against the Islamic Republic of Iran in an attempt to export their own culture and beliefs to our country. No one says anything when the US wants to export its culture to our country... If the export of revolution means that we proclaim the message that the dignity of Muslims depends on their return to Islam, then we accept that we export the revolution. But if it means intervention in the internal affairs and provocation of other countries, or that we intend to export arms to other countries, we deny this.[68]

Such statements recalled earlier remarks by *Majlis* Speaker 'Ali Akbar Hashemi-Rafsanjani and Iranian President Muhammad 'Ali Khameneh'i, disavowing the use of force in foreign policy, and asserting the "cultural" nature of Iran's "export" of Islam.[69] In the past, such statements had been interpreted by many observers as Iranian dissimulation, meant to erect a high wall of deniability between Iran and violent acts liable to bring retaliation. But in late 1985 and into 1986, such statements were subjected by US and Israeli officials to a systematic reinterpretation, and were read differently, as signals of a genuine Iranian willingness to improve relations with the US. And indeed, these three — Rafsanjani, Musavi, and Khameneh'i — directed the Iranian official who dealt with US emissary Robert McFarlane during his ill-fated mission to Tehran in May 1986. They were supposedly at the head of a "moderate" camp, and capable of enforcing restraint upon "radicals" who were otherwise prepared to terrorize and plot foreign revolution by any and all means. They reportedly enjoyed the backing of Khomeyni's son Ahmad, who played an increasingly important role in mediating the wishes of his ailing father.[70] But the "moderates" could not advocate their cause too boldly because, as McFarlane concluded, "they still cannot overcome their more immediate problem of how to talk to us and stay alive."[71]

The opposing "radical" camp was led by Ayatollah Husayn 'Ali Montazeri, Khomeyni's heir-apparent, who had taken upon himself the wider dissemination of the revolution's message in order to bolster his claim to the succession. (For Montazeri's role in the formulation of this policy, see *MECS* 1984–85, pp 151–53.)[72] One of Montazeri's principal aides in this task was Sayyid Mehdi Hashemi, head of the Liberation Movements' Department of the Iranian Revolutionary Guards Corps (IRGC). Mehdi Hashemi reportedly operated a training camp in North Tehran where Iranians as well as foreign Muslim volunteers and refugees underwent intensive ideological indoctrination in preparation for special operations. Before the revolution, Mehdi Hashemi was sentenced to death for the murder of an Isfahan cleric who had criticized Montazeri over a controversial matter of theology.[73] But his execution was stayed, and he was released following the revolution. Mehdi Hashemi owed his precipitous rise to his brother, Sayyid Hadi Hashemi, Montazeri's son-in-law and chief of Montazeri's bureau. Khomeyni himself reportedly paid frequent visits to Mehdi Hashemi's training camp, located only half a kilometer from the Imam's Tehran home. He also maintained bases of operation in his native Isfahan and in Qom.[74] Other advocates of an aggressive policy were Minister of Interior 'Ali Akbar Mohtashemipur, a former Iranian Ambassador to Syria who was recalled after Syrian complaints that he overstepped his bounds; and Ayatollah Fazlollah Mahallati, Khomeyni's special representative to the Supreme Council of the IRGC. (Mahallati perished in February 1986 in the downing of an Iranian airliner as it toured the Iranian-Iraqi war front.)[75] Also among the hard-liners was Hujjat al-Islam Muhammad Musavi-Kho'iniha, Prosecutor-General of Iran, former spiritual mentor of the students who seized US diplomats in Tehran, and past representative of the Imam to the pilgrimage. He had been removed from this last post as part of Rafsanjani's effort to improve relations with Saudi Arabia, since Kho'iniha had done much to incite Iranian pilgrims to confrontation (see *MECS* 1984–85, p 162). Montazeri also sponsored what various reports described as a Supreme Islamic Revolutionary Council, about which few verifiable details were known. It was said to operate under the direction of Hujjat al-Islam Muhammad Taqi al-Mudarrasi, the brilliantly eloquent leader of the Tehran-based Islamic Action Organization (*Munazzamat al-'Amal al-Islami*). (On the Council and Mudarrasi, see *MECS* 1983–84, pp 171, 173–74; 1984–85, p 152; and below). The Council's Committee for Europe, where it established most of its ties with foreign Muslims, reportedly used London and Rome as its principal bases.[76] Other reports mentioned Iran's embassy and consulates in West Germany as bases of operation.[77]

Divisiveness over the export of revolution was said to parallel the larger split between Montazeri and Rafsanjani over the future course of Iran's domestic and foreign policies — a split denied by both men, and difficult to measure, since Khomeyni's lingering presence inhibited any open airing of differences.[78] Rafsanjani himself dismissed rampant media speculation about the supposed split: "They cannot understand our relations with Ayatollah Montazeri as our former teacher, present successor to our leader, and our future leader. They think our relations are similar to their political relations in the West."[79] That may have been true, but Rafsanjani and Montazeri did nothing to present their own authoritative account of these relations, allowing free reign to speculation in Iran and abroad (see chapter on Iran). Certainly Montazeri, Rafsanjani, and many other persons in high positions of responsibility thought it essential that Iran should continue to develop close ties with Muslim movements abroad, and agreed that the sympathies and allegiances of other Muslims, Shi'is and Sunnis, constituted a valuable asset in the pursuit of any foreign policy. But they seemed to differ considerably over the ends which these alliances were to serve, and whether the international network created by Iranian efforts should employ violence as a matter of course.

This issue came to a head with the 12 October 1986 arrest of Mehdi Hashemi and many of his collaborators (numbering between 40 and 200). Much uncertainty surrounded the role of Mehdi Hashemi, who would eventually be accused of every kind of malfeasance, from murder and kidnapping to collaboration with the former secret police (SAVAK) and subversion.[80] Perhaps more important was the fact that Mehdi Hashemi had taken many independent (and violent) initiatives which cut across the grain of Rafsanjani's attempts to give nuance to Iran's regional and foreign policies.[81] These initiatives allegedly included an unauthorized attempt to disrupt the pilgrimage in a bid to thwart Rafsanjani's *rapprochement* with Saudi Arabia (see below); and the one-day kidnapping in Tehran of the Syrian chargé d'affaires, in apparent retaliation for Syrian-imposed restraints on Iranian activities in Lebanon.[82] By striking back at Mehdi Hashemi, Rafsanjani and his supporters sought to wrest control of Iran's regional network from Montazeri's personal office, and make it subject to collective decision-making. A central figure in this effort was Iran's Intelligence Minister, Muhammad Muhammadi-Reyshahri (son-in-law of the influential Ayatollah 'Ali Meshkini), who saw Mehdi Hashemi's operation as a competing bureaucracy, and who led the assault against him. During 1986, Reyshahri established an intelligence college, which reportedly enrolled 50–60 students from Bahrain, Kuwait, and Saudi Arabia, alongside some 200 Iranians.[83] This may have been created as a counterpoint to Mehdi Hashemi's operations in Tehran, Qom, and Isfahan. And it was Reyshahri who amassed the evidence against Mehdi Hashemi and orchestrated his arrest. Even a rare visit by Montazeri to Tehran failed to secure Hashemi's release,[84] and the arrests were generally interpreted as a blow to Montazeri's near-monopoly in the promotion of Islamic liberation abroad.

But Mehdi Hashemi's fall did not deliver his network straight into his rivals' hands. His supporters took their revenge by leaking word of US-Iranian contacts and the McFarlane mission. These revelations, made to a Lebanese weekly by Hadi Hashemi,[85] embarrassed Rafsanjani, who was compelled to conduct a public campaign of self-defense on his own behalf. Rafsanjani ultimately landed on his feet. According to reports, a December 1986 meeting attended by Montazeri, Rafsanjani, Khameneh'i, Musavi, and Reyshahri resolved to centralize all contacts with Iran's foreign Muslim supporters in Tehran, under the supervision of the Foreign Ministry.[86] (It was not clear whether this affected the position of Iran's Ministry of Islamic Guidance, entrusted by Khomeyni with disseminating Iran's "cultural" as distinct from "political" influence.) On the face of it, this strengthening of the Foreign Ministry appeared to undermine Montazeri's position. It was certainly resented by the radical students at Tehran University, who charged the Foreign Ministry with abandoning the revolutionary policy of seeking relations with peoples rather than governments. Islamic groups at the university issued a scathing critique of the Foreign Ministry after the revelations about US-Iranian negotiations, affirming that "the proper way to fight is through establishing relations with the liberation movements, building cadres and striking out against the US in all areas. The successful phenomenon in Lebanon called *Hizballah* supports this view. Three years ago, *Hizballah* did not exist in Lebanon, but at present, this movement is one of the most influential factors in the issues of Lebanon and the region."[87]

But later reports claimed that the Foreign Ministry's coordination with Muslim liberation movements elsewhere had been entrusted to Ayatollah Hadi Khosrowshahi, Iran's former Ambassador to the Vatican, who was suspected by Western intelligence circles of having established a clandestine European network of Muslim extremists based in Rome. (For Khosrowshahi's past activities, see *MECS* 1984–85, p 160.)[88] If Khosrowshahi had indeed succeeded Mehdi Hashemi, this seemed to represent a compromise between Montazeri and Rafsanjani. As a militant cleric, Khosrowshahi could be expected to pursue his task with the zealotry favored by Montazeri; but by placing Khosrowshahi in the Foreign Ministry, he could nevertheless be held accountable before Rafsanjani and Khameneh'i, through Foreign Minister 'Ali Akbar Velayati.

By the close of 1986, control of Iran's export of Islam had become a contested issue. Those favoring restraint in Iran's policy, such as Rafsanjani, had gained ground, but they could not exclude Montazeri from the enterprise. The possibility that their differences might spill over into the wider world of Iran's sympathizers also remained strong, and was realized during the year in Lebanon, the most important foreign proving ground for Iran's message of Islamic revival and revolution.

IRAN AND LEBANON'S ISLAMIC REPUBLICANS

Iranian leaders often boasted of their growing "influence" in Lebanon, an influence exercised primarily through Lebanese Shi'is who professed varying degrees of allegiance to the revolutionary message of Imam Khomeyni. That influence approximated direct control in the case of some Shi'is organized in the Iranian-inspired framework of *Hizballah*. Other Shi'is within *Hizballah* did not answer to Iran, but they did generally respond to Iranian moral and material incentives.[89] Indeed, even within the purely Lebanese *Amal* movement, with its formal professions of Lebanese

Nationalism and its alliance with Syria, there were many rank-and-file members who looked for guidance from Iran. Most remarkable of all, Iran had succeeded in extending its influence into the Sunni bastion of Tripoli, by assiduous cultivation of Shaykh Sa'id Sha'ban, leader of the Islamic Unification Movement (*Harakat al-Tawhid al-Islami*), who also advocated the transformation of Lebanon into an Islamic republic. (On the growth of Iran's influence in Lebanon, see *MECS* 1983–84, pp 171–73; 1984–85, pp 155–59.)

But Iran's Lebanese clients were sorely divided over whether they should work for this transformation immediately, in the teeth of opposition from Lebanese Christians and secularists, or base their appeal upon a gradual campaign of persuasion. The most impatient of Iran's friends in *Hizballah* went so far as to call for the open declaration of an Islamic Republic of Lebanon, centered in Ba'albak, the former resort town in Lebanon's Biqa' valley which had been transformed into a bastion of radical Shi'ism by the presence of an IRGC contingent. So eager were these zealots that they even printed postage stamps in the name of the Islamic Republic of Lebanon, and these began to appear on letters mailed from the town.[90] But no new regime was declared during 1986, due to the opposition of certain Lebanese Shi'i leaders who doubted whether *Hizballah* enjoyed the kind of support necessary to make a revolution. This view found its most articulate expression in the speeches and interviews of Sayyid Muhammad Husayn Fadlallah, the prominent Beirut-based Shi'i cleric who claimed a wide following (but no formal position) in *Hizballah*. This stand put Fadlallah at odds with Montazeri, but he remained in Rafsanjani's good graces. (On Fadlallah's views, see *MECS* 1984–85, pp 155, 157–58.)[91]

Iranian leaders in 1986 aimed at strengthening their hold over their Lebanese clients, and educating them to view their own predicament through an Iranian prism. One approach was to bring Lebanese sympathizers on political pilgrimages to Iran. The fourth annual Conference on Islamic Thought, which met in Tehran from 29–31 January 1986, provided just such an opportunity. In the past, the conference had served the general purpose of showing Iranian hospitality to sympathetic Muslims, in the expectation that they would speak well of Iran upon their return home. This time the event was aimed more deliberately at bringing some of Iran's Lebanese sympathizers into Rafsanjani's orbit.

Fadlallah attended; he had not been invited to Iran for some time because of his open disagreements with Montazeri. Shaykh Muhammad Mahdi Shams al-Din represented another important acquisition for Rafsanjani. As head of Lebanon's Supreme Islamic Shi'i Council, he could be said to represent the Shi'i community of Lebanon in a legal sense, although the extent of his real influence within the community was uncertain. Shams al-Din once maintained a steadfast independence from Iran. As recently as 1983, he had declared that "the Shi'i Muslims in Lebanon have always been Lebanese first... every sect in Lebanon at some time in its history has resorted to calling for help from an outside foreign power — with the exception of the Shi'i Muslims, who have always been loyal and sincere to Lebanon. Lebanon is their native land. When dealing with matters concerning Lebanon, their premises are always purely Lebanese."[92] This assessment now seemed hopelessly out of date, as Shams al-Din himself became a regular visitor to Iran, where he made three appearances in 1986. But while his own premises were no longer purely Lebanese, neither were they purely Iranian, and he carefully preserved his independent standing.[93] Also in attendance were Sayyid Ibrahim al-Amin, *Hizballah's* spokesman in Beirut, and Husayn al-Musawi, leader of the Ba'albak-based Islamic *Amal.*[94] These last two figures were self-avowed servants of Iran who openly disclaimed any predilection for independent judgment. As Ibrahim al-Amin explained, he owed his loyalty to Khomeyni exclusively. "Our connection with Imam Khomeyni regarding executive and practical matters is, of course, carried out through the command of the revolution, which is our command."[95] Shaykh Sa'id Sha'ban was also on Iran's guest list, but Syria apparently blocked his departure for the conference.

Fadlallah and Shams al-Din actually addressed the conference; several persons spoke on behalf of Iran, including Khameneh'i, Rafsanjani, and Ayatollah Ahmad Jannati, head of the Islamic Propagation Organization (*Sazmane Tablighate Islami*), who had visited Lebanon twice in 1985.[96] Montazeri's absence suggested that Rafsanjani, Khameneh'i, and Jannati saw this as their own forum for consolidating their influence in Lebanon, particularly through Shi'i leaders like Fadlallah and Shams al-Din who recoiled from Montazeri's appeals for the immediate establishment of an Islamic government in Lebanon. Although the final resolutions did call in a general way for the establishment of Islamic governments throughout the world, they made no explicit reference to Lebanon, while other causes — Palestine, the Iraqi-Iranian war, and the Soviet presence in Afghanistan — were all addressed in specific terms.[97] During the conference, Rafsanjani apparently assured Lebanese Shi'i leaders that they need not preach the immediate transformation of Lebanon into an Islamic Republic in order to enjoy Iran's continued support.

This found confirmation in remarks made during and after the conference. Fadlallah continued to preach patience. Establishing an Islamic republic would not be a "picnic," he said, for "the objective conditions do not exist for the implementation of an Islamic government in Lebanon." The majority of Lebanese, or at least the majority of Lebanese Muslims, first had to be won over to the idea.[98] Shams al-Din, talking of the plan for an Islamic government in Lebanon, defended the right of its advocates to speak their minds, but "concerning practical implementation, we must say that it is not presently practical to implement this plan."[99] Even Islamic *Amal* leader Husayn al-Musawi criticized "those excited brothers who want us to behave as if the conditions are like those after the revolution in Iran ... as if we have achieved victory. The conditions are different in Iran and Lebanon. The nature of the society in Lebanon and the nature of its Muslims are very different from those in Iran." On account of these differences, "no person, Lebanese or Iranian, believes that what can happen in Tehran can also occur in Beirut." In Musawi's view, "to present a plan for the formation of an Islamic republic is not proper at present."[100] This cautious realism represented an about-face for Musawi, prompted by Rafsanjani's personal encouragement. Montazeri perhaps now realized the need for a temporary retreat. When Fadlallah and Shams al-Din met with him during their stay, he did not admonish them to preach revolution, but simply urged them to foster unity.[101]

Rafsanjani received important Lebanese Shi'i support in return for his stand. During the year, Fadlallah declared Rafsanjani "undoubtedly the thinking head of state."[102] He also gave his endorsement to the admissibility of collective leadership by Muslim jurisprudents — a position known to correspond to that of Montazeri's critics. And even while professing a voluntary fidelity to Khomeyni, Fadlallah asserted that it was perfectly legitimate for the different regions of the Shi'i world to submit to the final authority of different jurisprudents.[103] By these statements, Fadlallah prepared his theoretical grounds for standing up to Montazeri, should Montazeri indeed succeed Khomeyni as Iran's "leader."

The long-term implications of these developments were unclear. However, they did confirm that Lebanon's Islamic Republicans had a tendency to factionalism along lines that coincided with the fissures in Iran's own Islamic Republican Party (IRP). Like the ruling IRP, *Hizballah* was a coalition with a single purpose, but it was a coalition nonetheless. It brought Fadlallah and his following, with their strong streak of independence, into an alliance with new converts to the cause who professed unflinching allegiance to Iranian emissaries. During the early years of Iran's involvement in Lebanon, Montazeri sought to channel all contacts with Iran's Lebanese clients through persons who answered to him, and particularly through Mehdi Hashemi. But the important visits to Iran by Lebanese Shi'i leaders in early 1986 broke Montazeri's virtual monopoly, and opened the Lebanese arena to a wider variety of Iranian players.

This development was abetted by the October 1986 demise of Mehdi Hashemi (see above). His disgrace, the consequence of his alleged (and later self-admitted) "deviation," seemed still further evidence of Montazeri's loosening grip on Iranian activities in Lebanon. Fadlallah welcomed this development. He announced that Mehdi Hashemi's demise did not mean that the Iranian institutions assisting the "liberation" of other Muslims would be disbanded. It did mean that Iran's "struggle against Imperialism" would proceed "in a studied and rational manner."[104] Immediately after Mehdi Hashemi's removal, his Beirut collaborator, Iranian chargé d'affaires Mahmud Nurani, was recalled to Tehran for consultations, and Iran announced that it would appoint Ahmad Dastmalchiyan its first Ambassador to Lebanon in four years.[105] This seemed to be yet another maneuver to circumscribe the influence of Montazeri in Lebanon, and to tighten Iran's grip on its Lebanese Shi'i clients.

But with Mehdi Hashemi's fall and the revelations about Iran's dealings with the US, other Lebanese Shi'is became furious, particularly the hostage-holders in *Hizballah,* who made it clear that they would no longer answer Iranian requests to yield hostages. The American hostages were held by 'Imad Mughniyya, a *Hizballah* military commander in Beirut, who was one of four persons indicted in the US for involvement in the June 1985 hijacking of a TWA airliner to Beirut (see *MECS* 1984–85, essay on armed operations).[106] He was also the brother-in-law of a Shi'i condemned to death in Kuwait for involvement in the December 1983 bomb attacks against the US embassy and other installations (see *MECS* 1983–84, pp 405–6). Mughniyya, operating under the cover of Islamic Jihad (*al-Jihad al-Islami*), had seized American hostages in Beirut in order to secure the release of the Kuwait prisoners. But by pressure and deception, Iranians involved in the dealings with the US had managed to part Mughniyya from some of his hostages without delivering any of the Kuwait prisoners. Once the details of the arms-for-hostages deal became public, an angered Mughniyya broke his ties with the Iranians, who had so obviously used his hostage-taking for their own ends. Mughniyya apparently took additional hostages (including would-be mediator Terence Waite), and reports had it that Iranian emissaries were no longer able to locate their disgruntled protégé.[107] As a result, Rafsanjani lost his leverage in the arms-for-hostages game. He still offered to use his exhausted "influence" for release of the remaining hostages in exchange for the continued flow of US arms. But he could no longer control the most radical of Iran's clients in Lebanon, who viewed his dealings with the US (and Israel) as so much treason against the creed of Islamic Republicanism.

The hostage issue also complicated Iran's and *Hizballah*'s relations with Syria. Throughout the year, Syrian President Hafiz al-Asad pressured *Hizballah* for the release of foreign hostages, discovering only belatedly that the hostages were being held by "a small group outside [*Hizballah*'s] control."[108] The resulting tension highlighted Iran's vulnerability in Lebanon: Iran's supply lines to its Lebanese clients ran through Syria, and Syria appeared increasingly anxious over the growth of *Hizballah*. Time and again, Syria and *Hizballah* found themselves on the brink of conflict, as the "war of the camps" pitted Syrian-backed *Amal* militiamen against Palestinian fighters in areas adjacent to *Hizballah* enclaves. Fearful of Syrian encroachment in Beirut, *Hizballah* tilted toward the Palestinians, and numerous Iranian mediators appeared in Lebanon to promote a settlement that would forestall a Syrian-imposed solution. In the middle of the year, Iran also dispatched a new Ambassador to Damascus, Hujjat al-Islam Muhammad Hasan Akhtari, as part of the intensification of diplomatic contacts between Syria and Iran regarding Lebanon. (The post of Ambassador had been vacant for nine months, as the Syrians reportedly turned down three of Iran's nominees for the post.) While Rafsanjani seemed anxious to keep Iran's disagreements with Syria under wraps, Khameneh'i spoke of them freely, and was particularly incensed over Syria's treatment of *Hizballah* and Syrian overtures to Jordan. Nor did he hesitate to raise the matter of Syria's unpaid oil debt to Iran, put at $1.675 bn. There was even a period during the summer when Iran suspended its oil shipments to Syria, in order to gain more diplomatic leverage.[109] That the distrust-ridden Syrian-Iranian alliance lasted for yet another year remained something of a miracle, explicable only by the animosity toward Iraq shared by the two States, and the role played by Iran in promoting a war of insurgency against Israel and Israel's Lebanese clients in South Lebanon. (See also chapters on Iran; Syria.)

The Islamic Resistance (*al-Muqawama al-Islamiyya*) represented to the southern struggle against Israel what Islamic Jihad represented to the campaign to purge Beirut of foreigners. In fact, these were both pseudonyms for *Hizballah*, which enjoyed much Iranian support in extending its reach to the South. *Hizballah* rallied around the rejection of resurrected United Nations' Resolution 425 (dating from March 1978). This it regarded as implicit recognition of Israel's right to exist, since the resolution explicitly recognized Israel's right to a secure Lebanese frontier. In this respect, *Hizballah* differed markedly from *Amal*, which accepted the need for security guarantees in return for an Israeli departure from the South.[110] This difference of opinion aggravated the tendency of *Amal* and *Hizballah* to clash.[111] More important, the *Hizballah*-backed Islamic Resistance launched numerous attacks against Israeli forces and the Israeli-backed South Lebanese Army, and also against the United Nations Interim Force in Lebanon (UNIFIL), which it regarded as an impediment to prosecution of the *jihad*. The growing frequency and effectiveness of these attacks were acknowledged by Israel and UNIFIL.[112] (See also essay on armed operations and chapter on Lebanon.)

But the IRGC contingent in Ba'albak, numbering about 800 persons, did not join in the southern fighting in 1986, confining its role to training and indoctrination.[113] On this account (and because of the possible presence of American hostages in its midst), the contingent enjoyed an immunity from Israeli retaliation. Iran also invited 158 southern Shi'i *mujahidun* freed from Israel's 'Atlit prison to visit Iran, where they made professions of devotion to their hosts.[114]

The resistance in the South did not depend entirely upon the support of Iran. Neither did the growth of *Hizballah*. Both drew upon the conditions of internal disorder and foreign intervention that had plagued Lebanon for over a decade. But the material and moral support of Iran hastened the ascent of Lebanon's Islamic Republicans, and inspired them with confidence in the inevitability of their own triumph, even as many of their rivals sank into despair. By the year's end, the combination of Iran and *Hizballah* had come to preoccupy Israel, Syria, and much of the West.

IRAN AND THE IRAQI SHI'I OPPOSITION

Iran's policies toward Shi'i communities elsewhere in the Arab world varied widely. Iran could not give support to Shi'i opposition movements on the Arab side of the Gulf without driving conservative Arab regimes completely into the Iraqi camp. But Iran had always given strong encouragement to Iraqi Shi'i exile groups based in Tehran. (For the groups referred to below and their differences, see *MECS* 1983–84, pp 170–71, 483.) Iraqi Shi'is associated with the exiles overstepped their bounds in 1985 by pursuing their campaign against Iraq into Kuwait, in a round of terrorism that ultimately embarrassed Iran (see *MECS* 1984–85, pp 153–54). In early 1986, the Iranian authorities sought to redirect the zeal of these groups to fighting the war itself, in part by mobilizing specifically Iraqi units for the battle. Hujjat al-Islam Muhammad Baqir al-Hakim, leader of the Iraqi Shi'i *al-Da'wa* movement and head of the Tehran-based Supreme Assembly of the Islamic Revolution in Iraq (SAIRI), planned to have such units placed in "liberated" regions of Iraq, and also sought recruits among the many Iraqi prisoners of war in Iranian camps.[115] This campaign was not unrelated to the difficulties faced by Iran in finding recruits for the war. SAIRI even extended its recruitment campaign to Damascus, where many Iraqi Shi'is lived in exile.[116]

But a disharmony could be detected in the Iraqi Shi'i opposition, over the question of who would lead the anticipated triumphal return to Iraq: Baqir al-Hakim or Islamic Action's Muhammad Taqi al-Mudarrasi. The former represented an autonomous Iraqi Shi'i revolutionism that predated Iran's own revolution: Baqir al-Hakim saw himself as an equal partner, not a servant, of the Islamic Republic of Iran. And in according the very highest priority to Iraq's liberation, he sought to channel his movement's resources into conventional warfare on the front. This served as his principal credential for future leadership. In contrast, Muhammad Taqi al-Mudarrasi placed himself at the service of any cause which his hosts assigned him, and his small following included all sorts of Muslim revolutionaries who had congregated in Tehran.[117] Bombings and assassinations constituted Islamic Action's contribution to the war effort. The group carried out its operations not on the front but in Baghdad and elsewhere in the Iraqi rear, where Islamic Action also distributed Khomeyni's speeches and photographs.[118]

During 1986, these two rivals exchanged subtle accusations. In particular, persons associated with *al-Da'wa* accused Islamic Action of fabricating events described in its military communiqués. The actions carried out by its "martyrs" allegedly never took place, and members of Islamic Action who claimed to be engaged in clandestine work were actually evading service at the war front.[119] Islamic Action replied by questioning the loyalty of *al-Da'wa* to Khomeyni and his designated heir, Montazeri. *Al-Da'wa*'s critics could point to the fact that a few members of *al-Da'wa* had even left the organization to establish an Iraqi *Hizballah*, more faithful to the "line of the Imam."[120] And it was undoubtedly true that some *Da'wa* activists found Tehran stifling. One of the Hakim brothers, Mahdi al-Hakim, a leading figure in *al-Da'wa*, left Iran for Britain, supposedly out of resentment against Iran's overbearing attitude toward his movement. These controversies left little doubt that the Iraqi Shi'i opposition based in Tehran also represented an uneasy coalition. Like the Lebanese *Hizballah*, its wings also aligned themselves with the various contending factions in Iran. Muhammad Taqi al-Mudarrasi was close to Montazeri and Mehdi Hashemi, through his former association with Montazeri's late son, Muhammad. Muhammad Baqir al-Hakim took an independent stand between Montazeri and Rafsanjani, and had a close relationship with Lebanon's Fadlallah, to whom Baqir al-Hakim was also linked by family ties.

The interrelated mesh of Shi'i alliances, which transcended all borders, came into play again following France's forced repatriation of two Iraqi Shi'i oppositionists to Iraq, in March 1986. The two had been arrested after the terrorist attacks in Paris on 12 February 1986, which led to the deportation of 13 persons to various countries.[121] False reports indicated that the Iraqi authorities had immediately executed one of the returned prisoners. The Tehran-based groups could do little in retaliation, but Lebanese Shi'is could, and they promptly claimed to have retaliated by executing Michel Seurat, a French academic taken hostage while conducting research in Beirut.[122] They also kidnapped a French television crew in Beirut, in order to secure the return of the two Iraqis to France.[123]

Iran made a serious effort to heal the divisions in the Iraqi opposition by having SAIRI convene a Conference of Solidarity with the Iraqi People, which met in Tehran from 24–27 December 1986. This gathering reportedly brought over 90 Iraqi dissidents, residing mostly in Britain and Syria, back to Tehran, in the hope of ending their differences with leaders of the Iraqi Shi'i opposition in Iran. Iraqi Shi'i and Kurdish activists abroad feared that Iran planned to annex Iraq to a greater Islamic Republic; one aim of the conference would be to alleviate their apprehensions. To assist in the effort, SAIRI also summoned its Lebanese Shi'i friends: Fadlallah, Shams al-Din, Husayn al-Musawi, Ibrahim al-Amin, and Subhi al-Tufayli all arrived in Tehran for the conference.[124] According to reports, 423 persons participated in the event. It was addressed by Khomeyni in the mosque next to his Tehran home. Khameneh'i gave the crucial assurances: following the victory of Iranian arms, "recognized international borders between us and Iraq would remain in effect, and the political future of Iraq, which is something that should be decided by the people of that country, should be settled in such a way that would guarantee its territorial integrity."[125] The resolutions, which called for "escalation" of Iran's war with Iraq until final victory, also stressed the need to preserve Iraq's "territorial integrity." The conference proceeded to establish a "special commission for evaluation of the future government of Iraq," composed of Iraqis and charged with drafting a future constitution for an Islamic Iraq.[126] When Montazeri met the delegates, he urged them to show "greater unity."[127]

The fact that Montazeri had to plead for "greater unity" from Iran's Lebanese and Iraqi Shi'i clients indicated that the factionalism that afflicted Iran had serious repercussions in Iran's own regional sphere of influence. As Iran drifted toward a struggle for succession, these clients could only wonder what the impending internal struggle portended for Iran's avowed commitment to the success of their bids for power. Among Iran's Shi'i admirers abroad, every tremor in Tehran was carefully registered, producing subtle but important realignments.

MEETINGS ON ISLAM'S MARGINS

MUSLIM BROTHERHOOD INTERNATIONAL IN EUROPE

One remarkable aspect of contemporary pan-Islamic activism was the absence of any regular and institutionalized exchange among Sunni Fundamentalist groups of the Muslim Brotherhood variety. There were many ties between these groups, but these remained informal or clandestine. Sunni Fundamentalists did occasionally meet under the auspices of the London-based Islamic Council of Europe. (For a previous instance, see *MECS* 1983–84, p 174.) It was in Europe that these groups operated and interacted with one another most freely. Geneva, city of refuge for Muslim activists for over half a century, provided a hospitable setting for a conference entitled "Islam, The Liberating Force," which met from 10–11 March 1986. Among those who addressed the gathering were Dr Necmettin Erbakan, leader of Turkey's outlawed National Salvation Party, and Ahmad Ben Bella, who, since his release from an Algerian prison in 1980, had adopted a Fundamentalist position.[128] But a number of scheduled speakers did not appear in the end. They included two Egyptian Muslim Brotherhood ideologues, Shaykh Muhammad al-Ghazali and Shaykh Salah Abu Isma'il, as well as Sudan's Sadiq al-Mahdi.[129]

The conference called upon the ICO to admit the Afghan resistance organizations to full membership, called for the liberation of Palestine in its entirety, denounced the Syrian regime for its human rights violations, and appealed for the establishment of an Islamic order, based on Islamic Law, throughout Muslim lands. It was unusual, however, to see such a gathering condemn Saddam Husayn as the aggressor in the Gulf war. This perhaps explained the decision of notable activists to absent themselves from the conference, and indicated a possible split in Sunni Fundamentalist ranks over who should bear the blame for the continuing conflagration in the Gulf.[130] One source claimed that Ben Bella later met secretly in his Lausanne apartment for a week with representatives of various Muslim opposition movements, in order to plan a common strategy.[131]

ISLAM'S CALL FROM LIBYA

Libya's Mu'ammar al-Qadhdhafi continued to lay claim to a position of primacy in Islam in his efforts to fend off international isolation. (For the wider context of Qadhdhafi's policy, see chapter on Libya.) Libya's embattled leader had accrued no discernible influence over Muslim movements in the heartlands of Islam. But in recent years the Libyan regime had built a substantial network of Muslim sympathizers in Europe, Black Africa and Southeast Asia, and these were now called upon to demonstrate their solidarity with Qadhdhafi in his moment of need.

The task of organizing and eliciting such demonstrations of support remained the responsibility of the Tripoli-based Islamic Call Society (*Jam'iyyat al-Da'wa al-Islamiyya*), under the guidance of Muhammad Ahmad al-Sharif. (On the Society, see *MECS* 1981–82, pp 293–94; 1982–83, p 245; 1984–85, p 161.) This Libyan-controlled international organization of Muslim activists had been established in 1970, but only in 1982 did it resolve to convene large-scale conferences every four years. Such a conference was due in 1986, and it met in Tripoli from 15–20 September 1986. Some 400 guests reportedly attended the proceedings. They included a deputy of Ugandan President Yoweri Museveni and Uganda's Minister of Information, who arrived in the wake of Qadhdhafi's own visit to Uganda earlier in the month.[132] Other noteworthy participants included Syria's Chief Mufti, Shaykh Ahmad Kiftaru, and American Black Muslim leader Warith al-Din (Wallace Deen) Muhammad.[133]

An address by Qadhdhafi marked the high point in the deliberations of the conference. In his remarks, Qadhdhafi portrayed the gathering as evidence of "the mass Islamic support" for Libya in its battle against the "crusader-Zionist alliance against Islam." Israel and the US had become one; US Secretary of State George Shultz was "also a Jew — a Jew and a Zionist." To meet the threat to Islam, Qadhdhafi called for a *jihad* "against the Americans everywhere, against the Zionists everywhere," and urged Muslim volunteers from around the world to come to Libya, "the first stronghold of Islam," in order to defend it against aggression. Qadhdhafi also called for the establishment of an Islamic bank or fund, supported not by Muslim governments but by individuals, which would finance the *jihad*.[134] The conference resolutions endorsed these appeals in a routine manner, and also called on all Muslims to withdraw their deposits from foreign banks in order to invest them in the service of Islam.[135] The conference in fact had more the character of a rally, for the conferees greeted Qadhdhafi with tumultuous revolutionary sloganeering.[136] They also visited Qadhdhafi's home, to see for themselves the consequences of the April 1986 American aerial "terrorist" attack against the Libyan leader (see chapter on Libya).[137] Typical of the delegates' enthusiasm was a comment by a South African Muslim who attended the gathering: "I found Qadhdhafi to be a very warm person who loves life. He enjoys the acceptance and affection with which people meet him."[138]

During the year, the Islamic Call Society also successfully promoted the establishment of a Union of Islamic Councils in East, Central, and South Africa, headquartered in Uganda. These were all areas where Libya had invested much effort in creating a sympathetic Muslim following.[139] Alongside the overt propagation activities of the Islamic Call Society, there were numerous reports of continuing Libyan involvement with Muslim activists in places as diverse as Senegal, Ghana, Pakistan, Malaysia, Thailand, and the Philippines.[140] American Black Muslim leader Louis Farrakhan also attended a conference in Libya in March 1986, prompting the US Justice Department to investigate the circumstances of the visit.[141] Farrakhan's stateside organization reportedly received a $5m interest-free loan from Qadhdhafi.[142] But such demonstrations of solidarity did not spare Qadhdhafi the criticism of Libyan Muslim opposition groups allied with the Muslim Brotherhood abroad. In one notable instance, these accused the Libyan *haj* mission of assassinating one of their exiled leaders during the pilgrimage to Mecca in 1985, after luring him to the mission's headquarters.[143]

It was difficult to know whether Qadhdhafi's influence in the Muslim world was enhanced or diminished by the US-Libyan confrontation of 1986. But the Libyan leader did not relent in declaring himself to be the visionary leader of all Islam and special patron of besieged Muslim minorities, even as he himself came increasingly under siege.

MUSLIMS FOR PEACE IN THE SOVIET UNION

The Soviet Union seemed an unlikely claimant to the title of defender of Muslim interests. But the Soviets had interests of their own in the Muslim world, and these they sought to defend by presenting Soviet policy as wholly compatible with the cause of Islam. This task, always difficult, had been complicated by the war in Afghanistan. As a result, the Soviets relied upon Soviet Muslims to sway Muslim opinion abroad. A success in this campaign was registered in an international conference of "Muslims for Peace," which met in Baku, Azerbaijan Soviet Socialist Republic, from 1–3 October 1986. A conference with the identical aim had been convened in September 1980 in Tashkent (see *MECS* 1980–81, pp 121–22). On that earlier occasion, Muslims from abroad were enticed to the Soviet Union by the (ultimately disappointed) expectation that the Soviets might be persuaded to withdraw from Afghanistan. That same expectation reappeared in 1986 in the wake of conciliatory statements made by Mikhail Gorbachev. Soviet exploitation of this expectation soon followed. The conveners of the conference in Baku meant to demonstrate that in the contest between the US and the Soviet Union for Muslim minds, the Soviets enjoyed a clear advantage, even as Soviet troops fought on Afghan soil.

It was essential that invitations to the conference be issued under Muslim auspices, a task fulfilled by Mufti Tal'at Tajuddin, Chairman of the Muslim Religious Board for the European Part of the USSR and Siberia. He played a growing role in representing Soviet Islam to Muslims elsewhere, and even led a group of Soviet Muslims on the pilgrimage to Mecca in 1985.[144] The conference itself gathered *c* 500–600 Muslim participants, 200 of whom came from abroad. Among those in attendance were Ministers of Islamic Affairs from Afghanistan, Iraq, Jordan, and Syria, a representative of Libya's Islamic Call Society, and the Secretary-General of the Muslim World League, 'Abdallah 'Umar al-Nasif, whose unexpected presence indicated Saudi interest in the proceedings. His participation was all the more remarkable as his predecessor had led a Muslim boycott of the Tashkent conference six years earlier.[145] The conference was greeted with a message from Soviet Prime Minister Nikolai Ryzhkov, who declared that "US bandit actions against Libya, Israeli refusal to withdraw its troops from South Lebanon, the threat of using force against Syria and other countries, are fraught with a direct danger to universal peace." The other threats to peace were the "bellicose imperialist circles" who were "pushing the world to a nuclear catastrophe."[146] During the conference itself, Muslim delegations joined their Soviet hosts in condemnation of Israel and support for the Soviet nuclear "peace initiative." As for Afghanistan, only Nasif raised his voice in measured criticism of his hosts. Nasif called on the Soviet Union to "reconsider its position on Afghanistan," because "the Soviet military presence in Afghanistan harms Moscow's relations with the Islamic world."[147]

The Baku conference evoked some favorable comment from sympathetic Leftists in the Muslim world.[148] But a Muslim critic lambasted "unknowing or complacent delegates who were impressed by Soviet hospitality, architectural monuments, restored caravanserais, mosques, the market square of Baku, or by the Soviet rhetoric against the Israelis."[149] The Soviets understandably counted the event a success, and even established a permanent committee assigned to publicize its resolutions and perhaps convene future conferences.[150] Whether there occurred a more substantial dialogue between Muslim activists and the Soviets could not be determined. But the Soviets had clearly succeeded in convening a major Muslim gathering simply on the promise of a reassessment of policy on Afghanistan, and a reiteration of old positions on the Palestine question.

THE PILGRIMAGE OF 1986

The pilgrimage, symbol of Islam's elusive unity, had become a setting of strife following Iran's Islamic revolution. (For the development of the pilgrimage controversy, see *MECS* 1981–82, pp 284–88, 301–3; 1982–83, pp 238, 249–51; 1983–84, pp 175–77; 1984–85, pp 161–64.) With the passage of time, Saudi Arabia and Iran reached a compromise that allowed Iran to conduct a tolerable measure of political propaganda during the pilgrimage. By this arrangement, Khomeyni's pilgrimage representative was permitted to organize two pilgrims' rallies, the first in Madina and the second in Mecca. Iranian pilgrims were also free to congregate in small groups with pilgrims from other Muslim lands, in order to explain the message and meaning of Iran's Islamic revolution. But two prohibitions applied. Pilgrims were not allowed to import printed materials of a political nature; and they were not to initiate spontaneous demonstrations. This understanding allowed Iran's pilgrims to vent their views, but enabled Saudi authorities to confine all demonstrating to two fixed events. The number of Iranian pilgrims also remained more or less fixed at 150,000. The Saudi authorities, concerned about terrible overcrowding, imposed quotas on the number of pilgrims from all countries, and Iran had no cause for complaint, since its pilgrims constituted 18 per cent of all foreign arrivals, the largest of all foreign pilgrimage groups.[151] But even if the ground rules and numbers were fixed, the Saudi-Iranian understanding was not a static one, and during each pilgrimage season it was subject to minor modification.

Montazeri again spelled out the obligations of Iran's pilgrims, in the customary gathering of Iranian pilgrimage functionaries that preceded the pilgrims' departure. Iranian pilgrims were to "stay away from conflict, not lose their tempers, and be ready at any moment to sacrifice and forgive; they should behave in such a way that they will earn respect for Islam and for the revolution." At the same time, they were to identify "influential and committed people" from other Muslim countries, and explain the revolution's achievements, thus "neutralizing the enemies' evil propaganda."[152] Khomeyni reiterated these themes in his annual pilgrimage message. He urged Iranians to tolerate any "mistreatment" and to carefully follow the instructions of Iranian officials at the permitted rallies. Khomeyni added to his usual points his instruction that Iran's pilgrims purchase no US-made articles and merchandise during their sojourn in Saudi Arabia: "Their purchase is tantamount to aiding the enemies of Islam."[153] It was difficult to determine whether this call for a boycott had any effect, as Iran claimed it did.[154]

In the holy cities, Khomeyni's representative, Hujjat al-Islam Mehdi Karrubi, supervised the activities of Iran's pilgrims for the second consecutive year. Karrubi had won Saudi respect for his avoidance of confrontation and his businesslike approach to settling differences with the Saudi authorities.[155] Karrubi aimed at preserving the pilgrimage peace, while extracting Saudi concessions that would enhance Iran's influence over the rites. He soon found an appropriate issue of contention. Shortly after his arrival in Madina on 25 July 1986, Karrubi announced that the Saudi authorities were preventing Muslims from visiting al-Baqi' cemetery in Madina, in violation of an alleged Saudi promise.[156] A few days later, Karrubi met with the Saudi Cabinet Minister responsible for the pilgrimage, to request that the cemetery be opened for visitations by pilgrims; the Saudi Minister announced that a plan for opening the cemetery was under serious consderation.[157] A short time later, the cemetery was opened for visitations, and Karrubi expressed his formal appreciation to Saudi King Fahd Ibn 'Abd al-'Aziz.[158]

What was the significance of the cemetery and its opening by the Saudi authorities? While the pilgrimage to Mecca holds the same significance for Sunnis and Shi'is, the visitation (*ziyara*) to Madina is of special significance for Shi'is. The cemetery of al-Baqi', near the city, is the reputed resting place of Fatima and four of the Twelve Imams, who are counted among Shi'ism's 14 intercessors. The Saudis, with their Wahhabi revulsion against all visitation, demolished al-Baqi' when they captured Madina 60 years ago. "The whole area, the resting place of so many of the Household of the Prophet, is but a desolate waste," wrote a contemporary scholar. "It remains a place of weeping, but the formal prayers invoking their intercession are no longer said at the tombs of the Imams in Madina."[159] After Iran's revolution, the formal prayers were reinstituted by Iran's pilgrimage supervisor, but only outside the perimeter of the cemetery, which was closed off by a high wall. The Saudi decision in 1986 to open the cemetery for visitations and prayer represented a major Saudi concession toward Iran's pilgrims; for while Iran tried to present the closure of al-Baqi' as offensive to all Muslims, it had constituted an insult only to Shi'is.

With this issue resolved, the pilgrimage seemed to unfold without incident. The Iranian-sponsored "Unity March" that took place on 1 August 1986 in Madina passed peacefully.[160] So too did the "Immunity from Pagans" march in Mecca on 11 August 1986.[161] Iran also sponsored a number of closed meetings, including a pilgrims' "seminar" for 200 Muslim scholars.[162]

Yet the understanding was breached on 8 August 1986, when 113 Iranian pilgrims from Isfahan were detained on arrival at Jidda Airport for "security reasons." The group was kept in detention throughout the pilgrimage, although they were allowed to observe the rituals in Mecca under police escort.[163] The continued detention of these pilgrims finally led Iranian Prime Minister Musavi to warn the Saudi Government that "if the problem is not rapidly solved, it may lead to a dangerous trend in relations between the two countries."[164] *Majlis* Speaker Rafsanjani also warned that "the incident might prove costly for bilateral relations."[165] But it did not, since all but ten of the detainees were released a few days later.[166]

Iran demonstrated remarkable restraint in this episode, for reasons which became known only later in the year. Some of the pilgrims on the flight carried concealed explosives — supplied by Mehdi Hashemi, according to his opponents, and by the IRGC, according to his supporters. The aim was allegedly to destroy the pilgrimage understanding between Iran and Saudi Arabia.[167] Iranian leaders were clearly embarrassed, and dissociated themselves from the plot by allowing the Saudis to detain the pilgrims for weeks without protest. (Sources in Iran may even have tipped off the Saudi authorities in advance of the plane's arrival.)[168]

With the pilgrimage concluded, Karrubi termed the year's observances "good,"[169] and thanked King Fahd for the opening of al-Baqi' and the release of most of the detained Iranian pilgrims. "Your efforts in these matters opened new doors to hope toward further understanding between the two Muslim countries," Karrubi cabled Fahd, adding that "we condemn any plot that threatens the security of the two holy shrines or the *haj* pilgrims. We consider ourselves committed to the emphatic recommendations made by the leader of the revolution, Imam Khomeyni, in connection with safeguarding the security and discipline in the two blessed holy shrines."[170]

The pilgrimage peace had been preserved, despite the plot devised by the pilgrims from Isfahan. This was a testament to the success of the diplomacy of reconciliation with Saudi Arabia, a policy largely masterminded by Rafsanjani. But Montazeri's resentment of the Saudis, while contained, could not be repressed. In receiving Karrubi after the pilgrimage Montazeri did not laud the Saudis, but ridiculed them as "a minority sect completely isolated among Muslims" still bent on imposing its "divergent notions" on others. He demanded that the Saudis permit visitations at al-Baqi' and other shrines "at any time."[171] The outcome of the internal struggle for Iran would ultimately decide whether cooperation or confrontation would prevail at Islam's great annual assembly.

NOTES

For the place and frequency of publications cited here, and for the full name of the publication, news agency, radio station or monitoring service where an abbreviation is used, please see "List of Sources." Only in the case of more than one publication bearing the same name is the place of publication noted here. Reference to JPRS publications is to the Near East edition, unless otherwise noted. The newspaper *Kayhan* cited here is the Tehran publication, unless otherwise noted.

1. R. Damascus, 8 January — DR, 8 January 1986.
2. MENA, 7 January — DR, 8 January 1986.
3. MAP, 8 January — DR, 9 January 1986.
4. Final resolutions, R. Rabat, 11 January — SWB, 14 January 1986.
5. MENA, 11 January — DR, 14 January 1986.
6. QNA, 30 July 1986.
7. Texts of statements, R. Rabat, 7 January — DR, 8 January; MAP, 11 January — DR, SWB, 13 January 1986.
8. INA, 7 January — DR, 8 January; AFP, 7 January — SWB, 9 January 1986.
9. AFP, 8 January — DR, 9 January; AFP, 10 January — DR, 14 January 1986.
10. KUNA, 30 December 1985 — DR, 2 January 1986.
11. INA, 10 January — DR, 10 January 1986.
12. Details of debate, *al-Sharq al-Awsat*, 12 January 1986.
13. Tariq 'Aziz statement, R. Rabat, 11 January — SWB, 14 January; Iranian view, IRNA, 12 Januray — SWB, 14 January 1986.
14. *Al-Sharq al-Awsat*, 15 January 1986.
15. Report on state of the committee, *al-Anba*, Kuwait, 25 September 1986.
16. *Impact International*, 14 February 1986.
17. Text of resolutions, R. Rabat, 22 January — DR, 23 January, SWB, 24 January 1986.
18. 'Arafat speech, R. Rabat, 21 January — DR, 22 January 1986.

19. See Martin Kramer, "Israel in the Muslim-Christian Dialogue," *IJA Research Report*, November 1986.
20. R. Rabat, 5 January — DR, 6 January 1986.
21. MAP, 6 January — DR, 7 January 1986.
22. Pirzada interview, *Impact International*, 27 February 1987.
23. R. Lagos, 28 January — SWB, 30 January; *Impact International*, 14 February; *LAT*, 15 February 1986.
24. *Arabia, The Islamic World Review*, June 1986.
25. *WP*, 15 April 1987.
26. Musavi interview, *Arabia, The Islamic World Review*, May 1986.
27. Pirzada's complaints over funding, *al-Riyad*, 29 December 1985; *al-Tadamun al-Islami*, June; *al-Bayan*, 4 October 1986.
28. Fu'ad 'Abd al-Hamid Ahmad al-Khatib interview, *Arabia, The Islamic World Review*, August 1986.
29. *'Ukaz*, 7 January 1986.
30. Pirzada interview, *Impact International*, 23 January 1987.
31. Pirzada interview, *Impact International*, 27 February 1987.
32. *Bernama*, 5 February — JPRS, 27 February 1987.
33. *Khaleej Times*, 19 March 1986.
34. Fu'ad 'Abd al-Hamid Ahmad al-Khatib interview, *Arabia, The Islamic World Review*, August 1986.
35. IDB statistics, *Arabia, The Islamic World Review*, April, May 1986.
36. Anatolia, 11 March — DR, 18 March 1986.
37. Detailed account of conference, *Impact International*, 11 April 1986.
38. R. Ankara, 15 March — DR, 18 March 1986.
39. Anatolia, 14 March — DR, 18 March 1986.
40. R. Ankara, 16 March — DR, 18 March 1986. In September 1986, the Standing Committee held a follow-up session; *Tercüman*, 11 September — JPRS (West Europe), 24 December 1986.
41. Pirzada interview, *Impact International*, 27 February 1987.
42. *Impact International*, 23 January 1987.
43. *MWL Journal*, November 1986.
44. *Akhbar al-'Alam al-Islami*, 10 February 1986.
45. *MWL Journal*, January-February 1986.
46. *Ha'aretz*, 23 September 1986.
47. Nasif interview, *al-Dustur*, Amman, 8 February; *'Ukaz*, 12 January 1986.
48. R. Israel, 3 May — DR, 5 May, SWB, 7 May; *Impact International*, 23 May 1986.
49. *Ha'aretz*, 23 March 1986.
50. SPA, 17 March — DR, 18 March 1986.
51. Accounts of conference and WAMY activities, *Impact International*, 14 March; *MWL Journal*, October 1986.
52. Account of committee's work, *MWL Journal*, December 1985-January 1986; account of Saudi and other Muslim relief, *Arabia, The Islamic World Review*, December 1986.
53. *WP*, 21 July 1986.
54. Announcements of awards, *MWL Journal*, January-February 1986.
55. Profile of Deedat, *Arabia, The Islamic World Review*, March 1986.
56. *Impact International*, 28 February 1986.
57. *MWL Journal*, January-February 1986.
58. *Arabia, The Islamic World Review*, March 1986; article also includes tables from DMI's fourth annual report.
59. *MEER*, April 1986.
60. *MEM*, October 1986.
61. See DTU's four-page advertisement, *Jeune Afrique*, 18 June 1986.
62. Debate over Islamic banking, *al-Ahram* (int ed), 23 December 1986, 7 January 1987 — JPRS, 26 February 1987.
63. Jadd al-Haqq news conference, supplement to *Majallat al-Azhar*, March 1987.
64. Jadd al-Haqq interview, *Akhbar al-Yawm*, 22 February 1986.

65. Article in *al-Mukhtar al-Islami*, July; reprinted in *Kayhan al-'Arabi*, 13 October — JPRS, 26 November 1986.
66. Jadd al-Haqq statement, *al-Ahram*, 7 April 1986.
67. For another account, with somewhat different emphases, see R.K. Ramazani, *Revolutionary Iran* (Baltimore: The Johns Hopkins University Press, 1986); and his article in *NYT*, 4 December 1986. For a (sensationalist) presentation of the other side of Iran's policy, see Amir Taheri, "The Fruits of Terror," *New Statesman*, 28 November 1986.
68. Musavi interview, *Arabia, The Islamic World Review*, May; cf IRNA, 2 May — SWB, 6 May 1986.
69. *MECS* 1983–84, p 167.
70. Ahmad Khomeyni's role, *Kayhan*, London, 8 January — JPRS, 24 February 1987.
71. McFarlane cable, *Report of the President's Special Review Board*, (Washington: US Government Printing Office, 26 February 1987), p B–102. For a profile of Rafsanjani as moderate, see Robin Wright, "Iran's Smiling Powerbroker," *New Leader*, 12 January 1986.
72. For a biographical profile, see Yann Richard, "Hoseyn 'Ali Montazeri," *Orient*, September 1985, pp 303–6.
73. This was the controversy over the tract entitled *Shahide Javid*, for which Montazeri had written an introduction. On the dispute, see Hamid Enayat, *Islamic Political Thought* (Austin: University of Texas Press, 1982), pp 190–94.
74. Details on Mehdi Hashemi's career, *al-Dustur*, London, 26 December 1983; *Le Figaro*, 11 January — JPRS, 14 March; *Lettre Persane*, June — JPRS, 24 September; *Le Monde*, 25 October — DR, 27 October; *al-Shira'*, Beirut, 3 November — DR, 6 November 1986. Hashemi had trained with Palestinians in Lebanon before the Iranian revolution; *The Times*, 23 October 1986.
75. On Mahallati see *al-Majalla*, 5 November 1983. According to *FR*, 30 January 1986, Mahallati was trained in Lebanon in the late 1960s, in a camp run by George Habash. Between 1970 and 1972 he reportedly ran a "school" in South Yemen, with a faculty composed of East German, Cuban, and Bulgarian instructors. For his death, see *WP*, 21 February; *LAT*, 21 February 1986.
76. *FR*, 27 February 1986.
77. *WP*, 21 April 1986.
78. Issue of Montazeri-Rafsanjani split discussed, *NYT*, 8 November; *WSJ*, 25 November 1986.
79. Rafsanjani speech, IRNA, 30 October — DR, 30 October 1986.
80. Account of charges by Intelligence Minister Muhammad Muhammadi-Reyshahri in letter to Khomeyni, R. Tehran, 27 October — DR, 28 October 1986.
81. For a general account of the affair's significance, see Robin Wright's piece in *CSM*, 5 November 1986.
82. *Le Monde*, 25 October; *MEES*, 3 November 1986, for analysis of kidnapping.
83. The Imam Muhammad Baqir Intelligence College; *FR*, 6 February; *Kayhan*, 29 September; *Impact International*, 10 October 1986.
84. *The Times*, 31 October 1986.
85. *Al-Shira'*, Beirut, 3 November — DR, 6 November 1986. The conduit for the leak was Shaykh Isma'il Khaliq, Montazeri's personal representative in Beirut; *al-Dustur*, London, 22 December; *WP*, 7 December 1986, where the editor of *al-Shira'* confirmed leak by Montazeri's office.
86. *FR*, 18 December 1986.
87. *Kayhan*, 18 November, cited by *Kayhan*, London, 4 December 1986 — JPRS, 3 February 1987.
88. Khosrowshahi's alleged appointment reported in *FR*, 22 January 1987; *Kayhan*, London, 25 December 1986 — JPRS, 5 February 1987 (possibly the basis of the *FR* report). For a reiteration of charges against Khosrowshahi (which first appeared in *ST*, 8 January 1984), see *WP*, 24 January 1986.
89. For new details on *Hizballah's* emergence, see *al-Shira'*, Beirut, 17 March, 1986.
90. *Al-Mustaqbal*, 13 September 1986.
91. See also Martin Kramer, "Muhammad Husayn Fadlallah," *Orient*, June 1985, pp 147–49;

and the full account of Fadlallah's differences with Iran in *al-Shira'*, Beirut, 4 August, 1986.

92. Shams al-Din interview, *al-Mustaqbal*, 5 March 1983.
93. E.g., Shams al-Din interview in Tehran, *Kayhan*, 8 February 1986. His second visit reported by IRNA, 31 July — DR, 31 July; IRNA, 2 August — DR, 4 August; third visit, IRNA, 29, 31 December — DR, 31 December 1986.
94. Amin interview, *Kayhan*, 9 February — JPRS, 16 April; Musawi interview, *Kayhan*, 9 February — JPRS, 16 April 1986.
95. Amin interview, *Kayhan*, 19 October 1985 — JPRS, 3 January 1986.
96. Texts of speeches by Khameneh'i and Rafsanjani, and papers by Fadlallah and Shams al-Din, *al-Tawhid*, 10 May; see also reports on conference, IRNA, 29 January — DR, 30 January; R. Tehran, 30 January — DR, 31 January; R. Tehran, 1 February — DR, 3 February 1986.
97. Text of resolutions, *al-Tawhid*, 10 May; R. Tehran, 31 January, 1 February — DR, 3 February 1986.
98. Fadlallah interview, *al-Shira'*, Beirut, 26 May; cf Fadlallah interview, *al-Tadamun*, 11 October 1986.
99. Shams al-Din interview, *Kayhan*, 8 February 1986.
100. Musawi interview, *Kayhan*, 27 July — DR, 18 August, JPRS, 30 September 1986.
101. Account of meeting, R. Tehran, 15 February — JPRS, 18 March 1986. Hostile Arab sources gave a completely different account of the conference and its significance. These claimed that Khomeyni met with the Lebanese participants after the conference to urge them to establish a provisional Islamic government, and asked that they draft an Islamic constitution for Lebanon. Khomeyni reportedly even authorized the establishment of revolutionary courts for Lebanon, and appointed 40 Lebanese as judges and prosecutors. Shams al-Din allegedly authored the draft constitution, which recognized Khomeyni as "ruler of the Muslims" but authorized Shams al-Din to act in his stead. The report named 63 supposed signatories to the draft, including Shams al-Din, Fadlallah, and Sha'ban. *Al-Siyasa*, Kuwait, 26 March 1986. Later in the year, in an address to Lebanese students in Qom, Montazeri did urge "learned men of religion [in Lebanon] to form courts and appoint judges who can impartially implement God's will according to Islamic law"; *al-Safir*, 5 October 1986.
102. Fadlallah interview, *La Vanguardia*, 9 November — DR, 17 November 1986.
103. Fadlallah interview, *al-Shira'*, Beirut, 26 May 1986.
104. Fadlallah interview, *La Vanguardia*, 9 November — DR, 17 November 1986.
105. *NYT*, 21 November 1986.
106. On his connection with the hijacking, which he was said to have masterminded, see *NYT*, 14 March 1986.
107. *US News and World Report*, 30 March 1987.
108. Asad interview, Damascus TV, 18 May — DR, 19 May 1986.
109. Syrian-Iranian relations surveyed, *al-Dustur*, London, 2 June — JPRS, 29 July; *WSJ*, 23 May; *WP*, 29 May; *Memo*, 26 June — JPRS, 14 August 1986. See also the reporting by Jim Muir in *MEES* during May, June, and July 1986.
110. Shi'i debate over Resolution 425 summarized in *al-Mustaqbal*, 13 September 1986.
111. Catalogue of clashes, *al-Mujtama'*, 28 October 1986.
112. *Hizballah* in South, *WP*, 28 September; general assessment of conflict with UNIFIL, *MEES*, 29 September 1986.
113. Rafiqdust interviews, *al-'Alam*, 18 October 1986; *Middle East Insight*, May-June 1987.
114. R. Tehran, 7 April — DR, 9 April; *JI*, 20 April — JPRS, 23 June 1986. According to Iranian opposition sources, they were to be recruited into a brigade for irregular warfare; *Kayhan*, London, 17 April — JPRS, 14 May 1986.
115. IRNA, 27 March — DR, 28 March 1986.
116. IRNA, 22 April — SWB, 24 April 1986.
117. E.g., his attacks on Saudi Arabia, Mudarrasi interview, *al-Thawra al-Islamiyya*, June 1986. This article also includes some biographical details.
118. Account of Islamic Action's activities, R. Tehran, 10 May — DR, 12 May 1986.
119. *Al-Masar*, 16 July 1986.
120. *Al-Masar*, 30 May 1986.

121. Account of deportation, *Le Monde*, 8 March 1986.
122. *NYT*, 6, 11 13 March 1986.
123. *NYT*, 7 September 1986.
124. IRNA, 22 December — DR, 23 December; *MEED*, 13 December; *WP*, 30 December 1986; *Impact International*, 9 January; *Jeune Afrique*, 14 January 1987.
125. Khameneh'i speech, R. Tehran, 24 December — DR, 29 December 1986.
126. Conference resolutions, IRNA, 28 December — DR, 29 December 1986.
127. IRNA, 29 December — DR, 30 December 1986.
128. Account of conference, *Impact International*, 9 May 1986. For Ben Bella's current positions, see the interviews collected in *Ben Bella...revient* (Paris: Jean Picollec, 1982).
129. Scheduled speakers listed, *Impact International*, 28 February 1986.
130. *Impact International*, 9 May 1986.
131. *October*, 8 June 1986.
132. Speech by Ugandan Minister, *al-Fajr al-Jadid*, 17 September 1986.
133. *Al-'Alam*, 26 September 1986.
134. Qadhdhafi speech, Tripoli TV, 17 September — SWB, 19 September; R. Tripoli, 17 September — DR, 18 September; *al-Fajr al-Jadid*, 19 September 1986.
135. Report of resolutions, JANA, 21 September — DR, 22 September; SWB, 24 September 1986. In another move, the conferees formally renamed their organization the World Islamic Call Society (*Jam'iyyat al-Da'wa al-Islamiyya al-'Alamiyya*), a usage the Libyans had already adopted with the apparent intention of stressing the organization's international composition. See also *Impact International*, 10 October 1986.
136. Report of Qadhdhafi's reception, *al-Fajr al-Jadid*, 19 September 1986.
137. Report of visit, *al-Fajr al-Jadid*, 17 September 1986.
138. *Grassroots* (Cape Town), October — JPRS (Sub-Saharan Africa), 4 December 1986.
139. *Impact International*, 28 November 1986.
140. Libya's African activities, *Washington Times*, 24 June; Asian activities, *Newsweek*, 28 July 1986.
141. *WP*, 13 April 1986.
142. *Impact International*, 14 March 1986.
143. *Arabia, The Islamic World Review*, May 1986.
144. Tajuddin interview, *al-'Awda*, 15 September 1986.
145. In fact, Nasif had been preceded in the Soviet Union by the MWL's Deputy Secretary-General, who spent two weeks in the Soviet Union as a guest of Muslim religious boards there; *Impact International*, 23 May 1986.
146. Text of Ryzhkov greeting, Tass, 1 October — JPRS (Soviet Union, Political and Sociological), 12 November 1986.
147. KUNA, 3 October — JPRS (Soviet Union, Political and Sociological), 12 November 1986.
148. E.g. *al-Ahali*, 12 November — JPRS, 29 December 1986,
149. *Impact International*, 26 December 1986.
150. R. Damascus, 3 October; Tass, 3 October — JPRS (Soviet Union, Political and Sociological), 12 November 1986.
151. Figures for 1986, *'Ukaz*, 20 August; *Arabia, The Islamic World Review*, October 1986.
152. Montazeri speech, R. Tehran, 4 July — JPRS, 4 August 1986.
153. Khomeyni message, R. Tehran, 7 August — SWB, 9 August; IRNA, 8 August — DR, 11 August; official text, IRNA, 9 August — DR, 12 August 1986.
154. R. Tehran, 7 August — SWB, 12 August 1986.
155. It would later be reported that his brother played a central role in dealing with both Americans and Israelis in the arms-for-hostages negotiations; *US News and World Report*, 30 March 1987.
156. R. Tehran, 27 July — DR, SWB, 29 July 1986.
157. R. Tehran, 30 July — DR, 31 July, SWB, 1 August 1986.
158. R. Tehran, 29 August — DR, 3 September 1986.
159 Dwight M. Donaldson, *The Shi'ite Religion* (London, 1930), p 151. For a description of the demolition, see Eldon Rutter, *The Holy Cities of Arabia* (London, 1930), pp 562–64.
160. R. Tehran, 2 August — SWB, 4 August 1986. Iran claimed that 150,000 pilgrims participated.

161. Accounts of march, IRNA, 12 August — DR, 15 August; (clandestine) Voice of the Pilgrims (to Saudi Arabia), 15 August — DR, 27 August 1986. Iran claimed that 20,000 pilgrims participated.
162. R. Tehran, 11 August — SWB, 13 August; seminar on Iraqi-Iranian war, IRNA, 20 August — DR, 21 August 1986.
163. IRNA, 10 August — DR, 11 August; SPA, 11 August — DR, 11 August 1986.
164. Musavi statement, IRNA, 25 August — DR, 25 August; R. Tehran, 25 August 1986.
165. Rafsanjani speech, R. Tehran, 24 August — SWB, 26 August 1986.
166. R. Tehran, 28 August — DR, 28 August 1986.
167. *NYT*, 29 August; *The Times*, 29 November; *al-Shira'*, Beirut, 3 November — DR, 6 November 1986.
168. *The Times*, 29 November 1986.
169. IRNA, 1 September — DR, 3 September 1986.
170. Text of Karrubi cable, R. Tehran, 29 August — DR, 3 September 1986.
171. R. Tehran, 9 September — DR, 9 September, SWB, 10 September 1986.

The Iraqi-Iranian War

URIEL DANN

The Iraqi-Iranian war in its sixth year made international headlines with the relevation that the US and Israel had been secretly delivering arms to Iran. It would appear that anti-tank (*TOW*) and anti-air (*HAWK*) missiles, as well as diverse spare parts, had been delivered on a considerable scale since some time in the summer of 1985 and throughout most of 1986. The effect of these deliveries on the progress of the war cannot as yet be assessed. While Iraq asserted that the deliveries played a significant role in limiting Iraqi superiority in the air, one of its chief assets so far, this must be treated with caution because of the obvious political intent.

The war on land remained the most spectacular manifestation of the contest, and the one where a breakthrough seemed most likely.

After an absence of major operations on land during more than ten months (see *Middle East Contemporary Survey* [*MECS*], 1984–85, pp 168–73), about 100,000 Iranians, mostly Revolutionary Guards (RG) and Basij volunteers, crossed the Shatt al-'Arab near its mouth, during the night of 9–10 February 1986. It was the seventh anniversary of Ayatollah Khomeyni's return from exile. These masses, half the Iranian forces deployed on the southern front, staged a surprise attack on the Iraqi Seventh Army which held the southern sector of the right bank. The Faw peninsula, bordered by the Shatt al-'Arab to the north, the Khawr 'Abdallah water arm (separating Iraqi territory from the Kuwaiti islands of Warba and Bubiyān) to the south and the open waters of the Gulf to the east, was quickly occupied, including the town of Faw — the only Iraqi settlement on the Gulf coast and virtually deserted since the first days of the war when the Iranians shut off Iraqi sea-going traffic. There were Iranian attempts at a follow-up — to break out of the peninsula northward in the direction of Basra, and west and northwestwards in the direction of the Iraqi river port of Umm Qasr, and of Bubiyan. The attempts soon foundered in the face of Iraqi opposition and the difficulties of the terrain, and probably were not meant from the outset to be serious efforts. Also, a simultaneous Iranian push 40 miles upriver which led to the conquest of the small island of Umm al-Rassas, is seen in retrospect as designed to confuse the Iraqi command. If so, it was successful. The Iraqi counterattack in the Faw sector took a fortnight to develop. By then the Iranians were well entrenched, and the Iraqi effort to retake the peninsula, though furiously pursued well into March and again including the use of poison gas, had little or no effect. By the end of 1986 the Faw peninsula was still in Iranian hands. It is difficult to assess the significance of *Val Fajr Eight*, the Iranian code name for the offensive. The casualty report of 30,000 Iranians and 15,000 Iraqis is probably no exaggeration and certainly horrendous. Since Iran has the advantage over Iraq in manpower, these heavy losses were worse for Iraq. Strategically the Iranians gained little: the Faw peninsula — mud, surrounded by desert — leads nowhere. Operationally the campaign once more showed up the death defiance and gift for improvisation of the Iranians — especially their irregulars — and the heaviness of the Iraqi command, although the Iraqi troops again courageously and tenaciously defended their home ground. However, the main impact at the time was the sheer victory achieved by the Iranians, the most spectacular since their reconquest of Khorramshahr in May 1982 (see *MECS* 1981–82, pp 311–12). It seems proved that the victory meant the loss of political strength for the Iranian former Prime Minister, Mehdi Bazargan, who during the previous year had openly advocated a negotiated end to the war. On the other hand, the Iranian victory did not cause a weakening of the Iraqi will (not just among the Ba'thi elite) not to surrender on Khomeyni's terms.

On 25–26 February the Iranians started another major offensive, long expected, in the north of the central front. This offensive, *Val Fajr Nine*, was poised in the direction of Sulaymaniyya and Chwarta in southern Kurdistan, and apparently aimed at destabilizing the already weak Ba'thi regime's hold on the Kurds. After initial gains, Iraqi counterattacks slowly pushed the Iranians back to near their starting positions. Again losses on both sides were heavy, and the attackers achieved nothing except, perhaps, that it drove home once more their determination to wage a war of attrition, forever, if necessary.

As on earlier occasions, these efforts slowed down the Iranians as regards offensive capability, for a considerable time.

On 17 May 1986 the Iraqi Army attacked the Iranian border town Mehran, east of Baghdad, which it had occupied at the beginning of the war and later lost in the exodus of June 1982. The Iranians were evidently taken by surprise and the town, long since reduced to shambles, was lost. To the Iraqis it was a propaganda victory, shown up with much fanfare as the revenge for Faw. After six weeks of Iranian counterattacks the Iraqis withdrew to their side of the border. While their local offensive now seems to have been an unconscionable waste of resources that never promised a real strategic gain, at the time it may have given Iraq a desperately-needed boost of morale, and a corresponding jolt to the belligerent faction among the rulers of Iran.

Iranian raids in strength further north in October, opposite Sulaymaniyya and Kirkuk, were part of an overall effort to weaken the Iraqi regime through exploitation of the Kurdish problem, and will be treated in this essay below.

On the other hand, *Karbala Four*, launched on 24 December on the southern front, might have been intended as another "final offensive", a threat which the Iranians have made often. If so, it was a failure — unless yet another hecatomb of Iraqis slain is regarded as an Iranian achievement regardless of the price paid by themselves. Of about 70,000 Iranians involved — overwhelmingly RG and Basij irregulars — many succeeded in crossing the Shatt al-'Arab on a front of about 30 miles north and south of Khorramshahr, only to be thrown back by the Iraqis. The Iraqi claims of a huge disproportion between Iranian and Iraqi losses, in the latter's favor, seem to be better substantiated than usually. However, the Iranians continued their offensive pushes into January 1987. *Karbala Five*, launched on 6 January between Iranian Khorramshahr and Iraqi Basra, succeeded in establishing an Iranian foothold on the Iraqi bank which the Iraqis were unable to dislodge but which, like others in that sector, was hemmed in by impassable stretches of water and swamp. *Karbala Six*, 250 miles further north in the sector of Qasr Shirin, was launched one week later and yielded limited Iranian gains of Iraqi territory. From then on the Iranian offensive spirit on the ground petered out for the rest of the Iranian year, ending on 21 March 1987.

Throughout 1986 Iraq preserved their superiority in the air and may have even increased it through the acquisition of fighters from the Soviet Union. It is difficult to assess how Iraq used that superiority. Independent observers agree that the tactical employment of the Iraqi Air Force was deficient in dash and skill, despite the critical need for those qualities especially during the Iraqi counteroffensive in the Faw sector. Also, in 1986, the Iraqi high command did not renew terror attacks on Iranian population centers — the "war of the cities" — possibly because it did not want to precipitate the "final offensive" on land (see above). However, the Iraqi leadership greatly increased the use of its Air Force against economic targets over Iranian territory and the Persian Gulf; it did so with tenacity, boldness and expertise that greatly surpassed previous offensives by the Iraqi Air Force, and even increased during 1986. In fact, the major part of Iraqi air activity was over the Gulf and its coastline. Generally, bouts of activity coincided with offensive thrusts on the ground, whether the offensive came from Iran or Iraq, but there was no total letup in the air. The most devastating bombings by Iraq in Iran were those of the oil refinery at Isfahan and the Ahwaz power station in March and, most important, the Shahr-e Rey refinery near Tehran, Iran's largest, on 7 May. The Iranian Air Force's response was, by necessity, feeble and restricted to ineffective attacks on Iraqi targets close to the front. These included the Daura refinery near Baghdad and the Umm Qasr port installations west of Basra. In addition, there were artillery shellings of Basra itself and occasional missile attacks on Iraqi population centers, including the Baghdad area, but on a smaller scale than in 1985.

The Iraqi objective was twofold. One was to threaten Iranian exports of crude oil — and therefore make it difficult to pay for the imports necessary to continue the war. The other aim was to cripple oil product imports on which Iran depended to supplement the capacity of its own installations which had been severely hurt at the war's outbreak, when the Abadan complex was put out of use, and by later Iraqi air bombardments (see above).

Iraqi bombers on missions over the Gulf aimed at targets of three kinds: one was the installations at Ganaveh and on the island of Kharg, chief outlets of the oilfields in southwestern Iran. A second target was the tankers shuttling between Kharg and the loading platforms on the islands of Sirri, Lavan and Larak, hundreds of miles down the Gulf. (The Iranians deferred the construction of a coastal pipeline from Ganaveh intended to obviate the shuttle service between Kharg and the lower Gulf terminals [see *MECS* 1984–85, p 171] because of the expenditure involved.) The last target was the newly installed terminals on those islands, a feat that at the end of 1985 was still considered beyond the capacity of the Iraqi Air Force. The results cannot be termed dramatic. No terminals were entirely put out of service for any length of time, and the totality of tankers hit was only a fraction of those which served the Iranian oil trade. Still, the performances of Iraqi pilots had impressively improved (particularly in the realm of midair fuelling rendered necessary by attacks on targets near the mouth of the Gulf). The undoubted lift to Iraqi morale must also be considered in drawing up the balance. Iranian air counterattacks on oil shipments to and from Kuwait and Saudi Arabia, presumably serving Iraqi needs, were much less formidable than Iraqi activities.

Although Iraq was superior in the air, Iran preserved its naval domination over the Gulf, and made no aggressive use of its advantage. The Iranian Navy's main job was to check vessels entering the Gulf for contraband that might be diverted to Iraq by road via Kuwait and Saudi Arabia. The procedure was considerate, by and large, and friction remained within bounds. In any case, Iraq had by then developed trade routes that avoided the Gulf Lane.

The Kurdish question played a more conspicuous part in the Iraqi-Iranian war in 1986 than before (see chapters on Iraq and Iran).

Generally, the initiative for exploiting the Kurdish potential lay with Iran. The greater flexibility that has distinguished Iran historically from Iraq in dealing with the Kurds played its role in this field, too. Throughout 1986 the Kurdish nationalist organizations on Iraqi soil, mainly the Barazanis' Kurdish Democratic Party (KDP) based in the north and Jalal Talabani's Patriotic Union of Kurdistan (PUK) based further southeast, kept up negotiations for joint action with Iranian authorities. The Iranian-based "Supreme Assembly of the Islamic Revolution in Iraq" was on occasion pushed forward to appear as arbitrator and guide; the claim was unconvincing because the interests of the Sunni Kurds were decidedly nationalist and not Shi'a-Islamic. Kurdish-Iranian cooperation was hardly evident. Kurdish Peshmarga took part in the various Iranian operations in the mountainous north, from Panjwin to Shaykh 'Umran; territorial gain was restricted from the outset, expensive, and mostly wiped out in Iraqi counterattacks. Kurdish guerrillas in northern Iraq, whether professing loyalty to either or none of the major movements, were more numerous and better armed during 1986 than since the Kurdish debacle of 1975 which followed the Iranian-Iraqi Algiers Agreement. They controlled much of the area adjacent to the Turkish border and thereby jeopardized Iraqi relations with Ankara. Above all, the Kurds kept the Iraqi Government in perpetual terror so they would not cut the pipeline from the northern oilfields to the Gulf of Alexandretta on which much of the financing of the war depended. Though the threats remained merely threats, the Iraqi High Command felt it necessary to keep combat troops and equipment (which it could ill spare) in Kurdistan.[1] As for political machinations, the Kurds were, as always, too deeply divided for an effective alliance with Iran, in spite of a reported understanding between the KDP and the PUK in November 1986. (An overall settlement between the Kurds and the Iraqi regime for which — unlike that of Tehran — Baghdad would have had to pay out of its own pocket, could not take place in 1986 because mutual suspicion, based on past experience, went too deep.)

In regard to the remaining aspects of the war, namely arms procurement; relations between the belligerents and the outside world, and the Gulf countries in particular; attempts at mediation; and respective war aims, all had one common denominator: no existing patterns were broken, though there were variations.

In the area of arms procurement, Iraq continued to be served mainly with deliveries based on contracts between governments, or under governmental auspices. As before, France, the Soviet Union and Brazil were the chief suppliers. Iran, on the other hnad, subsisted as before by feverishly fueling the international arms trade. Some foreign governments were conniving, others indifferent and a few obstructive. However, China and North Korea probably delivered arms to Iran according to official contracts. (As for the US and Israel, see above.) In the end both Iraq and Iran managed to acquire a sufficient quantity and quality of matériel to keep up the style of warfare that had characterized both countries for years, although there were shortages, diplomatic and legal barriers, and financial stringency. The general Iraqi superiority in armaments remained unimpaired.

The relations of Iran and Iraq with other countries, regarding the ongoing war, were modified little by developments on the whole. The Iranian occupation of the Faw peninsula in February 1986 was a shock for the Gulf Cooperation Council countries, besides being a spectacular invasion by non-Arabs of undisputedly "Arab" territory. This combination caused these countries, and Saudi Arabia and Kuwait in particular, to relax the stance of "nonintervention and coexistence" which they had affected, although not very credibly, for years, and declare their sympathy for Iraq. As the Gulf countries had been a vital mainstay financially of Iraq since early in the war, the practical upshot was nil. Fluctuations within the rest of the Arab world were insignificant, too. Syria and Libya remained hostile to Iraq, despite an effort by King Husayn to effect a reconciliation between Baghdad and Damascus, and Syrian uneasiness at the Iranian invasion of Faw. Egypt remained friendly, although problems connected with the 1m Egyptian workers in Iraq caused some irritation. As to the outside powers, relations between Iraq and the US, on the upgrade for years, were hardly affected by the revelation of the arms-to-Iran scandal, and those between Iraq and the Soviet Union improved less than might have been expected. When the year ended, the Soviet Union was maintaining an uneasy, though superficially "normal", relationship with both Iraq and Iran. Formerly France had allied itself with Iraq regarding arms supplies and general manifestations of sympathy, without much thought for Iranian reactions. In 1986 concern for French hostages taken by Shi‘a activists in Lebanon caused the French Government to abstain from identifying too closely with Iraq. A spectacular step in this direction was the expulsion from France in June 1986 of Mas‘ud Rajavi, leader of the Iranian *Mujahidine Khalq* (who took refuge in Baghdad). Iran was hardly responsive, and its seems that by the end of the year the flow of arms from France to Iraq had not changed.

The year 1986 saw attempts at mediation and conciliation to which the world was by now accustomed. They climaxed in the United Nations Security Council (UNSC) Resolution No 588 of 8 October which, by a unanimous vote in effect called on Iraq and Iran to end the war by negotiation.[2] The resolution was immediately rejected by Iran. The war aims of the belligerents had not changed, and hence the gap between them was still unbridgeable. The Iranian regime, directed by Ayatollah Khomeyni, did not budge from its stand that no negotiations were possible so long as the Ba‘th ruled Iraq; considerations of cost effectiveness, of suffering, even of religion as commonly understood (Tehran refused to accede to a request for a truce during Ramadan) were simply irrelevant. The Iraqi regime for its part was as eager now for a cessation of fighting as it had been since the summer of 1982 (at the latest), and presumably it would have been ready to make considerable sacrifices. It was not ready for willful self-destruction, and its security system throughout the country was strong.

In summary, the wisdom survived during 1986 that Iraq could not win the war and Iran could not lose it. But neither did Iraq lose nor Iran win. Moreover, the will to continue the war is essential for its continuation, and this will is not absolutely dependent on military operations. The most impressive phenomenon of the year was arguably the readiness of the Iraqi public, combatants and noncombatants, to go on with the war despite depressing losses on all land fronts. This phenomenon can by no means be explained only with the terror exerted by the Ba'th regime. Nor is there any guarantee that the will to go on may not collapse in either country at any time. It may be surmised that such a collapse will not be caused by financial or economic factors, but this is as far as we may go.

Should peace be established today, it would have a flying start in one respect: the belligerents' embassies in each other's capital have never been closed, though ambassadors were withdrawn well before the outbreak of war.

NOTES

For the place and frequency of publications cited here, and for the full name of the publication, news agency, radio station or monitoring service where an abbreviation is used, please see "List of Sources." Only in the case of more than one publication bearing the same name is the place of publication noted here.

1. According to *The Economist*, 15 February 1986, the Kurds at that time may have drawn as many as 160,000 Iraqi soldiers away from the Iranian front — though it is difficult to understand how any outside observer, however competent, could have arrived at a numerical estimate.
2. For the text, see UNSC S/RES/588 (1986), 8 October 1986. A similar SC resolution, No 582, had been unanimously passed on 24 February in the wake of the Iranian offensive against Faw.

PALESTINIAN ISSUES

The Palestine Liberation Organization

JOSHUA TEITELBAUM

Nineteen eighty-six was a difficult year for the Palestine Liberation Organization (PLO). It began with one last intensive effort in Amman to convince the PLO to accept United Nations' Security Council Resolutions 242 and 338 so it could participate in the US-sponsored peace process. The PLO was not prepared to make the necessary concessions, and thus ended a period of intermittent consultations with the Jordanians that began following the PLO's exit from Beirut in 1982. Jordan's King Husayn finally announced the end of political coordination in a speech on 19 February 1986.

The leadership of the Fath mainstream was intent on downplaying the seriousness of the move. It recognized that an outright split with Jordan would make contact with West Bank Palestinians more difficult and possibly endanger any chance of PLO representation in peace moves. Despite constant urging by high-ranking Fath officials and the leaders of other PLO factions, PLO Executive Committee Chairman Yasir 'Arafat refused to announce that the Jordanian-Palestinian Agreement of 11 February 1985 had been canceled.

The Popular Democratic Front for the Liberation of Palestine (PDFLP) and the Popular Front for the Liberation of Palestine (PFLP) believed that Husayn's move opened the door to possible internal Palestinian reconciliation, on condition that the agreement be unequivocally canceled and repudiated by 'Arafat. A series of meetings were held during the year, mostly between the PDFLP, Fath, and the Palestinian Communist Party (PCP). These culminated in the Prague Declaration of 5 September 1986, in which Fath consented to term the agreement "no longer operative." The PDFLP quickly interpreted this as amounting to a cancellation, but in 'Arafat's eyes he had not done so. The PFLP continued to insist on unequivocable cancellation.

Reconciliation was reached between Palestinian factions in one local arena — Lebanon. The Shi'i militia, *al-Amal*, feeling threatened by the rising armed Palestinian presence in the Beirut, Sidon and Tyre areas, resumed attacks on the Palestinians who were successful in breaking several sieges and even capturing the strategic town of Maghdusha which overlooked the refugee camps of Miya al-Miya and 'Ayn al-Hilwa near Sidon. The perceived threat was of such magnitude that all Palestinian factions fought together, much to the dismay of *Amal*'s Syrian patron.

PRELUDE TO A PARTING OF THE WAYS: THE LAST EFFORTS TO GET THE PLO TO RECOGNIZE 242 AND 338

As 1985 came to an end, it became clear that the significant differences between the PLO and Jordan, which had been papered over by the Amman Agreement of 11 February, still remained. The PLO continued to reject Resolutions 242 and 338 and was at loggerheads with Jordan over the relationship between the future confederated states of Jordan and Palestine, as well as over the nature of PLO representation at an international conference. While the Jordanians saw the joint accord as the first step in bringing the PLO to the negotiating table, the PLO saw it as the maximum concession, not the beginning of a process. Moreover, the accord, the PLO reiterated, dealt with the relationship with Jordan and not with possible peace with Israel (see *Middle East Comtemporary Survey*, [*MECS*] 1984–85, pp 195–200).

Efforts by US Assistant Secretary of State Richard Murphy to move the process along during his visit to Amman in August 1985, when 'Arafat was also there, proved futile. 'Arafat refused to accept US conditions for a dialogue with the PLO, namely, acceptance of Resolution 242, the recognition of Israel's right to exist, and the denunciation of terrorism. The US also indicated that it would perceive the proposed dialogue as a prelude to direct negotiations with Israel. Again, 'Arafat insisted that dialogue with the US be unconditional.

All this contributed to the ever-growing frustration of King Husayn. In his perception, 'Arafat was continuing to play for time, dragging the discussions out. Time was exactly what Jordan did not have on its side. That being the case, Husayn tried to pin 'Arafat down on Resolutions 242 and 338 by persuading Prime Minister Margaret Thatcher to insist that the PLO delegation recognize the resolutions at a meeting with Foreign Minister Geoffrey Howe scheduled to take place in London on 14 October. The PLO refused, and the meeting was not held. While the PLO blamed the British, the Jordanians placed the blame squarely on the PLO (see *MECS* 1984–85, pp 205–7).

Husayn and 'Arafat met again in late October in Amman, but it was reported that the King was already "fed up." The PLO Central Council meeting in Baghdad in late November 1985 refused even to relate to Resolution 242 in its final statement. As far as Jordan was concerned, it was "a five-page ambiguous statement which did not contain any direct answer." Jordan, said one official, was "still waiting for the PLO's answer." PLO radio, however, in a commentary during the Central Council's deliberations, noted that a "suspect media campaign has been going on for some time to make people believe that the Central Council meeting is to define a stand on Resolution 242, as if the Central Council or the Palestinian cause has no other topic to discuss and their only task is to accept it or reject it....The PLO's stand on Resolution 242 is not a tactical matter which may differ from one day to another. It is a known stand and there is nothing new that calls for changing it, positively or negatively."[1]

On 30 December, Husayn met Syrian President Hafiz al-Asad in Damascus. It was the first meeting between the two since 1979. The significance of the visit was not lost on 'Arafat, who noted that Syria intended to renew relations with Jordan in order to provoke a split between Jordan and the PLO. Al-Fath Central Committee member Salah Khalaf (Abu Iyad) stressed that "Jordan's goal is to pressure the PLO into concessions, while Syria's goal is to put a stop to the Jordanian-Palestinian connection."[2]

A definite break was thus only a matter of time. Apparently, however, King Husayn — perhaps with the active encouragement of the US — continued to try to push 'Arafat to give a definite yes or no to recognition of 242. 'Arafat continued to stall and delay his visit to Jordan. In the first week of January 1986 it was reported that 'Arafat had come down with flu. 'Arafat himself noted that his illness was preventing him from going to Jordan, having been ordered by his physicians to rest. He would go to

Jordan as soon as he was able to travel.[3] "Diplomatic sources" quoted in Tunis, however, said that 'Arafat's illness was "partly real and partly diplomatic." Although he was suffering from depression, it was not serious enough to prevent him from going to Amman.[4] His illness was not, apparently, serious enough to stop him traveling to Riyadh, where he arrived on 9 January. On the same day it was reported that the PLO Executive Committee would meet soon in Baghdad. The meeting would also include members of the Fath Central Committee and the permanent bureau of the Palestine National Council (PNC).[5]

The meeting of the Palestinian leadership began in Baghdad on 13 January. While it was clear that the most important topic on the agenda would be what to do about the Jordanian-Palestinian relationship in light of Jordanian pressure to recognize 242 and 338, 'Arafat on his arrival played this down and instead stressed that the meetings would concentrate on Israeli activities in the West Bank and Gaza Strip, the threats to the Palestinians in Lebanon, and the results of the visit of the head of the PLO Political Department Faruq Qaddumi, to the Soviet Union.[6]

On 14 January, PLO radio reported that the PLO had decided in Baghdad "to take enough time" to collect information on future steps. Similarly, the Jordanians "will have enough time to collect new information." This seemed like an additional delaying tactic, as Jordan certainly had no need for more time, and the PLO already knew that it would not accede to Husayn's demands. PLO radio continued in the same broadcast in a conciliatory vein, advising that the two sides should stress the "clear provisions of the agreement" and in a direct dialogue find "a joint interest in finding ways to confront US and Israeli moves to strike at joint Arab action by setting up ambushes, the most serious of which are those aimed at removing the PLO from the equation and creating alternatives to it and to its role."[7]

The final statement issued at the end of the meeting in Baghdad included nothing that would satisfy Husayn. It did not mention Resolution 242, yet it did mention that 'Arafat would lead a Palestinian delegation to Amman to "follow up all aspects of joint action with the Jordanian brother officials on the basis of the Jordanian-Palestinian Agreement and the joint understanding of the interests of the Jordanian and Palestinian peoples."[8]

'Arafat arrived in Amman on 25 January, and began his discussions with Husayn the next day. Even before his arrival, several PLO officials spoke skeptically in interviews with the Arab Press. Qaddumi echoed a theme that would appear more often. He downgraded the agreement to the status of "working paper," and explained: "I don't term it an agreement. It was an attempt to advance the peace process in the Middle East, but maneuvering by the US caused it to fail." Khalaf, who had opposed the agreement from the start, maintained that "the Amman Agreement had canceled itself due to the limits put on it by Washington. In my opinion, the agreement died in London."[9] 'Arafat, on the other hand, continued to strike a positive chord regarding relations with Jordan, stressing the importance of the agreement, its strength and durability. There was no reason why political differences could not exist between the two sides as long as the agreement continued to exist.[10] Yet it was evident that such statements were mere posturing prior to what was shaping up more or less as a final showdown. 'Arafat was about to tell Husayn that the PLO refused to accept 242 and 338.[11]

On 25 January, the day of 'Arafat's arrival in Amman, Husayn had received, according to his own account which was later confirmed by American officials, US assurances that if the PLO clearly accepted Resolutions 242 and 338, was prepared to negotiate with Israel and to renounce terrorism, the US would "accept the fact" that an invitation be issued to the PLO to attend an international conference.[12] This was definitely a change in the position of the Reagan Administration, which had consistently opposed an international conference. Moreover, while previously the US had insisted on PLO recognition of the resolutions as a precondition for even talking to the PLO, it was now offering to go even further and agree to invite it to an international conference. The stage was thus set; Husayn was going to offer 'Arafat a final ultimatum.

Several versions of the talks between the Jordanians and the Palestinians were published in the Press.[13] What is clear is that the talks assumed the character of indirect US-PLO discussions, with Husayn as mediator between 'Arafat and two US envoys, Walter ("Wat") Cluverius and Roscoe Suddarth. Husayn presented 'Arafat with the US concession, that it had agreed to accept an international conference with PLO participation if the PLO accepted 242 and 338.

To Husayn's dismay, the PLO remained entrenched in its position that acceptance of the resolutions would have to be conditional on US acceptance of the Palestinians' right to self-determination. The organization, said a "senior PLO official," wanted "ironclad guarantees."[14] Husayn, however, was concerned that time was running out for Jordan. Self-determination was a matter between Jordan and the Palestinians to discuss when they constituted their confederation. Husayn urged the PLO to act now since the priority was to get back the land. The Palestinians remained firm, so Husayn agreed to go back to the Americans with the PLO's offer. It seems, though, that both sides may have just been going through the motions. Husayn had probably already decided to break with the PLO after the ill-fated attempt at a meeting in London the year before. 'Arafat, from his point of view, could never recognize the resolutions. Even if he personally might have been prepared to do so, hard-liners within Fath would never have stood for it. In their eyes, acceptance of Resolutions 242 and 338 dealt with every problem except the Palestinian one. It turned the Palestinian problem into one of the borders of a country which they did not recognize. The national dimensions of the Palestinian problem were not addressed. Despite the feeling of an impending split, the PLO tried to maintain a positive tone. After the above-mentioned rejection of the US proposal, Khalaf told reporters in Amman that the talks were positive and that they had been conducted in an atmosphere of understanding and concern.[15]

The US rejected the PLO's counteroffer, maintaining that self-determination could be one of the issues raised by the PLO at the international conference. The US position remained the same. This was relayed to 'Arafat at a meeting on 28 January, but he insisted that Husayn try again. The American reply was negative.

On 29 January, the King informed 'Arafat of the US reaffirmation of its previous position. Since this meeting was held in an enlarged forum, several parts of the exchange between 'Arafat and Husayn were leaked to the Arab Press. What clearly emerged in the dialogue were the different perceptions of the importance of the time factor. 'Arafat argued that recognition of 242 would be considered treachery by the Palestinians. The PLO could not recognize Israel without a guarantee of the right to self-determination. He asked for more time to try to persuade other Arab countries to put pressure on the US. For Husayn, the return of land was most important. The Arabs were divided, Israel was tightening its grip on the West Bank, the Gaza Strip and Jerusalem. In such a situation, Husayn maintained, the Arabs should accept what was offered. Palestinian demands could be met later at the international conference. At this point, 'Arafat told Husayn that he had to consult the Palestinian leadership, a sentence which must have conjured up in the King's mind another prolonged absence and further delay. He asked 'Arafat to give him the PLO's final answer before he left Amman. If he left without a yes or no reply, then Jordan would consider the resolutions rejected. "Each of us," he emphasized — in what must have been a threatening tone of voice — "would then have the right to choose his own way of restoring the usurped Arab rights."[16]

Although the talks were to go on for another week, the seriousness of the differences between the parties was very apparent. Qaddumi condemned the US for causing the talks to fail, while "sources" in Amman said the talks had come to "a dead end."[17]

On the same day, the US told Husayn that, until such a time as the PLO saw fit to accept Resolution 242, the peace process could proceed with non-PLO Palestinians from the occupied territories. Jordan rejected this as being akin to a separate settlement, which it would not undertake under any circumstances. 'Arafat was informed of the Amerian offer and of the Jordanian rejection.[18]

On 30 January, Khalaf returned to Amman from Rabat, where he had gone at the behest of 'Arafat to request that King Hasan II intercede with the US. According to various reports, he came back empty-handed.[19] Husayn and 'Arafat did not meet again until 5 February. 'Arafat spent the intervening two days in intensive talks with Palestinian leaders in Jordan.

The Palestinian delegation remained in Amman, waiting for the beginning of the next round of talks. As usual, the Fath leadership spoke differently about the progress of the talks. In stark contrast to Qaddumi's negative assessment and lashing out at the US, Fath Central Committee member Hani al-Hasan, political adviser to 'Arafat, described the US proposal for an international conference as "reflecting a positive change in the American position." The US position represented progress, stated al-Hasan, but the PLO would never give up the demand for self-determination. For Fath Central Committee member Khalid al-Hasan, the Amman Agreement was by no means dead; it was a strategic agreement and not a tactical one. 'Arafat went so far as to say that the talks were heading in a positive direction.[20] What is clear is that, from the beginning of the talks until several months after Husayn's 19 February speech, the PLO for the most part remained positive about relations with Jordan, not wanting to burn its bridges. This, as will be shown later, was not Husayn's view at all.

On 1 February, Khalil al-Wazir and Hani al-Hasan met with Husayn and informed him that the PLO had "finally and totally" rejected Resolutions 242 and 338.[21]

The Jordanians, while still not talking openly about breaking off relations with the PLO, let it be known that Syrian President Hafiz al-Asad would soon come to Amman to reciprocate Husayn's visit to Damascus the previous December.[22] The announcement of the visit was obviously intended to put pressure on the PLO; while paying lip service to the Syrian-Jordanian reconciliation as a positive step toward Arab unity, the organization feared that it would come at its expense.

Although it was clear that the talks had broken down, the US continued to seriously try to involve the PLO in negotiations. On 5 February, the Americans presented

Husayn with another offer for presentation to 'Arafat, whereby the US would approve the convening of an international conference based on Resolutions 242 and 338 and the "safeguarding" of the legitimate rights of the Palestinian people. At this meeting 'Arafat handed Husayn three proposals; in the King's opinion, they were "three differently worded texts which were the same in substance, reaffirming the same PLO position which we had heard from the start of this round of meetings."[23]

The published texts of the proposals represented some change in the PLO position. The proposals were very similar to one another. All called for an international conference at which the PLO would be a part of an equal, joint Jordanian-Palestinian delegation; the conference would be held on the basis of securing the legitimate rights of the Palestinian people, including their right to self-determination; Resolutions 242 and 338 were specifically mentioned in the proposals as a basis for the conference, but along with the other UN resolutions "pertinent to the Palestine question." The PLO noted its rejection of terrorism, but the proposals stressed that this was as stated in the Cairo Declaration of November 1985. The PLO had always interpreted the declaration to mean that the armed struggle in Israel, the West Bank and Gaza would continue (see *MECS* 1984–85, pp 207–8).

The only significant difference in the proposals was that while the other proposals noted that the PLO would be present at the international conference along with the permanent members of the UN Security Council and "concerned Arab parties," the second proposal stated that "all the concerned parties, including Israel," would attend. In the version of the proposals given to the Chairman of the Subcommittee on the Middle East and Europe of the House Committee on Foreign Affairs, Lee Hamilton, by Secretary of State George Shultz, there appeared an additional section entitled "steps." In this section the PLO outlined a procedure whereby the organization's acceptance of Resolution 242 would be conditional on the affirmation by the US of the Palestinians' right to self-determination.[24]

These proposals certainly represented the outer limits of PLO concessions, and indeed, Fath leaders did not immediately reveal their content. Although 'Arafat repeatedly referred to the three proposals, he never referred to their content, even noting at one point that should he do so he would "burn them."[25]

On 6 February, 'Arafat, Hani al-Hasan and PLO Executive Committee member 'Abd al-Razzaq al-Yahya met with Jordanian Prime Minister Zayd al-Rifa'i. There had not yet been a US response to the new PLO proposals. The PLO noted that they could still not accept 242, as US recognition of the legitimate rights of the Palestinian people did not encompass the right to self-determination, which the organization wanted mentioned explicitly. On 7 February, 'Arafat left Amman. For Husayn, "thus came to an end another chapter in the search for peace."[26]

Even amid rumors of an impending crisis in relations between the PLO and Jordan,[27] up until Husayn's speech the PLO continued to downplay the seriousness of the breakdown of the talks. "All the rumors of Jordanian-Palestinian tensions," stated Hani al-Hasan, "were pipe dreams of those who were not pursuing what was best for the Palestinian cause and the Arab nation." 'Arafat stated that he "wished to pay tribute to the position of King Husayn," who "succeeded...in convincing America of the merit of an international conference."[28]

While Husayn had no compunctions about placing the blame squarely on the shoulders of the PLO, 'Arafat and others avoided placing any blame on Jordan.

According to 'Arafat, Jordan merely passed messages back and forth between the PLO and the US: "therefore there is no anger between Jordan and us [just] because we said 'no' to the American proposals Jordan passed on to us."[29] It was contended that no "last chance for peace" had been missed, since even though the PLO expressed a readiness to reexamine its position on 242 and 338, the US would not agree to self-determination. The US, therefore, was at fault.[30]

Reports on the Soviet role in the talks held in Amman varied. The Soviets had opposed the US-orchestrated moves for a Middle East settlement that began after the PLO withdrawal from Lebanon in 1982. In their view, this confirmed US dominance in the region. They had opposed the Jordanian-Palestinian agreement of February 1983 and all the contacts that followed.[31] A "Western diplomat" noted that the failure of the talks was largely the result of Soviet pressure on 'Arafat. 'Arafat had met with the Soviet Ambassador in Amman "at least three times" while the talks were going on. The Soviet Union feared the success of a US-led peace process and the further strains acceptance of 242 would cause between PLO factions. In exchange for the rejection of 242, Moscow promised to try to reunify the PLO by using its influence with the pro-Syrian and Marxist factions.[32] Following the collapse of the talks, Radio Moscow commented that reality had proved that the policy of operating alone and of submission to the Israeli-American strategic alliance had reached a dead end.[33] It is possible that 'Arafat may have paid heed to the Soviet urgings. Given the state of the talks with the Jordanians, he may have felt it worthwhile to ingratiate himself with Moscow and at the same time leave an opening for improved relations with those PLO factions opposed to him. Indeed, following Husayn's speech, internal reconciliation became the focus of his activities.

On 8 February, Israeli Prime Minister Shimon Peres declared that the talks had been a "devastating failure." He then noted that the inhabitants of the administered territories should be given more control over their lives until such time as a formal peace agreement was reached. He later stressed that he was not proposing unilateral autonomy, a concept which was once proposed by Moshe Dayan and which appeared to many Arabs to be a way of finalizing Israeli rule. He was, rather, proposing a "devolution of authority" (*ha'atzalat samkhuyot*) whereby civil matters would slowly and selectively be transferred to the control of the residents.[34]

The PLO failed to see a significant difference between unilateral autonomy and devolution of authority. For the organization, it was simply a unilateral implementation of autonomy as envisaged in the Camp David Accords. The plan was attacked by Muhammad Milhim, the deported former Mayor of Halhul and the PLO Executive Committee member responsible for the territories: he declared that it would meet the same fate as the Village Leagues, since it did not give the Palestinians the right to choose their own representatives. Wazir stated that the plan was a "Zionist attempt...aimed at polishing the image of the occupation."[35]

The US, apparently still trying to salvage something from the Husayn-'Arafat talks, made an announcement on 10 February that attempted to placate to some degree the PLO's animosity toward Resolution 242. State Department spokesman Charles Redman stated that:

> The Palestinian problem is more than a refugee problem. Beyond that, there should be no confusion between Resolution 242 and the legitimate rights of the

> Palestinian people. They deal with different issues and are in fact complementary....As a separate but related matter, negotiations regarding the final status of the West Bank and Gaza, in addition to resolving the location of boundaries and the nature of the security arrangement, must also recognize the legitimate rights of the Palestinian people. The full manner in which those rights will be exercised will become clear as the process of negotiations proceeds.[36]

The PLO continued to speak with different voices also in reaction to the Redman statement. Qaddumi declared outright that the statement contained "nothing new and did not reflect any change in the known US position." 'Arafat, however, who was in Cairo, where he had arrived on 13 February, termed the announcement a repetition of the Reagan Plan; but, on another occasion, he said it was "an important and positive step forward."[37] PLO radio commented that since the statement was given by a lower-level official, and not Secretary of State Shultz, Washington did not deem it particularly important. Moreover, the statement did not define legitimate rights, and was therefore vague and not useful. Finally, the statement was clear in demanding prior recognition of 242 and 338, something that the PLO refused to do. 'Arafat's comments were consistent with his general behavior. They were made in Egypt, where President Husni Mubarak stated that the US announcement was "encouraging."[38] 'Arafat did not want to offend his Egyptian hosts, who were engaged in trying to restore relations between him and Husayn. Furthermore, just as he had not rejected the Reagan Plan outright, he saw no reason to reject this latest statement.

Until Husayn's 19 February announcement, the PLO engaged in intensive diplomatic efforts in Baghdad, Cairo and Amman to try to ward off a public statement by the King. The PLO was confident — and rightly so — that Husayn would not enter negotiations without the PLO and violate the 1974 Rabat summit decision that the PLO was the sole, legitimate representative of the Palestinian people. PLO radio continued to broadcast statements affirming the positive aspects of the Jordanian-Palestinian relationship: "The mutual Palestinian-Jordanian understanding has won out over the tensions and the serious contradictions that usually bring about a split."[39]

THE AFTERMATH OF HUSAYN'S 19 FEBRUARY SPEECH

King Husayn's speech, announcing that he was terminating political coordination with the PLO, was a detailed historical *tour d'horizon* of his efforts to bring about the return of the West Bank. In his mind, the PLO had "lost a precious opportunity." The most immediate threat was to the land, he contended; self-determination was an internal matter between Jordan and the Palestinians that could be discussed once the land was returned.[40] The PLO lacked credibility, he added soon after the speech: "The speech was intended to lead to the appearance of a Palestinian side which reacts to its cause in a responsible manner." What was needed, affirmed Husayn, was "to find Palestinian forces that are concerned about liberating the land and the people on the land instead of looking forward to rule (*al-hukm*)."[41]

The immediate reaction of the PLO mainstream was to publicly express surprise over Husayn's moves and to downplay their seriousness. Fath leaders emphasized repeatedly the importance of the Jordanian-Palestinian relationship: "...the PLO insists that a difference of opinion need not mean a split or a negative impact on relations, nor need it mean engaging in propaganda battles."[42]

'Arafat was most concerned with damage control. Realizing the importance of the PLO presence in Jordan, a confrontation state, as well as what would continue to be gained from the relatively easy access to the West Bank, 'Arafat instructed all PLO offices to issue no statements in reaction to Husayn's speech, pending an official statement from the PLO Executive Committee.[43] He wanted to prevent unauthorized statements that would give Husayn an excuse to intensify his attack on the PLO. In Bucharest and Cairo he received similar advice: keep the door open to Jordan and react carefully and unemotionally.[44] This was the course he was to follow.

After the speech each side sought to publish expressions of support from the West Bank and Gaza. In his speech, Husayn had said that he would turn to those under occupation and ask them to decide. He therefore had a supreme interest in drawing out expressions of support. 'Arafat, for the same reason, had to show that he had the West Bankers behind him.[45]

'Arafat was the PLO leader who maintained the most conciliatory tone; in various interviews he blamed the US, not Jordan. "There are no differences or misunderstandings between myself and King Husayn," stressed 'Arafat. In his mind, even though Jordan had frozen joint action, "we would not think of abolishing the [Jordanian-Palestinian] agreement."[46] Khalaf, however, answered Husayn's speech by directly challenging its main points. While the King had tried to paint a picture in which the only obstacle to withdrawal was the PLO's refusal to recognize Resolution 242, Khalaf pointed out that from 1967 to 1974 the PLO did not present itself as the sole legitimate representative of the Palestinians, and the territories were not regained. All the pre-1974 political efforts noted by Husayn, including the Rogers Plan and the 1973 Geneva conference, had not succeeded. Khalaf vehemently denied that the PLO had ever consented to recognize Resolutions 242 and 338 in August 1985, as Husayn claimed. With regard to self-determination, Khalaf claimed that this could only be an internal Jordanian-Palestinian affair if an eastern front were established with Syria, Jordan and all the Arabs, and "when we regain the West Bank, more than the West Bank, and Gaza by arms."[47] Qaddumi noted that the talks in Amman had gone beyond what was included in the joint Jordanian-Palestinian "working paper"; they had dwelt on the recognition of Resolution 242, which was unacceptable.[48] Indeed, this point was a cardinal one, since Jordan had interpreted the agreement as at least implicitly recognizing 242 (see *MECS* 1984–85, p 199).

On 4 March, the PLO Executive Committee and the Fath Central Committee began deliberations in Tunis to produce an official response to Husayn's speech. There were serious disagreements among the Fath leadership, which became apparent soon after the meeting began. Several leading figures, notably Qaddumi and Khalaf, favored a harsh announcement and the public abrogation of the Amman Agreement. Such a stand, it was argued, would pave the way toward internal reconciliation. 'Arafat, on the other hand, wanted to maintain relations with Jordan, which had taken several years to build.[49] This argument took on a public expression when the official PLO spokesman, Ahmad 'Abd al-Rahman, called on Husayn to reconsider his policy toward the PLO because it was harmful to the interests of the Arab world. 'Abd al-Rahman went even further and accused Prime Minister Zayd al-Rifa'i of influencing the King to stop political coordination. Thus the King was not really at fault, al-Rifa'i was. 'Arafat responded quickly, just a few hours after 'Abd al-Rahman's statement was broadcast. The statement, he emphasized, did not represent the opinion of the Executive Committee. Moreover, "the PLO does not interfere in the internal affairs of Arab states and does not permit itself to interfere in Jordan's internal affairs."[50]

On 8 March, the PLO Executive Committee issued its official response to Husayn's speech. From an examination of the statement it is evident that 'Arafat's line won out. The statement was forthright and took issue with several points in the speech. Although the 11 February 1985 Agreement was mentioned, it was not reaffirmed in the statement. Instead, the statement noted only the PLO's "desire to realize a positive course for the Jordanian-Palestinian relationship." This language followed 'Arafat's "yes and no" (*la'am*) policy; an opening was left to Jordan, as the agreement was not publicly abrogated. On the other hand, since the agreement was not reaffirmed it left an opening toward efforts at internal reconciliation (see below). The statement rejected Jordan's effort to "separate the organization from the people." Just as the Algerian *Front de la Libération Nationale* (FLN) had used the slogan "The people are the FLN and the FLN is the people," the Palestinian people raised the same slogan: "The people are the PLO and the PLO is the people." Following the signing of the 11 February Agreement, noted the statement, the PLO agreed to let Jordan try to bring the US toward accepting an international conference with PLO participation, even though the PLO "was aware of the realities of the US stand." The PLO therefore "expresses deep regret that King Husayn's speech, which concentrated on directing the blame on the PLO, justified, in return, the US stand. Instead of blaming the US stand for foiling the move, the PLO was held responsible." The statement denied that the PLO ever agreed in August 1985 to accept Resolutions 242 and 338; if it had done so without the assurance that an international conference would be held on the basis of Palestinian self-determination as well, then the conference would have dealt only with border issues and thus consent would be akin to "agreeing to the cancellation of the Palestinian cause." The PLO also rejected outright Husayn's claim that it was interested only in ruling and not in the return of the land.[51]

In evaluating the attitudes of the PLO leadership and of Jordan, what is most apparent is the difference in their perception of the importance of the time factor. For Husayn, there was a real possibility that the Israelis would drive out the residents of the West Bank, thus causing the permanent loss of the land, and, more importantly, the destabilization of his regime.[52] The PLO was aware of this Jordanian conception, but had its own view. "Jordan's approach...is different concerning the rate at which matters progress," stated 'Arafat. "Jordan claims that time is short and we must move speedily.... We, on the other hand, will not stray from our principles...even at the expense of a delay." For 'Arafat, the issue of delay was a serious one, but it had its advantages: "There is no doubt that the time factor must be taken into account. We know that the time factor eats away at us, but there is a difference if it eats away at us and threatens us, or if it eats away at us and we benefit from it. I would maintain that time will not become a sword over our heads."[53]

In sharp contrast to 'Arafat's reaction to Husayn's speech, the PDFLP and PFLP saw it as a vindication of the futility of political action based on the Amman Agreement, which both had opposed. While al-Fath had blamed the US for the failure and had cast Husayn more or less in the role of messenger boy, the radical groups put the blame squarely on Husayn's shoulders. His speech "[was] actually a staunch defense of the US conditions for imposing a capitulatory solution for the Middle East crisis and the Palestinian problem," noted the Secretary-General of the PDFLP, Na'if Hawatima.[54] According to the PDFLP, what now was needed was the cancellation of the Amman Agreement by the PLO leadership; this would remove the Palestinian card from Husayn's hands and pave the way toward internal reconciliation.[55]

The PFLP seemed to be concerned mostly about a response on the part of the residents of the administered territories to Husayn's urging them to find an alternative leadership, and published warnings to them not to answer Husayn's call. Telephone threats were also made.[56] The most symbolic response of the PFLP to Husayn's speech was the assassination of Zafir al-Masri on 2 March. Al-Masri had been appointed Mayor of Nablus by Israel in coordination with Jordan and with the apparent consent of the PLO in November 1985. The post had previously been held by the pro-PFLP Bassam al-Shak'a, who had been deposed by Israel. In a PFLP Political Bureau release, the organization noted that al-Masri had been "executed" following "the people's judgment." His deeds constituted treason in that he was taking part in the "Zionist-Jordanian reactionary project...to liquidate the Palestinian cause by negating the PLO."[57] Within three days several mayoral candidates had withdrawn their candidacy (see essay on the West Bank and Gaza Strip). When the PLO leadership did not issue a statement for several weeks following Husayn's speech, they came in for increasing criticism from PFLP Secretary-General George Habash for not immediately canceling the Amman Agreement.[58] Habash noted that "[t]here are now suitable objective conditions for restoring the PLO's unity and national line.... It is an unparalleled opportunity."[59]

Al-Sa'iqa, representing the views of the pro-Syrian Palestinian National Salvation Front (PNSF), used Husayn's speech to launch an attack on 'Arafat and called on him to step down.[60]

The PLO leadership's official response to Husayn's speech met with criticism from both the PDFLP and the PFLP, mostly because it did not cancel the Amman Accord, a step which was regarded as a *sine qua non* for establishing internal unity.[61] Yet Husayn's speech had created opportunities for a dialogue between the PLO factions. Contacts between the factions began soon after the speech, and for the rest of the year they centered on attempts to move 'Arafat and the Fath leadership to cancel the Amman Agreement.

THE PLO ON THE DEFENSIVE: REACTIONS TO JORDANIAN ATTEMPTS TO LIMIT PLO INFLUENCE IN JORDAN AND THE ADMINISTERED TERRITORIES

Soon after his speech, Husayn initiated several steps to limit PLO influence in the administered territories (see chapter on Jordan and essay on the West Bank and Gaza Strip). The return to Jordan, which began in earnest after the 1984 PNC, was regarded by the PLO leadership, and particularly 'Arafat, as one of the major accomplishments of his policies since the withdrawal from Lebanon in 1982. The PLO had become ensconced in a confrontation state with relatively easy access to the two major Palestinian population centers: Jordan and the administered territories. Husayn therefore moved throughout 1986 to curtail the influence of the PLO in these two areas. In Jordan, a law was passed increasing the size of the Jordanian Parliament and thus its West Bank representation; PLO and Fath offices were closed; and Khalil al-Wazir, the PLO representative on the Palestinian-Jordanian Committee that was established in 1978, was deported. Husayn also supported an effort to undermine the PLO from within by aiding the "Rectification Movement" (*al-Haraka al-Tashihiyya*) of 'Atallah 'Atallah (Abu al-Za'im; see below). In the administered territories, where the PLO was very strong, he began an activist policy of funding pro-Jordanian figures and publications, and boycotted pro-PLO publications and journalists. Moreover, he announced an extensive Five-Year Development Plan for the West Bank; this would allow him to assert his responsibility and implied sovereignty over the area. The plan was to be funded from overseas and would not be under partial control of the PLO as were moneys transferred through the Joint Committee (see chapter on Jordan, and esaay on the West Bank and Gaza Strip).

What ensued was essentially an all-out battle for the hearts and minds of the residents of the West Bank and Gaza Strip. All these steps met with intense opposition across the PLO spectrum and forced the leadership to go on the defensive. Most of this activity centered on the West Bank. The massive outpouring of support for 'Arafat during the funeral procession of Zafir al-Masri, the brazen PLO attack at the Western Wall in October and various demonstrations in favor of 'Arafat were PLO successes in the face of the Jordanian effort (see essays on armed operations, and the West Bank and Gaza Strip). They put the King on notice that the undermining of grass-roots support for 'Arafat — in his role as a symbol of Palestinian Nationalism — was by no means an easy task.

The Jordanian steps against Fath and the PLO were anticipated by the leadership. Salah Khalaf mentioned that he had heard threats by certain Jordanian personalities — not necessarily the King — against the Palestinian presence in Jordan and against the Palestine Liberation Army (PLA) camps there. He belittled the importance of the PLA bases and the expressions of support for Husayn by Na'im al-Khatib, Commander of the Badr Forces of the PLA in Jordan.[62]

On 27 March, the Jordanian Parliament voted to expand its membership from 60 to 142, thus increasing Palestinian representation (see chapter on Jordan). The new Election Law provided — for the first time — for the election of representatives from the Palestinian refugee camps in Jordan. The law also allowed for the continued appointment of members to vacated West Bank seats, thus enabling Husayn to appoint pro-Hashemites to these positions. 'Arafat, while maintaining a correct tone, as was his practice in relations with Jordan, stressed PLO opposition to this step:

> Jordan has the right to expand its Parliament as it likes and in the manner it desires, but there is a serious violation in the new Election Law in that this is the first time an Arab country is incorporating the representation of camps in its Parliament. This is in total violation of the Arab resolutions adopted by the Arab League concerning the countries playing host to refugees.[63]

On 22 April, Husayn deported seven high-ranking Fath officers; an eighth officer, Salah al-Ta'amri (who had been the highest-ranking Fath operative captured by Israel during the 1982 war in Lebanon and was married to Husayn's ex-wife, Dina), was reported to have been deported on 15 May. In view of the deportations and the closing of the PLO-Jordanain liaison office in early April (see below), 'Arafat issued orders to all his officers and cadres not to travel to Jordan.[64] Reacting to the expulsion of the Fath officers, Khalil al-Wazir stated that they had conducted a meeting which "was in keeping with their legitimate activities." He added that all Palestinian fighters in Jordan were well aware of the delicate situation in Jordan and were careful not to make any moves that might be interpreted as dangerous to its national security.[65]

Riots broke out in mid-May on the campus of Yarmuk University in the Jordanian town of Irbid, supposedly to protest against high tuition costs (see chapter on Jordan). The Jordanians charged that Fath was behind the riots and had cooperated with both communist forces and the Muslim brotherhood, and that the office of Wazir was directly responsible for the outbreaks at the university. It was also contended that Wazir had tried to influence the outcome of parliamentary elections in Irbid by trying to buy votes for the Muslim Brotherhood candidate. Wazir vehemently denied the accusations, challenging the Jordanians to prove them.[66] The PLO, in reacting to the riots, noted that Yarmuk University had a large Palestinian student body from the West Bank, and therefore was particularly concerned with the implications of Husayn's 19 February speech. The students had acted on the basis of a patriotic tradition. According to the PLO, the demonstrations were put down brutally by the Hashemite regime.[67]

To further their effort to limit the influence of the PLO in the territories and increase their own influence, the Jordanians blacklisted 34 "pro-PLO" West Bank and East Jerusalem journalists in mid-June, prohibiting them from entering Jordan. The Jordanian media were forbidden to quote most of the Palestinian papers published in the territories. In order to counter the influence of the pro-PLO dailies, a pro-Jordanian weekly, *al-Nahar*, began publishing in March. These steps came on top of a general policy of preventing those deemed to be supporters of the PLO from entering the Hashemite Kingdom. Many West Bankers were called to the Jordanian Ministry of the Interior and questioned about their political affiliations and sympathies.[68]

Reactions on the part of the PLO to these Jordanian steps demonstrated a gradual loosening of the reins of self-restraint. 'Arafat accused Husayn of interference in internal Palestinian affairs with the aim of exerting pressure on Palestinians from the West Bank to abandon the PLO and pay allegiance to Jordan.[69] In a statement issued by the Fath Revolutionary Council in Tunis on 19 June, the leadership lashed out at the regime for its activities.

> While the US and Israel consider striking at the PLO...we notice...a series of measures adopted by the Jordanian Government which directly and seriously encroach on national Palestinian and basic Arab principles defining the correct stand toward the Palestinian issue, the Palestinian people's national rights and the national Palestinian struggle led by the PLO.

The statement further declared that the actions resorted to "remind us of similar measures adopted by the occupation authorities." The Jordanian decision to expand the Parliament came in for particularly harsh criticism. The Amman Agreement was not mentioned in the statement.[70] Khalaf raised the stakes by attacking the King personally: "King Husayn has pushed the PLO into opening a new front against him. At the beginning our reaction was mild because we did not really believe this was the King's position. But afterwards it became clear that he has serious plans to undermine us. He has no morals."[71]

In midyear, reports began to appear on a new, comprehensive Five-Year

Development Plan for the West Bank being prepared by the Jordanian Government (see chapter on Jordan and essay on the West Bank and Gaza Strip). It was obvious that the plan was aimed at building up the pro-Hashemite constituency on the West Bank and as a replacement for the Joint Palestinian-Jordanian Committee which had not met in months. It was widely characterized as the "carrot" part of the "carrot and stick" policy initiated by the King. According to Marwan Dudin, a member of a prominent West Bank family and Minister for Occupied Territories Affairs, Jordan hoped to spend — with international assistance — approximately $150m during each year of the plan.[72] The plan came in for intense ridicule by the PLO as did the television program entitled "With Our People in the Occupied Territories," which explained it to West Bank residents.

> Of course no one forgets that the so-called Development Plan...is the bribe the...White House is offering in implementation of Uncle Sam's well-known formula for transforming the daily concerns of our Palestinian people...into concerns dealing with daily livelihood to prevent them from enrolling in the Palestinian march of national liberation and rejecting and confronting the...occupation.

Wazir, the Palestinian representative on the Joint Committee, made it clear that the West Bankers understood that the PLO had no objection to funds put into the West Bank; but this should be done in coordination with the PLO and through the Joint Committee. Moreover, stated Wazir:

> The real question is what is the political goal behind the plan. Does it serve the citizens in the occupied land, or is it an attempt to set rules by which it would be possible to politically penetrate the occupied land, with the aim of building political support for the engineers of the plan?[73]

Much of the Jordanian activity on the West Bank was coordinated with Israel. Thus the Jordanian authorities welcomed the appointment by Israel on 28 September of Arab mayors to head committees to handle the municipal affairs of al-Bira, Hebron and Ramallah.[74] The PLO defined the appointments as "within the framework of [Israel's] continued attempts to promote the autonomy plan conspiracy and impose it on our steadfast people." The organization called for elected municipal councils. Interestingly, most of the PLO attack was reserved for the Israelis, despite the rousing Jordanian endorsement of the move. The PDFLP, the PCP, and the PNSF vehemently condemned the appointments. The PFLP, which had claimed credit for the murder of the Israeli-appointed Mayor of Nablus, Zafir al-Masri, demanded that the Mayors resign or be liquidated.[75]

The most severe blow to the PLO in the aftermath of Husayn's speech was the closing of Fath and PLO offices that began in April with the shutting of the PLO's liaison office and culminated in the closing of 25 Fath offices in July. The Jordanians were probably waiting for a PLO provocation and thus adopted a wait-and-see attitude concerning the offices following Husayn's speech. In fact, soon after the speech PLO Executive Committee member ʻAbd al-Razzaq al-Yahya was informed by Zayd al-Rifaʻi that despite the termination of political coordination, the PLO would be allowed to maintain its offices.[76] Reports in late March began to mention that the offices in Amman would soon be closed; but — again, to keep the atmosphere as positive as possible and not to provoke the authorities — Khalil al-Wazir and PLO radio forcefully denied these reports.[77] However, by 2 April 'Arafat confirmed that the PLO liaison office — originally established in 1984 to coordinate the entry and residence of PLO members in Jordan — had been closed by "joint agreement." It was also reported that the Palestinian News Agency, WAFA, had ceased to issue its daily bulletin in Amman.[78] Another office established in 1984, the Department of Popular Organization, which was headed by 'Abd al-Rahim Ahmad, an Executive Committee member from the pro-Iraqi Arab Liberation Front (ALF), also closed its doors. The department was responsible for the political organization of refugees in the camps.[79]

Wazir preferred to downplay the closing of the above offices, even going so far as to term them "unnecessary." Yet the other steps taken by Jordan (see above) in combination with the closing of the offices meant that "Jordan was slowly entering into a war with the PLO."[80] 'Arafat even noted publicly for the first time that he had proof of official Jordanian support for a revolt against him led by his former head of Intelligence (see below).[81]

As noted above, the Jordanian steps against the PLO evoked a harsh reaction in a Fath statement issued on 19 June. The Jordanians were accused of stabbing them in the back while they were under attack in Lebanon and by the Israelis on the West Bank. It is worth noting that a statement issued by the PLO Executive Committee on 16 June had dealt almost exclusively with the situation in Lebanon (see below); the problems with Jordan were not mentioned. This was indicative of 'Arafat's behavior, and was part of his "yes and no" policy. Statements that might be too strong for the particular moment, as in the case under discussion, were issued through Fath or leaders other than 'Arafat and not through the PLO. This was also the case with the Prague Declaration "canceling" the Amman Agreement; although Wazir had signed it for Fath, 'Arafat would claim that the agreement could only truly be canceled at a meeting of the PNC (see below). Such behavior gave 'Arafat the maximum room for maneuvering to maintain the best position *vis-à-vis* other PLO organizations or the Jordanians. Yet a policy of this type was not without risks; on 7 July, Jordan announced that it was closing additional Fath offices not affiliated with the PLO; it cited the 19 June Fath statement as the reason for the step. At the same time, the Government announced that it still recognized the PLO as the sole legitimate representative of the Palestinian people, thus emphasizing that it was acting against Fath and not the PLO *per se*.[82]

For 'Arafat, Wazir's continued presence in Amman had been a sign of sorts that relations with Jordan had not soured completely.[83] No sooner had Wazir commented on the closing of the Fath offices, noting the "revenge spirit" of the Jordanian announcement, than he was given 48 hours to leave the country.[84]

The PLO leadership referred to the closed offices as "PLO offices," thus characterizing the Jordanian move as one against the "sole legitimate representative" of the Palestinian people. The Jordanians went out of their way to stress that the offices closed belonged to Fath and "had no direct link to the PLO as a political body, and [their] contacts had been solely with Fath and some of its leaders. These offices carried out activities unrelated to the PLO." Prime Minister Rifa'i stressed that there were two PLO offices operating openly in Jordan which had not been closed. These included the offices of al-Yahya and the PNC office. Husayn linked the closed offices directly to interference in the parliamentary elections in Irbid and to the riots at

Yarmuk University. 'Arafat, on the other hand, maintained that only two of the offices closed belonged to Fath.[85] Among the most important Fath offices closed were Wazir's office, the elite Force 17 offices and the office of the "Western Sector" responsible for operations against Israel.[86]

The closure of the Fath offices — with all that the step implied for the PLO's freedom to act in the heart of Palestine, the West Bank — marked the apex of Jordanian moves against the PLO. This was reflected in the rise in the rhetoric level of the PLO mainstream's reactions to the move. Even 'Arafat, usually the most careful to maintain a positive atmosphere concerning relations with Jordan — which, after all, were the cornerstone of his post-Lebanon policy — reacted in the strongest terms: "Is this not a disgrace? Along with the oppression by Israel, the Palestinians are now starting to be oppressed by Jordan also." According to 'Arafat, the closing of the offices and the deportation of Wazir was an act "of revenge, which aims to implement a major plan directed at destroying strategic Palestinian-Jordanian relations." The Jordanian claim that the Fath Revolutionary Council statement of 19 June was the reason for the closure of the offices was belied, stressed 'Arafat, by the fact that only two of the offices closed were Fath offices. The Jordanians had closed his office in Amman, and he was Chairman of the PLO Central Council. Such statements were indicative of the self-identification by Fath and the PLO as being one and the same thing.[87] Khalaf was very bitter; he interpreted the Jordanian move as a slap in the face while attempts were being made to heal the rift between the parties.[88] Wazir stressed the emotional aspect of his expulsion, comparing it to similar expulsions from Beirut and Tripoli. However, Wazir emphasized that political disagreements should not mean cutting off contacts. The Jordanians, he maintained, were trying to isolate the PLO from the occupied territories.[89] Hani al-Hasan threatened the Jordanian regime:

> The Palestinian people usually ring the bells before entering a new stage.... If it is proven that there is a large-scale plot aimed at attaining a physical liquidation of this people we will undoubtedly defend ourselves using all legal and illegal means.[90]

One of the main concerns of the PLO leadership with respect to the Jordanian moves was that Jordan wanted to undermine its present leadership. This was strongly implied in Husayn's speech and explicitly stated by several Jordanian leaders, such as the Chief of the Royal Court, Marwan al-Qasim, who said that "Jordan will continue to recognize the PLO as the sole legitimate representative of the Palestinian people, but will try to change its current leadership."[91] 'Arafat recognized that, following Husayn's speech, and in light of the *rapprochement* between Asad and Husayn, the latter two now had a common enemy — 'Arafat.

Relations between Jordan and the PLO continued on a low-key basis, despite the severe setbacks following Husayn's speech. Public statements remained rather hostile, yet PLO figures (but not 'Arafat) continued to visit Amman. Moreover, a mediation effort led by Egypt with the aid of other Arab countries began soon after Husayn's speech.[92] 'Arafat, loyal to his policy of keeping options open, continued to be cautious about severing contact with Jordan. The Executive Committee's official statement following the closing of the offices and the deportation of Wazir only went so far as to express "deep regret" at the moves.[93] Although other PLO leaders were very blunt in their condemnation of the Jordanian-Palestinian accord, saying that it was now "in the graveyard,"[94] 'Arafat always insisted that, as far as the PLO was concerned, it could only be canceled by another session of the PNC. This was a perfect formulation. The cancellation was a carrot held before the radical groups to get them to attend the next session of the PNC; on the other hand, 'Arafat kept the door open to the Jordanians by not openly canceling the agreement. At one stage he even went so far as to state specifically that he still regarded the agreement as valid even though it had been abrogated by his own Fath movement in the Prague Declaration of September (see below).[95]

THE "RECTIFICATION MOVEMENT" OF 'ATALLAH 'ATALLAH

Following Husayn's speech, the Jordanians lent their support to the "Rectification Movement" (*al-Haraka al-Tashihiyya*) of the head of Fath Military Intelligence, 'Atallah 'Atallah (Abu al-Za'im), which went public soon after the speech. Both the Jordanians and 'Atallah denied that the movement had Jordanian support, but it was obvious that it could not have operated in such an open manner without the acquiesence of the Hashemite regime.

This Jordan-based movement against the PLO leadership actually originated before the King's speech, but the speech provided the pretext and the opportunity to gain Jordan's support since no such group of rebels could exist without some support from an Arab country. The political tone and direction of the rebels therefore took the form of attacks on 'Arafat's rejection of going along with Jordan.

The rebellion following the speech was built on two foci of dissatisfaction:

(1) Officers of the Badr Forces of the PLA, led by Na'im al-Khatib (see above — he had come out strongly on behalf of Husayn).

(2) Fath officers led by 'Atallah, many of whom were from the Karama Forces of *al-'Asifah*, Fath's military arm.

Although not officially linked, the timing of their appearance and Jordanian encouragement suggest coordination; Khatib, however, disassociated himself from the 'Atallah-led Fath rebellion, stating that there might be differences within Fath, but the PLA had nothing to do with them.[96] The PLA, established along with the PLO in 1964, was to have been its independent military arm. However, from the start the various PLA units were entirely subordinate to the various Arab countries in which they were stationed, although it was the PLO which officially paid the salaries. When the fida'i organizations — led by Fath — took over the PLO following the 1967 war, the PLA remained but was increasingly perceived as a burden on the "authentic" Palestinian guerrilla fighters. It represented a part of Palestinian history which involved subservience to Arab regimes and of which the fida'iyyin were not very proud. At the fifth PNC in 1968 they moved to disassociate themselves from the previous Shukayri-led PLO and revised the Palestinian National Charter to emphasize the armed struggle and the fida'i nature of the "new" PLO.

The PLA contingent in Jordan had been formed and stationed in Jordan in the early 1970s. There were indications that the PLO leadership was considering closing down the bases of the Badr Forces just before or right after Husayn's speech. Following Khatib's forthright support of Husayn after the speech, there were also reports that the PLO leadership was planning to retire or send several PLA generals to the reserves.[97] For Khalaf, Khatib was nothing more than "a prominent intelligence agent imposed on the liberation army since 1970."[98] In early April, it was reported that

'Arafat had decided to stop paying the salaries of the Badr Forces under Khatib's command.[99] In response, Khatib affirmed that the March salaries had been paid, but that "we will cut off the head of anyone who stops paying the salaries to the PLA in Jordan... The PLO is not 'Arafat — it belongs to the Palestinians."[100] A few weeks later, Khatib confirmed that the salaries had been terminated. In a letter to Wazir that reached the Press, he stressed that this meant the end of the armed struggle; he emphasized that the PLA was created by and based upon the Palestine National Covenant of 1964 — a statement intended to show that the PLA was even more legitimate than Fath since it existed before the latter became part of the PLO. Khatib maintained the traditional Hashemite position by stressing the unity of both Banks of the Jordan.[101]

The other — and by far the most significant — component of the revolt against 'Arafat was led by 'Atallah, who was born in Bayt Surayk, a village near Ramallah on the West Bank. A Jordanian citizen, 'Atallah had been an officer in the Jordanian Army but left it in 1970 to join Fath. He was a member of the Fath Revolutionary Council and the PNC. He later became head of Fath's Military Intelligence, a position that made him many enemies. During the war in Lebanon he was characterized as 'Arafat's "iron fist"; he stayed close to him during the siege of Beirut and accompanied him when he left the Lebanese capital. After leaving Beirut he moved to Cairo. 'Arafat eventually came under pressure to relieve 'Atallah of his duties, and this was done in 1984. 'Atallah was later named Fath representative in Jordan. It appears that 'Atallah's resentment against 'Arafat dates mostly from the time of this incident and that he used the Jordanian-PLO rift as a vehicle to challenge 'Arafat's leadership.[102] He was supported by at least several hundred soldiers of Fath's Karama Forces.[103] Prominent Fath personnel who sided with 'Atallah included Abu Khadr al-Lahham, Commander of Force 14, Fath's Air Force; 'Umran 'Awda, former General Prosecutor of Fath; Kamal al-Shaykh, adviser to the Commander in Chief for Military Research and Studies; and Muhammad Muslih Ya'qub, deputy head of Military Intelligence.[104]

The first indications of 'Atallah's movement came soon after Husayn's speech. 'Atallah began to tour the refugee camps in Jordan, making speeches against 'Arafat, Qaddumi and particularly Khalaf. Much of his time was spent at the Karama Forces' camp in al-Zarqa, where he tried to incite the troops against the Fath leadership. When 'Arafat demanded that 'Atallah come to see him in Tunis, he refused, claiming that the dispute could not be resolved by a meeting between the two as it was not a personal argument but an ideological problem that needed to be addressed.[105] 'Arafat then attempted mediation by sending 'Atallah's brother, Ghazi 'Atallah (Abu Hajim), Commander of Fath's al-Aqsa Forces based in Iraq, to try to convince his brother to give up. It was later reported that Ghazi had joined his brother's uprising.[106]

On 22 April, a shooting incident was reported at the PLO office in the Jabal al-Nuzha neighborhood of Amman between supporters of 'Atallah and 'Arafat. According to 'Atallah, several of his supporters who worked in the office arrived in the morning to find that the locks had been changed. He denied, however, that any shots had been fired.[107] The next day, at a meeting in Baghdad, the Palestinian Supreme Military Council decided to strip 'Atallah of all military rank. 'Atallah, who had refused to attend the session of the council, called the decision "illegal." He said that it was not the Supreme Military Council which had met, but rather "the council of the family from which our fighters and people have suffered.... The policy being practiced by...'Arafat is better suited to the running of a farm than to leading a revolution."[108]

On 28 April, 'Atallah convened a meeting of his supporters in Amman. This meeting declared the Baghdad meeting that had expelled 'Atallah illegal and issued statements praising 'Atallah's move.[109]

On 1 June, 'Atallah held another meeting of his supporters. It "suspended" the membership of 'Arafat and Wazir and "stripped" them of their powers as Commanders of the *al-'Asifa* forces. 'Atallah was named Commander of *al-'Asifa* until the convening of the fifth Fath General Congress. The gathering was attended by over 400 persons. 'Atallah was escorted by armed guards, a rare scene for a PLO personality in Amman. During the meeting, 'Atallah charged the Fath leadership with serious crimes of corruption and financial irregularities. It was claimed that all the funds of the revolution were in the personal accounts of 'Arafat; that he had given Salah Khalaf $40,000 for his silver wedding anniversary; that millions of dollars had been given to African states; and that 'Arafat's brother Jamal, the PLO representative in Sudan, had known of Israeli efforts in 1984 to spirit Ethiopian Jewish refugees out of Sudan to Israel.[110]

In mid-June, it was reported that 'Atallah had rented a large office building in Amman and had set up headquarters there. With the closing of 25 Fath offices in July (see above), 'Atallah remained the only Fath leader of any stature in Jordan. He began to publish a biweekly magazine called *al-Masir* (Destiny), containing details of his activities and professions of support. Pictures of 'Atallah were published, as were his various pronouncements.[111]

Toward the end of the year pamphlets supporting 'Atallah began to appear on the West Bank. In December, a supporter of 'Atallah from Hebron, 'Abd al-Muttalib Tahbub, held a press conference in East Jerusalem and outlined plans to open an office and to publish a newspaper.[112]

'Atallah emphasized that he was not seceding from Fath or the PLO, but was leading a "democratic movement" that was calling for reform. Politically, the movement echoed several themes from Husayn's speech. 'Atallah stated: "Since 1974, the year when 'Arafat raised the slogan of the weapon and the olive branch [in his speech at the UN], we have not progressed even one step.... All that is happening now ignores the requirements of our people in the occupied lands."[113] He urged that the PLO remain faithful to the Jordanian-Palestinian Agreement, and suggested that the residents of the West Bank and King Husayn should be given a chance to negotiate.[114]

'Atallah attempted to portray himself as representing the frustrations of the fighting man with the excesses of the political leadership: "The stage of the struggle in the view of Fath leaders is business travel, jet airplanes, tickets and always staying at the most luxurious hotels in the world."[115] He demanded a reexamination of the goals of the armed struggle and its role in the Palestinian effort. Here, he was echoing sentiments that had been expressed over the past few years by other PLO personalities (see *MECS* 1984–85, pp 210–11). In Lebanon, he argued, Palestinian blood had been wasted on involvement in internal Lebanese struggles, all of which brought the Palestinians no closer to Palestine. 'Atallah admitted that he had much in common with the Fath rebels, who were brothers-in-arms, particularly concerning the individualistic style of leadership exercised by 'Arafat. But, he stressed, they were unrealistic politically in that they expected to liberate Palestine all at once.[116]

'Atallah's most persistent demand was that the leadership hold a Fath General Congress. It had not met since 1980. Events such as the leaving of Beirut, the expulsion of the Fath rebels from the movement, the Jordanian-Palestinian Agreement, the negotiations and their suspension — any one of these would have been sufficient reason to call a General Congress. The same demands had been and continued to be made by the Fath rebels.[117]

Initial reactions of the Fath mainstream to 'Atallah and his movement were to downplay its importance, stressing that it was not worthy of attention. 'Atallah's claims never received serious consideration; his move was termed nothing more than a "television coup."[118] Khalaf, the target of much of 'Atallah's venom, reacted strongly: "The behavior of Abu al-Za'im is known. He used to have quite a nightlife, organizing parties which stood in contrast to the morals of the Palestinian revolution and its honor. He wasted millions; he is completely sick." In any case, added Khalaf, "he is the property of Jordanian Intelligence."[119] 'Arafat echoed the latter sentiment, stating that the whole episode was "a show put on by Jordanian Intelligence."[120]

Of course, both 'Atallah and the Jordanians denied any mutual involvement. 'Atallah asked pointedly: "Am I an agent [of the Jordanians] when I carry out an agreement which you signed, Yasir 'Arafat?"[121] The Jordanians stated that the whole affair was an internal Fath one, but 'Atallah enjoyed considerable freedom of movement in Jordan. In mid-May, he even met with King Husayn in what was certainly a show of support.[122] It was reported that 'Atallah had contacts with US officials in Amman; if true, it would suggest that the US and Jordan were engaging in initial exploration of his strength and ability to present a serious alternative to 'Arafat.[123]

The "Rectification Movement" within Fath led by 'Atallah never seemed to enjoy any great popularity and actually was more of an annoyance than a real threat to the Fath leadership. As ex-Chief of Military Intelligence, 'Atallah may have amassed significant information that could incriminate the leadership.[124] It was certainly not of the same magnitude or significance as the rebellion in 1983. Its importance was primarily in emphasizing once again that the PLO was still as vulnerable as ever to interference by Arab regimes who were capable of exploiting real or imagined internal PLO issues and turning them against the leadership when it suited them. If anything, 'Atallah brought home to the Fath leadership the importance of its Jordanian territorial base and the price of losing it.

INTENSIFIED EFFORT TOWARD INTERNAL RECONCILIATION

King Husayn's speech had a direct influence on efforts to reunify the fractured PLO. The intiative was taken by the PDFLP and Algeria, which offered to host a national dialogue and a PNC; at a later stage there were signs that the PFLP might become a party to the reconciliation efforts. Despite efforts by Moscow, the PFLP continued to play the role of spoiler, preventing, as the year closed, any across-the-board reconciliation meeting or PNC.

'Arafat was caught in a dilemma. He was intent on keeping the door open to Jordan — one could not "liberate" Palestine from Tunisia or Iraq. His relationship with Husayn, no matter how difficult, provided the PLO with an entrance to negotiations for a settlement — should such an opportunity arise, and facilitated his efforts to limit

Husayn's diplomatic leeway on the Palestinian issue. Furthermore, it provided him with access to the West Bank and Gaza Strip, his major constituency. Nevertheless, as leader of the PLO he suffered from the divisions that plagued the organization, which arose to a great extent from the very policy he sought to follow. His relationship with Jordan thus came at the expense of Palestinian unity. Husayn's speech opened new options, yet 'Arafat was hesitant. If he made a sharp and public break with Jordan, an act demanded by his opponents not only in the other PLO constituent organizations but also within his own Fath, he would lose his "Jordanian option." Moreover, those who demanded the cancellation of the Amman Agreement were also demanding closer relations with Syria, which in turn was demanding — at best — strict controls on 'Arafat's freedom of action and — at worst — his removal from power.

Even before Husayn's speech, PLO leaders, notably Khalaf and Qaddumi, who had opposed the Amman Agreement, emphasized repeatedly that for the sake of internal reconciliation all was negotiable, including the accord, the Cairo Declaration and the resolutions of the 17th PNC.[125] Such statements had the effect of maintaining an "all options are open" posture and served to counterbalance 'Arafat's efforts toward Jordan. Following the speech, Khalaf argued that the speech itself was the best evidence that 'Arafat "does not want to relinquish, sell, or leave the cause. On the contrary, he is a man who adheres to principles and who has flexibility without concessions."[126] Khalaf thus portrayed 'Arafat as an intelligent leader who examined all options; when Jordan demanded too much, 'Arafat stood firm.

As noted above, both Habash and Hawatima interpreted Husayn's speech as creating an atmosphere that was conducive to unity. Hawatima, however, was more flexible. Whereas Habash demanded an outright, clear and unequivocal cancellation of the Amman Agreement by Fath as a prerequisite for any reconciliatory dialogue, Hawatima was willing to begin the dialogue as long as there was a promise that the accord would eventually be canceled. This difference of opinion led to serious exchanges between the PDFLP and the more hard-line PFLP and effectively prevented the participation of the PFLP in the reconciliatory dialogue until late November. Until that time, the PDFLP was the main interlocutor with the Fath leadership in the national unity efforts. It is worth noting, however, that 'Arafat refrained from engaging in talks with leaders of the opposition factions; these were carried out on Fath's behalf by Qaddumi, Khalaf and Wazir. 'Arafat continued to play the Jordanian card, hoping that Egypt could facilitate a *rapprochement*. While this two-track policy was typical and probably even necessary, it slowed down efforts to effect a reconciliation, since, when other Fath leaders were promising an annulment of the Amman Agreement to Hawatima, 'Arafat was simultaneously trying to repair his relations with the Hashemite regime. By the end of the year, however, when an understanding appeared to have been reached with the PFLP, the PLO was closer to the holding of a PNC. After numerous delays, the 18th session of the PNC finally convened in Algiers on 20 April 1987.

All the non-Arab venues for the reconciliatory meetings were Soviet and East European — Moscow, East Berlin, and Prague. Indeed, the Soviets and the Algerians were the handmaidens of *rapprochement*. Having influenced 'Arafat into maintaining a firm position in his talks with Husayn (see above), they moved to convince the PDFLP, the PFLP and the Syrian masters of the other factions to reunify the PLO (for Soviet calculations, see essay on the Soviet Union and the Middle East).

The first reconciliation contacts came right after Husayn's speech. During the latter part of February, Wazir met in Prague with the deputy head of the PDFLP, Yasir 'Abd Rabbu, and a representative of the PCP.[127] While little was published about this meeting, according to 'Arafat these talks resulted in the formation of a Palestinian delegation headed by Qaddumi to the 27th Congress of the Communist Party of the Soviet Union.[128]

The PDFLP, which had not joined the PNSF as had the PFLP (see *MECS* 1984–85, p 216) and was therefore less clearly in the opposition, moved immediately to effect a reconciliation based on the cancellation by Fath of the Amman Agreement.[129] Hawatima also proposed that reconciliation take place at the 18th PNC which would supplant the controversial 17th PNC held in Amman in 1984 (on the 17th PNC, see *MECS* 1984–85, pp 181–94). The Aden Accords, ratified in the summer of 1984, which had limited 'Arafat's freedom of movement, would be debated at the PNC (on the Aden Accords, see *MECS* 1983–84, pp 218–21).[130] Khalaf, who had fought strongly within Fath against the signing of the Amman Agreement and for its abrogation following Husayn's speech, kept the track to reconciliation open by calling on all factions to attend a unifying PNC meeting where the cancellation of the agreement would be announced. The PNC could then annul the resolutions of the 17th PNC and even the Cairo Declaration.[131]

It was clear, however, that any convening of the PNC would have to be preceded by the arduous task of gaining a consensus between Fath, the PDFLP and the PFLP. The most significant impetus to this end occurred on 8 April when Algerian President Chedli Benjedid announced that he was prepared to host a new PNC.[132] This contrasted with Algeria's refusal to hold the 17th PNC. The announcement came after Benjedid returned from Moscow, where he probably received Soviet encouragement for the move.

'Arafat and Khalaf both announced Fath's acceptance of the Algerian initiative.[133] On 27 April, the PDFLP published a statement welcoming the initiative, as the pro-'Arafat Muhammad 'Abbas (Abu al-'Abbas) faction of the Palestine Liberation Front (PLF) had done earlier.[134] The reactions of the PFLP and the smaller Syrian-supported organizations of the PNSF were much more tepid. The PFLP paid lip service to the initiative because it did not want to alienate the Algerians. However, it let it be known that the abrogation of the Amman Agreement by Fath was a precondition for participation in any reconciliation meeting prior to a PNC.[135] The PNSF published the contents of a letter sent to Benjedid thanking him for his efforts but emphasizing that solving the PLO crisis had to be based on the "correcting of the deviation of the PLO leadership."[136]

By the end of April, it seemed that the initial optimism accompanying the Algerian initiative had faded. While Syrian opposition prevented the participation of the smaller Damascus-based organizations — the Fath rebels, the Popular Front for the Liberation of Palestine-General Command, the Palestine Popular Struggle Front (PPSF) and al-Sa'iqa, all of which insisted on the ouster of 'Arafat as a prerequisite for reconciliation contacts — there was the initial hope that the prior demands of George Habash would give way and that a reconciliation meeting could be held between Fath, the ALF, the 'Abbas faction of the PLF on the one hand, and the PFLP, PDFLP and PCP on the other.

Habash, however, remained firm. He cast doubt on the seriousness of PLO criticism of Jordan following Husayn's speech, since Fath had refused to abrogate the Amman Agreement.[137] While Khalaf and Qaddumi referred to the accord as something that had only been a "working paper" and not an "agreement," and that was now "dead,"[138] Habash recognized that Fath was not eager to cut relations with Jordan. He asked: "If the agreement is actually dead, then why has there not been an official declaration that it is dead?" Habash insisted that there could be no dialogue between the Fath Central Committee and the PFLP unless there was a previous abolition of the Amman Agreement. Otherwise, he concluded, "we will not be prepared to enter a useless dialogue." In addition to the cancellation of the accord, Habash demanded the establishment of a "truly collective leadership," and a full inquiry into PLO activity since the exit from Beirut.[139]

Habash's stubbornness was not without its positive features for some in the Fath leadership, notably 'Arafat, who continued efforts to repair relations with Jordan. Although he was willing to eventually cancel the accord, its actual official and public cancellation remained the bait for the PFLP. Khalaf maintained that Fath insisted first on a dialogue during which all factions could declare the abrogation of the accord and thereafter present their decision to a new PNC. He admitted that Fath's stand on the timing of the annulment of the agreement was a "tactical matter and [had] nothing to do with the stance toward the Jordanian-Palestinian Agreement."[140]

In mid-April, 'Arafat met with Soviet leader Mikhail Gorbachev at the Congress of the Socialist Union Party of the GDR in East Berlin. This was the first meeting between 'Arafat and a Soviet leader since the death of Yuri Andropov in 1984. PLO radio emphasized the significance of the meeting, stressing that previous problems between the two had not affected "the essence of the relationship between the PLO and Moscow. It can even be said that what had prevailed in the relations between the two aides were only incorrect deductions by those who fish in murky waters, or mere ambiguity necessitated by the situation in the Middle East."[141] It was reported, however, that while Gorbachev agreed to "attempt to contact the Syrian leadership" to persuade it to drop its demand that 'Arafat apologize to it, he seemed to support some of the more extreme preconditions of the Syrian-supported factions, such as the annulment of the Amman Agreement and the resolutions of the 17th PNC. 'Arafat replied that the Fath Central Committee had rejected prior conditions.[142] The meeting put the PLO leadership on notice that while there was Soviet support for 'Arafat as its leader, the USSR expected some concessions. If these led to reconciliation under the Soviet-supported Algerian auspices, then 'Arafat could expect an invitation to visit Moscow.

On 14 May, preliminary discussions were held in Algiers between Fath, the PDFLP and the PFLP. There was little publicity surrounding the meeting and the various groups were represented at a relatively low level. The PFLP representative insisted that the PLO issue an official statement that it no longer abided by the Amman Agreement; 'Arafat refused.[143]

One of the main characteristics of the negotiations was the continuous announcement that a date had been set to convene a PNC or a preliminary comprehensive dialogue. As each date passed, a new date was announced. The announcements came from Fath, which used this as a tactic designed to pressure the PFLP. such was the case in early May, when it was announced that a reconciliatory meeting would be held in Algiers during the middle of Ramadan (around

23 May). The meeting was never held since the PFLP stood by its preconditions.[144]

'Arafat's main goal was to break the Syrian-sponsored PNSF by convincing the PFLP to return to the fold. Indeed, while the PFLP was certainly subject to Syrian pressure because its headquarters were in Damascus, the organization exhibited enough freedom of movement for hope for a reconciliation still to remain. This was not the case with the other factions organized in the PNSF, whose relations with the PFLP grew more estranged as the latter began late in the year to move toward an agreement with Fath. The former Chairman of the PNC, Khalid al-Fahum, presented a program of his own which centered on the abolition of the resolutions of the 17th PNC (which he did not chair) and closer relations with Syria. Several factions within the PNSF insisted that 'Arafat be removed from the PLO leadership.[145] Ahmad Jibril, Secretary-General of the PFLP-GC, maintained that there had been no change in 'Arafat's line that warranted reconciliation and could serve as a basis for the efforts of the Soviets or President Benjedid. "I believe," added Jibril, "that the stories about the reunification of the PLO are nothing but wishful thinking." Referring to the efforts to involve the PFLP, he correctly perceived that the whole reconciliation attempt was aimed at "destroying the [PNSF] from within."[146] Syria also constantly put obstacles in the way of the reconciliation dialogue. In addition to pressuring its client factions to reject the efforts, it was reported that Syria had insisted that the new PNC be held in Damascus.[147] Such a step was inconceivable to 'Arafat, who would do all he could to preserve the PLO's "independent decision making" (*istiqlal al-qarar*).

The summer of 1986 saw intensified reconciliation efforts. In a conciliatory bow to Soviet wishes and in an attempt to strengthen his position in Moscow, 'Arafat signed an agreement in early June with the PCP, a group which at the time was not even represented in the PNC. 'Arafat had agreed to this step in principle in the Aden Accords of 1984 (see *MECS* 1983-84, pp 219-20). The two organizations agreed to coordinate efforts to oppose Israeli and US plans for the occupied territories and welcomed Algeria's call for unity dialogue. Later the same month, "secret" meetings were reported to have been held in Tunis with Fath, the PFLP, the PDFLP and the PCP. Progress was made, apparently, but only between the latter two and Fath, since Habash continued to insist on the cancellation of the Amman Agreement as a prerequisite for an expanded pre-PNC reconciliation meeting. "The abrogation of the Amman Agreement," noted the Political Bureau of the PFLP, "is the true litmus test of the seriousness and credibility of the Fath Central Committee."[148]

Hawatima took the position of mediator between Fath, the PFLP and the other groups in the PNSF. He maintained that if a reconciliation meeting in Algiers could be convened on the basis of the Aden Accords and the resolutions of the 16th PNC, then "automatically this would mean the rejection [by Fath] of the Amman Agreement." Calling upon all factions to attend the proposed meeting in Algiers, he stated that they could present all of their demands there. At the same time, he took 'Arafat to task for his visits to Cairo, which were part of his effort to renew relations with Amman.[149] Hawatima was motivated by his concern to maintain the unity of the PLO, despite his disagreements with the present leadership. Husayn's speech, he maintained, had shown that those who had supported US solutions — 'Arafat and colleagues — and those who had assumed that the current leadership was finished — Habash and the PNSF — were both wrong. This meant that reconciliation was possible if there were no preconditions and ways could be found to end the domination of Palestinian institutions by the Fath Central Committee in an alliance with the "Palestinian *haute bourgeoisie.*"[150]

In July, the Algerian Foreign Minister arrived in Damascus for talks with President Asad and leaders of Syrian-supported Palestinian factions. His goal was to convince the Syrians and the factions to attend a preparatory reconciliation meeting. These Algerian efforts proved futile. On 29 July, a meeting was held in Tunis without the Damascus-based factions. Participating were Fath, the Abu al-'Abbas faction of the PLF, the ALF, and the PDFLP and the PCP. The official spokesman of the PLO, Ahmad 'Abd al-Rahman, stated that the organizations had agreed to call for a PNC to be held "within 45 days."[151] While the meeting was acknowledged in separate statements by the PCP and the PDFLP, the latter denied that it had agreed to a deadline of 45 days for a PNC. It also stressed that it had informed Fath during the Tunis meeting that it would participate in any PNC as long as it was preceded by a comprehensive national dialogue during which the Amman Agreement would be canceled. It was this cancellation, noted the PDFLP, which was the central issue discussed in Tunis. The organization continued to call publicly for the abrogation of the Amman Agreement, but unlike the PFLP, was willing to engage in reconciliation discussions without the cancellation.[152]

The talks held in Tunis continued almost immediately in Moscow, where representatives of Fath, the PDFLP and the PCP held discussions which began on 4 August with Soviet participation.[153] This meeting resulted, apparently, in significant gains, because this time both the PLO spokesman and Hawatima portrayed the discussions favorably. 'Abd al-Rahman stated that the meeting had cleared the road for a dialogue to be held in Algiers, but he made no reference to the Amman Agreement. Hawatima, on the other hand, revealed that the Fath representative to the talks, PLO Executive Committee member Mahmud 'Abbas (Abu Mazin), had pledged to renounce the Amman Agreement. A PDFLP statement termed the meeting "an exceptional event" that had yielded "positive results." Moreover, the statement added, Mahmud 'Abbas had emphasized that the Amman Agreement would not be an obstacle to restoring PLO unity.[154]

The PFLP — in its reaction to the dialogue in Moscow — continued to demand exact formulations. "Palestinian national unity cannot be established, as viewed by some [i.e., the PDFLP], through formal and indulgent methods that are devoid of accurate specifications or through bypassing essential political and organizational issues," it stated. Fath would have to pledge, added the statement, to admit that the 17th PNC was illegal and to sever relations with Morocco and Egypt. Habash demanded that:

> The brothers in Fath must at least give the slightest hint that they will cancel the Amman Agreement and then all will see that the PFLP will open a comprehensive dialogue to define the political and organizational foundations on which Palestinian national unity will be built...We will not accept general and vague formulations in this respect since we are not interested in returning to the language of "yes and no"....[155]

The Fath rebels announced shortly after a meeting with President Asad that they refused to participate in any dialogue which had as its goal the return of 'Arafat to the "revolutionary camp." Jibril rejected the convening of a PNC in Algiers and announced that he differed with the Soviet Union on the Algerian initiative. On 22 August, a spokesman for the PNSF rejected outright the convening of a reconciliation meeting with 'Arafat in Algiers.[156]

The Fath-controlled Voice of Palestine reacted to the above objections by accusing those factions of putting forth "illogical conditions" such as the canceling of the Amman Agreement as a prerequisite for participating in a reconciliation conference in Algeria. "Until when will the factions residing in Damascus continue to act against Palestinian interests and to follow the destructive slogans of Damascus?" demanded the radio's commentator. Khalaf declared that if the factions continued to refuse to participate, the PNC would be convened with whoever showed up. Echoing a statement made often by 'Arafat, he maintained that "the legal formula for canceling the Amman Accord was in the hands of the PNC."[157]

Hawatima's readiness to enter negotiations with Fath necessarily led to tension with the PFLP and other PNSF factions. He reiterated that Fath had pledged in Moscow to abrogate the Amman Agreement, and maintained that some organizations were confusing setting the abrogation of the accord as a condition for initiating national dialogue with setting its abrogation as a condition for restoring unity. The PDFLP's magazine, *al-Hurriyya*, termed the small Syrian-supported factions "nihilistic" and claimed that they were prepared "even to stone the Dome of the Rock if [their] interests demanded it." The PFLP was termed the "hesitating party" which would not move until Arab (i.e., Syrian) approval had been received. A spokesman for the Fath rebels denounced the PDFLP's statements and accused it of being in line with "deviationist policy."[158]

Despite the conflicts with the PFLP and the other PNSF factions, the dialogue, which began in Tunis and was continued in Moscow, kept up its momentum and reconvened again for yet another round in Prague on 1 September. According to Hawatima, the goal of the Prague meeting was to transform what was agreed upon in Moscow into a complete political and organizational document.[159] On 6 September, the three parties to the Prague talks — Fath, the PDFLP and the PCP — issued a joint declaration. The "Prague Declaration" stressed the PLO's commitment to an international peace conference where the PLO would have "independent and equal" representation, a position never accepted by the Jordanians. The parties agreed to strengthen unity in the occupied territories and to fight the Jordanian attempts to find an alternative leadership. In an effort to placate the Asad regime, special mention was made of the need to maintain "brotherly relations" with Syria. With respect to organizational issues, the factions agreed to form the PLO's leadership "according to the organizational points" in the Aden Accords and called for "direct national dialogue in order to reach comprehensive national agreement which would serve as a basis for the convening of a new session of the PNC." This last point seemed a retreat for Fath, which had basically ignored the implementation of the restrictions on 'Arafat's leadership included in the accords. At the controversial 17th PNC, for instance, it was resolved that dialogue be governed by "the spirit" of the Aden Accords, rather than the accords themselves (see *MECS* 1984–85, p 192). The most significant point in the Prague Declaration dealt with the Amman Agreement. Fath emphasized that the Amman Agreement was "no longer operative" (*lam ya'ud al-'amal bihi qa'iman*), and that it "no longer constitutes a basis for the policy of the

PLO."[160] Khalaf expressed the hope that following the Prague Declaration, the PFLP would join the reconciliation talks.[161]

The richness and nuances of the language of diplomatic formulations lent themselves to 'Arafat's policy of leaving options open and saying yes and no at the same time. The Prague Declaration did not explicitly cancel the Amman Agreement, as demanded by most of the other PLO factions. It would have been simple to use the Arabic word for cancel — *ilgha'*— but this was not done. Instead, the agreement was declared only "no longer operative." This formulation was transparent to the factions of the PNSF. Al-Sa'iqa, terming the declaration a "failure" for the Democratic Alliance, said that there was still no decisive position on the Amman Agreement. The PPSF, among its other criticisms of the declaration, saw nothing new in the reference to the Amman Agreement. By declaring that it "was no longer operative" and that it was no longer a basis for the policy of the PLO, Fath had merely restated a reality: namely, that political coordination between the PLO and Jordan had stopped. "We find no signs that the Amman Agreement has been canceled," concluded the PPSF. It added that Fath had failed to cancel the principles mentioned in the accord, such as "territory for peace" and a confederation with Jordan.[162]

That the formulation of the Prague Declaration concerning the Amman Agreement was not decisive became immediately apparent. In an effort to signal 'Arafat that the door was still open, Jordanian officials publicly floated the possibility that the formulation did not come from 'Arafat's faction within Fath.[163] 'Arafat himself asserted a month later in an interview with the Egyptian weekly *October* that he regarded the accord as still valid: "On our side, the Jordanian Agreement stands because it cannot be abrogated except by the PNC, and neither I nor anyone else can cancel it."[164] These were just the type of statements which formed a part of the yes and no policy so bitterly resented by 'Arafat's opponents from within Fath and from without. For this reason they demanded controls on his behavior.

It was apparent that while what had been achieved in Prague was a step toward convening the 18th PNC, there was still much to be done. As noted above, the three sides that had signed the Prague Declaration interpreted it differently — a point that was duly noted by all and that threatened to undermine what had been achieved. Moreover, it was necessary to expand the circle to include — at least — the PFLP. Another round of talks was therefore held in Prague on 18 September at a higher level of representation than the previous round. Fath was represented by al-Wazir and Muhammad Ratib Ghunaym (Abu Mahir), the PDFLP by Hawatima, and the PCP by its Secretary-General, Sulayman al-Najjab. Talks with the same representatives continued in East Berlin in mid-October. Meanwhile, Algerian officials continued their attempts to convince Syria to become involved in the reconciliation process and they also had contacts with the recalcitrant PFLP.[165]

Towards the end of September meetings were held between the PDFLP and the PFLP in which the latter requested that the Prague Declaration be dropped since it was problematic. According to the PFLP the declaration did not cancel the Amman Agreement but only froze it, which was another example of the "yes and no" policy. Moreover, the declaration did not mention relations with Egypt or the Cairo Declaration. The PFLP added that, while the declaration rejected Resolution 242, 'Arafat had accepted it at the Non-Aligned Summit in Harare along with other UN resolutions.[166] The PDFLP and the PCP replied that they had a secret commitment signed by Mahmud 'Abbas that the Fath Central Committee and the PLO Executive Committee would cancel the Amman Agreement with the convening of a united PNC. According to the PDFLP, 'Abbas also agreed on behalf of Fath to implement the organizational reform of the Aden Accords and annul the resolutions of the 17th PNC. With respect to relations with Egypt, these would be up for discussion at the PNC, and Fath promised to abide by the PNC's decision. Hawatima stated that the PFLP promised "to study [the results of the Prague discussion] in a positive spirit."[167]

Yet, for the PFLP, it was just such "secret" commitments that were at the heart of the problem. In a statement following a special session of the PFLP Central Commitee which met from 27–29 September, Habash took issue with the same points that Hawatima had said were dealt with in 'Abbas's secret commitment. The Amman Agreement would have to be canceled publicly and officially, relations would have to be severed with Egypt and the 17th PNC declared divisionist and illegal. Once the Amman Agreement had been publicly canceled, a comprehensive national dialogue could begin. Habash also accused 'Arafat of acting for the past 20 years as if the PLO were his personal property. Clearly, the Prague Declaration, while acknowledged by Habash as "a step seeking national unity," was not to be the basis for national reconciliation. This stand received Syria's blessing, and the PFLP leader's statement was broadcast on Radio Damascus's special Palestine program.[168]

The PDFLP took issue strongly with the tactics of the PFLP. The PFLP's demand to "officially" abrogate the Amman Agreement was ridiculous, wrote *al-Hurriyya*, since that would have to be done by the Executive Committee elected at the 17th PNC — which had been boycotted by the PFLP and was perceived as illegal. Furthermore, argued the PDFLP, the present Executive Committee was overwhelmingly pro-Jordanian and would never abolish the accord; that is why there was a need to convene a new PNC in order to elect a new Executive Committee.[169]

The PFLP, therefore, continued to put off a reconciliation meeting in Algiers. In mid-October, it was reported that Fath was about to issue a call for a new PNC to be held in the second half of November.[170] The Amman Agreement would be discussed at that PNC. The PLO representative in Saudi Arabia, Rafiq al-Natsha (Abu Shakir), declared that the PNC would convene with the factions that presented themselves.[171] Such statements had the effect of being ultimatums as well as threats. If the PFLP stayed out of the pre-PNC negotiations, then it ran the risk of losing any control whatsoever over 'Arafat and of not being represented in the decision-making bodies of the PLO. It remained unclear at the time whether such pressure tactics would produce results.

Five Palestinian organizations (the PDFLP, Fath, the ALF, the PCP and the Abu al-'Abbas faction of the PLF) met again in Tunis on 22–23 October at the deputy-leader level, with the intention of devising a strategy to involve the PFLP. The meeting ended with a call to convene a PNC "as soon as possible." The parties agreed to dispatch a delegation to Moscow to ask the Soviet Union to mediate with Syria, the PFLP and the other Damascus-based organizations.[172] The absence of a fixed date for the PNC was interpreted by some as intended to leave an opening for the PFLP, but a "high-level Palestinian source" was soon quoted as saying that a pre-PNC reconciliation dialogue would take place in Algeria in November; if the Soviet efforts failed, then it would convene without the other factions.[173] Despite such ultimatums, various Fath officials made an effort to maintain an atmosphere of optimism and openness. Rafiq al-Natsha stressed that Fath was capable of taking steps that went beyond the Prague Declaration since the organization considered the Amman Agreement to "be nothing but a corpse."[174]

The efforts of Moscow and Algiers eventually began to pay off. Events in Lebanon, where the Syrian-backed *Amal* militia was engaging Palestinians of all factions in increasingly fierce fighting (see below), may also have finally convinced Habash that Syria could not be counted on. Habash, who had always tried to maintain some freedom from Damascus, could not afford to be perceived as a Syrian puppet when Syrian clients were killing Palestinians in Lebanon. Furthermore, with the Amman Agreement nearly dead as a result of his efforts, Habash, as a veteran Palestinian leader, could afford to ignore Syrian wishes. From 17–25 November, therefore, Habash consented and attended meetings in Prague and Moscow with Wazir. It was the first known meeting between the two in the last three years. Wazir described the meetings as "useful and fruitful."[175] A PFLP statement was less enthusiastic, noting only that Habash had presented the views of his organization to Wazir.[176] It was later reported, however, that the two leaders had agreed to concentrate on what Wazir termed "common denominators that could form a foundation for cooperation during the current difficult circumstances." These were coordination in the armed struggle in the occupied territories and in the camps war in Lebanon. The latter point, of course, had implications for the PFLP's relations with Syria.[177]

During the discussions, Wazir presented Habash with a four-point working paper:

1. The Prague declaration would be regarded in its entirety as a basis which committed all sides.
2. Fath's Central Committee promised to uphold the cancellation of the Amman Agreement on the eve of the comprehensive dialogue held just before the 18th PNC.
3. The arrangements for the PNC would be reached just before the comprehensive national dialogue.
4. The PFLP would announce during the dialogue its withdrawal from frameworks outside the PLO [i.e., the PNSF] and declare its commitment to attend the PNC.

Habash reiterated in reply that the Amman Agreement had to be canceled publicly as a precondition for a pre-PNC national dialogue, while Fath was demanding prior agreement to such a dialogue as the price for canceling the accord. Habash added that Fath's insistence on setting the date and place of the PNC before the pre-PNC dialogue showed that it was not serious about discussing PFLP demands such as organizational and political reform. The PFLP could not be expected to renounce its "national alliances" and to commit itself to a PNC before a national agreement was reached.[178]

The very fact that the PFLP even held such a meeting with Fath was enough to cause serious difficulties in the PNSF. The Fath rebels attacked the meeting and stated that such a step showed that there was no place for the PFLP in the PNSF. It was apparent that they were also worried that cooperation between the PFLP and the 'Arafat loyalists in Lebanon would put them in a difficult position.[179] The PFLP replied that, while no concrete gains had been made in the meetings, Wazir had agreed to present the views of the PFLP to the Fath Central Committee. The PNSF, it noted, was a temporary framework and the PFLP would not let its efforts for reconciliation be supervised by any other group. It was reported that as of 4 December the PFLP was boycotting the meetings of the PNSF.[180] Shaking the foundations of the PNSF was a gain for Fath, as without the PFLP the PNSF was worth little.

The importance of the meetings in Prague and Moscow became readily apparent when both Habash and Wazir continued on to Algiers. The visit was a gesture to Algeria by both organizations and an acknowledgment of its central role in the reconciliation process. Moreover, by visiting the initiator of the process, Habash signified that he was now taking the possibility of reaching an agreement very seriously. The Algerians were honored by the presence of both leaders in the central celebrations of the International Day of Solidarity with the Palestinian People held on 29 and 30 November. At a solidarity rally, the PLO representative to Algeria asked "brother Abu Jihad's permission that the Palestinian revolution's speech be one speech, delivered by Comrade Dr George Habash."[181] Habash gave the speech.

It was clear that the main breakthrough of the PFLP-Fath meetings in Prague, Moscow and Algiers was the fact that they took place. Algerian and Soviet pressure on Habash had worked, and the PFLP boycott of Fath had been broken. As the year drew to a close, the modalities for the convening of the 18th PNC remained to be worked out, but the Palestinian organizations were closer to convening it.

THE RETURN TO LEBANON AND THE WAR OF THE CAMPS

'Arafat's Fath had been returning to Lebanon in a steady trickle since the end of the 1982 war, but during 1986 the pro-'Arafat presence in that country reached new proportions as a result of a new alliance with its former enemy, the Lebanese Forces of President Amin al-Jumayyil. The fluid nature of Lebanese political relationships had brought about, once again, another covenant of convenience (see chapter on Lebanon).

The decision by 'Arafat to enter into an alliance with Jumayyil was a necessary evil which was a corollary of his primary goal: a return to Lebanon. The chaos that reigned in that country combined with the support he enjoyed in the Palestinian refugee camps to make Lebanon an attractive area in which to reestablish his presence. Although such considerations were constant and were indeed behind the permanent flow of his loyalists to Lebanon since after the war, developments in 1986 served as a catalyst to increase 'Arafat's desire to return. The break with Jordan made it more important that the Fath mainstream had a presence in a large Palestinian population concentration. Furthermore, relations with Tunisia were forcing a deployment of forces outside that North African country (see below). According to one report, Fath had established a committee comprising Khalaf, Wazir and Ha'il 'Abd al-Hamid which made several recommendations with respect to the return to Lebanon. In order not to provoke its enemies, Fath decided not to return well-known figures who were particularly objectionable to the Phalangists. Moreover, those "visible" Fath members, such as those on the Central Committee, would not make an appearance in Lebanon. The return would happen first in the Sidon area, where *Amal* was not so strong and where 'Arafat enjoyed the support of the local Sunni militia leader, Mustafa Sa'd. This was in order to give the return the appearance of something that was designed to continue the armed struggle against Israel, and not as being aimed at *Amal* or the Syrians.[182]

'Arafat loyalists returning to Lebanon during the year brought their numbers to an estimated 4,000.[183] Several routes — not without difficulty — were open to those wishing to return. Boats leaving from Cyprus brought loyalists to the port of Khalda, controlled by the Druze Progressive Socialist Party (PSP), and to the port of Sidon, controlled by Mustafa Sa'd's Sunni militia. Those arriving at Beirut International Airport with forged passports would either head north and pass through *Amal*-manned roadblocks for a high price or go through the eastern roadblock, manned by the PSP, as part of larger-scale arrangements involving groups of loyalists, military hardware and buildings in West Beirut.[184]

However, the main factor contributing to the increased loyalist presence in the Beirut camps and those around Tyre and Sidon was the opening of a new route through the Lebanese Forces-controlled port of Juniya, north of Beirut. The loyalists and Jumayyil had two common enemies: *Amal* and Syria. In two interviews in April, Khalaf denied having any contacts with the Phalangists and then only denied having "direct" contacts with Jumayyil.[185] Less than a month later, on 7 May, Khalaf met with Jumayyil in Tunis. According to 'Arafat, the meeting resulted only in the agreement to renew the travel documents of Palestinians resident in Lebanon. Yet there were reports, denied by the PLO leadership, that Jumayyil had provided Khalaf with 6,000 blank Lebanese passports to facilitate the entry of 'Arafat loyalists.[186] Other PLO leaders were less evasive about the nature of the return of Palestinians following the meeting with Jumayyil. Jumayyil, noted Qaddumi, had given refugee passports to Palestinains. "But he who comes with a weapon in his hand," he stressed, "needs no passport."[187] 'Arafat thanked Jumayyil profusely for what he had done "with respect to the tribulations of the Palestinians." On 11 November, the pragmatic *rapprochement* between the two leaders became manifest in the most public way: 'Arafat appeared in a broadcast of the television station of the Lebanese Forces. He admitted that the PLO had "made mistakes" in Lebanon, but now both the Palestinians and the Lebanese were threatened by Syria. The implication was that the two should make common cause against Asad.[188]

Palestinian leaders cited the danger faced by the Palestinian refugee camps in Lebanon as the reason and justification for the return of PLO forces. The "war of the camps" which began in 1985 between the Palestinians and the Syrian-backed *Amal* militia continued with varying degrees of intensity throughout 1986. *Amal* maintained that it should control the South and that the Palestinians were welcome — but not outside the camps and not if they were armed. If they wanted to fight Israel, said Da'ud Da'ud, an *Amal* leader in the South, "then let them enter [*Amal*'s] operations room."[189] *Amal*'s main concern was that the PLO presence should not reach the dimensions it had before the Israeli invasion.

'Arafat and his aides were feeling belligerent as a result of their increasing strength in Lebanon and were not beyond making trouble for the Syrians. Therefore, while sometimes stating that those who had returned to Lebanon were just being united with their families, PLO leaders were very frank about their goals and may have even exaggerated their presence to some extent. Khalaf, for instance, admitted that "under the slogan of preventing the displacement of the Palestinians our fighters fought to defend the camps. Every Palestinian who left Lebanon has returned."[190]

The problems faced by the Palestinians in Lebanon had the effect of unifying the various factions, at least militarily. The PNSF claimed to represent the Palestinians in Lebanon and constantly demanded that it be allowed by *Amal* to deploy throughout the camps. The *Amal* leader, Nabih Barri, correctly perceived that as far as the Palestinian predicament in Lebanon was concerned, "there is no difference here between the PNSF and Abu Ammar ['Arafat]." He rejected PNSF and Syrian proposals that he allow the PNSF to deploy in the camps, on the grounds that once they were allowed to do so, they would join 'Arafat.[191]

Fierce battles continued during the period under review between *Amal* and the Palestinians in the Beirut refugee camps of Sabra, Shatila and Burj al-Barajina. The deployment of a small force of 150 Syrian troops in the area along with Lebanese troops in early July did little to quieten things down. The primary new development in 1986 concerning the Palestinians in Lebanon was the increasing 'Arafat loyalist presence in the camps near Sidon and Tyre. The newfound unity betwen the PFLP and Fath as well as the other organizations brought on by the common threat posed by *Amal* allowed the Palestinians to undertake their first major operation outside of the camps, the capture of the town of Maghdusha which overlooked the refugee camp of 'Ayn al-Hilwa near Sidon. Maghdusha also controled the strategic coastal road.

The situation in the South was characterized by a high degree of tension exacerbated by constant mutual kidnappings and arrests by *Amal* and the Palestinians. Towards the end of September and the beginning of October, *Amal* began a siege of the Palestinians' camp of al-Rashidiyya near Tyre, fearing the growing strength of the Palestinians there. In a retaliatory move later in October, a squad of 'Arafat loyalists stormed the *Amal* base in al-Shawakir near Sidon, killing five militiamen.[192] Sporadic fighting for Maghdusha began in late October. On the night of 23–24 November the Fath-led Palestinians stormed the town and captured it after fierce fighting. This occurred during cease-fire negotiations which were being held in Damascus between *Amal* and the PNSF ('Arafat was not represented) with Syrian, Libyan and Iranian mediation.[193] Israel moved to prevent a consolidation of the Fath successes and attacked 'Arafat loyalist positions in 'Ayn al-Hilwa a day after the victory.

During the negotiations in Damascus, while fighting raged, PNSF representatives complained that *Amal* was not willing to let them keep their weapons and to recognize the Palestinian presence.[194] The main points of disagreement between *Amal* and the Palestinians remained over who went first: *Amal* was not willing to lift the siege of Rashidiyya unless the Palestinians retreated from the positions captured in Maghdusha; the Palestinians wanted assurances that the siege would be fully lifted before they left. Eventually, the PNSF agreed to an Iranian proposal which provided for *Hizballah* men to take over the Palestinian positions. The proposal began to be implemented on 14 December. However, it became immediately clear that the 'Arafat loyalists had no intention of abandoning their position, thus creating a situation where only the PNSF forces began to withdraw.[195] Moreover, the Fath loyalists insisted that any moves in the Sidon area be linked to a cease-fire around the Beirut camps, some of which had been 50–70 per cent destroyed. The Fath refusal to withdraw triggered a heavy artillery bombardment of Burj al-Barajina by *Amal*.[196]

By the end of the year, Fath still held positions in Maghdusha, and the siege of Rashidiyya had not been lifted.

THE PLO IN THE ARAB WORLD

During 1986 the PLO became increasingly isolated in the Arab world with the deterioration in its relations with Jordan (see above) and Tunisia. Relations with

Syria remained tense, and later worsened with the heating up of the war of the camps. Iraq, however, continued its positive relations with the PLO, and 'Arafat and the PLO leadership spent increasingly more time in Baghdad and less time in Tunis. Libya and the PLO began to improve their relations following a meeting between the Libyan leader, Mu'ammar al-Qadhdhafi, and 'Arafat at the Non-Aligned Summit in Harare in September. Libya was also involved in efforts to halt the war of the camps. With Egypt, which tried to mediate between Jordan and the PLO, relations remained correct despite Egyptian disappointment over the failure of the PLO to recognize Resolution 242 (see chapter on inter-Arab relations).

TROUBLE WITH TUNISIA AND IMPROVING RELATIONS WITH IRAQ

The Israeli attack on PLO installations in Tunisia in 1985 (see *MECS* 1984–85, essay on armed opeations) signaled the beginning of the end for the military presence of the PLO there. In May, it was reported that the PLO had closed its camp in the Wadi al-Zarqa area.[197] 'Arafat tried to portray the shrinking PLO presence in Tunisia as a mutually agreed upon step, although it was clearly stated by Tunisian officials that the PLO military installations in Tunisia had been banned.[198] Tunisian discomfort with the PLO grew into anger when in August a Fath Revolutionary Council member based in Tunisia known only as "al-Hawwari" was implicated in an attempt to blow up a synagogue in Casablanca, Morocco.[199] By October, the PLO military presence had reportedly been eliminated in Tunisia and the only offices remaining there were the PLO headquarters, the Information Department and the Political Department.[200]

The positive trend in PLO-Iraqi relations noted in 1985 (see *MECS* 1984–85, p 224) grew stronger in 1986. With the removal of PLO military installations from Tunisia, Iraq became the most important country for the organization's fighters. It was reported that several families of the PLO leadership had moved to Iraq. There were also reports that the PLO was on the verge of moving all of its major offices to Iraq.[201] Unlike several other Arab countries which had made commitments at the 1978 Baghdad summit, Iraq continued — despite the financial burden of the war with Iran — to allocate funds to the PLO.[202]

'Arafat continued wholeheartedly to support Iraq in its war with Iran and lost no opportunity to castigate the Arabs (and the implication was, specifically, Syria) for not coming to the aid of Iraq as specified by the Arab League Charter.[203] In the face of its estrangement from Syria and Jordan, the PLO needed the support of Iraq. By expressing support for Iraq's war efforts, it put itself in the majority Arab camp, opposite its main Arab enemies, Syria and Libya.

NOTES

For the place and frequency of publications cited here, and for the full name of the publication, news agency, radio station or monitoring service where an abbreviation is used, please see "List of Sources." Only in the case of more than one publication bearing the same name is the place of publication noted here.

1. VoP (Baghdad), 26 November — DR, 27 November 1985; *JT*, 15 January 1986; VoP (Baghdad), 25 November — DR, 26 November 1985.
2. AFP, 2 January — DR, 3 January; *al-Siyasa*, Kuwait, 4 January 1986.
3. *Sawt al-Bilad*, 15 January; AFP, 2 January — DR, 3 January 1986.

4. *Al-Usbu' al-'Arabi*, 6 January 1986.
5. R. Monte Carlo, 9 January — DR, 10 January; MAP, 10 January — SWB, 11 January; *al-Ra'y*, 9 January 1986.
6. INA, 13 January — DR, 14 January 1986.
7. VoP (Baghdad), 14 January — DR, 15 January 1986.
8. VoP (Baghdad), 15 January 1986.
9. *Al-Majalla*, 15 January; *al-Majalis*, 12 January 1986.
10. 'Arafat to *al-Bilad*, Cyprus, 15 January; 'Arafat to *al-Musawwar*, 24 January; VoP (Baghdad), 26 January — SWB, 28 January 1986.
11. R. Monte Carlo, 22 January — DR, 22 January 1986.
12. This assertion is contained in Husayn's landmark speech, Amman TV, 19 February — SWB, 21, 22, 24 February; *al-Ra'y*, 20 February 1986 (henceforth, Husayn's Speech). For the US confirmation of this offer, see *JP*, 23 February 1986.
13. For descriptions of the talks and of exchanges between Husayn and 'Arafat, see Husayn's Speech; *al-Sharq al-Awsat*, 21 February; *al-Majalla*, 12 February; *October*, 9 February 1986.
14. *NYT*, 27 January 1986.
15. VoP (Baghdad), 28 January 1986.
16. *October*, 9 February 1986.
17. VoP (Baghdad), 28 January; R. Monte Carlo, 29 January — SWB, 31 January; *JT*, 30 January 1986.
18. *Davar*, 31 January 1986; Husayn's Speech.
19. *Sawt al-Sha'b*, 31 January; *October*, 9 February 1986.
20. *JT*, 30 January; *al-Qabas*, 1 February; KUNA, 2 February — DR, 4 February; VoP (Baghdad), 3 February — DR, 4 February 1986.
21. VoP (Baghdad), 2 February — DR, 4 February; AFP, 2 February — DR, 4 February 1986.
22. *Al-Sharq al-Awsat*, 4 February 1986. On 9 February, Jordanian Prime Minister Zayd al-Rifa'i flew to Syria to inform Asad about the talks with the PLO and officially invite him to Amman.
23. Husayn's Speech.
24. For the text of the three proposals, see *Journal of Palestine Studies*, Vol 15, No 4, Summer 1986, pp 241–42; Vol 16, No 1, Autumn 1986, pp 234–38.
25. From remarks made at a symposium published in *al-Ahram*, 19 February 1986.
26. Husayn's Speech.
27. See, for example, *al-Qabas International*, 5 February; R. Monte Carlo, 8 February 1986.
28. Hani al-Hasan to *al-'Ukaz*, 5 February; 'Arafat to *al-Watan al-'Arabi*, 7 February 1986.
29. 'Arafat to *al-Akhbar*, Cairo, 2 February 1986.
30. *Filastin al-Thawra*, 8 February 1986.
31. See E. Primakov in *Izvestiia*, 28 October 1985.
32. *Al-Majalla*, 12 February; *IHT*, 12 February; *NYT*, 17 February 1986.
33. R. Moscow in Arabic, 10 February 1986.
34. *Ma'ariv*, 11 February 1986.
35. *Al-Sharq al-Awsat*, 11 February; VoP (Baghdad), 10 February — DR, 11 February 1986.
36. *JP*, 11 February 1986.
37. KUNA, 12 February — DR, 13 February; *Ha'aretz*, 16 February; *JP*, 16 February; R. Cairo, 14 February — DR, 18 February; MENA, 15 February — DR, 18 February 1986.
38. MENA, 13 February — DR, 18 February 1986.
39. MENA, 14 February; *al-Tadamun*, 14 February; VoP (Baghdad), 14 February 1986.
40. Husayn's Speech.
41. See Husayn's interview with *al-Siyasa*, 25 February, broadcast on R. Amman, 1 March — SWB, 3 March; *JT*, 1 March 1986.
42. *Al-Sharq al-Awsat*, 21 February; Khalil al-Wazir to *Filastin al-Thawra*, 22 February 1986.
43. R. Riyadh, 20 February; *al-Majalla*, 12 March 1986.
44. *Al-Majalla*, 12 March 1986.
45. *JT*, 22 February; *JT*, 27–28 February; *Ha'aretz*, 28 February; VoP (Baghdad), 20 February — SWB, 25 February 1986.
46. *Al-Dustur*, London, 24 February; *al-Qabas*, 10 March; *al-Yawm al-Sabi'*, 10 March 1986.

47. R. Monte Carlo, 25 February — DR, 26 February 1986.
48. Qaddumi to *al-Bayan*, 21 February 1986.
49. *NYT*, 8 March; *IHT*, 10 March; *al-Majalla*, 12 March 1986.
50. R. Monte Carlo, 5 March — DR, 6 March 1986.
51. PLO Executive Committee Statement, Amman TV, 8 March — DR, 10 March 1986.
52. See, for example, Husayn's statements in *JT*, 23 February; R. Amman, 11 March 1986.
53. *Al-Watan al-'Arabi*, 7 February; *al-Jumhuriyya*, 19-20 February 1986.
54. R. Monte Carlo, 26 February — DR, 28 February 1986.
55. R. Monte Carlo, 21 February 1986.
56. R. Monte Carlo, 20 February; *al-Hadaf*, Damascus, 24 February; *'Al-Hamishmar*, 11 March 1986.
57. *Democratic Palestine*, April 1986.
58. R. Monte Carlo, 24, 28 February 1986.
59. *Democratic Palestine*, April 1986.
60. R. Damascus, 23 February 1986.
61. R. Monte Carlo, 10 March — DR, 11 March; R. Monte Carlo, 10 March — SWB, 11 March 1986.
62. *Al-Qabas*, 17, 18 April; *JT*, 22 February; R. Amman, 21 February 1986.
63. *Al-Musawwar*, 30 May 1986.
64. MENA, 18 May; R. Monte Carlo, 19 May — DR, 20 May; *al-Majalla*, 7 May 1986.
65. *Al-Yawm al-Sabi'*, 19, 26 May 1986.
66. *Ha'aretz*, 1 August; *Ma'ariv*, 5 May; *al-Sharq al-Awsat*, 6 August 1986.
67. *Filastin al-Thawra*, 7 June 1986.
68. *Ha'aretz*, 5 May; KUNA, 6 May; *JP*, 16 June 1986.
69. VoP (Baghdad), 18 June — DR, 19 June 1986.
70. VoP (Baghdad), 20 June — DR, 23 June 1986.
71. *The Guardian*, 20 June 1986.
72. *CSM*, 24 June; details of the plan may be found in *al-Dustur*, Amman, 25, 26 October 1986.
73. VoP (Baghdad), 11 August — DR, 12 August; *al-Majalla*, 13 August; *Filastin al-Thawra*, 30 August 1986.
74. *JT*, 30 September 1986.
75. VoP (Baghdad), 30 September — SWB, 2 October; VoP (Baghdad), 2 July — DR, 3 July; *JP*, 3 July; *NYT*, 9 July; QNA, 30 September 1986.
76. *JT*, 25 February 1986.
77. R. Monte Carlo, 27 March — DR, 28 March; VoP (Baghdad), 28 March — SWB, 1 April 1986.
78. R. Monte Carlo, 2 April — DR, 2, 3 April 1986.
79. QNA, 3 April; *al-Anba'*, 4 April 1986.
80. Al-Wazir to *al-Afaq*, 5 June 1986.
81. 'Arafat to *al-Tadamun*, 14 June 1986.
82. JNA, 7 July — SWB, 9 July; *JT*, 8 July 1986.
83. 'Arafat to *al-Tadamun*, 14 June; and to *al-Siyasa*, Kuwait, 7 July 1986.
84. KUNA, 7 July — SWB, 9 July; R. Monte Carlo, 7, 8 July — DR, 8 July 1986.
85. Jordanian Information Minister, Muhammad al-Khatib, JNA, 21 July — SWB, 23 July; Zayd al-Rifa'i to *al-Majalla*, 23 July; GNA, 24 July; R. Cairo, 16 July 1986.
86. R. Monte Carlo, 7 July 1986.
87. *Der Kurier*, 9 July — DR, 9 July; VoP (Algiers), 10 July — DR, 15 July; R. BBC (in Arabic), 15 July 1986.
88. *Al-Majalla*, 23 July; VoP (Baghdad), 8 July — DR, 9 July; *The Guardian*, 10 July 1986.
89. VoP (Baghdad), 12 July; R. Monte Carlo, 8 July — DR, 10 July; *al-Majalla*, 16 July 1986.
90. *Al-Anba'*, 15 July 1986.
91. KUNA, 26 February — DR, 27 February 1986.
92. MENA, 5 November; Rafiq al-Natsha to R. Monte Carlo, 29 December — DR, 20 December 1986.
93. VoP (Baghdad), 10 August — SWB, 12 August 1986.
94. For example, see Salah Khalaf to GNA, 25 September — DR, 26 September 1986.
95. *JP*, 19 October 1986.

96. R. Monte Carlo, 7 April — DR, 7 April 1986.
97. *Al-Majalla*, 12 March 1986.
98. Khalaf to *al-Anba'*, 11 April 1986.
99. KUNA, 7 April — DR, 8 April 1986.
100. *Al-Siyasa*, Kuwait, 9 April 1986.
101. *Al-Anba'*, 21 April 1986.
102. For details on 'Atallah's biography and the background to the uprising, see *al-Qabas International*, 8 April; *Ha'aretz*, 22 April, 5 May; *The Guardian*, 25 April; R. Monte Carlo, 9 April — DR, 10 April; *al-Majalla*, 16 April; *al-Dustur*, London, 21 April 1986.
103. *Al-Shira'*, Beirut, 10 February 1986.
104. *Al-Hadaf*, Damascus, 7 April; *al-Bayan*, 9 April; *Ha'aretz*, 8 April; *al-Majalla*, 30 April; *Akhir Sa'a*, 4 June 1986.
105. *Al-Bayan*, 20, 26 March; *al-Jumhuriyya*, 14 April 1986.
106. R. Monte Carlo, 11 April; *al-Anba'*, 4 April 1986. Ghazi 'Atallah was one of the Fath officers promoted in 1983 in a move that was to spark the uprising led by Sa'id Musa (Abu Musa).
107. R. Monte Carlo, 22 April — DR, 23 April; MENA, 23 April; *al-Watan*, 23 April 1986.
108. QNA, 14 April; R. Monte Carlo, 24 April — SWB, 28 April; AFP, 24 April 1986.
109. R. Monte Carlo, 28 April — SWB, 28 April; QNA, 28 April; JP, 29 April 1986.
110. R. Monte Carlo, 1 June — DR, 2 June; *Ma'ariv*, 2 June; *al-Akhbar*, Cairo, 3 June; *Akhir Sa'a*, 4 June; *JP*, 20 June 1986. Accounts of PLO financial mismanagement are myriad; see, for example, *WSJ*, 21 July; *Newsweek*, 7 April; *FR*, 3 July 1986.
111. *Al-Ra'y al-'Amm*, 14 June; *al-Bayan*, 10 July; KUNA, 14 July; *al-Masir*, 15 April 1986.
112. *JP*, 12, 22, 26 December; *Ma'ariv*, 15 December; *Yedi'ot Aharonot*, 18 December; VoI, 21 December — DR, 22 December 1986.
113. *Al-Watan*, 18 April 1986.
114. *Al-Ittihad*, Abu Dhabi, 14 April 1986.
115. *Akhir Sa'a*, 11 June 1986.
116. *Al-Anba'*, 27 April; *Akhir Sa'a*, 7 May; *al-Usbu' al-'Arabi*, 28 April 1986.
117. *Al-Ittihad*, Abu Dhabi, 14 April; *al-Usbu' al-'Arabi*, 28 April 1986.
118. Salah Khalaf to *al-Anba'*, 11 April 1986.
119. Salah Khalaf to *al-Akhbar*, Cairo, 9 June 1986.
120. R. Monte Carlo, 4 June 1986.
121. 'Atallah to *Kull al-'Arab*, 12 November 1986.
122. *Al-Bayan*, 20 May; *al-Tali'a al-'Arabiyya*, 5 May 1986.
123. *Al-Qabas International*, 30 May; *al-Bayan*, 27 August 1986.
124. 'Atallah often boasted that "files contain a lot. When I find it necessary I will turn over these files." For this and similar statements see *al-Watan*, 18 April; *Akhir Sa'a*, 7 May 1986.
125. Salah Khalaf to *al-Siyasa*, Kuwait, 4 January; *al-Majalis*, 12 January 1986.
126. Khalaf to R. Monte Carlo, 25 February — DR, 26 February 1986.
127. *JP*, 26 February; *NYT*, 23 February, 2 March 1986.
128. 'Arafat to *al-Qabas*, 10 March 1986.
129. Hawatima to R. Monte Carlo, 26 February — DR, 28 February; *al-Hurriyya*, 3, 16 March 1986.
130. *MM*, 3 March 1986.
131. *Al-Anba'*, 4 April 1986.
132. VoP (Algiers), 9 April — DR, 10 April 1986.
133. VoP (Algiers), 9 April — DR, 10 April; KUNA, 10 April — DR, 11 April 1986.
134. QNA, 27 April; APS, 10 April — DR, 11 April 1986.
135. QNA, 10 April; KUNA, 13 April — DR, 14 April 1986.
136. R. Monte Carlo, 25 April 1986.
137. Habash to *al-Bayan*, 24 May 1986.
138. Khalaf to *al-Anba'*, 11 April; Qaddumi to *al-Anba'*, 15 April 1986.
139. Habash to *al-Bayan*, 24 May; Habash to *al-Shira'*, Beirut, 21 April 1986.
140. Khalaf to *al-Anba'*, 11 April 1986.
141. VoP (Baghdad), 20 April — DR, 21 April; VoP (Baghdad), 21 April — DR, 22 April 1986.
142. *Al-Qabas*, 22 April 1986.

143. KUNA, 15 May — DR, 16 May; KUNA, 19 May 1986.
144. QNA, 21 May — DR, 23 May 1986.
145. *Al-Bayan*, 28 May; *al-Shira'*, Beirut, 7 April; ENA, 30 May — DR, 30 May 1986.
146. Jibril to *al-Bayan*, 2 June 1986.
147. KUNA, 30 May — DR, 2 June 1986.
148. VoP (Baghdad), 3 June — SWB, 5 June; *al-Watan*, 1 June; *al-Bayan*, 23 June; R. Monte Carlo, 3 July 1986.
149. Tanjug, 5 June 1986.
150. Hawatima to *al-Hawadith*, London, 20 June 1986.
151. *Al-Majalla*, 9 July; QNA, 30 July; R. Monte Carlo, 30 July — DR, 31 July; VoP (Baghdad), 31 July — DR, 1 August; *JP*, 31 July; *The Guardian*, 1 August 1986.
152. R. Monte Carlo, 2 August — DR, 4 August; *al-Khalij*, 3 August 1986.
153. KUNA, 1 August; GNA, 3 August 1986.
154. QNA, 10 August — DR, 12 August; Hawatima to QNA, 15 August; Hawatima to R. Monte Carlo, 11 August — DR, 12 August; R. Monte Carlo, 8 August — DR, 8 August 1986.
155. R. Monte Carlo, 10, 11 August — DR, 11 August; Habash to *al-Khalij*, 20 August 1986.
156. *Al-Khalij*, 12 August; R. Monte Carlo, 13 August — DR, 13 August; R. Monte Carlo, 22 August; *IHT*, 26 August 1986.
157. VoP (Baghdad), 9 August; Salah Khalaf to *al-Jazira*, 6 August 1986.
158. GNA, 20 August — DR, 21 August; *al-Hurriyya*, 31 August; R. Monte Carlo, 21 August — DR, 22 August 1986.
159. QNA, 3 September — DR, 3 September 1986.
160. The full text of the Prague Declaration was published in the Fath-dominated PLO organ, *Filastin al-Thawra*, 13 September 1986.
161. KUNA, 7 September — DR, 9 September 1986.
162. R. Monte Carlo, 8 September — DR, 9 September; *Nidal al-Sha'b*, 22 September 1986.
163. QNA, 7 September 1986.
164. *JP*, 19 October 1986.
165. *Al-Bayan*, 20 September; ENA, 16 October — DR, 17 October; *al-Siyasa*, Kuwait, 17 October; QNA, 25 October; *JP*, 25 September 1986.
166. In a speech to the plenum, 'Arafat had announced that the PLO accepted 242 and 338 along with other relevant UN resolutions. This was similar to the formulation contained in the three proposals submitted by Husayn to the US in January (see above).
167. *Al-Ittihad*, Abu Dhabi, 21 September; *al-Bayan*, 21 September; *al-Riyad*, 18 September 1986.
168. R. Monte Carlo, 30 September; R. Monte Carlo, 4 October — DR, 6 October; R. Damascus, 5 October — SWB, 7 October 1986.
169. *Al-Hurriyya*, 12 October 1986.
170. *Al-Bayan*, 14 October 1986.
171. Al-Natsha to *al-Anba'*, 31 October 1986.
172. KUNA, 22 October; AFP, 23 October; MENA, 23 October; *JP*, 24 October; R. Monte Carlo, 24 October — DR, 27 October; ENA, 25 October — DR, 27 October 1986.
173. GNA, 30 October 1986.
174. KUNA, 12 November 1986.
175. R. Monte Carlo, 19 November — DR, 20 November; QNA, 20 November 1986.
176. KUNA, 21 November — SWB, 24 November 1986.
177. *Al-Anba'*, 26 November; KUNA, 25 November 1986.
178. *Al-Hadaf*, Damascus, 1 December; R. Monte Carlo, 22 November — DR, 25 November 1986.
179. R. Monte Carlo, 24 November 1986.
180. *Al-Hadaf*, Damascus, 1 December; *al-Ra'y al-'Amm*, 6 December 1986.
181. VoP (San'a), 1 December — DR, 2 December; *al-Ittihad al-'Usbu'i*, 27 November 1986.
182. *Al-Majalla*, 16 April; *The Economist*, 13 December 1986.
183. *Ha'aretz*, 29 January 1986, 13, 15 May 1987.
184. *Ha'aretz*, 27 April; Ahmad Jibril to *al-Shira'*, Beirut, 16 June 1986.
185. Khalaf to *al-Majalla*, 16 April; Khalaf to *al-Qabas*, 17 April 1986.

186. 'Arafat to *al-Watan al-'Arabi*, 30 May; ENA, 6 June — DR, 9 June; *al-Bayan*, 22 June 1986.
187. Qaddumi to *Svenska Dagbladet*, 29 October — DR, 3 November 1986.
188. 'Arafat to *al-Watan al-'Arabi*, 30 May; 'Arafat to Lebanese Broadcasting Corporation (Lebanese Forces TV), 11 November; *The Guardian*, 13 November; *JP*, 14 November 1986.
189. Da'ud Da'ud to *al-Qabas*, 22 August 1986.
190. Salah Khalaf to *al-Ittihad*, Abu Dhabi, 8 November 1986.
191. Barri to VoL, 23 June — SWB, 25 June 1986.
192. *JP*, 24 October 1986.
193. VoP (Baghdad), 24 November — SWB, 26 November; *JP*, 25 November; *IHT*, 25 November; *Ha'aretz*, 26 November 1986.
194. R. Monte Carlo, 1 December — DR, 2 December 1986.
195. VoL, 14 December — DR, 15 December; R. Beirut, 14 December — DR, 14 December 1986.
196. VoP (Baghdad), 15 December — SWB, 17 December; *JP*, 15 December 1986.
197. *Al-Majalis*, 31 May 1986.
198. 'Arafat to *al-Sharq al-Awsat*, 29 September; Tunisian Foreign Minister Hedi Mabrouk to *al-Ittihad*, Abu Dhabi, 17 October 1986.
199. KUNA, 14 September; *IHT*, 29 September; *al-Majalla*, 1 October 1986.
200. *Al-Qabas*, 9 October; Qaddumi to *The Guardian*, 23 October 1986.
201. *JP*, 14 February; KUNA, 14 September; ENA, 1 October — DR, 1 October 1986.
202. *Al-Watan*, 2 January; *al-Ra'y al-'Amm*, 12 October; *al-Yawm al-Sabi'*, 20 October 1986.
203. VoP (Baghdad), 25 February — DR, 26 February; 'Arafat to *al-Dustur*, London, 4 February 1986.

The West Bank and the Gaza Strip

ELIE REKHESS

THE ISRAELI GOVERNMENT AND THE LOCAL POPULATION

THE SECURITY SITUATION: TERROR AND RIOTS

In 1986 there was a marked decrease in terrorist activity against Israelis in the West Bank and the Gaza Strip. The number of Israelis killed dropped to two, from seven in 1985, while 62 were injured compared with 99 in 1985. The noticeable change was partly attributed to the authorities' success in stopping the smuggling of weapons over the Jordan river bridges. In three incidents, however, guns were used. It was believed that they had been stolen from Israeli soldiers and army camps and later sold to terrorists by Israeli Arabs acting as intermediaries. As in previous years, the lack of arms led local terror groups to carry out more sophisticated and audacious attacks. The more frequent and sporadic use of homemade bombs ("Molotov cocktails") and knives indicated that the new generation of Palestinian youth in the West Bank had managed to overcome the barrier of fear in confronting the Israel Defense Forces (IDF). Military sources in Israel pointed out that a substantial number of operations directed against Israeli targets were carried out by Palestinian security convicts released in the May 1985 prisoner exchange[1] (see *Middle East Contemporary Survey* [*MECS*] 1984–85, p 236).

The change in terrorist tactics was clearly demonstrated in the Gaza Strip. After a relatively lengthy period of quiet, the Gaza region witnessed a time of intensive armed operations against Israeli targets. The head of the IDF's Southern Command, while seeing the Gaza situation as "tolerable," nevertheless admitted that two types of renewed terrorist activity had caused particular concern. One was the planting of roadside bombs, which were activated against Israeli civilians and military vehicles in a preplanned and organized manner. The other involved indiscriminate knife attacks.[2] In late September and early October 1986 two Israeli taxi drivers, Haim Azran and Israel Kitaro, were stabbed to death by knife-wielding assailants at the Gaza city market and garage area.

Disturbances of public order by West Bank and Gaza Strip inciters and demonstrators declined significantly during the first three months of the year. Commuters in the area were less likely to be stoned or stopped by burning tires or roadblocks erected by local residents. The number of stone throwing incidents and similiar disturbances was believed to have dropped due to the stricter security policy imposed by the IDF in 1985 (see *MECS* 1984–85, pp 237–38). It was also the result of mass arrests of teenagers involved in this kind of activity and of stiffer jail sentences.

The situation changed drastically in March 1986 when Israeli troops were compelled to use force to control nationalist demonstrations to commemorate "Land Day."[3] In

Gaza, a teenager was shot and killed after he hurled a homemade petrol bomb at a passing Israeli patrol. In Bir Zayt, about 100 students gathered at the university campus, erected a roadblock, burned tires and threw stones at passing Israeli cars. When the students did not obey orders to stop, shots were fired at their legs and several of them were seriously wounded. In mid-May, security forces again opened fire at students, this time at al-Najah University in Nablus. They were protesting against an Independence Day march organized in the region by *Gush Emunim*, the Jewish settlement movement. The Arab demonstrators stoned cars and smashed the windshields of army vehicles. Troops opened fire in an attempt to contain the rioters. Two students suffered gunshot wounds. In September, violent clashes erupted in the Gaza Strip between security forces and demonstrators marking the fourth anniversary of the Sabra and Shatila massacre. As a result, a youth was wounded and subsequently died.

The most serious wave of riots swept the territories in December. On 4 December, two Bir Zayt University students were killed and 12 wounded when IDF troops opened fire in what was described as the "worst West Bank campus incident since 1967"[4] (for details of previous riots at Bir Zayt, see *MECS* 1984–85, p 237).

The killings set off six consecutive days of unrest and violence. On 5 December, Israeli troops shot and killed a 14-year-old boy in the Balata refugee camp near Nablus, after an army patrol was attacked by stone-throwers. Four days later another teenager in Gaza was shot and fatally wounded by the IDF. The week of rioting against Israeli forces resulted in three residents being killed and approximately 20 injured.

The immediate reason for the mounting tension in Bir Zayt was the introduction of a policy of tighter control by the military authorities. The Arab protest was focused against the roadblocks and checkpoints the Army set up in the neighborhoods around the university. West Bank Palestinian sources claimed that the newly introduced identification procedures caused continuous delays and, in fact, forced the total suspension of classes.

Israeli spokesmen attributed the unrest to the 25 November anniversary of the 1947 United Nations partition vote on Palestine. Observers noted that the riots also reflected growing support of the PLO, following the strategic gains of Palestine Liberation Organization (PLO) forces in fighting against the *Amal* Shi'i militia in South Lebanon. Brig Gen Ephraim Sneh, head of the West Bank Civil Administration, asserted that the eruption of simultaneous demonstrations throughout the territories indicated a concerted effort by local PLO supporters to exploit anger over the Bir Zayt killings to stir up anti-Israeli hostility. Israeli commentators further contended that the PLO was attempting to stage a comeback in the region following Israeli and Jordanian moves to increase Jordanian influence at the expense of the PLO[5] (see below).

The series of killings by IDF troops drew sharp criticism in Israel especially after Bir Zayt students claimed that the troops had treated them brutally, using live ammunition almost from the outset. "The soldiers shot to kill," they said. Left-wing politicians and the Press condemned the soldiers' conduct, asking whether the Army should have responded so fiercely. The Peace Now movement demanded that a commission of inquiry be set up to investigate the shootings. Maj Gen Ehud Barak, the commanding officer of Central Command, expressed regret over the fatal incidents but maintained that the soldiers "acted with the utmost restraint and did not shoot unless there was a real danger."[6] Military investigators reportedly found that the troops had followed military open-fire ordinance. Army spokesmen argued that the soldiers had shot only at the legs of the demonstrators, after firing warning shots in the air, tear-gas canisters and rubber bullets.[7]

After peace had been restored in the area, a high-level army source said that the IDF was intensively seeking alternative systems and improved equipment to help it deal with violent demonstrations and to avoid having to use live ammunition. However, he added, there was no intention of changing standing orders on when and how to open fire when soldiers faced situations that endangered their lives.[8]

STRICTER SECURITY MEASURES

Although the basic guidelines of Israel's security policy in the territories remained unchanged, the Government nevertheless pursued its August 1985 decision to renew deportation and administrative detention of subversive elements. The hard-line policy had been reintroduced in response to pressures from Jewish settlers demanding a harsher approach toward Arab law-breakers after a wave of West Bank violence (see *MECS* 1984–85, pp 236–37).

Since November 1985 nearly 100 people had been placed under administrative detention. They were mostly student leaders, trade union organizers and suspected PLO activists. In mid-March 1986, the authorities began to release some of the detainees because the periods fixed in their arrest orders had elapsed. Most were held for six months, the maximum period allowed by law. By late October, only 30 West Bank and Gaza Strip residents remained under detention.[9]

Special action was taken against trade unionists in an attempt to curb their growing influence. In August 1986 the authorities issued town restriction orders against three leading figures: Shihada Minawi, head of the General Federation of West Bank Unions; Adnan Kilani, head of the Construction Workers' Union in Y'abad; and Amal Wahdan, member of the Women's Work Committee. Minawi, the most prominent of the three, was accused of being an active member of Fath, while Wahdan was said to be a member of the Popular Democratic Front for the Liberation of Palestine (PDFLP).[10]

A few weeks later the Army closed down two trade union headquarters in Nablus. Military spokesmen claimed that the two offices were engaged in subversive activities, such as recruiting members for the PDFLP, organizing political rallies and distributing leaflets. In a separate raid in Hebron, Ahmad Ziyada, head of the local trade union, was served with a six-month administrative arrest order.[11]

On 31 January 1986, the Army expelled to Jordan three West Bank residents for having allegedly organized local cells of the PDFLP and conducting subversive activity. The three were Dr 'Azmi Shu'aybi, a dentist who had served as deputy mayor of al-Bira until the City Council was dissolved in 1982; 'Ali Abu Hilal, a leader of the Construction Workers' Union in Abu Dis; and Hasan 'Abd al-Jawad, a Duhaysha refugee camp activist. The expulsion date was set after they withdrew their appeals to the High Court claiming that they would not get a fair hearing. Another leading PLO supporter, Zaki Istatiyya, of the Jabaliya refugee camp in Gaza, was deported in late April, bringing to 34 the number of Palestinians expelled since August 1985.[12] Most of those expelled were former prisoners released in the May 1985 controversial exchange of 1,150 Arab prisoners for three Israeli soldiers captured in Lebanon.

The deportation orders generated wide criticism both locally and internationally. "This is one of the worst policies," protested Faysal al- Husayni, an acknowledged Fath supporter and head of the Jerusalem Arab Studies Society. "We are in our homeland and a foreign power is trying to uproot us," he maintained.[13] In response, Israeli officials argued that the number of deportees was small and that the Government was acting under the 1945 emergency regulations inherited from the British Mandate.

Shmuel Goren, the Coordinator of Government Activities in the Territories, justified the stricter policy by saying it had been put into effect to secure calm in the region. Since it was reintroduced, he claimed at the beginning of 1986, the number of disturbances had declined considerably.[14] However, the fatal events at Bir Zayt in December 1986 (see above) proved the opposite.

The Government also reacted firmly against the East Jerusalem Press. The growing importance of the Arab newspapers as a mobilized and partisan Press serving PLO targets had led to strained relations with the Israeli authorities. The military censorship often banned large parts of submitted material. Distribution of the papers was occasionally delayed because of suspected violations of censorship.

On 12 August, the East Jerusalem daily *al-Mithaq* and the biweekly *al-'Ahd* were closed by the Interior Ministry. Both publications were known to be expressing the views of the radical left opposition in the PLO. They were banned because they were allegedly directed and operated by the Popular Front for the Liberation of Palestine (PFLP). The owners petitioned the High Court of Justice against the closure. They enlisted Israeli public opinion, particularly among their colleagues in Jerusalem who regarded the shutdown as a violation of elementary right of freedom of expression. The Higher Court, however, ruled differently. The prime reason for revoking the papers' licenses, it said, was not "one or another opinion" but the "extensive organizational involvement of the Popular Front in the operations and financing of the publications."[15]

A similar debate was sparked at the end of 1986 when Akram Haniyya, the editor of *al-Sha'b*, was issued with a deportation order for engaging in hostile activity. Again, Israeli public opinion opposed the motive behind the deportation: it was argued that the measure had been taken because of Haniyya's political views. The authorities could not give a full explanation and the Military Government found itself in a bind: it could not publicize the evidence against Haniyya for fear of exposing the sources of the incriminating information and the manner in which it had been obtained. The classified material could only be presented to the court.

Shortly before his case was to be heard, Haniyya withdrew his petition to the High Court and accepted the administrative deportation order from the commanding officer of Central Command. He had apparently concluded that his chances of convincing the judges of his innocence were slim. Only after his deportation, at the end of December 1986, did the security services allow some of the evidence against him to be published.

It appeared that Haniyya had served as one of Fath's senior commanders in the territories. He had not been personally involved in terrorist acts but had allegedly attempted to strengthen the organizations locally by funneling money to them. The authorities also claimed that Haniyya had been in charge of formulating PLO policy in the territories. According to the security sources, he had latterly been trying to establish a local Fath headquarters which would coordinate reports, distribute funds and issue instructions.[16]

IMPROVING THE QUALITY OF LIFE

As in the previous year, the Defense Ministry continued to make considerable efforts to "improve the quality of life in the territories." Progress was achieved: new medical equipment was installed in West Bank and Gaza hospitals; free medical care was offered for children up to the age of three; new telephone systems were introduced; restrictions on direct dialing and telex communications were almost eliminated; some $3m was invested in providing electricity to Nablus and 30 neighboring villages; some $340m had been brought into the West Bank and Gaza Strip since the authorities lifted in May 1985 all restriction on the transfer of funds from Jordan and other Arab countries; greater flexibility was shown in approving economic projects that did not compete with Israeli industries; and international organizations were given permission to operate in the territories and maintain permanent representation there.[17] (For a similar list of projects see *MECS* 1984–85, pp 238–39).

In sharp contrast to the official viewpoint, which expressed reserved satisfaction with what had been done, West Bank public opinion suggested that the Government's achievements in improving the standard of living were ambiguous, at best. West Bank political circles asserted, *The New York Times* reported, that in some key aspects of daily life, such as administrative detention or the deportation of Palestinian activists (see above), there had been a change for the worse. Another area in which there had been a deterioration was in the issuing of permits for the reunion of the many West Bank families that have relatives in Jordan. In 1985, only about 300 such permits were granted, compared with more than 1,000 in 1984, apparently in an attempt to slow the rate of increase in the Arab population.[18]

Prime Minister Shimon Peres attached great significance to improving the quality of life in the territories. He was eager to prove to the American Administration that Israel was committed to bringing about a socioeconomic change in the area, despite the political stalemate. The Coordinator of the Government Activities in the Territories, Shmuel Goren, was dispatched in March to the US to discuss with Assistant Secretary of State Richard Murphy a new $500m development plan aimed at raising the standard of living.

The plan comprised three major elements: (a) construction of industrial parks near central West Bank and Gaza cities in order to provide local sources of employment for the population in the areas; (b) development of an infrastructure of public services, such as job-training programs, schools, and hospitals; (c) promotion of urban projects designed to modernize and develop water and sewerage systems.

Goren had also conferred with representatives of private and Government-supported US aid agencies such as the American Near East Refugee Agency, as well as with the directors of the UN Development Programme. He investigated the possibility of these organizations helping to finance or extend credit for the proposed socio-economic schemes.[19]

West Bank public opinion was skeptical about Israel's ability to raise the necessary funds and the international agencies' willingness to contribute the money. PLO supporters doubted the sincerity of the Israeli move, and pointed to the Likud's strong opposition to any substantial move to strengthen the Arab economy in the territories. Goren's trip was strongly criticized by the Arab Press. *Al-Fajr*, for example, wrote that his plan was only intended to "take away the legitimate Palestinian rights and replace them with social-material benefits." The paper predicted that the West Bankers "will defeat the Goren Plan in the same manner they defeated the Camp David Accords."[20]

THE APPOINTMENT OF ARAB MAYORS

The introduction of the new development plan coincided with growing attempts on behalf of the Israeli Government to further devolve power to the local leadership.

Following the successful appointment of Zafir al-Masri as mayor of Nablus in November 1985 (see *MECS* 1984–85, pp 240–42) and in the wake of the stalemate in negotiations between Jordan and the PLO, the Israeli Prime Minister, Shimon Peres, declared in February 1986 that the Government should "aspire to enable the Arabs [of the West Bank] to run their lives by themselves." Peres' statement was interpreted as a prelude to the implementation of "unilateral autonomy."[21]

However, the assassination of al-Masri on 2 March 1986 dealt a severe blow to the Israeli plan to appoint representatives of the local population as mayors. The murder was condemned in what one commentator described as "a rare chorus of unanimity" that seemed to cross political barriers. The PLO Chairman, Yasir 'Arafat, who had neither condemned nor condoned al-Masri's appointment, strongly denounced the killing. He reportedly sent a message of condolences to the family in which he expressed regret over the death of "our heroic martyr." An official PLO statement described al-Masri as a "nationalist symbol of the Palestinian struggle." Jordan, which had tacitly approved al-Masri's appointment similarily described the murder as a "new act of criminal terrorism directed against the Palestinian cause."[22]

In the West Bank all political groupings except the radical supporters of the PFLP reacted with shock and resentment. Most East Jerusalem dailies, excluding *al-Mithaq*, carried strongly worded editorials denouncing the killing. *Al-Sha'b*, for example, wrote on 3 March that the act was contrary to the Palestinian people's "revolutionary traditions." Bassam Shak'a, the deposed mayor of Nablus who had publicly opposed al-Masri's move, also declared his outright condemnation of the murder. More moderate figures such as Elias Freij, the mayor of Bethlehem, said that al-Masri's death could only have an adverse effect on the peace process. West Bank nationalist circles, however, though not openly supporting the murderous act, stated that it served as a warning to both Israel and Jordan not to exclude the PLO and its followers in the West Bank from the processes that determined their own fate.[23]

The pronounced sorrow expressed by tens of thousands of mourners at al-Masri's funeral was interpreted as a most powerful demonstration of West Bank solidarity with the PLO. In the procession, hundreds of youths wearing the traditional head-covering waved the banned Palestinian flag, chanted national slogans and carried portraits of Yasir 'Arafat. The funeral was like a referendum, said Hana Siniora, the editor- in-chief of *al-Fajr*: "The [West Bank] Palestinians voted overwhelmingly for 'Arafat."[24]

Al-Masri's death dealt a major blow to Prime Minister Peres' efforts to provide the inhabitants of the West Bank and the Gaza Strip unilaterally with a measure of political autonomy by allowing them a more active role in administering their municipal affairs. Brig Gen Sneh conceded that the murder had been designed to deter potential appointees from cooperating with the Israeli authorities.[25]

Shortly after the killing, individuals and groups who had been approved by the Israelis as future members of Municipal Councils in other West Bank towns began to retract their initial consent. Nadim Zaru, an ex-Jordanian Cabinet Minister who was expected to apply for the mayoral appointment in Ramallah, published a personal notice in the East Jerusalem Press denying that he had ever sought the mayoralty. In al-Bira, Jamil Tarifi, the deposed Deputy Mayor and a known Fath backer, also withdrew his candidacy. In Hebron, Muhammad Rashid Ja'bari, head of the city's Education Department, announced that press reports indicating his intention to apply for a mayoral appointment were "incorrect."[26]

Despite the public withdrawals, Peres announced that the fatal incident would not deter the Israeli Cabinet from carrying out its original plans. Several months later, contacts between Israel, Jordan and local representatives were resumed. In June 1986, three potential candidates, Ja'bari of Hebron, Khalil Musa Khalil of Ramallah, and Walid Mustafa of al-Bira, were summoned to Amman and asked to take over the municipalities. Jordan reportedly pledged support for their appointment. However, shortly after King Husayn closed the PLO offices in Amman and ousted PLO officials from Jordan (see below), Ja'bari and Mustafa withdrew. Their decision was viewed as a direct outcome of the anti-Jordan backlash in the West Bank, in reaction to the King's move.[27]

Nevertheless, contacts between local leaders, the Israeli authorities and the Jordanians continued to be held secretly. On 28 September 1986, the Civil Administration, in an unexpected move, announced the appointment of Arab mayors in Hebron, Ramallah and al-Bira, three towns which had been run by Israeli officials. The new apointees were Dr 'Abd al-Majid al-Zir, a physician who served as district health officer in Hebron; Khalil Musa Khalil, a Ramallah businessman and a former mayor of the city; and Hasan al-Tawil, an al-Bira businessman and community leader. None of the three was a prominent political personality and all were known for their moderately pro-Jordanian views. In order to avoid the fate of Zafir al-Masri, the newly appointed mayors played down the significance of their appointment, saying they were municipal leaders with no political ambitions.

The step was fully coordinated with the Jordanians. The three new mayors had traveled to Amman to receive Jordan's blessing before taking up their jobs. Marwan Dudin, the Minister in Charge of the Occupied Territories' Affairs, approved the appointments, saying that they came in response to "continuous severe pressures exerted by West Bank citizens who called for Arab national bodies to replace the Israeli Administration." He promised the new mayors assistance and aid.[28]

Commentators viewed the step as an apparent Israeli attempt to bolster pro-Jordanian leadership and claimed it was related to recent Israeli-Jordanian cooperation on the planned reopening of the Cairo-Amman Bank in Nablus (see below). Foreign observers noted that the Israeli move marked the initial granting of a limited degree of autonomy to the West Bank and Gaza Strip. Sneh, however, downplayed the political significance of the act. It was merely an extension of Israel's previously stated intention to return Arab mayors to towns from which they had been ousted in 1982, he said.[29]

Public opinion in Israel welcomed the move. *Ha'aretz* wrote on 1 October 1986 that it "marked an important step in the right direction." The fact that the three mayors were Arabs, the paper said, was more important than the manner in which they came to their position.

Several West Bank personalities reacted moderately. Mayor Freij of Bethlehem was pleased with the appointment. In the absence of municipal elections, he explained, it was better to have Arab mayors to run Arab towns. Support also came from the Israeli-appointed mayors of Dura, Rafa, and Yata. Nationalist circles and leftist labor unionists, on the other hand, opposed the move vehemently condemning it as a "Jordanian-Israeli conspiracy" aimed at bypassing the PLO. The appointment, the pro-PLO *al-Fajr* argued, came to reinforce the joint Jordanian-Israeli action, but was contrary to the desire of the residents.[30]

LOCAL POLITICAL DEVELOPMENTS

KING HUSAYN'S 19 FEBRUARY SPEECH AND ITS AFTERMATH

King Husayn's 19 February 1986 speech, in which he proclaimed an end to further Jordanian contacts with the PLO and blamed Yasir 'Arafat for the lack of political movement toward a settlement, drew sharp reactions in the West Bank and in Gaza. Israeli observers commented that, in the wake of the dramatic speech, PLO supporters had managed to recruit the bulk of the West Bank population to their side and against the King's position. The four East Jerusalem dailies, including the traditionally pro-Jordanian *al-Quds*, condemned the speech as an attempt to undermine the PLO. The speech should never have been made, wrote *al-Quds* in an editorial which marked a basic change in its political orientation: from unquestioned loyalty to the Hashemite regime to a growing allegiance to the PLO. The newspaper nevertheless maintained a semineutral stance, seeking to bring Jordanian and Palestinian views closer. Much less cautious was *al-Sha'b*, which reflected the views of Fath hard-liners. The paper's editor, Akram Haniyya, repeated the argument that Husayn should have blamed the US Administration and not Yasir 'Arafat. "Accusations against the PLO leadership of surrender and capitulation have proven completely false," stressed Haniyya, reflecting the view of PLO mainstream loyalists. He addressed himself to the West Bank followers of radical organizations such as the PFLP and the PDFLP who in the past had strongly denounced the Husayn-'Arafat *rapprochement*. *Al-Mithaq*, representing the latter factions' views, maintained that Jordan's position was a "powerful slap" at the PLO. It "did not come as a surprise," the paper said, since " 'Arafat's approach ignored the aspirations of the Palestinian people."[31]

An overall analysis of the new situation created by Husayn's speech was provided by Hanna Siniora, the most prominent West Bank representative of the PLO mainstream. To his credit, the King frankly identified the primary obstacle as disagreement between Jordan and the PLO over acceptance of UN Resolutions 242 and 338, Siniora wrote. But what Husayn failed to mention, noted *al-Fajr*'s editor, was that 'Arafat had, in fact, accepted the two resolutions, albeit only in the context of all UN resolutions relevant on the Palestinian issue. In defense of the PLO's official view, Siniora explained that to recognize the two resolutions unconditionally was to accept the notion that "the Palestinian people's struggle was nothing more than a problem of refugees, void of national rights to a homeland and the basic right of self-rule." He justified his leader's stance by saying that if 'Arafat had done so he would have lost not only popular support but possibly his position as "leader of the revolution." Siniora further argued that the King drew a dangerous distinction between the withdrawal of Israeli troops and the recovery of land, on the one hand, and the recognition of legitimate Palestinian rights on the other. While Husayn regarded the latter as less important, for the PLO leadership, the two went together.

Husayn's aim, Siniora concluded, was to drive a wedge between the Palestinian people and their legitimate leadership. The East Jerusalem spokesman did not, however, exclude the possibility that the Palestinian-Jordanian relationship would eventually improve. The crisis, he predicted, would be resolved, since "our destinies [are] intertwined." He also predicted that the King would not begin peace without the PLO. Proof of this, Siniora said, lay in Husayn's reaffirmation of his acceptance of the Rabat summit resolutions, recognizing the PLO as the sole legitimate representative of the Palestinian people.[32]

Prominent pro-Jordanian figures kept a low profile at first and were reluctant to speak openly in favor of the King's decision. They noted that not one Arab nation had endorsed the King's break with 'Arafat. Nevertheless, certain moderate circles echoed Husayn's view that the PLO had made unnecessary demands. The goal that had to take precedence over everything, they said, was the liberation of the land so it could remain Arab, thus ensuring that its own people would continue to live on it.[33]

Reserved support was also expressed by Mayor Freij, who said he was "deeply impressed" by the "frankness and seriousness" of the King's speech. Had the Arabs sat and waited "until the West Bank [was] Judaized," he said, "the situation would have become irreversible." He predicted that the speech would have a strong and positive effect on future developments in the region, and added that now the matter was in the hands of "the Americans, the Israelis and the people of the West Bank and Gaza."[34] Israeli observers linked Freij's remarks to comments made by Defense Minister Yitzhak Rabin immediately after Husayn's speech. Rabin called upon the residents of the territories to take their destiny in their own hands, "to divest themselves of the PLO and of outside forces...and to join Husayn in a move for peace negotiations with Israel [but] without the PLO."[35]

Israeli commentators noted that though the King had not expected massive Palestinian support for his move, he nevertheless anticipated solid backing at least from his loyalists. A considerable number of West Bankers, including Members of Parliament, and representatives of the Village Leagues, did, in fact, travel to Amman to express their support. The show of solidarity was believed to have been orchestrated by Jordanian emissaries. PLO followers in the West Bank, however, played down the significance of the delegations. For every message of support, they claimed, there were "hundreds of individuals and institutions" publishing anti-Husayn notices in the Palestinian Press. When Freij gave limited support to the King, *al-Fajr* contended, the rest of the Bethlehem City Council rallied behind the PLO.[36] The massive demonstration in support of the PLO during the funeral of Mayor Zafir al-Masri (see below), proved that 'Arafat enjoyed the backing of many West Bankers.[37]

According to *The Jerusalem Post*, the murder of al-Masri also led to the shelving of plans for a delegation of senior and prominent pro-Jordanian figures to go to Amman to express their loyalty to the King. Pro-Hashemite figures such as Freij were now saying that they would refrain from further comment until the PLO clarified its own decision.[38]

Anti-Jordanian sentiment grew markedly stronger in May when Bir-Zayt students protested against the killing of three Palestinian students by Jordanian security forces in clashes at Yarmuk University (see chapter on Jordan). The demonstrators burned pictures of Husayn at a mock funeral for the dead students and vehemently attacked him for his "repressive actions." For the first time in a long period, West Bank leftist circles issued calls for the overthrow of the "traitorous Jordanian regime."[39]

Husayn's decision to close 25 offices in Jordan of the Fath wing of the PLO in July 1986 and to severely restrict the freedom of movement of top 'Arafat aides, sparked another, more profound, wave of anti-Jordanian protest. West Bank Nationalists staunchly condemned the move, contending that Israel, Jordan and Syria had embarked on a conspiracy, supported by the US, to undermine the PLO and remove it as a potential partner for a peace settlement. Leaflets calling for direct action against pro-Jordanians and for an escalation of resistance to Israel were distributed in the West Bank by Fath supporters. The statements denounced the "abominable holy trinity of the enemies of our revolution embodied in US Imperialism... The lead of the bullets and the Molotov cocktails will always be the most categorical and effective way to eliminate lackeys," the Fath signed leaflets announced.[40]

At Bir Zayt University and the Islamic College of Hebron, students criticized the deportation of 'Arafat's military deputy, Khalil al-Wazir (Abu Jihad), by burning Jordanian flags and repeatedly denouncing Israel and the US. "Whoever considers backing the King," the demonstrators warned, "is destined to be liquidated."[41]

The daily *al-Sha'b*, known for its unreserved support of the PLO hard-liners, published a lengthy reply to Jordan's accusation that the PLO lacked credibility and trust. Credibility according to Jordan's standards, the paper challenged, meant that the PLO should have liquidated itself by accepting what stood in conflict with its philosophy, objectives and programs, and by "becoming a department affiliated with the Jordanian regime." The West Bankers chose to be Palestinian, *al-Sha'b* wrote, "now and forever."[42]

Moderate political quarters expressed deep disappointment and regret over the crisis. "We had been hoping," said Fa'iz Barakat, head of East Jerusalem Chamber of Commerce, "that the Palestinian-Jordanian sides would get along to the point of an agreement rather than reach a point of a major split. This was a tragedy," he concluded.[43] The pro-Jordanians did not come out openly against the PLO following the closure of Fath offices in Amman. They maintained that their main task was not to attack 'Arafat's followers but rather to convince them that Jordanian-PLO coordination was essential because the only way Israel was going to give up territories was through a deal with King Husayn.[44]

According to foreign observers, the pro-Jordanian circles felt that European and American public opinion was no longer prepared to tolerate PLO fence-sitting. Since the *Achille Lauro* affair, explained Freij, "the world's biggest superpower, the US, [had not only] cursed us with the stamp of terrorism [but also became] openly hostile." 'Uthman al-Khallaq, another known supporter of the King, similarly attacked the PLO leadership for its rigid stance: "We want movement, not rhetorics," he said. "You can feed people slogans for two or three years, but not for a lifetime."[45]

To sum up: the Jordanian-Palestinian *rapprochement*, highlighted by the 11

February 1985 Accord, led to the realignment of their followers in the West Bank and Gaza Strip. The closer relations between the Jordanian regime and the PLO provided their loyalists with a common cause and eliminated the uneasy question of whom to choose. Husayn's 19 February 1986 speech, however, put a drastic end to the comfortable situation in which West Bankers and Gazans were relieved of the necessity of choosing between the two forces.

GROWING JORDANIAN INVOLVEMENT IN WEST BANK AFFAIRS

Husayn's 19 February speech signaled the beginning of a new era in Jordan-West Bank relations. In 1985, Jordan, while preserving a certain amount of influence over West Bank affairs through various financial and administrative measures, refrained from openly undermining the PLO's position in the region. However, once Jordan's commitment to the Amman Accord was terminated, it launched a comprehensive and well-coordinated campaign to gain a stronger foothold in the area by significantly weakening the PLO's stature. The newly implemented Jordanian strategy included the following elements: a series of both punitive and constructive measures; a Five-Year Development Plan for the West Bank; the reopening of a branch of the Cairo-Amman Bank in Nablus; and the reinstalling of Arab mayors.

The change was felt immediately after Husayn's speech when action was taken against pro-Jordanians who failed to back the King, as well as against PLO activists who had condemned him. Sanctions directed at dissident circles included bureaucratic harassment, passport confiscation, and interrogation by security services. PLO loyalists were treated harshly when they arrived at the Jordan river bridges on their way to Amman. The passport of Jamil Tarifi, the prospective nationalist candidate for mayor of al-Bira (see above), was confiscated at the Allenby Bridge; he was detained for investigation and later sent back to the West Bank without being allowed into Jordan. Another prominent pro-PLO figure was taken to Intelligence headquarters in Amman and held under house arrest for several days. The Jordanian authorities also limited the duration of permits granted to West Bankers visiting the Kingdom. New regulations were issued for obtaining Jordanian passports, which all West Bank residents carried. From the beginning of 1986, passports were renewed for only six months and each renewal required a visit to Amman. After the town of Jenin's cooperative organization refused to sign a pledge of loyalty to Husayn, *Newsweek* reported, Jordanian officials prevented Jenin farmers from sending their goods to Jordan.[46]

In June 1986, the East Jerusalem Press reported that 34 Palestinian journalists had been blacklisted by the Jordanian Government and warned that they would be arrested and tried if they crossed the bridges into Jordan. The list included editors and writers who had taken a hostile stand against the King following his February speech. The Jordanian Government was particularly upset with the editor-in-chief of *al-Quds*, who, after Husayn's announcement, had written more favorably about the PLO (see above). The Palestinian Press also claimed that Jordan had imposed a media blackout on reports originating from West Bank periodicals and news agencies. "Unfounded allegations and sheer lies" was the reaction of Jordan's Information Minister.[47]

In another punitive move, the Jordanian Government instructed its Ministries not to acknowledge the signatures of several pro-PLO West Bank mayors who had been deposed by the Israeli authorities. Prior to the new orders the mayors used to certify applications for passports, birth certificates and other official documents. The list included Bassam Shak'a of Nablus, Ahmad Shawki of Jenin, Ibrahim Tawil of al-Bira and Wahid Hamdallah of 'Anabta.[48]

In yet another attempt to gain public support the Ministry for the Occupied Territories' Affairs launched a massive propaganda campaign. In August 1986 Jordan began to broadcast a special television and radio program directed at the West Bank and Gaza Srip inhabitants. The program, entitled "With our People in the Occupied Land," included clips from old speeches by Husayn in which he spoke of Jordan's commitment to the Palestinian people and pledged to continue supporting their just cause. Also broadcast were lengthy interviews with senior Jordanian officials who surveyed the financial and political support Jordan had provided to the West Bank, and with senior pro-Jordanian figures who had been visiting Amman, such as Elias Freij and Rashshad al-Shawa.[49]

The Jordanian Government allegedly backed the establishment in East Jerusalem of a new weekly newspaper with pro-Jordanian views. The new publication, *al-Nahar*, made its debut in March. The editor and publisher, 'Uthman al-Khallaq, said the inhabitants of the territories needed a moderate publication that would reflect the opinion of the "silent majority of Palestinians who support peace." *Al-Nahar* seemed to have taken the role of the East Jerusalem daily *al-Quds* as defender of Jordan policy.[50]

Other elements in the King's drive to reinstate his influence in the West Bank included the payment of regular salaries to some 10,000 teachers whose employment started under Israeli rule; the construction of new terminals on the Jordanian side of the Jordan river bridges; the setting up of new Chambers of Commerce in the West Bank; and the training of pro-Jordanian cadres in the trade unions and professional associations.[51]

THE FIVE-YEAR DEVELOPMENT PLAN

On 4 August 1986 Jordan officially announced the introduction of a "Five-Year Development Plan" aimed at investing approximately $1.3 bn in developing West Bank and Gaza economic and social projects. The plan, which constituted the first integrated Jordanian initiative to enhance the territories' economy since 1967, had set three major targets:(a) to reduce pressure on Arab laborers in Israel and thus curb the contribution to the Israeli economy; (b) to limit the permanent and temporary emigration of inhabitants from the West Bank and Gaza; (c) to create job opportunities for workers returning to the West Bank from Arab oil countries.

The aim, apparently, was to stabilize the West Bank economy by promoting the following:

1. Housing, by financing some 14,000 cooperative-managed housing units at nearly 100 sites; provinding $20,000 (per unit) home mortages to local home owners and cooperatives.
2. Education, by providing funds for new vocational schools and centers and 15 nurse-training centers, and approving plans for about 85 new elementary and secondary schools, mostly in rural areas.
3. Agriculture, by setting up new agricultural credit institutions, cooperative societies and a marketing company; providing additional credit facilities for the private sector and investment loans to individuals for new machinery; embark-

ing on reclamation, sinking new wells and introducing new irrigation systems.
4. Industry, by giving loans for new enterprises and approving new credit programs and nine development projects for the West Bank, including inter alia, limestone mines, a metal-industries complex, ceramic and porcelain factories, a textile dyeing plant, and pharmaceutical plants.
5. Health and welfare, by constructing new hospitals and rural health centers.[52]

The plan, widely viewed as a Jordanian attempt to bolster its image in the territories, was warmly welcomed by the King's followers. *Al-Nahar* praised it as "a qualitative leap." The implementatioin of the plan, the paper asserted, was a pan-Arab and national duty "in which everyone [should] participate regardless of his faction and beliefs." The plan could ease the suffering of the inhabitants, entrench their presence on their land and deepen their sense of affiliation with "a great glorious nation," *al-Nahar* concluded.[53]

PLO supporters, on the other hand, denounced the plan, contending that it was designed to reinforce Jordan's stance and minimize the PLO's influence. Such a development, they suspected, could lead to the emergence of a new Jordan-oriented political constituency, which might eventually form a credible Palestinian negotiating partner for Jordan. The King's failure to solicit West Bank political support, argued *al-Fajr*, made him "flex his monetary muscles to accomplish what his emotional appeals could not."[54] The move was a mere device to buy fealty by exploiting the deteriorating economic situation and the people's suffering under occupation, the paper maintained. The Development Plan, wrote *al-Sha'b*, was in reality calculated to "rob our people of their identity and use pressure and blackmail on them."[55]

PLO circles in the West Bank were nevertheless careful not to reject totally Jordan's initiative. Aware of the West Bank's financial problems, they were reluctant to negate a strategy that could alleviate their situation. Their ambivalent approach was illustrated in an *al-Fajr* editorial which explained that since most of the funds on which the plan relied were Arab, the contributing governments should, therefore, supervise the distribution of money through the joint Jordanian-Palestinian Committee.[56]

Israel's initial reaction was warm. Shmuel Goren welcomed the move, stating that the Government's policy was to encourage investments by outside sources, including Arab investments. He insisted, however, that Israel would take care to safeguard its own interests. Later in the year, however, the Israeli authorities refrained from evaluating the Jordanian projects, and doubted whether the money was actually likely to flow into the areas. Officials in Jerusalem noted that while the Jordanian Ministry of the Occupied Territories' Affairs had limited funds for specific projects, there was no evidence that Amman had allocated substantial sums for imminent transfer to the territories. Jordan, they added, simply had no money for such a large-scale external investment.

Jordan's direct contribution was indeed limited. In November, Marwan Dudin, the Minister in Charge of the Occupied Territories' Affairs, announced the introduction of a new JD4.8m emergency budget. Shortly afterwards, Crown Prince Hasan said that Jordan would help the West Bank with some $40m annually, a sum much lower than that originally promised.[57]

Jordan nevertheless stressed that the successful launching of the $1.3 bn plan depended on the availability of international aid from the West. The US had given

Jordan $5.1m in emergency aid for the 1986 fiscal year. An additional $15m had been allocated for 1987, and another $15 m had also been promised. The US also channeled a further $14m through the Agency for International Development. Preliminary commitments from Japan and Canada suggested that financing for the plan would fall far short of the original goal. The European Economic Community (EEC), for example, agreed to make available only $3.5m as a direct contribution.[58]

Palestinian observers asserted that Jordan was not likely to meet with much success in convincing other Arab countries to help finance the plan, since Arab leaders refused to violate the 1978 Baghdad summit resolutions which stipulated that contributions to West Bank development be solely administered through the joint Jordanian-Palestinian Committee. Direct Arab aid to Jordan dropped drastically, owing mainly to falling oil prices and the Gulf war. In an attempt to encourage foreign investment in the scheme, the Jordanian Government convened in November 1986 an international conference of economic and finance experts. The meeting had a limited success as many of the better-known figures stayed away, while those present did not agree that the plan was feasible.[59]

THE REOPENING OF THE NABLUS BANK

The second major Jordanian economic effort in the territories in 1986 was the reopening of a Jordan-controlled commercial Arab bank in Nablus. The issue had been discussed in previous years; in 1985, the bank and a group of Nablus businessmen took the initiative and were encouraged by the Israeli authorities, but the bank failed to open due to a Jordanian-Israeli controversy over the question of who would supervise its monetary function (see *MECS* 1984–85, p 239).

In mid-September 1986, Israeli officials announced that a branch of the Cairo-Amman Bank would soon be opened in Nablus. Shmuel Goren later added that the bank would be subject to Jordanian and Israeli regulatory authority. Goren made it clear, however, that for security reasons ultimate control would be in the hands of the Israeli Administration, which would keep a close check to make sure funds were not channeled to "hostile organizations." Reacting to the Israeli statement, Dr Mahir Shukri, the deputy governor of Jordan's Central Bank, claimed that Jordan would control and inspect branches established in the West Bank in accordance with the regulations in force in Amman. He added that his Government's decision to reopen bank branches in the West Bank applied only to banks that had operated there prior to the Israeli occupation. Jordan insisted, Shukri explained, that the new bank should not be allowed to grant services to Israeli citizens. Transactions involving remittances and credits in foreign currency would have to be supervised by the head office in Amman.[60]

The official opening of the bank kept being postponed as Israel and Jordan differed over whether to permit Israeli residents to open accounts at the bank.[61] The dispute related mainly to the inhabitants of East Jerusalem who, despite their Jordanian citizenship, were residents of the State of Israel. It was finally agreed that East Jerusalemites would be prohibited from using the services of the Nablus bank. On 3 November the Cairo-Amman Bank quietly opened its Nablus branch, becoming the first West Bank financial institution to resume business since the June 1967 war.[62]

The reopening was warmly welcomed by the local population. Nablus businessmen explained that it would solve the problems of currency exchange faced by Palestinians in the territories, since the bank was to operate in both Jordanian dinars — widely used in the West Bank — and Israeli shekels. Even the pro-PLO *al-Fajr* agreed that it was "a positive step on the path of supporting the residents' steadfastness and encouraging projects that protect their presence."[63]

According to Israeli sources, the reopening was made possible by a secret agreement signed in London by representatives of the Bank of Israel and the Bank of Jordan. Yehuda Litani, *The Jerusalem Post*'s Middle East editor, wrote that the London agreement was the first to be reached between official Israeli and Jordanian delegations since 1949. It was "the most dramatic evidence" of King Husayn's move toward an implicit form of establishing "an Israeli Jordanian condominium," he said.[64]

Foreign and local observers claimed that Israeli-Jordanian cooperation had also been achieved in other areas. Officials from Amman reportedly visited the West Bank and Gaza Strip to coordinate religious and educational matters with the Israeli Civil Administration. On the recommendation of the Israeli security services, *Newsweek* reported, Jordan dismissed Dr Mundhir Salah, the president of al-Najah University in Nablus. Jordan ordered the university's Board of Governors to replace Salah, a known PLO supporter, with figures who would be "acceptable both to the King and the Israelis." *Ha'aretz* added that Salah's removal signaled the "Jordanization" of the nationalist university. Israel and Jordan had allegedly consulted with each other before the reinstatement of Arab mayors. The two countries also cooperated in promoting the new Five-Year Development Plan (see above). Both *The Jerusalem Post* and *Newsweek* shared the view that the bilateral secret arrangements gave Jordan a large measure of administrative control over the West Bank. "Four or five years from now Jordan may be able to compete with the PLO for influence from an equal rather than an inferior position," concluded Yehuda Litani.[65]

PRO-JORDANIANS VERSUS PLO SUPPORTERS

After King Husayn's 19 February speech and after the murder of Zafir al-Masri, West Bank public opinion tended to support the PLO at the expense of the Jordanian regime (see above). We have mentioned the dilemma of many pro-Jordanians who had to choose between Jordan and the PLO. The Jordan-PLO crisis, which escalated in the summer after the closure of the Fath offices in Amman, caused a further deterioration in the relationship between PLO sympathizers and Jordanian loyalists (see above).

Despite vociferous expressions of support for the PLO leaders and the alleged weakening of the pro-Jordan camp, it seems that since Husayn began to implement his new comprehensive policy in the West Bank, the standing of his followers has significantly improved. Their strongest argument *vis-à-vis* their traditional nationalist opponents was anchored in pragmatic grounds. If the PLO had a way of getting rid of the Israeli occupation without Jordan, it was welcome to implement it, challenged 'Uthman al-Khallaq, the editor of *al-Nahar*; but so far, he added, there was no alternative to the Jordanian option. He fully accepted Husayn's view that the question of land must take precedence over that of representation. Addressing himself to the PLO chairman, Khallaq declared: "We want movement, not rhetoric...you can feed people slogans for two or three years, but not for a lifetime."[66]

The apparently coordinated action by Israel and Jordan dealt a serious blow to the pro-PLO camp in the West Bank. The East Jerusalem Press, representing the PLO view, was very frustrated by the course of events. "Desperate to see the PLO lose its power base in the West Bank and Gaza Strip, Israel granted Jordan most, if not all, of its requests," *al-Fajr* wrote. The joint activity, the paper added, was designed to curtail or eliminate PLO influence and put an end to Palestinian aspirations for independence and statehood.[67]

The growing Jordanian involvement seemed to substantially strengthen the political quarters associated with the King. Public statements by members of this group became more decisive and self-assured. "Why should we, Palestinians, deny our gratitude to Jordan?" asked Elias Freij. "Who stopped the Israelis from reaching the River Jordan in [the] 1948 [war]? Who kept East Jerusalem, Nablus, Bethlehem and Hebron Arab?" He also provided the answer: "We breathe through Jordan; it is our gate to the Arab world... the West Bank is totally dependent on Jordan, economically, politically, geographically [and] psychologically."[68]

The more pronounced and independent stance of the pro-Jordanian circles was clearly demonstrated in May, during a meeting in Jerusalem between a group of West Bank and Gaza personalities and the British Prime Minister, Margaret Thatcher, then on an official visit to Israel. Among the participants were Hana Siniora, 'Abd al-Nabi Natshe, Rashshad al-Shawa, 'Izat 'Alul, Zuhayr al-Rayyis, Fa'iz Abu Rahma, Basil Kan'an and Elias Freij. The pro-PLO representatives submitted to the British Prime Minister a petition that reflected the traditional views of the PLO mainstream. It stressed that the Palestinian problem was a national and political one and not a problem of refugees; it called for the right of Palestinians to exercise self-determination in their own independent state on their national soil. The petition also urged the British Government to launch a direct dialogue with PLO representatives without preconditions.

In previous years, and especially after the February 1985 Amman Accord, moderate PLO supporters and Jordanian loyalists had easily agreed upon the principles of a political program such as stated above. In May 1986, however, Freij declined to sign the memorandum presented to Thatcher. He first said that he had not been consulted on the contents; later he said that the protest ignored reference to the Jordanian-Palestinian accord, which, he argued, had been considered by "the majority of the Palestinians as the main pillar on which the peace efforts must rely."[69]

The rift between the conflicting parties widened in late July 1986 when Vice President George Bush visited Israel. Palestinian representatives were invited to meet with Bush at a reception in the American consulate in Jerusalem. Ten of the 30 invited decided to boycott the event. Among those who stayed away were 'Abd al-Nabi Natshe, Zuhayr al-Rayyis, and Ziyyad Abu Ziyyad — all known supporters of the PLO. Hana Siniora attended in order to make sure, as he explained, that the Palestinian cause was properly presented, and to express the West Bank's protest against the US. Reports in the Israeli Press said that, during the meeting, Jordanian and PLO supporters spoke separately. While the former stressed the need to advance economic projects for the improvement of the "quality of life," the latter called on the US to recognize the PLO under the leadership of 'Arafat as the sole legitimate representative of the Palestinians.[70]

The positions of PLO supporters in the West Bank and Gaza Strip were further eroded by the continued factional power struggle within the PLO. The growing fragmentation in the inner circles of the Organization was clearly mirrored in the territories. Not only were PLO backers divided between pro-'Arafat groupings and supporters of the more radical Democratic Alliance, but Fath activists themselves were also split. In an in-depth analysis of the pro-PLO camp's political structure, Joel Greenberg, the West Bank correspondent of *The Jerusalem Post*, first mentioned the more pragmatic wing in the local Fath leadership, centered on the Jerusalem-based Arab Council for Public Affairs.[71] The Council, which served as a Palestinian "think tank," included Hana Siniora, Fa'iz Abu Rahma, 'Abd al-Nabi Natshe, Zuhayr al-Rayyis and Ziyyad Abu Ziyyad (who later resigned). The participants had reportedly pronounced themselves in private meetings to be in favor of a Palestinian State in the West Bank and Gaza Strip, alongside the State of Israel. Senior military officials claimed that Siniora, the nominated West Bank representative for a future Palestinian delegation, was identified with the pragmatic stream in Fath headed by Hani al-Hasan. Siniora had taken the lead in issuing moderate statements, such as the proposal of an EEC-style association comprising the future Palestinian State, Jordan and Israel. On several occasions he stated that a desirable formula for a political solution of the conflict was based on mutual concessions: exchange of land occupied by the Israelis in 1967 for Palestinian recognition of the State of Israel. Explicit recognition of Security Council Resolutions 242 and 338, he said, was possible in return for a statement by the US recognizing the right of the Palestinian people to self-determination.[72]

But *Al-Fajr*'s publisher, Paul Ajluni, was reported to be more sympathetic toward Fath hard-liners. The more militant supporters of Fath were identified with the East Jerusalem newspapers *al-Sha'b* and *al-'Awda* and the Jerusalem Arab Studies Center directed by Faysal al-Husayni. These groups espoused 'Arafat's views but also took the more radical stance professed by Salah Khalaf (Abu Iyad). They were critical of America's West Bank policy and were much more hostile toward Jordan.

Supporters of the Democratic Alliance continued to uphold their radical positions. They were mainly active on university campuses. At Bir Zayt, for example, they accused 'Arafat and his local backers of showing inconsistency and of lacking a clear policy line. The radicals won 36 per cent of the votes in the 1986 student elections, and the Fath camp 38 per cent.[73] A Palestinian observer described the left-wingers as "ideological purists more committed to a rigid political line." *The Jerusalem Post*, however, held that the West Bank PFLP and PDFLP circles appeared to be maintaining a degree of tactical cooperation with Fath supporters in an effort to help reunite the PLO factions abroad.[74]

All PLO supporters in the West Bank, moderates and hard-liners alike, called for the restoration of Jordanian-Palestinian cooperation on the basis of mutual respect, rejecting "hegemony or domination." This, *al-Sha'b* wrote, was the right road to a just and comprehensive solution of the problem. In this respect they unanimously held a common view with the pro-Jordanians.[75]

LOCAL POLITICS IN THE GAZA STRIP

Gaza Strip politics in 1986 revolved around three major issues: the resurgence of Islamic Fundamentalism; the pro-Jordanian policy promoted by Rashshad al-Shawa; and the question of implementing autonomy. In April, Prime Minister Peres proposed that Israel and Egypt should jointly supervise an autonomous Palestinian administration in the Gaza Strip. Peres's call for an "interim Israeli-Egyptian condominium,"[76] was, in fact, a repetition of his previous suggestions concerning the "Gaza-first option", under which the area would gain limited political autonomy as a first step toward an overall settlement (see *MECS* 1979–80, pp 285–87). The Israeli Prime Minister discussed the matter several times with Rashshad al-Shawa, the former mayor of Gaza. Shawa revealed that Peres had proposed that Israel should turn over the running of Gaza to the local population, on condition that security matters and foreign relations be left in Israel's hands.[77]

While rejecting Peres' proposals, Shawa came up with ideas of his own which he presented to President Husni Mubarak in May 1986. During a meeting in Cairo in May 1986, the veteran Gaza leader proposed Egyptian-backed Palestinian self-rule in the Gaza Strip. Shawa suggested the establishment of Egyptian consular services, the reactivation of the Palestinian Legislative Council, which had existed in Gaza under Egypt's rule and the opening of an Egyptian bank in the area. "What I suggest[ed]," he said "[was] that Gaza be granted autonomy under Arab sovereignty, following an Israeli withdrawal from all occupied territories. Since Egypt is the closest Arab power to us, I suggested to President Mubarak that it be under Egyptian sovereignty." Shawa emphasized, however, that any autonomy arrangement "should not preclude the ultimate Palestinian objective of an independent homeland."[78]

Shawa's views reflected a marked Gazan tendency to cooperate with Egypt and seek greater Egyptian involvement in the Palestinian problem (see *MECS* 1983-84, p 257). Mubarak, however, rejected Shawa's proposals, saying he could not treat the Gaza issue separately and "behind the back of King Husayn" without having settled the West Bank problem first. The King himself was said to have vehemently rejected the idea, largely because he continued to regard himself as the representative of all Palestinians under occupation.[79]

Jordan acted independently to strengthen its positions and erode PLO influence in the Gaza area. In the summer, Husayn decided to give Jordanian passports to about 70,000 former Gazans living in Jordan. The Five-Year Development Plan (see above) referred to the Gaza Strip as well. In addition, a new adviser on Gaza affairs had been appointed within the Ministry of the Occupied Territories' Affairs. Gazans were also given the right to own property and operate businesses in Amman without any restrictions. They were, however, excluded the right to vote for Parliament.[80]

Husayn's initiatives toward Gaza seemed to have been coordinated with Jordan's most prominent supporter in the Strip, Rashshad al-Shawa. In mid-July, while in Jordan for consultations with the King, Shawa openly attacked the PLO and declared his unconditional support for the King's policies. Interviewed by Jordan television, Shawa echoed Husayn's February speech and said: "Exchanging land for peace is a means of saving kinfolk, ending the Israeli occupation and returning the occupied territories to Arab sovereignty under which the citizens may be able to breathe."[81] Shawa welcomed the notion of an international conference and called for the acceptance of Resolution 242. He left no doubt as to the nature of his political orientation: "Our self-determination is joining Jordan in a confederation under which all citizens, whether in the East Bank, the West Bank or Gaza, will be equal." Shawa criticized the PLO, which, in his opinion, "imposed its will over the occupied territories' inhabitants instead of taking into consideration their views." He repeated the argument made at the same time by prominent pro-Jordanians in the West Bank: "If the PLO [has] a substitute that [can] save us from this situation...the PLO [is] welcomed...but if the PLO [has] no way to end the occupation we believe that...Resolution [242] is the only serious way to end Israeli occupation."[82]

While Husayn was reportedly pleased with Shawa's harsh words against the PLO, the reaction in Gaza was quite different. Shawa came under blistering attack from his traditional opponents representing both Fath and left-wing radical activists. The "national institutions" in the Strip denounced his remarks saying he represented only himself. Their announcement rejected Resolution 242 and all "suspect plans starting with the autonomy and ending with the so-called development plan."[83] Fath leaflets calling Shawa a "traitor," a "liar," and "scum of the swamp" were distributed in Gaza. He received several death threats and a day after he was interviewed by Jordan television, his Gaza citrus packing plant was set on fire. Shortly after his return from Amman a bomb was planted near a Gaza building owned by him.[84]

Israeli military sources believed the attacks against Shawa were carried out by Gaza-based members of the left-wing PDFLP and the PFLP. The left-wing groups in Gaza were facing growing opposition not only from pro-Jordanian elements, but also from local Islamic Fundamentalists. Islamic activism in the Strip had been markedly on the rise (see *MECS* 1984–85, pp 249–50). Eight Islamic groups, all offspring of the Muslim Brotherhood, operated in the region. The largest organization was *al-Mujamma'* (the community), comprising approximately 1,200 activists and headed by Ibrahim Yazuri. Their spiritual leader, Ahmad Yasin, was imprisoned for terrorist activity and released in the May 1985 prisoner exchange (see *MECS* 1983–84, p 258). *Al-Mujamma'* adopted an extremist program that called for the uprooting of the "Zionist entity" by means of a holy war (*jihad*) against the State of Israel. Another group, the *Salafiyyun*, included extremist Sunnis who preached Islamic purism and a return to the customs of the time of the Prophet Muhammad. For example, they demanded that mosques be built of wood rather than cement. A third group, *al-Jihad al-Islami* (Islamic Jihad), consisted of four minor Khomeyni-inspired organizations. Islamic Jihad was considered the most radical of all the fundamentalist movements in the area. Members of the group were actively involved in terrorist activity. In late December, security forces uncovered an Islamic Jihad cell that was allegedly responsible for the murder of two Ashkelon residents in Gaza (see above).[85]

The growing influence of Islamic circles in Gaza was reflected in the large number of mosques constructed in recent years: in 1967 there were 75, while in 1985 the figure had risen to 150. Foreign observers noted that a growing number of local inhabitants began wearing conservative dress in accordance with the precepts of Islam. As the movements gained power, they became more provocative and militant in attempting to enforce the laws of Islam. The Israeli Press reported that Islamic extremists interrupted weddings in which men and women celebrated together and Western music was played. Stores that sold hard liquor or video cassettes were vandalized.[86]

Serious clashes erupted between radical Muslims and left-wing secularists who showed disregard for Islamic laws. Such incidents had also occurred in the past (see *MECS* 1983–84, p 257); but, according to military sources, disputes between the rival factions reached an unprecedented level in 1986. "Acid attacks, knife slashing, and fire bombing [directed at] secular elements as well as the destruction of mosques," wrote an Israeli observer, "[had] become commonplace with the upsurge of Islamic Fundamentalism in the Gaza Strip."[87] In late June 1986 membersof the *Mujamma'* violently attacked and injured Dr Rabbah Muhanna, a known Leftist and the deputy chairman of the Gaza Physicians' Association. The assault came in response to a similar attack against Ibrahim Yazuri, head of the *Mujamma'* group.

The Israeli authorities were deeply disturbed by the wave of religious violence. Senior officials in Gaza's Civil Administration who feared the outbreak of a "religious war" defined the changed situation as a "time bomb." When further incidents occurred, Brig Gen Shaike Erez, head of the Civil Administration, intervened. He summoned some 150 local leaders and asked them to stop the intercommunal strife; otherwise, he warned, the Army would intervene. Erez's threats seemed to have helped, and in the latter part of the period under review the local rivalries had quietened down.[88]

NOTES

For the place and frequency of publications cited here, and for the full name of the publication, news agency, radio station or monitoring service where an abbreviation is used, please see "List of Sources." Only in the case of more than one publication bearing the same name is the place of publication noted here. In the present essay, however, all references to *al-Fajr* and *al-Sha'b* are to the East Jerusalem editions of these newspapers unless stated otherwise.

1. *Davar*, 4 May 1986; VoI, 21 January 1987.
2. *Ma'ariv*, 16 January; VoI, 19 June 1986.
3. On that day ten years earlier, six Israeli Arabs were killed in Galilee in clashes with the Army over land expropriations.
4. *Ha'aretz*, *Ma'ariv*, 5 December 1986.
5. *Davar*, *al-Fajr* (in English), 5 December; *NYT*, 7, 10 December; *Newsweek*, 22 December 1986.
6. *The Times*, 6 December 1986.
7. *JP*, 5, 15 December; *IHT*, 8 December; *CSM*, 9 December 1986.
8. VoI, 2 January — SWB, 3 January 1987.
9. *NYT*, 5 January; *The Guardian*, 9 February; *JP*, 3 March; *Ha'aretz*, 19 October 1986.
10. *Ha'aretz*, 9 July; *al-Fajr*, 14 August 1986.
11. *Ha'aretz*, 22 October; *al-Fajr*, 24 October 1986.
12. *JP*, 2, 7 February; *The Guardian*, 9 February; *al-Fajr*, 2 May 1986.
13. *The Guardian*, ibid.
14. *JP*, 13 January 1986.
15. *JP*, 17 July, 13 August; *Ha'aretz*, 24 August 1986.
16. *JP*, 4 November; *al-Quds*, 5 November; *Ha'aretz*, 29 December 1986; *JP*, 22 April 1987.
17. *NYT*, 5 January; *JP*, 13 January; *Ha'aretz*, 9 March; *'Al-Hamishmar*, 16 July 1986.
18. *NYT*, ibid.
19. *'Al-Hamishmar*, 31 March, 11 April; *JP*, 3 April 1986.
20. *Al-Fajr*, 21 March 1986.
21. *FT*, 11 February 1986.
22. *Ha'aretz*, *JP*, 3 March; *al-Fajr* (in English), 7 March 1986.
23. *JP*, *Ma'ariv*, 3 March; *al-Fajr*, 7 March 1986.
24. *The Guardian*, 4 March; *Davar*, *JP*, 6 March 19086.
25. *Ma'ariv*, *JP*, *IHT*, 3 March; *al-Fajr*, 7 March 1986.
26. *JP*, 4 March; *IHT*, 5 March, 1986.
27. *JP*, 1, 13, July; *Davar*, 3 July; *al-Nahar*, 4 July; *al-Bayadir al-Siyasi*, 5 July; *Ma'ariv*, 12 July 1986.
28. R. Amman, 29 September — DR, 29 September; *The Economist*, 25 October 1986.
29. *Ha'aretz*, *Ma'ariv*, *JP*, *NYT*, *FT*, 29 September 1986.
30. *Al-Fajr*, 3, 10 October 1986.
31. *Al-Fajr*, *Ma'ariv*, *JP*, 21 February; *al-Fajr*, 28 February; *JP*, 3 March; *MEI*, 7 March 1987.
32. *JP*, 20 February; *al-Fajr*, 21 February 1986.
33. *Al-Quds*, 21, 28 February; *NYT*, 3 March 1986.
34. *JP*, 19 February 1986.

35. *JP*, *Ha'aretz*, 20 February 1986.
36. *MEI*, 14 March; *al-Fajr*, 14 March 1986.
37. *JP*, 3 March 1986.
38. *JP*, *Yedi'ot Aharonot*, 4 March; *MEI*, 21 March 1986.
39. *Al-Fajr*, 17 May; *Davar*, 22 May; *JP*, *Ma'ariv*, 23 May; *'Al-Hamishmar*, 29 May 1986.
40. *IHT*, 9 July; *Ha'aretz*, 16 July 1986.
41. *Ha'aretz*, 7, 13 July; *JP*, 13 July; *The Guardian*, 16 July 1986.
42. *Al-Sha'b*, 15 July 1986.
43. *IHT*, 9 July 1986.
44. *NYT*, 9 July 1986.
45. Ibid.
46. *'Al-Hamishmar*, 9 April; *JP*, 14 April, 2 May; *NYT*, 9 July; *Newsweek*, 10 November 1986.
47. *Al-Fajr*, 13 June; *JP*, 18 June 1986.
48. *Al-Fajr*, 14 August 1986.
49. *Al-Fajr* (in English), 14 August, 7 November 1986.
50. *JP*, 7 March 1986.
51. Ibid, 3 October 1986.
52. *JP*, 12 December 1986.
53. *Al-Nahar*, 26 September, 12 October, 7 November 1986.
54. *Al-Fajr*, *JP*, 16 May; *ME*, January 1987.
55. *Al-Sha'b*, 2 July 1986.
56. *Al-Fajr*, 13 August; *ME*, January 1987.
57. VoI (in Arabic), 6 August — DR, 7 August; *JP*, 10 November, 12 December; *'Al-Hamishmar*, 13 November 1986.
58. *JP*, 7 November 1986; *ME*, January 1987.
59. *JP*, 7 November; *The Economist*, 15 November; *Ha'aretz*, 20 November 1986; *ME*, January 1987.
60. *Ha'aretz*, *FT*, *The Guardian*, 18 September; *Sawt al-Sha'b*, 22 September 1986.
61. *The Guardian*, 18 September 1986.
62. *Al-Dustur*, London, 17 October; *Ha'aretz*, 19 October; *JP*, 4 November 1986.
63. Ibid, *al-Fajr*, 19 October 1986.
64. *JP*, 3 October 1986.
65. *Ha'aretz*, *JP*, 3 October; *Newsweek*, 10 October 1986.
66. *NYT*, 9 July; *Ha'aretz*, 5 July 1986.
67. *Al-Fajr* (in English), 7 November 1986.
68. *JP*, 18 April; *Sawt al-Sha'b*, 6 August — DR, 6 August 1986.
69. VoI, 27 May — DR, 28 May; *al-Quds*, 27 May; *al-Nahar*, 30 May 1986.
70. VoI, 29 July — DR, 30 July; *Ma'ariv*, 30 July; *al-Fajr*, 1 August 1986.
71. *JP*, 17 September 1986.
72. *Al-Fajr* (in English), 17 January 1986.
73. *Ha'aretz*, 7 March; *al-Fajr* (in English), 28 March 1986.
74. *JP*, ibid.
75. *Al-Sha'b*, 12 August 1986.
76. *JP*, 21 April 1986.
77. *IHT*, 23 August 1986.
78. *JP*, 22 May; *NYT*, 23 May; *al-Fajr* (in English), 6 June 1986.
79. *JP*, 21 May, 1 June; *NYT*, 23 May 1986.
80. *JP*, 10 October 1986.
81. Jordan TV, 15 July — DR, 16 July 1986.
82. Ibid.
83. *Al-Sha'b*, 17 July 1986.
84. *Ha'aretz*, 1 June, 18 July; Jordan TV, 24 July — DR, 25 July; *JP*, 25 July, 4, 20 August; *Davar*, 8 August 1986.
85. *Ha'aretz*, *JP*, *Davar*, 26 December 1986.
86. *Al-Fajr* (in English), 9 May; *JP*, 19 May, *Ma'ariv*, 25 May 1986.
87. *Counterpoint*, August 1986.
88. *'Al-Hamishmar*, 5 June; *Davar*, 25 June 1986.

MIDDLE EAST ECONOMIC ISSUES

Middle East Oil Developments 1986

BENJAMIN SHWADRAN

INTRODUCTION

The basic characteristics of a cartel are production control and price control. Production limitations imposed by members of the cartel enables them to set and control the price of their product. For the successful operation of a cartel, the members must be the exclusive or major suppliers of the product, and their interests must not conflict. The small members of a cartel, as a rule, benefit most from the organization, for through the limits set by the big producers, they obtain higher prices for their products. However, when the big producer sees great opportunities for the expansion of its market it abandons the small producers and floods the market, thus forcing the small producers out.[1]

The Organization of Petroleum Exporting Countries (OPEC), when it was established in October 1960, could not function as a regular cartel because its members were not companies but sovereign states. Resolutions had to be adopted unanimously, first by the delegates and 30 days later by their home governments. Moreover, there were serious conflicts of interest between the conservative great oil producers and the radical small producers. From the very beginning OPEC was not granted the power to either control production or set prices. As such, it did not — and still does not — have the power to enforce its decisions.

Even the original, very limited objective of the Organization — restoration of the price of oil to what it was before the companies cut it in 1959-60 — could not be achieved during the first decade of its existence, for the oil supply in the world market was greater than the demand. In the late 1960s OPEC practiced price setting in conjunction with the concessionary oil companies. The 1970s saw the emergence of OPEC as the most powerful force in the world oil market as the demand for oil was larger — for a number of reasons — than the supply. OPEC's uniform oil price — determined by itself — dominated the world oil market. In the late 1970s, primarily because of the Iranian revolution and the fear of a shortage that possessed the oil consuming world, the uniform price was practically eliminated. The official price was the minimum, on top of which each member placed a surcharge of its own as it saw fit. Saudi Arabia, which, for its own reason, adhered to the official OPEC price, tried to reestablish the uniform price. For three years its efforts failed and it was swept along by raising its own prices, from $12.70 a barrel at the end of 1978 to $32 in September 1981. Not until October 1981 did Saudi Arabia succeed in establishing a uniform price at $34 a barrel.

The drop in demand for oil compelled the other members to drop their price to $34 a barrel. This move did not halt the rapid drop in demand, and early in 1982 OPEC, meeting in Vienna, decided to resort to the cartel practice of controlled production. It adopted a total production level of 18m barrels a day (b/d). Yet Saudi Arabia declared: "We don't regard OPEC as the place to decide the level of Saudi production."[2] The attempt failed. In March 1983, OPEC took a momentous step. While meeting in London, it decided to reduce the price from $34 to $29 a barrel. The overall production ceiling was set at 17.5m b/d; the apportionment was modified to increase the levels of the weaker members, at the expense of Saudi Arabia, as it refused to grant OPEC the power to set its production level. However, as the dominant and biggest producer in the organization, Saudi Arabia assumed the role of swing producer. This meant that all members produced according to their quotas, and Saudi Arabia would produce the balance as determined by market conditions.

The system did not work. For most of the members, in order to increase, or at least maintain, the levels of their oil revenue, were cheating on both production and price levels. They produced more than their quotas and sold below the official OPEC price. Because of its nature the Organization could not compel its members to abide by its decision. OPEC named a Monitoring Committee to monitor members' production and price levels. Later it named a Ministerial Executive Council to check price and production levels. The members, however, devised various means of overcoming the limitations of production and prices. Saudi Arabia's production dropped from about 8.5m b/d in 1981 to a little above 2m b/d in August 1985. Although Saudi Arabia refused to continue as swing producer and accepted in September 1984 a quota of 4.35m b/d, it did not begin to produce at the quota level until September 1985. General cheating continued unabated. Indeed, Saudi Arabia itself resorted to some of the devices for increasing production and revenue, such as netback and countertrade. King Fahd, assuming direct leadership in the country's oil affairs, threatened publicly to resort to the cheating practices of the other members.

In its efforts to restore prices and increase demand for the oil of its members, OPEC faced harsh competition from the non-OPEC producers, especially Britain and Norway. Practically all non-OPEC producers and a number of OPEC members adopted spot market prices as the basis for their crude oil exports. Since the spot market prices in a glutted market are inevitably much lower than any official long-term price, OPEC prices were meaningless and so was the OPEC quota system.

Saudi Arabia became desperate. By the end of 1985 it threatened both OPEC and non-OPEC producers with a price war.[3] It was hoped that the producers of both groups would retreat from their positions and restore the OPEC prices. The maneuver failed.

In a frantic move, OPEC changed direction toward the end of 1985. It abandoned price control and decided "to secure and defend for OPEC a fair share of the world oil market consistent with the necessary income for member countries' development."[4] This was a surrender of OPEC's basic historic position as the price setting determiner of the world oil market. Morever, the "fair share" concept was undefined, hasty and unimplementable. The December 1985 Conference named a special committee — Saudi Arabia refused to join — and charged it to find ways of restoring OPEC's share of the free world's petroleum production.

OPEC's decision, combined with Saudi Arabia's defiant determination to rapidly increase its production rate produced consequences that were not foreseen by OPEC or the non-OPEC producers, the world oil industry or the world at large.

Oil prices throughout the world began to drop, and the major non-OPEC producers took the rapid developments in stride. They were not intimidated and continued with their production practices. OPEC, therefore, was forced to fall back on its own devices.

JANUARY-MARCH 1986

The majority, led by Saudi Arabia, backed the "fair share" policy to achieve the desired objective. A minority — Algeria, Iran and Libya, sometimes joined by Gabon — rejected the "fair share" decision. On 5 February, the Finance Ministers of the three met in Algiers and called for the restoration of OPEC's price structure and production programming. They also called for drastic curtailment in the production quotas of the big producers in order to maintain the price at $28 a barrel. Iran went so far as to advocate a total stoppage of production for four weeks.

The special ministerial committee named in December met in Vienna on 3–4 February 1986. It made no progress, and merely recommended that the "share" should be "higher than the self-imposed production ceiling" (16m b/d).[5] At the same time five Ministers, including the representative of Saudi Arabia, met there and discussed the problem of falling oil prices.

During February, crude oil prices continued to fall. In New York, prices plunged to below $15 a barrel; the same happened in London and Mexico. Kuwait's Oil Minister warned on 18 February that prices could drop as low as $5 a barrel. On 23 February, *The New York Times* reported that West Texas Intermediate crude (US benchmark) fell below $14 a barrel. On the following day the publication reported that the US imported between 25 and 30 per cent of its petroleum consumption, down from a peak of 46 per cent in 1977; reliance on Arab members of OPEC had been slashed by 85 per cent, the import from the Arab OPEC producers was about 500,000 b/d. On 2 March, the same publication reported that crude oil prices dropped to $13.25 a barrel. Three days later it was reported that the major oil grades in the US and Britain dropped below $12 a barrel. West Texas Intermediate went down to $11.63; British Brent dropped to $11.86.

EXTRAORDINARY OPEC GENEVA CONFERENCE

16–24 MARCH 1986

To deal with the rapidly deteriorating situation an extraordinary conference was convened in Geneva on 16 March. On the following day the Saudi Arabian Oil Minister predicted that prices might drop to $5 a barrel unless the non-OPEC producers cooperated with the Organization. He stressed that the help of Britain would be essential for the success of any OPEC-non-OPEC joint undertaking. He also made it clear to both OPEC and non-OPEC producers that his country had no intention of reducing its current oil output of about 4.35m b/d. "Our policy is not to cut production from the present level."[6] To this the British Chancellor of the Exchequer replied the following day in the House of Commons: "The most dramatic development on the world economic scene, one of considerable importance to this country, has of course been the collapse in the price of oil." Britain welcomed lower oil prices, despite the loss of revenue, because lower prices would bring more economic growth and lower inflation. He concluded by declaring: "There is no question whatever, and never has been any question of the United Kingdom cutting back its oil production in an attempt to secure higher oil prices."[7]

Saudi Arabia continued with the practice of netback deals,[8] about which Yamani said in March 1986: "I think it is the best system we can adopt with the least ups and downs and with the least speculative effects."[9] Saudi Arabia reportedly contracted to purchase 132 military aircraft from Britain at a total cost of $7 bn, payment for which, in great measure, was to be made by Saudi oil on a countertrade arrangement.[10]

The extraordinary conference faced, in addition to the deep division between the majority and minority about the "fair share" policy, three specific issues:

1. individual quota allocations;
2. second quarter production ceiling;
3. modification of the 14.5m b/d.

After eight days of futile discussions the Ministers decided to adjourn for three weeks and reconvene on 15 April, after they consulted with their governments, with each other and with other oil-producing countries.[11] Early in April it was estimated that the oil income of the 13 OPEC members would be $60 bn less in 1986 than in 1985.[12]

15–21 APRIL 1986

The reconvened extraordinary conference opened discussions on 15 April. After six days of heated debate, the ten-member group, defying the three-member minority group, decided that the production level for the entire year of 1986 be set at 16.7m b/d, and that the "fair share" objective would be pursued. The ten-member group formed a committee comprising the delegates of Indonesia, Kuwait, Nigeria, Saudi Arabia and Venezuela to make contacts with the non-OPEC producers and get them to agree to a joint effort to stabilize the oil market. The ordinary midyear conference was to convene on 25 June in Brioni, Yugoslavia.

By now Saudi Arabia had abandoned its threat of an oil price war. At a press conference in Geneva on 22 April, after the conclusion of the OPEC conference, Shaykh Ahmad Zaki al-Yamani was asked: "Do you consider [that] the price war policy is over and that it has been a failure?" He replied: "I don't consider there was a price war policy to start with. The whole matter happened when Saudi Arabia was not able to carry the burden. We just failed to carry that burden. You could call it competition in the market. A war in that sense has to be announced. No one announced the war. We all hate that war."[13]

The committee established to contact non-OPEC producers held discussions with Angola, Malaysia, Mexico and Oman. It reported that both sides had agreed to support an oil price structure targeted at $28 a barrel. On 23 May, the committee members met and reported that they had had talks with representatives of Egypt, Malaysia, Mexico and Norway, who had all indicated willingness to cooperate with OPEC. On 20 May, Yamani appeared on Saudi television and threatened the major non-OPEC producers with chaos in the oil market, after which prices would be fixed by OPEC.[14] The committee met again early in June and targeted the price at $17 to $19 a barrel. The willingness of the smaller non-OPEC producers to cooperate was not spelled out, except their support of an oil price structure targeted at $28 a barrel. Since the aim of OPEC was to obtain a fair share of the world oil market, which could be achieved only by competition, the targeted price could be only a desired objective. An immediate price increase of $17 to $19 a barrel and a "fair share" of the world market are contradictory aims.

MIDYEAR REGULAR OPEC CONFERENCE

25–30 JUNE 1986, BRIONI

Saudi Arabia pursued a policy of increasing output. During May, it offered customers an incentive discount on every barrel of crude provided they were lifting no less than the minimum volume specified in their contracts. The discount was to increase if the customers lifted up to the maximum volume specified in the contracts. The minimum discount was 50 cents a barrel. The discounts were granted on netback deals. Early in June, Saudi Arabia extended its incentive price discounts for June. On 14 June, the same was extended for July. In the middle of June it was reported that Saudi Arabia's General Petroleum and Mineral Organization (Petromin) was selling oil products from its export refineries on the spot market price basis.[15] It was also reported that the smaller non-OPEC producers — Angola, Egypt, Malaysia, Mexico and Oman — refused to attend the conference as observers, as did Britain and Norway.

OPEC's midyear conference opened on 25 June in Brioni, after the unsuccessful sessions of the extraordinary conference in March and April, the attempts of the special committee on the fair share of the market and the reports of the committee on non-OPEC producers cooperation. Facing the conference were the basic issues of the overall production ceiling, quotas for members, price increase targets and the sharp division between the majority and minority groups on policy.

While the recommended price target was $18–20 a barrel, the spot market price that practically dominated the crude oil market was $10.50–13 a barrel. The overall OPEC production ceiling was almost nonexistent. While the official ceiling was 16.7m b/d, it was reported that actual production reached over 19m b/d.

Bitter discussions were carried on for five days, and the majority faction — 10(9) — decided to set a price target of $17–19 a barrel, and an overall production ceiling of 17.6m b/d. The minority faction — 3(4) — targeted the price increase at $28 a barrel, the overall production ceiling was to be 14.5m b/d, with drastic reductions in the output of the big producers: Saudi Arabia, Kuwait and the United Arab Emirates (UAE). There were no discussions by either group on individual quotas. Rilwani Lukman of Nigeria was elected president. The conference broke up on 30 June without reaching agreement on all the issues, and it was decided to reconvene on 28 July in Geneva. During the interval, Ministers were to consult their Governments.

Two factors deeply upset the oil market during the interval. OPEC production rose and prices went down. Total OPEC production averaged 19.5m b/d and on 7 July, *The New York Times* reported that the price of crude oil had continued to drop to below $12 a barrel. Saudi Arabia, as mentioned above, continued to increase output. Up to June 1986 its quota was 4.35m b/d. In June, production rose to 4.6m b/d. During the first half of July, output was increased to over 5m b/d and was to reach 6m b/d by the end of the month. Saudi Arabia also notified its netback customers that the incentive price discount would be continued in August. Toward the end of July, Saudi Arabia was reported to have chartered three huge crude tankers for its Norbec[16] floating storage fleet. At the beginning of June, Norbec's floating storage fleet consisted of 16 tankers with a total capacity of 33m barrels. The additional chartered vessels were for ports in the Far East.

On 8 July, *The Wall Street Journal* reported that oil prices had tumbled to $11 a barrel on world markets. As the opening of the conference approached, it was reported that OPEC daily production had averaged 20.1m barrels, some 3m barrels above the projected third quarter consumption requirements.[17] Of the total, Saudi Arabia produced 5.8m b/d. On 23 July, it was reported that oil prices had fallen below $10 a barrel. British Brent sold at $9.78 a barrel. Two days later Brent sold at $8.45 a barrel. This was the lowest price since it was first produced from the North Sea a decade previously.

Before the conference opened, preliminary talks were conducted among the delegates which Yamani called "useful," and Dr Subroto of Indonesia said that there was some movement on a plan to cut output of total production. At first, Iraq demanded a quota equal to 13.1 per cent of OPEC's aggregate output; later, the Iraqi Oil Minister Qasim Taki demanded a quota equal to Iran's. The major issues facing the conference were reduction of the total OPEC production, which was reported to have been increased to 20.1m b/d, about 5m barrels over the world demand; Saudi Arabia was producing 5.8m b/d. The other issue was the individual quota allocation of the members.

28 JULY–5 AUGUST 1986, GENEVA

The conference was duly opened on 28 July in Geneva, but was adjourned for 24 hours. OPEC president Lukman and former president Subroto were given the task of obtaining pledges for voluntary production cutbacks on an interim basis for August and September. After nine days of discussions, the conference decided that for the months of September and October all member countries (except Iraq) would be bound by the individual quotas decided upon in October 1984. The total for the 12 member countries was to be 14.8m b/d; Iraq was not limited. Both antagonists in the Gulf war changed their positions. Iraq insisted that as long as the war continued, its quota was to be equal to that of Iran. On 4 August, the Iranian Oil Minister, Gholamreza Aqazadeh, proposed that Iraq should be excluded from the quota allocation. The general indication was that Iraq would produce about 2m b/d.

The agreement was temporary and not to be considered a precedent. Any confirmed quota violation by a member would release all other members from abiding by their quotas. High level marketing officials of all member countries were — as a group — to monitor the implementation of the agreement under the supervision of the president of the conference.[18]

As indicated above, Saudi Arabia gave up the price war but adhered to the "fair share" policy. By August, it appeared that it had practically given up the "fair share" aim for an OPEC-wide controlled production policy through the fixed price system. This was a total reversal of policy. For on 2 August, while the Geneva discussions were in full swing, Saudi Arabia issued the following statement of its position:

> Firstly, Saudi Arabia does not allow itself, nor does it cooperate with others, to inflict damage on any producing country, whether within OPEC or outside it. Secondly, Saudi Arabia's policy seeks to achieve fairness and balance. It rejects flooding the market with oil while supporting a gradual increase in prices, which have witnessed a major collapse in recent months. The Kingdom believes that achieving this goal has become an urgent necessity imposed by events, but that this should be done in a gradual manner so that prices can be brought to a specific level agreed upon, and adhered to by all.

> Thirdly, OPEC must respond to the facts created by market developments with the carefulness and flexibility which will ensure that the situation is dealt with step by step.[19]

The picture drawn by this statement belies the facts. After the meeting in Brioni (25–30 June), Saudi Arabia and Kuwait increased production which, combined, amounted to 7.3m b/d, about 80 per cent more than the average of 1985. This raised OPEC total production to more than 20m b/d. Obviously, the Saudi Arabian tactics failed. The market share policy, which was to be achieved by the threat of a price war, also failed. Max Wilkinson wrote in *The Financial Times*, "It has become obvious...even in the highly charged political atmosphere of recent OPEC conferences, that a price war in pursuit of market share is one which the group as a whole could not possibly win."[20]

The failure determinant in Saudi Arabia's reversal of policy did not, apparently, satisfy some of the State Department analysts. They maintained that Saudi Arabia responded to Iran's proposal — to reject the "fair share" and return to curtailed production and a fixed price in order to draw the Islamic Government of Iran to become more engaged in political and economic diplomacy. A State Department official explained: "Drawing Iran into various international networks has the potential benefit of making it more sensitive to the view of those countries it had to deal with, and if it works it would encourage Iranians in the leadership to be more outward looking."[21] This analysis would seem to be nothing but wishful thinking on the part of the State Department policymakers in their efforts to bring Iran into the Western or American camp and cooperate with Saudi Arabia.

Indeed, Iran's offer of the OPEC solution was a victory of the minority group. The major feature of the Iranian proposal was a cut of 4m b/d of total OPEC production at the expense of the big producers. Saudi Arabia's production in July averaged 5.427m b/d, and nominations for August anticipated a production level of 6.1m b/d.[22] To be sure, the Iranian proposal exempted Iraq from the production scheme not out of a sudden change of attitude but because the war measures against Iraq would prevent Iraqi export increases.

Again, following its own policy aims, the State Department official advised: "I think it's a mistake to see this as a big victory for Iran and a defeat for the Saudis, it was a genuine compromise."[23]

In line with the August OPEC accord, Saudi Arabia advised all its customers that it was ending the practice of granting incentive discounts on netback deals, as of 30 September, but the netback deals themselves were to continue. The extent of these deals in OPEC were estimated at 5–7m b/d.[24]

Reacting to the call of the conference on the non-OPEC producers to cooperate with OPEC, US Energy Secretary John Herrington said that "the establishment of the dominance of OPEC as we knew it in the 1970s is unhealthy for Americans and the free world; not only that, it is unacceptable." The State Department spokesman said: "We have long felt and continue to believe that the free market and the laws of supply and demand should determine oil price and supply levels."[25]

Market reaction to the Geneva August accord was prompt. British Brent went up on 1 September, from \$9 a barrel on 10 July to \$14.50. In New York, West Texas Intermediate reached \$15.25 a barrel.

6–22 OCTOBER GENEVA OPEC CONFERENCE

While the August accord demonstrated almost unanimous solidarity, the October conference revealed serious divisions. Some members advocated converting the two-month temporary production agreement into a permanent accord; Saudi Arabia and Kuwait pressed for immediate discussion of the issues of individual quotas, overall OPEC production ceiling, and prices which would lead to permanent solutions. Most members favored extending the existing arrangements to the end of the year, when the situation would be reassessed.

The conference named two ministerial committees, one on pricing (comprising Kuwait [chairman], Ecuador and Libya), the other on quota distribution (Nigeria [chairman], Indonesia and the UAE). The Experts' Committee was to submit its recommendations to the Ministerial Committees.

During September the UAE, Ecuador and Gabon surpassed their quotas set in August. Saudi Arabia and Kuwait demanded higher quotas.

On 13 October, while the conference was in session, the Saudi Arabian Cabinet issued a statement calling for the replacement of the two-month temporary accord by a permanent agreement "which will take into consideration the past sacrifices of Gulf Cooperation Council members of OPEC." It stressed that in determining quotas, compensation should be made for the "great sacrifices which the Kingdom of Saudi Arabia has made on OPEC's behalf from the Organization's foundation up to the present day."[26] Kuwait issued a similar statement on 12 October following a cabinet meeting.

Finally, on 22 October, the conference arrived at an agreement. The temporary accord was extended to the end of the year with the following modifications. The overall production ceiling for the 12 members (Iraq excluded) was increased from 14.8m b/d to about 15m b/d in November and about 15.1m b/d in December; Kuwait's quota was augmented by 21,000 b/d in November and 79,000 b/d in December, making an average of 60,000 b/d. Ecuador, Gabon and Qatar, because of their small basic outputs, were granted significant increases; Saudi Arabia and the UAE voluntarily agreed to forgo any increases. The others were allowed minor additions. The quota distribution was based by the Ministerial Quota Committee on the criteria — not of equal weight — of reserves, production capacity, historical production, population, dependence on oil, domestic oil consumption, cost of production and external debt.[27] The issue of fixing a price was discussed but not decided upon, and left for the pricing committee. The year-end conference was to meet on 11 December in Geneva.

11–20 DECEMBER GENEVA CONFERENCE

The major issue, after the October meeting, was the fixed price. While the targeted price adopted was $17 to $19 a barrel, the real price was about $15 a barrel. At the end of October, the Saudi Arabian Acting Oil Minister Hisham Nazer called for an emergency meeting of the Ministerial Pricing Committee to take "an immediate decision" on fixing a price no less than $18 a barrel as proposed by his country on 17 October. The UAE and Algeria supported Saudi Arabia.

On 14 November, the committee met in Quito, Ecuador, under the chairmanship of the Kuwaiti Oil Minister 'Ali Khalifa al-Sabah. Six days later, the committee recommended a prompt return to the system of fixed official pricing based on a reference price of $18 a barrel. However, instead of Saudi Arabian light serving as the benchmark crude, the committee selected a basket of seven crudes (six OPEC and Mexico) to set the price.

The Experts' Committee met in Vienna from 20–30 November and adopted a new method of setting up the differential structure.

When the conference opened the main issue was the fixed price of $18 a barrel. Iran pursued its old campaign to cut production. Six of the 13 — Algeria, Ecuador, Gabon, Iraq, Libya and the UAE — supported Iran's proposal to cut production by 10 per cent. As previously, the Iranian campaign was aimed at the major producers, especially Saudi Arabia. After three days of discussion, the Ministers were reaching agreement except for the clash between Iran and Iraq. Iraq demanded that it either be exempt from the quota as in the August accord, or be granted a quota equal to that of Iran. Iran, on the other hand, insisted that Iraq be given the same quota as in the 1984 division. On 15 December, Saudi Arabia proposed an across-the-board-cut of 7.5% per cent for all members.

On 20 December, the conference agreed to cut production by 7 per cent for the first six months of 1987, and fixed the price at $18 a barrel. The overall production ceiling was set at 15.8m b/d; this compared with the current production of 17m b/d. Iran's quota was cut from 2.75m b/d to 2.25m b/d; Iraq was assigned 1.5m b/d/, but it refused to sign the agreement.[28] Two days after the OPEC agreement was reached oil prices in the world markets jumped to $18 a barrel.[29]

Before assessing the Middle East oil developments in 1986 we should deal with two issues. The dismissal of the most outstanding and colorful OPEC leader in the history of the Organization, and its undisputed spokesman; and the impact of the lowered oil prices on the greatest oil consumer in the world, the US.

YAMANI'S DISMISSAL

Ahmad Zaki al-Yamani had been Saudi Arabia's Minister of Petroleum and Mineral Resources since 1962. He was responsible, over the years, for Saudi Arabia's oil policy; he was the most prominent force in the councils of OPEC, and known throughout the world as the most polished and smooth-tongued representative of the Middle East oil producers. At all international gatherings dealing with the question of energy, Yamani's words were the most listened to. Indeed, Yamani was "Mr Middle East Oil" and later "Mr Middle East Power" and "Mr Middle East Money". On 29 October 1986, King Fahd issued a royal decree dismissing "Mr Yamani" as Oil Minister.[30]

Al-Yamani, 56, was born into a wealthy family in Ta'if. His father was a judge and he himself graduated in law from the University of Cairo and studied at Harvard University. He became Minister when he was 31 years old.

Since no reason was given for his abrupt dismissal, there was much speculation. His relations with the Royal Family were mentioned, as he was a commoner. However, a man who had served under three Kings over a long period was not likely suddenly to develop difficulties with members of the Royal Family. The most likely reason for Yamani's dismissal was the failure of the Saudi oil policy. From early 1985 to the end of that year, Saudi Arabia's oil policy, forcefully and super-confidently presented by Yamani, threatened a price war against all oil producers and even threatened the world financial structure. The threat was of flooding the world oil markets, which only Saudi Arabia was capable of doing.

Yamani negotiated with OPEC and non-OPEC producers and delivered the threats. He reportedly advocated various devices to increase Saudi production and export. By August 1986 Saudi oil policy was an utter failure both in aims and in practical application, and it had to be changed radically. Yamani's dismissal was the repudiation of the old policy; and the naming of his successor, first as Acting Minister and then as Minister, was the beginning of a policy of controlled production and fixed prices.

Yet this single explanation does not make sense. When Fahd succeeded to the throne he took over the regime and personally involved himself in the affairs of state, and did not leave matters entirely in the hands of the Ministers. He was chairman of the Saudi Arabia Supreme Petroleum Council, and in the last two years it was Fahd rather than Yamani who made the official pronouncements about oil policies of the Kingdom. Moreover, never under the previous Kings did Yamani make statements of policy on oil in their names; only during Fahd's regime did Yamani often speak in the councils of OPEC and to the world at large in the name of the King. Indeed, Fahd often sent instructions to Yamani to change positions, and these instructions were made public. Yamani may therefore have been the scapegoat for the failure of policy that was as much his responsibility as the King's, and perhaps more the King's than Yamani's. The fact that Yamani was not a member of the Royal Family made it easier for Fahd to dismiss him.[31]

LOWER OIL PRICES' IMPACT ON THE UNITED STATES

The drop in oil prices from about $28 a barrel on 10 December 1985 to $9 a barrel in July 1986 was more than welcomed by the great number of oil consuming countries throughout the world. The drop of about two thirds in the price was a real revolution — after 13 years of suffering — in the economic and financial circumstances of these countries. On the other hand, the sharp drop in the oil price brought severe hardships to the oil producing countries: reduced revenues, curtailment of economic development programs, drastic decreases in financial reserves, increases in unemployment and sharp drops in the standard of living. The big Persian Gulf producers — Saudi Arabia, Kuwait and the UAE — could manage their economic life, though drastically curtailed, with the heavily reduced revenue. The small OPEC producers were the most seriously affected.

The non-OPEC oil exporters were differently affected. The Soviet Union, for which oil was *a*, if not *the*, major source of desperately needed foreign currency, was greatly upset by the huge drop in foreign currency earnings. Britain, as mentioned above, reconciled itself to the reduction of its oil income, and was consoled by the realization that the reduced oil prices would benefit the economy. Norway flirted with the possibility of cooperating with OPEC. Egypt was badly affected by the drop in oil prices as its economy was under great strain. Mexico was the most negatively affected, for its external debt reached over $90 bn and the oil resource was its major means of financing the economy and servicing the debt.

The US was uniquely affected. Being the greatest oil consumer, per capita as well as total, the public stood to save about $75 bn a year from the lowered oil prices. All the economic ills that resulted from the high oil prices imposed by OPEC would be removed. There would be greater resources for economic growth, increased employment opportunities, reduction in the negative balance of payment and perhaps no inflation. Above all, the price of oil would be determined not by manipulation but by a tenet of American capitalism: economic forces of the free market.

Although the US, especially the Republican Party, professed that it was always guided by the principle of free competition and that economic forces determined market prices, in reality, since the organization of the Standard Oil Company in 1870 by John D. Rockefeller, and until the current crisis, oil prices had never been determined by a free market. They were manipulated both domestically and internationally by cartel tactics and the actors were the same in both areas. Should the free market determine prices the entire oil industry structure would have to be radically changed.

The question was what could be done to prevent the so-called disaster facing the oil states and the oil companies?

A proposal which *The New York Times* and other publications enthusiastically supported, along with the oil states and the oil companies, was that the Government impose an import tax on oil equivalent to the difference between the price on the spot market and $28 a barrel (which was to be established as the permanent price). The advantages of such a measure would redound to the oil states and the oil companies. The consumers would gain nothing and pay the high prices as before. The advocates stressed that the increased revenue could reduce, if not wipe out, the Federal Government deficit. This would help the taxpayer, and it would prevent consumers from increasing consumption and maintain the conservation regimen. It would also preserve and even strengthen the service branch of the industry.

The Reagan Administration was divided as to what measures should be taken on the lowered oil prices. Some of the economic advisers advocated allowing the price to be determined by the free market without tampering. Very few members backed the import tax measure. The most outspoken opponent of the tax was Secretary of State George Shultz. On 10 February 1986 he reiterated his opposition to the measure and the opposition of the Administration to any attempt to prop up oil prices. The lower oil prices, he said "help a lot of people, including us."[32]

Reacting to the 2 April *The New York Times* advocacy of the oil-import tax, Energy Secretary John S. Herrington, in a letter to the editor on 6 April, stated the Administration's position on the issue. "If the energy story of the last five years tells us anything, it is that market-oriented energy policies are the answer to our nation's energy-security needs. This Administration has been steadfastly wedded to this course." He went on to list the advantages of the new situation. "There is no question that the US will reap enormous benefits from lower oil prices. They will slash inflation more, stimulate economic growth, cut the deficit and help American exports. Consumers are rightfully enjoying lower prices at the pumps." On the other hand, the oil-import tax "would send the energy prices upward. The resulting inflation would hold down economic growth, damage our allies and undercut our ability to sell exports in foreign markets."

The first reaction of President Ronald Reagan and the other members of the Administration to the lowered oil prices was that they were the product of the free market and not the result of manipulation, hence the decision to do nothing about them. However, if there was manipulation, measures would have to be taken to protect the domestic oil industry as a matter of national security. The basic need of the domestic oil industry is stability, which would guarantee price, operation and growth.

The manipulated drop of the oil price was primarily caused by Saudi Arabia's decision to increase production and flood the markets. After competing producers were eliminated, the major Persian Gulf producers would control the supply and raise prices to levels higher than ever before. To prevent such an eventuality Saudi Arabia would have to be persuaded, together with its other major Persian Gulf producers, to curtail oil production and stabilize the market.

The campaign was launched in March. On 31 March, Secretary Herrington called on Saudi Arabia and other OPEC members to consider the political consequences of falling oil prices. He declared: "It has got to be apparent to the Saudis and to the rest of OPEC what damage is being done to our industries...The Saudis have a lot of friends in the world, and forcing prices down by excess production has ramifications among their allies. I am sure they are conscious of this."[33]

The next day, Vice President George Bush, a former Texas Congressman and the head of an oil company in Odessa, Texas, from 1948–66, announced that he was taking a ten-day trip to the Middle East and visiting Saudi Arabia and other countries. His goal, he said, was to "tell Saudi Arabia that the protection of American security interests requires action to stabilize the falling price of oil." He warned against letting oil prices experience "a continued free fall like a parachutist jumping out without a parachute."[34] Bush apparently went too far and soon retreated, declaring that he was seeking stability. Some members of the Administration were disturbed by his remarks and hastened to assure the Saudis and the other producers that there had been no change in the stated policy.

Bush's meeting with Fahd in Dhahran forced the Vice President to retreat further and declare that he supported "the lowest possible prices consistent with the fact that we need a domestic oil industry for our national security." He had not tried to exert pressure for high prices. "I honestly can't set a price, I don't know where we find this balance."[35] He was reported to have told the King that the US did not blame Saudi Arabia for the collapse of the oil prices.

Herrington pursued the line of the danger of manipulating prices. In his letter to *The New York Times* he stated that "the dangers of manipulating oil prices in the 1980s can be as serious as it was in the 70s. It can severely weaken competing producers of other nations, allow OPEC to corner the market again, and, in the long term, drive oil prices back up."[36]

Bush's mission to the Middle East must have had the backing of the President, who apparently retreated from his position of support of the free market. For on 9 April the President said at a press conference in Washington that "the market in oil is not completely free" since in some cases governments rather than companies set production levels and prices. He added that maybe someone would think of driving it down to get rid of a lot of competition. Foreign producers might "do what comes naturally to monopolists" and drive prices up again. He warned that the US must be alert "to see that no one starts playing tricks for some kind of illicit future gain." He was obviously pointing to Saudi Arabia. Yet, when asked what the US might do if it determined that prices were being manipulated for such sinister ends, he replied: "Then we would have to see what our options were."[37]

His options were not numerous. For the US, after identifying the manipulator and clearly discerning his designs, could not do very much. The Bush mission was a failure, if not foredoomed. Three days later, on 9 April, the President stressed that the benefits of cheaper oil for the US economy far outweighed the drawbacks. Some would have "to make a difficult adjustment to these new lower prices, but overall less expensive oil represents a tremendous boon to our economy."[38]

The oil states and the oil companies have not succeeded in halting the deterioration of their position. Neither an oil-import tax nor Saudi Arabia's production reduction could be achieved. Politically, the President and the Republican Party found themselves in a deep quandary. The great drop in oil prices would make the Republican Party very popular with the oil consuming public.[39] On the other hand, the oil states and the oil companies would be estranged from the party. The Reagan Administration was, therefore, practically paralyzed on the issue.

THE 1990s

As oil prices began to drop rapidly and the inevitable impact was sharply felt in the US, a number of academic and research institutions, oil company specialists and other analysts began to issue reports predicting what the drastic reduction in price would do to the energy situation in the 1990s. Practically all predicted doom.

The high OPEC prices induced the consumers to change radically the pattern of energy consumption. There were basic life-style changes of conservation in home heating and air conditioning, in commercial establishments, and, through new technologies, the restructuring of industrial plants and the rearranging of patterns of the factors of production. In the same spirit governments and research institutions were feverishly working for the development of alternatives to oil. An intensive effort was made to increase oil production from wells that were not considered profitable prior to the 1973 oil crisis. The service sector of the industry was greatly expanded. The net result was a great decrease in the consumption of oil on the one hand and an increase in oil production on the other. The overall pattern of energy consumption, instead of increasing was either stationary or even decreasing.

On the other hand the major non-OPEC oil regions, such as the North Sea and Alaska, will shortly be exhausted. US production will continue to decline rapidly. The only major source for oil will be the Middle East. The Western world will then be at the mercy of the big producers in the Persian Gulf. The terms they impose will be much harsher and the prices much higher than ever before. The crucial time will be in the 1990s. The euphoria and reckless consumption of oil at low prices might continue during the 1980s, but with the 1990s the great energy crisis will come and overwhelm the consuming world. It will then be at the mercy of Saudi Arabia, Kuwait, the UAE, Iran and Iraq (the last two will no longer be at war), not only economically and financially, but worse — politically.

Most of these gloomy reports and predictions were based on assumptions and statistical projections that were doubtful to say the least.[40] For the oil development story was unique and, therefore, the authors had no knowledge nor experience from which to draw conclusions and make projections. The reports of doom of the mid-1970s were all proven wrong, for their assumptions were not based on facts. A plethora of books, reports and articles were based on the following major assumptions: in spite of some 13 years of suffering at the hands of OPEC and the resultant saner and more rational use of energy, as soon as the price came down all the past experience would be discarded overnight and the consumers would revert to the pre-1970 oil-waste orgy. All the new technological advances in the usage of energy would be dismantled and the old system would be restored.

It was assumed that all the achievements in the research for alternatives to oil would be totally abandoned for the old use of oil. It was also assumed, as in the reports of the mid-1970s, that the yearly energy increase would jump to 5 per cent to 7 per cent and even higher. At the same time the production level in the US would constantly and rapidly decline. In the mid-1990s, the US would have to import over 80 per cent of its consumption needs.

These assumptions and many others have no basis in fact. There is no evidence that all conservation advances and other achievements will be abandoned. It would seem that what all these reports aimed to do was to force the US Government to take measures to protect the "national security" interests of the domestic oil industry, namely the oil states and the oil companies. The Persian Gulf producers avidly adopted the conclusions of the doom reports. By the 1990s, they warned, they would dictate to the Western world oil prices and political conditions for the supply of oil.

The answer to the Persian Gulf producers was given by Belkacem Nabi, Algeria's Minister of Energy and Petrochemical Industries, in an interview with the Kuwait daily *al-Watan* on 22 April 1986. He said: "I believe we are making an obvious political mistake in believing that the future of this industry lies with the Gulf states alone. The Western countries will not wait from now until 1990, for example, to allow a group of Arab countries to dominate their destiny."

ASSESSMENT

1986 was no doubt the worst year in OPEC's experience. Between December 1985 and July 1986 the price of a barrel of oil dropped from $28 to about $9.[41] After six conferences — ordinary and extraordinary — the Organization was unable to establish a permanent, agreed system of production quotas and price levels. The ills that befell OPEC in the last four years, which became progressively more severe, are to be traced to the nature of the so-called OPEC cartel. OPEC as a cartel with a basic difference, as described by Ahmad Zaki Yamani, lost its difference when the chips were down; instead of a shortage of supply which disposed of the oil of all the members at premium prices, a glut set in in the oil markets, and members vied with each other to sell their oil, almost at any price. Although OPEC by its nature was not a cartel, it acted as one, and this led to the inevitable consequences of a cartel.

As the third crisis progressed, Saudi Arabia as the biggest producer, and the owner of the greatest reserves and production capacity, refused to carry the small producers on its shoulders. All Saudi Arabia's cajoling and dire threats failed to persuade the smaller producers to accept their inferior status and allow Saudi Arabia the big share of the "cake" it claimed it was entitled to because of its superior status. The smaller producers resorted to two means available to them. On the one hand, they demanded drastic curtailment in the oil output of the big producers in order to restore the former official prices; on the other hand, they cheated on production and price levels. They resorted to such tactics as barter, countertrade and netback deals to increase, or at least maintain, their oil revenue. Consequently, in 1986 Saudi Arabia defiantly increased production, which almost reached pre-third crisis levels.

By August, Saudi Arabia was willing to return, on a two-month temporary basis, to the October 1984 quota production apportionment. It abandoned previous objectives for a system of fixed prices with radical changes in determining the benchmark crude and the differentials structure. But a number of members did not abide by their quotas, and others — especially Kuwait — belligerently and threateningly demanded substantial increments in their production quotas. Minor adjustments were made in some of the quotas, but the differences remained and discontent prevailed.

The underlying cause of dissension in OPEC was the unbridgeable gap between the interests of Saudi Arabia as the big oil producer and the interests of the smaller producers. Despite all the Saudi protestations of devotion, loyalty and sacrifices for the Organization, the conflicting interests of the two could not be reconciled.

When the third crisis began at the end of 1981, OPEC did not realize or refused to admit that its very high prices were the inexorable cause of the crisis and its intensification. Instead, it blamed the consumers and their policies and devices, and the non-OPEC producers for stubbornly refusing to join the Organization to stabilize the market. Only on 20 May 1986, in a reference on Saudi television to the cause of the OPEC crisis, did Yamani admit, "First of all I would like to clarify that the mistake made by OPEC was that it raised prices between 1979 and 1981 to very high levels that prompted the consuming nations to pursue alternative sources of energy. This was OPEC's mistake."[42] But the blame was not entirely OPEC's. There were forces outside the Organization which must share the blame. At the end of April, after the conclusion of the Geneva conference, the Saudi Arabian Oil Minister was asked about the cause of the OPEC crisis. He said: "The main cause started in 1979 when OPEC revised its prices for two years, plus the huge build-up of stocks for consumers. This led to more conservation and less consumption, with the stocks coming back as an additional source of supply. The high price of oil helped non-OPEC producers to increase production, to explore and exploit. Thereafter, they kept increasing production and OPEC kept decreasing its production. I really cannot blame OPEC for what you call lack of discipline because it was too much to take. They were reducing production every year. Also I think there were concerted efforts by the major consumers to push the price down to what it is now."[43]

This sophisticated analysis, blaming the consumers and the non-OPEC producers after four years of crisis, did not help OPEC to devise policies and measures which the circumstances demanded. Instead, all efforts were concentrated on getting the non-OPEC producers to join the Organization outright and form a world cartel, or at least cooperate with it in stabilizing the market and bringing the price back to the level at the time of the outbreak of the crisis. However, all the attempts made in this direction with the major and crucial producers, especially Britain and the US, utterly failed. OPEC therefore turned to the minor non-OPEC producers such as Angola, Egypt, Malaysia, Mexico, Norway and Oman. The difficulty with the small non-OPEC producers was the same as with the small OPEC producers, for their oil revenue could not be reduced further by cutting production. Their commitment could not be more dependable than the commitment of OPEC members. After long hesitation Norway announced on 10 September that it would reduce exports by 10 per cent during November and December.[44] The minor non-OPEC producers promised to cut production, but the extent of their reduced output and the impact these reductions had on the overall oil supply in the world market and on the price level remained unclear.

The Soviet Union was, naturally, deeply disturbed by the drastic drop of oil prices, for it benefited enormously from the high OPEC prices. While it did not identify with OPEC, its oil export prices were determined by high OPEC prices. On 28 February 1986, the Soviet Ambassador to Venezuela told the Venezuelan news agency that the Soviet Union was interested in reaching agreement with OPEC and other oil exporters to stabilize the world oil market.[45] On 24 August, *The New York Times* reported that the Soviet Union had agreed to cut oil exports to the West by 100,000 barrels a day at the request of Iran, for the purpose of stabilizing oil prices. In 1985, the Soviet Union sold to the West 1.36m b/d, and derived from it 60 per cent of its hard currency. But the Soviet move was only for the months of September and October. Naturally, the Soviet Union would be interested in entering into oil agreements with OPEC as a whole and with individual members, as well as with non-OPEC producers, not only for economic and financial advantages but also for political reasons. Both Britain and the US rejected out of hand all OPEC attempts, under threats, to involve them in stabilizing — really monopolizing — the world oil market.

Thus, while OPEC may have achieved limited and temporary success with the minor non-OPEC producers and with the USSR, its major objective of aligning the major non-OPEC producers in restoring high oil prices in 1986 was a failure.

The reaction of the US to the drop in oil prices was ambivalent. There were attempts to take some action — from imposing an oil import tax to persuading Saudi Arabia to reduce production in order to protect the US oil industry. But in view of the dangers — both domestically and internationally — of any tampering with the existing oil structures, the attempts were bound to fail. The US took the oil-price debacle in its stride.

The upward movement of the oil price, from about $9 in July to about $18 by the close of the year, was taken by some analysts as an indication of the success of the new OPEC policy. The oil problem was on its way to a satisfactory solution. Prices would climb back to their previous levels.

A careful analysis reveals that the price advances were not the result of economic factors. There was no substantial increase in demand, and the glut did not dry up. The up and down price movements were the result of psychological and speculative reactions by traders to reports emerging from OPEC conferences and committees. Moreover, OPEC members were deeply disturbed by evidence of non-abidance by the decisions on production and other issues. The basic characteristics of internal OPEC conflicts were still operating.[46]

NOTES

For the place and frequency of publications cited here, and for the full name of the publication, news agency, radio station or monitoring service where an abbreviation is used, please see "List of Sources." Only in the case of more than one publication bearing the same name is the place of publication noted here.

1. At a symposium in Bonn on 14 October 1975 Ahmad Zaki al-Yamani, then the Saudi Arabian Minister of Oil and Mineral Resources explained the difference between a regular cartel and OPEC. The general rule in cartels is that the strongest member "has to carry weaker members on its shoulders. It will eventually tire of its burden and refuse to bear it any longer, and therefore any cartel will come to an end and collapse. However, this is not the case with OPEC. In most cartels, the strongest member seeks to sell as much of its

goods as possible, but Saudi Arabia's interests lies in selling less of its oil." *MEES*, 17 October 1975.

2. *MEES*, 29 March 1982.
3. It is not clear whether the father of the idea of a price war was the well-established former Minister of Oil and Mineral Resources, Ahmad Zaki al-Yamani, or King Fahd himself. See below the issue of Yamani's dismissal.
4. *MEES*, 16 December 1985.
5. *MEES*, 10 February 1986.
6. *MEES*, 31 March 1986.
7. *NYT*, 23 March; *MEES*, 24 March 1986. On 10 April, in addressing the Economic Club of New York, the Chancellor said: "It is in the interests neither of the UK nor of the world at large to curb UK production in an attempt to keep the price artificially high." *MEES*, 14 April 1986.
8. Since OPEC controls were limited to crude oil, Saudi Arabia negotiated netback deals with major oil companies in the US, Europe and the Far East. The netback price was based on the netback realization from product sales, minus refining expense and crude freight/insurance cost from port of loading. At the time, the price realized was about $2–3 lower than OPEC crude price. *PE*, July 1985; *MEES*, 27 January 1986.
9. *MEES*, 31 March 1986; *PE*, March 1986, p 105, reported that Aramco was aiming at 2m b/d westward, and 1m b/d eastbound for netback deals.
10. For a definition and practice of countertrade see Benjamin Shwadran, *Middle East Oil Crises since 1973* (Boulder: Westview Press, 1986), pp 200–1.
11. The March conference was assessed by the following professional publications. The *PE*, March 1986, p 74 summarized, "OPEC's desperate gamble, as we described two months ago the 'market shares' strategy adopted last December, has not proved a winner. It has failed in the sense that every member of the cartel, with the exception of Saudi Arabia, is now worse off than it would otherwise have been. Not surprisingly, the toothless committee which met early last month evolved no magic formula to counter the inexorable operation of economic forces. Unless this month's full-scale ministerial meeting is able to reinforce production discipline, 1986 will go down in the annals as the year in which the 25-year-old cartel finally fell apart, allowing oil prices to drop through the floor." *MEES*, 31 March 1986, said that the conference fizzled out in total failure to agree on the quota division of a targeted second quarter ceiling of 14m b/d, or even a modified version of 14.9m b/d.
12. *Petroleum Times*, April 1986.
13. *MEES*, 28 April 1986.
14. *PE*, June, 1986 reported that OPEC had signed a memorandum of understanding with the five non-OPEC exporters promising cooperation in production limitation. Yamani expressed the view that "an adequate contribution from them would be around 1m b/d."
15. The *Petroleum Times Price Report*, 21 June 1986 observed that "OPEC as a group, over the last three months, has increased its oil output and exports as prices have been falling. OPEC crude production is up some 30 per cent on the 14m b/d output levels of three months ago."
16. By the end of 1983, Saudi Arabia organized Norbec, a company which secretly acquired a number of very large crude oil storage tankers. In 1984, it had been estimated that Norbec stored 40m barrels of Saudi crude oil. The tankers were anchored outside the Persian Gulf, in ports in South America, the Far East and West Africa.
17. *MEES*, 4 August 1986 concluded: "The fact is that OPEC is now in a free-for-all situation in which the former quota limitations are no longer recognized by any member country."
18. The cooperation of the non-OPEC producers was summarized on 11 August. Mexico promised to cut 10 per cent of production, from 1.5m b/d to 1.35m b/d; Malaysia to cut 10 per cent, from 510,000 b/d to 459,000 b/d; Oman ready to cooperate but no specifics; Egypt ready to cooperate; Norway promised to study the situation. *MEES*, 11 August 1986.
19. Ibid.
20. *FT*, 6 April 1986.
21. *NYT*, 9 August 1986.
22. In the middle of November, Petromin was reported to have signed a one-year agreement for 30,000 b/d crude oil supply with Hispanoil on a netback price basis. *MEES*, 17 November 1986.

23. *MEES*, 18 August 1986. Saudi Arabia promised in the August accord to reduce production to 4.3m b/d; *NYT*, 16 August 1986.
24. *NYT*, 9 August 1986.
25. *MEES*, 11 August 1986.
26. *MEES*, 20 October 1986.
27. *MEES's* reporter noted, "Both Saudi Arabia and Kuwait have categorically made it clear that they will not countenance any further extension of the agreement after the end of December." *MEES*, 22 October 1986.
28. The vagaries of the oil market. On 15 December, it looked as if OPEC had reached agreement on price and production levels, and prices in the oil market went up from $15 to $16.60 a barrel. Three days later, when Iran called for the expulsion of Iraq from OPEC for refusing to accept the quota, prices dropped to $15.85 a barrel.
29. *NYT*, 21 December 1986 noted that "the agreement appears to reduce OPEC production by 1m b/d to roughly 16m." Referring to the change of the Oil Minister in Saudi Arabia, the publication observed, "Hisham M. Nazer, the acting Saudi Oil Minister, put strong pressure on his OPEC colleagues to limit production. Mr Yamani, who was dismissed by King Fahd this fall, had supported free market pricing as a way to force higher cost producers out of the market and stop OPEC members from cheating on the quotas." See below.
30. The decree: "We, Fahd Ibn Abd al-'Aziz, King of Saudi Arabia decree that: (1) Mr Ahmad Zaki Yamani, the Minister of Petroleum and Mineral Resources, is relieved of his post. (2) Mr Hisham Muhi al-Din Nazer, the Minister of Planning is charged with undertaking the work of Minister of Petroleum and Mineral Resources in addition to his own duties. (3) The Deputy Prime Minister shall implement the decree." *MEES*, 3 November 1986.
31. For further insights into the character of Yamani, see Shwadran, op cit, 127–30, 211–13, et passim.
32. *MEES*, 17 February 1986. When asked what the US should do if the price decline became so steep that it threatened to disrupt supplies, he replied, "Nothing, oil is a very important commodity, but I am a believer in the market and so I'll stay with it."
33. *MEES*, 7 April 1986.
34. *NYT*, 6 April; *MEES*, 7 April 1986.
35. *NYT*, 13 April 1986.
36. *NYT*, 6 April 1986.
37. *MEES*, 14 April 1986.
38. *MEES*, 1 April 1986.
39. In a radio broadcast on 11 January 1986, Reagan said that US economic measures had "shaken up oil prices and brought OPEC to its knees." *MEES*, 20 January 1986.
40. In a long report in *WSJ*, the reporter stated: "If the price of oil should rise to say $23 a barrel, according to a Congressional Budget Office study, US imports by 1990 would average 6m b/d. At an $18 price, close to the current level, that study found imports rising to 7.8m b/d by 1990. A separate report by the Library of Congress concludes that, at $20 a barrel, imports by 1990 would reach 7.7m b/d. At $15 a barrel, imports would be much higher by 1990, averaging 11m b/d. That would suggest cash outflows for oil of $56 bn to $60 bn a year." *WSJ*, 23 May 1986.
41. It was estimated in August that the price collapse cost OPEC members $100m a day in lost revenue during the first six months of 1986.
42. *MEES*, 2 June 1986.
43. *MEES*, 28 April 1986. Speaking in Geneva after the conference, Yamani was very conciliatory toward the OPEC members. But addressing Saudi Arabia, he blamed OPEC outright and added, "After OPEC committed this blunder Saudi Arabia issued warning after warning and stood practically alone...[except for the UAE]. Everyone was against Saudi Arabia and wanted to raise prices." *MEES*, 2 June 1986.
44. While in Oslo, the US Energy Secretary John Herrington said on 16 September that Norway was wrong to intervene in production decisions. "We would prefer decisions on production levels to be left to market forces, rather than governments...We are opposed to cartels, and do not want to see OPEC established as the power it was in the 1970s." *MEED*, 20–26 September; *MEES*, 22 September 1986. Herrington reported in London on 23

October that, while OPEC took Norway's decision to reduce exports by 10 per cent in November and December as support of OPEC's effort to stabilize prices, the Norwegian Prime Minister confirmed to him that "it was not a move to stabilize prices." *MEED*, 1–7 November 1986.

45. He added that his country was seeking bilateral and multilateral meetings with OPEC members for this purpose.
46. See Note 28 above.

The Middle East "Oil Decade" in Perspective

GAD G. GILBAR

Following the 16 October 1973 announcement by the ministers of the Organization of Petroleum Exporting Countries (OPEC) of their decision to double the prices of all types of crude oil, it became generally held that a profound social and economic change was about to occur in many societies, both developing and developed. There was particular hope among the Middle East oil-producing countries that a new era had opened, and that as it progressed fundamental changes would ensue in their economic and political circumstances. There were even those who envisaged an "oil century" with the economic and political world order being determined by the leading members of OPEC. It seems that the first period (some say the last) in which the oil states enjoyed great economic and political power terminated in the 1980s. The years 1973–81 are considered the "oil decade," with the economic power and political influence of the oil states being incomparably greater than in any previous period and greater than in the years immediately following that decade.

The surge in economic power was predicated, of course, on the steep rise in revenues from the export of crude oil, natural gas, and refined products. Income from oil exports by the seven Middle Eastern members of OPEC rose from $10 bn in 1972 to $207 bn in 1980 and $187 bn in 1981 (current prices). The total revenue of these governments in the decade under discussion amounted to $1,120 bn (current prices).[1] The immensity of this sum may be gauged if we recall, for example, that in 1981, when Saudi Arabian oil revenues reached their peak of $113.2 bn, this figure was 4.7 times greater than the Egyptian gross domestic product (GDP) that year and 5.5 times the Israeli GDP.[2]

The increased political power of the Middle East oil states derived largely from the tremendous increase in their economic resources. Petrodollars bought friends and in many cases mitigated hostility in the region and elsewhere. In addition, these countries became an important market for the industrialized economies and very welcome customers at Western money markets. Above all, it was the dependence of Western Europe, Japan, and the US on the import of Middle East oil that gave the exporters remarkable political leverage. We may note that in 1976 oil from Middle East Arab states constituted about 70 per cent of the total oil imports of France, 56 per cent of Japan and 38 per cent of the US.[3]

This article seeks to examine the changes Middle East OPEC countries underwent during the oil decade as a result of the unexpected influx of capital and advanced technology, of maneuverability and political power in the world arena on a scale Middle East rulers had never known in modern times. Put otherwise, we are asking how the oil states of the region exploited their extraordinary wealth. The examination of the influences and changes attributable to the oil factor is made in three contexts: (1) demographic effects; (2) economic and social results; and (3) political aspects. For the sake of brevity, only major changes are dealt with here. Statistical data relate mainly to a selected number of oil states.

DEMOGRAPHIC DEVELOPMENTS

Directly or indirectly, the economic forces generated by the "oil effect" gave rise to a number of demographic processes in the oil states themselves and in several neighboring countries. Three developments in this context are especially prominent.

The first is the process of settlement of nomads in the Arab oil-producing countries, Saudi Arabia in particular. While at the end of the 1960s nomads were estimated to account for about 50 per cent of the population, some 12 years later this figure had fallen to 10 per cent.[4] The smaller number of the Bedouin settled in villages. Most headed for the main cities of the Saudi Kingdom. Settlement in villages accorded with the official policy of encouraging the settlement of the nomads, while migration to the cities was the result of powerful, attractive forces generated by the rapid economic development of the major urban centers. The dramatic fall in the proportion of nomads in the total Saudi population had many results, of which the most important was the continued decline of tribal power in the political system.

Secondly, the process of urbanization, which began prior to the oil decade, continued in full force. Migration to the cities is connected with the settlement of nomads noted above, but not exclusively. Accelerated urbanization is a common phenomenon in the desert oil states such as Saudi Arabia and Libya as well as in other oil economies such as Iran and Iraq. The proportion of city-dwellers in the total population increased in Saudi Arabia from 30 per cent in 1960 to 69 per cent in 1982, in Libya from 23 to 58 per cent, in Iran from 32 to 52 per cent and in Iraq from 43 to 70 per cent, respectively.[5] It is thus evident that in these, as in the other Middle East oil countries, city dwellers became the majority of the population during the oil decade.

Thirdly, during this ten-year period, movement of workers between the Arab states increased greatly: from the poor states — Egypt, Yemen (North and South), Sudan, Syria, and Jordan — to the oil-rich states — Iraq, Saudi Arabia, Kuwait, Libya and the United Arab Emirates (UAE). At the peak of this movement in 1982, the number of migrant workers from the countries listed was estimated at about five million.[6] Most of them remained only a limited number of years in the oil countries. A movement on this scale was possible on account of the need by the oil states for more workers, either for the extensive development programs (Saudi Arabia, Libya, Kuwait) or to replace the workers recruited into the army to fight the war (Iraq). These workers transferred large sums of money to their families in their home countries. Billions of dollars were sent each year to the poorer Arab states in this way. In several of the latter, these transfers became a most important element in foreign currency revenues. In Egypt, transfers sent through official channels amounted to about $3 bn yearly in the early 1980s. In Jordan a (net) sum of $900m flowed in; and in Syria the figure was $700m–800m in both 1981 and 1982.[7] The movement of workers on so large a scale from one Arab country to another and the transfer of such great sums of money created for the first time since these states were established a real interdependence, particularly between the rich and the poor economies. A sharp drop in the scale of the transfers would severely damage the ability of such states as Egypt, Jordan and Syria to balance their expenditures in foreign currency. Beyond the economic relations, the inter-Arab migratory movement created additional reciprocal connections and influences, particularly in the social and cultural spheres.

ECONOMIC AND SOCIAL CHANGES

The enormous amount of resources that the oil economies disposed of from October 1973 permitted them simultaneously to increase both consumption (private and public) and investment by tens and sometimes hundreds of per cent annually. The rise in expenditure on consumption since the mid-1970s, particularly among the upper strata, is a matter of record. The consumption of the rulers of the oil states, their families and relatives came to symbolize their wealth. This spending was restricted only by the limits of Middle Eastern imagination and Western advanced technology. The consumption of the other social strata also greatly increased. Thus, for example, the volume of food, clothing and durable goods imported rose by hundreds of per cent in the period under study. A considerable proportion of these items was acquired by the middle and even lower classes.

In the field of public consumption the leap in military spending, especially the acquisition of weapons, was clearly evident. Iran under the Shah, Saudi Arabia, Iraq (already before the outbreak of war in 1980) and Libya each spent billions of dollars annually on rocket systems, aircraft, submarines, tanks, and similar sophisticated weaponry produced in the US and other Western countries, and the USSR.[8] There was also a substantial rise in spending on public administration, as a result of the expansion of the bureaucratic systems in the oil countries. In spite of the investment of many tens of billions of dollars during the oil decade by each of the oil states on hundreds of projects, no structural change occurred in any of them. A structural change in this context is expressed, among other things, in a noticeable drop in the relative share of the oil sector in the GDP and a parallel rise in the relative share of the non-oil sectors, primarily industry. A decrease in the dependency of these economies on oil revenues became one of the major economic goals of the oil states.

However, except for the petrochemical industry, which developed rapidly and was also an export-oriented branch, development in light and heavy industry was limited. At the end of the oil decade, not one of the oil states possessed an industrial sector that contributed 20 per cent or more of the GDP and employed a similar percentage of local workers. Iran alone approached this figure. At the end of the Pahlavi period the industrial product (excluding oil) constituted about 15 per cent of the GDP.[9] However, it should be stressed that a change in the structure of the Iranian economy had begun as early as the 1930s, and it received a great impetus during the oil decade. There are many reasons why the Arab oil economies did not undergo a structural change, the most significant being the lack of incentives for the establishment of industries over a wide range. In countries where foreign currency revenues were so great and which for most of the period were subject to the pressures of the industrialized economies to recycle their revenues, among other things through the massive acquisition of manufactured goods, no incentives to encourage local manufacturing were generated. It hardly needs to be stated that none of the Arab oil countries employed a policy of restrictive imports. There were almost no administrative restrictions or import quotas that could serve as a protective barrier for local production.

A decrease in dependence on oil revenues through rapid growth of the non-oil sectors was therefore only marginal. At the same time, a marked and important change did occur in two areas: in the development of physical infrastructure (especially in the desert oil states) and in human resources (investment in educational systems). In a few years there arose in states such as Saudi Arabia, Libya, and the UAE wide-ranging and high-quality systems of roads, means of transportation, networks of communication, power stations and electricity grids. Similarly, these and other oil states made heavy investments in building both for public purposes and for housing. New cities were built.[10] The central place that investments held in the infrastructure is not surprising, for they are not contingent on "preconditions"; the investments themselves are essential for the development of other economic sectors. For this reason the rulers of these states gave priority to the construction of infrastructure. Furthermore, the obstacles in the way of construction of infrastructure itself — whether highways and airports or hospitals and schools — were surmounted relatively easily: the scarcity of labor was solved by opening the gates of these countries to workers, skilled and unskilled, from abroad. The shortage of raw materials or any other item needed was made good by imports. Planning and completing complex projects were also not a problem: multinational corporations from the US, Japan and Western Europe competed for contracts in planning and constructing the various projects.

The most impressive development occurred in the educational systems. Very considerable sums — in absolute and relative terms — were allocated to this development. Saudi Arabia spent over $9 bn, and even Kuwait and Libya each spent over $1 bn on the development and operation of educational systems in 1982.[11] The funds went not only toward the construction of buildings and acquisition of equipment. Large sums were expended on teachers from Western and neighboring Arab countries. Similarly, governments paid the tuition fees of students at colleges and universities in Europe and the US.

The high priority given to education was the outcome of a "rapid growth" strategy. From the moment rulers and governments were motivated to modernize their economy and society, it became vital to give precedence to education.

The results of investment in educational systems have been considerable, particularly the large increase in enrolment rates of pupils in secondary schools (i.e., the percentage of pupils attending secondary schools, of the total of the relevant age group). In Saudi Arabia this rate rose in 1970-82 from 12 per cent to 32 per cent, in Iraq from 24 to 55 per cent, and in the UAE from 22 to 67 per cent. Illiteracy rates also decreased consistently as a direct result of increasing enrolment in primary schools. In 1982, enrolment rates in these schools reached 67 per cent in Saudi Arabia, 91 per cent in Kuwait, 97 per cent in Iran and 109 per cent in Iraq (above 100 per cent as many of the 11+ age group stayed on at primary school).[12] The expansion of education, which is gaining momentum, will be fully expressed in many spheres in the oil states. In a number of areas, not only economic but also military and political, the results are already evident.

The massive influx of economic resources into the oil economies naturally affected the mode of distribution of capital and income. From existing data it is possible to indicate the social groups and strata that improved not only their real but also their relative economic conditions. First, there was a huge growth in the accumulation of property and the amplitude of income of the ruling elites in the Arab oil states and in Iran until the Islamic Revolution. This arose from the fact that oil in these countries is state-owned, and revenues from its export flowed into government coffers — that is, the rulers' coffers. The figures we have on the "property portfolios" of the Shah of Iran, the Saudi house, and the al-Sabah family of Kuwait are of course only partial; but from the fragmentary information that has been published, it appears that these rulers joined the ranks of the small group of individuals who privately own the greatest holdings in our times.[13]

Another social group whose accumulated capital and level of income rose considerably comprised the private businessmen of the oil countries: company owners, suppliers of various services, etc. The growth of wealth of this group stemmed from the steep rise in demand for their services, from the significant increase in the import of goods, and from the encouragement given to private investors to participate in large-scale construction and development projects; in Pahlavi Iran there was government support for private enterprise in industry.[14] These groups also gained economically from the high inflation rates during the oil decade in the economies under review.

The condition of the other social groups — the civil service and salaried employees in the private sector — was different. The real income of most, if not all, of these groups rose. In some cases the annual rise in real terms reached 20-25 per cent. However, the gap between these strata and the elite and the upper-middle class increased considerably.[15] It appears, also, that at the bottom level of the oil societies there were those whose economic situation worsened: in real terms their income fell. An outstanding example was Iran, where there was a deterioration of the condition of the landless peasantry. As a result of the agrarian reform and the introduction of wide-scale mechanization in farming (the creation of the large farms), many of these peasants lost their livelihood, migrated to the big cities, but did not find permanent employment there. They formed the group that inhabited the shantytowns in Tehran, Tabriz and other cities.[16] The governments in many oil countries did not maintain effective fiscal mechanisms to reduce inequality in the distribution of wealth and income. Such an important tool as progressive income tax did not exist at all (Saudi Arabia) or was ineffective (Iran). The growth in resources was accompanied, therefore, by a widening of economic gaps. Proportionately, the upper tenths benefited more from the boom than the lower tenths. The harsh social consequences of this were mitigated by the rise in the real income of most of the strata and the opening of effective channels of mobility, particularly in private business.

POLITICAL ASPECTS

The "oil effect" left its mark in many parts of the political arena. Here we focus on three areas only: its effect on the stability of regimes; its impact on the vision of Arab unity and pan-Arab solidarity; and its influence on the nature of the relations between the oil economies and the West.

How far was the stability of regimes in the oil countries determined by the "Eldorado effect"? On the face of it, developments were polar. At one extreme there was a revolution in Iran comparable to the great revolutions of the modern age that brought to power a theocratic regime led by a new political elite of Shi'ite clerics. At the other extreme, in the Arab oil states, there was stability and continuity to a degree unknown since the 1950s. This stability is characteristic both of regimes that have undergone a military *coup d'état* (Iraq, Libya) and of "conservative" monarchies (Saudi Arabia,

Kuwait). This striking difference is due to several factors, only one of which is noted here in view of its obvious association with the "oil effect." It is the different manner in which, until 1979, petrodollars were used in Iran as compared with the Arab oil states. In Iran, the way oil revenues were used aroused opposition and increasing hostility toward the Shah and his regime. A powerful lever of rule — available economic resources — boomeranged. Instead of increasing support for the regime, it weakened it. First, because the glaringly uneven distribution of resources among the various sections of the Iranian population provoked much anger. The Arab regimes showed greater sensitivity in this respect, realizing the importance of distributing wealth in a way that would appear fair according to the criteria prevalent in their societies. Secondly, the Shah's massive expenditure on economic development aroused great hostility because of its very scope and what many considered its "over-rapid modernization." In the Arab countries, too, there was heavy investment in economic systems, but the rulers proved to be more concerned about their social costs. One should note, however, that in the Arab oil countries there were also developments that raised doubts about the immunity of the regimes. Regarding the monarchical oil states, several scholars have stressed the ever-growing gap between the rising social force and self-awareness of the middle class — in particular its medium and upper sections — and its low political status; that is, the lack of appropriate representation and influence at the centers of political power. This gap harbors a threat to the stability (and perhaps to the very existence) of these regimes.[17]

One of the predominant, even surprising, political developments in the oil decade was that the ideal of Arab unity and pan-Arab solidarity suffered heavy blows, the most severe since the idea of Arab unity became a political force in the Middle East. Two events stand out in this connection. The first is the separate peace Egypt made with Israel in 1979. The State that led the Arab world since the 1950s in its struggle to realize Arab unity transgressed both ideologically and politically against a basic injunction in the perception of Arab Nationalism by its very recognition of the neighboring Zionist State, let alone its willingness to live with it in peace. Secondly, in the Gulf war between Iraq and Iran, the latter won political, economic, and military support from Syria and Libya — two of the more radical Arab states regarding Arab unity and solidarity. In the oil decade, therefore, the Arab world became deeply divided against the background of its relations with non-Arab states — Israel and Iran. As with many of the developments noted above, the oil factor was not the sole cause of the deep crisis that undermined Arab unity. Revenues from oil exacerbated the differences in the economic conditions of the Arab states, particularly between the sparsely inhabited oil states of the Arabian Peninsula and the densely populated countries of the Nile Valley. The yawning gap in available resources for consumption and investment between Saudi Arabia or Kuwait, on the one hand, and Egypt or Sudan, on the other, put the concept of unity to a most difficult test. The poor Arab states demanded a significant share in the unexpected riches. As this demand was rejected, the attitude of the poor states toward the meaning and validity of the idea of Arab unity veered sharply. In the case of Egypt, serious economic and political constraints reinforced its call for economic assistance from its wealthy Arab neighbors. But when the oil states refused to countenance these demands Egypt embarked on a new and different path, no longer consonant with the ideology of Arab Nationalism as it had been crystallized since the First World War.[18] The tension betwen the two

Ba'thist regimes — the Syrian and Iraqi — was also fed to a considerable extent by the great gap in available resources and in the rate of economic development and military aggrandizement between these two states in the first years following the sharp rises in oil prices. Like Egypt, although the circumstances were different, Syria expected and requested a generous share of the oil revenues from its eastern neighbor.[19] The disappointment at Iraq's refusal to consider seriously these requests was one of the causes of the conflict that developed between them, to the extent of Syrian support for Iran in the Gulf war. Toward the end of the oil decade, the Arab states appeared to come increasingly to terms with the fact that realization of the vision of Arab unity was more distant than ever. Even pan-Arab solidarity was hardly in evidence.

Toward the end of the 1970s, when the dependence of the Western economies on Middle East oil reached its high point and the oil states in the region enjoyed their greatest economic power, it seemed to many that the ground was ready for a new quality of relations with the West. No longer would it be a relationship between unequal partners, with the West retaining the power to determine the course of events, but one between sides that were balanced, each with its own strengths and weaknesses, and mutually dependent on the economic welfare and political stability of the other. Oil was deemed to be the compensatory factor in an unequal system. It followed that in such a system the Middle East oil states would have the capacity to bring about (or even impose) a change in the attitudes, postures, and decisions of the Western states in areas that were important to the oil states.[20]

The change in official Western attitudes toward the oil states and their rulers was, in the latter half of the 1970s, indeed remarkable. It was expressed in the ceremonial aspect of the relationship and, far more important, in a willingness to supply advanced technology and weaponry to the oil states. Moreover, there was a shift in the actual policy of Western states in areas where the oil states pressed for change, primarily in their posture toward the Arab-Israeli conflict. In the economic sphere, partnerships between Western companies and Arab public as well as private firms were established, and the latter exerted much influence on the Western money markets.

However, there was not enough in these changes to alter the nature of relations between the West and the Middle East oil states. Oil indeed imparted to the latter a power they did not possess prior to the price revolution, but a balanced and weighted system of relations was not established. It is ironical that at the end of the oil decade the great oil exporters of the area recognized that their economic dependence on the Western countries had grown in comparison with the period before 1973-74. This was evident mainly in dependence on income deriving from the major consumers, as well as dependence on the supply of goods and technology. This development came against the background of the high levels of expenditure on consumption and investment that had become customary in the fat years of the oil decade. High levels of spending created a chain of expectations and habits which the elites of the oil states found difficult to break. In these conditions Western countries such as Britain and the US, themselves major oil producers, were able to influence oil prices on the world market and consequently to affect the revenues of the oil states. Regarding dependence on the supply of goods, it need hardly be stressed that in this decade there is no viable alternative to the technology offered by the Western economies and Japan. Moreover, the association with Western technology during the construction of infrastructure and the establishment of petrochemical industries made the transfer to alternative technologies economically almost impossible because of the costs involved. Politically, the dependence of the regimes in Saudi Arabia, Kuwait and the UAE on the US has grown as a result of the Iraqi-Iranian war and the Iranian threat to strike at these countries because of their support for Iraq.

The greater economic dependence of the oil states on the West in the years following the oil decade confirms the conclusion that no fundamental change has occurred in relations between the two sides. Ultimately, greater economic dependence resulted from the response of the oil states, primarily Saudi Arabia, to pressures by the consumer states, particularly the US, to produce oil in larger quantities than the oil states wished. This compliance set off a chain of developments and processes whose end was a deeper economic dependence. Obviously, compliance with pressures to produce such large quantities of oil arose from the weakness of the producers in the face of Western pressure.[21]

CONCLUSION

In its force and power, the "oil factor" came as a surprise not only to the consumer states but also to the major OPEC producers. In the absence of economic master plans to exploit the billions of dollars that flooded the oil countries, economic conceptions and plans were formulated at the same time as the "big boom" was proceeding. The expectations for change at the beginning of the oil decade were vast. But most of them did not materialize. The first cycle of plenty from the income of oil exports came with the governments and rulers of the oil states being unprepared for it.

However, it was in the political sphere that the change recorded was the most circumscribed. A survey of developments connected with the stability of regimes and inter-Arab and international relations shows that the "oil effect" acted to strengthen the forces of the status quo or the conservative forces in the region. To a certain extent, the Islamic Revolution in Iran was also an expression of this general tendency. Indeed, the power of the monarchical Arab regimes waxed; the status of the separate Arab nation-state was reinforced; there was a marked improvement in the position of the Western states in the area, and dependence on them grew.

Nor was there a revolution in the economic structure. As indicated, an economic revolution could not have occurred under the conditions that existed in the oil states; nor could it have occurred in a relatively short period of time. However, there was a far-reaching change in the physical infrastructure. In this respect the oil states altered their situation fundamentally, and the full result of this will be felt in years to come. In the long run, it seems that the social area will prove to be the one where the most significant change took place during the oil decade. The settlement of the nomads, the acceleration of urbanization, the rapid expansion of the educational systems, especially secondary and higher, as well as the quantitative growth and strengthening of the social and economic power of the middle class predominate here. These developments will undoubtedly have wide-ranging effects in the closing of years of the century.

Why did the oil states fail to register more impressive achievements, either in the economic or political sphere? That they themselves were surprised by the extent of their riches is only a partial answer. Regarding the desert oil states, the main explanation lies in some of their underlying characteristics, principally the stark imbalance between the excess of wealth and the shortage of local manpower. Moreover, the absorption of advanced technologies met several obstacles in terms of traditional production patterns and a technical-technological level that has not yet closed the gap with the West. As for Iran and Iraq, the Islamic Revolution in the former and the war between them struck hard not only at existing economic achievements but also at many programs that were supposed to be implemented. Developments in the desert countries as well as in the populated oil states show that there are no shortcuts. While the progress that was made is not to be belittled, these societies are still only at the threshold of the path leading to the goals they set themselves; and they have a long, arduous way to go.

The oil decade was a "short" decade. The recession came earlier and with greater force than the rulers of the Middle East oil economies expected. It was already in evidence in the autumn of 1981 and it reached its lowest point in mid-1986. The two foremost elements in the recession were obviously the sharp fall in revenues of the oil exporters from the export of crude oil and the substantial decline in the dependence of the industrialized West (including Japan) on Middle East oil.

The fall in revenues came in two main waves: the first was in 1982–84, when the revenues of the Middle East OPEC states came to approximately half the sum of the peak year — from $207 bn in 1980 to about $109 bn in 1984. The second was in 1985–86, when revenues fell a further 58 per cent: from $109 bn in 1984 to $46 bn in 1986 (all figures in current prices). Thus the 1986 revenues amounted to a mere 22 per cent of those of the peak year (1980). Of all the Middle East oil states the sharpest fall in both absolute and relative terms was suffered by Saudi Arabia: from $113 bn in 1980 to about $20 bn in 1986 — a drop of 82 per cent in six years.[22]

In the perspective of these years of recession several developments and characteristics that became apparent during the oil decade take on particular significance. Firstly, the interrelationship between the economic condition of the oil states and that of the neighboring economies became tangible. Just as there was "export of prosperity" so was there export of economic difficulties. Since the late 1970s the welfare of Egypt, Jordan and Syria has been largely connected with that of Saudi Arabia and Kuwait, and recession in the latter has caused serious economic difficulties in the former. Secondly, the years of recession have demonstrated the central importance of the effort to establish an extensive industrial sector that may replace part of the income accruing from the export of crude oil to maintain the levels of consumption and continued growth in the oil economies. Thirdly, the recession years again highlighted the great dependence of the oil economies on the Western states, economically as well as politically. Fourthly and finally, the recession period revealed once more the strength of the forces underlying the separate Arab state. Even in times of difficulties and recession there were no noticeable signs of greater economic cooperation among the Arab economies.

TABLE 1: OAPEC AND MIDDLE EAST OPEC – GOVERNMENT OIL REVENUES, 1973–81 (billions of US dollars, current prices)

	1973	*1974*	*1975*	*1976*	*1977*	*1978*	*1979*	*1980*	*1981*
Saudi Arabia	4.3	22.6	25.7	33.5	38.6	34.6	57.5	102.0	113.2
Iran	4.1	17.5	18.5	21.1	21.6	20.9	19.1	13.5	8.6
Iraq	1.8	5.7	7.5	8.5	9.8	9.6	21.3	26.0	10.4
Kuwait	1.9	7.0	7.5	8.5	7.9	8.0	16.7	17.9	14.9
Libya	2.3	6.0	5.1	7.5	8.9	8.6	15.2	22.6	15.6
UAE	0.9	5.5	6.0	7.0	9.0	8.0	12.9	19.5	18.7
Algeria	0.9	3.7	3.4	3.7	4.3	4.6	7.5	12.5	10.8
Qatar	0.4	1.6	1.7	2.0	2.0	2.0	3.6	5.4	5.3
Total OAPEC	**12.5**	**52.1**	**56.9**	**70.7**	**80.5**	**75.4**	**134.7**	**205.9**	**188.9**
Total ME OPEC	**16.6**	**69.6**	**75.4**	**91.8**	**102.0**	**96.3**	**153.8**	**219.4**	**197.5**

SOURCES: *PE*, May 1977, p 167; June 1981, p 232; July 1985, p 236.

TABLE 2: MIDDLE EASTERN ECONOMICS: DISTRIBUTION OF GDP BY MAIN SECTORS, 1982

	GDP (millions of US $)	*Agriculture (%)*	*Industry (%)*	*Manufacturing*[1] *(%)*	*Services (%)*
Saudi Arabia	153,590	1	77	4	22
Libya[2]	28,360	2	68	3	30
Kuwait	20,060	1	61	7	38
Jordan	3,500	7	29	14	64
Egypt	26,400	20	34	27	46
Turkey	49,980	21	31	22	48

SOURCE: *World Development Report 1984* (New York: Oxford University Press for the World Bank, 1984), Table 3, pp 222–23.

NOTES:

1 Manufacturing is part of the industrial sector; it does not include oil production.

2 Figures for 1981.

TABLE 3: ENROLLMENT RATIOS FOR THE FIRST, SECOND AND THIRD LEVELS OF EDUCATION IN MIDDLE EASTERN COUNTRIES, 1970–82 (various years; in percentages)

Country	*Year*	*First Level*	*Second Level*	*Third Level*
Egypt		**(6–11)**	**(12–17)**	**(20–24)**
	1970	72	34	8.0
	1975	73	43	13.7
	1981	78	54	14.7
Sudan		**(7–12)**	**(13–18)**	**(20–24)**
	1970	38	7	1.2
	1975	47	14	1.5
	1981	52	18	2.0
Bahrain		**(6–11)**	**(12–16/17)**	**(20–24)**
	1970	102	54	1.8
	1975	96	52	2.4
	1980	101	58	5.3
Iran		**(7–12/6–10)**	**(13–18/11–17)**	**(20–24)**
	1970	73	27	3.1
	1975	95	46	5.0
	1982	97	40	3.7

TABLE 3 (contd)

Country	*Year*	*First Level*	*Second Level*	*Third Level*
Iraq		**(6–11)**	**(12–17)**	**(20–24)**
	1970	69	24	5.2
	1975	94	35	9.0
	1982	109	55	10.1
Israel		**(6–13)**	**(14–17)**	**(20–24)**
	1970	96	57	20.0
	1975	97	66	—
	1982	95	76	30.4
Jordan		**(6–11)**	**(12–17)**	**(20–24)**
	1981	103	77	31.6
Kuwait		**(6–9)**	**(10–17)**	**(20–24)**
	1970	89	65	3.7
	1975	93	67	9.1
	1982	91	77	15.4
Lebanon		**(5–9)**	**(10–16)**	**(20–24)**
	1970	119	40	23.7
	1981	118	58	28.3
Oman		**(6–11)**	**(12–17)**	**(20–24)**
	1975	44	1	—
	1982	74	21	—
Qatar		**(6–11)**	**(12–17)**	**(20–24)**
	1970	102	39	—
	1975	111	54	4.2
	1982	116	74	16.5
Saudi Arabia		**(6–11)**	**(12–17)**	**(20–24)**
	1970	45	12	1.7
	1975	58	22	4.1
	1981	67	32	8.7
Syria		**(6–11)**	**(12–17)**	**(20–24)**
	1970	78	38	9.2
	1975	96	43	12.1
	1981	101	48	16.1
Turkey		**(7–11)**	**(12–17)**	**(20–24)**
	1970	110	27	6.0
	1975	108	29	6.7
	1981	102	38	5.2
UAE		**(6–11)**	**(12–17)**	**(20–24)**
	1970	98	22	—
	1975	102	33	—
	1982	132	67	6.8

SOURCE: *Statistical Yearbook 1984* (Paris: UNESCO, 1984), Table 3.2, pp III–20–71.

NOTES

For the place and frequency of publications cited here, and for the full name of the publication, news agency, radio station or monitoring service where an abbreviation is used, please see "List of Sources." Only in the case of more than one publication bearing the same name is the place of publication noted here.

1. Figures based on the *PE*, May 1977, June 1981 and July 1985. See Table 1.
2. For figures on GDP (current prices) in 1981 see *World Development Report 1983* (New York: Oxford University Press for the World Bank, 1983).

3. *Monthly Petroleum Statistics Reports*, various issues, 1977.
4. See and compare, R.F. Nyrope *et al*, *Area Handbook for Saudi Arabia* 3rd ed (Washington, DC: The American University, 1977), p 67; J.S. Birks, "The Impact of Economic Development on Pastoral Nomadism in the Middle East: An Inevitable Eclipse?" in J.J. Clarke and H. Bowen-Jones (eds) *Change and Development in the Middle East* (London: Methuen, 1981), p 84.
5. *World Development Report 1984* (New York: Oxford University Press for the World Bank, 1984), Table 22, pp 260–61.
6. *Mideast Report*, 15 August 1983; cf N. Chouri, "Migration in the Middle East: Transformation and Change," *Middle East Review*, Vol 6, No 2 (1983–84), pp 17–23; E. Kanovsky, "Migration from the Poor to the Rich Arab Countries," in *Occasional Papers*, No 85 (Tel Aviv University: The Dayan Center, June 1984), pp 56–77.
7. See and compare, *IFS*, December 1984, July 1985, July 1986; *QER:* Egypt, Annual Supplement 1984; *QER: Jordan*, Annual Supplement 1983; *QER: Syria*, Annual Supplement 1983.
8. SIPRI, *World Armaments and Disarmament Yearbook 1983* (London: Taylor & Francis for SIPRI, 1983), Table 7A.2, pp 162–63.
9. *Handbook of Industrial Statistics* (New York: UNIDO, 1982); *World Development Report 1984*, Table 3, pp 222–23. See Table 2 above.
10. For data on investments in physical infrastructure see, for example, *Annual Report 1399* (1979), (Jidda: SAMA, 1980); *Statistical Yearbook for Asia and the Pacific 1982* (Bangkok: UN, 1982), Tables 23, 27–28, pp 234–35.
11. *Statistical Yearbook 1984* (Paris: UNESCO, 1984), Table 4.1, pp IV–6–14.
12. Ibid, pp III–20–71. See Table 3 above.
13. See, for example, *NYT*, 10 January 1979; *FT*, 29 July 1980.
14. R. Graham, *Iran: The Illusion of Power* (New York: St Martin's Press, 1979), pp 47–49; R. M. Kavoussi, "Economic Growth and Income Distribution in Saudi Arabia," *Arab Studies Quarterly*, Vol 5, No 1 (1983), pp 74–78; 'I. al-Khafaji, "State Incubation of Iraqi Capitalism," and J. Paul, "The New Bourgeoisie of the Gulf," *MERIP Reports*, September-October 1986, pp 4–9, 18–22.
15. M.H. Pesaran, "Economic Development and Revolutionary Upheavals in Iran," in H. Afshar (ed) *Iran: A Revolution in Turmoil* (Hampshire, England: Macmillan, 1985), pp 29–31, 34. For a different view see N. Momayezi, "Economic Correlates of Political Violence: The Case of Iran," *MEJ*, Vol 40 (1986), pp 71–81.
16. F. Kazemi, *Poverty and Revolution in Iran* (New York and London: New York University Press, 1980), pp 35–42 and *passim*.
17. M. Heller and N. Safran, "The New Middle Class and Regime Stability in Saudi Arabia," *Harvard Middle East Papers*, Modern Series, No 3 (1985), pp 7–26.
18. See further G.G. Gilbar, "One Arab State, Many Arab States — The Impact of Population Growth and Oil Incomes," in E. Kedourie and S. Haim (eds) *The Middle Eastern Economy: Second Series*, (London: Frank Cass, forthcoming).
19. A.S. Baram, *National* [*wataniyya*] *Integration and Exclusiveness in Political Thought and Practice in Iraq under the Ba'th, 1968–82* (in Hebrew), Ph D Thesis (The Hebrew University of Jerusalem, 1986), p 230.
20. G.G. Gilbar, "The Economics of Interdependence: The United States and the Arab World, 1973–77," in H. Shaked and I. Rabinovich (eds) *The Middle East and the United States* (New Brunswick and London: Transaction Books, 1980), pp 209–40.
21. For a detailed discussion of this development, see A. Alnasrawi, *OPEC in a Changing World Economy* (Baltimore and London: The Johns Hopkins University Press, 1985), pp 112–16.
22. *PE*, July 1987.

PART TWO: COUNTRY-BY-COUNTRY SURVEY

Middle East Countries

Basic Data

Country	*Capital*	*Most Important Natural Resources*	*Area 1,000 sq kms*	*Population in millions (mid-1985)*	*GNP per capita ($US 1985)*
Bahrain	Manama	Crude Oil	1	0.417	9,420
Egypt	Cairo	Cotton, Crude Oil, Fruits, Vegetables, Iron	1,001	48.5	610
Iran	Tehran	Crude Oil, Natural Gas	1,648	44.6	NA
Iraq	Baghdad	Crude Oil, Dates, Cement	435	15.9	NA
Israel	Jerusalem	Citrus Fruits, Potash	21	4.2	4,990
Jordan	Amman	Phosphates, Vegetables, Fruits, Potash	98	3.5	1,560
Kuwait	Kuwait	Crude Oil	18	1.7	14,480
Lebanon	Beirut	Fruits, Citrus Fruits, Vegetables, Forests	10	NA	NA
Libya	Tripoli	Crude Oil, Vegetables, Fruits	1,760	3.8	7,170
Oman	Muscat	Crude Oil	300	1.2	6,730
Qatar	Doha	Crude Oil	11	0.315	16,270
Saudi Arabia	Riyadh	Crude Oil	2,150	11.5	8,850
Sudan	Khartoum	Cotton, Gum, Cereals	2,506	21.9	300
Syria	Damascus	Cotton, Crude Oil, Vegetables, Fruits, Livestock, Phosphates	185	10.5	1,570
Turkey	Ankara	Cotton, Wool, Tobacco, Chrome, Copper	781	50.2	1,080
United Arab Emirates	Abu Dhabi	Crude Oil	84	1.4	19,270
Yemen (North)	San'a	Coffee, Cotton, Sorghum, Fish	195	8.0	550
Yemen (South)	Aden	Cotton, Fruits, Vegetables, Tobacco, Fish	333	2.1	530

SOURCE: *World Development Report 1987* (New York: Oxford University Press for the World Bank, 1987).
NA = not available.

Currencies

Country	Currency Unit	US Dollar	Pound Sterling	Deutsche Mark	Swiss Franc	French Franc
		*Approximate Equivalent in Other Currencies**				
Bahrain	Bahraini Dinar = 1,000 Fils	2.65	1.80	6.16	5.19	19.60
Egypt	Egyptian Pounds = 1,000 Milliemes	(c) 0.73	0.50	1.70	1.43	5.40
Iran	Iranian Riyal = 100 Dinars	0.012	0.008	0.028	0.024	0.089
Iraq	Iraqi Dinar = 1,000 Fils	3.22	2.19	7.49	6.31	23.82
Israel	Israeli Shekel = 100 Agorot	0.67	0.46	1.56	1.31	4.96
Jordan	Jordanian Dinar = 1,000 Fils	2.91	1.99	6.77	5.70	21.53
Kuwait	Kuwaiti Dinar = 1,000 Fils	3.43	2.33	7.98	6.72	25.38
Lebanon	Lebanese Pound = 100 Piastres	0.04	0.027	0.09	0.08	0.29
Libya	Libyan Dinar = 1,000 Dirhams	3.19	2.17	7.42	6.25	23.60
Oman	Omani Riyal = 1,000 Baiza	2.60	1.77	6.05	5.10	19.23
Qatar	Qatari Riyal = 100 Dirhams	0.27	0.18	0.63	0.53	2.00
Saudi Arabia	Saudi Riyals = 100 Halalas	0.27	0.18	0.63	0.53	2.00
Sudan	Sudanese Pound = 1,000 Milliemes	0.25	0.17	0.58	0.49	1.85
Syria	Syrian Pound = 100 Piastres	0.25	0.17	0.58	0.49	1.85
Turkey	Turkish Lira = 100 Kurus	0.001	0.00099	0.0023	0.0020	0.0074
United Arab Emirates	Dirham = 100 Fils	0.27	0.18	0.63	0.53	1.99
Yemen (North)	Yemeni Riyal = 100 Fils	0.12	0.08	0.28	0.24	0.89
Yemen (South)	Yemeni Dinar = 1,000 Fils	2.92	1.99	6.79	5.72	21.60
$US rate $1		—	0.68	2.326	1.96	7.398

* As quoted by the Bank of America in London on 9 April 1986.

(c) = Commercial rate.

The Arab Republic of Egypt
(Jumhuriyyat Misr al-'Arabiyya)

AMI AYALON

DOMESTIC AFFAIRS

During 1986 the Egyptian Government faced increasing socioeconomic and political pressures that presented a serious challenge and at times jeopardized the stability of the State. By and large, however, the regime continued to control the political game, and the political institutions functioned effectively even in the face of mounting difficulties. Under the shadow of the oil crisis and diminishing resources, the Government's exchanges with its critics grew sharper. The regime had to contend with attacks in the opposition Press, strikes and demonstrations by students and workers, threats by underground groups of Muslim radicals, and, for the first time, an open revolt by units of the Security Forces in Cairo.

This last incident, in February, was the most remarkable event of the year in Egypt. It showed up, if only briefly, the curious phenomenon of a regime surviving in relative stability despite highly adverse material conditions. Faced with an unusually dangerous threat, the country's leadership responded with equally unusual severity by deploying large army units in the capital and imposing a curfew until the rebellion was quelled. Although the uprising was exceptionally violent and costly, it was also typical in its causes and consequences: the severe material and spiritual distress that erupted in desperate protest; the firm hand of the army-backed Government in suppressing it; and the eventual spectacle, by now all too familiar, of hundreds of men in iron cages on collective trial. By spring, the crisis was over and life in Egypt returned to its routine as both the Government and the people braced themselves for future crises and possible confrontations.

MOUNTING ECONOMIC PRESSURES

One of the chief victims of the collapse in world oil prices, and the least able to afford the consequences, Egypt in 1986 was subject to a further deterioration in its economic resources. Crude oil exports, which earned the country *c* $2.15 bn in fiscal year 1984–85 (a decline of some 14 per cent from the previous year's earnings), dropped by another 16 per cent to only $1.8 bn in 1985–86. Since the beginning of 1986, however, the decline was much steeper, and Egypt's revenues from oil in fiscal 1986–87 were expected to fall by 50 per cent or more to some $900m.[1]

Similarly, the decline in remittances from Egyptians working abroad persisted, as the economic crisis in the countries employing them forced many of the workers out. In February, Iraq, the biggest foreign employer of Egyptian labor (as many as 1.5m Egyptians had jobs there), imposed a ceiling of $100 per month on the export of foreign currency by aliens. This caused many Egyptians — tens of thousands a month in early 1986, according to some accounts — to return home from Iraq. They were among an estimated 10–15 per cent of the 3m Egyptians employed overseas who were compelled to return.[2] This dealt Egypt a double blow: first, remittances — which had already dropped from $3.9 bn in 1983–84 to $3.7 bn in 1984–85 — continued to fall to an estimated $3.5 bn in 1985–86;[3] and second, the return of these expatriates exacerbated domestic unemployment and increased imports.

Egypt's third major source of foreign exchange, the Suez Canal, was the only source of income to remain stable in 1985–86, producing *c* $1 bn — roughly the same as in the year before.[4] On the other hand, tourism, the country's fourth most important source of revenue, suffered a severe blow following a series of terror incidents in the region in summer and fall of 1985, and the February 1986 rebellion of the Security Forces. Earnings, expected to reach $1 bn in 1985–86, reportedly fell to *c* $800m. Further losses, estimated at about $100m, were incurred by the hotel industry as the result of sabotage during the riots.[5]

This trend of declining income left the Government with ever fewer means at its disposal to handle the grave economic problems. With the population growing by a million every 250 days (it reached 50m on 1 July),[6] and with more than half of the country's food purchased abroad, Egypt's import expenses continued to rise, reaching *c* $10 bn in 1985–86.[7] The country's foreign debt also rose to *c* $36 bn in 1986 (up from *c* $31 bn the previous year); the servicing of this debt swallowed about one half of Egypt's revenues in foreign currency.[8] And the budget deficit, *c* $5.9 bn in 1985–86, was expected to increase to $6.6 bn in 1986–87, a 12 per cent rise.[9] The country's economic leadership thus found it increasingly difficult to implement its Five-Year Plan, which entered its last year in July 1986, and to meet Egypt's basic economic needs.

These gloomy figures were not unknown to the Egyptian public, nor was their painful significance lost. President Husni Mubarak, faithful to his principle of disclosing the truth, however discouraging, to the people, discussed the situation in detail on numerous occasions. "You must know that we will be facing one of our most difficult years," he said in his May Day address, adding:

> We do not underestimate the severity and difficulty of the problem we are facing. The problem has been made more acute by two fundamental factors. The first was the amazing drop in oil prices. Some people are saying that the Government should have expected this. By God... are we angels possessed of the secrets of the universe, so that we know that the price would fall down? ... The second factor is that the size of the repayments resulting from our external commitment, which must be met, reach their peak in the current year and the next two years ... We will be under considerable pressure for these three years. We will be compelled to face them.[10]

Candidly acknowledging the difficulties, Mubarak insisted, however, that the Egyptian economy was not "in the intensive care unit nor...on top of a volcano." It was not true, he argued, that the country was "on the verge of bankruptcy," as some observers claimed — "that is preposterous. We will never go broke."[11] The crisis was temporary, a mere "bottleneck," out of which Egypt could remove itself through "discipline and serious endeavor" as well as "total resolve and insistence."[12]

There were other — more practical and distressing — signs of the deteriorating situation. There were periodical increases in the prices of many basic commodities, among them meat, sugar, cheese, detergents, electricity, cooking gas and clothing. The upgrading of prices was effected surreptitiously, in order not to generate public protest, and was reported mainly by the opposition Press.[13] There were also frequent shortages in the collective stores and markets of Cairo and the provinces.[14] Growing agitation and recurrent strikes by workers demanding pay increases to compensate for rising prices clearly reflected the vexation felt by many. In February some 42,000 textile workers in al-Mahalla al-Kubra went on strike, demanding a pay increase, and some 300 of them were arrested by the security police. In July, workers of the national railways went on a general strike. And in November there were further troubles in al-Mahalla al-Kubra.[15] Unrest and strikes were likewise reported elsewhere.[16]

In an article analyzing the country's mood at midyear, Ibrahim Nafi', editor of *al-Ahram,* depicted the atmosphere as unhealthy. "Many of us," he stated, "are struck by complete despair."

> Despite the tremendous work being done... there is no joy over the completion of a project, no smile of delight in a success, as if the achievements of our country were achieved elsewhere. People always talk about negative things only... There is profound lack of faith in the statements and decisions of leaders, and we always err in interpreting them... We suffer from widespread individualism and indifference... Frustration is prevalent among the people.[17]

The Government's record in tackling these problems in 1986 was modest at best. Whether long-term economic planning could lead to an eventual recovery was a matter of controversy; but that such planning was unable to prevent acute crises in the process was beyond question. The Government, therefore, was forced to seek palliatives, mostly in the form of foreign aid. It intensified its efforts to persuade the US Administration to increase financial support, or at least to reduce its interest rate on loans by as much as half. Several high-level Egyptian delegations went to Washington, including two that were headed by Deputy Prime Minister and Defense Minister Abu Ghazala, as a part of this special effort. And when US Vice President George Bush visited Cairo in August, rescheduling Egypt's debts was, likewise, a major item on his agenda (see further below).[18] Another source from which emergency aid was sought was the International Monetary Fund (IMF). Intensive negotiations with IMF officials were conducted during the second half of 1986 over Egypt's request of a \$1–1.5 bn IMF loan. In July, President Mubarak visited West Germany, England, France and Italy in an attempt to persuade their Governments to back his country's request for IMF assistance. In December he again went to Paris and Bonn to discuss the issue further.[19]

Meanwhile, at home, Mubarak tirelessly continued to call upon the Egyptians to "show greater responsibility" and "exert greater efforts to increase production." The country, he stated, could "no longer afford repetitious talking" about improvements; "the talk must turn into great and decisive deeds."[20] In a somewhat more practical vein, on 8 November Mubarak dismissed Prime Minister 'Ali Lutfi, an economist whose appointment to the post 14 months earlier was designed to reinforce the country's economic leadership with high professional talent. But Lutfi, though skilled and devoted, failed to devise answers for the dangerous deterioration of the economy

— in the words of one journal, because he adhered "to common and customary methods" and did not try to "produce unconventional solutions."[21] Lutfi was replaced by Dr 'Atif Sidqi, a 56-year-old professor of law and author of several books on economic subjects who had headed the Central Auditing Agency during the previous five years. A partial cabinet reshuffle followed, affecting mainly Ministers in charge of economic portfolios (see Table 1 below). Formulating the assignments of the new Cabinet, Mubarak indicated the mobilization of "all domestic and foreign resources for effectively tackling the economic situation" as its top priority.[22]

'Ali Lutfi had to go because he failed to produce unconventional solutions; but Mubarak's own approach to the crisis also contained little that was original or innovative. Lutfi's dismissal after 14 months — the same amount of time his predecessor occupied the post — and his replacement by a skilled economist with limited political experience created a strong impression of *déjà vu*. So did Mubarak's exhortations for more toil and sweat from the people. Nor were the efforts to enlist foreign assitance very successful. Further aid from Washington was not readily forthcoming, mainly because of a US effort to cut its own large budget deficit. And the IMF made its support to Egypt conditional upon structural changes in its economy which the Government found difficult to accept. "We have limits we cannot exceed," Mubarak remarked, referring to the Fund's demands. "I can never accept that the IMF comes and imposes on us more burdens than we can take."[23]

The Government's inability, or unreadiness, to comply with the IMF call for a "rationalization" of the country's economy seems to have highlighted the complexities of the situation. The unbalanced economic structure, especially the existence of a large public sector and the heavy dependence of the sizable poor classes on subsidies, severely undermined the regime's ability to meet problems and dangers as they arose. Yet any attempt to reform this structure, so as to render it economically healthier and persuade potential providers of aid of its viability, involved a serious risk of unrest, instability and perhaps eventual collapse. Thus, by the end of 1986, just as at the beginning of the year, the Egyptian economy, even if not on the verge of bankruptcy, was in deep trouble with no substantial relief in sight.

DISTURBANCES IN THE CAPITAL: THE SECURITY FORCES' MUTINY

The large-scale riots that broke out in Cairo on the night of 25–26 February presented the regime with its most serious challenge ever. The riots were initiated by men of the Central Security Forces (*al-amn al-markazi*), a police unit of some 280,000 draftees assigned to guard embassies, bridges and other sensitive sites in and around the capital. The Security Forces comprised mostly illiterate youths from the countryside; their service conditions were extremely poor, as was their public image. A rumor about a government intention to extend their three-year service by another year ignited the rebellion in a camp near the Giza pyramids, from which hundreds of policemen took to the streets and began to vandalize hotels, nightclubs, cars and other property in the vicinity. Men from other units of the Security Forces as well as small bands of civilian youths joined in the burning and looting. By morning the riots had spread to other parts of the city — to the Ma'adi suburb in the south, where the rebels broke into Tura jail and freed some 1,200 mostly non-political prisoners, to the Shubra neighborhood in the northeast and the Cairo International Airport area. Similar disturbances, although on a much smaller scale, erupted in the towns of

Hilwan, Suhaj and Asyut. Altogether, about 17,000 men of the Security Forces took part in the riots.

The Government reacted promptly. Upon learning of the nature of the rebellion, President Mubarak and Defense Minister Abu Ghazala decided to take no chances. Large army forces, including special commando units, tanks and artillery were called into the capital before dawn. They surrounded the rebels both inside and outside their camps and confronted them firmly. By the morning of 26 February there was a massive military presence in the city, at all major crossroads and other locations. The Government also took the unusual step of imposing a complete curfew on the Greater Cairo area beginning in the afternoon of that day. Under the circumstances, all universities in Cairo canceled classes.

Army and riot police units continued to clash with the rebels for the following three or four days. Some 2,000 central security men and several hundred civilians were arrested, and nearly all the prisoners freed from Tura jail were recaptured. The curfew was gradually relaxed during the following days, and was lifted completely on 8 March. Meanwhile, on 28 February, Interior Minister Ahmad Rushdi, who was in charge of all police forces, was made to resign. He was replaced by Maj Gen Zaki Badr, hitherto governor of Asyut. As it turned out, Rushdi was the only senior official who lost his post because of the riots.

An official statement put the number of casualties at 70 dead and 206 wounded. Five hotels, 42 police installations, 120 private installations and more than 2,000 cars were damaged.[24]

While nearly two weeks passed before life in the capital resumed its normal routine, by the end of the first day it was already quite clear that the regime was in complete control of the situation. Displaying unreserved loyalty to the Government, the Army acted effectively and quickly contained the insurgence. The media, both electronic and printed, gave open and detailed coverage of the events, making special efforts to prove their credibility and at the same time to convey the message that the rioters were an "isolated group of irresponsible troublemakers" who were trying "to murder the country's future."[25] The public at large, either out of fear and confusion or because of common dislike for the Security Forces, passively supported the regime and abided by the curfew instructions. And the opposition parties unequivocally condemned the rebels: in a meeting of all party leaders with Mubarak on 28 February, they expressed their full support of the Government's firm action against the insurgents and denounced the "criminal acts... of sabotage, riots and arson."[26] The opposition Press amplified this position.

In a broadcast address to a joint session of the People's Assembly and the Consultative Council, on 8 March, Mubarak admitted that the outburst took him by surprise. "I never imagined," he stated, "that such a treacherous blow would be struck as we carried out the most honorable actions and offered the purest sweat." The act of sedition (*fitna*), Mubarak said, was the work of "a few misled deviationist groups of the Central Security Forces and some outlaws," while the rest of the nation, "all groups, sects and ages... faced this terrible test with genuine wisdom, supreme courage and a sincere attachment to the land." He commended the Army for its "performance [which] was illustrated in the professional manner in which the sound plans of the armed forces were implemented within a few hours." Through the acts of the Army and of the rest of the people, who showed such a sense of responsibility, "national unity in Egypt revealed its strength and solidity." This reaction by the people was "an unprecedented collective referendum on the masses' full confidence in their regime, constitutional structure, government policy and commitment to the rule of law." Mubarak pledged to remain committed to democracy — "a lofty edifice and a firm pyramid in our lives" — and to be frank with the people "who have a right to know... about both the good and the bad." He promised he would act to improve the service conditions of the Security Forces, and announced his intention not to forgive those who created the crisis, for "the quick deterrence of legal punishment is the mercy for the right of millions to live."[27]

Several lessons could be drawn from the dramatic events of February. Above all, the outbreak was a dangerously clear sign of the exasperation felt by lower classes. That such *malaise* existed among a segment of the Security Forces, regarded as one of the regime's chief power bases, was especially ominous. While the Government was evidently caught unprepared by troubles erupting in an unexpected quarter, in retrospect, such a violent expression of protest against misery and maltreatment was scarcely surprising. On the contrary, it was perhaps amazing that outbursts of this kind did not occur earlier or more frequently; they would be a natural outcome of the country's harsh socioeconomic situation.

The measures by which the Government resolved the crisis served as a reminder that the regime depended, in the final account, on the loyalty of the Army. Its very existence palpably in jeopardy, the regime, in an instinctive motion of survival, fell back upon its military support. The country's leaders, who had taken special care to keep the armed forces content even in times of want, and thus interested in preserving the stability of the existing order, knew it could count on their constancy when the need arose. The crisis necessitated no change in the basic rules of the political game. A confident leadership, headed by former generals and backed by a loyal Army, proved a sufficient answer to the challenges presented by serious socioeconomic problems, at least for the time being.

By and large the regime emerged safely from the crisis. It not only suppressed the rebellion, but also retained popular support for itself, making the public share its view of the rebels as an irresponsible lot who had betrayed their country. Yet, although it failed seriously to shake the regime, the insurgence surely bruised it somewhat. Forced to abandon all other political instruments and resort to the use of sheer force, if only briefly, the Government was obliged to admit the inadequacy of other mechanisms it had worked so hard to foster. The February riots thus served to emphasize the limited range of options available to a leadership with problems as formidable as those of Egypt.

THE THREAT OF RADICAL ISLAM

The call of Fundamentalism and its subsidiary message of militant or millenarian Islam continued in 1986 to appear as an attractive alternative to the regime's somewhat obscure philosophy. It was an expected, perhaps natural, result of material deterioration and increasing sociopolitical pressures. No dramatic confrontation between the Government and Muslim radicals, such as the one of summer 1985 (see *Middle East Contemporary Survey* [*MECS*] 1984–85, pp 352–54) took place in 1986. But otherwise constant tension dominated their relations. The contention revolved around old and familiar themes: implementation of the Holy Law (*Shari'a*); the nature of Egypt's spiritual and moral values; and the compatibility of the Government's political and economic strategies, as well as its international alliances, with Islamic principles.

Small-scale outbursts of violence by impatient exponents of Islamic orthodoxy (the "groups" or *jama'at*), and periodic arrests of those viewed as their more dangerous members, became recurrent patterns of the regime's relations with the religious opposition. On 15 April members of Islamic radical groups clashed with the police in Minya during a violent demonstration, and nine were arrested.[28] Another clash took place in Minya on 28 April which led to the arrest of 70 demonstrators. On the following day Muslim Fundamentalists demonstrating in Aswan tried to storm a mosque and were confronted by police, who arrested 56, among them Shaykh 'Umar 'Abd al-Rahman, one of the ideologues of the radical *al-Jihad* group (cf *MECS* 1984–85, pp 349, 353).[29] In late June, a series of attacks and arson attempts on nightclubs, liquor stores, theatres and video rental shops occurred in the Greater Cairo area and a few other cities. This led to the arrest of scores of people (up to 300, according to some accounts), mostly affiliated with the *al-Jihad* organization. Seventy-five of them were prosecuted.[30] In early August, several members of Islamic groups suspected of an attempt to topple the regime were arrested in Cairo.[31] In mid-October, four groups of radicals who allegedly plotted to attack the Alexandria broadcasting station and set video rental clubs on fire were captured.[32] At the month's end, a clash between Muslim Fundamentalists armed with chains and knives and hundreds of policemen left one person dead and about 20 wounded in Asyut; more than 100 people were arrested.[33] And on 4 December it was announced that 33 people were to face trial for forming an extremist religious organization which "sought to overthrow the Government in power"; among them were four junior military officers — apparently the first known infiltration of the armed forces by Muslim extremists since President Sadat's assassination in 1981.[34]

The police kept a watchful eye on the activities of the radical groups, frequently harassing them and making clear its firm intention to check their plans and activities. A report submitted by Interior Minister Zaki Badr to Mubarak toward the end of the year indicated that in late 1985 and throughout 1986 some 2,500 members of Islamic groups had been arrested.[35] Badr, who for four years had been governor of turbulent Asyut — a stronghold of Islamic radicalism — brought to his new post a strong conviction that Islamic extremism should be confronted uncompromisingly. "The radical groups seek to impose their ideas on our society through violence and terror," he told an interviewer, "and whoever resorts to violence and terror should be met with deterring steps... we shall respond with resolve."[36]

The generally moderate branch of the Islamic Opposition, the Muslim Brothers, caused the regime much less concern than did the *jama'at*, not merely because of their relative moderation (they supported the Government during the February events and denounced "destruction, sabotage and terror"),[37] but also because in 1986 they were preoccupied with a transfer of leadership and with changes in their political orientation. On 21 May, the Brothers' "Supreme Guide" since 1974, 'Umar al-Tilmisani, died in Cairo after a long illness. Before his death a struggle for succession had already developed among the mostly elderly leaders of the movement. The controversy, which was bitter, continued for a while after Tilmisani's death.[38] By way of compromise a group of leaders resolved to elect the 73-year-old Muhammad

Ahmad Abu al-Nasr, the most senior man in the movement's "guidance bureau," as temporary "Supreme Guide."[39] Tension at the top seemed to be persisting, although by the first week of June a "senior source" in the movement's leadership was quoted as stating that Abu al-Nasr's election was permanent.[40] In an interview upon assuming the position, Abu al-Nasr pledged to "follow in the late leader al-Tilmisani's path, a path characterized by moderation, openness, and the handling of matters gently, sensibly and prudently."[41]

The Brothers, however, faced difficulties in their search for an organizational framework that would allow them to wield influence in the political arena. In late 1985 a rift occurred between the Brothers and the Wafd Party, with which they had joined forces in 1984 and under whose umbrella they had their representatives in the People's Assembly (cf *MECS* 1983–84, p 355; 1984–85, p 350). According to Salah Abu Isma'il, an outspoken representative of the Brothers in the Assembly, the cause of the differences was the Wafd's "advocacy of secularism and failure to call for the application of Islamic Law."[42] Prevented by law from establishing their own party, the Brothers began to look for an alternative partner among existing parties. They first negotiated a coalition with the small People's [*Umma*] Party, but this failed, apparently due to disagreement over the question of party leadership.[43] The Brothers then approached another small party, the Liberals (*al-Ahrar*), whose "only fault was that they approved of Camp David."[44] By midyear the two sides had reached an agreement of unity, according to which party leader Mustafa Kamil Murad was to serve as party president for life, Salah Abu Isma'il would be vice president, and the Brothers would have 50 per cent of the party's organizational apparatus. The Brothers thus attained their goal of becoming "the backbone of the party and its decision makers," and "the Liberal Party became an unobstructed avenue through which the Muslim Brothers and the Islamic tendency in Egypt can pursue their objectives."[45]

Predictably, the merger lent a strong Islamic color to the Liberal Party. Already during the merger negotiations the party dropped the word "Socialist" (*al-ishtirakiyyun*) from its name, which was thus shortened to "the Liberal Party"; and, under the influence of Muslim Brother ideologues, it decided to back down from its approval of the Camp David policy.[46] The party's newspapers, *al-Ahrar* and *al-Nur*, adopted an increasingly religious tenor and focused more on Islamic subjects. It was sure to become a more aggressive actor in the Egyptian multiparty game. From the regime's point of view, however, the Brothers had opted to spend their oppositional energy through the easily controllable channel of a political party. More radical Muslim Fundamentalists, to whom such a channel seemed too ineffective, were left to seek avenues of action other than the Muslim Brothers.

STUDENT UNREST

The atmosphere on university campuses, traditionally a highly sensitive indicator of the general climate, continued in 1986 to be as tense and nervous as it had been during the previous two years (cf *MECS*, 1983–84, pp 366–67; 1984–85, 355–57). The basic grievances of the student sector — tight police control of their activities, overcrowded classrooms, poor campus services — remained unresolved, while the national problems, about which they were used to voicing their views loudly, became increasingly complicated. Unhappy with their lot, and with the Government's performance on domestic and foreign issues, the students frequently protested and clashed with police on campuses throughout the country. Typically, the universities persisted as foci of Islamic Fundamentalism: radical students not only amplified the call for an "Islamic state," but were also eager to implement Islamic principles on campus right away, including the separation of sexes, modest dress for female students, and the prohibition of alcoholic drinks, movies and foreign music. This, naturally, encouraged greater police intervention in student activities and considerably contributed to unrest in this sector.

In early February students at Cairo University demonstrated against, and used force to cause the closure of, a Rotary Club exhibition on campus, since "Rotary is a branch of the Freemasons and hence a Zionist movement." Campus guard units were called in and clashed with the students.[47] Later that month, students in Damanhur demonstrated against "provocations by campus guards," ill-treatment by their professors, poor meals, the high cost of textbooks, and the absence of mosques.[48] In March a grave incident took place at the University of Asyut, when a student posting an announcement about a symposium on religious issues was shot by security men, and later died. This started a wave of severe agitation on that campus that lasted for several days, during which the embittered students repeatedly attacked the authorities and put forward a variety of demands.[49] Another clash occurred in mid-October in Bani Suwayf, where students, demonstrating against the rise in the cost of living, were confronted by the police, who arrested 40.[50] And at the month's end unrest resumed in Asyut, after another clash between students and the police in which 51 demonstrating students were placed in custody.[51] These events characterized the relations between the regime and the segment of the political public that was perhaps the most eager to react to the country's ills.

In November student union elections took place. As was often the case, the election campaign provoked open conflict and violent clashes between student groups on the one hand, and university officials and security units on the other. Students repeatedly protested against the authorities' meddling with candidate lists and preventing the students from stating their views. Such demonstrations sometimes led to intervention by campus guard units and to arrests. Student complaints in 1986 were also echoed by opposition party spokesmen who, at a press conference in Cairo after the elections, accused university and security authorities of having arrested 224 students and crossed 2,500 candidates' names off election lists in their attempt to influence the results.[52] Some of these accusations were undoubtedly true. These efforts on the part of the authorities notwithstanding, the Islamic groups — which had previously controlled the unions on all important campuses — again won a majority in most places, and even strengthened their presence in the unions.[53] Such results, scarcely surprisingly, were yet another source of concern for the Government.

THE MULTIPARTY SYSTEM: TENTH YEAR OF THE DEMOCRATIC EXPERIENCE

By 1986 Egypt had completed a decade of experimenting with political pluralism and freedom of expression. Having begun in 1976 under Sadat, the democratic experience had gone through various stages of progress and retrogression — under Mubarak it was mostly the former rather than the latter. It was a constant process and, despite crises and setbacks, it was never abandoned. 1986, like the year before, marked a relatively quiet period in the multiparty game, with no outstanding events such as parliamentarty elections or the formation of new parties. In this peaceful atmosphere Egyptian democracy continued to make significant strides.

The Opposition continued to criticize the Government through its own organs and the national daily press, as well as at public gatherings, referring basically to the same issues as in the past, presenting the same arguments and phrasing them in similar language. On the domestic front, the Government was attacked for its mishandling of the economy and for taking insufficient and often wrong measures, without bothering to consult the Opposition. Poor economic thinking, disregard for the needs of the lower classes, and corruption were presented as the reasons for the persistence of the crisis. "The failure of the Government's economic policy, if it has one at all, is evident," said Liberal Party leader, Mustafa Kamil Murad, who called upon the Ministers to "resign, and God will have mercy on you. Perhaps after you leave, without us regretting it, God will give us a new and wise government to bail us out of the severe distress."[54]

Another, traditional, area of criticism was democracy and freedom of speech. While acknowledging what had already been achieved in this field, spokesmen for the Opposition continued to express discontent with the limits that were still imposed on their freedom to organize, act and sometimes express their views. In 1986 this became the most important issue of contention between the Government and the Opposition parties (see below).

Opposition leaders backed the regime during the security forces crisis which, they felt, was as great a danger to the multiparty system as it was to the Government's survival. In the words of Khalid Muhyi al-Din, leader of the leftist National Progressive Unionist Grouping (NPUG), the riots "undermined not merely the economy and public security but also the democratic process."[55] But the event also provided grounds for criticsim. The outburst "demonstrated the risks inherent in the socioeconomic reality, and the absence of democratic channels and institutions to express the public will. It was a logical outcome of the formation of artificial bodies which falsified the wishes of the people," the NPUG organ *al-Ahali* charged.[56] The riots were a "result of Government impotence." *Al-Ahrar,* the Liberal Party weekly, welcomed the resignation of Interior Minister Rushdi and called upon Prime Minister Lutfi "to follow the example of the Interior Minister... and to allow the establishment of another government, more capable of handling [such] events," for the existing Government "proved unable to maintain security."[57]

The country's foreign policy also remained a target for opposition attacks. Criticism of the US and Israel was a matter of routine in the opposition Press, which lashed at the Government for its cooperation with both countries. The Opposition called for a boycott of the Israeli pavilion at the Cairo International Trade Fair in March, and charged the Government for "showing no consideration" for public sentiments and "insulting the people's holiest of holies... it brings us this provocative pavilion of our enemies... the Government is exposing the country's stability to danger and lacks the minimum of nationalist feelings when it allows the opening of the Zionist pavilion."[58]

Similarly, the opposition Press rejected the Egyptian-Israeli arbitration compromise over Taba that was reached in September; the subsequent visit by Israeli Prime Minister Shimon Peres to Alexandria; and the reappointment of an Egyptian Ambassador to Tel Aviv (see below). All these steps, it was stated, were "aimed at making the Egyptian role in the region subservient to US and Israeli designs":

> The Government declares its submission to US pressure for the completion of the agreement regarding Taba arbitration at the time specified by the White House, for the return of the Egyptian Ambassador to Israel, and for the reception of the enemy Prime Minister in the homeland...all that in return for a handful of dollars which, as past experience has proved, does not help but rather increases our loss of independent will and intensifies Egypt's economic crisis. Let today be the day of anger and rejection.[59]

In April, the Liberal Party — the only opposition party still recognizing the validity of the Camp David agreement — decided to withdraw its recognition. Its union with the Muslim Brothers seems to have been at least partly responsible for the change. Party leader Murad explained at a press conference that "the Party had initially supported the treaty but Israel's acts of aggression against Lebanon and the PLO and the obstacles it has been placing in the way of negotiations prove beyond any doubt that Israel does not want peace."[60]

The most common subject of exchanges between the Government and the Opposition in the tenth year of party pluralism was democracy. The Opposition continued to complain of insufficient freedom and of the slow pace of progress in the democratic process. There were repeated calls to amend the Constitution "to consolidate the power of the people," since the Constitution, which was "drafted [in 1971] under the one-party system... [was] pervaded by totalitarianism in word and spirit."[61] The Opposition also demanded the abolition of the emergency law and state of emergency, the amending of election laws for parliamentary and local councils, and the removal of restrictions still in effect on the freedom to form parties and to publish newspapers.[62] The language of these demands and charges was often harsh, and opposition critics used terms such as "the cancer of dictatorship" and "limitless suppression" to describe government policy toward their parties, and "a gang of base hypocrites" to depict leaders of the ruling National Democratic Party (NDP).[63] A new motif was bold criticism of Mubarak personally: Mubarak had hitherto been out of the range of opposition fire, but as party spokesmen grew more confident, they lashed out at him as well. "We cannot sell our principles just to avoid upsetting the ruler, nor are we capable of flattering the ruler at the expense of the Egyptian people and its interests," stated Mustafa Sharadi, chief editor of *al-Wafd*, who pledged to speak frankly "for the sake of freedom, even if the cost would be the hanging tree." In an "open letter" to the President, Sharadi stated:

> At the beginning of your tenure you emphasized you were neither Abd al-Nasser nor Sadat. But since then many changes have taken place, which have generated serious concerns. These concerns are growing daily in face of the acts performed by the Government. It seems that these changes are among the chief reasons for the present economic crisis. It also appears that the public has begun to feel confused about your views, ideas, statements and true intentions, Mr President... This profound confusion is further aggravated by your press interviews and speeches... We have chosen a 'Mubarak regime,' and have lovingly put it at the top of a new leaf, detached from the past; then we have been surprised to see this 'leaf' overcast by shadows which cause doubts and puzzlement.[64]

Another article in *al-Wafd* was more blatant:

> The oppressive and plunderous revolution [of 1952] created a situation whereby one person [Nasser] made himself the master of Egypt. Consequently the Egyptians lost their honor and rights. Egypt became a lord's colony, where he could act at whim. Egypt's ruler was in effect a king, similar to all other kings... The situation should have changed; but Egypt is still its ruler's property. True, the President does not contaminate his hands with Egyptian blood, and does not seek revenge of his opponents; but he still controls the Press and all authorities... Those who robbed the people of what was theirs and those responsible for all the crimes of torture and murder under the dictatorial regime should have been put on trial, rather than given state posts... This was not done.[65]

The Opposition, apparently, was energetically fulfilling the role assigned to it in the multiparty game. And Mubarak, who was committed to the gradual advancement of democracy, acknowledged with satisfaction that the democratic process was developing nicely. At the same time, however, he felt that Egyptian democracy still needed to be under the President's watchful eye, to ensure that criticism did not turn into dangerous incitement and that the demands for more freedom did not undermine the political order. This often led him to launch counterattacks against the Opposition. He repeatedly urged "those who play with fire to take a long and clear look beyond their own noses and discern something much nobler than party interests, self-benefit, political maneuvering and one-upmanship."[66] He accused opposition leaders and the Press of defamation, distortion of truth, and going "so far as to encroach on honor, values and fundamental principles with no compunction whatsoever."[67] Sometimes he issued implied warnings:

> I frequently ask myself: what will happen if this present course of events continues? What if the Opposition continues to twist facts, taking advantage of every opportunity to incite and provoke? I often ask myself: How long can Egypt put up with this nonsense? ...I do not think Egypt can take it any more, nor can the regime bear it any longer... [the opposition newspapers] have abandoned the problems of the people and devoted thamselves to a vendetta... They are wasting democracy. They are killing it ... I and others are fed up with practices that seek to bury democracy alive.[68]

Such accusations and warnings by the President not unexpectedly met with angry opposition reaction. His statements were viewed as further evidence of the claim that "Mubarak's democracy has so far remained tactical rather than strategic, so that it serves to contain the Opposition, not to expand its freedom."[69] Some went so far as to respond with an implied warning, reminding Mubarak of "the events that put an end to Sadat's rule, for there are elements that are interested in popular incitement against the President."[70]

The Consultation Council elections on 1 October provoked bitter opposition attacks on the Government. One half of the Council's 210 members, including 70 elected members and 35 who were appointed by the President, were replaced. As was the case in the previous two rounds of these elections (see *MECS* 1980–81, pp 435–36; 1982–83, pp 422, 424), the opposition parties decided on a boycott on the grounds that the electoral system, unchanged since 1980, was "undemocratic" and "unfairly benefited the ruling party at the expense of the smaller parties."[71] In addition to verbal assaults on the Government, opposition representatives approached an administrative court with a request that it invalidate the existing elections law as it "contradicted the Constitution and did not enable the citizens to elect their representatives in a free and democratic way." The court turned down the request on 23 September.[72] As a result of the opposition boycott, only the NDP staged candidates and won all 70 seats. An official statement put the number of those who voted at *c* 11 million, or slightly more than 80 per cent of eligible voters,[73] an impressive but somewhat dubious proportion.

As expected, the Opposition charged that the elections were a fraud, "a vulgar example of rigging, forging and assaulting the people's will, and of replacing political action by forgery."[74] Its leaders ridiculed the results announced by the Government, alleging that the polling stations were empty on election day, and announced their intention to prove their charges in court.[75] Such allegations notwithstanding, two opposition leaders, Murad of the Liberal Party and Ahmad al-Sabbahi of the People's *(Umma)* Party, accepted appointment to the Council by the President.[76] (Among the other members appointed were Interior Minister Zaki Badr and Prime Minister 'Ali Lutfi; the latter, after having resigned his post at the head of the Government, became Consultative Council Speaker.)[77]

The process of democratization had come a long way in its first decade. A remarkable degree of freedom to organize, act and criticize had become an integral part of political life, and a vital outlet for all kinds of pressures. In the estimate of some observers, the process may well have reached the point beyond which an attempt to reverse or curb it would be impossible without serious unrest, which would entail a painful price to be paid by both the Government and the governed. Party pluralism and free speech, having begun as an "experiment" (*tajriba*, in Sadat's usage), seemed to be emerging confidently from the experimental stage. Egyptian democracy, if still immature, was forging ahead toward further gains — or, possibly toward a mighty confrontation with forces whose position of power it potentially jeopardized.

FOREIGN AFFAIRS

EGYPT AND THE UNITED STATES

The 11 October 1985 incident, in which American aircraft intercepted an Egyptian plane over the Mediterranean and forced it to land, left a heavy load of Egyptian hard feelings to weigh on Cairo's relations with Washington. President Mubarak estimated then that full reconciliation would "take a long time" and involve great "efforts by both sides." (For details see *MECS* 1984–85, pp 362–63). Egypt's ties with the US were vital to the former's national interest, increasingly so with the deterioration of its economic conditions. But the dependence on massive American support was frustrating — to many even humiliating — because of the Egyptian dislike for Washington's attitudes and policies. Such sentiments continued to cast a long shadow on Egyptian-US relations in 1986. It was perhaps indicative that Mubarak did not visit Washington even once during the period under review — the first year that this happened since he became President. A visit was scheduled for late September, but it was postponed till the next year.[78]

There were other signs of disagreement. In March-April, during the American-Libyan crisis (see essay on the US and the Middle East, and chapter on Libya), Egypt was strongly critical of US acts, especially its use of force against Libya. The Government issued a statement indicating its "great disturbance and dissatisfaction" with the American attack on "fraternal Libya."[79] The national Press was even more vehement in condemning US "aggression," which confirmed that Washington "sees the region as a US protectorate."[80] The opposition Press likewise denounced "American gangsterism in the entire region" and "the barbarism and bestiality of Reagan and his Administration."[81] Similarly, in November, when the American arms deal with Iran became known (see essay on th US and the Middle East). Egypt, which was backing Iraq in its war against Iran, reacted with anger. The disclosure of the deal, said the chief editor of *al-Jumhuriyya,* "unmasked [Washington's] lies" and pointed to the existence of an "alliance against Arabism, the Arab world, and the real interests of the Arabs."[82] The US was charged with "encouraging terrorism and furnishing Iran with proof that terrorism is profitable." The result was bound to be "the loss of its trustworthiness in the Third World."[83] Mubarak, similarly dismayed, sent a message to President Ronald Reagan, calling on him "to do something so as not to lose [US] credibility in the Arab world as result of this action."[84]

Distaste for US policies was also expressed in other ways. In February, an Egyptian lawyer filed with a Cairo court "a suit against President Reagan and the US Administration," asking $10 bn in "indemnities for harming the feelings of the Egyptian people" in the October 1985 incident.[85] In early May, a young Egyptian opened fire on an American ship in the Suez Canal,[86] and later that month, a bomb exploded at the Egyptian-American bank headquarters in Cairo.[87]

Egypt, however, could afford to disagree with the US only up to a point. The financial support it was getting from Washington — *c* $1.3 bn in economic aid and about the same sum for military projects[88] — was too vital to be given up or risked by insisting on matters of national pride. So were the other advantages that Egypt enjoyed from this friendship. Thus, cooperation in the same broad scale as in the past, and diplomatic efforts to coordinate political strategies persisted.

A central issue on the agenda in 1986 was the heavy military debt to the US, amounting to *c* $4.5 bn and accounting for about one half of Egypt's total debt to that country. The servicing of all debts to Washington was to cost Egypt about $800m in 1986, of which more than $600m would go to servicing the military debt.[89] Such sums would consume a sizable share of US aid to Egypt. Partly responsible for these startling figures was the interest rate on the debts, set in 1979 at 14–17 per cent. Meanwhile, world interest rates decreased considerably and Cairo was now requesting that Washington cut the interest down to six or seven per cent. The request was brought up by Egyptian officials on numerous occasions. The Deputy Prime Minister and Minister of Planning, Kamal al-Janzuri, traveled to Washington twice, in June and September, to negotiate rescheduling of the debts. And the question was also discussed during the visit to the US in May of the Minister of the Economy, Sultan Abu 'Ali, during Abu Ghazala's two missions, in June and November, and US Vice President George Bush's visit to Cairo in August.[90] The Egyptian Press, too, often voiced this demand.[91] Washington, however, was slow to grant the Egyptian request: financial difficulties and a review of its foreign commitments dictated a more stringent policy of aid appropriation. By the end of 1986 the Egyptian request was still under consideration by the US Administration.

Another area of US-Egyptian relations was military cooperation. Adm William Crowe, Chairman of the US Joint Chiefs of Staff, visited Cairo in January, and his Egyptian counterpart, Lt Gen Ibrahim al-'Urabi, returned the visit in May. There were negotiations concerning joint military production,[92] and in August the two sides resumed joint military exercises,[93] a program the Egyptian Government had stopped temporarily following the October 1985 crisis (see *MECS* 1984–85, p 363). Around midyear there were reports of secret Egyptian-American contacts concerning an Egyptian proposal to lease two former Israeli air bases in Sinai to the US in exchange for full or partial offsetting of Cairo's military debt. As could be expected in view of the sensitivity of this issue, especially in Egypt, these reports were denied by both parties.[94]

Egyptian-American cooperation on broader Middle Eastern issues was given a low profile in 1986. Until September, talks between the two sides focused chiefly on the formulation of the Taba arbitration compromise (see below) — the US assisting Egypt and Israel in reaching an agreement — alongside nonspecific exchanges of views concerning the Middle East peace process. Once the arbitration question was settled, attention shifted to the idea of an international conference for peace in the region, which the Mubarak-Peres summit in Alexandria seemed to have rendered practical (see below, and essay on the peace process). The US was less enthusiastic than Egypt about the idea, Washington at that stage preferring to seek direct negotiations between the potential partners to peace. Discussion of this, and other possible ways of advancing the peace process, largely of broad principles rather than practical aspects, continued between Egyptian and American officials through the end of the period under review and beyond.

EGYPT AND THE SOVIET UNION

Egyptian-Soviet relations had a good year in 1986. Cairo continued to intensify its contacts with Moscow as a part of the ongoing effort to expand its international ties. It was a year of frequent exchanges of high-level visits: in March, a Soviet delegation led by Pavel Gilashvili, Deputy Chairman of the Presidium of the Supreme Soviet, came to Cairo. He was followed by the head of the Near Eastern Desk at the Soviet Foreign Ministry, Vladimir Polyakov, who visited Egypt twice, in April and October; the Soviet Deputy Foreign Minister, Vladimir Petrovsky, who came in August; and a large Soviet trade mission that visited Cairo in November. Egyptian officials reciprocated: the Minister of Economy and Foreign Trade, Sultan Abu 'Ali, traveled to Moscow in April at the head of an economic delegation; and the Minister of State for Foreign Affairs Butrus Butrus-Ghali, visited the Soviet capital in June.

These exchanges created opportunities for frequent statements by officials of the two countries emphasizing the "friendly" and "steadily improving" relations between them. The Egyptian Press, hitherto reserved and at times even hostile to the Soviets, now tended to treat the USSR more favorably. An editorial in *al-Musawwar*, for example, stressed Egypt's "profound interest" in "restoring correct relations" with the Soviet Union. To meet this objective, the paper suggested, Cairo had to cooperate with Moscow in "creating a healthy atmosphere"; the "road between Moscow and Cairo" had become "passable" with the emergence of "a new leadership in both Egypt and the Soviet Union ready to surmount the bitterness of the past for the sake of a better future."[95]

The main area of Egyptian-Soviet cooperation was the economy. In recent years Egypt had become sixth among the Third World countries and second among African countries in trade exchanges with the Soviet Union. By 1986 the annual volume of this trade had reached *c* $600m,[96] and the two countries were seeking to expand it. There were two outstanding problems in their economic relations: the large Egyptian military debt to the USSR, the size of which was a matter of controversy (it was estimated to have totalled between $3–4 bn in 1977, when repayments were suspended by Sadat); and the question of the artificially low exchange rate at which Egypt calculated its exports to Moscow.[97] These issues, and the enhancing of trade, were negotiated during the mutual visits of economic delegations, and in December the two countries signed a trade protocol for 1987 which envisaged a 20 per cent increase over the previous year. The problems of the debt and the exchange rate were left for further negotiations in 1987.[98]

The new life blown by Mubarak and Peres into the idea of an international conference for peace in the Middle East (see essay on the peace process) served to revive another area of Egyptian-Soviet cooperation. Moscow had always been in favor of this option, which would open the door for its return as a major partner to the political process in the region. Egypt had not rejected the idea in principle, but as long as alternative ways seemed more profitable it preferred to advocate them. Now, as the option was brought up again, Cairo and Moscow could find a new area of cooperation. The Soviet Union, Foreign Minister 'Abd al-Majid stated, had "a responsibility, as a superpower, to work for stability and peace in our region. There are signs of an increasing Soviet interest in fulfilling a positive role... We welcome that, and welcome the USSR participation in the international conference."[99]

EGYPT AND EUROPE

With its economy in serious trouble, the peace process stalemated, and the US less cooperative than Egypt would have liked it to be, Cairo remained very interested in fostering ties with Western Europe. Egypt wanted its chief European allies, France, Britain, West Germany and Italy, to lend it support where that rendered by the US was insufficient. It thus sought loans from these Governments and the rescheduling of its debts to them, tried to enlist their support for its request of an IMF loan, and endeavored to obtain their cooperation on the issue of an international peace conference. High-level visits between Egypt and these countries were frequent in 1986, and they always focused on both bilateral and broad Middle Eastern issues. In January, Mubarak went to France, where he addressed the European Economic Community (EEC) Parliament in Strasbourg on Egypt's Middle East peace strategy and its economic situation, and conferred with President Mitterrand. From there he went to visit Bonn.[100] In July, the Egyptian President again traveled to Europe, visiting four capitals — Rome, Paris, Bonn and London — in 48 hours to request their Governments' support in relieving Egypt's debt problem.[101] And, in December, he took another trip to France, West Germany, Italy and Greece.[102] Cairo often expressed satisfaction "with the results and with the spirit" of its dealings with West European states. "This spirit," Mubarak stated after his trip in July, "was such that we did not need to give exhaustive explanations. Rather, we sensed that all these leaders were ready to understand our point of view." Mubarak even went so far as to declare that "had we not had strong relations with them, no one would have supported us or realized the value of stability in our country." He singled out West Germany as the State with which Egypt had "strong friendly relations" and the one "which shows more understanding [of] the Middle East situation than any other European state."[103] These efforts met with European readiness to assist Egypt. Leaders of the States approached by Cairo undertook to intercede with the IMF on its behalf. And the EEC Commissioner-General, Claude Cheysson, pledged in July to increase the aid to Egypt by replacing EEC loans with grants and by making special efforts to boost the volume of Egypt's economic cooperation with Western Europe.[104]

Mubarak's Government also continued to invest efforts in improving relations with Eastern Europe, geared to serve mainly bilateral interest. For Cairo this meant expanding its trade exchanges with these countries and trying to enlist greater East European participation in Egyptian development projects. In May, the Polish Foreign Minister came to Cairo, returning a visit by his Egyptian counterpart a year earlier.[105] In June Egyptian Foreign Minister 'Abd al-Majid went to Czechoslovakia — the first visit at such a high level there in 15 years — and to East Germany.[106] Romania's Foreign Minister came to Cairo in July, and Mubarak visited Bucharest in December.[107]

EGYPT AND THE ARAB WORLD

"Every Egyptian follows conditions in the Arab world with pain, sorrow and bitterness; every morning that dawns on the Arab nation brings with it the darkness of a frightful sunset."[108] Thus lamenting the state of inter-Arab relations, Mubarak also hinted at the reason for Egypt's relief at no longer being the target of a coordinated Arab offensive. In 1986, Cairo's relations with the Arab world were basically the same as in the previous year: alliances and rivalries remained unchanged; none of the Arab states still without diplomatic relations with Cairo moved to renew them; and the Arab League continued to deny readmittance to an Egypt committed to peace with Israel.

Yet after years of formal ostracism by the regional system on the one hand, and of friendly relations in practice with many Arab governments on the other, Egypt had grown accustomed to this state of affairs and, so it seemed, felt comfortable with it. Arab world reality, Mubarak reminded his Egyptian audience, was marked by "division, infighting and fragmentation";[109] and Arab leaders were "drowning in a sea of error and... fighting and fumbling in the land of disability... going from one failure to the next and from division to deterioration."[110] Similarly, the Arab League was "a dead body... unable to solve any problems in this problem-infested part of the world."[111] Egypt, by contrast, was confident and sure of its way, knowing that even those Arab leaders most hostile to it, "deep in their hearts, wish they had the courage of the will for peace, which has liberated the land of Egypt."[112] Mubarak, therefore, insisted that he felt no need to "strive to regain Egypt's leading role" in a fragmented Arab world, for Egypt was still the predominant power in the region, whether others liked it or not."[113]

The scene of intraregional relations being so gloomy, no Arab summit took place in 1986, notwithstanding efforts to convene one in May (see essay on inter-Arab relations). Nor was there much progress in the Middle East peace process, mainly due to Jordanian-Palestine Liberation Organization (PLO) differences (see essays on the

Middle East peace process and on the PLO). Thus there was little room for a significant Egyptian role in the regional arena. Egypt participated in the January 1986 conference of Islamic Foreign Ministers in Fez, where it was represented by Foreign Minister 'Abd al-Majid, and in the fifth Islamic summit conference in Kuwait, in January 1987, which Mubarak attended. Cairo also continued with its mediation efforts between King Husayn of Jordan and PLO leader Yasir 'Arafat, seeking to emphasize its conscientious commitment to a solution of the Palestinian problem and its belief that a frozen peace process was detrimental to the Palestinian cause, since "time is not on the side of the hesitant and reluctant... time favors those who act and who are capable of shouldering the responsibility."[114] Similarly, Egyptian spokesmen continued to reiterate that Egypt's support for Iraq in its war with Iran (see below) reflected nothing but profound concern for "the Arab nation's ...strategic security" and interests.[115]

Apart from such declarative measures, Cairo's efforts in the Arab arena were mainly of a bilateral nature. While Egypt claimed it had "good relations with all Arab leaders, marked by mutual trust,"[116] its two chief allies remained Jordan and Iraq. Egypt and Jordan held similar views regarding the future of the peace process. Amman's disagreement with the PLO, which led to a standstill in the process, was a central item on the agenda of frequent high-level meetings, in which Cairo kept urging the Jordanian King to soften his position and resume the dialogue with 'Arafat. Egypt also offered to participate in Jordanian-Palestinian meetings as a third party in order to help restore their mutual confidence.[117] But such Egyptian efforts turned out to be of little consequence. Another matter of common concern was the war in the Gulf, and continuous "Iranian aggression," which the two sides viewed with increasing apprehension. "We support and back Iraq," King Husayn stated at a joint news conference with Mubarak, "because Iraq is defending the eastern gate of the great Arab homeland"[118] — a clear expression of the deep anxiety about the growing Iranian menace, which was shared by both. Mubarak conferred with Husayn in 'Aqaba on 11 May and 28 December, and the King went to Alexandria on 7 August and to Cairo on 23 November. Egyptian Prime Minister 'Ali Lutfi and his Jordanian counterpart Zayd al-Rifa'i likewise exchanged visits, in April and August respectively. Rifa'i also went to Cairo in October, heading an official delegation of eight ministers, to take part in a meeting of the joint Egyptian-Jordanian Higher Committee (for the forming of this committee in 1985 and its early activities see *MECS* 1984–85, p 367). The committee discussed areas of economic and technical cooperation, and the two sides signed a number of agreements in these fields.[119]

The fraternal spirit which had marked Egyptian-Iraqi relations in recent years persisted in 1986, and Cairo reiterated its support for Iraq's President "Saddam Husayn and the Iraqi Army which is bravely defending its land."[120] Egypt's Deputy Prime Minister and Minister of Agriculture, Yusuf Wali, visited Baghdad in February, and Iraq's Foreign Minister Tariq 'Aziz reciprocated the following month. A moment of tension occurred in these relations in May, when some 30 Egyptian citizens residing in Iraq, who were tried for forging their passports so that they could send home more foreign currency, were sentenced to death and the Iraqi Government insisted on executing them. Egyptian officials and the Egyptian Press strongly urged the Iraqis not to implement the court's decision, and Mubarak interceded with Saddam Husayn on behalf of the sentenced Egyptians. Husayn eventually agreed, out of "love for and appreciation of his brother, President Mubarak, as well as his love for the Egyptian people, who are dear to him and to all Iraqis," and commuted the sentences to life imprisonment.[121] With the incident over early in June, Foreign Minister 'Aziz could again depict his country's relations with Egypt as "firm and fraternal in the full, profound sense of these words," and Mubarak could respond by pronouncing Egypt's persistent friendship with and support for "our brother and friend, President Saddam Husayn, and... the fraternal Iraqi people."[122]

At the opposite end of the Arab spectrum as viewed from Cairo were Syria and Libya, the foes of Egypt as they were of Jordan and Iraq. Profoundly disagreeing with Egypt on every major regional and global issue, they constantly traded charges and abuse with Egyptian officials and the Press. When the security forces crisis broke out, Syria's ruling party organ *al-Ba'th* described it as an "armed popular upheaval against the Mubarak regime and the treasonous Camp David course." Having been humiliated and exploited by the Egyptian regime's domestic and foreign policies, the "Egyptian masses and their national forces...cannot but avenge their dignity." Radio Tripoli echoed the same message and called upon all Egyptians to "come out in these immortal hours... to the streets, join the popular revolution...and defeat the US and the Zionists in Cairo."[123] This outraged the Egyptians. Mubarak strongly rejected the Syrian intervention as "unacceptable to all Egyptians and... far removed from the way we feel and think," and denounced the Libyan call for popular revolt in Egypt as "sick voices [carrying]...a stupid call... These methods are childish."[124] The Egyptian media were much harsher in their condemnation of "these pygmies who rule from Damascus and who tyrannize the Syrian people," and of Qadhdhafi, who was "mentally deranged... helpless and wretched."[125] Such language typified Egyptian references to both countries throughout the year. Syria was attacked for its role and "plots" in Lebanon, which were "aimed at undermining and destroying Arab causes";[126] for "doing nothing to liberate" the territory occupied by Israel and "acting to impede peace efforts that are certain to lead to the liberation of its territory";[127] and for having "struck truly severe blows at the Palestinian revolution, producing a serious division within the revolution's ranks."[128] Libya was accused of "frequently sending Libyan and foreign terrorists to Egypt,"[129] while Qadhdhafi was described as "unable to fulfill the commitments of an alliance; he resorts to alliances in order to stab his friends in the back."[130] Both Syria and Libya were repeatedly assailed for assisting Iran in the war, thus standing "in the same trench with the aggressors and... participating in supplying weapons to strike at another Arab state, Arab army and Arab people." It was precisely this kind of position, Cairo charged, that was responsible for the "gaps in the Arab dialogue and [that] paved the way for selfishness, regionalism and maneuvers."[131]

While expressing hostile attitudes toward both States, Egypt's view of Libya was in a way different from its feelings about Syria. A close neighbor, Libya was regarded not merely as a political foe but also as an immediate peril. Its policies and moves always generated suspicion and often anxiety, as well as resentment; and the periodic uncovering of Libyan plots, of which Egypt was at times the potential victim, served to substantiate these fears. Mubarak on one occasion singled out "the one who sits across our western border" as "the only [Arab] leader whom I do not trust."[132] As against this, the negative attitude toward Syria mainly reflected ideological and political differences but not as much mistrust and disdain. In Egyptian-Syrian relations there was room for occasional guarded expressions of respect, such as Mubarak's open reference to his "dear friend Hafiz al-Asad, President of fraternal Syria... I am as proud of [our old] personal ties as he is."[133]

The tension which crept into Egypt's relations with Sudan following the April 1985 coup in Khartoum (see *MECS* 1984–85, pp 367–68) continued to mar their friendship in 1986. Much of the resentment the new Sudanese regime felt toward the deposed President Numayri was occasioned by his policy lines and his accomplishments during his tenure (see chapter on Sudan). Among these was the Sudanese-Egyptian Integration Plan, which, the new Sudanese Government now argued, was based on a system of "useless institutions" that Numayri had "inposed upon the Sudanese people" for the sake of "consolidating his hated rule."[134] Accordingly, on 30 March, the Sudanese Government announced its decision to "dissolve all the existing integration bodies," but later clarified that it was only "freezing, rather than abolishing" them.[135] In early April, elections for the Sudanese Parliament resulted in victory for the People's (*Umma*) Party which was headed by al-Sadiq al-Mahdi, a staunch critic of Numayri's heavy reliance on friendship with Egypt, and which had a strong pro-Libyan orientation. Al-Mahdi declared that relations between his country and Egypt had to be redefined: "Special relations are not something which should be rejected," he stated, but they had to be "based on Sudan's being an independent country with its own interests," unlike in the past, when the ties were "based on concepts that did not serve the interests of the Sudanese people."[136]

A particular point of contention was Egypt's persistent refusal to extradite former President Numayri, in exile in Cairo, to the new Government in Khartoum, This, the Sudanese felt, did not merely "constitute a stab at the Sudanese nation" but also amounted to "Egyptian recognition of the criminal role that was played by this man against his nation and homeland."[137] Hence, in August, the Sudanese Government started a legal process in Egypt's Supreme Administrative Court designed to lead to Numayri's extradition.[138]

Egypt, however, tried to play down the tension. When Sudan's decision about the Integration Plan was announced, Usama al-Baz reacted by asserting that what interested Egypt was "not the form but the spirit of relations between the two countries. These relations are very good and free of any tension."[139] Cairo continued to deliver arms and ammunition to Khartoum, "out of care for Sudan's safety and independence," and played up the news of their shipment and of other aid given to Sudan in its media.[140] Egyptian officials emphasized that work on joint projects "within the framework of the Integration Plan" was continuing, and that the plan was "still effective and it will not be canceled unless the two Heads of State issue a decision in this respect."[141] There were also exchanges of visits: a large delegation of Egyptian party leaders, headed by Deputy Prime Minister Yusuf Wali, went to Khartoum in May; Sudan's Foreign Minister al-Sharif al-Hindi visited Cairo in the same month, and Interior Minister Sayyid Ahmad al-Husayn came to Egypt in November. Official Egyptian public references to Sudan continued to project the same friendliness as in the past: Sudan, Mubarak stated, was "much more than an ally and a partner. It is our twin to whom we are tied by kinship and blood and common interests that know no political bounds or formalities or official considerations."[142] The new Sudanese regime, still fresh and highly sensitive, remained somewhat reserved. Its spokesmen chose to treat statements such as Mubarak's as little more than "harping on the old tune of good intentions, cordial sentiments and the common destiny."[143] Beyond the tension and points of disagreement, however, it seemed that both Governments acknowledged their strong mutual interests and were keen to maintain their friendly dialogue and close cooperation.

Egypt's relations with the PLO remained cordial in 1986. When there was an impasse in the PLO's dialogue with Jordan early in the year (see essay on the PLO), Cairo embarked on a conciliation campaign. PLO Chairman 'Arafat along with a delegation of Palestinian leaders, went to the Egyptian capital to discuss the situation, and that round of meetings was followed by intensive contacts between Egyptian and PLO (as well as Jordanian) officials. In April 'Arafat again visited Cairo, and many other PLO leaders followed suit. As the effort to break the Jordanian-Palestinian deadlock failed, Egypt, firmly and declaredly committed to the Palestinian cause, continued to seek ways of bringing the PLO into the peace process. Mubarak brought up the issue of PLO representation in a future Middle East peace conference in his September summit with Israeli Prime Minister Peres[144] (see below) as well as in his contacts with other parties directly or indirectly involved in the process.

EGYPT AND ISRAEL

1986 was an eventful year in Egyptian-Israeli relations. An agreement concerning the Taba arbitration was reached in September, to be followed by a Mubarak-Peres summit in Alexandria and the reappointment of an Egyptian Ambassador in Tel Aviv, after four years without one. All these events led to an improvement in the substance and style of Egyptian-Israeli exchanges in the latter part of the year.

During the first half of the year, however, such an improvement was still considered remote, even unrealistic. The harsh impact of the October 1985 Ra's Burqa' incident — in which Israeli tourists were killed in Sinai by an Egyptian soldier — and its sequel in early 1986 (for details see *MECS* 1984–85, pp 360, 371–72) dominated the atmosphere of relations between the two countries. A great many Egyptians stated openly that the soldier's deed reflected a widespread and authentic Egyptian feeling of resentment against Israel. The Israeli media, in turn, continued to express a strong public sense of shock at the act and disillusionment over relations with Egypt. The Israeli Government demanded compensation for the families of the victims; Cairo agreed in principle, but the question of the amounts became a subject of prolonged negotiations, which continued intermittently throughout 1986 and beyond.

The two sides continued to trade accusations and expressions of mistrust. Egypt was much more active in this, and its media lashed at Israel for its "rough treatment" of the population in the occupied territories; for attacking villages and refugee camps in Lebanon; and for its "expansionist" and "intransigent" nature, which made it a menace to the entire region.[145] It was this last characteristic, the Egyptian Press charged, which made Israel so difficult to deal with in the sensitive issue of Taba (see below).

A grave incident occurred on 19 March, when gunmen attacked Israeli diplomats in Cairo, as they were leaving the International Trade Fair, in which Israel participated. One woman was killed and three men were wounded. An organization calling itself "Egyptian Revolution," which claimed responsibility for the assault, had already killed an Israeli diplomat in Cairo in August 1985 (see *MECS* 1984–85, p 371), but had not been uncovered by the Egyptian police.[146] The Egyptian Government expressed its sorrow for the attack, and Mubarak pledged that his Government would find the perpetrators.[147] Being the third incident in seven months in which Israelis were assassinated on Egyptian soil, the attack greatly added to the burden of tension marking Egyptian-Israeli ties at that stage.

Meanwhile, negotiations on the Taba issue continued at a slow pace. The Egyptian and Israeli delegations to the talks exchanged working visits, meeting in Cairo or Tel Aviv once every few weeks and making repeated references, in their public statements, to the "serious difficulties" on the road to an agreement. Cairo continued to insist that a meeting between President Mubarak and Prime Minister Peres, as well as the return of the Egyptian Ambassador to Tel Aviv, depended on the settlement of the Taba problem.

By May the pace of the talks had begun to accelerate, and a US legal adviser joined in the efforts to bring them to a conclusion. On 10 August it was announced that the two States had reached an agreement on the basic principles of an arbitral compromise.[148] The Israeli Inner Cabinet approved the agreement on 13 August, and the Egyptian Government confirmed it, after it had been completed, on 10 September.[149] Three legal experts from Sweden, Switzerland and France, were agreed upon and appointed as arbitrators. The process of arbitration, expected to last for a year or more, began near Geneva on 8 December (for further details see essay on the peace process).

The conclusion of an agreement on Taba paved the way for the summit meeting which Prime Minister Peres had sought since he came to power in September 1984. On 11 September 1986 Peres went to Alexandria for two days to discuss with Mubarak and other Egyptian officials ways of reviving the peace process and improving Egyptian-Israeli relations. A joint communiqué at the end of the summit described the meeting as marking "the beginning of a new era in the relations between Egypt and Israel and in the search for a just and comprehensive peace in the Middle East." The two sides undertook to attempt to resolve "all aspects of the Palestinian problem," and proclaimed 1987 "the year of negotiations for peace." In a more practical vein, the two leaders agreed to act to convene an international peace conference and to form a preparatory committee for such a conference.[150] (See further in essay on the peace process.) On 12 September the Egyptian Government announced its decision to appoint Muhammad Basyuni, who had been Egypt's Chargé d'Affaires in Tel Aviv since the recall of the Ambassador in September 1982, as Egypt's new Ambassador to Israel.[151]

These developments contributed to a thaw in the atmosphere. With the Taba arbitral compromise signed, and the Egyptian Ambassador back in Tel Aviv, it was generally felt that two serious obstacles had been removed from the way to a better dialogue. There was a sense of much satisfaction, typical of moments when major achievements on a treacherous road prove that the road is nonetheless the right one. This was reflected in a series of friendly exchanges between high officials of the two countries and in optimistically phrased commentaries in the Egyptian and Israeli media. In this atmosphere, even Israel's new Prime Minister, Yitzhak Shamir, who replaced Peres in late October and who had in the past expressed serious reservations about the peace with Egypt, found it appropriate to praise Mubarak "who had demonstrated qualities of leadership and dedication to the cause of peace."[152]

Such a positive spirit, however, only partially reflected the Egyptian-Israeli scene in late 1986. Shamir's replacement of Peres was followed in Cairo with much concern. And when, upon assuming office, Shamir announced his intention to encourage more settlements in the occupied territories, Egypt reacted with anger: the semi-official *al-Ahram* termed the statement "a discouraging beginning" for Shamir, which gave rise to "many questions about his credibility regarding continued support for peace in the region"; a Radio Cairo commentator spoke of "this overriding danger hanging over the head of the Arab people."[153] Thus, while there were new efforts to collaborate more closely in the political process, Egypt's relations with Israel were also likely to be characterized by frequent expressions of criticism and disagreement.

TABLE 1: 'ATIF SIDQI'S CABINET, November 1986[154]

Prime Minister	Dr 'Atif Muhammad Najib Sidqi*
Deputy Prime Minister and Minister of Defense and War Production	Field Marshal Muhammad 'Abd al-Halim Abu Ghazala
Deputy Prime Minister and Foreign Minister	Ahmad 'Ismat 'Abd al-Majid
Deputy Prime Minister and Minister of Planning and International Cooperation	Dr Kamal Ahmad al-Janzuri
Deputy Prime Minister and Minister of Agriculture and Land Reclamation	Dr Yusuf Amin Wali
Minister of Social Insurance and Social Affairs	Dr Amal 'Abd al-Rahim 'Uthman
Minister of Housing, Utilities and new Urban Complexes	Hasballah Muhammad al-Kafrawi**
Minister of State for Foreign Affairs	Dr Butrus Butrus-Ghali
Minister of Justice	Ahmad Mamduh 'Atiyya
Minister of Transport, Communications, and Maritime Transport	Sulayman Mutawalli Sulayman
Minister of Electricity and Energy	Muhammad Mahir 'Uthman Abaza
Minister of State for War Production	Dr Jamal al-Sayyid Ibrahim
Minister of State for People's Assembly and Consultative Council Affairs	Muhammad 'Abd al-Hamid Radwan
Minister of Information	Muhammad Safwat al-Sharif
Minister of Irrigation	'Ismat Radi 'Abd al-Hamid Radi
Minister of Industry	Muhammad Mahmud 'Abd al-Wahhab
Minister of Petroleum and Mineral Resources	'Abd al-Hadi Muhammad Qandil
Minister of Cabinet Affairs and Minister of State for Administrative Development	Dr 'Atif Muhammad Ahmad 'Ubayd
Minister of State for People's Assembly and Consultative Council Affairs	Dr Sayyid 'Ali al-Sayyid
Minister of Culture	Dr Ahmad 'Abd al-Maqsud Haykal
Minister of Tourism and Civil Aviation	Fu'ad 'Abd al-Latif Sultan
Minister of Interior	Zaki Mustafa Badr
Minister of Supply and Internal Trade	Dr Muhammad Jalal al-Din Abu al-Dhahab*
Minister of State for Scientific Research	Dr 'Adil 'Abd al-Hamid 'Izz*
Minister of Health	Dr Muhammad Raghib Duwaydar*
Minister of Economy and Foreign Trade	Dr Yusri 'Ali Mustfa*
Minister of Local Government	Dr Ahmad Salama Muhammad*
Minister of Education	Dr Ahmad Fathi Surur*
Minister of Finance	Dr Muhammad Ahmad al-Razzaz*
Minister of Waqfs [Religious Trusts]	Dr Muhammad 'Ali Mahjub*
Minister of State for Emigration and Egyptians Abroad	'Ali 'Abd al-Shahid Bishay*
Minister of Manpower and Training	'Asim 'Abd al-Haqq Salih*

* New Ministers.

** Reshuffled to another portfolio.

NOTES

For the place and frequency of publications cited here, and for the full name of the publication, news agency, radio station or monitoring service where an abbreviation is used, please see "List of Sources." Only in the case of more than one publication bearing the same name is the place of publication noted here. In the present chapter, however, all references to *al-Ahrar, al-Akhbar, al-Jumhuriyya* and *al-Sha'b* are to the Cairo papers of these names.

1. Mubarak's May Day address, R. Cairo, 1 May — DR, 2 May; *JP*, quoting Reuters, 19 June, 24 November; *Memo*, 12 September, 21 November 1986.
2. *FT*, 12 February, 11 April; *NYT*, 6 July; *Memo*, 12 September, 21 November 1986.
3. Another estimate was that the country would lose as much as $1 bn from remittances in 1986; *FT*, 11 April; *Memo*, 14 March, 12 September, 21 November 1986.
4. *Memo*, 12 September 1986.
5. *NYT*, 12 January; MENA, 1, 5 March — DR, 3, 6 March; *IHT*, 6 March; *JP*, 1 July 1986.
6. *Al-Ahram*, 27 July 1986.
7. *Memo*, 12 September 1986.
8. *JP*, quoting Reuters, 1 July; *NYT*, 6 July 1986.
9. *JP*, quoting Reuters, 19 June 1986.
10. Mubarak's May Day address, R. Cairo, 1 May — DR, 2 May; Mubarak's speech to NDP Congress, R. Cairo, 20 July — DR, 22 July 1986.
11. Mubarak's speech to NDP Congress, R. Cairo, 20 July — DR, 22 July 1986.
12. Mubarak's May Day address, R. Cairo, 1 May — DR, 2 May; Mubarak's interview in *Der Spiegel*, 28 July 1986.
13. E.g., *al-Ahali*, 16 April, 16 July; *al-Sha'b*, 9 December 1986.
14. *Ruz al-Yusuf*, 28 April; *al-Jumhuriyya*, 23 November 1986.
15. *Al-Akhbar*, 11 February; *al-Sha'b*, 11 February, 4 November; *al-Ahali*, 12 February; R. Cairo, 8, 9 July; MENA, QNA, 8 July 1986.
16. E.g., *al-Sharq al-Awsat*, 29 April; *al-Sha'b*, 5 August 1986.
17. *Al-Ahram*, 9, 16 May 1986.
18. *Al-Ahram*, 18 June; *al-Musawwar*, 18 July; MENA, 1 August; *Ruz al-Yusuf*, 6 October; *al-Ittihad*, Abu Dhabi, 22 November; *al-Wafd*, 27 November 1986.
19. Mubarak's speech to NDP congress, R. Cairo, 20 July — DR, 22 July; *Memo*, 12 September; *Le Monde*, 14-15 December 1986.
20. Mubarak's May Day address, R. Cairo, 1 May — DR, 2 May 1986.
21. *Al-Musawwar*, 14 November 1986.
22. MENA, 9 November — DR, 10 November 1986.
23. Mubarak's interview in *Der Spiegel*, 28 July; *FT*, 4 December 1986.
24. MENA, R. Cairo, AFP, 25 February-7 March — DR, 26 February-8 March; *al-Ahram*, 26–28 February; *FT*, 27 February; *The Guardian*, 28 February, 7 March; *NYT*, 1, 3, 9 March 1986. The official statement on casualties and damages was made on 3 April; MENA, 3 April — SWB, 5 April 1986. Earlier accounts, however, gave higher figures: 107 dead and 719 wounded; *al-Ahram*, 5 March; *IHT*, 6 March 1986.
25. E.g., Information Minister Sawfat al-Sharif on R. Cairo, MENA, 27 February — DR, 27, 28 February; Usama al-Baz in MENA, 27 February — DR, 28 February; *al-Ahram*, 27 February 1986.
26. *Al-Akhbar*, 28 February; MENA, 3 March — DR, 4 March 1986.
27. Mubarak's address, R. Cairo, 8 March — DR, 11 March 1986.
28. MENA, 15 April — DR, 16 April 1986.
29. *Al-Ra'y al-'Amm*, 30 April; R. Cairo, 30 April, 1 May — DR, 1, 5 May; *al-Qabas*, 1 May 1986.
30. *Al-Ahali, al-Nur*, 2 July; *al-Wafd*, 10 July; MENA, 1 September — DR, 2 September; *al-Musawwar*, 5 September; *Akhir Sa'a*, 10 September 1986.
31. *Al-Akhbar*, 11 August, 3 September 1986.
32. *The Guardian*, 22 October; *IHT*, 24 October 1986.
33. MENA, 31 October; *IHT*, 1-2 November; *Ha'aretz*, quoting AFP, 4 November 1986.
34. MENA, 4 December — SWB, 5 December; *IHT, FT*, 5 December 1986.
35. *Al-Ahrar*, 24 November 1986.

36. Badr's interview in *al-Siyasa*, 13-14 September 1986.
37. 'Umar Tilmisani in *al-Sha'b*, 18 March 1986.
38. *Al-Musawwar*, 2, 23 May, 6 June; *Akhir Sa'a*, 28 May 1986.
39. *Al-Sharq al-Awsat*, 28 May; *al-Musawwar*, 6 June; *al-'Alam*, London, 21 June 1986.
40. *Al-Siyasi*, 8 June 1986.
41. *Al-Siyasi*, 22 June 1986.
42. Interview in *al-Khalij*, 14 June 1986.
43. *Al-Ahrar*, 27 January; *al-Khalij*, 14 June 1986.
44. *Al-Khalij*, ibid; Abu Isma'il's interview in *al-Yamama*, 23 July 1986.
45. Ibid; *al-Ahrar*, 7 April 1986.
46. Abu Isma'il's interview in *al-Yamama*, 23 July; *al-Ahrar*, 7, 14 April 1986.
47. *Al-Wafd*, 6 February; *al-Ahrar*, 10 February 1986.
48. *Al-Ahrar*, 19 February 1986.
49. MENA, 31 March, 1 April — DR, 2 April, SWB, 3 April; *al-Ahali*, 9 April; *al-Ahram*, 11 April 1986.
50. *Al-Qabas*, 21 October 1986.
51. MENA, 4 November — SWB 7 November 1986.
52. *Al-Wafd*, 27 November; *The Guardian*, 28 November 1986.
53. *Al-Jumhuriyya*, 21 November; *al-Sha'b*, 25 November 1986.
54. *Al-Ahrar*, 14 April 1986.
55. *Al-Musawwar*, 7 March 1986.
56. *Al-Ahali*, 19 March 1986.
57. *Al-Ahrar*, 3 March 1986.
58. *Al-Sha'b*, 18 March 1986.
59. *Al-Ahali*, 17 September 1986.
60. *Al-Ahrar*, 14 April 1986.
61. Fu'ad Siraj al-Din's interview in *al-Akhbar*, 19 February 1986.
62. E.g., ibid.
63. E.g. *al-Wafd*, 12 June, 7 August; *al-Sha'b*, 4 November 1986.
64. *Al-Wafd*, 12 June, 7 August 1986.
65. *Al-Wafd*, 13 February 1986.
66. Mubarak's address, R. Cairo, 20 July — SWB, 22 July 1986.
67. Mubarak's address, R. Cairo, 12 November — DR, 14 November 1986.
68. Mubarak's interview, *al-Musawwar*, 17 January 1986.
69. *Al-Ahali*, 29 October 1986.
70. *Al-Ahrar*, 20 January 1986.
71. *Al-Wafd*, 11 September 1986. For details on the elections law of June 1980, still in effect in 1986, see *MECS* 1979-80, pp 346-47.
72. *Al-Wafd*, 11 September; *al-Akhbar*, 24 September 1986.
73. *Al-Jumhuriyya*, 3 October; *FT*, 4 October; *Akhir Sa'a*, 8 October 1986.
74. *Al-Ahali*, 5 November 1986.
75. *Al-Sha'b, The Guardian*, 28 October 1986.
76. *Ruz al-Yusuf*, 6 October; R. Cairo, 30 October — DR, 31 October 1986.
77. R. Cairo, 30 October — DR, 31 October; MENA, 10 November — DR, 10 November.
78. *Al-Ahram*, 22 September 1986.
79. MENA, 15 April — DR, 15 April 1986.
80. *Al-Ahram*, int ed, 17 April 1986.
81. *Al-Ahali*, 16 April; *al-Sha'b* 29 April 1986.
82. Chief editor of *al-Jumhuriyya* interviewed by R. Cairo, 16 November — DR, 17 November 1986.
83. *Al-Akhbar*, 12 November; *al-Ahram*, 16 November 1986.
84. MENA, 23 November — SWB, 25 November 1986.
85. *Al-Ahram*, 22 February 1986.
86. R. Damascus, 13 May; *al-'Alam*, London, 24 May 1986.
87. Voice of Free Lebanon, 30 May — DR, 30 May 1986.
88. *FT*, 12 March; *NYT*, 31 August 1986.
89. *Al-Musawwar*, 18 July; *Ruz al-Yusuf*, 6 October 1986.

90. MENA, 30 May, 20 June; *al-Ahram*, 18, 21, 25 June, 1 August, 23 September; *al-Ittihad*, Abu Dhabi, 22 November; R. Monte Carlo, 26 November 1986.
91. E.g., *al-Ahram*, 21 March; *al-Musawwar*, 18 July; *Ruz al-Yusuf*, 6 October 1986.
92. *Al-Ahram*, 21, 28 June 1986.
93. MENA, 28 August — SWB, 30 August 1986.
94. *Al-Anba*, Kuwait, 24 May; *JP*, 25 May; *MM*, 23 June; *al-Ahram*, 25 June; *al-Dustur*, London, 7 July 1986.
95. *Al-Musawwar*, 4 April 1986.
96. MENA, 23 March, 8 April — DR, 25 March, 9 April 1986.
97. *FT*, 8 April, 17 December 1986.
98. *FT*, 17 December 1986.
99. 'Abd al-Majid's interview with *al-Ra'y al-'Amm*, 29 September 1986.
100. *Al-Ahram*, 27 January; MENA, 29 January — SWB, 31 January; R. Cairo, 30 January 1986.
101. *Akhbar al-Yawm*, 19 July; Mubarak's speech, R. Cairo, 20 July — DR, 22 July 1986.
102. *Al-Ahram*, 10 December; MENA, 14 December — SWB, 16 December 1986.
103. *Akhbar al-Yawm*, 19 July; Mubarak's speech, R. Cairo, 20 July — DR, 22 July 1986.
104. MENA, 14 July — SWB, 16 July 1986.
105. MENA, 3, 4 May — DR, 5 May 1986.
106. *Al-Ahram*, 4, 24 June 1986.
107. R. Cairo, 10 July; *The Guardian*, 19 December 1986.
108. Mubarak's May Day address, R. Cairo, 1 May — DR, 2 May 1986.
109. Mubarak's address, R. Cairo, 20 July — SWB, 22 July 1986.
110. Mubarak's May Day address, R Cairo, 1 May — DR, 2 May 1986.
111. Mubarak's interview with *Newsweek*, 19 May 1986.
112. Mubarak's May Day address, R Cairo, 1 May — DR, 2 May 1986.
113. Mubarak's interview with *Der Spiegel*, 3 February 1986.
114. Mubarak's address, R. Cairo, 20 July — DR, 22 July 1986.
115. E.g., ibid; Mubarak's May Day address, R. Cairo, 1 May — DR, 2 May 1986.
116. Mubarak's interview in *Akhbar al-Yawm*, 18 October 1986.
117. R. Monte Carlo, 11 May; R. Manama, 12 May — DR, 13 May 1986.
118. MENA, 23 November — SWB, 25 November 1986.
119. For details, see MENA, 25, 26 October — DR, 27 October 1986.
120. E.g., R. Cairo, 17 February 1986.
121. MENA, 22 May, 2 June — DR, 23 May, SWB, 4 June; *al-Ittihad*, Abu Dhabi, 26 May; R. Cairo, 29 May — DR, 30 May 1986.
122. INA, 2 June — SWB, 4 June; Mubarak's address, R. Cairo, 20 July — DR, 22 July 1986.
123. *Al-Ba'th*, 27 February; R. Tripoli, 28 February — DR, 28 February 1986.
124. Mubarak's speech, R. Cairo, 8 March — SWB, 11 March 1986.
125. R. Cairo, 28 February, 4 March — SWB, 3, 8 March 1986.
126. MENA, 22 June — SWB, 24 June 1986.
127. R. Cairo, 30 October — DR, 31 October 1986.
128. E.g., ibid.
129. MENA, 1 February — DR, 3 February 1986.
130. R. Cairo, 4 March — SWB, 8 March 1986.
131. R. Cairo, 28 April — DR, 29 April; Mubarak's May Day address, R. Cairo, 1 May — DR, 2 May 1986.
132. Mubarak's interview in *Akhbar al-Yawm*, 18 October 1986.
133. Mubarak's address, R. Cairo, 8 March — DR, 11 March 1986.
134. Al-Sadiq al-Mahdi's interview in *Ruz al-Yusuf*, 30 June 1986.
135. SUNA, 30 March, 3 April — DR, 1, 8 April 1986.
136. Al-Mahdi's interviews in *al-Sharq al-Awsat*, 27 June, and in *Ruz al-Yusuf*, 30 June 1986.
137. SUNA, 30 June — SWB, 2 July 1986.
138. *Al-Sha'b*, 19 August; *al-Sharq al-Awsat*, 22 August 1986.
139. MENA, 31 March — SWB, 1 April 1986.
140. E.g. MENA, 5, 16 April — DR, 8, 17 April; AFP, 6 April — DR, 8 April; *al-Ahram*, int ed, 8 April — DR, 10 April; SUNA, 9 April, 9 July — SWB, 11 April, 11 July 1986.

141. *Al-Ahram*, 8 April; SUNA, 17 October — SWB, 20 October 1986.
142. Mubarak's address, R. Cairo, 20 July — DR, 22 July 1986.
143. SUNA, 30 June — SWB, 2 July 1986.
144. *JP*, 12 September; MENA, 12 September — SWB, 13 September 1986.
145. E.g., *al-Akhbar*, 20 February, 8 April 1986.
146. *Ha'aretz, JP, NYT*, 20 March; VoI, 20 March — SWB, 21 March 1986.
147. R. Cairo, 20 March; MENA, 21 March — DR, 21 March 1986.
148. MENA, 10 August — SWB, 12 August 1986.
149. VoI, 13 August — DR, 14 August; MENA, 10 September — DR, 11 September 1986.
150. MENA, VoI, 12 September — DR, 12 September 1986.
151. MENA, 12 September — DR, 12 September 1986.
152. *JP*, 7 November 1986.
153. R. Cairo, 23 October — SWB, 25 October; *al-Ahram*, 24 October 1986.
154. R. Cairo, 11 November — DR, 12 November 1986.

The Gulf States

DORE GOLD

REGIONAL DEVELOPMENTS

It is the common understanding of analysts of regional international organizations that the emergence and intensification of a common threat should theoretically lead to a greater degree of integration between a given grouping's constituents. Since its inception in 1981, the external military and internal revolutionary capabilities of the Islamic Republic of Iran certainly served as one of the principal catalysts for the emergence of the Gulf Cooperation Council (GCC; for the origins of the GCC see *Middle East Contemporary Survey* [*MECS*] 1980–81, pp 458–65). In 1986, just as Iran achieved a major military and psychological victory in Iraq's southern Faw peninsula (see chapter on Iraqi-Iranian war), bringing the Islamic Republic's land armies practically up to Kuwait's border, with the Iranian Navy and Air Force considerably stepping up their campaign against all types of commercial shipping serving the Gulf states, the GCC did not appear to respond with a greater corresponding cohesiveness. Iranian attacks against oil tankers alone while numbering 16 in 1984 and 11 in 1985 now jumped to 38 in the course of 1986.[1] Kuwaiti alarm notwithstanding, the GCC seemed not only to have plateaued in terms of its unified action and progress but even to have lost some ground in comparison with its early years of steady growth.

Part of its lost momentum was connected to the range of responses each member state felt appropriate for handling the Iranian threat. Clearly Kuwait and Bahrain were the two GCC states most directly threatened by Iran: the former would first feel the implications of an Iraqi collapse in the south; the latter, with its majority Shi'i population, was an ideal target for the expansion of the Iranian Islamic revolution. Behind Kuwait and Bahrain stood the power of the largest GCC member, Saudi Arabia. Riyadh, which in late 1985 and early 1986 was prepared to explore some limited *rapprochement* with its Iranian neighbor, nonetheless made it clear on a number of occasions that it would assist any GCC state if it were attacked (see chapter on Saudi Arabia). This Saudi position became relevant again in mid-1986 as the influential Speaker of the Iranian Parliament, Hashemi Rafsanjani, threatened to attack those Gulf countries assisting Iraq financially and thereby enabling it to continue its war effort.[2] However, the direct Iranian threat did not seem to affect Oman, Qatar, and the United Arab Emirates (UAE) in the same way that it affected the other GCC members. Utilizing their greater diplomatic flexibility, they were better positioned to pursue their traditional diplomacy of accommodation with Tehran than their more threatened GCC partners.

The loss of forward momentum in the GCC's development was evident during 1986 in a variety of areas. The outbreak of the brief conflict between Bahrain and Qatar over the island of Fasht al-Dibal served as a reminder of the persistence of intra-GCC

The Persian Gulf

boundary disputes which, if left unsettled, could bring two GCC member states to the brink of open warfare, external Iranian threats notwithstanding (for details see Bahrain-Qatar dispute, below). The very existence of the GCC framework was apparently insufficient to dissuade Qatar from attempting a *fait accompli* in territory the control of which it disputed with another GCC state. Within the GCC itself, while military coordination continued between the member states in small-scale bilateral air and naval exercises, no *Dir' al-Jazira* multilateral six-state exercise was again held in 1986. There were reports that the *Dir' al-Jazira* force established in 1984 continued to be developed, but it was doubtful that the smaller GCC states could lend substantial contingents to this force for extended periods of time. Talk of the GCC states arriving at an agreement governing their cooperation in internal security affairs had by 1986 completely stopped. Nor were breakthroughs announced in the socioeconomic spheres of GCC activity. Many issues that had been raised in past years, such as joint GCC passports or a GCC currency, remained under study.

THE GULF COOPERATION COUNCIL INSTITUTIONS

At the very beginning of 1986, the outlook for improved GCC-Iranian relations looked good given the diplomatic exchanges that several of the Gulf states had had with Tehran during 1985 (see *MECS* 1984–85, chapters on Saudi Arabia, the Gulf States — Oman). Diplomatic sources in Abu Dhabi were expressing optimism in early January concerning new GCC efforts to bring the war to an end, especially after the visit of the UAE Minister of State for Foreign Affairs to Tehran at the very end of December.[3] There were also expectations that Oman's Minister of State for Foreign Affairs would shortly be following his UAE counterpart to the Iranian capital.[4]

Two very different sorts of events led quickly to an overall worsening of GCC-Iranian relations. The decision by the Organization of Petroleum Exporting Countries (OPEC) to allow members to boost revenues by maximizing their market shares was taken by Iran as a scheme to slash oil prices and thereby deny Iran of the necessary funds to continue its war against Iraq.[5] Radio Tehran's Arabic service referred to Iranian official views that described the recent oil policy decisions as "an oil price reduction conspiracy in which some GCC countries are participating" in collaboration with the US. The Iranian radio warned the Gulf leaders that support for Saddam Husayn and reduced oil prices angered the peoples of the GCC's member countries and — in an apparent reference to the potential for internal revolutionary disorder — that the Gulf leaders "were sitting on top of a volcano."[6]

From the GCC's standpoint the event that ended any chance for a *rapprochement* between the two sides of the Gulf was Iran's February offensive in the Faw peninsula at the tip of southern Iraq. The GCC Foreign Ministers, meeting from 1–3 March in a regular session of the Ministerial Council in Riyadh, concluded their discussions with a statement that was highly critical of Iran:

> The Council reviewed the dangerous situation in the region in view of Iran's occupation of parts of Iraqi territory which is a violation of international charters and principles of good neighborliness and an assault against Iraq's sovereignty and the integrity of its territories. *The Council condemns this occupation and calls on Iran to withdraw its forces immediately to the international borders* [author's emphasis].[7]

The Ministerial Council expressed its concern about Iranian threats to some GCC states as well. Worried about "the expansion of the area of the conflict," it plainly stated that "the Iranian threats have created a tense atmosphere." The Council called on Iran "to stop its threats." The remainder of the Ministerial Council's statement dealt with, among other things, a reminder of collective security obligations of all the GCC states as well as the GCC's *Dir' al-Jazira* force's readiness to assume its responsibilities in any area within the member states' territories that "might become affected by recent developments."[8]

The Ministerial Council met again in the Saudi city of al-Ta'if between 28–30 June for its second ordinary session of the year. The Council condemned the recent terrorist attack on Kuwaiti oil installations (see section on Kuwait). No state or organization was specifically identified as having supported the attack. The Council also heard a detailed report from Saudi Foreign Minister Prince Sa'ud al-Faysal about Saudi mediation efforts between Bahrain and Qatar (for details of their dispute, see below). The Council also discussed the Iraqi-Iranian war; in its final statement it noted "with regret that the Iranian side still insists on using the policy of force and that it does not respond to the good offices of the GCC and many other parties."[9]

The GCC Ministerial Council's regular meeting on 26–27 August in Abha, Saudi Arabia, was held against the background of Iraq's 12 August long-range attack against Iran's Sirri Island oil-terminal (see chapter on Iraqi-Iranian war) and Iran's subsequent threats against GCC states found to be furnishing facilities to Iraq. The meeting concluded with the following reminder of GCC collective security obligations:

> The Council has noted with great regret the escalation of Iranian threats directed at the security and sovereignty of some member states. The Council reaffirms its collective support for any member state that would be subjected to threats, inspired by the Charter of the Council and the decisions of the Higher Council [Supreme Council] and it would consider these threats as threats to all the Council member states, since the security of member states is one and indivisible.[10]

The Council also expressed its "extreme concern" over Iranian interceptions of shipping en route to and from the ports of the GCC states. Much of the discussion focused also on the 5 August OPEC price agreement (see chapter on Middle East oil developments).[11]

The GCC Defense Ministers met on 4–5 October in Muscat, at which time they continued to review the joint military strategy they had approved during the previous year.[12] According to a subsequent interview with UAE Defense Minister Shaykh Muhammad Ibn Rashid al-Maktum, the Ministers decided to initiate studies on developing the GCC states' arms production capabilities.[13] The GCC Interior Ministers met on 21–22 October in Riyadh. No new steps in the internal security coordination of the GCC states were announced. No references were made to the past issue of a Gulf security agreement (see *MECS* 1983–84, p 392).

The GCC Ministerial Council met in Abu Dhabi at the beginning of November in order to set the agenda for the GCC Supreme Council meeting on 2 November. While security issues again loomed high in the Ministerial Council's discussions, especially in connection with the intensifying tanker war, significant time was also spent on economic issues including further implementation of the GCC unified economic agreement. The establishment of a unified Gulf currency was reportedly still under study. The GCC planned to investigate the possibility of establishing a joint Gulf stock exchange. While the GCC Foreign Ministers met at the Ministerial Council meeting, GCC Oil Ministers met at the same time to prepare their positions for the OPEC Pricing Committee meeting, which was expected to be held on 6 November. No unified GCC oil position was announced, although UAE Foreign Minister Rashid 'Abdallah expressed the hope that the new OPEC policy would lead to increased prices of around $17–18 per barrel[14] (see chapter on Middle East oil developments).

The GCC Supreme Council held its seventh session on 2–5 November in the Abu Dhabi emirate of the UAE. According to later reports, Kuwait sought approval of a new joint GCC strategy for gaining superpower protection of Gulf shipping. The Kuwaiti plan did not win Council approval. The UAE and Oman, both of which enjoyed relatively stable working relationships with Tehran, cautioned that superpower involvement would only make Iran more hostile.[15] The final statement of the GCC summit, as the Supreme Council session is commonly called, did not indicate that any breakthrough had been achieved in the meetings or that any fundamental changes in policy — such as those sought by Kuwait — had been chartered (for the complete text of the GCC summit see Appendix I at the end of this section). The usual call for ending the Iraqi-Iranian war appeared with no explicit words of condemnation for Iran for its continuation of the war. Reference was not only made to United Nations Security Council Resolutions 582 and 588 calling for an immediate cease-fire to the conflict but also to Security Council Resolutions 540 and 552 supporting the freedom of navigation and passage of merchant ships in international waters. The Supreme Council continued to express its concern for the Palestinian issue, the territorial integrity of Lebanon, and the breakdown of the Arab consensus.

Without being specific, the Supreme Council approved certain recommendations in the area of military cooperation. Subsequent reports speculated that the GCC states had decided to further build up their individual Air Forces as part of an effort to establish an air patrol against attacks on merchant shipping heading for Gulf ports.[16] In a related development, the GCC was reported to be interested in receiving a formal relaxation of American regulations regarding the transfer of data collected from US-supplied Saudi AWACS aircraft to third parties.[17] None of these developments were particularly new as the GCC's joint defense strategy, which was developed during 1984 (see *MECS* 1983–84, p 393), focused essentially on the defense of GCC territorial waters from air attack by coordinating GCC air forces and their warning systems.

On the economic front, some progress was made on gradual implementation of the unified economic agreements in the areas of equal treatment of all GCC citizens in the fields of investment — creating equal access to bank loans and industrial development funds — and of retail and wholesale trade.

THE BAHRAIN-QATAR DISPUTE

The closest event to an outright conflict between two member GCC states occurred on 26 April when a token force of Qatari troops seized the Bahraini-controlled island of Fasht al-Dibal in an apparent attempt to assert Qaṭar's sovereignty over the disputed territory. The Qatari assault was conducted without any loss of life to citizens of either state. The undefended island was only occupied by 26 foreign workers who were taken prisoner by the Qatari force; they included two British subjects, a Dutch citizen, two Thais and 21 Filipinos. An initial force of 36 Qatari troops in four helicopters was later reinforced by heavier artillery units. The incident placed immediate pressure on Saudi Arabia to mediate between the parties (see chapter on Saudi Arabia). Qatar, which shared a common Islamic puritantical heritage with Saudi Arabia (the dynasties of both states had accepted the 18th century teachings of Muhamamad Ibn ‘Abd al-Wahhab), was a traditional close ally of Saudi Arabia; Bahrain, by virtue of its new land link to the Saudi mainland, was fast becoming one of the closest states to Riyadh in the GCC. The dispute was therefore essentially a quarrel between two Saudi clients. Ths situation assured Saudi activism in resolving the conflict as well as careful considerations by both Qatar and Bahrain of Saudi attitudes and policy.

Saudi mediation led first of all to the release of the foreign workers held by Qatar on 12 May.[18] On 19 May, Saudi Arabia announced that an agreement had been reached to end the crisis. The agreement was reportedly built around the following three points:

1. Withdrawal of Qatari forces from Fasht al-Dibal and the restoration of the military situation in all the disputed island areas and along the Qatari coast and waters to what it was previously.
2. No resort to the use of force by the two countries.
3. No media provocations or campaigns by either side.[19]

A Saudi arbitration committee was to be established to bring about a final solution to the dispute. A GCC supervisory committee was to be appointed to oversee the Qatari withdrawal. Qatar, reportedly, sought an addition to the agreement that reserved it the right to reject any ruling made by the proposed arbitration committee as well as the right to refer the dispute to the World Court. Bahrain rejected these latter Qatari requests and threatened to broaden the dispute, should Qatar turn to the World Court, by renewing its traditional claims to parts of the Qatari mainland.[20] Qatar finally completed its withdrawal of some 100–150 soldiers by mid-June.[21]

There was considerable speculation concerning Qatar's motives in initiating its seizure of Fasht al-Dibal. Formally, the Qatari Government issued a statement on 30 April which explained that Bahrain's actions in hiring a company to execute land filling and construction amounted to a transformation of Fasht al-Dibal into an "industrial island." Qatar claimed that Bahrain's development plans for the island violated a principle of previous Saudi mediation efforts that prohibited either party in territorial disputes from carrying out actions that could strengthen its position in the disputed territories. Moreover, this Saudi principle had been formally adopted as a resolution of the GCC Ministerial Council during its meeting in Riyadh in 1982. Subsequent reports stated that Qatar was concerned that Bahrain intended to construct a coast-guard station on Fasht al-Dibal. (For the complete text of Qatari and Bahraini official statements, see Appendix II below).

Another theory regarding the Qatari operation was that Qatar was not all that interested in Fasht al-Dibal. Rather, it aimed at reactivating Saudi intervention over its more important Hawar Island dispute with Bahrain (see *MECS* 1977–78, p 414, and 1979–80, p 424).[22] Behind the conflict over both islands, in fact, was the unsolved problem of establishing submarine boundaries separating Qatari and Bahraini territorial waters. Bahrain's possession of Hawar brought Bahrain's territorial waters right up to the Qatari coast. Further complicating any resolution of the disputes was the Bahraini claim to Zubara, on the northern coast of the Qatari Peninsula. Zubara became the home of the al-Khalifa rulers in 1766 before their conquest of Bahrain in 1783. Successive Bahraini rulers, even in the period of British hegemony, continued to claim sovereignty over large parts of Qatar and the allegiance of the Nu'aim tribe which came to settle in Zubara.[23]

APPENDIX I: FINAL STATEMENT OF THE GULF COOPERATION COUNCIL SUMMIT IN ABU DHABI

At the invitation of HH Shaykh Zayid Ibn Sultan al-Nuhayyan, Head of State of the UAE, the seventh session of the Supreme Council of the GCC was held, with God's assistance, in Abu Dhabi, during the period 30 Safar-3 Rabi al-Awwal 1407 AH, corresponding to 2–5 November 1986 AD with the attendance of: HH Shaykh Zayid Ibn Sultan al-Nuhayyan, Head of State of the UAE; HH Shaykh Isa Ibn Salman al-Khalifa, Emir of the State of Bahrain; the Servant of the Two Holy Places, King Fahd Ibn 'Abd al-'Aziz Al Sa'ud, King of the Kingdom of Saudi Arabia; HM Sultan Qabus Ibn Sa'id, Sultan of Oman; HH Shaykh Khalifa Ibn Hamad al-Thani, Emir of the State of Qatar; [and] HH Shaykh Jabir al-Ahmad al-Jabir al-Sabah, Emir of the State of Kuwait.

The Supreme Council discussed the overall development of cooperation and coordination and new developments in the political, security, military, economic and social fields since the sixth summit meeting in Muscat is Safar 1406 AH, corresponding to November 1985 AD.

The fraternal spirit existing between the member states was crystallized and the determination was stressed to continue the march for good which started in Abu Dhabi on 21 Rajab 1401 AH, corresponding to 25 May 1981 AD, for the realization of the hopes of the Council's member countries in consolidating security and stability, achieving the citizens' ambitions in providing prosperity and progress, and affirming the cohesion of the peoples of the region.

The Council discussed the Iraqi-Iranian war, its resulting destructive effects on two Muslim peoples, and the dangers it posed for the region's security and stability, and expressed its regret over the continuation of this war and its profound concern over the intense and continuous escalation and the developments which harm the interests of two Muslim peoples. It affirmed its adherence in the two UN Security Council Resolutions Nos 528 and 588 of 1986 AD which call for an immediate cease-fire and the withdrawal of forces to the international boundaries and for seeking the settlement of the conflict between the two countries by peaceful means.

It expressed its hope that Iran would respond to this international effort. The Council expressed its esteem for brotherly Iraq's response to the efforts which are aimed at putting an end to this destructive war through peaceful means. The Council renewed its determination to continue exerting all efforts and endeavors and its agreement with all international efforts and endeavors aimed at putting an end to this war and achieving a peaceful solution to it.

The Council affirmed its adherence with Security Council Resolution 540 of 1983 and Resolution 552 of 1984 which expressed the attitude of the international community with regard to freedom of navigation in international waters and freedom of passage of merchant ships to and from GCC ports. It expressed its hope that Iran would respond to this international effort expressed by these two resolutions. The Council expressed its determination to safeguard the legitimate interests of the member states and protect freedom of navigation to and from GCC ports.

Stemming the aims embodied by the basic Constitution, the Supreme Council stressed the need to clear up all differences between sisterly Arab countries and heal divisions. It reviewed the results of efforts which have been exerted toward clearing the Arab atmosphere and it affirmed the importance of continuing these endeavors to overcome the hurdles facing the convening of an Arab summit conference which would realize the unity of the ranks in order to confront the challenges facing the Arab nation.

The Council also reviewed the development of the Palestine question and reaffirmed its support for the Palestine Liberation Organization as the sole legitimate representative of the Palestinian people, and renewed its commitment to the resolutions of the Arab summit conferences which call for the Palestinian people's right to self-determination and the establishment of an independent state.

The Council also studied the situation in Lebanon. The Council reaffirmed its continuing support for legitimacy to preserve the unity, territorial integrity, sovereignty and independence of Lebanon. The Council called on all the sides involved in the conflict in Lebanon to stop the bloodshed and reach agreement in order to guarantee the national unity of the Lebanese people.

The Council expressed its regret for the deterioration in Syrian-British relations. The Supreme Council, while reaffirming anew its condemnation of terrorism in all its forms and types, expressed its rejection of the attempts to link the concept of terrorism to Arabs and to harm the Arab nation.

The Supreme Council had approved the recommendations which were submitted to it with regard to military cooperation. The Supreme Council praised the progress of this cooperation and the achievements of the *Dir' al-Jazira* [Peninsula Shield] Force in terms of its readiness as a symbol of the joint determination of joint defense and stressed the importance of continuing to bring about self-reliance gradually in order to make available the circumstances and capability to bolster defence capability and to effect the latter's development and modernization.

The Council expressed its satisfaction with the degree of cooperation and coordination reached in the field of security. It approved the intense contacts between the security organs of the member states in order to consolidate and guarantee the security and stability of the member states of the Council.

The Supreme Council praised the steps taken so far for the implementation of the unified economic agreement according to a timetable. It stressed the importance of completing the necessary measures for implementing this program. Out of its desire to realize [equal rights and opportunities] for all citizens [of the member states] in economic and trade activities, the Supreme Council had decided the following: (1) To permit investors from among the citizens of the member states of the Council to obtain loans from banks and industrial development funds in the member states and [to permit] their equality with the national investor [the local investor in any particular member state] from the point of view of qualifications and according to the regulations which have been approved, as from the first day of the month of Rajab 1407 AH, corresponding to 1 March 1987; (2) to allow GCC citizens to engage in retail and wholesale trade in any member state and to be treated equally with the country's nationals according to the rules agreed with effect from 1 Rajab 1407 AH corresponding to 1 March 1987, with regard to retail trade, and from 25 Jumadah al-Ula 1410 AH coresponding to 1 March 1990 *vis-à-vis* wholesale trade. The Supreme Council also agreed upon the united bases giving priority to government purchases concerning national products and locally-produced goods [as heard].

In order to achieve better cooperation with other countries and international economic circles in the interests of the economic development, social progress and cultural development of the GCC states and the welfare of their citizens, the Supreme Council agreed upon the continuation of contacts with other countries and international economic bodies. It has charged the Ministerial Council with drawing up the goals and cooperation policies that are the aims of these contacts. It has charged it to follow them up and implement them.

The Supreme Council agreed upon the GCC media charter and external media regulations as a unified basis for the media policy of the member states stemming from the desire to deepen the heritage and root it in the citizen's discipline, to deal with the external media in a way which would protect the heritage of the region, its Islamic virtues and its national interests.

The Supreme Council expressed its full gratitude and admiration to HH Shaykh Zayid Ibn Sultan al-Nuhayyan, the UAE Head of State, his Government and his people for the hospitality and the warm welcome accorded to GCC leaders and members of the participating delegations for the excellent organization which played a major role in achieving the results of the Supreme Council. The Council looks forward toward its eighth meeting in the Kingdom of Saudi Arabia in Rabi al-Thani 1408 AH corresponding to December 1987 in response to an invitation from the Servant of the Two Holy Places, King Fahd Ibn al-'Aziz Al Sa'ud, King of the Saudi Arabian Kingdom.

Issued in Abu Dhabi and dated 3 Rabi al-Awwal 1407 AH corresponding to 5 November 1986. Thank you, Your Highness the Chairman.

SOURCE: SWB, 6 November 1986.

APPENDIX II: OFFICIAL STATEMENTS OF QATAR AND BAHRAIN OVER THE FASHT AL-DIBAL CONFLICT

Statement of the State of Qatar

The State of Qatar deeply regrets the disagreement between it and the State of Bahrain concerning their maritime borders. It is a disagreement which Qatar has attempted to resolve through all fraternal and amicable means in a way that secures justice and restores rights to its owner. However, all of its attempts were fruitless as a result of Bahrain's insistence on continuing to violate the sovereignty of the State of Qatar over its maritime province.

Despite this continued violation of its sovereignty, the Government of Qatar maintained the greatest patience, tolerance, and self-control for long years to preserve fraternal relations. Bahrain, however, continued to violate the sanctity of good neighborliness which the State of Qatar takes the utmost care to preserve. It has carried out actions, which include transforming Fasht al-Dibal into an industrial island, an action which violates one of the principles of the mediation carried out by the fraternal Kingdom of Saudi Arabia — which has our gratitude and appreciation — and which provides for a pledge by each party not to carry out any action which could strengthen its legal position, undermine the legal position of the other party, or benefit the current situation concerning the issue disagreed upon.

Any such action is considered not to have happened and has no legal effect. This principle was asserted by a resolution adopted by the GCC Ministerial Council during its meeting in Riyadh in 1982.

Concerning this violation, the Government of Qatar has been compelled to stop the land filling and construction which Bahrain had carried out at Fasht al-Dibal designed to restore the situation to what it was previously, which is what the principles of mediation and the rulings of the GCC Ministerial Council's resolution were directed at and to which Qatar had totally committed itself.

On this occasion, the State of Qatar wishes to assert its continued commitment to these principles and rulings and to express its full gratitude and profound appreciation to His Majesty King Fahd Ibn 'Abd al-'Aziz Al Sa'ud, King of fraternal Saudi Arabia, for his good efforts in seeking to end the dispute between the two fraternal countries. It also expresses its full gratitude and great appreciation for their majesties and highnesses the leaders of GCC countries for the sincere care and great attention they have shown toward resolving the issue in a fair and just manner and for the good of the two fraternal peoples.

SOURCE: GNA, 1 May — DR, 1 May 1986.

Statement by the Government of Bahrain

The Government of Bahrain expresses its regret at the action carried out by a Qatari military force against Bahraini territory and the detention of unarmed civilian workers. The Government of Bahrain considers this action a departure from the principles of good neighborliness on which the GCC is based. Bahrain also expresses its great appreciation to His Majesty King Fahd Ibn 'Abd al-'Aziz and the Government of fraternal Saudi Arabia for their good efforts to bring the parties together, contain the crisis, and restore things to normal.

Bahrain affirms its support, blessing, and total responsiveness to these efforts.

Bahrain also appreciates the positive stands of their majesties and highnesses the leaders of the GCC countries for their sympathy with Bahrain's stand, which is aimed at self-control, the preservation of interests of the two fraternal peoples of Bahrain and Qatar, and the avoidance of violence; and their persevering quest to preserve the rights of the member countries to complete sovereignty over their territories, and the security and peace of their sons.

SOURCE: SPA, 29 April — DR, 30 April 1986.

NOTES

For the place and frequency of publications cited here, and for the full name of the publication, news agency, radio station or monitoring service where an abbreviation is used, please see "List of Sources." Only in the case of more than one publication bearing the same name is the place of publication noted here.

1. *US News and World Report*, 31 August 1987.
2. Reuters in *JP*, 5 August 1986.
3. *Al-Jazira*, 1 January 1986.
4. *The Guardian*, 13 January 1986.
5. *ME*, September 1986, p 8.
6. SWB, 7 March 1986.
7. SPA, 3 March — SWB, 5 March 1986.
8. Ibid.
9. SPA, 30 June — DR, 1 July 1986; *al-Siyasa*, 22 June — JPRS, 30 July 1986.
10. SPA, 27 August — DR, 25 August 1986.
11. Ibid.
12. GNA, 5 October — SWB, 7 October 1986.
13. *Al-Siyasa*, 23 November 1986.
14. GNA, 4 November — DR, 5 November 1986.
15. *IHT*, 16 June 1987.
16. *MM*, 24 November 1986.
17. *Jane's Defence Weekly*, 1 November 1986.
18. *FT*, 13 May 1986.
19. *Al-Khalij*, 3 June — DR, 4 June 1986.
20. Ibid.
21. *Al-Khalij*, 15 June — SWB, 17 June 1986.
22. *Al-Watan*, 15 May — DR, 19 May 1986.
23. For a full account of the historical and international legal background to these disputes, see Husain M. al-Baharna, *The Legal Status of the Arabian Gulf States: A Study of their Treaty Relations and their International Problems* (Manchester: University of Manchester Press, 1968.)

Bahrain

DORE GOLD

Simultaneous military and economic pressures on Bahrain, which had made themselves felt in recent years, only seemed to be getting worse in 1986. Iranian propaganda continued to pick on Bahrain — in addition to Kuwait — among the GCC states. But it was not Iran that actually seized Bahraini territory in 1986, it was Bahrain's old GCC rival, Qatar. Since the mid-1970s, Bahrain had aspired to convert itself into the newly rich Gulf's banking center, especially with the decline of Lebanon. With the financial slump in the Gulf during the year, the number of foreign banks based in Bahrain continued to decline for yet another year. The Kingdom of Saudi Arabia stood behind Bahrain in its difficulties. The Saudis served as persuasive intermediaries in the brief conflict between Bahrain and Qatar. Saudi budgetary support cushioned the effects of the regional recession on the Bahraini economy. The Saudi air umbrella continued to cover Bahraini airspace as well. In 1986 as the causeway linking the two countries was completed, these ties acquired a physical dimension as well.

DOMESTIC AFFAIRS

TEMPORARY CABINET

In December 1985, Bahrain's Prime Minister, Shaykh Khalifa Ibn Salman al-Khalifa suffered a heart attack and was rushed to Houston, Texas, for surgery. Subsequently he went to convalesce in London, where he was visited by his brother, Bahrain's ruler, Shaykh 'Isa Ibn Salman al-Khalifa. In Shaykh Khalifa's absence, the Bahraini Cabinet was headed by Shaykh Hamad Ibn 'Isa al-Khalifa, the heir apparent and Commander in Chief of the Bahrain Defense Force. Shaykh Khalifa returned to Bahrain on 22 April and promptly resumed his former duties, thus replacing the younger Shaykh Hamad at the head of the Government before the conflict between Bahrain and Qatar erupted in late April (for details see the Gulf States - "Regional Developments", above). Shaykh Hamad, according to one report, demanded reprisal operations against Qatar, but was overruled by the Cabinet.[1] Such an activist course contrasted with the quiet diplomacy Bahrain eventually followed in the crisis that led, through Saudi mediation, to a denial of Qatari ambitions. Whether Shaykh Hamad's actions during the conflict or his performance in his uncle's absence threatened or improved his chances of eventually becoming Bahrain's ruler could not be ascertained.

SUBVERSIVE ACTIVITIES AND REGIME RESPONSES

Reports from Bahraini opposition sources as well as from Tehran's overseas Arabic radio service highlighted the large number of arrests and deportations carried out by the Bahraini authorities during 1986. Among the more prominent detainees were

Shaykh Muhammad 'Ali al-'Askari, of the Bahraini *'ulama*, Shaykh Hasan Qaysi, a local activist cleric, and Dr Hashim Sayyid Isma'il al-'Alawi. The last was arrested in connection with a controversial documentary report he prepared on the death in prison of Razi Mehdi Ibrahim, one of the large number of Bahrainis imprisoned in the wake of the December 1981 attempted overthrow of the Government (see *MECS* 1981–82, pp 490–97). Dr al-'Alawi, like Razi Mehdi Ibrahim, reportedly died in detention.

As in the past, reports on opposition activities in Bahrain were hard to come by in the local and even international Press as the Bahraini authorities strove to prevent embarrassing news of subversive operations from being published. For example, in May, many of the international news services in Manama received anonymous calls claiming attempted attacks in Bahrain, but did not include any reference to them in their international reports. When the local Reuters representative failed to hold back such stories, he was told by the authorities that he would have to leave the country.[2] (For previous Bahraini crackdowns on the international and local Press, see *MECS* 1983–84, p 399).

FOREIGN AFFAIRS

REGIONAL POLITICS

(For a detailed review of the Bahraini conflict with Qatar, see "Regional Developments" above.)

Bahrain's special ties with Saudi Arabia were given an added physical dimension in 1986 with the opening of the 24-km Bahrain-Saudi causeway on 26 November. The inaugural ceremonies were held in Bahrain and attended by both Shaykh 'Isa Ibn Salman al-Khalifa and King Fahd Ibn 'Abd al-'Aziz. The implications of the causeway's completion were not yet clear in 1986. Bahraini merchants were concerned about the future of their import trade, fearing competition from Saudi counterparts who had the benefit of the Kingdom's import subsidy policies as well as lower unit costs resulting from the relatively large scale of the Saudi economy. These Bahrainis lobbied for high tariffs between the two countries. Other sectors of the Bahraini business community looked forward to the increasing use of Bahrain as a more comfortable and liberal base of operations for Western commercial interests operating in Saudi Arabia. Both Bahrainis and Saudis were concerned about the links that might be formed between subversive organizations in the two countries, especially among their Shi'i communities. How these various and sometimes even opposing interests would affect Bahrain's immigration and tariff controls along the causeway, and correspondingly the degree of political-economic integration between the two countries, will only become apparent with time.[3]

As in previous years, Bahrain continued to be a target of Iran's Arabic radio service. Nonetheless, diplomatic contacts were maintained between Manama and Tehran. On 19 February, for example, the Director-General for Political Affairs at the Iranian Foreign Ministry, Muhammad Husayn Lavasani, visited Bahrain and met with Acting Prime Minister Shaykh Hamad Ibn 'Isa. Lavasani carried a message for Bahrain's ruler, Shaykh 'Isa Ibn Salman, from Iranian President 'Ali Khamene'i.[4] Iraq's First Deputy Prime Minister, Taha Yasin Ramadan, met with Shaykh 'Isa in Manama on 23 July and brought a message from Iraqi President Saddam Husayn.[5] A similar message was brought by Iraqi Interior Minister Sa'dun Shakir in late October.[6] Close ties were maintained throughout the year with all the GCC states with the exception, of course, of Qatar.

Outside of the Gulf, Bahrain continued to value its relations with Jordan and even Egypt — despite the lack of formal diplomatic ties with the latter. King Husayn during his traditional yearly tour of the Gulf states arrived in Manama for a one-day visit on 14 October. The King headed a large delegation that included the Jordanian Prime Minister, Zayd al-Rifa'i, and the Commander in Chief of the Jordanian Armed Forces, Maj Gen Samir Farraj.[7] Bahrain, according to Egyptian diplomatic sources, was expected shortly to be the first of the GCC states to renew diplomatic ties with Egypt — outside of Oman that never cut them.[8] Egypt's Information Minister, Sawfat al-Sharif, heading an Egyptian delegation, was hosted in Manama on 25–30 October 1986. Al-Sharif brought Shaykh 'Isa a written message from Egyptian President Husni Mubarak.[9]

INTERNATIONAL POLITICS

The high point in US-Bahraini relations in 1986 was the three-day visit of a large American delegation to Manama led by US Vice President George Bush, which began on 7 April. The Vice President was accompanied not only by members of his personal staff but also by Deputy Assistant Secretary of State for Near Eastern and South Asian Affairs Marion Greekmove and Deputy Assistant Secretary of Defense Robert Pelletrau as well as a number of senior civil and military officials.[10] A Bahraini cabinet official subsequently explained that talks between American and Bahraini officials focused on ways of ending the Iraqi-Iranian war, the Palestinian issue, and the situation in the world oil market.[11] Foreign Minister Shaykh Muhammad Ibn Mubarak al-Khalifa, in a separate statement after the talks, noted that Bahrain and the US were satisfied over the development of their bilateral relationship. While hoping that the countries of the world would find a way to bring an end to the attacks on tankers in the Gulf, Shaykh Muhammad expressed his satisfaction with the overall US security policy: "We are endeavoring with the US and various countries to keep the Gulf a region of peace. There is conformity of opinion on this point."[12] A mildly critical note was sounded in connection with US policy on the Arab-Israel conflict:

> The Bahraini Minister demanded that the US take an acceptable positive stand on the Middle East cause and said: 'The US should take the view of the two sides into consideration.'[13]

While the Bahraini Press observed a similarly restrained critical style during the Bush visit, there were strong attacks on US policy particularly in *Akhbar al-Khalij*, after the April American air attacks on Libya (see chapter on the US and the Middle East). It was asserted that the US was pulling ahead of Israel as the primary source of aggression "against the Arab nation."[14] In July, the Bahraini newspaper rejected what it viewed as American pressure on the Arab world to enter into negotiations with Israel since it could not anticipate any future Israeli territorial concessions.[15] In November, revelations about US arms sales to Iran proved, according to the newspaper, that "US neutrality in the war and US endeavors to end it are mere lies..."[16]

Among other important official exchanges between the US and Bahrain was the visit of Gen George Crist, the Commander in Chief of the US Central Command (CENTCOM) on 5 July.[17] In mid-November, Shaykh Khalifa, heir apparent and Commander in Chief of the Bahrain Defense Forces, made an official visit to Washington where he met Secretary of Defense Caspar Weinberger, top officials in the Department of Defense, and the Joint Chiefs of Staff.[18]

Bahrain was expected in 1985 to become the next GCC state to establish diplomatic relations with the USSR; this development was still expected in 1986.[19] However, Moscow made no new diplomatic advances toward Manama. Shaykh 'Isa made it clear that Bahrain had not forgotten about the Afghan issue:

> We are against foreign intervention in countries' internal affairs and also against any invasion of other peoples' territories. Whatever the justification, we still urge that the Muslim Afghan people be given the opportunity for self-determination without any pressure or intervention. The GCC states side with the Afghan people and provide them with every possible support and assistance.[20]

Though Shaykh 'Isa did not link the Soviet presence in Afghanistan to the state of Bahraini-Soviet relations, as Saudi Arabia had done in the past, it could be predicted that, given Bahrain's increasingly close relations with Riyadh, any change in Bahraini policy toward the USSR would have to be in line with Saudi policy.

NOTES

For the place and frequency of publications cited here, and for the full name of the publication, news agency, radio station or monitoring service where an abbreviation is used, please see "List of Sources." Only in the case of more than one publication bearing the same name is the place of publication noted here.

1. *MM*, 1 September 1986.
2. *Al-Anba*, 22 July 1986.
3. *Al-Bayan*, 13 October 1986; "London Observer Service" in *JP*, 9 October 1986; *The Guardian*, 17 November 1986; *MM*, 24 November 1986; SPA, 25 November — DR, 26 November 1986; *Time*, 8 December 1986.
4. GNA, 19 February — DR, 19 February 1986.
5. GNA, 23 July — DR, 24 July 1986.
6. GNA, 30 October — DR, 31 October 1986.
7. GNA, 14 October — DR, 15 October 1986.
8. *Al-'Alim*, 8 November 1986.
9. GNA, 26 October — DR, 27 October 1986.
10. R. Manama, 7 April — DR, 8 April 1986.
11. GNA, 13 April — DR, 14 April 1986.
12. QNA, 8 April — DR, 9 April 1986.
13. Ibid.
14. GNA, 17 April — DR, 17 April 1986.
15. *Akhbar al-Khalij*, 27 July — DR, 29 July 1986.
16. GNA, 17 November — DR, 17 November 1986.
17. GNA, 5 July — DR, 8 July 1956.
18. *Al-Siyasa*, 19 November 1986.
19. *Al-Ra'y al-'Amm*, 26 June 1986.
20. *'Ukaz*, 1 November — DR, 6 November 1986.

Kuwait

DORE GOLD

Iran's successful Faw offensive in early 1986 brought the ground forces of the Islamic Republic of Iran practically up to the Iraqi-Kuwaiti border and nudged Kuwait that much closer into becoming the next country to be dragged into a widening Iraqi-Iranian war. That trend was strengthened by continuing Iranian accusations that Kuwait was in fact allowing Iraqi forces to use Kuwaiti territory: first in connection with the Faw offensive, and later in the year in connection with the Iraqi Air Force's successful long-range strikes at Iran's remote Sirri and Larak oil export terminals in the Lower Gulf.

As external pressures increased against Kuwait, internal pressures in no way diminished. Acts of sabotage continued, as in the previous year; in 1986, however, they involved Kuwait's own oil production and export facilities. With oil revenues further declining, the al-Sabah family did not feel it had a partner for handling these mounting problems in the Kuwaiti National Assembly. In an atmosphere of near national emergency, the recently elected Assembly was suspended for the second time in Kuwait's brief history as parlimanentary challenges against the Government became unbearable.

DOMESTIC AFFAIRS

SUBVERSIVE ACTIVITIES

In 1986, as in 1985, Kuwait was subjected to attempts at subversion and sabotage conducted largely by members of the foreign community — particularly by Iranian, Iraqi, and Lebanese nationals. The common denominator in each of these groups was a Shi'i religious affiliation and some connection with Iranian revolutionary circles.

There were several reports during the year of attempted acts of terror and subversion, many of which were intercepted by the Kuwaiti authorities in the planning stage. In March, a Lebanese citizen was convicted of conspiring to bomb a Kuwaiti refinery and electricity station.[1] An Iranian report described the discovery by the Kuwaiti authorities in February of a plot to stage a *coup d'état* involving Kuwaiti military personnel. The reported leader of the coup, Col 'Abd al-Rahim Fakhru, was arrested along with 20 officers from an armored unit and four pilots.[2] Another report stated that the Kuwait State Security Court had sentenced Col Fakhru to 10 years' imprisonment for openly calling for the overthrow of the Kuwaiti Government.[3]

THE ATTACK ON THE AL-AHMADI OIL TERMINAL

The most serious incidents of the year were the series of explosions set off by saboteurs at the al-Ahmadi oil terminal, Kuwait's principal oil export outlet, on 17 June. According to the Kuwaiti Minister of Oil and Industry, Shaykh 'Ali al-Khalifa, there were four separate explosions: outside of the northern collection center, along one of the pipelines connecting the northern center to the port outlet, and two explosions in the vicinity of the southern collection center. The first two were reportedly caused by 350-kg explosive devices, while the latter two appeared to have been caused by 12 to 15-kg devices. Secondary fires caused by the explosions in some cases lasted for two days. Shaykh 'Ali played down the extent of the damage. He stated that the explosion would in no way affect the country's oil production policies.[4]

An anonymous caller to a Western news agency in Amman claimed that an organization calling itself the "United Arab Revolution" (*al-Thawra al-'Arabiyya al-Muwahhada*) took credit for the attack. The organization, the caller said, was committed to Arab unity and to boycotting the US as well as its Arab allies.[5] According to the Abu Dhabi daily, *al-Ittihad*, the Kuwaiti authorities arrested the members of the unit that conducted the operation while they were waiting to board an aircraft at Kuwait's international airport. Most of the members of the unit were reported to be of Lebanese nationality.[6] A larger security sweep at the same time led to the arrest of 27 individuals — of various nationalities — in connection with the explosions.[7]

SUSPECTED PERPETRATORS OF 1985 TERRORIST ATTACKS APPREHENDED

The authorities apprehended suspects involved in three terrorist attacks of the previous year: the shooting of the editor-in-chief of the Kuwaiti daily *al-Siyasa*, Ahmad al-Jarallah; the bombing of two seaside cafes; and, above all, the attempted assassination of the ruler of Kuwait, Shaykh Jabir al-Ahmad al-Sabah (for details see *MECS* 1984–85, p 404–5). The Ministry of the Interior announced the arrests in July. Parliamentary sources reported that among those detained were five members of the pro-Shi'i Iraqi *al-Da'wa* organization and two Palestinians connected with Abu Nidal's terrorist network.[8] In the fall, the State Security Court passed sentences on the suspects. On 29 November one Iraqi national was sentenced to death for his role in the attack on Shaykh Jabir, while another was sentenced *in absentia* to life imprisonment. Three other suspects were found not guilty.[9] In early December, three of five Jordanian nationals were convicted for their involvement in both the shooting of *al-Siyasa*'s editor-in-chief and the bombing of the cafés. One defendant was sentenced to 20 years' imprisonment while two others were sentenced *in absentia* to life and ten years' imprisonment, respectively.[10]

DISSOLUTION OF THE KUWAITI NATIONAL ASSEMBLY AND THE IMPOSITION OF PRESS CENSORSHIP

In February 1985, Kuwait held elections for the sixth session of its National Assembly (*majlis al-umma*). (For a detailed account of the election returns and a breakdown by political orientation of the new Assembly, see *MECS* 1984–85, pp 398–400.) Perhaps the ruling al-Sabah family believed that by permitting a limited reintroduction of the Arab nationalist opposition — whose activities had led in 1976 to the dissolution of the Assembly for four years — it might acquire a hidden ally to counter the impact of the fundamentalist movements in Kuwait. But rather than cancel one another out in the new Assembly, the Arab nationalist and Islamic representatives made common cause against the Government and even sought to oust members of the Cabinet who were the hand-picked choice of the ruling family. In 1986, the Islamic Deputies focused their angry attention on the Minister of Education, Dr Hasan 'Ali al-Ibrahim who wanted to introduce liberal reforms in the universities. He offered his resignation in May but was persuaded by Shaykh Jabir to stay on.[11] As the Assembly's investigatory zeal turned on the Minister of Oil and Industry, Shaykh 'Ali al-Khalifa, as well as on the Minister of Finance, Jasim Khurafi, in late June 1986, the entire Cabinet preferred to resign.[12]

Under these conditions, and with increasing threats of subversion, as was demonstrated in the al-Ahmadi bombings in June, it was hardly surprising that Shaykh Jabir decided to dissolve the recently elected National Assembly and impose new restrictive laws. In his decree of 3 July, he gave his reasons as follows:

> ...The country has faced many ordeals and harsh conditions, the likes of which it has never experienced at the same time before. Thus its security has been exposed to fierce external plots, which threatened souls and almost destroyed the resources of this nation and the source of its livelihood. The flames of the war raging between its two Muslim neighbors have almost reached its borders. And it has faced a serious economic crisis. And instead of efforts coming together, and all parties cooperating in order to contain these crises, the word was split, opinion was divided, and blocs and parties emerged which have led to the shattering of national unity and the interruption of work to the point where the Council of Ministers has been unable to continue its task.

Shaykh Jabir did not specify for how long the Assembly would be suspended.

In addition to halting Kuwait's parliamentary life, Shaykh Jabir decreed new laws that tightened the Government's control of the Press. The Cabinet accordingly reserved for itself the right to suspend or cancel the license of any newspaper "if what it is publishing contradicts the national interest" (Article 35, Law No 3).[13] Publications obtaining "aid, assistance or benefit in any form, and for any reason" from any other state or party without permission from the Ministry of Information would be subject to a similar fate.[14] A decree from the Information Ministry subjected all periodicals in Kuwait to censorship.[15] Under these tight rules, it was not surprising that the Kuwaiti newspapers did not criticize these curtailments of freedom of the Press and parliamentary democracy. *Al-Ra'y al-'Amm* stated that the measures would actually "boost our democratic experience; it noted that "the aim is that Kuwait [will] remain an ideal of freedom of opinion and dialogue...." *Al-Siyasa* acknowledged that the Ruler's decision was difficult, but would ultimately serve the national interest.[16]

Opposition groups were critical of the Ruler's decrees and hoped that they were only temporary. The leading Kuwait Arab nationalist opposition figure, Dr Ahmad al-Khatib, in an interview in an Egyptian newspaper, claimed that the clashes that developed in 1985-86 between the Cabinet and the Assembly were engineered by certain elements — whom he did not identify by name — to serve as a justification for its eventual dissolution.[17] He argued that, instead of imposing anti-parliamentary measures the Kuwaiti ruling family could have selected a Government that was more agreeable to the Assembly. Al-Khatib said he believed there were two essential reasons why some elements were anxious to do away with the Assembly:

(a) As the Assembly investigated the Government's handling of the Suq al-Manakh stock market crisis of 1981, leading figures in the Kuwaiti Establishment risked being connected with corrupt practices — furthermore, the Assembly refused to approve the expenditure of state funds to compensate those who had lost money in the affair.

(b) Iranian military successes against Iraq since early 1986 required greater coordination between Kuwait and the GCC (the Kuwaiti nationalist and Islamic opposition forces in the Assembly both opposed too close a relationship with the GCC, especially in the security field).

From his perspective, there were good reasons why certain groups in Kuwait were not at all disturbed by the Assembly's dismissal.

THE APPOINTMENT OF A NEW KUWAITI CABINET

With the formal resignation of the Kuwaiti Cabinet on 3 July, Shaykh Jabir reappointed Shaykh Sa'd al-'Abdallah al-Sabah as Prime Minister. The latter proposed a new Cabinet that was accepted by Shaykh Jabir on 12 July:[18]

Prime Minister	Shaykh Sa'd al-'Abdallah al-Sabah
Deputy Prime Minister and Minister of Foreign Affairs	Shaykh Sabah al-Ahmad al-Jabir
Minister of Education	Anwar 'Abdallah al-Nuri
Minister of Social Affairs and Labor	Jabir Mubarak al-Hamad
Minister of Finance	Jasim Muhammad al-Khurafi
Minister of Religious Trusts and Islamic Affairs	Khalid Ahmad al-Jasir
Minister of Communications	Khalid Salim al-Jumay'an
Minister of State for Cabinet Affairs	Rashid 'Abd al-'Aziz al-Rashid
Minister of Defense	Shaykh Salim al-Sabah
Minister of State for Foreign Affairs	Sa'ud Muhammad al-Usaymi
Minister of Justice and Legal Affairs	Dari 'Abdallah al-'Uthman
Minister of Public Works	'Abd al-Rahman Ibrahim al-Huti
Minister of State for Minicipal Affairs	'Abd al-Rahman Khalid al-Ghunaym
Minister of Public Health	'Abd al-Rahman 'Abdallah al-Awdi
Minister of Oil	Shaykh 'Ali al-Khalifa al-Atubi al-Sabah
Minister of State for Services Affairs	'Isa Muhammad al-Masidi
Minister of Trade and Industry	Faysal 'Abd al-Razzaq al-Khalid
Minister of Planning	Muhammad Sulayman Sayyid 'Ali
Minister of Electricity and Water	Muhammad 'Abd al-Muhsin al-Rifa'i
Minister of State for Housing Affairs	Nasir 'Abdallah al-Rudan
Minister of Information	Shaykh Nasir Muhammad al-Ahmad
Minister of Interior	Shaykh Nawwaf al-Ahmad al-Jabir al-Sabah

Significantly, both the Minister of Oil and the Minister of Finance were retained in the new Cabinet, despite the criticism directed at them in the National Assembly before its dissolution. The former Minister of Education, Dr Hasan 'Ali al-Ibrahim, who was disliked by traditional Islamic elements, was replaced. The new Cabinet was somewhat larger than its predecessor. Several Ministers' dual portfolios were reduced to a single portfolio. Thus, Shaykh 'Ali was now only Minister of Oil and not Minister of Oil and Industry as before; and a new portfolio — Trade and Industry — was created. Similarly, a separate Housing Ministry was carved out from the former Ministry of Public Works and Housing. The former Cabinet included a total of 16 Ministers; the new Cabinet contained 21.

KUWAITI BUDGET CUTBACKS

Kuwait continued to run a deficit budget, and the expected fall in the State's oil revenues led to a virtual doubling of the anticipated deficit for 1986–87 as against 1985–86. Oil revenues were projected to fall in one year by 40.9 per cent from 2,801.9m Kuwaiti dinars (KD) in 1985–86 to KD1,656m in 1986–87. The latter figure was based on an anticipated further lowering of prices for oil in 1986. The Government succeeded in cutting its 1986–87 budget by only 14 per cent despite the fact that the expected drop in oil revenues, when taken together with Kuwait's other sources of income, was projected to lead to a total drop in state revenues of 38.6 per cent. The Government was expected to have to dip into its reserves to cover the deficit.[19] At the same time, it was expected that many services which had previously been offered free-of-charge by the Government would now require some payment.

FOREIGN AFFAIRS

REGIONAL POLITICS

Iran's offensive on Iraq's Faw peninsula in early 1986 (see chapter on the Iraqi-Iranian war) led to the worsening of an already bad relationship between Iran and Kuwait. Not only were Iranian ground forces that much closer to the Kuwaiti border, but the Faw battle also brought new Iranian charges in February (voiced by Deputy Foreign Minister 'Ali Muhammad Besharati) that Kuwait had let Iraqi forces use its territory and airspace. The Kuwaiti island of Bubiyan directly faced Iranian supply lines and was located only 15 miles from the front. These charges were strongly denied by Kuwaiti officials. Two Iranian helicopters flying over Kuwaiti territorial waters on 22 February harassed a boat belonging to the Kuwaiti Navy. The incident was followed by the summoning of the Iranian Chargé d'Affaires in Kuwait to the Foreign Ministry to receive Kuwait's condemnation and a warning regarding the "negative repercussions" of such incidents on relations between the two countries.[20]

There were further sources of tension between the two countries during the year. Kuwait's almost monthly expulsions of Iranian Muslim workers were reported in detail on Iranian radio usually with the following introduction: "The Kuwaiti Government, in continuation of its hostile actions against the Islamic Republic of Iran...."[21] A Kuwaiti registered vessel, the *Ibn al-Bitar*, confiscated by Iran in November 1985, remained in Iranian hands in 1986; Kuwait complained about the seizure to the UN Secretary-General on 29 April.[22] In September, Kuwaiti fishing boats manned by an Egyptian crew came under fire from the Iranian Navy; three Egyptians were killed in the attack. Many other Egyptian fishing crews were taken into custody by the Iranians.[23] On 16 September, an Iranian gunboat fired two missiles at the Kuwaiti oil tanker *Fintas*, 35 miles east of Kuwait. Again the Iranian Chargé d'Affaires was summoned to the Kuwaiti Foreign Ministry for "clarifications."[24] In October, Kuwaiti forces fired two missiles at a hostile aircraft that had violated its airspace.[25] The downed aircraft was believed to be Iranian. Later in the year, Iran renewed its accusations that Kuwait had allowed Iraq to use Kuwaiti territory and airspace for military purposes; the Iranian claim was made in connection with the Iraqi Air Force's successful long-distance bombing raid on the remote Iranian oil terminal at Larak (see chapter on the Iraqi-Iranian war).[26]

Kuwait continued to be a strong financial supporter of Iraq as well as a port of entry for goods destined for Iraq. Asked if war material got to Iraq through Kuwait, Deputy Prime Minister and Foreign Minister Sabah al-Ahmad al-Sabah evasively replied in a German periodical: "You cannot demand that I play the policeman and look into every container in our ports destined for Iraq."[27] Iraqi First Deputy Prime Minister Taha Yasin Ramadan and Interior Minister Sa'dun Shakir traveled to Kuwait for talks on 23 July and conveyed a message from President Saddam Husayn.[28]

Deputy Prime Minister and Foreign Minister Tariq 'Aziz made a surprise visit to Kuwait on 17 November and delivered a message from the Iraqi President to Shaykh Jabir.[29] Later in the year, as Iran criticized Kuwait for assisting Iraq in the Larak raid, the Iraqi Air Force Commander responded by stating that aggression against the Gulf states would be regarded by Baghdad as aggression against Iraq itself.[30] Coordination with Baghdad was thus important for Kuwait, whose leaders probably viewed the Iraqi defense lines as their own forward positions. Nonetheless, it seemed doubtful even under conditions of mutual threat, that the Kuwaitis could so easily forget Iraqi territorial aspirations *vis-à-vis* Kuwait as manifested in the crises of 1961 and 1973. For this reason it is unlikely that Kuwait allowed Iraqi troops to use strategic positions on its island territories across from the Faw battle, Iranian accusations notwithstanding.

Repeated Iranian military provocations made Kuwait's relationship with the GCC and, above all, Saudi Arabia, a vital element in its national security. Shaykh Jabir made at least two visits to the Saudi Kingdom in 1986, at which times he held bilateral talks with King Fahd Ibn 'Abd al-'Aziz. The first meeting took place on 19 March, and the second on 29 May, just as Shaykh Jabir completed a minor pilgrimage to the Holy Cities.[31] Saudi Arabia was not the only Arab state expressing concern for Kuwait. Jordan continued to maintain its special traditional ties with Kuwait; both states served as supply corriders to Iraq and perhaps were the most clearly identified supporters of Baghdad in the Arab world. Kuwaiti financial assistance and investment were important elements in the strength of the Jordanian economy. Although talk of a Jordanian rapid deployment force had subsided by 1986, the improvement of the Iranian military position in southern Iraq early in the year prompted King Husayn to make an unambiguous statement about what Jordan would do if Kuwait came under Iranian attack:

> We are responsible for Kuwait's security and I will not hesitate to deploy Jordanian forces to defend the Gulf states if I am asked to do so.[32]

On 18–19 October, bilateral talks were held between a delegation of Jordanians, led by Prime Minister Zayd al-Rifa'i, and their Kuwaiti counterparts. The discussions focused on issues of trade and banking. An economic, trade, and technical cooperation agreement was signed; it included an exemption of tariffs and other import fees on the commodities of both countries as well as capital investment incentives.[33] Kuwait was clearly willing to establish special trading arrangements with Arab states beyond the GCC. King Husayn paid a short visit to Kuwait on 21 December and held talks with Shaykh Jabir.[34]

Kuwait exhibited an unusually warm attitude toward Egypt — evident in both official and press statements — despite the fact that both countries continued not to have resident Ambassadors and to be represented only by "interest sections." President Mubarak spoke to Shaykh Jabir by telephone immediately after the June bomb attacks on Kuwait's al-Ahmadi oil facilities (see "Subversive Activities" above).

Mubarak reportedly offered Kuwait anything it might ask for to strengthen its security and stability.[35] The Kuwaiti Press showed considerable understanding of Mubarak's predicament regarding his obligations to Israel and the US. He was complimented for representing Arab interests and was not criticized for meeting Israeli Prime Minister Shimon Peres in late summer (see chapters on Egypt and Israel). The Kuwaiti Press generally called for the return of Egypt to the Arab fold.[36] On the Arab-Israeli conflict, Kuwait continued to take a firm position against any improvement of Israel's diplomatic standing; it was the only Arab state to recall its Ambassador to Spain for consultations in reaction to Madrid's decision to establish diplomatic relations with Israel. But, unlike the rejectionist states, Kuwait exercised considerable rhetorical restraint toward those Arab leaders interested in exploring political solutions to the conflict. This was not only the case toward Egypt, but also toward Morocco. Reacting to the news of the Peres visit to Morocco (see chapter on Israel and essay on the Middle East peace process), the Kuwaiti Cabinet voiced somewhat moderate criticism of the meeting, focusing on the principle that any treatment of the Palestinian issue must be handled in a collective Arab framework.[37] The attitude expressed in the Kuwaiti Press toward the meeting was more critical, although the establishment paper, *al-Siyasa*, praised the Moroccan King's initiative, noting that his previous controversial approach toward a political solution of the Arab-Israel conflict was proving historically correct.[38]

INTERNATIONAL POLITICS

Kuwaiti relations with the US underwent complex changes during 1986, but were ultimately undermined by the end of the year with the revelations of US-approved arms shipments to Iran. Earlier in the year, the US extended its previous offer of support for Kuwait's security in case of external attack, on condition that Kuwait requested assistance. This was at least one element in the talks between Richard Murphy, Assistant Secretary of State for Near East and South Asian Affairs, and Shaykh Sabah al-Ahmad al-Jabir, Kuwait's Deputy Prime Minister and Foreign Minister, on 5 April during Murphy's tour of the Gulf states.[39] Earlier in the year, the US naval force in the Gulf, MIDEASTFOR, began to escort US merchant shipping in a move against Iranian provocations; the US naval presence near Kuwait had increased during the first few months of 1986. The Kuwaiti Press was strongly critical of US military assistance to Kuwait, which it saw as interference in Gulf affairs; the rejection of US military involvement was frequently connected with US policy toward Libya — which the Kuwaiti Press condemned — or with Israeli operations against the PLO — which were perceived to have American backing.[40] Yet despite these public complaints, important security contacts were maintained during the year. Gen George B. Crist, Commander in Chief of the US CENTCOM, who had planning and operational responsibility for US military forces in Southwest Asia as a whole, visited Kuwait on 6 July and met with Shaykh Jabir.[41] One Egyptian report stated that the two decided on US assistance in establishing and training a Kuwaiti force to guard oil facilities.[42]

By the year's end, however, US-Kuwaiti relations at first seemed badly damaged by the revelations of US-approved arms sales to Iran. Shaykh Sabah al-Ahmad stated his personal attitude as follows:

> What the Americans have done is very painful and bitter for us. Everybody

> thinks only of his own interests and nothing else. Do not forget Afghanistan. The Americans want to establish new relations with Iran to set up some sort of a balance between Iran and the US on the one hand, and Afghanistan and the Soviet Union on the other. The Americans want to get closer to Afghanistan.[43]

Shaykh Sabah later denied a report attributed to Secretary of State George Shultz that US National Security Adviser Vice ADM John M. Poindexter had pressed Kuwait during 1986 to release Shi'i terrorists as part of the arms-for-hostages deal.[44]

The Kuwaiti Cabinet's official complaint focused on the need for the US to uphold its declared policy of seeking an end to the Iraqi-Iranian war: "The latest American stand did not accord with its declared policy."[45] The Kuwaiti Press was highly critical of the entire affair. *Al-Qabas* claimed that the US was mistaken in believing in the moderating influence of US arms: "...in our view such military supplies will only prolong the war...."[46] The paper was also disturbed by the apparent convergence of US and Israeli interests in keeping Iraq preoccupied with the war, so as to upset the Arab-Israeli balance and thus allow them to put forward peace plans in Israel's favor. Other newspapers focused on the irony that the US, which had so recently defended the war against terrorism, was now dealing with terrorists. American credibility on the whole was undermined by the incident.

Yet only a few weeks after the Iran-Contra story first became known, Kuwait seemed prepared to explore with the US unprecedented levels of strategic cooperation. A Kuwaiti probe of US policy in the Gulf came through a request by the state-owned Kuwait Oil Tanker Company (KOTC) to the US Coast Guard, on 10 December, for information regarding procedures for the reflagging of foreign-flag ships to US-flag vessels. On 23 December, the KOTC informed the US embassy of its interest in reflagging.[47] A careful, albeit low-level, process was thus set under way that would greatly restore the credibility the US appeared to have lost with its failed secret *rapprochement* toward Iran.

Kuwait-USSR relations improved during the year. On 11 January, the Soviet Deputy Defense Minister, Gen Vladmir Govorov, arrived in Kuwait at the head of a senior military delegation for a six-day visit. Govorov used his visit to express Soviet disapproval of any expansion of the US military presence in the Gulf in connection with the Iraqi-Iranian war: "We do not approve the US steps of sending their troops to the Gulf region because that is not their right."[48] Oil and Industry Minister Shaykh 'Ali al-Khalifa al-Sabah was in Moscow in February to discuss possible oil barter arrangements as well as the establishment of joint economic ventures. These discussions continued in July when Soviet Central Committee member and head of the Government Committee for Foreign Economic Relations, Konstantin Katushev, visited Kuwait. Political-military issues appeared to have been raised during the visit of Kuwaiti Foreign Under Secretary Sulayman Majid al-Shahin to Moscow in mid-September. Arriving soon after the Iranian attack on the Kuwaiti tanker, *Fintas*, the Kuwaitis expressed their concern that the Gulf war would soon spread. They apparently asked Moscow to pressure both Iraq and Iran to stop their respective attacks on commercial shipping, especially oil tankers.[49] By late November, Kuwait actually sought Soviet protection of Kuwaiti ships from the intensifying attacks of Iran.[50] Whether by design or accident, Kuwait placed itself by the end of 1986 at the center of a superpower rivalry for being its principal protector.

NOTES

For the place and frequency of publications cited here, and for the full name of the publication, news agency, radio station or monitoring service where an abbreviation is used, please see "List of Sources." Only in the case of more than one publication bearing the same name is the place of publication noted here.

1. *Al-Qabas*, 17 March 1986.
2. R. Tehran, 10 March — SWB, 12 March 1986.
3. *Al-Watan al-'Arabi*, 18 April 1986.
4. R. Kuwait, 18 June 1986.
5. R. Monte Carlo, Paris, 25 June — DR, 26 June 1986.
6. Reported in *Ma'ariv*, 19 June 1986.
7. *JP*, 20 June 1986.
8. *The Times*, 5 July; *FT*, 14 July; *IHT*, 5-6 July 1986.
9. SWB, 1 December 1986.
10. SWB, 9 December 1986.
11. *The Economist*, 12 July; *FT*, 3 July 1986.
12. R. Kuwait, 3 July — SWB, 5 July 1986.
13. R. Kuwait, 3 July — DR, 7 July 1986.
14. Ibid.
15. KUNA, 3 July — DR, 7 July 1986.
16. KUNA, 5 July — DR, 7 July 1986.
17. *Al-Wafd*, 30 October 1986.
18. R. Kuwait, 12 July — DR, 14 July 1986.
19. *Al-Nahar Arab Report and Memo*, 12 September 1986.
20. KUNA, 23 February — SWB, 25 February 1986; *The Guardian*, 3 March 1986.
21. R. Tehran, 31 March — SWB, 3 April 1986.
22. KUNA, 29 April — DR, 30 April 1986.
23. *Al-Sha'b*, Cairo, 2 September 1986.
24. KUNA, 17-18 September — DR, 18 September 1986.
25. *IHT*, 27 October 1987.
26. SWB, 4 December 1986.
27. *Der Speigel*, 24 November — DR, 25 November 1986.
28. INA, 23 July — DR, 24 July 1986.
29. KUNA, 17 November — DR, 17 November 1986.
30. SWB, 4 December 1986.
31. SPA, 19 March — DR, 19 March; SPA, 29 May — DR, 30 May 1986.
32. *Jane's Defence Weekly*, 5 April 1986.
33. R. Amman, 19 October — DR, 20 October 1986.
34. R. Kuwait, 22 December 1986.
35. *Al-Ahram*, 20 June 1986.
36. *Al-Ra'y al-'Amm*, 11 September 1986.
37. KUNA, 27 July — SWB, 29 July 1986.
38. *Al-Siyasa*, 23 July — DR, 25 July 1986.
39. KUNA, 5 April — DR, 7 April 1986.
40. KUNA, 7 April — DR, 7 April 1986.
41. SWB, 7 July 1986.
42. *Al-Wafd*, 10 July 1986.
43. *Der Spiegel*, 24 November — DR, 25 November 1986.
44. *NYT*, 27 January 1987.
45. KUNA, 23 November — SWB, 26 November 1986.
46. *Al-Qabas*, 16 November — DR, 18 November 1986.
47. Caspar W. Weinberger, "A Report to the Congress on Security Arrangements in the Persian Gulf," 15 June 1987.
48. KUNA, 15 January — SWB, 20 January 1986.
49. *Al-'Alim*, 2 October 1986.
50. *NYT*, 4 June 1987.

Oman

DORE GOLD

With the violent overthrow of the regime of President 'Ali Nasir Muhammad of the People's Democratic Republic of Yemen (PDRY) in January, Oman might have expected 1986 to be a year of heightened tensions in Southern Arabia. But the Omani Government very soon found itself back on the path of reconciliation with the new regime in Aden (see chapter on the PDRY). This diplomatic dialogue was undoubtedly helped by the newly emerging relations between Oman and the PDRY's major supporter, the USSR. The 1985 decision to establish diplomatic relations was implemented in 1986. On Oman's other front, Iraq's long-range strikes against Iranian oil facilities, while bringing the war closer to the Straits of Hormuz, did not alter Oman's accommodative approach to Iran.

DOMESTIC AFFAIRS

SUBVERSIVE ACTIVITIES

As in the past, evidence of subversive operations against the Omani regime were not reported in Omani or in most Gulf newspapers. Opposition activities as such were primarily evident from the literature produced by the organizations challenging the rule of Sultan Qabus or from newspapers based in countries hostile to Omani policy — i.e., Libya. A Palestinian newspaper in East Jerusalem, known for its sympathetic attitude toward al-Fath, reported on 31 January that Sultan Qabus had ordered the execution of six Omani citizens including two from the military, who had been accused of planning a *coup d'état*.[1]

Further evidence of the existence of Omani opposition elements emerged in the Sultanate's own announcement on 17 April that it was giving "the opportunity to opposition and misguided elements to return to the homeland." In this statement, the Omani Foreign Ministry implied that the Government was granting a general amnesty until 31 December 1986, for it explained that those responding would be provided with "suitable jobs" and be assisted in settling in Oman; no specific reference, however, was made to granting legal immunity from prosecution. A specific call was made to Omani students studying abroad "at the expense of foreign parties." They were told that they must return to Oman in order to submit applications "to further their studies at the expense of the Sultanate's Government."[2] An example of what the Government must have had in mind was the community of Omani students sponsored by Libya. The Oman National Union of Students held its fourth general congress in Libya in early August 1986, and saluted Libya's confrontation with "the forces of evil and aggression under the leadership of American Imperialism" as well as Tripoli's support of "liberation causes of our Arab nation."[3]

A spokesman for the Popular Front for the Liberation of Oman (PFLO) reported that the Omani authorities since December 1985 had initiated a sweeping campaign of arrests throughout the Sultanate. Eighteen detainees were mentioned by name; they included government officials, soldiers, and intellectuals.[4] A Palestinian source in East Jerusalem reported a large explosion that wounded several guards in one of Sultan Qabus' palaces in Muscat. Additional arrests were reported.[5] The same source revealed in July that in the aftermath of increased threats against his regime, Qabus had turned to several countries to assist him with Intelligence and internal security.[6]

CABINET CHANGES AND OFFICIAL APPOINTMENTS

In January 1986, Sultan Qabus made a number of appointments to the Foreign Ministry: Sayf Ibn Hamad al-Battashi was made Under Secretary for Financial and Service Affairs; and Haytham Ibn Tariq al-Sa'id was made Under Secretary for Political Affairs.[7]

In October, several Cabinet posts were reshuffled. Hamad Ibn Hamud was appointed Special Adviser to Sultan Qabus. Muhammad Ibn 'Ali al-Qatbi was appointed Chairman of the Civil Service Council with ministerial rank. Muhammad Ibn 'Abdallah Ibn Zahir al-Hana'i and 'Abdallah Ibn Hamad Ibn Sayf al-Bu Sa'idi were made Minister of Agriculture and Fisheries and Minister of Housing respectively. Sultan Ibn Hamad Ibn Faysal al-Sa'd was made State Adviser for Tribal Affairs.[8]

SOCIAL AND ECONOMIC DEVELOPMENTS

The Government, out of concern about the influence of the foreign labor community, decreed that Omanis could no longer intermarry with non-Omani nationals, except those from GCC states. Most of these mixed marriages were reportedly with citizens of Egypt, Syria, Lebanon and Jordan. The new law would not affect those already married to foreign nationals.[9]

The Ministry of Housing continued to implement a massive land distribution campaign throughout the Sultanate which, by February 1986, affected nearly 11,000 units of industrial, residential, commercial and agricultural property.[10]

The crash in oil prices in early 1986 cut deeply into Oman's yearly income. Oil production (maintained at approximately 550,000 barrels a day) made up 80 per cent of the Sultanate's revenue. Omani officials forecast a $500m shortfall in income and a shrinking of economic growth for the first time in years; annual growth had averaged 10 per cent a year since 1981. In January, the Government devalued its currency — the Omani riyal — and cut government spending including defense spending. Oman asked the United Kingdom to delay until 1992 the delivery of eight *Tornado* aircraft ordered for 1988.[11]

FOREIGN AFFAIRS

REGIONAL POLITICS

Oman was cautious in its approach to Iran, in continuation of a policy that first became apparent in 1985. Oman did not condemn Iranian search-and-seize operations in the Gulf and the Arabian Sea. Omani Under Secretary for Foreign Affairs Haytham Ibn Tariq explained that Oman was concerned primarily with what went on in its territorial waters and not with events in international waters. Moreover, he asserted that, under international law, Iran had the right to stop and search ships since it was in a state of war.[12] The Omani view contrasted with Kuwait's on this matter (see section on Kuwait, above.) High-level contacts were maintained during the year between Oman and Iraq. On 28 October, the Iraqi Deputy Prime Minister and Foreign Minister, Tariq 'Aziz, arrived in Muscat for two days of talks with Omani officials. He conveyed a written message from President Saddam Husayn.[13]

Oman continued to strengthen its security ties with the GCC and the Kingdom of Saudi Arabia. Omani fighter and transport aircraft were used in joint exercises with the Royal Saudi Air Force in the Kingdom itself between 18 and 27 September.[14] The Omani decision to postpone until 1992 the receipt of British *Tornado* aircraft (see above) was expected to mean that Oman, with no proper air defense aircraft of its own, would have to continue to rely on the Saudi defense umbrella, whatever its attitude toward security dependence on the Kingdom.[15] In late June, Sultan Qabus paid a private visit to Abu Dhabi, where he held talks with UAE President Shaykh Zayid. The Kuwaiti daily *al-Siyasa* reported that the two leaders had reached agreement on the Abu Dhabi-Oman border issue. No further details were supplied.[16]

Oman and the PDRY sought to renew the process of normalization between their two countries begun in 1982, just as the new regime in Aden consolidated its position after the intra-party civil conflict of January (see chapter on the PDRY). In February, a PDRY delegation arrived in Muscat headed by PDRY Minister of Transport and Yemeni Socialist Party Central Committee member Salih Abu Bakr Ibn Husaynun. The PDRY delegation, after reviewing the events of January, expressed its desire to see a renewal of bilateral negotiations which would include the issue of the undefined PDRY-Omani border.[17] High-level contacts were maintained throughout the year; there was also a letter from the PDRY President to the Sultan of Oman.[18]

Outside of the Gulf and the Arabian Peninsula, two countries were important in Oman's regional diplomacy: Jordan and Egypt. King Husayn paid a one-day visit to Oman on 5 October when he consulted with Sultan Qabus.[19] The Egyptian and Omani Foreign Ministers met in New York in late September at the opening of the new UN General Assembly session.[20]

INTERNATIONAL POLITICS

Britain remained one of the most important extra-regional actors in Oman's foreign policy in 1986. The British foreign community in Oman was estimated to number about 11,000 people — a substantially larger number than the nearly 1,000 Americans who also worked in the Sultanate.[21] With Britons placed in key military and advisory positions (see *MECS* 1984–85, pp 411–12), British commercial and even military access to Oman appeared at times to be preferred to that of the US. The British Foreign Secretary, Sir Geoffrey Howe, arrived in Muscat on 11 January on the first leg of a five-day official visit to the Persian Gulf. He held wide-ranging talks with the Omanis on subjects that included the Iraqi-Iranian war, the war on terrorism, and the Arab-Israeli peace process.[22] British military forces conducted a large joint exercise with Omani units in late November called "Swift Sword." The exercises entailed the landing of sea- and air-borne forces in a remote area of Oman; the island of Masira was used as a forward staging area for the British forces.[23] The publicity Oman permitted concerning this joint exercise contrasted with the American "Bright Star" Middle East exercises of 1985, during which Omani participation was not acknowledged. Whether the more favorable public attitude toward military cooperation with Britain as opposed to the US was a function of regional political constraints or of the influence of the Sultan's British advisers could not be ascertained.

The US attempted to upgrade its military presence in Oman in early 1986. As simultaneous crises in the Mediterranean and the Gulf overburdened the US Navy's deployment capabilities in the Middle East, the US reportedly offered Oman the temporary stationing of US ground-based fighter aircraft. The new US presence would make up for moving the *US Saratoga*, an aircraft carrier, from the Indian Ocean to the Mediterranean near Libya.[24] No such new US presence was reported during the year. US Vice President George Bush led a high-level American delegation to Oman on 9 April for a two-day visit.[25] During March, a delegation of the Omani State Consultative Council made a two-week official visit to Washington where it held talks with members of the Senate and House of Representatives.[26]

Given Oman's own dialogue with Iran in 1986, Muscat's reactions to the revelations of the Iran-Contra affair in November were relatively mild. Thus the Omani Minister of Information Abd al-'Aziz al-Rawwas explained:

> ...We must not be surprised if a country makes contact with Iran. The fact is that the entire world makes contact with Iran in one way or another. I do not wish to take the position of defending the US. The US can defend itself. I am underlining here a fact. Why should we busy ourselves with who stands with Iran and who stands against it when we find within the Arab framework those who stand with Iran?[27]

Oman and the USSR implemented their September 1985 agreement (see *MECS* 1984–85, p 414) to establish diplomatic relations. Both countries appointed their Ambassadors to Jordan as Non-Resident Ambassadors to each other's country. On 5 May, Aleksandr Ivanovich Zinchuk, the Soviet Ambassador to Jordan, presented his credentials in Muscat as the USSR's Non-Resident Ambassador to the Sultanate of Oman.[28] On 17 July, Khamis Ibn Hamad al-Bittashi, Oman's Ambassador to Jordan, presented his credentials in Moscow as Oman's Non-Resident Ambassador to the USSR.[29] During the earlier ceremonies in Muscat, Sultan Qabus raised some of the issues that were of common concern to both the USSR and Oman. Besides the issues of nonintervention in one another's internal affairs and support for peaceful coexistence and national sovereignty Qabus noted:

> We followed, with respect, the USSR's stand which supports the Arab causes in the Middle East conflict. This conflict, in our view, lacks international agreement which would help bring about a comprehensive and lasting peace based on justice and which would achieve security and stability for the peoples in the area.
>
> We believe that the Iraqi-Iranian war is a source of instability in the Gulf area. The continuation of this war threatens international security and peace and is a tool for wasting the human and economic potentials of the two countries. The Indian Ocean which borders our country has become a zone of international competition due to the regional problems around it. We are peacefully seeking with the international parties who have interests and concerns in the Indian Ocean area to find satisfactory solutions to these problems. We would be happy to hold consultations and exchange frank and

faithful opinions with your country, *as there are important points of concurrence in the stands of our two countries* toward regional issues of common concern [author's emphasis].[30]

It was not clear whether Omani and Soviet positions converged on these issues. If they did converge especially regarding international competition over the Indian Ocean, then the prospects for continued American military access to Oman in support of its peacetime naval presence did not appear to be good.

NOTES

For the place and frequency of publications cited here, and for the full name of the publication, news agency, radio station or monitoring service where an abbreviation is used, please see "List of Sources." Only in the case of more than one publication bearing the same name is the place of publication noted here.

1. *Al-Bayadir al-Siyasi*, 31 January 1986.
2. R. Muscat, 17 April — DR, 17 April 1986.
3. R. Tripoli, 12 August — SWB, 16 August 1986.
4. *Al-Huriyya*, 20 April 1986.
5. *Al-Bayadir al-Siyasi*, 3 May 1986.
6. Ibid, 19 July 1986.
7. R. Muscat, 2 January — DR, 3 January 1986.
8. R. Muscat, 14 October — DR, 15 October 1986.
9. AP in *Ma'ariv*, 3 February 1986.
10. *'Uman*, 27 February 1986.
11. Reuters in *JP*, 27 February 1986.
12. KUNA, 8 December — SWB, 9 December 1986.
13. R. Muscat, 30 October — DR, 31 October 1986.
14. GNA, 18 September — DR, 19 September 1986.
15. *MM*, 17 February 1986.
16. *Al-Siyasa*, 25 June — DR, 30 June 1986.
17. R. Salalah, 3 February — SWB, 5 February 1986.
18. *Al-Ittihad*, Abu Dhabi, 19 December 1986.
19. R. Amman, 6 October — DR, 7 October 1986.
20. R. Muscat, 30 September — DR, 10 October 1986.
21. *Le Monde*, 5–6 January 1986.
22. R. Muscat, 13 January — SWB, 15 January 1986.
23. *FT*, 24 November; R. Muscat, 27 November — SWB, 29 November 1986.
24. *LAT*, 18 January 1986.
25. R. Muscat, 9 April — DR, 9 April 1986.
26. QNA, 6 April — DR, 10 April 1986.
27. *Al-Hawadith*, 19 December 1986 — JPRS, 12 March 1987.
28. R. Muscat, 5 May — SWB, 8 May 1986.
29. R. Muscat, 17 July — DR, 18 July 1986.
30. R. Muscat, 7 May — DR, 9 May 1986.

Qatar

DORE GOLD

Qatar's bid to seize the disputed island territory of Fasht al-Dibal from Bahrain was clearly the outstanding event for this tiny Shaykhdom during the period under review. But outside of this incident and its immediate repercussions for Qatar's relations with both Bahrain and Saudi Arabia, Qatar remained relatively stable. It was by no means the same kind of target for Iranian pressures as was Kuwait or Bahrain. Internally, it did not face the same sort of challenges as its neighbors. The continued drop in oil income created increasing pressures on the Government to develop alternative sources of income, especially its substantial offshore gas reserves.

DOMESTIC AFFAIRS

SUBVERSIVE ACTIVITIES

In mid-February, five suspects were brought to trial for attempting to blow up Doha's water purification station. The ethnic and organizational links of the suspects were not reported.[1]

During the year there were repeated reports, which were subsequently officially denied, of assassination attempts against leading Qatari figures. In early May, Qatar's Information Minister, 'Isa Ghanim al-Kuwari, denied a report on Radio Monte Carlo that he had been shot and injured.[2] At about the same time a brother of the Ruler, Shaykh Nasir Ibn Hamad al-Thani, was admitted to a London hospital suffering from a gunshot wound.[3] Shaykh Nasir's son, Shaykh 'Abd al-'Aziz, while admitting that his father had in fact been shot and wounded, nonetheless denied that there had been any assassination attempt. But Shaykh 'Abd al-'Aziz did not say how his father had received the gunshot wounds.[4]

CABINET CHANGES

Commerce and Economy Minister Shaykh Nasir Ibn Khalid al-Thani died in August. A replacement was not immediately named.[5]

FOREIGN AFFAIRS

REGIONAL POLITICS

(For a full account of the dispute between Qatar and Bahrain over Fasht al-Dibal, see the section on "Regional Developments" at the beginning of the chapter on the Gulf states.)

At the end of 1985, Iran's Ambassador to Qatar said on Radio Tehran that Iran sought to maintain the security of the Gulf region and was interested "in expanding relations with other countries, particularly Qatar." Qatar, in brief, was one of the few

GCC states that was in a position to preserve a relatively less hostile relationship with Iran.[6] Considering Iranian ambitions in heavily Shi'i-populated Bahrain, it is little wonder that Iranian statements seemed to indicate an Iranian tilt toward Qatar in the latter's dispute with Bahrain over Fasht al-Dibal. However, not everything was smooth between Iran and Qatar. Iranian search and seizure operations against ships in the Gulf not only affected Qatar's overseas commerce but also sometimes directly involved vessels of Qatar's national shipping company.[7] Moreover, despite some Iranian overtures, Qatar maintained good relations with Iraq. Iraqi First Deputy Prime Minister Taha Yasin Ramadan led a delegation to Qatar for a one-day visit on 22 July.[8] Qatar continued to maintain close ties with its fellow GCC states, with the exception of Bahrain. It could not be confirmed whether relations with Saudi Arabia were damaged by the crisis it caused in the GCC by its seizure of Fasht al-Dibal, although such a development would have been predictable and logical.

Outside of the Gulf, Qatar maintained close ties with Egypt, despite the continued absence of full diplomatic relations between them. Jordan and Morocco were also important Arab partners in Qatari's regional foreign policy. The Chairman of the Palestine Liberation Organization, Yasir 'Arafat, arrived in Doha for talks with Qatari officials on 1 April.[9] He returned to Qatar on 19 September.

INTERNATIONAL POLITICS

The Qatari Press continued to be highly critical of US policy in the Middle East; in 1986 it focused on the growing military confrontation between the US and Libya and on the revelations concerning American arms transfers to Iran. At the UN, Qatar's permanent representative, Hamad 'Abd al-'Aziz al-Kuwari, rejected the US claim that its April air attack against Libya fell within the right of self-defense as guaranteed by Article 51 of the UN Charter.[10] US Assistant Secretary of State for Near Eastern and South Asian Affairs Richard Murphy arrived in Doha on 4 April for a brief visit as part of his tour of the Gulf countries.[11] There were reports during the year of Soviet-Qatari contacts over the establishment of diplomatic relations.[12] Despite the rumors, no firm decision was taken in this regard in 1986.

NOTES

For the place and frequency of publications cited here, and for the full name of the publication, news agency, radio station or monitoring service where an abbreviation is used, please see "List of Sources." Only in the case of more than one publication bearing the same name is the place of publication noted here.

1. *Al-Qabas*, 18 February 1986.
2. *Gulf Daily News*, 8 May — DR, 8 May 1986; R. Monte Carlo, 7 May 1986.
3. DR, 3 May 1986.
4. *Al-Qabas*, 11 June 1986.
5. QNA, 2 August — DR, 4 August 1982.
6. R. Tehran, 31 December 1985 — DR, 2 January 1986.
7. *Al-Akhbar*, 4 March 1986.
8. INA, 22 July — DR, 22 July 1986.
9. QNA, 1 April — DR, 2 April 1986.
10. GNA, 17 April — DR, 17 April 1986.
11. GNA, 4 April — DR, 7 April 1986.
12. *Al-Ra'y al-'Amm*, 18 June 1986.

The United Arab Emirates

DORE GOLD

Since the beginning of the "tanker war" between Iran and Iraq in early 1984, the UAE had been relatively unaffected by the attacks against the commercial shipping of the Gulf states. First, Kuwait and Saudi Arabia were the focus of Iranian ire — due to their substantial assistance to the Iraqi economy. Thus Iranian operations were concentrated on the Upper Gulf. Second, the UAE preserved a special trading relationship with Iran, chiefly through the Dubai Emirate. However, in 1986, the naval strategies of both Iran and Iraq led to increased hostile activity in the Lower Gulf as well. In mid-October, three unidentified missiles struck a Danish-French oil rig off Abu Dhabi.[1] Several days later a Kuwaiti tanker was attacked by Iranian gunboats in UAE territorial waters, just ten miles off the coast of Dubai.[2] UAE-owned ships found themselves subject to Iranian naval inspections as well during the year. But the principal event marking the escalation in the Lower Gulf was the attack on Abu Dhabi's Abu al-Bukush offshore oil rig (see below). The UAE's near immunity to the Iraqi-Iranian war appeared to have come to an end.

DOMESTIC AFFAIRS

REINSTATEMENT OF FEDERAL LEADERSHIP AND THE FORMER CONSTITUTIONAL SYSTEM

Domestic politics in the UAE over the last two years were conducted with an awareness that the UAE Federation operated in accordance with a Provisional Constitution that was set to expire at the end of 1986. Any speculation about possible changes in the distribution of federal powers among the Emirates or between the UAE Supreme Council (consisting of the heads of each Emirate) and the appointed Consultative Assembly was put to rest by mid-October, when the UAE Supreme Council unanimously decided to continue to work in accordance with the Provisional Constitution for the next five years, starting on 2 December. At the same meeting Shaykh Zayid Ibn Sultan al-Nuhayyan, Ruler of Abu Dhabi, was reelected as President, and Shaykh Rashid Ibn Sa'id al Makhtum, Ruler of Dubai, was reelected as Vice President — both for five-year terms from 2 December.[3] It was the first time the UAE Supreme Council had met since December 1985.

SUBVERSIVE ACTIVITIES

A source in the UAE Ministry of the Interior reported that a bomb had exploded on 16 January in an Abu Dhabi commercial office building. No one was injured in the explosion. Among the offices most affected by the blast were those of Syrian Arab Airlines and PDRY Airlines.[4]

A Palestinian source in Jerusalem reported that the UAE authorities had uncovered a terrorist unit under the direction of Syrian Intelligence. The unit reportedly intended to hit targets in Abu Dhabi.[5]

ATTACK ON THE ABU AL-BUKUSH OIL INSTALLATION

On 25 November, unidentified aircraft attacked the Abu al-Bukush offshore oil platform 100 miles northwest of Abu Dhabi — within its territorial waters. Five people were killed, including two French citizens, and 24 were wounded. It was not entirely clear who was responsible for the attack.[6] Iraqi aircraft had recently extended the range of their attacks against Iran's southern oil terminals (see chapter on the Iraqi-Iranian war); an accidental Iraqi air attack could not be dismissed as a possibility. Iran claimed the attack was Iraq's reponsibility and offered to help repair the damaged oil facility.[7] The UAE Council of Ministers, meeting in an extraordinary session on 26 November, did not blame either side; several days later Shaykh Zayid maintained the UAE's official ambiguity about who was to blame for the attack:

> We are not affected by what has taken place and our self-confidence has not been shaken. We do not want to see our brothers harmed because we are one body. What hurts one part will also hurt the other parts. These events have shown us who is the enemy and who is the friend. We will do our duty if this act is repeated *by any side or any country* [author's emphasis].[8]

On 27 April, the UAE Consultative Council approved a recommendation by its special committee that all youths aged between 18 and 20 should undergo military training.[9] No details were given about the length of training; nor was it clear whether foreign residents would also be drafted. Approval by the Council of Ministers was required before the proposal could become law.

Earlier in the year, it was reported that the UAE and Morocco had reached an agreement over the deployment of 5,000 Moroccan soldiers in the UAE.[10] The agreement was part of a general pattern in the Gulf states to look for ways of increasing military manpower by hiring foreign Islamic forces such as those of Pakistan or Jordan. After a visit by UAE Defense Minister Shaykh Muhammad Ibn Rashid to Islamabad, it was expected that Pakistani military units would soon arrive in Dubai to train UAE forces in the use of American and British equipment.[11]

THE BUDGET

According to the UAE Central Bank, the 1985 UAE budget was 16,633,700,000 UAE dirhams (UAEDh) as against 17,229,400,000 for 1984. The 1985 budget deficit came to UAEDh 7.5 bn, compared with UAEDh5.4 bn in 1984.[12] The UAE Minister of Finance and Industry, Shaykh Hamdan Ibn Rashid, expected that the 1986 budget would have to be 30 per cent less than that of the previous year.[13]

FOREIGN AFFAIRS

REGIONAL POLITICS

UAE-Iranian relations at the start of the year were better than Iran's relations with any other GCC state. In January, it was reported that the Speaker of the Iranian Parliament, Hashemi Rafsanjani, had been invited to visit the UAE.[14] However, as noted in the beginning of this section, the Iraqi-Iranian struggle over the movement of commercial shipping in the Lower Gulf eventually led to a number of incidents between Iran and the UAE. The general effect of these was to push the UAE toward a state of greater military preparedness, and closer coordination with its GCC partners as well as its potential allies outside the Gulf.

The UAE was a strong advocate of the return of Egypt to the Arab fold. On 21 April, Shaykh Hamdan Ibn Zayid, UAE Under Secretary of Foreign Affairs, met with President Mubarak in Cairo for talks. Shaykh Hamdan explained that Shaykh Zayid had called for an urgent Arab summit meeting attended by Egypt.[15] King Husayn arrived in the UAE on 1 August for a three-day visit. The UAE and Jordan continued to develop their traditionally close ties.[16] In late November, Shaykh Zayid made a personal visit to Morocco, where he held talks with King Hasan.[17] The UAE maintained close contacts with the non-conservative Arab states as well. Messages were exchanged during the year with Libya; in October, the PDRY Foreign Minister, Dr 'Abd al-'Aziz al-Dali, visited the UAE.

INTERNATIONAL POLITICS

As expected, the USSR dispatched its first Ambassador to the UAE in October 1986, in accordance with the November 1985 agreement between the UAE and the Soviet Union to establish diplomatic relations. The new Ambassador, Feliks Nikolagvich Fedotov, was a Resident Ambassador — unlike the new Soviet Ambassador to Oman (see section on Oman); and a new Soviet embassy was opened in the UAE during the year.[18] In 1986, the USSR substantially increased its merchant shipping presence in the UAE. In May, the first Soviet shipping line to Rashid Port in Dubai was inaugurated. Three additional shipping lines were established in June from Northern Europe to Dubai.[19]

UAE newspapers, which normally voiced Arab nationalist criticism of America's Middle East policy, had several opportunities during the year to lash out at Washington. All the major newspapers condemned the April raid against Libya.[20] In November, revelations of the Reagan Administration's secret arms sales to Iran caused a second series of attacks on US policy. The UAE Press focused particularly on the role of the US in keeping the war going.[21] The US's special Middle East envoy, Walter Cluverius, was in the UAE in November, when he met with Shaykh Hamdan Ibn Zayid. Developments in the Arab-Israeli peace process were discussed.[22] Earlier in the year, in February, ADM John Adams, Commander of US Naval Forces in the Middle East, paid a visit to the UAE.[23]

NOTES

For the place and frequency of publications cited here, and for the full name of the publication, news agency, radio station or monitoring service where an abbreviation is used, please see "List of Sources." Only in the case of more than one publication bearing the same name is the place of publication noted here.

1. AFP, 16 October — DR, 17 October 1986.
2. KUNA, 22 October — DR, 23 October 1986.
3. QNA, 15 October — DR, 16 October 1986.
4. KUNA, 16 January — DR, 16 January 1986.
5. *Al-Bayadir al-Siyasi*, 22 June 1986.

6. R. Dubai, 25 November — DR, 26 November 1986.
7. SWB, 9 December 1986.
8. *Al-Ittihad*, Abu Dhabi, 3 December — SWB, 6 December 1986.
9. GNA, 27 April — DR, 29 April 1986.
10. *Al-'Alim*, 11 January 1986.
11. *Al-'Alim*, 27 February 1986.
12. GNA, 13 May — DR, 13 May 1986.
13. *Al-Siyasa*, 24 April 1986.
14. *Al-Mustaqbal*, 25 January 1986.
15. GNA, 21 April — DR, 22 April 1986.
16. R. Dubai, 11 August — DR, 13 August 1986.
17. GNA, 1 December — SWB, 4 December 1986.
18. GNA, 20 October — DR, 21 October 1986.
19. *Al-Khalij*, 29 June — SWB, 5 July 1986.
20. ENA, 16 April — DR, 17 April 1986.
21. *Al-Bayan*, 15 November — DR, 18 November 1986.
22. *Al-Ittihad*, Abu Dhabi, 14 November — DR, 17 November 1986.
23. Voice of Kuwait, 8 February 1986.

Iran
(Jumhuriyye Islamiyye Iran)

DAVID MENASHRI

Three sets of problems preoccupied the Iranians in 1986: the war with Iraq; the continued economic downturn, and the fierce power struggle within the revolutionary Establishment. The problems were clearly interrelated and inseparable: the war added to the economic burden and gradually turned into an issue of controversy; the economic difficulties influenced the war strategy and were at the center of the internal rifts; the struggle for power evolved around the economy and the war as well as the most crucial question of the policy and — no less important — the leadership of Iran after the death of Ayatollah Ruhollah Khomeyni.

The intensification of the three sets of problems led to growing disillusionment within the ranks of the *mostaz'efin* (the "dispossessed") and thus added a new challenge for the regime. While since 1981 the new leadership had enjoyed relative stability, consolidated their power and preserved sufficient public support, grave threats to this stability emerged in 1986. Although all these problems did not yet produce a change of declared policies (toward the war, for instance), they clearly led to greater pragmatism in Iran's approach to domestic issues and foreign relations.

In the last quarter of the year internal developments were overshadowed by the revelations concerning the arms deals with the US. These led to an intensification of the internal power struggle — in fact they were revealed because there were rifts in Tehran. At the end of the year, while the arms deals continued to occupy public opinion in Iran and abroad, the war, the economy and the struggle for power continued to be the real problems facing the Government. For the first time since 1981, the revolutionary regime was faced with challenges threatening its stability.

TEHRAN AND THE AMERICAN ARMS

FROM POLITICAL NEGOTIATIONS TO TRADE OF ARMS FOR HOSTAGES

By the very nature of things, revolutionary movements are often led to deviate from their radical doctrines once they have made the transition from opposition to power. The Islamic revolution was no exception. As long as he headed an opposition movement, Ayatollah Ruhollah Khomeyni had depicted a "new Iran" as being modeled on early Islam. Once in power, he knew he could not rule by means of revolutionary slogans — certainly not slogans drawn from seventh-century thought. He and his disciples were now called upon to manage, rather than discuss, affairs of state. Soon they compromised with reality, not from a new-found moderation, but from a pragmatism responsive to the exigencies of their situation.

Evidence of this may be found already in the first years of the revolutionary regime.

How else is it possible to explain the close ties of Islamic Iran with the professedly atheist Ba'th Party of Syria? How else is it possible to reconcile Khomeyni's insistence on the elimination of the Ba'th Party in Iraq as a condition for ending the war with Iraq, while choosing as his closest ally Syria, a country led by a different branch of the same party? Also, how can one reconcile his pan-Islamic ideology and his abhorrence of nationalist divisions within the domain of Islam with his insistence that the Gulf must be called (and therefore be) Persian? How does his supranational ideology and assertion that there is no difference between Muslims anywhere, neither ethnically nor on account of their being Shi'is and Sunnis, accord with the Constitution's stipulation that only a Shi'i of Iranian origin can hold office as President.[1] Perhaps the best example is that even after six years of war with Iraq, the Iranians still ran their embassy in Baghdad and the Iraqis theirs in Tehran. A close scrutiny of the revolutionary regime's domestic and foreign policies points to a gradual retreat from doctrinaire purity to pragmatic considerations of expediency.

Appeals by revolutionary leaders to exercise a cautious pragmatism related first to specific and narrow issues, such as the employment of professionals even though they might have served the *ancien régime* or refrained from supporting Islamic rule in its early stage (see *Middle East Contemporary Survey* [*MECS*] 1981–82, pp 546–47). Later, when the regime felt more secure and became more mindful of areas of public resentment, voices calling for moderation came to deal with broader issues such as the administration of justice (see *MECS* 1982–83, pp 523–25). Finally, Khomeyni threw his weight behind a policy to slow down Islamization. Speaking to the Council of Guardians on 2 September 1984, he advised the clerics not to press "too hard" on the people and to "refrain from extremism." Encouraged by the Imam's guidelines, *Majlis* Speaker Hujjat al-Islam 'Ali Akbar Hashemi Rafsanjani elaborated on them in two Friday sermons in September 1984. He advised against pushing the revolutionary process forward too fast and against going further than "necessary." Wisdom, he said, "calls for moderation at this stage." Moderation became the keynote of his sermons (see *MECS* 1983–84, p 447). Extremism, Ayatollah Husayn 'Ali Montazeri — Khomeyni's successor-designate — said over and over again in 1986, was shortsightedness. He advocated moderation. "Take the middle way," he said, explicitly denouncing "extremism" (*efrat* and *tafrit*).[2]

By degrees, the same tendency emerged in foreign policy too. Here, again, the overall trend was first given legitimacy by Khomeyni and then spelt out in greater detail by Rafsanjani. In the early days of the revolution, Khomeyni had proclaimed the illegitimacy in principle of governments everywhere and in Muslim countries in particular. The Islamic Republic would ignore governments and deal directly with the various peoples. Iran then demonstrated its disdain for diplomatic conventions by seizing the diplomats of a country with which it had "normal" relations (the US) while maintaining "normal" relations with a country with which it was at war (Iraq). In 1981, Khomeyni held up isolationism as a new ideal for Iran's foreign policy: only through isolation could Iran become truly independent, he argued (see *MECS* 1980–81, pp 557–58) Gradually, the doctrinaire approach was whittled down by realities. In October 1984, Khomeyni announced that his country wanted "relations with all countries," with the exception of the US, Israel and South Africa. It was "against reason and Islamic law" not to do so. Ayatollah Reza Mahdavi-Kani added that it was "neither right nor possible" to insist on having relations "with peoples" (see *MECS* 1984–85, p 449).

Officially, the slogan "neither the East nor the West" continued to express Tehran's attitude toward Moscow and Washington. But, in day-to-day practice, repugnance against the US — "the great Satan" — was voiced more often, and slogans such as "Death to America" and "America cannot do just any damned thing" remained current. But here, too, signs of moderation became apparent by degrees.

Some low-keyed references to a possible future renewal of relations with the US were made soon after the 1982–83 crackdown against the *Tudeh* (Communist) Party. In a Friday sermon on 13 May 1983, Rafsanjani addressed "the Americans" directly to remind them that, in principle, Iran was ready for relations with all countries that were prepared to have "proper (*sahih*) relations with us," and to "honor our revolution." He now excluded only Israel and South Africa (see *MECS* 1982–83, p 541).

Rafsanjani had long been known for his appreciation of American weapons and his recognition of the necessity to buy American arms. Upon the delivery of French planes to Iraq in 1983, for example, he said that neither French nor Soviet arms (then delivered to Iraq) could change the course of the war, since Iran possessed American fighter planes. American weapons, he went on, were by and large much better than any others (see *MECS* 1982–83, p 541). At a press conference in July 1984, Rafsanjani went a step further, declaring that Iran would not reject buying American-made spare parts for the Army — preferably through a third party, directly if necesssary (see *MECS* 1983–84, p 454). In August 1985, when the first shipments of American-made arms had already been delivered to Iran but before the whole issue had become public knowledge, Rafsanjani disclosed that his country was in fact buying American arms, though he did not reveal their source. He said: "The situation in the West is such that it is very easy to buy weapons from arms dealers." Acknowledging that such purchases amounted to indirect dealing with the US, he said his country did not have much choice, since it was not wise for it to change its weapons systems, which would require new staff, training and logistics.[3] Early in 1986 he claimed that his country had never maintained that it would never have relations with the US. If Washington was ready to have relations with Iran "based on justice and equality," he said, Iran would have relations with the US.[4] Late in April 1986, Rafsanjani made it clear in a Friday sermon that Iran had to buy American arms and would do so from any source available. "It is not a shame" to buy American arms, he said, and added:

> We do not deny that *we will buy American weapons wherever they will be available* for us. All the world knows that the Iranian Army in the days of the Shah was equipped with American arms. All the world knows that we are currently fighting with American weaponry. We openly declare that our aircraft are American, a great part of our missiles are American and much of our artillery is American. All these require spare parts. [Author's emphasis.][5]

Two months later, after the trip of Robert McFarlane (Assistant to the President for National Security Affairs) to Tehran, Rafsanjani said: "We have never been determined to cut off relations with the West. For many reasons we prefer to have ties. But what we do not want is Western hegemony....We seek cordial and friendly relations, and we are endeavoring to establish better relations."[6] Even after the contacts were leaked, Rafsanjani did not close the door to *rapprochement* (see below). The Iranian Ambassador to the United Nations, Sa'id Raja'i-Khorasani, confirmed that his country was buying arms from the US and made it clear that it was ready — more so than in previous years — to reestablish ties with the US.[7] True, such statements were greatly outnumbered by many others denying that any *rapprochement* was possible. But often Iranian officials voicing even the most extreme anti-American slogans added the rider that the Iranian attitude might change if US policy did. Moreover, two lines of communication were kept open all along. One was the Hague Joint Committee, which dealt with mutual claims deriving from the 1981 Algiers Agreement. The other comprised American commercial firms, including oil companies and — most importantly — arms dealers. According to a senior Central Intelligence Agency (CIA)source, there were "probably 30 to 40 requests per year from Iranians and Iranian exiles" for American arms.[8]

Hostility toward the Americans, it must be remembered, had at no time toned down the ideological and political considerations that made the Soviet Union almost as objectionable to the new regime (see below). Khomeyni considered the USSR to be as imperialist as the US. (Russia's record of intervention in Iran throughout the 19th century as well as during the two World Wars are part of Iran's living historical memory.) In Khomeyni's words, "America is worse than the Soviet Union and the Soviet Union is worse than America." If America was "the Great Satan," the Soviet Union was "the Red Satan." In theological terms, Christian America was on a par with atheist Russia. In political terms, Iran criticized the Soviet Union for its ties with leftist groups and ethnic minorities in Iran; for its invasion of Afghanistan; and for its support of Iraq. Often enough, the new regime overreacted in its apprehensions of Soviet designs on Iran (see, for example, Iranian reactions following Saddam Husayn's visit to Moscow in December 1985, *MECS* 1984–85, p 450).

If the slow turn toward more pragmatic assessments, and the prevailing distaste for the Soviet Union were in themselves likely to lead to more accommodating policy toward the US, such trends were greatly reinforced by the country's deteriorating economic situation, the exigencies of the war, and the power struggle within the Establishment (for all three, see below).

By the second half of 1984, Iranian signals to Washington of a new willingness for some kind of accommodation had become more definite. But the American Administration was still the captive of its own concept of revolutionary Iran as a menace to American interests. According to a detailed interagency study completed in the US in October 1984, Khomeyni's death was probably a precondition for changes in Iranian policies and a realistic prospect of improved Iranian-American relations. The study "conveyed an impression of relative American powerlessness to affect events in Iran, powerlessness that would continue indefinitely."[9]

Failing to gain an attentive ear in Washington, the Iranians decided to approach Washington through Jerusalem. Their middlemen (Manuchehr Qorbanifar and 'Adnan Khashoggi) convinced them that the Israelis — keen to rebuild their bridges to Tehran for their own purposes — were the only ones capable of persuading the Americans to alter their policy with regard to Iran. The first practical steps in this direction were taken in March 1985, when Khashoggi contacted potential representatives of Israel.

Even now it is not sufficiently clear what led to the Iranian initiative. Different interpretations have been offered (cf below), but in broad terms it may be argued that the initiative signaled a pro-Western shift — either on the part of the Iranian Administration as a whole or of a significant group within the Establishment — and at the same time a bid to strengthen the more moderate and pro-Western (or perhaps more radical and anti-Soviet) elements in the internal power struggle. This was the way the initiative was presented by the Iranians at their initial meetings with their Israeli interlocutors. Clearly, the main issues discussed were political: to secure support for pragmatists in Tehran and, consequently, to weaken the pro-Soviet elements within the Administration and to block a possible Soviet threat. At that point, the sale of arms and the release of hostages were secondary issues.

The principal assessment of the domestic Iranian scene was passed on to Western interlocutors by Khashoggi. In a memorandum dated 2 May 1985 that reflected the assessment of Qorbanifar, he described what he called the "three lines," which, in his view, were struggling to monopolize power in Iran: a radical-leftist trend, a rightist-moderate one, and a "balancing" trend. He made it clear at this early stage that despite their differences all three "lines" supported the Islamic Republic, upheld the supremacy of Islam and the clerics and were opposed to any separation of religion and state.

He described the leftist hard-liners as advocating the "exporting of the revolution" and as the "generators" of terrorism. At home they supported the redistribution of land and strict Islamization in all spheres of life. The rightist group was presented as anti-Communist and anti-Soviet, opposed to exporting the revolution, desirous of friendly relations with Western states, and much more pragmatic in domestic policies. The third group held an intermediate position. He went on to plead for American support of the Rightists as being in best interests of both Iran and the West. If this was done, Iran would establish "mutually satisfactory relations with foreign countries in the field of politics and economics, and [follow] an open-door policy between Iran and the outside world." He went on to warn, however, that a government formed by the pragmatists would still be Muslim, "even fanatically so." But it would not be as fanatical as those of the other two trends and more open to reason: "*By Iranian standards* they will be moderate [author's emphasis]." In any case, the main and immediate target was the elimination of the pro-Soviet and radical group.

The emergence of a government of the moderates would be followed — according to Khashoggi, Qorbanifar and their colleagues — by a pro-Western shift in Iranian policy as a natural consequence of failing "Soviet design" and of eliminating the radicals. This point was stressed by Ayatollah Hasan Karubi at a meeting with Israeli representatives in Hamburg on 8 July 1985. (Karubi is a leading cleric from Qom, closely associated with Khomeyni and even more so with his son Ahmad and with Rafsanjani. His brother, Ayatollah Mehdi Karubi, is the head of the Foundation of the Martyrs.) He told the meeting:

> We are interested in cooperation with the West — exactly so — [because] we have common interests with the West...There has been a diversity of [pro-Western] movements which need coordination...We are ready for a detailed and practical (*'amali*) debate, and willing to put at your disposal all our powers and to discuss how to restore Iran to the West, on an honorable basis, not as a surrender, but as [necessitated by] our mutual interest. It should not be said that nothing can be done — on the contrary, one should concentrate on the actions.

He added that both the US and "our region" were subject to a "real physical threat from the Soviet Union," and that unless the West acted decisively it would "lose Iran definitely."

In a letter from Tehran dated 15 July, Karubi — urging his Western partners to support his "line" — elaborated further:

> If our Western friends are not resourceful and will not care to organize the [Iranian] forces that support their line, and if they do not give a prompt positive response to our demands — and after, all we do have similar aims, ambitions and interests — after the death of Ayatollah Ruhollah Khomeyni ...[and considering the Russians' historical designs on Iran] our country may expect one of two fates: either it becomes a second Lebanon in greater, more dangerous dimensions, or in a few months — two years at the most — [it]...will turn into a satellite of Communist Russia.

The argument that there was an anti-Soviet interest shared by the US and the Iranian moderates ran like a red thread throughout the negotiations. In late 1984 Qorbanifar had told former CIA officer Theodore Shackley that he "feared that Iran would become a Soviet satellite within the near term — three to five years."[10] Similarly, on 20 February, 1986, Mohsen Qangarlou (an assistant to the Prime Minister) told Oliver North that "the Government of Iran is terrified of a new Soviet threat."[11] Even stronger emphasis on Iran's declared desire to balance its relations with the two superpowers was expressed at the Tehran meetings in May 1986. The main figures on the Iranian side were, according to available sources, Qangarlou and the deputy chairman of the *Majlis* Committee on Foreign Relations, Hadi Najafabadi. At the first meeting they stated: "We are open to a stable relationship with the US but it will not be easy to overcome a bitter history." At another point in the negotiations they added: "Iran does not just want to discuss spare parts." But they again made it clear that "to rebuild a bridge of confidence will take time."[12] The Americans were similarly interested in building a bridge; and they also chose to (over)emphasize the Soviet threat.[13] In a meeting with Qorbanifar in Paris in March 1986, North told him that "the real problem facing Iran — that of Soviet intervention — was becoming a reality and that the Iranians are in no position to deal with this problem. We can help — and are willing to — because a free independent Iran is in our best interest." And while preparing the May trip to Tehran the Americans made sure to convince the Iranians "of a significant near-term and long-range threat from the Soviet Union," as well as the fact that "we have real and deceptive intelligence to demonstrate this threat during the visit."[14]

It is difficult to avoid the impression that both sides — given their own perception of the other side's apprehensions of the Soviet threat — often exaggerated the dimensions of the Soviet danger in order to further their negotiations. Yet, even if we allow that such perceptions were being played up deliberately by both sides, and although the issues of arms and hostages had been discussed from the early stages of the negotiations, there remains the fact that, to begin with, the main issue at stake in the negotiations was political. Thus, McFarlane testified to the Tower Committee: "I was very precise in saying: The purpose here is a political agenda; the vulnerability and risk is a perception of something far different, which is arms for hostages."[15] Yet, at some stage during the negotiations, the political agenda was lost sight of and what remained was mainly an attempt to trade off arms for hostages.

THE GOVERNMENT VERSUS THE REVOLUTIONARY ORGANIZATIONS

Who were those pragmatists in Iran willing to negotiate with the US? Who opposed them? And how did their contacts with the US affect the domestic power struggle?

Western opinion by and large viewed the struggle as being between a faction of "moderates" and a faction of "extremists." In fact the situation was much more complex, and identification of individual leaders with this or that group was no easy matter. For one thing, the various competing groupings were not organized in clear-cut factions, let alone political parties (most of them were members of the ruling Islamic Republican Party), and had no coherent collective ideology. All proclaimed themselves loyal to Khomeyni and his "line." As usual in Iran, personal rivalries and ideological controversy were impossible to separate. Also, some actors on the domestic scene appeared moderate on one issue yet extremely radical on another[16] (for the earlier rivalries within the revolutionary Establishment, see *MECS* 1984–85, pp 435–38).

To illustrate: in May 1985, Qorbanifar (through Khashoggi) handed the Israelis three lists — of moderates, extremists and middle-of-the-roaders. In July, Ayatollah Hasan Karubi provided his own list of moderates. A comparison between them indicates considerable inconsistency. Moreover, some of the leading figures in Qorbanifar's list of radicals later proved instrumental in the negotiations with the Americans and the Israelis (including Prime Minister Mir Husayn Musavi and President Muhammad 'Ali Khameneh'i). Also, the original Israeli and American negotiators claimed that they were dealing with "moderates," yet Amiram Nir (special adviser to the Israeli Prime Minister on counterterrorism who became the chief Israeli negotiator in January 1986) claimed that their contacts had been with some of the most radical clerics.[17] Obviously, one man's radical was another man's moderate.

Well aware of the pitfalls of error and inaccuracy, I would propose the following distinction: those who hold executive power (including, for this matter, the *Majlis* Speaker) and share the burden of running the State are generally more pragmatic. Those outside the Administration (such as the key figures in most of the revolutionary organs) provide the bulk of the radicals. But it must be remembered that the former, too, started out as radicals fully aligned with Khomeyni's doctrines. It was only the practical problems of the day-to-day running of the Government and the perpetuation of Islamic rule that gave their thinking a belated pragmatic tinge. As Qorbanifar put it, they were moderates "by Iranian standards" and only if compared with the other groups.

In time, and as the problems facing the regime grew, the ranks of the pragmatists expanded and their tendency toward pragmatism became more marked. Yet many revolutionaries continued to preach the old ultraradical policies. A prominent example among the latter — eventually to become the token figure of opposition to deals with the US — was Mehdi Hashemi (the brother of Montazeri's son-in-law, Hadi), who was in charge of the revolutionary office coordinating Iranian support for liberation movements abroad. Run under the overall supervision of Montazeri, it was active mainly in support of the Muslim movements in Lebanon and Afghanistan. At home, the group's chief strength was in the Isfahan-Najafabad area — the Montazeri family homeground, where he was also believed to have a group of armed retainers. (For other prominent members in this ultraradical group, see the list of names in the Appendix.)

Ayatollah Montazeri himself distinguished between the state apparatus and the revolutionary organizations. The Beirut paper *al-Shira'*, which first leaked the story of McFarlane's trip to Tehran, also reported that Rafsanjani and Montazeri disagreed about the rule of the revolutionary organizations. Referring to Rafsanjani's intention to disband Hashemi's office, Montazeri said: "This office is under my patronage. Its philosophy is different from yours. You are a State [*daulah*] with relations that you must preserve. The office is a revolution [*thaurah*] and it has relations [of its own which] it must preserve," and, the paper added:

> Whatever the outcome, there are now two opposing logics in Tehran: the logic of the State and the logic of the revolution. If it is difficult for either of them to back away from their ideas, it is still more difficult for either of them to stop leveling the worst accusations against the other to make their logic prevail.[18]

This duality had characterized the Islamic regime since its early days. At first, under Mehdi Bazargan's Premiership and Abul-Hasan Bani Sadr's Presidency, the revolutionary organizations had supremacy over the Government. Later, under Musavi, the Government — then controlled by the radical clerics themselves — tightened its control over the extragovernmental bodies. While Bazargan had good reason to complain that he had been given "a knife without a blade" (see *MECS* 1979–80, pp 438-39), later Governments wielded a sharp knife indeed. The recent incident was further proof of the Government's supremacy.

The establishment of the Government's supremacy led generally to greater pragmatism, particularly in foreign relations. The following assessment by Prof R. K. Ramazani, a leading expert on Iran's foreign policy, best sums up the new trend: "On the whole, Iran's foreign policy shows a growing retreat from a confrontational stance. Its policies have been returning to a degree of "normalcy" as a result of its efforts to shed its pariah status in world affairs." While the rhetoric of the Islamic revolution continued, national intersts were accorded the highest priority.[19] The fact that the most vocal opposition to the arms deals came from those advocating the export of the revolution — where the retreat from dogma was clearly marked — may help to pinpoint the basic disagreements between the two groups. The victory of the "State" over the "revolution" — inasmuch as it can be considered an established fact at the time this volume goes to print — may also contain pointers to the strength of those advocating a greater degree of pragmatism.

Officially, Iran speaks with a single voice, echoing the line set by Khomeyni. Rafsanjani and his men insist that in their contacts with the US there were no discussions about improving political relations.[20] This brings them into line with the official version. Yet, beneath the surface, disagreements abound, sometimes even becoming public knowledge.

What does the arms affair teach us about the relative strength of the different groups so far? Clearly the pragmatists, led by Rafsanjani, won the first round. Though publicly accused of dealing with the "Great Satan," none of their number was arrested, lost his job, or was personally criticized by Khomeyni. Even Montazeri did not go so far as to directly accuse Rafsanjani. On the other hand, of the more radical group, which leaked news of the arms deals, Mehdi Hashemi and some 40 others were detained and had to "confess" to a long list of crimes (see below). Even Montazeri came out against them.

Attacked in October 1986 (after being charged with kidnapping the Syrian Chargé d'Affaires in Tehran, Ayyad Salim al-Mahmud, on 3 October), supporters of Hashemi went onto the offensive. They first leaked the story of the arms deals. Then, in mid-November, another round was started when eight *Majlis* members set out to undermine Rafsanjani's position. The eight had the support of a conservative-rightist faction grouped around the newspaper *Resalat* as well as of Montazeri's men. They planned to put an embarrassing parliamentary question to Foreign Minister 'Ali Akbar Velayati, but retreated following Khomeyni's intervention and only had it printed in *Resalat*. They prefaced their question by saying that it had come to their knowledge that "persons outside the framework of the Foreign Ministry contacted and negotiated with [an] American delegation." They asked whether the persons "were sanctioned by the Foreign Ministry, and if not, what was the legal authorization of their contacts?" They went on to inquire who had made the decision about the contacts, at what level they were conducted, who negotiated with the Americans in Iran, what they discussed, and what the outcome was.[21]

A direct confrontation between the two groups could have led to a dangerous split in the revolutionary camp. Aware of the danger, Khomeyni stepped in to stop them. He did so by means of a speech on 20 November in which he made it perfectly clear that he was satisfied with the Speaker. He instructed both sides to remain united, or at least to prevent disunity from becoming a danger to the revolution. He went on to say that those who raised such questions were either ignorant of developments or were pretending to be. He expressed disappointment with "certain individuals" who instead of "shouting against America...shout against our officials." These people, he added, were influenced either by foreign propaganda or by "their own selfish ambitions." He accused them of causing dissension among the leaders of the nation and concluded: "Why do you wish to cause schism? ...This is contrary to Islam...Do not do such things."[22] As on so many previous occasions, his word was law.

Both sides complied, partly because Khomeyni had ordered it, partly because they wanted to reexamine their relative positions and prepare themselves for the next round. The first round had gone to the pragmatists: it was the radicals who had to desist. They continued to distribute pamphlets criticizing the negotiations with the US, but Rafsanjani's position was not hurt. In his public statements, he was forced to express more critical views of Washington. But even in doing so, he managed to address himself to Washington and Moscow simultaneously. In mid-December, for instance, he warned that Iranians must "not be deceived" by the "apparent kindness" of the superpowers because, both in Moscow and in Washington, "behind these smiles are hearts filled with animosity, greed, and hostility toward the Islamic revolution."[23] Also, in mid-December, in his capacity as the Imam's representative in the Supreme Council of Defense, he inspected the naval maneuvers in the Straits of Hormuz thereby demonstrating that his position was as firm as before. Considering the nature of the accusations against him, the fact that he did not lose power was a great victory for Rafsanjani and his group.

The outcome for him must be compared with the fate of his opponents. Mehdi Hashemi and his colleagues were arrested and Khomeyni himself permitted an investigation of their group. At a press conference on 14 December, the Minister of Intelligence, Muhammad Reyshahri, made charges against them of a kind hitherto reserved for outright enemies of the Islamic regime rather than rival groups within the Establishment. He said that their aim had been to contaminate the religious seminaries, the clerics and the revolutionary system "with their deviationist ideologies." For good measure, he added murder, kidnapping, past collaboration with the State Intelligence and Security Organization (SAVAK), secret illegal activities, possession of explosives, and plotting to subvert the Islamic revolution.[24] In a letter read over Radio Tehran, Montazeri urged Khomeyni to have the investigation pursued "remorselessly and with utmost care ...whatever the cost." He added that the fact that Hashemi was a relative of his should not stand in the way of a proper investigation.[25] He even offered to resign as successor designate, but his resignation was not accepted by Khomeyni. Sa'id Montazeri (the Ayatollah's son) and Hadi Hashemi (Mehdi's brother and the Ayatollah's son-in-law) also called for an "impartial" investigation of all charges.[26] Mehdi Hashemi was eventually released, but not before he had appeared on television to confess his crimes (as had been the practice in the past with other opponents of the regime: Ayatollah Kazem Shari'atmadari, Sadeq Qotbzadeh, the *Mujahidine Khalq* and the *Tudeh*). As other "enemies of the revolution" had done, Hashemi said that the "right attitude of prison interrogators and officials" had enabled him to give deep thought to his past deeds. He had become convinced that he fully deserved Khomeyni's description of him as a "deviate and plotter."[27] His trial was scheduled for 1987.

The domestic developments following the arms deals, as described here, allow one of the following conclusions to be drawn:

First, it was not a matter of a few individual moderates but rather of a significant group (in fact most of the leading politicians) who turned to the West in an attempt to strengthen their country and their regime. Most of them were motivated by fear of the Soviet Union and were seriously interested in better ties with Washington.

Second, the Iranians in contact with the Americans wished only to secure arms for the front, without any serious consideration of a pro-American shift in Iranian foreign policy. All they wished to do was to trick the Americans and Israelis into shipping them weapons without giving anything in return.[28]

Third, some of the people involved (on both sides) viewed the arms shipments as a lever to organize a coup and put the "moderates" into exclusive power in Iran.[29]

It is, of course, possible that different actors had a different — or even more than one — aim in mind. But an analysis of all known facts points to the conclusion that the second and third interpretations take too narrow a view of the Iranian situation. If the first interpretation is correct (or at least was the dominant one), the issue of arms sales can hardly teach us much about the power struggle. After all, that struggle was not between Hashemi (and revolutionaries of his cast of mind) on the one hand and men like Rafsanjani and Khameneh'i on the other. Hashemi and his ultraradical associates may yet become important and their ideology may turn out to be pivotal. But, at present, they are certainly subsidiary figures, on the margin of the main struggle within the Establishment in which President Khameneh'i and Speaker Rafsanjani are the protagonists.

At the core of the controversy — alongside, if not subject to, the personal rivalry for power — are social and economic policies. Consistent with his previous statements (see *MECS* 1984-85, p 436) Rafsanjani spoke of "two relatively powerful factions" with different views "on the way the Government should be run." These two streams, he said, existed "in the *Majlis*, in the Government, within the clergy, within the universities and across the society as a whole." They may in fact be regarded, he added, as "two parties without names."[30] The Prime Minister, while admitting that two wings in fact existed, said they were not engaged in *inteqad* (criticism) but in *inteqam* (vengeance) against each other.[31] Judging from his many speeches over the last eight years, it seems that Rafsanjani is the most pragmatic among the leaders of the first rank. As noted above, he has frequently come out in favor of moderation and gone on record as being willing, under certain circumstances, to consider improving relations with the US. According to most sources, it was he who was behind the contacts with the Americans. When preparing the Tehran meeting, the Iranians indicated that Rafsanjani would personally "come as the head of the Iranian side."[32] When the story was leaked, he had to admit that negotiations had in fact taken place, but he neither apologized nor gave an order to break off the contacts altogether.[33]

It is this author's view that Rafsanjani continues to be the most powerful leader of revolutionary Iran, second only to Khomeyni. At least since his renomination as Prime Minister in 1985, Musavi has been his protégé, and Rafsanjani is clearly in the ascendancy. By contrast, Khameneh'i's position seems to have weakened since his reelection in 1985 (see *MECS* 1984–85, pp 425–29). One way for him to strengthen his position again could be to identify with the extremists, but this would involve an all-out confrontation with Rafsanjani, the outcome of which he could not predict.

THE STATUS OF MONTAZERI

While the arms affair has thus not appreciably altered the relative strength of the protagonists in the current power struggle, its effect on the succession issue and the status of Montazeri as the designated future "leader" of Iran may well turn out to be important. Under the principle of *Velayate Faqih* (the rule of the jurist-consul), as developed by Khomeyni and incorporated into the 1979 Constitution, Khomeyni assumed all spiritual and temporal authority. That poses the question of whether Montazeri (or any other successor, for that matter) will be capable of doing so to the same extent. Montazeri lacks Khomeyni's standing as a religious scholar and has neither his charisma nor his popular support. Now public opinion is likely to group him together with Hashemi, and the fact that he was forced to offer his resignation as the successor-designate has undoubtedly affected his status. He can no longer claim to be above the struggling camps, and what is more the group he was identified with turned out to be the weaker one.

Even since Montazeri's nomination in November 1985 (see *MECS* 1984–85, pp 433–35) many Iranians have had second thoughts about the wisdom of nominating him as the sole successor. Some students and supporters of the other Grand Ayatollahs (mainly of Reza Golpaygani and Abul-Qasem Kho'i),[34] who had not supported his selection in the first place, now came out openly against him, among them Shaykh Lotfollah Safi and Seyyed Hasan Taheri Khorramabadi (from among Golpaygani's followers) and Ayatollah Shaykh Hasan Vahid-Khorasani and Ayatollah Seyyed Kavakebi (both disciples of Kho'i's).[35] These clerics — men from the second and third rank of the religious Establishment — are also important figures among the pragmatists (see the attached list). Some other clerics — prominent in their own right, although not Grand Ayatollahs — had also challenged Montazeri's nomination all along. One of them, Ayatollah Sadeq Ruhani, has declared that he considers himself no less qualified than Montazeri. Some other Ayatollahs (for example, Hasan Azari-Qomi) may also see themselves as candidates for the future leadership.[36]

All these and a few other Ayatollahs now seem to favor the formation of a Council of Leadership, rather than a single successor. The idea was publicly raised by Ayatollah Muhammad Shirazi. Some of the clerics-turned-politicians, including Rafsanjani, may now also prefer this solution (although in 1985 Rafsanjani supported Montazeri's nomination; see *MECS* 1984–85, pp 433–34). Some more prominent clerics probably support the idea in the expectation of becoming members of the Council (e.g. Ayatollah 'Ali Meshkini).[37] Another challenge may come from other communities elsewhere. Some experts, for example, believe that Shaykh Fazlollah, the *Hizballah* leader from Lebanon, by virtue of his religious scholarship and revolutionary posture, is no less qualified than Montazeri. But it is unlikely that the Iranians will agree to a non-Persian assuming the position of *Velayate Faqih*, which is almost always held by an Iranian. (There was, however, one recent exception when Ayatollah Hakim, an Arab, held the position in the 1970s.) In addition, those inclined toward the *Hujjatiyyah* have always preferred the principle of collective leadership (see *MECS* 1981–82, pp 535–40). One way or another, establishment support for a Council of Leadership has grown ever since the news of the arms deals leaked in November 1986. Moreover, unrelated to that affair, Montazeri had made more enemies for himself when he began, soon after his nomination, to carve out a personal power base and to behave, as his detractors put it, like a "young Khomeyni." As a Muslim diplomat who has met him several times put it: "He is his own man and has grown with the job."[38]

If the issue of Khomeyni's succession was a major challenge facing the regime even before the events of 1985–86, the latter made it more visible and even more crucial. If Khomeyni wishes to spare Iran the upheavals of a contested succession, and if he remains convinced that the future of the Islamic Republic is better served by a single successor than by a collective leadership that is bound to engage in infighting, he can still bolster Montazeri's chances. An unequivocal and outspoken endorsement of his candidacy by Khomeyni in his lifetime, or even in his testament, could well tip the scales — Montazeri's recent loss of status notwithstanding — at least for his initial period in power. However, although Khomeyni has made it known that under the circumstances Montazeri is his favorite candidate, he has never shown any marked enthusiasm for him. To ensure an uncontested succession, Khomeyni would have to throw his full weight behind Montazeri and back him unreservedly.

As long as he is alive, Khomeyni can probably rely on his hold over the masses and the leadership alike to prevent open conflict within the Establishment. To quote from Qorbanifar, he is "beyond the law of nature." In his memorandum of May 1985, Khashoggi added that all those mentioned in domestic and foreign media as individuals with power and influence should be considered only as "pawns" who have the support of Khomeyni at a given time and on a specific case. But if it is permissible to speculate, one might argue that the Islamic revolution has already passed its peak. The authority of the *Velayate Faqih* as currently exercised by Khomeyni will probably not survive him. With regard to one of its basic elements the future regime — even if led by his disciples — will no longer function in keeping with Khomeyni's doctrine. If and when that occurs, internal strife is bound to assume threatening proportions.

Even if one faction of his disciples wins, it seems likely that its rule will be considerably different from that of Ayatollah Khomeyni.

(For a tentative listing of the comparatively pragmatic and the more extremist groups, see the Appendix.)

THE ECONOMY, THE WAR AND THE GROWING OPPOSITION

ECONOMIC REPERCUSSIONS

The economy continued to be beset in 1986 by the same major problems that had affected it in previous years, some of them dating to the emergence of the revolutionary regime. First was the revolutionary process and the insecurity it had engendered since 1977–78, which had led to a serious deterioration of the economy. Since 1980, the war with Iraq had compounded these problems and added others. Finally, the world oil glut and the sharp decline of oil prices made it difficult for Iran to augment its oil revenues as a means of financing the economy. The rapid population growth (see below) made all these factors increasingly more threatening. (For similar problems in the first years of the revolution, see: *MECS* 1981–82, pp 545–49; 1982–83, pp 527–31; 1983–84, pp 450–53; and 1984–85, pp 441–45). In 1986, growing public resentment became noticeable — both among the upper-middle classes and, more significantly, among the masses. For Khomeyni's regime, which had pledged to serve the *mostaz'efin*, this was not only frustrating but also potentially dangerous. Signs of growing disillusionment among the lower strata of society, already visible in previous years, appeared in greater magnitude in 1986.

The drop in oil prices constituted the main immediate problem. As in many fields, the Government's reaction was on two different levels: in its public declarations for foreign and domestic consumption it denied that there was any significant problem; behind the scenes, however, it tried to control the problem and limit its implications. How important this issue was one can learn not only from the heavy dependence of the economy on oil income, but also from the place allocated to the issue in the media and in the speeches of revolutionary leaders.

Outwardly, Iran claimed that the drop of oil income was not likely to harm it. The Prime Minister said that his country could survive without exporting oil at all. Rafsanjani added that Iran had other economic resources and, anyway, the people were willing to suffer economic hardships for the sake of their revolution.[39] Nevertheless, there were clear indications of economic repression, many development projects were postponed or canceled, and a new economic policy was formulated (see below).

The decline of oil income was a twofold problem: one was the result of the war (difficulties in production, shipment and securing markets); the other had to do with the sharp decline in oil prices in the international market. The solution for the first was still partly in Iranian hands; over the second they had only marginal control. To "solve" the second problem they could only criticize the Organization of Petroleum Exporting Countries (OPEC) and non-OPEC countries for allowing such a drop in prices. For example, in an interview late in January, Husayn Kazem-pur Ardebili (the Deputy Oil Minister for International Relations) criticized Britain and Norway and called for cooperation between all oil exporters. The main reason for the continued decline in oil prices, he said, was psychological; therefore, oil exporters should strive to change the conviction that prices would continue to fall.[40] It was not sufficiently clear how critical the Iranian situation was, but there were growing indications that it was creating greater pressure than previously.

To solve the first problem the Iranians (still unwilling to end the war) took a variety of steps to adjust their economy to face the new realities and to secure public support. Outwardly, the Government tried to make it appear as if it was "business as usual." The leaders claimed that Iran could survive (and continue the war) even if "one drop of oil" was not exported. At the same time they tried — more than in the past — to lower expectations (and called on people not to seek quick material rewards) and not to indulge in "consumerism"; they also blamed foreign countries for conspiring to lower the price of oil in order to weaken the revolution.[41] It mainly blamed the US and its regional "slaves" (i.e., Saudi Arabia and Kuwait), other OPEC members, oil importers (mainly Japan, Israel and West Germany), and non-OPEC oil exporters (Britain and Norway). Typical was the claim by the Prime Minister that "today, we are stronger than ever." He added: "We declare today that despite the economic pressure, the imposed war and despite these countries' conspiracies ...none of these conspiracies will halt our movement toward a self-sufficient economy...They had the futile hope that economic pressure would harm us. But it did not happen."[42] In a different vein, admitting that in fact the country was experiencing economic difficulties, Iranian leaders called the people to be ready for material sacrifice for the sake of Islam.[43] Montazeri went so far as to say that the growing economic difficulties may mean that "we will all have to fast."[44]

To meet the challenge of diminishing income, Tehran also used diplomatic channels — sometimes using the "carrot" and on other occasions the "stick" — to persuade Saudi Arabia and other regional OPEC members to support its policies. Tehran even announced its readiness to halve its oil sales to prop up prices. The Deputy Minister of Foreign Affairs, Shaykh al-Islam, who went in March to Saudi Arabia to deal with the oil crisis, among other things, declared his country's readiness to stop exports altogether to force the price down.[45] At the same time, Tehran endeavored to coordinate its oil policy with revolutionary OPEC members (mainly Libya and Algeria). More practically, it decided to continue with its plan to construct a pipeline to bypass Kharg; labored to reconstruct the damage caused by Iraqi air raids and to prevent further raids; pressured exporters of goods to Iran to buy more of its oil; warned Iraq not to attack its oil terminals; and strove to reach an understanding with Iraq, through friendly states, to avoid further damage to oil terminals. However, it did not have much success in any of this.

Iran also did its utmost to sell as much oil as it could at the highest possible prices. Thus, while initially Tehran accused Riyadh of selling out by agreeing to a market-price mechanism, Iran itself agreed to sell oil under a netback agreement.[46] Also, it started (without much publicity) to review its economic plans and to postpone some projects. Thus it subsequently had to drop its plan to build a pipeline to bypass vulnerable Kharg Island because it could not produce the financing.[47] At the same time, it put more pressure on its debtors, such as France, to repay the sums owed (see Foreign Relations, below).

Faced with a decline in oil income as well as non-oil exports, and huge expenses (financing the war, among other things), the Government sought to increase taxation.

However, like its other major economic moves in the past — involving land reform and the nationalization of foreign trade — this initiative created fierce internal controversy. Some of the arguments for and against the proposed legislation were social and economic (the need to finance the war and strengthen the economy, against apprehension that the tax burden would fall mainly on the lower strata); some were political (reflecting attitudes toward the private sector and the middle class in general); and others doctrinal (revolving around contradictory interpretations of Islamic concepts of taxation).

Aware of the need to secure the proper running of the State, Musavi's Government (backed by Khameneh'i, Rafsanjani and apparently Khomeyni himself) supported the bill, which they had already presented in 1985 (see *MECS* 1984–85, pp 443–44). They argued that, in order to achieve the goals of the Islamic revolution, the economy's dependence on oil had to be terminated, and this was possible mainly through taxation. Moreover, they argued, while the issue of taxation was in fact controversial in Islam, taxation in time of war is undoubtedly permitted. The religious rulings against taxation, they added, were announced under usurper and anti-Islamic governments (including that of the Shah); but since the regime was now Islamic and the income would serve the people, the measure was undoubtedly legal. The Minister of Economy said that the aim was to gain — in five to ten years — some 80-90 per cent of the Government's income from taxes. Musavi explained that one of the basic goals of the proposed law was to "provide social justice" — through the law, "the Government wants to put the distribution of revenues on its proper course, based on Islamic religious law and the Constitution." He also emphasized "the counterinflationary effect" of taxation and went on to explain: "Our expenditures are for the defense and expansion of Islam, we have a global aim in spreading Islam" (see sources, below).

The opponents of the proposed legislation claimed that, according to Islamic law, the only legal taxes were the dues paid to the religious Establishment. To prove this they cited religious decrees by prominent clerics in the past, as well as contemporary religious authorities and the writings of Khomeyni himself (while he was still in opposition). Moreover, they argued, although taxation under emergency conditions was permitted, its provisions (i.e., duration, purposes and amount) had to be specified. They also claimed that, given past experience, the burden would fall only on the dispossessed and that, in any case, the Government had enough income from other sources (oil, mines, etc).[48]

After a long silence, the Government tried once again to push the legislation through in May 1986. It held seminars and explained further the need for taxation. But as was the case with similar laws, this piece of legislation reflected the ongoing doctrinal-political controversies within the ranks of the clerics (including opposition from the *Hujjatiyyah*), as well as the growing need for alternative sources of income to compensate for lower amounts coming in from oil. Although the *Majlis* discussed the bill and approved some of its clauses,[49] it did not become law in 1986. The 1986–87 budget, however, was already based on greater taxation and immediately became yet another cause for resentment by the public in general and the Bazaar and the private sector in particular. The Government itself admitted that, compared with the private sector, the wage earners already paid much more tax than their share. But such statements only antagonized the wage earners and the private sector.

The Government continued to claim that the economic problems were not critical and were certainly unlikely to affect the war or the supply of goods for the *mostaz'efin*.[50] But by the summer of 1986, it had to admit that some basic modifications in the budget and the economic plans were essential. On 24 June, the Prime Minister announced a "new" economic policy.

Presenting his plan, Musavi once again blamed all the economic difficulties on superpower conspiracies and expressed the hope that "not only will the fall in price of oil not defeat our system, but it will create new directions for our economy and move us more rapidly toward achieving [our aims]." Nevertheless, he added that Iran's foreign exchange earnings for the current Persian year (from March 1986) were estimated after three months at only half of what had been anticipated when the budget was first drawn up. He said that due to the drop in oil prices the budget for 1986–87 has been pared by $7.8 bn. Although he made it clear that the economic situation was "serious," he stressed that the Government's new policy would enable the country to cope with the crisis.

The new economic policy — like previous ones — emphasized the following points: the war would remain the Government's top priority; greater attempts would be made "to cut off dependence on oil and keep the level of productive employment as high as possible"; priority would be given to agriculture; in order to provide the minimum basic requirements of the people, subsidies, rationing and price controls would be maintained and additional products would be added to the list of rationed goods; there would be greater control of imports, and many items regarded as "luxuries" would not be imported. Musavi also promised that the Government would continue to operate and invest in the major industrial projects. But he also appealed for cooperation:

> We would like you [the people] to calculate your minimum requirements for essential goods, bearing in mind the revolution, the war and the Government's expenditure...We have to save and economize in order to be able to stand on our own feet. We have to cut down our consumption, particularly of imported goods.[51]

One paper summarized the plan as "more rationing, fewer luxuries."[52] The Minister of Finance and Economic Affairs, Muhammad Javad Irvani, using more positive terms, said "the policy is to economize." He admitted that under the new policy "the development projects will inevitably go through a shrinking phase."[53] The Minister of Heavy Industry, Behzad Nabavi, was not satisfied with the new policy either. He claimed that the Government was "unable to carry out many of its revolutionary programs and it acts cautiously." He went on to explain: "Part of the caution is because of opposition; and some of the fear of opposition causes us not to go after uncertain things. Our policy has [also] been to stay away from those areas that might cause ideological [i.e., doctrinal] clashes in society." Personally, he believed that Iran could not afford to send 150,000 pilgrims to Mecca only to "hold the record for the number of pilgrims sent there." Also, under the restraints of hard currency, he said, "it does not make sense for us to spend $400m annually for some of our young people to study abroad." Referring more generally to the Government's economic policy to confront the decline in oil income, he claimed: "In this regard I have to tell you frankly that the Government has no plans...The Government is not following a clearly defined economic policy."[54] A former governor of the Central Bank, reviewing the general economic trends, was no less critical. He said that "the attempts by the executive bodies... to put our affairs in...order have not yet borne fruit."[55]

Aware of the growing public discontent and criticism of the Government (provoked mainly by the economic situation and the war), Khomeyni came to its support. In a speech on 30 August, he warned critics of the Government's record and said it had done "great work." He advised critics to think of the difficulties the Government was facing.[56] Responding to resentment in the Bazaar circles, Montazeri — much to the distaste of Musavi — advised giving the private sector more room for economic activity. All in all, he preached — as he had many times previously — for greater tolerance of individual differences, and called on officials to serve the people, eliminate their difficulties and meet their requirements. In short, "try to keep the people satisfied." But such speeches, which revealed the mounting criticism against the Government, could not calm tensions.[57] Some people, Khomeyni stressed, had even claimed that "the economy is such that Iran is bankrupt." However, even official studies of the economy often described mounting difficulties.[58]

The foreign media disclosed from time to time information on demonstrations in Tehran against the difficult economic conditions. Thus, according to one source, Muslim militants on motorcycles protested in mid-May against high food prices in Tehran and presented a petition calling for the use of force against "bloodsucking middlemen." Quoting Khomeyni as saying that "the powerful only understand the language of force," the protesters said that given his permission, they would ransack the shopkeepers' warehouses. The paper *Abrar*, carrying the petition, also attacked high prices in an editorial entitled "Wolves Have No Mercy, even for Fasting People" — it was Ramadan at the time.[59]

Clearly, the economic problems left their mark on morale. The drop in oil income affected the services the Government was able to provide. Nonetheless, the Government continued to express optimism. In October, the leaders pointed to the removal of Zaki Yamani (from his post as Saudi Arabia's Oil Minister) as a turning point in the battle for a dramatic increase in oil prices. But they were forced to admit that serious problems did in fact exist. Musavi said that the country's enemies "had exerted economic pressures on Iran" in order "to push it to compromise."[60] His occasional rosy descriptions of the economy notwithstanding, he termed the current year as "the year of a great test" as far as the economy was concerned.

Tangible evidence of the crisis was the decision, in October, to reintroduce fuel rationing. The Ministry of Energy warned that, "due to restrictions on energy production at certain power stations, the national grid will face power shortages."[61] It must be stressed that such problems in the past (both under the Monarchy and again under the Islamic Republic) had caused much resentment and even led to demonstrations. Not only were the economic problems more tangible now, but their connection with the continuing war had become more evident. Moreover, the *mostaz'efin*, who had sacrificed most (both to the success of the revolution and to the war effort), were now the first to suffer again.

The constant increase of the population and accelerated urbanization made the Government's work more difficult. The 1986 census (the first under the Islamic regime) showed a population growth of 11m since the revolution — from 37m in 1979 to 48m in 1986. The current rate of population growth is 3.5 per cent a year. More than half of the population were under the age of 20. The prospect for the future was even more ominous.[62] A sociologist in one of the leading Iranian universities gave the author the following statistics of births in Iran: in 1978, there were 1.338m births (and 127,857 deaths); in 1981, there were 2.421m births (178,099 deaths); because of the war there was a temporary decrease in the number of births (2.101m in 1982) and since then a renewed growth was registered. The process of urbanization was similarly pressing hard, with all Government's plans to curb it clearly having failed.

Iraq's successful attacks on Iranian economic targets in general and on oil installations in particular (mainly since August 1986) considerably aggravated these problems. According to *The Middle East Economic Survey*, between August and October 1986 Iranian oil exports dropped from 1.6m barrels per day (b/d) to 0.8m b/d. In Kharg, only one berth was then operative; the attacks on Sirri in August forced the Iranians to move further south, to Larak, which was also attacked later.[63]

From the above, the following conclusions can be drawn: first, Iran was facing serious economic problems; second, there was growing popular resentment; third, and even more serious, was the fact that people were now aware of the link between their economic distress and the war. Although the regime still seemed strong enough to meet such challenges, the economy was in serious trouble.

THE WAR WITH IRAQ

After a long interval and following repeated threats to launch the "final and decisive attack," Iran embarked on a major offensive, "Dawn [*Fajr*] Eight," on the eve of the seventh anniversary of the establishment of the Islamic regime. Although it took Iran a step further into Iraqi territory (where it occupied Faw) and gave it psychological and tactical gains, it fell short of securing a decisive strategic advantage. Iranians themselves proved reluctant to refer to this attack (and the subsequent "Dawn Nine" launched a couple of weeks later) as the long-awaited "final attack." The only other major military attempt in May, in the Mehran area, did not give them a significant breakthrough either. In a way, these operations were only a continuation of the fairly constant pattern of the war, which first became discernible in spring 1982: while the initiative remained almost entirely with the Iranians, it was nevertheless in line with the pattern of intermittent Iranian offensives — vigorous though local in character and separated by rather long intervals. True, this time the operations were much more impressive and the gains more strategically important. But like the previous sporadic operations, they did not prove decisive in terms of war-winning strategies.

While in earlier years the war was regarded as an asset for revolutionary Iran (see *MECS* 1981–82, pp 543–45), in 1986 there were growing signs that it had already turned into a burden. But in its public statements, Iran continued to cling to its old slogans, rejecting any compromise. Certainly no new policy had the blessing of the Ayatollah himself. They all continued to support the idea of "war, war until victory." Yet, clearly, Iran was now experiencing more military and economic difficulties. At the end of the year it was in no better position to win the war than it had been at its outset. Moreover, Iraq, which had long failed to carry out any serious military operation, succeeded in upsetting the Iranians, mainly with its air raids on oil terminals and oil installations, its use of chemical weapons,[64] its attacks against civilians and such "operations" as shooting down a Fokker plane in March and killing 46 people.[65]

The lack of breakthrough in the war, its resultant economic burden and the casualties seemed finally affecting — more seriously than before — Iranian public opinion. Now it was not only the opposition which criticized the continuation of the war (including the Freedom Movement and the *Hujjatiyyah*), but also prominent clerics (including, reportedly, Ayatollah Kho'i)[66] and apparently other segments of society (including many of the *mostaz'efin*).

The Freedom Movement, which had previously criticized the continuation of the war (see *MECS* 1984–85, pp 439–40), stepped up its opposition. In a "plan" it formulated to end "the endless war" it stated: "This vicious war will produce only the destruction of Iran and the ruin of Islam and Shi'ism...Because of the war our country has lost its independence; this war has distorted our image in the world; we have become [viewed as] a group of terrorists who enjoy killing, destruction and devastation." It argued that after the recapture of Khorramshahr, Iran should have ended the war "in a way pleasing to God and to the Iranian people. But those who want the war as a cover for their actions found in its continuation a means to preserve their power."[67] In a statement issued on 22 June, the movement added that since the capture of Khorramshahr "we had one through nine *al-Fajrs* [i.e., Dawn operations] each was supposed to end the dark nights and establish our flags of victory ...But the movement is still continuing and it seems like we are still where we started and have a long way to go."[68] Similarly, *Mujahidine Khalq* and other opposition movements criticized the regime for failing to end the war. The National Council for Resistance published a plea for peace, signed by 5,000 politicians from 57 countries supporting its 1983 peace plan.[69] Many Iranians had come to believe that it was a mistake not to end the war; all of them pointed to the recapture of Khorramshahr as the golden — but lost — opportunity.

Confirmation of the growing resentment at home was provided by Khomeyni himself. In a speech on 24 March, he referred to "those criticizing" the continuation of the war. Defending charges that it was unIslamic to fight Muslims — as was often argued by opponents of the war — he made three points: the Imam 'Ali himself led wars against Muslims; the Iraqi regime was not truly Islamic; and Iran was not attacking anyone but only defending itself.[70] Admitting that some groups — mostly of the educated class — were "asking for a peace of conciliation," he made it clear that his country was determined to continue the war until victory.[71] Rafsanjani also claimed that "the liberals at home" were calling to terminate the war in terms even worse than those pressed by Washington.[72]

The ongoing war and the growing number of casualties (coupled with other social, economic and political hardships), intensified the disagreements within the Establishment and, most profoundly, between the Army and the Revolutionary Guards (RG). Aware of a potential threat from the Army, the revolutionary leaders had extolled the parts played by the RG and the *Basij*, Islam and Allah himself in the victories, but were careful not to give the Army too much credit — a deliberate policy to prevent it from becoming a political threat to the regime. Similarly, no individual general was given the opportunity to appear as a hero or to posture as a savior of the nation. Also, the Islamization of the Army and the constant purges had significantly changed its composition. However, gradually, Khomeyni called upon the people to support the Army, which he claimed had already proven its loyalty to Islam and the revolution. It was, he said, "our divine duty" to support the Army.[73] Yet he appealed to the Army and the RG to unite and not allow disagreement among them to threaten the revolution.[74] There have been many unsubstantiated reports of frictions between these two military bodies, because the RG were concentrating too much power, and because the Army advocated more careful military operations to avoid casualties. The very fact that the Imam himself summoned officers, and aired the frictions publicly, suggested that the problem had gradually grown more serious.

Another challenge was presented by diminishing revolutionary zeal and the greater difficulties Iran was experiencing in recruiting volunteers. Khomeyni repeatedly called on all able-bodied men to go to the fronts.[75] Similar appeals were made by Rafsanjani, Musavi and Khameneh'i.[76] There was also a special appeal for women to join up; in July, the first group of women completed military training.[77] The media subsequently reported an "enthusiastic popular response" and the dispatch of volunteers to the fronts. But revolutionary zeal was unmistakably flagging. Such a conclusion was further supported by the clerics' attempts to encourage support for the war. For example, in a Friday sermon appealing for mass conscription, which he delivered in Tehran in April, Ayatollah Kashani reminded the people that "weakening the war is tantamount to the weakening of Islam and the Prophet."[78] Warnings against draft dodgers also attested to similar difficulties. In August, the public relations office of the Gendarmerie announced that those failing to report for service would be "punished" by having their period of service extended.[79] If such measures were in fact needed, it was clear that the revolution was experiencing more problems in recruiting volunteers than it previously had.

Despite all this, however, Tehran continued to cling to the slogan "war, war until victory"; it was unwilling even to entertain the idea of *rapprochement*. Khomeyni made it clear that "as long as this 'Aflaqi [Ba'th] Party exists, we will fight to remove this cancerous tumor."[80] Rafsanjani echoed this, stressing that the downfall of Saddam Husayn himself would not be sufficient reason for ending the war — the Ba'th Party should be toppled.[81] Rejecting any mediation, he claimed that "cease-fire is worse than war."[82] Rafsanjani was undoubtedly speaking for the entire leadership when he said in May that the only way to end the war was to destroy the Ba'th regime in Iraq.[83] Other leaders followed suit.[84] Early in the year they had claimed that that particular Persian year (ending on 20 March 1987) would be the last year of the war. Rafsanjani said in March 1986: Last year was the "year of resistance" and this year will be "the year of victory."[85] Mohsen Reza'i, the Commander of the RG, added in May that "the fate of the Iraqi-imposed war will be determined this year," and that on orders from Khomeyni Iran had decided "to implement an extensive program for the continuation of the war and achievement of a quick and ultimate victory."[86]

Although in their official declarations the leaders of Iran tried to play down the pressure of the war, it was clear from their announcements that they were worried — much more so than in previous months. In several speeches during June, Rafsanjani, Khameneh'i, Shirazi (the Commander of the Ground Forces), Reza'i and other leaders acknowledged that there was in fact a clear improvement in the Iraqi posture. Moreover, while previously they had asserted that time was on the side of the Iranians, they now hinted that time was running out. Rafsanjani admitted in June that the Iraqis had recently launched a series of "suicide operations" (i.e., attacks) against Iran. He expressed confidence that these attacks were doomed to fail, but nonetheless revealed some concern. He therefore called for massive recruitment to prepare for a final strike against the Iraqis, with the aim of ending the war "immediately," or, as he said in another Friday sermon, "this year." He added that Iran "should no longer allow any time to our enemies," and that "the political conditions and the other problems oblige us to bring the war [soon] to a desired point."[87] Although he claimed that Iran could in fact prolong the war "forever," it was the first time the Iranians stated it as their goal to end the war "this year." Moreover, Rafsanjani claimed that Iran was now "at a juncture where this issue [the war] must be settled."[88] President Khameneh'i expressed (again, for the first time) exasperation with the absence of any light at the end of the tunnel. He said: "We must break out of this no-war, no-peace situation which is definitely harming us." He went on to advocate "another blow like the Faw offensive [in February]."[89] He, and Mohsen Reza'i, also called for an end to the war "once and for all."[90] Col Shirazi (who was generally given the credit for shifting Iranians tactics in 1982–83 from massive, bloody, offensives to smaller scale attacks) also sounded a note of impatience. He stressed, in June, that Iran should launch offensives "to determine the outcome of the war as soon as possible." He added: "We should not be satisfied with limited military operations under the present circumstances. *Time is an important factor for Iran* [author's emphasis]."[91]

Aware of the devastating effects of such statements, but also of the difficulties of gaining a clear-cut victory "this year," Rafsanjani tried (on 31 July) to lower expectations. At a press conference he said that the declarations regarding "the year of victory" did not mean "that the war will come to an end" this year but rather that "we hope to gain more considerable victories this year." Elsewhere, he added that although "there is no reason not to end the war this year," the previous statements only meant "that more remarkable victories are already planned."[92]

The stubborn Iranian policy notwithstanding, some difficulties were now having a greater effect on Tehran than they had earlier. The economic difficulties, the lack of a significant breakthrough at the fronts and the heavy casualties led to growing public resentment and disillusionment. While, previously, views against the war had been limited to opposition circles, more and more people from the lower strata were now voicing their dissatisfaction.

Faced with growing public resentment the leadership came out with declarations of confidence during "War Week" (in late September). They made it clear that their conditions for terminating the war remained unchanged; that they were gaining strength, and that Iraq was on the verge of final collapse. Typical were the words of Rafsanjani, who said that the Iranian "military situation, combat readiness, logistics and mobilization ...are the best they have been" since the beginning of the war. Elsewhere he claimed that people's "enthusiasm and eagerness to go to the fronts...is at an excellent level." Referring to the long-awaited offensive, he added: "We are ready for something big." The President, who also claimed that "people's preparedness to continue [the war]...is even greater" than in 1980, concluded that victory "is near."[93]

But the popular resentment continued. An interview with Khameneh'i, broadcast over Radio Tehran, revealed some of the questions worrying the people. Here are three of them presented as questions to the President:

> Another point of ambiguity that we wish to clear up is the statement that our objective in the war is to achieve a lasting peace. The question arises [among people]: How could a war lead to a lasting peace?

> Considering that the people's motivation in participating in war efforts is strengthened daily, how long do you believe this readiness on the part of the people will continue?
>
> [Some groups claim] that following the recapture of Khorramshahr ... and [at least after] the liberation of Faw, Iran had the opportune moment for negotiations; that is to say that Iran could have... [imposed] its conditions had negotiations taken place at these junctures. These parties state that similar occasions will not occur in the future, and that Iran will eventually have to accept negotiations under much worse conditions.[94]

Such highly critical questions were undoubtedly meant to provide Khameneh'i with an opportunity to remove some of the people's doubts — not to challenge the President. Yet they revealed — as the interviewer himself admitted — the kind of questions people were now asking.

While the first stages of the war had contributed to the consolidation of the regime, the fighting had now become a major cause of public resentment and turned into an important issue in the ongoing internal power struggle. Thus there were signs of disagreement over war strategy, not only between the RG and the professional Army, but also between leaders of the revolution themselves. Although none had given up the military option, some were nevertheless more willing to gain its political goal with a minimum of military risks. Rafsanjani, for example, seemed to have adopted a new strategy, aimed mainly at persuading Iraq's regional and international allies to end their support for President Saddam Husayn. To this end he increased his reassuring statements that his country was not willing to use force to export its revolution. Although many radicals (such as Mehdi Hashemi and his group) viewed such statements as "defeatist" and accused him of "treachery," many others supported such a modification in their country's war policy.[95]

Until a year or two previously, the war had been a source of "blessings" to strengthen clerical rule: it offered a focus for public attention and helped to inflame revolutionary-religious zeal; it served as a "good" excuse to explain (or, rather, explain away) the economic hardship; it kept the Army far from Tehran; and it encouraged unity among the revolutionary leadership. In 1986, however, it seemed that the benefits had been exhausted. The war had turned into a burden, and was no longer an asset.

THE OPPOSITION

Taken all in all, the consolidation of the regime went hand in hand with the steady weakening of the opposition. They continued to be divided and sterile, and, eventually, a growing helplessness became noticeable in their ranks. The domestic opposition could not go much beyond verbal criticism; their sporadic acts of terrorism — harmful as they were — could not influence the Government's policy let alone topple the regime. From abroad, they could hardly advance such a goal at all. Yet, the deteriorating economy, the endless war and its human cost, and the fierce internal struggle for power all breathed new life to the various opposition movements in 1986. At the end of the year, it was news of the arms deals with the US that turned into a focus of the opposition movements' criticism of the Government.

All movements stepped up their activities, but none seemed capable of capitalizing on the growing discontent to improve its position significantly. More critically, even the shared hatred of the clerics in power did not produce even a tactical alignment between them. Ideological divisions and personal conflicts were so deep that no single expatriate leader looked capable of unifying the groups for concerted action. Personal factors remained as divisive as ideological differences, if not more so. Group leaders tended to think of themselves as the future saviors of the nation to the exclusion of all others. Moreover, many expatriates claimed that 85–90 per cent of Iranians had now had enough of Khomeyni,[96] but none of their leaders knew how to take advantage of this situation, assuming it was so. None of the expatriate factions seemed to give any cause for real concern to the clerics in Tehran. If they were worried at all it was about the flagging revolutionary zeal within the *mostaz'efin* and the rifts within their leadership.

Late in February, Shahpur Bakhtyar left for the US (his third visit since the revolution), but the local media hardly mentioned it. He tried hard in his public lectures (mainly to Iranian dissidents) to play on the traditional American fears of spreading Communism. He said that most people (and "80 per cent" of the clerics) had had enough of Khomeyni, and that they might even turn to Communism "to liberate themselves from Khomeyni's tyranny."[97] But his audience remained mostly indifferent; and he did not do much to change the realities at home. In a message broadcast over a Baghdad-based radio station he asked the Iranians to help him overthrow "the present decadent regime." To achieve such a goal, he said, there should be "a complete unity of internal forces and their coordination with extraterritorial activities"; also, people should distance themselves "from indifference and despair."[98] But the opposition movements remained divided, and the people mostly indifferent.

As far as can be established, Reza Pahlavi did not go much beyond verbal criticism either. On 4 August, a meeting was held in Paris and attended by Reza. 'Ali Amini (a former Prime Minister and the leader of the Front for the Liberation of Iran), and Shahpur Bakhtyar joined in an attempt to unite Khomeyni's opponents and plan a concentrated action to topple the regime and restore a constitutional monarchy. The two former Prime Ministers were appointed initial members of the Council of Advisers to Reza Pahlavi. Their statement pointed to a major alliance among the groups favoring constitutional monarchy, but no major act was reported during the rest of the year.[99] While the meeting itself was important, the general posture of these groups was not seriously improved. Their main "success" in 1986 was to interrupt the state-controlled television service and get a ten-minute program on the air. Iranians watching television (on 5 September) were reportedly startled by the unauthorized appearance of Reza giving them the glad tidings that he would return to Iran and with their assistance save the country from Khomeyni's backward rule.[100] Tehran, however, denied the whole story.[101]

The *Mujahidine Khalq*, still the most organized opposition group, showed signs of fatigue. Yet, the growing disillusionment of the Iranian people and the need to move the group's headquarters from Paris (see Foreign Relations, below) encouraged greater activity on their part.

In June the *Mujahidin* leader, Mas'ud Rajavi, was pressured to leave France and moved his headquarters to Iraq. Tehran claimed a success in the very fact that Rajavi had been forced out of France. But concerning its actual gains, there have been different views. Some believed this would weaken the *Mujahidin*: first, because

Baghdad was a remote site from which to run an international movement; and second, because close ties with Iraq would, inevitably, disgust the Iranians (even those opposing Khomeyni), who had a strong hatred for Iraq (and they would be regarded traitors and collaborators.) Others believed that this would boost the *Mujahidin*: it would bring the leadership closer to Iranian territory and to their fighters. Yet others thought it would make no difference at all: their cooperation with Iraq was previously known to the Iranians, and their inactivity would not be affected by their transfer to Iraq. In the second half of the year it was not possible to draw a definite judgment although some signs of growing activity had become noticeable.[102] Their former ally, Abul-Hasan Bani Sadr, was mainly engaged in granting interviews (especially about the arms deals). He continued, however, to promise: "I will return triumphant."[103]

The Freedom Movement, led by former Prime Minister Mehdi Bazargan, continued to be the only important opposition movement within Iran that was still tolerated by the regime, but only to a degree. Early in the year Bazargan characterized the situation in the following terms: "We are in opposition and struggle, or perhaps it would be better if I say that the Government is struggling with us." The only freedom they still had, he added, was their Press, which had been attacked several times; the movement's contact with the people had not been cut off but was significantly reduced and closely guarded.[104]

In March, Bazargan announced the formation of a new opposition group named "The Association for the Defense of Freedom and Sovereignty of the Iranian Nation." Its 20-member Central Council was led by Bazargan and consisted of veteran politicians, most of them members of the Central Council of the Freedom Movement and seven members of Bazargan's 1979 provisional Government. The association made it clear that it resented the continuation of the war, the lack of freedom and the Government's economic policy.[105] They continued to voice criticism, and were often brutally attacked by the *Komitehs*.[106]

Toward the end of the year all opposition movements concentrated on ridiculing the arms deals with the US and Israel.

Other challenges came from the growing, yet disorganized, public dissatisfaction with the Government and its policy, and from some professional groups. Despite the increasing resentment in Bazaar circles, in July it was the physicians who challenged the Government. The Iranian Medical Association (IMA) called on its members throughout the country to strike for 24 hours on 14 July, to protest against "a campaign of intimidation" by the Government against the medical profession. In a harsh unprecedented announcement, the IMA said that the strike was necessary because of the Government's decision to appoint a new head for the organization (former Health Minister Dr Hadi Manafi) in violation of the IMA charter; it was also to protest the arrest and detention of four physicians, among them the elected president of the IMA, Dr Muhammad 'Ali Hafezi. The IMA also complained against the Government's failure to support medical schools and provide the number of physicians needed,[107] to build new hospitals and clinics, or even to improve existing facilities. They charged that, since the revolution, government funding for health care had been reduced to only 43 per cent in real terms of the amount devoted to it previously. Another sore point was the Government's monopoly on pharmaceutical imports; the physicians claimed that money was spent on "unnecessary or even harmful drugs" because a handful of *Hizballahi*s with no professional knowledge ran the import program. They further contended that in some cities local officials had confiscated hospitals in order to use them as dormitories for the RG or Qur'an schools. They bitterly complained of "mullahs interfering in medical matters beyond their competence," which in some cases had led to "grievous injury or death." The statement deplored the fact that many physicians had been arrested and others had been prevented from leaving the country with their families, who were thus kept as "hostages." (See sources, below.)

The 24-hour strike was successful enough to force the regime and the government-controlled media to acknowledge it publicly. The latter said that the strike was strong in north Tehran (the richer part of the city), but claimed that it was not observed by doctors elsewhere.[108] However, the fact that the authorities and the media reported the strike at all — the only strike covered prominently in the media since the revolution — indicated that it was so broad that it could not be ignored. Official statements confirmed that the strike was more than professional — it was of a political nature. Musavi said that the strikers had been incited by a "handful of opportunists and counterrevolutionary doctors." The Minister of the Interior said that the striking physicians were "agents of international Imperialism." Manafi claimed that their aim was "to confront the revolution," and Kho'iniha added that the strike was "a political move to confront the Islamic regime and not a guild movement."[109]

The strike and the nature of the accusations made by the physicians revealed the growing resentment among certain professional groups. Similar attitudes also existed among many university professors, lawyers, and even soldiers. The Government used typical revolutionary methods to deal with the problem: it made no concessions to its rivals; it portrayed independent action as antirevolutionary and anti-Islamic; and it incited the masses against the protesters on social and religious grounds. Yet the resentment felt by professional groups and their open criticism of the Govenment caused the regime just as much concern as the opposition movements in 1986.

FOREIGN RELATIONS

The revolutionary drive and the war with Iraq continued to mold Tehran's foreign relations in 1986. In ideological terms, continuity prevailed. The concept of "Neither the East nor the West" continued to guide relations with the superpowers. In regional policy, the objectives of "exporting" the revolution, mainly to neighboring Muslim states, and Muslim solidarity — even unity — persisted as primary goals. With regard to Iraq, the declared aim remained unchanged: "War, war until victory." In practice, however, there was a greater willingness to tone down the revolutionary spirit and allow more room for improving bilateral relations.

Contradictions between ideology and actual policies had, of course, characterized the foreign policy of the Islamic regime since its initial stages. In 1986, however, there were more signs of willingness to compromise, even on matters of doctrine. Iran had negotiated with the US (the "Great Satan") and Israel (its "illegitimate son") and even hosted their officials in Tehran (see above); and Iranian leaders, quieted their insistence on exporting the revolution. The conduct of foreign policy was guided in 1986 by more pragmatic considerations. Instead of rejecting both superpowers, Iran now tried to reduce tension with them. Downplaying aggressive policies toward the Muslim states, Iran now tried to buy their cooperation.

THE EAST AND THE WEST

Iranian "relations" with the US are covered elsewhere in this volume; partly above in this chapter in the section "Tehran and the American Arms," and partly in the essay on the US and the Middle East. This section deals with relations with the Soviet Union and France.

THE SOVIET UNION

As in the first seven years of the Islamic Republic, Iran's anti-American stand in 1986 did not produce a corresponding pro-Soviet turn: ideological tenets and political considerations made Moscow almost as repugnant as Washington. The main issues which overshadowed bilateral relations were the Soviet invasion of Afghanistan and arms shipments to Iraq. However, expediency dictated that relations with the Soviet Union should be less strained than those with the US. Therefore, Iranian policy toward the USSR was generally more cautious, and anti-Soviet sentiment was far less vigorous than were anti-American expressions. Bilateral relations in 1986 continued along similar lines of political tension, mistrust and mutual accusations, accompanied at the same time by an attempt to improve relations, mainly in the economic sphere (for Iranian anti-Soviet sentiments, see above).

After the strains created by Saddam Husayn's visit to Moscow in December 1985 (see *MECS* 1984–85, p 450) both sides tried to reduce tension. Early in February 1986, the Soviet Deputy Minister of Foreign Affairs, Georgy Markovich Kornienko, visited Iran. Tehran viewed the visit not only as a means to improve economic ties, but also to expand political dialogue. 'Ali Besharati, the Iranian Deputy Foreign Minister, explained that the visit had taken place "in view of the common historical background, good neighborly relations, good economic relations and...the long borders." Rafsanjani said in an interview that the visit was important not only for economic-technological relations "but also in conjunction with the war." After the visit, Rafsanjani said that the Soviets now better understood Iranian war policies. He added, however, that while there was improvement in economic relations between the two countries, several problems still existed in bilateral relations. Among them he specified the war, Afghanistan and the agreement for gas exports to the Soviet Union.[110]

In June, economic talks were held in Tehran. Among the topics discussed were Soviet plans for hydroelectric projects on the Arras river which forms part of the border between the two countries, the return of Soviet technicians pulled out by the Soviets two years earlier because of Iraqi air attacks, and the resumption of gas sales to the Soviet Union. The talks were described by both sides in highly positive terms but did not bear immediate results.[111] The discussions were followed up in August during visits to Mocow by two Iranian high-level economic delegations. The first delegation, early in the month, was led by Muhammad Javad Larijani, Deputy Foreign Minister for International and Economic Affairs; the second, two weeks later, was headed by Gholam Reza Aqazadeh, the Oil Minister. Both discussed expanding cooperation between the two countries in the issues concerning oil production and price. The conferees agreed on the formation of a joint commission for economic and trade cooperation to be convened in Tehran later in the year. Larijani reported that the two sides learned that "there are no major problems in the way of expanding mutual relations." He added that the Soviets "expressed an inclination" for finishing the projects they had earlier undertaken. Yet with regard to Afghanistan and Iraq, all the Iranians did was to make "our views known to them."[112] Of special importance were the discussions on resumption of gas sales to the Soviet Union and through it to Europe. Both countries were, by now, willing to work out an agreement for the resumption of gas exports, but they were divided on the question of the price. In their meetings they decided that experts of both countries would study the possibility of supplying the southern Soviet Union with Iran's gas and that Soviet experts would be involved in the Iranians' studies for the exploitation of gas and oil reserves in the Caspian Sea.

The discrepancy between economic and political relations became even more evident during the visit of the Iranian Oil Minister to Moscow in August. The two countries decided on renewal of exports of natural gas to the Soviet Union within a few months, though neither of them revealed how much the Russians would pay for the gas.[113] Two weeks later, Iranian gunboats intercepted two Russian ships for cargo inspection off the United Arab Emirates' shores. They were released two days later. It was the first time Iran, which routinely stops suspected ships in the Gulf, had acted against Soviet vessels. The Soviets strongly protested such "violation of freedom of navigation."[114]

Later in 1986, amidst the public debate on the Iranian deals with the US, Iran and the Soviet Union signed an important economic protocol at the conclusion of the tenth session of their joint economic committee in Tehran. Signed on 11 December, the protocol included Tehran-Moscow cooperation in the fields of trade; banking; transportation; construction of power stations; fisheries; house building; and other technical and industrial activity. It stipulated that high-level delegations representing the two countries would meet every six months and review the understandings reached and the methods by which they would be carried out. The protocol was signed by the visiting Soviet Chairman of the State Committee for Foreign Economic Relations, Konstantin Katushev, and the Iranian Minister of Finance and Economic Affairs, Muhammad Javad Irvani. During his four-day visit Katushev discussed expansion of Tehran-Moscow political and economic relations, among other topics, with Khameneh'i, Rafsanjani and Musavi.

Undoubtedly, the signing of the protocol, its stipulations, its timing and the very convening of the committee after a long interval were all significant. Yet, it is questionable whether this signals any political preference in favor of the USSR. Its significance seems mainly economic, not political. In his meeting with Katushev, Rafsanjani expressed hope that the Soviets would be serious "in strengthening and activating the two countries' relations and would seriously act in accordance with the content of the talks between the delegations." He went on to criticize Soviet support for Iraq, the way the Soviet media responded to the revelations of American arms shipments to Iran, and "massing up things in Afghanistan." He made clear that to "seriously" improve relations, such obstacles should be first removed: "If you really have a message for expanding relations, kindly do be serious and rest assured that the Islamic Republic in that case will be fully prepared to expand relations."[115] At the end of the period discussed, such problems still overshadowed bilateral relations.

FRANCE

Relations with France in 1986 were characterized by their ebbs and flows. Following some trends toward improved relations in the spring and summer of 1985 (see *MECS* 1984–85, p 451), tension returned to dominate the picture in the autumn. The main points of friction were — as in the previous years — French military shipments to Iraq, France's harboring the Iranian opposition, and France's debt of more than $1 bn (see below). Both sides were eager to improve relations. But — as was the case with Moscow — although economic relations seemed to be improving, political ties remained strained.

Early in January an official mission from Paris arrived at Tehran to seek ways to improve relations. The head of the Iranian delegation, Dr Mehdi Navab, pointed to some achievements but made clear the problems were too many and too complicated to be solved in one round of talks. Both sides were interested in improving their relations — mainly, but not only, for economic reasons — but the gap in their positions was still wide.[116] The talks continued the following month in Paris, concentrating on a long-standing source of friction. This was France's non-repayment of a $1 bn loan made by the former regime of the Shah. France's Atomic Energy Commission received the loan in 1974 to help pay for the construction of a uranium enrichment plant by the French consortium, Eurodif. But after the 1979 revolution, Tehran scrapped plans for a large-scale nuclear power industry and canceled its contracts with France. The loan plus interest was estimated at about $1.5 bn in 1982, when a French Appeal Court ruled that Eurodif had illegally withheld interest payments.[117] The Iranians made it clear in 1986, as Musavi put it — that France should "unconditionally return its debts" as a prerequisite for improving relations.[118] The Iranian Chargé d'Affaires in Paris made it clear that since it was France that caused the deterioration of relations, it should also take the first step toward normalization. The "unconditional repayment of Iran's loan" was specified as the Iranian precondition for improving relations.[119]

To remove such an obstacle, a French delegation headed by the Deputy Foreign Minister arrived in Tehran in April. While the French delegation expressed interest in improved relations, Iran again listed the "hostile" policy of France toward Iran: its support for Iraq, its debt to Iran, its hosting of the Iranian opposition, and its "basic animosity" to the revolution.[120] Both sides expressed willingness to bridge the gap, but this was still wide. Paris was willing to go far in its conciliatory tone and even "admitted" some mistakes in its relations with Iran in the past. But the Iranians were still waiting for "practical and positive steps" to prove French good intentions. Late in May, the Iranian Deputy Prime Minister for Political Affairs, Mo'ayeri, went to Paris to discuss bilateral relations. Tehran now laid down three main conditions for normalization: the return of the debt; blocking of arms shipments to Iraq; and extradition of Iranian "terrorists." Mo'ayeri made clear that, in addition to the payment of its debt, "France must prove its neutrality in the war." He added that "public opinion in Iran cannot accept that people who have killed their children [i.e., Iranian opposition leaders] ...be accepted in France." As always, Paris was willing to voice conciliatory positions, but the Iranians wanted proof rather than talk. Tehran made clear that the three conditions were inseparable, but it knew that France would find it difficult to change its policy toward Iraq. Repayment of the debt became the main issue for Tehran, which badly needed the money. France was more forthcoming on this point and promised to "solve the problem as soon as possible." Tehran continued to claim that this would not be enough. In the meantime, although the basic elements of friction — and mainly with regard to the war — were not removed, the atmosphere in bilateral relations was improving and economic ties prospering.[121] Prime Minister Chirac declared that his country was "ready to normalize relations" but emphasized France's determination to continue its close ties with Baghdad and his Government's unwillingness to extradite Iranian dissidents being sought by Tehran, most prominently, Mas'ud Rajavi. "France is not accustomed to expelling political refugees," he said. "It is absolutely out of question that it would take such measures."[122]

Soon after, that was exactly what France did. In June, after another round of negotiations in Paris, France forced Rajavi to move his headquarters from Paris to Baghdad; in return, two of the French hostages in Lebanon were released.[123] (See the chapter on Lebanon.)

Negotiations for settling the mutual financial claims were also in progress. Several rounds of talks took place during the summer and autumn, both in Paris and in Tehran.[124] To review the complexity of mutual relations the Foreign Ministers of the two countries convened in October in New York where they were attending the UN General Assembly. It was the highest level diplomatic meeting between the two countries' officials in recent years. This indicated that the two countries' policies aimed at resolving the problems hindering the normalization of relations. Referring to this meeting, Foreign Minister Velayati said: "Considering its unrealistic past relations, the present French Government has subjected the relations between the two countries to a process of readjustment and greater understanding."[125] Earlier, in mid-September, the Iranian Chargé d'Affaires in Paris met the French Foreign Minister and declared that the French Government had shown "a degree of goodwill" over the financial dispute. He expressed optimism that the problem would be solved in "a few weeks." Similarly, Paris expressed optimism over the fate of the hostages in Lebanon.[126] In mid-November, the two countries reached partial agreement on their financial differences. It stipulated a reimbursement of $330m as part of the loan. This sum was deposited in Iran's account on 22 November.[127] This was an important step forward in improving bilateral relations, but it did not resolve the financial dispute between the two countries, let alone their other differences — most profoundly the disagreement concerning Iraq and the war.

RELATIONS WITH THE MUSLIM AND THE ARAB WORLD

In its relations with the Arab world, Iran continued to combine the pragmatic considerations of national interest inherited from the past with the ideological spirit of the Islamic revolution. Over time, balance had clearly shifted in favor of pragmatic, national aims. (For earlier illustrations of such policies see *MECS* 1979–80, pp 485–86; 1980–81, pp 562–63; 1981–82, p 566; 1982–83, pp 542–44; 1983–84, p 456 and 1984–85, pp 452–53.)

In 1986 the war and the world oil glut were the main issues in Tehran's bilateral relations with the regional Arab states. As in 1985, this meant, above all, to keep as many Arab countries as possible from actively supporting Iraq, and to prevent a further decline of oil prices. To achieve such goals, Tehran intensified its diplomatic efforts and moderated its public declarations in an attempt to calm tempers among the Gulf states. Tehran did not abandon its radical ideology, nor did its neighbors believe it was willing to do so. The basic ideology prevailed, yet the tone changed considerably.

THE PERSIAN GULF

The war and the world oil glut convinced Tehran that it needed to improve its relations with the Gulf states. As since the early years of the new regime, in its relations with these states (mainly with Saudi Arabia and Kuwait) Iran continued to combine the carrot and the stick, but it was by now more willing to offer the carrot, while making clear that it carried a long stick as well.

In a Friday sermon on 28 February, Rafsanjani threatened Saudi Arabia, Kuwait and Iraq that Iran would "direct the war toward the oil regions," if they continued "their conspiracies." While Iraq attacks Iranian oil installations, he said, the other two were lowering oil prices. For Iran, he emphasized, that meant that the three "have a common policy."[128] Two weeks later he added, "Iran will no longer accept that your ports should receive arms shipments bound for Iraq...and that Iraqi oil pipelines should pass across your territory."[129] In another week, on the occasion of the Persian New Year, 21 March, he repeated his charges but also offered "good neighborly relations" if they would avoid supporting Iraq.[130] In July, he added that if they continued backing Iraq, his country "will consider them responsible for Iraq's acts of wickedness."[131] Referring to these countries in mid-August, Rafsanjani again threatened that if they continued their support for Iraq, Iran would consider them as activists in the war and reserve the right to take any revenge on them.

The President, blaming them for providing facilities for Iraq, similarly warned: "We will not let these facilities lie idle forever. When it becomes necessary we will deliver more decisive blows against those without whom Iraq could not carry out these wicked deeds."[132] In September, referring to Iraqi air raids on Iran's oil installations and the Gulf states' support for the disruption of Iranian oil exports, he warned: "Where necessary, we shall deal more resolute blows to those without whose help Saddam cannot carry out his mischief." He reiterated accusations that "certain regional states" had assisted Iraq in raids on the offshore oil terminal at Sirri. Similarly Rafsanjani warned Saudi Arabia and Kuwait, not to "overdo it." He added: "They must not think that Iran will not wage war against them because of its war with Iraq...All their installations are within range [of our weapons]."[133] The Prime Minister added that "the Gulf will be safe for Iran or for nobody."[134]

Yet, the leaders of revolutionary Iran have often coupled such threats with declarations of good intention. Khameneh'i made clear in March: "We are not desirous of extending the war beyond Iraqi territory."[135] A week later he added: "We do not want to spread the war beyond Iraq. It is no one's turn after Iraq, it will be the turn of peace and security."[136] Rafsanjani, disclaiming any Iranian threat to these states, said Iran was "ready to ignore the past ...if they amend their policy, it is forgivable."[137] Alluding to Iranian warnings, he said these should be considered as "counsels," not as "threats." He added, however, that "if we notice that our counsels, messages and practical warnings are of no avail" Iran will have to use power.[138]

The successful offensive in Faw was also used as a reminder that the war was going in Iran's favor and was likely to end in Iranian victory, sooner or later. Consequently, Iranians claimed, by supporting the Iraqis the Gulf neighbors were only throwing good money after bad, artificially prolonging Saddam Husayn's life and causing more bloodshed on both sides. In fact, the very location of "Dawn Eight," which brought Iranian troops close to Kuwaiti strategic centers, was intended to warn Kuwait and other littoral states to avoid supporting Baghdad. Rafsanjani declared that this was in fact one of the targets of the offensive.[139]

Yet, practically, Iran continued to show restraint. It sent conciliatory messages to the Gulf states declaring that it had no territorial ambitions on the Arab side of the Gulf and was seeking good neighborly relations.[140] In March, it sent high officials (including the Deputy Minister of Foreign Relations for Political Affairs) to the Gulf states to explain Iranian positions. At the same time, when some 2,000 students marched to the Saudi and Kuwaiti embassies on 12 March to protest against these countries' "conspiracies" in the war and their oil policy, they were blocked by policemen with truncheons and tear gas.[141]

Although tension with Saudi Arabia reached a peak during the annual *haj* (pilgrimage) to Mecca, compared with the tension during the pilgrimages in 1982 and 1983, Iran showed much self-restraint. Again and again, Tehran advised its people to refrain from independent initiatives and strictly follow the instructions of Iranian officials. Montazeri advised pilgrims to obey the group leaders and Muslim morale; he made clear that "violating the Islamic Republic's law is forbidden."[142] Khomeyni called on his countrymen to treat other pilgrims in an Islamic manner and "exhibit their revolutionary patience toward any misbehavior."[143] Moreover, when the Iranian authorities learned about a plan (by a radical circle close to Mehdi Hashemi) to smuggle propaganda material and explosives to Saudi Arabia, they informed the Saudi authorities.[144] This is not to say that there were no demonstrations disliked by Riyadh, clashes with Saudi authorities, detention of Iranian pilgrims, or provocative statements. Thus, for example, Montazeri even criticized Saudi control of the holy shrines.[145] But, by now, the Iranians were clearly unwilling to let differences with Saudi Arabia develop into an open rift.

RELATIONS WITH SYRIA AND LIBYA

The member states of the Steadfastness Front (mainly Syria and Libya) were the only Arab countries with whom Tehran had relatively good relations. However, while sharing some basic policies and certain values — such as hostility to the US, Israel and Iraq — they also had their differences. Some signs of incipient differences with Syria, the leading state in the front and the closest ally of Iran, appeared in 1986. They revolved around two main issues: the war in the Gulf and the civil war in Lebanon.

After the recapture of Khorramshahr in May 1982 (see *MECS* 1982–83, p 568) it was already clear that the two countries did not view the continuation of the war in the same light. As against Iran's uncompromising stand, there were growing signs of Syrian support for a negotiated cease-fire. Damascus did not share Iran's war goal, resented constant Iranian criticism against the Ba'th ideology and could not remain indifferent to Tehran's ambitions to set up an Islamic regime on its borders or even (given its own Arab national ideology) to invade Arab territory. The civil war in Lebanon, in which groups supported by Tehran and Damascus often confronted each other, contributed another area of disagreement.

Syria's dialogue with Iraq was the main cause of tension in Tehran-Damascus relations in 1986. After having impaired its relations with Jordan the year before,

Damascus was now improving its ties with the more moderate Arab countries. With their blessing — and mediation — Syria also mended fences with Iraq. In his visit to Kuwait and Saudi Arabia, late in May, Iraq Foreign Miniser Tariq 'Aziz admitted that King Husayn was active in bringing the two countries closer, though he admitted that there were several obstacles to achieving substantial immediate results.

For Syria, its isolation in the Arab world and the economic problems it was facing suggested the advisability of improving its relations with other Arab countries. Jordan took it upon itself to bring Baghdad and Damascus closer, and some negotiations — mostly subterranean — took place during the year. During his visit to Tehran, the Syrian Foreign Minister declared his Government's support for Iran. But, at the same time, attempts were made to set a meeting between Saddam and Asad.[146]

All in all, in summer 1986 the way for reconciliation between Syria and Iraq still seemed long, but the initial discussions were enough to cause concern in Tehran. During the year Iranian officials were regularly received in Damascus with considerable fanfare. In a meeting in June with the Iranian Deputy Minister of Foreign Affairs, 'Ali Besharati, President Asad said the relations between the two countries were "firm and strategic." But this did not calm Iranian apprehensions either.[147]

For its part Tehran made intensive attempts to buy back Syrian fealty. The price for this was the signing of a pact with Syria. After negotiations between economic delegations of the two countries in Tehran, Iran agreed to sell the Syrians 100,000 barrels of oil a day at a reduced price over the next six months. Both sides refused to give details on the new price, nor did they indicate whether Iran had also undertaken to supply Syria with some free oil, as was the case under the previous agreement.[148] Intensive negotiations were also held on other — mostly economic — issues with three Syrian Ministers visiting Iran in one week in mid-July. During July, relations between Syria and Iraq also became extremely tense. Although Iran was successful in keeping its alliance with Syria alive, the real gain was for the Syrians. The basic disagreements between Damascus and Tehran have continued. The disagreement over policy in Lebanon, and the subsequent kidnapping of the Syrian Chargé d'Affaires in Tehran in October, are other demonstrations of the strange-bedfellows quality of Iranian-Syrian relations.

Relations with Tripoli have been always problematic for revolutionary Iran. The very nature of Qadhdhafi's regime, his personal image, and his presentation of Libya's policies as an Islamic revolution, were all disturbing to Iran. However, with the growing tension between Libya and the US early in 1986 (see chapter on Libya), Tehran felt obliged to support Tripoli, but its declarations sounded more anti-American than pro-Libyan.

Iran had made clear that it "understands" the motivations of the "freedom fighters" who had attacked the airports of Vienna and Rome late in December 1985. Iran praised the suicide-type operations as being inspired by the Islamic revolution. Tehran saw this as an opportunity to incite tension against the US, to demonstrate to developing countries and others "the evil character of America," to point to Washington's impotence to act against "independent leaders" like Qadhdhafi, and to show its support for Libya. These points fit well into Iranian propaganda purposes. In backing Libya, Iran expressed its own revolutionary ideology, but it also hoped thus to secure Qadhdhafi's continued support for Iranian war aims. Khameneh'i called

Qadhdhafi to convey his country's support for Libya. Yet, Tehran was hesitant to promise any active support in case the US attacked Libya. Ardebili, making it clear that his country was itself engaged in war, promised only that Tehran would help Libya "within the limits of its possibilities." Meeting with the Libyan Chargé d'Affaires, Defense Minister Jallali was no more explicit.[149]

Iranian "support" remained essentially verbal after Libya was attacked by the US in April. Iran vehemently denounced the American attack, voiced unconditional support for Qadhdhafi and indirectly expressed support for terrorism. Immediately after the attack, the Foreign Ministers of Iran, Syria and Libya convened for their regular meeting, this time in Tehran. They condemned the US and expressed support for Libya.[150] All in all, Tehran again seemed more willing to criticize Washington than to support Tripoli.[151] As in previous years, the frequent exchange of visits of high-ranking officials highlighted the already close — though problematic — relations between the two countries in 1986.

APPENDIX: SOME LEADING PRAGMATISTS AND EXTREMISTS

Below are two lists, one of some leading pragmatists and another of some of the leading radicals. One caveat is essential: some of those listed as pragmatists may on one occasion or another express extremist opinion and some of those listed as extremists may come out with moderate views. The list was formed by the author on the basis of their public statements over a decade or more.

Leading Pragmatists

Ayatollah 'Ali Akbar Hashemi Rafsanjani: Speaker of the *Majlis*.

Ayatollah Hasan Karubi: Main operator behind the "moderates." Met several times with the Americans and the Israelis. When he found out that in the first meeting there were also Israelis (and not only Americans), he did not refuse to deal with them, although he said (as one of the participants told the author), that it would be very dangerous for him if this fact were disclosed. Worked closely with Khomeyni and has close ties with his son Ahmad Khomeyni. His brother, Mehdi Karubi, is head of the Foundation of the Martyrs.

Ayatollah Muhammad Reza Mahdavi-Kani (55, born in Tehran): Studied theology under Borujerdi and Khomeyni, has been a member of the Council of the Revolution (1979–80), has held the sensitive position of the Minister of the Interior in 1981, and served as an interim Prime Minister in September-October 1981 (just before Musavi). Since the early days of the new regime (mainly as a member of the Council of the Revolution), he has expressed relatively moderate views. He did not join the Islamic Republican Party and refrained from making the kind of uncompromising speeches characteristic of the other clerics. Serves as the head of the Association of Active Clerics.

Ayatollah Mirza Hasan Azari-Qomi: Member of the *Majlis*. Has often expressed moderate views and openly criticized the modus operandi of the Islamic regime.

Seyyed Mehdi Ruhani (65): From a family of prominent clerics in Qom (cousin of Ayatollah Sadiq Ruhani), studied under Borujerdi and Damad. Before the revolution he denounced Khomeyni, claiming that he lacked religious qualification for leadership. After the formation of the new regime, he was incorporated into it. Serves as member in the Council of Experts.

Jallal al-Din Farsi (55): was born in Afghanistan to Persian parents from Meshhed. Due to his opposition to the Shah he had to go into exile, to Lebanon, where he came close to the Fath Movement. He was a candidate in the first presidential election (1980) but was disqualified because he was not "of Iranian origin" — a condition the Constitution prescribes for Presidents. Member of the *Majlis*. Maintains close ties with the RG.

Habibollah Asghar-Owladi Musalman (57): Served as Minister of Commerce but was forced to resign because of public criticism (some even claimed then that he supported the *Hujjatiyyah*). He presented his candidacy for the 1981 presidential elections, but finally did not run. In 1985 he ran for the Presidency, but gained only 2% of the votes.

'Ali Akbar Parvaresh (57): Was active in the *Hujjatiyyah* at least before the revolution (and as such extremely anti-Soviet and anti-Bahai), and was tolerated by the Shah. *Majlis* member from Isfahan and formerly Minister of Education who lost his position in 1985. Maintains close ties with Bazaar circles in Isfahan.

Shaykh Lotfollah Safi (70): Former student of Ayatollah Golpaygani and his son-in-law. Chairman of the Council of Guardians, and in this capacity was instrumental in rejecting some of the radical laws approved by the *Majlis* (including land reform).

Shaykh Muhammad Javad Hujjati-Kermani (55): From a family of clerics in Kerman. Studied in Qom under Khomeyni and Borujerdi and engaged in oppositionary activities against the Shah (and spent many years in jail). Was member of the first *Majlis* and maintained close ties with Bani Sadr. Later he served as special aide for President Khameneh'i.

Shaykh Mahmud Halabi: The religious leader of the *Hujjatiyyah*.

Col Sayyad Shirazi: Until very recently he was the Commander of the Ground Forces of the Army. One of Khomeyni's representatives in the Supreme Council for Defense (the other is Rafsanjani).

Col Sohrabi: Commander of the Gendarmerie.

Leading Extremists
Seyyed Mehdi Hashemi: See above in the text.

Ayatollah Mirza 'Ali Meshkini: President of the Council of Experts and acting Jum'ah Imam of Qom. He advocates the exporting of the Islamic revolution. At one stage he even suggested turning Arabic into the international language of all Muslims.

Ayatollah Muhammad Reyshahri: (Son-in-law of Ayatollah Meshkini); the Minister of Intelligence.

Hujjat al-Islam Muhammad Kho'iniha: Member of the Council of Experts. His radical views were clearly exposed while supporting the students who captured the American embassy in Tehran (1979–80) and while serving as the Imam's representative on the *haj*. In 1986 he was removed from this last post (apparently as a gesture of goodwill toward Saudi Arabia) and has served since as the revolutionary prosecutor-general.

Hujjat al-Islam Sadiq Khalkhali: Member of Parliament and member of the Council Experts. In the first year of the revolutionary regime, he was the head of the revolutionary courts and ordered the execution of many supporters of the Shah's regime, drug-dealers, etc. His position has significantly deteriorated since 1981.

Ayatollah Ahmad Jonati: Head of the Islamic Information System and member of the Council of Guardians. (His son, *'Ali Jonati*, also belongs to the same camp.)

Ayatollah Fazlollah Mahalati: Member of the High Council of the RG. (Died in February 1986.)

Hujjat al-Islam 'Ali Akbar Mohtashemipur: Former Iranian Ambassador in Damascus; Minister of Interior.

NOTES

For the place and frequency of publications cited here, and for the full name of the publication, news agency, radio station or monitoring service where an abbreviation is used, please see "List of Sources." Only in the case of more than one publication bearing the same name is the place of publication noted here.

1. For the disqualification of a presidential candidate (Jallal al-Din Farsi), in the 1980 presidential campaign, because his father was an Afghan, see *MECS* 1979–80, p 447.
2. For some of many such expressions, see: *KH*, 15 January, 2 July; R. Tehran, 15 June — SWB, 17 June; *Kayhan*, Tehran, 26 July 1986.
3. *The Guardian*, 9 September 1985.
4. *KH*, 19 February 1986.
5. *KH*, 30 April 1986.
6. R. Tehran, 10 June — SWB, 12 June 1986.
7. *IHT*, 14 November; R. Tehran, 16 November — SWB, 18 November 1986.
8. The White House, Office of the Press Secretary, *The Tower Report* (Washington, DC: 1987), p B/3.
9. See similarly a memorandum, written early in 1984 by Geoffrey Kemp, Senior Director for Near East and South Asian Affairs on the staff of the National Security Council and submitted to Robert McFarlane, Assistant to the President for National Security Affairs,

which suggested the resumption of covert operations against Iran. Both are quoted in the *Tower Report*, p B/2–3.

10. *Tower Report*, p B/3.
11. Ibid, p B/76.
12. Ibid, pp B/101, 104, 110.
13. See, for example, the *Tower Report*, pp B/6, B/8, B/10, B/104.
14. Ibid, pp B/82, 88.
15. Ibid, p B/21.
16. See, for example, the words of the Prosecutor-General, Hujjat al-Islam Muhammad Kho'iniha (one of the biggest extremists), in support of freedom of the Press (*Kayhan*, Tehran, 26 July) as against his appeals for the strict Islamization of women's dress (*KH*, 28 May 1986).
17. *WP*, 7 February 1987.
18. *Al-Shira'*, Beirut, 3 November 1986.
19. *IHT*, 15 December 1986.
20. For full account of Rafsanjani's version on the negotiations with the Americans, and particularly McFarlane's visit to Tehran, see: *Ettela'at*, 5, 15, 24, 29 November 1986.
21. Quoted by *IHT*, 21 November 1986.
22. *Ettela'at*, 22 November; R. Tehran, 20 November — SWB, 21 November 1986.
23. R. Tehran, 14 December — DR, 15 December 1986.
24. *Ettela'at*, 14 December 1986.
25. R. Tehran, 15 December — SWB, 16 December 1986.
26. R. Tehran, 18 December — SWB, 19 December 1986.
27. R. Tehran, 9 December — SWB, 11 December 1986.
28. Such a view was most profoundly expressed by *US News and World Report* which speculated that Khomeyni summoned the entire leadership and told them to secure arms by deceiving the Americans and Israelis. The title of the article reveals its content: "Masters of Deceit: How the Iranians Manipulated the US, Israel and the Soviet Union," *US News and World Report*, 30 March 1987.
29. In a report to the American President dated 12 December 1986, Qorbanifar said he had at one point asked the Americans for "certain drops" to kill Khomeyni. His US counterpart, Michael Ledeen, replied that the US did not have such "drops." At other stages of the negotiations similar intentions were expressed by the Iranians. Whether they were serious or merely wished to impress their American and Israeli partners in order to further the negotiations, cannot yet be established. Ledeen, it must be stressed, told the author that he had never been asked to supply such "drops." Yet it is not entirely clear from his statement or from those of others involved in the negotiations, that demands for something like that (though not necesssarily for "drops") were not made. In another article the *US News and World Report* (29 June 1987) argued that there was a plot shared by the Americans, the Israelis and some Iranians to kill Khomeyni.

    Some of those involved on the American-Israeli side also viewed the arms deals as an instrument for promoting "radical change" in Iran. According to one theory, the profits from the arms deals would be sent to Iran to support the "moderates" (and in fact throughout the negotiations, the Iranians asked for financial support for such purposes). In this way, some of them eventually brought themselves to believe Khomeyni would himself finance his own overthrow.
30. R. Tehran, 10 June — SWB, 12 June; *KH*, 18 June 1986.
31. *KH*, 18 June. See similarly, statements by Khomeyni (*KH*, 18 June, 30 July) and Montazeri (*KH*, 25 July 1986).
32. *Tower Report*, p B/85.
33. *Al-Shira'*, Beirut, 3 November 1986, which first leaked the news of the negotiations, also implied that Rafsanjani was the moving spirit in the affair.
34. Opposition circles have often quoted Kho'i as challenging Khomeyni's status as the Shi'i world's (or even Iran's) supreme religious authority: Voice of the Liberation of Iran, 22 September — SWB, 25 September 1986.
35. The death, on 3 April, of Ayatollah Kazem Shari'atmadari removed from the scene the

main contender for leadership after Khomeyni. His followers — who disputed Khomeyni's leadership qualifications — came out against Montazeri (see below).

36. Azari-Qomi (who publishes the conservative paper *Resalat*) wrote that the nomination of Montazeri by the Council of Experts was merely a prediction of possible incidents in the future, but the Council would be obliged to ratify its decision when Khomeyni passed away. Without such a ratification its choice would not be valid. Azari-Qomi has also disclosed that while the nomination was discussed in 1985 the question arose as to whether Montazeri should be addressed as Ayatollah or (in recognition of his scholarship) be referred to as Grand Ayatollah. There were, he said, only ten who voted in favor of Grand Ayatollah: *Resalat*, 9 March — *IPD*, 10 March 1986.
37. Meshkini, Chairman of the Council of Experts (empowered to select the Leader or Leaders) and son-in-law of Intelligence Minister Reyshahri, launched a campaign against Montazeri toward the end of the summer, stating that there was a large body of opinion in favor of setting up a Leadership Council. The council he was heading, it must be stressed, had nominated Montazeri as the sole successor in November 1985: *Le Monde*, 25 October 1986. In February, however, referring to rumors about the validity of Montazeri's nomination, he said that since all members of the Council had signed the final communiqué, it must be regarded as valid: *IPD*, 11 February 1986.
38. *The Guardian*, 5 January 1986.
39. *KH*, 5, 12 February 1986.
40. *KH*, 5 February 1986.
41. See typical advice against consumerism by Montazeri: *KH*, 25 June 1986.
42. R. Tehran, 1 April — SWB, 3 April 1986.
43. See, for example, such an appeal by Khameneh'i calling on the *Jum'ah Imams* to prepare the people "to accept economic hardships": *KH*, 25 June 1986.
44. *IT*, 18 July 1986.
45. *KH*, 19 March 1986. In February it was Kazem-pur Ardebili, the Deputy Oil Minister for International Relations, who visited Saudi Arabia and other Gulf states to coordinate oil policy.
46. For such Iranian sales, see: *IT*, 14 March 1986.
47. *IT*, 28 February 1986.
48. *JI*, 7 May; *Kayhan*, Tehran, 9 May; *KH*, 14, 21 May 1986.
49. *Kayhan*, Tehran, 20 July 1986.
50. See, for example, words of Musavi in this regard in *KH*, 18 June 1986.
51. R. Tehran, 24 June — SWB, 26 June; *KH*, 25 June; *IT*, 27 June 1986. Similarly, an interview with the Minister of Commerce, 'Abedi Ja'fari: *Kayhan*, Tehran, 1 December 1986.
52. *IT*, 27 June 1986.
53. R. Tehran, 29 June — SWB, 1 July 1986.
54. *Kayhan*, Tehran, 7 September 1986.
55. *Ettela'at*, 6 July 1986.
56. R. Tehran, 30 August — DR, 2 September; *Ettela'at*, 30 August 1986.
57. R. Tehran, 20, 22 September — SWB, 23 September 1986.
58. While presenting his Government's new economic plan, Musavi referred to a study released by the Ministry of Planning and Budget which contained unpromising prospects. "It is like assessing the situation along the same lines that America is trying to impose on us." Its publication, the Prime Minister said, created among the people "an atmosphere of ambiguity and fear": R. Tehran, 24 June — SWB, 25 June 1986.
59. *Abrar* — *The Guardian*, 14 May 1986.
60. *Kayhan*, Tehran, 30 September 1986.
61. R. Tehran, 2 October — DR, 2 October 1986.
62. R, Tehran, 29 October, 1 November — SWB, 31 October, 5 November 1986.
63. *MEES*, 25 August, 13, 27 October 1986.
64. Late in February, the Iranian authorities disclosed that during the operations the same month some 8,500 Iranians were wounded or killed by chemical weapons. This was the first time that Tehran accused Iraq of using chemical weapons against civilians: *IT*, 28 February, 7 March 1986.

65. Among them were eight members of the *Majlis* and Hujjat al-Islam Mahalati (Khomeyni's representative in the RG): *IT*, 28 February 1986.
66. Voice of the Liberation of Iran, 22 September — SWB, 25 September 1986.
67. *Al-Dustur*, London, 3 February — JPRS, 1 April; *Le Monde*, 4 March 1986.
68. *Kayhan*, London, 17 July 1986.
69. *The Guardian*, 15 May 1986.
70. R. Tehran, 24 March — SWB, 25, 26 March 1986; *IT*, 28 March 1986.
71. R. Tehran, 24 August — DR, 25 August 1986.
72. *KH*, 7 May; *Kayhan*, London, 17 July 1986.
73. *KH*, 1 January 1986. See similar expressions by Khameneh'i (ibid, 23 April) and the Commander of the Ground Forces (until August 1986) Sayyad Shirazi (ibid, 9 April 1986).
74. For a typical such appeal see: *IT*, 25 July 1986.
75. *FT*, 1 April; *KH*, 9 April 1986.
76. R. Tehran, 2 April — SWB, 4 April; *KH*, 9 April 1986.
77. *The Guardian*, 3 March; *JI*, 16 April; *Kayhan*, Tehran, 23 July 1986.
78. *KH*, 16 April 1986.
79. *Kayhan*, Tehran, 5 August 1986.
80. R. Tehran, 24 March — SWB, 25, 26 March 1986. Similarly: *Ettela'at*, 22 April, 9 November 1986.
81. *KH*, 19 February, 7, 14 May; *IT*, 18 July; R. Tehran, 9 July — SWB, 11 July 1986.
82. *KH*, 7 May 1986.
83. *KH*, 7, 14 May 1986.
84. See words to this effect by Khameneh'i in *KH*, 19 February and *Ettela'at*, 6 November; by Montazeri on R. Tehran, 11 September — DR, 12 September; and by Velayati, *Ettela'at*, 30 March 1986.
85. *IT*, 28 March; similarly: R. Tehran, 24 March — SWB, 26 March 1986.
86. R. Tehran, 31 May — DR, 2 June 1986.
87. R. Tehran, 6 June — SWB, 9 June; *KH*, 11, 25 June, 16 July 1986.
88. R. Tehran, 8 June — SWB, 10 June 1986.
89. *IT*, 20 June 1986.
90. R. Tehran, 30 May — SWB, 2 June 1986.
91. *IT*, 20 June 1986.
92. *Ettela'at*, 2 August 1986.
93. *Ettela'at*, 22 September 1986.
94. R. Tehran, 22 September — DR, 22 September 1986.
95. For details of such rivalries within the Islamic institutions, see: *Le Monde*, 25 October 1986.
96. See, for example, a typical interview with Shari'atmadari's representative in the FRG, Ayatollah Va'ezi, in which he claimed that most of the people and "more than 95 per cent" of the Iranian religious leaders opposed the regime: *Kayhan*, London, 15 May 1986.
97. *IT*, 7 March 1986.
98 "Radio Iran," 6 February — SWB, 11 February 1986.
99. Free Voice of Iran, 14 August — SWB, 16 August 1986.
100. Voice of the Liberation of Iran, 7 September — DR, 8 September; *IHT*, 8 September 1986.
101. R. Tehran, 12 September — DR, 12 September 1986.
102. For the *Mujahidine Khalq* moving from Paris and its background, see: *IT*, 6, 13 June; *NYT*, 8 June; *IHT*, 9 June; *The Guardian*, 10 June 1986.
103. *Al-Nahar al-'Arabi wal-Duwali*, 1-7 December 1986.
104. See an interview with Bazargan in *Kayhan*, London, 20 February 1986.
105. *Kayhan*, London, 27 March (which also gives the list of the members of the Central Council); *MEED*, 10–16 May 1986.
106. For the attack on them on the occasion of the anniversary of the establishment of the Freedom Movement, in May, see: *Qiyame Emruz*, 29 May — JPRS, 30 July 1986; *Kayhan*, London, 5 June 1986.
107. According to its estimation, Iran needed at least 50,000 doctors to provide the population with minimally acceptable standards of health care. There are in Iran an estimated 14,000 doctors — fewer than before the revolution.

108. According to the IMA, 90 per cent of the nation's doctors, 85 per cent of the nurses and more than 70 per cent of the pharmacists observed the strike.
109. *Ettela'at*, 15 July; *Kayhan*, Tehran 26 July; *IT*, 25 July; R. Tehran, 15, 23 July — SWB, 16, 26 July 1986.
110. R. Tehran, 2, 3, 4 February — SWB, 4, 5, 6 February; *KH*, 12, 19 February 1986.
111. *IT*, 27 June 1986.
112. *The Times*, 4 August; R. Tehran, 9, 10 August — SWB, 11, 12 August 1986.
113. *IHT*, 26 August 1986.
114. *IHT*, 5 September; *NYT*, 7 September 1986.
115. R. Tehran, 9 December — SWB, 11 December 1986.
116. *KH*, 15 January 1986.
117. *JP*, 16 February 1986.
118. *IT*, 28 March 1986.
119. *Ettela'at*, 19 April 1986.
120. *KH*, 23 April 1986.
121. R. Tehran, 22, 23 May — SWB, 24, 26 May; *NYT*, 24 May; *Le Monde*, 24 May; *KH*, 28 May 1986.
122. *NYT*, 24 May 1986. See similarly, *The Guardian*, 23 May 1986.
123. *IT*, 6, 13 June; *IHT*, 13 June 1986.
124. Thus, for example, an Iranian delegation visited Paris in June; a French delegation visited Tehran in July.
125. *Le Monde*, 12 September 1986.
126. *Le Monde*, 14-15 September 1986.
127. R. Tehran, 23 November — SWB, 25 November 1986.
128. *IT*, 7 March 1986.
129. *IT*, 28 March 1986.
130. R. Tehran, 20 March — SWB, 22 March 1986.
131. R. Tehran, 27 July — SWB, 29 July 1986.
132. R. Tehran, 22 August — DR, 22 August 1986.
133. R. Tehran, 28 August — SWB, 1 September 1986.
134. R. Tehran, 22 September — SWB, 22 September 1986.
135. R. Tehran, 7 March — SWB, 10 March 1986.
136. *IT*, 14 March 1986.
137. R. Tehran, 20 March — SWB, 22 March 1986.
138. R. Tehran, 4 April — SWB, 7 April; *KH*, 16 April 1986.
139. *KH*, 26 February 1986.
140. See a speech by the President quoted by *KH*, 19 February 1986.
141. The students said they did not seize the embassies because some *Majlis* members said they were not "worth the effort."
142. R. Tehran, 4 July — SWB, 8 July 1986.
143. R. Tehran, 7 August — DR, 7 August 1986.
144. The Saudi authorities confirmed that a group of Iranian pilgrims was arrested on board Iran Air: R. Riyadh, 11 August — DR, 11 August 1986.
145. R. Tehran, 9 September — SWB, 10 September 1986.
146. *KH*, 21 May 1986.
147. For this and the Syrian-Iraqi negotiations in June, see: *IT*, 6, 13, 20 June; R. Tehran, 7 June — SWB, 9 June 1986.
148. *IT*, 4, 18 July; R. Tehran, 11 July — SWB, 22 July 1986.
149. *KH*, 8, 15 January 1986.
150. R. Tehran, 15 April — SWB, 17 April; *KH*, 23, 30 April 1986.
151. See, for example, Khameneh'i's statement to leaders of Islamic countries: R. Tehran, 21 April — SWB, 23 April 1986.

Iraq
(Al-Jumhuriyya al-'Iraqiyya)

OFRA BENGIO

A combination of military, economic and political factors made 1986 a very difficult year for Iraq, in fact the most difficult since the beginning of its war with Iran. In many respects, Iraq's predicaments in 1986 resembled those faced in 1982 (see *Middle East Contemporary Survey* [*MECS*] 1981–82) albeit in a much more aggravated form due to the cumulative effect of six years of fighting, the military setbacks on Iraqi territory, and the fact that the prospects for ending the war seemed as remote as ever.

Most demoralizing were the military setbacks. The high points in the fighting can be summed up as follows: the Iranian offensive of February, which resulted in the occupation of the strategic area of Faw in the south and some pockets in the Kurdish north (see map: Iranian Military Achievements by the End of 1986); the Iraqi occupation of Mehran in May and its reconquest by Iran only six weeks later; and the new Iranian offensive in December in the Basra area. After August, the Iraqi Air Force succeeded in mounting long-range attacks on Iranian oil outlets far removed from the area of fighting; in addition, "the war of the cities" was resumed in the fall with full vigor.

The military setbacks brought pressure to bear on the political system. The military leadership demanded greater freedom of action; the political elite around President Saddam Husayn pressed for a bigger share in the decision-making process, while some politicized but still amorphous groups began to show signs of restiveness toward the authoritarian system. There were indications of some liberalization, but it remained to be seen whether these were merely cosmetic changes or the beginning of a deep-rooted process.

Iraq's difficult economic situation was complicated further in 1986 by its accumulating external debts, the high cost of the war and the world oil crisis which drastically curtailed its income. This situation alarmed the regime because it was likely to hamper the war effort and to undermine the social basis on which it rested. Pressures also began to increase for a liberalization of the economic system. But this trend met with strong opposition from groups that have had vested interests in the socialist system, and the Government had to steer very carefully between the opposing trends. Another internal problem made more intractable by the war was that of the Kurds. Not only was the Iraqi Army's hold on the Kurdish area precarious, but the two main Kurdish opposition groups allied themselves with Iran and thus increased the threat to the country.

The difficult military and economic situation had its repercussions on Iraq's foreign relations and its ability to mobilize support for its cause. Baghdad's inability to pay its debts on time threatened to undermine its credibility and made new deals highly risky.

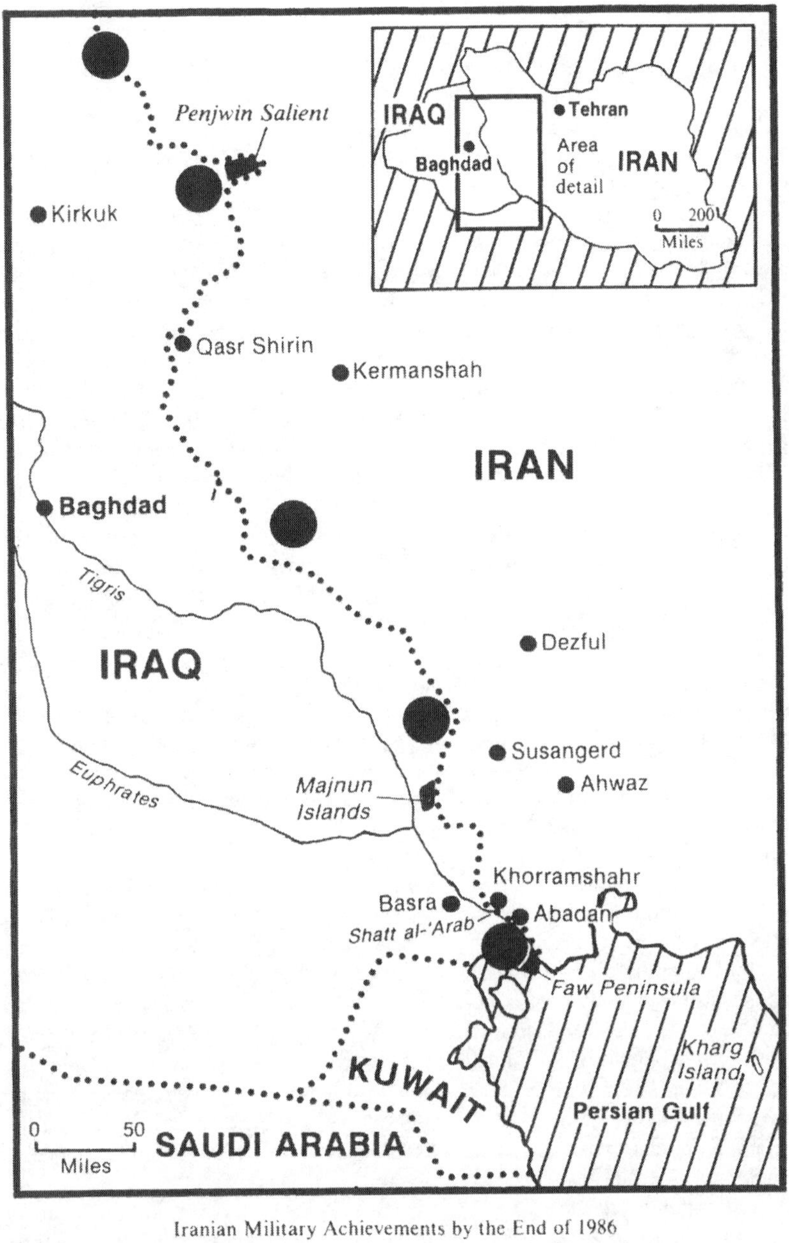

Iranian Military Achievements by the End of 1986

Moreover, the danger of its military collapse prompted some of Iraq's staunchest supporters to open channels of communication with its rival.

To balance this dark picture, the following points may be made. First, Iran's economic predicament was not less serious than Iraq's. Second, while the Iranian Army enjoyed superiority in terms of the morale and dedication of its soldiers, Iraq had superior military equipment. Third, although some of Iraq's supporters began to hedge their bets in the war, their huge investments in Iraq and the prospects of an engulfing Iranian victory dictated a cautious policy of balancing one antagonist against the other. To sum up, although Iraq was on the defensive militarily, politically and economically, 1986 was not a "year of decision"; rather, it marked another swing of the pendulum.

THE REGIME

THE ENTRENCHMENT OF PRESIDENT HUSAYN

The military setbacks in the first part of 1986 had destabilizing effects on the regime. A certain crisis of confidence began to develop after the fall of Faw in February, reaching its climax following the fall of Mehran in early July. However, although it affected all centers of power, namely the President, the military leadership, the Ba'th Party and the security forces, the crisis remained under control.

The first to be affected by the military upheavals was President Husayn, who in addition to being Commander in Chief of the Armed Forces had also come to be personally associated with the war. The hostile Iranian and Syrian media reported assassination and coup attempts against him immediately after the setbacks, but these reports could not be corroborated. What seemed quite certain, however, was that Husayn's popularity was declining, that questions were raised regarding the way he conducted the war, and that there were incipient attempts to challenge his authoritarian rule. It was perhaps a symptom of his own feeling of insecurity that he ordered the media to repeat the blessing "May God preserve him" whenever they mentioned his name. In another defensive reflex Husayn strengthened further the hold on power of his close relatives, and of those Tikritis[1] who were loyal to him personally, thus further narrowing his basis of support. By 1986 most sensitive posts were in family or Tikriti hands. Husayn's paternal cousin, Hasan 'Ali Majid, was Director-General of Security (*Mudir al-Amn al-'Amm*), while his maternal cousin and brother-in-law, Khayrallah Talfah, was Minister of Defense. In 1986, Husayn, added an influential officer to his entourage when his son Qusay married the daughter of Mahir 'Abd al-Rashid, Commander of the Third Army Corps. At the same time, Husayn took cautious steps to strengthen the standing of his son 'Uday. Thus, in March, 'Uday was made head of the prestigious Olympic Committee; however, it put him at loggerheads with the Minister of Youth. In addition, two key posts were in the hands of Tikritis: Hamid Sha'ban was Commander of the Air Force and Fadil Barrak was head of Intelligence (*Mukhabarat*). But although Tikrit formed an important base of support for Husayn, not all the Tikritis supported him — in fact, many of his opponents came from this town. Thus, there were reports of an armed confrontation in Tikrit (date not given) between Husayn's bodyguards and a particularly vindictive group of Tikritis headed by 'Umar Hazza', a close associate of the late President Ahmad Hasan al-Bakr and Commander of the Republican Guard in 1969, and

Deputy Minister of Defense in 1977. Reports vary about the causes of the conflict and its outcome; some even claimed that Hazza' had been executed with two other members of his family.[2]

No less problematic were Husayn's relations with the top political leadership, namely the Ba'th Party Regional Command (RC) and the Revolutionary Command Council (RCC) which is the highest legislative and executive body in the country (except for one, all RCC members belonged to the RC as well). While most members of this group regarded their fate as closely linked with Husayn's, some of them considered themselves contenders for power and tended to question his authoritarian rule. To counteract disaffection, Husayn sought to attenuate his authoritarian stance without relinquishing real power. At the same time, he reinforced the "divide and rule" formula among members of this group. There were also indications of a certain attenuation of Husayn's aggressive personality cult and a tendency to stress the importance of collective leadership. Probably at Husayn's instance, the RCC introduced in March the golden "leadership badge" which was to be worn on special occasions by all members of the RCC and the Ba'th Party RC. Such token gestures were accompanied by talk of democracy in the party and the State, of the importance of the "collective institution" and of the emphasis Husayn placed on consulting his colleagues.[3]

More tangible was the fact that after the setback at Faw, Husayn, for the first time since the war began, allowed a member of the political leadership, his Deputy 'Izzat Ibrahim al-Duri, to participate in discussions with the military command. After Mehran, he extended the circle to include other members such as the Foreign Minister, the Culture and Information Minister, and the Head of Security. While this development indicated the end of the monopoly Husayn had on contacts with the military leadership, it also pointed to his political cunning and ability to maneuver in times of extreme pressure. Including these people in the discussions was a way of controlling potential rivals, such as Taha Yasin Ramadan (al-Jazrawi), First Deputy Prime Minister and the Commander of the Popular Army, or checking the powers of over-ambitous military commanders. Another development was that reports of cabinet discussions became much more detailed. And for the first time cabinet decisions were referred to the National Assembly or Parliment for discussion. Although the Assembly remained a rubber stamp, the impression was that Husayn felt the need to take into consideration the opinion of assembly members.

In one interview Husayn expressed his dislike of the title of "ruler," suggesting that he considered himself a "historical leader." Whatever his view of himself, Husayn excelled in the art of survival. Given the fact that each power center was, by definition, a two-edged sword, Husayn's ability to manipulate them all for his own purposes was indeed remarkable.

THE MILITARY BID FOR GREATER FREEDOM OF ACTION

The defeat at Faw was traumatic for Iraq for several reasons. Although Faw had ceased to serve as an oil terminal at the start of the war, its occupation underlined Iraq's difficult strategic position because it was left with no potential outlet to the sea. The fall of reportedly 10,000 soldiers[4] in that one battle was an enormous loss for a country whose population was one-third that of its enemy. Most demoralizing of all was the fact that Iraq had used its best forces including elite units of the Presidential

Iraq's Army Corps on the Front Line

Guard, and the Air Force, as well as chemical weapons in the failed attempt to reconquer Faw. The impasse at Faw and the fall of Mehran later in the year brought to light latent problems between the military and political leadership concerning the military strategy that should be adopted and the relationship between the military and the political command. There were indications that the military command had pressed for an offensive strategy, while the political leadership had opted for a defensive one. After the fall of Faw, the Commander of the Third Army Corps voiced publicly the idea to retaliate by occupying Khorramshahr.[5] Similarly, the Air Force pressed for more aggressive attacks on Iran, including the bombing of populated areas. The political leadership sought to restrain the military, either because it had no confidence in its performances or because it sought to limit casualties and prevent retaliatory measures against its own population.

These differences pointed to the heart of the problem: to what extent should the political leadership control military activities and who was to be held responsible for failures? Obviously, Husayn aspired to achieve absolute control to prevent the Army from becoming independent and turning against the regime. However, he did not hesitate to blame the military command for failures. Shortly after the fall of Faw, he dismissed 'Ata Shawkat, Commander of the Seventh Army Corps (see map: Iraq's Army Corps on the Front Line) responsible for the Faw area.[6] After the failure of the counteroffensive, Husayn initiated a wide-scale reshuffle, including at least four commanders. One of them was Tali' Khalil (Arhim) al-Duri, Commander of the Presidential Guard, who less than a year earlier had been singled out for heroism and the contribution of his guard in stemming the spring 1985 offensive. Al-Duri was appointed Commander of the Fifth Corps in the North (see map: Iraq's Army Corps on the Front Line), while the command of the Republican Guard went to Husayn Rashid Muhammad, a Kurd. Another important change was the appointment of the influential officer Mahir 'Abd al-Rashid as Commander of the Seventh Army Corps. At the same time, there were reports of summary executions of officers responsible for the rout at Faw.[7] These reports could not be verified; what was clear, however, was that disenchantment was mutual. The military reportedly began to blame meddling by the party's civilian officials for the setbacks. Even Husayn did not escape criticism.[8] The most critical were said to be the "Mosulian officers," those who had been trained at the Mosul Military Academy and were more bound by their *esprit de corps* than by loyalty to the Ba'th Party.[9] It was probably to ward off pressures from these officers and to rehabilitate the prestige of the Army that Saddam Husayn gave the green light to the "mobile defense strategy" that led to the occupation of Mehran in mid-May. However, the reoccupation of Mehran by Iran on 2 July precipitated a crisis of confidence more severe than that which occurred after Faw. It was reported that Husayn had ordered the occupation of Mehran against the advice of the Commander of the Second Army Corps, Diya Tawfiq Ibrahim,[10] who, however, acquiesced in the occupation and even received a medal of valor. Also, during the Iranian counterattack at Mehran, the Iraqi field commanders asked for air support which was delayed because of the clumsy structure of the armed forces. Thus, the political leadership would not allow direct contact among the different forces but insisted that such requests should first pass through Baghdad.[11]

After Mehran, the military commanders began to demand greater freedom of action on the battlefield. Husayn took measures to tackle the crisis. He first convened the Ba'th Party Regional Congress (see below) and received its backing. Then he initiated another reshuffle of the Commanders (see Table 1). Diya Tawfiq Ibrahim, the demoralized Commander of the Second Army Corps, was removed from the Army, and Mahir 'Abd al-Rashid was promoted to the rank of Lt Gen. More important was the permission given to the Air Force, and only to the Air Force, to pursue far more aggressive attacks on Iran, accompanied by a greater degree of freedom on the operational level.[12] Concurrently, Husayn made symbolic gestures to appease the military, such as the granting of Medals of Valour. After Faw, some commanders were awarded two or three medals of valor at one time. After Mehran, Husayn named Hamid Sha'ban Commander of the Air Force an "Al-Qadisiyya hero," an honor he bestowed on others as well. Sha'ban generally increased his influence in the second half of 1986, as was evidenced by his extensive exposure to Iraqi and foreign media. Sha'ban's ascendance can be attributed to the growing importance of the Air Force in the attacks on Iran, but also to Husayn's need to balance Tikriti officers against the Mosulis.

THE BA'TH PARTY EXTRAORDINARY REGIONAL CONFERENCE

The Ba'th Party Extraordinary Regional Conference, held on 10 July 1986, epitomized the crisis which the system had undergone in the first half of 1986. The circumstances leading to the extraordinary conference resembled, in many respects, those of the Ninth Regular Conference held in June 1982 (see *MECS* 1981–82, pp 588–90). The Regular Conference was also held against the background of a military defeat (at Khorramshahr) and Husayn's need to mobilize support for himself in the Army and the Ba'th Party. There was, however, one essential difference: while the Regular Conference thoroughly discussed a wide range of ideological and political issues winding up with the adoption of a new, even revolutionary line for the party, the Extraordinary Conference ignored these questions. Instead, Husayn delivered a long speech about the plot (*mu'amara*) against the party and the nation.[13] This difference symbolized the party's loss of vitality as well as Husayn's struggle for survival. In his speech, Husayn repeated the word "plot" no less than 25 times. However, it does not appear that there was a plot in the real sense. The Extraordinary Conference reflected the pressure Husayn was being subjected to by the military and political leadership and his attempts to deal with it.

Explaining the reason for the extraordinary session, a Ba'th party statement claimed that it was to renew the vote of confidence in the RC as well as to enlarge its membership from 15 to 17, which had been made necessary by the increasing burdens on the party. The statement stressed that the elections were in line with the principles of democracy in the party. However, it soon emerged that the list of candidates had been prepared in advance and the conference had to vote for it *in toto*. The conference reelected Saddam Husayn as the party Secretary-General, and other members of the outgoing command, with one exception. (For the outgoing command, see *MECS* 1981–82, p 611). This in itself was meant to be a signal to the military that Husayn had the backing of the party and that the political leadership was as strong and as cohesive as ever. What was conspicuous, however, was the expulsion from the command of Na'im Haddad, a Shi'i and a Ba'thi leader of long standing who, as late as October 1984, had combined the post of Speaker of the National Assembly with that of Secretary-General of the Patriotic and Progressive National Front (PPNF —

originally an alliance with Communist and Kurdish parties); he was also a member of the RCC as well as a member of the Regional and National Command of the Ba'th Party. No reason was given for the explusion. Non-Iraqi sources speculated that he had failed to rally the PPNF around the regime, or that he incurred Husayn's wrath when he was mentioned as a substitute for him. In fact, Haddad's powers had already started declining in October 1984 when he ceased to be Speaker of the Assembly. It is therefore possible that he fell out of favor because he had been critical of the war and Husayn's conduct of it. This was hinted at in Husayn's speech, when he blamed a "minority" in the party for betraying Iraq through its attempts to intermingle "with the enemy in matters of religion and religious school [*madhhab*]."[14] Given the fact that Haddad is a Shi'i, it is possible that Husayn chose this particular issue in order to indirectly tarnish his image and facilitate his removal. Indeed, after the conference, the RCC expelled Haddad from the RCC and later also stripped him of the post of Secretary-General of the PPNF.[15] Sa'dun Hammadi, a Shi'i and the Speaker of the Assembly, replaced Haddad in the RCC (for its composition see *MECS* 1981–82, p 611), while Hasan 'Ali (al-'Amiri), also a Shi'i and a member of the RCC and the Ba'th Party Regional Command, became the Secretary-General of the PPNF.

No less significant was the inclusion of the six new members and reserve members in the command (for the composition of the new command, see Table 2). A key new member was Latif Nusayyif al-Jasim, the Minister of Culture and Information since July 1979, who was considered a close associate of Husayn. Shortly before the conference, Husayn decorated al-Jasim with the Rafidayn Medal, praising the "great role" played by the media in general and Jasim in particular during the war. Husayn explained that "whenever armies were defeated...certain elements appeared and returned to the rear of the Army and entrenched themselves like nails in the ground." It was Jasim, Husayn stressed, who had played that role after the difficult battle of Khorramshahr in 1982 by directing the media "in a manner that restored people's morale and helped entrench our forces in the face of the aggressive Iranian invasion."[16] Other key figures were the new member Hasan 'Ali Majid, Director-General of Security, and reserve member Fadil Barrak, Head of Intelligence. The need to stuff the party's high echelons with security men was evidence of the erosion in Husayn's standing. The President needed these men to keep a close eye on his political entourage as well as to warn both the political and military leadership against any attempts to act against him.

THE ASCENDING ROLE OF THE SECRET SERVICES

The role of the secret services, always important for the survival of the regime, had become crucial in 1986. One indication was the incorporation in the party's RC of Majid and Barrak. Another indication was the regular participation (in the second part of 1986), of Majid in the meetings between Husayn and the military command. This development highlighted the growing involvement of the secret services in political and military affairs as well as their exposure to publicity, which was a new phenomenon. Both Barrak and Majid published books dealing with security affairs. Barrak himself was awarded two medals of valor in June.[17] For his part, Majid gained publicity, through his weekly meetings with citizens[18] and his discussion of security problems in the media. In one interview, Majid disclosed the unearthing of two sabotage networks and the public execution of 15 of their members. At the same time, he mentioned a wide range of issues which the secret services dealt with, so that citizens could lead a "normal life."[19] Indeed, in addition to their task of keeping a vigilant eye on political and military affairs, the secret services now had to deal with negative economic and social phenomena; they accordingly formed a special section to deal with problems of smuggling, forgery and the black market. The extent to which the secret services had infiltrated daily activities in Iraq was described in an anthropological study of a village in the south where the citizens had been mobilized into the secret services and were thus able to keep a watchful eye on the village and help prevent dissident acts.[20]

At the beginning of the year, Husayn singled out the activity of the security forces for special mention, calling their members "struggling fighters" (*munadilun mujahidun*). In his speech before the regional conference he praised the special apparatuses for their contribution in thwarting the "plot" against Iraq. At the same time, however, it appeared that the regime had become increasingly worried about friction between the public and the security forces, and the excesses of the latter. This could be inferred, among other things, from complaints directed to Husayn against these institutions, from Majid's need to devote a special day of the week to answering citizens' complaints and his insistence on the "educational" rather than "terrorizing" nature of these services. But apart from alienating the people, the secret services also posed a potential threat to the regime by accumulating too much power. (There was a precedent in 1973 when the then Director-General of Security attempted to topple the regime.) Referring to these dangers, Husayn said that the leadership would prevent the services from turning into "oppressive organs" or "a bogey which would frighten the masses." The duties and the scope of authority of the services should be well-defined, he said, and the services should be under the Government's "constant supervision" — in fact, they should be "transparent" before it. Husayn affirmed that the Ba'th's aim was to build a "State of principles" and not a "State of the secret services."[21]

In December, an Iraqi airliner was hijacked on its way to Amman. The plane exploded on Saudi territory and 62 passengers were killed. Non-Iraqi sources and a Jordanian official suggested that members of Iraqi security were involved in the affair, either passively or actively.[22]

THE ASSAULT ON CORRUPTION AND BUREAUCRACY

In one of his speeches during the year, Husayn declared: "For some time now, I have been instigating the citizens against the State [*al-dawla*, in this case the Administration or bureaucracy] whenever they find it committing an offense against a citizen." He further stated that he had directed the media to allow citizens to criticize various social and economic phenomena, including those in the state apparatus.[23] While such a stance might indicate an underlying tension between Husayn and the governing apparatus, it served Husayn's various motives. His prime motive was to draw a dividing line between himself and the misdeeds of the various state organs, and thus direct criticism against them. Another motive was to use public criticism as a pretext for purging unreliable elements. Indeed, the war had highlighted various social and economic phenomena that might be harmful to the regime. These were the enlargement of the private sector (see below); the rapid acquisition of wealth by certain groups, especially those with access to public funds and resources; and nepotism and corruption. Especially damaging was corruption in the governing apparatus, which was something quite new in the Ba'th regime. Aware of public criticism of such developments, Husayn appeared keen to combat them. In January, five high-ranking officials were executed for bribery and forgery.[24] On 22 June, a Republican decree dismissed 'Abd al-Wahhab Muhammad Latif (al-Mufti) as Mayor of Baghdad and appointed Khalid 'Abd al-Mun'im Rashid (previously Chief of the Presidential Office) to the post. The decree explained that Latif had been dismissed because of the "betrayal of his responsibility toward the money of the State."[25] Significantly, only six months earlier, Husayn had decorated Latif with the Rafidayn and the Valor Medals "in appreciation of his sincere and great endeavor in assisting the armed force."[26] It is to be noted that Latif, who was a civil engineer, had among his other responsibilities the task of helping the Army build defenses along the border with Iran and deciding how British supply credits were to be spent. Latif was known as a doer, as a good organizer and as a person who enjoyed Husayn's trust. During the fighting in Faw he organized the construction of several roads and concrete hardstands for vehicles in the marshland and he completed the job in double-quick time. It was not known what specific act of corruption he was guilty of, but it appeared that other people in the governing machinery were also involved, as others were dismissed and arrested, including his deputy and — according to some sources — up to 30 of his associates.[27] Another "assault" on corruption took place in early October when the Oil Ministry Under Secretary 'Abd al-Mun'im Hasan 'Alwan and six businessmen were executed for "dealing with a number of foreign companies and providing them with information about project tenders in Iraq and getting commission."[28] In November the RCC decreed up to ten years' imprisonment and the confiscation of the property of any state official guilty of accepting bribery during the war. It promised ten per cent of the amount "stolen" from the State to people who helped to reveal such acts.[29] Another Iraqi innovation for keeping a close watch on officials was to order senior officials to fulfill the tasks of their juniors for two weeks or more, a method that was initiated by Husayn and became routine in the various ministries and offices.

Opposition papers regularly accused Husayn of corruption, rapid enrichment and nepotism, claiming that the whole of his "enlarged" family had committed such misdeeds. Whatever the truth was, Husayn appeared extremely sensitive to such charges. Husayn reacted by defending the right of rulers and officials to own private property, saying that even the orthodox caliphs (*al-Khulafa al-Rashidun*) had property. Regarding his treatment of his relatives, the President said that while he did not object to talented people (in this context, his relatives) assuming responsibility, he at the same time kept a close eye on them, and nipped in the bud any negative conduct by them. He further said that he punished his relatives, including his sons, brothers and nephews, more severely than he did other people.[30] *Le Monde* reported that the President had stepped in personally to end certain dishonest operations that his family members were engaged in, such as the smuggling of currency by his maternal uncle Khayrallah Talfah, nicknamed "Mr Five Per Cent."[31]

Since the beginning of the year, a latent struggle for power had been developing between Husayn's son 'Uday, then head of the Iraqi Soccer Federation, and Nuri Faysal Shahir, Minister of Youth (since December 1983) and head of the Olympic Committee. Indirectly justifying his son's stand, Husayn said that the State (meaning the Minister) should not put its weight on sports activities but rather make room for individual enterprises.[32] In February, the two competed for control of the Olympic Committee and ‘Uday came out on top. In May, probably following further friction between ‘Uday and the Minister of Youth, the former threatened to resign from his posts; however, he withdrew his threat after “pressures” were applied on him. Meanwhile, Shahir had been under attack from the leading sports daily, *al-Ba‘th al-Riyadi*, which was owned and edited by ‘Uday.[33] On 17 June, a republican decree dismissed Shahir from his post and appointed him Director-General at the Ministry of Labor and Social Affairs. The decree did not mention the reason for the dismissal, but it appears that the struggle for power with ‘Uday was the main cause. Only two months later, ‘Abd al-Fattah Muhammad Amin al-Yasin was appointed to the post of Minister of Youth. On the same day, Sadiq ‘Abd al-Latif (Yunis al-Witari), who had been Minister of Agriculture since June 1982, was dismissed from his post and replaced by ‘Aziz Salih Hasan al-Numan.[34] No reason was given for this dismissal either, but it appeared that it was due to friction with Husayn on the question of socialist policies in the agricultural sector. *Le Monde* reported that ‘Abd al-Latif had already fallen into disgrace in March because of his strict adherence to “etatist” policies.[35]

THE WAR EFFORT

THE MOBILIZED SOCIETY

1986 witnessed the most forceful campaign to mobilize Iraqi society since the war began. The Iranian attacks, and their partial success were one cause; another was the need to combat demoralization and prevent dissent by “organizing” the people for various “projects” and thus keeping them under tighter control. A third cause was the need to balance Iraq’s demographic inferiority *vis-à-vis* its enemy, which, although not a new factor, appeared more menacing than ever in 1986. Commenting on the problem, Husayn stressed that “for every Iranian who wages one battle, the Iraqi wages four battles because the Iranians outnumber the Iraqis four to one....”[36] At the same time, however, he attempted to play down the problem by saying, “If the enemy is boasting of its ignorant mob, we challenge it with the 15m Iraqi men and women. Our capability for a serious and efficient mobilization was and still is greater than the capabilities of those retarded people....”[37] Indeed, regimenting the population involved different spheres of life from birth to death.

One way of dealing with the demographic problem was to introduce a nationwide campaign to encourage procreation. It was President Husayn himself who started this campaign when he declared: “We believe that our motto must be that each family produce five children...and that the family which does not produce at least four children deserves to be harshly reprimanded.” He added that female students should prefer procreation to university degrees.[38] Immediately afterwards, the General Federation of Iraqi Women, headed by Manal Yunis, organized meetings to explain the need to procreate, and to give presents to “fertile” (*waluda*) women. On one such occasion, gifts were awarded to women who had given birth to more than 15 children. In November, Husayn ordered that apartments be given to a group of mothers of large families who did not own one.[39]

If such campaigns had any value whatsoever, it was in terms of their psychological, reassuring effect. More to the point, however, was the drive to mobilize women into the Popular Army (*al-Jaysh al-Sha'bi*), the Ba'th party militia, and to train them to use arms. While aimed at balancing Iraq's demographic inferiority, this move was to counteract a similar Iranian measure and to prepare the population for every eventuality. Women were encouraged to volunteer for nursing jobs, so crucial to the war effort, as well as for men's jobs.

All Iraqis were called upon to contribute money, blood and working hours for the war effort. RCC member and Popular Army Commander, Taha Yasin Ramadan emphasized that "there is also a continuing organization of citizens who are not included in these services" (the Army and Popular Army).[40] By the end of 1985, the authorities had enlisted 85,000 men, women and children to cut reeds in the marshes in the south, with a view to facilitating the Army's activities. Commenting on the campaign, Husayn said: "In only a few days and under heavy enemy artillery shelling, the Iraqi men and women, while facing hardships and difficulties, transformed the difficult marshland into a suitable theater for military operations."[41] Terming the campaign a "slaughter," the opposition paper *Risalat al-'Iraq* claimed that thousands of these people had either been killed by Iranian or Iraqi bullets or had died as a result of difficult climatic conditions and hard work.[42]

On 22 June, the authorities took, according to Husayn, "an unprecedented and unique" step by mobilizing 100,000 students and 15,000 university teachers for five months of military training. In previous years students had been called up, during the summer vacation, for the Popular Army or other jobs in factories and in the field. However, this was the first time that all university students and their teachers had been mobilized en bloc; some of them were sent to the front.[43] Preparing the ground for this, Husayn had declared in April: "Everyone who is capable of walking on Iraqi land...must carry a weapon and go to fight."[44] Later, he said that mobilization was general and that, except for the blind nobody could exempt himself, not even the sons of officials "who were the first to escape training." When visiting a students' training camp, he stressed that his own son, Qusay, was among the students and that he had already been through other training courses.[45] This step attested to the strong psychological and physical pressures inflicted by Iran. Iraqi officials and the media gave various reasons for the move. Asserting that it was a "national and historical necessity," they said that it was a preemptive measure that would at the same time inculcate feelings of patriotism among students, discipline them and prepare them better for the military life that was expected of them after they completed their studies. Husayn gave the two most important reasons for training students. The first was to fight demoralization among soldiers at the front, for "if the young fighters return from the front and find other youths of their age hanging around in the streets...this will reflect negatively on their zeal and relationship with the front." The second was to prevent dissent because "from the educational viewpoint it is incorrect for students to continue to walk aimlessly in the streets during the summer holidays and to be exposed to negative influences."[46]

It seems that the mobilization of students was quite controversial, causing unrest among them.[47] The campaign unleashed by the media to justify the "militarization" (*'askara*) of students was only one indication of this. Discussing the benefits of training, a high-ranking officer disclosed that both the question of training and participation in the fighting were controversial issues among students.[48] Echoing this unrest, Husayn said teasingly that students should be aware of the fact that, like them,

Iraqi women are also trained in the use of arms. However, he stressed "I am confident that Iraq's men are numerous enough and will not need Iraqi women to fight on the battlefield."[49] Nonetheless, Husayn who had personally initiated the move, began to fear alienating this important sector of society, which had always been a hotbed for "revolutionary" activities. Hence the urgent need to appease the students. In a bid to allay their fears about participation in the fighting, Husayn disclosed in October that the political and military command had discussed the issue and reached the conclusion that the Army was strong enough to defeat Iran by itself. "Accordingly, we do not have to send the students whom we prepared in the training camps to the battlefields."[50]

In the aftermath of a conflict between a commander of a training camp in Dhi-Qar and a member of the National Union of Iraqi students (controlled by the Ba'th) the RCC decided not only to expel the commander from the Army but also to arrest him and to punish other commanders.[51] By publicizing this incident, which was exceptional, the leadership clearly intended to signal to the students that it was on their side. In an attempt to boost the students' morale, the authorities organized throughout the country parades of students returning from the training camps. In one of these parades the students presented Husayn with a "deed" written with their own blood, whereby they promised to be "his loyal sons."[52] On 22 November the colleges and universities were reopened with the slogan "We turn the rifles' muzzles into lances which write the history of great Iraq and we also turn the pens' edges into lances in the chests of the invading enemies."[53]

By the end of the year, the Culture and Information Minister could announce that 677,541 fighters had been trained in arms since the Faw battles.[54]

COMBATING DEMORALIZATION

The problem of demoralization both at the front and in the rear became acute in 1986. Husayn himself betrayed this fact when he declared in August: "If we assume that on a certain day we closed our eyes until you [Iranians] reached the eastern tip of Baghdad, God forbid, then we will have the factors of zeal, honor, vigor, faith and dignity that enable us to drive you out of our borders...."[55]

Especially unnerving was the setback at Faw. The high number of dead weighed heavily on the Iraqis who already suffered from numerical inferiority *vis-à-vis* Iran. On the other hand, the Iraqis were less prone to martyrdom (*shahada*) than the Iranians. With a view to reducing disaffection, the authorities ordered for the dead to be transported at night and for the bodies to be delivered in "installments" after being kept in huge refrigerated store houses sometimes for weeks. In addition they forbade the use of black calicos on the houses, a traditional sign of mourning.[56] They had banned public funerals since the beginning of the war. Indeed, concern for casualties had become a greater factor than ever in Iraq's military decisions, which the President himself admitted: "We had to deal with the details of the war with patience and rationalism to reduce our losses [and] safeguard the blood of our sons."[57]

The unpopularity of the war was reflected in desertions from the battlefield and attempts to escape conscription altogether by fleeing abroad, for example. *Le Monde* reported that by October 1986 there were 30,000 deserters hiding in the southern marshes alone.[58] One way of fighting desertion was to impose the death sentence on those who attempted it; this measure had already been introduced at the beginning of the war. In an apparent attempt to "speed up" the process and make it more effective, the authorities reportedly formed an "execution brigade," generally stationed right behind the frontline, which had the task of executing "cowards" and "backsliders" on the spot.[59] In addition, the RCC ruled that a wife could leave her husband if he deserted to the enemy or escaped conscription for a period of six months. The "divorce" would be revocable if he rejoined the Army, but would be considered final if he deserted a second time.[60] Similarly, the media published "stories" from time to time about deserters; one was about a father who killed his son because he had refused to join the Army. Declaring this father a model for all Iraqis, President Husayn decorated him with the Rafidayn Medal.[61] Art was also used as a tool to fight desertion. Thus, the national theater company produced a play about a mother who burned her son alive because he had deserted from the Army. She did this as she sang the song, "Better fire than disgrace" (*al-nar wala al-'ar*).[62] At the same time, Husayn attempted to raise the specter of an Iranian invasion, which would be facilitated by the cowardice of the Iraqi soldier. "Every mother will tell her son: 'May you not drink my milk if you let the aggressors cut off your mother's breast. They will cut it off if you do not fight.' "[63]

The exposure of the big cities — Baghdad, Basra, Mosul and Kirkuk — to Iranian shelling was of great concern to the authorities because it brought the war to the very homes of the people and underlined the Government's helplessness. Basra, which was the closest to the fighting, suffered the most. Dubbed "the city of the million fighters," Basra had always been the target of shelling. In the second half of 1986 the residents showed increasing signs of weariness, and a large exodus began to take place. The authorities attempted to prevent this, but had to give up. However, they warned those leaving that the Government would not provide assistance for resettlement elsewhere.[64] Husayn himself visited the city at the end of the year in an attempt to stem the flight, but to no avail. The exodus from Basra caused severe pressures on Baghdad, so much so that the Government passed a law allowing only those who had been born in Baghdad before 1977 to live there.[65] No less worrying were the missiles that began to strike Baghdad — the capital and the most densely populated area in Iraq — in September. There was pressure on the Government for retaliation, but the Government feared the consequences of such a move, which might have affected the other cities and increased the general demoralization, while only adding to the determination of the Iranians to fight. Hence Husayn and other officials advised restraint and patience, justifying this stance by mentioning the need to achieve international support, and to prove that Iraq was "a civilized country."[66] At the same time the regime sought to exploit the shelling to fan the flames of hatred against Iran and increase Iraqi motivation to fight.

The shelling was also used as a safety valve for the expression of feelings of exasperation about the war. Thus, while the regime kept completely silent about its dead soldiers and banned public funerals for them, it gave wide publicity to the victims of shelling. It also encouraged public funerals for these victims, with thousands of participants calling for revenge.[67] But despite declarations that Iraq would not be dragged into the "war of cities," the Government finally had to give in to pressure and resumed bombing Iranian cities despite the severe consequences.

THE IMPLICATIONS OF THE OIL CRISIS AND THE ACCUMULATING DEBTS

The country's economy, which began to deteriorate in 1982, reached a critical point in 1986 as a result of the cost of the war and the fall of oil prices on the world market. By the end of 1986, Iraq's foreign debts totalled between $50 bn and $65 bn, according to different estimates,[68] and its oil exports (1.5 m barrels per day) was still down by 50 per cent from the pre-war level because of the closing of the pipelines through the Gulf and Syria. Yet Iraq's predicament was such that although it had managed to boost its oil exports by one half since it had opened the new pipeline through Saudi Arabia in September 1985, its income from oil in 1986 was approximately $6–7bn, down by almost one-half that of 1985. This paradox can be easily explained by the fall of oil prices, whose impact on war-torn Iraq was keenly felt.

The Government was deeply concerned about developments in the oil market that threatened to turn upside down all its calculations and programs. Referring to it all as a "plot," Husayn nonetheless tried to reassure the people that the Government had the ability to weather the crisis. He stressed repeatedly that the situation was "temporary" and that the war had prepared Iraq to better absorb the shock: "This is because, at least since 1982, the war has compelled us to establish a correct balance in our social and economic policy based on expecting the worst." Recalling that Iraq had reduced its number of giant projects, he stressed: "The fall did not take place from the top of the ladder downward but from the middle or the lower rungs of the ladder. Our ribs were not broken; we only sustained some bruises."[69] However, despite Husayn's assurances, the picture continued to look bleak.

The difficult economic situation had an adverse effect on Baghdad's foreign relations. A very thorny problem was its inability to pay debts on time, which undermined its credibility and jeopardized new deals. In March, the Iraqi state-owned bank, Rafidayn Bank, unilaterally suspended debt repayments to banks in France, Japan and other countries, an act which deeply worried the financial community. (Iraq actually wanted to defer debt repayment for six years.)[70] Similarly, uncertainties regarding the strength of the Iraqi economy increased the restiveness of its trading partners. Thus, in the summer, New Zealand cut off supplies of dairy products when Iraq fell $30m behind in payments.[71] Indian companies reportedly ceased taking on new commitments in Iraq after they failed to receive payment of 1983 debts rescheduled for 1986. Similarly, banks in France ceased financing new trade with Iraq in May.[72] The Iraqi Government found it difficult in 1986 to persuade its main partners — France, India, Turkey, West Germany and Japan — to reschedule debts, sometimes for the second or third time. Although by the end of the year Iraq did succeed in rescheduling most of its debts, its prestige was seriously affected.

THE ADVERSE EFFECTS OF AUSTERITY

The Government was forced to abandon all development projects during the year. It had to give priority to military imports and cut down civilian ones while at the same time attempting to reduce as much as possible the flight of hard currency abroad. The war crippled the growth of the industrial and agricultural sectors; inflation stood at 50 per cent annually;[73] and simple commodities were lacking; and a policy of austerity was implemented. The first to be affected were foreign workers, especially Egyptians who constituted the major group in the country — about 1.5m persons. During the first five years of war, the number of Egyptian workers in the country increased. This trend came to a halt at the end of 1985, and then reversed itself from the beginning of 1986 when Egyptian workers started to leave. It was reported that by the summer of 1986, 200,000 Egyptians had left,[74] and by the end of the year the number had risen to 750,000.[75] Although the numbers could not be corroborated, the trend was obvious. There were two main reasons for the exodus, which appears to have taken place with the tacit encouragement of the Iraqi authorities. The first was the reduction in the number of jobs available, which, according to *al-'Iraq*, prompted the authorities to "freeze" the work permits for foreigners.[76] Although the Iraqi Government had encouraged Egyptians to settle in Iraq with a view to increasing its population, it could no longer do so at the expense of unemployment for Iraqis and at the risk of social instability. Second, to keep hard currency, the authorities reduced by about 55 per cent the amount a foreign worker was allowed to send abroad — from $175 a month to $75. These limitations left the Egyptians with fewer incentives to stay in Iraq and gave rise to attempts to smuggle money abroad. At the end of 1985, the authorities arrested 112 Egyptians accused of forming "bands specializing in forgery, currency smuggling and economic sabotage." Ten of the 112 were sentenced to death by the Revolutionary Court "for carrying out sabotage against the economy more than once,"[77] but were later amnestied (see below).

Not only foreigners but also Iraqi businessmen and wealthy citizens who were becoming increasingly worried about the prospects of the war tried to smuggle hard currency abroad. The Government attempted to combat this phenomenon by imposing a ban on travel abroad except for official or urgent medical reasons.[78] (The aim of this ban was also to prevent desertion from the Army.) It seems, however, that Iraqis attempted to bypass the ban by forging passports of foreign countries and other official documents. In fact, at the beginning of the year, the RCC decreed that death or life imprisonment would be the sentence for persons who forged the passport of another country, or official papers "for the sake of acquiring financial benefits which might harm the national economy."[79]

Another means of preserving hard currency was to cut civilian imports. Luxury goods had been completely banned since 1982 while allocations for other civilian imports were cut down from $13 bn in 1985 to $10 bn in 1986.[80] These measures resulted in a shortage of consumer goods, foodstuffs and spare parts and precipitated price rises. The Government itself attempted to raise the price of bread by 20 per cent but the National Assembly rejected this proposition.[81] The shortage of various commodities resulted in an increase of black-market activities, hoarding and profiteering to the point where the secret services had to be mobilized to combat them. The newspapers published articles and caricatures criticizing these practices. Non-Iraqi sources claimed that the country's financial crisis had become so acute that the Government was forced to cut various benefits granted to bereaved families since the beginning of the war.[82] If true, this meant that the Government had been obliged to renounce the very mechanism it had developed for absorbing public indignation toward the war. On the other hand, lowering the standard of living would have affected morale and undermined the social basis of the regime.

INFITAH

One of the developments with potentially far-reaching implications not only on the economic but also on the social and political levels was the continued expansion of the private sector. This policy of economic *infitah*, or the open-door policy, which had received impetus with Husayn's advent to power in 1979,[83] continued its upward trend during the war. *Infitah* was applied to industry, agriculture and foreign trade. To cite one example, in 1980–82, the private sector increased its share of exports (excluding oil) ten times, from 4.4 to 45.9 per cent.[84] In 1986 appropriations for the export of the private sector were increased by 27 per cent for industry and 8 per cent for agriculture.[85] The same upward trend was also noticed in manufacturing, construction and transportation. Husayn disclosed on one occasion that there were companies in the private sector "with capital of more than 3m dinars" and that a citizen could establish "a company with capital of 50m dinars"[86] It seems, however, that it was in the field of agriculture that the private sector received the greatest incentives. Since 1979, price policy, agricultural credit and new marketing arrangements appeared to have been consciously designed to expand private-sector activities.[87] According to the President, the Government leased "vast areas" to an individual or a group of people, sometimes "thousands of dunams [4 dunams = *c* 1 acre]," on the understanding that they would be put to good use.[88]

What were the motives behind this policy? Husayn, the main driving force behind it, explained that leaving economic activity exclusively in the socialist sector hampered development and creativity and encouraged bureaucratic and routine-like processes.[89] A Western analyst suggested that the motive was not only economic, namely to get rid of shortcomings of the socialist economy, but also political: it aimed to consolidate Husayn's power following his accession to the Presidency. Thus, his encouragement of the private sector has weakened the hold of the Ba'th Party on the public sector of the economy and "paved the way for the emergence of a new, as yet amorphous group, rather than a class upon which an increasing amount of the President's political base and legitimacy rest."[90] The war has added new incentives to *infitah* as a result of the need to cut expenditures in the public sector on the one hand, and the desire to attract foreign entrepreneurs and encourage trade and economic relations with Western countries, on the other.[91]

For all the progress it had made, *infitah* still appeared to be highly controversial, both on ideological and practical grounds. The expansion of the private sector appeared to be clashing with a main Ba'thi tenet, namely Socialism (for the controversy in 1982 see *MECS* 1982–83, pp 568–69). On the practical level, privatization threatened to undermine the hold of the party apparatus on one of the country's most important centers of power. The fact that only in 1983 was privatization of agriculture given an official blessing through legislation was seen as a sign of this controversy.[92] Moreover, opposition to *infitah* continued well into 1986. This was inferred from a talk in which Husayn went to great lengths to explain the importance of the private sector, to justify it, and to encourage its expansion. Stressing that the state of conflict between the socialist and the private sectors had disappeared and that the private sector had come to be considered a "part of the national wealth," Husayn attempted to attract more people to become active in the private sector. He said that the private enterprise in Iraq was "fortunate" for "there are people who did not have a piaster...and have come to own a lot now." At the same time, echoing criticism on profiteering in the private sector, he warned "We want private enterprise to develop, but private enterprise must help us by not taking a short-term view of profit."[93] Indeed, for all its blessings, *infitah* was not without risks. First, there was the danger that the private sector would get out of hand and crystallize into a class with its own identity and solidarities and oppose the regime. Second, the quick expansion of this sector, especially in wartime, tended to encourage quick enrichment, to highlight the clash of interests between the public and private sectors, and to underline social inequalities, thus increasing tension among the different social strata. Moreover, the engagement of certain members of the ruling elite in private enterprise[94] was liable to split the elite, on the one hand, and alienate it from its bases of support, on the other. Lastly, liberalization of the economy was likely to bring about pressures to also liberalize the political system, a prospect highly undesirable for the regime. Hence the regime had to tread very cautiously on this issue and to apply checks and balances along the way. A Western analyst summed up the limits of *infitah* as follows: "Iraqi *infitah* has been designed to stimulate economic performance and the popularity of the political elite, and not to transform the economic system from a state capitalist into a free enterprise one... nor politics from authoritarian to liberal democratic."[95]

THE OPPOSITION

The various opposition groups did not exploit the erosion in the regime's standing; they did not unite or act in concert against the Ba'th. The ideological gulf remained the main stumbling block toward establishing a viable national front of Communists, Kurds and Shi'is. The Ba'th remained well entrenched in the center and the south of the country so that the opposition did not make significant headway there. On the other hand, the regime's hold on the north was more tenuous, and that was why the various opposition groups tended to act against the regime via the north. In adddition, the vitality of the Kurdish opposition in the north had convinced Iran not only to turn them into the main vehicle for destabilizing the Ba'th but also to attempt to unite all Kurdish groups (see below), as well as to form an alliance between them and the Iraqi Shi'i opposition. Toward the end of the year, Iran did succeed in bringing the Kurds and the Shi'is to negotiate methods of cooperation between them (see below). It also convened, at the end of December, "a conference of solidarity with the Iraqi people" in Tehran, with the participation of various dissident Iraqi groups, excluding apparently, the Communists. However, despite the Iranian endeavors, a genuine alliance among the Iraqi opposition parties was not formed. Also despite the cooperation between Iran and the Kurds, the two parties did not overcome their mutual suspicions; Iran feared a too independent and strong Kurdish national movement, while the Kurds suspected a sudden Iranian betrayal.

One party that suffered from fragmentation and growing isolation was the Iraqi Communist Party (ICP). Its fourth congress, held in November 1985 in the Kurdish north, aimed at uniting its ranks but actually deepened internal rifts (see *MECS* 1984–85, p 468). The conflicts evolved around the line the party should adopt on the war, the legitimacy of the congress, and the party leadership. One splinter group criticized the deepening gulf between the leadership and the rank and file, as well as its domination by Kurds, claiming that they constituted 50 per cent of the leadership.[96] In the political report published after the congress the main group remained silent on such internal conflicts. However, it did express frustration about the possibility of establishing a National Front. The report explained that the Patriotic Union of Kurdistan (PUK) not only opposed any alliance with the ICP, but also went so far as to launch propaganda and even physical attacks on Communists. Nor were prospects of cooperation with the Islamic groups any better, for, as the report pointed out, in spite of all ICP endeavors and "its positive stands" toward "the Islamic forces," they "continued to oppose any form of alliance."[97] Although the ICP appeared to have lost its vitality, the authorities' apprehensions of it did not diminish. At the beginning of the year, Fadil Barrak, the head of Intelligence, published a book *Alliance of Opposites* about the ICP and *al-Da'wa* parties' "treasonous stand" on the war and gave instructions to Ba'this on how to treat these parties, warning them to take precautions against them. On the ICP he wrote: "Check this cursed party, it is dangerous."[98]

RELIGION AS A POLITICAL VEHICLE

The military threat sharpened Baghdad's sensitivity toward religion. The Iranian success at Faw and the fact that the most important offensives were from the Shi'i south raised fears that further successes might precipitate a surrender en masse of Shi'i soldiers or of the Shi'i segment of the population, which was more susceptible to Khomeyni's Islamic appeals than the Sunnis were. Although it did not abandon its strict secular ideology, the Ba'th attempted to show more deference to Islam, mainly with symbolic gestures. In an attempt to emulate Iranians and to raise the motivation of the Iraqi soldiers, Saddam Husayn encouraged his soldiers with calls such as "God is Great." One Iraqi Army unit was named "The God-is-Great Force" (*Quwwat Allah Akbar*), while military communiqués started quite often with a Qur'anic verse. In addition, the authorities dispatched men of religion to visit soldiers at the front. Summarizing the activity of his Ministry of *Awqaf* and Religious Affairs, 'Abdallah Fadil disclosed that 4,250 men of religion were government employees, and that his Ministry also handled welfare projects such as building hospitals, schools and markets. Lauding the President's role in this field, he said that Husayn was concerned with the reconstruction of religious sites, that he contributed money for the purpose, and that eight new mosques in different parts of the country were named after him.[99] In another gesture of piety, Husayn made the small pilgrimage to Mecca at the end of the year.

By far the most important concession toward religion was the move to enforce public observance of Ramadan. Restaurants and cafés were instructed to close during the fasting hours, while all nightclubs were ordered to close throughout the holiday period. Internal security forces were entrusted with supervising implementation of the decision.[100] In addition to pacifying the religious segments of the population, the exceptional move was introduced for economic reasons too. With the closure of the nightclubs, several thousand foreign bar girls were asked to leave the country; this helped to preserve hard currency.[101] On the other hand, it became necessary to prepare the public for new austerity measures. The closure of nightclubs and bars was also intended to reduce tensions between rich and poor and increase identification with the mourning families.

The Government was far more strict when religious rites clashed with its interests. Thus, fears that the pilgrimage to Mecca would be exploited either to escape military service or smuggle money abroad, or establish contacts with Islamic Fundamentalists from other countries, prompted the authorities to place more obstacles than before in the path of pilgrims. In 1986, only men over the age of 55 who had never performed this duty were entitled to go to Mecca (in 1985, the age limit was 50). Also, while in 1985 all bereaved parents were entitled to go on pilgrimage, in 1986 the right was restricted to those going for the first or second time.[102]

Although Husayn genuinely feared the impact of Shi'i Fundamentalism on Iraq, he also used the threat of it as a means of combating disaffection within the Ba'th and shoring up support for himself. Thus, in his speech before the Ninth Extraordinary Regional Congress, he raised the specter of Shi'i Islamic revolution, saying that "the most dangerous aspect of this conspiracy...was the religious intermingling between Iraq and Iran."[103] Nonetheless Shi'i opposition did not constitute a serious challenge to the regime. The most vocal group was the Supreme Assembly of the Islamic Revolution in Iraq (SAIRI), an umbrella organization based in Tehran and financed and supported by it. However, in spite of this backing, SAIRI's contribution to the destabilization of the Ba'th was inconsequential. The Iranian Prime Minister, Husayn Musavi, indirectly expressed his frustration with the group while addressing its general session in early January. Alluding to internal differences, Musavi said: "The oppressed Iraqi people expect more of you, and their expectation demands that your activities have greater variety and diversity and be based on greater expertise."[104] During the session, SAIRI elected a new leadership. Muhammad Baqir al-Hakim, the outgoing spokesman, was elected president, Sayyid al-Hashimi became spokesman, and Abu Ahmad al-Ja'fari became secretary. However, it appears that the results of the session were disappointing to *al-Da'wa*, the main Shi'i opposition group in Iraq. *Sawt al-'Iraq*, one of its organs, attacked SAIRI for the way it had conducted the elections, for its inactivity, and for not allowing "Iraqis and Islamic cadres" to take responsibility on "their issue,"[105] probably implying that SAIRI had become a mere tool in the hands of the Iranian Government. Throughout the year, SAIRI issued communiqués supporting Iran in the war; it sent a delegation to Faw and claimed that it had sent volunteers to fight with the Iranian Army. In November in Tehran, a tripartite meeting was held with the participation of Muhammad Baqir al-Hakim, Mas'ud Barazani, head of the Kurdish Democratic Party (KDP), and Jalal Talabani, head of the PUK, to coordinate activity against the Iraqi regime. After the meeting, Baqir al-Hakim said that agreement had been reached on general issues.

The Iraqi authorities continued to consider *al-Da'wa* the most dangerous Shi'i opposition group, probably because of its authenticity and its roots in Iraqi society. The fact that Fadil Barrak singled it out for special mention in his book was only one indication of this. However, *al-Da'wa* also apparently remained inactive during the period reviewed. (For the deportation of two *Da'wa* members from France, see below.) *Al-Da'wa* was one of four groups that claimed responsibility for the hijacking of the Iraqi airplane in December (see above). The authorities themselves blamed *al-Da'wa* and Iran.

THE KURDISH MENACE

The Kurdish opposition's potential to hamper the Iraqi war effort grew even stronger in 1986 than at any time during the previous six years. For the first time, the two main Kurdish opposition groups, Barazani's KDP and Talabani's PUK, were cooperating with Iran concurrently. Moreover, these two historical rivals made an effort to patch up their differences and coordinate activities against the Ba'th. These new factors, added to the precarious hold of the regime on the north, the vulnerability of the area because of the presence of the oil fields and the oil pipeline to Turkey and the threat of an Iranian offensive coordinated with Kurdish forces from within, alarmed the regime. Sometimes even the President betrayed such feelings: "With God's help we will be victorious, and all the other conspiracies, be they from the Kurdistan mountains or from other places, will be of secondary or tertiary importance."[106] Referring to Kurdish opposition, he said on another occasion, "Regrettably, some of these people were corrupted by the late Barazani" (the Kurdish national leader until the mid-1970s). However, he stressed, "The Kurdish people are not represented by those who stab Iraq in the back and stand by the enemy."[107] Indeed, the regime was so alarmed by these developments that it formed special units called the "Light Battalions" (*al-Afwaj al-Khafifa*). They were manned by Kurds who were being paid by the Government and whose task was not only to fight Kurdish guerrillas but also Iranian troops. This force, which according to one estimate accounted for 150,000–250,000 persons,[108] was an adjunct to the Popular Army (*al-Jaysh al-Sha'bi*) and the Ba'th party militia. Its members were exempted from army conscription.

The "Light Battalions" were tested on 25 February when Iranian forces launched the "Dawn Nine" attack in the Sulaymaniyya region with a view to diverting the Iraqi Army's attention from Faw. Iran claimed it captured the town of Chwarta and 37 abandoned villages. (According to an unconfirmed report, Iranian forces were initially aided by the PUK, which, however, changed sides in the middle of fighting.)[109] The opening of the new front in the north compelled the President, whose main preoccupation was the southern front, to delegate some power to one of his associates. Husayn dispatched 'Izzat Ibrahim al-Duri, Assistant Secretary of the Ba'th and RCC Vice Chairman, to supervise the situation in the north. He became the official responsible for the region and contacted army commanders on his own, while he also attempted to mobilize Kurdish civilians to support the war, or at least to prevent demoralization and desertion from the Army. Admitting some Iranian success, al-Duri said in a meeting with officials in Sulaymaniyya: "The Iraqi armed forces will purge Iraqi territory from the filth of the invading Iranian forces in a decisive victory that will soon take place."[110] The Iraqi military magazine, *al-Yarmuk*, also admitted the initial Iranian success, which it ascribed to difficult topographic conditions and the inability to use tanks in the mountains.[111] However, by early April, the Army could declare the recapture of the area of Chwarta and 29 mountain peaks of "tactical and strategic importance" which had been in Iranian hands "since 1983."[112] It should be noted that all the communiqués and reports referred to the important assistance the "Light Battalions" had given the Army in these battles. The President himself honored members of these battalions "for their effective role in aiding the armed forces in liberating several mountainous vantage points east of Chwarta."[113] A non-Iraqi source citing military experts attributed the success to large payments made to local tribes for the capture of individual peaks.[114]

But even money and Baghdad's backing could not guarantee absolute loyalty to the regime. The volatility of the situation in the north was illustrated by the revolt in May of an official in the strategic town of Mangeesh, 40 km south of the Turkish border (near the pipeline). The official, who had been a supporter of the Government, changed sides and facilitated the ten-day capture of the town by KDP forces. The KDP claimed to have killed 50 soldiers and captured 800. However, Baghdad was reported to have sent units of the elite Presidential Guard to recapture it.

One way of placating the Kurdish population was to stress its unique position in Iraq, maintaining that only in Iraq were Kurds entitled to autonomy and to democratic elections for their own institutions. The embodiment of this autonomy was the Legislative Assembly which was elected for its first term in September 1980 and for the second in August 1983. Elections to the new Assembly took place on 13 August in a "democratic atmosphere," as the authorities said. However, wartime pressures and doubts regarding the loyalty of assembly members prompted the Government to scrutinize new members more carefully. (For the limitations of this body, see *MECS* 1979–80 pp 511–12). An amendment to the Assembly Law stipulated that a candidate "should have played a well-known role in fulfilling the [Ba'th Party] principles and aims."[115] In other words, only proven Ba'thi Kurds were permitted to be members in an Assembly which was expected to represent the autonomous will of the Kurdish population. Fifty members were elected out of 146 candidates, 20 of whom were in the outgoing Assembly. The number of women elected was doubled from two to four. Most members, aged between 30 and 40, were Government officials, and none had higher education. Three members who had held the key posts in the outgoing Assembly continued to hold them in the new one: Ahmad 'Abd al-Qadir al-Naqshbandi, the Speaker; Hikmat Haji Salim (al-Atrushi), his Deputy; and Jamal Jalal, the Secretary. Following the elections, President Husayn appointed Sirwan 'Abdallah Husayn (al-Jaf) head of the Executive Council, replacing Yahya al-Jaf.[116]

To demonstrate the importance Husayn attached to pacifying the Kurds, he attended, for the first time, the Assembly's opening session. In his speech to the Assembly, he emphasized that autonomy was "indispensable both for Iraq and the Kurdish people." He also announced his intention to turn Irbil into the summer capital of Iraq. Despite these assertions, autonomy still seemed a highly controversial issue in the Ba'th. Husayn himself noted that some officials thought autonomy would result in the partition of Iraq. Similarly, the "Arabs in Baghdad" resented the regime's endeavors to implement autonomy at a time when Kurds were barely participating in the war and instead were engaging in sabotage actvities. Attempting to justify autonomy to its Arab critics, and portray himself as the main guarantor of its implementation, Husayn said that autonomy did not mean the partition of Iraq, that the Kurds' special background was the reason for their behavior, and that in their minds "they are part of the Iraqi mind."[117]

On 15 August, Turkish air force planes crossed the Iraqi border and bombed 22 camps where Kurdish insurgents from Turkey had found refuge, apparently under KDP protection.[118] Although directed mainly against Turkish Kurds, the attack alarmed both Iran and the KDP, who interpreted it as an attempt to assist the Iraqi Government in breaking the power of the Iraqi Kurds in the north. Moreover, they feared that such an action might serve as a precedent for deeper Turkish involvement in an attempt to protect the oil pipeline which passed through Turkey, against a joint Iranian-Kurdish action.

The Turkish attack on Kurdish bases appeared to have expedited an alliance, albeit a tactical one, between Iran and the PUK. Contributing to the alliance was the fact that following the break of talks with the Iraqi Government (see *MECS* 1983–84, pp 481–82), the PUK looked for new alliances, and despite inherent mutual distrust, a convergence of interests united the PUK and the Iranian Government. Cooperation between the two first bore fruit in the attack on Kirkuk oil facilities in October in which about 100 Iranian commandos and 2,500 PUK Kurds reportedly participated.[119] It appears that contrary to Iranian claims, the attack did not cause serious damage to the installations or the pipeline. However, it did have a psychological impact on Iraq proving as it did that its most strategic area was no longer immune to Iranian or Kurdish operations. Following the attack on Kirkuk, the PUK escalated its attacks on administrative and military targets, including targets of the secret police, in its zone of operations.[120] Iran took a further step in its bid to destabilize Baghdad by convening in October in Tehran the Assembly of Iraqi Kurdish (Sunni) *'ulama*. Although a representative of the SAIRI participated in the session, it is not known whether there was cooperation between Sunni and Shi'i *'ulama*. However, Iranian mediation efforts did bear fruit in another area. In early November, Mas'ud Barazani and Talabani held a joint meeting in Tehran and agreed to mend fences between their two groups. Immediately afterwards the "Fath III" offensive was launched in Zakho, Mosul and Irbil[121] with Iranian, KDP and PUK forces participating. To stem the offensive the Iraqi Army launched a huge counterattack, which was masterminded by 'Izzat Ibrahim al-Duri and 'Abd al-Jabbar Shanshal, Minister of State for Military Affairs. In the ferocious fighting, which went on for the rest of the year, the Iraqi Army had recourse to forces of the "Light Battalions," but it appeared that many of them deserted to the rebels. Furthermore, it was reported that Kurdish women had joined guerrilla ranks.[122] By mid-December, the Iraqi Government claimed to have purged the north of guerrilla forces and to have occupied all their bases.[123] Even if this were true, the joint Kurdish-Iranian challenge to the north was not over.

THE IMPACT OF THE WAR ON FOREIGN RELATIONS

THE ARAB COUNTRIES' CONFLICTING ATTITUDES

Iraq's hopes of turning the occupation of Faw into a lever for mobilizing all-Arab support in the war were not fulfilled. (For a detailed discussion, see essay on inter-Arab relations.)

Most exasperating for Baghdad was the stance of Syria, which remained Iran's main supporter in the war. Prior to the occupation of Faw, Syria's officials let it be understood that if Iranian forces were to occupy an inch of Iraqi territory, Syria would change its stance and break its alliance with Iran. Nothing of the kind happened, and embittered Iraqi officials repeatedly reminded Damascus of its promises as well as of the fact that Iraqi forces had come to its rescue when it was in a critical military situation in the 1973 Yom Kippur war. Damascus' position looked even more harmful against the background of the severe economic crisis which swept Iraq in 1986 and which could have been alleviated significantly if Syria agreed to reopen the Iraqi-Syrian pipeline it had closed in 1982. In fact, intensive efforts were invested from October 1985 until June 1986 in mediating between Syria and Iraq, and one of the aims was to open the pipeline. Throughout the mediation attempts, in which the Soviet Union, Saudi Arabia and Jordan took part at different stages, relations between Syria and Iraq developed on two opposing levels. While reconciliation talks went on discreetly behind the scenes, the two countries exchanged vitriolic attacks, each blaming the other for treason and for interfering in the other's affairs. However, because of Damascus' isolation in the Arab world, its worsening relations with Iran, and strong pressures, especially from King Husayn of Jordan, expectations ran high that a meeting scheduled for 13 June between an Iraqi and a Syrian representative would lead to a breakthrough; but Damascus canceled the meeting at the last moment. Meanwhile it transpired that Damascus was aiming only toward achieving a better bargain with Iran. The collapse of the negotiations, which constituted an economic, political and strategic blow for Iraq, prompted it to declare that the Iraqi-Syrian pipeline would be closed forever, and that Baghdad would develop alternative pipelines which would free it from dependence on Syria.[124] In the aftermath of the abortive negotiations, relations between the two became more strained than ever. Hafiz al-Asad's call in September for Iraqi-Syrian unity was met with derision in Baghdad. In fact, at the beginning of the year, on two different occasions, Saddam Husayn had voiced skepticism regarding the possibility of uniting the Arab countries under one Arab leader[125] when he said: "The Arabs are today 22 countries, 22 situations, 22 rulers or leaders, 22 economic and social situations and 22 special national [*watani*] situations [*wad'*]."[126]

No less disheartening for Baghdad was the position of Libya which, like its ally Syria, was one of Iran's main supporters and arms suppliers. As with Syria, attempts were made at end of 1985 and in early 1986 for a reconciliation between Baghdad and Tripoli, but nothing materialized. In March, Tariq 'Aziz called on the Arab League to review Syrian and Libyan membership in the League in view of their anti-Iraqi stands. Iraq took the opportunity to retaliate against Libya in April. In the aftermath of the American raid on Tripoli (see chapter on Libya), Libya called for an Arab summit conference to condemn the US and to prepare sanctions against it. While Iraq paid lip service by condemning the American attack, it used the occasion to attack Libya for its "treasonous" stance on the war, and to prevent the convening of a summit that would deal solely with the attack. In fact, Iraq's insistence that the summit should also deal with the Iraqi-Iranian war, a request which was backed by other Arab countries, frustrated the convening of the Arab summit altogether (see essay on inter-Arab relations).

Relations with Egypt, one of Iraq's staunchest supporters in the war, underwent a minicrisis in the first part of 1986. This crisis developed independently from the strong backing Egypt provided to Iraq during the offensive on Faw, which reportedly included an airlift of weapons and ammunition.[127] The minicrisis evolved around the trial of 112 Egyptians and the death sentences given to ten of them (see above). The incident caused an uproar among the Egyptian public and in the media. At the time, there were still 1.5m Egytpians working in Iraq;[128] and there were fears of an exodus of Baghdad's Egyptians, which would exacerbate the economic situation in Egypt. Baghdad's intention to execute ten Egyptians elicited strong criticism from the Egyptian Bar Association, which blamed the Iraqi authorities for attempting to apply capital punishment retroactively, and emphasized that the "war should not be used as a license to violate human rights."[129] Iraqi officials responded by expressing their indignation over the "unjust" attack on Iraq in the Egyptian media. The National Assembly Speaker emphasized: "We...officially protect the Egyptian community against any friction or challenge."[130] On 1 June, President Husni Mubarak contacted President Husayn in person and asked him to commute the death sentences to life imprisonment. Husayn acquiesced and the crisis was over. Both parties were satisfied that this side issue would not jeopardize the important relationship they had. In July, two agreements were signed for cooperation on information and for economic, trade and technical relations. In August, the Iraqi Minster of Defense went to Cairo to discuss a stronger military relationship, and requested military support and weapons manufactured in Egypt. Politically, though, there was no breakthrough. While Iraqi officials proclaimed their eagerness to see Egypt back in the Arab fold, they were reluctant to renew diplomatic relations.

Jordan remained Iraq's main supporter in the war. King Husayn visited Baghdad four times in 1986, and added to his tasks that of mediating between Baghdad and Damascus. Although he failed in his first round of talks, he reportedly renewed his attempts in the fall, but failed again. On the other hand, it was reported that the strong economic Jordanian-Iraqi relations had come under a cloud because of the latter's inability to honor its debts.[131] Another potential source of friction between the two countries was the fact that Baghdad had become the main supporter of the 'Arafat faction in the Palestine Liberation Organization (PLO), following the rupture in relations between him and King Husayn (see chapter on the PLO).

The position of the Gulf states, which from the very beginning of the war had been caught between hammer and anvil, became even more complicated in 1986. The occupation of Faw seriously alarmed these countries — especially Kuwait — because it brought the war to their doorstep. Also, pressures by both belligerents increased significantly: while Iraq pressed the Gulf states to increase political, economic, financial and strategic support, on the ground that it was fighting their war, Iran said it would punish them if they continued to support Iraq and would only spare them the horrors of war if they stopped this support. Since the Gulf states were also facing economic difficulties because of the oil crisis, they found it more difficult now to allocate huge sums of money to help Iraq. Above all, the Gulf states feared that Iran would have the upper hand in the war and turn its Army against them. Trapped in this difficult situation, the Gulf states were very cautious in their attitude toward the belligerents. Saudi Arabia attempted to mediate between Baghdad and Damascus, both at the beginning and the end of the year, while it also increased its pressure on Syria to stop aiding Iran; but nothing happened. In March, Kuwait and Saudi Arabia renewed the three-year agreement under which they would jointly sell 350,000 barrels of their own oil on Iraq's account.[132] Both countries were also providing Iraq with some important logistical support, including shipment services in Kuwaiti harbors and the transport of oil through the Iraqi-Saudi pipeline (which became active in the fall of 1985). Saudi Arabia was also believed to be financing Egyptian military equipment to Iraq.[133] Similarly, Kuwait, Saudi Arabia and other countries in the Gulf were mentioned in connection with the servicing of Iraqi planes in their long-distance attacks on the Iranian Sirri and Larak oil terminals in the second half of 1986. At the same time, however, Saudi Arabia was attempting to open new channels of communication with Tehran. There was an exchange of visits by officials. In August and October, Saudi Arabia intervened within the Organization of Petroleum Exporting Countries to produce a surprising accommodation with Iranian cutback proposals. There were also claims that Saudi Arabia had been an intermediary between Iran and the US in their arms deal, through the businessman 'Adnan Khashoggi. In addition, Saudi Arabia had reportedly allowed oil products refined in the Kingdom to be sold through intermediaries to Iran.[134] It was apparently against the background of Saudis' wavering stand, the Iranian offensive in December and the approaching Islamic conference scheduled for the beginning of 1987 that President Husayn paid a surprise visit to Saudi Arabia on 27 December. Officially, the aim of the visit was "to perform the minor pilgrimage and visit the tombs of Muhammad and his righteous companions." While this aspect of the visit was emphasized for domestic considerations, it was the need to discuss relations with Saudi Arabia that was uppermost. Husayn, apparently, sought to prevent Saudi Arabia from supporting Iran and to request more military assistance. The Iraqi Air Force Commander accompanied Husayn on the visit.

INCREASED DEPENDENCE ON THE SOVIET UNION

Baghdad's dependence on the Soviets increased during the period under review. Iraq and the Soviet Union had in 1972 signed a Treaty of Friendship, and Baghdad must have hoped that if the worst came to the worst in the war, it might invoke this treaty to ask for Soviet assistance. The Soviet Union had been Iraq's main arms supplier, so it had become extremely important to retain Soviet goodwill in order to ensure a steady shipment of arms. Another important factor in the relationship was the large debt owed to the Soviet Union. One estimate put it at \$5 bn,[135] and Baghdad needed to defer payments. Baghdad also hoped that Moscow would exert pressure on Damascus for a reconciliation. Lastly, Iraq sought to prevent a Soviet tilt toward Iran, or at least to reduce the sale of Soviet-made arms to Iran by way of its allies.

The Soviet Union, too, was alarmed by the military developments, and its statements against the continuation of the war were apparently quite genuine. The USSR was put in a difficult position following the occupation of Faw because it began to fear that Iraq would invoke the treaty for assistance. Clearly the USSR was unwilling to become involved militarily, especially after its involvement in Afghanistan. In addition, the USSR feared that Iraq's difficult military situation would throw it into the arms of the Americans and help the US to consolidate its still precarious position in Iraq. Moscow also feared that the vulnerable position of the Gulf states would boost the US position in this strategic area. Nor were the prospects of an Iranian victory or an American return to Iran less disturbing for the Soviets. Hence Moscow's policy was to attempt to prevent an Iraqi military collapse or even a severe setback, and at the same time to widen channels of communication with Tehran.

Shortly after the beginning of the offensive at Faw, the Iraqi Foreign Minister, Tariq 'Aziz, went to Moscow for consultations. The topics of the talks were not revealed but later it was reported that the Soviet Union had dispatched 1,000 military advisers in response to Iraq's call for aid.[136] It was further reported that the Soviet Deputy Minister of Defense had made a secret visit to the Iraqi front, and that other high-ranking Soviet officials had gone to Baghdad to discuss the military situation at the front. Concurrently, the Soviets attempted to mediate between Baghdad and Damascus, but without success. Asked if the Soviet Union had exerted enough pressure on Syria to change its relations with Iraq, Tariq 'Aziz answered diplomatically, "I do not believe that the Soviets fail to act when they are convinced of something, but what can you do about a side [Syria] which does not respect the wishes of its strategic friends?"[137] In April, another high-ranking Iraqi official, Taha Yasin Ramadan, went to Moscow, but the results of the talks only became clear in May when five-year agreements on economic, scientific and commercial cooperation were signed in Baghdad. The USSR had undertaken to construct the first section of a trans-Iraq natural-gas pipeline and the main canal systems of the Tigris-Euphrates drain. While Iraq was known in the past to have criticized the Soviet technological know-how, it now felt "compelled" to increase cooperation in this field for the following reasons. It needed to buy Moscow's goodwill; Moscow provided easy loans for these projects; and Iraq sought to deepen Moscow's obligations toward it. Another sign of Iraq's eagerness to strengthen relations was that Husayn, who had occasionally criticized Moscow, now went out of his way to praise ties with the Soviets and to meet with nearly every Soviet official who visited Baghdad. In August, the USSR was reported to have urged Syria to persuade Tehran to accept a compromise in the war, but Tehran rejected the move. Although Soviet officials continued to stress the need to end the war and settle the conflict peacefully, Iraqi officials were not convinced that Moscow was exerting enough pressure. Tariq 'Aziz asked: "Is this attitude [of the USSR] enough? We say that this attitude and other similar attitudes are not enough. This is not a criticism of the Soviet Union, which is our friend...we respect what it tells us about its limited capabilities."[138] However, Iraq's frustration over the Soviet inability or unwillingness to help find a political solution to the conflict was more than balanced by the vital military assistance it received. A Soviet official commented: "had it not been for...Soviet arms supplies to Iraq, matters would have been extremely difficult."[139] Indeed, immediately after the start of the December offensive, the USSR was reported to have activated an airlift to Iraq which included modern tanks and missiles.

While the Soviet Union was strengthening its relations with Iraq, it was also increasing its efforts to acquire a foothold in Iran. One of the most important ways of doing this was through military supplies, which were channeled to Iran secretly through third parties, such as East Germany, Bulgaria, Czechoslovakia, North Korea, Syria and Libya. It was even reported that Iran had bought about half of its weapons from Soviet allies.[140] No doubt Iraq was deeply worried by this, but in the circumstances had to turn a blind eye to it.

FRANCE'S MORE "BALANCED" STANCE

The "special" relations with France underwent a crisis in 1986 for various political, diplomatic, economic and financial reasons. While France did not cease to be Iraq's main supporter in the West, it did, however, attempt to achieve some normalization with Iran and to strike a certain balance in its stance on the war, which had previously been pro-Iraqi. Ironically, this change came under the new Government of Jacques Chirac who came to power in 1986 and who ten years previously had been the main architect of the special relationship between Paris and Baghdad.

The French drive to normalize relations with Iran had various motives, but there was no doubt that fears over Baghdad's ability to withstand the war and the need to open channels to its enemy was a prime factor. In fact, there were developments in French-Iranian relations which alarmed Baghdad. The most important was the report in March of a secret sale of French arms to Iran.[141] When Iraq protested that such a policy constituted "a serious deterioration" in relations not only with Iraq, but also with other Gulf countries, Paris tried to clarify the issue by saying that the deal had been carried out without the Government's knowledge. Iraq was also concerned about the strengthening of political relations through exchanges of visits between French and Iranian officials as well as the expulsion in June of an Iranian dissident leader, Mas'ud Rajavi, and some of his supporters, which was one of the Iranian conditions for normalizing relations with Paris. Further cause for Iraqi concern was the agreement in November to repay part of the French debt to Iran. Another development that complicated French-Iraqi relations and encouraged Paris to placate Iran was the problem of the nine French hostages kidnapped in Lebanon by a pro-Iranian fundamentalist group following the expulsion in February of two *al-Da'wa* members to Baghdad. The kidnappers' main demand was that Iraq release the two *al-Da'wa* members and allow them to return to France. Strong pressure by France secured an Iraqi amnesty for the two in March, but it was only in September that they were allowed to leave the country. Although Iran denied any connection with the kidnappers, the French assumed that the key for releasing the hostages was in Tehran's hands and this was another incentive for ameliorating relations with Iran. Iraqi officials attempted to gloss over these developments by saying that it was only "natural" for France to seek to normalize its relations with Iran; that France had informed Iraq about the talks with Iran; and that Iraq "was not worried" because "France's policy is clear and firm and there will be no change."[142] Nevertheless, Iraqi officials demonstrated concern regarding the possibility of arms supplies to Iran, but their French counterparts assured them that things would not go as far as that.

Beyond the complications on the trilateral level, there were severe problems on the bilateral level as well. The most pressing problem was the economic one, as Iraqi debts to France reached $3.1 bn in early 1986.[143] What worried France was that Iraq was unable to repay debts due in April 1986. Following tough negotiations, France agreed to reschedule these debts for two to four years, but there was no doubt that these financial problems left a negative impact on relations. Another economic problem was caused by the fact that France had reduced the amount of oil it was buying from Iraq, because of the parties' inability to reach agreement on its price. This made it more difficult for Baghdad to finance its arms deals with Paris. Another bone of contention was Iraq's demand to rebuild its French-made nuclear reactor bombed by Israel in 1981. France refused to do so. Iraq, however, had more pressing requests, namely for French hardware. It was reported that, in April, Iraq and France had signed a FFr1 bn deal for mortars and ammunition. Another contract for several dozen *Dauphin* and *Super-Puma* helicopters as well as *Mirage* 2000 combat fighters was being negotiated, but financial problems apparently prevented the completion of the deal and even the supply of arms agreed upon some years earlier. On the other hand, it was reported that 12 French specialists had helped the Iraqi pilots to refuel the *Mirages* in the air on their way to long-distance attacks.

In an attempt to prevent the further erosion of Iraqi-French relations, Iraq dispatched Tariq 'Aziz to France in June, and he held talks with high-ranking officials including the President and the Prime Minister. They both assured 'Aziz that relations with Iraq would not be affected by the normalization of relations with Iran; but the fact that he went again for the same purpose in October proved that Iraq was extremely worried about the repercussions of Franco-Iranian relations. However, Iraq was not in a position to stop this tilt. It could only hope that it would not be too far-reaching.

COVERT AMERICAN TILT TOWARD IRAN

Relations with Washington, always intricate, became even more so following the revelations in November 1986 concerning the secret deal to sell American weapons to Iran which had been initiated in August 1985 (for details, see essay on the US). The deal was a severe blow to Baghdad, which felt betrayed and deceived by Washington. While American officials kept declaring their neutrality in the war and their eagerness to see it end quickly, their covert actions had the effect of both breaking this neutrality and prolonging the war. Baghdad's sense of betrayal was underscored by the memory of an earlier experience, namely the covert American-Iranian aid to Iraqi Kurds against the Ba'th in 1972–75. Worst of all, the American deal with Iran was a slap in the face of the leaders in Baghdad, especially Saddam Husayn, who had engineereed the restoration of relations with Washington in October 1984. The feeling was that Baghdad had made an important ideological and political sacrifice for this controversial move, which had not gained it strong American support, the stoppage of Western arms supplies to Iran,[144] or an end to the war. But despite all its frustrations and anxieties, Baghdad's official reaction was cautious. First, Iraq could not afford to antagonize one of the superpowers and throw it into the arms of Iran, which was considered a bigger prize than Iraq. Second, Iraq believed that in any negotiated end to the war, the superpowers should play a leading role. Third, Iraq did not wish to jeopardize American political, economic and military support, however limited they might be. Finally, if Iraq condemned Washington too harshly, it might boomerang on that same group in the Government that had supported the restoration of relations in the first place. Accordingly, Iraq did not threaten any sanctions against Washington, let alone break off relations with it. Husayn himself reacted a little belatedly "to the special and dirty cooperation" between US organs and the "Zionist entity."[145] However, the thrust of his attack was against Iran and the Zionist entity. Statements by other officials or state organs such as the RCC, the Ba'th Party or the National Assembly, also stressed the "dirty" plot against Iraq and the duplicity, as well as the inherent contradiction, in Washington's posture. However, they, too, appeared to be seeking to mitigate the attack on the US, among other things, by deflecting it toward Israel and Iran. It was argued that "as a responsible country" Iraq did not object to any state establishing normal relations with Iran, "as long as these relations do not threaten Iraq's security."[146] On the other hand, officials stressed time and again "the role played by Israel in forcing the US to indulge in policies that are hostile to the Arabs."[147] Furthermore, it was argued that Israel's main aim was to drive a wedge between Baghdad and Washington, but Baghdad would not satisfy Israel by breaking relations with the US.[148] Other arguments claimed that the US had "fallen" into the "trap of the Iranian blackmail." By focusing on Israel and Iran, Baghdad sought to absolve the US and thus justify the continuation of relations with it. Iraq also hoped to tarnish the image of Tehran (which had collaborated with Israel while purporting to liberate Palestine), and to mobilize stronger support for Baghdad's cause in the Arab world. But while Iraq itself did not take any measures against the US, in December it called on the Arab League, the Islamic Conference Organization and the Non-Aligned Movement to take "appropriate measures" against arm deals involving the US, Iran and Israel.

The restrained Iraqi reaction could also be explained by the revelation in December that, at the same time that it was shipping arms to Iran, Washington was sharing intelligence data, vital for the conduct of the war, with Iraq. This intelligence assistance, which started in 1984 (see *MECS* 1983–84, p 488), was stepped up in August 1986 on the initiative of the Central Intelligence Agency (CIA), which established a direct top-secret Washington-Baghdad link to provide the Iraqis with better and more timely satellite information. It was reported that CIA Director William Casey had met twice, in October and November, with senior Iraqi officials to ascertain that the link was functioning and to urge Iraq to escalate its attacks on Iranian installations. Following the disclosure of the Iranian deal, Casey met again with the Iraqi official; he did not apologize for the deal but pledged that the secret channel for satellite data would continue functioning.[149]

On another level, US-Iraq trade was believed to amount to $915m in 1986 with Washington importing mainly crude oil and exporting farm products.[150] However, apart from cooperation in these areas, relations were low-key throughout the year and did not develop significantly on the military or political level.

ISRAEL AND THE IRAQI-IRANIAN WAR

In 1986, Iraq tended to focus its rhetorical attacks against Israel by portraying it as the source of all evil. The attacks on Israel, which invariably referred to it as "the Zionist entity" or "Israel" in quotation marks, were at times permeated with anti-Jewish undertones. The causes for the renewed emphasis[151] were manifold. They were partly ideological and partly political, but mostly of a propagandist nature — to deflect attention from difficulties at home. In the middle of the Faw offensive, Husayn declared: "Our main enemy is the Arab Nation's enemy...that is, Zionism" which is found "in occupied Palestine" and elsewhere in the world, "for since they are Zionist Jews they must hate the Arabs." Answering a question regarding a possible war between Syria and Israel and Iraq's stand on it, Husayn said that Iraq had never, and would never, stay away from any battle on any Arab land.[152] While this stance constituted a main Ba'thi ideological tenet, flaunting it at that particular time served the immediate political goal of attempting to lure Syria away from its alliance with Iran. Iraq sought to persuade Syria to support it in ending the war so that the two would be able to concentrate their energies on the Palestine question. Following the occupation of Faw, Iraqi officials and media put increasing emphasis on "the Iranian-Israeli connection," among other things, as a way of explaining to their own public the failure at Faw. Thus, Taha Yasin Ramadan explained that Israel "participated in the planning of this aggression because the military cadres in Iran are not sufficiently qualified to prepare for this aggression in the manner in which it was carried out."[153] Propaganda apart, Baghdad seemed to genuinely fear the "collusion" or "the unholy alliance" between Israel and Iran, fears which came to a head with the revelation of Washington's involvement in the secret arms shipments to Iran. From the beginning of the year the Iraqi media published reports on secret Israeli arms shipments to Iran, and the hiring of Israeli pilots by the Iranian Air Force for combat as well as military assistance in other fields. It also put into relief Israeli statements to the effect that the prolongation of the Iraqi-Iranian war served Israeli interests. An entire theory was developed concerning Israel's "part" in the opening of the war and its prolongation. It was argued that "the essence of the conflict [with Iran] was the Persian-Jewish alliance" that was based on their historical enmity toward the Arabs, and their "common goals against the Arab Nation." It was explained that "the Zionist entity is a strategic component in the war against Iraq" because this war served its main strategic aim, namely, "to prevent Iraq from fulfilling its duty for the Palestinian cause." Furthermore, not only was Israel the element that incited Iran against Iraq, but it was also the one that "activated Syria against Iraq from the beginning of the Iraqi-Iranian war."[154] Thus, a strategic triangle was formed with Israel, Iran and Syria comprising the three states.[155] Developing this theory further, it was argued that Israel was behind the American tilt toward Iran. Thus, the Iraqi Ambassador to France explained, "It is clear that Washington no longer controls its Middle East policy... and that Israel's expansionist policy regarding the Arab world has become the driving force even for the Americans."[156] In short, "It became clear that the Khomeyniite war...was masterminded by Zionist circles."[157] Together with this stance there was apparently a somewhat more moderate one. In March, there were reports to the effect that Iraq had made a secret appeal to Israel, first via Cairo and then through direct contact with an Israeli representative at the United Nations, requesting military equipment and information about the Iranian forces.[158] Both Iraq and Israel vehemently denied these reports, but the denials could have been only a camouflage. It is possible that the request was made; but nothing materialized. On another front, Iraq violently attacked King Hasan of Morocco for hosting Israeli Prime Minister Shimon Peres, in July. However, beyond its verbal lashing, Baghdad did not take any steps to "punish" Morocco, such as breaking off relations with it, the way Syria did. (For a discussion on the Arab world's reactions to the visit, see essay on inter-Arab relations.)

TABLE 1: ARMY COMMANDERS AS OF JANUARY 1986 AND SUBSEQUENT CHANGES

Post	*Name*	*Remarks*
The Chief of Staff	Gen 'Abdallah Jawad Dhanun	
Armed Forces Assistant Chief of Staff for Operations	Lt Gen Hisham Sabah al-Fakhri	
Armed Forces Assistant Chief of Staff for Training	Lt Gen Sa'di Tu'ma 'Abbas al-Jaburi	
Commander of the Presidential Guard Forces	Lt Gen Husayn Rashid Muhammad	Until April, the Commander was Maj Gen Tali' Khalil Arhim al-Duri. Muhammad is a Kurd.
Air Force and Air Defense Commander	Lt Gen Hamid Sha'ban (Khaydar) al-Tikriti	
Commander of the Naval and Coastal Defense Forces	Maj Gen 'Abd Muhammad 'Abdallah	
Commander of the First Special Army Corps ("*Allah Akbar* Forces")	Lt Gen Isma'il Tayih al-Nu'aymi	
Commander of the First Army Corps	Maj Gen Shawkat 'Abdallah	His predecessor was (at least until the end of April) Maj Gen 'Abd al-Karim al-Khazraji.
Commander of the Second Army Corps	Lt Gen 'Abd al-Sattar (al-Ma'ini)	His predecessor, Lt Gen Diya Tawfiq Ibrahim, was dismissed after the fall of Mehran in July.
Commander of the Third Army Corps	Maj Gen Tali' Khalil Arhim al-Duri*	His predecessors were Lt Gen Mahir 'Abd al-Rashid and Lt Gen Diya al-Din Jamal (al-Shaykh).
Commander of the Fourth Army Corps	Lt Gen Thabit Sultan Ahmad*	
Commander of the Fifth Army Corps	Lt Gen Diya al-Din Jamal (al-Shaykh)*	During the year he exchanged duties with Duri as Commander of the Third Army Corps.

Post	Name	Remarks
Commander of the Sixth Army Corps	Maj Gen Sultan Qasim Hashim Ahmad	
Commander of the Seventh Army Corps	Lt Gen Mahir 'Abd al-Rashid	His predecessor Maj Gen 'Ata Shawkat was dismissed, probably at the end of February.

* Indicates he was given a medal of valor.

TABLE 2: THE COMPOSITION OF THE BA'TH PARTY REGIONAL COMMAND AS OF JULY 1986

Name	Remarks
Saddam Husayn	President of the Republic; RCC Chairman; Secretary-General of the Ba'th Party RC; Commander in Chief of the Armed Forces; Deputy Secretary-General of the Ba'th National Command (NC); Chief of the Executive Authority.
'Izzat Ibrahim (al-Duri)	Vice-Chairman of the RCC; Assistant Secretary-General of the RC; member of the Ba'th NC.
Taha Yasin Ramadan (al-Jazrawi)	Commander in Chief of the Popular Army; member of the RCC and NC; First Deputy Prime Minister.
'Adnan Khayrallah Talfah	Member of the RCC; Deputy Prime Minister; Deputy Commander in Chief of the Armed Forces; and Defense Minister.
Sa'dun Shakir	Member of the RCC; Minister of Interior; Secretary-General of the Ba'th Central Vocational Bureau.
Tariq 'Aziz	Member of the RCC and NC; Deputy Prime Minister; Foreign Minister; Official in Charge of the Arab Liberation Movement Bureau of the RCC. Christian.
Hasan 'Ali (al-'Amiri)	Member of the RCC; Trade Minister; as of August Secretary-General of the PPNF; Shi'i.
Muhammad Hamza al-Zubaydi	Secretary of the Ba'th Party Northern Bureau.
'Abd al-Ghani 'Abd al-Ghafur	Adviser of the President with the Status of Minister.
Samir Muhammad 'Abd al-Wahhab al-Shaykhli	Minister of Higher Education as of July 1985.
'Abd al-Hasan Rahi Fir'awn	Adviser to the President with the Status of Minister; Shi'i (?)
Sa'di Mahdi Salih	Secretary of the Youth and Students' Bureau in the Ba'th Party.
Mazban Khadr Hadi	Adviser to the President with the Status of Minister.
Sa'dun Hammadi	Member of the RCC as of August 1986; Speaker of the National Assembly as of October 1984; Shi'i.
'Ali Hasan al-Majid*	Director'General of Security; reserve member in the former RC.
Kamil Yasin Rashid*	Director of the RC Secretariat Office.
Latif Nusayyif Jasim*	Minister of Culture and Information as of July 1979.
Fadil al-Barrak Husayn**	Director of the Baghdad Organization's Office; Head of Intelligence as of February 1984.
Radi Hasan Salman**	Official in Charge of the Party in Najaf Governorate.
'Adnan Dawud Salman**	Minister of Local Government.

* New member.

** New reserve member.

NOTES

For the place and frequency of publications cited here, and for the full name of the publication, news agency, radio station or monitoring service where an abbreviation is used, please see "List of Sources." Only in the case of more than one publication bearing the same name is the place of publication noted here. In the present chapter, however, all references to *al-Thawra* and *al-Jumhuriyya* are to the Baghdad newspapers of those names.

1. Husayn was born in 'Auja village near Tikrit but he is considered a Tikriti.
2. *Al-Masar*, 4 September; *al-Safir*, 12 September — DR, 15 September; *The Guardian*, 21 September; *Le Monde*, 15 October 1986.

3. I.e., *al-Thawra*, 22 August 1986.
4. *Time*, 21 April; *FT*, 30 May 1986. One should be cautious with regard to these numbers.
5. *Al-Thawra*, 11 February; al-Anba, Kuwait, 14 February 1986.
6. There were reports that he was executed, but later *MM* reported that he became military secretary to the President. *MM*, 4 August 1986.
7. *WP*, 7 March; *Le Monde*, 15 October 1986.
8. *Jeune Afrique*, 28 May; *Le Monde*, 15 October 1986.
9. *Le Monde*, 15 October 1986.
10. *Le Monde*, 23 September 1986.
11. *Insight*, 22 September 1986.
12. Commentators attributed the air force success in the long-range attacks as of August, to this newly acquired greater freedom of action. However, *Jeune Afrique* attributed them to the reported using of mercenary pilots. It claimed that in the attack on Sirri only two out of the 23 pilots and technicians were Iraqis. *Jeune Afrique*, 15 October 1986.
13. For the text, see *al-Jumhuriyya*, 12 July 1986.
14. *Al-Jumhuriyya*, 12 July 1986.
15. Various reports claimed that Haddad was executed but this could not be verified.
16. R. Baghdad, VoM, 28 June — DR, 30 June 1986.
17. *Al-Thawra*, 24 June 1986.
18. *Alif-Ba*, 19 November 1986.
19. *Alif Ba*, 5 February 1986.
20. 'Abd 'Ali Salman 'Abdallah, *Rural Community in Iraq* (in Arabic; Iraq: *Manshurat Wizarat al-Thaqafa wa-al-A'lam*, 1980) pp 100–1.
21. *Al-Thawra*, 23 August 1986.
22. *NYT*, quoted by WF, 29 December; *The Guardian*, 31 December 1986.
23. *Al-Thawra*, 21 January 1986.
24. *Al-Thawra*, 20 January; *Le Monde*, 29 March 1986.
25. *Al-Thawra*, 23 June 1986.
26. *Al-Thawra*, 16 January 1986.
27. *MM*, 4, 18 August; *Insight*, 22 September 1986.
28. INA, 2 October — SWB, 4 October 1986.
29. *Al-'Iraq*, 27 October 1986.
30. *Al-Thawra*, 23 August 1986.
31. *Le Monde*, 15 October 1986.
32. *Al-Thawra*, 21 January 1986.
33. APS, 14–21 June 1986.
34. In December six governors were reshuffled. On the other hand, no replacement was announced for the Minister of Light Industry, Tariq Hamad 'Abdallah, who died in the same month after a serious illness.
35. *Le Monde*, 29 March 1986.
36. R. Baghdad, VoM, 15 September — DR, 16 September 1986. The proportion is, in fact, 16m to 47m.
37. R. Baghdad, VoM, 16 July — DR, 17 July 1986.
38. *Al-Jumhuriyya*, 4 May. Iraq's underpopulation has led the authorities to officially prohibit the use of contraceptives and abortions as a means of birth control. Camillia Fawzi el-Solh, "Migration and the Selectivity of Change: Egyptian Peasant Women in Iraq," *Peuples Méditerranéens*, No 31–32, April-September 1985, p 258.
39. *Al-Thawra*, 30 May; *Alif Ba*, 26 November 1986.
40. *Al-Majalla*, 3–9 September — DR, 10 September 1986.
41. R. Baghdad, VoM, 6 January — DR, 6 January 1986.
42. *Risalat al-'Iraq*, No 58, January-February 1986.
43. APS, 21–30 June 1986.
44. *Al-Thawra*, 30 April 1986.
45. *Al-Thawra*, 25 June 1986.
46. R. Baghdad, VoM, 4 October — SWB, 6 October 1986.
47. *Le Monde*, 15 October 1986.
48. *Al-Thawra*, 2 July 1986.
49. *Alif Ba*, 15 October 1985.

50. R. Baghdad, VoM, 4 October — SWB, 6 October 1986.
51. *Al-Thawra*, 30 October 1986.
52. *Al-Thawra*, 19 October 1986.
53. R. Baghdad, VoM, 4 October — SWB, 6 October 1986.
54. R. Baghdad, 3 November — SWB, 5 November 1986.
55. R. Baghdad, VoM, 2 August — DR, 4 August 1986.
56. *NYT*, 2 March; *Le Monde*, 13 March; *FT*, 30 May; *MM*, 4 August 1986.
57. R. Baghdad, VoM, 16 July — DR, 17 July 1986.
58. *Le Monde*, 15 October 1986.
59. *The Guardian*, 21 September 1986.
60. *Al-Thawra*, 22 January 1986.
61. *Al-Thawra*, 12 January 1986.
62. *Risalat al-'Iraq*, No 58, January-February 1986.
63. R. Baghdad, VoM, 2 August — DR, 4 August 1986.
64. *FR*, 23 October 1986.
65. *Al-Thawra*, 9 December 1986.
66. Taha Yasin Ramadan to *al-Majalla*, 3–9 September — DR, 10 September 1986.
67. I.e., APS, 6-13 September; *The Guardian*, 27 November 1986.
68. *Memo*, 29 August; *Middle East Times*, 14 September; *CSM*, 12 December 1986.
69. INA, 1 June — DR, 3 June 1986.
70. *MM*, 18 August; *Middle East Times*, 14 September 1986.
71. *Insight*, 22 September 1986.
72. *MM*, 18 August 1986.
73. *Middle East Times*, 14 September 1986.
74. *Insight*, 22 September 1986.
75. *Newsweek*, 22 December 1986.
76. *Al-'Iraq*, 1 May 1986.
77. Tariq 'Aziz, to MENA, 2 June — SWB, 4 June 1986.
78. *FT*, 8 March 1986.
79. *Al-Jumhuriyya*, 24 February 1986.
80. *Memo*, 29 August; *CR*: Iraq, No 3, 1986.
81. *FT*, 8 March 1986.
82. *MM*, 4 August 1986.
83. For a thorough discussion on the policy of *infitah* see, Robert Springborg, "Infitah, Agrarian Transformation, and Elite Consolidation in Contemporary Iraq" in *MEJ*, Vol 40, No 1, Winter 1986, pp 33-52.
84. Ibid, p 50.
85. Minister of Trade, Hasan 'Ali, to *al-Thawra*, 4 February — JPRS, 16 April 1986.
86. *Al-Thawra*, 21 January 1986.
87. Springborg, op cit, p 40–41.
88. *Al-Thawra*, 21 January 1986.
89. *Al-Thawra*, 11 February 1986. In the same interview, Husayn hinted that he had advocated *infitah* as early as 1975.
90. Springborg, op cit, p 34.
91. Husayn disclosed that the incentive to Arab entrepreneurs was a governmental loan amounting to 60 per cent of the entrepreneurs' own capital. *Al-Thawra*, 11 February 1986.
92. Springborg, op cit, p 37. It should be noted that this legislation took place following the Ba'th party ninth congress, which discussed the matter thoroughly and in which President Husayn's approach had the upper hand.
93. *Al-Thawra*, 21 January 1986.
94. Springborg, op cit, p 44; *MM*, 4 August; *Le Monde*, 15 October. Husayn indirectly admitted it in one of his interviews — *al-Thawra*, 23 August 1986.
95. Springborg, op cit, p 51.
96. *Al-Nashra*, 7 April; *al-Shira'*, Beirut, 1, 15, 29 September 1986.
97. *Al-Thaqafa al-Jadida*, February 1986.
98. *Risalat al-'Iraq*, No 6, March-April 1986.
99. *Al-Thawra*, 26 September 1986.

100. *Al-Thawra*, 8 May 1986.
101. *FT*, 24 May 1986.
102. *Al-Thawra*, *al-'Iraq*, 22 April 1986.
103. *Al-Thawra*, 12 July 1986.
104. R. Tehran, 7 January — SWB, 9 January 1986.
105. *Sawt al-'Iraq*, February 1986.
106. *Al-Thawra*, 11 February 1986.
107. R, Baghdad, VoM, 15 January — DR, 16 January 1986.
108. *JP*, 13 June 1986. The number appears exaggerated.
109. *FR*, 23 October 1986.
110. INA, 3 March — DR, 4 March 1986.
111. *Al-Yarmuk*, 9 March 1986.
112. *Alif Ba*, 9 April 1986.
113. *Al-Thawra*, 13 March 1986.
114. The rate for a mountain was said to be 500,000 Iraqi dinars (£1.5m). *FT*, 28 May 1986.
115. *Al-Thawra*, 17 June 1986.
116. It is not known whether they are relatives, but they certainly belonged to the same tribe.
117. *Al-Thawra*, 29 August 1986.
118. R. Ankara, 15 August — SWB, 16 August; *Pulse*, 25 August 1986.
119. *The Observer*, 30 November 1986.
120. *The Observer*, 30 November 1986.
121. *The Guardian*, 19 November 1986.
122. *The Observer*, 30 November; *Ma'ariv*, 17 December 1986.
123. INA, 11 December — DR, 12 December; R. Monte Carlo, 12 December 1986.
124. *CR*: Iraq, No 3, 1986.
125. *Al-Thawra*, 11 February, 5 May 1986.
126. *Al-Thawra*, 5 May 1986.
127. *Al-Ra'y al-'Amm*, 16 February; *Ma'ariv*, 17 February; R. Tehran, 17 February — SWB, 19 February; *al-Dustur*, Amman, 18 February 1986. According to *al-Dustur*, Cairo was believed to have boosted ten times its arms shipment in comparison with earlier months.
128. According to the National Assembly Speaker, Sa'dun Hammadi the number of Egyptians working in Iraq was 2m; *al-Tadamun*, 31 May–6 June — DR, 3 June 1986.
129. R. Cairo, 29 May — SWB, 31 May 1986.
130. *Al-Tadamun*, 31 May–6 June — DR, 3 June 1986.
131. *CR*: Iraq, No 3, 1986.
132. *The Economist*, 15 March 1986.
133. *FT*, 23 September 1986.
134. *The Guardian*, 18 December; *AfricAsia*, No 37, January 1987.
135. *Akhir Sa'a*, 28 May 1986.
136. *Newsweek*, as quoted by *Le Monde*, 13 March 1986. The number seems exaggerated.
137. *Al-Tadamun*, 7–13 June — DR, 11 June 1986.
138. *Al-Hawadith*, 25 April — DR, 7 May 1986.
139. KUNA, 23 October — SWB, 24 October 1986.
140. *Al-Mustaqbal*, 6 September; *al-Usbu' al-'Arabi*, 30 June; *IHT*, 1 December 1986.
141. *Le Monde*, 6 March 1986.
142. Iraqi Ambassador to France to *Le Figaro*, 30 April — DR, 12 May 1986.
143. *MM*, 18 August; *CR*: Iraq, No 3, 1986.
144. Iraqi Ambassador to Washington, Nizar Hamdun, explained that the weapon sales struck at the heart of Iraq's purpose in reestablishing full diplomatic relations: to press Washington to use its diplomatic muscle to dissuade Western countries from selling weapons to Iran, *IHT*, 24 November 1986.
145. R. Baghdad, VoM, 1 December — SWB, 3 December 1986.
146. INA, 15 November — SWB, 17 November 1986.
147. Tariq 'Aziz to INA, 21 November — DR, 21 November 1986.
148. *WP*, 10 December 1986.
149. *IHT*, 16 December 1986.
150. *NYT*, 4 November 1986.

151. It seems that there was a certain lull in 1984–85.
152. *Al-Thawra*, 11 February 1986.
153. INA, 25 March — DR, 25 March 1986.
154. *Al-'Iraq*, 2, 27, 30 January 1986.
155. *Al-Thawra*, 1 July 1986.
156. *AfricAsia*, No 37, January 1987.
157. R. Baghdad, VoM, 9 November — SWB, 11 November 1986.
158. *FR*, 6 March; *JP*, 10, 21 March; VoI, 21 March — SWB, 24 March; *Davar*, 21 March 1986.

Israel
(Medinat Yisrael)

YAEL YISHAI

1986: THE TURBULENT STABILITY

Nineteen eighty-six was a turbulent year for Israel. There were recurring dramatic events which confounded the orderly conduct of politics and threatened the stability of the political system. A few highlights of the drama were Peres' visit to Morocco, Finance Minister Yitzhaq Moda'i resigning from the Government, the Herut convention and the General Secret Services (GSS) Affair. Peres' visit was designed to hasten the peace process; Moda'i's resignation put a question mark over the continuation of the Unity Government; Herut, a leading coalition party, publicly exposed its vulnerability and came very close to a virtual split; and the GSS Affair jeopardized the rule of law. While the events sowed the seeds of turmoil, nothing further developed. Peace has not been concluded, the Unity Government has remained intact, Herut continued to be united and the rule of law was not hampered. The National Unity Government continued to shape Israel's foreign and domestic policies. The partners in this Government continued to bridge their ideological and political gaps and reached a consensus which, although sometimes shaky, proved better than the alternative. Furthermore, the Israeli system seems to have developed a mechanism for self-correction; while not impeding the outbreak of crises, it prevented their expansion and escalation. Stability was maintained to the extent that motivated a renowned journalist to complain that one could "die of boredom."[1]

THE GOVERNMENT: THE PITFALLS OF COHABITATION

The transition of government poignantly reflected the turbulent stability. As the date of rotation approached, crises developed which could have doomed its existence. A last-minute solution, however, prevented a collapse. The governmental crises centered mainly on foreign and economic views and interests, but also on personal rivalries and animosities.

The first crisis in 1986 concerned the fate of Taba which was disputed by the major coalition partners. Likud accused Labor of artificially seeking to turn the Taba issue into a pretext to break up the Unity Government and evade the rotation agreement. The cause of this accusation was Peres' insistence on an inner cabinet vote on arbitration about Taba's future.[2] The interparty controversy resulted from the clauses dealing with the linkage between Israeli agreement to arbitration and Egyptian implementation of normalization. Likud Ministers demanded that Israel must attach conditions to the package deal with Egypt before agreeing to arbitration. Likud feared that, even after Israel agreed in principle to arbitration, Egypt would continue to stall and Israel would receive nothing concrete in terms of normalization and conciliation. Labor claimed that the clauses voted on already contained linkage between Israeli agreement to arbitration and Egyptian implementation of normalization.

Differences of opinion persisted but the case did not bring down the Government. After a full night's dramatic cabinet session both parties claimed victory.[3] Both parties had good reasons to be satisfied: after four years of resistance Herut had finally capitulated, and Peres secured the Likud's agreement to submit the Taba dispute to binding international arbitration. The Premier attained a 14-point document confirming all major points of the initial draft based on the Israeli-Egyptian undertakings reached in bilateral talks. For Shamir the decision was a mixed blessing. On the one hand, he failed to persuade Labor to compel Egypt to accept conciliation as a means of solving the Taba dispute. On the other hand, he had secured the inclusion of four clauses which were not included in the original draft: first, a clause regarding the report on the Ra's Burka murders and reparation to the bereaved families; second, a clause including a pledge by both countries to be "faithful to the peace treaty and the Camp David agreements"; third, a clause committing both countries to prevent terrorist presence and activity and, finally, a clause forbidding mutual hostile propaganda.[4] In addition, Shamir also gained strength within his own party. Both his opponents, Levy and Sharon, opposed Labor's draft proposal but finally voted for it, thus acknowledging their leader's authority.

The Cabinet's vote on Taba did not settle the friction within the coalition. The possibility of breaking up the rotation agreement was not abandoned by anti-Likud Laborites. A group within the party (headed by Health Minister, Mordechai Gur, and including Economic and Planning Minister Gad Yaacobi; Immigration and Absorption Minister, Yaacov Tzur; and Minister without Portfolio, Ezer Weizman) conducted an anti-rotation campaign which attempted to topple the Government.[5] Since Labor had given up the idea of establishing a narrowly based Government it now faced two choices: rotation or early elections. Many Laborites seemed to favor the second option. Preparations for the party convention planned for April (including membership census, holding of local elections and convening committees for drafting the platform) were regarded as providing opportunities to prepare for early elections. It was thus not surprising that shortly after the Taba issue had been settled the Government was embroiled in yet another crisis — this time over economic affairs.

The first hint of a crisis occurred when a group of Laborites (including Uzi Baram, Labor's secretary-general and Yisrael Keisar, the Histadrut's general secretary) opposed Moda'i's budget proposal. The rotation opponents called for the dismantling of the Government on the grounds that its economic policies were "incompatible with Labor principles."[6] The dispute resulted when the Government gave financial aid to Histadrut affiliated enterprises, including Kupat Holim and Solel Boneh. Initially the Labor Ministers accused the Treasury of halting funds and blocking an agreement on a "recovery plan" for these enterprises out of political motives.[7] Subsequently, however, the terminology (as well as the strategies of conflict) underwent change. Labor became the major advocate for "economic growth" and recovery. The Likud held fast to its economic version of "stability." Behind these slogans, specific demands were put forward. Labor demanded the establishment of a committee of five Ministers, headed by Peres, to administer the allocation of a $500m growth investment fund; Likud categorically rejected this demand, perceiving it as an infringement of Moda'i's authority. Likud also described it as a Labor attempt to monopolize the economy since the proposed committee contained a built-in Labor majority.

The issue was cloaked in ideological overtones. Peres told Labor's central committee he would not serve in a government which "destroys industry, agriculture and the settlement movement."[8] At stake, however, was not ideology but a political rift that reflected the mistrust between the two parties. The Likud feared that Labor was intensifying the crisis in order to prevent the rotation. Labor suspected that the Treasury was holding funds for distribution after the rotation while blaming Labor for retrenchment and its hardships. The putative collapse of the Histadrut enterprises fueled the flames of conflict. Labor feared that the Likud's goal was to erode Labor's economic foundations. The debate, then, between the two parties did not center on values, but on political power and the economic fortunes which ensured the implementation of this power. Instead of debating the real economic principles which divided the major coalition partners, the "rotation fever" gave rise to squabbles over "who is to pay the price for the recovery program and who is to enjoy its benefits."[9]

The crisis reached its peak when three Ministers — Moshe Shahal, Gad Yaacobi and Yaakov Tzur — demanded the break-up of the Government if the Likud did not accede to Labor's demands. The mechanism of self-correction was at work when a compromise was reached — to let private and Histadrut-controlled firms raise $450m on the capital market, at the expense of government revenues from short-term bonds. Labor Ministers decided to freeze their demands for the disputed committee. This decision cooled the crisis but did not end it. Since the Likud did not veer from its objection to a Labor-dominated economy, it was up to Labor to decide whether the Unity Government would be maintained. It was not easy to decide: on the one hand, the economic plight of the Histadrut enterprises, especially the construction company Solel Boneh, contributed to reconciliation. It was generally agreed that Solel Boneh was in dire need of financial support. On the other hand, antirotation sentiment within the Labor Party grew considerably.[10] Peres responded to his party constituency by stating he regarded "economic recovery" as more important than avoiding a coalition crisis.[11] Yet he refrained from taking decisive measures because of a compelling public objection to the breakup of the unity government. At a Labor central committeee meeting convened specifically to discuss the desirability of new elections, the Premier himself preempted a resolution to break up the Government's unity.[12]

Only a few days passed before intracoalition relations reached unprecedented peaks of tension. The event that sparked the renewed crisis was a collision between Moda'i and Peres on the basis of personal recriminations.[13] Peres was put under heavy pressure to dismiss Moda'i for the following reasons:

1. Buttressing the Premier's authority. Moda'i's disloyal and offensive statements to the media were a clear violation of the rules of the coalition game of politics. Peres had a right (or even a duty) to punish the recalcitrant Minister.[14]
2. The combination of wide public support for Labor[15] and the tarnished image of Herut in the wake of its convention (see below) prompted Peres to seek alternatives to the National Unity Government, i.e., to declare new elections.
3. New elections could establish Labor's prominence and enable the party to accrue all the fruits of victory, including economic benefits for Labor-affiliated enterprises.

There were also reasons against Moda'i's dismissal:

1. Peres could have been projected as one who nullifies agreements. Shamir, who unequivocably backed Moda'i, stated that the coalition agreement morally overrode the Prime Minister's constitutional authority to dismiss any Minister from the Likud camp.
2. Firing Moda'i implied bringing down the Government. There could be disadvantages to such a move. For example, the Likud Finance Minister, in the Transition Government, could use his position to block the aid promised to Histadrut enterprises.
3. There was no assurance that Labor would win the election. Furthermore, elections could wreak havoc with the economic stability that had been tenuously maintained. The public could punish those responsible for destroying stability.[16] Peres was thus left on the horns of a painful dilemma. He did not wish to be held responsible for the demise of the National Unity Government. But he could not, without loss of face, absolve Moda'i and continue with business as usual.

The Moda'i crisis coinciding with the Labor convention fanned the flames of the conflict. Peres publicly stated he would fire Moda'i, a statement which quashed all hopes that the crisis would dissipate. The Likud, for its part, found it difficult to back down from its commitment to oppose Moda'i's removal. It seemed that both parties would go over the brink in the interparty confrontation. At the same time, however, each party insisted that it did not want elections. Peres said that although he was determined to dismiss Moda'i, he also strongly supported the continuation of the Unity Government. His adherence to unity was prompted mainly by the Likud's threat to make Peres' credibility the main issue of the election campaign. Shamir also shunned elections. To go to the polls shortly afer the Herut convention was not too promising, especially since the party's internal conflicts had not been settled.[17] Agreeing on rejection of the electoral option, the two major parties reached an arrangement which ensured an end to the crisis.

The solution was found in the exchange of offices between Moda'i and Moshe Nissim, the Justice Minister. Nissim was acceptable to everybody. Since he was a Liberal, the party did not cede the finance portfolio. The Likud's inherent weakness in the coalition was exposed, yet the Treasury was still controlled by one of its members. Labor believed that the minister-designate would be cooperative and attentive to its demands. The crisis was thus ended when Nissim reluctantly bowed to the strong pressures exerted on him and accepted the job.[18]

Moda'i served as Minister of Justice for about three months. In July he again made insulting remarks about the Premier.[19] Once again the parties were caught on the horns of a dilemma. Peres could not publicly swallow abuse, nor did he wish to mar his credibility by impeding rotation. Likud could ill afford to do anything that would jeopardize the rotation; at the same time, it could not shy away from a colleague-minister. From a legal standpoint, both Peres and Shamir had a just claim. The Prime Minister was granted statutory powers to dismiss a minister; Shamir could have invoked the clause in the coalition agreement to make this right conditional on the consent of the other party's leader.

It was evident, however, that Peres could not overlook Moda'i's behavior without a substantial loss of prestige. This time it was Shamir's turn to yield. Moda'i's willing resignation on 22 July, half-heartedly agreed to by the Likud, ended the crisis. The justice portfolio was handed to the Tourism Minister, Avraham Sharir, who was expected to be a temporary custodian, until Moda'i's anticipated post-rotation return.[20]

Rotation took place almost on its designated date (10 October 1986), but not before last-minute obstacles cast doubt on the transfer of power. The hurdles in the way of rotation were mainly personal. Likud insisted on including Moda'i in the Government; Labor demanded the appointment of Weizman as "Minister of the Foreign Office"; Likud rejected Labor's candidates to the US embassy and other important positions; Labor opposed the intention to appoint Arens to deal with Soviet Jewry.

Division of power was also at stake. Labor demanded that Peres have the right to put issues on the Cabinet's agenda and to have a "minirotation" after Shamir's 25 months in office. Both demands were rejected by Likud.[21] All these issues were settled by a compromise. The agreement between the two parties stipulated that there would be no changes in responsibility within the Government without prior agreement between Peres and Shamir. A number of Peres' appointees would stay in office.[22] Both clauses were prone to be subject to interpretation and negotiations. They were, however, the only compromise that could have been reached with the Likud eager to hold power, and Labor reluctant to withhold it in defiance of a signed agreement.

Shamir took office on 20 October 1986. The transfer of power was conspicuously smooth. The Press described Peres' farewell speech in the Knesset as being "geared to ensuring as smooth as possible a rotation and as amiable a working relationship as possible between himself and Vice Premier Shamir in the coming 25 months."[23] Premier Peres pointed to diffused social tensions, revived international goodwill, an economy that was recovering from a deep malaise, brightening prospects for peace and the excellent record of relations with the US. Peres handed over to Shamir a government that palatably marked its achievements. In his inauguration speech in the Knesset, Shamir committed himself to the spirit of unity. A new note was nevertheless introduced. In a post-vote ceremony Shamir stated that with the Likud at the helm of the Government, "the policies of Greater Israel" would be more strongly implemented.[24] During the first period of his incumbency Shamir has done nothing to validate this statement.

The spirit of conciliation was congruent with public mood. Support for the National Unity Government (always highly pitched) continued to rise as rotation neared. As much as 63% of a national poll's respondents in September 1986 thought the Government was, in general, fairly successful or mainly successful compared with 61% in May (and only 35% in August 1985). No other government has enjoyed such high public support over the past decade. Implementation of the rotation pact was also acceptable to the public, with 60% favoring it in September 1986 compared wth 57% in May.[25]

Israel has marked a political precedent: in no other parliamentary democracy have the main rivals ever entered into a deal such as that between Likud and Labor. The parties were not honeymoon lovers but were coerced into temporary cohabitation in which each had experienced losses and gains. During the first half of the Government's life, it was mostly Labor which secured the benefits, getting an immediate return for its political investment. Likud took the helm anticipating similar rewards.

THE KNESSET: INEFFECTIVE OPPOSITION

The Israeli Parliament operated in the shadow of the National Unity Government. On the one hand, all important issues were settled outside the legislature so the Knesset lost much of its clout. Members of the Knesset were criticized for not attending sessions and for giving priority to private affairs over public commitments. In fact, the Knesset did not produce much legislation of substance. The antiracist bill (see below) dragged its feet before it was approved and made law.

Electoral reform, which had long been tabled on the Knesset's agenda, passed its preliminary hearing on 7 August in the last session of the Knesset summer term. According to the reform bill, 80 of the 120 Members of Knesset (MKs) will be elected according to a constituency system, with five seats for each of the 16 constituencies. The remaining 40 seats will be elected using the same system of proportional representation presently in force for all 120 seats. The major objectors to the bill are the small parties which anticipate their demise. Likud has also not been enthusiastic about reform. The prospects of its final adoption are thus rather low,[26] and the legal hurdles have not been cleared. The Coalition Committee for Electoral Reforms (chaired by Gad Yaacobi) made no progress owing to the Likud's objection. In December the committee did reach a consensus on limiting the period of electoral campaigning to 30 days.[27] It remains to be seen if this consensus will result in Knesset legislation.

On 27 July the first hearing of the minimum wage bill was carried and passed to the committee. Another important bill presented to the Knesset in a preliminary hearing (on 5 November) concerned equal employment opportunities for men and women. The establishment of a postal authority (on 1 January) may also be regarded as one of the Knesset's legislative accomplishments.

More conspicuous, although futile, was the activity of the smaller opposition parties. The predominance of the coalition parties, coupled with the Government's lack of legislative initiative, gave rise to intensive opposition in the form of no-confidence motions — the only strategy left for the Opposition by which it could raise its voice and be heard by the public. The frequency with which this strategy was employed indicates its usefulness for the opposing parties.

During 1986, thirty no-confidence motions were submitted, voted upon and defeated.[28] *Kach* was the most active party in tabling these motions, responsible for one third of the total. The Knesset, however, usually ignored Kahane's moves. Occasionally, parties situated far apart on the political spectrum submitted a motion of no-confidence on the same grounds. Such strange bedfellows acted together in submitting no-confidence motions regarding the issues of the "senior official" (see below);[29] the delay in enacting the antiracist bill;[30] and the Government's intention to levy taxes on pensions.[31]

Issues concerning internal affairs triggered opposition parties to submit most of the no-confidence motions (57% of the total). These included the relation between Jews and Arabs, the GSS Affair (see below), police conduct, and the Nakash affair.[32] While the no-confidence motions have not toppled the Government, the Knesset often turned into a battleground for MKs accusing each other. The feuds were not confined to members of the Opposition. One of the more severe clashes occurred between MK Menachem Porush (*Agudat Israel* — a coalition party) and Knesset Speaker, Sholomo Hillel. Porush was banned from attending five consecutive sessions of the plenum because he was abusive to the Speaker and subsequently refused to apologize.[33]

POLITICAL PARTIES: COUNTING FORCES

THE HERUT CONVENTION

The year of partisan conventions was 1986. Approaching the turnover of government, the parties of both coalition (Herut) and opposition (*Hatehiya*), large parties (Labor Party) and minor parties (*Ometz*) gathered their elected delegates and convened public meetings. Partisan convention is a two-edged sword. It is designed to increase support both within its ranks and in the public at large by rallying adherents around its flag. At the same time it may expose partisan vulnerability and weakness. This was the case of Herut, visibly plagued by deep rivalries and internal dissensions.

The events that took place at Herut's 15th convention indicated that the leadership crisis following Begin's resignation had not yet been settled, and that the intraparty rifts were deep and almost could not be bridged. Herut was divided into three factions ("camps"). The first, headed by Shamir, included mainly veteran party leadership and its descendants. The second, headed by David Levy, was supported mainly (though not exclusively) by membership of development towns. The third, headed by Ariel Sharon, mobilized support among the two constituencies. The rift within the party had various manifestations including ethnic origin, historical affiliation and personal rivalry. Such rivalry sharpened as the date drew closer for elections when the two leading contenders, Shamir and Levy, were fiercely struggling for control of the convention. All factions aimed at controlling the central committee (whose membership was to be determined at the convention), designed eventually to choose the party's new leader and its Knesset list. It was to Sharon, or alternatively to strategic devices employed by either leader, to determine who would rule the party. By virtue of his position as a party head, Deputy Premier and candidate for Premiership, Shamir had an advantage over his opponents which he skillfully employed.

Both the timing of the convention and its composition made matters tense. While Levy insisted on convening the party "as soon as possible," Shamir linked the convention to an immediate merger with the Liberal Party, which presumably contained his supporters.[34] As to the composition — Shamir insisted that delegates representing "party sectors" be co-opted, since they were unlikely to gain "rightful" representation through branch elections. Indeed the central committee decided (in February) to co-opt 150 extra delegates with the party's 1,400 delegates. The key committee nominating these delegates was to be composed of Shamir's supporters or Herut's veteran statesmen. Shamir won another victory when the central committee approved the co-option of the small *La'am* faction, most of whose delegates were his supporters. Finally, Shamir disqualified some 9,000 bogus names, seen as Levy supporters, added at the last minute to the party-voter rolls. These devices were regarded by the Levy camp as a violation of the Herut Party's Charter. Frustrated by these measures, Levy threatened to boycott the convention and appealed to the party's court which nullified the decision to allow extra delegates to be co-opted. In the same vein, however, the court decided to increase the number of "notables" nominated to the convention.[35]

Although the judicial resolution bolstered Shamir's dominance he faced severe opposition from his co-leaders. The party election gave Shamir a majority of 45%. His rivals, Levy and Sharon, however, if united could overrule him, gaining 35% and 20% respectively. This constellation added fuel to the party's factional fire. The differences that racked the party were evident even at the convention's festive opening on 9 March. As one reporter put it: "The Herut factions enter their party's convention gloves off and poised for battle."[36] All attempts to mitigate the internal strife were futile. The first contest occurred over the election of the convention presidium and its chairman. The candidates running were Eliyahu Ben Elissar (Levy-Sharon camp) and Moshe Katzav (Shamir camp). The intraleadership relations exacerbated the strife: Levy accused Shamir of undemocratic practices;[37] Shamir, for his part, refused to meet with Levy claiming "there is nothing to discuss."[38]

By the opening of the convention the disputed issues had not been solved. The actual number of delegates remained unknown because of appeals made by all camps. Even the factional makeup of the party was not clear-cut. What was clear was that Levy challenged Shamir and cooperated with Sharon for control of the convention. At the same time, Levy was also Sharon's rival; each aspired to be chairman of the party. In addition, there were intracamp ambiguities. Some groups within both Sharon's and Levy's camps were opposed to the deal between the two leaders because it lessened each leader's support. In the next few days this turned into a physical battle, fist fights, shouting and shoving. Levy exhorted his supporters to "act as soldiers in a war against conquest."[39]

The violence reached its climax when Deputy Foreign Minister Ronnie Milo, attempting to rebuke Levy's charges of disqualifying delegates numbered among his supporters, was knocked to the floor. It was ironic that this occurred after he had said, "Everyone has the right to speak here." As the attacker (Gaston Malka)[40] grabbed the microphone and hurled it from the podium, hundreds of delegates surged forward in what threatened to become a major stampede.[41]

While no blood was shed at the Herut convention, there was also no end to the fierce rivalry. The fate of the party's leadership was also not clearly resolved.

A few votes would determine the winners: the chairmanship of the mandates committee was contested by Benny Begin (Shamir camp) against Sharon, and the steering committee was contested by Levy against Arens (Shamir camp).[42] The winners of these posts were to have a crucial role in determining the makeup of the new central committee, which was to select the party's next Knesset list. The issue, however, would not be resolved at the polls. In its third day the convention was brought to a standstill when its top leaders were locked in a furious fight for party control. The personal enmity between Shamir and Levy was so blatant that reconciliation appeared remote.[43] In the first vote, Sharon scored a victory over Begin by winning 54 to 46 per cent of the vote. The rejection of Begin's name by the Herut voters marked the crashing of a psychological barrier by sending a message that the party no longer "belonged" to the veterans of the revisionist party, but had become an open organization attracting new forces.[44] In the short run, however, Sharon's victory contributed very little to the convention's orderly conduct. While it strengthened the Levy-Sharon alliance (at least during the convention), it also reinforced the opposition against Shamir. The latter, appearing on a television news program, used harsh words in characterizing his rival's camps, which added fuel to the already heated conflict. Consequently, the continued wrangling brought the convention business to a standstill.[45]

The vote taken at the convention proved that Herut is a two-pronged party, divided between the veteran establishment, mostly of European origin (headed by Shamir) and the "newcomers" (most of them born in Israel) mainly of non-European origin, who aimed at becoming leaders. Furthermore, the events of the convention also indicated that Herut had not yet overcome its leadership crisis caused by the withdrawal of Begin, the uncontested authoritative leader. The rivalry among the three contenders for control (Shamir, Levy and Sharon) was clear proof that the game of power was not yet settled and the big prize of leadership was not yet won.

Since no agreement could be secured, the 15th convention thus adjourned, putting a question mark over Herut's continued survival as a united party. The internal rift was deep, wide and unmistakable. Neither did the tainted personal relations hold out much hope for the party's integrity. Herut thus faced three options. The first was to establish an official system of factions on the basis of internal elections. This alternative had only a slim chance of being chosen since it was incompatible with the party's long tradition of centralized rule. Second, it could split into two or three parties. This would obviously prevent the fulfillment of the rotation agreement, so desired by the party which was already enjoying the spoils of power. Third, Herut could propose new elections, believed to be a suicidal move, which was rejected out of hand. Consequently, Herut had no alternative but to patch up its dissensions and present a facade of unity, which was a challenge. Levy continued to demand an immediate second session of the convention and maintained that the party institutions and office holders had no authority. Shamir, for his part, demonstrated a more conciliatory frame of mind willing to make peace — obviously on his terms. The compelling circumstances brought about a degree of moderation. A series of face-to-face meetings between Shamir and Levy enabled the absorption of the deep internal power struggle which had surfaced violently at the party convention. While the storm has now subsided, the question remains: what does it portend both for Herut and the Israeli political system?

An analysis of the events leads to equivocal conclusions. Herut was regarded by media commentators as a party which made a mockery of the democratic process. The mutual insults between the leaders of the contending factions and their followers turned democracy into a shambles.[46] There is, however, another side to this story. It was widely agreed that the Levy and Sharon camps were deprived of their rights in the convention. The fact was that, in the branch election, their factions had won a clear majority. It was the Shamir camp that attempted to pad the convention with its own appointees. The victory of Sharon over Begin, as well as Levy's ruling power, may be regarded as signs of populist, grass-roots party democracy. There are also two sides to the external effects. On the one hand, David Levy instigated populist ethnicism at a time when ethnic gaps were being palpably reduced.[47] The oriental upheaval was conceivably a "genie" of ethnic politics that could not be put back into the bottle. Although intraparty strife did not develop along clear ethnic boundaries (Katsav, for example, belonged to the Shamir camp and Micha Reiser was part of Levy's camp), it was nevertheless imbued with deep ethnic sentiment. On the other hand, the Herut convention reaffirmed what had already become a common practice. One of the positive developments in Israel's politics of the last decade has been a substantial increase in the number of politicians from Arab-speaking countries. The turbulent convention proved they are an integral part of the Israeli political process.

THE LABOR PARTY CONVENTION

The Labor Party's convention (held on 8 April) was calm and peaceful in comparison to Herut's. The delegation (a third of whom were reportedly young new faces of North-African origin)[48] overwhelmingly supported their leadership headed by Premier Shimon Peres. The composition of the convention's appointments, steering committees and presidium were approved unanimously. No power struggles were evident since the selection of the new central committee was deferred to a later convention session to be held in May. The spirit of unity was also evident in the second session (held on 18 May); neither was this disrupted by factional feuds.

The Labor Party, enjoying the fruits of power and public popularity, approved a revolution in its internal politics by adopting a new procedure to put the Knesset list together.[49] The new system was designed to broaden the franchise of choosing the party's Knesset members so that the choice would no longer be left to an appointment committee. However, the new procedure was not put into practice, since the central appointment committee nominated almost half of the membership instead of the third designed by the new regulation.[50]

Ideology played a minor role in the two convention sessions. One potential problem was the religious plank. However, this was solved when the Labor Party dropped its previous commitment to equal status for all streams of Judaism in favor of a vague "recognition" of religious pluralism.[51] The section on human rights, including a clause condemning Apartheid in South Africa, was also watered down. Obviously, the party was united around its leadership and in no mood for ideological polemics.

THE NATIONAL RELIGIOUS PARTY CONVENTION

The National Religious Party (NRP) held its convention for the first time in 12 years. The party continued to play the double game — condemning factional activity as disastrous to the party and providing the factions legal opportunities to amass power. Three major factions were contesting for votes in the internal elections preceding the convention: Zevulun Hammer's Young Faction, Yosef Burg's *Lamifne* and Hanan Porat's *Matzad*, consisting of *Gush Emunim*'s adherents. Each of these factions claimed 40% of the vote in polling for the 1,000 convention delegates.[52]

The NRP was in urgent need of unity and rehabilitation, but the conduct of the convention's affairs demonstrated that the two objectives were mutually exclusive. The long-overdue convention got off to a stormy start when the approved new party constitution (formulated by the NRP rehabilitation committee) was put on the agenda.[53] Controversy centered mainly over the composition of the central committee designed to obliterate factional representation. A split was narrowly averted as the Young Faction yielded to *Lamifne* (Burg's faction) and backed down from its demand that elections for the post of political secretary be held.[54] The NRP emerged united from its convention.

LIBERAL CENTER CONVENTION

In 1986 a new party resulted when a faction ceded from the Liberal Party to form a separate political organization. The founders of the new Liberal Center headed by Tel Aviv Mayor Shlomo Lahat held its first convention on 20 May. However, internal dissensions which were made public at the founding convention cast doubt on the viability of the party. The delegates failed to elect a party executive and the session adjourned amidst stormy pandemonium.[55]

A CLASH BETWEEN LAW AND SECURITY: THE CASE OF THE GENERAL SECRET SERVICES

The most serious crisis in Israeli politics concerned its most covert domain — the GSS. Like widening ripples in a pool, the stone cast into Israel's policy by the GSS Affair has caused underlying tensions to surface. It has also exposed Israel's Achilles' heel regarding the linkage between its security and its constitutionalism. Israel has been described as a "garrison democracy" involved in a protracted armed struggle with its neighbors while at the same time attempting to maintain the rule of law.[56] The GSS Affair vividly exposed the incompatibility of the two objectives. The clash between the security needs (as defined by political leaders) and the constitutional writs (as defined by legal representatives and their supporters within the political community) uncovered the two faces of the Israeli society — the face of the "garrison" involved in perennial conflict with bitter enemies, and the face of the constitutional democracy.

As usual, the Israeli public was the last to know the details of the event. Toward the end of May the media reported that a "senior official" was about to come under investigation for committing a serious crime. Shortly it became known that the "senior official" was no less than Avraham Shalom, the head of the GSS. The alleged crime concerned the highjacking of a Tel Aviv-Ashkelon bus (known as Bus 300) by Arab terrorists on 12 April 1984. The GSS head was suspected of having directly ordered the deaths of two terrorists after their interrogation, and of having susbsequently tampered with evidence and subpoenaed witnesses. The affair had already been subject to investigation by two committees, the Zorea Commission in 1984 and the Blattman Commission in 1985. The committees did not reveal the facts Instead paratroop commander Tat-Aluf Yitzhak Mordechai was blamed for killing the two terrorists. On 18 May, the Attorney-General Yitzhak Zamir issued a complaint to the Police Inspector-General demanding an investigation of the whole affair.

The political community's reaction to this demand resulted in what became known as the GSS Affair. The majority of the inner cabinet members opposed the investigation demanded by Zamir who, according to Israeli law, must act independently of the political authorities. The opposition parties jumped on the bandwagon of public interest (and controversy) and presented four no-confidence motions in the Knesset.[57] The Knesset rejected these motions, but the affair continued to snowball, deepening the imbroglio. While Peres denied that pressures were exerted on Zamir to bar a police probe it was evident that there was no clear-cut legal solution to the crisis. The Attorney-General urged the GSS head and his aides to resign to enable a "quiet" investigation to take place. The political authorities strongly objected to such a move.

Initially the crisis was confined to the confrontation between the Attorney-General and the Inner Cabinet, neither budging from its position. Zamir was conceivably the watchdog of Israel's legal system and moral integrity. The Cabinet was ostensibly the custodian of Israel's security needs. The deadlock between the Attorney-General and the majority of the Inner Cabinet continued with both sides appealing to the public for support. Zamir, meanwhile, seemed ready to consider two other options to a police investigation of the GSS's head: the establishment of a judicial commission of inquiry with full powers to investigate the whole affair, or alternatively, the waiving of the GSS officials' prosecution after which they resign and become private citizens.[58] The first option was attractive to the cabinet members because it did not involve a criminal investigation. The major impediment to its materialization, however, was Zamir's insistence that the GSS head and his aides implicated in the affair be suspended from duty, a demand rejected by the Cabinet.[59]

The crisis was not confined to the relationship between the judicial and the government authorities; it also exended to the partisan arena. Speculation was rife about the possible connection of the top leadership with the GSS Affair. Israel TV reported that a senior Likud Minister claimed that Shamir, Premier at the time of the incident, gave the order to kill the two captured terrorists and that Peres, who was then opposition leader, subsequently supported the decision.[60] Both Labor and Likud officially stood behind their leaders although there was some criticism. The affair did not become a political struggle. No Labor-Likud recriminations were evident to develop into a coalition rift. In fact, Peres, Shamir and Rabin have cooperated closely in the handling of the case and assumed collective responsibility.

Nevertheless, a partisan element was interjected into the affair when Shamir, conceivably responsible, was blamed at least ministerially for the affair. The Deputy Premier, who denied any charge against himself, said that "reporters and editors were exploiting the fact that out of discretion motivated by concern for state security, Shamir was maintaining silence over the affair."

Having realized, though, that an investigation of any type was unavoidable,[61] there seems to have been a preference within the Cabinet for a judicial inquiry. The advantage of such an investigation was that once it was launched the GSS officials need not be suspended. Furthermore, being composed of prominent jurists, senior defense personnel and senior officials, such a committee could formulate "a code of behavior" for the GSS and would be able to maintain secrecy in its proceedings. The advantages of a judicial committee of inquiry were also its handicaps. It was feared, especially by the Likud, that it would not confine itself to GSS personnel but would also look into the role of the politicians in the affair.[62]

A major development of the crisis was the replacement of Yitzhak Zamir by Yosef Harish. Zamir insisted that his resignation was not linked to the GSS Affair. The Press reported it differently. The new appointment ensured a respite since Harish was given time to learn the details of the event. The respite, during which the issue was dropped from the top of the political agenda, was interrupted by a legal brief presented by Energy Minister Moshe Shahal to the Premier and the Attorney-General. According to Shahal the instruction of the police to investigate the GSS was irreversible, since it had set in motion an irreversible process.[63] The obligation of the police to continue the investigation cannot be canceled or superseded "even if the Attorney-General requests that his instruction be reversed." The Attorney-General was thus prohibited from investigating the affair. The legal options were, according to Shahal, only a police or a judicial enquiry.

Another dramatic turning point in the crisis occurred on 26 June, when President Herzog granted a pardon to GSS head Avraham Shalom and four of his aides. The President attributed his decision to security exigencies. The unequivocal announcement of the Attorney-General that it was impossible to halt a police investigation of the affair had created a situation in which the GSS personnel would have had to face examination without being able to defend themselves, unless they disclosed classified security data. These arguments were hardly convincing and led to criticism on two grounds. First, doubt was cast on the President's authority to grant a pardon to those who had not been sentenced. Herzog's claim was that he relied on the arguments of "the great legal experts in Israel," including Professor of Law, Communications Minister Amnon Rubinstein,[64] the opinions of former Supreme Court Justices, and two High Court precedents.[65] The second ground for criticism was ethical. The pardon was described as "political maneuvering" and "a slap in the face" to the Israeli judicial system. The objectors claimed that although the letter of the law had not been violated, constitutional convention and established norms had been compromised.[66] Clemency was regarded as an instrument for circumventing the courts and a threat to the standing of the Attorney-General.[67]

Political reactions to clemency were more ambiguous. The Labor Knesset faction decided, at Peres' request, that its members would make no more statements to the media about the deal, thus letting it drop from the political agenda. At the same time, leading politicians (chief of whom was Shahal) continued to demand the establishment of a full-scale commission of inquiry.[68] The general feeling, however, was that clemency had put an end to the crisis.

Shortly, however, it became evident that the crisis over the clemency was deepening. Criticism took various forms. First, over 100 attorneys called for the Attorney-General's resignation.[69] Second, the political community also had to acquiesce. Peres was under massive pressure from the majority of Labor Ministers and MKs to set up a judicial commission of inquiry to probe the affair and learn about the role of "the political echelon" (i.e., Shamir) in the killing and its cover-up. It was precisely for this reason that a motion (tabled by Moshe Shahal and Amnon Rubinstein) to this effect, had dim prospects of being approved by the two-pronged (Labor-Likud) Cabinet.[70] The only realistic hope for a commission to be set up emerged from a new direction: a few, separate, appeals were submitted to the Supreme Court. One, submitted by two MKs of the Citizens' Rights Movements, asked for an investigation of the events surrounding the bus highjacking and insisted that the High Court was empowered to overrule Herzog's pardon. Subsequent appeals echoed demands that the Court investigate all those involved in the GSS Affair.[71]

The crisis deepened as the three Ministers — Shahal, Rubinstein and Weizman — threatened to resign if a commission of inquiry was not established. In fact, a majority of Labor's Ministers publicly declared their support for a serious probe. The Labor Knesset faction also voted 22-6 in favor of holding an inquiry.[72] The Likud, though, remained adamant that there should be no investigation and strongly hinted it would not mind going to the polls on the GSS issue. Peres was in a dilemma. On the one hand the threat of resignation of three Ministers convinced him to order an investigation; on the other hand, this move was bound to end the National Unity Government and force elections over an issue in which the Likud might score higher than Labor. The general public, so it was assumed, had no sympathy with the call for an investigation, which would have allegedly led to the ruin of the GSS. While the possibility of general elections had been seriously discussed by the two parties, the Likud had a clear advantage.[73] It issued an official statement accusing "some Labor Ministers of neglecting important national issues, while harping in a tendentious and malicious manner on the GSS Affair."

Peres was looking for a compromise. In the Knesset he called for an investigation without specifying what sort, by whom, or what it would be called upon to probe. It was vague enough to suit everyone.[74] While eagerly waiting for the Court's final ruling he made attempts to acquiesce to his co-party leaders.[75]

The Government, though, did not demonstrate a spirit of compromise since the cabinet vote highlighted interparty differences. All 11 Labor Ministers and the *Shinui* Minister voted for a commission of inquiry. They were defeated by the 14 Likud Ministers, the religious parties and *Ometz*. A split was, however, averted by Harish's promise (about to be announced in the High Court hearings) that a police investigation would be carried out. The Attorney-General told reporters that "the police would probe 'all aspects' of the affair, including the possible involvement of the 'political echelons'." The statement enabled him to eat his cake and have it, too. First, it reinstituted the prestige of the Attorney-General who was praised for his courage and sense of justice.[76] The recalcitrant Ministers, chief among whom was Amnon Rubinstein, withdrew their threat to leave the coalition. Likud regarded this resolution as the least of two evils, preferring it over any other form of investigation. The Labor Party, while criticizing Harish's position (fearing it would cover the political echelon) was satisfied with the approval of inquiry. Furthermore, it was learned that President Herzog would not automatically grant advance pardons to other GSS officers.[77]

The final scene in the GSS drama occurred in the High Court of Justice which upheld the President's pardon of the four officials and took note of the Attorney-General's instructions to the police to investigate the affair.[78] Two (out of three) judges indicated that, for purposes of the Basic Law, anyone who allegedly committed a crime, not only those convicted in court, may be considered offenders and therefore eligible for pardon. The decision, which was regarded as a milestone in Israel's constitutional law,[79] reduced the prospects of the GSS Affair turning into a renewed political dispute. It was unanimously agreed that the Court's decision must be honored and that the police be allowed to continue their investigation.

On 18 September, the Police Inspector-General handed the material regarding the investigation to Harish who appointed a special "examination team" to complete the inquiry. Part of the final report was made public.[80] The committee found that the GSS officials were responsible for the killing of the two terrorists and had attempted to sabotage the investigation. It also unequivocally concluded that the "political level," i.e., Yitzhak Shamir, then Premier, was not responsible for the act. He did not order the killing, nor did he back the falsification of evidence by the GSS officials. From the judicial aspect, the GSS Affair ended by clearing the statesmen who were in charge of the security services. It indicated, though, that "security" is no longer a sacred cow in Israeli politics and that security affairs can no longer be settled behind thick curtains of secrecy. While the public, in general, still shied away from civilian intervention in security affairs, there have been voices in the media, in the judicial system and in the public at large which demanded justice and morality. One problem, however, remained unsolved. The committee has not designed the ways and means to submit the GSS to a strict civilian political authority and to ensure its proper management. In this regard the GSS Affair exposed Israel's vulnerability without providing a proper remedy.[81]

The implications of the GSS crisis relate to three domains: the Government, political parties and the polity at large.

1. The governmental arenas. The issue had different effects on each of the major parties. To begin with, it vividly exposed the distribution of power within the National Unity Government. The vote in the Cabinet was a clear-cut manifestation of the Likud's hegemony over the religious parties. Peres failed to mobilize religious support for his proposal of a commission of inquiry. The religious parties may have been persuaded to vote as they did because of the Likud threat to bring about a coalition crisis and force new elections, for which Labor was not ready. Yet their alliance with the Likud seemed to hold true beyond temporary considerations.
2. The partisan arena. Peres confronted trouble within his own party. He has been criticized for not having seized the opportunity to bring down the Unity Government and for not insisting on involving a judicial investigation. At the same time the Premier feared that his credibility would be dealt a severe blow if the GSS Affair were to serve as a means of hindering the rotation.[82]

   In contrast to Labor, Likud benefited from the crisis. The feuding leadership united behind Shamir, whose personal popularity rose. Even David Levy, Shamir's greatest rival, denied rumors that he would challenge Shamir for the top position on the party's Knesset list. One of the reasons for the Likud's unity was its confidence that most of the public was fed up with the damage inflicted on the secret services.[83] It appeared furthermore as a guardian of national security as opposed to Labor, which was described as being anxious to gain political advantages.
3. The third implication related to Israel's legal and moral structure. The GSS Affair revealed a clash between law and security, a clash which Israel had continually attempted to ignore. Division of opinion was unequivocal. On the one hand, there were those assuming that the interests of state security should prevail over any legal consideration. This point of view is poignantly summarized by Deputy Premier Shamir, who staunchly objected to any kind of investigation:

> No one says that in this country anyone or anything is above the law. But there are certain norms, certain modes of operation for which the people engaged in the State's security are responsible... There are certain procedures which the security forces have followed since the establishment of the State and they have proved themselves... Secrecy shrouds everything about the GSS — the identity of its men, its structure, its mode of operation, its means of operation. The minute you disclose this the damage is enormous.[84]

According to this view, Israel's democracy stops short of security affairs. There was another version to this theme: Israel is indeed a democracy; however, Peres said, "In no democratic country did legal institutions and legal considerations treat operational situations involved in state security in the same light as ordinary civil cases."[85] Put differently, the problem was not whether or not democracy prevailed, but what are its boundaries. The security domain, it was argued, was outside these boundaries.

The other view advocated that (a) adhering to the word and letter of the law is an essential requirement in a working democracy, and (b) that Israel is and should remain a democracy in which this requirement is fully applicable. Abba Eban maintained ironically that "we have to draw a list, like a protocol list, of officials not bound by the law. Should the law bow before power? Should it abdicate?"[86] It was not "arid legality" which the promoters of investigation were seeking, but the fair application of the profound democratic norm of equality before the law and the superiority of the judicial process over all other considerations.

The compromise that finally settled the GSS Affair was a typical compromise of a State that has evinced a turbulent stability. Those who demanded investigation were mollified by the Attorney-General's decision to launch a police investigation. Those who rejected such an option took consolation in the fact that the investigation was to be carried out behind a heavy curtain of secrecy that would not reveal the differential role of those conceivably involved in the affair. Neither would the investigation harm the chief GSS officials who already enjoyed the benefits of the President's clemency. The concerted activity of two state authorities, the Presidency and the Judiciary, both enjoying the trust of the Knesset, resulted in the unraveling of many tangles and the overcoming of obstacles that a few weeks earlier had seemed to be insurmountable.

SOCIAL AFFAIRS: TENSIONS UNDER CONTROL

Social tensions within the Jewish community have largely decreased, especially with regard to the strained relations between the *Ashkenazim* and *Sephardim* in Israel. The ethnic factor did not play a role in the turbulent events of Herut's convention (see below). In fact the spirit of unity was vividly expressed when Anatoly Shcharansky was released from the Soviet jail and arrived in Israel. Greeted by the Premier and his Deputy, Chief Rabbis, MKs and a large crowd, the famous new immigrant upheld the notion of "one people, one state."[87]

Ferment was evident, however, on three other fronts — labor relations, the secular-orthodox relationship and Jewish-Arab relations.

LABOR RELATIONS

In January, the 650 employees of Haifa's shipyard found themselves locked out of work.[88] After bitter protests (supported by the Histadrut which called for a general strike), the ministerial economic committee decided that the shipyards would remain open. While the shipyard's workers used violent means such as blocking roads, and occupying government and Histadrut offices, their activity did not hurt the public at large. This was not the case regarding the second major strike of the year in the medical services.

The labor dispute between the nurses and government Ministries of Health and Finance also started in January 1986, but took ten months to settle. The long (though intermittent) strike pitted the nurses who claimed that they worked hard without adequate remuneration, against the Finance Ministry, which was determined to uphold the stringent wage policy in effect. The nurses' strike triggered intensive emotions. While the media constantly exposed the suffering of hospital patients, the nurses became more militant as the strike continued. They only returned to work on 30 October after the Government had applied to the courts for an injunction against the strike. Despite the high-pitched emotions that were attached to the strikes in the shipyards and in the hospitals, there were no changes in labor relations. This was not the case regarding secular-orthodox relations.

SECULAR-ORTHODOX RELATIONS

The secular-religious rifts occupied the public more often than any other social issue in 1986. Tension mounted both in the street and in political institutions. One of the contentious issues was the sanctity of the Sabbath. In what became almost common practice, the religious parties disrupted cinema shows on Friday night. There were fervent demonstrations in Petah Tikva against the reopening of the controversial Heichal Cinema.[89] The major area of opposition was, however, in Jerusalem where the extremely religious community, *Neturei Karta*, held a major campaign against what it termed "obscene posters." From April to June zealots attacked bus shelters where the posters were displayed and burned them. The religious-secular tension reached its climax when an unprecedented event occurred: a synagogue was set on fire and Torah scrolls desecrated. Reactions were charted throughout the country. Leading public figures, such as the President and the Premier, urged moderation. A rally organized by the various kibbutz movements, both the religious and secular, also called for restraint.[90] Negotiations held with the zealots brought about the removal of the "obscene posters." The mechanisms of self-correction mitigated the secular-religious tensions which were threatening to disrupt the social cohesion.

The Knesset also provided an arena for religious-secular confrontation. Laws were enacted to bolster the orthodox features of the State. One prominent example is the law prohibiting the display of bread or bread products for sale during Passover.[91] Three other items on the political agenda fanned the flames of orthodox-secular tension: summer time, the law against racism and the perennial problem of "Who is a Jew?" The right to order the introduction of daylight-saving time (usually known as summer time) is vested in the Interior Minister; in 1986, this was Yitzhak Peretz, a member of *Shas*, the extreme orthodox party and, himself, an opponent of summer time. Religious opposition was based on the inconvenience that summer time causes observant workers who may not have the time to pray in the morning. Another objection is that business establishments that are scheduled to open at the close of Sabbath may be tempted to open before sundown. Anticipating public pressure, Peretz appointed a seven-member committee to study the issue.[92] Since the committee was caught in a deadlock (with three favoring, three opposing and one withholding his opinion), the Minister froze the issue and thus avoided a decision. However, mounting public pressure brought the issue to the Cabinet, whose members voted by 11–6 (with one abstention) to introduce summer time from 17 May to 6 September.[93] Peretz did not enjoy the support of the whole religious community. In fact, the NRP, *Morasha* and individual religious citizens supported summer time, yet the orthodox/secular aspect was predominant in the deliberations of the issue.

The law against racism also highlighted tension on religious grounds. It was actually intended to cope with the problems presented by Kahane and his *Kach* party to the Knesset. The law purported to express a wall-to-wall conviction that racism is not to be tolerated. At the same time it both exposed and reinforced the religious-secular rift. The Penal Code Amendment (No 24) on Incitement on Racism was prepared by the Knesset Committee on Law and Legislation on 21 January. Only on 5 August was it approved in a version markedly different from the original. The reason for the change was based on "religious politics." The religious parties (*Shas*, NRP, *Agudat Israel* and *Morasha*) supported the proposal to narrow down the amendment's definition of "racism" and to apply the prohibition on publication of racist incitement which had already been shown to have caused racist effects. The religious were apprehensive because they felt that the law would lay open to prosecution charges of racism against those who cite biblical passages referring to the "chosen quality" and separateness of the Jewish people. The distinction between Jew and Gentile enshrined in Jewish tradition could therefore be interpreted according to the proposed law as a form of racism. In fact, approval of the law by the Knesset was delayed many times because of orthodox opposition fearing a racist law could create the impression that Judaism is racist.[94] MK Avraham Shapira, for one, claimed the bill would make him a criminal for reciting the prayer at the conclusion of Sabbath.[95] The religious parties thus decided to support the bill only on condition that a sentence be included to the effect that Jewish law (*Halacha*) would not be considered racist. Once again the religious community was divided between the extremists who obstructed the passage of the law and the moderates who endorsed it.[96] Thus, legislation was deadlocked. Although both Labor and Likud were committed to the bill, they were seeking to reduce friction with the orthodox. In order to placate the religious factions, an element of intent was added by inserting the word *"B'Matara"*— ("with an object of") to the bill, to ensure that bona fide quotations of religious writings would not be actionable under the law. While this addition would have made it much harder for the prosecution to prove incitement the religious parties were not mollified.[97]

The bill which became law[98] was a watered-down compromise that did not satisfy any of the contending groups. The law failed to appease the Liberals on three grounds. First, the approved law required intent to incite to racism whereas under the original draft, the publication of something likely to incite racism constituted adequate grounds for prosecution. Secondly, the law's definition of racism speaks of the persecution, degradation, etc, of a group because of its color, racial affiliation, or national-ethnic origin. The previous definition was "...on account of its racial affiliation, nationality *or* religion." The religious factions were thus quelled by omitting the word "*or*." Thirdly, a new clause was added to the law excluding the publication of something "that aims at preserving the character, uniqueness or worship of a religion, provided that this was not done with the object of inciting to racism."

Despite these changes the ultraorthodox coalition members (*Shas* and *Agudat Israel*) abstained from the vote. Ironically the majority which supported the law was joined by Meir Kahane himself, against whom the original bill was conceived. The religious angle of the bill thus prevented the endorsement of its undisputed goal by the total Knesset membership.

The problem of "who is a Jew?" was put to the test in the case of Suzanne Miller. Israel's civil courts recognize as Jews all converts arriving in the country under the Law of Return. The rabbinical courts, however, do not approve conversions abroad by Conservative or Reform rabbis. This creates a problem for the marriage registrars who are under rabbinical jurisdiction. The traditionally orthodox-ruled Interior Ministry has been trying a number of devices to solve this problem, among them encouraging reconversion. Refusing to accept this advice, Suzanne Miller, a Reform convert, appealed to the High Court of Justice, which ordered the Interior Minister, Yitzhak Peretz, to register her as a Jew. The Ministry responded by suggesting that all converts would be designed as such in their identity cards, to ensure that conversion was in accordance with the *Halacha*. The proposed procedure was opposed by religious and secular circles alike. Orthodox rabbis cited the precept that converts are not to be reminded that they were not born Jews and the secular Jews abhorred the idea of stigmatizing converts.[99] The Court's order to the Interior Minister to register Miller as a Jew was never obeyed; it left unresolved at the end of 1986, the troublesome question of "who is a Jew?" and added tension to the widening secular-orthodox gap.

JEWISH-ARAB RELATIONS

The police annual report revealed that in 1986 there was a marked decrease in terrorist activities in Israel and the occupied territories.[100] Tensions, however, between Jews and Arabs living beyond the "Green Line" have not relaxed. A few times during 1986 interethnic relations in Israel deteriorated to the point of explosion. Both sides (though not to the same extent) contributed to the escalation. In January tempers flared on Temple Mount, when a Knesset delegation under the leadership of Dov Shilansky toured the area. The MKs, whose visit was arranged with the *Waqf*, were confronted by hundreds of agitated Muslims. Moods were calmed by joint efforts of the Knesset and the Jerusalem municipality to assure Muslim authorities that there were no hostile intents in the committee's visit. Violence nevertheless broke out on the second visit when MK Eliezer Waldman (*Hatehiya*) held public prayers.[101] When the issue was brought to the Government, the Premier asserted Jewish sovereignty over Temple Mount and begged for moderation.

Violence was more conspicuous in the incidents following the murder of the Yeshiva student, Eliyahu Amedi, by terrorists. This triggered high-pitched emotions of vengeance: Arab-owned shops were damaged and Arab people were harassed by Jewish rioters who shattered at one swoop the peaceful image of a united Jerusalem.[102] The riots against the Arabs, claimed the Press, undermined Israel's claim to act as guardian of a city that is holy to all three religions. The mounting interethnic tension proved that time alone does not build peaceful coexistence. What had been built in nearly two decades of living together was seriously threatened by the incidents of 1986.

THE ECONOMY: THE END OF STABILITY

Since the package deal agreement, signed in 1985, was not due to expire until the end of 1986, this year has been stable. In his farewell address Shimon Peres regarded the state of the economy as one of the major achievements of his Government.

The budget presented to the Knesset in January 1986 highlighted the major components of the planned economy. The NIS30.194 bn state budget was distributed roughly between debt payment (40%) and defense (25%) on the one hand, and pensions, compensations and allotments (18%) and non-military spending (10%) on the other. Only 7% remained for investment. Social services were intended to bear the brunt of the proposed budget cuts. The extent of the reduction in spending on social services became clear when it was compared to the gross national product (GNP). In 1985 this expenditure was 20% of the national income. In 1986, it would be only 17.6%. The implications of the budget cuts were: reduction in the number of teaching hours, slowdown in the construction of classrooms and less allocation for health care.

The whole budget represented a real cut in spending of 5.3% compared with the 1985 budget. The cuts were not aimed at reduction of public sector spending but at shifting expenditure to the public through a further decrease of subsidies on basic commodities (by 40%) and through the imposition of fees for government services.[103]

Consequently, the budget (approved by the Knesset at the first hearing on 22 January) was unpopular among many public sectors. Government workers, secondary school teachers and nurses among others, held strikes and organized work stoppages to protest the Government's social policy as expressed in the proposed budget.

The most significant outcome of the budget cuts was the crisis that threatened to bring down some of the country's largest firms and public bodies such az Zim, Elscint, Solel Boneh and Kupat Holim. Providing financial support to these bodies had become a serious bone of contention within the coalition. Peres hinged the existence of the National Unity Government on aid to the public enterprises. As noted earlier, Finance Minister Moda'i adamantly opposed such aid. A compromise $350m aid package was approved along with the extension of the levy on private cars, education and pensions. The trade-off (aid for taxes) between the Prime Minister and the Finance Minister enabled the Knesset to approve the budget.[104] Two months later, however, the Government officially abandoned its plans to tax education and pensions.[105] Furthermore, as a result of apparent economic stability, large economic organizations, especially the Histadrut and the industrialists, continued to protect the interests of their constituencies. Under these circumstances, one might ask if the budget's objectives have been achieved.

Although final statistics for 1986 were not available at the time of writing, data available indicate that the major economic goals have been realized. The achievements of the July 1985 Stabilization Program in the areas of inflation and financing of the balance of payments were maintained. Inflation was reduced from 304% in 1985 to about 48% in 1986, the lowest in the past eight years. Various indicators of the balance of payments (such as the external debt, foreign currency reserves, as well as the black market exchange rate) indicate stability and even improvement. These developments largely resulted from the continued policy of keeping the exchange rate stable and of maintaining price controls. Although price controls were gradually lifted during the year, there were no signs of renewed skyrocketing inflation. Devaluation of the shekel was avoided when the Israeli currency was linked to a basket of currencies composed of the weighted average of the currencies of Israel's major trading partners.[106]

The positive developments were a result of three major factors. First, external developments included the continued strengthening of the European currencies and the Japanese yen against the US dollar, and the fall in oil prices.[107] Continued American aid was another important external factor. The second reason was the continued cooperation between the Government, the employees (the Coordinating Bureau of the Economic Organization) and the Histadrut. Third, the public supported the new economic trend. Since the majority of Israel's workers are salaried employees, the public had indeed a good reason to be satisfied.[108] In 1986 income distribution shifted in favor of such employees with the share of wages in national income rising at the expense of the share of profits. The reduction of taxes on salaries urther raised the income of the employees. Consequently consumption increased by 12% in comparison to -0.4% in 1985. There was also a sharp rise in demand for durable goods. This increasing demand (toward the end of the year) has been pushing up prices and has made Israel once again a paradise for consumers. A comparison between the patterns of consumption in the first nine months of 1986 and 1985 indicates a rise of 61% in the purchase of private cars, 59% in buying home equipment and electrical appliances, and 22% in acquiring furniture.[109]

What does all this mean to the economy? The most obvious implication was the continued decline in investment which, with regard to industry, decreased by some 5% in comparison to the previous year.[110] The combination of rising consumption with stable income also implied a significant fall in savings. The implication was a near stalemate in economic activity and concomitant rise in unemployment. Israel's GNP rose in 1986 only by some 2% in comparison with 2.8% in 1985. Unemployment increased from 6.7% in 1985 to 7.1% in 1986.[111] Another outcome of the wave of consumption has been a fast-growing deficit in the trade balance, which surged by 50% in the last three months of 1986. The rise was due to an increase of 15.7% in imports that was only partly covered by a rise of 13.8% in exports.[112]

The Government, nonetheless, took measures to limit further deterioration. Toward the end of 1986 it presented a new economic plan envisaging far-reaching structural economic changes. The plan called for an overall reduction of the Government's involvement in the economy; that is, reduction of the size of public sector employment, liberalization of the capital market and tax reform. The maintenance of stability and the encouragement of growth were adopted as major economic targets by Shamir's National Unity Government. There were, however, some partisan overtones in the new economic plan which reflected a "liberal" mood predicating, as has already been noted, less state intervention in economic affairs.

In his inauguration address, Premier Shamir defined his economic plans, in terms of "Zionist economy," an economy in which there would be no place for subsidies, grants or free services.[113] At the same time, however, Shamir added that the "Zionist economy" would be based "not only on economic principles or social considerations on which there is a clear national consensus. It would also be based on Zionist values, namely the supreme value of settlement through *Eretz Israel.*"[114] Shortly after the presentation of the 1987 draft budget, there were sharp interparty disputes about the principles of the "Zionist economy."

THE BEJSKI REPORT

While 1986 as a whole may be regarded as a rather stable year, in terms of economic development, the Bejski Report was like an earthquake which ended in crashing silence. On 20 April the report of the Bejski Commission of Inquiry into the 1983 bank shares scandal was made public. The commission, nominated after manifest public pressure, not only dealt with a major economic problem; it also defined its terms of reference to a far-reaching extent — the very foundations of Israel's economy.

Generally speaking, the commission's recommendations fell into four sections:

1. The report recommended that definite standards of accountability be established for senior figures both in public service and the banking system.
2. The report reviewed the role of the people involved in the bank-share scandal. Those who were still holding power at the time of the report were called to resign within 30 days.[115]
3. The commission came out in favor of moving towards equality of voting rights for publicly issued shares, the voting rights of which were to be equal to those of the superior class of shares already issued.
4. The most far-reaching recommendation was that the banks be banned from managing share-oriented mutual funds or provident funds. The banks should

> also be prohibited from trading in shares on their own account. Furthermore, the commission recommended that legal restrictions be placed on banks to prevent conflict of interest regarding investment counseling given by their employees.

In short, the report called for basic changes in the banking system, the capital market, the powers of the Bank of Israel and the Treasury. It put special emphasis on the relations between the Government and the banks. The Treasury, according to the Bejski Report, should have no power to approve or deny capital share issues. At the same time, however, it demanded an increase in the powers of the Securities Authority and of the Examiner of the Banks. The banks were called upon to stop dealing as brokers, and as managers of funds, and to stop trading in shares for their own account. The report's contribution was not confined to economic-technical aspects but also carried social-moral implications. The Bejski Report established norms of individual responsibility rather than putting the blame on the "system." In the report's words, "The existence and application of rules of responsibility, and recognition of the fact that those who transgress the law and those who fail in their jobs cannot carry on as if nothing has happened, are vital to the effective functioning of Israel's society."[116]

The report was hailed by politicians and the public alike. Peres pledged to carry out its recommendations. The Press praised the commission for the rigor and courage it had displayed.[117] There were nevertheless delays in implementation with respect to both policies and individuals. While three banks (Hapoalim, Hamizrachi and Leumi) acted in accordance with the recommendations regarding the managers' responsibility, Raphael Recanati, Discount Bank's chairman, refused to comply. Only after the Cabinet decided (on 13 July) to authorize the Bank of Israel to suspend Recanati did he resign from his position in the Bank.

FOREIGN AFFAIRS

INTERNATIONAL RELATIONS

The year under review was a good year for Israel's foreign relations. Israel broke its isolation by resuming ties with countries in other parts of the world. On 17 January 1986, Israel and Spain announced the establishment of diplomatic relations. For Spain the move was an outcome of membership of the European Economic Community (EEC). The fall in the price of crude oil, Spain's desire to affiliate with the North Atlantic Treaty Organization, as well as the personal friendship between the Israeli and Spanish Premiers also played a role. For Israel the move was more than routine diplomatic procedure. It also implied an encounter with a weighty historical legacy. There were signs of *rapprochement* in other parts of the world as well. In February, the Ivory Coast renewed its diplomatic relations with Israel.[118] There were also signs of the start of a dialogue with the Soviet Union. Talks between Israel and the USSR began in Helsinki in mid-August, the first official meeting since the Soviets broke relations with Israel in the wake of the 1967 war. Although the talks ended as abruptly as they started, they signaled a Soviet interest in *rapprochement* with Israel.[119] The widening of Israel's foreign relations culminated in President Herzog's 19-day tour of Asia and the Pacific, including Australia, New Zealand, Fiji, Tonga, Singapore and Sri Lanka. Special significance was attached to the visit to Sri Lanka, which had severed its diplomatic relations with Israel.

The foreign arena also had its pitfalls. First, Israel reacted fiercely to the election of Kurt Waldheim as President of Austria on 8 June (by 53.9%). While Peres seemed eager to ease the friction between the two countries he had to consider the Jewish characteristics of Israel's foreign relations. Waldheim's Nazi past and alleged role in the killing of Jews and Yugoslavs made it impossible for Israel to continue business as usual. At the same time, however, Israel could not sever its relationship with this important European State. Consequently, Israel's Ambassador to Vienna, Michael Elitzur, was called home for consultations and remained in Israel leaving the supervision of the embassy to a chargé d'affaires. This unpalatable compromise indicated that Israel could not deny its central role in world Jewish affairs; at the same time, however, it could not ignore universal diplomatic modes of behavior.

The Pollard Affair has been another stain on the generally bright scene of foreign relations. Jonathan Jay Pollard and his wife Ann were alleged and convicted of spying for Israel in the US. Suggestions of a more massive Israeli espionage network have been reported in the US news media since Pollard's plea of guilty was announced (on 4 June). *The Washington Post* reported[120] on page one that Israel has run "intelligence operations in the US for years despite Israeli assertions that Pollard was an isolated incident." It has been argued that the information received from Pollard involved Arab military threats to Israel, and that US national security was never really compromised. Although the chairman of the Senate's Select Committee on Intelligence, David Durenberger, insisted that there was not yet enough evidence to suggest that Israel was conducting widespread espionage against the US, the incident created tension in the relationship between the two States.

The "Israeli connection" regarding the arms sale to Iran was also initially a source of strain in US-Israel relations. As the crisis continued, it became evident that the tension was more within the American domestic political system, and that Israel did not play a leading role in the event. Peres' statement at his Knesset farewell speech that the record of the relations with the US is excellent[121] indicated that the incidents were subdued because of the nature of the common interests and relations of both countries.

REGIONAL DEVELOPMENTS

On the regional front there were positive developments though no breakthrough was achieved, and the stalemate in the peace process continued. The most dramatic event of the year was Peres' meeting with King Hasan in Morocco in July 1986 which attracted much media and public attention. It was compared to Sadat's astounding visit to Jerusalem (on 19 November 1977), but Peres' visit in effect bore no tangible results. Israel and Morocco have enjoyed intimate connections for years. While Morocco has denied Israel formal recognition, many Israeli tourists and statesmen have been allowed to visit this Arab country previous to the summit meeting. Nevertheless, the visit was expected to benefit Israel on the following grounds.

First, it could have encouraged Mubarak to advance in his *rapprochement* with Israel, especially to have the summit meeting with Mubarak so desired by Peres before the end of his term. Secondly, the Rabat meeting was conceivably one more step along the road to legitimacy by the Arab world. It could encourage other moderate states such as Jordan (and perhaps even Iraq) to acknowledge Israel, *de facto* (as Jordan has already been doing) if not *de jure*. Thirdly, the Rabat visit was seen as enhancing Israel's image as "always ready to talk to Arabs everywhere," by blaming any stagnation in the peace process on the Arabs. Finally, Peres himself could accrue political domestic benefits from his visit to Morocco. His widely televised royal meetings enhanced his personal prestige, especially among the Moroccan community in Israel, which is the largest ethnic Jewish group in the country.[122] The support of the Moroccan constituency which has traditionally voted for the Likud[123] is regarded as essential for winning the elections.

The joint communiqué,[124] issued on 23 July, which was described as "the first major official Arab-Israeli document since the Camp David Accords," was rather non-committal. It merely stated that discussions had taken place and it mentioned the Fez Plan.[125] Peres reportedly agreed to the participation of the Palestinians in a prospective joint Jordanian-Palestinian negotiating team and rejected Hasan's proposal for the creation of a West Bank "homeland for the Palestinians" in confederation with Jordan.

A more significant development occurred in the Peres-Mubarak summit meeting of 12 September 1986. Both Israel and Egypt attempted to arrive at the most possible common denominators in view of their genuine differences of opinion. Declaring the year 1987 as a year of "negotiations for peace," and calling upon all parties concerned "to dedicate this year to an intensive effort to achieve the common and noble objective of a just, lasting and comprehensive peace," the two leaders negotiated agreement based on vague principles. Peres and Mubarak were not satisfied, however, with symbolic declarations but made progress on three material issues. First, Egypt agreed to return its Ambassador to Israel. Secondly, Mubarak implicitly agreed to a Palestinian solution within a Jordanian-Palestinian context, without mentioning the Palestine Liberation Organization. Thirdly and most important, Peres committed himself towards an international peace conference as a framework for future peace talks. Mention of the agreement on an international conference was not included in the official declaration, however, because Israel and Egypt could not agree on if and how the Soviets would participate, and also on the issue of Jordanian or possibly Palestinian membership in the preparatory committee to this conference.

While the Premier's aides belittled the importance of an international conference, the Likud clearly opposed his initiative, upholding its demand for direct negotiations with Jordan. With only a month to go before rotation, the formal Likud reaction was nevertheless considerably restrained. The party found it could live with the contents of the joint communiqué, since it did not mention an international conference. More worrisome were the two leaders' opinions about the statement to establish a preparatory committee for the conference. Shamir described the statement as "in the realm of fantasy. The Government, and not Peres, will make the decision."[126] The short time left until the rotation did not allow for implementation of the summit's decisions. The idea of advancing toward peace through an international conference was, however, included in the arsenal of Israel's strategies. It remained to Shamir to implement or, alternatively, to reject his predecessor's policy.

The search for a common denominator for the various political crises which occurred in 1986 reveals the intricacies of the peculiar political arrangements of the era; the so-called "unity" between traditional rivals and enemies produced recurrent crises. The exigencies of reality, however, restrained the destructive tendencies and ensured, perforce, the maintenance of stability.

NOTES

For the place and frequency of publications cited here, and for the full name of the publication, news agency, radio station or monitoring service where an abbreviation is used, please see "List of Sources." Only in the case of more than one publication bearing the same name is the place of publication noted here.

1. *Ha'aretz*, 21 November 1986.
2. *JP*, 9 January 1986.
3. The drama was supplied by Ezer Weizman and Ariel Sharon who exchanged recriminations and accusations. *Ha'aretz*, 4 January 1986.
4. The full text of the Taba Resolutions may be found in *JP*, 14 January 1986, p 8.
5. Ibid, 17 January 1986.
6. *Ha'aretz*, 21 January 1986.
7. *JP*, 17 February 1986.
8. Ibid, 21 February 1986.
9. Ibid; editorial, "The Nitty Gritty," 23 February 1986.
10. A petition signed by 100 central committee members, including leading figures, asked for the convening of the whole committee to vote on a motion calling for the dissolution of the Government and holding new elections. Ibid, 28 February 1986.
11. *Ha'aretz*, 6 March 1986.
12. *Ma'ariv*, 24 March 1986.
13. Moda'i attacked Peres' trip to the US calling him "a flying Premier" and accused him in an interview to *Ha'aretz* (4 April 1986) of squandering funds on institutions connected with the Labor movement, at the expense of economic growth.
14. In November 1985, Peres refrained from dismissing Sharon who also publicly attacked him. Peres put it on record that, in the future, punishment for a ministerial outburst would be dismissal, regardless of belated apologies.
15. In March 1986 Labor scored high at the polls, gaining (with *Yahad*) 42% of the Jewish vote, in comparison to the 39% in the 1984 elections. Smith Poll, *JP*, 19 September 1986.
16. Ibid, 8 April 1986.
17. Ibid, 11 April 1986.
18. *Ha'aretz*, 14 April 1986.
19. Moda'i said that Peres "knows as much about law as he knows about economics," *Ma'ariv*, 21 July 1986.
20. *Ha'aretz*, 25 July 1986.
21. Ibid, 12 October 1986.
22. *JP*, 19 October 1986.
23. Ibid, 8 October 1986.
24. Ibid, 21 October 1986.
25. Smith Poll, in Note 15.
26. *Ha'aretz*, 16 July 1986.
27. The TV campaign was shortened to 21 days. Ibid, 12 October 1986.
28. The average annual number of no-confidence motions tabled between 1968–78 was 5.3. Amnon Sella and Yael Yishai, *Israel: The Peaceful Belligerent 1967–79* (London: Macmillan, 1986), p 104.
29. The parties were *Mapam, Hatehiya, Ratz* and *Hadash*.
30. *Ha'aretz*, 1 July 1986.
31. Ibid, 5 November 1986.
32. Ibid, 4 January 1984.
33. *JP*, 15 July 1986.
34. The Liberals, for their part, threatened that the Likud Knesset list would be split if no Herut move toward unification became evident. Ibid, 1 January 1986.
35. *Ma'ariv*, 16 February 1986.
36. *JP*, 10 March 1986.
37. The committee which was empowered to co-opt notables as convention delegates had approved 150 pro-Shamir names, 20 from the Sharon camp, and only ten from Levy's. Ibid, 9 March 1986.

38. Ibid, 10 March 1986.
39. Ibid, 11 March 1986.
40. The delegate's credentials were suspended the next day by a unanimous vote. One day later, having written a letter of apology, he was reinstated. *Ha'aretz*, 12 March 1986.
41. Ibid, 11 March 1986.
42. Moshe Katzav of the Shamir camp was elected as the presidium chairman, defeating Eliyahu Ben Elissar, of the Levy camp.
43. Shamir called the convention a "circus" and derogated Levy, who indicated he might withdraw his support from Shamir and obstruct his Premiership. *JP*, 13 March 1986.
44. Ibid.
45. Deadlock resulted from the procedures adopted in selecting a new central committee, which would eventually select the party leader. The formula proposed was to declare the convention itself a central committee. Ibid.
46. Ibid, 12 March 1986.
47. Ibid, 14 March 1986.
48. Ibid, 9 April 1986.
49. According to the new system, 26 nominees are to be elected by the central committee, with 23 others nominated by the branches and sectors. *Davar*, 10 April 1986.
50. *Ha'aretz*, 18 May 1986.
51. *JP*, 2 April 1986.
52. Ibid, 5 June 1986.
53. Ibid, 21 July 1986.
54. *Lamifne* threatened to split the four-man Knesset faction. Ibid, 25 July 1986.
55. The major cause of the uproar was former MK Yitzhak Yitzhaki, who was ostensibly deprived of adequate representation in the party's council. Ibid, 21 May 1986.
56. J.C. Hurewitz, *Middle East Politics: the Military Dimension* (New York: Praeger, for the Council on Foreign Relations, 1969), ch 20.
57. *JP*, 27 May 1986.
58. Zamir maintained that any investigation would be hampered if the suspects remained in their posts.
59. Ibid, 29 May 1986.
60. On 28 May 1986.
61. The Police Inspector-General David Kraus was abroad. His safe contained a letter from Zamir, instructing him to open an investigation. The police thus had no alternative but to pursue investigation, which could not have been withdrawn. *JP*, 30 May 1986.
62. *Ha'aretz*, 1 June 1986.
63. *JP*, 18 June 1986.
64. Herzog quoted from Amnon Rubinstein's book *Constitutional Law*. (Jerusalem: Schocken, 1969), p 264. According to Rubinstein the law does not restrict the President's authority to pardon offenders; it entitles him to grant clemency even before they have been convicted. This ruling was also upheld by Chief Justice Berensohn.
65. The cases were Reuven vs the State (1950) and Matana vs the State (1960).
66. *JP*, 26 June 1986.
67. Harish denied he had anything to do with this initiative. Later, it became known that he had been consulted prior to the deal.
68. *Shinui* threatened it would "weigh" leaving the coalition if an inquiry were not instituted. Ibid.
69. Former Tel Aviv District Court President openly criticized clemency in a TV interview on 26 June 1986.
70. Even if a cabinet majority favored a probe, Shamir had the right, by coalition agreement, to transfer the matter to the ten-man Inner Cabinet, where there was a built-in 5-5 standoff between Labor and Likud.
71. Supreme Court Justice (SCJ) 428/86. See also *JP*, 27 July 1986.
72. Ibid, 2 July 1986.
73. Ibid, 29 June 1986.
74. Ibid, 2 July 1986.
75. In the political bureau's meeting Peres failed to delay a debate on the issue until after the

conclusion of the proceedings in the High Court, although no decisions were adopted at the close of a stormy meeting. Ibid, 4 July 1986.

76. See for example, ibid, 15 July 1986.
77. Only new pardons had to be approved by the Inner Cabinet and the Attorney-General, if the President concluded there was no reason to discriminate against the new application for pardon. Ibid, 16 July 1986.
78. Ibid, 7 August 1986.
79. Ibid.
80. For the full version of the report see *Ha'aretz*, 30 December 1986.
81. Ibid, 2 January 1987.
82. *JP*, 29 June 1986.
83. Ibid, 30 June 1986.
84. Ibid, 30 May 1986.
85. Ibid, 3 June 1986.
86. Ibid, 29 May 1986.
87. *Ha'aretz*, 12 February 1986.
88. *Ma'ariv*, 22 January 1986.
89. *Ha'aretz*, 6 April 1986.
90. Ibid, 1 July 1986.
91. The law excluded those areas populated by non-Jews. *JP*, 6 August 1986.
92. Ibid, 2 April 1986.
93. The vote strained Labor-*Shas* relations as the former Ministers unanimously favored the introduction of summer time. Ibid, 21 April 1986.
94. The Likud also opposed the law, demanding to "balance" it by outlawing any contact with terrorist organizations.
95. *JP*, 19 February 1986.
96. Yosef Burg, for example, said that "anyone who argues...that this bill will hurt Judaism has an inferiority complex." Ibid, 7 April 1986.
97. Ibid, 22 May 1986.
98. The bill was approved only after Labor agreed to the Likud's condition to support a bill banning an unauthorized contact with PLO. *Ha'aretz*, 6 August 1986.
99. *JP*, 29 June 1986.
100. *Ha'aretz*, 21 January 1987.
101. Ibid, 9–17 January 1986.
102. *JP*, 21 January 1986.
103. One coalition member, Yaacov Shami, who leads the Likud faction in the Histadrut, voted against the budget. The secretary-general, Yisrael Keisar, did not vote at all. Ibid, 30 March 1986.
104. Ibid, 22 May 1986.
105. *Ha'aretz*, 31 July 1986.
106. One has to note, though, the difficulties in international markets for some Israeli export branches, especially in the electronics industry, caused by the same factors.
107. *Israel Statistical Abstract 1986*, p 305.
108. *Ma'ariv*, 16 January 1987.
109. *Ha'aretz*, 28 January 1987.
110. Ibid, 9 February 1987.
111. Ibid, 11 January 1987.
112. Bank of Israel Research Department, *Recent Economic Developments*, 40, Jerusalem, September 1986.
113. *JP*, 21 October 1986.
114. The list included the Governor of the Bank of Israel and the general heads of the four major banks — Hapoalim, Leumi, Hamizrahi and Discount.
115. Quoted in *JP*, 21 April 1986.
116. Ibid.
117. Ibid, 15 July 1986.
118. *Ha'aretz*, 13 February 1986.
119. Ibid, 18 August 1986.

120. *WP*, 5 June 1986.
121. *Ha'aretz*, 8 October 1986.
122. In 1984 Jews of Morocco and Tangier constituted 13.6% of the total Jewish population in Israel. *Israel Statistical Abstract*, 1985, p 74.
123. Yael Yishai, "Hawkish Proletariat: The Case of Israel," *Jewish Journal of Sociology*, 13 (1985), pp 53–73.
124. For the full text of the communiqué see *JP*, 24 July 1986.
125. Ibid, 14 September 1986.
126. *Ha'aretz*, 8 October 1986.

Jordan
(Al-Mamlaka al-Urdunniyya al-Hashimiyya)

ASHER SUSSER

The year 1986 ushered in a new phase in relations between Jordan and the Palestine Liberation Organization (PLO) and in Jordan's Palestinian policy. Since late 1982, King Husayn had sought to forge an alliance with Yasir 'Arafat in order to achieve a breakthrough in the peace process. This phase came to an end in February 1986, when Husayn announced that he was suspending coordination with the PLO leadership. From this point on, Jordan embarked on a new peace strategy, the thrust of which was a concerted offensive in the occupied territories against the PLO as relations with the organization returned to their normal state of conflict. Jordan's objectives in regard to the Palestinians were made unmistakably clear — the ultimate incorporation of the Palestinians, in Jordan and the occupied territories, into a Jordanian-dominated political entity. Jordan's new Election Law was yet another obvious indication of this vision of the future.

The new Election Law was also a response to the steadily growing demands for the democratization of the Jordanian political system, but it introduced no significant change in the country's guided and controlled form of democracy. Political unrest during the year was the most serious since the civil war of 1970–71. It was dealt with harshly and was curtailed quickly. Generally speaking, the Rifa'i Government that came into office in April 1985 had been repressive in its unflinching pursuit of domestic political stability. It made no concessions to the Opposition, it cracked down on the Muslim Fundamentalists, and it increased government control of what was already a well-supervised Press.

Zayd al-Rifa'i seemed to have a firm grip not only of a somewhat troubled domestic political scene, but also of the country's economy, which was still in the throes of a recession, and had clearly averted a disaster. Rifa'i was proving to be a real asset to Husayn, head and shoulders above his mediocre contemporaries who had preceded him in the Premiership.

POLITICAL AFFAIRS

PARLIAMENT, PARTIES AND THE NEW ELECTION LAW

The draft of the new Election Law approved by the Cabinet in December 1985 (see *Middle East Contemporary Survey* [*MECS*], 1984–85, p 512) was brought before Parliament for ratification in January 1986. The regular four-month session of Parliament was extended in early March for two more months, mainly to enable the Government to obtain parliamentary ratification for the Election Law. On 27 March the law was passed by the Council of Deputies with an overwhelming majority[1] of 50 against two — Layth Shubaylat and Riyad al-Nuwayisa. Both these Deputies, the former a Muslim Fundamentalist and the latter a Ba'thi, had been elected in the 1984 by-elections (see *MECS* 1983–84, pp 512–13) and were stalwarts of the Opposition (see *MECS* 1984–85, pp 506–12).

The new law increased the number of Deputies in the Council from sixty, evenly divided between the East and West Banks of the Kingdom, to 142, also divided evenly between the two Banks. However, as opposed to the old law, the new one allocated one seat to each of the 11 refugee camps on the East Bank, thus providing for Palestinian representation on the East Bank for the first time. These 11 seats were added to the 60 seats allocated to West Bank constituencies and were considered part of the West Bank representation of 71, i.e., half of the total. The new law was intended to reflect the growth in population and other demographic changes that had taken place since the previous law was enacted in 1960. However, while the increased number of Deputies was more or less commensurate with the increase in population, it did not accurately reflect the real population distribution. Though there were actually to be 82 representatives from East Bank constitutencies and only 60 from the West Bank, this did not adequately reflect the fact that the East Bank population was about three times that of the West Bank. The number of Palestinian delegates from the East Bank (11) did not correspond with the fact that Palestinians made up about half of the East Bank population. Nor did the overall number of Palestinian delegates coincide with the fact that the Palestinians were certainly a majority in both Banks combined. The manner in which the seats were distributed did, however, clearly represent the political aspirations of the regime, i.e., the creation of an integrated Jordanian-Palestinian political entity, ostensibly based on equality, but in fact preserving East Bank supremacy.

As in the previous law, the seats were distributed on a regional and confessional basis. Representation was thus guaranteed for minorities in those constituencies which included sizable minority communities. Jordan's population, on both Banks, is predominantly Arab and Sunni Muslim (*c* 90 per cent). Various Arabic-speaking Christian denominations, mainly Greek Orthodox, constitute less than 10 per cent of the population. There is also a very small non-Arab, ethnic, but not religious, minority of Circassians and Chechens on the East Bank who comprise less than 1 per cent of the overall East Bank population. Though Muslims, the Circassians and Chechens, who migrated to the East Bank from Caucasia in the last quarter of the 19th century, still preserve a certain measure of ethnic distinctiveness. Over the years they have become increasingly Arabized and have played an important role in Jordanian politics, far greater than their small number (*c* 25,000) would warrant.[2] In the new Election Law, as in the previous one, the Circassian and/or Chechen minority, and the Christians, were over-represented. Both of these communities, with some notable exceptions, have generally been very loyal subjects. The Christians were thus to have 19 seats (ten West Bank, nine East Bank) and the Circassians and/or Chechens were to have three, giving the minorities 15.5 per cent of the seats, one-and-a-half times their percentage in the population.

The regional distribution of seats also clearly favored the rural and provincial populations over the metropolitan center of Amman and Zarqa. While these two centers included about half of the East Bank population, the entire Governorates of Amman and Zarqa, which included some rural areas as well, were only to have 27 of the 82 East Bank seats. This seemed to be a calculated effort to reduce the representation of the potentially more radical urban population. The new law also required that candidates pay a non-refundable "nomination fee" of JD500 (Article 22). This was a relatively high amount, which would tend to exclude many political candidates from even the middle income groups, not to mention the poorer sections of society. It thereby tended to favor those whose political proclivities would generally be more conservative. The law did not provide for the legalization of political parties, banned since 1957, and forbade the candidacy of anyone who belonged to any "illegal or other party" which had "aims, objectives and principles" that contradicted the Jordanian Constitution (Article 18e).[3] Though this article still left considerable room for the Government to seek the disqualification of undesirable candidates, it was an improvement on the original draft that had explicitly disqualified all members of illegal political organizations. This article was the main point of controversy raised by Shubaylat in the debate over the law; he therefore regarded the amendment as an achievement, even though he still opposed the law. He and Nuwayisa were also critical of the seat distribution, which they said was based on "sectarian, racial, tribal and regional considerations" instead of purely demographic factors. Shubaylat also opposed the inclusion of the West Bank because it was still under Israeli occupation, and Nuwayisa criticized the restrictive nature of the nomination fee.[4]

Palestinian sources were quick to condemn the law for its emphasis on the incorporation of the West Bank and the Palestinian refugees on the East Bank into the Jordanian body politic in a manner that undermined the representative status of the PLO.[5] Particularly interesting, however, was the criticism of this same point in the Senate by former Premier Ahmad 'Ubaydat. 'Ubaydat, an East Banker and former Director of General Intelligence (internal security), did not welcome the incorporation.[6] But one may safely assume that his opposition was motivated by apprehension about the possible long-term Palestinian threat to the predominance of the Trans-Jordanian political elite, rather than any concern for the PLO and its representative status.

New general elections were not due until 1988. The implementation of the Election Law was therefore not an issue in the period under survey. But two Deputies from Irbid passed away in 1986, and by-elections were required. In January, a veteran parliamentarian of one of the most prominent East Bank families, Na'im al-Tall, died. The by-election took place in June and did not seem to have enjoyed the same measure of freedom that had characterized the by-elections of 1984. The regime had most probably been deterred by the results of the by-election in which Muslim fundamentalist candidates had done particularly well (see *MECS* 1983–84, pp 512–13). Of the nine candidates who originally filed nominations, seven actually ran in the elections on 19 June. The winner was Jamal 'Ubaydat, a member of one of the largest tribes in the north and also the Director-General of the Irbid Cooperative Organization and a supporter of the Government. Voter turnout was very low in the city of Irbid and did not exceed 10 per cent, while in the rural areas of the Irbid Governorate it reached about 40 per cent. This was particularly helpful to 'Ubaydat, whose support was stronger in the villages, as opposed to his main rival, Dr 'Abd al-Majid Nusayr, whose main support was in the city itself.[7] Nusayr, a former mathematics professor at Yarmuk University and a Muslim Fundamentalist who had lost his position at the university in the November 1985 crackdown against

Fundamentalists (see *MECS* 1984–85, pp 508–9) complained that his defeat at the polls was due to government intervention and unfair practices. He complained that "the only political party [in Jordan was] the *Mukhabarat*," i.e., General Intelligence, the domestic security apparatus. Nusayr contended that security police had intimidated his voters and stuffed ballot boxes for the successful government-favored candidate.[8] He filed a formal complaint to the Council of Deputies, seeking the annulment of the elections.[9] By the end of the year the council had yet to deal with Nusayr's complaint. In the meantime, in December, Nusayr was reportedly arrested together with other Fundamentalist activists,[10] thus severely reducing the chances of his case ever being reviewed.

Shortly before the elections, the Governor of Irbid met with the candidates in an unsuccessful attempt to persuade them to forgo the process of election and agree between themselves on a single candidate who would automatically be elected. This was followed by yet another bid toward this end by the Minister of Interior, Hasan al-Kayid. After this measure had also failed, the Minister expressed his regret that his efforts had been "misunderstood...as government intervention." He explained that his only intention was to spare the citizens "trouble and expenditure" and to save the Government the effort of holding the by-election.[11] It did appear, however, that the Government was trying to apply pressure to secure the unopposed election of its own candidate. Nusayr even claimed that government officials had offered to reinstate him in the university position he had lost in November 1985, if he agreed to drop out of the race. Since these tactics failed, it is very likely, considering past practices, that the Government did resort to unfair and fraudulent procedures to ensure 'Ubaydat's election. The fact that the police detained reporters and questioned two Western journalists who tried to cover the by-election[12] seemed to reinforce this appraisal.

A second by-election was held in Irbid on 14 August following the death of the Christian Deputy Ya'qub Mu'ammar in June. As Jordanian law provided for a fixed number of minority representatives in various constituencies, a by-election to replace a Christian Deputy would require all candidates to be Christians, just as Muslims would have to run for Muslim seats. This by-election did not, therefore, arouse the specter of Muslim fundamentalist candidature, and did not give rise to any government intervention either. The date of the by-election, 14 August, happened to be the first day of the *'Id al-Adha* public holiday. It aroused little public interest and voter participation (some 21 per cent) was even lower than that in the previous by-election. The fact that the by-election was for a Christian seat may also have contributed to the low turnout. The victorious candidate was Dr Nadir Abu al-Sha'ar, a local surgeon. He did not appear to have strong political views, and his main concern, he said, was to improve services for the people.[13]

Parliamentary activity in 1986 followed what had become a regular pattern since the restoration of Parliament in 1984. The Government enjoyed an overwhelming majority, which was never seriously challenged. The main opposition on all issues continued to come from the two most outspoken Deputies — the Muslim Fundamentalist, Shubaylat, and the Ba'thi, Nuwayisa, with Shubaylat being the more successful of the two in gaining the support of other Deputies. In February, 33 Deputies supported a motion to introduce a *zakat* law (*zakat* is the alms tax prescribed by religious law), and 22 supported legislation to prevent the production and sale of alcohol.[14] Though these motions were not acted upon during the year under survey, they were indicative of the influence of the fundamentalist trend. Shubaylat, who in the past had complained that the Speaker of the House, 'Akif al-Fa'iz, often restricted his right to speak (see *MECS* 1984–85, p 505), challenged Fa'iz for the Speakership when the new session of Parliament opened in November. Fa'iz won easily by 47 votes to 13, but the fact that Shubaylat received 13 votes was significant. The same number of Deputies had abstained or opposed Fa'iz at the opening of the previous session (see *MECS* 1984–85, p 506). Apparently the same 13 had now voted for Shubaylat.[15] This suggested that he had a sizable and consistent body of supporters in his fight against Fa'iz which, according to Shubaylat, was intended to "reinforce the principle of democracy... and to prove that Deputies still have the right of self-expression".[16] Though Shubaylat lost, one of the two Deputy Speakers elected was 'Ati Abu al-'Izz,[17] also a Muslim Fundamentalist, the first to be elected to this position since the revival of parliamentary life in 1984.

Shubaylat, other Fundamentalists and Nuwayisa continued to assail the Government on various issues. In early December, Yusuf al-'Azm followed up on a written complaint that Shubaylat had distributed among the Deputies against the Government's information policy. This came in the wake of a very heated exchange, outside the Chamber, between Shubaylat and the Minister of Information, Muhammad al-Khatib, in which Shubaylat accused the Minister of not allowing sufficient coverage of parliamentary debates in the Press. 'Azm addressed this issue from the rostrum of the House and called for a special session to discuss it. Prime Minister Rifa'i dismissed Shubaylat's complaint as a personal quarrel between him and the Minister of Information and suggested that his motion be dropped. Rifa'i's position was accepted by the House and this matter was laid to rest.[18]

Later in December, both the Council of Deputies and the Senate approved the 1987 budget (for details on the budget, see below), the former with an overwhelming majority and the latter unanimously.[19] The debate in the Lower House, however, provoked further heated exchanges between Fundamentalist Deputies and the Government. Those who aired their opposition to the Government's economic policies during the debate were its consistent hard-core opponents: Nuwayisa, Shubaylat, 'Abdallah al-'Akayila and Ahmad al-Kufahi. Shubaylat had yet another verbal clash with a Minister, this time with the Minister of Labor, Khalid al-Hajj Hasan. Shubaylat had hardly begun his speech when the Speaker began ringing his bell to signal Shubaylat to stop. The Minister of State for Parliamentary Affairs, Sami Jawda, and the Minister of Labor complained that Shubaylat's statements were offensive to Deputies and Ministers and, therefore, disallowed by the laws of the House. Shubaylat was not permitted to continue.

The other spokesmen of the Opposition focused their criticism mainly on the Government's foreign debt, the problem of unemployment and the Government's development plan for the West Bank and Gaza (for details of which, see below). Kufahi and 'Akayila both suggested Islamic methods to deal with the foreign debt. They proposed that the Government increase its own revenue by introducing the *zakat* tax and that it resort to foreign loans from Islamic banking institutions that did not take interest.[20] Rifa'i did not reply directly to these suggestions, but forcefully dismissed much of the criticism of Jordan's foreign debt as baseless and factually incorrect. He was particularly harsh on Nuwayisa, who had suggested that the development plan for the West Bank and Gaza was an "American-Zionist" idea and that the Government's privatization policy was similarly inspired by recommendations from foreign financial institutions. Rifa'i described Nuwayisa's allegations as "some form of outbidding and nonsense" that was not really worthy of any response at all.[21]

Opposition to the Government's privatization policy and its foreign borrowing was also expressed outside Parliament by Jamal al-Sha'ir's Unionist Democratic Alignment (see *MECS* 1984–85, p 503), which sent a memorandum to Husayn expressing these views.[22]

More significant, and indeed extraordinary, was the nucleus of opposition to the Rifa'i Government that formed around Rifa'i's predecessor, 'Ubaydat. It was not unusual for former Prime Ministers to be critical of those who had replaced them. 'Ubaydat, however, did not confine his criticism to parliamentary debates, where he expressed his opposition from the Senate floor (see above); nor did he seek the King's ear to air his complaints as others had done before him. In mid-September, 'Ubaydat, together with a group of other former Ministers and officials sent a memorandum to President Husni Mubarak of Egypt in which they criticized the joint commitment by the Egyptian President and the Israeli Prime Minister Shimon Peres, to make 1987 the year of negotiations for a comprehensive Middle East peace. This, they feared, would be counterproductive, due to the regional balance of forces and US support for Israel. It would support the "plot to normalize Arab-Israeli relations" on the West Bank and Gaza Strip. This latter reference could only have been understood as an allusion to Jordan's own new policy of intensive involvement in West Bank and Gaza affairs with Israel's acquiescence (see below). This was not just a criticism of Rifa'i but of the King himself, and it was made in the most derogatory fashion.[23] Stating the above in a memorandum to the Ruler of another state added insult to injury, especially since the contents of the memorandum became public knowledge when dispatches from Amman were broadcast in Arabic on Radio Monte Carlo.[24] King Husayn responded quickly and decisively, forcing 'Ubaydat to resign his seat in the Senate.[25] In his Speech from the Throne in early November, Husayn referred disparagingly to those who had "perfected the art of changing positions with the change in their posts." He would not be deflected from his course by those whose "[personal] motives are apparent" and whose "strange utterances" would not prevent the regime from carrying out its responsibility by preserving the Palestinian Arab identity of the West Bank and Gaza by "deeds rather than [by] claims and pretensions."[26]

'Ubaydat's motives may have been personal, as Husayn had implied, but there was a certain consistency in 'Ubaydat's opposition which also suggested something more profound. 'Ubaydat's opposition to the new Election Law, because of its emphasis on the incorporation of the Palestinians into Jordan's political structure (see above), his opposition to Jordan's involvement in the peace process and negotiations with Israel, and his opposition to Jordan's West Bank development plan were all facets of a coherent political position. One source, referring to the 'Ubaydat group, spoke of many East Bankers who resented spending money on the Palestinians.[27] Another spokesman of the 'Ubaydat group, Hani al-Khasawna, a former Minister and Ambassador to Moscow and Paris, said that they feared Husayn was moving toward a suicidal separate deal with Israel that would never satisfy the Palestinians.[28] These views were clearly representative of an important, but hitherto not decisively influential, body of Hashemite loyalist East Bankers that began to emerge in the late

1960s and early 1970s. They believed it to be in the Kingdom's best interest to disengage itself from the Palestinian problem. This, however, was not what the regime had in mind. On the contrary, the state-controlled Press welcomed the Government's Palestinian policy as an embodiment of the "sacred unity" between the two Banks.[29]

EXTRAPARLIAMENTARY OPPOSITION — THE YARMUK UNIVERSITY INCIDENTS

The extreme sensitivity shown by the Government to the candidacy of a Muslim Fundamentalist in the Irbid by-election may well have resulted not only from the success of fundamentalist candidates in the 1984 by-elections, but also from a much more recent event. On 15 May, an official spokesman of the Ministry of Interior announced that three students had been killed in riots at the Yarmuk University campus in Irbid.[30] The immediate cause of student disaffection was the Faculty of Engineering's decision in March to charge its students an extra fee for practical training. Following student protest the university authorities reduced the fee but student unrest did not cease.

In mid-April, students had also demonstrated against the US air strike against Libya; later in April, student activists met to form a representative body to present their various demands to the university authorities. On 3 May, in an apparent effort to nip this political organization in the bud, the university administration decided to expel 32 students as of the end of the academic year. On 13 May, possibly as many as 2,000 students demonstrated on the campus. On the following day, according to the Ministry of Interior, students began to riot, to damage property and to intimidate other students and faculty members. The university authorities, "at the behest of a large number of professors and students," in the words of the Ministry, called in the police. In the ensuing ferocious clashes between the police and the students, three (and, according to rumors, many more) students were killed, and 18 policemen and between 60 and 200 students were injured.[31] The Government blamed an unidentified "sabotage group" for fomenting the sedition, but, according to numerous sources, the two groups who had been most active in organizing the student protest were the Muslim Brotherhood and the Communist Party.[32] Other sources maintained that pro-Fath elements had also been active in promoting the unrest, to protest against Jordan's policy toward the PLO,[33] since Husayn's break with 'Arafat in February 1986 (see below). Immediately after the incident, the authorities arrested about 20 members of the Communist Party leadership, all of whom were released in early September.[34] Several Muslim Fundamentalists were also arrested, and some members of the university staff were reportedly suspended.[35] The central role of Muslim Fundamentalists in the student protest was attested to by the fact that, when the students sought mediation with the police, they called in the Mayor of Irbid and the Muslim Fundamentalist Deputy from Irbid, Ahmad al-Kufahi, to negotiate on their behalf. It was well known that the Muslim Brotherhood and left-wing groups had gathered wide support on the campus; of the 14,000 students registered in 1986, many were from middle class and poorer backgrounds, with a large proportion from the West Bank and Gaza. The campus had a reputation for being more volatile than the country's other universities and colleges. Students there also had a variety of grievances on which political groups could capitalize with relative ease. These grievances included not only the newly imposed fees, but also more stringent academic standards (which had resulted in the dismissal of low-scoring undergraduates), and the rigid control of political and social life on campus.[36] Students and faculty complained that the student body was kept under close surveillance by the Students' Affairs Department which was run by former military and domestic intelligence officers. They made regular reports on student activities and compiled lists of activists, submitted to the university administration and to the security authorities.[37]

The violence at Yarmuk University was the most serious the country had witnessed since the civil war of 1970–71, and was said to have "disrupted Jordan's relatively calm domestic scene." The use of extreme force by the police aroused widespread criticism and resentment, even within the upper echelons of the Establishment. There were rumors that children of some high-placed officials had been among the casualties of the police onslaught. The Government had clearly overreacted to the student protest. It had demonstrated a hypersensitivity to any manifestation of political opposition and a fear that, at a time of economic recession and growing unemployment (see *MECS* 1984–85, pp 497–502, and below), campus protests could overflow into more general discontent.[38] The widespread disapproval of the police action was probably the factor that had prompted Husayn to appoint a ministerial commission of inquiry to examine the Yarmuk University incidents. In early July, the committee filed a report which neatly avoided blaming either the Government or the security forces, while faulting militant students with political party affiliations and the expendable president of the University, Dr 'Adnan Badran. Badran, the report said, had shown a persistent insensitivity to student requirements and had mismanaged the whole crisis when it came to a head in mid-May.[39] The president was presumably forced to resign and was replaced by Dr Muhammad Ahmad Hamdan. Fifteen faculty members and six members of the administrative staff were also dismissed.[40]

The after effects of the events at the university lingered on for months. Both the King and the Prime Minster alluded to them in public. In a letter to Rifa'i in early July, Husayn noted that Jordan had enjoyed a "state of stability and security...[for] the past 15 years," i.e., since the end of the armed struggle with the PLO, and the regime had every intention of keeping it that way. Husayn would not allow "this handful" of students to succeed in their "treacherous and odious attempt" to "harm this State, change its nature and turn it from its course." Husayn made it clear that he would view anyone who tried to instigate political unrest on the campuses as an "aggressor against the entire people."[41] Rifa'i assured the King that the Government would do everything to secure the "sound course" of the universities.[42] The Yarmuk University incidents were not repeated elsewhere, and law and order prevailed. Even so, Husayn placed special emphasis, in his Speech from the Throne on 1 November, on the fact that the first priority of his Government was to preserve national security, "both on the domestic and the foreign levels." The "supremacy of law and order" was the sine qua non for any kind of development and progress, he said.[43]

Shortly after the events at Yarmuk University new legislation was introduced by the Government to further tighten its control over the universities. The existing law on higher education was amended in a manner that invested the Government, through the Minister of Higher Education, with complete authority to regulate the affairs of the country's four universities (the University of Jordan in Amman, Yarmuk University, Mu'ta University and the new University of Science and Technology in Irbid that was to begin operating in the 1986-87 academic year). University affairs had hitherto been under the control of the Council for Higher Education, which was established in 1980. This council, chaired by the Prime Minister, included the Ministers of Higher Education (a position created in 1985, see *MECS* 1984–85, pp 510–11), the Ministers of Education and Planning, the presidents of the universities, two members representing private and public community colleges, six specialists appointed by Royal Decree, and the Commander in Chief of the Armed Forces. This body, which had dealt not only with general policy guidelines but also with such matters as senior faculty appointments, was not abolished by the amendment, but the supreme authority was now transferred to the Minister of Higher Education. The Minister was empowered to make decisions without necessarily having recourse to the council. This further curtailed the influence of the universities in determining education policy, which even prior to the new law was constrained by the Government by virtue of the composition of the Council for Higher Education. The new legislation was passed in both Houses of Parliament in July and August, but not without some opposition. During the debate in the Council of Deputies, one of the Fundamentalist Deputies, 'Abdallah al-'Akayila, assailed the law as an instrument to curtail the independence of the universities, to politicize them, and to transform them into "government schools." His view was reportedly shared by many faculty members in the universities who thought that the law would give too much authority to the Minister of Higher Education rather than to a collective body, like the Council for Higher Education, which included people with a wide spectrum of opinion on higher education.[44]

Assurances by Prime Minister Rifa'i and the Minister of Higher Education, Dr Nasir al-Din al-Asad, that the universities would still maintain their independence, did not satisfy the opponents of the law. During the debate in the Senate, nine of the 25 Senators present abstained in the voting. This was an exceptionally high number for the Upper House, which was not elected by the populace but appointed by the King.[45]

The 1986–87 academic year began without incident in all four universities. In October, during a visit to the University of Science and Technology, Crown Prince Hasan urged restraint upon the students, suggesting that they "adopt an approach of constructive dialogue in presenting and discussing their problems."[46] The authorities, however, resorted to other means as well to ensure campus tranquillity. There were reports of Yarmuk University students from the West Bank not being allowed back into Jordan to resume their studies.[47] Further arrests of fundamentalist faculty and students in Yarmuk and Jordan Universities were similarly reported.[48]

The most serious opposition to the regime clearly came from two sources — the Fundamentalists and the radical Left. It was certainly the former who, in recent years, posed the greater threat. As in the recent past, the regime continued to deal with its religious opponents with a combination of conciliation, control and repression. The radical Left, however, rarely met with any form of toleration. The regime always unhesitatingly declared its hostility to the radical Left whose very existence represented at least an ideological, if not a serious political, challenge to the existing political order. Its attitude to religious activism, however, was far more complex and ambivalent. Spokesmen for the regime took pains to explain that its confrontation with the Muslim Brothers was not due to their religious fervor but to their political activity.[49] Considering the inextricable relationship between religion and politics in Islam, this, of course, was not an easy distinction to make.

The growing influence of religion in Jordanian society had certain advantages for the regime in that it tended to weaken the appeal of Communism and other ideologies of the radical Left. The Hashemites, as descendants of the Prophet Muhammad, enjoyed a measure of legitimacy based on their ancestry, which was very prestigious in religious terms. As Rifa'i put it, "the King is the scion of the Prophet." There was therefore "no room for religious outbidding" with the Hashemite regime.[50] Rifa'i pointed out that Islam was the religion of the State. The Government, he said, had no quarrel with anyone over Islam. The regime coexisted with the Muslim Brotherhood, which was a licensed and recognized group — indeed, the only such political group in the country. After all, Rifa'i explained, Islam as a creed or a way of life was the "only indigenous creed," as opposed to the "imported" Marxist or pseudo-Marxist radical left-wing or other secular ideologies. All political thought that was not Islamic was "imported," he said. The regime, therefore, had no problems with the "so-called fundamentalist current."[51] Rifa'i's statements reflected the measure of tolerance the regime displayed towards the Fundamentalists. It certainly did not wish to appear to be antireligious, and it was not. But as Rifa'i knew only too well, the regime's relations with the "fundamentalist current" were hardly harmonious. He himself warned of the danger of "any faction" exploiting religion for political ends "far removed from Islam." Such groups would be dealt with not as religious groups, but as any other political movement, in accordance with the requirements of "national security." This had indeed been the case when a connection was evident "between what might be called religious extremism and the [Yarmuk] university incidents."[52] In a regime that made no distinction between real opposition and threats to "national security" there was bound to be friction with the "fundamentalist current" that did, in fact, challenge the existing political order. The Fundamentalists raised serious questions pertaining to the very existence of the basically secular nation-state. Their ideology related not only to individual piety and the observance of Islamic social norms, but also to the structure of the State and the fundamental political questions of authority and legitimacy. It was on these issues that the Fundamentalists were bound to clash with a Westernizing, modernizing, pragmatic, non-ideological and essentially secular regime over such crucial questions as legislation and the ultimate source of authority. There was a great difference between the regime's desire to employ religion as an instrument to legitimize its own control over the Jordanian nation-state, and the Fundamentalists' perception of a state governed and controlled by religious law.

The regime demonstrated its own dedication to religious piety and observance, but severely restricted fundamentalist intervention in affairs of state. In his Speech from the Throne on 1 November, Husayn outlined his Government's care for the *Awqaf* (religious endowments) and the Holy Places. The Government had also put forward a clear policy for mosque construction and maintenance throughout the Kingdom. It had completed the necessary design work of five new mosques to honor the memory of the companions of the Prophet Muhammad, which were to be constructed in 1987. The Government, he said, had similarly facilitated the *haj* procedure and had begun to place memorial plaques at Islamic historical sites. It was particularly important for the King to clarify precisely who was in real control. He therefore reminded his listeners of the new Law of Preaching, Guidance and Teaching enacted in late 1985 (see *MECS* 1984–85, p 509), according to which the Government and no one else, could regulate religious guidance and instruction and ensure "the proper functioning of the mosque,"[53] i.e., mosque activity was to be controlled by the Government and not by unauthorized fundamentalist preachers. Islamic organizations were, however, allowed a measure of politically innocuous freedom not permitted to others. Thus, the Council of Islamic Organizations in Amman was allowed in mid-April to denounce the US air raid on Libya in the Jordanian Press,[54] while the Ba'th Party in Jordan could only do so over Radio Damascus.[55] A demonstration organized by Jordan's professional associations, in which opponents from the Left figured prominently, was dispersed by the police in front of the US embassy.[56]

On the other hand, as attested to by the Yarmuk University incidents, the Government's intervention in the by-election in Irbid, the dismissal of Fundamentalists from the universities, and the reported removal of a number of fundamentalist officials from the Ministries of Education and Religious Affairs,[57] anything that even remotely challenged the Government's authority was not tolerated.

As in the past, Husayn continued to argue in favor of what he regarded as a moderate and balanced approach to the relationship between religion and state and religion and modernity. Addressing the annual conference of the *Al al-Bayt* Foundation (see *MECS* 1984–85, pp 507–8), he called for a synthesis between religious and scientific thinking for Jordan to "get along in modern life." Such a synthesis, no doubt to be determined by the regime itself, would, he said, help the nation to progress materially while, at the same time, "firmly binding people to their religious and cultural heritage." That, after all, was the objective of the *Al al-Bayt* Foundation. There could be no mistake, however, in interpreting Husayn's view that religious and spiritual factors, important and relevant as they might be, were nonetheless auxiliary and subordinate to the purely rational and scientific in Jordan's pursuit of modernity and progress. He contended that the national and cultural institutions of the Muslim world had "remained frozen over the years because they [had] been linked only to the past, lagging behind the advances of today's scientific progress; for this reason they [had] failed to contribute to modern science and modern civilization...Modern science remain[ed] totally alien to us, rendering us incapable of probing its depths...It has no roots in our culture and has not taken root in our environment." Having delivered such a scathing critique of Islamic society, Husayn, however, was, it seemed, genuinely in agreement with an important point often made by exponents of the fundamentalist approach. He conceded that the scientific progress of the West had taken an anti-religious course that had established modern societies, in both the Communist and Capitalist worlds, which were characterized by materialism and greed and were sorely lacking in moral and spiritual values. He therefore concluded with an appeal to the scholars at the conference to "embark on the task of helping the younger generations to absorb modern science and to blend it with spiritual values and beliefs."[58]

While religion clearly had a spiritual, though not a political, role to play in modern society, the regime had an extremely low threshold of tolerance for radical Leftists. Their ideology was culturally repugnant and politically hostile. They were totally unacceptable and were treated accordingly. The organs of the more radical factions of the PLO, the Popular Front for the Liberation of Palestine (PFLP) and the Popular Democratic Front for the Liberation of Palestine, repeatedly complained about the systematic harassment of their supporters by the regime. The Committee for the Defense of Democratic Freedoms, which operated under the auspices of the two groups and the Jordanian Communist Party (see *MECS* 1978–79, p 631; 1979–80, p 576; and 1984–85, p 504), frequently reported on the imprisonment of political activists and on government intervention and intimidation in alumni, student, professional and trade-union affairs. According to the committee, there were over 200 political prisoners in Jordan.[59] In early November, the "Jordanian Popular Forces," a euphemism for the leftist opposition, issued a statement, broadcast by Radio Damascus, in which they condemned all efforts to negotiate a peaceful settlement with Israel.[60] Though Jordan was not explicitly referred to, the statement was clearly directed against Husayn's efforts to coordinate his West Bank policy with Israel and to convene an international peace conference. The statement was signed by over 50 people, including well-known anti-Establishment figures like Bahjat Abu Gharbiyya and Sulayman al-Hadidi (prominent Ba'this); Mahmud al-Mu'ayta (former leader of the Syrian Ba'thi-controlled al-Sa'iqa faction of the PLO); Yahya Hammuda and 'Abd al-Jawad Salih (former chairman and member of the PLO Executive Committee, respectively); Husayn Mjalli (chairman of the Jordanian Bar Association); 'Ali Abu Nawar (a former Chief of Staff involved in the plot against Husayn in 1957); and some former officials who had been associated with the oppositional activities of Ahmad 'Ubaydat, such as Sulayman 'Arar (a former Minister in the Badran, Sharaf and 'Ubaydat Cabinets) and Hani al-Khasawna. Over 30 of the signatories were summoned for interrogation by the Minister of Interior, Raja'i al-Dajani, and warned not to indulge in such activity lest they find themselves confronted by the domestic security apparatus.[61]

Husayn's Palestinian policy and his break with 'Arafat, which included punitive measures against the PLO in Jordan (see below), must have aroused considerable indignation among at least part of the Kingdom's very large Palestinian population. But the measures did not provoke open protests or demonstrations against the regime as may have been expected. One Western diplomat made what appeared to be very pertinent observations in this respect. He explained that the Palestinians in the country not only had "a healthy respect for the police and security forces," but had also, to a large extent, been integrated into Jordanian society. They felt at home there, and would "think twice about opposing the King."[62] A striking example of this integration was Raja'i al-Dajani's appointment as Minister of Interior in Rifa'i's Cabinet in October. (For cabinet changes, see Table 1.) Dajani, a member of a very prominent Palestinian family, was given a portfolio that was very rarely placed in the hands of a Palestinian, because it involved responsibility for domestic security. Dajani's loyalty, however, was apparently beyond any doubt; he had served as the Assistant Director of General Intelligence until 1982, when he retired from that position with the rank of Major General.[63] Interestingly enough, the Palestinian who had last served as Minister of Interior was another member of this family, Kamil al-Dajani, who was appointed by Premier Wasfi al-Tall in 1962.

The King was able to pursue policies that were unpopular to some, or maybe even to many, due to a widely held feeling among Jordanians that other Arab regimes were far worse, and that there was no viable alternative. Jamal al-Sha'ir, himself quite outspoken in his criticism of the regime, in an apparent allusion to Islamic Fundamentalism noted that whatever "alternative people can think of [was] very frightening. Even the most harshly critical of the system, say the Communists, believe[d] this...The King [had] carried things on from 1953 to 1986 in the midst of a mad Arab world."[64] The Opposition was at present no more than an irritant, but the regime nevertheless found it necessary to tighten its control over all spheres of the political process.

THE REINFORCEMENT OF GOVERNMENT CONTROL OVER THE PRESS

Under the Government of Zayd al-Rifa'i numerous steps had been taken to reestablish government control over religious affairs and the election process, and very firm action had been taken against any form of opposition to the regime. In late 1985, there were various indications that the Government was also planning measures to further increase its control of the Press (see *MECS* 1984–85, pp 504–5). During the decade of tranquillity and prosperity, from the early 1970s to the early 1980s, the Government had allowed increasing private ownership of the daily newspapers, although it still maintained firm control of the Press by means of the Press and Publications Law (see *MECS* 1984–85, p 505). Now, with an economic recession, somewhat greater opposition and rising demands for democratization of the system (see *MECS* 1984–85, pp 503–6), the regime responded with a comprehensive reassertion of government control rather than make any concessions of substance to its opponents. This was particularly so in reference to the Press. In early 1986, steps were taken by the Government to increase its share in the ownership of the three dailies, *al-Ra'y*, *al-Dustur* and *Sawt al-Sha'b*, by transforming them all into joint stock companies controlled by the Government. This, in effect, nationalized the daily press. In *al-Ra'y* and *al-Dustur*, hitherto privately owned, 35 per cent of the shares were to be held by the original owners, 25 per cent by public subscription, 15 per cent by a government fund, 20 per cent by government-controlled corporations and public institutions, and 5 per cent by the paper's staff. In *Sawt al-Sha'b*, hitherto a joint stock company, the Government was now to control over 60 per cent of the shares.[65] In mid-May the Government removed Muraywid al-Tall, the chairman of the Board of Directors, and Tariq al-Masarwa, the editor-in-chief, from their positions at *Sawt al-Sha'b*.[66] This measure reportedly followed their refusal to write editorials backing the Government in the wake of the Yarmuk University incidents.[67] During the first half of 1986 about a dozen local journalists were, in effect, banned from writing in the local papers on sensitive issues, after the Government found their work to be too critical. The leading editors of the local dailies were given a list of these reporters, whose work was to be "closely watched." As a result, most of them did not write on political issues for a while. One of these reporters, it was said, had failed to praise Husayn for his speech in February announcing the break with 'Arafat (see below). Another, or possibly the same one, was even jailed for a few weeks. The Government, as one of its Ministers conceded, was "very committed to discipline."[68]

A number of foreign journalists were also blacklisted. But at the end of July, after reports of restrictions on local journalists reached the foreign Press, the bans were lifted. A number of foreign journalists who had been detained and deported after covering the Yarmuk University incidents, were allowed to return to the country.[69] Husayn went out of his way to make amends with the foreign Press. In mid-July he held a press conference in his palace gardens to "smooth over animosities...and to polish Jordan's image as a progressive pro-Western country."[70]

In his Speech from the Throne on 1 November, the King underscored his Government's commitment to "freedom of the Press within the Law." The freedom upheld by the regime, Husayn explained, was "responsible freedom," that which did "not threaten the national security of the State" or undermine "the ultimate national interest." Freedom of expression could not be allowed to become "freedom to subvert."[71]

Nothing in Jordan's authoritarian tradition had changed, as attested to by the regime's attitude to the Opposition and the Press. There could be no "loyal Opposition" in a political tradition that so clearly equated opposition with subversion. Zayd al-Rifa'i made a most revealing comment on this subject in one of his interviews. Noting that all political thought that was not Islamic was "imported" and therefore, by implication, not authentic (see also above), Rifa'i remarked that these "imported" ideas included democracy.[72] Rifa'i, like the King, obviously did not believe that democracy, as understood in the West, should or could be applied in Jordan. Clearly, in their view, it was a luxury the country could not afford.

THE ECONOMY AND THE NEW FIVE-YEAR PLAN

Jordan in 1986 was still in the throes of an economic recession, spurred by the slump in the economies of Saudi Arabia and the Gulf states; a sharp decline in Arab economic aid; the decline of prices of raw materials and commodities like phosphates, potash and cement, which were Jordan's main exports; and the economic ramifications of the Gulf war. But the Government did appear to be managing the situation. At least for the time being, financial disaster had been averted and the Government was engaged in planning for an essential revitalization of the economy. The biggest threat was that of unemployment, which had steadily increased in recent years. In early 1986 the number of unemployed, according to government sources, was said to have risen from the 1984 figure of 27,000 to between 30,000 and 40,000, or some 6–8 per cent of the locally employed work force.[73] In his budget statement to the Council of Deputies in December, the Finance Minister, Hanna 'Awda, admitted that unemployment had reached the "alarming rate of nearly 8 per cent."[74] According to other sources, unemployment was as high as 10–12 per cent, and it was feared that by 1990 the number of unemployed might be as high as 100,000. A 1984 World Bank study had forecast a 30 per cent level of unemployment in the 1990s but had modified the figure after Jordanian objections.[75] Due to the recession in Saudi Arabia and the Gulf states, the demand for Jordanian workers there had dropped considerably; fewer Jordanian workers were leaving to work in their economies and a growing number were also returning permanently to Jordan every year. In 1985 the number of Jordanian expatriate workers was estimated at 328,000. If correct, this figure was only slightly higher than previous figures and was expected to level off or even to decline. It was estimated that 10-15 per cent of the expatriate workers had returned or were in the process of returning to Jordan.[76] The Government, however, contested these figures on returning workers. According to the Minister of Supply, Industry and Trade, Raja'i al-Mu'ashshir, the number of workers returning from the Gulf did not represent a significant increase compared with previous years, and the Prime Minister declared that there had been no "group exodus" of workers from the Gulf. He said that reports to this effect were exaggerated. Khalid al-Hajj Hasan, the Minister of Labor and Social Development, visited several countries in the Gulf and received official assurances that Jordanians employed in the public sector would not lose their jobs.[77] It was in this sector that most Jordanians were employed. Many of those returning to

Jordan were people employed in the public sector who had reached retirement age and were, presumably, replaced by others. Other returning workers had been employed in private companies, particularly in construction. One may assume that most, or even all, of these workers were not replaced by other Jordanians, because of the slump in the construction industry in the Gulf states.[78] What was clear, however, was that the outflow of workers from Jordan to Saudi Arabia and the Gulf was decreasing from *c* 15,000 in the boom years to *c* 5,000 a year.[79] Particularly noteworthy was the sustained increase in the percentage of Jordanians in the overall expatriate Arab labor force employed in Saudi Arabia and the Gulf states. This percentage rose from 14.3 in 1975 to 14.7 in 1980 and to 17 in 1985.[80] This confirmed previous assessments that the relatively highly skilled and well-educated Jordanian workers were still needed in the Gulf states (see *MECS* 1984–85, pp 497–98). These figures suggested that the very pessimistic projections of an imminent mass return of Jordanian workers were indeed exaggerated. The Government did, nevertheless, have to contend with a substantial fall in worker remittances, which dropped from JD475m in 1984 to the 1983 level of JD403m in 1985.[81] Similarly, it had to deal with rising unemployment. While worker remittances could possibly stabilize, more or less, at the 1985 level, as the Government projected, due to the stability in the number of workers,[82] unemployment was bound to increase. The number of school and university graduates entering the job market was approximately 30,000–35,000 a year. Since a much smaller ratio of the surplus was now being siphoned off by the job markets in the Gulf, unemployment could only go up. Unemployment was particularly severe among physicians, and engineers. In some cases, joblessness in the professions exceeded 30 per cent.[83] Although the Government denied that it had any intention of forcing students to study in certain fields, it did have plans to "guide students" to study areas of specialization that were required in the local market.[84] Rifa'i said that the fact that there had been no link in the past between university education and job opportunities was a "major problem." The Government therefore intended to take various measures, including a "radical reconsideration of education methods" at the elementary, preparatory and secondary levels, to focus more on vocational training and less on purely academic education, except in accordance with the country's needs.[85] In August and September legislation to this end was passed in both Houses of Parliament.[86]

Though there was increasing unemployment there was no decrease in the number of foreigners (mainly Egyptians) employed in Jordan. The Government introduced stricter regulations to monitor the employment of foreigners and to ensure preference for Jordanian nationals.[87] These, however, did not have a much greater effect than previous regulations. The number of foreign workers remained steady at 150,000.[88] The major obstacle to the Government's efforts in this regard was the fact that most of the foreign workers were employed in low-paying menial jobs which many of the Jordanian unemployed did not want and for which they were overqualified.[89] The Government therefore sought to bring about a change in social values in an effort to alter people's attitudes to manual labor.[90] But that was easier said than done. Addressing a group of students at the University of Science and Technology, Crown Prince Hasan complained that the country suffered from unemployment partly because graduates refused certain jobs offered to them. This, he said, should be avoided as it was not worthy of "dedicated and faithful citizens."[91] One could hardly expect such an appeal to change much, unless market forces made menial jobs far more rewarding financially.

The country did not have an elaborate social security system and did not provide unemployment benefits, and the Government was concerned about the possible sociopolitical effects of widespread unemployment. In August, Parliament passed the National Aid Fund Law, which authorized the provision of state assistance to needy families from a JD1.5m fund and was designed to help people find jobs by offering them vocational training. The projected fund was also to finance studies to suggest ways of overcoming poverty and helping needy people become self-reliant. This was to be in addition to the financial aid of JD750,000 per year being offered by the Ministry of Labor and Social Development to some 8,000 families. As usual, special attention was paid to the needs of servicemen in an effort to maintain their economic security and well-being. Parliament thus amended the Military Housing Fund Law and increased the amount of interest-free loans for servicemen's housing from JD4,500 to JD5,000.[92]

The overall performance of the Jordanian economy during the recession, according to the Minister of Supply, Industry and Trade, had "run completely counter" to some of the more pessimistic projections. During Jordan's decade of growth from 1973 to 1982, the gross domestic product (GDP) had increased at an unusual average of 10.5 per cent. In 1984, it was down to about 4 per cent. This kept in step with Jordan's annual rate of population growth (3.8–4 per cent) and Jordan, the Minister contended, remained a "relatively prosperous developing economy." Inflation in 1985 was down to 3 per cent; there had been a continued modest narrowing of the large trade deficit from 1984, which persisted through the first half of 1986; and remittances had remained steady in the first half of 1986.[93] Oil consumption increased from 2.76m tons in 1984 to 2.82m tons in 1985, but due to a drop in prices the cost of Jordan's energy imports dropped slightly, from $612m in 1984 to $603m in 1985.[94]

In seeking to revitalize the economy the Government laid special emphasis on developing the private sector. Its main objectives were:

1. To maintain and replenish its foreign currency reserves (which had dropped in early 1985 to JD147m[95] — their lowest point since 1976).
2. To create as many jobs as possible.
3. To encourage and protect domestic production from severe foreign competition and dumping.
4. To make full use of its relatively well-educated manpower and geographical location to build the country as a regional center for services, maintenance and banking.[96]

Jordan's new Five-Year Plan for 1986-90 was approved by the Cabinet in August[97] and shortly thereafter the Cabinet set up an Economic Consultative Council. The Council was to be chaired by the Prime Minister and to include the Ministers of Supply, Industry and Trade, Finance and Planning, the governor of the Central Bank and a number of key figures from the private sector.[98]

The plan projected a modest, but hopefully sustainable, 4 per cent annual growth rate of the GDP. (This was the figure given in a briefing by the Minister of Supply, Industry and Trade in early September. Subsequently, the targeted annual growth rates of both the GDP and the gross national product were given as 5 per cent.) This was expected to alleviate the country's economic problems, the most serious of which was looming unemployment. The planned growth rate was a function of increasing pressures and financial constraints caused by the continued drop in financial aid, budget support and workers' remittances from the Gulf. These flows were all expected to be further affected by the forecast continuation of the economic slowdown in the oil-producing countries, sustained by a depressed oil market. But to achieve the planned growth rate required the implementation of an ambitious investment program of JD3.115 bn.

The basic objectives of the plan were:

1. To achieve the planned growth rate.
2. To reduce dependence on external grants and to cut down the trade deficit.
3. To balance the Government's budget.
4. To expand basic social services in all regions of the country in order to achieve a more balanced distribution of the fruits of development and thereby to reduce internal migration to the cities.
5. To reduce the proportion of consumption in the GDP and to increase domestic savings.
6. To create sufficient jobs to absorb the expected gradual return of workers from the Gulf and a much higher ratio of the Jordanians entering the labor market, far fewer of whom were expected to find employment abroad.[99]

Economic policy was designed to foster a business climate conducive to private enterprise. Investment in the private sector was expected to reach JD1.482 bn, or 48 per cent of the overall planned investment. These investments were to be concentrated mainly in agriculture, industry, housing and construction. The public sector that would account for the remaining JD1.633 bn, or 52 per cent of investment, was to focus on infrastructural projects that would include water and irrigation systems, and communication and transport projects, as well as on social services. Most important of all was the fact that the plan was expected to create over 200,000 new jobs, partly as a direct result of the new investments and partly by having Jordanians replace foreign workers in the local economy.[100]

The 1986–90 Five-Year Plan represented a coming-to-terms with new economic realities. The high hopes that the 1981-85 Plan would maintain the levels of GDP growth achieved in the late 1970s, i.e., 11–12 per cent, had been dashed. The Jordanians were now being compelled to lower their expectations and to strive only to maintain the much lower growth rate of about 4 per cent that had actually been achieved in the 1981–85 plan. A potential problem in attaining even this relatively modest objective, which did no more than keep growth in step with the population increase, was the country's heavy dependence on external sources to finance its investments. Government-to-government loans and external commercial loans were expected to provide 57.7 per cent of the total of funds needed during the plan's period. Of the total of some JD4 bn that were expected to be available under the new Five-Year Plan, just over JD3 bn were to be used in actual investment. Another JD222m were to be used to replenish reserves and some JD660m would go to meet principal and interest payments on previous loans.[101]

Jordan's accumulated external debt already amounted to JD1.053 bn at the end of 1985, according to figures from the International Monetary Fund. Jordan, however, continued to enjoy a good credit rating and had experienced no difficulties in the past in servicing its foreign loans. With the recent drop in foreign earnings the situation could become more difficult. But the hope was that as the new plan's targets of increasing domestic savings and government revenue from domestic sources were realized, the country's dependence on external loans and assistance would also be reduced, albeit by a limited margin. The Jordanians also pinned some hopes for a significant improvement in their overall economic situation on the discovery of oil in commercial quantities.[102] So far, oil discoveries in the Kingdom had been modest and of marginal consequence (see *MECS* 1984–85, p 500).

In an effort to promote international interest and financial assistance for the 1986–90 Plan, a special Development Conference was held in November in Amman, to which representatives of over 30 Western and Arab states were invited. In his opening address to the conference, the King placed particular emphasis on the need for regional and international cooperation, "to spread stability and development," which were the "two sides of the same coin." Stability, he noted, was the basis for development, just as balanced development was the basis for stability.[103] It seemed that Husayn was trying to convey both a political and an economic message to his audience: that it was also in the interest of the Western industrialist nations and Jordan's Arab neighbors to sustain Jordan's economic development and to cooperate on questions of finance and labor migration in the cause of regional stability.

Though the Jordanians stressed that the conference was "not a pledging one,"[104] they were obviously seeking at least general commitments for financial support. The US, Britain, West Germany, the World Bank, the European Investment Bank, the Arab League Educational, Scientific and Cultural Organization, the Kuwaiti-based Arab Fund for Economic and Social Development, the Kuwaiti Fund for Arab Economic Development, the Abu Dhabi Fund for Arab Economic Development and the Islamic Development Bank all pledged to support the development plan.[105] Notably absent were the Saudis. Since Jordan's development program included a controversial plan for the West Bank and Gaza (see below), the Saudis, characteristically, preferred to stay away from the conference.[106]

Jordan's budget of JD1.018 bn for 1987 was presented to Parliament in December and approved without any difficulty. The deficit, estimated at JD39.6m, exceeded that of 1986 by only JD2m even though the budget was nearly JD95m larger than that of 1986 (JD923.7m).[107] What was of special significance was that, for the first time, domestic revenues equalled current expenditure. During the debate in the Council of Deputies, some Deputies had suggested that the Government reduce its dependence on foreign loans by imposing on itself a predetermined ceiling of foreign debt. This was rejected by the Prime Minister, who explained that such a limitation would retard the country's development. Most of the foreign loans were for long and easy terms. Moreover, the cost of servicing these loans was only 12.4 per cent of the country's exports in 1986, well below the internationally accepted "red line" of 20 per cent.[108]

JORDAN, THE PALESTINIANS AND THE MIDDLE EAST PEACE PROCESS

THE BREAK WITH THE PALESTINE LIBERATION ORGANIZATION

By the end of 1985, relations between Jordan and the PLO had deteriorated considerably. Husayn had failed to induce the organization to endorse Security Council Resolution 242 unequivocally and unconditionally. In the Jordanian view such a PLO endorsement was the sine qua non for any breakthrough in the peace process. The King was clearly exasperated by 'Arafat's maneuvers on this matter (see

MECS, 1984–85, pp 514–18), but, in early 1986, yet another effort was made to extract this concession from the PLO. 'Arafat arrived in Amman in late January, and intensive negotiations were held until early February, between the PLO leadership and the Jordanian authorities. These talks, however, did not produce the desired breakthrough. The PLO still refused to accept Resolution 242, unless the US recognized the right of the Palestinians to self-determination and statehood within the framework of a Jordanian-Palestinian confederation and unless the PLO was guaranteed a seat at a future international conference to negotiate Middle East peace. The US, whose positions were communicated to the PLO by Jordan, would not, however, agree to PLO participation in any such international conference, unless the organization accepted Resolution 242 unconditionally.[109] The US, according to the Jordanians, had, in fact accepted the principle of PLO participation in the talks, if the organization would only accept Resolution 242, which was to be the basis for any future Middle East peace conference. A US offer along these lines was transmitted by the Jordanians to the PLO, but was turned down by the organization. The PLO leadership was not prepared to settle for anything less than US recognition of Palestinian rights to self-determination and statehood (see also chapter on PLO), a concession the US was not prepared to make. The PLO and the US remained firm in their respective positions.[110] The deadlock was therefore complete, and the peace process had reached an impasse.

On 19 February, Husayn expressed his deep disappointment in a long address to the nation in which he clearly blamed the PLO and not the US for the failure of the negotiations. Husayn laid particular emphasis on his success in bringing about an evolvement in the US position toward the PLO and the idea of an international conference. The Americans, who had hitherto opposed PLO and Soviet involvement, now accepted the participation of all five permanent members of the UN Security Council in such a conference in addition to all the local parties concerned. Two serious problems still remained: that of the nature, mandate and powers of intervention of the participating Great Powers in the negotiations; and that of the basis for PLO participation. As for the first, no agreement was reached; but on the question of PLO participation, said Husayn, the Americans had taken an important step forward. In January 1986, following talks Husayn had in London with the US Assistant Secretary of State for Near Eastern and South Asian Affairs, Richard Murphy, the US informed Jordan, in a written undertaking, that it would agree to the PLO being invited to participate in the international conference, if the organization declared its unequivocal acceptance of Resolution 242; declared its readiness to negotiate for peace with the Government of Israel in the framework of the international conference; and condemned terrorism.[111] This, Husayn pointed out, was a significant change in the US position. When the negotiations with the US began, after the signing of the Husayn-'Arafat accord of February 1985 (see *MECS* 1984–85, pp 201–4), the US position had been that it would only enter into a dialogue with the PLO once the organization had accepted Resolution 242. Now, however, the US was prepared to go a step further, and it had agreed to have the PLO invited to the international conference if the organization accepted the Resolution. Nevertheless, Husayn complained, despite this progress, the PLO refused to accept the resolution and was thus wasting an opportunity for an historical breakthrough. The PLO leadership remained adamant on the question of self-determination as an essential quid pro quo for their acceptance of 242. On 27 January, the US embassy in Amman notified Husayn of the American position. The US reiterated its support for the legitimate rights of the Palestinian people, as stated in the Reagan Plan of September 1982, and agreed that the PLO, like any other party, had the right to bring up any question it wished at the international conference, including that of self-determination. On 5 February, according to Husayn's account, the US presented a new text containing its agreement to the convening of an international conference that would be based on Resolution 242 and on the assurance of the legitimate rights of the Palestinian people.[112] 'Arafat notified Zayd al-Rifa'i on the following day that the US position was still inadequate, in that it did not specifically include a US commitment to recognize the Palestinians' right to self-determination. 'Arafat left Amman on 7 February, still insisting that unless the US did so, the PLO would not accept Resolution 242.[113]

Husayn accused the PLO of having reneged on previous commitments, made during 1985, to accept Resolution 242 in exchange for US agreement to deal directly with the organization and thereby accord it official recognition. Husayn recalled that when he visited the US in May 1985 he had issued a statement to that effect, after having obtained 'Arafat's prior approval of the text. This same commitment, Husayn added, had subsequently been reaffirmed by 'Arafat on more than one occasion, in his talks with the Jordanians.[114] In these circumstances, Husayn concluded, Jordan was no longer able to continue its political coordination with the PLO leadership, at least until such time as their "word became their bond" and cooperation was governed by "commitment, credibility and consistency."[115]

Husayn's contention that the PLO had reneged on previous commitments was not really in accordance with the facts. 'Arafat may well have agreed to Husayn's issuing of the statement he had made in Washington. But there was an important difference between agreeing to Husayn making a statement and directly committing the PLO to the text, which 'Arafat, in fact, subsequently refused to do. Before and after the signing of the accord of February 1985, the PLO leadership had consistently maintained that it had not, and would not, accept Resolution 242 unless the US recognized the Palestinians's right to self-determination (see *MECS* 1984–85, pp 199–200). Following Husayn's statements in the US to the effect that the PLO was indeed willing to accept 242, in exchange for dialogue with the US, 'Arafat and other PLO leaders all refused to endorse them (see *MECS* 1984–85, p 203). Husayn could not therefore have been as "surprised" as he claimed to be[116] when the PLO simply reiterated its longstanding position on Resolution 242 during the last round of negotiations in early 1986. Throughout the negotiations the Jordanians had tried in vain to pressure the PLO to accept the resolution unconditionally and without linking it to Palestinian self-determination. Husayn was exasperated in this effort by 'Arafat's maneuvers and prevarications, but he could hardly have been "surprised."

The Jordanians, as opposed to the PLO, had no real interest in pressuring the US to recognize Palestinian rights to self-determination and independent statehood. The Jordanians regarded a fully independent, PLO-controlled state as a threat to themselves and sought to secure a settlement for the West Bank and Gaza that would give Jordan as much control and influence as possible in these territories. Universal recognition of the Palestinians' right to self-determination could have severely reduced the measure of Jordanian influence in determining the future of the West Bank and

Gaza and might very well have delivered the exercise of self-determination entirely into the hands of the Palestinians, regardless of Jordanian preferences and fundamental interests. For Jordan, coordination with the PLO was a means of transforming the organizaton into a legitimizing instrument of Jordanian political objectives. For the PLO, on the other hand, this coordination was designed to transform the Jordanian role into that of an auxiliary, to pave the way for the establishment of an independent Palestinian state. The coordination, therefore, was between two historical rivals with diametrically opposed objectives, each seeking to subordinate the other. As a result, the failure of the coordination was almost a foregone conclusion.

Husayn had argued all along, and again in his speech of 19 February, that the question of self-determination in the framework of a Jordanian-Palestinian confederation was a purely Jordanian-Palestinian issue which had nothing to do with anyone else.[117] The Jordanians had deliberately skirted the issue of self-determination in all their dealings with the US (cf *MECS* 1984–85, p 516), arguing with the PLO that the first priority ought to be Israeli withdrawal,[118] after which all other issues could be addressed. This, of course, was a self-serving argument. Shifting the emphasis to withdrawal was clearly intended to circumvent the problematic issues of Palestinian representation and self-determination. These were the most difficult preliminary obstacles to overcome in the peace process. Moreover, they tended to weaken rather than to reinforce the Jordanian role in the settlement process. Precisely for this reason the PLO sought to direct the process toward US acceptance of PLO representation and Palestinian self-determination. This PLO thrust, Husayn contended, was a "confusion of priorities" which resulted directly from the Rabat resolutions.[119] These resolutions, which had recognized the PLO as the "sole legitimate representative of the Palestinian people," had never been willingly accepted by the Jordanians. And in his speech, Husayn cautiously restated his long-held view, that, in essence, they were misguided (cf *MECS* 1984–85, p 513). He implied that the resolutions had allowed the PLO to identify its own narrow organizational interests with those of the Palestinian people as a whole. "Some Palestinians" went so far as to consider "the organization to be the land and the rights, and the land and the rights to be the organization." The retrieval of the land was no longer seen as the top priority that would pave the way for the restoration of the national rights of the Palestinian people.[120]

The difference in priorities was, however, only a function of the fundamental issue of contention, i.e., the ultimate political control of the West Bank and Gaza, over which a gulf of mistrust separated Jordan and the PLO. Husayn, therefore, accused the PLO of being more concerned with the question of who would rule the occupied territories after liberation than with the problem of liberation itself.[121] But it was equally obvious that Husayn's tactic of deferring the question of future rule on the West Bank and Gaza Strip was designed primarily to leave Jordan sufficient leeway to impose its own control over these territories in the future. Husayn himself suggested that the PLO's desire to involve the US and others in the question of self-determination was motivated by a lack of confidence in Jordan's good intentions.[122] Jordan, however, according to Husayn, had already taken the necessary steps to dispel such mistrust. As far back as 1972, he had published his federation plan as the basis for future relations between Jordan and Palestine.[123] But Husayn's plan fell far short of accepting the notion of a fully independent and sovereign Palestinian state and could hardly have reassured the PLO. It referred to a federation between the Jordanian and Palestinian "regions" of what was to become the Jordanian dominated "United Arab Kingdom." Recently expressed Jordanian views on confederation did not differ greatly from Husayn's original plan and referred to the Swiss or US federative structure as relevant examples to follow. The Palestinian State in the Jordanian-Palestinian confederation, according to 'Adnan Abu 'Awda, the Minister of Court, and one of Husayn's closest advisers, was to be "something like the states in the US"[124] (see also *MECS* 1984–85, pp 517). Such ideas would never have sufficed to assure the PLO of Jordan's good intentions. One can, however, safely assume that it was not the PLO that Husayn was trying to convince, but rather the people on the West Bank and Gaza Strip, to whom his speech was addressed to a very large degree. Husayn was making a calculated effort to discredit the PLO as an unrealistic, dogmatic and untrustworthy organization that was insensitive to the basic interests of the people in the occupied territories and overly preoccupied with its own self-serving organizational interests. Husayn was clearly trying to drive a wedge between the PLO and the West Bankers with the message that Jordan was more attentive than the PLO to their immediate desire for Israeli withdrawal. Moreover, purely in terms of political realism, if Israel were to give up any territory at all, it would do so to Jordan rather than to the PLO.

Though extremely critical of the PLO leadership, Husayn did not withdraw Jordan's recognition of the organization as the "sole legitimate representative" of the Palestinians. Husayn and Rifa'i repeatedly explained that Jordan's conflict was with the PLO leadership and not with the organization itself.[125] This was an artificial distinction which was symptomatic of the ambivalence that had characterized the Jordanian position toward the PLO since the Rabat resolutions had been adopted in 1974. Husayn could not afford to denounce the Palestinian and general Arab consensus on the PLO, in which he grudgingly acquiesced. But, at the same time, he could and did question its political wisdom, in a calculated effort to erode this consensus. For Jordan, despite the lip service it paid regularly to the PLO's exclusive representative status, Palestinian representation was actually divided among three parties: Jordan, the PLO and the West Bankers. Now, following the break with the PLO, Husayn sought to alter the relative weight of these components by encouraging a Palestinian and Arab reassessment of the PLO role. As Husayn put it in his speech, having given a public explanation of all that had taken place, the time had come to "transfer the matter again to the Palestinian platforms of discussion (*manabir al-hiwar*)" in the occupied territories and the diaspora and to these "platforms of discussion" in the Arab world as well.[126]

In statements to Western and Arab media after his speech, Husayn was more explicit on this score, openly challenging the PLO's leadership and questioning whether it really did represent the interests of the Palestinian people. His speech, Husayn said, was intended to lead to the emergence of a "Palestinian side" which related to its cause "in a responsible manner."[127] He urged the Palestinians in the occupied territories to "define what they want." If they were unhappy with Israel's creeping annexation of the West Bank and Gaza, they ought to tell the Jordanians what they wanted Jordan to do about it. They could "create an apparatus to express themselves," Husayn said. If it was the PLO, Jordan would accept that; but if they chose another apparatus to express their wishes, that would also be welcomed by Jordan.[128] Addressing delegations from the West Bank in late February and early

March, Husayn emphasized that it was up to them to decide whether they supported the stands of the PLO, because it was they who "should be the decision-makers in this particular issue."[129]

After all, the PLO leadership was detached from the conditions of the people under occupation and was "not in touch with the facts." The PLO had not done much in terms of liberation so far, Husayn argued, even though Jordan had paved the way for the organization to play its role.[130] Jordan would therefore focus on the Palestinians in the occupied territories as it was they who were the "principal constituency."[131]

These were all facets of a policy that was designed to shift the balance of power in the Palestinian arena, according greater influence and importance to the West Bankers in the formulation of Palestinian policy, at the expense of the PLO. Jordan aimed to create a climate of public opinion in the occupied territories that would come out openly and express disapproval with the PLO's handling of their interests. This in turn was intended, at the very least, to bring pressure to bear on the PLO to change its policies, and, at most, to lead to the eventual emergence of an alternative Palestinian leadership. In view of the widespread support that the PLO still enjoyed in the occupied territories, promoting an alternative leadership was indeed a tortuous venture. One may assume that it was the disappointing measure of support that Husayn had initially obtained for his anti-PLO policy in the occupied territories which had motivated the Jordanians to deny that they had any intentions of promoting an alternative Palestinian leadership.[132] But the Jordanians were clearly making a very serious effort to erode the hold of the PLO over the people on the West Bank and Gaza Strip.

In his speech on 19 February, Husayn had restated the four constant foundations on which Jordan's policy in the peace process rested. These were:

1. Security Council Resolution 242.
2. Security Council Resolution 338, which reaffirmed Resolution 242 and called for negotiations between the parties concerned "under appropriate auspices." This Jordan understood to mean an international conference.
3. The Rabat resolutions, without, however, losing sight of all the diplomatic difficulties and "confusion of priorities" that they had given rise to.
4. The Arab peace plan adopted at the Fez summit in September 1982.[133]

Despite the suspension of political coordination with the PLO leadership, Husayn repeatedly stated that Jordan's Palestinian policy and Jordanian-Palestinian relations would still be governed by the principles of the February 1985 accord (see *MECS* 1984–85, p 523), in respect of the "equality of rights and duties in facing the one common destiny."[134] In his speech, and repeatedly thereafter, Husayn and other senior spokesmen made it abundantly clear that Jordan would not enter into any separate settlement with Israel. Husayn revealed that during the last round of negotiations in January the US had suggested that, since the PLO would not accept Resolution 242, the peace process could proceed with Palestinian representatives from the occupied territories instead. Once the PLO accepted 242 it could immediately join the international conference. Jordan had turned down the US offer, Husayn said, because of its unwavering rejection of the notion of a separate settlement.[135] In early April, Husayn was quoted as having said in an interview that the sharp reduction in Arab economic aid to Jordan would force him to bow to American pressure to make a separate peace with Israel, in order to obtain vital assistance.[136] If this was, in fact, what Husayn had said, it would appear to have been directed more to the wealthy Arab states than to anyone else, in an effort to induce them to increase aid to Jordan; it was hardly the expression of a genuine intention to enter into separate negotiations. In any event, the report was immediately and emphatically denied by a palace spokesman.[137] Israeli disclosures of "quiet contacts" with Husayn were also denied in Amman and Husayn was reported to have conveyed his anger to Israeli Prime Minister Peres for having himself been the source of these revelations.[138]

The Jordanians were not prepared to engage in negotiations without broad Arab backing and credible Palestinian support. Husayn was quite willing to make every effort to undermine the PLO, even in cooperation with Israel, but he was not prepared to negotiate without the PLO, unless he could obtain Palestinian and Arab backing to do so. Jordan, Husayn said, "cannot talk on behalf of the Palestinians. We have to have a clear mandate."[139]

After the break with the PLO, Husayn declared on numerous occasions that Jordan would not deputize for or serve as a substitute for the Palestinian people and their "sole legitimate representative" — the PLO.[140] This, of course, did not preclude the theoretical possibility of having Jordan cooperate with a Palestinian substitute for the PLO, if the Rabat resolutions were to be sufficiently eroded. Husayn argued, maybe somewhat over-optimistically, that the question of who would ultimately represent the Palestinians was still open.[141] Jordan, he maintained, could only cooperate with the PLO if it chose to address itself "to saving the Palestinians from occupation,"[142] i.e., if it accepted Jordan's order of priorities and peace strategy. This implied that until such time as the PLO did so, Jordan would do all in its power to pressure the PLO, or even promote an alternative leadership. However, unless a credible alternative representation emerged, with the necessary Palestinian and Arab backing, Jordan would still have to seek eventual cooperation with the PLO. This was clearly for lack of a better choice, rather than a product of any genuine sense of commitment to the organization, but it placed Jordan in a position fraught with internal contradiction — that of rejecting and accepting the PLO at the same time.

As a corollary of Jordan's objection to a separate settlement, Husayn and other senior spokesmen repeatedly rejected direct negotiations with Israel, except within the framework of an international conference. As in the past, Jordan maintained that such a conference would have to be attended by the five permanent members of the Security Council and all the local parties to the conflict, including the PLO.[143] Zayd al-Rifa'i even went so far as to insist that Jordan could not imagine a conference without the PLO.[144] Any talk, he said, about a US solution, a separate move, or "an attempt to find alternatives [was] incorrect and [did] not reflect the truth." The conference, the Jordanians noted, would have to be based on Resolutions 242 and 338. Consequently, as Rifa'i pointed out, no party could attend the conference, if it rejected the basis on which the conference was to be held.[145] As Jordan would not attend such a conference without the PLO, and the PLO could not attend because of its continued rejection of Resolution 242, there was still no way out of the diplomatic impasse. As Rifa'i put it, unless Jordan could get the PLO to accept 242 and Israel to accept an international conference, the Palestinians on the West Bank and Gaza Strip would remain under occupation. The suspension of coordination with the PLO had not changed much in this respect, at least not in the short term.

Though there was no progress over the question of Palestinian representation, the idea of an international conference was gaining increasing acceptance internationally, as well as in the US and in Israel. Serious differences still remained in regard to the precise definition of the nature and the mandate of such a conference. The US and those Israelis who supported the idea regarded the conference as a forum for direct negotiations in which the Great Powers would be allowed only minimal intervention. The PLO, on the other hand, regarded the conference as a means of avoiding direct negotiations and as a venue for a settlement to be imposed by the Great Powers. It did not want a peace conference that had no "binding arbitration powers" and would serve "as a mere mediation forum."[146] Jordan's position was somewhere in the middle between these two. Husayn had publicly accepted the notion of direct negotiations within the framework of the conference (see *MECS* 1984–85, p 515). The aim of the conference, according to the Jordanians, "should not be the imposition of a settlement, but the manipulation of the leverage of influence [of the Great Powers] to induce constructive results."[147] The conference would not be expected to "solve deadlocks," but it was not to be just a symbolic venture either.[148] It would have to be "real" and not merely "ceremonial."[149] A "senior Jordanian official" rejected the Israeli position, noting that Jordan would not agree to a conference that did not have "decision-making powers and binding authority."[150]

In his Speech from the Throne on 1 November, Husayn declared that Jordan would "not allow stagnation to prevail, nor [would it] act unilaterally." This indeed was the gist of Jordanian policy. However, this policy suffered from some immediately apparent flaws. Negotiating unilaterally was one sure way out of the impasse. Once this option was ruled out, a new Jordanian strategy toward the Palestinians became imperative in order to "avoid stagnation" and to create the required conditions for a future Jordanian-Palestinian partnership, on Jordan's terms. The all-out offensive against the PLO was the cornerstone of this strategy, but this tended to alienate many of the Palestinians in the occupied territories and to deepen the chasm between them and Jordan, instead of driving a wedge between them and the PLO. The short-term consequences of Jordan's policy seemed to be undermining its long-term objectives. All the same, the Jordanians kept up their offensive with considerable determination, presumably on the assumption that the initial setbacks could be overcome in the longer term by sheer perseverance.

In the meantime, the rupture with the PLO leadership returned Jordan-PLO relations to their normal state — that of overt rivalry and confrontation. Even the brief period of coordination had been governed by deep mistrust, as each of these two historical rivals sought to neutralize and subordinate the other. The deep hostility between Jordan and the PLO, which had been temporarily submerged, now resurfaced in full force. Immediately after Husayn's speech on 19 February, Jordanian officials asserted that, though the door to renewed dialogue remained theoretically ajar, in practice the King wanted nothing more to do with 'Arafat,[151] if only for the time being.

THE WEAKENING OF THE PLO PRESENCE IN JORDAN

During the period of coordination between Jordan and the PLO, particularly since the 17th session of the Palestine National Council, held in Amman in November 1984, Husayn had permitted the organization to bolster its political presence in Jordan (see *MECS* 1984–85, p 206). This concession, however, was granted in expectation of the PLO agreeing to enter into a political partnership with Jordan on Husayn's terms.

Once the Jordanians had finally ascertained that this objective was not going to be realized, and had consequently suspended their coordination with the PLO, the expanded PLO presence in the Kingdom became an intolerable incongruity. The PLO's presence in Jordan was an important asset to the organization for maintaining access to the two largest Palestinian communities, those on the East and West Banks of the Jordan. Having decided on an all-out offensive against the PLO, Husayn had every reason to withdraw the concession, which, as it now transpired, had been made gratuitously.

Immediately after Husayn's announcement of the suspension of a coordination with the PLO leadership, Zayd al-Rifa'i informed the PLO's representative in Amman, 'Abd al-Razzaq al-Yahya, that the PLO offices in Jordan would be allowed to continue to function.[152] Husayn, it seems, was biding his time, waiting for a reasonable pretext to take sterner action. In the first few months after Husayn's February speech, a number of PLO offices were closed down in Amman, under pressure from the authorities, and the Palestinian News Agency, WAFA, also ceased issuing its daily bulletin in Amman.[153] In early April, 'Atallah 'Atallah (Abu al-Za'im), a disenchanted former head of Fath's military intelligence, launched a "corrective movement" in Amman against Yasir 'Arafat's leadership (see chapter on the PLO). Abu al-Za'im and the Jordanians both denied that there was Jordanian support for this. But the very fact that the movement was launched and allowed to operate in Jordan indicated at least the implicit approval of the authorities.[154] Some 'Arafat loyalists were also said to have been deported by the Jordanians following the emergence of Abu al-Za'im's "movement."[155]

On 19 June, the Fath Revolutionary Council issued a statement denouncing Jordan for its anti-PLO policy, and suggesting collusion with the US and Israel. On 7 July, the Jordanian Cabinet issued a statement announcing its decision to close down the offices opened by Fath in Jordan in the past two years. These offices, the statement said, could not continue to operate in accordance with policies made by a party that had "chosen to pursue this negative approach towards Jordan." Though this was quite obviously a strike against the PLO, the Jordanians persisted in their fictitious distinction between the PLO leadership and the PLO as an institution. The Fath offices that were closed down were therefore described as not officially affiliated with the PLO and its institutions, and the Cabinet also went to the trouble of declaring that these measures did not mean that Jordan would cease dealing with the PLO as the sole legitimate representative of the Palestinians.[156]

The Minister of Information said that the step was taken in the interests of Jordan's national security.[157] Though nothing in this regard had been mentioned in the cabinet statement, Husayn later accused the PLO of having meddled in Jordan's domestic affairs. Zayd al-Rifa'i even accused 'Arafat personally of having done so.[158] Husayn said that there was conclusive evidence that the PLO had intervened in the Irbid by-election by giving financial support to the Fundamentalist candidate who had lost there. The PLO had also been involved in the Yarmuk University incidents (see above) in what Husayn called a "rather strange, unholy alliance" between a faction of the PLO and Islamic radicals.[159]

The decision to close the Fath offices that had been opened since 1984 affected those of 'Arafat and his deputy Khalil al-Wazir, as well as the offices of Force 17 and the "Western Sector," which supervised operations against Israel. On 8 July, Khalil al-Wazir, who had been living in Amman, was ordered out of the country. Twelve offices not associated with Fath but with the PLO as a whole were allowed to remain open. Though some PLO officials still remained in Amman, and at times met with Husayn or Rifaʿi, the Jordanian-PLO relationship was, in reality, devoid of any meaningful content.

JORDAN'S WEST BANK OFFENSIVE

Jordan's break with the PLO ushered in a new phase in Jordan's Palestinian policy, governed by a fundamental change of strategy and a totally different time frame. Husayn's coordination with the PLO had been intended to achieve a rapid breakthrough in the peace process. The status quo was seen by the Jordanians as a source of ominous development that could have disastrous consequences for the Kingdom. Time was of the essence and a settlement had to be achieved soon if disaster was to be averted.

Following the collapse of the coordination attempt, chances of a breakthrough in the peace process seemed extremely remote. Jordan's appraisal of the dangers inherent in the status quo did not change, but the strategy for contending with them underwent a profound transformation. Instead of striving for a quick settlement Jordan now embarked on a long-term policy that was designed to create the conditions for a settlement by an incremental process. This was to be achieved by a combination of political and economic measures that would undermine the PLO; enhance the political prominence and influence of the Palestinians under occupation; increase their dependence on Jordan; and, simultaneously, counter the potentially dangerous consequences of the status quo.

Since the early 1980s the Jordanians had consistently expressed their fear that the growing strength of the right wing in Israeli politics would lead to prolonged occupation of the West Bank and Gaza, increased Jewish settlement, and the possible annexation of these territories by Israel. This, the Jordanians feared, might in turn lead to the massive emigration or even the eviction of hundreds of thousands of Palestinians to Jordan which would have catastrophic socioeconomic and political consequences for that country (see *MECS* 1981–82, p 679; 1982–83, pp 631–32; 1983–84, p 517).

As Husayn emphasized in his speech of 19 February, Jordan fully recognized "the danger inherent in the situation of no war and no peace, firstly to the Palestinian people and Jerusalem, secondly to Jordanian national security and to the Arab nation thereafter."[160] It could not be faced with empty slogans and idle talk. Time was not on the Arabs' side. Israel was rapidly approaching a serious dilemma if it did not give up the occupied territories. It would lose its Jewish character if it granted citizenship to the Arabs of the West Bank and Gaza; if it did not, it would lose its democratic character and be forced to adopt the apartheid model of South Africa. Israel might therefore seek to solve this dilemma by evicting the inhabitants to Jordan. This last option, Husayn said, was gaining support in Israel, "coloring the current Israeli political vision with an extremist right-wing hue."[161] The Jordanians, according to one of Husayn's key advisers, were "very worried about these demographics."[162] These factors also motivated Jordan to give priority to the question of withdrawal over all other issues; and it was on this order of priorities that it clashed with the PLO. Husayn explained that he wanted to get results "before it was too late." But, in an implicit reference to the PLO, he complained that the Arabs "talk much and do little" wasting time on "impossible issues," while the Arab territory was "disappearing in a fast, frightening way."[163] Husayn thus sought to emphasize the community of interests between Jordan and the West Bankers, which the PLO, he intimated, did not share. He also wished to draw their attention to the inseparable bonds between the Jordanian and Palestinian peoples which, Husayn said, were not only a matter of "history, experience, culture, economy and society but also [of] destiny." The destinies of Jordan and the Palestinians were very closely linked, for better or for worse,[164] and Husayn sought to make the most of the West Bankers' dependence on Jordan and their shared interest in a rapid Israeli withdrawal. He sought to encourage the emergence of a significant body of opinion that would express itself in support of his thesis and pressure the PLO to do likewise.

The initial response on the West Bank to Husayn's anti-PLO policy was a sore disappointment for the Jordanians. Various West Bank delegations went to Amman to express their support for Husayn, but these were invariably composed of political nonentities. Some of them had not come from the West Bank at all, but were Palestinians from the East Bank, urged or ordered by the authorities to make an appearance at the Royal Palace.[165] The general response on the West Bank was one of anti-Jordanian sentiment, coupled with a reaffirmation of allegiance to the PLO (cf chapter on the West Bank and the Gaza Strip). The fact that both Houses of Parliament, which included representatives from the West Bank, expressed their support for Husayn and for the constitutional unity between Jordan and the West Bank[166] was not really of great consequence as it did not truly reflect the climate of opinion where it really counted, i.e., on the West Bank itself. Politicians of stature did not come out publicly in favor of Husayn's policies. There were, however, a few notable exceptions. The former Mayor of Gaza and that area's leading personality, Rashshad al-Shawa, appeared on Jordanian Television during a visit to Amman just after the closure of the Fath offices in Jordan. Shawa endorsed Husayn's policies and accepted the King's priority for liberation. He criticized the PLO for not having accepted Resolution 242 and for having imposed its will on the population in the occupied territories instead of representing their immediate interests.[167] Shawa was not followed by others of similar stature. But the Mayor of Bethlehem, Elias Freij, was quoted in the Jordanian Press as having said that even though the PLO remained the sole legitimate representative of the Palestinians, that did "not mean that West Bankers and Gazans have to freeze their minds and not criticize the organization."[168] Statements such as these served the Jordanian argument that the PLO had to take into consideration the desires of the people under occupation instead of just "issuing them with orders" that the PLO leadership may decide upon, for reasons quite unrelated to the "Palestinian arena and its priorities." The PLO, Rifa'i explained, had been created by an Arab decision. They were not elected by the population, and should therefore pay more heed to "the people's desires."[169] Though Jordanian sources at times reported pro-Jordanian leaflets being distributed by the self-proclaimed "silent majority" on the West Bank and Gaza Strip,[170] the PLO's firm grip on the population had not been seriously weakened. In early September, the pro-Fath, East Jerusalem daily *al-Fajr* published the results of a poll it had conducted in conjunction with the New York paper *Newsday* and an Australian television network. The poll showed overwhelming support on the West Bank and Gaza Strip for the

PLO, its leadership and its policies and only a marginal 3 per cent support for Husayn.[171] The Jordanians claimed that the poll was neither neutral nor academic and was indeed planned to be unobjective.[172] Considering that *al-Fajr* was behind the poll, it may have been biased or improperly conducted; nonetheless, it did seem to give a more or less accurate indication of the climate of opinion in the occupied territories.

But Husayn was not deterred by this poor showing. It is reasonable to assume that, while disappointed by the initial West Bank reaction, the Jordanians were familiar enough with the West Bank and PLO popularity there not to have anticipated an immediate transformation of the local political scene. Husayn's objectives were now governed by long-term calculations and the belief that the PLO's position could be weakened in the long run if dependence on Jordan could be enhanced and if the people became more desperate about their future. Jordan's hopes rested on the assumption that it was not impossible to envisage a situation in which the Palestinians of the occupied territories could be induced to cooperate with Jordan, not because of pro-Hashemite sympathies, but through the eventual realization that, for political and economic reasons, they had no better choice. Jordan's constituency, according to Husayn, was the "silent majority" that had yet to speak up.[173] The poll conducted by *al-Fajr* included a disproportionately high percentage of students and young, well-educated urban professionals, who constituted the hard core of the PLO supporters. Jordan's "natural constituency," according to one of Husayn's key advisers, was the bourgeoisie, "the realists, the more mature, especially in the countryside, among the merchants and farmers."[174]

The Jordanians, however, had a long way to go. Jordanian influence had declined considerably on the West Bank in the last decade and Jordanian involvement had been relatively low-key. In the last few years, as Jordan sought to draw the PLO into its orbit, it would have been bad tactics to actively antagonize the PLO on the West Bank and thus undermine the process of coordination. These considerations were no longer relevant as the Jordanians embarked on their intensive campaign not only to discredit the PLO, but also to force the population into the realization that they were politically and economically dependent on Jordan. A combination of "carrot and stick" measures were adopted to drive home the message that Jordan could no longer be taken for granted.[175]

The open bridges across the Jordan gave the Jordanians a considerable measure of control over the daily lives of the West Bankers and the residents of the Gaza Strip in such spheres as travel, the maintenance of family ties, and trade. The bridges, according to Husayn, were the "veins that pump life and Arabism" into the occupied territories,[176] and it was through these "veins" that Jordan sought to exercise influence and demonstrate its authority. The Jordanians did not hesitate to take punitive measures against its opponents in the occupied territories, while simultaneously rewarding its supporters. Some PLO sympathizers were blacklisted and consequently harassed and interrogated at the bridges when traveling to Jordan. Some were not allowed to cross over into Jordan, and others had their passports confiscated, or encountered difficulties having their passports renewed.[177] In June, *al-Fajr* reported that the Jordanian Ministry of Information had instructed the Jordanian media not to carry any reports that originated in the pro-PLO Press on the West Bank. It also compiled a list of 34 journalists whose entry into Jordan had been forbidden and who could even be arrested on trying to enter the country.[178] The Minister of Information,

Muhammad al-Khatib, categorically denied this report.[179] Whether true or not, the report indicated that there now was a general awareness of the rules of the game.[180]

The Jordanians made it quite clear that the future of the Gaza Strip, "the Gaza of Hashim" (see *MECS* 1982–83, p 636), was to be tied to that of the West Bank.[181] Whatever aspirations they had for the West Bank therefore applied equally to the Gaza Strip. In June, the Jordanians decided to forgo all customs duty on goods imported from the Gaza Strip.[182] Shortly after his favorable appearance on Jordanian Television, Rashshad al-Shawa and his family were given Jordanian citizenship,[183] and a member of the Shawa family, Hisham al-Shawa, was appointed as an adviser to the Ministry of Occupied Territory Affairs.[184] Gazans residing in Jordan were also allowed to own property,[185] and some 70,000 of them were also to be allowed to obtain Jordanian passports.[186]

Numerous measures were taken to cultivate support on the West Bank. It was decided to improve retirement benefits for civil servants (who received salaries from the Jordanian and Israeli authorities);[187] to channel more funds into a variety of philanthropic societies and into pro-Jordanian agricultural associations;[188] and to pay regular salaries to some 10,000 teachers on the West Bank whose term of employment began after 1967.[189] Payments to lawyers who had been on strike since the beginning of the occupation in 1967 were also to be resumed.[190] Since the establishment of the Jordanian-PLO Joint Committee to Support the Steadfastness of the Occupied Territories in 1979 (see *MECS* 1978–79, p 296), these strike funds had been channeled through the Joint Committee. The Committee had become inoperative, both because of a lack of funds and the state of Jordanian-PLO relations. Jordan now acted independently on this as on other matters.

Addressing the Arab Economic and Social Council in Amman in September, Crown Prince Hasan appealed to the Arab states to increase their imports from the occupied territories,[191] and it was subsequently reported that Jordan had relaxed some of its own import restrictions. For the first time since 1967 the Jordanians had allowed West Bank and Gaza industries exporting to Jordan to bring in raw materials through Israeli ports.[192]

Jordan also began to compete directly with the PLO's organizational infrastructure in the unions, the universities and the local Press. It was reportedly encouraging the formation of new chambers of industry, and building its own cadres of political activists in the trade unions and professional associations. The lawyers' and doctors' associations were said to be "heavily influenced" by pro-Jordanians. Pro-PLO administrators were dismissed, under Jordanian pressure, from the Najah University in Nablus, the largest on the West Bank.[193] Moreover, the Jordanians were even said to have let the Israeli authorities know that Jordan would like to see them crack down on PLO supporters.[194]

In mid-1986, a new pro-Jordanian weekly, *al-Nahar*, began to appear on the West Bank, financed by Jordan.[195] In August, Jordanian Television and Radio began broadcasting new weekly programs dealing specifically with the affairs of the occupied territories. The programs were full of praise for the steadfastness, heroism and patriotism of the people in the occupied territories and emphasized the Jordanian role in providing assistance to the West Bank and Gaza.[196] In the first of these programs, the Minister for Occupied Territory Affairs Marwan Dudin (himself a Palestinian from the West Bank), criticized the pro-PLO Press on the West Bank because of its anti-Jordanian stand. He made the quite remarkable contention that the fact that Israel had not shut these papers down proved that they served Israel's interests.[197] The Jordanians also laid special stress on their concern for the Islamic Holy Places in Jerusalem. They gave special prominence to their allocation of funds for the maintenance and repair of the Holy Places and to the efforts of the Ministry of *Awqaf* and Religious Affairs to continue paying the salaries of the religious officials on the West Bank, as they had done since 1967.[198]

However, the centerpiece of Jordan's West Bank offensive was a very ambitious and much publicized Five-Year (1986–90) Plan for the development of the West Bank and Gaza. The plan, the first of its kind since 1967, was already in the initial preparatory phase in late 1985 (see *MECS* 1984–85, p 518), i.e., before the final breakdown of Jordan's coordination with the PLO. After the rupture with the PLO, however, the plan was destined to become a major instrument to erode the PLO's position on the West Bank and Gaza Strip. Its implications were just as political as they were economic. On the one hand, the Jordanians explained that the plan, which envisaged the investment of JD362.5m in the five-year period was intended to stem emigration from the occupied territories and to keep the people on their land, by improving the standard of living, reducing Arab dependence on the Israeli economy and creating more job opportunities. Jordan had consistently provided aid to the West Bank since 1967, but the present plan marked a new approach. It was the first comprehensive effort towards economic development instead of charitable and stop-gap measures.[199] As Crown Prince Hasan put it, Jordan now had to plan "to contain the demographic implications of the occupation." If the Jordanians did not plan for themselves, then they would "be planned for."[200] These statements reflected genuine Jordanian concerns. But their insistence that the plan had no other political objectives and that Jordan was not competing with the PLO,[201] could not be taken at face value. The plan's purpose was twofold: to contend with the status quo, and to pave the way for eventual Jordanian-Palestinian political cooperation, in seeking a settlement and Israeli withdrawal.

The PLO had not been consulted about the plan; its implementation was not to involve the Jordanian-PLO Joint Committee for Steadfastness; and Rifa'i was quite candid about Jordan's having no intention of "sharing activities" that were "within the competence of the Jordanian Government."[202] The plan, according to the Minister of Occupied Territory Affairs, was to bring about the eventual economic integration of the West and East Banks. Everyone had to "be made to remember that this is one country, the Hashemite Kingdom of Jordan." The plan was clearly designed to enhance Jordanian influence in the occupied territories and "to make the people on the receiving end accountable to [Jordan]."[203] The plan was to establish a network of dependence and patronage in which Jordan would be the conduit for large sums of money pumped into the West Bank and Gaza.

The plan placed particular emphasis on housing, education and agriculture, thus following Jordan's pre-1967 practice of preferring the East Bank for major industrial projects. The overall outlay of JD362.5m was distributed as follows: housing and construction — JD 155 m; education — JD 78.7m; agriculture — JD 61.7m; health services — JD 34.4m; industry — JD22.5m; social services — JD 10.2m.[204] The plan favored supporting the rural population and agriculture rather than promoting industrialization and urbanization, thereby bolstering that sector of the population that was potentially more supportive of Jordan. About one third of the total aid was to be disbursed as personal grants or loans for new home mortages and supplements to teachers' salaries, thereby tying a large number of individuals to the Jordanian Government by their purse strings.[205]

The major problem was that despite the plan's impressiveness on paper, the Jordanians by their own admission had no available resources to finance it.[206] Considering the plan's controversial political objectives and the fact that it had been condemned by the PLO, the Jordanians had difficulty obtaining funds in the Arab world. This was true even in respect to the Saudis, who were the only really consistent providers of financial support to Jordan. These not very bright prospects had induced the Jordanians to scale down the planned investment from the original amount of JD461.5m (*c* $1.27 bn) to JD 362.5m (*c* $1 bn), and Zayd al-Rifa'i said that in fact the Jordanians were aiming for $750m.[207]

The US committed itself to channel only $4.5m through Jordan for the plan in 1986.[208] The international conference the Jordanians held in November, to launch the Five-Year Plan for both the East and West Banks (see above), did not yield any firm commitments other than one from the US for 16m in 1987.[209] The Jordanians therefore decided to allocate JD10m a year from their own budget as of 1987 for the plan, in addition to JD4.8m they had earmarked in November 1986 for "urgent projects" that were not part of the plan itself.[210] This left the Jordanians with some $45m for the plan in fiscal 1987, which was not insignificant but a lot less than planned.

Channeling funds into the West Bank required an institutional set-up in the area through which the plan could be implemented. This, the Jordanians pointed out, required that Arab mayors be restored in those towns run by Israeli officers[211] and that Jordanian banks, which had not been in operation since 1967, be reopened.[212] This would enable the Jordanians to avoid the most blatant forms of collaboration with the Israelis in executing the plan while allowing the elevation of pro-Jordanian personalities to positions of influence. In late September and late October four pro-Jordanian Arab Mayors were appointed by the Israelis, in cooperation with Jordan, to the towns of Hebron, Ramallah, al-Bira and 'Anabta. Coming not very long after the assassination by the PFLP of the Mayor of Nablus, Zafir al-Masri (see chapter on the West Bank and the Gaza Strip), this was a minor coup for the Jordanians, particularly since the appointments were expressly opposed by the PLO. Israel and Jordan also came to a written agreement, the details of which were made public in Israel in October,[213] on the reopening of branches of the Cairo-Amman Bank on the West Bank.

Thus, despite PLO opposition, the Jordanian Plan was getting off the ground, in what began to look like a tacit Jordanian-Israeli power-sharing agreement and a joint effort to undermine PLO influence in the occupied territories. Jordan now faced the accusation from PLO sources that it was normalizing relations with Israel to pave the way for a separate peace. However, as Husayn was quick to explain, Jordan's West Bank policy was an interim measure to deal with the effects of the status quo, and it did not constitute, and could not be a substitute for, a "just and comprehensive solution."[214]

Jordan's West Bank policy, seen in conjunction with the new Election Law (see above) and stepped-up efforts to improve conditions in refugee camps on the East

Bank, were all components of a grand strategy, i.e, to incorporate the Palestinians — refugees and non-refugees alike, on the East Bank, the West Bank and the Gaza Strip — into one, Jordanian-dominated political entity.

JORDAN AND THE ARAB WORLD

The disarray in the Arab world had long been a cause for complaint by the Jordanians. Though Jordan's Arab relations remained on an even keel in 1986, the Jordanians had nothing to show for their efforts to forge a consensus favorable to themselves on key issues such as the war in the Gulf or the Palestinian question. Jordan's consistent calls for an Arab summit[215] went unheeded. The Arab reaction to the rupture between Jordan and the PLO bordered on indifference. This was equally disheartening for Jordan and the PLO. Jordan did not face a barrage of condemnation, but neither did it gain any support for its offensive against the PLO.

Jordan had the good fortune of maintaining favorable relations with Syria, Iraq, Egypt and Saudi Arabia at one and the same time. This was no mean feat for the Hashemite regime, or for any Arab regime for that matter. But Husayn also had reason to be disappointed with all four. Syria, of course, had no qualms about Jordan's rupture with 'Arafat, but it still remained suspicious of Husayn's peace policy. Jordan's relations with Syria had improved considerably since late 1985 (see *MECS* 1984–85, pp 519–20). During the year, frequent high-level meetings were held, including an official visit in May by President Hafiz al-Asad to Jordan, his first such visit in nine years.

Husayn's efforts in midyear to effect a reconciliation between Syria and Iraq made no progress. The Jordanians, fearful of the possible political consequences of an Iranian victory in the Gulf war, already suffering from some of its economic ramifications, and seeking to establish a broad Arab front to support them either in peace or war with Israel, were really interested in bringing about a thaw in Iraqi-Syrian relations. The divide between these two was still unbridgeable and Husayn was unable to penetrate "the wall of ideological differences."[216] Syria and Jordan still remained on opposing sides of the fence in respect to the Gulf war, with Syria supporting Iran and Jordan supporting Iraq.

Relations with Egypt were characterized by intensive political coordination at the highest level, and Husayn and Mubarak exchanged visits frequently during the year. But even Egypt did not openly side with Jordan in its clash with the PLO. The Egyptians, as part of their Arab relegitimization policy, remained publicly committed to the PLO, often more emphatically so than other Arab states. Egyptian efforts to reconcile Jordan and the PLO made no headway in Amman. The Jordanians wanted Mubarak to take their side, not to mediate.

Equally disappointing were the Saudis. They too, as always, would not take sides. Their apparent unwillingness to finance Jordan's controversial West Bank Development Plan was a setback for the Jordanians, but very much in keeping with the Saudi practice of shying away from any inter-Arab controversy.

JORDAN AND THE GREAT POWERS

JORDAN AND THE UNITED STATES

Jordan's relations with the US, though relations between allies, were, as in the past, not devoid of serious difficulties. However, when it came to the American role in the Middle East peace process, the Jordanians, in contrast to their reactions in the not too distant past, mainly praised the US position. In his speech of 19 February, Husayn noted the positive changes that had taken place in the US attitude towards an international conference and laid the blame for the impasse on the PLO and not on the Americans (see above). This differed markedly from Jordan's reaction after the failure of the first round of negotiations on political coordination with the PLO, in 1983. At that time, Husayn had been unusually outspoken in his condemnation of US policy in the Middle East (see *MECS* 1983–84, pp 527–28). Though the Jordanian Press consistently criticized the US Administration and its alliance with Israel,[217] Husayn himself refrained from doing so.

In June, Husayn paid an unofficial visit to the US, during which he had talks with President Ronald Reagan and Secretary of State George Shultz. As expected, these did not produce any new ideas about the Middle East peace process, but Husayn made an effort to impress upon his hosts the necessity for the US to play a more active role in Middle East diplomacy in order to keep the peace process alive.[218]

While Jordan's relations with the US Administration remained generally favorable, those with the US Congress did not. Congressional disapproval of a $1.9 bn arms deal with Jordan, because of Husayn's reluctance to enter into direct negotiations with Israel, finally scuttled the deal. After the difficulties in Husayn's cooperation with the PLO had become apparent, Reagan wrote to the King on 31 January, explaining his inability to proceed in his efforts with Congress for the conclusion of the arms deal.[219] The Administration preferred to postpone the deal indefinitely rather than see it voted down by Congress. Under earlier arrangements on Capitol Hill, the deal would have gone through on 1 March unless Congress voted to block it. By late January, however, it was clear that congressional opposition was overwhelming.[220] Husayn expressed his deep disappointment with this turn of events, noting that they were bringing to an end a period of 30 years of close association, during which the US had been Jordan's main arms supplier. Jordan, he said, would now have to look to other countries, including the Soviet Union, for arms.[221] Zayd al- Rifa'i and the local Press condemned Congress for submitting to "Israeli-Zionist influence," by setting impossible and humiliating conditions for the deal.[222] However, both Rifa'i and Husayn were anxious to point out that Jordan's disappointment on this matter did not imply that the Kingdom was about to change its great-power orientation. Rifa'i explained that distinction had to be made between the US Congress and the US Administration. Relations with the Administration were good, but Jordan's dealings with Congress were subject to "various pressures."[223]

This neat distinction between the Administration and Congress was, however, brought into question by the revelations at the end of the year about the US-Israeli-Iranian arms deal. Husayn described the US action as a "shock and a great disappointment." It was, he said, an insult to all Arabs. He was "perplexed because he could not understand the US thinking on what had happened and because what did happen would not bring [the Gulf] war to an end."[224] The Jordanians were clearly dismayed by the US action. All the same, considering the regional interests still shared by the two countries and Jordan's need for continued US political and economic support, it was hardly likely that the Iran affair would have a lasting effect on Jordanian-US relations.

RELATIONS WITH THE SOVIET UNION

Jordan and the Soviet Union were not allies but their relations were cordial and friendly and were based on agreement on some crucial issues. Jordan welcomed Soviet support for an international Middle East peace conference to be attended by all five permanent members of the Security Council.[225] The Soviets for their part recognized Jordanian centrality in the peace process and held regular consultations with Jordan on this and other regional issues. Vladimir Polyakov, head of the Middle East Department of the Soviet Foreign Ministry, Yuli Vorontsov, Soviet First Deputy Foreign Minister, and Mikhail Sytenko, Ambassador at large at the Soviet Foreign Ministry and Mikhail Gorbachev's envoy, all visited Jordan during the year for talks with the country's leaders.

Jordan continued to purchase arms from the Soviet Union (cf *MECS* 1981-82, p 693 and 1984–85, p 522) to bolster its air defenses. It was reported that Jordan had begun to receive unspecified additional quantities of SAM-8 anti-aircraft missiles.[226] Husayn said that an agreement had been reached with the USSR for additional weapons to complement systems previously acquired from the Soviet Union.[227] According to an Israeli source, there were Soviet advisers in Jordan — mainly anti-aircraft experts.[228] Husayn, however, hoped that it was clear to the Soviets that any Jordanian request for weapons was merely that, and that "no realignment of Jordan's position will result" from a Soviet agreement to sell weapons to Jordan.[229]

JORDAN AND WESTERN EUROPE

Jordan's concept of an international conference accorded an important role to Britain and France in the Middle East peace process. In June, Husayn visited Paris and London for talks with President François Mitterrand and Prime Minister Margaret Thatcher. The Jordanians had drawn particular satisfaction from a statement by Mrs Thatcher, during a visit to Israel in May, to the effect that the PLO could not play a role in the peace process unless it recognized Resolution 242 and renounced terrorism.[230]

Jordan also entered into negotiations with the Europeans for the purchase of 25–40 fighter aircraft instead of those it had failed to obtain from the US. During the year there were frequent reports that Jordan was negotiating with the British to purchase *Tornado* fighter planes and with the French for the *Mirage* 2000. Although there was a report that Jordan had opted for the French plane, this was still not certain by the end of the year; it was also not clear whether Jordan could obtain the necessary financing to conclude such a deal. The Saudis, who were expected to foot the bill, were said to prefer the *Tornado*, which they themselves had ordered, because of their interest in standardizing Jordanian and Gulf weaponry.[231]

TABLE 1: JORDANIAN CABINET CHANGES — 1986*

Portfolio	*Cabinet as of 27 April*	*Cabinet as of 4 October*
Prime Minister and Defense	Zayd al-Rifa'i	Zayd al-Rifa'i
Deputy Prime Minister	'Abd al-Wahhab al-Majali[2]	'Abd al-Wahhab al-Majali[2]
Education	'Abd al-Wahhab al-Majali[2]	Dhuqan al-Hindawi
Minister of State for Premiership Affairs	Dhuqan al-Hindawi[1]	'Abd al-Wahhab al-Majali[2]
Minister of State for Parliamentary Affairs	Sami Jawda (P)	Sami Jawda (P)

Portfolio	*Cabinet as of 27 April*	*Cabinet as of 4 October*
Interior	Hasan al-Kayid	Raja'i al-Dajani (P)
Labor and Social Development	Khalid al-Hajj Hasan	Khalid al-Hajj Hasan
Communications	Muhyi al-Din al-Husayni (P)	Muhyi al-Din al-Husayni (P)
Foreign Affairs	Tahir al-Masri (P)	Tahir al-Masri (P)
Municipal, Rural and Environmental Affairs	Marwan al-Humud	Yusuf Hamdan
Awqaf, Religious Affairs and Holy Places	'Abd al-'Aziz al-Khayyat (P)	'Abd al-'Aziz al-Khayyat (P)
Public Works	Mahmud al-Hawamida	Mahmud al-Hawamida
Supplies, Industry and Trade	Raja'i al-Mu'ashshir	Raja'i al-Mu'ashshir
Transport	Raja'i al-Dajani (P)[1]	Ahmad Dakhqan
Finance	Hanna 'Awda (P)	Hanna 'Awda (P)
Energy and Mineral Wealth	Hisham al-Khatib (P)	Hisham al-Khatib (P)
Planning	Tahir Kan'an (P)	Tahir Kan'an (P)
Higher Education	Nasir al-Din al-Asad	Nasir al-Din al-Asad
Agriculture	Ahmad Dakhqan	Marwan al-Humud
Information, Culture, Tourism and Antiquities	Muhammad al-Khatib	Muhammad al-Khatib
Justice	Riyad al-Shak'a (P)	Riyad al-Shak'a (P)
Health	Zayd Hamza	Zayd Hamza
Occupied Territory Affairs	Marwan Dudin (P)[1]	Marwan Dudin (P)
Youth	'Id Duhayyat[1]	'Id Duhayyat

1 Not in previous Cabinet.
2 Majali held two portfolios.
(P) Palestinian origin.
* For Cabinet formed in April 1985, see *MECS* 1984-5, p 523.

NOTES

For the place and frequency of publications cited here, and for the full name of the publication, news agency, radio station or monitoring service where an abbreviation is used, please see "List of Sources." Only in the case of more than one publication bearing the same name is the place of publication noted here.

1. R. Amman, 27 March — DR, 28 March 1986.
2. Uriel Dann, "Regime and Opposition in Jordan Since 1949," in M. Milson (ed), *Society and Political Structure in the Arab World* (New York: Humanities Press, 1973), p 147.
3. For the text of the law, see *JT*, 29 March 1986.
4. *JT*, 29 March 1986.
5. *Al-Hadaf*, Damascus, 17 February; *al-Hurriyya*, 6 April 1986.
6. R. Beirut, 27 April 1986.
7. *JT*, 31 May, 21 June; *al-Ra'y*, 20 June 1986.
8. *NYT*, 9 July 1986.
9. *JT*, 3 July 1986.
10. *Al-Ahrar*, Cairo, 8 December 1986.
11. *Al-Ra'y*, 1 June; Jordan TV, 17 June — DR, 18 June 1986.
12. *AP* quoted in *JP*, 2 July 1986.
13. *JT*, 13, 19 August 1986.
14. *Al-Dustur*, Amman, 10 February 1986.
15. *JT*, 2 November 1986.
16. Ibid.
17. *Al-Ra'y*, 13 November 1986.
18. *Al-Ra'y*, 7 December; *JT*, 24 December 1986.
19. *JT*, 24 December; R. Amman, 31 December — DR, 31 December 1986.
20. *Al-Ra'y*, 24 December 1986.
21. *JT*, 24 December 1986.
22. *Al-Hurriyya*, 14 December 1986.

23. *The Guardian*, 10 October; *al-Hurriyya*, 26 October 1986.
24. R. Monte Carlo, 23, 24 September — DR, 24, 25 September 1986.
25. AP quoted in *JP*, 6 October 1986.
26. Jordan TV, 1 November — DR, 3 November 1986.
27. *NYT*, 2 November 1986.
28. *The Guardian*, 10 October 1986.
29. E.g., *al-Dustur*, Amman, 28 March; *al-Ra'y*, 29 March 1986.
30. R. Amman, 15 May — DR, 15 May 1986.
31. Ibid; *al-Fajr*, East Jerusalem, 16 May; *NYT*, 21 May; *al-Dustur*, London, 26 May; *ME*, July 1986.
32. R. Amman, 15 May — DR, 15 May; *NYT*, 21 May; *The Guardian*, 21 May; *ME*, July 1986.
33. *JP*, 16, 18 May; *Filastin al-Thawra*, 7 June 1986.
34. R. Monte Carlo, 19 May, 6 September — DR, 19 May, 8 September 1986.
35. *ME*, July; *al-Shira'*, Beirut, 11 August 1986.
36. Ibid.
37. *The Guardian*, 21 May 1986.
38. *NYT*, *The Guardian*, 21 May; *FT*, 12 June; *ME*, July 1986.
39. *Al-Watan*, 3 July 1986.
40. *Sawt al-Sha'b*, 8 July; KUNA, 14 July 1986.
41. Husayn's letter to Rifa'i read on Jordan TV, 5 July — DR, 7 July 1986.
42. Rifa'i's reply to the King read on Jordan TV, 7 July — DR, 8 July 1986.
43. Jordan TV, 1 November — DR, 3 November 1986.
44. *JT*, 26 July, 6 August 1986.
45. *JT*, 28 July, 6 August 1986.
46. *JT*, 14 October 1986.
47. *Al-Sha'b*, East Jerusalem, 13 September; *al-Fajr*, East Jerusalem, 31 October 1986.
48. *Al-Fajr*, East Jerusalem, 11 December 1986.
49. Rifa'i to *al-Majalla*, 23 July 1986.
50. *Al-Hawadith*, 22 August 1986.
51. Rifa'i to *al-Hawadith*, 22 August and to *al-Tadamun* as reported in *JT*, 1 November 1986.
52. Ibid.
53. Jordan TV, 1 November — DR, 3 November 1986.
54. *Al-Dustur*, Amman, 17 April 1986.
55. R. Damascus, 16 April — DR, 17 April 1986.
56. *JT*, 16 April; R. Monte Carlo, 16 April —DR, 16 April 1986.
57. *NYT*, 9 July 1986.
58. *JT*, 24-25 April 1986.
59. *Al-Hadaf*, Damascus, 13 January; *al-Urdunn al-Dimuqrati*, February; *al-Hurriyya*, 15 March, 14 December 1986.
60. R. Damascus, 5 November — DR, 6 November 1986.
61. *Al-Hurriyya*, 14 December 1986.
62. *CSM*, 31 October 1986.
63. *Al-Dustur*, Amman, 28 April 1986.
64. *CSM*, 31 October 1986.
65. Mahmud al-Kayid, head of the Journalists' Union, in an interview with *al-Majalla*, 23-29 April 1986.
66. *Al-Bayan*, 18 May 1986.
67. *Al-Hurriyya*, 1 June 1986.
68. *Al-Bayan*, 18 May; *FT*, 12 June; *NYT*, 9 July; *al-Ittihad*, Abu Dhabi, 30 July 1986.
69. *Al-Watan*, *al-Ittihad*, Abu Dhabi, 30 July 1986.
70. *IHT*, 17 July; *Baltimore Sun*, 20 July 1986.
71. Jordan TV, 1 November — DR, 3 November 1986.
72. *Al-Hawadith*, 22 August 1986.
73. *Khaleej Times*, 28 January; *al-Dustur*, Amman, 24–25 March; *al-Liwa*, 2 Aprii 1986.
74. *JT*, 7 December 1986.
75. *Al-Dustur*, Amman, 24–25 March; *FT*, 12 June 1986.
76. *Al-Dustur*, Amman, 24–25 March; *JT*, 18 May; *al-Liwa*, 2 July; *FT*, 12 June; *al-Khalij*, 22 November 1986.

77. *JT*, 2 September, 1 November 1986.
78. *Al-Khalij*, 22 November 1986.
79. *Al-Ra'y*, 29 July 1986.
80. Ibid.
81. *JT*, 18 May; *FT*, 12 June 1986.
82. The figure for 1984 was exceptionally high considering the fact that the number of workers had remained more or less constant. It may have reflected "balloon payments" of returning workers.
83. *FT*, 12 June; *al-Ra'y*, 29 July 1986.
84. Minister of Higher Education Nasir al-Din al-Asad in *JT*, 28 July 1986.
85. Rifa'i to *al-Tadamun*, quoted in *JT*, 1 November 1986.
86. *JT*, 9 August, 13 September 1986.
87. *JT*, 8 March, 1 June 1986.
88. *JT*, 10 November 1986.
89. *FT*, 12 June; *al-Ra'y*, 29 July 1986.
90. Rifa'i to *al-Tadamun*, quoted in *JT*, 1 November 1986.
91. *JT*, 14 October 1986.
92. *JT*, 5, 31 August 1986.
93. *JT*, 6 April; *al-Ra'y*, 30 August; *JT*, 2 September 1986.
94. *Al-Dustur*, Amman; *JT*, 10 May 1986.
95. *Al-Liwa*, 2 April 1986.
96. *JT*, 2 September 1986.
97. R. Amman, 24 August — DR, 25 August 1986.
98. *JT*, 14 September 1986.
99. *JT*, 2 September 1986.
100. R. Amman, 24 August — DR, 25 August; *JT*, 2 September, 8 November 1986.
101. *Memo*, 26 September 1986.
102. Ibid.
103. R. Amman, 8 November — DR, 10 November 1986.
104. Crown Prince Hasan in *JT*, 11 November 1986.
105. *JT*, 9, 10, 11 November 1986.
106. *MM*, 8 December 1986.
107. *JT*, 1 December 1986.
108. *JT*, 24 December 1986.
109. *JT*, 28 January; R. Monte Carlo, 28 January — SWB, 30 January 1986.
110. *JT*, 30–31 January, 3 February 1986.
111. Dayan Center Archives, Official Arabic Text of King Husayn's Speech of 19 February 1986 (The Hashemite Kingdom of Jordan, Ministry of Information), pp 101–3.
112. Ibid, pp 103–12.
113. Ibid, pp 112–13.
114. Ibid, pp 83–91.
115. Ibid, p 119.
116. Ibid, p 105.
117. Ibid, pp 106–7.
118. Ibid, p 107.
119. Ibid, pp 50–54.
120. Ibid, p 54.
121. *Al-Siyasa*, Kuwait, 1 March; *JT*, 13 July 1986.
122. Husayn's speech of 19 February, ibid, p 108.
123. Ibid, p 49.
124. *Moment*, January-February 1986. I wish to thank my colleague Bruce Maddy-Weitzman for having drawn my attention to this source.
125. Husayn quoted on R. Amman, 27 February — DR, 27 February and Jordan TV, 3 March — DR, 4 March; Rifa'i to *al-Hawadith*, 22 August 1986.
126. Husayn's speech of 19 February, ibid, p 115.
127. *Al-Siyasa*, Kuwait, 1 March 1986.
128. *NYT*, 23 February; Husayn in interview to the American CNN, reported in *JT*, 23 February 1986.

129. *JT*, 27–28 February, 2 March 1986.
130. *Al-Siyasa*, Kuwait, 1 March 1986.
131. Crown Prince Hasan quoted by R. Amman, 29 May — DR, 30 May 1986.
132. Husayn at a news conference in Amman, *JT*, 13 July; Rifa'i quoted by KUNA, 9 August — DR, 11 August 1986.
133. Husayn's speech of 19 February, ibid, pp 38–58.
134. Ibid, p 116; R. Amman, 1 December — DR, 2 December 1986.
135. Husayn's speech of 19 February, ibid, pp 110–11.
136. *Jane's Defence Weekly*, 5 April 1986.
137. R. Monte Carlo, 2 April 1986. The date of the denial precedes that of the interview. The text of the interview had obviously become available before the cover date.
138. *JP*, 29 April 1986.
139. Husayn to CNN, reported in *JT*, 23 February 1986.
140. *JT*, 12 March; Husayn in his Speech from the Throne, R. Amman, 1 November — DR, 3 November 1986.
141. *Al-Siyasa*, Kuwait, 1 March 1986.
142. *JT*, 27–28 February 1986.
143. Husayn quoted in *JT*, 30 July and MENA, 21 November — DR, 24 November 1986.
144. *Al-Hawadith*, 22 August 1986.
145. *Al-Mustaqbal*, 19 July 1986.
146. *JT*, 28 January 1986.
147. Crown Prince Hasan in *JT*, 8 January 1986.
148. Hasan in *JT*, 9-10 January 1986.
149. Tahir al-Masri to *Der Kurier*, 4 September 1986.
150. *JT*, 3 February 1986.
151. *The Guardian*, 20 February 1986.
152. *JT*, *NYT*, 25 February 1986.
153. R. Monte Carlo, 2 April — DR, 3 April 1986.
154. *NYT*, 9 April; *al-Majalla*, 11 June 1986.
155. *JP*, 23 April; *al-Ittihad*, Abu Dhabi, 11 May; *CSM*, 24 June 1986.
156. JNA, 7 July — SWB, 9 July 1986.
157. *Sawt al-Sha'b*, 8 July 1986.
158. *JT*, 3 August 1986.
159. Husayn at Amman news conference, *JP*, *FT*, 16 July 1986.
160. Husayn's speech of 19 February, ibid, p 7.
161. Ibid, pp 16–21.
162. *NYT*, 14 July; similarly *WSJ*, 16 July 1986.
163. *Al-Siyasa*, Kuwait, 1 March 1986.
164. Husayn's speech of 19 February, ibid, p 25; Speech from the Throne, R. Amman, 1 November — DR, 3 November 1986.
165. *NYT*, 5 March 1986.
166. R. Amman, 22, 23 February — DR, 24 February; *JT*, 24 February 1986.
167. R. Amman, 15 July 1986.
168. *JT*, 3 August 1986.
169. *Al-Hawadith*, 22 August 1986.
170. Jordan TV, 31 July — DR, 1 August; JNA, 14 September — DR, 16 September 1986.
171. Jordan TV, 19 September — DR, 22 September 1986.
172. *Sawt al-Sha'b*, 21, 27 September; *al-Dustur*, Amman, 22 September 1986.
173. *JP*, 16 July 1986.
174. *NYT*, 2 November 1986.
175. *NYT*, 8 July 1986.
176. *JT*, 15 July 1986.
177. *'Al-Hamishmar*, 9, 13 April; *JP*, 2 May; VoP (Baghdad), 18 June — DR, 19 June; *CSM*, 24 June 1986.
178. *Al-Fajr*, East Jerusalem, 12 June 1986.
179. R. Monte Carlo, 17 June — SWB, 19 June 1986.
180. *Al-Quds*, East Jerusalem, 19 June 1986.

181. Tahir al-Masri to *al-Majalla*, 6–12 August 1986.
182. KUNA, 7 June 1986.
183. QNA, 25 August—DR, 26 August 1986.
184. VoP (Baghdad), 22 August — DR, 26 August 1986.
185. R. Amman, 12, 13 July — DR, 14 July 1986.
186. *Sawt al-Sha'b*, 30 September; R. Amman, 4 October — DR, 6 October 1986.
187. *Al-Quds*, 29 April 1986.
188. *JP*, 2 May; *al-Dustur*, Amman, 7 October 1986.
189. *JP*, 3 October 1986.
190. R. Amman, 29 September — DR, 30 September 1986.
191. R. Amman, 9 September — DR, 10 September 1986.
192. *JP*, 3 October 1986.
193. *Ma'ariv*, 26 September; *JP*, 3 October 1986.
194. *Ma'ariv*, 17 September 1986.
195. *JP*, 2 May, 3 October 1986.
196. Editorial report, DR, 18 August 1986.
197. *JP*, 10 August 1986.
198. R. Amman, 12 August, Jordan TV, 15 August — DR, 21 August; *Sawt al-Sha'b*, 20 October 1986.
199. Husayn quoted in *JT*, 13 July; Minister of Information, Muhammad al-Khatib, quoted by JNA, 21 July — DR, 22 July; Minister of Planning, Tahir Kan'an in *JT*, 17 September 1986.
200. Jordan TV, 10 November — DR, 12 November 1986.
201. E.g. Rifa'i to *al-Mustaqbal*, 19 July and to *al-Majalla*, 23–29 July 1986.
202. *Al-Dustur*, Amman, 5 August; Rifa'i to *al-Hawadith*, 22 August; Marwan Dudin to *al-Ra'y*, 16 October; Rifa'i to *CSM*, 31 October 1986.
203. Dudin in *The Observer*, 29 June 1986.
204. *Al-Ra'y*, 2 December 1986.
205. *JP*, 12 December 1986.
206. Rifa'i to *al-Majalla*, 23–29 July 1986.
207. *JT*, 6 August 1986.
208. *NYT*, 1 August 1986.
209. *MM*, 8 December 1986.
210. Jordan TV, 6 November — SWB, 8 November; *JT*, 10 November 1986.
211. *WP*, 24 July; Tahir al-Masri to *al-Majalla*, 6-12 August 1986.
212. Tahir Kan'an to *JT*, 17 September 1986.
213. VoI, 2 October — SWB, 3 October 1986.
214. Speech from the Throne, R. Amman, 1 November — DR, 3 November 1986.
215. Tahir al-Masri to *al-Sharq al-Awsat*, 29 March; Husayn on R. Amman, 13 December — DR, 15 December 1986.
216. *Al-Ittihad*, Abu Dhabi, 16 August 1986.
217. Eg. *Sawt al-Sha'b*, 19 January; *al-Ra'y*, 1 February, 19 July, 10 December 1986.
218. *NYT*, 10 June 1986.
219. Husayn in his speech of 19 February, ibid, p 111.
220. *FT*, 3 February 1986.
221. *IHT*, 12 June 1986.
222. *Al-Dustur*, Amman, 3 February; Rifa'i to *al-Hawadith*, 22 August 1986.
223. Husayn at news conference in Amman, Jordan TV, 13 July — DR, 14 July; Rifa'i to *al-Majalla*, 23–29 July 1986.
224. MENA, 23 November — SWB, 25 November; *JT*, 23 November 1986.
225. Husayn at a press conference in Amman, Jordan TV, 13 July — DR, 14 July 1986.
226. ENA, 24 August — DR, 25 August 1986.
227. *JT*, 15 June 1986.
228. *Ha'aretz*, 17 December 1986.
229. *Jane's Defence Weekly*, 5 April 1986.
230. *JP*, 30 May 1985.
231. *MM*, 31 March, 23 June; *Aerospace Daily*, 9 September 1986.

Lebanon
(Al-Jumhuriyya al-Lubnaniyya)

YOSEF OLMERT

The year under survey was another bad one for Lebanon, marked as it was by stalemate, raging violence and terrorism, and a rapidly declining economy. Political stalemate was the inevitable outcome of the collapse of the "Damascus Agreement" of December 1985 (see *Middle East Contemporary Survey* [*MECS*], 1984–85, pp 530–37). That failure left the political system in a far graver situation than was usual even in the Lebanese chaos. The Government did not meet for most of the year. Influential political leaders boycotted the President, and so did the Syrian regime. The Maronite community, a traditional backer of the Presidency, was torn apart in a violent internecine struggle. Other important communities, except the Druze, were also seriously fragmented. Above all, Syria, traditionally the final arbiter of Lebanese politics, proved unwilling to enforce a political solution in that country. Syria's problems in Lebanon coincided with its other external and domestic difficulties during the year, thus eroding its ability to play an effective role in the Lebanese arena (on Syria's policy in Lebanon, see chapter on Syria in this volume). Syria's low profile policy encouraged other actors to increase their activities. President Amin Jumayyil, while boycotted in Damascus, made an extensive effort to attract Arab and international attention to the Lebanese predicament. By so doing, he hoped to find an alternative to the "Syrian option," but his efforts were futile. The Vatican was active during the year, trying to bring about a political settlement. This initiative failed, as did the United Nations' attempts to initiate a settlement. More successful were two other actors: Iran and the Palestine Liberation Organization (PLO), whose efforts during the year were not aimed at fostering reconciliation but at further destabilizing the situation in the country. The Iranians backed their local clients, the fundamentalist Shi'i organizations, whose stated aim was to turn Lebanon upside down and establish there an Islamic Republic. The Fundamentalists, for their part, challenged the authority of the mainstream *Amal* militia in the Shi'i community, increased their campaign of terror against local political rivals, and foreigners, and stepped up their armed operations against the Israeli-backed Security Zone in South Lebanon (for more on the Security Zone, see *MECS* 1984–85, pp 547–51). The Iranians also interfered in *al-Amal*-PLO fighting, which continued throughout the year and came to a climax toward the end of the year (for a description of this fighting in the previous year, see *MECS* 1984–85, pp 543–44). The Iranian activities antagonized Syria as well as some Lebanese factions, especially the Lebanese Forces (LF) and the Druze who perceived them as a Shi'i attempt to dominate local politics.

The Shi'i threat was seen by important Lebanese elements as more dangerous than the PLO attempt to reestablish its presence in Lebanon, which was severely affected during the Israeli operations in summer 1982. Only *al-Amal* presented a counter-challenge to the PLO, without support from even its self-styled political allies, such as the Druze (on Shi'i-Druze tensions, *MECS* 1984–85, pp 544–45). The outcome of the fighting was a defeat for *al-Amal*, which lost some territory to its Palestinian adversaries. This was the only important territorial change in a year which was characterized by rampant terrorism rather than large-scale fighting. This terrorism was initiated mainly by Shi'i organizations inspired by the desire to destabilize Lebanon as much as possible.

The fear of rising Shi'i power, as well as suspicions regarding Syria's policy in Lebanon, led also to new dialogues: first, between the PLO and the LF and the Jumayyil Administration (hitherto bitter enemies of the Palestinians); second, between the Druze and the Maronites. The latter community had a particularly bad year. Following the collapse of the Damascus Agreement, the community was in turmoil. The LF, the main military wing of the Maronites, disintegrated; President Jumayyil's authority was widely challenged; the Phalangist Party was torn apart by splits; and an overall atmosphere of indifference and frustration prevailed in the community.

Casting a huge shadow over all this was the economic crisis, which reached unprecedented proportions during 1986. The Lebanese currency was dramatically devalued, inflation skyrocketed, along with unemployment, and people were starving in various parts of the country. The country sorely needed a strong effective governing power and a large measure of national unity in order to cope with such a dangerous situation. In their absence, the normally difficult reality became a desperate one.

FUNCTIONING OF THE STATE INSTITUTIONS

THE GOVERNMENT AND THE CHAMBER OF DEPUTIES

Following the collapse of the Damascus Agreement, the pro-Syrian elements started a campaign of political pressure against President Jumayyil. The Druze leader, Walid Junblat, and his Shi'i counterpart, Nabih Barri, declared that the President was a traitor and called for his removal.[1] The prominent Sunni leader and Minister of Education, Salim al-Huss, called for a boycott of the President,[2] as did the Prime Minister Rashid Karami.[3] The Greek-Catholic representative in the Government, Josef Skaf, joined the anti-Jumayyil boycott,[4] while former President Sulayman Faranjiyya called for a sustained political struggle to remove the President.[5] The Lebanese Government had never been an effective governing body, but at least it met and maintained the semblance of formality and legitimacy. Now, even that did not exist. Only on 2 September 1986 did Rashid Karami reconvene his Ministers (see below). The Chamber of Deputies (CD) was also paralyzed for most of the year. Late in January, the CD extended its mandate for another two years.[6] (The last parliamentary elections in Lebanon were held in 1972.) It reconvened when the Government resumed its sessions (see below) and shortly afterwards reelected the Speaker, Husayn Husayni, for another two-year term.[7]

PRESIDENT AMIN JUMAYYIL

Since the abrogation of the Israeli-Lebanese Agreement of 17 May 1983 (see *MECS* 1983–84, pp 545–46), Amin Jumayyil enjoyed Syrian support for his Presidency. This support mitigated the hostility toward him of the Druze and Shi'i allies of Damascus, and also deterred the President's Christian rivals from trying to overthrow him. Jumayyil was, therefore, Damascus' man in Beirut, providing the Syrians with a measure of legitimacy to their policy in Lebanon. For his part, the President upheld the "Syrian option," which meant that the Lebanese problem was a Syrian-Lebanese affair, not a pan-Arab or an international one. The Damascus Agreement signaled the end of the Syrian-Jumayyil alliance, since the former decided to throw in their lot with the Commander of the LF, Elie Hubayka, who was Jumayyil's archrival in the Maronite community (see *MECS* 1984–85, p 536).

When the Syrian-led initiative failed, the Syrians distanced themselves from the Lebanese President, blaming him for the failure. Jumayyil's reaction was twofold: on the one hand, he tried to expand his diplomatic contacts with Arab and non-Arab leaders, and on the other, he tried to mend his fences with the Syrians.

February was a particularly busy month for Jumayyil. He visited Rome, where he met Pope John Paul II and Italian Premier Bettino Craxi.[8] Soon afterwards, the Vatican started a mediation effort in Lebanon, but failed to produce a solution (see below). Jumayyil also visited Paris, where he disagreed with his host, President François Mitterrand. Jumayyil referred to the Damascus Agreement as null and void, while Mitterrand viewed it as a good basis for a solution.[9] Jumayyil also met with Arab leaders: the Prime Minister of Tunisia and the Egyptian Minister for Foreign Affairs.[10] Later on, he proceeded to Morocco, where he met King Hasan II.[11] Late in March, Jumayyil visited Austria, where he met the West German politician, Franz Josef Strauss, who had earlier visited Damascus in an attempt to mediate between Asad and Jumayyil.[12] The meeting produced no breakthrough in the relationship between the two Presidents. In April, Jumayyil received a message from President Husni Mubarak of Egypt concerning Egyptian policy towards Lebanon, which was to stabilize the country on the "basis of political and democratic dialogue among the various Lebanese citizens." There was no mention of Syria's role in Lebanon.[13] A few days later, it was reported that Jumayyil had secretly visited Cairo and conferred with Mubarak.[14] The report could not be verified. In May, Jumayyil was hectically engaged in diplomatic activity. He visited Tunisia again, where, according to reports, he asked the General Secretary of the Arab League, Chedli Klibi, to mediate between him and Asad.[15] During this visit, Jumayyil embarked upon a new diplomatic initiative, resuming political dialogue with the PLO. The two sides had no positive common interests to warrant such a dialogue. Their perceptions regarding the future of Lebanon were different. Their previous relations had been tense, acrimonious and violent. However, in 1986, they shared two negative common interests: they resented Syria and its presence and policy in Lebanon, and they feared the rising power of the Shi'i community. While in Tunisia, Jumayyil met Salah Khalaf (Abu Iyad), one of the senior leaders of the PLO, and handed him 5,000 Lebanese passports to be used by Palestinian fighters returning to Lebanon.[16] It was also reported that the PLO intended to invest money in the construction of a new, Christian-controlled airport in Halat, north of Beirut, to facilitate the arrival of Palestinians in Lebanon.[17] According to another report, the PLO started to smuggle arms to Lebanon via the Christian-held port of Junieh, but this was denied by Khalaf, who also denied getting the Lebanese passports.[18] Also the Administration of General Security in Lebanon denied making special arrangements to facilitate the return of Palestinians to Lebanon.[19] Nonetheless, it became clear that Jumayyil had established the "Palestinian option" as part of his efforts to replace his former "Syrian option."

In June, Jumayyil visited the Gulf area, where he met with the leaders of Abu Dhabi,[20] Oman,[21] Qatar[22] and Kuwait, where he publicly castigated Syrian policy in Lebanon, but also denied reports of a mass return of Palestinians to his country.[23] According to one report, Jumayyil visited Iraq secretly during his official visit in the Gulf.[24] In June, Jumayyil also visited Romania, where he met the leaders of that country and the Foreign Minister of Iraq,[25] as well as a Soviet envoy who handed him a special message from the Soviet leader, Mikhail Gorbachev.[26] The contents of this message were not divulged. Damascus was not included in Jumayyil's busy schedule during the year. However, his envoys did visit the Syrian capital on several occasions, trying to organize a summit between Jumayyil and Asad, but to no avail. Officially, Jumayyil declared that relations between Syria and Lebanon were "natural,"[27] but the Syrians insisted that the Lebanese President had to be more specific regarding Syria's "special" relations with Lebanon.[28] Syria also criticized Jumayyil's *rapprochement* with the PLO (see above) and demanded that Lebanon sever its diplomatic ties with Britain, following the crisis between Syria and Britain in October[29] (see chapter on Syria in this volume). Lebanon did not do so, and this was one of the reasons why a summit between Asad and Jumayyil did not take place.

In 1986, Jumayyil was a flying President, desperately trying to bring about Arab and international involvement in Lebanese affairs. He failed to achieve that, or to use his extensive contacts as leverage on Syria to change its policy and once again recognize Lebanon's President as its supreme client in Lebanon. However, Jumayyil's flying diplomacy served to emphasize his position as a key figure in the Lebanese arena. Not the most dominant politician in the country, perhaps, but surely one to be reckoned with. The point was also brought home in the Maronite community, where the President found himself confronting a series of challenges to his authority (see below).

PEACE INITIATIVES IN LEBANON

THE VATICAN INITIATIVE

Following Jumayyil's visit in Rome, two envoys, Luciano Angeloni and Monsignor Gatti, were sent from the Vatican to Lebanon.[30] On 9 March, the Vatican Foreign Affairs Secretary, Cardinal Silvestrini arrived in Lebanon as well.[31] Officially, the Vatican envoys did not spell out any specific peace plan, but unofficially it was reported that they had outlined the following main points: (a) Lebanon is an integral, sovereign and unified state; (b) Syria ought to play a role in ending the conflict in Lebanon; (c) the Asad-Jumayyil personal dialogue ought to resume; (d) strong opposition to any partition plan; (e) consultation with the US in order to put pressure on Israel to withdraw its forces and influence from the "Security Zone"; (f) within the Maronite community, the supreme authority should be in the hands of the religious hierarchy.[32]

Silvestrini met with many Lebanese leaders, Christian and Muslim alike, and visited Damascus, where he conferred with Vice President 'Abd al-Halim Khaddam.[33] Silvestrini himself rated the response to his initiative as "favorable" and remarked that Damascus gave his plan a "positive reception."[34] However, the initiative failed:

Silvestrini left, and Angeloni and Gatti were called back to Rome.[35] As so often in the past, this initiative was thwarted by an unholy alliance of all those who felt damaged by it. The Syrians insisted on a "special" role in Lebanon, and resented the internationalization of the problem. The LF resented the role assigned to the Maronite Church, and so did Jumayyil. Muslim elements, both Sunni and Shi'i, resented in principle the interference of the Vatican.

THE LEBANESE-CHRISTIAN PEACE PLAN

On 14 May 1986, a "Christian Peace Initiative" was promulgated. The plan had been devised by a wide range of Christian parties and organizations — the National Liberal Party (NLP) of Kamil Cham'oun, the Phalangist Party, the "Union of Independent Maronite Deputies," members of the LF, Armenian Deputies and others — and contained the following main points: (a) Lebanon is a free, sovereign and independent state; (b) Lebanon is an Arab state and a full member of the League of Arab States; (c) the parties totally object to any partition plan; d) Lebanon is a state of minorities representing different civilizations; therefore, the formula of "political confessionalism" ought to remain the basis for the future of Lebanon; (e) wide administrative decentralization is desirable; (f) an economic regime based on free enterprise is best for the country; (g) the "strong" relationship and common interests of Syria and Lebanon are defined and stressed.

Regarding the principles of the political reform, the plan emphasized the following points: (a) distribution of seats in the CD on an equal basis between Muslims and Christians (as opposed to the 6:5 ratio in favor of the Christians in the current system); (b) abolition of the confessional system in public posts, except for the senior administrative and military posts; (c) there will be six Vice Presidents, representing the main religious communities; (d) the Prime Minister will sign, together with the President, decrees and new laws; the Premier will also sign decrees regarding the dismissal of Ministers and can force his opinion on the President regarding the selection of a new government, provided he has a majority of 55 per cent in the CD (these measures would add to the powers of Sunni Premier and reduce the authority of the Presidency); (e) the number of Deputies wil be increased from 99 to 108.[36]

The new plan included changes in the political system that were designed to appease the Muslims. Still, it fell short of the basic Muslim demand for a complete abolition of the confessional system, even on a gradual basis. The plan insisted on the dominant position of the Presidency, which was in Christian-Maronite hands, and rejected Syria's demand for a "special" relationship with Lebanon as envisaged by the "Damascus Agreement."

There were some negative reactions to the plan, such as Barri's[37] which referred to it as a "farce," and Faranjiyya's.[38] Yet, the plan was not without a follow-up in the coming months.

THE WEST BEIRUT SECURITY PLAN

On 3 June, as the "camps war" raged (see below), fierce street battles broke out in West Beirut between the Shi'i *Amal* militia and some Sunni militias. The battles culminated in a total Shi'i victory.[39] A few days later, on 13 June, a new Syria-sponsored security plan for West Beirut was devised in Damascus. The agreement called for a cease-fire, to be supervised by a force comprising the Lebanese Army's mainly Shi'i Sixth Brigade, the Druze militia and the Syrian-sponsored Ba'th Party militia. The new plan went into effect on 24 June.[40] (See also the chapter on Syria in this volume.) Thus in a relatively peaceful West Beirut, the effort to achieve reconciliation in Lebanon was given an impetus.

THE CHRISTIAN-MUSLIM DIALOGUE

On 1 August, Jumayyil made an important speech, appealing for a new relationship with Syria, which, he said, should be "special and privileged." The President also called for a gradual phasing out of the confessional system, and mentioned that the CD was empowered to amend the Constitution to introduce equal representation for Muslims and Christians. The speech was well received in the Christian camp, with the exception of the LF, but Syria was not at all impressed, stressing the need to reenact the Damascus Agreement. Still, the speech ignited a positive momentum. The Premier, Rashid Karami, dropped his demand for Jumayyil's resignation; and Druze leader Walid Junblat, interviewed by a television station run by the LF, called for a dialogue. On 2 September the Government convened for the first time in months (see above). The meeting agreed on the following points: (a) An immediate cease-fire; (b) equal representation of Muslims and Christians in the CD; (c) reforms in the Army; (d) "the need to liberate the South."[41]

This was a broad framework, enough to begin a new political dialogue, but, as was proved shortly afterwards, not specific enough to bring about a comprehensive new settlement. The dialogue took place in the Beirut Hippodrome, and two Ministers — the Maronite supporter of Jumayyil, Josef Abu Hashim, and the Sunni and pro-Syrian Salim al-Huss prepared more specific plans for national reconciliation. Soon, the differences between them became obvious. They revolved around the issue of the special relationship with Syria, the complete end of political confessionalism, the question of the renewed unity of the Army, and the Arab identity of Lebanon. These were no minor problems but the very ones that had wrecked the Damascus Agreement and now loomed again as insoluble. Indeed although there were changes of tone and tactics in the behavior of some Lebanese factions during the summer of 1986, they did not amount to changes of substance and strategy. Reaching an agreement meant mutual concessions, which in turn could be precipitated by an effective outside pressure, i.e., Syrian commitment to do more in Lebanon than it was ready to do. This commitment was lacking, and other forces, such as the PLO, Shi'i Fundamentalists and Christian factions spoke and acted against a political settlement. As was the case on so many other occasions in the past, this opportunity too was overshadowed by the forces of violence and destruction.

DISINTEGRATION, VIOLENCE AND ECONOMIC DEPRIVATION IN LEBANON

TERRORISM

Terrorism has constantly plagued Lebanon since the outbreak of the civil war in 1975. But in 1986 it reached proportions unknown even in that country. Terrorist actions had three distinct targets: Lebanese politicians; Lebanese Jews; and foreign citizens, diplomats, academics and others. A close examination of most of these actions indicates that they were committed by militant Shi'i organizations — the identity of the victims, the justification given for the actions, the names of the organizations that claimed responsibility, the timing of many of the actions, and the general interest of these organizations in destabilizing the country even further (see below), supported this assumption. Among Lebanese politicians, special attention was given to Nabih Barri, the leader of *al-Amal.* During the year, Barri's house was attacked five times: on 31 March, a rocket-propelled grenade was fired at the house. Three members of *al-Amal* were behind the attack,[42] which took place few days before the *Amal* convention (see below), when Barri was under attack from more militant elements in his own movement. The second attack took place on 27 May. This time, the Sunni Murabitun movement claimed responsibility, allegedly to avenge *Amal* atrocities against the Palestinians in West Beirut[43] (see below). Early in August, a booby-trapped car was discovered near Barri's house.[44] This time no one claimed responsibility. Early in November, a Shi'i movement called the "Youth of 'Ali" attacked Barri's house.[45] From the text of the movement's communiqué it was clear that this was an anti-Syrian Shi'i group. Such anti-Syrian Shi'i groups were generally pro-Iranian. On 30 November, there was another rocket attack on Barri's house.[46] Barri was not hurt in these attacks, but he was forced to go into exile in Damascus (see below), and this undermined his political stature in the Shi'i community. Other Shi'i leaders were also not spared the wrath of the Fundamentalists. On 11 March, Shaykh 'Abd al-'Aziz Faqih, the brother-in-law of the moderate Shi'i leader, Shaykh 'Abd al-Amir Kabalan (the Ja'afari Mufti of Lebanon), was assassinated.[47] In December, Rabab al-Sadr, the sister of the revered Imam Musa al-Sadr (for more on Imam Musa, see chapters on Lebanon in previous volumes of *MECS*), narrowly escaped an explosion in her house.[48] It is significant that both Kabalan and Sadr were at an Iranian-inspired Islamic Conference in Tehran early in 1986 (see below). Also Sunni religious leaders fell victim to terrorism. On 9 February, Shaykh Khalil 'Akawi, a prominent Sunni leader, was assassinated in Tripoli. His supporters accused the followers of the pro-Iranian Shaykh Sa'id Sha'ban of being involved in the murder[49] (for additional material on Shaykh Sha'ban, see chapters on Lebanon in previous volumes of *MECS*). Shaykh Sha'ban participated in the above-mentioned conference in Tehran. On 7 October, Shaykh Subhi Salih, deputy chairman of the Higher Islamic Council (the Sunni Council) was assassinated. According to some reports, the murder was linked to the visit to Lebanon of Mahmud Hashemi. It was rumored that the Iranians were angry with Shaykh Salih because he refused to attend Islamic meetings in Tehran.[50]

Another target of the Shi'i terrorists was the Lebanese Communist Party (LCP), a pro-Syrian, anti-Iranian group that made some inroads into Shi'i population concentrations, for instance in Beirut, as well as in South Lebanon. For these reasons, the Communists provoked the anger of both *al-Amal* and the fundamentalist *Hizballah.* On 20 February, Khalil Na'us, a member of the LCP's politburo, was assassinated in Beirut. The Communists warned *al-Amal* that it would be dealt a double blow in retaliation.[51] A few days later, another prominent Communist, Suhayl Tawila, a member of the Party's Central Committee, was assassinated near the Iranian embassy in West Beirut. This time, the Communists blamed *Hizballah* and the two parties clashed in the streets of West Beirut.[52] On 3 March, *Hizballah* applied "Islamic justice" against 11 people, among them two women, who were accused of collaborating with Israel and the US. All the accused were executed.[53] Three other prominent Lebanese politicians were assassinated during the year — 'Isam al-'Arab, leader of the pro-Syrian Nasserite group, the "Forces of Nasser";[54] 'Azabin Jarbatian, the chairman of the right-wing Armenian Party, Tashnak;[55] and Nasib al-Khatib, the former leader of the pro-Syrian Red Knights militia.[56]

Other prominent personalities escaped attempts on their lives — the deposed LF leader, Elie Hubayka, on 31 January,[57] and the serving Commander of the LF, Samir Ja'ja' late in May and in July.[58] The Commander of Syrian Intelligence in Lebanon, Ghazi Kana'an (for more about him, see chapter on Syria), escaped an attempt on 28 June.[59] Rashid Karami, the Sunni Prime Minister, was a target on 9 January,[60] and Gen Antoine Lahad, Commander of the South Lebanese Army (SLA), on 8 November and 5 December.[61] An easy target for the Shi'i terrorists were some of the few remaining Jews of Beirut. Jews were regarded by the terrorists as potential collaborators with Israel. Killing them was supposed to put pressure on Israel and also to avenge Israeli activities in the South. Late in December 1985, two Jews, Haim Cohen and Isaac Trab, were executed.[62] In February 1986, two more Jews, Ibrahim Benesti and Elie Halak, were murdered.[63] Three more Jews were found dead on 30 December.[64] One Shi'i organization, the "Oppressed on Earth" (*Mustad'afin Fil Ard*) claimed responsibility for all these attacks.

The main burden of terrorism was aimed at foreign embassies, institutions and citizens. During the year, many foreign embassies and individual diplomats were attacked in what seemed to be a systematic effort to force diplomats out of Lebanon and inflict yet another blow on official Lebanese legitimacy and the prestige of the Jumayyil Administration. This was the oft-repeated goal of militant Shi'i organizations. The Soviet embassy was attacked four times: in February, twice in October, and in November. There were no casualties in all these attacks.[65]

A South Korean diplomat was kidnapped on 1 February by a hitherto unknown group called the "Green Brigades."[66] Following the American attack on Libya in April (see chapter on Libya and essay on the US and the Middle East), the home of the British Ambassador was attacked,[67] and soon afterwards, many foreigners, including staff of the British embassy, left Lebanon.[68] In April, the Netherlands decided to close its embassy in West Beirut.[69] In May, the Turkish and Senegalese embassies and the South African consulate were attacked,[70] and the Austrian embassy in West Beirut evacuated its staff.[71] Belgium followed suit in June,[72] and Portugal did likewise in October.[73] Spain, on the other hand, vowed not to close down its embassy.[74] In October and November, the French and Romanian embassies were attacked.[75] The Lebanese Government proved unable to deal with the situation. It was Walid Junblat who established a special Druze unit to defend East European embassies, chief among them the Soviet embassy.[76]

A special effort was made by *Hizballah* to terrorize the personnel of the American University in Beirut (AUB), in order to bring about its closure. Once the center of scholarship in the Middle East and a hotbed of Arab Nationalism, the AUB had never had such a rough time since its inception in 1866.[77] From the point of view of the Shi'i terrorists, it was a foreign institution, spreading foreign values and preaching communal solidarity, tolerance and dialogue. This was exactly what *Hizballah* was against. Late in February, the AUB decided to close its branch in Christian East Beirut[78] and remain only in West Beirut. Soon afterwards it was reported that the

AUB had decided to move completely to Morocco.[79] April was a particularly troublesome month: two British professors were kidnapped and the students started a strike in protest.[80] A few days later, an Irish professor was kidnapped.[81] On 20 April, 19 foreign members of the AUB's staff returned to their countries.[82] On 28 April, two Cypriot students were kidnapped, to be released two months later.[83] On 19 July, a bus carrying doctors from the AUB was attacked — three were killed and several were wounded.[84] On 24 September, the Islamic Organization of Revolutionary Justice claimed responsibility for the kidnapping of an American accountant at the university, Josef Cicippio.[85] In October, a dean at the university was forced to resign after receiving threats from *Hizballah*.[86] However, there was also some good news for the AUB when a kidnapped professor, Nabil Matar, was released on 21 October.[87] Late in October, the board of trustees of the AUB, convening in New York, threatened to close the university for the first time in its long and glorious history. When the communiqué was issued, the university had about 5,000 students and 400 academic staff,[88] and was still the finest academic institution in Lebanon.

During the year, Shi'i terrorists intensified their campaign of abductions and killings of nationals of countries with which Iran was at odds. A French hostage, Michel Seurat, was assassinated on 5 March by the Islamic Jihad.[89] Following the American attack on Libya in April (see above), two Britons and an American were executed in Beirut. A pro-Libyan group, the Arab Fidayyin Cells, claimed responsibility.[90]

By the end of the year, various terrorist groups in Lebanon were still holding French, British, American, Italian and South Korean citizens and diplomats hostage. Some Lebanese Jews were also being held, as well as two Israeli soldiers (see below).[91] On the other hand, two American hostages, Laurence Janko and David Jacobson, were released by their Shi'i captors in July and November,[92] as part of the American-Iranian arms deals (see chapter on Iran and essay on the US and the Middle East). These two released hostages notwithstanding, Lebanon in 1986 was plagued with terrorism and the fanaticism that made terror a daily occurrence in the streets of Beirut and other cities. As if to exemplify the deterioration, there occurred the most astounding kidnapping of all: on 20 January 1987, Terry Waite, the personal envoy of the Archbishop of Canterbury who had been involved for years in negotiations to free hostages, was abducted in Beirut, apparently by one of the Shi'i terror organizations.[93]

THE ECONOMIC DETERIORATION

Lebanon's economy was regarded for years as a success story, almost a miracle. Despite the various disturbances, wars and political conflicts, there had been a significant economic advance. In 1983–84, it was observed that the miracle fizzled out (see *MECS* 1983–84, pp 555–60), and 1985 was also a disastrous year economically. The objective conditions were terrible, with more than 620,000 people living as refugees in their own country. Out of a population of some three million, 2.5 million have at one time or another been forced to leave their homes to escape the terrors of violence. More than half a million Lebanese have emigrated. Hundreds of thousands of people still live in dilapidated neighborhoods, half-built trade centers and religious institutions.[94] Still, the figures for 1985 showed at least one ray of hope: the overall balance of payments recorded a $380m surplus. The improvement stemmed from a big decline in government imports of military equipment, an influx of funds for the militias, and cuts in consumption and foreign travel.[95] But this was the only encouraging figure. Foreign exchange reserves fluctuated and affected government borrowing. In the first nine months of 1985, inflation increased by 55 per cent. According to a Labor Ministry report published in August 1985, unemployment in the Greater Beirut area stood at 28 per cent. Also, the prices of petroleum products went up.

There was more bad news in 1986. Early in January, the rate of exchange of the Lebanese pound was $1=£L18.[96] By the end of December 1986, it stood at $1=£L90, recovering slightly to $1=£L87.25 by the end of the following month.[97] Anti-Jumayyil sources charged that huge arms purchases, made by the President, were responsible for the dramatic collapse.[98]

The Executive Committee of the LF tried to be more positive in its approach. It formulated a four-point plan calling for: (a) A social and economic state of emergency in order to ensure the provision of basic food and medical supplies at reasonable prices. Subsidies should also be provided so that these supplies could be sold at less than cost price. (b) A social and economic salvation plan to be drafted in cooperation with the various state organizations. (c) Reduction in unnecessary public expenditure. (d) Encouragement for banks to rechannel their investments into production, particularly in the industrial and agricultural sectors.[99]

The governor of the Lebanese Central Bank ascribed the difficulties to "hatred between certain members of the Lebanese communities." He expressed the hope that Lebanese deposits abroad, which were valued at between $25–30 bn, could be repatriated.[100] This was some hope; in reality things happened differently. The Government adopted several measures, but they were far from what was necessary. The salaries of Lebanese diplomats abroad were cut by half.[101] Two embassies in Africa and some consulates were closed down,[102] and the Government searched for foreign aid. Its success was very limited: Czechoslovakia promised a loan of $150m for 1987,[103] and the Federal Republic of Germany promised to give £L1.5 bn.[104] The US, on the other hand, demanded that Lebanon pay what it owed for the arms ordered by Jumayyil.[105] In the absence of effective action to stop the deterioration, popular anger expressed itself. It was anger and hunger that unleashed protest by both Muslims and Christians. On 3 July, a general strike united Beirut.[106] On 22 November, Lebanon's Independence Day, there was a partial strike in West Beirut. A grim picture of economic deprivation was presented by a resident of Tripoli who offered his eight children for sale.[107] On 2 December another general strike paralyzed the country.[108] New organizations protesting against the situation mushroomed in Beirut. Among them were the "Eagles of the South," the "Underground Military Forces," and the "Black Panthers."[109] Their protests and the situation itself brought Lebanon to the brink of a "war of starvation." This war did not break out in 1986. But nor were the fears of the population sufficient incentive for the warring factions to close ranks to save the country. An atmosphere of chaos prevailed, as members of the numerous militias took pains to retain their sources of income in the face of a paralyzed economy. Banks were broken into, and the Government had to devise an emergency security plan to protect them.[110] Militia members were given a free hand by their leaders to extort money from individuals, to burst into restaurants, and to increase taxation in areas under their control.[111] Under these circumstances, militias tried to tighten their control of seaports as well as airports, in order to collect the revenues on incoming and outgoing goods. The Christians built a a new airport near Beirut, in Halat, but problems between the LF and the Government prevented its operation until the end of the year.[112] During the sessions of the governmental dialogue committee (see above), a decision was taken to close all the "illegal" seaports used by the various militias,[113] but nothing was done as the Government was hardly functioning (see above).

LEBANON'S MAIN COMMUNITIES AND THE CRISIS

THE CHRISTIAN COMMUNITY

STRUGGLE OVER CONTROL OF THE LEBANESE FORCES

By the end of the year, a Christian-Lebanese delegate at an international Christian conference claimed that the Christians of Lebanon still constituted a majority of the population (51 per cent as against 49 per cent Muslims).[113] Bearing in mind the consistent assessment that the Christians were only a minority, and a dwindling one to boot, this was indeed an optimistic view of the Christians' position in Lebanon.

The signing of the Damascus Agreement in December 1985 (see above and *MECS* 1984–85, pp 530–37) unleashed a violent struggle among the Maronites, the largest Christian community in Lebanon, which continued unabated throughout 1986. The struggle focused on the LF, but its ramifications engaged all the main interest groups in the community: President Jumayyil, the Phalangist Party, the supporters of Kamil Cham'oun, and the Maronite Church. By far the most ferocious and significant clash was between Samir Ja'ja' and Elie Hubayka, the two leaders of the competing wings of the LF. The outcome of the January 1986 fighting between them (see *MECS* 1984–85, p 537) dictated the course of events during the rest of the year. Four hundred people were killed in the bloody clashes of 15 January 1986,[114] many of them Hubayka's men who were massacred after they had turned themselves in to Ja'ja''s units. People were taken from their homes and summarily executed, and bodies were found mutilated.[115] Hubayka himself and some of his senior assistants were saved only after mediation by senior commanders of the Lebanese Army.[116] Most of Hubayka's men left for Paris; Hubayka himself was in France for a short while before returning to Lebanon via Damascus. Upon his arrival in Lebanon, he vowed to fight back against Ja'ja' and destroy him and his supporters.[117] What first seemed to be the pledge of a desperate man soon became a troubling reality in the Christian enclave of East Beirut and Mount Lebanon. Backed by Syria and driven by a spirit of revenge, Hubayka conducted his operations against Samir Ja'ja' along three lines: political activity, terror actions and a full-scale military attack to regain full control of the enclave.

Eight days after his forced departure from East Beirut, Hubayka met former President Faranjiyya, another old rival of Jumayyil and Ja'ja'.[118] There was no immediate political follow-up to the meeting, but hundreds of Christian youngsters from villages under Faranjiyya's influence were dispatched to the Biqa' valley, where Hubayka had established training camps for his loyalists.[119] The Biqa' was under strong Syrian influence, and its main city, Zahla, was a center of the Greek-Catholic community. It was noted when Hubayka arrived there that the reaction of the local population was far from enthusiastic.[120] However, Hubayka had Syrian backing and with it he established a radio station and prepared to set up a television station.[121] He also established branches of the LF in the Biqa' area, financing his activities with the millions of dollars he managed to smuggle out of Beirut after his defeat in January 1986. Early in September it was reported that he commanded a force of 2,000 men.[122] While all this happened, his loyalists conducted a terror campaign against Ja'ja''s strongholds. On 21 January, a car bomb exploded in East Beirut, killing 22 people.[123] Early in February there was a wave of blasts in East Beirut, killing nine people.[124] A few days later, another bomb killed two more. This time, Ja'ja's men reacted by launching a campaign of arrests against hidden Hubayka supporters.[125] But the severe security measures failed to stop the terror campaign: a car bomb exploded in East Beirut on 8 March, killing five,[126] another on 26 March, killing ten,[127] and on 8 April, the residents of the port city of Junieh were subjected to terrorism when a car bomb exploded there and killed nine people.[128] On 23 May, six were killed in East Beirut[129] in another car bomb explosion, and two were killed on 1 August.[130] On 14 August, 14 people were killed when a particularly huge car bomb exploded in East Beirut.[131] No organization linked with Elie Hubayka claimed responsibility for these attacks, but the Hubayka connection was nevertheless obvious. All the explosions took place in Ja'ja'-held territory and were targeted against buildings and offices operated by Ja'ja''s and Amin Jumayyil's supporters. The sustained terror campaign demonstrated Hubayka's resolve to oust Ja'ja', but it failed to achieve its goal. Life in the Christian enclave became miserable and tormented, Ja'ja''s hold proved fragile and vulnerable, but he remained in control. Also two large-scale military operations against him failed, but highlighted the precariousness of his situation. The first took place on 10 August and did not involve Hubayka's loyalists. Units of the LF, loyal to two Commanders of the Christian militia, Marun Mash'alani and Fu'ad Abu Nadir, revolted against Ja'ja'. Of the two, Abu Nadir was the more important. He was a nephew of the President and had served as chairman of the Command Council of the LF from September 1984 until March 1985, when he was demoted following an insurrection in the LF led by Samir Ja'ja' (see *MECS* 1984–85, pp 538–40).

Since then, Abu Nadir and Ja'ja' had been at odds; and on 10 August, the former narrowly escaped an assassination attempt.[132] Mash'alani's revolt came after an attempt by Ja'ja''s men to force LF soldiers to take extra training in a camp known for its rigorous regime.[133] The clashes subsided early in the morning of 11 August,[134] but resumed on 12 August,[135] and continued until 14 August.[136] The rebels were prevented from taking over East Beirut, but Ja'ja' was denied a final, complete victory, as both Mash'alani and Abu Nadir were allowed out of East Beirut. The former was held under house arrest in the Christian town of Jubayyil.[137] The latter moved to the village of Brumanna, where he established a training camp.[138] His house there was attacked by Ja'ja''s men but Abu Nadir survived.[139] Toward the end of the year, it was reported that Ja'ja' and Abu Nadir were reconciled.[140]

Following the August events, Ja'ja' gained some time to organize his loyalists — mainly by promoting people who, like him, were Maronites from North Lebanon. But shortly afterwards he faced another violent challenge to his authority. This time, it was Elie Hubayka who struck at East Beirut. On 26 September, he formed a new Command Council for his wing of the LF and formulated again his political platform. Two main points were prominent on his agenda: (1) Relations between Syria and Lebanon "must be established on firm and permanent historical and geographical facts, which dictate that cooperation with Syria be given priority over cooperation with other Arab states." (2) The "liberation of the South is a national responsibility."[141]

The two points were very much in line with Syrian policy in Lebanon. The announcement was just a prelude to a full-scale military attack against East Beirut by Hubayka's forces with the support of pro-Syrian elements on 27 September. The operation was the result of high-level Syrian consultations with Hubayka and it was aided by the following pro-Syrian factions: the Ba'th Party Militia, a battalion of the Syrian Army, *al-Amal*, and the Syrian Social Nationalist Party (SSNP).[142] The battle was fierce and brutal, and Ja'ja''s forces managed to overcome the attackers. On the morning of 28 September, the situation in the eastern sector of Beirut was declared "normal." Thirty-seven people, most of them attackers, were killed in the clashes.[143] Immediately after the fighting ended, Ja'ja''s men started a campaign of terror in East Beirut against those suspected of "collaborating" with Hubayka. Scores of bodies were found in various parts of Beirut.[144] One of the victims of the Ja'ja' vendetta was a senior officer in the Lebanese Army, Col Khalil Kana'an, Commander of the Fifth Brigade. He was assassinated after a clash involving his men and some LF fighters.[145] The assassination, as well as the clash that preceded it, were inevitable developments in the atmosphere of confusion and terror that prevailed in East Beirut. The Army supported Ja'ja' in the fateful events of 27 September, following strict orders from President Jumayyil.[146] Nonetheless one of its senior Commanders was murdered by the very people he was instructed to support. As the dust settled, it became clear that Hubayka's gamble had not paid off. He vowed to continue the struggle[147] and stated that, despite the military failure, he had gained political success,[148] but his Syrian patrons thought otherwise. They took over Hubayka's centers in Zahla[149] and accused his followers of leaking the plan to attack East Beirut.[150] Officially, the Syrians denied any role in the Christian in-fighting.[151] By the end of the year, Hubayka still had 800 loyal fighters,[152] but in Zahla there was increasing opposition to his continued presence, including that of influential local Shi'i leaders.[153]

Samir Ja'ja' was the victor, but late in the year, as well as at the beginning of the year, he was not alone in his struggle against Hubayka. He had to share the spoils of his victories with a grudging coalition, including Jumayyil, the Phalangist Party and Kamil Cham'oun. On 24 January, he was elected head of the LF Executive Committee. Karim Bakraduni, an Armenian-Catholic lawyer, was elected a deputy chairman.[154] (For more about him, see *MECS* 1983–84, p 559; 1984–85, pp 537, 541). It was reported that Ja'ja' had received Israeli arms shipments,[155] and that he had conducted negotiations with Israel regarding the reopening of the Israeli liaison office in the Christian enclave,[156] which had been closed in summer 1984 (see *MECS* 1983–84, p 550). The office was not opened during 1986; nor was there any official confirmation of any links betwen Ja'ja' and Israel. However, Ja'ja''s basic positions were well known: he was pro-Israeli and anti-Syrian (see *MECS* 1984–85, p 539). Yet, the "Israeli option" as opposed to the "Syrian option" was not the dividing line between Ja'ja' and Jumayyil. They competed for political domination of the Maronite community and political maneuvering and military power were used by both sides. While Ja'ja' commanded the LF and insisted on a unified Christian power under his command, Amin Jumayyil counted on the support of the Christian units of the Lebanese Army stationed in East Beirut (see above), and also forces loyal to the Phalangist Party and a special personal militia, loyal to him, known as the "Matn Forces" or "Force 75."[157] Jumayyil also enjoyed some support in the LF itself.[158] The forces of Jumayyil and Ja'ja' never engaged in a large-scale fighting during the year, but were involved in an endless number of small clashes. The two leaders understood that any major fighting between them would play into the hands of Elie Hubayka and his Syrian mentors. Again, it was proved that the only effective political coalition in Lebanon was one based on a negative common denominator. In the absence of overt fighting, Jumayyil and Ja'ja' struggled for domination of the Command of the LF and the Phalangist Party. Regarding the LF, the victory was in Ja'ja''s hands. In the party, the situation was different (see below).

On 5 December, following long discussions between various Christian elements, the Executive Committee of the LF, "seeking more comprehensive representation and greater efficacy within the LF," decided to become a Command Council including representatives of all Christian parties.[159] On 8 December, the new Command elected Ja'ja' as chairman and Bakraduni as his deputy.[160] The new Command included fewer Jumayyil supporters than the previous one.[161] One of the missing members was Abu Nadir (see above). By the end of the year, it reaffirmed the LF political platform, emphasizing (a) the need to establish "natural friendly relations between Lebanon and Syria," based on equality and on mutual respect for the two countries' independence and territorial integrity; (b) a call for Syria to withdraw its forces from Lebanon; (c) a call for international support to Lebanon in its struggle to regain its sovereignty.[162] This was clearly an anti-Syrian document, reflecting Ja'ja''s political concepts. Indeed, 1986 was the year of Samir Ja'ja' in the Christian community. His leadership was frequently challenged, but he managed to survive, thus becoming a key figure in his community.

THE PHALANGIST PARTY

During the year under review, the Phalangist Party, a traditional claimant to political leadership of the Christian community, had to face a growing challenge to its authority. The challenge was posed by internal rivalries, the growing stature of Kamil Cham'oun (see below), and, above all, the ambitious leadership of the LF under Samir Ja'ja'. This was the time when the party needed strong, charismatic leadership. Yet this type of leadership had beeen lacking since the death of the founder and leader of the party, Shaykh Pierre Jumayyil, and the election of Dr Elie Karami as his successor (see *MECS* 1984–85, p 538). The stormy events of the last two years proved that a political party used to a personality cult and an internal authoritarian regime could hardly function when they were missing. The party failed to democratize itself and adapt to changing circumstances. Amin Jumayyil and Karami, his appointee in the party, did not rise to the occasion, and the Phalangists faced a deep crisis. The LF tried to establish a new Christian front comprising various non-partisan organizations, and at the same time tried to infiltrate the party in order to take it over.[163] The moment of truth came on 16 June, when the party held its leadership elections.

For the first time in the history of the party, there were two candidates competing for its leadership. Pierre Jumayyil, on the other hand, had always won unanimous renomination for the post. The elections produced a new leader, Dr George Sa'ada (for details of his past activities, see *MECS* 1983–84, p 571; 1984–85, p 538) formerly the deputy leader, who defeated the former leader Karami. The new deputy leader was George Umayrah, who defeated Fu'ad Abu Nadir (see above). The 12-member Political Bureau of the party was also elected. This time, Abu Nadir received the largest number of votes.[164] When the results were announced, Samir Ja'ja' expressed his satisfaction, claiming that "there will no longer be any reason to differentiate between the LF and the Phalangists. Now, there is only one community and one people."[165] His elation no doubt stemmed from the fact that at least six out of the 12 in the new Political Bureau were LF supporters.[166] The election of these people, it was rumored, became possible only after a campaign of coercion by Ja'ja''s men against Phalangist voters.[167] Soon after the election, it became clear that Sa'ada was not at all a pawn of Ja'ja''s. He was a veteran Phalangist who was friendly toward Amin Jumayyil and ruled over a Political Bureau in which there was no majority for the LF. This was so because Sa'ada was entitled, ex officio, to add new, unelected members to the Bureau. (It is interesting that one of the new members was Ja'ja' himself.) Sa'ada had moderate opinions regarding the role of Syria in Lebanon and was in constant touch with former President Faranjiyya, himself an avowed foe of Ja'ja'.[168] One of Sa'ada's first initiatives was to meet with Faranjiyya.[169] Although the meeting produced no dramatic result, it nevertheless indicated Sa'ada's desire to pursue his own political agenda, not necessarily Ja'ja's. Sa'ada also kept under his control some party military units, such as the "Special Phalangist Force" and the "Matn Forces" of the party,[170] while Ja'ja' wanted all Christian units to be subjected to him (see above). All this was not done in order to ignite trouble with the LF but to reassert the leading role of the party, preferably through cooperation. On 6 September, Sa'ada announced in the presence of Ja'ja' that an arrangement had been arrived at between the party and the LF to regulate their future relationship. The details of the new arrangement were not specified, but Sa'ada was more generous in providing information regarding organizational changes within the party itself. Steps would be taken to achieve centralization in order to strengthen the overall control of the leader.[171] Sa'ada's ceremonial statement was soon put to the test when the forces of Hubayka and those of Ja'ja' clashed in East Beirut (see above). Referring to the fighting, Sa'ada expressed full support of the LF.[172] However, until the end of the year, the LF and the Phalangist Party did not completely settle their differences. Ja'ja' did not subject himself politically to the party, and George Sa'ada did not abolish the Phalangist military forces. A tense, but non-violent, form of coexistence prevailed between the two powers.

Late in November, the party held its 18th conference, commemorating its silver jubilee. This was supposed to be a big celebration, a rallying point for the party that claimed to be the Christians' hope for a better future. But the Christian areas reacted with overt indifference to the event, thus providing another grim reminder of the abysmal state of affairs in the Christian community at large and in the Phalangist Party. In his speech, Sa'ada called upon Syria to establish normal relations with Lebanon, demanded the total withdrawal of armed Palestinians from the country and called for Israeli withdrawal from the South, while offering to safeguard Israel's security interests. Sa'ada also reiterated his party's objection to the complete abolition of political confessionalism in Lebanon.[173]

KAMIL CHAM'OUN'S ACTIVITIES

The internal tensions in the Christian community played into the hands of the almost eternal politician Kamil Cham'oun. At the age of 87, Cham'oun loomed again as a prominent figure, exploiting fully the internal splits in the LF and the Phalangist

Party. In his return to a central role in Christian politics, Cham'oun had some disadvantages to overcome; but he also had advantages. On the credit side was his untarnished image as a traditional bearer of the Lebanese-Christian ethos of struggle against pan-Islamic and pan-Arab aspirations, compared with the vacillating image of President Amin Jumayyil regarding these issues. Also, Cham'oun had the social standing of a traditional Lebanese leader (*za'im*), whereas Hubayka and Ja'ja' were social upstarts with no background of significance, a serious drawback in the generally traditional Maronite society. Cham'oun had the additional advantage of being the middleman in the almost endless conflict between Samir Ja'ja' and Amin Jumayyil. On the debit side, Cham'oun did not command large and effective military forces, as did Ja'ja'; and unlike Jumayyil he did not have the powers of state of the President. Before the events of January 1986, Cham'oun coordinated his moves with Ja'ja'; and his son, Danny, warned Jumayyil not to betray Ja'ja' after the removal of Hubayka.[174] Soon afterwards it was reported that Ja'ja' had asked Cham'oun to reestablish training camps for a militia of the latter's party, the NLP.[175] Late in April it was reported that the party had made preparations for a military parade in East Beirut.[176] However, the full military comeback of the NLP did not materialize. Samir Ja'ja', who resented the existence of partisan military forces, went back on his agreement to reestablish Cham'oun's militia. It was rumored that Cham'oun went too far in his attempts to win Ja'ja''s support and the latter did not deliver on his promises.[177]

During the year Kamil and Danny Cham'oun were also engaged in independent diplomatic activity. Danny Cham'oun met with Jordan's King Husayn, the PLO leader Yasir 'Arafat, and Iraqi leaders,[178] as well as the Director-General of Israel's Foreign Ministry and Gen Antoine Lahad, Commander of the SLA.[179] It was reported that the NLP promised financial support to the SLA.[180] The Cham'oun family was also involved in an interesting dialogue with a bitter political rival, Walid Junblat, leader of the Druze of the Shuf mountains. In September 1983, the Druze under Junblat had evicted the LF, commanded by Samir Ja'ja', from the Shuf, which was a traditional stronghold of the Cham'oun family (see *MECS* 1982–83, pp 676–84).

Thus, in the rapidly changing circumstances of 1986, Cham'oun cooperated with Ja'ja', and at the same time his family and Junblat found enough common ground to start a political dialogue. In August, Junblat called for a reunification of the Shuf in a common effort with the Cham'oun family.[181] The latter were only too pleased to hear this. It was evidence of their growing stature in Lebanese politics in general and the Maronite community in particular.

THE MARONITE CHURCH

In December 1985, the head of the Maronite Church, Patriarch Antonios Butrus Khuraysh, resigned his post, and a contest developed to find his successor. Each one of the various Maronite political factions had its own candidate. The Phalangist Party and Cham'oun preferred Archibishop Ibrahim al-Hilu, the permanent Apostolic Delegate in Lebanon. The LF proposed Archibishop Yusuf al-Khuri of Tyre. Elie Hubayka and Sulayman Faranjiyya preferred Archibishop George Iskander of Zahla.[182] On 19 April the Electoral College, comprising 20 senior Maronite clergymen, elected Archibishop Nasrallah Sfeir, 66, as the new Maronite Patriarch.[183] His election was seen as a victory for the moderate elements in the community.[184] When the Patriarch was officially appointed, both Samir Ja'ja' and Karim Bakraduni boycotted the ceremony.[185] The antipathy was apparently mutual. Following the 27 September events (see above), the Maronite Bishops chaired by Sfeir issued a statement referring negatively to the role of the LF. This time, Ja'ja' felt obliged to meet the new Patriarch, in order to discuss their relationship. Following the meeting, the two leaders publicly stated that their misunderstandings were over.[186] Soon afterwards, Ja'ja' publicly stated that "it was natural" for the LF to authorize Patriarch Sfeir to speak on its behalf in the Vatican and in Paris.[187]

THE SHI'I COMMUNITY

In 1986 as in previous years (see chapters on Lebanon in previous volumes of *MECS*), the Shi'is were in the forefront of tension, agitation and fighting. This was so because they sought a prominent role for themselves under the Lebanese sun. They were the up-and-coming community, the largest single religious group in the Lebanese mosaic, the community credited with the great victory over the Israeli occupation forces in South Lebanon (see *MECS* 1984–85, pp 541–45).

Historically, Lebanese politics were characterized by the opposition of various communities to attempts by a single group to dominate the Government. In such a situation, coalitions were formed to stop one group or another from fulfilling its goals. This was especially the case with the Shi'is, whose drive to centrality seemed extremely dangerous to the other Lebanese communities because they were backed by formidable external forces, such as Syria and Iran. Consequently, during the year under survey, Shi'is were involved in fighting with Christians, Druze, Sunnis and Palestinians, and among themselves.

AL-AMAL CONVENTION AMID SPLITS

The last convention of *al-Amal* ended its sessions on 15 April 1983 with the election of Nabih Barri as chairman of the movement. The new convention was scheduled for 4 April 1986,[188] but before it began reports indicated that the movement was split into two main factions. One was led by Barri, the other by Hasan Hashim, chairman of the Executive Committee (for the history of the conflict between them, see *MECS* 1984–85, pp 541–43).

Barri controlled some suburbs in West Beirut and the Biqa' valley's branches of *al-Amal*. His associate, Mahmud Faqi, was the dominant personality in the Nabatiyya area in South Lebanon. Hashim's support was concentrated in some suburbs of West Beirut and South Beirut, where another *Amal* leader, 'Aql Hamiyya, was also very influential. The Tyre area in South Lebanon was dominated by Dawud Dawud, an ally of Hashim. It was reported that Barri's rivals accused him of being too soft toward some enemies of the Shi'is because he was interested in an alliance with leftist parties.[189]

On 22 March, supporters of Hashim clashed in Beirut with supporters of Barri, and four people were killed.[190] On the eve of the convention, Iran warned Barri not to adopt "anti-Islamic" resolutions.[191] At the convention itself, Barri outlined *al-Amal's* main policies: (a) support of the Damascus Agreement; (b) acknowledgment of the need to prevent anti-Christian activities in Beirut as well as in other regions of Lebanon; (c) confirmation of an alliance with Syria, and support of the Islamic Republic of Iran; (d) support of the Palestinian cause, while preventing the Palestinians from reestablishing their presence in Lebanon under conditions similar to the pre-1982 situation; (e) demand for the complete abolition of political confessionalism in Lebanon; (f) launch a political and military campaign to liberate the South; (g) form an alliance with the Druze and other nationalist and leftist parties.[192]

After a day of deliberations, the convention reappointed Barri as leader of *al-Amal* for two more years. Mufti Kabalan was elected chairman of the Islamic Jurisprudence Committee, and Dr Mustafa al-Hajj was made president of the Islamic Court. ‘Akif Haydar was elected deputy leader and chief of the Research Bureau. The convention also elected the members of the Political Bureau, and the Executive Committee and officers for various positions. The two most important functionaries were ‘Aql Hamiyya who was elected Military Officer, and Mustafa Dirani, the Security Officer.[193] The convention did not end without disputes: Dawud Dawud refused to accept the position of chairman of the Executive Committee; and Hasan Hashim was not elected to any position and vowed to establish an alternative leadership to Barri's.[194] Hashim was not Barri's only rival; Hamiyya was also a rival, and disobeyed his orders during the fighting with the PLO (see below).[195] The Biqa‘ members in the new Political Bureau also boycotted the bureau's sessions.[196] It was reported that a member of the bureau from the Biqa‘, Abu Yahya, led a revolt against Barri early in September, but *al-Amal*'s leadership denied that.[197] Denials notwithstanding, *al-Amal* was evidently plagued with internal splits. While the fighting with the PLO was at its height, Dawud Dawud demonstrated his independent line: he refused to cooperate with Ghazi Kana‘an — Syria's chief man in Lebanon — to settle the problems in the Tyre region.[198] And Hasan Hashim continued to criticize Barri, who retaliated by attacking Hashim's house and a convoy of cars escorting him. Hashim survived the attacks.[199] It was reported that Mustafa Dirani also disobeyed Barri during the war with the PLO.[200] According to an unverified report, Barri himself uncovered an Iranian plot to assassinate him.[201] For this and other reasons (see above), he moved to Damascus in the middle of November, and stayed there for the remainder of the year under review. This was indeed an unprecedented move: Nabih Barri was the elected leader of a movement that was engaged in a battle against external enemies and internal rebels. The fact that he opted to leave his men behind underlined the fragility of his personal position and the overall weakness of *al-Amal* in facing up to formidable challenges, the chief among them in 1986 being from the PLO.

AL-AMAL AND ITS ADVERSARIES — THE "CAMPS WAR"

The indecisive outcome of the *Amal*-PLO fighting in 1985 (see *MECS* 1984–85, pp 543–44) paved the way for the battles of 1986. Already in late October 1985, ‘Arafat's loyalists predicted that the fighting, which died down in the summer, would resume,[202] and it did. During January there were reports about movement of PLO fighters around the camps in the Sidon area,[203] where there were said to be 50,000 Palestinians — in Sidon itself and in two large camps.[204] In February, there were reports of a deteriorating security situation in the camps of West Beirut, following the withdrawal of Syrian observers from the area.[205] (About their stationing there, see *MECS* 1984–85, p 533).

The tense situation in Beirut erupted in open fighting on 28 March, on the eve of *al-Amal*'s convention. In several days of uncompromising fighting, 50 people were killed and 80 wounded, and the PLO managed to extend its control in and around the Palestinian camps in West Beirut.[206] Anti-‘Arafat Palestinian elements also participated in the defense of the camps, and disobeyed the line of their patron, Syria.[207]

After the first round of the fighting, a pattern was established whereby *al-Amal* and anti-'Arafat elements from the Palestinian National Salvation Front (PNSF; see essay on the PLO) convened in Damascus and agreed upon a cease-fire, only to see the cease-fire crumble after a short while. 'Arafat's loyalists did not feel bound by the agreements, Syria did not have the manpower to enforce them in Beirut or with *al-Amal*, and there were some elements who wanted to continue the fighting. The next flare-up occurred late in May.[208] Again an agreement was reached in Damascus,[209] and again it was not long before it was violated. This time Barri lashed out at the PNSF, saying that there was "no difference" between it and 'Arafat's PLO.[210]

'Arafat for his part claimed that the campaign waged by *al-Amal*, with the support of the Shi'i Sixth Brigade of the Lebanese Army, had left 2,000 dead and wounded, and later sent an "urgent memorandum" to international bodies concerning the plight of the Palestinian camps in Lebanon.[211] The fighting with *al-Amal* resumed in full force in October and continued until the end of the year. West Beirut, Sidon and Tyre[212] were the battlefields. The battles in Tyre were initiated by the PLO, and when *al-Amal* retaliated there, the Palestinans reacted by attacking Shi'i positions east of Sidon,[213] in an area which had been in Christian hands until the events of April 1985 when a Shi'i-Druze onslaught removed the LF from there (on these events, see *MECS* 1984–85, pp 549–50). The fighting also engulfed the camps in West Beirut, and it became an all-out *Amal*-PLO battle. Yet this was not a Shi'i-Palestinan war, as *Hizballah* abstained from the fighting, and its patron, Iran, tried to mediate between the warring factions.

This was clearly an anti-Syrian and pro-PLO step, and was contrary to conventional wisdom, since Iran was officially allied with Syria and anti-PLO. The PLO was pro-Iraq and transmitted its messages to its fighters in Lebanon from a radio station in Baghdad. But this was just one paradoxical element in the complex situation created by the camps war. It seemed that the *Amal*-PLO conflict and Syria's role in the background of the fighting provided the setting for a realignment of politics in Lebanon. 'Arafat appeared on the television station run by the LF, once his most bitter enemies, and castigated Syria and *al-Amal*.[214]

Israel took part in the fighting, but indirectly. The Israelis intensified their attacks on the PLO while the fighting was on: there was an aerial attack in Sidon on 10 September,[215] another aerial attack in Tripoli on 6 October,[216] an attack against a PLO ship in Sidon on 20 November,[217] an interception of two PLO ships loaded with fighters and arms in the Sidon area,[218] a naval bombardment of the PLO's position in the Sidon area,[219] and another aerial attack on a PLO building in Tripoli.[220] Within the Palestinian ranks, 'Arafat's men were supported by most of the pro-Syrian Palestinian factions from the PNSF, despite the anti-'Arafat Syrian line.[221] Lebanese politics were also shaken by the fighting: Junblat issued an ultimatum to the PLO to withdraw from its positions in the Sidon region, but soon withdrew his ultimatum and did nothing to support the cause of his former ally, Barri.[222] The Christian leadership refrained from any official comment in support of the PLO, but favored the latter's drive against *al-Amal* and Syria. *Al-Amal*, the mainstream Shi'i organization, was isolated and consequently *al-Amal* was defeated.[223] A small Christian village east of Sidon, Magdusha, became a symbol of the bitter fighting: it was strategically located above the coastal road to Beirut and the port of Sidon. After the two months of fighting, Magdusha, an LF stronghold before coming into *al-Amal*'s hands, was still controlled by the PLO. Also symbolic were the Palestinian camps in West Beirut, especially Shatila (for the report on the massacre there in 1982, see *MECS* 1981–82, pp 647–48). Palestinian sources claimed that *al-Amal*'s offensive was helped by Syria, which at one point used "chemical substances" against the camp. Most of the buildings in the camp were destroyed in the *Amal* offensive, in which tanks operated by the Shi'is and Syrian commanders took part.[224]

The result of the fighting was a military victory for the PLO, which by the end of 1986 had over 8,000 fighters in Lebanon, including 2,500 in the Sidon-Magdusha region, 300 in Tyre, and 2,300 in the Beirut area.[225] In terms of sheer numbers, the Shi'is in Lebanon outnumbered the Palestinians five to one. *Al-Amal* was heavily backed by Syria and indirectly supported by Israel, whereas the PLO did not enjoy much outside support. *Al-Amal* also had an advantage over the PLO in terms of equipment, especially in armored vehicles. In 1985, *al-Amal* received about 50 tanks from Syria,[226] while the PLO had none. All this puts in perspective the extent of *al-Amal*'s defeat: it was a psychological, political and military setback whose repercussions were bound to affect *al-Amal* as an organization, the Shi'i community at large, and Lebanese politics in general.

The fighting in the Sidon area was temporarily stopped on 10 December when a cease-fire achieved through Iranian mediation came into force. According to the agreement, the PLO had to evacuate Magdusha and *Hizballah* units were supposed to take control there, and *al-Amal* was supposed to relax the siege on Palestinian camps in the Tyre region.[227] The PLO announced that its losses in the campaign were "2,500 martyrs and wounded."[228] The cease-fire did not resolve the situation in West Beirut, nor did it deal with the root causes of the clash in South Lebanon.

It was abundantly clear, therefore, that the *Amal*-PLO war had been frozen for a short while but was bound to resume.

AL-AMAL AND ITS ADVERSARIES FROM THE LEFT

The incidents between *al-Amal* and Walid Junblat's Progressive Socialist Party (PSP) that began the previous year continued in the year under review. Early in April, there were clashes in the Khalda area, south of Beirut.[229] On 8 June, three rockets were fired by *al-Amal*'s men at Junblat's house in Beirut, and *al-Amal* men tried to burst into the house. It was reported that Junblat gave Barri the keys of his house so that *al-Amal* fighters would not have to force their way into his residence.[230] Junblat, according to some reports, warned against the Shi'i influx from the South to the mountain area and predicted that this would touch off bloody fighting between *al-Amal* and the PSP along the coast and in West Beirut.[231] Barri, for his part, accused Junblat of collaborating with *Hizballah* against *al-Amal*.[232] Toward the end of the year, Barri accumulated more grievances against Junblat, since the latter did not commit his forces to the struggle against the PLO. During the year under survey, *al-Amal* clashed also with the SSNP a small, but well-motivated and organized pro-Syrian party. Early in October, they clashed in the western Biqa'.[233] A month later, the two sides fought again in the same region.[234] Later on, they also fought in West Beirut.[235]

During the year, *al-Amal* was also on a collision course with the LCP. Both parties were pro-Syrian, yet they clashed frequently (see also above). The LCP's leader, George Hawi, accused Barri of preventing his men from penetrating South Lebanon. To this the latter retorted that the South "is ours only."[236] In April and May there were clashes in the western Biqa' between the LCP and *al-Amal*, which this time was supported by the *Hizballah*[237] (see also below). While the fighting between *al-Amal* and the PLO raged in November, Hawi called upon the Palestinians to stop the fighting and expressed support for *al-Amal*.[238] However, on the ground, the Communists did not join the Shi'is, and the tension between them continued.

AL-AMAL AND ITS SHI'I ADVERSARIES

While *al-Amal* was engaged in fighting its many enemies outside of the Shi'i community, it had to look over its shoulders and watch of its adversaries from *Hizballah* rise to a position of prominence among the Shi'i and in Lebanese politics in general. The tension between the two organizations revolved around a wide range of issues and policies. *Al-Amal* was pro-Syrian, *Hizballah* pro-Iranian. *Al-Amal* resented the PLO presence in Lebanon, *Hizballah* was ready to tolerate it. *Al-Amal* wanted to pacify the South and retain there the UN Interim Force (UNIFIL), while *Hizballah* strongly objected to it. *Al-Amal* did not entertain any plans regarding the "liberation of Palestine," while *Hizballah* made this goal a chief item on its political and ideological agenda. *Al-Amal* still adhered to a pluralistic society in Lebanon, whereas *Hizballah* wanted to serve a worldwide, pan-Islamic cause and establish an Islamic Republic in Lebanon. *Al-Amal* was officially part of the political establishment, by virtue of the fact that Nabih Barri was a member of the Government, and *Hizballah* was by definition a revolutionary organization.

In sum, the two factions were diametrically opposed to each other in their respective policies, and, above all, they competed for domination of their community. During the year under review, the struggle sharpened, mainly due to *Hizballah*'s increased activities in the country (see below). *Al-Amal* thus faced a severe challenge to its supremacy among the Shi'is. Tensions and crises notwithstanding, the two sides seldom used violence against each other to settle their disputes. On two occasions there were armed clashes. The first clash was in February in Beirut, when *al-Amal* was backed by the mainly Shi'i brigade of the Lebanese Army.[239] On 8 September, there was another armed clash in Beirut. The Iranian embassy intervened to stop the violence.[240]

HIZBALLAH AND ITS ACTIVITIES

During 1986, much of the curtain of secrecy surrounding *Hizballah*, its organizational structure, the identity of its leaders and its military power, was lifted, thus making it possible to give a portrait of the movement. The supreme leader of *Hizballah* was Imam Khomeyni, whose instructions were transmitted through Iran's embassies in Damascus and Beirut and special Iranian envoys visiting Lebanon. In Lebanon itself, the movement was commanded by a council comprising 12 men, mostly religious leaders. There were three organizational regions: Beirut, the Biqa', and South Lebanon. The council operated seven functional committees. The propaganda department was particularly active, publishing a weekly (*al-'Ahd*) and a monthly (*al-Sabil*).

Hizballah received regular and very generous financial support from Iran. The main leaders of the movement were religious figures, and notable among them was Shaykh Muhammad Husayn Fadlallah, who was born in Najaf (Iraq) in 1936.[241] Alongside him, there was a series of younger leaders, prominent among whom were Abbas Musawi, Hasan Nasrallah, Subhi Tufayli and Ibrahim al-Amin, who was also the official spokesman of *Hizballah*. All of them were in their thirties.[242] According to unverified reports, Fadlallah's position in the movement eroded during the year. He himself made it clear that he did not belong to any particular party.[243] According to another report, he and al-Amin competed for power in *Hizballah*.[244] It was also reported that al-Amin was engaged in a struggle with another aspirant for power, Shaykh Zuhayr Kanj, who resided in South Beirut and was considered a most militant and staunch supporter of Iran.[245]

Hizballah's military power was estimated at 4,000 fighters, of which 2,500 were in the Biqa', 1,000 in West Beirut and 500 in the South, mainly in the villages of Jibshit, Zadikin and Ma'araka. It was observed that there was a gradual movement from small clandestine units to large, semi-regular military formations. The soldiers were well paid and wore uniforms.[246] *Hizballah*'s ideology was widely circulated during the year and its main articulators were Fadlallah and other prominent leaders. In a series of interviews, Fadlallah stressed that the CD was illegal; that the political system in Lebanon ought to be replaced by an Islamic system; that Arab Nationalism was a framework but not substantial, because only Islam offered the authentic source of solidarity. Israel, the Shaykh claimed, ought to disappear through armed struggle. Violence was not Islam's way of expressing itself, but a reaction to limitations on Islam imposed by others. The cause of violence in the Middle East was the establishment of Israel. The Shaykh also took pains to dissociate himself from the rampant Shi'i terrorism in Lebanon (see above).[247]

Another important factor in *Hizballah*'s ideology was a book written by 'Ali Kurani, which was exceptional in so far as it outlined *Hizballah*'s role in Lebanon since its inception. The book emphasized the need to "liberate Palestine and Jerusalem" as *Hizballah*'s main strategic target. To that end, all Muslims, Shi'is and Sunnis alike ought to close ranks.[248]

Another central item on *Hizballah*'s agenda was the call for the establishment of an Islamic Republic in Lebanon. Late in January 1986, Iran's President Muhammad 'Ali Khameneh'i opened in Tehran the "Fourth Conference on Islamic Thought." The list of Lebanese participants included prominent Shi'i and Sunni leaders. At the end of the conference, 60 people signed a draft Islamic Constitution for Lebanon (two of the signatories had reservations). Its main points were: (1) The Muslims constituted a majority in Lebanon, therefore there ought to be an Islamic Republic in the country. (2) Khomeyni represented Allah's will on earth, and he was the supreme religious leader of all the Muslims in Lebanon.(3) Since he was physically absent from Lebanon, his powers in Lebanon were delegated to Shaykh Muhammad Mahdi Shams al-Din, the deputy chairman of the Supreme Islamic Shi'i Council (SISC) whose chairman — officially at least — was Imam Musa al-Sadr (for more on Shams al-Din, see chapters on Lebanon in previous volumes of *MECS*). (4) The President of the Republic will be elected for four years in a popular vote and there will be a revolutionary Islamic Council replacing the existing CD.[249] During the year, there were various petitions by religious leaders and thousands of citizens, calling for the establishment of an Islamic Republic.[250] It became clear that *Hizballah*'s agitation to that end was enjoying some success in Shi'i population concentrations. For a revolutionary movement such as *Hizballah*, ideology, petitions and words, important as they were, constituted just one component of its activities. The movement was also engaged in terrorism (see above); fighting in the South (see below); and small-scale fighting with Syrian forces in the Biqa' on 12 March,[251] again on 1 May,[252] and during early June with Syria's staunch ally, the SSNP, in the western Biqa'.[253] The one major battle in which *Hizballah* did not take part was the *al-Amal*-PLO war (see above). From *Hizballah*'s point of view, this was an unneccessary confrontation, since it pitted Muslims against each other instead of against Israel.[254] Earlier it was reported that *Hizballah* had signed an agreement of cooperation with the PLO in Lebanon.[255]

THE DRUZE COMMUNITY

On the eve of the year under review, Walid Junblat personally and the Druze Community generally had many reasons to be content with their position in Lebanon: the Shuf region was practically a Druze canton, and within its boundaries lived most of the Druze population in the country. The canton had its educational institutions, an economic infrastructure based on a port in Khalda (south of Beirut), political bodies such as a Political Bureau and Executive Committee, and a strong military force which had proved its effectiveness (see chapters on Lebanon in previous volumes of *MECS*). Above all, the canton had in Junblat a legitimate leader who had faced no significant challenge from within the community since the death of Amir Majid Arsalan, chief of the rival Arsalani clan (see *MECS* 1983–84, pp 560–61). Yet, Junblat was a worried man during the year. His problem was how to retain all his assets and achievements in the face of pressures from outside forces. There were three sources of pressure. The first was Syria, which resented Junblat's growing stature and wanted to subjugate him, while strongly supporting *al-Amal* as its chief client in Lebanon. *Al-Amal* was Junblat's second problem. The rise of the Shi'is, moderates as well as Fundamentalists, frightened the Druze, as it did other communities in the country. Third, Junblat was worried about the reemergence of the PLO in Lebanon, which could be a positive factor in checking the Shi'is but could also develop into a major danger if the Palestinians scored too big a victory and reasserted their positions as they did in the pre-1982 situation.

Junblat's relations with the Syrians did not develop into an open and serious rift, but signs of tension were evident. One of Junblat's senior assistants in the PSP, Riyadh Ra'd, was removed for being too pro-Syrian. That happened after clashes between Junblat's men and Syrian units in the Hammana area.[256] There were also clashes between the Druze and Syria's surrogates, the SSNP, in the 'Aley-Bahamdun area and in the upper Matn.[257]

Yet this was small-scale violence. The conflict between Syria and Junblat was largely political; the Syrians wanted Junblat to withdraw his forces from Iklim al-Kharub, a coastal region between Sidon and Khalda with a largely Sunni population. Junblat viewed this area as vital strategically and part of the Shuf.[258] Traditionally, Iklim al-Kharub was a relatively peaceful area, but during 1986 tensions erupted between the Druze and the Sunnis there. On 7 April, two soldiers of the Druze militia were killed in a Sunni village, Basaba. In retaliation, the Druze killed 14 local villagers.[259] Junblat vowed at the funeral of his two slain men to "cut off the hands of saboteurs." He also vowed to stop the communal fighting,[260] and until the end of the year there was no more violence in the region. But tension prevailed. Early in May a mass grave was discovered, which led to counteraccusations between Junblat and Christian sources regarding the identity of the victims. The Christians believed the remains were those of coreligionists murdered by the Druze, who, for their part, charged that the dead were Muslims.[261] Junblati-Syrian differences also revolved around the Shuf itself, since the Syrians wanted to apply the West Beirut security plan (see above) there as well. Junblat, for his part, believed that the Syrians wanted to create separation between the Shuf and the Druze population of the South and West Biqa'.[262] All these tensions did not prevent Junblat from visiting Damascus during the year, but he also pursued an independent diplomacy.

Special attention was devoted to his relations with the USSR. On 1 March, Walid Junblat addressed the delegates to the 27th Congress of the Soviet Communist Party. He highlighted the following points: (a) Israel must withdraw from South Lebanon and must do so completely and unconditionally; (b) a serious dialogue must be started in Lebanon; (c) there will not be a settlement of the Arab-Israeli conflict unless the Palestinians obtain their "just and legitimate rights."[263] Later it was reported that Junblat took upon himself the task of protecting the Soviet embassy in Beirut (see above). In return, the Soviets reportedly gave Junblat political and military help. According to the reports, Soviet dialogue with Junblat was direct, and all their dealings took place without the participation of the Syrians.[264] Junblat also started a dialogue with the Christians. The Cham'oun family were natural partners to such a dialogue (see above), but Junblat's contacts went beyond them. Early in April, Junblat visited the Vatican and met Silvestrini (see above).[265] Following the election of the new Maronite Patriarch (see above), Junblat sent him a letter, the contents of which were not made public. It was rumored, though, that Junblat's message was of "historic" significance.[266] Later on came the governmental dialogue in which Junblat also took part (see above), but after it failed, the Druze leader lashed out at Jumayyil and Ja'ja', arguing that there could not be a "true" peace with them. Still, Junblat argued, political dialogue with the Maronites ought to continue.[267] But there was no dramatic breakthrough in this dialogue in the remaining part of 1986.

During the year, Junblat was also engaged in a dialogue with the PLO. While in Moscow, he met Faruq Qaddumi, the man in charge of the PLO's foreign affairs. He later met Qaddumi in Sofia.[268] It was rumored that Junblat met with Abu Iyad, when the latter visited Beirut secretly.[269]

Meetings notwithstanding, Junblat remained adamant that the PLO would not be able to regain its pre-1982 status in Lebanon.[270] But he refrained from actively combating the Palestinians. Junblat's calculation was that, although an *Amal* and Syrian victory was undesirable, the PLO should not emerge victorious either. At any rate, Junblat's fundamental policy was not to commit Druze soldiers to a war which was not directly linked to Druze interests. What emerged out of all these deliberations was a two-pronged policy; rhetorically, Junblat castigated 'Arafat, vowed to lead a joint force to fight the PLO,[271] called upon 'Arafat to resume relations with the Syrians,[272] and confiscated heavy arms used by the PLO in the Shuf region.[273] All this was just one side of the coin; the other side was a systematic effort not to fully participate in the war between *al-Amal* and the PLO. Both Syria and *al-Amal* did not fail to take note of the message conveyed by Junblat, once their devoted partner in the coalition that successfully undermined Amin Jumayyil's Administration and scored many other victories in Lebanon.

THE SUNNI COMMUNITY

Traditionally, the power of the Sunni community in Lebanon was based on three large Sunni population centers: Tripoli, West Beirut and Sidon. Through a process that lasted some years (see chapters on Lebanon in previous volumes of *MECS*), the local Sunni leaders lost control of these cities. The weakness of the community was highlighted when the Sunni Premier was not involved in the Damascus Agreement. Some Sunni religious leaders threw in their lot with the Iranian revolution and that further weakened the cohesion of the community (see above, on the participation of Sunnis in the Islamic conference in Tehran). The Sunnis could hardly count on the support of any external Arab power, and they lacked a significant military force to protect their communal interests. The PLO was, by and large, a Sunni-dominated force, and, as such, supported Sunni interests and was supported by Lebanese Sunnis; yet the PLO was also engaged in alliances and relationships with other actors in Lebanon. The PLO was not, therefore, a Sunni militia and it was not like *Hizballah* and *al-Amal*, which were Shi'i, or the PSP, which was Druze, or the LF, which was Maronite. This state of affairs did not change during the year.

THE SITUATION IN TRIPOLI

The main Sunni militia in Tripoli, the Tawahid Movement, led by Shaykh Sa'id Sha'ban was paralyzed for most of 1986, following its defeat in fighting during 1985 (see *MECS* 1984–85, pp 546–47). Clashes occurred in a village near Tripoli late in June between the SSNP and the Tawahid. Following the clashes, Syrian forces deployed in the area at the request of the Sunni Premier, Rashid Karami, himself from Tripoli.[274] The peace and quiet were soon undermined. Late in September it was reported that PLO fighters had sneaked into Tripoli.[275] Soon afterwards there were reports of a deterioration in the security situation in Tripoli.[276] Thus, a familiar scene unfolded in Tripoli; Syrian units were provoked, then the Syrian Army reacted violently, the local Sunni militia was soundly defeated, and Shaykh Sha'ban made another pilgrimage to Asad to ask him to have mercy on the poor Tripolitanians. The battle erupted on 18 December, and the Syrians, using a large force, were particularly harsh. According to one report, 500 residents were killed.[277] Two Syrian battalions were dispatched to the rural environs of Tripoli in the 'Akkar region.[278] The atrocities in Tripoli put Karami under pressure; he was asked by Sunni leaders in Beirut to resign in protest against Syrian behavior.[279] Shaykh Sha'ban, for his part, rejected Arab mediation and met with an Iranian delegation in Tripoli.[280] Sha'ban also paid his dues to the Syrians by publicly criticizing 'Arafat before proceeding to Damascus to meet with Asad.[281] Late in December it was reported that the Syrians had completed the "cleaning up" of subversive elements in Tripoli.[282] Judging from past experience, there was no doubt it was just a break in the ongoing struggle in and around Tripoli.

THE SUNNIS IN WEST BEIRUT

The Sunni suburbs of West Beirut continued to be dominated by non-Sunni forces: *al-Amal* and the PSP. Other political-military groups there were the Arab-Socialist Union (largely Sunni); the Arab-Socialist Union — the Nasserite organization (largely Sunni); the 6 February Movement (Sunni); the LCP (non-sectarian, largely Christian and Shi'i); the Ba'th Party (non sectarian, Syrian-dominated); and *Hizballah* (Shi'i, pro-Iranian).[283] The strongest Sunni movement in West Beirut in previous years, the

Independent Nasserites (Murabitun; see chapters on Lebanon in previous volumes of *MECS*), were greatly weakened during the year and hardly played a meaningful role in that part of the city. Late in the year, the Murabitun announced the formation of a new military-political structure for the movement in an attempt to regain its position in West Beirut.[284] A former Murabitun leader, Samir Sabagh, announced the formation of his own organization, the "Movement of Unionist Action," which was supposed to be non-sectarian. He also called for all "foreign" forces to leave West Beirut.[285] Early in June, *al-Amal* inflicted a blow on the 6 February Movement (see above), and afterwards a public debate developed between Sunni and Shi'i religious leaders. The Sunni Mufti, Shaykh Hasan Khalid, criticized those who raised supposedly Islamic slogans which were in fact false and not Islamic. A Shi'i leader, Mufti Kabalan, retorted by castigating those who wanted "to be leaders of Islam in Lebanon, but...we found them to be leaders of Tariq al-Jadida [a Sunni area in West Beirut],"[286] when the camps war raged in West Beirut (see above). Mufti Khalid rejected a return to the pre-1982 situation with regard to the PLO, but objected also to a unilateral disarmament of the PLO while the Israeli occupation of South Lebanon continued and other military forces were still armed.[287]

THE SITUATION IN SIDON

Following Israel's withdrawal from South Lebanon in spring 1985, Sidon's politics were relatively quiet (see *MECS* 1984–85, pp 548–51). All political and military forces there established a joint "Supreme Political Committee" to monitor developments. The existence of this committee neutralized many potential problems in the city itself, although tensions continued to exist in the Jizzin area (see below) and in other adjacent areas.

In the early months of 1986, the committee was paralyzed and the situation in Sidon gradually worsened. The main military force there was the "Popular Liberation Army" led by Mustafa Sa'd. There was also a "security police," whose tasks were maintenance of law and order. The "Islamic Grouping," a Fundamentalist Sunni group, was in touch with the Palestinians in the camps around Sidon.[288] The Deputy from Sidon, Nazih al-Bizi, was an influential figure and was considered pro-Syrian. Another important element was the organization established by the wealthy pro-Saudi businessman, Rafiq al-Hariri, who was, originally, from Sidon. According to one report, Hariri established a militia comprising of 3,500 fighters, and they were on bad terms with Sa'd's men.[289] Throughout the year, there were many reports of attacks against Hariri's men and institutions. According to one report, the Lebanese Army's Intelligence was behind the attacks.[290] According to another report, Shi'i Fundamentalists launched the attacks as part of their campaign against Saudi influence in the Muslim areas of Lebanon.[291] As tensions increased in Sidon as part of the general deterioration of relations between *al-Amal* and the PLO, it was reported that Hariri's men had located long-range artillery in the Sidon area.[292]

Sa'd, one of Hariri's adversaries, was also very active during the year. On various occasions he made it clear that he objected to the renewed PLO presence in Sidon (see above);[293] yet when the *Amal*-PLO fighting flared up, there was not much that Sa'd could do about it. Both forces were more powerful than his militia and this underlined the fact that in Sidon, too, the local Sunni leadership was weaker than other forces.

Another problem which Sa'd had to deal with was that of Jizzin, the Christian town

20 km east of Sidon. The fighting in spring 1985 between the LF and the leftist and nationalist forces (see *MECS* 1984–85, pp 549–50) left Jizzin under the control of units loyal to the Commander of the SLA, Gen Antoine Lahad. The truce between Lahad and his enemies was shaky. It was believed in Sidon that Lahad would try to reassert Christian control in the eastern suburbs of Sidon and their environs. There was a state of alert in Sidon in January,[294] February and April.[295] No military clash occurred but there was also no political settlement of the problem of Christian refugees, despite rumors to the contrary.[296] From Lahad's point of view, Jizzin was something of an additional burden, as remaining there stretched his lines of communication and strained his limited reservoir of manpower. Nevertheless, he insisted on staying because Jizzin was the only remaining Christian outpost in the southern half of Mount Lebanon and its population (30,000) was a potential source of manpower for his militia. Therefore, there was no change in the status quo in the Jizzin area, despite the fact that troubles in other parts of South Lebanon required Lahad's closest attention.

THE SITUATION IN SOUTH LEBANON

Before the beginning of 1986 there was a sharp rise in operations by *al-Amal* and other Lebanese organizations against Israel's Security Zone in South Lebanon and the SLA. On 23 November 1985, it was disclosed that UNIFIL had monitored 90 incidents since the start of the month in its own zone, which lies to the north of the SLA strip. On 3 December, a substantial Israeli army column carried out a raid on a position of the Popular Front for the Liberation of Palestine-General Command, several kilometers north of the SLA strip. Five Palestinians were killed in the attack. Late in December 1985 and early in January 1986, troubles intensified in the South, and the Israeli border town of Qiryat Shemona came under attack by Katyusha rockets.[297] Thus the stage was set for a stormy year in South Lebanon. Officially, there was one umbrella organization in charge of attacking the Security Zone: the Lebanese National Resistance Front (see also chapter on armed operations). In effect, there were four different organizations, sometimes acting in cooperation with each other, and at other times separately:

(a) The "Believers' Resistance" — under *al-Amal* supervision.
(b) The "Islamic Resistance" — under *Hizballah*.
(c) The "Comprehensive Resistance" — under the SISC.
(d) The "National Resistance" — under Syrian control and comprising elements from the Ba'th Party, the LCP and the SSNP.[298]

There was also the Palestinian factor which included both pro-'Arafat and anti-'Arafat elements.

Outside of Israel's Security Zone there was UNIFIL, the force that was established according to UN Security Council Resolution 425 of March 1978, following Israel's "Litani Operation" in South Lebanon (see chapters on Israel, and Lebanon, in *MECS* 1977-78). In the beginning of 1986, UNIFIL operated seven full battalions from Nepal, the Fiji Islands, France, Ireland, Ghana, Finland and Norway. There were also auxiliary units from Italy and Sweden, comprising altogether 5,842 soldiers and officers. The force was mandated to achieve three goals: (1) To ensure complete Israeli withdrawal from South Lebanon. (2) To ensure security and peace in the region. (3) To support the Lebanese Government's attempts to restore its full sovereignty over the region.[299]

In the Security Zone itself, the SLA was backed by an Israeli contingent totalling fewer than 1,000 men.

It followed, therefore, that South Lebanon was a powder keg: full of forces hostile to each other and trying to achieve conflicting goals simultaneously in a small area densely populated by Shi'is, Christians, Sunnis, Druze and Palestinians.[300]

Late in January, the situation in South Lebanon became explosive. On 23 January, Katyusha rockets were fired into Western Galilee from the area south of Tyre, provoking an artillery barrage from Israeli and SLA forces.[301] Later, rumors spread that Israel intended to annex parts of the Security Zone. President Jumayyil charged that a new Israeli electronic fence was designed to detach Lebanese territory from the South. Gen Lahad and Israel denied this charge.[302] On 17 February, there was an escalation in the situation: two Israeli soldiers and an SLA soldier were kidnapped. The "Islamic Resistance" claimed responsibility.[303] Immediately afterwards, a substantial Israeli force started a large-scale search operation outside of the Security Zone in order to find the kidnapped soldiers. During the operation, scores of suspected members of Lebanese militias were detained, bases and headquarters of these militias were demolished and four *Hizballah* men were killed; but the kidnapped soldiers were not found, and one Israeli soldier was also killed. After six days of violent and intensive searches, the Israeli units pulled back to the Security Zone.[304] The Israeli action was designed to indicate to the various hostile elements in South Lebanon that, despite the Israeli withdrawal in 1985, Israel was still strongly dedicated to the concept of the Security Zone, which was considered a success.[305] On the other hand, the harsh retaliatory measures were risky because they could ignite strong anti-Israeli feelings among the local population, and push them to support *Hizballah* instead of the relatively moderate *Amal*. On 26 February another Israeli soldier was killed in the northern part of the Security Zone. Again, the Israelis conducted a large-scale operation to locate the attackers, but it was not as massive as the previous operation.[306] The intense violence in the South prompted Marrack Goulding, the UN Under Secretary-General for special political affairs, to go to Beirut in an attempt to ease tensions and discuss UNIFIL's role.[307] French reservations about the role of the international force in the South comprised the biggest problem facing UNIFIL; the French were concerned about the safety of their units. Another blow to UNIFIL was the decision by the American Congress to cut the US subsidy by $18m.[308] On 19 April, the UN Security Council extended UNIFIL's mandate for three months only, instead of the usual six months.[309] The reason for the shorter extension was the French demand to review again, and as soon as possible, the role of UNIFIL. The sense of urgency injected by French policy did not change matters in the South, where business continued as usual — and that meant more violent skirmishes. On 29 June, five SLA men were killed in an ambush. The SLA retaliated by leveling a nearby Shi'i village.[310]

In mid-July, the UNIFIL mandate was again renewed; this time, the USSR, which had hitherto abstained on votes relating to UNIFIL, voted in favor of renewal. This was in sharp contrast to the American decision regarding UNIFIL (see above). According to a Lebanese source, the Soviets were ready to go a step further in their support of UNIFIL, as their ally, Poland, agreed in principle to provide more troops.[311] Still, the South was simmering. In July, eight rockets were fired into Israel. In August, there were 15 cross-border rocket attacks and 27 against the SLA. In September, the respective figures were 14 and 32. In addition, there were numerous attacks on SLA positions by gunmen.[312] On 12 August, *al-Amal* clashed with French soldiers near Tyre: five Shi'is were killed and 12 Frenchmen wounded.[313] It was not *al-Amal*'s policy to harass UNIFIL and the whole incident was a local affair. *Hizballah*, on the other hand, pursued a different strategy with regard to UNIFIL in general and the French force in particular. *Hizballah* resented the French role in the Iraqi-Iranian war (see essay on the Iraqi-Iranian war and chapters on Iraq, and Iran); besides, it wanted to destabilize the situation altogether as part of its drive to establish an "Islamic Republic" and "liberate" Palestine (see above). *Al-Amal* resented the existence of the Security Zone, but did not want to drive UNIFIL out and did not have any plans to attack Israeli territory proper. The conflicts between the two Shi'i organizations were bound to aggravate tensions and fuel violence in the South. The victims of the next incident were again UNIFIL soldiers. On 4 September, three French soldiers were killed by a remote-controlled bomb. Another French soldier died in a similar explosion on 14 September.[314] Both *al-Amal* and Mufti Kabalan denounced the attacks,[315] and *al-Amal* organized huge demonstrations in favor of UNIFIL staying on. In Tyre, almost 300,000 people joined *al-Amal*'s procession.[316] Troubles, however, continued. *Hizballah* attacked four SLA positions in the eastern section of South Lebanon and took them over while inflicting numerous fatalities on the SLA. Then the Israelis intervened and drove them out.[317] The Fundamentalists attacked the Nepalese battalion east of Tyre. The UNIFIL Commander, Gen Haaglund of Sweden, stated; "I will be the first to recommend UNIFIL's withdrawal if the attacks continue."[318] The deteriorating situation prompted hectic diplomatic activity: Goulding traveled again to Beirut and was quoted as saying that the UN would continue to put pressure on Israel to leave Lebanon completely and allow UNIFIL to replace the SLA in the Security Zone.[319]

In line with this opinion, the UN Security Council approved on 23 September a French draft resolution affirming Resolution 425, calling for the withdrawal of all foreign forces from Lebanese territory, to which the Lebanese Government objected, and urging the deployment of UNIFIL up to the international border. Only the US abstained from voting.[320] This resolution did nothing to improve the situation in South Lebanon. Israel did not leave the Security Zone; Iran, and with it the Shi'i Fundamentalists in South Lebanon, continued to reject Resolution 425. And the French did not stand behind their own initiative. They decided to reduce their contingent from 1,380 to only 520 soldiers, making it the smallest — instead of the largest — element in UNIFIL.[321] On 20 November, a booby-trapped car exploded on the fringes of the Security Zone. Three Fijian soldiers, three Lebanese locals and the two attackers were killed.[322] The man who operated the remote-controlled car bomb was a Shi'i religious leader from the Sidon area, Mahmud Muhammad Farhat.[323] Early in December, *Hizballah* again attacked SLA positions in the eastern sector of the Security Zone. Four SLA men were killed. Afterwards, the SLA conducted a revenge raid on a pro-*Hizballah* Shi'i village and killed some *Hizballah* fighters.[324] The *Hizballah* attacks signaled a new phase in its offensive: the use of relatively large units, well trained and motivated, against SLA positions. *Hizballah* had some local successes, but the SLA did not lose any of its positions and did not disintegrate, despite persistent reports to the contrary in the Lebanese Press.[325]

From the perspective of Israeli policy in South Lebanon, the SLA's performance was satisfactory. The situation in the Security Zone was not ideal, but it could be far worse. The economic situation in this region was far better than in the rest of Lebanon,[326] and the level of facilities and services available to the local population was also far higher than in other parts of South Lebanon.[327] Thus, the local population had sufficient incentives to maintain law and order in their area. In the circumstances of Lebanon in 1986, this was something to write home about.

NOTES

For the place and frequency of publications cited here, and for the full name of the publication, news agency, radio station or monitoring service where an abbreviation is used, please see "List of Sources." Only in the case of more than one publication bearing the same name is the place of publication noted here.

1. *Ha'aretz*, 19 January 1986.
2. R. Beirut, 20 January 1986.
3. R. Beirut, 20 January 1986.
4. *Al-Kifah al-'Arabi*, 27 January 1986.
5. *Al-Nahar*, Beirut, 26 January 1986.
6. *Al-Anwar*, 29 January 1986.
7. VoL, 21 October 1986.
8. VoL, 21 February — DR, 25 February 1986.
9. *Al-Hawadith*, 28 February 1986.
10. VoL, 18 February 1986.
11. MAP, 22 February — DR, 25 February 1986.
12. *Al-Anwar*, 30 March 1986.
13. VoL, 28 April — DR, 29 April 1986.
14. *Al-Qabas*, 27 May 1986.
15. *Al-Qabas*, 14 May 1986.
16. *Al-Shira'*, Beirut, 26 May 1986.
17. Voice of the Revolution, 8 May 1986.
18. *Al-Bayan*, Dubai, 10 June 1986.
19. *Al-Nahar*, Beirut, 15 November 1986.
20. KUNA, 15 June 1986.
21. R. Muscat, 18 June — DR, 19 June 1986.
22. R. Doha, 22 June — DR, 23 June 1986.
23. *Arab Times*, 23 June 1986.
24. *Al-Qabas*, 21 June 1986.
25. Voice of the Mountain, 14 June 1986.
26. *Al-Sayyad*, London, 27 June 1986.
27. VoL, 17 December 1986.
28. *Al-Safir*, 11 November 1986.
29. Voice of Free Lebanon, 31 October 1986.
30. VoL, 4 March — DR, 5 March 1986.
31. R. Beirut, 9 March — DR, 10 March 1986.
32. *Al-Kifah al-'Arabi*, 10 March 1986.
33. VoL, 13 March — DR, 14 March 1986.
34. Ibid.
35. *Al-Nahar*, Beirut, 1 April 1986.
36. For the full text of the plan, see *al-Anwar*, 15 May 1986.
37. R. Beirut, 16 May — DR, 19 May 1986.
38. Voice of the Homeland, 20 May 1986.
39. *CR*: Lebanon, No 3 — 1986, p 7.
40. *CR*: Lebanon, No 3 — 1986, pp 7–8.
41. *CR*: Lebanon, No 4 — 1986, pp 9–10.
42. Voice of Free Lebanon, 1 April 1986.
43. Voice of Free Lebanon, 28 May 1986.
44. *Al-Watan al-'Arabi*, 8 August 1986.

45. *Al-Nahar*, Beirut, 7 November 1986.
46. VoL, 1 December 1986.
47. VoL, 11 March 1986.
48. *Al-Shira'*, Beirut, 15 December 1986.
49. *Al-Watan al-'Arabi*, 14 February 1986.
50. *Al-Dustur*, London, 13 October 1986.
51. Voice of Free Lebanon, 20 February — DR, 21 February 1986.
52. *Al-Shira'*, Beirut, 25 February 1986.
53. *Ma'ariv*, 4 March 1986.
54. *Al-Nahar*, Beirut, 25 February 1986.
55. VoL, 3 March 1986.
56. Voice of Free Lebanon, 8 May — DR, 9 May 1986.
57. VoL, 1 February 1986.
58. *Al-Safir*, 14 June; *al-Ittihad*, Abu Dhabi, 18 July 1986 (respectively).
59. VoL, 28 June 1986.
60. VoL, 9 January — DR, 10 January 1986.
61. *Al-Ittihad*, Abu Dhabi, 9 November; R. Beirut, 12 December — DR, 12 December 1986 (respectively).
62. *Ma'ariv*, 1 January 1986.
63. *IHT*, 12 February: *Ha'aretz*, 22 February 1986 (respectively).
64. AFP, 30 December — DR, 31 December 1986.
65. Voice of Free Lebanon, 14 February — DR, 8 February; VoL, 22 October — DR, 22 October; Voice of Free Lebanon, 6 November — DR, 7 November 1986 (respectively).
66. Voice of the Homeland, 2 February 1986.
67. Voice of Free Lebanon, 17 April 1986.
68. R. Beirut, 21 April 1986.
69. VoL, 26 April — SWB, 30 April 1986.
70. Voice of Free Lebanon, 20 May — DR, 21 May 1986.
71. *Al-Ra'y al-'Amm*, 12 May 1986.
72. *Al-Safir*, 19 June 1986.
73. VoL, 22 October — DR, 22 October 1986.
74. VoL, 7 November — DR, 10 November 1986.
75. R. Beirut, 21 October — DR, 22 October; R. Beirut, 5 November — DR, 6 November 1986.
76. *Al-Bayraq*, 31 May 1986.
77. On the AUB, see G. Antonius, *The Arab Awakening: The Story of the Arab National Movement* (New York: Praeger, 1965), pp 35–51; K.S. Salibi, *The Modern History of Lebanon* (New York: Capricorn Books, 1965), pp 120–48.
78. *Al-Hawadith*, 28 February 1986.
79. *Al-Liwa*, 13 March 1986.
80. AFP, 2 April — DR, 2 April 1986.
81. AFP, 11 April — DR, 14 April 1986.
82. VoL, 20 April — DR, 21 April 1986.
83. Voice of Free Lebanon, 28 April — DR, 29 April; R. Nicosia, 21 June — DR, 23 June 1986 (respectively).
84. VoL, 19 July 1986.
85. AFP, 21 October — DR, 21 October 1986.
86. Voice of Free Lebanon, 12 October 1986.
87. Voice of the Homeland, 22 October 1986.
88. *IHT*, 26 October 1986.
89. *IHT*, 6 March 1986.
90. Voice of Free Lebanon, 17 April — DR, 17 April 1986.
91. *Ha'aretz*, 11 November 1986.
92. Voice of the Homeland, 26 July; AFP, 2 November — DR, 3 November 1986 (respectively).
93. *CR*: Lebanon, No 1, 1987, p 12.
94. *JP*, 17 December 1986.
95. *CR*: Lebanon, No 4, 1986, p 13.
96. *CR*: Lebanon, No 4, 1986, p 14.

97. *CR*: Lebanon, No 1, 1987, p 12.
98. See statements by Junblat, *al-Anwar*, 23 June; and Karami, *al-Liwa*, 18 November 1986 (respectively).
99. Voice of Free Lebanon, 2 July — SWB, 4 July 1986 (respectively).
100. AFP, 19 November — SWB, 21 November 1986.
101. *Al-Ra'y al-'Amm*, 7 April 1986.
102. *Al-Nahar*, Beirut, 16 November 1986.
103. *Al-Nahar*, Beirut, 19 July 1986.
104. *Al-Shira'*, Beirut, 15 September 1986.
105. *Al-Halij*, 18 June 1986.
106. *FT*, 4 July 1986.
107. *Ha'aretz*, 23 November 1986.
108. R. Beirut, 2 December — DR, 2 December 1986.
109. *Al-Liwa*, 20 November 1986.
110. *Al-Nahar*, Beirut, 13 July 1986.
111. *Al-Shira'*, Beirut, 19 May 1986.
112. KUNA, VoL, 2 October 1986.
113. *Al-Yawm al-Sabi'*, 2 November 1986.
114. *Al-Liwa*, 18 January 1986.
115. *Al-Kifah al-'Arabi*, 27 January 1986.
116. *Al-Shira'*, Beirut, 27 January 1986.
117. *Ma'ariv*, 24 January 1986.
118. *Al-Anwar*, 25 January 1986.
119. *Al-Kifah al-'Arabi*, 17 March; *al-Qabas*, 3 October 1986.
120. *The Guardian*, 27 January 1986; *al-Nahar*, Beirut, 28 January 1986.
121. *NAD*, 10 March 1986.
122. *Al-Shira'*, Beirut, 8 September 1986.
123. *NYT*, 22 January 1986.
124. *The Guardian*, 4 February 1986.
125. *The Guardian*, 13 February 1986.
126. Voice of the Homeland, 8 March 1986.
127. *NYT*, 27 March 1986.
128. VoL, 8 April 1986.
129. VoL, 23 May — DR, 23 May 1986.
130. R. Beirut, 4 August — DR, 4 August 1986.
131. Voice of Free Lebanon, 14 August — DR, 14 August 1986.
132. VoL, 11 August 1986.
133. *Al-Nahar*, Beirut, 11 August 1986.
134. VoL, 11 August 1986.
135. *Al-Safir*, 13 August 1986.
136. R. Beirut, 14 August 1986.
137. *Al-Sharq*, 20 October 1986.
138. *Al-Kifah al-'Arabi*, 29 September 1986.
139. *Al-Safir*, 2 November 1986.
140. *Al-Hawadith*, London, 26 December 1986.
141. R. Beirut, 26 September — DR, 30 September 1986.
142. VoL, 27 September — DR, 29 September 1986.
143. VoL, 28 September — DR, 29 September 1986.
144. *Ma'ariv*, 3 October; *al-Safir*, 8 October 1986.
145. R. Beirut, 29 September — DR, 29 September 1986.
146. *Al-Safir*, 6 October 1986.
147. Voice of the Mountain, 1 October — DR, 2 October 1986.
148. *Al-Khalij*, 22 October 1986.
149. VoL, 28 September — DR, 29 September 1986.
150. Voice of Free Lebanon, 28 September — DR, 29 September 1986.
151. R. Ihdin of Free and Unified Lebanon, 28 September — DR, 29 September 1986.
152. *Al-Sharq*, 10 October 1986.

153. *Al-Liwa*, 12 December 1986.
154. VoL, 24 January — DR, 27 January 1986.
155. *Al-Ra'y al-'Amm*, 20 January 1986.
156. *Al-Watan al-'Arabi*, 14 February 1986.
157. *Al-Safir*, 8 January 1986.
158. *Al-Shira'*, Beirut, 27 July 1986.
159. VoL, 5 December — DR, 8 December 1986.
160. Voice of Free Lebanon, 8 December 1986.
161. *Al-Anwar*, 15 December 1986.
162. VoL, 30 December — SWB, 3 January 1987.
163. *Al-Nahar*, Beirut, 12 May 1986.
164. VoL, 16 June — DR, 17 June 1986. For biographical notes on Sa'ada, see *al-Liwa*, 17 June 1986.
165. Voice of Free Lebanon, 17 June — DR, 17 June 1986.
166. *Al-Anwar*, 17 June 1986.
167. *Al-Qabas*, 17 June 1986.
168. *Al-Yawm al-Sabi'*, 30 June 1986.
169. *Al-Nahar*, Beirut, 5 July 1987.
170. *Al-Nahar*, Beirut, 13 August, 17 November 1986 (respectively).
171. VoL, 6 September — SWB, 8 September 1986.
172. Voice of Free Lebanon, 29 September — DR, 30 September 1986.
173. VoL, 20 November 1986.
174. *Al-Hawadith*, Beirut, 31 January; *al-Sha'b*, 19 January 1986 (respectively).
175. *Al-Anba*, 10 February; *Kull al-'Arab*, 5 March; *al-Kifah al-'Arabi*, 10 March 1986.
176. *Al-Kifah al-'Arabi*, 21 April 1986.
177. *Al-Kifah al-'Arabi*, 22 December 1986.
178. *Al-Kifah al-'Arabi*, 17 March 1986.
179. Voice of the Mountain, 13 February 1986.
180. *Al-Kifah al-'Arabi*, 24 February 1986.
181. *Al-Nahar*, Beirut, 4 August; *La Revue du Liban et de l'Orient Arabe*, 23 August 1986.
182. *Al-Watan al-'Arabi*, 28 March 1986.
183. For biographical notes on Sfeir, see *al-Nahar*, Beirut, 20 April 1986.
184. *Monday Morning*, 28 April; *NAD*, 28 April 1986.
185. *Al-Kifah al-'Arabi*, 5 May 1986.
186. Voice of Free Lebanon, 1 October — DR, 2 October 1986.
187. R. Beirut, 22 October — DR, 23 October 1986.
188. *Al-Safir*, 22 March 1986.
189. *Al-Anwar*, 30 March 1986.
190. VoL, 2 April 1986.
191. *Ma'ariv*, 2 April 1986.
192. R. Beirut, 5 April 1986.
193. R. Beirut, 4 April — DR, 7 April 1986.
194. *Al-Safir*, 5 April; R. Free Lebanon, 5 April 1986 (respectively).
195. Voice of Free Lebanon, 19 June 1986.
196. *Al-Watan al-'Arabi*, 11 July 1986.
197. Voice of the National Resistance, 3 September — SWB, 5 September 1986.
198. VoL, 1 November; *NAD*, 10 November 1986.
199. *Al-Nahar*, Beirut, 20 October; Voice of Free Lebanon, 2 November 1986 (respectively).
200. *Al-Anwar*, 9 November 1986.
201. *Al-Dustur*, London, 3 November 1986.
202. *Al-Jumhuriyya*, Beirut, 25 October 1985.
203. *Yedi'ot Aharonot*, 28 January; VoL, 1 February 1986.
204. *Al-Bilad*, Jidda, 1 October 1986.
205. *Al-Anwar*, 9 February; *NAD*, 24 February 1986. On the Palestinians in Beirut, see *al-Shira'*, Beirut, 7, 27 July 1986.
206. *Ha'aretz*, 6 April 1986.
207. *Al-Watan al-'Arabi*, 11 April 1986.

208. R. Beirut, VoL, Voice of Free Lebanon, 27, 28 May — DR, 28 May 1986.
209. *Al-Anwar*, 18 June 1986.
210. VoL, 23 June — SWB, 25 June 1986.
211. VoL, 29 June — DR, 30 June; VoP (Baghdad), 4 August — SWB, 6 August 1986 (respectively).
212. On the Palestinian presence in Tyre, see *NAD*, 13 October 1986.
213. *Davar*, 24 October; *Yedi'ot Aharonot*, 27 October 1986 (respectively).
214. VoL, 11 November — SWB, 13 November 1986.
215. VoP, 10 September 1986.
216. *Ma'ariv*, 7 October 1986.
217. *Ma'ariv*, 21 November 1986.
218. *Ma'ariv*, 20 November 1986.
219. *Ha'aretz*, 5 December 1986.
220. *Tanjug*, 11 December 1986.
221. *Al-Safir*, 26 November 1986.
222. *Ma'ariv*, 25 November, 4 December 1986.
223. JANA, 29 November — DR, 1 December 1986.
224. *Ma'ariv*, 4, 14 December 1986 (respectively).
225. *Ha'aretz*, 30 December 1986.
226. *Al-Difa' al-'Arabi*, 6 October 1986.
227. R. Beirut, VoL, Voice of the Homeland, 10 December 1986.
228. VoP, 15 December — SWB, 17 December 1986.
229. Voice of Free Lebanon, 5 April 1986.
230. VoL, 8 June; *al-Watan al-'Arabi*, 20 June 1986 (respectively).
231. Voice of Free Lebanon, 26 September — DR, 26 September 1986.
232. *Al-Watan al-'Arabi*, 3 October 1986.
233. VoL, 2 October 1986.
234. Voice of Free Lebanon, 2 November — DR, 3 November 1986.
235. VoL, 11 December — DR, 12 December 1986.
236. *Al-Yawm al-Sabi'*, 24 February 1986.
237. *Al-Anwar*, 19 April; *al-Nahar*, Beirut, 21 April; R. Beirut, 15 May — DR, 16 May 1986 (respectively).
238. R. Beirut, 24 November 1986.
239. Voice of Free Lebanon, VoL, R. Beirut, 16, 17 February — DR, 18 February 1986.
240. Voice of Islam, 9 September 1986.
241. M. Kramer, "Muhammad Husayn Fadlallah," *Orient*, Vol XXVI, No 2, June 1985, pp 147–49.
242. For data on *Hizballah*, see *al-Shira'*, Beirut, 17 March 1986; Ehud Ya'ari in *Monitin*, February 1987.
243. *Al-Shira'*, Beirut, 15 September 1986.
244. *Le Point*, 17 April 1986.
245. *Al-Qabas*, 29 September 1986.
246. Ze'ev Schiff, a prominent Israeli military analyst in *Ha'aretz*, 22 September 1986.
247. See Fadlallah's interviews, *Middle East Insight*, 5 March; *NAD*, 10 March; *Jumhuriyye Islami*, 20 May; *al-Shira'*, Beirut, 26 May 1986.
248. 'Ali Kurani, *The Road of Hizballah in Islamic Action* (*Tarikat Hizballah Fi'al-'Amal al-Islami*), (Beirut, np, 1986).
249. *Al-Siyasa*, Kuwait, March 1986.
250. *Al-Nahar*, Beirut, 30 August, 8 September; *al-Mustaqbal*, 13 September 1986.
251. VoL, 12 March — DR, 12 March 1986.
252. *Al-Nahar*, Beirut, 6 May 1986.
253. *Al-Safir*, 16 June 1986; *al-Liwa*, 18 July 1986.
254. Voice of Islam, 26 November 1986.
255. *Yedi'ot Aharonot*, 8 June 1986.
256. *Al-Watan al-'Arabi*, 8 August 1986.
257. Voice of Free Lebanon, 30 June, 8 September — DR, 9 September 1986 (respectively).
258. VoL, 9 September; Voice of Free Lebanon, 1 October 1986.

259. VoL, 8 April; *al-Nahar*, Beirut, 9 April 1986.
260. *Al-Sharq*, 9 April 1986.
261. Voice of Free Lebanon, 6 May — DR, 7 May 1986.
262. *Al-Qabas*, 15 September; *al-Nashra*, 22 September 1986.
263. R. Beirut, 1 March — DR, 3 March 1986.
264, *FR*, 2 October 1986.
265. *Al-Nahar*, Beirut, 6 April 1986.
266. *NAD*, 5 May 1986.
267. *L'Orient le Jour*, 23 September 1986.
268. *Al-Majalla*, 14 May 1986.
269. *Al-Watan al-'Arabi*, 12 June 1986.
270. Voice of the Mountain, 5 June — DR, 6 June 1986.
271. SWB, 30 October 1986.
272. *Al-Liwa*, 30 October 1986.
273. R. Beirut, 22 November 1986.
274. VoL, R. Beirut, AFP, 29, 30 June — DR, 30 June 1986.
275. Voice of Free Lebanon, 26 September — DR, 29 September 1986.
276. *Ha'aretz*, 3 November; *al-Sayyad*, Beirut, 21 November 1986.
277. *Yedi'ot Aharonot*, 21 December 1986.
278. VoL, 22 December 1986.
279. VoL, 24 December 1986.
280. Voice of Free Lebanon, 24 December 1986.
281. R. Beirut, 24 December; R. Damascus, 28 December 1986 (repectively).
282. R. Beirut, 31 December 1986.
283. *Al-Shira'*, Beirut, 14 April 1986.
284. *Al-Nahar*, Beirut, 10 November 1986.
285. VoL, 25 November 1986.
286. VoL, 8 June — SWB, 10 June 1986.
287. *Al-Anba*, Kuwait, 20 November 1986.
288. *Al-Hawadith*, Beirut, 1 August 1986. On the "Islamic Grouping" see also *al-Safir*, 1 September 1986.
289. *Al-Yawm al-Sabi'*, 29 January 1986.
290. *Kull al-'Arab*, 5 March 1986.
291. *Al-Dustur*, Beirut, 10 March 1986.
292. *Al-'Amal*, Beirut, 28 September 1986.
293. Voice of Free Lebanon, 26 May; *al-Majalla*, 3 September; *al-Usbu' al-'Arabi*, 8 September 1986.
294. *Al-Liwa*, 5 January; *al-Sharq al-Awsat*, 10 January; *al-Usbu' al-'Arabi*, 13 January 1986.
295. *Al-Liwa*, 26 February; *al-Siyasa*, Kuwait, 12 April 1986.
296. *Al-Bayraq*, 8 April; *al-Yawm al-Sabi'*, 22 September 1986.
297. *CR*: Lebanon, Cyprus, No 1, 1986, p 9.
298. *NAD*, 9 June 1986.
299. *Ha'aretz*, 17 February 1986.
300. For population estimates concerning the South, see *al-Shira'*, Beirut, 21 April 1986.
301. *CR*: Lebanon, Cyprus, No 2, 1986, p 9.
302. *Ma'ariv*, *Ha'aretz*, 13 February 1986.
303. *Ha'aretz*, 18 February 1986.
304. For full coverage of the search operation, see *Ha'aretz*, 19, 20, 21, 23 February. Also other Israeli newspapers, and UNIFIL report, *al-Nahar*, Beirut, 2 March 1986.
305. Ze'ev Schiff, *Ha'aretz*, 21 February 1986.
306. *Ha'aretz*, 28 February 1986.
307. On Goulding's meeting in Beirut, see *al-Anwar*, 7, 10 March; *al-Sharq*, 11 March 1986.
308. *Al-Liwa*, 5 April 1986.
309. VoL, Voice of the Mountain, 19 April 1986.
310. *CR*: Lebanon, Cyprus, No 3, 1986, p 9.
311. *CR*: Lebanon, Cyprus, No 3, 1986, pp 9–10.
312. *CR*: Lebanon, Cyprus, No 4, 1986, pp 11–12.

313. *CR*: Lebanon, Cyprus, No 4, 1986, p 12.
314. Ibid.
315. R. Beirut, 5 September; *al-Sharq*, 6 September 1986 (respectively).
316. R. Beirut, 17 September 1986.
317. *Ha'aretz*, 21 September 1986.
318. *Ha'aretz*, 25 September 1986.
319. *Al-Nahar*, Beirut, 11 September 1986.
320. R. Beirut, R. Damascus, 24 September — SWB, 26 September 1986.
321. *CR*: Lebanon, Cyprus, No 1, 1987, p 10.
322. VoI, 20 November — DR, 21 November 1986.
323. *Ha'aretz*, 24 November 1986.
324. *Ma'ariv*, 4 December 1986.
325. See for example, *al-Sharq*, 24 March, and a denial by Gen Lahad, Voice of Hope, 23 December — SWB, 29 December 1986.
326. *JP*, 13 May 1986.
327. *Ha'aretz*, 20 October 1986.

Libya

(Al-Jamahiriyya al-'Arabiyya al-Libiyya al-Sha'biyya al-Ishtirakiyya)

YEHUDIT RONEN

Libya's domestic and foreign affairs throughout 1986 were dominated by the conflict with the US, which culminated in the air bombing of Tripoli and Benghazi in mid-April. The attacks and military threats, whether actual or perceived, by the US against the *Jamahiriyya*, provided a new focus for national identification. The Libyan leader, Mu'ammar al-Qadhdhafi, with political cunning exploited the newly created circumstances to mobilize his people's support and to rekindle their "revolutionary" zeal, thus strengthening his hold on the country.

His seemingly smooth and orderly handling of the "People's Power" system during the period under review also enhanced his political prestige.

The annual conference of the General People's Congress (GPC), which convened in February-March in Benghazi, was permeated by a predictably strong anti-American atmosphere. It was almost exclusively devoted to discussions about American "aggressive terrorism." This focus on the dispute with Washington helped to unite the people and provided a welcome distraction from troubling domestic issues.

However, in the period immediately after the American attacks, it seemed that Qadhdhafi's personal and political position had been affected. The Libyan leadership was apparently panic-stricken and stupefied. The capital city reportedly reached the verge of anarchy, and there was much speculation about the status of Qadhdhafi and his close associates. There were rumors of a power struggle between Qadhdhafi and 'Abd al-Salam al-Jallud, a close aide and the Number Two man in the country. It was extremely difficult to gauge the real political strength of Qadhdhafi and the other members of the leadership. However, the opposition, both internal and external, was ineffective. And dissatisfaction in the armed forces was successfully curbed, mainly through the built-in system of close surveillance by the regime's devoted Revolutionary Committees. The sharp drop in oil revenues and the growing discontent of the population did not endanger the regime for the time being.

While the *Jamahiriyya's* foreign affairs were governed by the dispute with the US, which eclipsed all other external events, it did not result in the strengthening of political and military ties with the USSR, though Libya had hoped to project that impression.

Libya's persistent efforts throughout the period reviewed to seek closer ties with Algeria, which included repetitive calls for a formal union, were at the center of Tripoli's inter-Maghrib policies. The *rapprochement* with Algeria made for additional tensions with Morocco, reaching a peak in the summer when Rabat announced the

Egypt, Libya and Sudan

cancellation of the 1984 Federation Agreement with Tripoli. Relations with Tunisia continued along the same trained pattern of earlier years.

Libya remained hostile toward Egypt, but worked strenuously to reinforce its political standing in Sudan. The major importance which Qadhdhafi attributed to his relations with Khartoum was demonstrated by his visit there in the fall during a trip to other African countries.

Tripoli was apprehensive about Chad. The renewed fighting in the fall-winter of the year, stemming from a dramatic realignment of the political allies in Chad, became at the end of 1986 the major concern in Libya's foreign affairs.

INTERNAL AFFAIRS

THE SMOOTH RUNNING OF THE "PEOPLE'S POWER" SYSTEM

THE ANNUAL CONFERENCE OF THE GENERAL PEOPLE'S CONGRESS

Changes in the Top Formal Political Institutions

Even before the American air bombing of Libya on 15 April (see below), the conflict with the US overshadowed internal affairs. Real fear of an imminent American military assault had prevailed at the turn of 1985-86 among the Libyan leadership and population. Qadhdhafi had exploited fully these alarming circumstances to secure important political gains. The dispute with America, the "enemy," had long ceased to be a mere rational reason to contrast different interests and ideologies and had also become a deeply emotional platform to mobilize popular support. Almost every Libyan could sympathize with a small, ostensibly innocent, Arab country facing a serious military threat from an "imperialist" superpower. The almost obsessive preoccupation with the American dispute not only unified the people but also served as a convenient diversion from their economic problems, which had also potentially threatened Qadhdhafi's grip on power.

It was not surprising, therefore, that meetings of the Basic People's Congresses, which had convened throughout the *Jamahiriyya* in early 1986 to debate, and ostensibly determine, the broad guidelines of Libyan domestic and foreign policy that were to be discussed a short while later in the topmost forum of the GPC annual conference,[1] were dominated by a virulent anti-American atmosphere. Qadhdhafi himself had set the tone for dealing with the "US's provocative terrorist acts" against "our great struggling Arab nation,"[2] in his address on 14 January to the meeting of the Basic People's Congress in Tripoli.[3] The Libyan media further inflamed the anti-American and pro-Qadhdhafi sentiments. For instance, the state-controlled television had screened every night during January, when the Basic People's Congresses had been held, pictures from these forums, all of which had verbally assaulted the US and staunchly supported Qadhdhafi and the Revolution.[4]

Against this background the GPC annual conference held from 25 February–2 March in the city of *al-Bayan al-Awal* (Benghazi), was necessarily preoccupied with the conflict with the US, which as stated by the GPC Secretary, "confronts us like a devil."[5] The GPC resolutions mirrored that issue. The central resolution, hardly new, was the "condemnation of Imperialism, Zionism, Racism and Fascism in all their forms in any part of the world." Another resolution referred to the "setting up of suicide squads to hit American and Zionist interests wherever they may be...."[6] (For the economic issues dealt with during the GPC forum, see below.)

Qadhdhafi's political prestige benefited because his "revolutionary" political system, "People's Power," ran smoothly. Boosting the people's belief in the future of the "Revolution" had become increasingly important in previous years because of the significant decline in "revolutionary" brio. Qadhdhafi himself referred to this issue during the GPC conference, expressing his awareness that "for the time being [the Revolution] might not be fully appreciated by us...and even by the contemporary world." Nevertheless, he went on, it was only a matter of time before all would be convinced of its real significance. Qadhdhafi wished to strengthen his argument by referring to the case fo the French philosopher Rousseau: "[At the time of his death] only two of his friends were at his funeral, but after the passage of tens of years, millions...have become assured of the value of his great contribution to humanity."[7]

According to tradition, the GPC conference served also as the forum for administrative and personal changes in the country's top establishment. First, a new General Secretariat was elected to the GPC. There was no substantial departure from the earlier composition in terms of pattern. The new General Secretariat included:[8]

Secretary of the GPC	Dr Muftah al-Usta 'Umar
Assistant Secretary of the GPC	'Abd al-Razik al-Sawsa
Secretary for the Affairs of Congresses	'Umar Iskhal
Secretary for the Affairs of People's Committees	Ibrahim Bukhzam
Secretary for the Affairs of Professional Congresses	Bashir Huwayj
Chairman of the Auditing Bureau	Rajab al-Misallati

At the GPC conference, comprehensive changes were announced in the General People's Committee (GPCom; the equivalent of a Cabinet). These changes were significant, yet they were entirely expected. In fact, they had virtually been anticipated since early summer 1985, when Qadhdhafi had first publicly criticized what he felt was a bad performance of the GPCom, especially its handling of the country's economic affairs (see *Middle East Contemporary Survey* [*MECS*] 1984–85, p 559). Whatever the GPCom's alleged or real failures, Qadhdhafi blamed the country's highest executive body for the deteriorating economic conditions (see below). By blaming it and trying to make it a scapegoat, Qadhdhafi himself evaded responsibility. Accordingly, the GPCom's Secretaries (Ministers in Libyan terminology) had been officially and repeatedly asked since the end of 1985 to account for their actions on television. The Revolutionary Committees — the powerful organs of the "Revolution" which devotedly supported Qadhdhafi in the implementation of his "revolutionary" and political policies — also shielded him from criticism and pressures. The Committees launched strong attacks against the GPCom's Secretaries "for enjoying special cars, drivers, medical treatment, food and servants."[9] The changes made in the GPCom were, therefore, not unexpected.[10] (See Table 1.)

The drastic changes in scope and substance were aimed at improving the GPCom's performances, and also at enhancing the regime's prestige by presenting its leadership as responsible and devoted to the proper handling of the country's internal affairs, while at the same time courageously facing a serious challenge in its foreign relations: the American political, economic and military threat (see below). A salient change was the reduction in the number of the Secretariats from 19 to 11. Apart from wishing to make the GPCom more efficient[11] by cutting the number of portfolios, this was also an effective propaganda move because it was an example of financial restraint for the

TABLE 1: THE COMPOSITION OF THE GENERAL PEOPLE'S COMMITTEE

Portfolio	*Incumbent (as of 7 May 1985)*	*Incumbent (as of March 1986)*
Secretary of the GPCom	Muhammad al-Zaruq Rajab	Zaydallah 'Azuz al-Talhi
Justice	Muftah Muhammad Ku'ayba	
Health	Murad 'Ali Lanqi	'Abdallah Husayn Khaddura
Light Industries	Musa Ahmad Abu Furaywa	Hasan 'Abd al-'Ati al-Barghati
Heavy Industries	'Umar Mustafa al-Muntasir	Hasan 'Abd al-'Ati al-Barghati
Treasury	Muhammad Qasim Sharlallah	Unchanged
Atomic Energy	'Abd al-Majid al-Mabruk al-Qa'ud	—
Electricity	Jum'a Salim al-'Arabash	—
Economic Planning and Acting Secretary of Petroleum	Fawzi al-Shakshuki	Ibrahim Muhammad al-Bishari
Planning	—	Fawzi al-Shakshuki
Education	'Abd al-Hafiz Mahmud al-Zalaytani	—
Social Security	Ibrahim al-Faqi Hasan	—
Public Services	Muhammad 'Abdallah al-Mabruk	Unchanged
Agriculture	Abu Zayd 'Umar Durdah	—
Utilities and Acting Secretary of Housing	Muhammad 'Ubayd al-Shukri	
Foreign Liaison Bureau	'Ali 'Abd al-Salam al-Turayki	Kamal Hasan al-Mansur (al-Maqhur)
Universities	Yusuf Hamed al-Shin	—
Communications and Maritime Transport	Mubarak al-Samikh	Unchanged
Sport	Muhammad Abu Bakr 'Uqaylah	—
Scientific Research Centers	Musa Muhammad 'Umar	Ahmad Ibrahim
Information and Culture	Muhammad al-Fayturi	Unchanged

public. It should be recalled that during recent years, Qadhdhafi and his political bodies had persistently lectured the people on the need for austerity and the reduction of private consumption (see, e.g., *MECS* 1983–84, p 580 and 1984–85, p 558, and below). This was further evidence of his striving for more efficiency and austerity, and for a greater hold over the executive body.

The most noteworthy changes were the replacement of Muhammad al-Zaruq Rajab, hitherto the General Secretary of the GPC, by Zaydallah 'Azuz al-Talhi, and the replacement of 'Ali 'Abd al-Salam al-Turayki, the Secretary of the Foreign Liaison Bureau (or Foreign Minister) by Kamal Hasan al-Mansur (known earlier as Kamal Hasan al-Maqhur). The literal meaning of al-Maqhur is "the vanquished." Qadhdhafi had reportedly asked al-Maqhur to change his name to al-Mansur — "the victorious," since, the Libyan leader argued, "in the Libyan Revolution there is nobody who is vanquished; all are victorious."[12] These changes did not, however, herald a substantial new departure in the country's political buildup; all the newly appointed officials were well-known veterans in Libyan politics. Al-Talhi, the new General Secretary of the GPCom had already served in that post in 1979–84, when he was replaced by Rajab. Al-Talhi was considered a most trusted man and served until his new appointment in 1986 as the head of the Libyan leader's personal Secretariat within the Bab al-'Aziziyya barrack headquarters in Tripoli.[13] (Qadhdhafi's Secretariat, it should be noted, was an entirely separate organ from the formal scheme of the "People's Power" system.) Rajab was not appointed to any other formal office, but his "disappearance" from the formal hierarchy did not necessarily mean the end of his political career. While this possibility cannot be ruled out at this stage, it is equally possible that Rajab was put aside for a while as part of Qadhdhafi's shrewd tactics to prevent senior political figures from accumulating political strength which might later threaten his own power.

The other conspicuous change was the replacement of al-Turayki by al-Mansur (al-Maqhur). The latter, a former Petroleum Secretary, served as the Libyan head of the Arab-African Union — the body formed after the 1984 signing of the Federation Agreement with Morocco (see below). The dismissal of al-Turayki, a veteran politician who had served from 1982–84 as his country's permanent representative at the United Nations and as Qadhdhafi's personal envoy for special foreign missions, was due to "health reasons," as claimed by sources in Tripoli.[14] It should be noted that Turayki's health problems had been referred to in public in previous years,[15] as well as several weeks before his dismissal in early March. A foreign source claimed that al-Turayki had been flown to Europe for medical treatment for either kidney failure of diabetic complications.[16] Whatever the true reason for Turayki's removal, in the immediate had been flown to Europe for medical treatment for either kidney failure or diabetic country's delegate to the UN.[17] This served as clear evidence of Qadhdhafi's confidence in and special appreciation of his diplomatic skills. Late in November, Turayki became the *Jamahiriyya's* envoy to Canada.[18] Another new appointment was that of Ahmad Ibrahim to the post of Education Secretary. Ibrahim is Qadhdhafi's nephew and a leading ideologue in the Revolutionary Committees.[19] Qadhdhafi perhaps hoped to achieve through Ibrahim greater control in the shaping of Libya's ideological and political face.[20]

THE POLITICAL SCENE (from the American Attack until the End of the Year)

A smoke screen covered Tripoli's political affairs in the period immediately after the American air bombing on 15 April 1986. Qadhdhafi's failure to appear in public and, even more significant, to give any sign of life for nearly 48 hours after the attack only added vagueness and uncertainty to the scene. Rumor had it that Qadhdhafi had been seriously hurt, physically or mentally, and rushed out of the country. The death of his adopted daughter and the severe injury of two sons, as well as the heavy casualties and the damage to his residence and headquarters in Bab al-'Aziziyya,[21] had lent credence to statements that the Libyan leader was injured. At the same time, however, one could not rule out the possibility that Qadhdhafi had chosen to disappear to prevent, or at least significantly reduce, any possible threat to his personal and political position, either from the Americans or the domestic opposition, especially from the Army. No official explanation was given for Qadhdhafi's mysterious disappearance. However, one foreign source reported that Qadhdhafi had been in South Yemen, apparently to meet Soviet officials and organize support for his regime. Twenty hours after he returned, reported the same source, Qadhdhafi went to Sebha, his home province, instead of Tripoli.[22] Libyan official sources denied, however, all the "stories" about Qadhdhafi's absence, noting mockingly that they made the Libyans "burst out laughing in the streets."[23]

Official statements notwithstanding, it was hardly surprising that the shooting that broke out on 16 April around Qadhdhafi's headquarters and residence in the 'Aziziyya barracks was interpreted by foreign sources as an attempted coup by dissident army personnel.[24] This claim was further reinforced when Maj Qadhdhaf al-Damm, Qadhdhafi's cousin and a senior official in the Libyan secret services, referred to security problems in Tripoli at that time.[25] Nevertheless, the state-controlled media, which had played a crucial role in that sensitive period rallying support for Qadhdhafi's leadership, quickly denied any military uprising, and claimed that the firing had been directed at US reconnaissance aircraft.[26] Whatever the actual truth, it seemed that Tripoli had undergone a state of "near anarchy" in the wake of the attack, as one foreign report described it, with the Army, politicians and security services issuing diverse instructions.[27] In addition, it was reported that Libyans had fled their capital city in panic.[28] The dismissal of 'Umar Latif, the head of Internal Security, two days after the attack,[29] strengthened the impression that the Libyan leadership and establishment were acutely confused, perhaps partly paralyzed, immediately after the attack.

Qadhdhafi appeared for the first time since the attack on the night of 16 April to address the nation on television. He did not refer to his mysterious absence. Predictably, he strongly condemned the American attack, emphasizing that he would not stop inciting "revolution whatever raids [the Americans] carried out." Qadhdhafi further urged his people to dance in the streets. "Turn on the lights [and] dance...We were not afraid of America...We have Allah on our side and Allah is stronger than America," he said during a 20-minute address. It could not be ascertained whether Qadhdhafi had spoken live or on videotape.[30] Qadhdhafi's statement was immediately echoed and amplified by the other media, which played a decisive role in calming down the nervous capital and boosting Qadhdhafi's political prestige. "Let us stick together against the American savages..." and "let us stress our unshakable, firm faith in our principles and aims...our insistence on our leader, thinker, teacher and guide...Qadhdhafi," the media repeatedly stated.[31] The media's endeavor to strengthen the patriotic feelings of the populace was reinforced by the use of new terminology. On 20 April, five days after the attack, it was officially announced that "from now on" and "in accordance with popular demand," the word "Great" is added to the official name of the country "because the great *Jamahiriyya* has withstood the biggest power in the world...."[32] Another decision that should be viewed within the context of enhancing nationalistic sentiments was the return, in June of that year, "to [the use of the] Arabic names of [the] solar year months" in accordance with "Arab values" and in a "rejection of imperialist cultural piracy...."[33]

Meanwhile, the authorities' awareness of the dangers inherent in a static situation, especially since popular resentment of economic hardships was increasing (see below), prompted them to feverishly activate the media. The American attack and threat of further attack occupied a dominant place in the media throughout this whole period, almost entirely eclipsing all other internal affairs. Qadhdhafi used all his rhetorical talent to mobilize the people against the US, and indirectly to inflame their nationalistic and "revolutionary" fervor, to reinforce their support of the "Revolution" and his leadership. The American raids "cannot cancel the revolutionary principles even if the US undertakes to drop its nuclear bombs on our territories," said Qadhdhafi. "We are ready to adhere to our principles and to die defending our land."[34] On another occasion he said: "Let the [US] aircraft carriers come. If there is a landing on Libyan shores, it will be annihilated because we and the fish are awaiting them."[35]

These haughty statements conflicted sharply with the prevailing rumors in the summer that the Libyan leader was physically or mentally ill, or was even facing a serious challenge to his power.[36] Moreover, the authorities' abrupt cancellation in mid-June of an annual public holiday marking the 16th anniversary of the evacuation of US troops from Libya[37] created further speculation and mystery. Eventually, instead of delivering the speech in public, as was promised earlier by his aides and as was the tradition, Qadhdhafi spoke from a telelvision studio at a secret location. Unlike his other TV appearances there was no audience present to cheer him.[38] It was not known whether the speech was broadcast live or videotaped earlier. Qadhdhafi reportedly looked "tired," "sickly" and even "drugged," as some who watched the appearance thought.[39] The public reaction to his sickly appearance was so strong that Qadhdhafi felt compelled to react immediately. He dismissed the rumors that he was ill, psychologically unbalanced or no longer in daily control of the Government, as "untrue." In his first meeting with a Western reporter since the American attack, he said: "As you can see, I am fine." He admitted, however, that he was "very tired," but attributed this to fasting during the month of Ramadan.[40]

Qadhdhafi was eager to convey the impression that he had a strong grip on the country. This sharply contradicted claims by foreign sources that there were tensions and even violent rivalaries between Qadhdhafi and the Army's Command, as well as within the core of the Libyan leadership. Several reports alleged that Qadhdhafi had dismissed a "large number" of military commanders for failing to confront the US air raids in April.[41] Another (hostile) source even reported the placing of a number of senior officers under house arrest.[42] Regarding the alleged power struggle in the Government's top ranks, it was reported that Qadhdhafi's Number Two man, 'Abd al-Salam Jallud, had "narrowly" escaped being assassinated at his home in Tripoli in mid-May. Jallud was reported unhurt, but one gunman from the tribe of Qadhdhafi's wife was killed and a cousin of Qadhdhafi was injured.[43] The "false story" was categorically denied in Tripoli and was termed a "cheap joke."[44] However, there were persistent reports of a serious power struggle between Qadhdhafi and Jallud in the autumn of 1986.[45] At the end of July, other foreign sources reported that an attempt had been made on Jallud's life.[46] It was not clear, however, whether they were referring to the abortive attempt in May or to another one. Qadhdhafi's transfer of his command post from Tripoli to al-Bayda, near Tobruk, an area inhabited by his wife's tribe,[47] could also be interpreted as a sign of his lack of confidence in Jallud, although this was not officially hinted at. But there could have been other reasons. In the summer there was a new wave of rumors, mostly by hostile sources, claiming that Qadhdhafi faced additional serious threats to his political position and his very life.[48]

By the end of August, Qadhdhafi's behavior had changed remarkably. On the eve of the 17th anniversary of the 1 September Revolution that brought Qadhdhafi to power, he emerged publicly after several months of self-imposed withdrawal. He led a comprehensive tour of various coastal villages and municipalities greeting large crowds of "young followers" and turning meetings into demonstrations of support for the Revolution and his leadership.[49] The tour culminated in a rally in Tripoli on 31 August, when he addressed nearly 5,000 leaders of Revolutionary Committees from throughout the country. In his speech, he virulently attacked the US.[50]

Following the celebrations, Qadhdhafi went on a relatively long tour of Africa, his first since the American attack. That tour, and later visits to various centers in Libya, were intended to counter speculation that he was losing his grip over the *Jamahiriyya*. The relative ineffectiveness of domestic and expatriate opposition (see *MECS* 1984–85, pp 562–63) had undoubtedly contributed significantly to his success in retaining control. Yet it should be noted that by the end of the period under review, it was difficult to gauge the strength of Qadhdhafi's position.

CONTINUING ECONOMIC DIFFICULTIES: A POTENTIAL THREAT TO QADHDHAFI'S LEADERSHIP

Libya's economy was hard hit in 1986 by the continuing drop in world oil prices.[51] The *Jamahiriyya's* annual oil income fell from a peak of $22 bn in 1980 to $10 bn in 1985,[52] and it was expected to be almost half that in 1986.[53] The aggravating economic conditions were felt at both the national and local levels. The state budget for 1986, which had been ratified in early March at the GPC conference (see above), clearly reflected the difficulties. For example, the import budget, the most effective instrument to control the rate of economic development, was reduced by 6.3 per cent from LD 1.5 bn ($5.07 bn) to LD 1.411 bn ($4.77 bn) in 1986, with a recommendation "to import only essential goods — basic commodities, medicines, medical equipment, foodstuffs, spare parts and equipment needed to operate factories for agriculture."[54]

Nor did other economic data brighten the bleak picture. Foreign reserves in cash and gold were down to between $5.9 bn and $2-3 bn[55] (from the 1980 peak of about $13 bn).[56] The external debt was estimated at about $6.5 bn at mid-1985.[57]

The deteriorating economic situation, combined with the authorities' mismanagement,[58] resulted in more and more dissatisfaction. Acute shortages of food and other essential products affected daily life. There were shortages of a wide range of commodities, including meat (which some wealthy Libyans were reportedly flying to the neighboring island of Malta to buy)[59] and fresh produce. The chain of state-sponsored supermarkets, opened in 1980–81,[60] had relatively few items to sell. The Government tried to ease the hardship by opening a farmers' market outside Tripoli where farmers could sell fresh fruit and vegetables privately at higher prices, instead of through government monopolies.[61] The shortage in agricultural products was reportedly so acute that "at least" two Libyans died early in the year in a violent scramble for Nicaraguan bananas.[62]

The country's development, including the "Great Man-Made River," the *Jamahiriyya's* ambitious infrastructure project,[63] had been curtailed. Austerity was imposed on the people while tankers filled with oil were moored, without anywhere to go, in Libyan harbors.[64] (For further details of the economic hardships, which led, *inter alia*, to the expulsion of thousands of foreign workers in autumn 1985, see also *MECS* 1984–85, pp 560–61.)

The enormous scale of economic hardship troubled Qadhdhafi, especially since the economic recession had negatively affected the military — the most serious potential threat to Qadhdhafi's power. A number of military construction projects were canceled or curtailed, and some military commissary privileges were withdrawn. The waste and diminished privileges had in turn reportedly increased resentment.[65] Being highly aware of the danger presented to his regime's stability by the deteriorating economic conditions, Qadhdhafi downplayed, at least in public, the severity of the crisis. The Libyan leader tried to create the impression that the country's financial squeeze was merely a temporary situation, which could be overcome if Libyan citizens adjusted to austerity and increased productivity. In his festive speech to the GPC conference, and by extension to the whole Libyan populace, Qadhdhafi stated: "The important thing is that we will not be hungry, thirsty, [and] without clothing until the end of the oil problem." Qadhdhafi continued his speech in an encouraging tone, saying: "It is possible, in a simple way, to overcome [the] crisis. No matter how much we lost in the [oil] price drop, the loss was only in terms of luxury and extravagant items we used to buy." Qadhdhafi concluded his speech optimistically: "The price of oil will increase again [and] we have reserves of oil and gas for scores of years."[66]

Although he appeared to brighten the relatively bleak picture, Qadhdhafi did not underestimate the severity of the economic problem. He demonstrated his concern by advising his representatives to the forum of the Organization of Petroleum Exporting Countries (OPEC) to convince the member countries to reduce their oil production and contribute, thereby, to the stabilization of oil prices. OPEC's reluctance to meet the Libyan demand[67] was strongly condemned by Tripoli, which saw the OPEC policy as endangering Libya's "vital interests." Qadhdhafi even went so far as to term OPEC's policy a "declaration of war against the *Jamahiriyya.*"[68] It is a "real war, no less significant than the war of planes and warships that destroy factories and the economic effort of any country," Qadhdhafi noted on another occasion.[69] OPEC's policy and his country's increasing financial problems preoccupied the Libyan leader, who later said, "the continuing state of not reducing oil production is a waste of the principal national wealth of the Arab people and [it is] tantamount to conspiring against the Arab nation."[70] One might assume that the popular anger over the lack of goods, which allegedly resulted in "minor riots"[71] at the end of the fast of Ramadan, increased Qadhdhafi's comprehension of another, and perhaps even more serious, eruption of popular anger over the same problems. Qadhdhafi's repeated exhortations to his people, to take further austerity steps and add to their contribution for the sake of their country, were entirely expected. The Libyan leader called on every Libyan to donate about one month's salary to buy weapons to arm Libyan cities "to destroy any future American aggression."[72] Under these circumstances, it is easy to understand why Qadhdhafi allowed the reappearance of "unrevolutionary" phenomena, such as small private food stores, especially bakeries. His repeated calls for the adoption of a barter system in the *Jamahiriyya*, which would lead to "an end in dealing with money,"[73] should also be seen within the context of the country's financial crisis.

Nevertheless, despite the alleged riots at the end of Ramadan, there was no other overt evidence to indicate at the close of the period reviewed that economic pressures had been translated into a significant threat to Qadhdhafi's control.

FOREIGN AFFAIRS

THE UNITED STATES

Libyan-US tensions significantly escalated during the period under review. The US officially accused Qadhdhafi of complicity in the terrorist attacks that took place at the Rome and Vienna airports on 27 December 1985.[74] Libyan officials were quick to deny any responsibility for the attacks.[75] At the same time, however, Qadhdhafi reiterated his sympathy for those who had carried out the attacks, which he justified. "What took place [in Rome and Vienna] cannot be carried out by a UN member-state [such as Libya?]." Nevertheless, he elaborated, "what a group of Palestinians had carried out was a different thing, for Palestinians...[are] forced to act outside the law...."[76] The Palestinians, Qadhdhafi continued, "do not have aircraft to hit military targets... [therefore] they express [themselves] by hitting at Israelis everywhere."[77]

Qadhdhafi's provocative statements were compounded by vitriolic propagandist assaults by his media on the "Black House" in Washington[78] and the "Israeli dog barking in the Zionist farm."[79]

Bilateral tensions increased sharply during the first week of January when Qadhdhafi declared "a state of maximum alert" in his armed forces because the US had reinforced its forces in the Mediterranean "offshore of Libya."[80] Tripoli's growing sense of fear that an American attack was imminent was also echoed in Qadhdhafi's repeated threats to "turn the waters of the Gulf of Sidra into blood" and its territory into "a graveyard for any invaders."[81]

Meanwhile, the American Administration contributed to the seriously aggravating friction. On 7 January, President Reagan stated that Libya constitutes "a threat to the national security and foreign policy of the US." The next day, he severed economic ties with Libya and ordered the 1,000–1,500 Americans in Libya "to leave immediately."[82] Then he ordered a freeze on hundreds of millions of dollars of Libyan assets in American banks and their subsidiaries.[83] Tripoli reacted by announcing that the American economic sanctions were being considered as "tantamount politically to a declaration of war."[84] (It should be recalled that the US had used such punitive measures during earlier crises with Libya; see e.g., *MECS* 1981–82, p 741.)

The American economic sanctions, which went into effect on 1 February,[85] were colored by Washington's virulent attacks on the Libyan leader. Qadhdhafi "is not only a barbarian but he is [also] flaky,"[86] stated Reagan. Qadhdhafi responded a day later: "I did not hear that Reagan is a doctor or psychiatrist. I know that he was a bad actor." Qadhdhafi further accused the American President of being a "fool" and "a poor fellow" who "has arteriosclerosis due to old age."[87] This bitter war of words exacerbated the tension, and culminated in the middle of January in a clash between Libyan and US aircraft over the Mediterranean.[88] (A similar incident occurred in the fall of 1980 and full-scale aerial combat occurred in summer 1981. For more details on both events, see *MECS* 1980–81, pp 700–1.) Libya's growing concern that it might be attacked by the US was mirrored by Qadhdhafi's warnings to Washington not to attack or provoke Libya militarily. "Had [the Americans] continued their advance [to the Gulf of Sidra], war would have broken out,"[89] he said. "We were waiting for the [US] ships to cross the 32° 30′ degree line of latitude that marks the beginning of the Gulf of Sidra. This was the 'red line' which, if they had crossed it, would have had clashes begin between us and them,"[90] Qadhdhafi further stated. Libya combined its warnings with threats to activate suicide squads "to combat the US everywhere."[91] The American Administration retaliated by ordering on 24 January extensive naval flight operations off Libya for a week.[92] This further increased tensions; Libya branded the American move as "power mania," describing the US as "a moth that cannot keep away from the flame until it is completely burnt up,"[93] and warning it not "to play with fire."[94]

On 25 January, during a peak in the war of nerves, Qadhdhafi boarded a Libyan missile boat and sailed into the Gulf of Sidra for what he said was a confrontation with the US. "Libya is not going to be content to live under international terrorism forever," he stated dramatically. "I am now going on board this patrol boat to parallel 32° 30′ to stress that this is the gate to the Gulf of Sidra... the death line where we shall stand and fight with our backs to the wall...."[95] (Libya and the US had been at odds over Libyan's persistent claims to the Gulf of Sidra since 1973, when Libya announced that it considered the territorial waters and airspace from parallel 32° 30′ southwards to be an integral part of its territory. The US maintained, however, that the disputed area was international.)[96] Tension kept mounting in February. On 8 February Libya announced one week of maneuvers. Four days later, the US Sixth Fleet began a series of exercises off the Libyan coast, referred to by Tripoli as "terrorist aggression."[97] Libya's growing suspicion that "a criminal plan has been drawn up against the people of the *Jamahiriyya*..."[98] was further strengthened on 19 March, when US warships led by aircraft carriers began new exercises in the Mediterranean, near the disputed waters of the Gulf of Sidra.

On 24 March, there was a military clash. On the morning of that day, the Libyans announced: "The US Air Force began violating the airspace over the Libyan Arab territorial waters [in the Gulf of Sidra]. Our air defenses combated it and shot down three aircraft... [which] fell into the sea."[99] Tripoli stipulated on that occasion its determination to "teach the US a lesson worse than the lesson of Vietnam."[100] The White House claimed the clashes began because Libya had fired two long-range SA-5 surface-to-air missiles from Sidra at US aircraft "operating in international waters in the Gulf." The official American announcement added that US naval aircraft had retaliated by attacking two Libyan vessels and a missile site on Libyan soil.[101] On 25 March, US naval aircraft again attacked a Libyan missile site near Sidra. A Pentagon spokesman said the strikes were made because it appeared that the Libyan patrol ships were maneuvering to attack US ships.[102] The two-day clash resulted in the death of between 56 and 72 Libyans.[103] Nevertheless, these data were neither confirmed nor denied by Tripoli, which did not release any official figures of casualties and damage.

Whatever the scope of the damage, it was apparently serious enough to motivate Libya, at least as reported by American and other foreign sources, to attempt to open a dialogue with Washington. Qadhdhafi reportedly sent two high-ranking emissaries to Saudi Arabia to meet Vice President George Bush, who was scheduled to arrive in Riyadh.[104] Libya, however, categorically denied this.[105]

The bombing aboard an American Trans-World Airlines jet on 2 April 1986 in Karachi elicited the White House announcement that it viewed Qadhdhafi as "a suspect."[106] Libya released an immediate official denial.[107] On 5 April a West Berlin nightclub, frequented by American soldiers, was bombed; more than 150 people were wounded and two were killed, one of them an American soldier. The US Administration accused Qadhdhafi of being linked to the event though it admitted that it had no hard evidence to implicate him directly. The Administration said that the incident appeared to be part of a "pattern of indiscriminate violence" against Americans by Qadhdhafi.[108] Tripoli protested over what it called "the American state of hysteria" and "obsession" with Qadhdhafi, which it added, stemmed from the "spreading of the cancerous tumor" throughout the American President's "frail body."[109] Tripoli accompanied its protest with repeated denials of any connection with "the recent wave of [terrorist] attacks."[110] Tripoli continued to fear an imminent American military strike and again threatened that it would attack American targets with suicide squads if the US attacked Libya.[111] Tripoli prepared for that eventuality by taking measures to reduce possible damage in case of attack.[112] However, on the eve of the American air raids, Libya virtually waited passively for an attack.

On the morning of 15 April 1986, the long-feared American attack occurred. During the day, the Libyan media released reports of the "treacherous and barbarous air raid" saying in its first announcement to the "Libyan and Arab people" that the "residence of the brother leader of the Revolution" had been attacked. "A number of members of [his] family were injured," the announcement continued, adding that the "American barbarous air raid is continuing against populated and civilian quarters of Tripoli." A short while later, Tripoli announced the shooting down of three aircraft of "the American enemy." The radio also reported the death of the American pilots "in accordance with the principle of reciprocal treatment" for the "American aggression" on the crew of a Libyan boat after it was hit on 24 March in the Gulf of Sidra.[113]

Whether the Libyan media lacked at that stage a clear picture of the events, or whether they deliberately avoided dispersing the prevailing fog, remained unclear. Whatever the case, Tripoli's media took the "safe course" of channeling all its efforts that day and on subsequent days to launch fierce anti-American verbal attacks, and at the same time to further inflame the people's rage and incite them to take revenge on the US. By suggesting this outlet for indignation, it kept the public from possibly turning against the regime. This clearly helped Qadhdhafi in the fragile circumstances. Following the same line, the media intensively urged the Libyans, as well as "all Arab brothers," to avenge the American attack. "Every drop of blood... must be avenged. We here are drinking [the American] blood. But every one of you [Arabs] can in his own place also drink from the blood of the Americans: there are their embassies... companies, offices... [and] there are Americans living in the Arab capitals... Oh Arab[s], slaughter [the Americans] like sheep."[114] While broadcasting martial music and national songs, Tripoli's media also tried to boost morale. The repeated announcements of the "heavy damages" which "our brave sons" inflicted upon the "enemy" should be viewed within this context. "At least" 20 F-111 American aircraft were shot down by the *Jamahiriyya's* armed forces,[115] Radio Tripoli announced on 15 April. Later that day, it announced the "total destruction" of an American-manned communication installation on the Italian island of Lampedusa in retaliation for the US raid.[116] While the Libyan media refrained from giving details of the attacked targets, the American Administration did. They included Qadhdhafi's headquarters in *Bab al-'Aziziyya* barracks in Tripoli (which also served as his family's residence); the military section of Tripoli airport; the Sidi Bilal port military complex; the *Jamahiriyya* barracks in Benghazi, and the Benina military airfield there.[117]

The attack, with its officially admitted 37 dead and 93 wounded,[118] corroborated the well-rooted Libyan perception of being persecuted. "The American aggression does not aim in reality at anything but the destruction and demolition of the stronghold of freedom and the struggle against Imperialism, Zionism and Racism in the world, and the frontline of resistance in the Arab homeland represented by the *Jamahiriyya*."[119] Tripoli had vehemently dismissed at the same time the notion that "the issue of terrorism was the basis of the attack."[120]

Military tensions remained high during the whole second half of 1986, as Libya feared another attack. In mid-June, Libya announced a three-day missile-firing exercise in an apparent response to renewed US Sixth Fleet activity off its coast. One month later, both countries held rival maneuvers in the Gulf of Sidra.[121]

The joint US-Egyptian military exercises on 25–29 August near the Libyan border provoked renewed suspicion of Washington (and Cairo).[122] Libya demonstrated an increased level of nervousness in late summer 1986, which was expressed *inter alia* in Tripoli's definition of the American President as the "Hitler of the 20th century wanting to destroy the world."[123] Among other slanderous names used by the Libyan media when referring to Reagan were "mad dog,"[124] "rabid dog,"[125] and "leader of terrorism."[126] The US retaliated by significantly intensifying its verbal war against Qadhdhafi.[127] The latter responded by sternly warning that he would "fight America everywhere."[128]

The hijacking on 5 September of a Pan American plane in Karachi elicited an immediate Libyan denial of any involvement in the event. This, too, reflected Tripoli's fears of an American military strike. Libya accused the US of trying to attribute the hijacking to Libya in order "to create feeble pretexts for aggression and justifying it."[129] This trend continued to dominate Libya's attitude toward the US at the close of the period reviewed.

WESTERN EUROPE

BRITAIN

British-Libyan relations, already strained, underwent a severe crisis when the British Government authorized US F-111s to fly from bases in Britain to attack Libya on 15 April, and the British Government's subsequent justification of the American attack further inflamed Libya. Libya denounced Britain very clearly by saying: The "killer of children"[130] was not content with being "a rotten lackey to terrorist Reagan by allowing the use of US bases and aircraft on British territories to strike at the Libyan Arab people... but the old Thatcher assumed the role of advocate to defend terrorist Reagan... and to allege that the *Jamahiriyya* is a center for terrorism."[131]

From that point on, mutual recriminations increased. On 18 April, London announced that it had "firm evidence of direct Libyan involvement" in the kidnapping of two British teachers who were killed in Lebanon a day earlier in an apparent reprisal for the bombing raid by F-111s flying from British bases.[132] Libya denied any connection with the whole affair.[133] Either way, on 22 April, the British authorities ordered the deportation of 21 Libyan students who were said to constitute a threat to national security. The Libyans were not accused of any specific crime, but were known, according to the Home Office spokesman, as "revolutionary" activists in the UK.[134] Two days later, more than 300 Libyan pilots and aviation engineers training in Britain were banned from handling civilian aircraft and were expected to leave Britain. Their restriction had reportedly been under consideration since early April, when the Tripoli radio station reportedly broadcast a telephone call from one of them who volunteered for "suicide missions" against US installations in Britain.[135] Libya characterized the British moves against its citizens as "extremely barbarous and savage," and "devoid of any human and civilized principles."[136] It should be noted that the British deportation orders followed the decision of the European Economic Community (EEC) to curb the presence and activities of Tripoli's representatives in their countries. On 31 April Libya retaliated against the EEC decision by expelling more than 100 Britons, Spaniards and Italians.[137]

The next move came from Britain in early October when London announced that its air services agreement with Libya, which was to expire on 31 October, would not be renewed because of Libya's alleged support of terrorism.[138] Libya responded angrily by challenging Britain (to which it referred as America's "stationary US aircraft carrier") to produce evidence to back the accusation.[139] Later in October, Tripoli further responded by announcing its decision to teach the "stupid woman" a lesson,[140] and on the 25 of that month, it closed its airspace to British aircraft, in support of what Tripoli referred to as "Syria's breaking of relations with Britain."[141] That crisis atmosphere continued unabated until the close of the year.

ITALY

A new source of strain was injected into Libyan-Italian relations after 15 April 1986, when Libya launched a retaliatory attack against an American military installation on the Italian island of Lampedusa (see above). Bilateral tension continued to grow steadily. Libya reacted to the expulsion in late April of ten Libyan diplomats from Rome by expelling 25 of Italy's diplomatic personnel from Libya.[142] (The expulsions were not directed exclusively against Italy but were part of the broader Libyan reaction to the EEC decision of late April to support a US campaign against alleged Libyan-backed terrorism; see above). On 13 May, Rome expelled a diplomat from Libya's consulate in Palermo; ten days later, Italy ordered Libya, once again, to reduce its diplomatic staff in Rome.[143]

Another crisis between the two countries developed in October following Qadhdhafi's reference to Italy as Libya's "enemy Number One" because it was a base for the "official terrorism" of the US.[144] It was odd that Qadhdhafi's verbal attack on Italy coincided with an exchange deal by the two countries, according to which Libya freed four Italians for three Libyans convicted of the murder and attempted murder of Libyan opponents of Qadhdhafi in Italy.[145]

THE SOVIET UNION

Soviet efforts to reinforce Libya's military strength, particularly its air defense systems,[146] against what Tripoli considered an imminent American air attack (see also *MECS* 1984–85, pp 571–72), increased at the beginning of 1986. Moscow's military support was accompanied by political backing.[147] Qadhdhafi expressed his gratitude to the Soviets "for their supporting stand against the US."[148] At the same time he repeatedly mentioned Tripoli's plan to consider joining a military alliance with the Soviet Union (see below). However, his talks of closer relations with the USSR and his repeated statements about joining the Warsaw Pact should be viewed as much in the context of his relations as of his conflict with the US. Qadhdhafi wished to deter an attack from Washington and at the same time boost his political prestige and his people's morale in the face of America's alarming threat. The visit to Moscow by Abu Bakr Yunis, the Libyan Commander in Chief of the Armed Forces, on 24 January, which was followed a month later by that of 'Abd al-Salam Jallud, Qadhdhafi's closest aide, who was known for his close personal ties with the Soviet leadership, corroborated Libyan threats that it would draw politically and militarily closer to the Soviet Bloc.[149]

In late March, immediately following the outbreak of military hostilities between Libya and the US, the Kremlin voiced its support, which it limited to words. Furthermore, as claimed by an American source, the Soviets did not even pass on satellite data or other intelligence from Soviet ships in the Mediterranean as clashes occurred between Libya and the US.[150]

The American air attack on 15 April created a new measure of tension in Libyan-Russian relations. Though Moscow strongly condemned the US, it once again reportedly avoided passing on information to Libya regarding the imminent attack, which, according to American Intelligence, the Soviets surely knew about.[151] Another source, however, claimed that the USSR had warned Libya one hour in advance.[152] Whatever the truth, one foreign source reported that during the attack itself, Russian military advisers in Libya stayed in their underground bunkers, despite Libyan entreaties to help put up new launching pads.[153] Moreover, yet another foreign source reported that Moscow had pulled out several hundred military advisers from Libyan missile bases only two days before the US attack.[154] In light of these reports, it was not surprising that Tripoli was disappointed and disturbed by what it considered insufficient support from the Soviet Union. Qadhdhafi expressed publicly, though indirectly, his criticism of the Soviet stand during the American attack.[155] At the same time, however, Libya continued to warn (the West, and particularly the US) of its intention to join the Warsaw Pact. Qadhdhafi himself stated in late April that the American attack was forcing Libya "to become another Cuba and to declare its full alignment with the Warsaw Pact."[156] The official decision announced later in May to "end the teaching of English at all educational stages and the beginning of teaching the Russian language instead,"[157] lent further credence to Qadhdhafi's threats to "get out of our neutrality" and move closer to the Soviet bloc.[158]

Jallud's five-day official visit to the USSR, which began on 26 May, was aimed at discussing Libya's joining of the Warsaw Pact.[159] Jallud himself stated soon after the visit: "Libya is currently negotiating the practical arrangements for a future collaboration with the Warsaw Pact," and added that "Libya had come to believe that neutrality is the same as naïveté."[160] Whether this issue had indeed been seriously discussed by the two countries during Jallud's visit remained unknown. Nevertheless, Tripoli described the visit as "most successful," and announced the signing of an agreement for "economic, scientific, technical and commercial cooperation...until the year 2000."[161] Foreign sources claimed, however, that Jallud's visit was not as successful as Tripoli had presented it. According to one of them, Jallud did not receive the kind of impressive support that Libya had received in the past. In addition, it was reported that Moscow used Jallud's visit to exert further pressure on Tripoli to get its ramshackle economy under tighter control, if only to ensure that the $5 bn it owed the Soviets for arms would be paid.[162] Another foreign source added that Jallud had failed in his attempt to get Soviet aid to build a nuclear plant in Tajura city.[163]

In summer-fall 1986, high-ranking political, military and religious Soviet delegates were spotted in Libya. It was not known if they were there in an attempt to placate Tripoli. The visit by Libya's Foreign Liaison Secretary, Kamal Hasan al-Mansur, in mid-December to Moscow closed the intensive series of mutual contacts for 1986.[164]

AFRICA

NORTH AFRICA (MAGHRIB)

Algeria

Qadhdhafi met with Algeria's President, Chedli Benjedid, on 28 January in 'Ain Amenes (a small Algerian town about 50 km from the border with Libya) to pave the way for an improvement in relations between the two countries (see *MECS* 1984–85, pp 565–66). The meeting ended without issuing a joint communiqué. Although there were differences in emphasis,[165] the meeting was significant for Libya. Not only did it shatter the enmity between Tripoli and Algiers, but it also showed both the Libyan people and foreign governments, especially in the West, that Tripoli was not as isolated and rancorous as was generally thought. The fact that Qadhdhafi could demonstrate political affinity with another state, let alone with its militarily strong neighbor Algeria, was especially important to him against the background of escalating military tension with the US.

From 10–13 February, Jallud visited Algiers, concentrating his talks there on "political and economic cooperation...toward the achievement of the ideal and scientific form of unity." In addition, aspects of the international oil market were discussed.[166] During the visit, a foreign source claimed that the two countries had signed an agreement on military coordination with regard to monitoring airspace along the Mediterranean against possible Israeli-American air attack.[167] There were increased contacts between top officials from Tripoli and Algiers in early spring 1986. The most noteworthy visit was that of the Algerian Prime Minister to Libya from 21–23 March. But the press communiqué released in Tripoli at the conclusion of the visit was of a general and routine nature, and did not signal a significant change in ties between the two countries.[168]

When the Americans attacked in mid-April, Algeria supported Libya.[169] Tripoli praised Algeria's stand, and two months later, when Jallud visited Algeria again, he reiterated to his hosts the importance of creating a union between the two countries.[170] Following the same line, Radio Tripoli said in a commentary that unity between the *Jamahiriyya* and Algeria was the "survival weapon for the Arab revolution, Arab unity and pan-Arabism." The commentary continued to say that the combined human resources and industrial and agricultural capacities of Libya and Algeria would lead their union to superpower status.[171]

On 25 October, Jallud arrived for a one-day visit to Algiers, his third in 1986. The official Libyan version said he went "to continue the efforts for unity between the Arab people in the two fraternal countries."[172] After his visit, there were high-level exchanges between the two capitals.

On 3 December, Algeria's President Benjedid arrived on a "surprise"[173] visit to Libya, en route to Tunisia. The Libyans stressed the fact that he met Qadhdhafi in Sidra, in "the Gulf of Defiance" (*Khalij al-Tahada*),[174] wishing thereby to demonstrate Algeria's support of Libya against the US. The Algerian President's visit should, however, be viewed not so much within the context of bilateral relations as within the broader context of Maghrib affairs, and more specifically, within the context of Algeria's attempts to achieve reconciliation between Libya and Tunisia.[175]

Morocco

The year under review was characterized by increasing tensions between Libya and Morocco, especially as a result of the Libyan *rapprochement* with Algeria which threatened to disrupt the hitherto clear-cut alignment in the Maghrib between the competing camps of Libya-Morocco and Algeria-Tunisia-Mauritania (see *MECS* 1983–84, pp 587–89).

Tension increased between Libya and Morocco following the American attack in April. Libya criticized Morocco for its allegedly weak stand against the attack.[176] There was further tension after King Hasan II called off the proposed extraordinary meeting of Arab Heads of State in early May, because the Arab Foreign Affairs Ministers failed to agree on an agenda when they met in Fez on 3 May. The proposed summit, which aimed at presenting a united Arab front against the US attack, foundered after Libya insisted that only the raid against it be on the agenda. Morocco (and other countries) wanted the Gulf war and the broader context of the Libyan-American conflict to be discussed also.[177]

Tension reached a new peak following the visit of Israeli Prime Minister Shimon Peres to Morocco from 21–23 July. Qadhdhafi referred to the event as "treason" and termed the Moroccan move "a serious violation" of the Libyan-Moroccan Federation Agreement.[178] (For details on the agreement, see *MECS* 1983–84, p 587). A foreign source claimed that Qadhdhafi decided at that stage to cancel the agreement.[179] Whether Qadhdhafi intended to do so or not remained unknown. In any case, there were no visible indications of such a move. Moreover, when Qadhdhafi spoke on the second anniversary of the signing of the agreement, he emphasized the *Jamahiriyya's* adherence to it.[180] It was the Moroccan King who made a surprise announcement on 29 August that he was canceling the agreement with Libya. King Hasan said that the break was the result of the joint statement of condemnation by Libya and Syria, who had branded the visit as "treason."[181] Libya reacted by condemning Morocco's "illegal [and] unilateral abrogation" of the "union,"[182] and Qadhdhafi stated he still considered the union "with the Moroccan people" valid.[183] It was surprising that Qadhdhafi did not appear strongly insulted by Morocco's abrogation. Perhaps the fact that Morocco had initiated the agreement, which was bereft of any real significance, softened Qadhdhafi's reaction. Furthermore, since the abrogation of the agreement resulted from the meeting of Israeli and Moroccan leaders in Ifran, it emphasized Qadhdhafi's apparent devotion to the Arab cause and also formally released him from any political commitment to Morocco. This, in turn, enabled him to increase his efforts to improve relations with Algeria. A sharp deterioration in relations between Tripoli and Rabat soon followed. The latter announced in late August the exposure of a group of terrorists who were sent by Qadhdhafi to instigate sabotage in Morocco,[184] and recalled its Ambassador home. The arrival in that week of Muhammad 'Abd al-'Aziz, the senior Polisario leader, to attend the 1 September "Revolution" day celebrations, marked his first visit to Libya since the 1984 Agreement with Morocco,[185] and served as a clear indication of the break in ties between Morocco and Libya.

Tunisia

Libya's relations with Tunisia were severely damaged in summer-fall 1985 (see *MECS* 1984–85, pp 564–65). By the spring of 1986, there was a new crisis when the Libyans accused Tunisia of allowing American aircraft to use its airspace in order to attack their country.[186] Despite Tunisia's categorical denial of the Libyan charge, mutual suspicion increased. Bashir al-Gumgum, the Libyan representative to the Arab League in Tunis, was deported in the spring on the charge that he was in contact with the Tunisian opposition.[187]

Tensions appeared to abate between fall and the end of the year. In September, Tunisia's Premier, Muhammad Mazali, a sworn opponent of Qadhdhafi,[188] was fired. This reduced the tension. Libya was reported to have released some of Tunis Air's assets, valued at nearly $10m, which it had frozen after the 1985 break, and promised to pay most of the balance by spring 1987.[189] Algerian mediation seemed to play a central role in improving relations, though diplomatic ties were not restored by the end of the year.

CHAD

In early February 1986, after a lull of more than a year, fighting resumed between Libyan forces and those of the anti-Libyan Government of Hissène Habré in Chad. As the latter claimed, Libya attacked his forces stationed at Kouba-Olanga, 450 km northeast of the capital N'Djamena, on the road to the Libyan stronghold of Faya Largeau.[190]

While Tripoli denied any complicity in the renewed fighting,[191] the Habré Government announced that Libya had opened a second front by attacking Oum Chalouba, just south of the 16th parallel known as the "red line." This split the country into the "rebel"-held north under the Libyan-backed forces of Goukkouni Wuedei and the government-controlled south, under Hissène Habré. Fighting between Habré's troops (with the active military support of France) and the "rebel" Goukkouni (backed actively by the Libyan "annexationists," as the Chad Government termed them) continued throughout the second and third weeks of February.[192] On 16–17 February the fighting intensified when a Libyan Tupolev-22 Bomber attacked N'Djamena airport[193] in apparent retaliation for an air strike by French bombers a day earlier on a newly-built military airfield at Wadi Doum[194] in the rebel-controlled area north of Chad, where Libya's military presence was strong. At the same time, Libya adhered to its traditional tactics of denying any military intervention in the fighting.[195] Libya added to its denials strong denounciations of the "internationalization of the internal conflict in Chad."[196] N'Djamena responded by publicly displaying Libyan prisoners, who had allegedly been captured during the fighting in February and March.[197] Toward early spring 1986, however, the fighting petered out, only to resume in the late fall.

The renewed eruption was prompted by a dramatic change of inter-Chadian political alliances following a serious split in the Libyan backed *Gouvernment d'Union Nationale de Transition* (GUNT). Libya's ally and the head of GUNT, Goukkouni Wuedei, was engaged since the summer in a sharp dispute with another senior figure in GUNT, al-Shaykh Ibn 'Umar, the leader of a breakaway faction — the *Conseil Démocratique Révolutionnaire*. In early October, the Libyan forces sided with al-Shaykh's faction,[198] thereby switching their "puppet" leader in Chad. Goukkouni was reportedly "wounded seriously" during a shooting incident in mid-October when he resisted arrest by Libyan soldiers in Tripoli.[199] At the same time, while Goukkouni's group appeared to be seeking a *rapprochement* with the N'Djamena Government,[200] it was reported that Libya had attacked Goukkouni-controlled areas in north Chad and rounded up Goukkouni's followers.[201] On 14 November, N'Djamena reported a three-day battle with Libya, following the "uninterrupted bombardment" of positions in the north. The Habré Government announced the downing of a Libyan jet fighter and the killing of 200 Libyan soldiers.[202] Libya "vehemently denied" bombing Chad.[203]

In mid-November, al-Shaykh Ibn 'Umar was reportedly elected the President of GUNT,[204] replacing Goukkouni who was believed to be in a Tripoli hospital — or as another source said, in a prison in Sebha.[205]

In late November, Habré warned of Libya's reinforcement of its military forces in Chad in preparation for "a new advance" into the depths of Chad's territory.[206] It remained unclear, however, whether the Libyans actually planned at that stage to intensify their involvement in that country. Perhaps Habré wished to use the special new circumstances to prepare the ground to advance north of the 16th parallel and link up with Goukkouni's forces against Libya and its new ally's forces.

In early December, al-Shaykh Ibn 'Umar visited Tripoli. The Libyan reports on his arrival included a denunciation of the "French-American-Zionist colonialist intervention on the side of agent Habré."[207]

On 12 December N'Djamena announced that a major Libyan offensive on Bardai in the northeast had failed.[208] The attack reportedly involved both ground forces and aircraft. Several days later, N'Djamena announced that the Libyan forces had launched large-scale ground and air attacks in northeast Chad, near the Tibesti mountains and the border with Niger.[209] The end of 1986 witnessed a massive Libyan offensive in North Chad, directed principally against the Tibesti mountain towns in an apparent effort to crush anti-Libyan forces.[210] It should be noted that the significant escalation in fighting in North Chad at the close of the year was an extremely troubling development for the Libyans. They risked losing control of North Chad, which was important strategically, politically and economically. In addition, a serious defeat in Chad could undermine the already damaged position of the Libyan leader at home.

SUDAN AND EGYPT

Sudan

The *rapprochement* with Sudan was consolidated in 1986 (for the first stages, see *MECS* 1984–85, p 567). In mid-February, a trade deal was signed between the two countries. Libya had to supply 100,000 tons of oil a year to Sudan in exchange for Sudanese food.[211] A short while later, Libya reportedly gave Sudan 300,000 tonnes of oil, and there was talk of employing Sudanese citizens in Libya.[212] Militarily, Libyan Tupolev-22 bombers were "loaned" to Sudan, which used them for the first time in March to carry out attacks against the rebels in South Sudan.[213] Libya was also reported to have dispatched about 300 trucks manned by 700 troops and loaded with weapons and ammunition to help Sudan's Army in its war in the south.[214] (For Khartoum's reciprocating attitude, see chapter on Sudan.)

Another high point in relations, although mainly symbolic, was the trip by an official Libyan delegation to Khartoum on the first anniversary of the Sudanese 6 April upheaval. During that visit the Libyan made "the Sudanese people" a unity proposal.[215] The Sudanese leadership did not have any special difficulty evading further discussion of the unity offer. The American attack on Libya, launched about ten days later, dramatically shifted Libyan attention to its conflict with the US, and the unity offer was shelved for the time being. Nonetheless, cooperation continued. On 10 August, Sudan's Prime Minister, al-Sadiq al-Mahdi, paid a two-day official visit to Libya and signed a trade agreement valued at $60m.[216] Qadhdhafi returned the visit on 9–13 September, when he offered to mediate between Khartoum and Addis Ababa (the major supporter of the Sudanese rebels in South Sudan) in order to end the civil war in Ethiopia.[217] Qadhdhafi had apparently also acted to defuse the crisis simmering between Sudan and Uganda,[218] where he had been before he arrived in Khartoum (see chapter on Sudan). Although the two countries continued to cooperate, at least on the surface, their relations were not without tension, although Libya did not officially refer to it (see chapter on Sudan).

Egypt

Qadhdhafi did not change his chronic pattern of fierce hatred and complete rejection of the Egyptian regime of the President he called "Husni *al-Bariq*" (the sick) during the period reviewed.[219] Qadhdhafi and his media repeatedly urged the Egyptian people "to set [their regime] on fire"[220] and "rise up and put an end to the era of tutelage and capitulation"[221] by overthrowing the Mubarak regime.

NOTES

For the place and frequency of publications cited here, and for the full name of the publication, news agency, radio station or monitoring service where an abbreviation is used, please see "List of Sources." Only in the case of more than one publication bearing the same name is the place of publication noted here.

1. For details regarding the principles and functioning of the "People's Power" system, see all earlier chapters on Libya in previous volumes of *MECS*.
2. R. Tripoli, 10 January — DR, 13 January. See also R. Tripoli, 2 January, 25 February — DR, 8 January, SWB, 27 February 1986.
3. See Tripoli TV, 14 January — DR, 15 January 1986.
4. E.g., Tripoli TV, 14 January — DR, 16 January, a live broadcast from the Basic People's Congresses in Zlitan and in Tripoli. See also *Ha'aretz*, 24 February, quoting a report from Tripoli by the German *Der Spiegel* and *NYT*, 19 January 1986.
5. JANA, 25 February — DR, 26 February 1986.
6. For the full list of resolutions, including foreign issues, see R. Tripoli, 3 March — DR, 4 March 1986.
7. Qadhdhafi's speech, JANA, 2 March — DR, 3 March 1986.
8. As announced by R. Tripoli, 3 March — SWB, 5 March 1986.
9. *QER*, No 1, 1986, quoting *al-Zahf al-Akhdar* ("The Green March"), the mouthpiece of the Libyan Revolutionary Committees.
10. R. Tripoli, 3 March — SWB, 5 March 1986.
11. JANA, 2 March — DR, 3 March 1986. The case of the Secreteriat of Petroleum served as a clear case of striving for efficiency. The acting Secretary of that portfolio was a titular head who represented Libya at OPEC, but did little else. The main oil business and policy were conducted by the Libyan National Oil Company, headed by Muhammad 'Abdallah Badri, in conjunction with Qadhdhafi himself.
12. *Al-Hawadith*, 21 March 1986.
13. *MM*, 17 March 1986.
14. Quoted by *al-Mustaqbal*, 8 March 1986.
15. See e.g., *MECS* 1980–81, p 689.
16. *The Guardian*, 10 Feburary 1986.
17. *Al-Tadamun*, 26 April 1986.
18. JANA, 6 November — DR, 7 November 1986.
19. *MM*, 17 March 1986.
20. Qadhdhafi was reportedly disappointed with the new Education Minister since the latter had allegedly failed to effectively handle the situation in the immediate aftermath of the American attack. As further reported by the same source, the Libyan journalist Fawziya al-Shalabi was scheduled to substitute for him. *Al-Dustur*, London, 19 May 1986. Until the end of the year, however, no details were available on this change, if it occurred at all.
21. For more details regarding the attack's casualties and damage, see section on relations with the US in this chapter.
22. *DT*, 22 April 1986.
23. A Libyan senior official to DPA, 15 April — DR, 15 April; JANA, 24 June — DR, 25 June 1986, respectively.
24. E.g., *FT*, 17 April; *NYT*, 18 April, quoting a senior White House official; *Africa Now*, May 1986.
25. Al-Damm was quoted by *La Stampa*, 29 April — DR, 5 May 1986.

26. JANA, 16 April; see also a reference by Libya's Ambassador in France, AFP, 16 April 1986.
27. *DT*, 22 April 1986.
28. *CR*, No 4, 1986.
29. *DT*, 22 April; *al-Siyasa*, Kuwait, 16 June 1986.
30. For more details on his speech, see *NYT*, 17 April; *FT*, 18 April 1986.
31. R. Tripoli, 16 April — DR, 16 April and Tripoli TV, 7 May — DR, 8 May 1986.
32. Tripoli TV, 20 April — JPRS, 17 June 1986.
33. R. Tripoli, 21 June — SWB, 26 June 1986.
34. Qadhdhafi in an interview with *al-Mawqif al-'Arabi*, as quoted by *al-Ittihad al-'Usbu'i*, 1 May 1986.
35. Qadhdhafi's speech quoted by JANA, 13 May — DR, 14 May 1986.
36. MENA, quoting a French source, 20 July; *al-Dustur*, London, 21 July 1986.
37. On 11 June 1970, the Wheelus air base near Tripoli was transferred to the Libyans. King Idris al-Sanusi granted the US the right to use that base in September 1954, and the agreement was scheduled to expire in 1971.
38. *IHT*, 14–15 June; *NYT*, 15 June. For the full text of the speech, see *al-Jamahiriyya*, 13 June 1986.
39. *IHT*, 14–15 June; *Time*, 23 June 1986.
40. *IHT*, 20 June 1986.
41. *Al-Bayan*, 27 May; *al-Tali 'a al-'Arabiyya*, 2 June, 7 July; *al-Siyasa*, Kuwait, 12 June and *al-Dustur*, London, 21 July 1986.
42. *Al-Dustur*, London, 21 July 1986.
43. *Der Stern*, 26 June, quoting Libyan opposition source — DR, 26 June 1986.
44. JANA, 24 June — DR, 25 June 1986.
45. *Jeune Afrique*, 3 September; *al-Dustur*, London, 15, 22 September 1986.
46. APS, 2 December; *New African*, December 1986.
47. See *Der Stern*, 26 June — DR, 26 June; *al-Dustur*, London, 30 June 1986. His commando headquarters was a luxurious Mercedes Benz caravan.
48. *Al-Dustur*, London, 21 July; *al-Akhbar*, Cairo, 28 August; *Le Matin*, 11 September 1986.
49. For Qadhdhafi's emerging from his seemingly self-imposed isolation, see e.g., R. Tripoli, 27 August — DR, 27 August; APS, 29 August 1986.
50. For the text of the speech, see *al-Fajr al-Jadid*, 1 September 1986.
51. By early 1986 the price of oil had fallen to $15 a barrel. Non-oil exports were negligible.
52. *CR*, No 2, 1986.
53. E.g., see *The Times*, 27 January and *WP*, 15 June 1986.
54. *CR*, No 2, 1986.
55. *MEED*, 12 April and *NYT*, 2 May 1986, respectively.
56. *MEED*, 12 April 1986.
57. Ibid.
58. *Al-Zahf al-Akhdar*, 7 July 1986, a stern criticism of mismanagement, which in turn had brought about acute shortages of various commodities.
59. *NYT*, 13 January; *The Times*, 27 January 1986.
60. For Qadhdhafi's campaign against private trade and the replacement of private retail business with state-sponsored supermarkets, see *MECS* 1980–81, pp 692–93.
61. *Guardian Weekly*, 2 February; *NYT*, 2 May 1986.
62. *NYT*, 13 January; *The Guardian*, 22 January 1986, reports from Tripoli.
63. For details of the grandiose project of the "Great Man-Made River," which aims to bring water 1,000 miles from an inland reservoir in the south to the coast in the north for agricultural and industrial use, see *MECS* 1983–84, pp 579–80.
64. *NYT*, 2 May 1986.
65. *NYT*, 4 April 1986.
66. R. Tripoli, 2 March — DR, 5 March 1986.
67. For example, Libya asked OPEC to fix the ceiling of production at 15m, 14.5m and 16.8m barrels per day (b/d) for the 2nd, 3rd, and 4th quarters of 1986, while the decision eventually reached in OPEC's meeting in April was to fix the ceiling at 16.7m, 16.3m and 17.3m b/d during the same period. See statement by al-Badri, Libya's senior official for oil affairs, to KUNA, 9 May — DR, 16 May 1986.

68. In a statement quoted by R. Tripoli, 2 March — DR, 5 March 1986.
69. Qadhdhafi's interview with *al-Kifah al-'Arabi*, 24 February 1986.
70. R. Tripoli, 17 July — SWB, 19 July 1986.
71. *AC*, 3 September 1986.
72. E.g., R. Tripoli, 11 June — SWB, 13 June; *WP*, 15 June; *al-Majalla*, 18-24 June; *al-Dustur*, London, 21 July 1986.
73. *AC*, 3 September; Tripoli TV, 26 September — SWB, 29 September; *al-Dustur*, London, 6 October; *al-Fajr al-Jadid*, 12 December 1986.
74. Nineteen people were killed in the attacks, including five Americans, and more than 110 were wounded. For the American accusations, see Reagan's statement in a nationally televised news conference reported by *NYT*, 8 January 1986.
75. A top official in Libya's Foreign Affairs Ministry, ANSA, 1 January — DR, 2 January; al-Turayki in an interview with *al-Qabas*, 10 January 1986.
76. In a press conference with US journalists, *IHT*, 6 January; in a series of interviews with Tripoli TV, 9 January — SWB, 11 January; American ABC TV, as quoted in JANA, 15 January — DR, 15 January 1986.
77. Qadhdhafi in an interview with *al-Nahar al-'Arabi wal-Duwali*, 20–26 January 1986.
78. E.g., R. Tripoli, 2, 10 January — DR, 8 January, SWB, 13 January 1986, respectively. The term "Black House" was repeatedly used by Tripoli throughout the year when referring to Washington — see, e.g., R. Tripoli, 27 March, 7 April — SWB, 28 March, 9 April; JANA, 24 August — SWB, 27 August, *al-Fajr al-Jadid*, 5, 16 December 1986 and many others.
79. E.g., R. Tripoli, 8 January — SWB, 9 January 1986.
80. Qadhdhafi at a press conference in Tripoli with American media representatives, R. Tripoli, 5 January — SWB, 7 January 1986.
81. R. Tripoli, 3, 4 January — DR, 6 January 1986.
82. For additional details, see *NYT*, 8 January 1986.
83. *WP*, 9 January. For more details on Libya's assets in the US, see *MM*, 20 January 1986.
84. R. Tripoli, 8 January — SWB, 9 January 1986.
85. On the difficulties of implementing the American sanctions, see *FT*, 1 February; *The Guardian*, 9 February and *al-Nahar Arab Report and Memo*, 14 February 1986.
86. Reagan in a speech to the nation, *NYT*, 8 January 1986.
87. R. Tripoli, 9 January — SWB, 11 January; for other venomous attacks on the American President, see also R. Tripoli, 10 January — SWB, 13 January 1986.
88. For details, see *NYT*, 15 January 1986.
89. E.g., in an interview with West German TV, quoted by *IHT*, 16 January; MENA, quoting Qadhdhafi, 20 January — DR, 21 January 1986.
90. Qadhdhafi's interview with *al-Nahar al-'Arabi wal-Duwali*, 20-26 January 1986.
91. R. Tripoli, 2, 16 January — DR, 4, 17 January 1986.
92. *NYT*, 25 January 1986.
93. JANA, 24 January, R. Tripoli, 25 January — DR, 30, 27 January 1986, respectively.
94. R. Tripoli, 24 January — SWB, 25 January 1986.
95. Tripoli TV, 26 January — SWB, 28 January 1986.
96. For further details on the dispute, including its legal aspects, see *NYT*, 25 March 1986.
97. R. Tripoli, 12 February — SWB, 14 February 1986.
98. *Al-Zahf al-Akhdar*, 10 March 1986.
99. R. Tripoli's announcements, 24, 25 March — SWB, 26 March and DR, 25 March 1986, respectively. According to Washington's official statement, there were no reports on US casualties and loss of US aircraft or ships. See *NYT*, 25 March 1986.
100. R. Tripoli, 24 March — DR, 25 March 1986.
101. The White House announcement, *NYT*, 25 March 1986.
102. *NYT*, 26 March 1986. For a detailed account of the attack, including a map, see *ARB*, 15 April 1986.
103. Data given by *al-Sha'b*, Cairo, 8 April, quoting a top Libyan military commander and a businessman returning from Benghazi, respectively.
104. *WP*, 2 April; *al-Ittihad*, Abu Dhabi, 5 April 1986.
105. R. Tripoli, 3 April — SWB, 5 April and JANA, 6 April — DR, 7 April 1986.
106. *NYT*, 4 April 1986.

107. R. Tripoli, 3 April 1986.
108. *NYT*, 6 April; the US allegedly intercepted two messages that pointed to Libyan involvement in the West Berlin bombing, see *NYT*, 23 April 1986.
109. R. Tripoli, 7 April — DR, 8 April 1986.
110. JANA, 9, 10 April — SWB, DR, 11 April 1986.
111. *Al-Fajr al-Jadid*, 10 April; *al-Zahf al-Akhdar*, 14 April 1986.
112. For details, see R. Tripoli, 10 April — DR, 11 April; *al-Ittihad*, Abu Dhabi, 13 April; *The Guardian*, *Ma'ariv*, 14 April; *NYT*, 15 April 1986. The preparation included the transfer of most of the Libyan Air Force into Sudan's territory. See *al-Siyasa*, Kuwait, 17 April 1986.
113. R. Tripoli, 15 April — SWB, 17 April 1986.
114. Ibid.
115. R. Tripoli, 15 April — DR, 15 April; *al-Ittihad al-'Usbu'i*, 17 April 1986, quoting an interview with a senior Libyan official. According to *CR*, No 2, 1986, 33 US fighter aircraft took part in the attack.
116. R. Tripoli, 15 April — DR, 15 April 1986.
117. USIS, 8 May 1986. It should be emphasized that the chapter on Libya did not deal at all with the American side of the "story." For more details on the military aspects of the attack, see *ARB*, 15 May 1986.
118. Jallud in an interview with *al-Safir*, 29 April 1986.
119. R. Tripoli, 15 April — SWB, 17 April 1986. That message was further reiterated by the Libyan media from April 1986 on.
120. R. Tripoli, 9 May — DR, 9 May 1986.
121. JANA, 11, 12 July — DR, 14 July 1986, respectively.
122. See JANA, 21 August — DR, 22 August; *al-Zahf al-Akhdar*, 25 August 1986.
123. In a statement released by Tripoli's Foreign Affairs Ministry, R. Tripoli, 30 August — SWB, 1 September 1986. Reagan was repeatedly called "Hitler mark two", and "a new Nazi" by the Libyan media as well as by Qadhdhafi during the period that followed the April attack. See, e.g., JANA, 22 April; Tripoli TV, 7 October — SWB, 9 October 1986.
124. E.g., JANA, 2 October — DR, 3 October; *al-Fajr al-Jadid*, 8, 18 November; 4, 20, 27 December 1986 and many more.
125. E.g. JANA, 13 July — DR, 14 July; R. Tripoli, 20 July — DR, 21 July 1986 and many more.
126. E.g., JANA, 18 July — DR, 18 July; JANA, 5 October — DR, 6 October 1986.
127. At that time the Reagan Administration reportedly launched a secret campaign of deception designed to convince Qadhdhafi that he was about to be attacked again by US bombers and perhaps be overthrown in a coup. For details, see *WP*, *NYT*, 3 October 1986.
128. E.g., R. Tripoli, 31 August — DR, 2 September. See also Qadhdhafi's fierce anti-American speech in Zimbabwe, as quoted by *The Guardian*, 5 September 1986.
129. JANA, 5 September — SWB, 6 September 1986.
130. That terminology was persistently used by the Libyan media from April 1986 onwards, e.g., R. Tripoli, 12 June — DR, 12 June; *al-Fajr al-Jadid*, 7, 25 December 1986.
131. JANA, 21 April — DR, 22 April 1986.
132. *FT*, 19 April 1986, quoting a statement by Sir Geoffrey Howe, the Foreign Secretary.
133. JANA, 18 April 1986.
134. *FT*, 23 April 1986.
135. *IHT*, 25 April 1986.
136. Tripoli TV, 25 April — DR, 28 April 1986.
137. *The Guardian*, 1 May 1986.
138. For further details, see *The Guardian*, 3 October 1986.
139. R. Tripoli, 13 October — DR, 14 October 1986.
140. *Al-Zahf al-Akhdar*, 20 October 1986.
141. *NYT*, 26 October 1986.
142. JANA, 12 May — SWB, 14 May 1986.
143. *FT*, 16 May and *NYT*, 24 May 1986, respectively.
144. Qadhdhafi's speech on the occasion of the anniversary of "the revenge feast of expelling the remnants of the fascist Italian invaders" from Libya.
145. *FT*, 8 October 1986.

146. The Soviet military factor included four radar IL-38 planes together with Soviet crews and long-range SA-5 missiles. See *al-Ra'y al-'Amm*, 7 January; R. Cairo, 15 January 1986, respectively.
147. E.g., the repeated announcements by the spokesman of the Soviet Foreign Ministry, Vladimir Lomeyko, in Tass, 9 January, and as quoted by R. Tripoli, 25 March — DR, 26 March. See also the interview of the Soviet Ambassador in Libya with R. Tripoli, 11 January — DR, 13 January 1986.
148. In an interview with *al-Nahar al-'Arabi wal-Duwali*, 22–26 January 1986.
149. Tripoli did not release significant details of the aims or results of these two visits.
150. *NYT*, 29 March 1986.
151. *Ma'ariv*, 18 April 1986, a report from Washington.
152. *JP*, 27 April 1986 quoting the Egyptian *October*. Malta announced it had given Libya advance notice of the American air raid about 30 to 45 minutes before it took place, 6 August 1986.
153. *The Guardian*, 23 April 1986.
154. *IHT*, 7 May 1986.
155. Qadhdhafi in an interview with *al-Mawqif al-'Arabi*, Cairo, 30 May 1986. See also *al-Qabas*, 17 April 1986.
156. Qadhdhafi in an interview with *al-Ittihad*, Abu-Dhabi, 1 May 1986.
157. JANA, 22 May — DR, 23 May 1986.
158. Qadhdhafi in an interview with *The Times of India*, 27 April — SWB, 28 April 1986.
159. *Al-Ittihad*, Abu Dhabi, 4 June 1986.
160. Jallud in a statement to DPA, 15 June — DR, 17 June. For a similar statement by Qadhdhafi, see his interview with *Der Spiegel*, 18 June — DR, 19 June 1986.
161. *JM*, 4 June 1986.
162. *The Guardian*, 17 June 1986.
163. *Le Point*, 18-23 June 1986.
164. For details regarding the most noteworthy visits, see R. Tripoli, 16, 26 June — DR, 17, 27 June; *JM*, 25 June; R. Tripoli, 22 July — SWB, 5 August; R. Tripoli, 31 August — DR, 2 September; JANA, 13 December — DR, 15 December and *al-Fajr al-Jadid*, 16 December 1986.
165. See both versions, R. Tripoli, R. Algiers, 28 January — SWB, 30 January 1986.
166. See R. Tripoli, 10 February — SWB, 12 February and APS, 13 February — DR, 14 February 1986.
167. *Al Shira'*, Beirut, 17 February 1986.
168. See JANA, 23 March — SWB, 25 March; for further details on the meeting of the Algerian Premier and Qadhdhafi, see *Le Monde*, 25 March 1986.
169. R. Algiers, 21 April — DR, 22 April 1986.
170. *JM*, 25 June 1986.
171. R. Tripoli, 25 July — SWB, 28 July 1986.
172. R. Tripoli, 25 October — DR, 27 October 1986.
173. *Al-Sharq al-Awsat*, 4 December 1986.
174. *Al-Fajr al-Jadid*, 4, 6 December 1986.
175. *Al-Sharq al-Awsat*, 5 December; R. Algiers, 6 December — SWB, 9 December and *al-Bayan*, 9 December 1986.
176. The Libyan newspaper *al-Jamahiriyya* published a letter from "an Arab citizen" criticizing Morocco's stand. Quoted by JANA, 3 May — SWB, 6 May 1986.
177. *CR*, No 3, 1986.
178. JANA, 26 July, 22 July — SWB, 28 July, DR, 22 July 1986, respectively.
179. *Al-Liwa*, 27 July 1986.
180. *Al-Fajr al-Jadid*, 13 August 1986.
181. King Hasan II's address to the nation, R. Rabat, 29 August — DR, 2 September 1986.
182. R. Tripoli, 31 August — DR, 2 September 1986.
183. Qadhdhafi's anniversary speech on the occasion of the 1 September "Revolution," *al-Fajr al-Jadid*, 1 September 1986.
184. *Ma'ariv*, 1 September, quoting an official announcement by Morocco. See also *al-Watan al-'Arabi*, 5 September 1986.
185. APS, 30 August — DR, 6 September 1986.

186. R. Tripoli, 16 April 1986.
187. *Al-Qabas*, 15 May 1986.
188. See Libyan references to the impact of Mazali's dismissal on relations with Tunisia by JANA, 17 September — DR, 19 September, and by MENA, 20 October 1986, quoting a senior Libyan official.
189. *CR*, No 3; KUNA, 11 November — SWB, 13 November; *al-Qabas*, 5, 6 December and *al-Sabah*, Tunis, 23 December 1986.
190. Chad's Foreign Minister, Goura Lassou, in a statement released on 10 February, broadcast by R. N'Djamena, 12 February — SWB, 14 February 1986.
191. JANA, 11 February — DR, 12 February 1986.
192. R. N'Djamena, 14, 15, 16, 17 February — DR, 18 February 1986.
193. *Le Monde*, 18 February 1986.
194. According to AFP, 18 March — DR, 19 March 1986, that airport was repaired by the Libyans several days later.
195. For the repetitive denials, see e.g., JANA, 14, 18 February — DR, 16, 18 February 1986.
196. The Libyan delegation to the Organization of African Unity Council of Ministers meeting on 4 March in Addis Ababa, see PANA, 6 March — SWB, 8 March 1986.
197. AFP, 21 February, 20 March — DR, 24 February, 20 March 1986.
198. R. N'Djamena, 7 October — DR, 8 October 1986.
199. AFP, 1 November — DR, 3 November 1986.
200. AFP, 19 October — DR, 20 October 1986.
201. AFP, 30 October, 1 November — DR, 31 October, 3 November 1986.
202. *IHT*, 15-16 November 1986, quoting a military communiqué from N'Djamena.
203. JANA, 12 November — DR, 13 November 1986.
204. *Al-Fajr al-Jadid*, 19 November and *Le Monde*, 20 November. For more biographical details on al-Shaykh Ibn 'Umar, see AFP, 18 November — DR, 19 November 1986.
205. *The Economist*, 22 November and *al-Dustur*, London, 17 November 1986.
206. Habré's interview with AFP, 29 November — DR, 1 December 1986.
207. *Al-Fajr al-Jadid*, 7 December 1986. France and the US had indeed significantly aided Habré's forces. For example, on 22 December, the US delivered military supplies valued at $15m to N'Djamena. See *CR*, No 1, 1987.
208. R. N'Djamena, 12 December — SWB, 15 December 1986.
209. R. N'Djamena, 15 December — SWB, 17 December 1986.
210. *IHT*, 24-25 December 1986.
211. AFP, 22 February — DR, 29 February 1986.
212. *NYT*, 29 April 1986.
213. *WP*, 28 March; *al-Siyasa*, Kuwait, 26 March; *ARB*, 15 April; R. SPLA, 16 April — DR, 17 April; *ME*, June 1986.
214. *Newsweek*, April; *IHT*, 18 April 1986.
215. For more details, see JANA, 6 April — DR, 7 April; *al-Ittihad*, Abu Dhabi, 9, 10 April; R. Tripoli, 12 April — DR, 14 April 1986.
216. *CR*, No 4, 1986.
217. Qadhdhafi, quoted by SUNA, 13 September — DR, 15 September; Libya had reportedly been involved in mediatory activity between Sudan and Ethiopia since early 1986. See, e.g., SUNA, 17 March — DR, 18 March; *al-Shira'*, Beirut, 29 March; *al-Mustaqbal*, 12 April 1986.
218. For further details on Qadhdhafi's trip see JANA, 9 September, Tripoli TV, 11 September — DR, 10, 15 September, respectively. See also *al-Siyasa*, Khartoum, 10 September 1986.
219. E.g., JANA, 9 October, 9 November — DR, 10 October, 9 November; *al-Fajr al-Jadid*, 13, 19 November, 6, 11, 13, 27 December 1986.
220. R. Tripoli, 28 February — SWB, 3 March 1986.
221. JANA, 28 August — DR, 29 August 1986.

The People's Democratic Republic of Yemen
(Jumhuriyyat al-Yaman al-Sha'biyya al-Dimuqratiyya)

JOSEPH KOSTINER

Events in the People's Democratic Republic of Yemen (PDRY) in 1986 evolved in the shadow of the two-week civil war that erupted in Aden on 13 January 1986. The disputes among elite groups, notably between 'Ali Nasir Muhammad and his opponents who regrouped during 1985 (see *Middle East Contemporary Survey* [*MECS*] 1984–85, pp 577–81), reached its peak in a clash on 13 January. Following this incident, fighting quickly spread among tribal groups and units of the armed forces loyal to the disputing factions. The last days of January witnessed the decisive victory of the Opposition over 'Ali Nasir's loyalists. But the results of the fighting were horrible: destruction and death in Aden; deep-rooted regional and tribal divisions surfaced both among the new leaders and in society at large; the PDRY's veteran leadership was eliminated; and inexperienced and less prestigious politicians came to power. The question arose as to whether the victorious leaders would be able to cope and consolidate their position and rebuild the country. The fighting and subsequent change of the guard in Aden generated similar problems in foreign affairs, a field in which 'Ali Nasir's pragmatic attitudes gained him notable achievements. It remained unclear whether the new leaders would follow 'Ali Nasir's well-accepted policies in the Arab world and whether Arab leaders, or even the Soviet Union, would be ready to cooperate with 'Ali Nasir's rather obscure successors. The question was particularly intriguing because the deposed PDRY President was still traveling from one Arab capital to another trying to get help for his return to South Yemen.

The new leaders' approach to these problems was to avoid dramatic and controversial changes in internal and foreign affairs. By maintaining the status quo in these fields, the new elite sought to establish an image of stability and teamwork in the PDRY's policies, which would help it over the difficult post-civil-war period. Hence, the new leaders set out to repair the immediate damage wrought by the civil war, to consolidate their rule, and establish their legitimacy.

The attempts made to carry out these policies and the perils encountered generated the events noted in this chapter.

INTERNAL AFFAIRS

VIOLENT JANUARY

The escalating tension among the factions of the PDRY's ruling body, the Yemeni

The Arabian Peninsula and the Horn of Africa

Socialist Party (YSP), culminated in a showdown on 13 January 1986. Apart from partisan accusations which both ʻAli Nasir and his opponents voiced against each other, there was no impartial and decisive evidence to suggest that either of the factions had plotted a coup against the other. The evidence rather suggests that the dispute surfaced once it became evident that the inter-Arab mediation initiative of October 1985 (see *MECS* 1984–85, p 581) had failed, and both parties started preparing for a moment of decision. On 13 January a shoot-out erupted at the Central Committee's meeting. According to one version, ʻAli Nasir's men shot first, while the President himself was absent, secure at his home. Another version maintains that the fighting was prompted by one of the opposition leaders, either ʻAli ʻAntar or ʻAli Shayʻ Hadi, who drew a pistol and shot ʻAli Nasir in the arm. Loyal guards of both factions rushed into the room to defend their leaders. Clashes eventually spread to different parts of Aden. After two days, ʻAli Nasir's group seemed to have gained the upper hand, a development that was lauded in the country's media. Eight opposition leaders, including two former Ministers of Defense, ʻAli ʻAntar and Salih Muslih Qasim, as well as another top party leader, ʻAli Shayʻ Hadi, were reportedly executed for plotting against the Government.[1] There were conflicting reports on the fate of ʻAbd al-Fattah Ismaʻil, a former PDRY President, whose return to Aden after five years of exile in Moscow in February 1985 (see *MECS* 1984–85, pp 577–80) had precipitated the fighting. He was either killed or injured when the clashes broke out, and then taken to a Soviet ship in Aden. In any case, his leadership was also denied to the Opposition, who lost the first round.

The basic nature of the PDRY's polity resulted in continuing clashes. A mixture of tribal-kinship bonds, professional loyalties and Marxist-doctinaire comradeship tied each of the elite's members to a different tribal group and unit in the armed forces. These ties had been cultivated for years (see *MECS* 1984–85, pp 580–81) as a means of enlisting support for the central Government. However, the personalized, primordial nature of these bonds also reinforced the power of each member, which he could use to his personal advantage. Consequently, in the clashes that ensued, tribal and army units both massed in Aden to assist their leaders, and engaged in clashes among themselves in their regions — but along the lines of the continuing dispute in Aden. After a Soviet-initiated cease-fire attempt collapsed on 16 and 17 January (see below), heavy fighting broke out in different regions in the PDRY, clearly taking the shape of a civil war. The parties split as follows: in Aden, the popular militias, the Navy and the artillery forces sided with ʻAli Nasir; the armored forces sided with the Opposition; and the Air Force split between the factions. The parties bombarded each other heavily; the pro-opposition air force units even strafed the President's palace. In the provinces, ʻAli Nasir's forces were mainly based in Abyan (northeast of Aden in the second Governorate), whose local Governor, Muhammad ʻAli Ahmad, was ʻAli Nasir's ally and Commander of his forces. From there, ʻAli Nasir attempted to control the routes to Aden and Lahaj. His forces got supplies from North Yemen through the Mukiras route. The Opposition relied on the loyalty of tribes in the Daliʻ, Yafiʻi and ʻAwlaqi regions, northwest and northeast of Aden, respectively, who had been loyal to ʻAli ʻAntar since he commanded the guerrilla war against the British in the 1960s in these regions. They succeeded in controlling the western area of the PDRY as well as Hadramawt in the east, whose people were loyal to ʻAli Salim al-Bayd, a Hadramawt native and another Politburo member of the Opposition.[2] After several days of renewed clashes it became evident that the opposition forces, which outnumbered 'Ali Nasir's loyalists, had gained control over most of the provinces and made inroads into Aden from both the Lahaj and Dali' regions. Between 20 and 22 January their forces took over the boroughs of Shaykh 'Uthman, Tawahi and Little Aden, and from there established their prominence throughout the capital.[3] A second mediation initiative, by North Yemen and the Palestine Liberation Organization (PLO), which could have given 'Ali Nasir's forces time to regroup, was turned down by the Opposition.[4] The Opposition announced their victory to the media on 25 January and in the last week of January they continued eliminating 'Ali Nasir's forces in Aden and all over the country, including his main stronghold at Abyan.[5] At the end of January the Opposition took over the leadership of the PDRY. It included the remaining members of the opposition faction, such as 'Ali Salim al-Bayd, the former Deputy Prime Minister and Minister for Local Government, who had recovered from a stomach injury received on 13 January to become the new General Secretary of the YSP's Central Committee, and Salim Salih Muhammad, a former Secretary of the YSP's Ideological Committee, who became the General Secretary's assistant. Both were formally elected in a YSP Central Committee meeting on 7 February 1986. They collaborated with Haydar al-'Attas, the former Prime Minister, who had been on a tour of India and had gone to the Soviet Union during the critical period of the fighting, returning to Aden on 25 January to be elected by the Central Committee as Interim President of the PDRY (or, as it is officially called, President of the Supreme People's Presidium).[6] 'Ali Nasir and his top colleagues conceded their positions to the Opposition by leaving for Ethiopia and the YAR.[7]

CONSOLIDATING THE NEW LEADERSHIP

PROBLEMS AND POLICY PRINCIPLES

The civil war resulted in different kinds of problems for the PDRY, which the new leadership had to face and which seemed to cast a shadow over the process of its consolidation. One major problem was the new leadership's relative weakness. This problem stemmed from the fact that the veteran leaders who had ruled the PDRY until 13 January, either with 'Ali Nasir or with the Opposition, were almost completely eliminated. 'Ali Nasir's group in exile included 48 top functionaries, among them the former Minister of Health and Agriculture, the Chief of Staff of the Army, 'Abdallah 'Ali 'Ilaywa, his deputy, the Commanders of Military Intelligence, the Navy and the popular militias, the governors of Shabwah and Abyan, leading Politburo members such as 'Abd al-Raziq ba-Dhib, the party's ideologue, and Anis Hasan Yahya, a former leader of the Ba'th faction incorporated within the YSP.[8] The former Minister of the Interior, Muhammad al-Battani, and his deputy were arrested in Aden.[9] The Government that was formed in February 1986 included only four members of the earlier one. The YSP's Politburo, which consisted of a balance between both factions (see *MECS* 1984–85, pp 577–81) and whose members engaged in the 13 January shoot-out, was practically defunct. In the wake of these developments the new leadership had to replace a whole group of top-ranking leaders with people depicted by different observers as "second echelon," whose reputation, personal caliber and experience could not match their predecessors' qualities.[10]

Moreover, these leaders hardly formed a cohesive and determined group, but rather a coalition of different individuals emerging from a variety of tribal-geographical and ideological backgrounds, who accidentally survived the fighting and teamed up to try to provide the initial remedy to the war-weary PDRY. While Bayd and Salih Muhammad were known as doctrinaire hard-liners who had been opposed to 'Ali Nasir's compromising policies (see *MECS* 1984–85, pp 580–81), 'Attas was an engineer who came to power as a result of the incentives given to professionals by 'Ali Nasir and was perceived as a moderate and compromising politician. He maintained good relations with both internal factions and with different Arab rulers. It might have been his pragmatism, as opposed to the hard line of the earlier two, that convinced them to have 'Attas as a moderating and image-improving President, who would, however, be only a figurehead under their influence.[11] Al-'Attas probably found comfort in the aid of 'Abd al-'Aziz al-Dali, 'Ali Nasir's Minister of Foreign Affairs, who was left in this post. Salih Mundir al-Siyayli, the new Minister of Interior, was a former head of internal security, who had previously displayed no ideological leanings.[12] The ideological diversity of the new leadership was reflected in their tribal and geographical differentiations; while 'Attas, Bayd and Siyayli were from Hadramawt, Salim Salih came from Yafi'i in the central mountainous parts of the PDRY, a fact which further generated different interests among the new elite.

The factor of different backgrounds affected not only the elite, but also the entire society, generating animosity among various groups. This was another problem the new leadership had to face. The variety of striking gaps among tribes, tribal-states (or sultanates), and urban and rural areas, as well as between Hadramawt and the western parts, were ongoing factors in shaping political attitudes of traditional South Yemen.[13] The Marxist regime that had governed the PDRY since 1967 strove to attenuate tribal and geopolitical factors in South Yemeni politics, mainly by ignoring their existence and augmenting the role of ideology as the main motivating force in political participation. However, as mentioned earlier, the political leaders never stopped enlisting support on these grounds. Finally, the dynamics of the January 1986 civil war, which involved both army units and tribal groups in the fighting, stressed the importance of parochial motivations and relegitimized their activation. Furthermore, the animosity among groups of different backgrounds, which had taken opposing sides during the civil war, became a prevailing political factor. Reports mentioned proclamations and protests made by the Yafi'i and Dali' tribes against the dominance of the "Hadrami group,"[14] as well as divisions among the armed forces, parts of which kept on supporting 'Ali Nasir even after his deportation.[15] The reinstatement of social uniformity under such circumstances was definitely a difficult task.

The problem of societal divisions was inextricably linked with the reactivation of opposition to the regime. 'Ali Nasir was reported to command 40,000 men, undoubtedly comprising both his own supporters, who had fled from the PDRY into the Yemeni Arab Republic (YAR) and estimated to number 12,000, and earlier opposition groups (such as the Front for the Liberation of the Occupied South Yemen, which had participated in the struggle against the British in the 1960s but lost power to the victorious Marxist rulers of the PDRY). They settled in the southern YAR just north of the PDRY frontier and were a constant threat to the new leadership. Moreover, 'Ali Nasir still commanded support among the urban-educated population of South Yemen who thrived under his reforms, tribal groups of his home region, and pockets within the YSP and the armed forces. A group of exiled administrators and YSP members, who were reported to have viewed the new leadership as illegal, was indicative of this trend.[16] Hence, 'Ali Nasir's ability to inspire and lead an opposition was a danger the new leaders had to tackle.

The new leaders were also faced with the problem of reconstituting the PDRY's infrastructure, which had been damaged in the civil war. The number of casualties in and around Aden, where the fighting centered, was estimated at between 9,000 and 13,000;[17] the death toll among YSP cadres and activists was put by 'Ali al-Salami, Secretary of the People's Presidium Presidency, at between 1,700 and 2,000.[18] Thousands of houses were reportedly ruined, the electricity system ceased to function, and the refineries and port facilities were severely hit. 'Attas estimated the overall damage at $120m.[19]

Facing splits within the elite and the entire society, the lack of leadership experience and legitimacy, as well as a deteriorating position in the Arab world (see below), the new leaders apparently opted to avoid difficult decisions which might increase internal disputes and impede reconstruction. A new doctrinaire ideology and hard-line policies which would reflect the ideas of the anti-'Ali Nasir members in the elite, and were expected after their victory, were either avoided or, at least, not recommended. The new leaders focused, rather, on team work aimed at rehabilitating the State's basic institutions. They formulated their principles in a manner consistent with what seemed to be the public good and the party line. This was the basis of their new policies.

POLICIES OF RECONSTRUCTION, REHABILITATION AND CONSOLIDATION

The activities and declarations of the new leaders formed a set of principles which governed the policies of physical reconstruction and political consolidation:

(a) Prevention of foreign intervention during the fighting. In the new leaders' opinion, intervention by a PLO mediating force and/or the YAR would have kindled frontier clashes, and given 'Ali Nasir's forces precious time and even territorial sanctuary.[20] After such intervention was proposed by the above bodies on 20 and 21 January 1986, the new leaders, probably with the Soviet Union's support (see below), succeeded in forestalling the initiative, which facilitated complete victory over 'Ali Nasir's forces.

(b) Discrediting 'Ali Nasir. This policy had two major goals. First, to absolve the new leaders of any accusations that they had precipitated the January clashes by putting the whole blame on 'Ali Nasir. Second, to demonstrate that the new leaders were not mere "radicals," but that they followed a line of pragmatism and reason. They did so by explaining that it was really 'Ali Nasir who had deviated from the YSP's policies, while they had pursued the accepted party line in a reasonable and persistent manner. Hence, since February 1986, the new leaders depicted 'Ali Nasir as a schemer who had sought to carry out an imperialist plot instigated by the Central Intelligence Agency to ruin the PDRY's historical leadership.[21] In interviews given to Arab newspapers, the new leaders took pains to discredit 'Ali Nasir's deviationist policies and thereby show the logic, coherence and persistence of their own line. Hence 'Attas, the new Prime Minister, Yasin Sa'id Mu'man, al-Bayd and other leaders not only repeated the accusations that 'Ali Nasir was too soft on implementing Marxism (see *MECS* 1984–5, pp 580–81) which could have portrayed them as fanatic hard-liners, but also gave details of 'Ali Nasir's obstruction of justified and agreed-upon principles. He was accused of initiating lavish construction projects; of favoring people from his home region in the armed forces and the Administration; of reviving tribalism; of encouraging consumerism rather than social justice; and most of all, of disregarding the people, i.e., ignoring "the cause of the party." Rejecting these "deviations" and restoring the party line, it was implied, was an accepted and reasonable goal, a part of the "YSP's general orientation" which should earn the new leaders credit and support.[22]

(c) The new leaders tried hard to influence various groups in society, explaining their version of the "plot" of 13 January, and gaining their support. Leaders visited different party branches and made speeches to their members; special attention was paid to the major branches in Hadramawt and Abyan, 'Ali Nasir's home ground.[23] Military militia and police units held numerous parades to hail those groups that had sided "with the revolution" during the fighting.[24] The new leaders called elections for the local peoples' councils and for the People's Supreme Presidium in October. The aim was to gain official support for the new leaders, both by electing their candidates on the local party level and in legitimizing their roles at the level of the Supreme Presidium. This aim was expressed by the YSP's Central Committee as follows: "A referendum through which the masses...expressed anew the depth of their faith in their democratic nationalist regime."[25] According to the YSP's Central Committee report, voter turnout was high, with 89 per cent casting a ballot; new key leaders, who had previously not been members of the Presidium, were elected, and 'Attas was officially made President. The Presidium then elected a Council of Ministers under Nu'man's chairmanship, which included Siyayli and other members who seemed loyal to the new elite.[26]

(d) To secure their position the new leaders also had to overpower possible pockets of support for the Opposition. They did so in two main ways. First, by replacing key functionaries in the Administration and the armed forces. In March, new Commanders were appointed in the Air Force and Navy, and there was a new Deputy Chief of Staff.[27] Over the year, several Vice Ministers, Provincial Governors and Ambassadors were replaced.[28] Second, the Government arrested and detained for investigation thousands of people suspected of being 'Ali Nasir's supporters. This was intended to "purify" or rid different organs of unwanted elements, to seek out 'Ali Nasir's supporters and, if possible, to punish them. During the weeks that followed the fighting, Gulf-based and Egyptian newspapers reported that 10,000 had been detained, tens of secret trials and executions had been held, journalists had been "removed," and hundreds had been sent into exile in Suqotra.[29] Under pressure from various Arab states (see below), the new Government announced an amnesty both for the detainees kept in the PDRY and for most of 'Ali Nasir's supporters exiled in the YAR. In June 1986, the Government announced the release of 2,700 detainees. According to the Government's final plan, only 'Ali Nasir and 47 of his close associates would ultimately be denied amnesty and be charged and tried even in absentia, for hatching the January 1986 plot.[30]

THE PERILS OF CONSOLIDATION

In interviews with Arab papers, PDRY leaders focused mostly on 'Ali Nasir's deeds and tried to play down the effects of shock in the South Yemeni society and economy after the civil war.[31] However, the new leaders' attempts to reorganize society and consolidate their position encountered numerous difficulties. It became evident as the year progressed that the country faced administrative and economic problems which the Government could hardly solve. Several months after the civil war, reconstruction projects were reported in Aden. However, declining aid from Gulf states and/or foreign hesitation to renew financial activities in the war-stricken PDRY resulted in several development projects being halted, at least temporarily. These included the enlargement of Aden's port and a new road network. There were several minor exceptions: thanks to a donation from the International Development Association of the World Bank, interim stages of the projects designed to develop Aden's water supply system and fisheries were completed. Due both to the damage the Aden refineries had sustained and Iraq's successful bombardment of Iranian transport facilities, which curtailed the frequency of Iranian oil shipments for refining in Aden (see essay on the Iraqi-Iranian war), Aden's refineries worked at only 20 per cent of their capacity.[32] Foreign reports indicated that the PDRY's foreign currency reserves were drastically declining, but this assessment had no additional confirmation.[33] The YSP Central Committee's complaints of "objective complications," "lack of creative cooperation" and a "bourgeois layer" in PDRY society[34] indicated that the leaders were not very successful in solving their country's economic problems.

Another major problem that hampered the new leaders' attempts to consolidate their power and reimpose stability was the dominance of the interests of the groups of different descent in politics. The importance of this factor increased during and after the January 1986 incidents. Various reports noted that the new leadership was divided into several groups, all vying for power — notably the Hadrami group, comprising 'Attas and al-Bayd; the Yafi'i group lined up behind Salim Salih, who cooperated with a notoriously violent Politburo member, Muhammad Sa'id 'Abdallah; and the Radfan-Dali' group, who supported the Minister of Defense, Salih 'Ubayd Ahmad.[35] Accordingly, group rivalry erupted on 8 February when Siyayli assumed his position as Minister of the Interior, and was manifested in futile attempts to prevent his entrance into the Ministry.[36] In July, there were reports of three previous futile attempts on 'Attas's life and of divisions among army ranks.[37]

One major source of rivalry among these groups, which also destabilized society, were the activities of 'Ali Nasir's group. 'Ali Nasir succeeded in remaining a formidable rival to the new elite, by maintaining both personal friendship with several Arab leaders (see below) and keeping camps of opposition in the YAR, north of the PDRY frontier. These activities were in themselves damaging to the new leaders, as 'Ali Nasir's reputation and power were a way of luring dissatisfied elements from the PDRY's elite to his camp. Hence, during 1986, four important army officers (lieutenant-generals), as well as 'Abdallah Talib, a senior YSP member, defected to 'Ali Nasir's side; and thousands of citizens continued to flee to his camps in the YAR.[38] Moreover, several Arab leaders friendly to the PDRY, such as 'Ali 'Abdallah Salih of the YAR and Mengistu Haile Mariam of Ethiopia, kept pressing the new leaders to effect a reconciliation with 'Ali Nasir,[39] a demand which had to be taken into account.

For all these reasons the new leaders' attitude toward 'Ali Nasir reflected intra-elite divisions and ambivalence. According to different Arab sources and to 'Ali Nasir's own reports, PDRY officials, first al-Bayd and then Siyayli, met with him and his aides, in both Addis Ababa and San'a in June and July, respectively. 'Attas was said to be ready to negotiate and possibly be reconciled with 'Ali Nasir. But others, notably al-Bayd and Haytham Qasim, the new YSP Secretary-General and the new Commander of the armored forces and Deputy Minister of Defense, respectively, whose ideological differences with 'Attas overshadowed their common Hadrami descent, objected to any reconciliation with 'Ali Nasir and prevailed.

FOREIGN AFFAIRS

CONTINUITY OF FOREIGN POLICY

The tendency of the new leaders to avoid a drastic radicalization of PDRY policies and to portray a moderate and reasonable image was particularly evident in foreign affairs. This policy was motivated not only by the need to prevent intra-elite divisions (see above), but also for the following reasons. First, the new leadership had to prevent a complete loss of legitimacy in the Arab world. Since 'Ali Nasir came to power in 1980, he devised a foreign policy that earned the PDRY and himself personally an improved position with the pro-Western states in the Peninsula, with the radical states in the Arab world, and with the Soviet Union. 'Ali Nasir's sudden downfall was not justified in the Arab world, and his subsequent visits to Arab capitals to explain his version of the January 1986 events further improved his position.[40] The new leaders in Aden were therefore forced to create an acceptable image and foreign policy that would distance them from 'Ali Nasir and earn them support and legitimacy with the Arab states and with the Soviets. In addition, the PDRY's dire economic situation forced the new leaders to resume 'Ali Nasir's policies of improving relations with the Gulf states, in order to try to obtain financial assistance. For all these reasons the new leaders opted to continue the PDRY's pragmatic foreign policy.

However, following the civil war, they had a difficult task in resuming relations with states that favored the deposed leader. In addition, Arab leaders wanted to see how the new leaders would establish themselves in the PDRY, and what kind of foreign policy they would adopt, before making any gestures toward them. As a result of the devastating clashes of January and the emergence of a new regime, most contacts between Aden and the Arab states were frozen.[41]

The new leaders focused on appeals to the Arab Press and on visits to Arab capitals and the Soviet Union to explain their views. The main lines of this campaign were that 'Ali Nasir had distorted their true policies by portraying them as "Communists," "atheists," and "tribal."[42] The PDRY, they claimed, was in favor of "internationalist solidarity" and "peaceful coexistence."[43] They made it clear that they sought to resume the PDRY's friendship with the Soviet Union, while at the same coexisting with and befriending all of the PDRY's neighbors, especially the states of the Gulf Cooperation Council (GCC).[44] That 'Ali Nasir's Minister of Foreign Affairs, 'Abd al-'Aziz al-Dali, had remained in office, was another indicator that the new leaders aimed at continuing the PDRY's moderate policies. Upon resuming his office he was quoted as saying that "we have learned from our experience [that] you cannot export revolution,"[45] a principle expressing the YAR's intentions of good neighborliness.

RELATIONS WITH THE YEMENI ARAB REPUBLIC

The January clashes and the subsequent change of guard in Aden cast a serious shadow over inter-Yemeni relations. After several years of slow but steady improvement accompanied by the introduction of a unity program between the PDRY and the YAR, the civil war created two serious obstacles. First was the YAR's assistance to 'Ali Nasir, during and after the clashes. As a result of the good personal chemistry generated between 'Ali Nasir and his counterpart in the YAR, 'Ali Abdallah Salih, and from the YAR elite's sincere sympathy for 'Ali Nasir, who had turned a previously subversive South Yemeni policy toward the YAR into one of cooperation and unity, San'a was prepared to host 'Ali Nasir and even to intervene on his behalf in Aden. Hence, after 19 January, when 'Ali Nasir arrived in the YAR, San'a attempted to assist him both by mobilizing forces on the PDRY's frontiers and by calling for a cease-fire in Aden to be supervised by the PLO, a move which might have stopped the deterioration of 'Ali Nasir's forces and stabilized his position.[46] This attitude could have resulted in worsening relations between the two Yemens.

Second, it was feared in San'a that the new South Yemeni elite would once more provoke insurgency in the YAR, and thus rekindle animosity between the two states.

Given the emotional and unstable nature of inter-Yemeni relations in the past, Aden's leaders presumably realized that improved ties with the YAR would not only help to weaken 'Ali Nasir, but would also constitute a test case that would serve to improve relations with other Arab states.[47] Hence, while Aden sought to neutralize San'a's pro-'Ali Nasir interventionist attempts in the short run, it also aimed at allaying the YAR's fears in the long run, and at reinstating improved relations between the two states. 'Attas's call to the YAR on 21 January to abstain from intervention, which was made from Moscow and was supported by the Soviet Union,[48] indeed put a halt to anything San'a was contemplating in this direction. The new PDRY leaders were quick to announce their good intentions toward Arab states in general, and the YAR in particular. Thus, Salih's policies were depicted by Aden's leaders as manifestations of "nationalist reponsibility," and 'Attas reiterated the PDRY's hope of resuming unity negotiations with the YAR.[49] The combined effect of these statements and of San'a's growing realization that the new PDRY's leadership was firmly in power, led the YAR to adopt a more conciliatory and cooperative attitude to Aden. In early February 1986, San'a's radio reiterated Salih's "sincere commitment to fraternal and national unity,"[50] and on 19 February a mission of the new leaders arrived in San'a for discussions with local authorities.[51]

The following months witnessed an improvement in inter-Yemeni relations. Both sides declared their readiness to resume the unity talks;[52] land transportation and air communication between the two states, which had been halted since the fighting, reopened in February and March.[53] It became evident, however, that the problems arising from the change of regime in Aden had turned into residual impediments in relations between the two states. The flow of South Yemeni fugitives into the YAR grew to over 12,000, most of whom settled in camps near the PDRY's frontier,[54] and the continuous pressure of 'Ali Nasir made the YAR leaders demand repeatedly that the PDRY announce a complete amnesty and accept 'Ali Nasir again in the PDRY. Negotiations ensued during the summer; behind them loomed the possibility of renewed tension and violence between the two Yemens. A meeting between the PDRY's new Minister of Interior Siyayli and Salih took place in June 1986 (when, according to Arab sources, Siyayli also met 'Ali Nasir); the PDRY leader refused to accept Salih's demands.[55] Moreover, in a meeting between 'Attas, Salih and Libya's leader Mu'ammar al-Qadhdhafi in early July in Tripoli, 'Attas insisted that the PDRY would carry out its own plan of amnesty (see above), but would not agree to 'Ali Nasir's return. He also welcomed the resumption of unity negotiations, but did not agree to abandon any of the PDRY's principles or institutions, a policy which 'Ali Nasir apparently had been ready to forgo; namely, conceding that Islam would be the religion of the united Yemen (see previous volumes of *MECS*).[56] The aborted negotiations generated an escalation of tension along the YAR-PDRY frontier. According to Lebanese and Egyptian sources, minor clashes ensued along the frontier in September 1986.[57]

In the following weeks, leaders in both states tried to reduce tension and made soothing announcements about future unity; Ministers in both States also exchanged visits. However, the basic problems between the two Yemens obviously did not fade away, and would probably overshadow their relations in the future.

RELATIONS WITH OTHER REGIONAL STATES

ATTITUDES TOWARD THE GULF STATES

The PDRY's attitude toward the Gulf states was particularly indicative of the new leaders' aims. Aden sought to improve relations with these states, both to obtain financial assistance from the oil-rich monarchies, and as a manifestation of Aden's desire for regional stability and good neighborliness.

The PDRY leaders' initial statements to this effect were widely quoted by Gulf papers and won the approval of the leaders of the Gulf states.[58] PDRY leaders, notably 'Attas and Dali, set out to visit Manama, Kuwait and Riyadh. With the exception of Saudi Arabia's help in the construction of a hospital in Aden,[59] independent sources did not note any other significant contribution.[60] Gulf leaders may have been suspicious of the new regime or were still hoping for 'Ali Nasir's return. However, this fact did not deter PDRY spokesmen from attempting to cultivate Aden's relations with the Gulf states, probably as a policy that would pay off in the long run. Hence, toward the end of 1986, Aden praised the GCC as a "new asset of prosperity and progress for the Arab nation," and supported the GCC's policy of putting a halt to the Iraqi-Iranian war.[61]

Aden's diplomacy was relatively successful with regard to Oman. The PDRY had improved relations with Oman only in the last few years, during 'Ali Nasir's reign. Perpetuating this course served as a means of preventing tension with the state bordering the PDRY on the east, and as another manifestation of good neighborliness, which would add to the PDRY's prestige with other Arab states.

Oman's Minister of Foreign Affairs, Yusf al-'Alawi, visited Aden on Dali's invitation on 15 June 1986. From announcements made at the end of the visit and from subsequent commentaries, it seemed that Oman was ready to fully legitimize the new PDRY regime and cooperate with it. "Positive steps" to boost bilateral relations were taken, notably a decision to exchange Ambassadors during 1987, and a pledge to prevent either state's intervention in the internal affairs of the other. Oman's Deputy Minister for Foreign Affairs, Haytham Tariq, even indicated that his state would consider extending aid to the PDRY, but he did not indulge in specifics.[62]

ATTITUDES TOWARD RADICAL PARTIES

Improved relations with parties depicted as "revolutionary" or "radical" also constituted one of Aden's major goals. There were two reasons for this. First, like 'Ali Nasir in previous years (cf *MECS* 1984–85, pp 284–85), the new leaders viewed a state of improved relations with radical parties as a main instrument in preserving the PDRY's radical image, which had become attenuated in light of Aden's improved relations with the GCC states. Second, in the days immediately preceding the clashes of January 1986, it was 'Ali Nasir who had made the best of his relations with the radicals — by visiting Ethiopia, Syria and Libya and giving the local leaders his version of events. The new leaders in Aden therefore deemed it necessary to improve relations with radical parties as a means of establishing their own legitimacy and of overcoming 'Ali Nasir's influence in the Arab world.

Aden directed its initial efforts after January to dealing with the initial support 'Ali Nasir enjoyed among radical parties in the region. These attempts had only marginal success. There were overt tensions with the PLO, which had attempted to mediate during the fighting. According to Gulf sources, the new leaders even expelled 'Abbas Zaki, the PLO's representative in Aden.[63] Short of extending military aid to 'Ali Nasir, the Ethiopians were ready to host him and some of his aides in Addis Ababa and, according to an Egyptian source, refused a Soviet demand to dispatch the latter to Moscow.[64] A PDRY spokesman alluded later to the difficulties between the two states, by saying that during the first days after the clashes the Ethiopians had "misunderstood things."[65]

Muhsin Ibrahim, the leader of the Lebanese-based Communist Action Organization, visited Aden in February 1986 and expressed his confidence in the YSP's ability to regroup and reestablish its power in the PDRY.[66] This announcement enhanced the new leaders' image in Syria.

However, in the next months, the PDRY leaders launched a diplomatic campaign to improve the PDRY's position with radical states. 'Attas voiced Aden's identification with Libya after the US bombing raid in April.[67] In May, 'Attas reiterated his country's adherence to the "Tripartite Alliance" of August 1981 with Libya and Ethiopia.[68] Siyayli visited Ethiopia in May and 'Attas visited Syria in June.[69] Na'if Hawatima, the leader of the Popular Front for the Liberation of Palestine and a traditional ally of the PDRY elite, tried to maintain close contacts with both Aden and 'Ali Nasir,[70] a policy which still kept the PLO apart from the new leaders in Aden.

The relatively improved relations that followed this campaign did not turn the various radical parties from their friendship with 'Ali Nasir and from trying to persuade the PDRY into a settlement with him. In the next few weeks, they tried to generate several mediation attempts between the parties. In early July, Libya invited both 'Attas and Salih to Tripoli to discuss the fate of 'Ali Nasir and the South Yemeni fugitives, but to no avail (see above). This attempt was preceded, in May, by a visit of what was described as a joint mission of "progressive parties" from Egypt, Lebanon and the PLO, to explore the PDRY's position over such a settlement.[71] In November 1986, there were reports from 'Ali Nasir's camp that Syria had extended to the PDRY leaders new proposals for a settlement,[72] which, however, bore no immediate results.

During the last months of 1986, a continuous series of meetings ensued between PDRY officials and those of Ethiopia, Libya and the PLO, which attested to the improved status of the PDRY regime. The activities of 'Ali Nasir, however, continued to be an obstacle to closer relations.

RELATIONS WITH THE SOVIET UNION

CHANGING SOVIET ATTITUDES: EMERGING SUPPORT FOR THE NEW ELITE

In the view of a US analyst, there was "circumstantial but compelling" evidence that the Soviet Union had not been part of any premeditated attempt to overthrow 'Ali Nasir, and that it had actually been surprised not only by the outbreak of the clashes but also by their dimension and severity. The Soviets had supported the 1985 attempts to balance 'Ali Nasir's power and policies by reintegrating 'Abd al-Fattah Isma'il in the leadership (see *MECS* 1984–85, pp 577–80), but had not anticipated a coup and the subsequent civil war. Hence, the Soviets had engaged in efforts, not coordinated with the rebels, to evacuate their nationals from the PDRY; had not been able to prevent firing on their embassy in Aden during the January fighting; and had had to accept the loss of almost the entire PDRY leadership — all of which attested to the surprise and confusion of the Soviets.[73]

During the first week of the clashes, the Soviets preferred to wait and see, focusing mainly on mediation attempts conducted from their embassy in Aden (mostly on 16 and 17 January) in conjunction with the PLO, the YAR and Algeria.[74] According to Gulf sources, there were even differences of opinion among top Soviet decision-makers over which side to support, and these differences resulted in a policy of initial passivity and mediation.[75] However, after the first week of fighting, Moscow's leaders seemed to have made up their minds to support the new elite no doubt mainly because of the new leaders' superiority on the battlefield. But there were additional reasons for this decision. The continued fighting, the heavy tribal involvement, and the futile North Yemeni and PLO attempts to mediate, created a lasting civil war (made worse by foreign intervention), which could change the entire socialist character of the PDRY and thereby loosen the Soviet grip on the country. The Soviets therefore decided to stop the fighting as soon as possible, by aiding the stronger party to achieve final victory and by forgoing their previous policy of mediation in favor of a call for a stop to all foreign intervention, a move that paved the way for the Opposition's victory.[76] Moreover, the Soviets also sought to gain by influencing the new elite to accept 'Attas as the new President. The moderate politician from Hadramawt, who had the good sense to cut short a visit to the Far East after the fighting in Aden erupted and to go to Moscow instead, could serve as a moderating force among the more radical members of the Opposition and as a legitimizing factor in the Arab world.[77] In Moscow's view, 'Attas' influence would enable the new leaders to follow a relatively pragmatic foreign policy, similar to 'Ali Nasir's line, which the Soviets had basically favored. 'Attas returned to Aden on 24 January to assume the role of President.

Soviet aid soon started to flow to the Opposition. It came in the form of arms, intelligence information, and tactical combat assistance. By pursuing this policy, the Soviets in effect abandoned 'Ali Nasir and ignored his immediate pleas for an audience in Moscow. They were ready to bring him to Moscow, but only as an exile. This did not happen, however, thanks mainly to Ethiopia's leader Mengistu, who stood by 'Ali Nasir (see above).[78]

RENEWED SOVIET-PDRY COOPERATION

Once the new leaders were fully in control in the PDRY, both parties were interested in resuming cooperation of the kind that had prevailed between the PDRY and the Soviet Union before January 1986. While Aden sought economic and military assistance, the Soviets wanted to restaff their military positions on Suqotra Island and other bases in the PDRY, which gave them an important strategic advantage near the Gulf Bab al-Mandab Straits. Hence, as early as 18 February 1986, several Soviet Communist Party experts arrived in Aden to train new YSP cadres.[79] On 8 March, a Soviet military mission led by Peter Marcovitz arrived in Aden, presumably to examine the possibility of Soviet military experts returning to the PDRY; but he also gave Aden Moscow's guarantee that it would stick by its commitments in the treaty of cooperation of November 1979, and this was greatly appreciated by Aden.[80] A trade exchange treaty for 1986–90 was signed by the two states in June, which gave Aden the possibility of exporting its hides, fish and perfumes in exchange for Soviet goods, notably oil to be refined in Aden.[81] In addition, there were several visits by PDRY leaders to Moscow over the year. If the Soviets made demands concerning 'Ali Nasir's fate during the year, they were not reported.

NOTES

For the place and frequency of publications cited here, and for the full name of the publication, news agency, radio station or monitoring service where an abbreviation is used, please see "List of Sources." Only in the case of more than one publication bearing the same name is the place of publication noted here.

1. *The Guardian*, 14 January; *al-Yawm al-Sabi'*, 20 January; *Fourteenth October*, 22 January; *LAT*, 30 January; *al-Siyasa*, Kuwait, 25 January 1986.
2. *Al-Sharq al-Awsat*, 26 January; *NYT*, 18 January; *al-Majalla*, 22 January; MENA, 16 January — SWB, 16 January 1986.
3. *Al-Yawm al-Sabi'*, 20 January; *NYT*, 22 January; *al-Qabas*, 22 January 1986.
4. R. Monte Carlo, 21 January 1986.
5. *NYT*, 30 January; R. Monte Carlo, 25, 31 January 1986.
6. *Al-Siyasa*, Kuwait, 10 February; *al-Nahar*, Beirut, 14 February 1986.
7. R. Monte Carlo, 27 January 1986.
8. *Al-Majalla*, 20 August 1986.
9. *Al-Anba*, Kuwait, 9 February 1986.
10. Cf *al-Anba*, Kuwait, 27 January 1986.
11. *Al-Mustaqbal*, 1 February; *al-Nahar Arab Report and Memo*, 14 February 1986.
12. *Al-Qabas*, 23 January 1986.
13. Cf J. Kostiner, *The Struggle for South Yemen* (London: Croom Helm, 1984), chapters 1 and 2.
14. *Al-Wahda*, 15 March 1986.
15. *Al-Yawm al-Sabi'*, 3 February 1986.
16. GNA, 27 January — DR, 28 January 1986.
17. Cf R. Riyadh, 19 January; *FT*, 21 January; *NYT*, 16 February 1986.
18. 'Ali al-Salami's interview with *al-Watan*, 12 March 1986.
19. *LAT*, 30 January; *FT*, 30 January; al-'Attas's interview with GNA, 6 July — DR, 7 July 1986.
20. R. Monte Carlo, 20, 21 January 1986.
21. Cf R. Aden, 4 February — DR, 5 February; R. Aden, 5 February — DR, 6 February 1986.
22. Al-'Attas's interview with *al-Mustaqbal*, 22 February; Salim Salih's interview with *al-Ittihad al-'Usbu'i*, 22 May; al-Siyayli's interview with *al-Anba*, 19 September 1986.

23. Cf R. Aden, 26 April — SWB, 28 April 1986.
24. Cf R. Aden, 5 August — SWB, 8 August; R. Aden, 28 August — SWB, 30 August 1986.
25. R. Aden, 5 November — SWB, 8 November 1986.
26. R. Aden, 1 November — SWB, 5 November; R. Aden, 5 November — SWB, 8 November; R. Aden, 6 November — SWB, 8 November 1986.
27. R. Aden, 8 April — DR, 10 April 1986.
28. Cf R. Aden, 20 March — JPRS, 8 May 1986.
29. Cf *Al-Qabas*, 13 March; *al-Ra'y al-'Amm*, 18 March; *al-Tali'a al-'Arabiyya*, 11 August 1986.
30. SWB's announcement, 4 December 1986.
31. Cf Nu'man's interview with *al-Anba*, Kuwait, 10 September — SWB, 16 September; and al-Bayd's interview with *al-Majalla*, 22 October 1986.
32. *QER*, No 1, 31 March; *CR*, No 2, 20 June; No 3, 19 September; No 4, 22 December 1986.
33. *Al-Tali'a al-'Arabiyya*, 18 October 1986.
34. SWB's announcement, 22 September 1986.
35. *Al-Tali'a al-'Arabiyya*, 26 May; *al-Watan al-'Arabi*, 25 July 1986.
36. *Al-Mustaqbal*, 21 March 1986.
37. *Al-Mustaqbal*, 14 June; *FR*, 31 July 1986.
38. *FR*, 31 July 1986.
39. Cf *al-Siyasa*, Kuwait, 27 June; KUNA, 21 July — DR, 22 July 1986.
40. 'Ali Nasir's interview with *al-Watan al-'Arabi*, 23 October — DR, 27 October 1986.
41. QNA, 6 February — DR, 6 February 1986.
42. *Al-Nahar*, Beirut, 14 February 1986.
43. Salim Salih interview with *al-Anba*, Kuwait, 8 February 1986.
44. *Khaleej Times*, 30 January — DR, 1 February 1986.
45. Dali's words quoted by *NYT*, 9 February 1986.
46. R. San'a, 17 January; *Akhir Sa'a*, 22 January 1986.
47. Al-'Atta's interview with *al-Anba*, Kuwait, 7 February — DR, 10 February 1986.
48. *NYT*, 18 January; R. Monte Carlo, 22 January 1986.
49. Al-'Attas' interview with *al-Anba*, Kuwait, 7 February — DR, 10 February; Rashid Muhammad Thabit's (PDRY's Minister of Unity Affairs) interview with *al-Watan*, 23 February — DR, 25 February 1986.
50. R. San'a, 3 February — DR, 4 February 1986.
51. See Thabit's interview with *al-Watan*, ibid.
52. Cf al-Dali's interview with *al-Watan*, 19 March; and 'Abd al-'Aziz al-Ghani's (the YAR Prime Minister) interview with *al-Sharq al-Awsat*, 27 February 1986.
53. Ibid, and *al-Ittihad*, Abu Dhabi, 17 March — DR, 18 March 1986.
54. *Al-Khalij*, 4 June — DR, 5 June 1986.
55. *Al-Nashra*, 2 June; GNA, 26 June — DR, 27 June 1986.
56. *Al-Ittihad*, Abu Dhabi, 3 July; *al-Majalla*, 23 July 1986.
57. *Al-Safir*, 23 September; MENA, 23 September — DR, 24 September 1986.
58. Cf *Khaleej Times*, 30 January — DR, 1 February 1986.
59. R. Aden, 3 August — SWB, 12 August 1986.
60. *CR*, op cit.
61. R. Kuwait, 15 July — SWB, 17 July; Dali's interview with *al-Ittihad*, Abu Dhabi, 8 October — DR, 10 October 1986.
62. R. Salala, 17 June — DR, 19 June 1986.
63. *Al-Ittihad*, Abu Dhabi, 4 February 1986.
64. *Al-Jumhuriyya*, Cairo, 4 February 1986.
65. Quoted by *al-Majalla*, 30 September 1986.
66. R. Aden, 23 February — DR, 24 February 1986.
67. R. Aden, 16 April — DR, 17 April 1986.
68. 'Attas quoted by *al-Watan*, 2 May 1986.
69. *Al-Khalij*, 22 May — DR, 23 May; R. Aden, 28 June — DR, 30 June 1986.
70. *Al-Yawm al-Sabi'*, 14 April 1986.
71. *Al-Ittihad*, Abu Dhabi, 26 May — SWB, 29 May 1986.
72. R. Monte Carlo, 23 November — SWB, 25 November 1986.

73. David Pollock, "Moscow and Aden: Coping with a Coup," *Problems of Communism*, Vol 35, May-June 1986, pp 50–70.
74. *Al-Ra'y al-'Amm*, 18 January; *al-Majalla*, 22 January; *al-Ittihad*, Abu Dhabi, 22 January 1986.
75. *Al-Qabas*, 28 January 1986.
76. *Al-Qabas*, 21, 23 January; R. Monte Carlo, 25 January 1986; Pollock, op cit.
77. Ibid; *Guardian Weekly*, 2 February; *Jeune Afrique*, 5 February 1986.
78. Pollock, op cit; *al-Jumhuriyya*, Cairo, 4 February 1986.
79. *Al-Qabas*, 18 February 1986.
80. R. Aden, 8 March — SWB, 12 March 1986.
81. QNA, 10 October — DR, 10 October 1986.

The Saudi Arabian Kingdom
(Al-Mamlaka al-ʻArabiyya al-Saʻudiyya)

JACOB GOLDBERG

The sharp and quick drop in the price of oil in 1986 from over $25 a barrel to less than $10 in about four months resulted in economic havoc in Saudi Arabia. Economic conditions domestically were already deteriorating. With the fall in oil prices, a coherent economic strategy could not be formulated. Abroad, Saudi Arabia's regional and international standing were eroded, highlighting not only Saudi weaknesses and vulnerability but also the limits of Saudi oil power.

An extremely high level of uncertainties affected economic activity in the Kingdom in 1986. The sharp drop in oil prices had a snowball effect. It was impossible to project oil revenues, therefore an acute prediction of expenditures could not be made, thus preventing the formulation of a clear economic policy. The unstable conditions resulted in Saudi Arabia operating without a national budget for almost ten months. As the recession and the deflation of the economy continued and deepened, there was a further deterioration in business conditions and corporate liquidity. To counteract the economic and financial crisis, the Saudi leadership continued its policy of a two-pronged strategy: it cut deeply into expenditures, especially in infrastructure and construction, and drew on monetary reserves to cover budgetary deficits of over $15 bn a year. Beyond this immediate, short-term response, however, a long-term conceptual strategy was not developed. It became likely that the crisis would peak at the end of the decade when the Kingdom's reserves would be completely depleted.

Nevertheless, contrary to previous years, Saudi leaders were aware that the crisis was a long-term, comprehensive phenomenon, encompassing all sectors in their society. They were ready to communicate to their citizens that the boom years were over. All Saudis would now have to go through the painful process of adjustment and belt-tightening. The leaders became more conservative in their calculation of the Kingdom's projected oil income and more realistic about future developments in the oil market. They also saw advantages in the recession. The economy was more competitive; some of the extravagances of Saudi society were curbed; one million alien workers left the Kingdom; and the economy was becoming normal after the "abnormal" boom years.[1]

In foreign affairs, developments were more ominous and military threats increased. King Fahd lamented, "We are surrounded by the most critical conditions we have ever faced."[2] In view of the Iranian disposition toward a more aggressive posture *vis à vis* all the Gulf Cooperation Council (GCC) states, Saudi anxiety heightened regarding Persian Gulf security. The Saudis failed to bring about an end to the Iraqi-Iranian war, and they failed to effect a Syrian-Iraqi reconciliation.

Riyadh was still unable to convene the long-delayed Arab summit. An air of pessimism in the Persian Gulf arena and the inter-Arab framework resulted. In the Organization of Petroleum Exporting Countries (OPEC), Saudi Arabia decided not to have a confrontation with its opponents, mainly Iran, Libya and Algeria. Rather, the Saudis agreed to adopt production curbs and fixed prices. In addition, the "special relationship" with the US eroded, resulting in the British-Saudi Tornado arms deal.

The chain of external threats and problems made it difficult to form a coherent foreign policy. Contradictions were built into various Saudi policies. The attempt to arrive at a *rapprochement* with Iran contrasted with the massive support of Iraq. Effecting a Syrian-Jordanian reconciliation which, by definition, weakened 'Arafat, contradicted the Saudi wish to strengthen 'Arafat and his leadership. And assistance to the Contras in Nicaragua clashed with Saudi-backed Palestine Liberation Organization (PLO) support for the Sandinista regime. With the inherent limits and constraints, Riyadh was gradually returning to its former pattern of low-profile, backstage roles characterized by increasing passivity.

INTERNAL AFFAIRS

VICISSITUDES OF THE SAUDI OIL MARKET

The 12-month period ending in December 1986 was a stormy time for the Saudi oil market. The fluctuations seemed to result in a loss of control by the Kingdom, which had to adjust to patterns and policies shaped by others. The fluctuations, affecting both oil production levels and oil prices, were of an unprecedented magnitude for any such short period in recent history. Oil production reached a record low of 2m barrels a day (b/d) in the summer of 1985 going up to over 6m b/d by mid-1986 and then declining again to about 3.5m b/d towards the end of 1986. Oil prices, as high as $25 a barrel in December 1985, dropped to less than $10 a barrel within a few months, finally stabilizing at $18 a barrel towards the end of 1986. Since oil income accounted for a high percentage of the Kingdom's revenues, the frequent fluctuations prevented the formulation of a satisfactory economic plan and ultimately resulted in the dismissal of the veteran Oil Minister, Ahmad Zaki al-Yamani. (For a comprehensive analysis of the oil situation, see essay on Middle East oil developments.)

RAPIDLY SHIFTING PRODUCTION AND PRICES

OPEC oil production had been declining since 1981. Saudi Arabia had assumed the role of the "swing producer," meaning that it had to prevent a glut in the oil market. To accomplish this, it had to decrease oil exports in order to prevent a fall in oil prices. The result was that Saudi oil production declined by 80%: from 10.5m b/d in 1981 to 2m b/d in the summer of 1985. Since OPEC had set the Saudi quota at 4.35m b/d, it was obvious that other OPEC members were making up the difference.

Since their threats and warnings in OPEC meetings had gone unheeded, the Saudis decided in the summer of 1985 to bring this state of affairs to an end. "Saudi Arabia," said Finance Minister Muhammad Aba al-Khayl, "has always sought to restore stability to oil prices at its own expense; we have learned our lesson and this will not happen again. We will not make any more sacrifices by cutting our oil output in order to prop up world oil prices."[3] Oil Minister Yamani poignantly added that "we abandoned forever the role of a swing producer; we just want to get more money into the Treasury because we are facing an intolerable recession. There is no going back to lower Saudi production — ever."[4]

With this change in policy, Saudi oil production shot up from 2m to over 6m b/d within a few months, while oil prices declined from $25 to less than $10 a barrel. The Saudis aimed to gain with the new policy in both the short term and the long term. They sought to maximize their revenues which had fallen drastically in recent years. They hoped to drive the message home to OPEC and non-OPEC (especially Britain) oil producers that it was in their capacity to flood the world with cheap oil and in order to drive their competitors out of the market. They strove to force OPEC members into some agreements on production cuts. Finally, they figured that the only way to stimulate world oil demand — which was the crucial long-term Saudi goal and interest — was by significantly cutting oil prices.

By increasing oil production however, the Saudis unleashed a more dramatic price collapse than they themselves had intended. In addition, Iran, Libya and Algeria were virulently critical of Saudi Arabia, holding it responsible for the price war. The result was that the Saudis became frightened and retreated. The Ministry of Oil announced that the Kingdom "is making efforts to correct the situation and to ensure the return to just and acceptable price levels, as it always rejected wide fluctuations in oil prices, either up or down."[5] This statement did not solve the problems in Riyadh which was pressed by a conflicting set of considerations to increase oil production even at the risk of a drop in prices, i.e., the need to inject more money into the Saudi economy. Indeed, Saudi Arabia declared to other OPEC members that it was revenue requirements which would determine the level of Saudi oil production.[6] This prompted Saudi Arabia to increase its production to over 6m b/d in July and August (according to some reports, to 7m b/d), significantly above its official quota of 4.35m b/d. When OPEC Ministers convened in Geneva in late July, the Saudis informed them that the Kingdom could not reduce production below the level needed for its economic development.[7]

Meanwhile, the political pressure from Iran and Libya increased. Iran threatened the security of Saudi Arabia and its neighbors. A senior Iranian official said that Iran regarded "unrestrained oil production that leads to lower oil prices as a hostile act, a declaration of war against us, aimed at reducing our ability to carry on the war against Iraq."[8] Since the Saudis were disillusioned with the magnitude of the fall in oil prices, since there were strong indications that the US would like to see higher oil prices, and since other OPEC members promised to respect their quotas, the Saudis shifted their position once again at the end of the summer of 1986. They reduced their output to around their official quota of 4.35m b/d, and sought a return to a fixed-price system of $18 a barrel. Once again Saudi Arabia became the swing producer. Three stages were needed to arrive at a price of $18 a barrel. First, in August, OPEC reached a temporary agreement designed to strengthen prices. In October, the agreement was extended for two more months, prompting the dismissal of Yamani (see below). Finally, after OPEC had reimposed quotas on its members it officially adopted this policy in its December 1986 meeting in Geneva.[9] Saudi Arabia's implied role as swing producer was to ensure that there was room for Kuwait's higher production quota and for continued overproduction by the United Arab Emirates (UAE), a role it could ill afford. Moreover, according to many oil analysts, at $18 a barrel, the price of oil was artificially high. Thus, it seemed that the OPEC agreement set the same economic forces in motion that had caused OPEC to break up throughout 1986. If Saudi Arabia had to reassume the primary burden for cutting OPEC output, perhaps even as early as the spring of 1987, it would again face a severe decline in revenues.

The pattern of oil trends in general and OPEC's dynamics in particular in 1986, resulted in a mixed balance for Saudi Arabia. On the one hand, Riyadh managed to make use of its ability to flood the market and to persuade the other OPEC members to abide by the quota and pricing policy. On the other hand, however, the Saudis' room for maneuvering became restricted. They realized that the scope of the price collapse hardly served their short-term goal of maximizing revenues. If they were disappointed with 2m b/d priced at $25, they soon realized that 5m b/d priced at $10 fetched precisely the same revenues. It is against these restrictive circumstances that one has to judge Saudi oil policy zigzags in 1986.

THE DISMISSAL OF OIL MINISTER YAMANI

After a meeting between King Fahd and Oil Minister Yamani on 29 October, a Royal Decree announced "Ahmad Zaki Yamani, Minister of Petroleum and Mineral Resources, is relieved of his post" and Hisham Nazer, Minister of Planning, would become Acting Oil Minister. Two weeks later it was reported that immediately after his dismissal, Yamani's passport had been confiscated and that King Fahd had ordered him not to leave the country. Though Yamani himself denied these reports, it seemed that restrictions had indeed been imposed on him, accompanied by a media campaign to denounce him. In mid-December, the Royal Family announced the retirement of the Governor of the Petroleum and Minerals Corporation, Dr 'Abd al-Hadi Taher,[10] who was considered Yamani's right hand in the execution of Saudi oil policy.

Yamani, who became the Kingdom's Oil Minister in 1962, was considered the omnipotent architect of Saudi oil policy. Often described as "Mr Oil," Yamani could seemingly drive oil prices — and the global economy — up or down at will. His abrupt and unceremonious dismissal, therefore, calls all the more for an explanation.

During the past four years, two key Saudi oil strategies, with which Yamani was closely associated, failed. The first concerned the period from 1982 until the summer of 1985. As demand for OPEC oil declined, Saudi Arabia, guided by Yamani's advice, agreed to assume the role of swing producer. In practice it meant that whenever it looked as if quota cheating by member-states would breach OPEC's overall ceiling, Saudi Arabia had to decrease its own output. The most conspicuous example of Yamani's pursuing this strategy came during a 1984 OPEC meeting. Despite instructions from the Royal Family to lower the Saudi production ceiling to "not a gallon less than 6m b/d," Yamani proceeded to agree to a 4.5m b/d quota, apparently convinced that only a concession of that magnitude could hold OPEC together. The decision enraged the Royal Family which had formulated the Kingdom's budget predicated on the 6m b/d figure. Yamani assured the King that prices would go up, but this didn't happen; instead, Saudi oil production continued to fall for the next two years.[11]

This strategy cost Saudi Arabia an 80% decline in production and revenues, which resulted in budgetary deficits, depletion of financial reserves, and recession and criticism at home. Yamani was accused of subordinating Saudi national interests to those of OPEC and of putting the survival of OPEC above the priorities of the

Kingdom. One disenchanted official remarked, "While Yamani treated OPEC members' signatures as the holy Koran, they laughed at us, cheating on prices and production and offering discounts."[12]

So Yamani had to change tactics in the summer of 1985. The second strategy that he adopted was the reversal of the first one: increasing Saudi oil production dramatically in order to pull oil prices down. By keeping oil prices down for a long time, he hoped to expand the demand for oil, and remove from the market oil producers (such as Britain, Mexico, etc) who would not be able to sustain such low oil prices. However, this strategy could succeed only if applied to the long term, rigorously and systematically until, perhaps, the mid-1990s. Yamani also calculated that the Saudis would gain through high sales volume more than what they would lose through lower prices.[13]

But Yamani, obviously, did not expect that prices would plunge as low (from $25 to less than $10) and so fast (within a few months) as they did. Moreover, he failed to appreciate the consequences — domestically, regionally, and internationally — of this plunge in oil prices. Domestically, Yamani came under increasing criticism that his oil policies made it impossible to predict the volume of oil revenues, and hence to engage in serious economic planning and budget formulation. Regionally, Iran started to mount increasing pressures on Saudi Arabia (see above and below) aimed at reversing the Saudi strategy. Internationally, the US indicated that its own oil industry was badly hurt as a result of the Saudi strategy.

Royal Family support for Yamani had been systematically withdrawn throughout 1986 with messages from King Fahd to OPEC conferences leaving Yamani particularly exposed. Yamani had predicted falling oil prices, and before OPEC's meeting in March he warned in a well-publicized interview of a fall to as low as $8 a barrel. This resulted in an immediate rebuke in the form of a statement by an official spokesman of the Kingdom who claimed that "There is no truth in what was attributed to Yamani."[14] Although this was not the first time that Saudi officials contradicted Yamani, nor was it the first time that there were rumors about Yamani's retirement, it seemed that a government semi-official campaign to undermine Yamani's stature was under way.

As a result of the domestic, regional, and international damage, the Royal Family decided to shift course and return to a fixed-price system which, it hoped, would raise oil prices to $18 and set new quotas. Yamani rejected this line arguing that producers could control and fix either prices or output but not both at once.[15] Yamani's advice was ignored, and on 5 August OPEC adopted an interim agreement stipulating for temporary production quotas and measures to strengthen prices, steps that Yamani had steadfastly opposed.

In October, before and during OPEC's session in Geneva, when King Fahd was pushing toward a price of $18 a barrel, Yamani made it clear that demand for OPEC oil would not increase at a price above $15. As a result, during the 17-day OPEC meeting, King Fahd repeatedly intervened from Riyadh and contradicted Yamani on several key issues. Finally the King sent a message to the OPEC meeting empowering Yamani to agree to a two-month extension of the August agreement but only on condition that "the per barrel price should be set at no less than $18 and that everyone should adhere to this price." Although Yamani accepted a final resolution that extended the August agreement, he flouted the King's orders by making no reference to the $18 figure. Yamani was dismissed ten days later.[16]

There were also Royal Family politics connected with Yamani's ouster. Throughout the post-1973 period, an increasing number of Princes developed an antipathy towards Yamani. They resented his overexposure, high profile and star role in the foreign media, which often portrayed him wrongly as the sole arbiter of Saudi oil policy. They especially disliked the fact that he exceeded the limits of his position as a technocrat and behaved as if he were part of the inner core of the Royal Family. Some of his opponents included conservative, influential figures who resented Yamani's overtly Westernized patterns of conduct, style and three-piece European-tailored suits. There were other opponents who questioned the economic, financial and political costs of his policies. This coalition of rivals waited for the opportunity to press for his removal.

As long as oil prices and volumes of Saudi production were satisfactory, Yamani was virtually immune from public criticism. His was a success story from which the Kingdom benefited. However, when the new realities in the oil market, which did not basically depend on Yamani's policies, forced a change in the Saudi oil situation, his opponents seized the opportunity and demanded his dismissal. For the Royal Family, Yamani was an excellent scapegoat; if the Family wanted to distance itself from real and perceived failed policies, it could blame Yamani. The irony of Yamani's ouster was that he had been blamed for both — the consequences of a policy aimed at keeping prices up by keeping production down, and also for the consequences of a strategy aimed at keeping production up by depressing prices.

Yamani presided over the era of oil power — especially Saudi oil power. In one way, he had fallen victim to the demise of that era; in another, his ouster was a symbol and a microcosm of the decline in the stature of OPEC and Saudi Arabia. The new economic realities meant that Saudi Arabia no longer dominated oil pricing, and Yamani became the personification of that change. Yamani's dismissal signified a Saudi willingness to be less unilateralist and more cooperative within OPEC and perhaps even to seek regional accommodation with Iran. But it did not seem to indicate, as some argued, a basic reassessment of Saudi Arabia's security and foreign policies.[17]

HISHAM NAZER APPOINTED OIL MINISTER

Hisham Nazer began his career in government in the Oil Ministry, and was Yamani's Deputy from 1962-68. Then he was appointed Head of the Central Planning Organization, and in 1971 became Minister of Central Planning in charge of the formulation and implementation of the Five-Year Plans. In that job he presided over Saudi Arabia's growth during the boom years of the post-1973 era. Nazer, a longtime rival of Yamani, had coveted the latter's job and was critical of his approach to oil policies.[18] Their differences, reportedly, stemmed from the mid-1970s when Yamani pushed for higher oil production, while Nazer wanted production to be curtailed. Nazer was described as "an effective communicator who cuts less of a dash than Yamani, but is more tuned in to domestic realities."[19]

Although Hisham Nazer was nominated as Acting Oil Minister, there were persistent rumors that the King would give the job to a member of the Royal Family. But Nazer satisfied the King when he managed to achieve what Yamani failed to. In December, OPEC endorsed King Fahd's proposal to return to a fixed-price system of $18 a barrel. In addition to stabilizing the oil market, this enabled the Saudi

Government to publish its proposed budget for 1987 (see below). Only days after OPEC had adopted the plan, Nazer was appointed Oil Minister.[20]

DEEPENING ECONOMIC CRISIS AND RECESSION

THE ABSENCE OF A 1986 BUDGET AND THE DRAFTING OF A 1987 BUDGET

Given the vicissitudes of the Saudi oil market, forecasts about the Kingdom's revenues had become an exercise in guesswork. As a result, the Finance Ministry found it impossible to draft a realistic budget for the fiscal year 1986–87, which was to begin on 11 March 1986. The uncertainties prompted King Fahd to take the unprecedented step of postponing the publication of the 1986-87 budget for five months, until August. "I am confident," the King told his people, "that you will put your hands in ours to spare our country the drawbacks of the oil market trepidations." In the meantime, the King stated, government spending would continue each month at a rate of one-twelfth of what it was a year earlier.[21]

The postponement was variously described as "sensible" and "a panic measure." To the Saudis, the delay was a sign of indecision and uncertainty at the Kingdom's highest level. Saudi bankers feared the postponement might further erode confidence in Saudi Arabia's economic prospects. Some predicted an increase in the outflow of capital because of doubts about the Government's ability to handle the financial crisis. But, in general, the measure was viewed as inevitable given the uncertainties about oil revenues, and was accepted with calm in business circles.[22]

As the chaos in the oil market persisted into the summer, King Fahd announced in August a second budget postponement of five months till the end of 1986. He also said that the fiscal year would change to one based on the Western Gregorian calendar, and would begin on 22 December.[23] Obviously there would be no budget for 1986. When OPEC adopted King Fahd's proposal for fixed production levels and an $18 a barrel fixed price in its December 1986 session, it became possible to project revenues and, hence, draft a new budget. On 29 December the King officially announced a budget for 1987.[24]

There was a mystery, however, about the low level of anticipated oil revenues — $17.4 bn — since OPEC's accord promised the Kingdom revenues around at least $22.7 bn (export availability of around 3.55m b/d sold at *c* $17.5 a barrel). One possible explanation is that having been disillusioned previously with low levels of income which had disrupted all Saudi budget projections, the new Saudi Oil Minister decided to be ultracautious. If the OPEC agreement failed to insure its success, Saudi Arabia might have to revert to its former role as swing producer. In that case, Saudi revenue expectations ($17.4 bn) would be met even if production were to be cut to 3.3m b/d. Alternatively, if the OPEC accord collapsed, the revenue level would be reached even if oil prices fell to $13.5 a barrel. A second explanation is that the Saudis wanted to impress upon OPEC that the Kingdom's finances were really tight and that the Kingdom was making sacrifices. A third explanation for the discrepancy is that, for the first time, the Saudis acknowledged in the budget that a proportion of Saudi-generated oil income will not end up in the Kingdom's coffers. Known for years as "Princely Crude," this oil was sold for the private gain of senior members of the Royal Family.[25] Whatever the reason, the low projected income indicated that the

Saudi Government was determined to be more realistic and cautious. (For an analysis of the budget's projected expenditures, see below.)

DETERIORATING ECONOMIC AND FINANCIAL CONDITIONS

The sharp decline in oil production and prices led to a most dramatic fall in oil revenues; from $110bn in 1981 to less than $20 bn in 1986. But there were also factors which contributed to the decline in the Kingdom's revenues from non-oil sources and which prompted a rise in its expenditures. First, as interest rates fell in the West, Saudi earnings from foreign investments declined sharply. Secondly, since a large portion of Saudi foreign earnings are derived from dollar investments, the fall in the value of the American dollar in 1986 (about 25–35%) significantly eroded those earnings. Thirdly, though Japan and Western Europe are the major buyers of Saudi oil, its sales are priced in American dollars. Thus, not only did oil revenues decline so dramatically in recent years, but their real value shrank by one fifth because of the fall of the dollar.

In addition, Saudi Arabia's purchasing power has been further eroded by the falling dollar. Thus its expenditures on imports from Japan and Western Europe rose by at least 20%. Given that Japan was the number one supplier of goods to Saudi Arabia, and that Germany, Italy, Britain and France were number three, four, five and six, respectively, the Saudi balance of trade worsened considerably. There was an irony built into Japanese-Saudi trade. Japan was the largest source of both Saudi imports and exports (oil). But whereas the Saudis had to pay for their imports in ever-appreciating Japanese yens, they were paid for their oil in ever- depreciating US dollars. In addition, the European Economic Community dealt Saudi exports a blow, when it imposed customs duties on various imported Saudi petrochemical products. It became questionable as to whether or not Western Europe would continue to be a market for up to a quarter of Saudi Arabia's petrochemical exports. The new tariffs would make Saudi products less competitive and could prompt a decline in Saudi exports and earnings.[26]

Because of declining revenues and despite budgetary cutbacks, the Saudis had to dip deeply into their dwindling reserves to finance budget deficits of staggering proportions (see below). The volume of Saudi financial reserves remained shrouded in mystery. Many versions abounded to explain its size and liquidity. According to International Monetary Fund (IMF) figures Saudi revenues declined from $141 bn in 1982 to $109 bn in February 1986, but at least $30–40 bn were believed to be in illiquid categories, such as "loans" to Iraq and dicey investments in neighboring states.[27] According to another source, the balance of Saudi deposits with international banks in March 1986 was not more than $46 bn. This would appear to give the Kingdom only three to four years to run deficits at the projected 1987 level before depleting its reserves.[28] A third view put the reserves at $65 bn, down from $145 bn in 1982, a figure that included Saudi "loans" to Iraq, which were unlikely to be repaid in the foreseeable future. The most far-reaching view held that the Kingdom counted not only its "loans" to Iraq, Egypt, Sudan and Morocco among its assets, but also its $15 bn contributions to the World Bank and the IMF. By this calculation, the Saudis had about $20-30 bn left in liquid assets, which might run out at the end of 1987 in view of the large deficit built into the 1987 budget. But even according to the most optimistic, liberal calculation, which maintained that "loans" to Iraq were not counted, liquid assets totalled no more than $60 bn, much less than the $150 bn of four years earlier.[29]

Given the Saudi dispensation, articulated by the Government and evident by the 1987 budget, to draw even more upon the reserves in order to cover deficits, it was likely that the reserves would be depleted at as fast a rate, at least, as in the previous four years.

The economic and financial crisis led to a decline in the Kingdom's stature abroad. International banks were cutting credit lines to Saudi companies en masse, while trade boards were facing increasing claims for Saudi non-payment. Foreign companies were withdrawing from joint ventures in the Kingdom, among which was a leading German contracting company in hospital management, but the Government denied that any of them were being forced out by late payments.[30] Several international insurance companies covering exports to the Kingdom were beginning to register claims, warning exporters to take particular care in trading with the Saudis. In June, a large British insurance company demoted Saudi Arabia from category A to category B for medium- to long-term business cover. American lawyers confirmed that more than $2 bn was owed to US companies by the Saudi Government. There was evidence that the whole uncertain situation about contract payment was beginning to cost Saudi Arabia the willingness of contractors to bid for business in the Kingdom. In the summer, two tenders for hospital management attracted fewer bids than expected and at higher prices. Companies admitted to "loading" their bid prices to take into account the likelihood of cash flow problems caused by payment delays.[31]

The banking sector in Saudi Arabia was also hard-hit by the recession. All commercial banks, once among the most profitable in the world, suffered sharp profit drops, and some were actually taking losses. This was mainly attributable to the need to build up provisions against likely loan losses and the rescheduling of debts incurred by debtor-companies. In addition, the banks suffered a series of defeats in court when trying to win repayment of overdue loans. Since the concept of interest payment is prohibited by Islamic law, delinquent borrowers made it a habit to resort to the *Shari'a* courts and be absolved of their interest obligations. On occasion, the banks have even been ordered to return past interest payments already made. It was estimated that a third of all outstanding loans were non-performing. In some cases, the Saudi Arabian Monetary Agency (SAMA) had to intervene in order to forestall a bank failure and prevent a loss of confidence in the banking system. In one such rescue operation, SAMA was believed to have filtered nearly SR1 bn in deposits to the Saudi Cairo Bank, after it had incurred losses of over $400 bn.[32]

In other sectors, the recession deepened further. About 150,000 apartments and houses in the Kingdom were believed to be empty, and estimates put the surplus in office space in Riyadh at 50%. The overbuilding in past years was the result of not only public sector construction but primarily the fact that the system of incentives that the Government had devised offered practically free loans to any Saudi wishing to build a home.[33] Hotels, especially in the major cities, also suffered a serious recesssion, having an average annual vacancy of about 60,000 rooms. A new regulation allowed them to lease up to 50% (as opposed to the previous 5%) of their rooms to companies for their employees.[34]

Government expectations for more private sector investments, one of the characteristics of the fourth Five-Year Plan (1985–90), did not materialize. Various Ministers continuously stated that the era of heavy government investments was over and that it was now up to the private sector to play an increasingly central role in the economy. "Individual Saudis had accumulated money in abundance," said Finance Minister Aba al-Khayl, "but because of a certain state of mind they are reluctant to channel their capital to the main stream of the economy, which is completely unjustifiable."[35] It seemed that Saudi Arabia found itself in a vicious circle: the deepening recession made individuals reluctant to invest, and the absence of such investments further exacerbated the recession.

Another manifestation of the economic crisis, obscured in previous years and much more conspicuous in 1986, was increasing unemployment in general and among university graduates in particular. The authorities rejected any notion of existing unemployment and argued that jobs were available in abundance.[36] But after various newspapers overseas had continuously referred to the subject,[37] the regime finally admitted the existence of the problem and outlined some measures to remedy it. In addition to the general recession, the private sector was singled out and blamed for "not fulfilling its role in absorbing Saudi workers and solving the problem of unemployment." The other major reason for the phenomenon was the complete lack of correlation between the demands of the Saudi economy and the policies of admissions and enrollments of the universities. Finally, the authorities argued, many Saudis refused to accept jobs that they deemed inappropriate and demeaning. Thus, the recurring theme in government statements about the problem was that Saudis had to understand that the economic boom was over and they had to adjust to the new circumstances.[38]

THE REGIME'S POLICIES AND RESPONSE TO THE CRISIS

The same dilemma that had plagued the Kingdom since 1982 continued in 1986. It had to choose between two evils — slash expenditures so they conform to dwindling revenues even at the expense of public dissatisfaction or run the risk of considerable budgetary deficits even at the expense of depleting the Kingdom's reserves. As in previous years, the Saudi leaders opted for a combination of both. They had slashed budget outlays considerably, from $90 bn in 1981–82 to $70 bn in 1984–85 and continued slashing in 1985–86 to $55 bn to a projected $45 bn in 1987. Thus, even the "modest" annual expenditure target of the 1985–90 Five-Year Plan — of about $55 bn — had to be abandoned. Despite the massive cutbacks of 50% in five years, there were still large-scale deficits because the Kingdom's revenues declined by no less than 80%. The projected deficit built into the 1987 budget was the best case in point: $14 bn out of an expenditure target of $45.3 bn, or 31%; almost one third of all Saudi outlays were derived from non-revenue sources.

The deficit could be covered by imposing more taxes, fees, duties, etc; slashing the generous subsidy system; and obtaining loans. Senior members of the Royal Family decided to reject all three, and instead to continue to draw on the financial reserves of the Kingdom. These reserves provided, in the words of Finance Minister Aba al-Khayl, "the necessary cushion to carry on the development of the society despite the unfavorable direction of the oil market."[39]

Actual outlays in 1986 and those projected for 1987 exposed distinctly a shift in spending priorities. Whereas expenditures in infrastructure, construction and development were more drastically reduced, the policy of cutbacks in subsidies and services was stopped and, to some extent, even reversed. Such new emphases revealed shifting priorities: preventing popular unrest and social strains took precedence over the risks involved in deficits and further depletions of the reserves. At the time that the budget was first postponed, March 1986, King Fahd made it clear that he planned to keep the Saudi welfare state system intact. He pledged to continue free education and medical care for all Saudis and to maintain generous subsidies for such services as transportation, communications and electricity.[40] He reinforced this policy when he announced a new budget on 29 December 1986: "Subsidies on food, animal fodder, medicines and petroleum products will remain unchanged. We do our best in these difficult circumstances to keep the welfare of our citizens a top priority while not burdening the Kingdom with loans." The issue of subsidized electricity was a case in point. In late 1984 the Government raised electricity tariffs; in December 1985 these increases were substantially reversed.[41] In explaining this change of heart, the authorities claimed they were anxious to relieve citizens' financial burdens. "We are committed," said Minister of Planning Nazer, "to providing every Saudi with a minimum standard of living."[42] In fact, spending on subsidies and social services remained such a high priority that it the 1987 budget, expected to be no larger than $38 bn, it wound up with over $45 bn as the expenditure target.

Capital expenditure was substantially reduced in the fiscal year 1985–86. The Government awarded only $4 bn in new construction contracts. In the new 1987 fiscal year, said Finance Minister al-Khayl, no major government contracts would be awarded.[43] Indeed, infrastructure and development expenditures — the largest item in the budget during the boom years, reaching $50 bn in 1981 — dropped to no more than $8 bn in the 1987 budget. Spending on the ports of Jidda and Dammam and the new cities of Jubayl and Yanbu‘ were substantially reduced. In addition, the Government precluded a number of industries from new loans on the grounds of existing overcapacity in specific subsectors, mainly in the building materials industries.[44]

Delays in payments to contractors, a standard Saudi measure in recent years, continued. In fact, there were signs of escalation in the running battle over payments between construction companies, particularly foreign ones, and the Government. The committee of ministers set up to investigate claims of late payments reported in early 1986 that it found no evidence of government wrongdoing. It said that, as before, all delays were attributable to noncompliance with contractual obligations. It suggested that the companies were using such claims as an excuse to their banks and shareholders. When such claims did not stop, the Government threatened to ban firms which made false claims of late payments from further work in Saudi Arabia. The authorities also stopped advance payments to contractors, after having cut them progressively from 20% to 10% and finally to 5%.[45]

The major cutbacks in expenditures were reflected in the level of Saudi imports which fell 28% in 1985, compared to 1984, and probably another 20% in 1986.[46] The implications of these cutbacks were far-reaching. It would seem that the Saudi import market, after holding up for several years, suddenly began to plunge. The biggest falls were in the area of iron, metal and transport equipment. The infrastructure and urbanization boom was at an end. The effective devaluation of the Saudi riyal against the Japanese and West European currencies proved great enough to deter imports. Still, on 1 June, SAMA announced a 2.7% devaluation of the riyal against the US dollar — from SR3.65 to SR3.75 to the dollar.[47] It was not as high as expected because the dollar also fell during 1986. The effective devaluation against the yen and European currencies in 1986 was about 25-35%. This was the second devaluation of the riyal in less than a year: in June 1985 the riyal was devaluated from SR3.61 to SR3.65 to the dollar.

The Government also cut the substantial subsidies it had allocated to wheat production. As the latter reached 2m tons in 1985 (domestic consumption is less than 1m tons), the authorities announced that they would pay only SR2,000 for each ton of wheat, instead of SR3,500 which was five times the world price. When wheat farmers did not appear to be discouraged enough by the measure, Minister of Agriculture al-Shaykh informed them that the Government would buy only 60% of the output of large farms and only 70% of that of medium-sized farms.[48] It remained to be seen whether these measures would cut the excess production of wheat.

Other government efforts aimed to reduce the number of foreign workers in Saudi Arabia. To encourage their departure, and also to prevent unemployment among indigenous Saudis, a new regulation stipulated that an expatriate work permit would only be renewed if the ministries concerned were satisfied that no Saudi could fill the relevant job.[49] A major employer which cut down its foreign personnel was Aramco. It planned to cut its expatriate staff by 9,000 during 1986, and to reduce the number of its operational divisions from seven to five. All in all, it was estimated that during 1985 and 1986, about 1.5m alien workers had left the Kingdom.[50]

Deepening unemployment among university graduates forced the Government to adopt a more vigorous policy regarding higher education. As a result, 75,000 high school graduates, about half of all graduates who had applied to universities in the Kingdom, were turned down. This was a directive from King Fahd who wanted to restrict the number of new students because of the widespread unemployment among university graduates.[51] Acting along the same lines, the Minister of Higher Education stated that the civil service bureau had projected its requirements for the next ten years regarding graduates needed by the Government in various fields. He said that those who were denied admission to the universities would be asked to join technical and vocational training institutes. In order to cut expenditures, reach coordination between the job market and higher education, and prevent unemployment, the Minister stated that certain departments in the universities, "which produced more than the required number of graduates," might be closed.[52]

Even in the largest single item in the budget, defense, there appeared to have been a cutback, though the issue was shrouded in mystery. There was still a distinct bias towards defense expenditure, although allocations were practically cut from $19 bn in 1984–85 to $17.7 bn in 1985–86 and to a projected $16.2 bn for 1987.[53] In percentage terms, however, defense expenditures actually increased from 27% of total outlays in 1984–85 to 32% in 1985–86 to a projected 35.7% in 1987. Thus, while cutbacks in the military spending were implemented, they were of a smaller magnitude than other items.

INTERNAL CHALLENGES

ROYAL FAMILY POLITICS

The increasing concentration of power in the hands of the Sudayri branch of the Royal family in general, and in King Fahd's sons in particular (see *Middle East Contemporary Survey* [*MECS*] 1984–85, p 596), reportedly led to a serious split within the ruling family. This process was further highlighted during 1986 by the increasing prominence of Defense Minister Sultan, who was the second of the seven Sudayri brothers and second in line for succession, and the promotion of his sons. In mid-1986, Sultan created a fourth branch in the armed forces — an air defense force — and saw his son Khalid promoted to the rank of major general to command the new force.[54] His other son, Prince Bandar, who was the Saudi Ambassador to Washington, was reportedly lobbying intensively for the position of Foreign Minister, a move adamantly opposed by the other branches of the Royal Family. But after Oil Minister Yamani had been dismissed, Bandar was reported to have started lobbying for the Oil Ministry. Once again, the anti-Sudayri front in the Royal family, headed by Crown Prince 'Abdallah, resisted the move.[55] Both Sultan and Bandar, however, suffered a setback and were embarrassed by the failure of Saudi plans to procure weaponry from Washington (see below), the former as the one in charge of arms purchases and the latter as the Ambassador under whose jurisdiction the lobbying campaign was. His failures to get either the Foreign or Petroleum Ministries notwithstanding, Bandar was apparently well off even in such times of economic hardships: it was reported that he awarded a $30m contract to build himself a palace in Riyadh.[56]

Aware that such simmering power struggles projected negatively regarding the unity of the Royal Family, both camps strove to contain the rift, and stop the unpleasant publicity. In a publicized statement, King Fahd called on the Princes "to respect the close ties binding the sons of Saudi Arabia."[57] But such a call only confirmed the actual tensions and frictions. Another effort at projecting family unity backfired on 23 September, Saudi Arabia's National Day marking the 54th anniversary of the unification of the Kingdom. In a rather unusual and only recently established act of protocol, both King Fahd and Crown Prince 'Abdallah were scheduled to give a joint address to the nation. The televised speech was, however, delivered on their behalf by the Information Minister. If the idea of a joint address was calculated to remove the persistent rumors of a rift between the two top leaders of the Kingdom, the effect was spoiled.[58]

Despite the persistence of the power struggle, both camps were united over one issue of keeping all powers exclusively in the hands of the Royal Family. Thus, when the Governor of Madina, Prince 'Abd al-Muhsin, died, Prince 'Abd al-Majid moved to Madina from Tabuk, and Prince Mamduh was appointed Governor of Tabuk.[59] This confirmed the hold that the sons of the founder of the Kingdom — 'Abd al-'Aziz Ibn Sa'ud — enjoyed over governorship posts all around the country. Prince Mamduh, born in 1941, is one of the youngest sons of Ibn Sa'ud, being born in 1941.

The year reviewed in this volume also witnessed a change in the official title of the King. While delivering a speech at the opening of the Madina television center on 26 October, Fahd announced that the title of "His Majesty" would be replaced by "Servant of the Two Holy Shrines" (*Khadim al-Haramayn al-Sharifayn*). Majesty, explained Fahd, was a holy attribute of God, and using it for a temporal ruler could be offensive to the feelings of Muslims.[60] While it was clear that the new title was intended to give King Fahd greater standing in the Muslim and Arab world, it was unknown why Fahd felt it was necessary to introduce this change at this time. Perhaps he did so because of the forthcoming meeting of the Islamic Conference Organization in Kuwait in January 1987.

SECURITY PROBLEMS

During the year reviewed in this volume there was a distinct decline in reports about coup attempts, explosions and incidents in the Kingdom. Fewer such reports occurred even in overseas publications by opposition groups which usually reported extensively about such real, or imaginated, incidents. It was only at the end of the year that the monthly *al-Thawra al-Islamiyya* which appears in London, carried a story about an abortive coup attempt in December. According to the story, a group of army officers, headed by Defense Minister Sultan's son, tried to carry out a coup. The attempt was foiled when some Americans who worked with the Air Force grew suspicious of certain irregularities and reported them to the authorities.[61] It was impossible to corroborate or deny the story.

The perennial security problem posed by the annual pilgrimage to Mecca continued to plague the security authorities, with the Iranians being the greatest risk. Iranian pilgrims constituted the largest group to arrive from overseas, and their number increased in 1986 from 150,000 to close to 155,000. As in previous years, the Ministry of Interior warned the pilgrims against "carrying books, pictures and pamphlets that have political and propaganda goals which contravene the noble goal of the pilgrimage." Interior Minister Na'if specifically warned Iranian pilgrims not to "exploit the sanctity of the *haj* for political purposes," and declared that violators would be "severely dealt with and punished as a deterrent" by the Saudi authorities.[62]

There were, however, signs that the Saudi leadership was in contact with the Iranian authorities before the pilgrimage season, and that the issue became part of the secret dealings between the two countries (see below). Furthermore, it appeared that the issue became a bone of contention between the two rival camps within the Iranian regime (for details, see chapter on Iran). It came as a surprise when on 8 August the Saudis arrested a group of 113 Iranian pilgrims on board an Air-Iran jet at Jidda's airport before they even managed to disembark the plane, citing "fundamental reasons under investigation." It was argued, several months later, that the Saudis acted on information they had received from the Rafsanjani camp in Iran. This suggested that Ayatollah Montazari, Mehdi Hashemi and their supporters, determined to disrupt the *rapprochement* between the two countries, were sending a group of pilgrims carrying explosives to Mecca to stir up disturbances in Mecca. As a sign of goodwill, the Saudis had allowed the Iranians to perform the pilgrimage under the full supervision of their security units, before they released them and sent them back to Tehran at the end of the pilgrimage season.[63]

The Shi'ite-populated areas of the Eastern Province continued to remain tranquil. In early 1986, the Dammam area municipality was upgraded into a mayoralty which would encompass the cities of Dammam, al-Khobar, Dhahran and Qatif. The change was to increase effectively the extent of government attention paid to providing services to this part of the Eastern Province and to counter some of the social and economic tensions that had emerged in the area. The change also reflected the increasing importance of this region in government spending priorities. This shift started following the disturbances of late 1979 and early 1980, and gathered more momentum after the appointment in early 1985 of King Fahd's son, Muhammad, as the Governor of the Province (see *MECS* 1979–80, pp 688–90; 1980–81, pp 733–34; 1981–82, pp 785–86; 1984–85, p 596).

FOREIGN AFFAIRS

SAUDI POSITION IN THE INTER-ARAB FRAMEWORK

Throughout 1986, the Saudi leaders' plea for an Arab summit, postponed since 1983, persisted. Such a summit, they repeatedly emphasized, would help terminate interregional rivalries and conflicts and bring about reconciliation among various Arab and Islamic states. Also highlighted was the fact that only "Israel and other enemies of the Arab nation" were the real beneficiaries of the perpetuation of such inter-Arab struggles and frictions. The Saudi leadership and media went out of their way to stress that the summit could convene either in Riyadh, as was scheduled since 1983, or in any other capital agreed upon by the Arab states; that it could be on the level of experts, ministers, or heads of state; and that though it should eventually be an all-Arab summit, it could be preceded by "mini" summits which encompassed only a limited number of participants. At the beginning of the year, the Saudis were confident that a summit would convene shortly, and many of their statements suggested that its convening was just "a question of days."[64]

Saudi optimism rested on the success of the efforts to effect a reconciliation between Syria and Jordan, the credit for which they took themselves. "The normalization of the situation between Jordan and Syria is the natural outcome of the policies carried out by the Saudi leadership in general, and Crown Prince 'Abdallah in particular." The Syrian-Jordanian *rapprochement*, and hence Saudi success, was regarded as reaching its peak in June when the two countries exchanged Ambassadors for the first time since 1981.[65] (For assessment of the Saudi role in the *rapprochement*, see *MECS* 1984–85, p 601.) Such perceived success created in Riyadh the hope that the Syrian-Jordanian reconciliation could be turned into the first link in a multistage process which would culminate in an all-Arab summit.

In the second stage, they figured, a Syrian-Iraqi *rapprochement* was a top priority, given Syrian support of Iran in the Gulf war and the Saudi willingness to end the war. Therefore, they doubled efforts in the direction of Syria and Iraq, and hoped for success when representatives of both countries agreed to meet on 13 June. Even when the meeting was postponed, the Saudis still expressed optimism, arguing that this would give them "more time to make better preparations" for the meeting: "It is not the very meeting which is the most important; it is better to postpone it to assure positive consequences."[66] In October they launched another campaign of mediation, with Crown Prince 'Abdallah shuttling between Damascus and Baghdad. Their success in effecting a *rapprochement* between the latter two, the Saudis hoped, would pave the way for an all-out attempt, through small-scale, bilateral summits, to terminate the Gulf war. This, in turn, would herald the third stage: the convening of an Arab summit conference.[67]

It was easy, against this background of expectations, to understand the extent of Saudi frustration following the failure of their efforts. The Saudi leaders themselves realized by the end of the year that all three goals — an Iraqi-Syrian reconciliation, termination of the Gulf war, and the convening of an Arab summit — were impossible to attain. The best reflection of their disillusionment was conveyed in an editorial in *al-Jazira*: "The tragedy of the Arab world is embodied in its inablity to reach either resolutions or agreements with regard to any issue affecting the Arabs. The Arab nation is badly split on all these issues, the result being a series of tragedies — in the

Gulf war, in the war for the camps in Lebanon, in the split within the PLO, and in the simmering Palestinian problem."[68] But there was very little the Saudis could do in order to change this pattern of inter-Arab politics. King Fahd, indeed, suggested the revision of the Arab League Charter "so that it can respond to the changes and enable Arab action to proceed unobstructed,"[69] a formula that had been advanced by King Husayn long before. But Fahd was not bold enough to reiterate the second half of Husayn's formula, i.e., that the revision entailed a shift from "consensus" to "majority" as the principle governing the decision-making process in the League's meetings. However, to say so would have alienated Syria.

RELATIONS WITH SYRIA

Several developments in the Middle East appeared to have suggested that Saudi leverage on Syria, very negligible despite its assistance to Damascus, might have increased in 1986. The severe economic conditions in Syria, the draining of Iran in the war and the sharp decline of its revenues, and the growing internal crisis in Libya all opened the door for Saudi Arabia to be more influential on the policies of President Asad. Indeed, as the economic recession in Syria deepened, Damascus became more dependent on Riyadh's financial assistance.

Nevertheless, the pattern of Saudi-Syrian relations in the last decade seemed to have remained intact (see previous chapters of *MECS*, especially 1984–85, p 602). Though Saudi leaders intensified efforts to budge Syrian leaders from the positions they maintained, the two countries continued to differ on almost every major policy issue in the region: the Iraqi-Iranian war, a Syrian-Iraqi reconciliation, the split within the PLO, the Jordanian-PLO dialogue, and the internal struggle in Lebanon. Moreover, it appeared that the Saudis acted on many foreign policy issues in clear deference to Syrian positions, most notably over the question of restoring Eygpt to the Arab ranks. In general, Riyadh was anxious not to appear to be alienating Damascus. Thus, when some news agencies reported that Saudi Arabia had been ready to guarantee an IMF loan of $1 bn to Syria only if Damascus reconciled itself with Iraq and the PLO and ensured the security of the camps in Lebanon, the Saudi Government flatly denied the report.[70]

RELATIONS WITH EGYPT

The slow, gradual *rapprochement* between Saudi Arabia and Egypt that had evolved since 1982 gathered much more momentum in 1986 both in quality and quantity. The scope, level and frequency of Egyptian-Saudi contacts and visits were, indeed, of such magnitude that it was taken for granted that a full-fledged resumption of diplomatic relations was imminent. This, however, failed to materialize, indicating that the Saudis were still reluctant to formalize the *rapprochement* as long as there was no Arab summit decision (i.e., Syrian consent) reversing the 1979 resolution to break diplomatic relations with Egypt.

In the first interview of a Saudi King with an Egyptian newspaper since 1979, King Fahd told *al-Ahram* that "Egypt, the core of the Arab world, is our big sister and always in our heart and thoughts." Fahd hailed President Mubarak for his efforts to improve economic conditions in Egypt and called upon him to reassure "Egypt's natural and leading role in the Arab world." A few days later, King Fahd sent a message to President Mubarak informing him of a present of 200,000 tons of Saudi wheat "as a symbolic gift of the Kingdom to Egypt."[71] In December, President Mubarak, on an official visit to Paris, met with Prince Salman, the Governor of Riyadh and a full brother of the King. After the meeting, Salman stated that the ties between the two countries were "eternal," while Mubarak announced that the Saudi exhibition "Riyadh — Today and Tomorrow" would be held in Cairo in July 1987. It was also announced that following the meeting, Mubarak and King Fahd had a lengthy conversation on the phone. As an immediate follow-up, the Mayor of Riyadh arrived in Cairo a few days later to finalize all the necessary arrangements for the exhibition.[72]

It appeared that two senior Saudi Princes were instrumental in carrying out contacts between the two countries. The fact that they did not occupy any official post in the Saudi Government relieved Riyadh of the Arab (i.e., Syrian) pressure that such *rapprochement* was bound to generate. Prince Tallal (the King's half brother), chairman of the United Nations Children's Fund program for Gulf development, visited Egypt twice in 1986 and met with senior Egyptian officials, including Foreign Minister 'Abd al-Majid. He described his visit as aimed at "promoting bilateral relations between the two countries," and he called on "all Arabs to establish political, trade and economic relations with Egypt" because this was an "Arab interest." It was also reported that Prince Tallal was trying to arrange for all Gulf states to provide Egypt with a long-term loan for the construction of 3m apartments in order to alleviate the acute housing problem in Cairo.[73] Prince Turki (King Fahd's full brother) visited Cairo in October and had a meeting with President Mubarak, following which the latter spoke on the phone with King Fahd. Turki spent most of his time in discussions with Egyptian intellectuals and university professors. The identity of his interlocutors prompted rumors that his discussions were connected to his long-expected appointment as chairman of the projected consultative council (*shura*). In February, Prince Turki offered a personal contribution of $2m towards a fund designed to repay Egypt's foreign debts.[74]

The *rapprochement* was manifested, however, in the economic sector more than anywhere else. Again, it was easier for the Saudis to deviate from the official boycott of Egypt in the areas of economics and finance than in politics; the latter would have, undoubtedly, drawn severe Syrian criticism. It seemed as if the Saudi and Egyptian markets found each other in 1986 and discovered a mutual need. Egypt needed foreign investment capital to help it implement its five-year economic plan. Saudi investors found in Egypt an open field in which to use their mammoth construction equipment idled by the economic recession at home.

It was against such a background that an Egyptian-Saudi investment conference took place in Cairo in October. The Saudi delegation consisted of 40 businessmen, headed by Abu Dawood, president of the Jeddah Chamber of Commerce and vice president of the Federation of Saudi Chambers of Commerce. Among its many resolutions, the conference recommended that the Egyptian Government prepare a list of the projects required and feasibility studies made on them for the guidance of potential investors. It called for the formation of a permanent Saudi-Egyptian Committee to tackle any difficulty facing Saudi investments in Egypt. In November, a delegation of top Saudi contractors arrived in Cairo to undertake a number of priority investment projects in the fields of housing, land reclamation and the manufacture of building materials. More Saudi investors were expected in Cairo in early 1987 with additional investment plans. Another major step towards attracting Saudi and Gulf investors was made by Egypt when it lifted the ban on the possession of real estate by foreigners, allowing them to own apartments or land not more than 1,000 sq meters in size.[75]

Several statements by Saudi Chamber of Commerce officials revealed another angle to the subject. These implied that many Saudi businessmen were disillusioned with their investments in Europe and the US, and had begun to gradually shift them to the Arab world in general, particularly Egypt. Moreover, in the past, they were anxious lest their investments were nationalized. Now they regarded Egypt as, with the exception of the Gulf states, the most stable country in the Arab world. In addition, the Egyptian Government apparently promised to compensate any investor for damages incurred during disturbances and unrest.[76] With these steps and in such a conducive atmosphere for investments, it was expected that Saudi investments in Egypt, which stood at 27% of total investments at the end of 1986, would rise steeply. Besides, the Saudis could prove to act as a pathfinder to guide other Arab states toward investing in Egypt.

Though the net effect of all the Saudi activity pointed to a willingness to change the pattern of its relations with Egypt which had prevailed since 1979, the Saudis were obviously reluctant to formalize the change politically and diplomatically. Thus, when the Egyptian news agency reported that a Saudi military delegation had arrived in Cairo to discuss cooperation with the Egyptian military, the Saudi Government was embarrassed and denied the reports. The Saudis felt it was sufficient that they praised the central role played by Egypt in "promoting the Palestinian participation in the peacemaking process."[77]

ATTITUDE TOWARD JORDAN AND THE PALESTINE LIBERATION ORGANIZATION

The success of the Saudi-sponsored *rapprochement* between Jordan and Syria heralded a period of increasing cooperation and coordination between Riyadh and Amman. The two countries had similar perceptions about most major regional issues and, moreover, sought the same three goals: to effect a Syrian-Iraqi reconciliation, to terminate the Iraqi-Iranian war, and to convene an Arab summit conference. Thus, King Husayn and Crown Prince 'Abdallah actively pursued, and coordinated, mediation efforts between President Asad and Iraq's Saddam Husayn, hoping that an Iraqi-Syrian reconciliation would terminate Syria's support of Iran and, hence, prompt Iran to stop the war. In addition, King Husayn and King Fahd coordinated efforts toward convening an Arab summit, the latter adopting Husayn's call for a revision of the Arab League's Charter in a way which would base resolutions on majority voting and not consensus. For that purpose, Husayn visited Riyadh twice, in July and December. Both efforts, however, failed.[78]

The one issue on which the two countries did not see eye to eye was the Jordanian-PLO dialogue. The Saudi position continued to be characterized by ambivalence. On the one hand, since 1982 Riyadh had been expecting a joint Jordanian-Palestinian coalition that would join the political process. On the other hand, the Saudis could not publicly support and endorse any dialogue, let alone an agreement, between King Husayn and 'Arafat in the face of Syria's adamant rejection of the whole dialogue. The Saudi dilemma was, to a large extent, mitigated after King Husayn had announced on 19 February the end and failure of the process (see chapter on the PLO). The Saudis did not formally react to Husayn's speech, but the termination of the dialogue relieved them of the necessity to make a clear-cut stand on the issue. To reconcile these conflicting considerations, Riyadh adopted a compromise formula according to which "the Palestinians themselves are responsible for their fate and they should be allowed to determine what is good and what is bad for them; all Arabs ought to stop intervening in their affairs, except when such intervention is welcomed by the Palestinians themselves."[79]

Saudi Arabia continued to view 'Arafat as representing the PLO, perhaps the only issue on which the Saudis publicly disagreed with Syria. They demonstrated increasing anxiety about the splits within the PLO, particularly within al-Fath, and repeatedly called on all PLO factions to return to a unified organization under 'Arafat's leadership. The Saudi media stressed that these splits accounted for the "war for the camps" in Beirut from which only Israel benefited, and for the deadlocks in the political process which enabled Israel to perpetuate "its occupation of Arab lands."[80] 'Arafat, for his part, strove to ensure the Saudi support of his leadership of the PLO, especially after the breakdown of his negotiations with King Husayn. He was also concerned that the Saudi-sponsored Jordanian-Syrian reconciliation would not only be at his expense but that it would also deprive him of Saudi support. To preempt such a contingency, he was in continuous contact with the Saudi leadership and made three trips to Riyadh in January, March, and November 1986.[81]

RELATIONS WITH LIBYA

Saudi Arabia's relations with Libya were distinctly less strained than in former years. This resulted from different sets of interests that guided each of the two. Since Qadhdhafi had come under severe general criticism for his purported sponsorship of international terrorism, he sought to obtain Saudi political and diplomatic support to counter the criticisms and threats. His interest peaked in the aftermath of the American bombing raid on Libya on 14 April (see chapter on the US and the Middle East), when he expected Riyadh to come to his support by adopting a clear and public anti-American stand. The Libyans were extremely disappointed when the Saudis, in Tripoli's view, merely paid lip service to "Arab solidarity" without translating it into any concrete political action. The Libyan media commented that if Saudi Arabia was incapable of stopping the Americans' arrogant behavior, it should at least bring an end to its silence — before it was too late.[82] This criticism was, however, short-lived; it was apparent that Libya did not wish to cause any escalation in its relations with Riyadh. Indeed, in contrast to previous years, there were no reports during the pilgrimage season about any incidents involving Libyan pilgrims.

Saudi Arabia, for its part, sought to diffuse crises relating to Libya. Moreover, after the American raid Qadhdhafi called for the convening of an emergency Arab summit, and the Saudis supported it, hoping that such a summit meeting would pave the way for the long-delayed summit conference that they had been requesting since 1983. Alternatively, they suggested that the emergency summit deal not only with the American attack but also with "all external attacks directed against the Arab nation."[83] The reference to Iran's war against Iraq was clear, as was the Saudi interest in placing the war on the summit's agenda, something that had been frustrated by Syria's opposition.

Another context in which Saudi-Libyan contacts took place was the question of OPEC and oil production and prices. Libya, Iran and Algeria were at the forefront of OPEC members' striving to pressure Saudi Arabia to reverse its policy of doubling oil production which had led to a dramatic decline in oil prices. The number of Saudi-Libyan contacts was unusually high: there were no less than ten exchanges of messages between King Fahd and Qadhdhafi during 1986.

PERSIAN GULF CHALLENGES

ATTITUDE TOWARD THE IRAQI-IRANIAN WAR AND RELATIONS WITH IRAN

Saudi anxiety about the ongoing war between Iraq and Iran, which entered its seventh year, increased considerably during 1986. Iranian threats against Saudi Arabia, to begin with, were much more direct, unequivocal, and menacing than at any time since the beginning of the war. Following Iran's conquest of the Faw peninsula in February (see essay on the war), the Iranian media intensified their criticism of Riyadh, claiming that there were strong indications that the Saudis had renewed agreements with Iraq involving the sale of neutral zone oil. In July, in response to reports that Saudi Arabia had been selling 300,000 barrels of oil a day for Iraq, the Iranian Assembly Speaker Rafsanjani stated that if "reactionary regimes in the region continued their support for Iraq, Iran would hold them responsible for Iraq's wickedness." If Iraq used weapons paid for with Saudi or Kuwaiti oil money, these two countries would have "to pay for their aggression." In addition, Iranian leaders accused Saudi Arabia of passing on information and intelligence gathered by the AWACS to the Iraqi Air Force, thus enabling Iraq to attack the oil terminal on Sirri Island.[84]

Iran backed up its threats when it began to attack vessels belonging to Saudi Arabia and other Gulf states. In mid-March, after Iran's success in Faw, an Iranian helicopter gunboat fired a missile into a Saudi oil tanker in the Gulf, leaving four crewmen missing and seven wounded. In May, two Iranian helicopter gunboats struck two missiles at the Saudi oil tanker *al-Nasr al-'Arabi* 70 miles off the coast of Qatar. The attack was apparently a reprisal for an Iraqi attack on a supertanker heading for an Iranian oil terminal a few weeks earlier. In June, several Kuwaiti refineries were wracked by bomb explosions, and in late November installations at the Abu al-Bukush oil field in northwest Abu Dhabi were attacked.[85] It was never established who directed the attacks, but the explosions had underscored the potential for Iranian subversion in the region.

The strong, anti-Saudi Iranian posture was not only related to the ongoing war but also to the crisis in the oil market. Given its rising military expenditures, Iran was one of the main losers from the Saudi strategy of flooding the market which resulted in a decrease of oil prices. Thus, the Iranian leadership let the Saudis know that it considered their policies as "a hostile act" and as "a declaration of war" aimed at reducing Iran's ability to carry on the war.[86] Such statements and warnings abounded, especially on the eve of OPEC meetings in Europe, obviously designed to apply more pressure on Saudi Arabia to agree to an oil production pact to increase falling prices. But Iran also sought to implement its warnings; on the eve of OPEC's conference in October, in the Straits of Hormuz, Iranian jets attacked a Kuwaiti oil tanker carrying 18,000 tons of oil. In the meeting which convened 24 hours later, Yamani made a concession and agreed to continue the interim production accord that he had steadfastly opposed earlier.[87]

To counter such threats, Saudi Arabia adopted a two-pronged strategy. On the one hand, it issued continuous retorts — some of them more aggressive in nature than at any time since 1980. It pledged to defend its integrity at all costs, even war. "We will immediately exercise our legitimate right of self-defense with all our potential if we are faced with an aggression against our homeland or any of our sister countries. We have the means to respond to any aggression; the military and material resources at our disposal can silence any source of danger to our integrity." The Saudi media also accused Iran of inciting anti-Saudi sentiments among Iran's youngsters, something that violated the "noble tenets of Islam." Finally, Saudi leaders made it clear that any attack on any GCC member-state would be considered an attack on Saudi Arabia. When Kuwait became continuously subjected to Iranian threats, Crown Prince 'Abdallah declared that "Kuwait will not stand alone should the war expand and spill over its boundaries."[88]

On the other hand, the Saudis strove — at times publicly, but mostly secretly — to establish some channels of communication with various Iranian leaders in order to improve relations and change the Kingdom's negative perception in Tehran's eyes. This was the set of circumstances underlying the Saudi involvement in the American-Iranian-Israeli arms deal, known as Irangate (see essay on the US and the Middle East). Reluctant, however, to be perceived as playing a double game and unwilling to expose themselves to Iraqi criticism, the Saudis operated in a clandestine manner, using mainly the private channels of businessman 'Adnan Khashoggi, who acted as a surrogate for the Royal Family. But, according to a number of sources, a personal envoy of King Fahd — 'Ali Musallam — also participated in various parts of the deal, especially the financial ones. Other sources suggested that Muhammad Ayas, the business manager of King Fahd's son, Muhammad, was instrumental in channeling royal family money into the Iranian arms deal.[89] This policy of appeasing Iran also manifested itself in OPEC meetings in the second half of 1986 when Riyadh abandoned its previous position and accepted a production accord to stabilize the price of oil. Thus, when Yamani was dismissed (see above), there was much speculation that it had also been done in deference to Iranian wishes because Tehran held him responsible for the collapse of oil prices.

The net result of such a dual strategy was a very mixed and confusing state of relations between the two countries. On the one hand, a certain *rapprochement* evolved, reflected in the continuation of a peaceful pilgrimage season because of the good behavior of the Iranian pilgrims (see above, and *MECS* 1984–85, pp 506–6). It was also reflected by an increasing number of visits by Iranian and Saudi officials. On the other hand, Saudi fear of Iran and anxiety that the war was gradually spilling over to the Gulf states became tangible. Thus, when the first newly-purchased *Tornado* aircraft arrived in the Kingdom, the Saudis stationed them in Dhahran on the Gulf coast, thereby reflecting the Kingdom's perception of its security priorities.[90] But the overriding Saudi goal remained intact: to avoid any involvement or entanglement in the war. With its political and military leverage *vis à vis* Iran extremely limited, all that was left for the Saudis was to continue to press their mediation efforts; to dissuade Syria from its continuing support of Iran; to point to the absence of any rational reason to pursue the war; to instill the message that only "the enemies of Islam and

Arabism" benefited from the war; and to impress upon Iran the notion that the war could not ever end in a complete Iranian victory. However, all this was to no avail.[91]

ATTITUDE TOWARD THE GULF COOPERATION COUNCIL

In view of the intensification of the Iranian attacks, Saudi Arabia strove to improve cooperation and coordination among GCC members. It placed much more emphasis on turning the armed forces of the member-states into a military coalition capable of providing a viable, solid defense, actually a deterrent, against Iran. The original goals of the organization, to improve internal security and intelligence coordination, were now overshadowed by the priority given to military cooperation. The annual "Peninsula Shield" military exercises, encompassing land and air forces, navies and air defense units of all GCC members, were further expanded. New emphasis was laid in 1986 on the efficiency and mobility of the forces; Riyadh repeatedly stated that these forces could easily intervene in any Gulf state in times of crisis.[92] The predominant position of the Saudis in the GCC was systematically demonstrated in all these military exercises.

What became more conspicuous during 1986 was Riyadh's repeated assertion that it would regard an attack on a GCC state as an attack on Saudi Arabia. Such statements were made by the most senior members of the Royal Family such as Crown Prince 'Abdallah and Defense Minister Sultan.[93] The saliency of these declarations was a direct result of the attacks and explosions in various Gulf states that occurred frequently in 1986. In addition, there was a feeling in Riyadh that Iran underestimated the preparedness and willingness among GCC members to embark on a military action against Iran; hence they sought to make it absolutely clear that they intended to live up to their commitment and come to the support of any GCC member subjected to an Iranian attack. The Saudi readiness to help defend other GCC states was based on the traditional Saudi perception of these principalities as constituting the "soft belly" of the Kingdom and, as such, of no less importance to defend than Saudi territories themselves. (For details, see chapter on the Gulf states.)

THE INTERNATIONAL ARENA

RELATIONS WITH THE UNITED STATES

Relations between Saudi Arabia and the US at the beginning of 1986 were strained because of the cumulative impact of the crises of 1985: the failure of King Fahd's visit to Washington; US refusal to play a more active role in the peace process; US rejection of the Saudi request for more F-15 jets; the imposition of more restrictions on the delivery of the AWACS; and the general decline in Saudi stature in Washington. The damaged relations between the two countries were further exacerbated by a series of events and incidents in 1986.

It was hoped that Vice President Bush's trip to Riyadh in April would constitute a political signal of renewed "special relations" between the US and Saudi Arabia. But troubles had begun to mount even before he arrived in Riyadh. Before his departure, Bush addressed himself to the sharp decline in oil prices by declaring in Washington that Saudi Arabia had to take into account the damage being done to the US oil industry by the "free fall" in oil prices, thus implying that the Saudis were largely responsible for it. Already irritated by the US attitude regarding their arms requests, the Saudis were more angered by Bush's implied accusation. The first deliberate snub to the Vice President came upon his arrival at Riyadh Airport when it turned out that both King Fahd and Crown Prince 'Abdallah, Bush's official host, had left the capital earlier for Dhahran. The Saudi royal protocol office apparently had decided that Bush's three-day visit could be treated as a two-day official visit, which eliminated the necessity of having 'Abdallah greet him. It was therefore up to the Governor of Riyadh, Prince Salman, and lesser Royal dignitaries to greet Bush. The Saudis also decided that there would be no opportunity for news photographers to photograph Bush's meeting with King Fahd. But a worse diplomatic snub was to come when what was supposed to be the main demonstration of US-Saudi security cooperation — a fly-by in the Eastern Province of American-made F-5s and F-15s — was substituted with a European-made *Tornado* attack jet, the first of which had arrived just days earlier.[94] The significance of these snubs should be judged against the backdrop of Bush being the highest ranking member of the Reagan Administration ever to visit the Kingdom.

But the real bone of contention was what was perceived by the Saudis as the Reagan Administration's generally indifferent attitude toward the security needs of the Kingdom. The Saudi arms request that had been on Washington's agenda since late 1984 suffered several setbacks. First, President Reagan yielded in the summer of 1985 to congressional opposition to the sale of 60 additional F-15s to the Saudis, part of an arms deal valued at $3.5 bn. Then in March, a month before Bush's arrival in Riyadh, Reagan requested Congress to approve an arms package for the Saudis worth $354m, which included 1,700 *Sidewinder* air-to-air missiles, 800 *Stinger* ground-to-air missiles, and 100 *Harpoon* surface-to-air missiles. The Saudis felt that Reagan put very little effort into promoting the sales, since both houses of Congress voted against it. The Senate vote was 73-22 against, while the vote in the House was 356-62. It became clear that the only way to salvage at least part of the deal was to drop the *Stinger* missiles from the package. Thus, Prince Bandar, the Saudi Ambassador to the US, withdrew the request for 800 *Stinger* missiles, bringing the package's value down to $265m. Consequently, Reagan made good on his threat and vetoed the congressional votes. But even after eliminating the *Stinger*s, in addition to the F-15s and the combat helicopters withdrawn earlier, Reagan managed to uphold his veto by the slenderest possible margin: 34 Senators voted for the deal, precisely the minimal number required.[95] The approval of the limited, well depleted package, therefore, could hardly improve the strained relations between the two countries. Indeed, it became a cause for further accusations and recriminations.

Still another crisis in US-Saudi relations evolved over the delivery of the AWACS, which was to begin in late 1986. In the spring, there was growing evidence that Congress intended to stop the delivery of the aircraft on the grounds that certain preconditions to the sale's stormy passage through Congress in 1981 (see *MECS* 1981–82, pp 785, 788, and 800–1) had not been met. These included presentation to Congress of certain texts restricting Saudi use of the AWACS, ensuring security of AWACS technology, and confirming Saudi support for the Arab-Israeli peace process. A crisis was averted when Congress decided to accept at face value Reagan's letter of certification that security agreements were in place protecting AWACS technology and restricting Saudi use of the aircraft to within the Kingdom's airspace, and that Saudi Arabia had since 1981 assisted in the search for peace in the Middle

East. Four of the five AWACS were delivered by the end of 1986, and the last was due in late March 1987.[96] One factor in congressional acquiescence to completion of the deal was the large prepayment made by the Saudis, the return of which would have created both budgetary problems for the US and further strains with Saudi Arabia.

Another area of frictions and divergent perceptions was the problem of the stalled Arab-Israeli peace process. The Saudi leadership continued to criticize the US Administration for not playing a much more active role in the process and for not putting more pressure on Israel to modify its positions. The Saudis argued that such US inaction would inevitably undermine the American position in the Middle East and seriously erode US reliability and credibility as a superpower and broker. The Saudi media highlighted the fact that Washington had vetoed the Security Council resolution condemning Israel for the interception of the Libyan aircraft (see essays on Arab-Israeli relations, and armed operations), claiming that such a vote deprived the US of its role as an honest mediator.[97] Though the Arab-Israeli and Palestinian problems were one of the three major topics in the talks with Vice President Bush, both sides failed to arrive at any understanding on this issue.[98] The Saudis argued that US policy being pro-Israeli made it all the more difficult for Saudi Arabia to maintain good relations with Washington in view of the general anti-American atmosphere prevailing in the Arab world. Consequently, Saudi Arabia did condemn the US raid on Tripoli and Benghazi in Libya which occurred only ten days after Vice President Bush's visit to the Kingdom. The official Saudi reaction was that "the UN, rather than the battlefield," was the correct forum for such disputes, and it expressed support for the Libyan people.[99]

Underlying such strains and crises was the Saudi anxiety that two major developments, both inimical to the Kingdom's interests, were gradually shaping up. One involved the growing reliance on West European rather than exclusively US weapons and armaments. The Saudis hailed the principle of the "diversification of our sources of arms", and highlighted their ability to obtain sophisticated weapons from sources other than the US, which did not subject the arms deal "to extortion of any kind." But they realized that on balance this development entailed numerous disadvantages and risks and that they were pursuing it not out of their own will but rather as a result of US reluctance to comply with their requests.[100] By purchasing 132 aircraft from Britain (see below), the Saudis had to gear themselves up to operating and maintaining a very different type of jet from the F-15 they had expected to obtain and with which they were familiar. In addition, Saudi defense planning posed the greatest long-term problem. For a long time Saudi defense strategy had been based on the key principle of the interchange of its air defense equipment with that of the US. The switch to non-US hardware would create problems in strategies since there could no longer be interchangeability of US and Saudi air defense equipment.[101]

The second ominous development involved the obvious decline in the Saudi stature in the US. The enormous Saudi-British deal marked an eclipse in the level of US involvement in the Saudi defense market. Also, the general recession in Saudi Arabia resulted in a major decline in the volume of US business in the Kingdom. Moreover, there was an 85% decline in US imports from the Kingdom: from $14.4 bn in 1981 to $2.02 bn in 1985. The cumulative impact of these three trends meant that the US in general and American companies in particular had a much lesser stake in the economics, and hence politics, of Saudi Arabia. This was bound to have serious repercussions on future Saudi requests from the US. During the oil boom years, when military, economic and strategic cooperation reached record levels, numerous major American corporations lobbied the Saudi case in Washington. Under the new circumstances the Saudis would have to learn to do their own lobbying.[102]

Finally, the Saudis were anxious that the American perception of their financial, economic, and political weakness would result in Washington taking the opportunity to redress perceived compromises made by the US in the 1970s and early 1980s as a result of the Saudi oil power. From the Saudi perspective, this could have accounted, at least partly, for the increasing American reliance on and strategic cooperation with Israel since 1983 as a means for ensuring US interests in the Middle East. To counter such a dangerous trend, the Saudis sought to demonstrate their usefulness to Washington and to gain sympathetic treatment of their requests by offering their support to the rebels in Afghanistan, fighting the Soviet presence there, and to the Contras fighting the Sandinista regime in Nicaragua.[103] It was obvious, however, that given the new economic and political realities, the Saudi range of options was very limited.

ATTITUDE TOWARD THE SOVIET UNION

The previous pattern of Soviet overtures to Saudi Arabia, ambiguous Saudi responses, and the absence of any breakthrough in relations between the two countries persisted in 1986. The Saudi leadership remained, in the final analysis, reluctant to establish diplomatic relations with the USSR. However, the preconditions for considering ties with the Soviet Union were stated in broad, vague terms: "The Kingdom of Saudi Arabia wants to see a nonbelligerent Soviet attitude towards Islam in order to consider the question of diplomatic relations." When pressed to elaborate on such a statement, Defense Minister Sultan declared that "the future of relations depends on the extent of the Soviet response to Islamic causes in Afghanistan and elsewhere." Indeed, it appeared that most Saudi criticisms of the Soviets centered around the issue of Afghanistan.[104]

The USSR intensified its overtures towards Riyadh in 1986. Following the establishment of diplomatic relations between Moscow and the UAE and Oman in 1985 (see *MECS* 1984–85, pp 414, 421), the next Soviet targets were Qatar and Bahrain with the ultimate goal being Saudi Arabia. The Soviet media and "Soviet diplomatic sources" in the Gulf embarked on a campaign aimed at convincing the Saudi leadership that as Kuwait, the UAE and Oman had already established diplomatic relations with Moscow, it was only natural for Saudi Arabia to follow. Moreover, Moscow suggested that the most suitable candidates to mediate between the two conutries were the Gulf states themselves — Kuwait, Oman and the UAE.[105]

Soviet media pointed to a major advantage likely to result from Saudi relations with Moscow: it would enhance the Arab-Israeli peace process in a manner "more favorable to the Arab side and to the Palestinians' rights." The Soviets emphasized that while the US conditioned its support of Saudi Arabia on Riyadh's granting the US bases on its soil, the USSR respected Saudi sovereignty and integrity and was not asking for anything in return. Still another Soviet overture was made in the context of OPEC and oil prices. As Saudi Arabia came under increasing criticism regarding its role in the sharp decline of oil prices (see above), a Soviet spokesman stated in August that Saudi Arabia could not be regarded responsible for the decline; on the contrary, other oil producers should account for the adverse turn oil prices took.[106]

The Saudis responded in kind. When Oil Minister Yamani visited Moscow to discuss questions of prices and production, the visit was also described as a milestone in Saudi-Soviet relations. In February, the Saudi authorities lifted the ban on Soviet airplanes using the airspace of the Kingdom, explaining that the temporary ban had been caused by technical problems.[107] The Saudi leadership offered also a favorable interpretation of the coup in the People's Democratic Republic of Yemen (see the chapter on that country in this volume) as far as the Soviets were concerned. Dissenting from the common view that the USSR had played a major role in the coup, the Saudi media argued that the Soviets had not been involved in the execution of the coup, nor did they intervene until it became clear which faction was in command.[108] Finally, the Saudis praised the Soviet call for an international conference involving the Palestinians as the only means to solve the Arab-Israeli conflict. Riyadh, however, registered its dissatisfaction with Israeli-Soviet contacts which centered on the resumption of diplomatic relations between the two countries and Israel's demand for free Jewish emigration. These contacts, the Saudi media suggested, would only complicate the political process rather than enhance it. Such criticism notwithstanding, the Saudi and Soviet Ambassadors in London met in December to discuss the question of the international conference.[109]

Despite all the overtures, contacts and meetings, the Saudi leaders were united in viewing the issue of diplomatic relations as premature. As was the case in 1985, Prince Tallal, one of the King's brothers who did not hold any position in the Saudi hierarchy, was the only Prince calling outrightly for the establishment of diplomatic relations.[110] Moreover, the Saudis felt they had to avert a repetition of the embarrassing phenomenon of the UAE's and Oman's establishing relations with Moscow as far as Qatar and Bahrain were concerned. Thus, as the Soviets directed their efforts in the direction of these two principalities, Riyadh announced that "the GCC political entity does not stipulate the establishment of diplomatic relations by any GCC state with the Soviet Union."[111]

RELATIONS WITH BRITAIN

The British-Saudi arms deal involving 132 aircraft survived all the crises that had accompanied it (see *MECS* 1984-85, pp 609-10) and was finally signed on 17 February in Riyadh. The first six *Tornado*s arrived in March and April and were stationed in Dhahran on the Gulf coast. The deal included 48 *Tornado* strike aircraft and 24 *Tornado* air-defense jets, 30 *Hawk* advanced jet trainer aircraft, and 30 *Pilatus* basic trainers. The total value of the deal was estimated at over $7 bn, the largest arms deal ever concluded by Britain; other sources estimated the deal would be worth close to $12 bn over the longer term. In addition to the jets, the deal also involved the supply of weapons, an extensive training program, construction and improvement of bases, replenishment of spares and future modifications to the aircraft.[112]

The deal was to be paid for almost entirely in oil under arrangements involving Shell, British Petroleum (BP) and Aramco. According to the initial agreement, Saudi Arabia was to provide Shell and BP with 300,000 b/d for three years, the proceeds of which were to pay for the arms deal. However, as oil prices collapsed during the year, it became apparent that the rate of 300,000 b/d would not suffice. The Saudis agreed, therefore, to increase the amount to 400,000 b/d retroactive to February 1986. Some Western sources noted that such oil supplies would cause the Kingdom to exceed its quota of 4.35m b/d; but this was denied by Saudi officials who claimed that the 400,000 barrels would come out of their existing OPEC quota.[113]

Though the agreement did not stipulate that Saudi purchases from Britain would be offset, the Saudis made it clear that they expected such offset British investments in high-technology projects in the Kingdom. Several senior Princes, including Defense Minister Sultan, indicated that they expected Britain to recycle some 35% of the arms deal expenditure into investments in Saudi Arabia. The fact that the issue of offset investments was not explicitly mentioned in the agreement was bound to generate controversy. Indeed, while the British noted that both the agreement, signed in February 1986, and the memorandum, signed in 1985, did not contain any specific arrangements nor was any figure quoted, the Saudis pointed to a statement of intent in the memorandum stating the desirability of such offset investments. In May, it was reported that the British were "unenthusiastic" about investing in Saudi Arabia, and that they preferred to enter into coproduction agreements on other British armaments. The Saudis, however, demanded high-technology joint ventures involving comanufacturing of new military items.[114]

The successful conclusion of the *Tornado* deal created a kind of "honeymoon" between the two countries. Thus, the Saudi condemnation of the US raid on Libya made no mention of British involvement, though Britain was the only European country to cooperate with the US in the planning and execution of the attack. Likewise, Riyadh chose to ignore the news of a senior Saudi Prince facing trial in London for drug offenses. The British Foreign Office was concerned that the prison sentence on the Prince might create a hiatus in British-Saudi relations as happened in 1980 over the screening of *Death of a Princess*. But the fear did not materialize.[115]

The "honeymoon" seemed to have considerably cooled towards the end of the year. Already in May, the Saudi media expressed anger at Prime Minister Thatcher's visit to the "Zionist entity," pointing out that it was the first visit by a British Prime Minister "since the Zionist occupation of Arab Palestine in 1948." Reminding London of the Balfour Declaration, the media called on the British to "play an effective role in finding a solution for the problem" which they had created.[116] Then, in October, the Saudi Government expressed unhappiness with the British decision to cut off diplomatic relations with Syria over an issue "whose dimensions and facts are not clear so far." (For the Hindawi affair, see essays on Arab-Israeli relations, and armed operations in this volume.) It criticized the British Government for taking a "hasty, unjustified step and for not resorting to the usual diplomatic means to resolve all differences, especially that Syria has categorically denied the British charges."[117] Only days later, the Saudis expelled dozens of hospital workers, mainly nurses, after the raid on a birthday party and the subsequent arrest of some 100 people for drinking alcohol. The British sought to play down the incident, arguing that the nurses had not been deported by the Saudi authorities but rather sent home by their Saudi employers.[118]

But the worst incident was yet to come. It turned out that in June, the outgoing British Ambassador to Saudi Arabia, James Craig, wrote a confidential letter — his valedictory dispatch — to Foreign Minister Geoffrey Howe, summing up his tenure in the Kingdom. The letter was, apparently, leaked to the Press and published in

October by the *Glasgow Herald*, in Scotland, after the British Government had obtained an injunction banning the *New Statesman* magazine from publishing it. Though the letter was full of eloquent, positive comments about the Saudis, there were many characterizations of Saudis and Saudi society that would cause offense. Describing Saudi society and the country by three epithets — incompetence, insularity and Islam — Craig stated that incompetence was reflected in that the Saudis were disorganized, unconscientious, lacked any organizing capabilities, and did not want to work. These characteristics were further exacerbated, in Craig's opinion, by their being accompanied with arrogance and a reluctance to admit the need for guidance and reform.[119]

The British Government, extremely embarrassed, feared that "irreversible damage" to British-Saudi relations would ensue, and that the bad diplomatic relations that followed the *Death of a Princess* incident might reoccur. They hoped, therefore, that the November visit of the Prince and Princess of Wales to Saudi Arabia would provide a perfect opportunity to ease the strains and smooth any problems, crises and incidents that had marred relations between the two countries. The visit, however, created another incident when it turned out that Crown Prince 'Abdallah, the guests' counterpart and host, had left the country on a previously unscheduled private trip to the Canary Islands.[120] This royal snub made relations more tense; but so far it did not seem to have affected the critical issue of the *Tornado* arms deal.

RELATIONS WITH FRANCE AND GERMANY

Saudi Arabia's relations with France and Germany centered on Riyadh's attempt to purchase arms and military equipment and obtain military instruction from both countries. This effort was part of what the Saudis referred to as "the diversification of the Kingdom's sources of weaponry and armaments." French-Saudi contacts were clearly affected by the Saudi decision to opt for the *Tornado* rather than the *Mirage* 4000. Contacts with Germany were influenced by the German decision not to sell the *Leopard* II tank to Saudi Arabia.

In October, the French Defense Minister, Andre Giraud, signed in Riyadh a follow-up agreement on the already completed naval supply deal of 1980. The new agreement stipulated that supplies and technical help would be given to the Saudi Navy, especially to the four frigates that were fitted out with *Exocets* and *Shahine-Crotale* missiles. The French were also to ship AMX-40 tanks to the Kingdom for tests. Finally the French offered the *Mistral* shoulder-fired anti-aircraft missile, which could substitute for the US *Stinger* missile that Congress refused to sell to Riyadh (see above). Following Giraud's visit, there were numerous reports about a massive French-Saudi arms deal valued at $2 bn, which would also include surface-to-air missiles and other arms for the National Guard.[121]

Though the Government of Chancellor Kohl announced that it could not sell the *Leopard* II tanks to Saudi Arabia, German spokesmen repeatedly emphasized that they wished to sell the Kingdom other types of weapons. It seemed that the visit to Riyadh in November of Franz Josef Strauss was a turning point. Known to favor arms sales to Saudi Arabia, Strauss reportedly concluded the sale of eight patrol boats to the Saudi Interior Ministry and proposed the sale of eight submarines of a type used by the German Navy.[122] In a second field of cooperation, the head of Germany's counterterrorism forces was entrusted with the formation of counterterrorism squads in Saudi Arabia.[123]

NOTES

For the place and frequency of publications cited here, and for the full name of the publication, news agency, radio station or monitoring service where an abbreviation is used, please see "List of Sources." Only in the case of more than one publication bearing the same name is the place of publication noted here.

1. *FT*, 20 April 1986.
2. *Time*, 21 April 1986.
3. Interview with the *JT*, 23 March 1986.
4. *WSJ*, 27 January 1986.
5. *QER: Saudi Arabia*, No 1, 1986, p 11.
6. *CR*, No 3, 1986, p 8.
7. *MM*, 15 September; SPA, 25 July — DR, 27 July 1986.
8. *WSJ*, 31 October 1986.
9. *IHT*, 11 December 1986.
10. SPA, 29 October — SWB, 31 October; *FT*, 25 November; *Der Spiegel*, 8 December; R. Riyadh, 16 December — SWB, 18 December 1986.
11. *Newsweek*, 10 November 1986.
12. Ibid.
13. Yamani's two lectures: at Harvard University — *MM*, 15 September 1986, and at the Swiss-Arab Chamber of Commerce — *The Guardian*, 31 October 1986.
14. *Sunday Telegraph*, 16 March; SPA, 17 March — SWB, 19 March 1986.
15. *NYT*, 31 October 1986.
16. *CR*, No 4, 1986, p 6.
17. *IHT*, 4 November 1986.
18. Ibid, 31 October and *The Guardian*, 30 December 1986.
19. Assessment by the editor of *MEED*, quoted in *The Guardian*, 31 October 1986.
20. *IHT*, 30 December 1986.
21. R. Riyadh, 9 March — SWB, 11 March 1986.
22. *FT*, 11 March 1986.
23. R. Riyadh, 4 August — SWB, 6 August 1986.
24. SPA, 29 December — DR, 31 December 1986.
25. *MM*, 19 January 1987.
26. Ibid, 20 January 1986.
27. *The Economist*, 8 November 1986.
28. *ME*, January 1987.
29. *MM*, 31 March 1986.
30. *QER*, No 1, 1986, p 9.
31. *CR*, No 3, 1986, p 9.
32. *Middle East Times*, 21 September 1986; *ME*, January 1987.
33. *Arab News*, 29 March 1986.
34. *CR*, No 3, 1986, p 19.
35. *Al-Siyasa*, Kuwait, 30 September 1986.
36. *'Ukaz*, 2 July 1986.
37. For instance, *al-Thawra al-Islamiyya*, August 1986.
38. *Al-Yamama*, 12 November 1986.
39. Interview with Sultan, in *al-Qabas*, 6 January 1987; public speech by Aba al-Khayl, quoted in *MM*, 14 April 1986.
40. *Time*, 21 April 1986.
41. R. Riyadh, 3 December — SWB, 5 December 1985.
42. *Time*, 21 April 1986.
43. *NYT*, 1 October 1986.
44. *The Economist*, 8 November 1986.
45. *Al-Jazira*, 4 February 1986.
46. King Fahd's speech, SPA, 11 March — SWB, 13 March 1986.
47. R. Riyadh, 1 June — DR, 3 June 1986.
48. *MM*, 20 January 1986.

49. R. Riyadh, 14 December — DR, 16 December 1986.
50. *ME*, January 1987.
51. *Al-Thawra al-Islamiyya*, October 1986; *Emirates News*, 21 May 1986.
52. SPA, 19 May — DR, 21 May 1986.
53. *Time*, 21 April; WP, 21 July; SPA, 31 December — DR, 2 January 1987.
54. *Al-Majalla*, 4 June 1986.
55. *Newsweek*, 10 November 1986.
56. *CR*, No 3, 1986, p 7.
57. *QER*, No 1, 1986, p 3.
58. R. Riyadh, 23 September — DR, 25 September 1986.
59. R. Riyadh, 25 January — DR, 27 January; *al-Sharq al-Awsat*, 10 February 1986.
60. R. Riyadh, 26 October — SWB, 29 October 1986.
61. *Al-Thawra al-Islamiyya*, January 1987.
62. SPA, 23 April — DR, 24 April; R. Riyadh, 2 June — DR, 4 June 1986.
63. IRNA, 10 August — DR, 11 August; *The Times*, 29 November; SPA, 11 August — DR, 13 August; IRNA, 29 August — DR, 30 August 1986.
64. SPA, 2 April — SWB, 4 April; R. Riyadh, 20 April — DR, 23 April; *al-Riyad*, 26 April; *al-Bilad*, Jidda, 19 April 1987.
65. *Al-Riyad*, 29 May; R. Riyadh, 11, 19 June — DR, 13, 21 June 1986 respectively.
66. R. Riyadh, 18 June — DR, 19 June; *al-Yamama*, 18 June 1986.
67. *Akhbar al-Usbu'*, 9 October; R. Monte Carlo, 19 October — SWB, 20 October 1986.
68. *Al-Jazira*, 7 December 1986.
69. Interview with *al-Siyasa*, Kuwait, 2 June 1986.
70. R. Riyadh, 15 June — DR, 16 June 1986.
71. *Al-Ahram*, 6 July; R. Riyadh, 9 July — DR, 10 July 1986.
72. *Akhir Sa'a*, 17 December; R. Riyadh, 17 December — DR, 19 December 1986.
73. MENA, 1 April, 14 July — DR, 2 April, 15 July; *al-Masa*, 1 August 1986.
74. *Al-Sharq al-Jadid*, October; *al-Akhbar*, 24 February 1986.
75. *Al-Ahram al-Iktisadi*, 5, 10 October; *Ruz al-Yusuf*, 24 November; *Middle East Times*, 28 December 1986.
76. *Al-Ahram al-Iktisadi*, 20 October 1986.
77. *Al-Jazira*, 19 February 1986; MENA, 4 January — DR, 5 January; R. Riyadh, 5 January — DR, 7 January 1987.
78. R. Riyadh, 8 July, 20 December — DR, 10 July, 22 December 1986.
79. *'Ukaz*, 5 February 1986; R. Riyadh, 1 January — DR, 3 January 1987.
80. *Al-Jazira*, 7 August; R. Riyadh, 1 October — DR, 30 October 1986.
81. R. Riyadh, 12 January, 16 March, 22 April — DR, 14 January, 18 March, 4 April 1986, respectively.
82. JANA, 5 June — DR, 7 June 1986.
83. *'Ukaz*, *al-Riyad*, *al-Jazira*, 20 April 1986.
84. R. Tehran, 20 February, 27 July, 1 September — DR, 22 February, 29 July, 3 September, respectively; R. Riyadh, 2 September — DR, 4 September 1986.
85. *Time*, 21 April; *Gulf Daily News*, 8 May; R. Riyadh, 26 November — DR, 28 November 1986.
86. *WSJ*, 31 October 1986.
87. *IHT*, 31 October 1986.
88. SPA, 30 July — DR, 1 August; *al-Jazira*, 5 August, 9 November; KUNA, 16 March — DR, 17 March 1986.
89. *The Times*, 29 November; *NYT*, 30 November, 18 December; *The Guardian*, 1 December; *Time*, 15 December 1986; *Afric-Asia*, January 1987.
90. *MM*, 20 January 1986.
91. SPA, 10 February — DR, 12 February; *'Ukaz*, 25 December; *al-Sharq al-Awsat*, 13 February 1986.
92. *Al-Madina*, 11 February; KUNA, 9 February — DR, 11 February 1986.
93. KUNA, 27 March — DR, 29 March; *al-Yawm*, 19 June 1986.
94. *WP*, 21 April 1986.
95. *NYT*, 12 March, 8, 22 May, 6 June; SPA, 20 May — DR, 21 May 1986.

96. *CR*, No 3, 1986, p 6.
97. R. Riyadh, 21 January — DR, 3 January; *al-Riyad*, *al-Bilad*, 1 February 1986.
98. R. Riyadh, 7 April — DR, 9 April; *WP*, 21 April 1986.
99. *Al-Jazira*, 17 April 1986.
100. *'Ukaz*, 7 May; Sultan's interview with GNA, 8 May and with *al-Majalla*, 13 May 1986.
101. *MM*, 17 February 1986.
102. *MM*, 3 March; *WP*, 10 May 1986.
103. *The Times*, 29 November; *NYT*, 30 November, 18 December; *The Guardian*, 1 December; *Time*, 15 December 1986.
104. *Al-Jazira*, 17 December 1985; SPA, 3 January — DR, 5 January 1986.
105. *Al-Ra'y al-'Amm*, 17 June; *al-'Alam*, 9 August 1986.
106. *Najdonarodnia*, January; *Akhbar al-Usbu'*, 24 July; *al-Nahar Arab Report and Memo*, 1 August 1986.
107. *Al-Ra'y al-'Amm*, 15 January; *al-Watan*, 28 February 1986.
108. *'Ukaz*, 27 January 1986.
109. *Al-Yamama*, 16 July; *'Ukaz*, 2 August; *al-Tadamun*, 12 December 1986.
110. *Al-Watan*, 8 March 1986.
111. R. Riyadh, 10 January — DR, 12 January 1986.
112. *FT*, 14, 18 February 1986.
113. Ibid, *al-'Alam*, 20 September 1986.
114. *MM*, 17 March; *FT*, 6, 8 May 1986.
115. *The Guardian*, 18 January, 29 April 1986.
116. *'Ukaz*, 24 May 1986.
117. R. Riyadh, 27, 30 October — DR, 28 October, 1 November 1986, respectively.
118. *The Guardian*, 4 November 1986.
119. *Glasgow Herald*, 9 October 1986.
120. *The Guardian*, 4 November 1986.
121. *Al-Qabas*, 17 October; SPA, 19 October — DR, 21 October; R. Monte Carlo, 19 October — DR, 21 October; *al-Ahram*, 6 November; *Ha'aretz*, 21 November 1986.
122. SPA, 23 November — DR, 25 November; *Ha'aretz*, 2 December 1986.
123. *Jane's Defence Weekly*, 29 November 1986.

The Republic of Sudan
(Jumhuriyyat al-Sudan)

HAIM SHAKED and YEHUDIT RONEN

The major domestic process in Sudan in 1986 was the return to political democracy. The election campaign of April 1986, which led to the first democratically elected Constituent Assembly in 18 years, and the subsequent formation of a new Government, marked the peaks in the relatively short process which began in the immediate aftermath of Ja'far al-Numayri's overthrow in the spring of 1985 and changed the character of politics in Khartoum.

The *Umma* Party (UP; the political organ of the *Ansar* sect), led by its veteran and renowned leader, al-Sadiq al-Mahdi, won most of the assembly seats, thus becoming the main effective power in Sudanese politics. The Democratic Unionist Party (DUP), which derived its support mainly from the *Khatmiyya* sect, came second. The National Islamic Front (NIF), weakened by a split almost a year earlier from the Muslim Brothers, emerged somewhat surprisingly as the third significant political force. The success of the traditional parties could not but lead to the conclusions that the Sudanese body politic of 1986 bore a remarkable resemblance to that of the second half of the 1960s, notwithstanding almost two decades of Numayri's persistent and harsh suppression of political life.

The setting up of newly elected democratic institutions in late April and May was the next high point in the country's resumption of democratic life (excluding large areas in the South where fierce fighting was going on). The formation of the new Government, headed by al-Mahdi, triggered high expectations among the population, as well as within the Government itself. Hopes ran high that the new Government would bring about a rapid and tangible amelioration of the country's problems, especially the ailing economy and the devastating civil war in the South.

Nevertheless, as 1986 drew to a close, and the new Govenment's period of grace elapsed, the euphoria that had prevailed in Khartoum since April 1985 was largely dissipated. The new Government's failure to solve or relieve the problems, or even to produce a progress that could lead to solutions, created a serious crisis of expectations in Sudanese society. The lackluster Government, its low profile, and undaring policies *vis-à-vis* almost every problematic area in Sudan's domestic affairs, stemmed from a number of reasons, some of which were not related to the Government or its policies, but to the country's objective circumstances. A significant factor that undermined the Government's ability to function was its mounting conflict with the powerful NIF (which most effectively led the opposition to al-Mahdi's Government). The new Establishment's ineffectiveness and its failure to bring about a breakthrough in the armed conflict with the South, was especially alarming. The civil war between the Khartoum Government and the Sudanese People's Liberation Movement (SPLM) and its dominant military arm, the Sudanese People's Liberation Army (SPLA), escalated during 1986, representing a full scale resumption of the civil war which beset Sudanese life between 1955 and 1972.

The lack of tangible progress toward the eradication or amelioration of internal hardships, indeed their exacerbation during the second half of 1986, triggered growing economic and political unrest. There was also a sense of *déjà vu*, which made matters worse. The violent riots in the western and the Khartoum area as 1986 ended and 1987 began, were reminiscent of the Numayri era and, more significantly, served as a clear indication that nothing had basically changed for the better in Sudan.

In stark contrast to the generally ineffective handling of domestic affairs, Sudan's foreign policies were conducted intensely and dynamically and on a rather large scale.

The most salient aspect of Sudan's foreign policy was the preoccupation — throughout the period under review, but perhaps with less empahsis in the last quarter of 1986 — with the strengthening of links with neighboring Libya. Tripoli's persistent support — political, economic and even military — of the Khartoum Government, was essential for the latter's strengthening of its grip on power. At the same time, however, Khartoum had to pay a heavy price for the *rapprochement* with Qadhdhafi — distancing itself from both the Egyptian and American orbits.

Another major source of preoccupation for Khartoum's policymakers was its neighbors to the east and south — Ethiopia and Uganda. With both, but especially with the first, Sudan was at pains to iron out mutual difficulties. Hoping that this would lead to the halt, or even to a weakening, of Addis Ababa's support of the rebels fighting in southern Sudan, and, at the same time, to Addis Ababa goading the rebels to establish political contacts with Khartoum, the Sudanese made a number of overtures toward Ethiopia. Hostility toward Ethiopia did not abate, however; on the contrary, it increased, reaching a new peak of tension at the end of 1986. With Uganda, mutual tension gradually subsided and the crisis ended in the fall of 1986.

Relations in the third major circle of foreign affairs, that is, with the superpowers, followed throughout most of the year the same basic lines that had been shaped in 1985 by the Transitional Government. Khartoum continued to make efforts to bring about a change in its relations with the Soviet Union, while continuing to limit the scope and effectiveness of the US position in Sudan. Al-Mahdi's visit to Moscow in the summer of 1986 marked a climax in the two countries' process of *rapprochement*. Nevertheless, the visit did not lead to any substantial change. Al-Mahdi's visit, in the autumn, to the US (within the framework of a more comprehensive tour of the West) signified an improvement in Khartoum's relatively shelved relations with Washington. The change reflected Sudan's growing financial dependence on its foreign backers in general, and its efforts to mobilize urgent economic aid from the US in particular.

The gradual but steady improvement in relations with Iran, symbolized by al-Mahdi's visit to Tehran at the end of 1986, should be viewed, *inter alia*, within the same context of mobilizing economic support.

Thus, activism in the foreign arena served, to some extent, as compensation for the gloomy and frustrating state of affairs domestically.

INTERNAL AFFAIRS

THE PRE-ELECTION PERIOD

Domestic affairs during the first quarter of 1986 were not marked by any new significant development. Khartoum's political activities were deliberately handled in a relatively low key. The country's transitional leadership, under General (*al-Fariq Awal*) 'Abd al-Rahman Muhammad Hasan Siwar al-Dahab, as well as the other political circles in Khartoum, and in the South, were mainly preoccupied with the scheduled elections in April. Even the economic and social unrest, sometimes violent and with political overtones, which swept the country during these months and paralyzed major sectors of its economy, did not galvanize the Dahab leadership into action. Its pace was relatively slow, and in some spheres it appeared to be stalled. The same was true with regard to Khartoum's handling of the conflict with the South. Though the conflict was politically the country's most destabilizing issue, the Dahab Government did not make any dramatic move to achieve a political settlement. In that fragile period on the verge of a new era of democracy, the Dahab Government could not risk launching any course which might cause negative vibrations in Khartoum.

THE NEW DEMOCRATIC ERA

THE ELECTIONS

Elections to Sudan's first democratically elected Constituent Assembly in 18 years were held from 1 through 12 April 1986 — one year after the toppling of Numayri's regime. About six million Sudanese — out of a population of *c* 22 million — voted throughout the country,[1] except for large areas in the South. Despite many difficulties — primarily the civil war in the South, the parlous state of the economy, and poor transportation and communications — the elections were conducted without serious disruptions. Final results were announced later in the month, as follows:[2]

Party	*Seats*
UP	99
DUP	63
NIF	51
Sudanese African National Union (SANU — a Southern party)	11
People's Progressive Party (PPP — a Southern party)	9
Sudan National Party (SNP — a Nuba party)	8
The Southern Sudanese Political Association (SSPA — a Southern Party)	7
Independents	6
Communist Party	3
Beja Conference (connected with the Beja tribes in the Red Hills)	1
Sudan Federal Party (SFP — a Southern party)	1
Sudan African Congress (SAC — a Khartoum-based Southern party)	1
Southern results which had not been declared	4
Constituencies where elections were postponed	37
Total number of seats in the Constituent Assembly	301

The UP — the political organ of the *Ansar*, the Mahdi followers — won most of the assembly seats and became the major power in Sudanese politics. The DUP came second, with 63 seats. In the two earlier rounds of democratic elections in Sudan, in 1965 and 1968, the UP and the DUP had also won the highest number of assembly seats. (In 1965, the UP led with 76 seats out of 173, while in 1968 the DUP came first, with 101 seats out of 218, due to a split in the UP which weakened it significantly.) Despite the fact that almost two decades had passed since the earlier round of democratic elections, and despite Numayri's harsh suppression of these two traditionalist right-wing parties, they managed to maintain their powerful position within the Sudanese body politic.

The UP gained its victory under the able leadership of al-Sadiq al-Mahdi, the descendant of the Sudanese Mahdi, an Oxford graduate and one of the richest men in Sudan. Al-Mahdi, born in 1936 in Omdurman, had played a very prominent role in Sudanese politics since independence in 1956. A leading figure in the UP, he served as Sudan's Prime Minister in 1966–67. In 1969, in the wake of Numayri's *coup d'état*, al-Mahdi's UP (as well as the other traditionalist politico-religious parties) were outlawed. About a year later, in April 1970, following Numayri's crushing of the *Ansar* on Aba Island, the authorities deported al-Mahdi to Egypt and confiscated his property. During a long period of exile al-Mahdi launched a series of subversive activities against Numayri's regime, including the serious coup attempt of July 1976. Al-Mahdi then responded positively to Numayri's reconciliation initiative of 1977 and returned home in the fall of that year. Yet he persistently refused to collaborate with the Numayri regime, with which he established a "cold peace." A major departure from this *modus vivendi* was al-Mahdi's well-publicized rejection of Numayri's application of the *Shari'a* (Islamic law) in the country in September 1983, which led to his imprisonment. He was released in early 1985, mainly as a result of pressure imposed upon Numayri by an important Kuwaiti financial figure.[3]

Al-Mahdi's political prestige surged when he was unanimously reelected by his party,[4] in late February 1986, to lead it in the forthcoming election. His powerful position stemmed primarily from his own experience and centrality in Sudanese politics. In addition, the removal of his two main rivals in the UP leadership — Ahmad al-Mahdi and Wali al-Din al-Hadi — contributed to consolidate his position in the UP leadership. Ahmad al-Mahdi, who had collaborated politically with the Numayri regime, was arrested in early 1986 by the new Sudanese authorities on the charge of receiving a large sum of state money from the defunct regime.[5] The other contender to the party leadership, Wali al-Din al-Hadi, for reasons unclear at the time of writing, faded away from UP politics.

As evidenced by the election results, al-Mahdi and the UP had succeeded in retaining their political strength and even enjoyed a boost in their power despite the political vicissitudes which Sudan underwent during Numayri's 16-year period of military rule. The UP continued to derive its political strength from the party's traditional base of power — the *Ansar* religious sect — whose strongholds were in Kordofan, Darfur, and the central Gezira region.[6]

The second largest political party — the DUP — was headed by its spiritual and religious leader Muhammad 'Uthman al-Mirghani, of the famous Mirghani family, and by its political leader, Sharif Zayn al-'Abidin al-Hindi, a member of the Hindi family and the brother of the late Sharif al-Hindi (see *Middle East Contemporary*

Survey [*MECS*] 1981–82, p 823). The DUP derived its strength mainly from the *Khatmiyya* religious sect as well as the business and merchant class in the East and North of the country.[7]

The NIF emerged as a significant third political force, with 51 seats. The Muslim Brotherhood, under the leadership of the veteran political figure, Hasan 'Abdallah al-Turabi, who established the NIF in May 1985 (see *MECS* 1984–85, p 632) had won only three seats in the 1968 election. Drawing its support from petty traders in the urban areas in general and the capital in particular,[8] and enjoying political support among student circles, the NIF in 1986 won almost half the seats in the Khartoum area — turning out to be a key feature of Khartoum's political map. Apparently the best organized party in the election campaign, the NIF allegedly used its wealth to buy votes in the Gezira and in Khartoum.[9] (The NIF's financial backing came from the party's wealthy establishment and, reportedly, from Saudi and Iranian sources.)[10] Apart from its traditional base of political support, in 1986 the NIF also enjoyed strong support within the military. As reported by a foreign source, it won every constituency in which there were military barracks.[11] One possible explanation for the military's support of the NIF was the party's hard-line attitude toward the South, which tallied with the military's growing enmity toward the Southern rebels (see below). Interestingly, Hasan 'Abdallah al-Turabi, the founder and leader of the NIF, was defeated in his own constituency of Khartoum South (al-Sahafa neighborhood), after the other leading parties joined forces to back the DUP candidate there.[12]

The election results also reflected the weak political base of the Communist Party in the Sudanese population. During the 1960s, the Sudanese Communists constituted the largest and best organized Communist Party in Africa, to the extent of threatening — in the late 1960s — the position of the strong traditionalist right-wing parties. Later, in the early 1970s, they challenged Numayri's position, after he had seized power in 1969 with the significant help of the Communists and other leftist elements. Soon afterwards, Numayri felt threatened by the growing political strength of the Communists (and other leftist elements). Finally, after foiling in July 1971 a Communist-engineered coup attempt, he launched a crackdown against them, inflicting a critical blow from which they were unable to recover. Acting as an underground movement, the Communists engaged in subversive activities aimed at toppling Numayri's regime. They constituted a troublesome element by instigating industrial unrest in the country (see e.g., *MECS* 1977–78, pp 703–4; 1980–81, pp 771–72). Drawing its political strength mainly from urban-based trade unionists and intellectuals, the Communist Party had an efficient organization. It was led by Secretary-General Muhammad Ibrahim Nuqud[13] and by another veteran leader, al-Tijani al-Tayyib, formerly editor-in-chief of the Communist Party mouthpiece, *al-Maydan*. Notwithstanding the salience of the Communist presence on the Sudanese political scene, its test in a free election showed that the party had a relatively weak footing among the population and that its political weight and effectiveness had surpassed the actual number of its supporters.

Among the parties from the South taking part in the election, the SANU won the largest number of seats. The SANU was headed by the veteran administrator and politician Andrew Wieu, who served, *inter alia*, as Minister of Education in the regional Cabinet in the South from August 1980 until its arbitrary dissolution by Numayri in October 1981 (see *MECS* 1981–82, p 824). The SANU, which enjoyed strong support mainly in the Upper Nile region,[14] presented itself as a reincarnation of the original SANU, founded in 1962 by Southern exiles who supported a loose federal system with the North.[15]

The Southern PPP was formed in August 1985 under the leadership of Eliaba Surur, one of the earliest advocates of regional rule (which was enacted in Sudan in March 1972 within the framework of the Addis Ababa peace agreement between the Khartoum Government and the South). The PPP drew its support from the Equatoria region, and believed that the most suitable system of government for Sudan was federalism.[16]

The SSPA, whose base of support was in the Bahr al-Ghazal region,[17] was actually an association of Southern Sudanese political parties, formed after Numayri's downfall. The SSPA was led by Samuel Aro Bol, a veteran political figure who had participated in the activities of the anti-Numayri political organization called the Council for the Unity of Southern Sudan (see *MECS* 1981–82, p 825). Other noteworthy political figures of the SSPA were Peter Gatekouth Gual, Hilary Paulo Logali, Toby Madout, Samuel Abu John — all served in the June 1980 and August 1981 Southern Cabinets (see *MECS* 1980–81, p 768). The SSPA vehemently called for the cancellation of Numayri's redivision of the South in 1983, and of his September 1983 *Shari'a* laws, as well as for adherence to the Addis Ababa agreement.[18]

The SAC, formerly known as the Southern Sudanese in Khartoum, was led by Lam Akol. Like the SSPA, the SAC also called for the cancellation of the 1983 redivision of the South,[19] urging the Khartoum Government to negotiate directly with the SPLM-SPLA in order to reach "a permanent peaceful solution."[20] Later, in summer 1986, Lam Akol joined the SPLM, accusing al-Mahdi's Government of adopting a military solution to the Southern conflict.[21]

The SFP, formerly the Upper Nile Political Association, was established in December 1985.[22]

Of the two "tribal" parties, the SNP received disproportionate publicity thanks to its veteran leader, the Anglican priest, Philip 'Abbas Ghabbush. A senior and most active Nuba leader before and during the Numayri era, Father Ghabbush was accused several times of "racial" plots against Sudan's "unity" (see e.g., *MECS* 1976–77, p 589; 1984–85, p 616). The Dahab Government, too, accused Ghabbush in September 1985 of taking part in a coup attempt in Khartoum (see *MECS* 1984–85, pp 633–34). Ghabbush's party supported a federal system for Sudan with the Jabal Nuba area forming a region within the system.[23]

The other tribal party, the Beja Conference, appeared for the first time (alongside the Nuba Mountains Independents) in the 1965 elections, winning ten seats of the 173-seat assembly. The majority of the Beja people are nomads or seminomads who live in the Red Sea hills around Kassala. Their role in Sudan's politics has been marginal.

THE NEW GOVERNMENTAL INSTITUTIONS SET UP

The Constituent Assembly

Soon after the official announcement of the election results, the setting up of new governmental institutions intensified. On 26 April, Sudan's new Constituent Assembly (*al-Jam'iyya al-Tasisiyya*) convened in Khartoum for its first session. The Assembly's members were sworn in and the one-year transitional period of Gen al-Dahab's

Government formally ended (though it actually remained in office until 6 May). The event was a highly emotional one,[24] and the speeches delivered on the occasion emphasized the fact that, for the first time in Sudan's modern history, a military leader was voluntarily giving up power.[25] Sudan's political history during the whole era of independence since 1956 had witnessed hitherto only cases of removing military leaderships by force: of 'Abbud's in 1964 and of Numayri's in 1985. Al-Dahab transferred his position as Commander in Chief of the Armed Forces (which he had held since March 1985, the eve of Numayri's downfall) to Gen Taj al-Din 'Abdallah Fadl, his deputy in the Transitional Military Council (TMC) and a powerful military figure. The latter decided to continue to serve at the top of the military command with Muhammad Tawfiq Khalil, another key member of the TMC and the Chief of Staff since July 1985, even after the end of Dahab Government's term.[26] (In September 1986, both were dismissed from their posts. See below.)

The Council of Sovereignty

On 6 May, the second convention of the Constituent Assembly took place in Khartoum. The Assembly elected the Chairman and members of the Council of Sovereignty (*Majlis al-Siyyada*), known also as the State Supreme Council. (A similar council was dissolved by Gen 'Abbud when he took power in November 1958. When he was forced down in 1964, a similar council again replaced his Government.) Though virtually without any executive authorities, the council was formally considered the highest authority in the country. Allegedly, al-Dahab turned down an offer to serve as Chairman of the council.[27] Ahmad 'Ali al-Mirghani, the brother of Muhammad 'Uthman al-Mirghani, the leader of the *Khatmiyya* politico-religious sect and its DUP political organ, became the Chairman of the council. Notwithstanding al-Mirghani's stigma of being linked with the deposed Numayri regime, he was appointed to the second most important post in the country. His election reflected the position which the DUP gained in the elections. Mirghani, a senior and central leader in his party, had served from early 1978 until early 1979 as a member in the Central Committee of the Sudanese Socialist Union — the only legal political party in the Numayri era. From 1982 until Numayri was ousted, Mirghani served as a member of the Nile Valley Parliament (established in October 1982 by the Integration Charter between Egypt and Sudan). Another member of the Council, Muhammad al-Hasan 'Abdallah Yasin, a wealthy building contractor who prospered under Numayri,[28] was also a DUP man. The other three members of the council were Idris al-Banna and 'Ali Hasan Taj al-Din, both from the UP, and Pacifico Lado Lolik, a Southern politician born in 1938 in Juba, the capital of the South, and a Khartoum University Faculty of Medicine graduate.[29]

Constituent Assembly Speaker and Prime Minister

On 6 May, the Constituent Assembly also elected Muhammad Ibrahim Khalil, a law professor and UP member, to the position of Assembly Speaker. Khalil had held ministerial portfolios during the second half of the 1960s, and was arrested after Numayri's advent to power in 1969.[30] The Constituent Assembly also elected on that occasion al-Sadiq al-Mahdi as Sudan's new Prime Minister.

The New Government

On 15 May, al-Mahdi's feverish efforts to set up a Government[31] were successfully concluded.

TABLE 1: THE COMPOSITION OF THE CABINET[32]

Portfolio	*15 May 1986*
Prime Minister and Defense Minister	al-Sadiq al-Mahdi (UP)
Deputy Prime Minister and Foreign Affairs	al-Sharif Zayn al-'Abidin al-Hindi (DUP)
Interior	Ahmad al-Husayn (DUP)
Attorney-General	'Abd al-Mahmud al-Hajj Salih (UP)
Local Government	Joshua Dewal (SFP)
Finance and Economic Planning	Bashir 'Umar (UP)
Housing and Public Works	Muhammad Tahir al-Jaylani (DUP)
Industry	Mubarak 'Abdallah al-Fadil al-Mahdi (UP)
Agriculture and Natural Resources	'Umar Nur al-Da'im (UP)
Animal Resources	Isma'il Abaker (UP)
Commerce and Supply	Muhammad Yusif Abu Hurayra (DUP)
Transport and Communications	Fransino Wani (PPP)
Irrigation	Aldo Ago Deng (SSPA)
Energy and Mining	Adam Madibu (UP)
Information and Culture	Muhammad Tawfiq (DUP)
Health	Husayn Sulayman Abu Salih (DUP)
Education	Bakri Ahmad 'Adil (UP)
Cabinet Affairs	Salah al-Din 'Abd al-Salam al-Khalifa (UP)
Labor	Wal Kunijwok (SAC)
Peace and National Constitutional Conference	Muhammad Ahmad Yaji* ("Modern Forces")

* Resigned from his post in early November; see below.

The establishment of the first democratic Government in a long time did not herald any dramatic departures from the almost traditional composition of earlier governments. A certain innovation was, however, the formation of a new portfolio for Peace and National Constitutional Conference, aimed at making progress toward a solution of the armed conflict with the South. In fact, the new Ministry did not succeed in making any significant headway toward the fulfillment of its objectives. Perhaps it was against this background that its Minister, Muhammad Ahmad Yaji, resigned in November from his post, allegedly for health reasons.[33]

The NIF, the third major political power in Sudanese politics after the UP and the DUP, became the leading opposition force.[34] Taking its role very seriously, striving to increase its political influence, the NIF launched a campaign of intensive and consistent criticism against the Government's mode of operation. NIF leaders, with al-Turabi at the head, condemned what they termed the Cabinet's "constitutional violations."[35] They also emphasized their doubts about the survival of the Government: "Recent history has taught us that this type of combination [of the political parties composing the Government] has no chance of success," stated al-Turabi in one of his many interviews given between the Cabinet's formation in May 1986 and the end of the period under review.[36]

THE GOVERNMENT FAILS TO COPE WITH THE KEY POLITICAL AND ECONOMIC PROBLEMS: INCREASED CONFLICT WITH THE NATIONAL ISLAMIC FRONT

Eruption of Riots in Western Sudan and the Khartoum Area

Toward the end of 1986, after the period of grace of the Mahdi Government elapsed and the euphoria that accompanied the changing of the guard in Khartoum diminished, it became clear that the new Government was not fulfilling expectations that it would solve, or even ease the country's major problems. The main reason for the Government's unwillingness to move boldly to solve the central and controversial domestic issues was its fear that a daring step might trigger political instability, which in turn might undermine not only the Mahdi Government's grip on power, but also the whole political order in Khartoum. The relatively weak coalition Government was preoccupied with the consolidation of its position, which was seriously threatened by the NIF, which had launched a persistent verbal war of attrition against it. Increased conflict with the NIF had, undoubtedly, a decisive bearing on the Government's low key and unimpressive performance and, in turn, on the erosion of its political prestige. The main issues of contention between the Mahdi Government and the NIF were connected with the further validation of the *Shari'a* Islamic laws imposed by Numayri three years previously and the different attitude of both sides toward the handling of the armed conflict with the South. While al-Mahdi — who had declared his objection to the application of the *Shari'a* laws in the fall of 1983 — now reiterated his wish to promulgate new legislation to replace the laws,[37] the NIF did not agree to relinquish legislation to replace existing legislation.[38] The NIF and al-Turabi had been the architects of the application of the *Shari'a* laws, and their demand to maintain their validity in the country was a major reason for remaining in opposition. Since al-Mahdi wished to avoid a serious clash with the NIF, fearing the breakdown of the fragile political structure, and did not want to be branded the leader responsible for abrogating "God's Law," the controversial issue remained in abeyance. The stalemate, on the other hand, hampered the opening of a dialogue between Khartoum and the rebels in the South. In turn, their different attitudes toward the handling of the conflict with the South constituted another source of division between the Government and the NIF. The NIF demanded a more hard-line and decisive attitude toward the SPLA, gaining the support of wide circles in the Army. Tension between the Government and the NIF grew steadily, reaching a peak at the beginning of November when the Khartoum authorities claimed that the NIF was responsible for, or at least played an important role in, the riots that had swept Khartoum in September.

Aside from al-Mahdi's failure to inject a constructive, enthusiastic mood into Sudan's domestic politics, he also failed to make significant progress in the economy. The Government's inherited $13.3 bn foreign debt,[39] together with other damaging economic constraints, including the huge short- and long-term financial burden generated mainly by the continuing civil war, virtually thwarted any chances of making economic progress. The Government's failure to check the economic deterioration and raise the standard of living had serious implications, including the eruption into the open of latent tensions.

WAVES OF UNREST IN THE WEST AND IN KHARTOUM

Commander in Chief and Chief of Staff Dismissed

On 4 September 1986, perhaps in order to preempt a subversive move by the Army, or in an attempt to inject "new blood" into the high command while boosting his position, al-Mahdi announced the "dismissal and retirement" of the Commander in Chief, the Chief of Staff, and three Lieutenant Generals. Maj Gen Fawzi Ahmad al-Fadil was appointed Acting Commander in Chief and 'Abd al-'Azim Sadiq Muhammad was appointed Chief of Staff.

On 6 November, Fawzi Ahmad al-Fadil was promoted to General (backdated to 4 September) and appointed Commander in Chief of the Armed Forces. Al-Fadil, 49, had graduated from the Sudan Military College and later studied in Egypt and Pakistan. He had been the Director of Supplies in the General Army Command before his new appointment. The new Chief of Staff was a 50-year-old lecturer at the Sudan Military College and the Kuwait Military College. Before his appointment to his new post, he was the Director of Operations in the Army General Command.[40] This reshuffle of the Army High Command was a preventive measure, taken against the background of the Government's weakness, and the growing restiveness in the country in general and in the Army in particular.

Unrest in the West

On 13 September 1986, a wave of violent riots swept the town of Nyala, in the Darfur region in western Sudan. An earlier outburst of violent disturbances erupted in al-Abyad (El Obeid), also in the Darfur region, in January 1986, in protest against increasing prices and deteriorating public services.[41] Student demonstrations which now occurred in Nyala resulted in the death of two people and the injury of several dozen. Some shops were looted and burned and the Darfur Regional Government building was destroyed, as was the Governor's house. The Army intervened and suppressed the riots on the day of their eruption. A day later, Prime Minister al-Mahdi arrived in Nyala in an attempt to appease the grievances of the local population.[42]

Western Sudan — an arid, extremely poor and largely undeveloped area, suffering from its considerable distance from the country's political and economic centers — has been one of the most neglected regions in the country, hence, the recurrent riots which swept the region from time to time. (Especially serious was the turbulence at the turn of 1980–81: see *MECS* 1980–81, pp 763–64). In recent years, the harsh conditions in the region were further aggravated by two developments: a disastrous drought and consequent famine which hit most acutely the western parts of the country, and the influx of a huge number of refugees from the neighboring war-torn Chad, which placed a further burden on the already collapsing system (see also *MECS* 1984–85, p 621). Repeated incursions by the SPLA into both southern Darfur and neighboring southern Kordofan[43] further undermined the area's general security. While the riots in Nyala were — probably — economically motivated, the Khartoum authorities implied that they had, in addition, a political motivation. "There are several [political] elements who are trying to exploit the sentiments and conditions of the citizens," stated the Interior Minister, Ahmad al-Husayn, two days after the suppression of the riots.[44] A foreign source was more specific, stating that the Government suspected NIF complicity, especially in the secondary schools, where it was very influential, and in West and Central Sudan.[45]

Riots in Khartoum

The end of October-beginning of November witnessed riots in the area of the capital. On 28 October, following two days of intermittent riots,[46] a huge student demonstration was staged near the headquarters of the UP in Omdurman (one of three areas constituting the capital, Khartoum). During the event, which rapidly turned into a violent riot, a member of the UP was stoned to death. More than 100 students were subsequently arrested by the police and flagellated. The official Sudanese News Agency (SUNA), which reported the events, added that anti-Government leaflets were circulated by the students in the course of the demonstrations and that "the style and contents of the leaflets [were] above the students' cultural and political level."[47] The authorities stated further that "political forces" were "behind the sabotage."[48] Admitting that the protest was primarily motivated by the distressing economic conditions, the Khartoum authorities accused political elements of exploiting the students' discontent for their own political ends. "To use a partial shortage of commodities to mislead...students [and get them to engage in] sabotage [will have] drastic consequences" stated al-Mahdi in one official reference to the wave of unrest.[49] The Premier still refrained at that stage from explicitly pointing a finger at the NIF. He made, however, an obvious hint when he said that the political aim of the instigators of the riots was "to move the current discussions in the constitutioinal institutions...to the streets in order to make matters impossible for the democratic authorities...."[50] Despite the authorities' stringent security measures, such as the arrest of 296 students and 27 citizens,[51] the riots resumed several days later in a more vigorous and violent manner.

On 2 November, between 3,000 and 4,000 students, mainly from Khartoum University and the Cairo University branch in Khartoum (where NIF influence was highly dominant), staged a "'march" toward the Prime Minister's office. Their declared aim, as announced a day earlier by the President of the Khartoum University Students' Union, was to hand al-Mahdi a memorandum explaining the student's views on "the current situation in the country," with emphasis on the urgent need to tackle the high cost of living.[52] The memorandum also called for the enactment of the formally existing *Shari'a* laws, a clear echo of the NIF's persistent demand. At a certain stage — it was not clear whether before the students' march turned into a violent riot or perhaps even earlier — the police intervened, using tear gas and weapons. The event resulted in nine casualties, among them two students who were "shot and seriously wounded" by the police.[53] At that stage, circles in the Government blamed the NIF openly for the riots.[54] The NIF, for its part, denounced "the Government's handling of the students' demonstrations,"[55] and tension between the Government and the NIF reached a new crisis point. The October-November riots highlighted the fact that the situation in Sudan was again highly explosive. The Government's indecisiveness and inability to advance a solution or at least mitigate the serious problems, provided the backdrop for the unrest. This, in turn, served as a clear reminder of many similar waves of violence which had plagued the Sudanese scene during the Numayri era. To that bleak political and economic background, the civil war in the South added a particularly negative element.

FIERCE CIVIL WAR AND A POLITICAL STALEMATE

The turn of 1985–86 witnessed a significant increase in the fighting between Sudan's armed forces and the SPLA, which was rekindled in 1983 and rapidly escalated into full-scale civil war. The SPLA's capture of two towns in the Bahr al-Ghazal region — Yirol in late December 1985, and Rumbek in early March 1986,[56] signified a clear turn for the worse in the Government's position, and heralded the escalation in the war. In addition to the fighting in Bahr al-Ghazal, the SPLA launched during the same months a series of intensive military assaults in the two other regions of the South —

the Upper Nile and Equatoria. Especially fierce fighting took place in East Equatoria, around Torit and Kapoeta. The SPLA, despite the distance from its bases of power in the Dinka-dominated lands of the Bahr al-Ghazal and Upper Nile regions, succeeded in cutting the road from Torit eastwards, a vital link to Kenya, and westwards, to Nimule.[57] On 10 March, even the airport in Juba — the capital of the South — was threatened when about 100 government troops allegedly mutinied within the airport area, disobeying an order to go by air to the SPLA-captured town of Rumbek in order to fight for its recapture.[58] The affair, as reported by a foreign source, was a "close shave" to the Khartoum Government, for the SPLA was apparently on the verge of exploiting the chaos to take over the airport itself.[59]

Despite the rapid escalation of the conflict, neither the Khartoum Government nor the South made a serious effort to reach a negotiated settlement. While the Government was not engaging in a dialogue with the South, the Alliance of National Forces for the National Salvation of Sudan had opened in early 1986 a series of talks with the SPLA. The Alliance — a grouping representing the professional elite and various political parties which emerged on the political scene on the eve of Numayri's overthrow, played a most important role in his downfall (see *MECS* 1984–85, p 628). Garang's attitude was positive, as clearly attested to by his reference to the Alliance as the "vanguard of the mass movement in the towns, in the same way (and [with] the same sacrifices) that the SPLA is the vanguard of the mass movement in the bushes."[60] It was not clear whether the Alliance had the approval or even perhaps the backing of the Khartoum Government. The alliance representatives and the SPLA representatives met for their first round of talks on 24 March in Ethiopia, in the town of Koka Dam, 60 miles south of Addis Ababa. The meeting produced the "Koka Dam Declaration," which stipulated the two parties' agreement on the "prerequisites which will foster an atmosphere conducive to the holding of the proposed national constitutional conference" to pave the way toward achieving a solution to the conflict. The Declaration was signed for the SPLA by Lt Col Carabino, considered Garang's number-two man, and for the Alliance by Khalid Yaji, who was later appointed (in May 1986) Minister for Peace and National Constitutional Conference in al-Mahdi's Government. Its main points were:

(1) Repeal of the September 1983 (*Shari'a*) law and all other laws that were restrictive of freedom.
(2) Adoption of the 1956 Constitution as amended in 1964 with the incorporation of a Regional Government and all other such matters on which a consensus opinion of all the political forces would be reached.
(3) The abrogation of military pacts concluded between Sudan and other countries (apparently Libya and Egypt) which impinged on Sudan's national sovereignty.
(4) A continuous endeavor by the two sides to take the necessary steps and measures to effect a cease-fire.[61]

Meanwhile, fighting did not cease and the SPLA announced that it would disrupt the national elections scheduled for the beginning of April. The SPLA rejected what it termed the "fake and partial elections," and charged that they "deprived the SPLA from participation according to Khartoum's decision that those who carry arms have no right to take part in the elections."[62] Indeed, elections were officially suspended by Khartoum in 37 (out of 68) constituencies in the South because of the "continuing fighting" there.[63] Large parts of the SPLA-controlled regions of Bahr al-Ghazal and the Upper Nile, as well as certain parts of Equatoria, were affected.[64]

During its first days in power, al-Mahdi's Government showed a noteworthy willingness to bring about a political settlement of the war. In late April, even while he was preoccupied with the formation of his Government, al-Mahdi sent a delegation to Addis Ababa — the headquarters of the SPLA — to offer Garang a share in the new Government.[65] The SPLA flatly rejected al-Mahdi's offer, referring to it as "putting the cart before the horse."[66]

Meanwhile, in an unrelated set of contacts, a second round of talks was held between SPLA and Alliance representatives on 7 May in Ethiopia.[67] This meeting did not produce any tangible results, and coincided with the Sudanese Army's recapture of the town of Rumbek from the "outlaws,"[68] after inflicting "heavy casualties," including the killing of six senior SPLA officers.[69] Fighting over the control of the town continued intensively later in the month.[70]

A week after the recapture of Rumbek, which boosted the Army's morale, al-Mahdi formally assumed the Premiership of Sudan. He committed himself to do everything he could to bring about a settlement to the armed conflict, describing it as "the most serious problem" his new Government was facing.[71] That al-Mahdi did take it seriously was evidenced by the fact that he set up a Ministry to bring about a political solution of the conflict (see above), and presented the public with a new comprehensive plan, which he thought would advance the end of the war. Al-Mahdi's three-track program was detailed as follows:

> The first is the political channel, where we should urgently hold a national constitutional conference to discuss the main issues, grievances, differences, and complaints with a view to finding political solutions to them...The second is the security channel. It has to do with equipping the Sudanese armed forces with what is necessary to enable them to protect the lives, property, and honor of the Sudanese people. The third is the diplomatic channel. The differences which emerged between us and our neighbors and were intensified by the former regime must be resolved on the basis of good-neighborliness and cooperation to promote security and development in the Horn of Africa.[72]

At that stage — in May 1986 — al-Mahdi also stressed his readiness to meet Garang "at any time and at any place," providing he were assured that Garang believed the political option was "the only way to solve the Southern problem."[73] However, a measure of impatience in al-Mahdi's position toward the SPLA could be discerned in his statement that "Garang should either resort to dialogue or he would regarded as an outlaw."[74] The SPLA, for its part, underlined its adherence to the Koka Dam Declaration, emphasizing that it could not "be a party to any dialogue conducted outside the declaration."[75]

Following the advent to power of the new Government in Khartoum, the fighting between the SPLA and the Army escalated and a number of military aircraft were shot down by SPLA SAM-7 missiles over the Rumbek area.[76] The incidents constituted a dangerous development for Khartoum, since air supply was the only way of maintaning isolated military garrisons in many parts of the South, especially in the Bahr al-Ghazal region. Additional fighting was noticed in June, with a new advance of the SPLA toward Juba.[77] The military tension in the South reached such an alarming level that al-Mahdi decided to call off a visit to the South planned for early June.[78] (A foreign source reported that al-Mahdi secretly visited the South a month later).[79]

Meanwhile, contacts between the SPLA and the alliance representatives continued, but their third round of talks in Addis Ababa, held from 24-28 June, did not produce any breakthrough.[80]

During July, a further intensification of the war was reported. SPLA reports claimed the destruction of bridges and the blocking of important roads, as well as the destruction or siege of important towns.[81] One of the most acute problems caused by the spread of the fighting was the worsening famine in the South. In the summer of 1986, Juba became the center for emergency food distribution for the town and neighboring villages; there were many displaced people, including 150,000 refugees who had reportedly fled in July from various areas in Equatoria to Juba.[82] There were also reports that, during July, hundreds of thousands of destitute people were pouring into Uganda and Ethiopia.[83] The situation was more and more reminiscent of the first round of civil war, which plagued Sudan between 1955 and 1972.

Though the real state of affairs regarding the course of the fighting and the military position of each of the conflicting parties was unclear, it appeared in the summer of 1986 that the Army was unable to cope with the SPLA challenge. According to a foreign source, the Sudanese Army barely moved out of the garrison towns, while the SPLA increased its control over large sections of the remote and underpopulated rural regions.[84] This impression was enhanced by the SPLA's offensive, launched in mid-July on Jabel Lado, a prominent rock about 27 km north of Juba,[85] as the rebels advanced toward Juba airport on the town's northern outskirts. Jabel Lado controlled the main air routes into Juba from Khartoum and the North. On 25 July, the SPLA reported the occupation of Jabel Lado, adding that the Khartoum authorities had therefore been forced to close Juba airport as of 17 July.[86] Khartoum denied the SPLA claim, and ascribed the closure of the airport to "technical reasons." Al-Mahdi was quoted several days later as saying that the airport was closed because of "the presence in the area of a large number of cows," thus denying local and foreign reports that Juba was besieged.[87] The SPLA insisted, however, on 25 July, that Juba "has now been effectively besieged."[88] Whatever the truth, Juba airport was reopened on 30 July "after being completely secured."[89]

The military effectiveness of the SPLA and its links with the new President of neighboring Uganda (see below), apparently goaded al-Mahdi to increase his efforts to hold negotiations with the SPLA. On 31 July, while in Addis Ababa for the summit of the Organization of African Unity (OAU), al-Mahdi met Garang. The meeting, the first since al-Mahdi became Prime Minister, signaled some change on the part of the SPLA which hitherto had refused to talk directly with the newly elected Government of "al-Mahdi and al-Mirghani families."[90] The meeting did not produce an improved climate, and, as al-Mahdi said, the talks "did not go beyond the clarification of some points relating to the explanation of the Koka Dam Declaration and how to implement it."[91] The joint communiqué issued at the end of the Garang-Mahdi meeting stated, however, that "consultations, contacts and peace efforts shall continue through meetings of the [SPLM-SPLA and Alliance] follow-up committee."[92] Indeed, from 5 to 11 August, the fourth round of talks between the SPLA and the Alliance took place in Addis Ababa, but again without any progress.[93]

Meanwhile, further escalation in the war was noted on 15 August, when the SPLA released a warning that it would shoot down every plane, military or civilian, that flew over the war zone in the South. The SPLA explained that its stern warning resulted from what it saw as Khartoum's intention to take advantage of an international food airlift to Southerners to hurt the SPLA.[94] Just one day later the SPLA carried out its threat. Using SAM-7 anti-aircraft missiles, the SPLA shot down a Sudan Airways plane shortly after it took off from the town of Malakal, the provincial capital of the Upper Nile region, about 690 km south of Khartoum. All 60 passengers were killed.[95] Although pre-warned, the shooting of the civilian aircraft caused shock in Khartoum and a significant hardening of attitudes toward the SPLA. Al-Mahdi immediately suspended all talks with the SPLA. All relief flights were also suspended and a series of protests and virulent denunciations of the SPLA by various circles in Khartoum, including the Alliance, followed soon.[96] Three days after the incident, the SPLA released a new warning, aimed at civilians in the South, this time urging them to evacuate immediately the four major towns of Juba, Wau, Malakal and Bentiu, which it said it was about to attack (the latter was strategically important as the site of the country's principal oil field).[97] Al-Mahdi referrred to the SPLA warning as "sheer nonsense," adding that SPLA propaganda "is larger than the movement itself." Al-Mahdi further said that "Garang's movement" had proved "beyond any doubt that it is a terrorist rebel movement" and that "dealings with it will be [henceforth] based on this principle." To lend additional substance to Khartoum's toughening line, al-Mahdi also announced the "general mobilization at all levels to confront the terrorism of John Garang's movement."[98]

Meanwhile, as many as two to three million people in the South, including Army garrisons in the besieged towns, were facing malnutrition or even starvation.[99] Land, river and air supply routes to the South were cut by the SPLA, and in late August were also affected by the closure by Uganda of the important route from the Kenyan port of Mombasa to South Sudan (see below). Foreign relief supplies to the area were also hampered by the SPLA, which accused international relief agencies of neglecting rebel-held areas, and demanded that most relief aid should go through the SPLA since it allegedly "controlled 95 per cent of the population of South Sudan."[100] With both sides using food supplies as a weapon, the situation in the South became extremely grim, marking a vicious state in the war. (Two attempts to airlift relief supplies to the South, in October and November, failed. The operations were sponsored by about a dozen Western countries and private and international relief agencies.)[101]

During the last quarter of 1986, following the reshuffle of the top military command in September (see above), new vigor marked Khartoum's military operations against the SPLA. Also the dry conditions favored the Army more than the guerrillas, and an improvement, albeit perhaps only temporary, of security conditions in the South was noticeable. "The situation is much better," announced the Acting Commander in Chief, Gen Fawzi Ahmad al-Fadl, in a series of statements[102] which reflected the new military leadership's confidence — or at least its pretended confidence — in its ability to change the course of affairs in the South.

Persistent rumors spread by Khartoum sources during October-November about Garang's "serious wounding," and, a short while later, his "killing" by rivals in the SPLA,[103] significantly reinforced the impression of a decline in the SPLA's position and of serious internal divisions. The SPLA, for its part, denied Khartoum's "fabrications" concerning Garang's death, saying they were aimed at undermining morale within the SPLA.[104] On 5 December, Garang made a public appearance at a press conference in Addis Ababa.[105] While the cause of Garang's mysterious two-month absence remained unclear, his reappearance did not herald a new development in the course of the armed conflict, which had virtually reached an impasse at the end of the year.

The Mahdi Government, for its part, continued to face the same serious dilemma which exercised it throughout the period under review: whether to launch an all-out war with the SPLA (with a slender prospect of success, a possible military clash with Ethiopia, and — in any event — prohibitive financial cost), or to meet the SPLA demands articulated in the Koka Dam Declaration as a precondition for a dialogue. The latter course of action entailed a heavy short- and long-term political price. It was clear that al-Mahdi could not afford — personally or politically — to meet the declaration's two major demands: repealing the *Shari'a* laws of 1983 and canceling the military agreement with Egypt and, more important, with Qadhdhafi. He was prepared to promulgate new laws instead of the *Shari'a* ones (see above). As far as the cancellation of Sudan's military agreement was concerned, al-Mahdi could not afford that either, especially since Ethiopia was strengthening its political and military grip on the SPLA. (On Sudan's 1985 military agreement with Libya and its 1976 military agreement with Egypt, see *MECS* 1984–85, pp 635–36, and 1976–77, p 597, respectively). The severity of the dilemma somehow diminished as 1986 came closer to its end, as al-Mahdi realized that even the fulfillment of the declaration's demands would not lead to the immediate opening of negotiations between the conflicting parties. There could only be a dialogue with the SPLA, al-Mahdi repeatedly stated, if the SPLA received "the green light from Ethiopia to negotiate or liberated itself from Ethiopia's hegemony."[106] He further stated on various occasions in fall-winter 1986 that the rebel movement was "a foreign Ethiopian aggression" against Sudan[107] and that "Sudan will settle the question of war either by peace and justice if it is possible or by force."[108]

The SPLA persistently adhered to the Koka Dam Declaration, challenging al-Mahdi to take the "path of peace" by "adhering strictly to both the letter and spirit of the declaration," emphasizing that "neither [al-Mahdi] nor other political groupings should be scared of the Koka Dam Declaration as if it were a ghost." The declaration was "not going to oust the present Government overnight. All that it is intended to achieve is to lay the groundwork for a dialogue."[109] Garang's call for a dialogue was intertwined, however, with militant statements promising to continue fighting until the Mahdi Government stopped trying to impose Islamic customs on the Christians and animists of the South. "Religion must no longer be used for political aims," said Garang, adding that the SPLA was not "a Christian movement" or "an African movement. We are a Sudanese movement. We are a unionist movement dedicated to the creation of a united new Sudan." Garang vowed that the SPLA would extend the fight until its objectives were met: "As someone once said, war is better than a bad peace."[110]

FOREIGN AFFAIRS

LIBYA

Throughout 1986, *rapprochement* with Libya continued to be the most salient feature of Khartoum's foreign relations. (For details regarding the first stages of the process, which began in the immediate aftermath of Numayri's overthrow, see *MECS* 1984–85, pp 635–36). The beginning of 1986 witnessed a significant boost of the two countries' political, economic and military ties. Clear evidence of this trend was provided by Sudan's strong support of Qadhdhafi's regime during the latter's period of tension with the US (see chapter on Libya). The *rapprochement* with Tripoli was primarily shaped by Sudan's urgent interest in stopping Libyan support for the SPLA. Tripoli's political, economic and military support of the Khartoum Government was also important to the new Sudanese regime. Its drastic realignment in the regional setting fell in line with its need to legitimize power and broaden its base of popular support. Khartoum's tightening ties with Tripoli did not stem merely from ideological convictions or a different perception of Sudan's desirable foreign policy but primarily from political expediency. Sudan's Foreign Minister, Ibrahim Taha Ayyub, put it very plainly when he stated that "our relations with Libya are only designed to attain mutual interests in the same way as with all Arab and African countries."[111] Statements of that kind should be also viewed within the context of other factors of foreign, and possibly also domestic, affairs aimed at calming the apprehensions of the US, Egypt and perhaps even pro-Egyptian circles in Sudan, led by the DUP.

The growing links with Tripoli led to a series of visits to Libya by top Sudanese leaders during the first months of the year, and, in particular in March to two successive trips by Sudan's Defense Minister 'Abdallah 'Uthman Muhammad and a visit by Prime Minister Daf'allah Juzuli (see chapter on Libya). The dramatic American air attack on Libya on 15 April (see chapter on Libya) served as an additional catalyst for strengthening Sudan's solidarity with the Qadhdhafi regime. Sudan issued a spate of staunch pro-Libyan statements,[112] underlined by a huge pro-Libyan and anti-American demonstration in Khartoum.[113] Another demonstrative act of support was the visit paid by Sudan's Defense Minister to Libya on 19–20 April — being one of the first high-ranking foreign leaders to visit the country in the immediate aftermath of the American assault. Al-Mahdi issued a declaration of solidarity with the Qadhdhafi regime,[114] at a time when he was widely expected to become Sudan's next Prime Minister. (He had visited Libya a month earlier[115] and was known for his good ties with the Qadhdhafi regime, which had provided him during his exile in the 1970s with a base for launching his anti-Numayri activities.) Soon after his election as Prime Minister, al-Mahdi reiterated Sudan's support of Libya "with all [of Khartoum's] potential."[116]

Nevertheless, some tension reportedly crept into the two countries' ostensibly cordial relationship, although this was not confirmed or even referred to by either side. Foreign sources claimed that, in mid-1986 and later, tension revolved around two main issues: the continuing presence of Libyan troops on Sudanese territory; and the activities of the Libyan-backed Sudanese Revolutionary Committees which were supposed to promote Qadhdhafi's "Third Universal Theory" in Sudan.[117] Foreign sources reported during the summer of 1986 that about 800–1,000 Libyan soldiers were camping within the boundaries of the Sudanese airport of al-Fashir, the capital of Darfur in West Sudan.[118] The troops arrived in March 1986 under the guise of a "relief mission" to the backward and famine-struck area, and remained there under nominal Sudanese supervision.[119] The Sudanese authorities demanded that the Libyans leave, but they refused.[120] Sudan's sensitivity stemmed from the potential dangers inherent in the presence of Libyan troops among the restive population in West Sudan. Not only could the Libyans, if they so wished, instigate the already disaffected population against the central Government in Khartoum, but they could also create "pockets" of pro-Libyan support. No less alarming was the potential threat posed by the Libyan troops *vis-à-vis* Sudan's relations with Chad. This issue was not discussed in public, and the steady stream of Sudanese denials of such a presence, released in the fall of 1986,[121] could be interpreted as an indication of Khartoum's attempt not to escalate relations with Tripoli, while trying discreetly to solve the problem.

The other source of mutual friction was reportedly the growing activity of the Sudanese Revolutionary Committees in Sudan. Sudan reportedly asked Tripoli to curb the activities of the committees.[122] It was alleged by a foreign source that Libya had budgeted, in an attempt to influence Sudanese politics, $76m to support the committees, and had recruited to the committees' ranks about 4,000 people, most of them Sudanese exiles who had returned after April 1985 from Libya.[123] Allegedly, the committees' activities in Sudan were controlled by a Libyan operations team activated by the Libyan embassy.[124]

At least on the surface, the alleged tension did not seem to hurt the further fostering of ties with Libya. On 10 August, al-Mahdi, heading a high-level delegation, ended a two-day trip to Libya. The Sudanese official version described the list of topics discussed by the two sides as concentrating on "common issues and concerns — Arab, Islamic and African — as well as bilateral cooperation...."[125] The visit resulted in an agreement between Sudanese expatriates in Libya and the Libyan and Sudanese authorities on using the expatriates' savings to finance the acquisition of petroleum products. The Sudanese authorities were to reimburse these sums to the families of the expatriates in Khartoum.[126] On 9 September, Qadhdhafi reciprocated by paying a three-day visit to "sisterly" Sudan, on his way home from a visit in Uganda (where he apparently acted, *inter alia*, to defuse the crisis betwen Kampala and Khartoum; see below). Another important area of foreign relations — actually of much greater importance to Sudan's urgent interests — in which Libya also got involved for Khartoum's sake concerned Sudanese-Ethiopian relations (see chapter on Libya).

EGYPT

Relations with Egypt continued to suffer in 1986 from political stalemate, despite numerous references by top Sudanese leaders concerning the two countries' "special," "strong," and "eternal" relations, "tied by blood and common destiny."[127]

The process of gradual but consistent distancing from Cairo, which began immediately after Numayri's downfall, was the direct and inevitable result of Khartoum's accelerated process of *rapprochement* with Libya. Since Libya and Egypt bitterly opposed each other Sudan could not, even if it so wished, maintain close political ties with both. However, in order to minimize damage to their relations with Egypt, the Sudanese Governments of al-Dahab and of al-Mahdi tried to make it clear, from time to time, that closer relations with Libya would not come at the expense of

Khartoum's ties with Egypt.[128] These statements could not conceal the deterioration of Sudan's relations with Egypt, which caused Khartoum noticeable uneasiness. After all, Egypt had been a consistent source of support during the last decade, and the new Government in Khartoum still considered it potentially a most important asset. Khartoum tried to absolve itself of responsibility for the damaged relations with Egypt by pointing to the latter's refusal to fulfill its official request for the extradition of deposed President Numayri, as a major reason for the deterioration. Numayri was living in a guest house in Heliopolis, a residential suburb north of Cairo, as a political refugee since his downfall in the spring of 1985.[129] Though not of any special importance to Sudan's prime interests, the extradition affair was not dropped from Sudanese public attention during the whole period reviewed,[130] being deliberately blown up beyond its real significance. The Egyptian refusal to extradite Numayri was "a stab at the Sudanese nation,"[131] stated Khartoum.

Khartoum's clear-cut shift from Cairo to Tripoli was further demonstrated, albeit symbolically, by the announcement on 30 March of the dissolution of the integration institutions established in 1982 under Sudan's Integration Charter with Egypt (for details of the charter and the process of integration, see *MECS* 1982–83, pp 780–81; 1983–84, p 662; and 1984–85, p 626). Khartoum explained its move in terms of the integration's "irrelevance", saying that the process "was an act imposed from above which did not express the joint interests of the two peoples."[132] In the same breath, however, the Sudanese authorities hastened to declare that the dissolution act did "not mean or imply the abrogation of the principle of integration." In fact, they explained, the dissolution decision stressed "the soundness of the principle of integration and the need to apply [it] to production and development."[133] Khartoum's verbal maneuvers reflected its uneasiness *vis-à-vis* Cairo, the pro-Egyptian DUP and Washington (which preferred a Sudanese-Egyptian link to one between Sudan and Libya). They were aimed at warding off pressure from these three directions, especially since the dissolution act came at the same time as the furtherance of the *rapprochement* with Libya (see chapter on Libya). Practically, the Sudanese decision meant that the integration bureaucracy formally ceased its work. As the integration process had been shelved since the overthrow of the Numayri regime, if not before, Khartoum's decision had merely a propagandist effect, and should be construed primarily as a part of the price Khartoum had to pay for its *rapprochement* with Tripoli.

While its political ties with Egypt cooled, Khartoum was careful not to entirely sever its routes of communication with Cairo. Political links were kept mainly through the pro-Egyptian DUP leaders, headed by the Chairman of the State Council, Ahmad 'Ali al-Mirghani, and the Deputy Prime Minister and Foreign Minister, Sharif Zayn al-'Abidin al-Hindi. Following the setting up of the Mahdi Government in April-May 1986, both al-Mirghani and al-Hindi made several trips to Cairo. In late May, al-Hindi stopped over at Cairo airport (en route to New York), and, in mid-June, he went again to Cairo, on a one-week official visit.[134] On 6 July, al-Mirghani became the most senior Sudanese leader to pay an official visit to Egypt since the establishment of the Mahdi Government. However, his visit did not lead to any significant change in bilateral relations.[135] Moreover, a new crisis soon occurred when, in early August, Sudan suspended all exports to Egypt, citing a growing trade imbalance between the two countries. The Sudanese action amounted to a freezing of the protocol of commercial cooperation signed between the two countries a month earlier.[136] Al-Hindi's visit to Cairo, which began on 6 August and included a meeting with President Husni Mubarak, was apparently aimed at bringing about some relief of the newly created strain; but it was unsuccessful.[137]

A slight improvement towards the end of 1986 was indicated by the coming and going of top-level officials between Khartoum and Cairo, but it was not clear if these trips heralded a turning point in Sudan's bilateral relations with Egypt, or merely a limited development.

ETHIOPIA

In early 1986, Sudan claimed that Ethiopia was not satisfied with supplying the SPLA with backing, arms, training and — most effectively — Radio SPLA, but had also become actively involved in warfare alongside the rebels in the South. Specifically, Sudan argued that Ethiopian pilots had flown, early in 1986, transport helicopters in the service of the SPLA,[138] and that Ethiopian long-range artillery had been used from within Ethiopian territory to shell targets within Sudan.[139] Khartoum's apprehension of what it termed "direct Ethiopian aggression"[140] significantly increased at the beginning of the period under survey. Being aware of Ethiopia's key role in the escalation of the war in the South, and having, therefore, an essential interest in reducing tension in its relations with Ethiopia, Khartoum handled with great caution the issue of granting political asylum to an Ethiopian Air Force pilot who defected to Sudan in mid-January 1986.[141] While signaling to Addis Ababa that it had its own ways of hurting Ethiopia's interests, Khartoum hastened to emphasize at the same time that the asylum was granted on a "human basis"[142] and on condition that the pilot "would not embark on anti-Ethiopian activities."[143] The asylum affair had, however, only marginal impact on the two countries' relations. Of much greater significance, though seemingly of insufficient effectiveness, were Sudan's close ties with the Eritrean rebels, particularly the Eritrean People's Liberation Front. Khartoum hoped that Addis Ababa would drop, or at least significantly reduce, its support of the SPLA if Sudan, for its part, would stop serving as a base for the activities of the Eritrean rebels. Khartoum's series of statements, released in the first quarter of 1986, about its efforts to curtail the activities of the Eritreans in Sudan,[144] did not elicit a commensurate reaction by Ethiopia. On the contrary, mutual tension continued to mount. On 15, 17 and 31 March, Ethiopia allegedly violated Sudan's airspace. The Ethiopian aircraft, as Khartoum claimed, dropped food supplies to the southern Sudanese territory and carried out reconnaissance flights over the region.[145] Sudan regarded "the Ethiopian violations" as a most serious development, and a prominent figure from the TMC, which led Sudan in the wake of Numayri's toppling, even threatened that similar moves would compel Sudan "to take political, diplomatic and even military measures against Ethiopia."[146]

In late spring 1986, immediately after he assumed office, al-Mahdi placed renewed emphasis on his Government's wish to open "a new page" in its relations with Ethiopia. Al-Mahdi's reference to the issue in his very first speech before the Sudanese Constituent Assembly, on 6 May, plainly reflected the major importance he attributed to the removal of obstacles in the two countries' relations.[147] The two visits — in early May and in late June 1986 — by high-ranking Ethiopian officials to the Sudanese capital,[148] after a relatively long period without direct contacts between Addis Ababa and Khartoum, clearly attested to Sudan's endeavor to defuse mutual tensions.

Though the Sudanese media did not dwell on the visits' aims or on their results, one may assume that the Sudanese repeated their request that Ethiopia stop supporting the SPLA, and possibly also urged the latter to enter into negotiations with Khartoum. Whatever the issues discussed in the talks, they did not produce any tangible progress. The same was true with regard to al-Mahdi's meeting on 30 July in Addis Ababa on the occasion of the OAU summit, with the Ethiopian leader, Mengistu Haile Mariam. Sources close to the two leaders said that al-Mahdi repeated the offer to end Sudan's support for the Eritreans, in return for Ethiopia's curbing its support of the SPLA. According to the same sources, Mengistu refused on the grounds that Sudan would be unable to deliver its part of the bargain.[149]

Since a halt in Ethiopia's support of the SPLA was a crucial factor in advancing the chances of achieving either a political or a military solution in the South, al-Mahdi did not cease his efforts to persuade Ethiopia to cut its backing of the SPLA.

As 1986 came to an end, a new peak of tension marred Sudan's relations with Ethiopia. Khartoum accused Addis Ababa of staging, in November-December, repeated air attacks on a number of villages in the east of the country, where a large concentration of Eritrean refugees was located. The Sudanese authorities reported the killing and wounding of a number of people.[150] Sudan reacted strongly, lodging a complaint with the OAU[151] and recalling its Ambassador to Addis Ababa.[152]

UGANDA

Relations with Uganda, another country contiguous to the war-torn South, were marred by suspicion and strain during the major part of the period reviewed. A significant turn for the worse occurred immediately after the advent to power of President Yoweri Museveni's National Resistance Army in Kampala in late January 1986. The new Ugandan regime claimed that Tito Okello, the deposed Ugandan President, and his military forces had escaped to Sudan and found sanctuary there.[153] The Sudanese authorities hastened to deny the allegation, assuring Kampala that not "an inch of Sudanese territory will be used by any dissidents to disturb the peace and stability of Uganda."[154] Khartoum's reaction reflected its apprehension that escalation of tension with Uganda could do a great deal of harm to Sudan's essential interests. Uganda could block the single and most vital land route connecting southern Sudan with Kenya's port of Mombasa through Ugandan territory (as it actually did later in the summer; see below). Even more seriously, Uganda could allow the SPLA to use its territory as a base for the launching of a new, second front against Khartoum. During the first civil war between the South and Khartoum (from 1955–72), when the original Southern Anyanya guerrilla movement fought Khartoum's Army, it was Uganda rather than Ethiopia that provided bases for the rebels.

Not surprisingly, therefore, Sudan made a considerable effort to ease tension with Uganda. In February-March, notwithstanding its official admission that Ugandan dissidents were present on Sudanese territory,[155] Khartoum succeeded in ironing out its difficulties with Kampala, at least for the time being.[156] The trend of improvement, however, did not last long. In June, a tour of Uganda made by the SPLA leader, Col John Garang, rang alarm bells in Khartoum, especially in light of the friendly relations between Museveni and Garang.[157]

The simmering tension along the common border, which was totally lawless and impossible to police, culminated in late August in an open crisis. The Ugandan

President accused Sudan of supporting 3,000 Ugandan rebels who returned to attack towns in northern Uganda. Museveni further claimed that Sudanese troops had armed the "Ugandan rebels" and provided them with transport.[158] Sudan responded quickly, denying "categorically" the Ugandan accusation, and stressing that "Ugandan refugees in southern Sudan are not practicing any military or political activities" against Kampala.[159] Museveni was not impressed by Khartoum's denials, and on 27 August announced the closure of the Ugandan-Sudanese border. Simultaneously, he reportedly fortified the border area with between 10,000–15,000 troops.[160] Consequently, the movement of traffic carrying relief supplies from Mombasa via Uganda to southern Sudan was immediately stopped. The cutting off of the main route of supply to the starving population in the South, especially when other routes of supply were entirely blocked by the Southerners, signified a most detrimental development for Khartoum. Hence the feverish efforts by Khartoum to bring about a rapid termination of the crisis. Khartoum's attempts proved successful. On 20 September, both countries reached a reconciliation agreement. Sudan undertook to "remove genuine Ugandan refugees from the [common] border [area and to] stop rebel Ugandan soldiers [from] invading [Uganda] again," while Kampala announced "the reopening of the common border," allowing the transfer of "relief supplies only."[161] From the signing of the agreement until the end of the year, bilateral relations were not marred by any new crisis.

THE UNITED STATES

Tensions in Sudan's relations with the US since the April 1985 change of the guard in Khartoum, which were a result of Khartoum's *rapprochement* with the Qadhdhafi regime, were further heightened in 1986.

A sharp increase in the anti-American sentiments in Khartoum was clearly noticed immediately after the "savage American aggression,"[162] as it termed the military attack on Libya in April (see chapter on Libya). Dahab's interim Government, being in its last days in power, hastened to release, on the day of the American attack, a special statement denouncing the "brutal military action."[163] That night a US embassy official was shot and seriously wounded in Khartoum by an "unidentified person," as the Sudanese authorities hurried to emphasize.[164] Though an unknown organization calling itself "The Martyrs of Islam" claimed responsibility,[165] the identity of the assailant(s) remained unknown, or at least undisclosed. The shooting, apparently in retaliation for the US raid on Libya, was followed the next day by a huge anti-American demonstration in the streets of Khartoum.[166] The rapidly growing hostility toward Washington was mirrored in a series of verbal attacks by top Sudanese officials. Especially virulent among them was the denunciation by Defense Minister 'Uthman 'Abdallah Muhammad, a key member of the TMC who called on his Government to "expel all the staff in the US embassy and to liquidate all US interests in Sudan."[167] The US embassy, concerned about the anti-American violence, announced on 17 April the evacuation of between 200–500[168] American officials and their families from the Sudanese capital. Additional evidence of the mounting tension was the two countries' decision to recall their Ambassadors for consultations.[169]

Though relations deteriorated swiftly immediately after the American attack on Libya, the American action should not be mistakenly considered the reason for the eruption of the crisis. In fact, the American operation served merely as an excuse for the further improvement of Khartoum's already close political ties with Qadhdhafi — a process which inevitably increased strains with Washington. Sudan's *rapprochement* with Libya occupied, throughout 1985-86, the most prominent place in Khartoum's foreign policy, while it did not fall in line with the continuation of the traditional pattern of close political cooperation with the US. Another factor which played a role in distancing Sudan politically from the US was the determination of the Dahab and al-Mahdi Governments to abandon Numayri's pro-American orientation in favor of what Khartoum called the policy of "non-alignment and balance"[170] in international affairs.

Grievances against the US were also nourished by the US's "aggressive plots"[171] with regard to the smuggling of Ethiopian Jews via Sudan to Israel (see *MECS* 1984–85, pp 620–21),[172] and by the US's formal suspension, in late March 1986, of $158m in economic and military assistance for fiscal 1986, because of Sudan's failure to meet its debt repayment.[173] More reasonably, this move was designed as pressure on Sudan to change, or at least to slow down, its *rapprochement* with Libya. Khartoum responded angrily to the "foul" American behavior, stating that Washington "has the right to suspend aid...but has no right to decide Sudan's foreign relations" or "to impose its hegemony and patronage over Sudan."[174]

Since its inception in May, al-Mahdi's Government continued to toe the same anti-American line as its predecessor, despite its awareness that US economic support was vital if Sudan wished to salvage its seriously ailing economy. Al-Mahdi did not make, during his first months in the Prime Minister's office, any demonstrative move to placate the American Administration. His statement that Sudan had taken the "non-aligned course," hoping that "this policy would be acceptable to the US since this was the best option for Sudan,"[175] indicated that Khartoum's basic assumption was that while the *rapprochement* with Libya was in keeping with the country's essential interests, the softening of tension with the US could await for a more convenient time, without threatening Khartoum's long-term relations with the US.

In the fall of 1986, when Sudan's financial situation reached a new "red line," Khartoum searched for urgent injections of financial aid. The US, a traditional and major backer, became, therefore, a prime target for Khartoum's endeavor to mobilize desperately needed funds. In early October, al-Mahdi arrived in Washington, on a ten-day visit; he was accompanied by a high-level economic delegation. The visit proved fruitful and "culminated in a complete agreement with the US to activate bilateral relations."[176] The release of $71m and a food grant of $7.5m by the US were announced.[177] Al-Mahdi also signed several agreements for "military cooperation."[178] In November, an additional US grant of $18m to fund agriculture in the Kordofan region (western Sudan) was also reported.[179]

THE SOVIET UNION

During the period under review, the Sudanese authorities took pains to bring about a breakthrough in Khartoum's relations with the USSR, which had long been hostile. Following an official tour of the Soviet Union (from 11–15 August 1986), al-Mahdi stated that the visit had removed "the effects of the defunct era's stupid policy" toward Moscow, and concentrated on the "opening of a new chapter within the framework of non-alignment and balance."[180] Detailing the visit's gains, al-Mahdi announced that Moscow "agreed to revive projects" it had been associated with in Sudan from the late

1960s until mid-1971, when Numayri made a dramatic change in his country's international orientation, moving from the Soviet orbit into the American one after an abortive Communist coup. Moscow also agreed, according to al-Mahdi, to "repair the old Soviet civilian and military equipment in Sudan."[181] Of especial importance was the willingness to repair military equipment, since Sudan still had a substantial arsenal of Soviet weaponry acquired by the pre-Numayri regime and Numayri himself during his first two years in office. The bitter fighting in the South necessitated an urgent reinforcement of the Army's equipment. Another issue of major importance reportedly included in al-Mahdi's talks in Moscow was the armed conflict in southern Sudan.[182] Apparently, al-Mahdi asked his hosts to use their influence on Ethiopia's leadership to urge it to halt its significant backing of the SPLA. However, al-Mahdi denied that he had discussed this issue in Moscow.[183]

Another important feature of the visit, mainly for the enhancement of al-Mahdi's political and religious image at home and in the Arab world, was his tour of the Uzbek Soviet Socialist Republic — "a very important region in the sense that its inhabitants are Muslims," as al-Mahdi put it to the Sudanese public. The tour, he elaborated, was "an opportunity to renew relations with those Muslims of our Islamic family."[184]

Al-Mahdi's trip to the USSR — the first by such a senior Sudanese leader in a long time — constituted a personal and political success for the Sudanese Prime Minister. Moreover, it brought important gains for the country: it opened new routes of military and economic aid (at least as presented by the Sudanese authorities), while at the same time putting some pressure on the US to resume its suspended military and financial aid to Khartoum (see *MECS* 1984–85, p 637). Indeed, American financial assistance to Sudan rapidly ensued (see above). But there was no substantial momentum in Sudan's relations with the USSR and the Soviet bloc in general in the fall or later in the year.

AL-MAHDI'S COMPREHENSIVE TOURS ABROAD

During the last quarter of 1986, the Khartoum Government spared no effort to improve ties and acquire economic assistance in Western Europe, Saudi Arabia and Iran. This trend was clearly reflected, *inter alia*, by the intensive series of visits paid by top Sudanese officials. The most noteworthy among them were al-Mahdi's brief official visit to Saudi Arabia on 1 October;[185] al-Mahdi's comprehensive trip, directly from Riyadh, to the US (see above), Turkey, Britain and France, which ended on 20 October;[186] al-Mahdi's visit to Italy on 11 December;[187] and his visit to Iran about ten days later.[188] In the course of these visits, the Sudanese Prime Minister acted to bolster bilateral ties and mobilize economic aid. The visit to Iran showed, in an especially demonstrative manner, the success of al-Mahdi's diplomatic and economic mission. While there, he announced the reopening of the Sudanese embassy in Tehran, which had been closed since 1981, and an Iranian pledge to provide Sudan with substantial economic aid, while writing off Khartoum's $70m debt to Iran. In addition, the visit brought about the release of approximately 40 Sudanese prisoners-of-war in 1982–83 to help Iraq in the Gulf war[189] (see *MECS* 1982–83, p 784).

NOTES

For the place and frequency of publications cited here, and for the full name of the publication, news agency, radio station or monitoring service where an abbreviation is used, please see "List of Sources." Only in the case of more than one publication bearing the same name is the place of publication noted here.

1. *Al-Sahafa*, 1 April and *CR*: Sudan, No 2, 1986, respectively.
2. *CR*: Sudan, No 2, 1986. For a detailed survey on the election results, see also *al-Tadamun*, 31 May–6 June and 7–13 June 1986.
3. *Africa Now*, May 1986.
4. SUNA, 1 March — SWB, 7 March 1986.
5. *Al-Khalij*, 17 February 1986.
6. *Africa*, June 1986.
7. *ARB*, 15 May 1986.
8. *CR*: Sudan, No 2, 1986.
9. *Le Monde*, 10 July 1986.
10. *AC*, 12 March; *Africa*, June; *CR*: Sudan, No 2, 1986.
11. *CR*: Sudan, No 2, 1986.
12. *Africa*, June; *CR*: Sudan, No 2, 1986.
13. For a detailed interview with him see *al-Ahali*, 5 February 1986.
14. *Africa*, March 1986.
15. See Andrew Wieu's interview with *al-Sharq al-Awsat*, 17 January; see also press conference of the party, SUNA, 5 May — DR, 6 May 1986.
16. *Sudanow*, November 1985, for a detailed survey on the Southern political parties. *Al-Sharq al-Awsat*, 17 January 1986.
17. *Africa*, March 1986.
18. For a detailed presentation of the SSPA's political program, see *The Guiding Star*, 17, 24 July — JPRS, 2 September 1986.
19. *Sudanow*, July and November 1985.
20. See interview with Lam Akol in *al-Sharq al-Awsat*, 28 January; see also *al-Sahafa*, 19 June 1986.
21. Akol to *al-Sahafa*, 19 June 1986.
22. SUNA, 28 December — SWB, 1 January 1986.
23. See interview with Ghabbush, *al-Sharq al-Awsat*, 26 January — JPRS, 26 March 1986. See also an official statement issued by the General-Secretariat of the SNP, SUNA, 5 May — DR, 6 May 1986.
24. *CR*: Sudan, No 2, 1986.
25. According to a top official of the UP in a statement to *al-Khalij*, 28 April 1986.
26. *Al-Jazira*, 23 April 1986.
27. See Note 25.
28. *AC*, 7 May 1986.
29. SUNA, 6 May — DR, 7 May 1986.
30. For further biographical details regarding the new Speaker, see SUNA, 6 May — DR, 7 May 1986.
31. See for example reports in *al-Siyasa*, Kuwait, 19, 29 April; *al-Jazira*, 23, 29 April; the Sudanese media of the last ten days of April and the first half of May 1986.
32. As announced in *al-Sahafa*, 16 May 1986. The same source detailed the biographical background of each of the Ministers.
33. SUNA, 9 November — SWB, 13 November 1986.
34. For the NIF's reasons for not joining the Cabinet, see e.g., Turabi's interviews with *al-Majalla*, 11–17 June; *al-Ayyam*, 20 April and *al-Sahafa*, 30 April 1986.
35. R. Omdurman, 21 May — SWB, 23 May 1986.
36. Turabi's interview with *Le Monde*, 13 May — DR, 16 May. See also *al-Sharq al-Jadid*, 1 October 1986.
37. E.g., al-Mahdi's first speech before the Constituent Assembly on 7 July, SUNA, 7 July — SWB, 11 July; al-Mahdi's interview with *al-Sharq al-Awsat*, 9 October; in a press conference, *al-Siyasa*, Khartoum, 20 November 1986.

38. E.g., al-Turabi's interview with *al-'Alam*, 6 September; *al-Sharq al-Jadid*, 1 October; an interview of the NIF leader, 'Ali Ahmad Taha, with *al-Ahrar*, Cairo, 3 November 1986.
39. Al-Mahdi in his first speech before the Constituent Assembly, SUNA, 7 July — SWB, 11 July; in an interview with *Sawt al-Sha'b*, 24 November 1986. In its 1986–87 budget, Sudan earmarked $520m for debt servicing, a sum the economists said was sufficient to cover one quarter or one fifth of its obligation for that year. The official exchange rate in the fall of 1986 was £S2.50 to the dollar. For more economic details, see *Middle East Times*, 12 October 1986.
40. For additional details regarding the change in the Army's leadership, see *al-Siyasa*, Khartoum, 5, 8 September, and *CR*: Sudan, No 4, 1986.
41. For additional details on the January riots in Darfur, see *al-Sahafa*, 16 January and *FT*, 17 January 1986.
42. SUNA, 15 September — SWB, 17 September 1986.
43. *AC*, 17 September 1986.
44. SUNA, 15, 16 September — SWB, 17, 18 September 1986.
45. See *CR*: Sudan, No 4, 1986.
46. *Al-Siyasa*, Khartoum, 28 October 1986.
47. SUNA, 28 October — SWB, 30 October 1986.
48. *Al-Siyasa*, Khartoum, 29 October 1986.
49. SUNA, 28 October — DR, 29 October 1986.
50. Al-Mahdi at a meeting with the Sudanese media, SUNA, 1 November — SWB, 3 November 1986.
51. SUNA, 29 October — SWB, 31 October 1986.
52. The President of the Khartoum University Students' Union, Qaribullah al-Khadr, to SUNA, 1 November — DR, 3 November 1986.
53. *Al-Siyasa*, Khartoum, 3, 5 November 1986.
54. R. Omdurman, 2 November — SWB, 3 November, a statement by the DUP; see also *al-Siyasa*, Khartoum, 5 November 1986.
55. SUNA, 3 November — SWB, 5 November; *al-Siyasa*, Khartoum, 6 November 1986.
56. For details regarding the fall of Rumbek, see *ME*, June 1986.
57. *AC*, 7 May 1986.
58. R. SPLA, 17 March — DR, 18 March; *AC*, 7 May 1986.
59. *AC*, 7 May 1986.
60. R. SPLA, 3 March — DR, 4 March 1986.
61. For the full text of the declaration, see R. SPLA, 28 March — SWB, 1 April 1986.
62. Garang's interviews with *al-Ittihad*, Abu Dhabi, 5 March — DR, 7 March; *Africa*, May; SPLA's spokesman to *al-Sahafa*, 29 March 1986.
63. SUNA, 1 April — SWB, 3 April 1986.
64. *Al-Sahafa*, 28 April 1986.
65. *Al-Sahafa*, 28 April 1986.
66. *The Guardian*, 26 April; R. SPLA, 8 May — DR, 9 May 1986.
67. For more details, see SUNA, 7 May — DR, 8 May 1986.
68. *Al-Sahafa*, 8 May 1986.
69. *Al-Siyasa*, Kuwait, 16 May 1986.
70. E.g., R. SPLA, 1, 2, 6, 14, 22 May — SWB, 3, 5, 8, 17, 24 May 1986.
71. Al-Mahdi's interview with *Akhir Sa'a*, 14 May 1986.
72. Al-Mahdi's series of interviews with *al-Qabas*, *al-Tadamun*, and *Newsweek*, 11, 10-16 and 19 May 1986, respectively.
73. Al-Mahdi's interview with *al-Mawqif al-'Arabi*, Beirut, quoted by *al-Sahafa*, 20 May 1986.
74. *Al-Sharq al-Awsat*, 23 May 1986, a report from Khartoum.
75. *Al-Siyasa*, Kuwait, 16 May; R. SPLA, 17 May — DR, 19 May 1986.
76. SUNA, 18 May — SWB, 20 May; *AC*, 21 May 1986.
77. R. SPLA, 2, 6, 18, 25 June — DR, 6, 10, 24, 26 June; SUNA, 2, 6 June — DR, 3, 9 June 1986.
78. SUNA, 2 June — SWB, 4 June 1986.
79. *Al-Sharq al-Awsat*, 14 July 1986.
80. For the joint statement released at the end of the talks, see R. SPLA, 29 June — SWB, 10 July 1986.

81. E.g., R. SPLA, 2, 7, 9, 23, 29 July — SWB, 4, 10, 11, 26 July, 1 August 1986.
82. SUNA, 19 July — SWB, 21 July 1986.
83. *ARB*, 15 July 1986.
84. Ibid.
85. *The Guardian*, 18, 19 July 1986.
86. R. SPLA, 25 July — SWB, 28 July; *New African*, September 1986.
87. In an interview with *Sharq al-Awsat*, 23 July 1986. See also R. Omdurman, 7 August — SWB, 11 August 1986.
88. R. SPLA, 25 July — SWB, 28 July 1986.
89. SUNA, 30 July — SWB, 1 August 1986.
90. The SPLA representative in Addis Ababa to *al-Sahafa*, 26 May 1986.
91. Al-Mahdi in an interview with SUNA, 1 August — SWB, 4 August 1986.
92. A joint statement, R. SPLA, SUNA, 1 August — SWB, 4 August 1986.
93 For the joint statement released at the end of that round of talks, see R. SPLA, SUNA, 12 August — SWB, 14 August 1986.
94. R. SPLA, 15 August — SWB, 18 August 1986.
95. SUNA, 17, 18 August — SWB, 19 August 1986.
96. E.g., SUNA, 19, 24 August — DR, 20, 25 August; *al-Siyasa*, Khartoum, 21 August 1986.
97. R. SPLA, 19 August — SWB, 21 August 1986.
98. SUNA, 21 August — SWB, 23 August; same points in *al-Siyasa*, Khartoum, 22 September 1986.
99. *Africa Now*, September; *Time*, 22 September; *Africa*, October 1986.
100. R. SPLA, 27 August — SWB, 29 August 1986.
101. For further details on the two operations, see SUNA, 14 October — SWB, 17, 18, 27 October; *Le Monde*, 14, 22, 29 October; *ARB*, 15 November 1986.
102. Statements to *al-Khalij*, 7 October; to SUNA, 16 October — DR, 17 October and in an interview with *al-Quwat al-Musallaha*, quoted by SUNA, 30 October — SWB, 3 November 1986.
103. SUNA, 12 October — DR, 14 October; SUNA, 19, 25 November — SWB, 21, 26 November; *al-Siyasa*, Khartoum, 29, 30 October, 8 November 1986. Several reports claimed that Garang had been flown to Romania to receive treatment for serious wounds.
104. R. SPLA, 31 October — DR, 3 November 1986.
105. R. SPLA, 6, 8, December — SWB, 8, 11, December 1986.
106. *Al-Siyasa*, Khartoum, 19 October; see also similar references by al-Mahdi: interview with *al-Sharq al-Awsat*, 9 October and SUNA, 15 October — DR, 16 October 1986.
107. Al-Mahdi's interview with *Sawt al-Sha'b*, 24 November 1986.
108. SUNA, 10 September — DR, 11 September 1986.
109. R. SPLA, 13 September — DR, 19 September 1986.
110. Garang's interview with *Time*, 22 September 1986.
111. Interviewed by *al-Ittihad*, Abu Dhabi, 6 March 1986.
112. E.g., a statement by Sudan's Foreign Ministry, R. Omdurman, 15 April — DR, 16 April 1986.
113. SUNA, 16 April — DR, 17 April 1986.
114. Ibid.
115. SUNA, 23 March — DR, 26 March 1986.
116. SUNA, 29 May — DR, 30 May 1986.
117. Qadhdhafi's "Third Universal Theory," as set forth in his *Green Book*, stipulated that power, wealth and arms — the three factors determining, in his view, the freedom of man — must be in the hands of the people.
118. *AC*, 4 June; *al-Dustur*, London, 4 August; *al-Hadaf*, Kuwait, 9 August 1986.
119. *AC*, 4 June; AFP, 11 August — DR, 12 August 1986.
120. *AC*, 4 June and *al-Akhbar*, Cairo, 14 July 1986.
121. E.g., al-Mahdi in a press conference, SUNA, 21 August — SWB, 23 August; a top Sudanese politician quoted by AFP, 26 August — DR, 27 August; *al-Majalla*, 3–9 September; *al-Ittihad*, Abu Dhabi, 7 October 1986.
122. *Al-Tali'a al-'Arabiyya*, 26–27 January 1986.
123. *WP*, 28 March 1986.

124. *Al-Dustur*, London, 20 March 1986.
125. JANA, 9 August — DR, 11 August 1986.
126. *Al-Siyasa*, Khartoum, 9 August 1986.
127. E.g., al-Mirghani in a statement to *al-Ahram International*, 7, 24 May; al-Mahdi to *al-Musawwar*, 18 April; to *al-Akhbar*, Cairo, 8 May; to *al-Ayyam*, 6 June 1986.
128. E.g., Juzuli to *al-Sahafa*, 3 April; al-Mahdi to *al-Sahafa*, 20 May; Idris al-Banna, Deputy Chairman of the State Council, R. Omdurman, 18 September — SWB, 20 September; al-Mahdi, in the wake of Qadhdhafi's visit to Khartoum, SUNA, 21 September — DR, 22 September 1986.
129. Reports that he was staying at Kubbeh Palace and had an office at Abdin Palace were denied. *Middle East Times*, 14 September 1986.
130. Among the many statements and interviews of top Sudanese politicians, see, e.g., *al-Ahali*, 21 May; *al-Siyasa*, Khartoum, 3 June; *al-Akhbar*, Cairo, 17 June, 6 July; *al-Tali'a al-'Arabiyya*, 25 August; *Middle East Times*, 31 August — 6 September; SUNA, 8 September — DR, 9 September; *al-Watan*, 15 November 1986.
131. SUNA, 30 June — SWB, 2 July 1986.
132. *ARB*, 15 May 1986, quoting SUNA.
133. A statement by the Foreign Minister, Ibrahim Taha Ayyub, MENA, 2 April — SWB, 4 April. Similar statements were made by Prime Minister Juzuli in *al-Sahafa*, 3 April and by the Chairman of the State Council, al-Mirghani in *al-Ahram International*, 13 April 1986.
134. For al-Hindi's statements following his two arrivals in Cairo, see *al-Ahram*, 24 May and R. Cairo, 15 June — SWB, 17 June respectively. See also his interview with *Sawt al-Sha'b*, 30 June 1986.
135. For a report on al-Mirghani's visit and meeting with President Mubarak, *al-Qabas*, 6 July; *Akhir Sa'a*, 9 July and *al-'Alam*, 12 July 1986.
136. For a detailed survey see *Middle East Times*, 14 September; see also *al-Sahafa*, 9 July; *al-Ayyam*, 14 July and *al-Siyasa*, Khartoum, 10 August 1986.
137. For details regarding the visit, see *al-Ahram International*, 7 August 1986.
138. Sudan's Defense Minister and a key member of the TMC, 'Uthman 'Abdallah Muhammad, in an interview with *al-Musawwar*, 31 January 1986.
139. *Al-Sahafa*, 8 February 1986.
140. Ibid, and *al-Sahafa*, 24 March 1986.
141. *Al-Ayyam*, 30 January 1986.
142. The TMC Deputy Chairman, Taj al-Din 'Abdallah Fadl in a statement to *al-Sharq al-Awsat*, 31 January 1986.
143. *Al-Ayyam*, 30 January 1986.
144. E.g., a series of interviews with Sudan's high-ranking leaders: SWB, 17 January — DR, 24 January; *al-Sharq al-Awsat*, 1 February; *al-Jazira*, 4 March; KUNA, 27 March — DR, 28 March 1986.
145. SUNA, 20 March — SWB, 22 March; *al-Sahafa*, 24 March, 1 April 1986.
146. Fadlallah Burma Nasir, a member of the TMC, as quoted by SUNA, 24 March — DR, 25 March 1986.
147. SUNA, 7 May — SWB, 9 May 1986.
148. For general information regarding the two visits, see SUNA, 6, 26, 28 May — SWB, 8 May and 1, 3 July 1986, respectively.
149. *ME*, September 1986.
150. SUNA, 30 November, 4, 6 December — DR, 1 December, SWB, 5, 8 December 1986.
151. SUNA, 8 December — SWB, 10 December 1986.
152. *Al-Sharq al-Awsat*, 25 November 1986.
153. R. Kampala, 2 February — DR, 6 February 1986, quoting *The Standard*, Kampala.
154. E.g., SUNA, 31 January — SWB, 3 February; *al-Sahafa*, 8 February; R. Omdurman, 6 February — DR, 16 February 1986, al-Dahab's statement to the special Ugandan envoy who visited Khartoum in February 1986.
155. A statement by Sudan's Prime Minister, al-Juzuli, SUNA, 3 March — SWB, 6 March 1986.
156. SUNA, 13 February — SWB, 15 February; SUNA, 8, 16 March — DR, 11, 17 March; SUNA, 20 February, reporting on Uganda's wish to mediate between Khartoum and the SPLA, 20 February — DR, 21 February 1986.

157. Al-Dahab's statement to MENA, 12 February — DR, 14 February 1986.
158. Briefing journalists and diplomats in Kampala, *The Guardian*, 25 August 1986.
159. SUNA, 26 August — SWB, 28 August; SUNA, 27 August — DR, 27 August 1986.
160. *Al-Bayan*, 29 August 1986.
161. R. Kampala, 22 September — SWB, 24 September; *al-Siyasa*, Khartoum, 24 September and *al-Ittihad*, Abu Dhabi, 18 October — DR, 21 October 1986.
162. SUNA, 16 April — SWB, 18 April 1986.
163. R. Omdurman, 15 April — DR, 16 April 1986.
164. SUNA, 16 April — DR, 16 April 1986.
165. VoL, 16 April 1986.
166. SUNA, 16 April — DR, 17 April 1986.
167. *Al-Ayyam*, 17 April 1986.
168. The data were provided by the *NYT*, 18 April and *CR*: Sudan, No 2, 1986, respectively.
169. SUNA, 16 April — DR, 17 April; *The Guardian*, 18 April 1986.
170. Al-Mahdi's interview with *al-Siyasa*, Kuwait, 22 September 1986.
171. SUNA, 31 March — SWB, 2 April 1986.
172. See also *QER*: Sudan, No 1, 1986.
173. *CR*: Sudan, No 2, 1986.
174. *Al-Sahafa*, 30 March 1986, a statement made by Sudan's Defense Minister and key member of the TMC, 'Uthman 'Abdallah Muhammad.
175. SUNA, 1 June — SWB, 3 June 1986.
176. SUNA, 9 October — DR, 10 October 1986.
177. R. Omdurman, 5 October — SWB, 8 October 1986.
178. *Al-Siyasa*, Khartoum, 9 October and SUNA, 10 November — SWB, 18 November 1986, respectively.
179. SUNA, 10 November — SWB, 18 November 1986.
180. Al-Mahdi in a special statement on his return home, R. Omdurman, 15 August — SWB, 18 August and al-Mahdi's interview with *al-Siyasa*, Kuwait, 22 September 1986.
181. Al-Mahdi's statement in R. Omdurman, 15 August — SWB, 18 August; *al-Siyasa*, Kuwait, 22 September 1986, respectively.
182. As stated by Sudan's Minister of Finance and Economic Planning, Bashir 'Umar, in an interview with *al-Sharq al-Awsat*, 8 September; see also *Majalla*, 26 August, and *ME*, September 1986.
183. Al-Mahdi argued his alleged refusal to discuss that issue because of its being "a purely internal issue." *Al-Siyasa*, Khartoum, 22 August 1986. Nevertheless, towards the end of 1986 he was persistently claiming that the conflict with the South was no longer an internal problem but rather "a foreign aggression"; see above, section on the South.
184. R. Omdurman, 15 August — SWB, 18 August; al-Mahdi's interview with *al-Tadamun*, 18 October 1986, respectively.
185. On the visit's aim, see *al-Siyasa*, Khartoum, 29 September and 2 October 1986.
186. For details, see *al-Siyasa*, Khartoum, 12, 16, 20, 21 October 1986.
187. For details, see R. Omdurman, 13 December — SWB, 15 December 1986.
188. SUNA, 19, 21 December — SWB, 20, 23 December 1986.
189. Ibid.

The Syrian Arab Republic
(Jumhuriyyat Suriyya al-'Arabiyya)

YOSEF OLMERT

On the eve of 1986, the Syrian official organ, *al-Thawra*, expressed its confidence that, as in the past, also in the coming year, Syria's decisions would be crucial regarding peace and war. It was confidently stated that 1986 would be a year of major victories and achievements.[1] Official expectations notwithstanding, 1986 was a year of crisis. Both internally and externally, Syria under Hafiz al-Asad suffered a series of distressing setbacks. Some of them originated in previous years but were aggravated during 1986; others resulted from difficulties created during the year.

Syrian politics continued to be dominated domestically by the ongoing struggle within the Ba'th regime and the rapidly deteriorating economic situation. There was nothing new in the power struggle, which has been characteristic of Syrian life ever since November 1983, when President Asad collapsed and nearly died (see *Middle East Contemporary Survey* [*MECS*] 1983–84, pp 673–79; 1984–85, pp 643–47). The resumption of large-scale violent opposition activities against the regime aggravated the power struggle. Occurring four years after the Hamah massacre (see *MECS*, 1982–83, pp 847–55), these activities indicated that the opposition had not been completely crushed, political dialogue between Government and opposition was impossible, and violence had become inevitable in its absence.

Syria's economy has been steadily deteriorating in recent years because of a combination of factors: rampant corruption, the military build-up, the cost of maintaining military forces in Lebanon, and the structural failings of the socialist system. During 1986, all these factors were largely augmented by the effects of the declining prices of oil and other commodities, and adverse weather conditions for agriculture. The overall impact of these problems created a dramatic crisis and forced the regime to take drastic steps on the one hand, and to explain the predicament to the public in an apologetic tone, on the other.

Syria fared no better on the external front than it did domestically. Close to home, Lebanon proved more of a burden than an asset, as the warring factions, among them some of Damascus' own protégés, prevented any political settlement. Thus Syria's attempts to revive the Damascus Agreement of December 1985 were foiled (see *MECS*, 1984–85, pp 652–54).

Yet another problem facing Syria in Lebanon was its failure to stop the Palestine Liberation Organization (PLO) from reestablishing itself in some of its pre-1982 strongholds.

In the Arab system, the Syrian-Iraqi-Iranian triangle continued to be a source of problems for Syria. Relations with Iran worsened and relations with Iraq showed no signs of improvement. The dialogue with Jordan continued, although it produced no

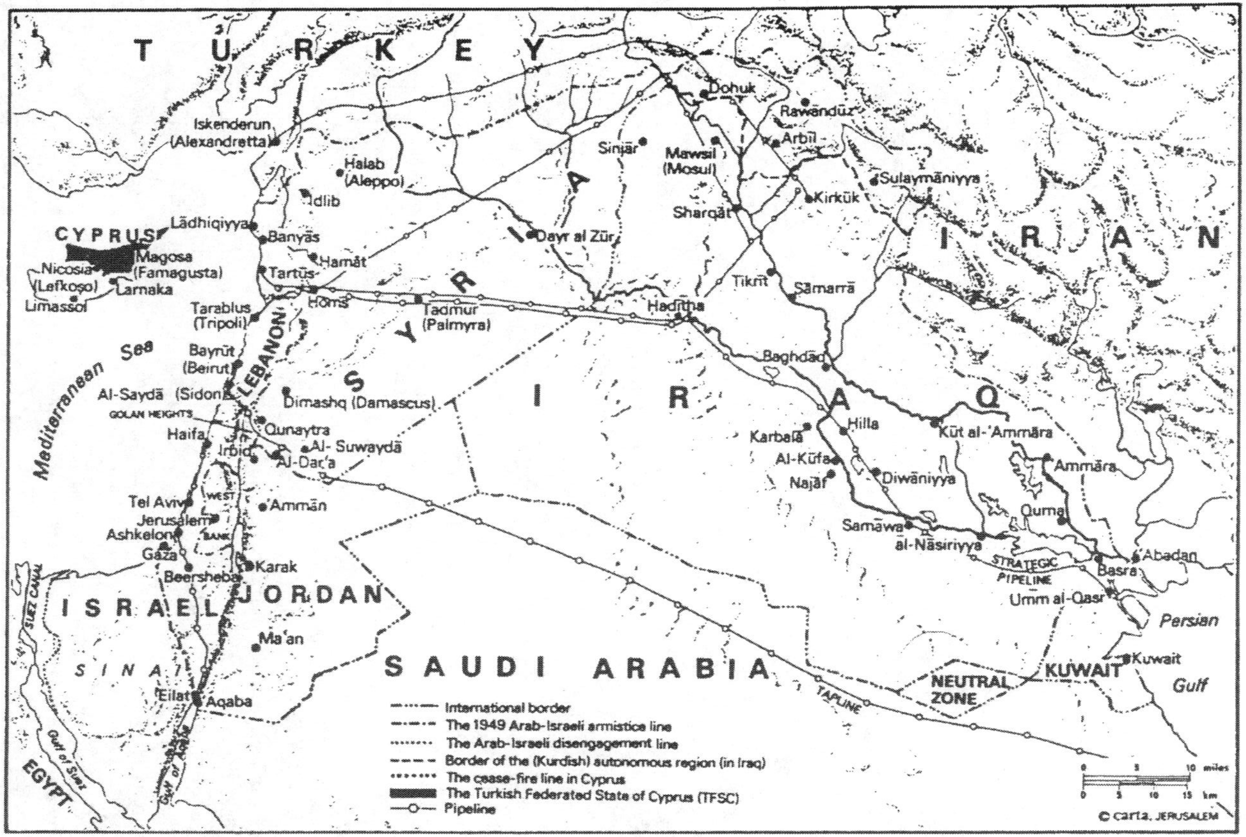

The Fertile Crescent

dramatic results. Overall, Syria remained in a position of "unsplendid isolation" in the Arab world, which was particularly painful to Damascus against the background of the gradual readmittance of its archenemy, Egypt, to the Arab system (see essay on inter-Arab relations).

Tensions between Syria and Israel heightened during the first half of 1986. At times, it seemed as if war was imminent in the region, mainly because of Syrian rhetoric and Israeli reaction. The question of Syria's goals in its relentless pursuit of "strategic parity" with Israel cast a persistent shadow between the two countries (see *MECS* 1982–83, pp 684–88; 1983–84, pp 656–58). Another source of tension between the two countries was the situation in Lebanon and Syrian involvement in anti-Israel terrorism.

The issue of terrorism led to crises in Syria's relationships with Western countries, particularly Britain, the Federal Republic of Germany, and the US. Syria's international image was greatly damaged by this crisis, which also affected the country's economy. Although relations with the USSR remained basically friendly and close, they too showed signs of strain.

DOMESTIC AFFAIRS

THE POWER STRUGGLE IN THE REGIME

The power struggle within the Ba'th regime continued unabated for the third consecutive year. The main elements closely resembled those of earlier years: (1) rivalry between Rif'at al-Asad, who was nominally a Vice President and practically a political exile, and his many opponents; (2) tensions between army commanders and chiefs of the various intelligence and security agencies; (3) Hafiz al-Asad's personal involvement in internal struggles; and (4) the President's continuing health problems.

The last point was crucial since the uncertainty regarding the President ignited the problems and fueled them throughout the crisis.

Rif'at al-Asad was first forced into exile in late May 1984 after the first round of the power struggle in Damascus. His enemies were determined to prevent him from becoming the official heir apparent to the Presidency. Six months later, Rif'at's older brother, the President, allowed him to return to Damascus, as part of a deal with the President, who sent a special plane to bring his younger brother. Rif'at was also named, in a special presidential decree, as the Vice President in charge of the security apparatus in Syria. Soon afterwards, he was elected as a member of the Regional Command of the Ba'th Party.[2] It remained to be seen how Rif'at would handle his many rivals in his new position. The list of his rivals was very long. Among the politicians, it included 'Abd al-Halim Khaddam, the Vice President for foreign policy in general and the "Lebanese portfolio" in particular. In summer 1984, Rif'at's men had attacked Khaddam's car on its return from Lebanon to Syria.[3] In the military, Rif'at's rivals included Gen Mustafa Talas, the Defense Minister; Gen Hikmat Shihabi, the Chief of Staff, who also narrowly escaped an attempt on his life by Rif'at's men in 1984;[4] Gen 'Ali Haydar, Commander of the "Special Forces"; Gen Shafiq Fayyad, the Commander of the Third Armored Division; Gen 'Ali Duba, Head of Military Intelligence; Gen Muhammad Khuli, Commander of Air Force Intelligence; and Brig Ghazi Kana'an, head of Syrian Intelligence in Lebanon.

While this was a formidable combination, it was not necessarily united. The fact that Rif'at had returned from exile indicated that the regime was concerned about Rif'at's accessibility to Syria's enemies in Europe. The anomaly of a Vice President being forced to be out of his country was a source of embarrassment and potential diplomatic incidents. Also, Hafiz al-Asad had family obligations toward his brother, and he wanted to establish a power base to counter the influence of the anti-Rif'at faction.

By bringing Rif'at back, the President hoped to be able to retain his traditional position as the final arbiter in feuds among his subordinates. He could then prevent any of them, including Rif'at, from becoming the number-two figure in the regime. In September 1985, the President successfully reconciled Rif'at and Gen Fayyad by arranging the marriage of the former's daughter to the latter's son.[5] But that was as far as Hafiz al-Asad would go to help his brother. He would not appoint him as his only deputy because he realized that such a step would ignite an immediate reaction on the part of the anti-Rif'at coalition. Rif'at al-Asad felt his brother had not done enough, and since Rif'at was impatient and immensely disillusioned, he went again into exile on 5 December 1985 and established headquarters in Paris.[6] But this was not a forced exile as the first one was. Rif'at did not lie low in Paris, and soon became a source of rumors and intrigues. It was reported that at a meeting with Hafiz al-Asad's son, Basil, Rif'at demanded the removal of all the Army and Intelligence Commanders, known as the "Group of 'Alis," headed by Duba and Haydar.[7] In May 1986, there were reports of pro-Rif'at demonstrations in Tartus and Ladhiqiyya.[8] It was reported in June that Rif'at had visited Damascus secretly to discuss the terms of his return with the President.[9] Shortly afterwards, the old Rif'at-Khaddam rivalry recommenced. Khaddam said that Rif'at was in Europe for medical reasons, while Rif'at's spokesman said that he was conducting diplomatic contacts designed to support the Palestinians and improve Arab-European relationships.[10] Rif'at denied that there was a rift between him and the President, and declared that he would return to Syria when "necessary."[11]

Rif'at's return was apparently "unnecessary" despite persistent rumors to the contrary. He started to publish a weekly in London, called *al-Fursan* (the Knights), in which he expressed his opinions on the situation in Syria. The publication sympathized with Syria as a State, but strongly criticized the policies of the regime. It alleged that Hafiz al-Asad's policies were responsible for Syria's economic predicament, its troubles in Lebanon, isolation in the Arab world, and problems with the West. It was, indeed, strange to have a Syrian Vice President in London expressing opposition to his country's policies, represented by his own brother, President Hafiz al-Asad. Other members of the Asad family were also in the news during the year. Jamil al-Asad, another brother of the President, was elected to the People's Assembly.[12] The President's son, Basil, was appointed the Security Officer of the Presidential Palace by his father.[13]

Another person who became prominent during the year was Gen Muhammad Khuli, the Air Force Intelligence Chief. Khuli's close association with Hafiz al-Asad dated back to 1968, when Asad asked him to command the security network of the Air Force. Over the years, this security network developed into one of the most influential intelligence and security agencies in the country. Khuli became responsible for Syrian Arab Airlines, the protection of distinguished foreign guests, and the personal protection of the President. Khuli also conducted secret meetings between Syria and various terrorist organizations, including the Abu Nidal group (see essays on the PLO, and on armed operations), and Kurdish, Armenian and other groups. Khuli's involvement in terrorism was exposed in trials in London and West Berlin during the year (see below). It was reported early in June that Khuli had been nominated head of the President's hitherto moribund "military council."[14] According to reports, Khuli was allied with Gen Shihabi, Foreign Minister Faruq al-Shar', and Gen 'Ali Aslan, Asad's adviser on military and intelligence matters and also Deputy Chief of Staff. It was reported that among Khuli's rivals were Mustafa Talas, 'Ali Haydar, 'Ali Duba and Ghazi Kana'an.[15] Early in 1987, there was an unconfirmed report that Khuli had been jailed.[16] He was either being punished for his involvement in the unsuccessful terrorist operations that complicated Syria's relations with Western countries (see below), or he was paying for his alleged good relations with the Soviets, since the latter possibility aroused Asad's suspicions. At this time, it was clear that the internal cohesion of the Asad regime was under pressure, and mistrust, intrigue, and fear were on the rise in Syria.

THE PEOPLE'S ASSEMBLY

Syria's Parliament, called the People's Assembly, was last elected in November 1981. In January 1986, President Asad called for new elections on 10 February.[17]

The elections are personal and regional for 195 seats in the People's Assembly. Membership is divided between Sector "A" (workers and *fellahin*) and Sector "B" (all other professions). Only the Ba'th Party and the small leftist parties belonging to the ruling National Progressive Front (NPF) are allowed to field candidates.

There were 2,875 candidates from Sector "A" and 1,949 from sector "B". Altogether there were 4,824 candidates.[18] According to an official communiqué, about 42 per cent of the electorate voted, and the results were as follows: 123 seats for the Ba'th Party (66 per cent), nine for the Communists (with no representation before), nine for the Socialist Union, eight for the Unitarian Socialists, and five for the "Arab Socialists." The rest were Independents.[19]

THE SYRIAN COMMUNIST PARTY

Mention should be made of the role of the Syrian Communist Party (SCP) in the NPF. Its relative success could not overshadow internal problems in the party, which was split into two wings. One was led by General Secretary Khalid Bakdash, the historical and perennial leader of the SCP, and the other was led by his deputy, Yusuf Faysal. According to some reports, their disputes focused on personal animosities and organizational matters.[20] Other reports emphasized that the rivalry in the party focused on the question of its relationship with the Ba'th regime. Faysal was considered to be pro-Ba'thi and close to the security and intelligence apparatus of the regime.[21] Some of Bakdash's opponents left the party and established the Central Committee of the SCP, but Moscow continued its support of Bakdash, whose wing of the party convened a conference in July 1986. The conference reasserted the party's cooperation with the Ba'th regime while emphasizing the independent line of the SCP in principal policy matters.[22]

One of the splinter groups of the SCP was the Communist Labor Party, a Marxist-Leninist organization founded in 1976. Since the party's creation, Syrian security agencies launched nine major series of arrests, each aimed at liquidating the organization. One such series reportedly took place in 1986, when more than 200 party members and sympathizers were imprisoned.[23]

VIOLENT OPPOSITION ACTIVITIES

Soon after the Hamah massacre of the Muslim Brothers in February-March 1982, it was rumored in Damascus that when the Governor of Hamah reported the events to the President, Asad asked him only one question, "Can the Muslim Brothers ever revive"? (See essay on Syria in *MECS*, 1981–82, p 852.) This could not be verified, but there was no doubt that the regime's counterattack in Hamah went far beyond the requirements of self-defense and the need to restore law and order. The regime's unprecedented action should be seen in the context of years of continuing, uncompromising violence on the part of the Muslim Brothers. It was Asad's desire to liquidate the opposition once and for all and to warn any other Syrian cities that might be tempted to challenge his authority. This major defeat of the regime's enemies was vividly demonstrated in 1983-84 when a sick Asad proved more dangerous to stability in Syria than the activities of the Muslim Brotherhood. Although they issued many long and cursory communiqués and engaged in terrorist activities, these hardly constituted an effective threat to the regime. Also the establishment of the National Alliance for the Liberation of Syria (see *MECS*, 1981–82, pp 854–55), consisting of Muslim Fundamentalists, Ba'th dissidents and Arab nationalist factions, was unable fundamentally to change this state of affairs. The demoralization within the opposition ranks was manifest early in 1985 when one of the fundamentalist factions, 'Adnan Uqla's vanguard group, reached an agreement with the regime to cease armed activities in return for full pardon of its members (see *MECS*, 1984–85, p 648).

In 1986, Asad's rhetorical question (see above) was answered in the affirmative when the Muslim Brothers dramatically resurfaced as a potent force. Late in January, there was a huge explosion in Dera'a in southeast Syria, followed by a series of arrests.[24] On 13 March, a huge explosion shook al-'Abbasiyya Square in Damascus. The number of dead and wounded came to 200, and extensive damage was done to buildings and cars.[25] The Government's reaction to the explosion was confusing: first, it blamed the Iraqi regime, then the Israeli "Mosad," and finally the Iraqis again. The man accused of operating the booby-trapped truck was identified as Ahmad Hasan 'Id, a Lebanese national.[26] Soon afterwards there was another spectacular attack in Damascus, when a booby-trapped car deliberately collided with a tramcar full of passengers. Another incident was averted when a booby-trapped car was discovered in front of the studios of the Syrian radio and television authority.[27] April saw another wave of explosions focusing on the northern cities of Homs, Tartus and Ladhiqiyya. Buses loaded with Syrian cadets were attacked, and there were 150 casualties. A previously unknown group called the "Military Wing of 17 April" (Syria's Independence Day) claimed responsibility.[28]

A few days later, there were more explosions in the Tartus area.[29] At about the same time, a new front was opened for the regime as the security forces prevented Kurds from celebrating their spring festival (*Norus*). People were reportedly killed.[30]

The campaign of explosions intensified during May, at a time of mounting tension with Israel (see below). The most spectacular attack was on the railroad linking Aleppo and Ladhiqiyya. One hundred and forty people were reported dead and 155 wounded.[31] According to one report, the man behind the spate of explosions was Tayasir al-Taba'a, whose family had been slaughtered in Hamah in 1982.[32]

In June, the violent campaign continued and Damascus was hit hard. There was an explosion in a restaurant and an attempt on the life of the pro-Syrian Palestinian leader Abu Musa.[33]

Unknown groups claimed responsibility for some of these attacks. Among them were the "Army for the Liberation of Syria"[34] and the "Islamic Liberation Organization — the Confident Ones," an allegedly secret Palestinian group backed by the Syrian Muslim opposition.[35] In addition to violent activities, the opposition also embarked on a political campaign against the Ba'th regime. The Muslim Brotherhood elected 'Adnan Sa'ad al-Din as their new "General Supervisor."[36] (For his past activities, see essay on Syria, *MECS* 1981–82, pp 853–55). He lashed out against the Asad regime in an interview,[37] vehemently attacking the 'Alawi (Asad) alliance with Shi'i Iran, describing it as a form of "sectarianism" stemming from "hatred for the Arab and Islamic creed." The Syrian regime retaliated by again besieging the defiant city of Hamah.[38] There was a wave of arrests against Palestinians,[39] and officers of Sunni origin were purged.[40]

These steps appeared to have little impact. In September, there were more explosions in Aleppo and Damascus.[41] Some sources reported that the regime had foiled an attempted *coup d'état*, in which supporters of Salah Jadid took part. (Jadid was Asad's 'Alawi rival for leadership between 1966 and 1970). Other reports linked the increasing unrest to troubles inside the 'Alawi community.[42] The violent anti-regime campaign in 1986 was notable for being sustained and for its achievements in terms of claiming casualties, causing nervousness and instilling fear in the country. From a technical point of view, the explosions demonstrated a large degree of sophistication. The campaign raised important questions. Who was behind it? Was it ignited by the deteriorating economic situation (see below), or was it due to other, more deep-seated reasons? Jordan was known to be a traditional backer of the Syrian Muslim Brotherhood, particularly in the late 1970s and early 1980s.

At the beginning of the Syrian-Jordanian *rapprochement* in 1985, Jordan officially admitted its support of the Muslim Brotherhood. King Husayn vowed to engage no longer in such activities (see *MECS* 1984–85 pp 652, 655–56). Now Jordan was dropped from the list of potential supporters of the Brotherhood. Syria blamed Iraq for the attacks. Evidence to confirm these allegations was flimsy. Though Iraq hated Syria and would have liked to undermine it, there was doubt that the Iraqis had sufficient resources to spare for that task, considering their difficult situation in the Gulf war.

The PLO, under Yasir 'Arafat, was constantly accused by Damascus of being involved in the anti-Syrian campaign. From Lebanon, the PLO could provide arms to elements inside Syria. The PLO was motivated to do this because of its ongoing rivalry with Syria (see below), and the latter's support of the PLO's enemies in Lebanon (see essay on Lebanon). Besides, the Syrian opposition — both the Fundamentalists and the Ba'th dissidents — always expressed support for the PLO. It was perceived as a model of "true" steadfastness as opposed to Asad's "false" raising of this banner. Other potential backers of the Syrian opposition were the Lebanese Forces (LF) under Samir Ja'ja', Syria's archenemy among Lebanon's Christians. Although the opposition received external support, its activities had to be seen against a wider backdrop. The fact that there were so many successful attacks against military targets indicated possible collaboration between the attackers and elements within the armed forces. Besides, the opposition also relied on solid bases of popular support, especially in the northern parts of the country, which were traditional centers of opposition activities. The main reason for these activities was the unbridgeable gap between the Ba'th regime and its opponents, who in 1986, as in past years, challenged the very legitimacy of the regime. For the Muslim opposition, this was a regime of "infidels," 'Alawis versus Sunni Muslims. For the Ba'th dissidents, it was a "deviationist," anti-Arab regime (which supported Iran against Iraq); also it was anti-Palestinian. The Government could, under these circumstances, use an iron fist, as it did in Hamah, in 1982, but it found it extremely difficult to coopt the opposition or parts of it, into the system. The inclusion of 'Adnan 'Uqla's group (see above) was the exception, not the rule. Political co-optation of the opposition also became increasingly difficult under the deteriorating economic conditions. In a year that witnessed a dramatic economic decline, the regime had little to offer its rivals but counterviolence.

THE ECONOMIC CRISIS

Syria's economic troubles, which first became manifest in 1982,[43] gradually worsened until 1986, which was a year of major crisis. In 1985, the gross domestic product (GDP) fell in real terms. The GDP rose by about 11 per cent, but this increase was far below the inflation rate, estimated by independent sources at 20 per cent.[44] The year under review brought with it more bad news. The collapse of oil prices greatly damaged the economy since crude oil constituted over 60 per cent of Syria's exports.[45] (Syria is both an exporter and an importer of crude oil.) The remittances of Syrian workers in the oil-producing countries to their families decreased accordingly. Foreign aid, mainly from Saudi Arabia, and to a lesser extent from Kuwait, also dwindled. The aid given by Iran, by supplying subsidized oil, fell short of Syria's needs. The effects of all this were quick and painful. The value of Syria's currency plunged dramatically. The main pressure on the pound was felt in January and August. During a 24-hour period in early August, the pound's value slumped from $1=£S18 to $1=£S30. New, strict currency regulations were imposed, but the black market and its dealers proved more capable of handling the situation than the authorities.[46] Foreign currency reserves were nearly depleted, and without them the Government could not import the necessary raw materials for industry. Consequently, many factories could not operate. The state of foreign currency reserves also forced the Government to stop the transfer of funds through the Central Bank to Syrian students abroad.[47] Shortages of basic commodities, frequent and long power cuts and growing inflation exacerbated the plight of millions of Syrians. The regime responded to the challenge with a combination of policy changes, administrative-disciplinary actions, apologies and explanations. The Government also tried to expand the role of the private sector,[48] especially under the influence of the US-educated Minister of the Economy, Dr Muhammad Imadi, who initiated some liberal reforms. Ordinarily Syrians were allowed to deposit foreign currency with the Commerical Bank of Syria to be used after three months to purchase foreign goods. Few questions were asked about the source of the currency.[49] President Asad himself publicly called for greater encouragement of the private sector.[50] In 1986, as in previous years, the Government cracked down on smuggling, especially from Lebanon, black marketeering and other manifestations of corruption. The fact that this campaign had become a yearly ritual indicated the authorities' inability to cope effectively with the problems. This was due mainly to the fact that high-ranking officers and politicians were involved in smuggling and the black economy. Therefore, a purge of the lower echelons of the Army and Government proved to be insufficient. Rif'at al-Asad was a notable example of corruption in the top echelon of the regime; but there were other such examples, though less conspicuous. In fact, Lebanon has become in recent years a base from which some officers have benefited hugely by supervising illegal imports. Although the scale of the black market in goods was hard to estimate, it was put as high as $1 bn per year, i.e., more than one half of Syria's recorded exports and one quarter of its recorded imports in 1985.[51] The huge profits from smuggling enabled some of the army and security chiefs to establish their own well-paid forces, thus consolidating their political power base.[52] Confronted by all of this, the regime had to explain matters and make promises to the people, as well as admit the existence of some of the problems. The official Press reported problems with harvests[53] and industrial production, mainly of iron and steel.[54] President Asad himself stated that although Syria was in difficult economic straits, it was not experiencing a major crisis. In 1970 the population was six million; this figure had doubled by 1986. Therefore, Asad declared, the country had to produce more by efficiently exploiting the existing infrastructure. Asad also blamed bad management and negligence. He promised that the future would be better since diamonds had been discovered in the country.[55] Asad also emphasized the importance of military expenditures and vowed to continue them. Syria's budget, announced in July 1986, allocated 55 per cent of public spending to the armed forces.[56] The military build-up in recent years had devastated the country's economy. While nearly every source of income decreased, the military budget increased greatly. The regime faced a dilemma: to continue with this trend and risk the possibility of a total collapse of the economy, or to change course by reducing military expenditure and diverting more resources to rescue the crumbling economy. During most of 1986, the armed forces continued to swallow up huge sums of money, and at the same time, the Government promised to deal with the economic problems and improve the situation. This was clearly an unrealistic policy. Another dilemma concerned the much-promised economic liberalization; could such liberalization occur without a similar political liberalization and change in the overt anti-Western foreign policy? As 1986 progressed, it became clear that there was no relaxation of the authoritarian nature of the regime, and there was a dramatic crisis in its relationships with the West (see below). The combined effect of all this was to worsen the economic crisis, which fueled the already tense domestic atmosphere.

EXTERNAL AFFAIRS

THE CONFLICT WITH ISRAEL

The Arab-Israeli conflict, the peace process, the Lebanese situation, and Israel's nuclear capability continued to be top Syrian priorities during 1986 (for details of these issues in 1985, see *MECS* 1984–85, pp 656–58). Terrorism became a new source of tension between Syria and Israel as direct Syrian involvement in anti-Israeli operations threatened to unleash actual hostilities. Meanwhile, both countries stepped up their rhetoric, thereby creating an atmosphere of near war. Syrian warmongering was perceived with growing concern in Israel. President Asad himself seemed to be in the forefront of the war of words. In view of Asad's reticence and restraint in the past, his militant public statements were carefully scrutinized in Israel and caused lively discussion in government, military, academic, and media circles. Syrian rhetoric took place against the backdrop of continued military build-up. Syrian apprehension regarding Israeli rhetoric was exacerbated by increasing feelings of isolation in Syria, the existence of pressing domestic difficulties, and mounting external threats, particularly the possibility of American-Israeli collaboration against the State.

The year under review opened with a conflict left over from 1985. Syria pulled back its mobile surface-to-air missiles deployed in Lebanon in late December[57] (see *MECS* 1984–85, p 658). A new source of tension developed on 4 February when Israel intercepted a Libyan plane carrying high-ranking Syrian officials to Damascus from Tripoli (Libya). Israel suspected that Palestinian leaders were on board and wished to detain and interrogate them. When none were found, the plane was allowed to fly to Damascus. The top Syrian official an board was 'Abdallah al-Ahmar, Deputy Secretary-General of the Ba'th Party. Syria felt humiliated and reacted with indignation and calls for revenge and diplomatic action. Israel was called the "true terrorist nation"[58] and was threatened with an "unforgettable lesson."[59] Syria called for an immediate meeting of the United Nations Security Council, and convened Arab Ambassadors in Damascus to get their support.[60] There was no military retaliation, but Syrian-Israeli tensions sharply increased. On 27 February and 8 March, President Asad delivered two speeches that were unprecendented in both tone and substance.[61] The main points in the speeches were:

(a) A promise to liberate the Golan Heights by force.
(b) A veiled threat to attack Israel itself, as was implied by his promise to put the "Golan in the center of Syria."
(c) Official, unqualified support to anti-Israeli actions in South Lebanon.

At the strategic level, the speeches revealed much about Asad's thinking regarding the conflict with Israel:

1. The Arab effort against Israel has to be military, leading to a series of wars against Israel to crush it completely.
2. Political and diplomatic effort cannot be a substitute for military effort but will complement it.
3. Syria will liberate the Golan in a military move, or force Israel to do so while Syria will not be required to make political concessions to the Israelis.
4. Total rejection of any political settlement of the Arab-Israeli conflict.
5. The need to rely on a superpower, like the USSR, to help the Arabs balance American support of Israel.
6. Time is on the side of the Arabs, not Israel. Consequently, the Arab world has to uphold the military option against Israel and use it at an opportune moment.

Immediately following these speeches, Israeli commentators and politicians started to assess them. The key question was whether the speeches were a prelude to an imminent war against Israel, or were supposed to rally public support of the regime at a time of deep economic crisis, and Arab support of Syria's firm policies. There was no consensus in Israel regarding the main message of the speeches. There was complete agreement, however, that the military option was under serious consideration, and Israel must be alert and ready. Syria realized that Israeli concerns could lead to uncontrolled deterioration toward war. On 10 March, an official Syrian commentary on Radio Damascus tried to reduce the tension.[62] However, talk of war intensified in both countries. Defense Minister Mustafa Talas stated that Syria could launch a surprise military attack against Israel. The Arabs would find a solution for Israel's alleged nuclear capability.[63] Early in April, Syria's air defense system brought down an Israeli pilotless plane.[64] Soon afterwards, there was an attempt to smuggle a bomb onto an El Al plane in London. In June there was an attack on an El Al counter in Madrid and 13 people were wounded (see essay on armed operations). In both cases, the evidence indicated direct Syrian involvement. These incidents triggered off another round of warmongering.

In late April, Syrian forces in Lebanon were put on a state of high alert, expecting a quick Israeli attack.[65] President Asad, while visiting Jordan (see below) early in May, warned that an Israeli offensive was "inevitable." It was reported that Asad had asked Husayn to help Syria in case of a war.[66] Publicly, Asad warned that the Middle East was on the brink of a new war, while Israel's Prime Minister, Shimon Peres, denied any intention to attack Syria.[67] Still, Israeli leaders and the media made it clear that had the Israeli plane been brought down, a war would have been likely. Clearly, Syria and Israel were on a collision course. Since the two countries did not wish to engage in a war at that particular juncture, the tension had to be dissipated. Hafiz al-Asad took the initiative. On 16 May, he told American newspapers that Syria was not planning a war, was not about to attack Israel, and had not been involved in terrorist actions against Israel. In fact, he said, Syria objected to terrorism and intended to punish terrorists.[68] Asad usually used Radio Monte Carlo, Arab journalists and even non-Arabs to convey subtle political messages to Israel, the US, and any other country in conflict with Syria. This time, because of the severity of the situation, he appealed directly to Americans and Israelis with a conciliatory and moderating message.

There was less tension between the two countries in the second half of the period under review. However, Israeli commentators and leaders stressed that the Syrian military threat was real and emphasized Syria's efforts to acquire chemical weapons.[69]

Syria continued to stress its determination to achieve strategic parity with Israel, especially in view of Israel's alleged nuclear plan,[70] which was publicized by former nuclear technician Mordechai Vanunu. When King Hasan hosted Israel's Prime Minister, Shimon Peres, Syria was the only Arab country that severed diplomatic relations with Morocco.[71] Referring to the possibility of an international peace conference on the Middle East, Hafiz al-Asad made it clear that the Arabs could succeed in such a meeting only if they had military superiority over Israel.[72]

The notion of "strategic parity" with Israel continued to loom large in Syrian media and official statements. Still, throughout the year, as in previous years, it was not clear what the phrase meant. Was it a defensive concept, or, perhaps, an offensive one? Was it meant to force Israel to make political concessions, even without a war, or was it meant to force Israel into making such concessions after a war? Was it a military-political concept only, or did it encompass all walks of life, implying that Syria had to be on a par with Israel at a societal level? While the uncertainty existed, and possibly also served Syrian intentions to keep its policy as unpredictable as possible, it was abundantly clear that Syria was paying a very heavy economic price (see above), which could well impede its military effort and damage its political credibility.

While the talk about "strategic parity" was not new, the exposure of Syria's direct involvement in anti-Israel terrorist operations outside the Middle East was new. Following Israel's withdrawal from Lebanon in spring 1985, it became difficult for Syria to maintain the momentum of terror actions against Israel. It was clear to the Syrians,that open, all-out support for attacks on the Israeli "Security Zone" in South Lebanon, or on targets inside Israel itself, could well ignite an untimely conflict. Yet it had been proved in 1982–85 that using terror tactics against Israeli and other targets was fruitful, as it claimed many lives. Therefore, the question for Syrian policymakers after June 1985 was how to keep the pressure on Israel while not risking a confrontation. Under these circumstances, Europe seemed a possible alternative to the Middle East. The success of the terrorist attacks in Rome and Vienna in December 1985 (see chapter on armed operations in *MECS* 1984–85) demonstrated the potential of such activities. Then came the interception of the Syrian plane by Israel (see above), which was particularly injurious to Syrian prestige and unleashed feelings of revenge. Asad himself praised the suicidal attacks against Israel in Lebanon, and called upon his country's youth to dedicate themselves to martyrdom saying, that "we shall teach our sons to sacrifice themselves."[73] The London operation and the one in Madrid were thus part of a pattern. They failed, and Syria was forced to pay a political price (see below). These were just two in the long list of Syrian failures in 1986.

SYRIA IN LEBANON

1985 was not the year of the much-heralded "Pax Syrianna," and neither was 1986. The fact that another year had passed in Lebanon without a Syrian-backed settlement of the crisis highlighted the realistic perspective of Syria's position in the battered country. Syria had been successful in precipitating the Israeli and American withdrawals from Lebanon. Syria could put effective pressure on Yasir 'Arafat's PLO in Lebanon, and was able to establish local coalitions to fight its enemies there. However, all that was not enough when Syria had to find a positive formula to settle things in Lebanon. The year under review provided ample evidence to confirm this.

Syria found itself with bad options and particularly difficult dilemmas in Lebanon. On the one hand it was keen to preserve its dominant position there, but on the other hand it was reluctant to deploy significant military forces to implement its plans. Only in July 1986 was Syria ready to send a small unit of "observers" to enforce its security plan in West Beirut. Tripoli was an exception, but even there, the Syrian show of force came only toward the end of the year (see chapter on Lebanon). During the year, Syria faced these major difficulties in Lebanon:

1. In the *Amal*-Palestinian clash, two Syrian allies, the Shi'is and the Palestinian National Salvation Front (PNSF, see essay on the PLO), fought against each other. Moreover, Syria's main enemy, Yasir 'Arafat's PLO, seemed to have the upper hand in the fighting, thus creating the conditions to reestablish itself in parts of Lebanon. Syria expressed its support of *Amal* by supplying it with arms, but refused to take an active part in the fighting.
2. Syrian passivity existed against the background of Iranian activity in Lebanon.

The latter supported the militant Shi'i *Hizballah* (the Party of God), which the Syrians viewed with suspicion. The radical Shi'is were strongly entrenched in the Biqa' valley, an area considered by Syria to be in its immediate sphere of interests. *Hizballah* was also active in South Lebanon, where its activities could unleash an Israeli reaction (see essay on armed operations).

3. After Amin Jumayyil joined the rivals of the Damascus Agreement, Syria lost its claims to legitimacy in Lebanon. Amin Jumayyil was, of course, a weak and ineffective President, but he was the legal authority in Lebanon, and Syria had no other effective Christian partner. Elie Hubayka, the deposed leader of the LF, failed to mobilize the Maronite community, and former President Sulayman Faranjiyya was based in the north, unable to affect politics in the Christian enclave north and east of Beirut.

While politically the Syrians failed miserably to impose a settlement, they continued to solidify their security interests *vis-à-vis* Israel, particularly in the Biqa' valley. They intensively fortified the southern Biqa' and for a short while moved ground-to-ground air batteries to this area (see above).

Syria's immediate reaction to the collapse of the Damascus Agreement was to apply military pressure on the LF. The Christian enclave was shelled from Syrian positions in the Matn,[74] but President Asad himself made it clear that full-scale military intervention was out of the question.[75] As it became clear that such an offensive would not be forthcoming, Christian leaders intensified their anti-Syrian rhetoric, and Dr Elie Karami, the Phalangist Party leader and protégé of Amin Jumayyil, defined the Syrian presence in Lebanon as "illegal."[76]

In late April, it was reported that, due to the deteriorating security situation in Syria itself (see above), the Syrian Army in Lebanon was forced to move some troops back to Syria.[77]

There was no letup, though, in the sensitive Biqa' valley. Following anti-Syrian activities there,[78] and battles between the *Hizballah* militia and the Syrian Social Nationalist Party, the Syrian Army took over the village of Masghara, just a few miles from the eastern end of Israel's Security Zone.[79] In mid-July, after Syrian "observers" entered West Beirut to impose a security plan,[80] 'Abd al-Halim Khaddam stated that Syria's presence in Lebanon was perfectly legal.[81] Early in August, the Syrians extended their presence in West and South Beirut, and upon entering areas under *Hizballah* control were welcomed with flowers. Nonetheless, it was noted that the Syrian "observers" and soldiers did not enter those parts of Beirut, where some Western hostages were allegedly being held.[82] Toward the end of the year, Damascus' main preoccupation was the *Amal*-PLO clash (see chapter on Lebanon and essay on the PLO), when it seemed that Syria's allies were defeated militarily, and Syria itself was defeated politically, as the arrangement that finally put an end to the battles around Sidon, especially in the village of Magdusha, was achieved through Iranian mediation (see chapter on Lebanon and essay on the PLO). It was true to say that Sidon had defeated Damascus with Tehran's help. In the Biqa', though, Syria intensified its efforts to consolidate its position, in order to put an end to the petty fights between rival militias, as well as to limit *Hizballah*'s freedom of action and to be able to control the Beirut-Sidon-Tyre highway.[83]

SYRIA AND THE REGIONAL SYSTEM

SYRIA-IRAQ-IRAN

The direction of Syria's policy regarding the Gulf war did not change during the year. Syria remained a declared ally of Iran and an avowed enemy of Iraq. Yet the alliance with Iran was not without its strains, and the enmity toward Iraq not as implacable as in recent years.

Relations with Iran were subjected to pressures due to several factors. Iran threatened to take over Iraqi territory, thus forcing Syria to state its objection to the loss of any Arab territory. Iran's war needs necessitated urgent shipments of arms, which could be delivered only by the West since Iran's Army used American-made equipment. Syria had trouble with pro-Iranian elements in Lebanon (see above and chapter on Lebanon), and its economic predicament made it more dependent on Iranian shipments of subsidized oil. Consequently, Syria lost some of its leverage on Iran. In the beginning of 1986, Syria's Foreign Minister, Faruq al-Shar' stated that his country had a written commitment from Iran not to seize any Iraqi territory. He also defined the war, which Iran so firmly refused to end, as a "crazy" war.[84] Soon afterwards, Iran occupied the Iraqi peninsula of Faw (see essays on the Iraqi-Iranian war, and chapters on Iran and Iraq), thus undermining Syria's credibility. A similar situation occurred when Iran launched its offensive against the Iraqi city of Basra toward the end of 1986 and early 1987 (see essays on the Iraqi-Iranian war, and chapters on Iran and Iraq). Greater strains in the relationship were felt in May-June 1986, when, through Jordanian and Saudi mediation, there was a dialogue between the two rival Ba'thi regimes in Damascus and Baghdad. Asad's immediate incentive to launch this dialogue was Tehran's decision to cut off its supply of 1m tons of oil to Syria because the latter could not pay the already subsidized price. Facing this development, Hafiz al-Asad made it known to Jordan and Saudi Arabia that he was interested in a dialogue with Iraq. The Saudis, as well as other Arabs had been patiently trying to persuade Asad to reach an agreement with Iraq, and to reopen Iraq's pipeline to the Mediterranean which runs through Syria. (On its closure, see *MECS* 1981–82, pp 865–66).[85]

Following a border meeting between Syrian and Iraqi security officers, the Foreign Ministers of the two countries were supposed to meet on 13 June. The meeting did not take place. The Iraqis claimed that Syria had demanded an immediate union between the two countries as a precondition for the meeting. The Syrians, indeed, made it clear that they were interested in a binding political relationship with Iraq, and they refused to cut off their Iranian connection, arguing that Iran had been an ally of the Arabs for the last 800 years.[86] Syria's demand for a union with Iraq was no doubt motivated by the classic Ba'th doctrine of Arab unity, but under the circumstances prevailing in 1986 it was a shrewd way of torpedoing the dialogue with Iraq. The reason was simple: Iraq was locked in a desperate war, and therefore in an inferior position *vis-à-vis* Syria. For Iraq, under these circumstances, to accept Syria's dictate would have been an act of subjugation, something which Saddam Husayn was not ready to do. A few years before, in the aftermath of Sadat's visit to Jerusalem, Hafiz al-Asad, facing a new and troublesome situation, went to Baghdad to seek a *rapprochement* with Iraq. The two countries agreed to "seek arduously the closest form of unity ties," but all that disappeared after only a new months (see *MECS* 1978–79, pp 236–40). Walls of hatred and mistrust separated the two Ba'thi regimes, as well as tangible economic and political interests. Syria was well rewarded by Iran for its decision not to pursue the dialogue with Iraq. Iran resumed its oil supply to Syria, and softened its demand that Syria should service its debt to it;[87] Iran also signed an agreement with Syria whereby the number of Iranian tourists visiting Syria would be increased from 200,000 to 700,000 on a yearly basis.[88] The outcome of the affair was not completely favorable to Syria, however. The Saudis and the Jordanians were dissatisfied with Syria's moves, and the latter's isolation in the Arab world was not mitigated. On 30 September, Asad resumed his call to Iraq to unite with Syria under a "charter binding the two countries."[89] The possibility of resuming the Iraqi-Syrian dialogue was also mentioned in January 1987.[90] From Syria's point of view, the need to keep the option of a dialogue with Iraq open was greatly motivated by its dissatisfaction with Iran's arms deals with the US,[91] as well as the Iranian handling of the question of hostages held by pro-Iranian groups in Lebanon.[92]

SYRIA AND JORDAN

The Syrian-Jordanian *rapprochement* of fall 1985 started at a quick pace (see *MECS* 1984–85, pp 655–56), including high-level meetings and a resumption of normal trade relations. The pace in 1986 was considerably slower, although Asad and Husayn met and the facade of good and cordial relations prevailed. The root cause of the relative cooling down of the dialogue was to be found in a series of strategic disagreements between the two countries.

They differed sharply in their attitudes toward the Gulf war. Regarding the Palestinian question, they shared a common mistrust of the PLO under Yasir 'Arafat, but they lacked a positive common denominator. Nor did they have one regarding the peace process. While Jordan and Syria adhered publicly to the idea of calling an international peace conference, their positions were dissimilar in terms of the substance of a peace settlement. Syria firmly backed the military option against Israel, while Jordan strongly objected to this option. King Husayn and President Asad met for two days in Damascus, late in December 1985.[93] No joint communiqué was issued after the meeting; this appeared to indicate that wide differences of opinion separated the two countries. The two leaders met again in early May 1986, this time in Amman, despite the fact that the differences of opinion between the two countries remained as they were. The official Syrian reaction to the visit was polite and friendly, but far from enthusiastic.[94] This was, indeed, the state of the bilateral relations; the two countries decided to normalize their relations, but did not form a new political axis in the Arab world.

SYRIA AND LIBYA — RELATIONS ARE STABLE

Syria's relations with Libya continued to be friendly during the year. While Libya emphasized the closeness of the political orientations of the two countries, it also served notice on Syria's overall isolation in the Arab world as well as in the international arena. Libya under Mu'ammar al-Qadhdhafi was seen more and more as a pariah state. When the US and Libya clashed in late March off the Libyan coast (see essay on Libya), and when the Americans staged an aerial attack on Tripoli in mid-April,[95] Syria strongly denounced the US.[96] Late in August, Asad visited Libya, and the joint communiqué issued at the end of the visit reaffirmed the solid bonds between the two countries.[97]

SYRIA AND EGYPT

The main outlines of the relationship between the two countries that were shaped after the peace treaty between Egypt and Israel remained unchanged during the period under review. Syria continued to condemn the peace treaty, and called upon opposition elements in Egypt to rise up against the regime. It was made clear that Egypt could be readmitted to the Arab world if it abrogated the Camp David Accords. Since Egypt did not succumb, Syria scorned those Arab countries that had improved relations with Egypt (see chapter on Egypt and essay on inter-Arab relations), but there was not much else it could do. Syria continued a dialogue with Jordan (see above), although the latter enjoyed warm and friendly dialogue with Egypt. In February, Syria had an opportunity to score some propaganda points at the expense of the Mubarak regime, following the riots in Cairo (see essay on Egypt). Asad praised the rioters, and viewed the eruption as a vindication of Syria's contention that the Egyptian "masses" resented their Government's policies. Interestingly, Asad spoke warmly about Mubarak personally. He mentioned their common background as former pilots, and Commanders of their respective Air Forces.[98] A year afterwards, in February 1987, at the Islamic summit conference in Kuwait (see essay on inter-Arab relations), Asad and Mubarak met briefly. Syria said the meeting was spontaneous, but it really followed on from Syrian-Egyptian contacts in 1986,[99] a fact which was also hinted at by Mubarak himself.[100] The Syrians, for their part, took pains to reassert their fundamental objections to Egypt's policy.[101] Nevertheless, while no change in policy occurred, the meeting, accidental or not, may have laid the groundwork for a more civilized dialogue between the two.

SYRIA AND TURKEY

During the period under survey, some tension existed between Syria and Turkey. In March, Syria's Prime Minister, 'Abd al-Ra'uf al-Kasm, visited Ankara,[102] and shortly afterward, it was reported that Turkey and Syria had agreed to cooperate in seeking out Kurdish separatists.[103] But only a few months later it became clear that there were problems between the two countries. As economic difficulties mounted in Syria, Turkey decided to increase its use of the Euphrates river waters flowing from Turkey into Syria and then to Iraq and the Gulf. Syria complained that Turkey was not releasing enough water. Meanwhile the Turks were filling up a reservoir behind a new dam, and were building another dam that would also have a reservoir to be filled. When Syria complained, the Turks responded by saying that terrorists of the Armenian Secret Army for the Liberation of Armenia were trained under Syrian supervision in the Biqa' valley.[104] Following an attack on a synagogue in Istanbul (see essay on armed operations) in September 1986, there was a deterioration in Syrian-Turkish relations. Turkey closed 42 crossings along its border with Syria.[105] Shortly afterwards, the Governors of Sanliurfa in southeastern Turkey and Hasaka Province in Syria, agreed on the "reciprocal extradition of separatist rebels, who fled to Syria after committing violence in southeastern Turkey and smugglers shot on the border."[106] However, this local agreement did little to improve relations between the two countries. Late in November, in a Turkish court, eight foreigners and a Turk faced charges of killing a Jordanian diplomat under orders from Syrian Intelligence. The story began nearly 17 months earlier, when a group of Arabs hired a car in Ankara and fatally shot Ziad Sati, the First Secretary at the Jordanian embassy.

Among the accused was Darwish Baladi, the Second Secretary in the Syrian embassy in Ankara, but he left Turkey before he could be indicted. He appeared on the Turkish wanted list for murder and activities threatening security.[107]

SYRIA AND THE PALESTINE LIBERATION ORGANIZATION

Syria's conflict with the PLO in the surveyed period had a military and a political dimension. Militarily, there was no direct clash between Syria and the PLO under Yasir 'Arafat; yet, the *Amal*-PLO clash was also a reflection of Syria's determination to stop the PLO from coming back to Lebanon in force. Syria was *Amal*'s chief military and political backer and had encouraged *Amal* to attack the PLO in 1985, in the first round of the "camps war" (see *MECS* 1984–85, pp 543–44). In 1986, there was another round of the "camps war," a sign of the *Amal* and Syrian failure in the previous round. The PLO managed to hold on to its strongholds as it did in 1985. The ramifications of this state of affairs were not only military, but also political. Other anti-Syrian elements in Lebanon were encouraged to continue their opposition to Syria. Furthermore, the PLO's relative success in Lebanon dealt another political blow to Syria when its own Palestinian protégés, including members of the PNSF, closed ranks with 'Arafat's men against the common Shi'i enemy (see chapter on Lebanon and essay on the PLO). That left Syria aligned with the discredited Fath rebels led by Abu Musa and groups like Ahmad Jibril's Popular Front for the Liberation of Palestine-General Command and Abu Nidal's group. Yet Syria also had gains: while, in 1982–85, the PLO's main political advantage in its confrontation with Syria had been its close cooperation with Jordan, all that changed in the latter part of 1985 and in 1986 as a result of Syria's *rapprochement* with Jordan (see above). Yet this was no more than a tactical gain. The Syrian intention to substitute a pro-Syrian leader for 'Arafat was unlikely to be realized. Under those circumstances, it seemed that the conflict with the PLO would persist.

SYRIA IN THE INTERNATIONAL ARENA

THE QUESTION OF TERRORISM

In 1986, Syria's relations with some Western countries deteriorated mainly because of its proven involvement in acts of terrorism in Europe.

The first crisis erupted in London in April when there was an attempt to plant a bomb in an El Al plane (see above). While the Intelligence Attaché in the Syrian embassy in London left willingly to evade an expulsion order by the British, three other Syrian diplomats had to be instructed to leave. Syria retaliated by expelling three British diplomats.[108] When a London court established a direct link between the convicted Nizar Hindawi and Syria's embassy in London and intelligence services in Damascus, Britain decided to sever diplomatic relations with Syria. Syria responded in kind.[109] Soon afterwards, Britain initiated anti-Syrian measures which were adopted by the European Economic Community (EEC). From Syria's standpoint, the damage was twofold: it cast a shadow over its image, and it had economic and political consequences. The EEC political sanctions included a ban on high-level visits to and from Syria, limits on the number and activities of Syrian diplomatic representatives, strict control over Syrian airliners at European airports, and an an embargo on arms sales. Previous to that, the EEC announced its intention to cut the special subsidies paid to Community grain traders who concluded deals with Syria. EEC grain exports to Syria totalled 350,000 tons by the end of October, compared with 850,000 tons in 1985 and 480,000 tons in 1984.[110] Britain also vetoed the renewal of the EEC's five-year $140m aid package to Syria. Furthermore, it exerted pressure on EEC members and introduced by majority on 13 November an amendment calling on EEC Finance Ministers to block payments to Syria under the EEC's 1987 aid budget for seven Middle Eastern countries.

Coming on top of Syria's mounting economic difficulties, these sanctions hit hard. In addition, France decided to halt arms deliveries to Damascus (see below).[111] Belgium recalled its Ambassador from the Syrian capital,[112] and Canada and the US recalled their Ambassadors as well (see below); Bonn expelled five Syrian diplomats, froze its economic aid to Syria and decided not to appoint a new ambassador to Damascus to replace its outgoing Ambassador.[113] In retaliation, Syria withdrew its Ambassador from Bonn and expelled German diplomats.[114] The expulsions from West Germany came after a German court charged Syrian agents, acting under instructions from the Syrian embassy in East Berlin, with the bombing of the German-Arab Friendship Club in West Berlin in late March. Among those convicted was the brother of Nizar Hindawi.[115] According to some reports, the Syrians were also linked to the bombing early in April of a discotheque in West Berlin where American soldiers met. Two were killed and 230 wounded in that attack.[116] At the time of the bombing, the US held Libya responsible and later bombed Tripoli (see essay on Libya).

Syria's relations with France during the year were also overshadowed by the question of terrorism, and the existence of French hostages in Lebanon. In March, Mustafa Talas secretly visited Paris and is believed to have asked for French arms, while raising the possibility of Syrian support for France in its efforts to release French hostages in Lebanon.[117] (On the question of hostages, see essay on armed operations and chapter on Lebanon). Late in June, two French hostages were released in Lebanon after an intensive Syrian mediation effort which prompted a friendly telephone conversation between Asad and French Prime Minister Jacques Chirac.[118] While visiting Paris in July, Khaddam promised that Asad was personally concerned about the fate of French hostages;[119] in November, the Syrians were involved in the release of more French hostages.[120] The timing of this particular exchange suited Syria, which was under heavy pressure from the EEC regarding the London and Berlin cases. Facilitating the release of hostages was one of the ways Syria coped with mounting international pressure over terrorism. Syrian official explanations regarding terrorism focused on three main points:

1. A denial of any Syrian involvement in acts of terror, as well as a denial of the charge that Lebanese territories held by Syria were a hotbed of international terrorism.
2. An attempt to explain that what was defined in the West as "terrorism" was in effect a "legitimate struggle for national liberation."
3. An assertion as international pressure on Syria intensified, that it was Britain, Israel and the US that were the "true" terrorist nations.

Asad charged that the London incident had been fabricated by Israeli Intelligence. He suggested an international conference to discuss the issues of "terrorism" and "legitimate" liberation struggles.[121] Asad's explanation notwithstanding, Syria suffered from the allegations and trials.

But Syria still had some friends in Europe, despite its behavior. During the year, Asad visited Yugoslavia, Romania and Greece.[122]

RELATIONS WITH THE SUPERPOWERS

RELATIONS WITH THE UNITED STATES

Syria's relations with the US gradually deteriorated during 1986. Early in the year, Syria expressed concern about American threats to Qadhdhafi; and, later, it strongly denounced the American aerial raid on Libya (see below). Syrian masses "spontaneously" demonstrated against the US in Damascus, and police had to intervene to prevent an attack on the US embassy.[123] While the official media were anti-US, Asad met Richard Murphy, Assistant Secretary of State for Middle Eastern Affairs,[124] but the meeting yielded no significant results. At about the same time, there were Syrian-American negotiations to include Damascus in Vice President George Bush's itinerary when he visited the region.[125] According to some reports, Murphy and other American officials believed it was pointless to ignore Syria, despite its tough political and diplomatic posture. Although Bush did not visit Damascus, two other senior American officials did in June. These were Gen Vernon Walters, American Ambassador to the UN, and William Casey, Director of the Central Intelligence Agency. According to one report, the Americans came to Damascus after Asad discovered a plot by some Communists to overthrow him.[126] According to another report, the discussions included the fate of the American hostages in Lebanon. America demanded that Syria close all its training bases and other facilities for terrorist organizations. The Americans expressed concern about the possibility of an Israeli-Syrian war;[127] and it was believed that the State Department wanted to facilitate a *rapprochement* between Syria and the US.[128] In September, Murphy visited Damascus again,[129] but following the Hindawi trial in London, the US recalled its Ambassador from the Syrian capital. The official reason was Syria's continued support of international terrorism. The US also retaliated by abrogating an air transport agreement and reducing the staff of the US embassy in Damascus. The US tightened its control on the export of items related to national security purposes. It expanded the list to include related technical data, along with all aircraft, helicopters, and their components. The US terminated the availability of Export-Import Bank programs for Syria. American oil companies were informed that continued involvement in Syrian oil operations was now inappropriate.[130] The US also stopped issuing entry visas to holders of Syrian service-passports.[131]

The American Government had already imposed, in June, an embargo on the export to Syria of materials used to produce chemical weapons.[132]

The crisis in late 1986 climaxed a tense period in US-Syrian relations. The root causes of the problem between the two countries emanated from disagreements on several issues, including the desired course of the peace process, the question of Palestinian representation in peace talks, the Camp David Accords, the Lebanese question, and terrorism. For Syria, the US was the mainstay of Israel, its archenemy. For many Americans, specially in the Reagan Administration, Syria was the chief villain in the Middle East, responsible for the American fiasco in Lebanon and serving as Moscow's outpost in the region. Under these circumstances, the crisis of 1986 could be seen as a continuation of a trend rather than a new development.

SYRIA AND THE SOVIET UNION

Contrary to the adversarial nature of US-Syrian relations, the dialogue between Syria and the Soviet Union remained friendly during 1986, although there were strains and pressures.

During the year, the USSR continued to supply arms to Syria. T-80 tanks[133] and two submarines[134] were delivered to Syria. MiG-29 planes were promised as well, but were not delivered till the end of the year.

According to one report, Syria had secret talks with the USSR in which the possibility of building a nuclear reactor in Syria was raised.[135]

In June, a report surfaced about a secret proposal made by Khaddam in Moscow to extend the Syrian-Soviet Treaty of Friendship and Cooperation (see *MECS* 1980–81, p 800) to include Syrian forces in Lebanon.[136] There was no confirmation of this report, but it should be analyzed against the backdrop of the Syrian-Israeli tension in May (see above). As in previous years, there were reports in 1986 about secret visits by Hafiz al-Asad to Moscow, especially at times of tension. Toward the end of the year, when Syria was under pressure regarding the question of terrorism, the USSR gave full public support to Syria. However, according to some reports, there were also tensions between the two countries because of Syria's support of Iran against Iraq. Moscow also wanted Syria to mend its fences with 'Arafat's PLO.[137] Whether or not these reports were correct, it was clear throughout the year that Syria and the USSR had enough common interests and concerns to overcome their differences.

NOTES

For the place and frequency of publications cited here, and for the full name of the publication, news agency, radio station or monitoring service where an abbreviation is used, please see "List of Sources." Only in the case of more than one publication bearing the same name is the place of publication noted here.

1. *Al-Thawra*, Damascus, 2 January 1986.
2. On Rif'at Asad's activities in 1985, see *MECS* 1984–85, pp 643–45; Amos Gilbo'a, *Ma'ariv*, 11 April 1986. The writer was deputy head of Israel's Military Intelligence.
3. Gilboa, ibid.
4. Ibid.
5. Ibid.
6. Ibid.
7. *Al-Nashra*, 10 February 1986.
8. VoL, 3 May 1986.
9. *Al-Tali'a al-'Arabiyya*, 23 June 1986.
10. VoL, 19 July 1986.
11. *Al-Sharq al-Jadid*, October 1986.
12. *Al-Musawwar*, 21 February 1986.
13. *Al-Tali'a al-'Arabiyya*, 21 July 1986.
14. *Al-Dustur*, London, 2 June 1986.
15. *FR*, 9 October 1986.
16. *Al-Bayadir al-Siyasi*, 31 January 1987.
17. *Al-Thawra*, Damascus, 10 January 1986.
18. *Tishrin*, 18 January 1986.

19. R. Monte Carlo, 12 February 1986. For the full list of the elected members, see *al-Ba'th*, 12 February 1986.
20. *Al-Shira'*, Beirut, 2 June 1986.
21. *Al-Tali'a al-'Arabiyya*, 28 July 1986.
22. *Al-Watan al-'Arabi*, 8 August 1986.
23. *Al-Dustur*, London, 14 July 1986.
24. *Al-Bayadir al-Siyasi*, 1 February 1986.
25. VoL, 17 March 1986 — UPI, 18 March 1986.
26. Syrian TV, 17 March 1986 — DR, 18 March 1986.
27. *Ma'ariv*, 19 March 1986.
28. VoL, 17 April 1986.
29. VoL, 24 April 1986.
30. *Al-Tali'a al-'Arabiyya*, 14 April 1986: there are 800,000 Kurds in Syria, concentrated in Damascus, the Aleppo area and the northeastern province of the Jazira, which is their main stronghold. On Kurds in Syria, see *al-Guraba*, June 1986.
31. *Al-Watan al-'Arabi*, 16 May 1986.
32. Ibid.
33. *Ma'ariv*, 5 June 1986.
34. *Al-Watan al-'Arabi*, 6 July 1986.
35. VoL, 11 July 1986.
36. *Al-Qabas*, 4 July 1986.
37. *Mayo*, 12 May 1986.
38. *Ha'aretz*, 25 June 1986.
39. *Al-Tali'a al-'Arabiyya*, 16 June 1986.
40. Voice of Free Lebanon, 10 June 1986.
41. VoL, 12 September, 22 September 1986.
42. *Al-Nashra*, 22 September; Voice of Free Lebanon, 11 October 1986.
43. For an excellent analysis of Syria's deteriorating economy, see E. Kanovsky, *What's Behind Syria's Current Economic Problems?* (Tel Aviv: The Dayan Center for Middle Eastern and African Studies, Occasional Papers, May 1985).
44. *CR*: Syria, No 3, 1986.
45. *Al-'Alam*, Rabat, 31 May 1986.
46. *CR*: Syria, No 4, 1986.
47. *Al-Yawm al-Sabi'*, 30 June 1986.
48. *Al-Bayan*, 30 January 1986.
49. *MM*, 3 March 1986.
50. *Tishrin*, 17 November 1986.
51. About the anti-corruption campaign in 1986, see *MM*, 3 March 1986; KUNA, 1 July 1986; *Tishrin*, *al-Ba'th*, 5 August 1986.
52. *MM*, 3 March 1986.
53. *Tishrin*, 1 July 1986; *al-Ba'th*, 2 July 1986.
54. *Tishrin*, 6 July 1986.
55. *Tishrin*, 17 November 1986; for more details on the discovery of diamonds, see *Tishrin*, 26 November 1986.
56. *Al-Ba'th*, 16 July 1986.
57. *IHT*, 6 January 1986.
58. Al-Ahmar's statement, R. Damascus, 5 February 1986.
59. Gen Shihabi's statement, R. Damascus, 4 February 1986 — SWB, 6 February 1986.
60. R. Damascus, 4 February 1986 — SWB, 6 February 1986.
61. SANA, 27 February; R. Damascus, 8 March 1986 (respectively).
62. R. Damascus, 10 March 1986.
63. *Al-Shira'*, Beirut, 17 March 1986.
64. *The Observer*, 6 April 1986.
65. *Ma'ariv*, 29 April 1986.
66. *FR*, 15 May 1986.
67. *Ma'ariv*, 11 May 1986.
68. *WP*, *IHT*, 16 May 1986.

69. *Ha'aretz*, 18 June; *Ma'ariv*, 1 December 1986. Also, Peres' statement, *Ma'ariv*, 8 August 1986. About Syria's military ability, see the 1986 report of the London-based International Institute for Strategic Studies, published on 6 November 1986.
70. See Shihabi's statement, *Ma'ariv*, 7 October 1986. For other references to the concept of strategic parity, see Talas' interview, *Der Spiegel*, 22 September 1986, and Asad's interview, *al-Qabas*, 24 January 1987.
71. R. Damascus, 22 July 1986.
72. *Ma'ariv*, 2 October 1986.
73. R. Damascus, 8 March 1986.
74. *Yedi'ot Aharonot*, 21 January; *Ha'aretz*, *Davar*, 22 January 1986.
75. Asad's interview, *Libération*, 19 January 1986.
76. Voice of Free Lebanon, 12 April — DR, 15 April 1986.
77. *Al-Watan al-'Arabi*, 25 April 1986.
78. See the report about an attack on a Syrian base there, *Ha'aretz*, 12 March 1986.
79. *Ma'ariv*, 16 June; *al-Nahar*, Beirut, 2 July 1986.
80. About the plan, see *al-Ba'th*, 15 June 1986.
81. R. Damascus, 18 July — SWB, 19 July 1986.
82. *Ma'ariv*, *JP*, 5 August 1986.
83. *Ma'ariv*, 7 November 1986.
84. KUNA, 29 January 1986.
85. *FR*, 19 June 1986.
86. *Al-Majalla*, 25 June 1986.
87. *FR*, 19 June 1986.
88. *Al-Dustur*, London, 23 June 1986.
89. KUNA, 30 September — SWB, 2 October 1986.
90. *Al-Qabas*, 29 January 1987.
91. *Al-Qabas*, 22 November 1986.
92. MENA, 21 November 1986.
93. *NYT*, 4 January 1986.
94. R. Damascus, 6 May — DR, 7 May 1986.
95. *Al-Ba'th*, 16 April 1986.
96. R. Damascus, 27 March — DR, 28 March 1986.
97. R. Damascus, 26 August — SWB, 28 August 1986.
98. See Asad's speech, SANA, 27 February 1986.
99. *Al-Sharq al-Awsat*, 2 February 1987.
100. See Mubarak's speech, 1 February 1987, as published by MENA.
101. *Al-Ba'th*, *Tishrin*, 2 February 1987.
102. On the visit, R. Ankara, 3, 5 March — SWB, 7 March 1986.
103. *Günes*, 12 March 1986.
104. *FR*, 19 June 1986.
105. Voice of Free Lebanon, 12 September — SWB, 15 September 1986.
106. R. Ankara, 17 October — SWB, 20 October 1986.
107. *Briefing*, 1 December 1986.
108. R. Damascus, 12 May — SWB, 14 May 1986.
109. R. Damascus, 24 October — SWB, 27 October 1986.
110. *Memo*, 21 November 1986.
111. *The Guardian*, 30 October 1986.
112. *JP*, 4 November 1986.
113. *Ha'aretz*, 28 November 1986.
114. R. Damascus, 28 November — SWB, 29 November 1986.
115. For a full description of the "Syrian Connection," see *Der Spiegel*, 12 May 1986.
116. *IHT*, 7 May 1986.
117. *Al-Watan al-'Arabi*, 6 June 1986.
118. R. Damascus, 22 June — DR, 1 July 1986.
119. R. Monte Carlo, 17 July 1986.
120. R. Damascus, 11 November — SWB, 13 November 1986.
121. Asad's speech, *Tishrin*, 17 November 1986.

122. *Tanjug*, 29 April; KUNA, 10 May; Syrian TV, 26 May — SWB, 28 May 1986 (respectively).
123. JANA, 28 March 1986.
124. R. Monte Carlo, 12 April 1986.
125. *Al-Qabas*, 20 March 1986.
126. *FR*, 7 August 1986.
127. *Al-Qabas*, 27 June 1986.
128. *Ha'aretz*, 5 August 1986.
129. *Al-Qabas*, 10 September 1986.
130. WF, 14 November 1986.
131. *Ha'aretz*, 5 December 1986.
132. *Al-Sharq al-Awsat*, 7 June 1986.
133. KUNA, 3 January 1986.
134. *Al-Ittihad*, Abu Dhabi, 26 April 1986.
135. R. Salala, 21 March — DR, 24 March 1986.
136. *Al-Watan*, 19 June 1986. On Khaddam's visit, see R. Damascus, 29 May 1986.
137. *Ma'ariv*, 22 September; *NAD*, 13 October 1986.

Turkey
(Türkiye Cumhuriyeti)

WALTER F. WEIKER

DOMESTIC AFFAIRS

The year under survey was another tumultuous one for Turkish domestic politics. In two important respects the developments continued their 1985 trend of disappointing those who had hoped that the 1983 constitutional reforms would change the pattern of political life. The first was the proliferation of political parties. The other was the reemergence of pre-1980 party leaders despite their being banned from formal party membership until 1992. The most important single event was the by-election for 11 vacant assembly seats in September.

TURMOIL IN THE PARTY SYSTEM

The political party system in 1986 was characterized by the dissolution of several parties, the formation of several new ones, and strife within both the right- and left-wing groupings. As a result, the line-up of parties in the Assembly changed frequently and it became virtually impossible to enforce Article 84 of the Constitution, which forbade Deputies who had resigned from their parties from joining other parties in the Assembly. Let us review the parties individually.

THE MOTHERLAND PARTY

The Motherland Party (MP; *Anavatan Partisi*), led by Prime Minister Turgut Özal, continued to hold a majority in the Assembly. In fact, it increased the number of its seats from 206 at the beginning of the year to 249 at the end. This was due mostly to the dissolution in May of the National Democratic Party (NDP; *Milli Demokrat Partisi*), one of the three parties that ran in the 1983 election but which had become a powerless rival to the MP. Twenty-two of its 52 Deputies went to the MP. The others formed the Free Democrat Party (FDP; *Hür Demokrat Partisi*), which merged with the MP in December and gave it 11 more seats. The MP also won six of the 11 seats contested in the by-election.

The MP was not without its troubles, however, which came from two major sources: continuing inflation; and competition from the True Path Party (TPP; *Doğru Yol Partisi*) with the reemergence of former Prime Minister Süleyman Demirel in close association with it.

Dissatisfaction with the Özal Government was expressed frequently. In January, for example, the important newspaper *Milliyet* reported results of a survey of political and economic leaders which showed widespread criticism from workers, whose buying power had been sharply eroded despite average wage increases of 35 per cent since 1984 (see Economy section below); and from some sectors of industry, because of

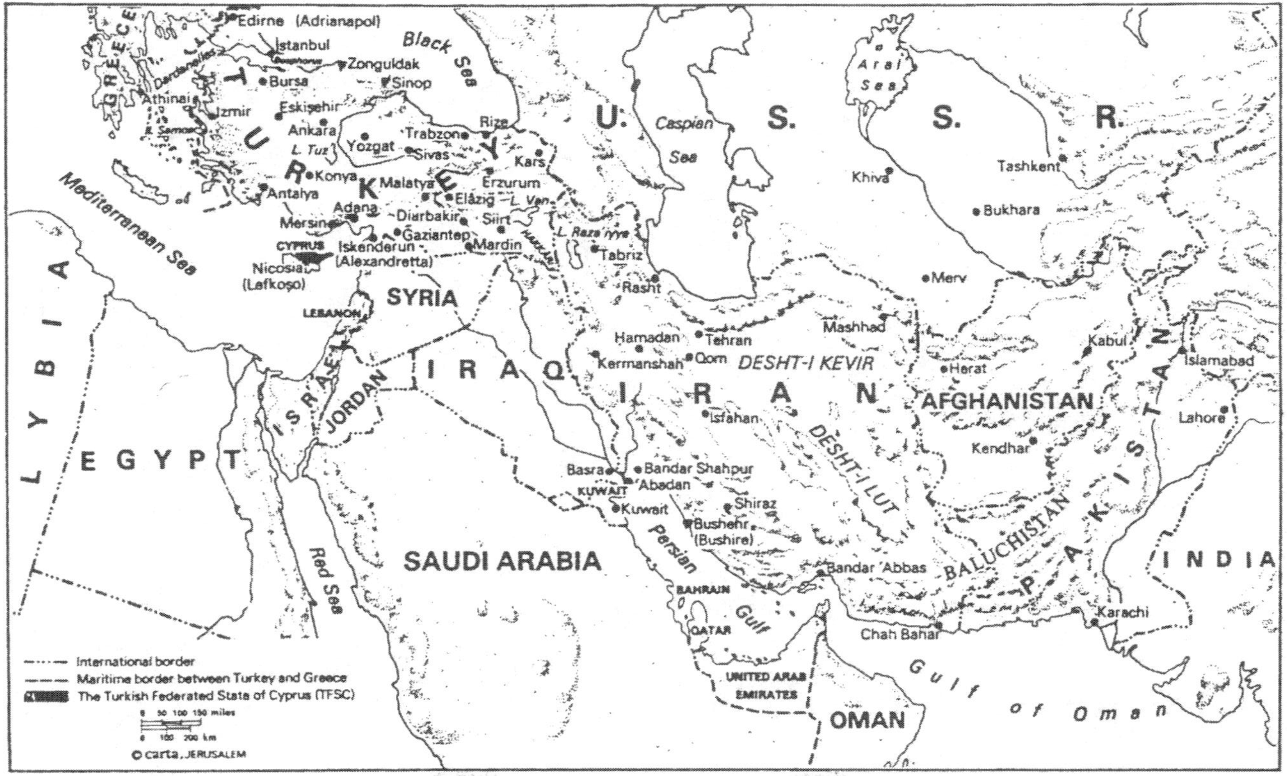

Turkey and Iran

Özal's policy of opening the Turkish economy to outside competition, and because of his alleged subservience to the International Monetary Fund and its austerity demands. There was also general criticism of such things as Özal's personal life-style, which was considered unnecessarily ostentatious.[1]

A study done for the Turkish Industrialists' and Businessmen's Association showed similar results. "Only about 25 per cent of the heads of Turkish households consider the economic well-being of their households to have improved over the last five years. Fifty-four per cent contend that their economic well-being deteriorated, while 20 per cent maintain that it did not change over the last five years. The same study indicated that only 26 per cent of the heads of Turkish households expected their economic well-being to improve over the next five years."[2] Another poll was somewhat better news for Özal, however. In July, the newspaper *Hurriyet* asked what the public thought of the performance of various party leaders, and on the basis of calculations of "very good, good," etc, the results were: Özal 67.2; Social Democratic Populist Party (SDPP; *Sösyal Demokratik Halk Partisi*) leader Inönü 60.1; TPP leader Çindoruk and Rahsan Ecevit, the leader of the Democratic Left Party (*DLP; Demokrat Sol Partisi*) 35.9; Mehmet Yazar, the leader of the FDP, 28.7; Vural Arıkan, the leader of the Citizens' Party (CP; *Vatan Partisi*), 19.4; and Ahmet Tekdal, leader of the Welfare Party (WP; *Refah Partisi*) 13.4.[3]

There were also reports of considerable internal strife within the party. It was due partly to the economic issue and the "liberals' questioning of Özal's wisdom," partly to religious issues (via followers of Deputy Chairman Mehmet Keçeciler, formerly a close associate of Necmettin Erbakan of the pre-1980 fundamentalist National Salvation Party [NSP; *Milli Selamet Partisi*]), and partly to the clashes between Özal and several important and strong personalities such as Istanbul Mayor Bedrettin Dalan.[4] One analyst summed up the situation thus:

> It appears to be the case...that the MP is in the process of being transformed from a catch-all party to just a right-wing (more precisely, a nationalist, conservative or religious) party. This transformation seems also to be disenchanting various groups of voters who had earlier supported it. Furthermore, it was quite difficult, if not impossible, for the liberal-nationalist-conservative-social democratic coalition of MP voters to persist [in the 1986 by-election] under the stresses and strains of Turkish politics. Issues concerning the allocation of resources and benefits, the educational policies of the State, political corruption, and civil liberties, have precipitated an erosion of the voter coalition that brought the MP to power in 1983.[5]

Apparently the MP is suffering significantly from the responsibility of governing, and many analysts believe that there will be considerable policy modification to appeal to the voters before the next general election, which must be held no later than 1988.

THE TRUE PATH PARTY

The TPP won almost a quarter (23.5 per cent) of the votes in the by-election, and four of the 11 contested seats. Led by Hüsamettin Çindoruk, a veteran politician whose experience goes back to the days of the 1960 military intervention and the Yassiada trials of the fallen Democrats, the TPP's major slogan in the by-election was that "the people want true democracy."[6] The specific issue in this regard was Temporary Article 4 of the Constitution imposing a ban on former political parties and on formal political activity by the pre-1980 leaders of those parties. The TPP's main asset in 1986 was the presence of former Prime Minister Demirel.

Demirel (as well as other former party leaders) had started to return to visibility in 1985, and during 1986 became perhaps the most colorful political personality after Özal and President Kenan Evren; Demirel was certainly the one who received the most attention from the Press. As required by the 1982 Constitution, he did not hold formal party office or act in such a way as to directly support a political party, but his association with the TPP was crystal clear and the leaders of the TPP did not attempt in any way to hide their admiration for the former leader of the Justice Party (JP; *Adalet Partisi*). Demirel began the year by giving a series of interviews to the English-language *Turkish Daily News*. He tested the waters by including in his complaints about the undemocratic prohibition on his political activity a more general (though mild) attack on some of the actions of the 12 September 1980 Military Junta.[7]

The failure of the Government or the courts to react strongly — in fact Demirel's activities received legitimacy when the prohibition against former leaders making formal speeches was lifted in March[8] — apparently emboldened him, and during the rest of the year he became increasingly active. By the time of the by-election campaign his picture appeared frequently in the newspapers, and he made numerous speeches and whirlwind tours around the country. His criticism of the Özal Government's economic policies focused to a considerable extent on his own record of having provided benefits for many voters in contrast to Özal's austerity program (though, as one publication put it, he displayed "selective memory" since his record also included massive balance-of-payments deficits and the near-collapse of Turkish credibility in the world financial markets).[9] Nonetheless, this tactic added to the TPP's popularity.

In relation to the Constitution, Demirel appears to have been correct in his apparent judgment that, as his activity continued, it would become harder and harder to stop the momentum of his reemergence with its all but direct challenge to the prohibitions that had been included in the Constitution on the direct initiative of National Security Council leader Evren, who was now President. Demirel always drew large crowds, especially at provocative events such as the 25th anniversary of the founding of the JP.[10] In much of the foreign Press, the results of the by-election were described mainly as a triumphant Demirel return.[11] In the spring of 1987 the Assembly agreed to schedule a referendum on Temporary Article 4, the first time this procedure for amending the Constitution would be used. The Opposition opposed the referendum idea strongly on principle, however, and President Evren opposed it on substance, and at this writing it is not at all clear whether it will in fact take place.

THE LEFT

The democratic Left was also in some disarray. The main fissure was between the two left parties, the SDPP and the DLP, though the former also had serious internal problems.

The Social Democratic Populist Party

The SDPP underwent a bitter leadership struggle during the first half of 1986. It pitted against each other the leaders of the two parties that had merged to form the SDPP in 1985: Erdal Inönü, son of former Atatürk colleague, President and Prime Minister Ismet Inönü and former head of the Social Democratic Party versus Aydin Güven Gürkan, formerly head of the Socialist People's Party. Factionalism within the SDPP came to its first 1986 showdown in March when three members of the Executive Board were replaced in what some observers saw as a victory for a group headed by former Republican People's Party (RPP; *Cumhuriyet Halk Partisi*) activist Deniz Baykal. There were also overtones of a Sunni-Alevi split. The contest seems to be substantially over personal ambitions rather than basic doctrines. In the party's first national convention in June there were early reports of an impending floor fight, but Gürkan declined to run for the post of Party Chairman and Inönü was elected with 733 out of 870 votes. Gürkan also decided against a post-election revolt and accepted a post on the Executive Board.

The convention sounded a decidedly militant note when it booed Ambassadors from several countries, including the US and Britain, and strongly applauded those from the Soviet Union, Cuba, China, and Afghanistan. There was also prolonged applause for former President Abdullah Baştürk of DISK (the Confederation of Revolutionary Trade Unions, a radical organization outlawed by the military; its leaders are still on trial for subversion). The rhetoric at the convention was strongly weighted in social-class terms.[12]

Although the factional strife continued for the rest of the year, the party maintained its 84 assembly seats until January 1987, when some 19 Deputies resigned to join the rival DLP, bringing the latter's number of seats to 24. In the by-elections the SDPP showed itself to be the strongest left-wing party with 22.7 per cent of the votes, and Inönü entered the Assembly on the strength of victory in the second electoral district of Izmir.

During the entire year Inönü was a vigorous spokesman for the Left, and the party's program stressed criticism of economic and social policies, human rights violations, the curtailment of political liberties (particularly the constitutional prohibition against political activity by trade unions and other private associations), and political corruption.[13] Inönü is recognized by Evren as the leader of the left-wing Opposition and is included in the regular briefings which the President gives to opposition leaders.

The Democratic Left Party

The DLP did not fare as well. Formed in 1985 by Rahsan Ecevit, the wife of former RPP leader and Prime Minister Bülent Ecevit, it has been very outspoken on both socioeconomic and political issues (with particular emphasis on political liberties), as well as in attacking the SDPP for being insufficiently committed to Socialist policies. In the by-election it polled a disappointing 8.5 per cent of the votes, less than half the number of the SDPP. There were several reasons for this:

1. The party was too new to have had time to build organizations in enough provinces to compete with the SDPP.
2. Rahsan Ecevit took a militant stance against any merger of the left parties, in contrast to the more realistic attitudes toward such action which were displayed by other left groups and which resulted in the formation of the SDPP in 1985 and

that party's becoming the second largest in the Assembly. After the by-election SDPP leader Inönü is reported to have said that "we will not forgive the DLP."[14]

3. The DLP became the vehicle for the political comeback of Bülent Ecevit. In contrast to the situation of Süleyman Demirel, however, Ecevit has been far less successful in his political recovery. This is partly because the Left has a far smaller base than the Right (see below), but it is also because "the majority of the leadership of the [former] RPP and/or elite sided with the SDPP."[15]

The DLP's electoral showing was particularly frustrating because it did not reach the 10 per cent threshold that was necessary for the election of any Deputies in the 1988 election.

THE BY-ELECTION

The first electoral test since the 1983 assembly election took place on 9 September in eleven constituencies where there were vacancies. Twelve parties presented candidates after the MP enacted a "suspension" of the Electoral Law to permit all existing parties to compete even though they had not complied with the regulations enacted earlier in the year which tightened the requirements.

Amendments to the Political Parties and Election Laws were passed in late March to prevent the proliferation of parties and the recurrence of the need for constant coalitions, which had been one of the causes offered for the political instability and paralysis that characterized pre-1980 Turkish politics. Among the most important amendments was the one that raised the number of provinces in which a party was required to have organizations from 34 to 45 (there are 67 in the country). A proposed amendment, to raise the "barrier" a party would have to meet in order to elect members to the Assembly from 10 to 17 per cent, was sent to the Constitutional Court by President Evren and was eventually dropped, after bitter attacks by the Opposition.[16]

The main issues of the by-election were the economy and the restoration of the political rights of pre-1980 party leaders. Charges of political corruption were made. The campaign was waged by the national leaders of the parties, although it was ruled that their platforms and statements could be presented on national radio and television only by regular media personnel, since the election was to take place in only a few provinces. This did not prevent the parties from using personal appearances, cassette tapes, and most other forms of mass communication, and from dwelling on national issues. The results were regarded, therefore, as significant indicators of voter opinion. The most important features were:

1. Voter turnout was 87.9 per cent. This was probably partly due to the possibility of voters being fined for nonparticipation. But the fact that participation varied significantly in the various constituencies indicated that there was also some connection to voter interest and response to vigorous campaigning. It is interesting that the lowest turnout was frequently significantly lower in the most urbanized areas (Istanbul's District 6 with 77.8 per cent, Ankara's District 2 with 82.8 per cent, the city of Gaziantep with 84.7 per cent, which was the lowest of all the districts in that province), thus confirming patterns in earlier elections.[17] However, the turnout does not seem to have varied markedly in relation to location or socioeconomic status.

2. The moderate right-wing parties received about 56 per cent of the votes. This was not far from the amount the moderate Right obtained in most of the elections before 1980.[18] Within the moderate Right, however, the MP suffered a defeat in that its vote of 32.1 per cent was a sharp drop from the 45.1 per cent it had polled in 1983. As mentioned above, a major part of the loss was attributed to the fact that, although inflation was down, it was still running at close to 30 per cent annually, and to the reemergence of former Prime Minister Demirel. Also, there were the numerous grievances that comprised the burden of the governing body.
3. The moderate Left received 31.2 per cent of the votes. This was its third lowest showing since the beginning of the multiparty period and a quarter lower than the 42.4 per cent the RPP gained in 1977. This figure may indicate that despite a generally upward trend after 1969, about one third is the plateau over which the Left may find it difficult to go. Within the Left the more established SDPP achieved a dominance over its rival DLP, as just mentioned; and it seems that the moderate Left's ability to be a significant Opposition, if it is not put into power in 1988, will depend largely on the ability of the various parties and factions to end the internal bickering that has long characterized their part of the Turkish political spectrum.
4. It was also significant that the radical Right did poorly. The best performance was by the WP with 5.5 per cent of the vote, an Islamist party led since 1985 by Ahmet Tekdal. None came even remotely near the 10 per cent threshold required to seat a member in the Assembly.
5. The personality and recognizability of individual candidates seems to have made some difference. Those elected included "two Cabinet Ministers and a Minister-to-be, two ex-Ministers who are quite popular in their home districts, the leaders of the SDPP and the TPP, and two provincial party chairmen."[19]

In sum, it appears that the Turkish political system is settling into its old pattern of two general blocs, both moderate, with a more radical rival within each bloc of the two largest parties. In terms of the desire of President Evren for an essentially two-party system, this is both promising and discouraging. It is promising in that, if neither of the two largest parties, the MP and the SDPP, will be able to gain a majority in the 1988 election, each of them will have the incentive to merge with the next largest in its bloc (the TPP and DLP), or at least to try to become a broader-based party which can aggregate many potential wings. It is discouraging because many of the parties are built around strong personalities and factions whose record of moderation and subordinating their personal or group interests in the name of a larger stability has not been good.

The complete results of the by-electoral districts are given in Table 1.

THE COMPOSITION OF THE ASSEMBLY

As mentioned earlier, enforcement of the article of the Constitution that forbids Deputies who resign from their party to join another and allows them only to remain in the Assembly as Independents, has been less and less rigorous. An important part of the reason for this was the recognition that it was not proper that major organized segments of the electorate should not be able to take part in legislative activity. Since it was also not forbidden for Deputies to join parties not previously in the Assembly, there were numerous changes in the overall Assembly composition, and at the end of 1986 the Assembly reflected the relative strength of the parties in a very general way. The big gainer in 1986 was the MP, which increased the number of its seats in the 400-member Legislature from 206 to 249 by picking up 22 members from the dissolved NDP, winning six of the by-election seats, and in December gaining another 11 when Mehmet Yazar (formerly chairman of the Union of Chambers of Commerce and aspirant for leadership of the TPP) failed in his attempt to found a new party (the FDP) around the remaining Deputies of the former NDP. (In a similar maneuver to bypass party-shift prohibitions a group of Deputies resigned from the TPP and formed a new Populist Party, which in turn dissolved itself and gave 18 of its members to the DLP, enabling that party to form a Party Group.[20] (A Party Group may be formed by any party with 20 or more seats, and gives the party added privileges in assembly debates and other business.)

At the end of the year the Assembly make-up was: MP — 249; SDPP — 65; TPP — 35; DLP — 24; Independents — 25; Vacant — 2.[21]

(Of the other parties running candidates in the by-election, the only one which had been in the Assembly was the CP of Vural Arıkan, a dissident from the MP, which merged with the TPP late in the year.[22]

ADDITIONAL NOTES

Other former party leaders were also active, but none so prominent as Demirel and Ecevit. Necmettin Erbakan, former leader of the religious-based NSP and now identified as a backer of the WP, visited Turkish workers in Germany in April.[23] And in October it was reported that leaders of the former NSP were planning to resume activities and that Erbakan would participate without waiting for expiration of the period during which he was banned from formal political party activity.[24] He also appeared at a Friday mosque service in Gaziantep as part of the election campaign.[25] Alparslan Türkeş, former leader of the ultranationalist National Action Party, participated in February in a panel discussion sponsored by a small Istanbul newspaper, and warned of "domestic and external dangers" from "cultural and ideological aggression."[26] His activities were at least partly limited by poor health. But he was also under threat of further punishment for his pre-1980 activities: in April 1987 he was convicted of sponsoring armed gangs and sentenced to 11 years in prison. A third former leader, former Turkish Labor Party head Mehmet Ali Aybar, was reported in March to be preparing to form a new "Socialist Party."[27]

PRESIDENT EVREN

President Kenan Evren continued his practice of earlier years, i.e., frequent appearances at events around the country, close contact with government leaders as well as periodic meetings with opposition leaders, a careful review of legislation, and public statements on both social and political issues and on constitutional matters. He also took a number of foreign trips (see Foreign Affairs section) and presided over some meetings of committees of the Islamic Conference which were held in Istanbul.

In reference to current issues, Evren concentrated on secularism (see Religion, below), defense of the 1980 military takeover, and the need for the highest quality in education. On constitutional matters he was particularly firm in opposing any change in Temporary Article 4, which banned leaders of pre-1980 political parties for five and ten-year periods.[28] He also expressed the wish for fewer political parties, as he had done many times during the 1980–83 period of military rule, and he supported most of the proposed amendments to the Electoral Law mentioned earlier.[29] In December, however, he vetoed two additional changes in Electoral Laws which were part of the Constitution, for which document he took personal responsibility. One change would have repealed the article that provided for penalties for not voting, and the other would have allowed paid broadcasts by political parties during election campaigns — a violation of Article 133, which stated that television commercials could not be used for political purposes. In reference to the latter, Evren asserted that the amendment would have discriminated against most of Turkey's political parties because the MP had far more financial resources than the others.[30]

The veto of the electoral changes was the 15th which the President cast. In all the previous 14, the bills were amended in line with Evren's objections, even though some were on matters important to the ruling MP, and the Assembly had the constitutional authority to reenact its own version.[31]

TABLE 1: RESULTS OF THE BY-ELECTIONS OF 26 SEPTEMBER 1986 (MAJOR PARTIES)

District	*% voting*	*MP*	*TPP*	*SDPP*	*DLP*	*WP*
Ankara 2	82.8%	37.3%	19.8%	20.0%	7.7%	4.2%
Bingöl	90.5	33.9	20.8	22.7	2.1	14.3
Burdur	94.2	37.1	25.2	18.8	5.2	3.5
Gaziantep	86.8	35.4	17.6	30.1	3.4	5.9
Istanbul 6	77.8	38.1	13.2	20.4	13.8	8.6
Izmir 2	89.3	29.3	19.5	34.5	9.2	2.2
Manisa 1	94.0	27.3	33.0	22.5	6.2	4.8
Manisa 2	95.2	27.3	36.4	19.7	6.3	3.9
Niğde	89.0	31.3	27.2	17.7	5.1	9.0
Samsun 2	91.4	29.7	33.3	16.5	8.6	3.9
Zonguldak 2	92.7	25.5	26.8	13.6	18.3	5.9
Total	**87.9**	**32.1**	**23.5**	**22.7**	**8.5**	**5.5**

SOURCE: *Milletvekili Ara Seçimi Sonuçlari* (Results of Assembly Deputy By-Elections), (Ankara: State Institute of Statistics, November 1986), Publication No 1213.

TABLE 2: OTHER PARTIES' BY-ELECTION RESULTS

Flag Party (*Bayrak Partisi*)	0.4
Great Anatolia Party (*Büyük Anadolu Partisi*)	0.6
Great Motherland Party (*Büyük Vatan Partisi*)	1.3
FDP	1.4
Reformist Democracy Party (*Islahat Demokrasi Partisi*)	0.6
Nationalist Labor Party (*Milli Çalişma Partisi*)	2.2
CP	1.0
Independents	0.2

SOURCE: *Milletvekili Ara Seçimi Sonuçlari* (Results of Assembly Deputy By-Elections), (Ankara: State Institute of Statistics, November 1986), Publication No 1213.

THE ECONOMY

The overall single description of the performance of the Turkish economy in 1986 was "disappointing." Inflation remained high; the balance of payments suffered because of static or reduced export earnings in almost all major sectors; a high growth rate increased demand for imports and raised general fears that the economy might become "overheated"; and fears began to be voiced that the approach of elections in

1988 would tempt the Government to seek short-term gains at the expense of continuation of long-term development plans. In the midst of all this, Turkey made a formal application in early 1987 for admission to the European Economic Community (EEC).

INFLATION

The final figure by the State Institute of Statistics was that consumer prices rose 34.6 per cent in 1986.[32] This was down from the 45–50 per cent rates of the previous two years, but still well above the 25 per cent which the Government had announced as its 1986 target, and inflation continued to be regarded by the public as the most important economic problem.

BALANCE OF PAYMENTS

Closely related to the problem of inflation was that of the balance of payments, which deteriorated sharply in 1986. This was particularly important because a great deal of the Özal Government's basic economic program was geared to opening up the economy to world influences, to reorienting the focus of the private sector to an export economy (instead of the import-substitution policies and practices that had prevailed for many years before the 1980s), and to eventual Turkish entry into the EEC.

The export side showed a decline or at best remained static in all major sectors. It was estimated that total commodity exports fell to $7.456 bn in 1986 compared with $7.958 bn in 1985,[33] a decline of 6.3 per cent. The most important single cause was the sharp decline in purchases by the Middle East oil countries as a result of the severe drop in world oil prices. In exports by commodity groups, agriculture had a better year than in 1985 ($1.886 bn in 1986, $1.719 bn in 1985),[34] up slightly under 10 per cent. A slight drop in the crop total, accounted for in large part by reduced foreign demand for tobacco, was more than offset by a substantial increase in the export of livestock and animal products. Mineral exports also rose slightly. The largest drop, therefore, was in manufactured goods, including a decline of more than 50 per cent in the export of petroleum products, and in the light and semi-finished products which had enjoyed especially large growth in the Middle East and other Third World countries in the last few years.

Analyzed by destinations, exports to the EEC countries rose by about 4 per cent ($3.263 bn in 1986, $3.133 bn in 1985). (The share of Turkish exports to the EEC countries rose from 40.5 per cent to 43.8 per cent.) Exports to the US were up 8.5% ($549.3m in 1986, $505.9m in 1985). Sales to Japan were significantly higher, though still very small in the overall picture, $32m as compared to $28.4m in January-September 1985. For the Islamic countries, however, Turkish sales dropped by almost a quarter (to $2.607 bn in 1986 from $3.407 bn in 1985). By far the largest drops were in purchases by Iran ($564m from $1,079m), Iraq ($553 from $961) and Saudi Arabia ($357m from $430m). This was partially offset by increased sales to Libya ($135m from $59m) and Algeria ($178m from $109m).

Regarding other sources of foreign exchange, there was also great disappointment in tourism. While revenues rose, they were far from the expected "explosion" that had been much heralded. The main causes were the Chernobyl nuclear disaster, terrorism in the Mediterranean, and the high prices of Turkish facilities.[35] Workers' remittances were also down a projected 10 per cent.

On the import side, the economy's 7.8 per cent growth rate for 1986 fueled a sizable increase in import demand. It more than offset the benefits which Turkey received from the drop in world oil prices. In terms of commodity groups, imports of agricultural goods were down about 4 per cent and 27 per cent in industrial goods. Among the latter there was a particularly large increase in the import of machinery (over 50 per cent). The largest sources of the increased imports were the European countries, whose sales to Turkey rose by about one third. The situation was only partially offset by reduced world oil prices.

BUDGET

Another source of inflation was the continuing budget deficit. For 1986 it was projected that the deficit would be about TL500 bn, to be met by domestic borrowing. The 1987 budget, as introduced in the Assembly in October, proposed almost doubling that figure to TL920 bn, although the percentage of the budget to be covered by borrowing would rise only from 6.8 to 8.4 on the expectation that tax revenues would also rise sharply with an increase in the value added tax (VAT).

AGRICULTURE

Turkish agriculture enjoyed a better year in 1986 than in 1985. Production of most major crops increased, even though, because of price factors, the overall agricultural growth of 3.7 per cent was somewhat below the 1984–85 average of 4.3 per cent. However, this was well above the target of 3.6 per cent.[36]

Much of the increase in production was the result of favorable weather. Among the most important were bumper harvests in wheat (19m tons in 1986, 17m in 1985), barley (7m tons in 1986, 6.5m in 1985), and sugar beets (11m tons in 1986, 9.8m in 1985). The large crops created storage difficulties since no new silos had been built in Turkey since 1954.[37] It also caused the Ministry of Agriculture to look actively for increased export markets for grain. The major markets that were being examined at the end of the summer were the USSR and the North African countries.

Other crops of special importance were tobacco, where output was about the same as in 1985, 170,000 tons; but this was significant because it represented a shift to better quality tobacco, which was important for export and because in the past the Government had had to buy and burn poor quality tobacco, at considerable cost.[38] Sunflower production also rose, from 810,000 tons in 1985 to 1 million tons in 1986, making Turkey the fifth largest sunflower producer in the world. Much of the increase was due to the use of hybrid seeds.[39]

There was a major drop in cotton production, but this was largely because it was continuing to be replaced by soya, something the Government encouraged. In the Çukurova region, the area planted with soya rose from 42,000 dekars in 1981 to 540,000 dekars in 1986.[40] (1 dekar = 1,000 square meters.)

At the end of the summer it was estimated that there would be increases in at least 35 other crops, including fruit, vegetables and nuts, many of which were also important for export.[41]

In a more developmental connection, fertilizer consumption dropped sharply, due to both rising prices and lower production. (January-September production in 1986 came to 2.24m tons of nitrogen fertilizer, compared with 2.66m tons in the same period of 1985; and the figures for phosphate fertilizer were 1.52m and 1.58m tons, respectively.)[42] The average application of fertilizer in Turkey is 15 kg/ha of nitrogen fertilizer and 12 kg/ha of phosphate fertilizer, compared with 74 kg and 39 kg, respectively, in EEC countries.[43]

There was also concern because agricultural investment lagged far behind expectations, being only 32 per cent of what had been projected for ten large projects in the first half of the year.[44]

INDUSTRY

Industrial production rose in a number of key sectors in 1986. Among the largest were iron and steel (3.596m tons in 1986, 3.080m in 1985), and cement (20m and 17.6m tons, respectively).[45] The cement industry was operating at nearly 95 per cent of capacity,[46] with almost all going to domestic consumption. Construction registered an increase of 44 per cent in building licenses (101,687 in 1986, 70,438 in 1985), and an increase of 46 per cent in occupancy permits (70,053 and 47,755, respectively).[47] The output of the automotive industry rose by about 2 per cent, with major shifts in its composition, apparently due to demand — i.e., a sizable increase in passenger-car production, a large drop in the production of tractors, and a smaller decline in truck output.[48] The overall growth in the industrial sector for the first nine months of the year was 10.9 per cent,[49] but as a whole the industrial sector was still operating at only about 60 per cent of capacity. Among the important causes were high interest rates and a lag in both foreign and domestic investment in industry. As was the case in 1985, there was emphasis on energy and transportation-communication. Several new dams were planned, and construction on projects to increase electrical output advanced. Construction on the new Fatih Bridge across the Bosporus was begun with the planned completion date of 1988.

STATE ECONOMIC ENTERPRISES

Some progress was made in rehabilitating the status of the State Economic Enterprises (SEES), a matter that had long been deemed of great importance for reducing government deficits and improving the quality of public sector industrial production. As a group, the SEEs again increased their profits, earning TL1.323 bn in 1986, compared with TL1.274 bn in 1985. They still varied greatly from one industry to another, however.[50] Profit rates also increased, reaching about 25 per cent in 1986, compared with 21 per cent in 1985 and 14 per cent in 1984.[51]

An important step was taken in June when the Morgan Report was submitted to the Government. The analysis that had been commissioned from the Morgan Guaranty Company, a major New York investment bank, concluded that several SEEs were in a fit condition to be sold immediately (including Turkish Airlines, the Etibank, and several production companies), and that many others could be brought to a suitable condition (after taking such measures as reducing excess personnel) in a relatively short time. A bill to authorize the Government to implement many of the recommendations was introduced in the Assembly later in the year.[52]

THE EUROPEAN ECONOMIC COMMUNITY

Early in 1987, Turkey formally submitted its application for full membership in the EEC. Its intention to take this step had been clear for many years, and all of the major political parties endorsed the policy. The application was the subject of much discussion both in Turkey and in Europe over the years, and the debate was pursued in 1986.

There were several controversies during the year from which Turkey emerged both a winner and a loser. Turkey was a winner when an Association Meeting of the members of the EEC was held in September over the strong objections of Greece. Turkey did not prevail, however, on an issue which had been widely discussed in the Turkish Press, the "free circulation" of Turkish nationals. This was a particularly bitter matter for Turkey because it was assumed that the EEC had at least implicitly committed itself earlier to allow complete mobility for Turkish workers at the end of 1986. But the EEC members refused to grant the Turkish demand.

In general, however, the discussions revolved around economic matters. Most observers urged Turkey to go slowly in its application schedule, on the grounds that the impact on Turkey would be severe once it opened up its markets to EEC competition, and that if Turkey insisted on too fast a pace the Europeans would put up stronger resistance to the subsidies and other forms of help that would be required to make the integration of Turkey successful. It was clear that long and hard negotiations lay ahead.[53]

MISCELLANEOUS

It was announced that Turkey would have to repay $5.150 bn in external debts in 1987, after paying $4 bn in 1986. This was disappointing because the Government had been expecting some diminution in the amount, and because it was feared that short-term debts might raise the total of repayments required to $5.5 bn.[54]

INTERNAL SECURITY

A variety of problems connected with internal security continued to plague Turkey during 1986. The main sources of trouble were Kurdish separatists, radical leftists, and some religious fundamentalists. The trials of persons accused of security and political violations before the 1980 military takeover also continued. In reference to all of these, Turkey continued to receive criticism from various European bodies on the grounds of the tarnishing of Turkish democracy, and as a result of allegations of torture of prisoners.

The process of gradually lifting martial law continued. In March, martial law was suspended in four eastern provinces (Bingöl, Elaziğ, Tunceli, Urfa) and replaced by the less stringent State of Emergency; the State of Emergency was lifted in Adiyaman, Artvin, Bursa, Erzurum, Gaziantep and Malatya; and martial law was extended in five of the most troubled eastern provinces (Diyarbakir, Siirt, Hakkari, Mardin and Van).[55] In July the State of Emergency in Sivas, Ordu and Icel was terminated, but it was extended in Istanbul, Ankara, Izmir, Adana, Hatay, Urfa, Elaziğ, Tunceli, Bingöl, Ağri and Kars.[56] In November it was lifted in Ankara, Izmir and Kars.[57] The areas in which restrictions remained were affected by both Kurdish separatism and the continuing pattern of arrests of radicals that took place in virtually all of Turkey's largest cities in 1986.

THE KURDISH PROBLEM

The problem of Kurdish separatism grew more serious in 1986. Incidents and clashes involving members of the Kurdish Communist Party (KCP) continued to occur at great frequency. To give only examples, in January, the police reported pirate Arabic and Kurdish broadcasts in eastern and southeastern Anatolia, the sources of which had to be constantly hunted.[58] In clashes in March, four policemen were killed in the Adiyaman area,[59] and three secessionists died in battles in Siirt.[60] In the same month a Kurdish guerrilla spokesman claimed that 1,500 soldiers had been killed in the past 19 months in eastern Turkey,[61] though that number was clearly exaggerated. A government report in April gave the number of policemen killed as 438.[62] In June, five Kurdish rebels were killed in a clash with village guards in Hakkari and Siirt; a policeman was killed and another wounded by drug traffickers in Siirt; Turkish newspapers carried several reports of infiltrations into Turkey through Syria and Iraq; and a trial of 638 persons accused of KCP separatism began in Adana with death sentences demanded by the Government for 48 of them.[63]

The Government took increasingly stringent steps to curb the incidents. The residents of 11 villages on the Iraqi and Iranian frontiers were moved inland, for example, and plans were announced for a buffer zone in several large areas including much of Turkey's 877 km border with Syria.[64] Interior Minister Yıldırım Akbulut admitted, however, that it was impossible to stop terrorist and secessionist activities entirely, even though much progress had been made.[65] There was also growing concern that the porous border was becoming increasingly used by drug smugglers, and there were a number of references in the foreign Press to the possible recurrence of the serious problem of Turkey being used as a transit point for narcotics supplies to Western countries.

The authorities were particularly sensitive about Kurdish operations from across the borders, and there was frequent discussion of the right of "hot pursuit." Turkish forces twice struck rebel bases in Iraq. The first incident was in August, when the Turkish Air Force bombed "defined hideouts of rebels" in Iraq in retaliation for an ambush in which 12 Turkish soldiers were killed. Prime Minister Özal stated that the estimated death toll was between 150 and 200. The attack attracted considerable attention in the world Press.[66] The second incident was in March 1987, after a Kurdish attack on a Turkish border village which took 14 lives. The Turkish Government stated that the Iraqi Government had been told in advance of the operation, in accordance with a 1984 agreement that permitted Turkey to carry out antiguerrilla operations on Iraqi territory,[67] but the incident caused negative comment nonetheless.

On a wider international level a new publication called the *Kurdish Times* appeared in 1986. Its first issue included both political and sociocultural articles, and four of the six main articles were about Turkey.

POLITICAL RADICALS

The problem of political radicals was more complex. A large number of radicals, both from the Right and the Left, had been arrested since the military takeover of 1980, and many trials were held. These actions led to considerable criticism from civil liberties organizations in Europe and the US on the basis of allegations that many of the charges did not distinguish between terrorism, violent crime and legitimate political dissent. There were also accusations of torture, of the dragging out of trials for several years, and of continuing arrests long after the alleged violations had been committed.

There were numerous arrests of radicals, particularly Leftists, throughout the country, although the number was smaller than it had been in 1985. (The problem of religious Fundamentalists will be discussed in a separate section below). To cite only a few examples: in January, six members of an "illegal organization" were captured in Mersin, and a Turkish People's Liberation Party-Front militant was sentenced to death by the Aegean Martial Law Tribunal.[68] Also in January, three members of an "illegal terrorist organization" were arrested in Kayseri "with automatic guns they had buried in the soil."[69] On 22 February, six people were arrested for distributing a leftist declaration during a rally by *Türk-İs* (the Turkish Confederation of Trade Unions) in Izmir.[70] In March, nine "high officials" of the Turkish Communist Party-Birlik were captured in Istanbul after they returned to Turkey from Europe, where they had allegedly been active among Turkish workers. In the same month, the trial of 291 members of the revolutionary organization *Dev-Yol* ended with nine death sentences for actions which "created the disturbances leading to [the events of] 12 September 1980."[71] On 22 May, "militants," 16 of whom were students, were arrested in Izmir for subversive activities.[72] In a house raid in Kartal (near Istanbul) in July, eight leftist and three secessionist terrorists (including three women) were arrested; they had all allegedly received training in Syria.[73]

While it was apparently not too difficult to justify action in most cases such as these, other arrests and trials caused more controversy. One was the Peace Association case, which had also caused controversy the previous year. It was particularly troublesome because of what many regarded as highly dubious assertions that several prominent defendants were not pressing for more conciliatory policies towards world peace, but were in fact making Communist propaganda. And it again attracted foreign attention. In March, a Military Appeals Court ordered the release of six of the main defendants, most of whom had been in prison for about three years.[74] In November, the military prosecutor recommended the acquittal of about half of the 71 defendants, but demanded prison terms of up to 12 years for the others.[75]

Equally troubling were a number of cases dealing with what many regarded as legitimate political activity. In February, a case concluded with the acquittal of 59 intellectuals who had been prosecuted for "demanding broader democratic freedoms."[76] In May, the heads of eight student associations in Izmir were put on trial "for publicizing problems in student hostels without official permission."[77] In the same month the editor of an Istanbul newspaper, *Sabah*, was taken to court on charges of insulting Prime Minister Özal.[78]

The most publicized case was that of former Prime Minister Ecevit. Indicted for a speech he made to the founding meeting of his wife's DLP, Ecevit put up an ingenious defense. "In the 6 November elections, I had to vote. If I didn't, I faced a fine. Since I cannot vote for the party I will support, I can only vote for the party I currently support. And now I am accused of supporting a party. This means that if I support, it's a crime, and it's a crime if I don't. This is just like La Fontaine's fairy tale of the wolf and the sheep." The case attracted widespread attention from abroad as well as from former RPP supporters, and Ecevit received messages of support from organizations like the Socialist Group of the Council of Europe. The trial was also attended by Western diplomatic observers and received wide press coverage in Turkey and abroad. Ecevit's acquittal in September was greeted with some relief.[79] In January 1987, however, Ecevit was convicted of illegal political activity for two speeches made earlier at public meetings in support of his wife's party, and was sentenced to 11 months in prison. The case was being appealed at the time of this writing.[80]

These and other cases were enough to keep relations strained with institutions such as the Council of Europe. Turkey had been suspended from several European bodies after the 1980 military takeover on the grounds that it was not currently a democracy, and on the basis of the view that the 1983 election had been less than fully democratic since many potential parties and candidates had been excluded. Even though Turkish politics has been lively and increasingly open since 1983, there remain some constitutional restrictions which observers deem unacceptable; consequently, many Europeans hesitated to declare Turkey fully "rehabilitated." Another problem was created by continuing reports of torture of political prisoners, and there was also criticism that the trials of those accused of political offenses were dragging on inordinately (even though this is not unusual in Turkish legal practice).

In the formal sense, there were a number of positive developments in 1986. One of the most important took place in March when the United Nations Human Rights Commission "decided to close the four-year-old Turkish File" dealing with reports of human rights violations. The vote was 30 countries in favor, two against (Costa Rica and the Greek Cypriot Administration), and five abstentions (Mexico, Mozambique, Nicaragua, Peru and the Congo). Six countries were "absent" (Liberia, Cameroon, the Soviet Union, Bulgaria, Byelorussia, and East Germany).[81]

Another positive development was Turkey's election to the Deputy Chairmanship of the Council of Europe for a six-month term from May through November, to be followed by a term as full Chairman. The endorsement was only lukewarm, however, as six of the 21 members voted against the motion (Norway, Denmark, Luxembourg, Malta, Greece and Greek Cyprus), and there was one abstention (Sweden).[82] Turkey took up its positions as both Deputy Chairman and Chairman on schedule.

Nevertheless, on the more informal level there were still numerous indications by European leaders that they were not entirely happy. This was made clear not so much by what the leaders said as by the fact that they felt it necessary to include a reference to the topic on almost any occasion. In January, for example, Council of Europe Speaker Karl Ahrens went out of his way to note that "Turkey has made significant progress in the field of democracy in recent years."[83] In February, during a lecture at the Middle East Technical University in Ankara, British Conservative Member of Parliament Sir John Biggs-Davison included the remark that, "In time, when police misconduct, denounced and punished by the military administration, martial law and the Turkish civil authorities, is buried in history, as long as Turkey proceeds toward a stable and durable democracy, her membership in the EEC, which is linked with the Ankara Association Agreement, will become more desirable."[84] In May, French Minister of Foreign Affairs Jean-Bernard Raimond, in a speech to the French Parliament, stated that "since the civilian Government took office [in Turkey] in 1983 important improvements toward democracy...had been recorded," and that this would be an important basis for "the restoration of relations between the two countries."[85] Even the report to the Council of Europe which was the basis of Turkey's election, was less than totally laudatory when it concluded that "political life showed positive developments and Turkey was making progress on the road to democracy."[86]

A potential setback occurred at the end of the year, however. In mid-December the long drawn-out trial of 1,477 trade unionists who had belonged to DİSK before the 1980 military takeover was concluded with 264 being given prison sentences. The Turkish Government defended the verdicts and was outspoken in asserting that it would not compromise the independence of Turkish courts in the face of foreign criticism. But many observers feared that relations with Europe would suffer nevertheless, because the DİSK case had long been followed there with special interest. *Türk-İş* was put in a quandary, and most of its leaders met the issue by saying that they were critical of the trial in general even though they did not support DİSK's ideas.[87]

Even the foreign Press normally friendly to Turkey picked these topics frequently in 1986. Two *Wall Street Journal* articles were headlined "Persuading Turks to Free Political Prisoners is a Delicate Art,"[88] and "Turkey's Rights Image Still Tarnished Despite Efforts to End Prison Brutality."[89] The British magazine *New Statesman* wrote that the fact that Özal was invited to visit Britain shows "how defense and commercial considerations take priority over human rights abuses."[90] An Amnesty International Report said that the "situation was improving." But Amnesty was still very critical, as was a Helsinki Watch analysis which cited numerous allegations of torture.[91] The official US State Department human-rights report for 1985 sounded a similar conditional note, saying that recent developments point to "the restoration of normal political activity and full democracy" in Turkey, and that the "overall status of human rights in Turkey showed continuing improvement, but there are important shortcomings," notably the persistence of reports of torture "usually at the hands of poorly educated police."[92]

In this connection, an incident occurred which supported both points of view — that there was police brutality and that it was being rooted out whenever it was discovered. In February, Sedat Caner, a former policeman, told the weekly newsmagazine *Nokta* that torture and maltreatment of prisoners was frequent and possibly even routine, and he backed his story with numerous details. Despite the fact that Caner was a prison escapee who had been convicted of the same kind of offenses and sentenced to four years' imprisonment, the Turkish Press was not impressed with the Government's vigorous rebuttal that Caner was not only self-serving but that he was also a tool of the radical left *Dev-Yol* organization.[93] In another case in May, six policemen in Erzurum were convicted of causing death through torture.[94] There was also controversy over whether government statistics showed diligence in rooting out the problem, and whether or not it was present to an "alarming" extent: "over the past eight years, 107 police or security officials have been sentenced to various terms of imprisonment for using torture which, in some cases, resulted in the death of detainees. In the same period, martial law authorities and the Public Prosecutor investigated 781 allegations of torture, but of these only 135 were considered serious enough to be brought to trial. Out of a total of 511 security officials who went on trial, however, only 107 were found guilty and sentenced."[95]

The problems of the aftereffects of some of the situations that led to the 1980 military intervention appear likely to continue for some time.

There were no attacks by Armenians against Turkish officials in 1986. Two old cases were disposed of when the last of five Armenians on trial in Los Angeles for planning an attack on the Honorary Turkish Consul there was convicted,[96] and when the three Armenians accused of conspiracy to murder the Turkish Commercial Counselor in Ottawa, Canada, were sentenced to prison terms.[97] In the US, both Turkish-American associations and Armenian groups continued to press their cases actively, against and for another attempt to put a resolution through Congress recognizing a memorial day for the 1915 incidents in Turkey. Such a resolution had been considered (and only narrowly defeated) in 1985, and did not come up again in 1986 (although one did get preliminary approval in a Congressional Committee early in 1987 — see section on US below). In Europe, however, such a resolution was narrowly passed (25 to 23) in February 1987 by the Political Commission of the European Parliament. It called on Turkey to "abide fully by the provisions for the protection of the non-Muslims as stipulated by Articles 37 to 45 of the 1923 Treaty of Lausanne."

LABOR

Like 1985, the year under review was not an easy one for Turkish trade unions. It began with a continuation of the outspoken activist statements that had been occasioned by frustration with the Government in 1985 when the unions won only a small part of the economic concessions they had sought (see *Middle East Contemporary Survey* [*MECS*] 1984–85, pp 670–72). In January, *Türk-İş* leader Şevket Yılmaz spoke out strongly against limitations on the political activity of labor (and other private institutions). In addition to asserting that the restrictions tarnished Turkey's reputation as a true democracy, he noted that some of them also conflicted with principles of the International Labor Organization, to which *Türk-İş* had brought some complaints in 1985.[98] More specifically, he declared that labor was particularly interested in gaining the right to call a general strike, and that a bill to that effect would be introduced in the Assembly.[99] However, there were no further reports during the year of such an action.

Türk-İş also held several rallies, some of which were less than great successes. In Izmir in February "hardly 10,000 people" attended the "Bread, Peace and Freedom Rally," despite the fact that groups were bused in from many parts of the country.[100] A June rally in Eskişehir was somewhat larger, and was given added importance when it was put under police helicopter surveillance.[101]

Türk-İş also sought to play a role in the by-election campaign by holding meetings in several of the constituencies. In July, it announced its intention to do this in ten of the 11 districts, as well as its intention to campaign against the MP.[102] But it ran into trouble. The rally secheduled for Samsun on 6 September was banned by that province's Governor on the grounds that it could be infiltrated by subversive elements, which brought bitter statements by Yılmaz that the laws were "being used against workers and that Turkey was becoming a 'police state.' "[103] The Government also canceled the planned Gaziantep rally.[104] Rallies were held in Izmir and Eskişehir and press conferences in Samsun, Manisa and Zonguldak, in which areas Yılmaz claimed that *Türk-İş* had "greatly influenced" the election.[105]

In other activities, *Türk-İş* held the first "march" (*yürüyüs*) since the 1980 military takeover in Balikesir in February.[106]

Factions in *Türk-İş* were not content with this record, and at the end of the year Yılmaz, representing the traditionally moderate positions for which *Türk-İş* has long been known, retained his position by only a small margin. He received 152 votes; Cevdet Selvi, the leader of the Social Democratic faction, received 140; and Mustafa Özbeck, the leader of the Conservative wing, got 104.[107]

Another reason why it was a noisy Congress was that Prime Minister Özal not only declined to appear but also chose to charge that *Türk-İş* "did not represent the entire working people of Turkey."[108]

It appears that *Türk-İş* will be in for serious internal strife in 1987; and, because its ability to win political and economic concessions does not appear to be great, it is likely that its tone will become increasingly militant, particularly as the 1988 elections approach.

RELIGION

Religion became a matter of political controversy in late 1986, specifically with a regulation issued by the Supreme Education Board (SEB; *Yüksek Öğretim Kurulu*) that female students in the universities would not be allowed to wear turban-like head coverings. But this issue was only a part of what many saw as a growing resurgence of Islamic Fundamentalism, which could pose serious problems for Turkey as a secular State.

Religion has been an important subject of public policy since the beginning of the Republic. Secularism was one of the central foundations of the Atatürk revolution, and during his Presidency (1923–38) numerous reforms in the role of religion in public life took place. He nationalized education and ended the teaching of religion in public schools, abolished religious courts, placed religious foundations under government supervision, required that imams meet certain educational standards, prohibited the wearing of clerical garb outside mosque property, etc. Unofficially, he also discouraged public religious observance, especially such things as Ramadan observance which seriously reduced productivity for an entire month. Violations of regulations were severely penalized.

When the multiparty period began in 1946–50, secularism became a major issue. The RPP actually made initial concessions, such as allowing religious instruction in the schools if parents requested it, so when the Democrat Party (DP; *Demokrat Parti*) came to power it was only a small step to require religious instruction unless parents specifically requested that their children be excused. The Democrats also relaxed some of Atatürk's policies by giving sizable funds for new mosques and introducing a generally much more relaxed attitude. This was one of the bases of their electoral popularity (though by no means the only one). It is agreed, however, that the concessions made by the DP did not seriously compromise secularism as a basic public policy.

Religion became a more direct political matter at the end of the 1960s when a political party based on religion was founded. The National Order Party was quickly closed by the Constitutional Court on the grounds that it violated the ban on religious-based parties, but it was succeeded by the NSP which ran in the 1973 election. It received 11.8 per cent of the votes, which was thought by some to be a great deal, although most observers were surprised it did not get more. In the 1977 election, its vote declined to 8.6 per cent. In 1980 the NSP was abolished, together with all the parties.[109]

A more informal "revival of religion" has been visible in the last few years, however. Religious publications have reappeared and have grown rapidly in popularity; Qur'an courses (both legal and illegal) have flourished; mosque attendance has increased greatly (especially at the Friday noon services); fasting on Ramadan has become a good deal more widespread. In part, this has occurred in response to the many social changes with which Turks have had to deal, and the absence of social institutions which could effectively take the place of the mosque. But many believe that this is also partly due to the deliberate actions of Islamic leaders, that it is encouraged by government officials who are sympathetic to religion and who are not supervised, and that the process is encouraged from abroad, specifically by Iran, and more generally through Turkey's increasing closeness to Islamic nations in its foreign policy. (Saudi Arabia, for example, regularly makes sizable financial contributions to Islamic cultural institutions in Turkey; and it was recently reported that Iran was sending a large amount of religious material into Turkey via the many trucks which use Turkey as a transit route.)

In 1986 there were several developments that caused particular concern. One was the reemergence of several fundamentalist sects, specifically the Nurcu, Nakshkebendis and Suleymancis. Another was the high degree of interest in religion shown by young people. This was particularly true among university students. In addition to the general causes such as personal-adjustment problems, and financial hardship, which often resulted in students living under very difficult conditions, it is attributed by some to the long-expected impact of large numbers of *imam-hatib* school graduates qualifying for admission to the universities. Islamic organizations on the campuses are also said to be unusually well organized and to be providing their members or adherents with many material and social services. Thus it appears to be more than a passing phenomenon.

In 1986, the number of incidents concerning religious activities seemed to have risen. In December, for example, the list included the arrest of 30 people charged with sect activities in Ankara; the revelation that a high State Planning Organization official was using his position to further "covert Islamic activities" (although this was apparently little different from the building of mosque chapels in numerous Government Ministries in recent years); demands from female students in Kahramanmaraş that they travel in separate school buses; the closing of a Qur'an course and a student aid hostel in a village in Trabzon when "local residents were split into two camps because of increasingly reactionary movements."[110] There were also reports, which were denied by the Government but which persisted nevertheless, that 60 cadets had been expelled from military academies because of fundamentalist activities.[111]

In response to growing concern about the universities, the SEB in December issued a regulation that female students at universities could no longer enter the campus wearing kerchiefs and traditional "turbans" (a broad kerchief-scarf combination covering the whole head as well as the neck). The reason given for the regulation was that these garments were being worn for "other than religious purposes." It was reported that the order had been issued at the specific request of President Evren. The order led to widespread protests by students at several universities, and the appearance of headgear that was ingeniously arranged to be different from those that were banned, but whose purpose was perfectly clear.

The reaction to the order led to statements by both Evren and Özal. The President said in his 1987 New Year message: "Those who are hoping and expecting to take our nation backward in order to make a profit out of it will, as always, find against them the Republican laws and this nation's Atatürkist forces."[112] The Prime Minister struck a different note, however, asserting that the universities could solve the "turban problem" by making concessions and accepting a "contemporary-looking" kerchief. He added that he was against a "double standard."[113] Thus proponents of more religious observance were given an opportunity to play the two leaders off against each other. (In May 1987, an incident occurred that alarmed many people in Turkey: a university student in the northeast city of Van was beaten to death because he did not fast on Ramadan.)

With the approach of the 1988 election it seems likely that the parties on the Right will seek to exploit the religious issue, very much like in the 1950s.

FOREIGN AFFAIRS

Both Prime Minister Özal and President Evren continued their travels abroad in 1986, and several foreign Heads of State or of Government visited Turkey. This section will deal with those countries where there were contacts at these high levels. Relations with the US, the USSR, Greece, Cyprus, and Middle Eastern countries are considered in separate sections. The composition of the list of countries visited by the Turkish leaders emphasized the importance of regional orientations in their country's foreign policy.

BRITAIN

In February, Özal paid a four-day official visit to Britain, where he was warmly received by Prime Minister Margaret Thatcher but got a cooler reception from the opposition Labor Party. In addition to meeting with government leaders, Özal also had discussions with numerous businessmen.

Relations between Britain and Turkey have on the whole been warm in recent years, particularly under Conservative Governments. Some Turks recall the support Britain gave the Ottoman Empire during much of the 19th century. Links to Turkey were also strengthened by Britain during the Atatürk period; and since World War II military cooperation between the two countries has increased steadily. The Turks were also affected by the EOKA rebellion against British rule in Cyprus in 1955–59, during which bilateral links were strengthened. Turkey has been unhappy that Britain did not take this relationship further and recognize the Turkish Republic of Northern Cyprus (TRNC), but Britain has decided to maintain an officially neutral policy between the two North Atlantic Treaty Organization (NATO) allies; nonetheless this has not significantly cooled British-Turkish ties.

The most important issues discussed during Ozal's visit were military cooperation and trade. In regard to the former, there were talks with various companies, though few agreements were reached. One problem was that British manufacturers wanted to sell equipment to Turkey directly, while Turkey preferred to stress joint investment and coproduction. The Turkish Defense Ministry delegation also stressed that it wanted arrangements that did not look to Turkish needs alone but were in a wider context of common NATO supply and production, in which Turkey could play a large role.

Trade between the two countries has grown significantly over the last few years. It is particularly significant for Turkey because of the large growth in its exports to Britain, which resulted in a sizable surplus in Turkey's favor for the first time in 1985. (Turkish imports from Britain have remained steady: $429m in 1981, $434m in 1982, $441m in 1983, $443m in 1984, and about $450m in 1985. Turkish exports to Britain, on the other hand, grew from $148m in 1981 to $189m in 1982, $247m in 1983, $261m in 1984, and a spectacular $512m in 1985.[114]

Two agreements were signed, one to eliminate double taxation, and the other to encourage and protect investments.

The issue of human rights did come up, but to a lesser extent than it had in most other European countries, and when it did it was mostly on the part of the Labor Party. Özal did, however, spend a good deal of time defending Turkey's record in this regard, as part of his campaign to restore Turkish ties with European institutions generally and the EEC in particular.[115] In regard to the EEC, Thatcher was reported to have told Özal that Britain would support the Turkish request for a new Association meeting to discuss steps toward eventual Turkish EEC membership: but she also advised Turkey to proceed slowly in this area. The visit was considered generally successful by both sides and relations between the two Governments are solid.[116]

WEST GERMANY

German President Richard von Weizsacker visited Turkey in May, the first Head of State of a Western country to do so since the military takeover of 1980. The discussions were wide-ranging because of the many-faceted relations between the two countries.

A topic of particular importance was the status of Turkish workers in Germany. Currently numbering well over one million, and constituting the largest group of foreign workers there, the Turks have had problems for some time. German official policy has always been supportive, but on the popular level they have often encountered the displeasure of some elements in the German population. In recent years there have been numerous attacks on Turks, and the Turks have remained the most ghettoized of all the foreign workers. They have also continued to do most of the lowest-level jobs, and have remained at the bottom of the economic and social ladder. On the other hand, very few Turks have expressed a desire to return to Turkey, even when they were offered quite generous incentives by Germany, which in recent years has had serious unemployment problems. Given the unemployment in Turkey as well, and the fact that workers' remittances constitute one of the largest components of Turkey's foreign exchange receipts, the Turkish Government had not made significant moves to cooperate with Germany to reduce the number of workers there.

In addition to a variety of issues, such as better insurance (in particular, transferability of workers; social insurance payments), educational facilities, and social issues, the most controversial topic of the 1986 discussions was "free circulation." The free movement of workers was provided for in the 1970 additional protocol to the agreement under which association between Turkey and the EEC is governed, but it has never been implemented. Turkey has insisted on it more and more strongly, but all the European countries have resisted it. In the Turkish-German talks there was no breakthrough; and later in the year the EEC as a whole formally rejected the Turkish demand. It was widely believed that some of the increased aid and economic support that Turkey would receive from Germany was at least partially in compensation for its attitude concerning the circulation issue.

The second major topic was economic. West Germany is Turkey's largest trading partner, and it is significant for Turkey that in 1984 and 1985 the balance was in Turkey's favor, with $1.391m in Turkish exports compared to $1.369m in imports from Germany in the latter year. The major Turkish exports to Germany are textiles (32.3 per cent), citrus (15.1 per cent) and leatherware (11.1 per cent).[117]

There seem to be no signs that trade will not increase even further, but the Turks are even more interested in German investment. Direct German investment in Turkey in 1985 was DM20m, for a cumulative amount of DM260m, and many of Germany's most important manufacturing firms have moved into the Turkish scene. The German presence is also prominent in terms of aid — Turkey was the second largest recipient with a total of DM4.7 bn in 1985. And there has been a German contribution to almost every large Turkish venture, such as the Keban Dam, the Bosporus Bridge, and manufacturing and mining development. German tourism is also a major foreign exchange earner for Turkey. In 1985, approximately 300,000 German visitors were received, and German tour operators reportedly estimated that an increase of as much as 20 per cent could be expected in 1986.[118] Von Weizsacker indicated that economic cooperation could be expected to remain at least at these levels.

A third area of major concern was Turkey's status in Europe. The German Government has been one of the strongest supporters of Turkey's "rehabilitation" after the 1980-83 period of military rule, and von Weizsacker made a particular point of mentioning that "the schedule for a return to democracy following 12 September was being kept...impressive political and economic achievements had been made..." and that Germany "wanted to support Turkey's demarches to develop democracy 'at the desired level.' "[119] He was more cautious, however, about Turkey's movement toward the EEC, advising that it would be best for all concerned if the process moved with careful consideration of each step. In the military sphere, Germany is one of the strongest emphasizers of the importance of Turkey's role in NATO. All in all, as one Turkish publication put it, "it can fairly be assumed that both countries will continue to need each other, this year and in the years ahead."[120]

INDIA

Özal paid a six-day official visit to India in April. Relations between Turkey and India were cordial in the early years of the Turkish Republic, in considerable part because of strong mutual admiration between Gandhi and Atatürk. However, since World War II, relations have frequently been cool, as a result of general and specific international issues. Among these have been India's leading role among the non-aligned countries, and Turkish friendship with Pakistan.

A large part of the talks concerned international issues. Both countries expressed concern over the Iraqi-Iranian war and the security of the Persian Gulf. India put special stress on the problem of Afghanistan as well. (Özal was asked by Pakistan to take a message to India on its behalf, which apparently was generally conciliatory in tone.) Turkey for its part pressed India for more support on the Cyprus issue. Indian policy has been to support the efforts of UN Secretary-General Pérez de Cuellar, but it also favored a "unitary, independent and non-aligned" Cyprus with less stress on guarantees for the Turkish minority than Turkey would prefer to have included in policy statements. After the talks, Özal said that he "did not expect India to change its Cyprus policy, but there would be a softening in the Indian policy about it."[121]

Economic issues were less prominent in the talks than they were in the other visits Özal made. Trade between Turkey and India is relatively small-scale. In 1985, Turkey exported $21.6m of goods to India, with chick-peas accounting for $17m, and imported $5.6m of Indian goods, with iron ore accounting for $2m. Turkish businessmen accompanying Özal "did not express optimism about the quick increase in mutual trade," with the exception of Muammar Şahin, President of the Pulse

Exporters' Union, who said he believed that the 400,000 tons of pulses which Turkey exported to India in 1985 could be increased to 600,000 in 1986.

India was reported to be favorably inclined to Özal's suggestion that India allow Turkey to use its unused textile export quota to the US. Two agreements were also signed during the visit, in reference to airline and broadcasting cooperation.[122]

ROMANIA

Özal's three-day visit to Romania at the end of June was his first official one to a Socialist country. Turkey has always had a foreign policy orientation with a strong regional component, though the fact that most of the Balkan countries are in the Soviet bloc has made relations with them a problem often requiring a careful balance. At the outset of his visit, Özal sounded what some took as a strong cautionary note when he said, "Turkey favors sound Balkan cooperation based, before anything else, on mutual trust, without any ulterior motives, cooperation that is not propaganda-oriented."

The major political dimension of the Özal talks in Romania concerned the Bulgarian issue (discussed elsewhere). Özal pressed Romania strongly to move more toward the Turkish side, but nobody was surprised that the Romanians remained courteous but non-committal. On the other hand, Romania has not hesitated to accept the transfer of a considerable amount of transit trade between Europe and the Middle East via Turkey, which Turkey has been seeking to divert in order to isolate Bulgaria. Since President Evren's visit to Romania in June 1985, some 12,000 of the 34,000 transports which passed through Bulgaria each year have been transferred to Romania. In addition, expansion of the Constanza-Trabzon ro-ro (car ferry) line will be expanded.

Economic issues were also important in the talks. Trade with Romania has not reached the levels projected earlier, largely because of a lag in Turkish exports, attributed by Turkey to Romania's failure to make promised purchases. Turkish exports of $50-60m in 1985, projected to reach $80m in 1986, were far below the $500m target established by Evren. A concomitant problem for Turkey is that there is a large trade gap; Romanian exports to Turkey are $360–370m because of a large amount of industrial goods exported in connection with certain investments. Romania is building two hydroplants in Turkey, and would like to build more.[123]

HUNGARY

President Evren paid an official visit to Hungary in June. Agreements were signed for cooperation in agriculture and energy research, and in regard to a $100m Hungarian loan in connection with the Catalgazi thermal plant. There was also some reference to the continuing imbalance in trade. But the main issues discussed were political, specifically Turkish complaints about Bulgaria and Greece. Evren spoke out strongly against what he regarded as insufficient support for the Turkish case in disputes with both those countries; but, in spite of warm official statements, it appears that there was not much real progress.[124]

YUGOSLAVIA

Evren spent three days in Yugoslavia in October. As was the case in Hungary, he emphasized Turkey's problems with Bulgaria and Greece. Yugoslavia could be expected to be sympathetic because of its own minority problems. "It was announced at the end of the talks...that Turkey had explained to Yugoslavia the Cyprus problem and that of the Turkish minority in Bulgaria, and Yugoslavia explained the Macedonian and Kosova questions."[125] But no significant policy changes were reported.

On economic matters, the two countries agreed to expand bilateral trade from about $150m to $200m, to attempt to correct the trade imbalance, which is now greatly against Turkey, and to advance preparations for opening truck-ferry transit trade between the Turkish port of Mersin and the Yugoslavian port of Koper. In addition, it was decided that an extradition agreement would be negotiated because many Turkish drivers in Yugoslavia caused accidents with their trailertrucks.[126]

ALGERIA

In May, Algerian Prime Minister Abdel Hamid Brahimi returned the visit Özal made in 1985. The discussions centered on economic issues. One of the main ways in which trade will increase from its 1985 level of $270m to $500m is through Algeria supplying Turkey with liquefied natural gas and contributing to the construction of facilities in Turkey for reconverting it to gas. In return, Turkey will send Algeria a variety of commodities. Algeria also agreed to sell Turkey 600,000 tons of crude oil in 1986. Agreements for air and maritime cooperation, increased joint investments, and infrastructure projects were either signed or prepared. In addition, arrangements were made for Turkish experts to assist in the restoration of Ottoman period monuments in Algeria.[127]

PAKISTAN

Pakistani Prime Minister Muhammad Khan Junejo paid an official visit to Turkey in July. The two countries agreed on virtually all the major issues that were brought up. In addition to general agreements to expand and diversify bilateral trade, it was announced that Pakistan would provide $50m in revolving credit to Turkey for the import of Pakistani products, in response to an earlier similar move by Turkey.[128]

CHINA

In July, Chinese Prime Minister Zhao Ziyang returned a visit made to his country by Özal in 1985. The main topics of discussion were economic. Bilateral trade increased from $48m in 1984 to about $100m in 1985 (Turkish exports to China were $33.5m, imports $64.1m, considerably below the $500m objective.) Turkish exports are mainly cotton and chromium. Among the products whose exchange can be expanded are Turkish steel and high quality coal, and automotive industry products and Chinese oil. General international political problems were also mentioned, and Turkey, as usual, brought up the Bulgarian problem.[129]

THE FAR EAST

Özal's final foreign trip of 1986 took him to Bahrain, Bangladesh, Hong Kong, South Korea, Malaysia, and Oman. In each country economic issues were stressed, though discussion of general international issues also took place, and Turkey, as elsewhere, emphasized its desire for support on the Bulgarian and Cyprus problems.

In Bahrain there was stress on regional issues. Bahrain expressed strong support of the Turkish position on Bulgaria, and it was agreed that a Turkish mission would be opened, affiliated with a consulate in some nearby country.[130]

Bangladesh will be the recipient of $60m in Turkish export credits, of which half will be a long-term loan with low interest, and half will be short-term. Agreements were signed on the encouragement and protection of investments, and Bangladesh agreed to bring up Turkey's cases regarding Bulgaria and Cyprus at the next session of the South Asian Regional Cooperation Conference.[131]

South Korea was, from the economic point of view, the most important stop on Özal's tour. Turkey has a large negative balance of trade with South Korea (in 1985 Turkish exports to that country totaled $3.6m compared with $28.8m in South Korean exports to Turkey.[132] South Korean officials said that they were sure this imbalance would be corrected "in the long run."[133] Turkey suggested that the overall situation could be adjusted more quickly if there were more South Korean investment in Turkey, including the transfer of "know-how and experience." While no specific agreements were reached, it was agreed that there would be activity on the basis of the interests each counry has in growth *vis-à-vis* the other's region, i.e., that Turkey would help South Korea expand its role in the Middle East in exchange for South Korean efforts to enable Turkey to enter more deeply into Far Eastern markets. One of the ways of doing this would be to make Turkey a transit point or reexporter (on commission) of Korean goods to other Middle Eastern countries, since an obstacle to interregional trade is the problem of distance. It was agreed that studies of all of these possibilities would begin soon. Turkish businessmen accompanying Özal also had numerous conferences with representatives of leading South Korean companies.

Özal's other stops — in Hong Kong, Malaysia and Oman — were short and unofficial, and no major developments were reported.[134]

Members of the Turkish National Assembly also visited a large number of countries in 1986.

THE BULGARIAN PROBLEM

There was no significant progress during 1986 on the problem of the oppression of the Turkish minority in Bulgaria, even though Turkey was able to elicit expressions of anger over Bulgarian policy from a large number of governments and private associations. In the area of sanctions, Turkey continued to try to divert transit trade between Europe and the Middle East to other routes, and in February 1987 ended electricity imports from Bulgaria.

THE MIDDLE EAST

Turkish foreign policy in regard to the Middle East continued to try to find a balance between the opposing parties in various situations: Arabs vs Israel, Iraq vs Iran, the US vs Libya, and Islamic countries vs the basic Turkish policy of being a secular State.

THE ARAB-ISRAELI CONFLICT

Turkey continued to be the only Muslim State other than Egypt to maintain diplomatic relations with Israel. The pattern of public criticism of Israel and support of the cause of the Palestinians persisted, however. This pattern was stressed on several occasions. The first was the strong Turkish condemnation of the Israeli bombing of the Palestine Liberation Organization (PLO) headquarters in Tunis in 1985, which continued to have reverberations in the Turkish Press for some months after the event. It had been the ostensible reason for the cancellation of a planned meeting between Israeli officials and Turkish Foreign Minister Vahit Halefoğlu, and even between the two countries' Prime Ministers, at the UN General Assembly in October 1985.[135] The raid was also described as an incident of international terrorism, so that it fitted into the Turkish policy of being one of the main spokesmen against such policies. The Israeli raid was also mentioned during Evren's visits to Tunisia and Egypt in mid-January.[136] The PLO also sought to capitalize on a December 1985 Turkish initiative to have a PLO delegation take part in Middle East peace talks, but it faded in the face of strong US opposition.[137]

The second incident involved an attack by an Israeli patrol boat on a Turkish fishing boat off Gaza, but this did not develop into a major dispute.[138]

Among the most publicized events was an official visit by PLO Chairman Yasir 'Arafat to Turkey in late February. He was received by both Prime Minister Özal and President Evren. The Turkish leaders stressed that their policy continued to be one of advocating that all countries in the region should live within recognized and secure boundaries, and that Turkey supported the 1985 Husayn-'Arafat understanding,[139] but the symbolism of the visit was clear, and the visit was highlighted in the Turkish Press.[140] In April, a seminar organized by the Palestinians' Inalienable Rights Committee, held annually on a different continent, took place in Istanbul.[141] In December, Özal sent warm messages — as he had done in previous years — on Palestinian Solidarity Day.[142] It is particularly notable that all of these statements were prominently featured in official Turkish government news publications.

On the Israeli side, trade with Turkey continued at an estimated $30m. In early October, there was a "bombshell" in Ankara when it was announced that 14 Turkish Parliamentarians had been invited for a week's visit to Jerusalem. The trip, kept secret until the weekend, was revealed by a Deputy, "unwittingly."[143] In the end, only four members of the Populist Party went. A more successful step toward better relations with Israel occurred when both countries sent more senior diplomats to their respective legations than had previously been assigned there, though Foreign Minister Halefoğlu described it as among "certain positive steps for the attainment of peace in the Middle East, rather than a change in policy or approach."[144] There were also increasingly frequent visits of Turkish journalists to Israel, and *Cumhuriyet* printed several articles on impressions of Israel by Cengiz Candar, and long interviews by him with Israeli Defense Minister Yitzhak Rabin, Minister Ezer Weizman, and several prominent West Bank leaders. A private visit to Turkey by former Defense Minister Ariel Sharon elicited from the Foreign Ministry only the comment that there was "no need to exaggerate it."[145]

Certainly the most dramatic incident in regard to the Arabs and Israelis was the bombing of the Neve Shalom Synagogue in Istanbul on 6 September. Twenty-two Jews were killed in the Sabbath morning massacre. The Turkish Government and the Press reacted not only with sympathy but with indignation that such an action was carried out against Turkish citizens, and numerous officials participated in the funeral services, which were also attended by representatives of Jewish communities around the world. In order to avoid political overtones, the Turkish Government turned down an Israeli request that Israeli government representatives take part.

The gunmen who staged the attack blew themselves up to avoid identification, but an intensive investigation by Turkish, American and Israeli police established beyond doubt that they were Arabs. Although evidence suggested that the raid had been supported — if not directly staged — by Syrian and Libyan government-sponsored groups, much speculation in Turkey centered on the theory that it was the work of the Abu Nidal group, thus enabling Turkey to avoid complications in its relations with those two Arab countries. For some months Turkish newspapers were full of stories that asked "Who is Abu Nidal?"[146] The embarrassment of the Turkish Government was acute, however, and its condemnations of the raid were loud and clear.[147]

LIBYA

Another tightrope act was required in relations with Libya, which have been close, in particular because of the large number of Turkish workers in that country. A major problem arose when both Libya and the US sought Turkish support after the American bombing raid of April 1986. In addition to calls for Turkish support of Libya from Arab states, there was pressure from Turkish contractors who pointed out that they did $3.5 bn in business in Libya, while the US was applying quotas on Turkish textiles.[148] Turkish incentives to support Libya were weaker than in earlier years, however, as a result of disputes about Libyan foot-dragging on payment of debts to Turkey; and although oil imports continued in 1985 at about $600m, Turkish exports to Libya dropped to around $50m from their high of $450m in 1985.[149]

On the other hand, there was increasing evidence that Libya was engaged in state-sponsored terrorism — and Turkey considers itself one of the most outspoken opponents of this phenomenon in the world. In the end Turkey refrained from taking sides, confining itself to urging that neither party should escalate the dispute. This Turkish policy pleased neither the US nor Libya. A related event was the June conviction of two Libyans charged with attempting to blow up the American Officers' Club in Ankara in April. Two Libyan diplomats were also implicated, but were not tried because they had diplomatic immunity.[150]

SYRIA

Syria presented Turkey with yet another dilemma. On the one hand, relations with Syria had long been bad. Terrorist infiltration (both Palestinian and Kurdish) and smuggling across the Syrian-Turkish border had been irritants for many years. Syrian maps also continued to show the province of Hatay as part of Syria, even though it had been part of Turkey since 1939. Syrian radicalism also concerned Turkey. On the other hand, Turkey saw closer ties to Syria as a possible way of alleviating these conflicts, as well as showing support for general Arab political causes.

Syrian Prime Minister 'Abd al-Ra'uf al-Qasim paid an official visit to Turkey in March. There was speculation that the visit was undertaken when Syrian concerns were raised after 'Arafat's visit to Turkey. Both Turkey and Syria have some cards to play against each other. On the Turkish side is control of the headwaters of the Euphrates river, which Turkey is harnessing as part of its intensive energy development and irrigation programs. Syrian cards include the porousness of the long border with Turkey.

Despite warm statements by both sides, it remains to be seen whether Syrian irritants against Turkish security will be moderated. Tensions were heightened again in November at the opening of the trial of a group of Arabs accused of assassinating the First Secretary of the Jordanian embassy in Ankara in July 1985. Allegations of involvement by both the Syrian and Iranian Governments were made. The trial was continuing at the end of 1986.[151]

IRAN AND IRAQ

Perhaps the thorniest issue for Turkey in the Middle East is the Iraqi-Iranian war. Over several years Turkey has developed extensive relations with both, especially in the economic area. The official Turkish position is that it favors neither side, and it is clear that both have an important place for Turkey. At various times there have been reports that President Evren would be interested in a role as mediator in the war, but he has usually distanced himself from such reports.

In 1985, Turkey imported over two thirds of its oil from Iran and Iraq, divided almost evenly (5,744,972 tons or 36.88 per cent from Iran, 5,206,420 tons or 32.61 per cent from Iraq).[152] On the export side, Turkey sent around $3 bn worth of goods to Iran in 1985, and earned a large amount from the transit of Iraqi oil to Mediterranean ports. Any disruption of relations with either country could therefore prove a heavy blow. The situation was complicated, however, by a variety of political and security issues which could threaten Turkey.

Özal visited both Iran and Iraq in 1986. His January trip to Tehran covered a wide variety of issues. In addition to Turkey's desire to increase oil imports and the export of Turkish goods, and to maintain the sizable transit earnings that have developed, its major preoccupation was frontier security.

This problem has several aspects. One is the long border, which is difficult to secure and has enabled Turkish separatists to operate out of the reach of Turkish forces. The porousness of the border has also continued to enable Iranians to flee into Turkey; estimates of over one million Iranians in eastern Turkey, which were first heard in 1985, became more frequent in 1986. The refugees posed several problems. One was the burden of welfare and support costs, particularly in the eastern provinces which are Turkey's poorest. Another was the fact that, among the Iranians, there are fundamentalist Khomeyni supporters who could give support to the Fundamentalists in Turkey (see Religion). The Iranians were also moving in increasing numbers to cities in more western parts of Turkey, where they frequently remained while seeking visas for other countries, visas which were becoming increasingly difficult to obtain. A specific case in 1986 involved Greek government complaints that Iranians were seeking to cross the Turkish border with that country illegally.[153] In addition to financial and religious concerns, reports in 1986 mentioned that some of the Iranians were drug traffickers, smugglers, etc. There were also increasing reports of feuds among rival Iranians, including an incident at the beginning of the year in which an Iranian colonel was shot in Istanbul.[154]

Another major concern was that Turkish interests could suffer because of the war. Iran in particular had threatened actions against Iraq which were inimical to Turkish interests. High among these, of course, was the possibility of the disruption of oil supplies. Part of the problem was that a considerable part of those supplies still came through the Persian Gulf, which the Iranians regularly threatened to close. Moreover, in 1986, at least one Turkish tanker was hit by Iranian guns. More serious was the oft-repeated Iranian threat to sabotage the pipelines from Iraq that supplied Turkey not only with oil but also with sizable transit earnings. Specifically, there were several threats to knock out the Kirkuk (Iraq) oil terminal and to cut the pipeline, a threat (in October) that reportedly caused alarm in Ankara and prompted hurried trips to the Turkish capital by both the Iranian Deputy Foreign Minister, Husayn Shayk al-Islam and the Kuwaiti Defense Minister.[155] Shaykh al-Islam was reported to have said at the time that Iran could not "give guarantees" that Iranian troops would not attack the pipeline."[156]

Yet another issue was Iran's support of Kurdish separatists. While this was not always directed against Turkey, it was nevertheless important because Iranian support for Kurds who were making trouble for Iraq — which also has a sizable Kurdish minority that has been at odds with the Iraqi Government for many years — is considered by Turkey to have grave spillover implications. (See section on Internal Security.)

Other economic issues included the paradox that the decline in world oil prices favored Turkey but also threatened to have an effect on Iran's ability to contract for Turkish cooperation in such projects as roads, bridges, dams and irrigation works, in which Turkish firms have been increasingly involved in recent years. The large delegation accompanying Özal to Tehran included the president of the Istanbul Union of Chambers of Commerce, and 150 businessmen.[157] (An incident reflecting the risks of the war took place when a Turkish Airlines Boeing 727 that was to bring back most of the delegation was intercepted by jet fighters and could only reach Tehran via Soviet airspace. It has not been established whether the fighters were Iranian or Iraqi, but the implications of either possibility were considered ominous by the Turkish authorities. If they were Iraqi, they showed how easy was the penetration of adjoining areas; if they were Iranian they indicated that serious internal strains existed in Iran which could make any agreements between Turkey and Iran shaky.)[158]

In regard to Iraq, which Özal visited in March, economic problems were central, with both positive and negative aspects. The difficult aspects stemmed mainly from the fact that Iraq had been severely affected by both the costs of the war and the drop in oil prices. As a result, Özal was presented with demands that Turkey should not only agree to a rescheduling of Iraqi debts (at least for a short time), but should also pay for oil imports in cash. The prospects of losing the developing Iraqi markets impelled Turkey to agree to some of the demands, though it was understood that Turkey could not afford many long-term credit sales, and that trade volume was likely to fall from the *c* $12 bn of 1985.[159] Agreement was reached in July, however, for phased repayment over two years of the Iraqi debt of $1.5 bn.[160]

The Kurdish issue also arose. Twice in 1986, Turkish forces pursued Kurdish separatists into Iraq (see Internal Security).

THE UNITED STATES

Relations with the US were again a major preoccupation of the Turkish Government. As was the case in previous years, the main topics were military cooperation and Turkey's role in NATO, the level of American aid, American quotas on the importation of Turkish textiles, and the Armenian issue in the US Congress. In May 1987 relations reached a low point when President Evren postponed his scheduled visit to Washington.

MILITARY COOPERATION

As was the case in 1985, much attention was focused on negotiations for a renewal of the Defense and Economic Cooperation Agreement (DECA). The negotiations were long and difficult, partly because many of the other issues of concern to Turkey and the US were connected with it. Negotiations for another five-year extension of the agreement had been going on for some time; and while there never was any doubt that the results would eventually be positive, there were many occasions during 1986 when Turkish-American relations were at a low ebb.

The year's activities began with the first of what would be three visits to Turkey by American Deputy Secretary of Defense Richard Perle. Among the topics discussed in long talks with high Turkish officials were American requests for additional military facilities at Turkish bases, American concern about the then pending visit of PLO leader ‘Arafat, and the terms of an American offer of more Turkish participation in arms manufacture and supply for American and NATO forces.[161]

The Perle visit was followed by a three-day visit to Ankara by Secretary of State George Shultz, which attracted a great deal of press attention. The visit was not altogether a happy one. In addition to the issues mentioned above, a number of new topics came up. One was American concern over the implementation of the Montreux Convention of 1936 governing passage of foreign ships through the Bosporus. Under its provisions, Black Sea powers can send ships of unlimited tonnage through the Bosporus to the Mediterranean, whereas non-Black Sea powers are limited in the size of warships they can send to the area and the amount of time they can stay there. The US, long concerned with the build-up of Soviet naval forces in the Black Sea, requested that Turkey limit Russian passage through the Straits, and pointed out the lack of symmetry in the fact that Russian aircraft carriers were allowed to pass but American ones, being larger, were not. The US also rejected a Russian protest to both Washington and Ankara that recent sailings into the Black Sea by American cruisers were provocative and aggressive.[162] Turkey rejected both the American request and the Russian protest.

The final day of Shultz's stay was marked by the US-Libyan crisis in the Gulf of Sidra, which led to pressure on Turkey by both the US and Libya for endorsement of their side of the dispute (see section on the Middle East). The US was rebuffed when, shortly after Shultz's departure, Evren issued one of his strongest statements to date expressing dissatisfaction with American policies, pointing in particular to reported American "soundings" for the use of air bases in eastern Turkey for the American Rapid Deployment Force. Evren was quoted in reference to this subject as saying that "countries which profess to be friends of Turkey...should be 'more realistic in their attitudes.' "[163] Evren also expressed renewed annoyance with the textile quotas issue and with the 10:7 ratio of aid to Turkey and Greece, respectively, which had been placed in congressional appropriations for many years.

Turkish statements of dissatisfaction with American positions continued in May when Foreign Minister Halefoğlu visited Washington. New issues at that time included a proposal by the US and NATO to add the Greek base at Lemnos to NATO's defenses (see section on Greece and Cyprus).[164] The US for its part expressed annoyance with Turkish criticism of its actions in possible violation of the SALT-II Treaty, and with Turkey's reluctance to agree to joint action against Syria.[165]

Talks continued on numerous occasions in meetings between officials of the two countries in Ankara and Washington, and following contacts in Europe and at the UN. In late September, Turkey increased its pressure by invoking the DECA termination clause, averting an automatic one-year extension "which would mean that the US would have had another comfortable year."[166] This was followed not long afterward by Perle's two additional visits to Ankara (one for the North Atlantic Assembly's autumn meeting which was held in Istanbul in mid-November, and an official visit in December), shortly after which negotiations were concluded. The five-year extension was signed at the end of the final visit. In addition to specific provisions for the use of Turkish bases, a key compromise was reached in which the American Administration committed itself to make its "best efforts" to increase military aid to Turkey. The Administration also outlined a general program of restructuring foreign military sales credits to make it easier for American allies to repay loans for military cooperation and modernization.[167] It was unofficially reported that for Turkey this would mean cancellation of about $800m of the $3.5 bn owed over the next 20 years, and that the surplus weapons plan would allocate to Turkey two squadrons of F-4E *Phantom* fighters and other equipment with a total value of $300m.[168] The agreement is good until 1990.

FOREIGN AID

On a number of occasions in 1986 Turkish officials expressed disappointment at the levels of American military and economic aid. Turkish Ambasssdor to Washington Şükrü Elekdağ pursued this theme, for example, at the University of New Hampshire in October.[169] In addition to their unhappiness about the absolute levels of aid, the necessity of which was continually stressed by pointing out the strategic importance of Turkey in view of the Iraqi-Iranian war and other regional dangers that resulted from the 1979 fall of the Shah of Iran, Turkish leaders also continued to voice their irritation at the provision in all recent aid appropriations that Greece received $7 in aid for every $10 given to Turkey. Halefoğlu sounded a familiar note when he told a Washington dinner for Secretary Shultz that, "unfortunately, we do not have Turkish-Americans in sufficient numbers in this country to counterbalance certain influences of the ethnic politics."[170]

American aid to Turkey in 1986 was about $739m, down significantly from $879m the previous year. The cuts were largely due to fiscal strictures in the American budget and did not reflect dissatisfaction with Turkish policies. The aid enabled Turkey to remain the third largest recipient of American assistance (behind only Israel and Egypt), with about 5.8 per cent of the total congressional appropriation. It was expected that the Administration request for 1987 would be about $974m. In October, Congress set the figure at $490m, however.[171] Part of the burden of the reduced aid was relieved by revisions in the ratio of grants to credits, and in easing of terms for repayment.

IMPORT QUOTAS

There was also continued friction about import quotas on Turkish products, and Turkish officials regularly linked this issue to the DECA negotiations and other talks. Shultz expressed particular irritation about this linkage during his visit to Ankara, observing that while it was regrettable that there were such restrictions, which the Reagan Administration regularly opposed, Turkey would have to recognize the realities of American politics.[172] Turkish officials, for their part, liked to counter by pointing to the contradiction between American policy of strongly urging free trade on other countries while restricting imports into the US. One American newspaper described it as a "supercharged emotional issue" for Turkey, and it was one of the most headlined topics in the Turkish Press during the Shultz visit.[173]

Part of the problem arose because of Turkey's increased production and exports in recent years. According to one analysis, at the end of 1985 Turkish textile exports were increasing at an annual rate of 37 per cent in dollar terms as compared, for example, with 8 per cent for Sri Lanka and 15 per cent for Portugal. This made Turkey an especially vulnerable target within the framework of an overall worldwide quota that had to be distributed among numerous potential importers. Agreement was reached in May to raise the 1986 quota to 113.5m square yards (from 96.8m square yards in 14 specified textile items in 1985). The value of Turkish textile imports for 1985 was $121.3m, up sharply over the $71m in 1984, and a State Department spokesman suggested that "Turkey should increase the quality and style of its textile production and sell less but earn more."[174]

Quotas imposed by EEC members continued in 1986 similar to the pattern of the previous year (see *MECS* 1984–85, p 689).

American concern with Turkish imports also extended to other items, particularly iron and steel. In February, the US International Trade Commission imposed antidumping and countervailing duties on imports of standard line pipe from Turkey and Thailand on the basis of a finding that the two Turkish producers of those items had received subsidies which unjustifiably injured American domestic producers.[175]

On other matters, Turkey expressed disapproval of President Reagan's arms deals with Iran.[176] While on the whole Turkish officials stressed the continuing solid relations between the two countries, Turkey nevertheless undertook a campaign to improve its image in the US. Included in these efforts were visits by numerous Turkish politicians, businessmen and others to the US; the hosting of several American Congressmen; several business conferences; numerous public appearances by Ambassador Elekdağ;[177] and increased activity by the Assembly of Turkish-American Associations. The overall campaign was summarized by Minister of State Mesut Yılmaz, who said: "We aim at declaring 1987 as 'promotion of Turkey year' in the US."[178] The crowning event in this context was the preparation of the Suleiman Exhibition of more than 200 art objects from the reign of Suleiman the Magnificent. It was the first time such objects had been allowed to leave Turkey. The exhibition opened in Washington in January 1987, and was scheduled to go to Chicago and New York in conjunction with numerous other cultural events.

POSTPONEMENT OF EVREN'S VISIT

Despite what appeared to be agreements on most of the above issues, however, dissatisfaction built up over what many Turks considered bad deals. There was continued frustration over export quotas, as Congress became increasingly protectionist, and the allegation in regard to DECA that Turkey had committed itself for five years while the US had only become obligated for one year at a time. The latter point became particularly contentious in late April 1987 when a congressional committee recommended a steep cut in the Reagan Administration's foreign aid request for Turkey. Tensions were heightened when at almost the same time another congressional committee approved a resolution on an Armenian remembrance day. After an intense discussion in the Press, Evren felt it appropriate to postpone his official visit until late in the year.[179]

THE SOVIET UNION

Turkish-Soviet relations in 1986 were highlighted by Özal's official visit to Moscow at the end of July. While in their official statements both countries stressed that it was possible for those even in different camps to have good relations, Özal probably put it most succinctly when he declared at a press conference on his return that "Turkey is very careful toward Russia in general political terms."[180]

Opinions on the results of the visit were very mixed. The most important topics were economic, and here there were both positive and negative results. In the positive column were the following: an agreement that the gas pipeline from Russia to Turkey via the Bulgarian frontier would become operable in April 1987 and that Turkey would receive sizable quantities of natural gas, which are important for reducing air pollution in some of Turkey's major cities; a Soviet promise to increase opportunities for Turkish contractors; and statements of Soviet willingness to increase loans and investments in Turkey. It was also projected that the trade volume between the two countries would reach $6 bn by 1990.

The item that received the most attention in the Turkish Press was a negative one, however. This was the failure to sign the so-called "highway agreement" whereby a stretch of Soviet road would be connected with a section of Turkish highway near the Turkish town of Hopa, so that there would be Russian road access to the Gulf. The apparent obstacle to the conclusion of the agreement, which has been pending for 20 years, was the inability of the two countries to agree on the line that governs territorial waters and airspace in the Black Sea. (In December, Turkey declared a 200 mile exclusive economic zone in the Black Sea; but in February 1987 the issue was settled when it was agreed that the borderline for both Turkish and Russian exclusive economic zones would be the Continental Shelf.)[181]

Another matter that caused many to see the visit as less than a diplomatic success was the fact that Özal was "unable to be received" by General Secretary Mikhail Gorbachev. This was regarded in Turkey as a deliberate snub. It came as no surprise that there was little agreement on two issues particularly sensitive to Turkey. One was the Russian position on Cyprus (that there should be an international conference, whereas Turkey insists that the only acceptable formula must state that no solution can be recognized that will result in Greek domination of Cyprus). The other was Russian reluctance to pressure Bulgaria on the issue of that country's ethnic Turks (see section on Bulgaria). It was also reported that the delegation of about 80 Turkish businessmen who accompanied Özal had great difficulty in making contacts and spent a good deal of time in their hotels.[182]

Other visits and exchanges also occurred. Turkey took a prominent part in the Moscow International Trade Fair at the end of 1985;[183] Turkish Finance Minister Ahmet Alptemocin was in Moscow in February; the Soviet Chief of Staff visited Ankara in September; and a special Soviet Ambassador was sent to Turkey in December to discuss disarmament topics and to reiterate Russian unhappiness with Turkey's supportive position on President Reagan's "Star Wars" project.[184]

At the end of the year the Soviet Union announced that a delegation would be sent to Ankara in January 1987 to arrange for construction by Turkish contractors of five hotels in the USSR at a cost of nearly $100m; and talks on other economic steps continued at intervals.[185] On the whole, however, relations between the two countries did not advance much in 1986.

GREECE AND CYPRUS

Tensions with Greece continued high during 1986, both over the Cyprus issue and over conflicts regarding the Aegean sea area.

On the Cyprus question there were several developments. One was involvement of the US and the USSR, with the two superpowers coming down on opposite sides. In January, a Pentagon report prepared in response to a congressional request concluded that the fault for the continuing deadlock lay primarily with the Greek Cypriots. It advocated the formation of an interim Federal Government pending final negotiations, a position which was essentially that of the Turkish Cypriots.[186] The Soviets entered the dispute the same month. After having been relatively quiet about the problem for some years, Moscow put forward a plan for Cyprus that called for the creation of a single, territorially whole and united state; the demilitarization of the island; and the resolution of outstanding issues through a UN-sponsored international conference.[187] It was not clear why the Russians chose to present this new initiative, but some sources speculated that, in the Russian view, the TRNC was consolidating its position as time passed. Observers were also puzzled that the Soviet Government should do something so overtly antagonistic to Turkey, a country which they had been courting in other ways. In any event, Turkey rejected the plan out of hand as "heated-up old food."[188]

In April, UN Secretary-General Pérez de Cuellar made another attempt to break the deadlock. He put forth a revised plan; but it was so similar to the draft of January 1985, which had been accepted by the Turkish Cypriots but rejected by the Greek Cypriots, that both these communities took the same positions again.[189] In April, Greek Cypriot Prime Minister Spyros Kyprianou made counterproposals, but the Secretary-General characterized them as unhelpful because they were obviously unsatisfactory to the Turkish Cypriots.[190]

Another flare-up occurred in July. Turkish policy, which had until then been strongly on the Turkish Cypriot side while remaining "diplomatically cautious," changed when Özal made an official visit to the TRNC. With the UN efforts at a "total, total, total impasse," as a senior official put it, observers agreed that Özal's move was to consolidate the position of TRNC President Rauf Denktaş. Immediately after Özal's departure, Denktaş moved to apply direct pressure on the UN to act, by closing the border between the Greek and Turkish zones to members of the UN peacekeeping force as well as to all other travelers. Among the statements that Denktaş made in conjunction with this action was the one that he was unhappy with many nations — in particular the US and Britain — for not pressing strongly on the TRNC's behalf.[191] The blockade was eased after about two weeks, when Denktaş felt he had made his point. The Turkish Press jubilantly hailed Özal's visit; one newspaper called it the "Third Turkish Landing" (the first two being the 1974 invasion and an unofficial 1982 visit by Prime Minister Bülent Ulusu).[192] At year's end the only change had been to further increase tension on the island.

Tensions between Greece and Turkey on other issues remained high as well. Part of the reason was that Greek Prime Minister Andreas Papandreou took every opportunity to oppose Turkish interests in various European institutions, in particular the EEC of which Greece had become a full member at the end of 1985. Communications between Özal and Papandreou were reported in the Turkish Press almost weekly, and emotions in Turkey proved easy to stir up. In addition to the general atmosphere, there were a number of specific incidents that caused concern in NATO. The first was a renewed dispute in May over a Greek proposal to militarize the Aegean island of Lemnos. The Greeks originally proposed in 1984 that Lemnos be made a NATO-connected facility. Turkey objected in the strongest terms, however, threatening military action, and the plan was dropped, though only after a considerable stir in NATO circles. The US came under Turkish verbal fire when it was revealed that American General Bernard Rogers, the NATO Commander, had drawn up a "contingency plan" for the use of Lemnos in case of war with the Soviet Union.[193]

A second crisis took place in December when there was a border clash involving a small number of Greek and Turkish soldiers. Two soldiers on each side were killed. Although it was eventually concluded that this was an isolated incident, it increased nervousness on both sides and again brought expressions of concern from European countries and the US.[194]

A third crisis occurred in March 1987, when Turkey announced that it would send the *Sismik I* research ship, together with a naval escort, to drill for oil in Aegean waters claimed by Greece. The Greek response included a pledge to resist, as well as a demand that the US suspend operations at its Nea Makri military base on the grounds that the US had "not exercised enough vigor diplomatically with the Turks to end this crisis."[195] The crisis eased when Özal agreed to pull back his ship, under considerable NATO and US pressure, but also with assurances that Greece would not attempt to drill in those waters.[196]

OTHER ITEMS

NATO Secretary-General Joseph Luns was awarded the first Atatürk International Peace Prize.

Celal Bayar, Turkey's third President, died on 22 August at the age of 104.

A second television channel was inaugurated by Turkish Radio and Television in October.

In Istanbul, important progress was made in the work of cleaning up both the waters and the shores of the Golden Horn.[197]

In the Netherlands, ten Turks were elected to Municipal Councils during local elections in March. All were members of Dutch political parties. An estimated 65 per cent of the 150,000 Turks living in the Netherlands voted in the first election in which foreigners were given the vote.[198]

NOTES

For the place and frequency of publications cited here, and for the full name of the publication, news agency, radio station or monitoring service where an abbreviation is used, please see "List of Sources." Only in the case of more than one publication bearing the same name is the place of publication noted here.

1. *WSJ*, 24 January 1986.

2. Ersin Kalaycioğlu, "The By-Elections of 1986: A Scrutiny of the Turkish Electoral Politics," *Current Turkish Thought*, No 60, Fall 1986, pp 13–14.
3. *Hürriyet*, 2 July 1986.
4. *Briefing*, 13 October 1986.
5. Kalaycioğlu, op cit, p 11.
6. *Briefing*, 13 January 1986.
7. Ibid.
8. *Hürriyet*, 14 March 1986.
9. Ibid.
10. *Briefing*, 17 February, 7 April, 5 May, 3 November; *Pulse*, 5 May, 23 June 1986.
11. E.g., *NYT*, 30 September; *WP*, 29 September; *The Economist*, 17 May 1986.
12. For a report of the convention see *Pulse*, 2 June 1986.
13. Kalaycioğlu, op cit, p 12.
14. *Hürriyet*, 8 October 1986.
15. Kalaycioğlu, op cit, p 20.
16. *Pulse*, 7, 21 April; *Briefing*, 31 March 1986.
17. Ergun Özbudun, *Social Change and Political Participation in Turkey* (Princeton, NJ: Princeton University Press, 1976) Ch 5.
18. See table in Walter F. Weiker, *The Modernization of Turkey* (New York: Holmes & Meier, 1981) p 145.
19. Kalycioğlu, op cit, p 14.
20. *Newspot*, 9 January 1987.
21. Ibid.
22. Ibid, 5 December 1986.
23. *Pulse*, 14 April 1986.
24. Ibid, 6 October 1986.
25. *Hürriyet*, 22 September 1986.
26. *Pulse*, 10 February 1986.
27. *Hürriyet*, 18 March 1986.
28. See, for example, *Hürriyet*, 18 March 1986.
29. Ibid, 29 March 1986.
30. *Briefing*, 12 January 1987.
31. Ibid.
32. Ibid, 11 May 1987.
33. Ibid.
34. Ibid.
35. Ibid, 29 December 1986.
36. *Pulse*, 24 November 1986.
37. Ibid, 1 September 1986.
38. Ibid, 24 November 1986.
39. Ibid, 3 November 1986.
40. Ibid.
41. For a full list see *Pulse*, 25 August 1986.
42. *Briefing*, 19 January 1987.
43. *Pulse*, 8 September 1986.
44. *Pulse*, 3 November 1986.
45. *Briefing*, 29 December 1986.
46. *Pulse*, 3 November 1986.
47. *Briefing*, 19 January 1987.
48. Ibid.
49. *Newspot*, 28 November 1986.
50. *Pulse*, 20 October 1986.
51. Ibid, 27 October 1986.
52. For details of the report, see *Briefing*, 2, 16 June 1986.
53. For a sample of articles which discuss the details, see *WSJ*, 22 April, 3 December 1986; *JP*, 12 April 1987; *Briefing*, 16 June, 8 December 1986; *Pulse*, 22 September 1986.
54. *Pulse*, 13 October 1986.

55. *Newspot*, 7 March 1986.
56. Ibid, 25 July 1986.
57. Ibid, 21 November 1986.
58. *Pulse*, 27 January 1986.
59. *MEJ*, Vol 40, No 3, 1986, p 504.
60. *Pulse*, 10 March 1986.
61. *MEJ*, loc cit.
62. *Pulse*, 14 April 1986.
63. Ibid, 23 June 1986.
64. Ibid, 17 February 1986.
65. Ibid, 14 July 1986.
66. See, for example, the *WP*, 16, 21 August 1986.
67. *NYT*, 5 March 1987.
68. *Pulse*, 8 January 1986.
69. Ibid, 20 January 1986.
70. Ibid, 10 March 1986.
71. Ibid.
72. Ibid, 16 May 1986.
73. Ibid, 14 July 1986.
74. Ibid, 17 March 1986.
75. Ibid, 24 November 1986.
76. *MEJ*, Vol 40, No 3, 1986, p 504.
77. Ibid, 1986, p 718.
78. Ibid.
79. *NYT*, 24 September 1986; *Facts on File* 1986, p 729.
80. *Pulse*, 19 January 1987.
81. *Newspot*, 7 March 1986.
82. Ibid, 2 May 1986.
83. Ibid, 31 January 1986.
84. Ibid, 28 February 1986.
85. Ibid, 2 May 1986.
86. Ibid.
87. *Briefing*, 29 December 1986.
88. *WSJ*, 2 April 1986.
89. Ibid, 22 April 1986.
90. *New Statesman*, 14 February 1986.
91. For a detailed report see *The New York Review of Books*, 27 February 1986.
92. *WSJ*, 22 April 1986.
93. *Pulse*, 3 February 1986.
94. Ibid, 12 May 1986. For a full report of reactions to the Caner case, see *Briefing*, 3, 10 February 1986.
95. Interior Ministry report as cited in *Briefing*, 3 February 1986.
96. *Newspot*, 21 February 1986.
97. Ibid, 20 June 1986.
98. *Briefing*, 27 January 1986.
99. *Pulse*, 6 January 1986.
100. Ibid, 24 February 1986.
101. *Hürriyet*, 14 July 1986.
102. *Pulse*, 14 July 1986.
103. Ibid, 8 September 1986.
104. Ibid.
105. *Pulse*, 3 November 1986.
106. *Hürriyet*, 10 February 1986.
107. *Pulse*, 5 January 1987.
108. *Briefing*, 29 December 1986.
109. On the NSP see Weiker, *The Modernization of Turkey*, op cit, pp 138–39, and Jacob Landau, *Radical Politics in Modern Turkey* (Leiden: E.J. Brill, 1974).

110. *Briefing*, 8 December 1986.
111. Ibid, 5 January 1987.
112. Ibid.
113. Ibid.
114. *Pulse*, 24 February 1986.
115. *Facts on File* 1986, p 186.
116. For reports on the visit see *Briefing*, 17 February; *Pulse*, 24 February; *Newspot*, 21 February; *Facts on File* 1986, p 186.
117. *Briefing*, 26 May 1986.
118. Ibid.
119. *Newspot*, 30 May 1986.
120. *Briefing*, 26 May 1986. For other detailed reports of the visit, see *Pulse*, 2 June; *Newspot*, 30 May 1986.
121. *Pulse*, 14 April 1986.
122. For full reports on the talks see *Pulse*, 14, 21 April 1986.
123. On the Romanian visit see *Newspot*, 4 July; *Pulse*, 7 July 1986.
124. On the visit see *Newspot*, 27 June; *Pulse*, 30 June 1986.
125. But no significant policy changes were reported.
126. *Pulse*, 27 October; *Newspot*, 24 October 1986.
127. *Pulse*, 5 May; *Newspot*, 2 May 1986.
128. *Newspot*, 11, 18 July 1986.
129. See *Newspot*, 18, 25 July; *Pulse*, 21 July 1986.
130. *Newspot*, 7 November 1986.
131. Ibid.
132. *Pulse*, 3 November 1986.
133. Ibid.
134. For reports on the Far East tour see *Newspot*, 7, 14 November; *Pulse*, 3, 10 November 1986.
135. *Briefing*, 7 October 1985.
136. *Pulse*, 20 January 1986.
137. Ibid, 3 February 1986.
138. *Newspot*, 21 February 1986.
139. Ibid, 28 February 1986.
140. *Pulse*, 3 March 1986.
141. *Newspot*, 4 April 1986.
142. Ibid, 5 December 1986.
143. *Briefing*, 27 October 1986.
144. *Cumhuriyet*, 14 October 1986.
145. *Günaydın*, 28 July 1986.
146. See, for example, *Hürriyet*, on several dates in November 1986.
147. For a full account of the investigation and its tentative findings, see the *NYT Magazine*, 4 January 1987.
148. *Pulse*, 21 April 1986.
149. *Briefing*, 5 May 1986.
150. Ibid, 5, 19 May; *WP*, 7 June 1986.
151. *Briefing*, 1, 8 December; *Pulse*, 24 November 1986.
152. *Briefing*, 31 March 1986.
153. *Pulse*, 10 November 1986.
154. *Briefing*, 20 January 1986.
155. Ibid, 20 October 1986.
156. *NYT*, 16 March 1987.
157. *Briefing*, 6 January 1986.
158. Ibid, 6 January 1986.
159. *Pulse*, 27 March 1986, p 2.
160. *Briefing*, 21 July 1986.
161. *Pulse*, 3 March 1986.
162. Ibid, 24 March 1986.
163. *Briefing*, 31 March 1986.

164. *Pulse*, 26 May 1986.
165. Ibid, 8 December 1986.
166. Ibid, 29 September 1986.
167. *NYT*, 17 December; *Briefing*, 15 December 1986.
168. *Briefing*, 15 December 1986.
169. *Newspot*, 3 October 1986, p 3.
170. *Newark Star-Ledger*, 17 March 1987.
171. *Pulse*, 20 October 1986.
172. See, for example, the *WSJ*, 26 March 1986, p 30.
173. Ibid.
174. *WSJ*, 1 April, 3 May 1986.
175. *American Metal Market*, 14 February 1986.
176. Interview by Özal with an associate of American columnist Jack Anderson, *Newark Star-Ledger*, 3 December 1986.
177. See, for example, "Turkey Focuses on Its Image," *NYT*, 20 January 1987.
178. *Newspot*, 30 May 1986.
179. *NYT*, 9 May 1987.
180. *Newspot*, 8 August 1986.
181. Ibid, 20 February 1987.
182. For a detailed report of the visit, see *Pulse*, 4 August 1986, pp 1–11.
183. *Briefing*, 7 October 1985.
184. *Pulse*, 8 December 1986.
185. Ibid, 5 January 1987.
186. *Newspot*, 3 January 1986.
187. *Pulse*, 27 January 1986.
188. Ibid, 27 January; *Briefing*, 27 January 1986, which gives the full text of the Soviet plan.
189. For the full text of the plan, see *Briefing*, 7 April 1986.
190. *Newspot*, 16 May 1986.
191. *NYT*, 5, 6, 13 July 1986.
192. *Pulse*, 7 July 1986.
193. *Briefing*, 26 May 1986.
194. Ibid, 29 December 1986.
195. *NYT*, 26 March 1987.
196. Ibid, 29 March 1987.
197. For descriptions see the *WP*, 24 September; *NYT*, 1 June 1986.
198. *Newspot*, 28 March 1986.

The Yemeni Arab Republic
(Al-Jumhuriyya al-'Arabiyya al-Yamaniyya)

JOSEPH KOSTINER

In 1986, the Yemeni Arab Republic (YAR) continued to focus on internal economic and administrative reforms, taking advantage of the relative internal tranquillity that followed two decades of internal war. The goals were to rehabilitate the economy and reinforce cohesion among the different segments of the YAR's population. President 'Ali 'Abdallah Salih tried to create improved economic organizations and to strengthen government institutions. In foreign affairs, the YAR sought mainly to preserve optimal conditions in the region, in order to prevent unwarranted foreign influences from shattering the Republic's newly acquired stability and interfering with internal affairs. Salih was particularly careful to neutralize the effects in his country of the civil war that broke out on 13 January 1986 in the People's Democratic Republic of Yemen (PDRY). The YAR's strategy in foreign affairs was to continue its non-alignment policy as the best possible means of survival.

INTERNAL AFFAIRS

REINFORCING POLITICAL SUPPORT

THE GENERAL PEOPLE'S CONGRESS

The General People's Congress (GPC) held its third session between 25 and 30 August 1986. Established in 1982, the GPC was created to enlist popular support for the Government and to spread its political line in the provinces (see *Middle East Contemporary Survey* [*MECS*] 1981–82, pp 932–33; 1984–85, pp 705–6). Under the circumstances of relative internal stability threatened by the impact of the revolutionary tide in the PDRY, the GPC convention seemed again to bear out these aims. First, it tried to get support for Salih's plans for economic development and administrative reorganization which had already been initiated (see *MECS* 1984–85, pp 706-8), but which Salih was anxious to accelerate during the relatively peaceful year. Second, Salih sought to foster his Government's hold over the YAR's once turbulent tribal peripheral provinces; under the conditions of relative tranquillity, fuller government control was considered possible.

In order to achieve these aims, the following steps were taken. A detailed report of the Government's plans for economic development was presented to the GPC's members, to enlist their support. As Salih presumably anticipated, he received the approval of the GPC, which enabled him in October 1986 to instruct his Cabinet to implement what had become the "GPC's decisions on economic development."[1] Under this label, Salih's policies carried wider legitimacy and influence.

The attempt to achieve a greater hold over the provinces was already discernible in

February 1986 during a meeting of the leaders of local councils, a body that had been elected in late 1985 (see *MECS* 1984–85, pp 706–7). Salih's own chairing of this meeting, along with the participation of four Cabinet Ministers and nine Directors-General of Cabinet Ministries, secured the channeling of the local councils' leaders along the Government's positions.[2] Moreover, the gathering of GPC members from all over the country reinforced the attempt to control the provinces. Salih himself gave vent to this trend by stating during the GPC's opening session that this institution "acquired a political line for our country...it began to cover all the provinces."[3] And in a later interview he asserted that tribalism merely denoted the population's descent rather than a separatist force in the YAR's provinces.[4] Salih's own reelection as the GPC's Secretary-General consolidated his control over this body. The fact that 700 GPC members (out of 1,000) were elected, gave an aura of legitimacy and massive support to the GPC's decisions and to Salih's preeminence in the Republic.

THE OPPOSITION

Salih's firm control also marked a lull in the activity and power of the opposition groups. There were no reports of leftist National Democratic Front activities. Following an unsuccessful assassination attempt on a staff member of the US embassy in San'a in April 1986, the Government closed down the leftist-nationalist weekly *al-Amal*, a step that further weakened leftist groups.[5] A lawsuit against this paper, which had been brought before a court in San'a in April 1985 and was still being prosecuted in early 1986, resulted in the influence of Muslim-Fundamentalist elements in the YAR to come to the surface. It was a group of religious clerics, incorporated within a body called the "Institutions for Religious Studies," who filed the suit against *al-Amal* for incitement to topple the Government, which the clerics denoted as heresy.[6] Although the Government succeeded in weakening the clerics in 1985 (see *MECS* 1984–85, p 707), and although they sided with the authorities in the above lawsuit, the clerics' inclination to support radical groups of Muslim Brothers[7] and their direct rivalry with the Leftists could encourage both opposition groups to embark on fiercer anti-Government activities.

Escaping from the heavy hand of the new PDRY Government, which came to power in January 1986, over 10,000 refugees (many more according to some reports) fled to the YAR. Most were tribal groups loyal to the former President of the PDRY, 'Ali Nasir Muhammad, but there were also former high-ranking South Yemeni officials and officers (see the chapter on the PDRY in this volume). These refugees were not only crowding villages and disrupting daily life in the southern parts of the YAR, but through old established contacts with YAR officials were trying to influence policy-making. The consequences still remain to be seen.

ECONOMIC DEVELOPMENT AND ADMINISTRATIVE REORGANIZATION

THE OIL OF MA'RIB AL-JAWF

There were conflicting reports on the value of the oil struck in the Ma'rib al-Jawf area (see *MECS* 1984–85, p 707). In December 1985, YAR sources stressed that the oil in the region was of commercial value and quantities and that a pipeline, which would become operational in late 1987,[8] would transfer the oil from Ma'rib to the Red Sea. A Western report in March 1986 was skeptical about the prospect of finding oil of commercial value particularly when oil prices were depreciating. According to this report, the Ma'rib field only included hydrocarbon gas for cooking and fertilizing.[9] However, during the year, Salih and other YAR spokesmen kept on stressing the discovery of a huge oil field which would produce about 200,000 barrels per day that would be shipped through a $300m pipeline to Salif on the Red Sea. The discovery was portrayed by Salih as a major boost for the YAR's economy,[10] although the lack of authoritative estimates of the commercial value of the Ma'rib oil and the problematic funding of the pipeline cast a shadow over these prospects.

FACING ECONOMIC DIFFICULTIES

The prospects of profitable oil sales could not offset the problems in other spheres. The budget for 1986 was based on an expenditure of YR9.94 bn; but with revenues of only YR7.179 bn, there was a deficit of *c* YR2.7 bn. It was not made clear how the deficit would be covered.[11] In addition, the Government made a great effort to develop the agricultural sector, which constituted 25 per cent of the YAR's gross domestic product and employed 70 per cent of the country's manpower. Moreover, the development of agriculture and fisheries was high on the Cabinet's priorities, since these were fields in which Yemenis had experience.[12] In order to facilitate this development, a reorganization of the sector was required, which occurred in July 1986, when the Ministers of the Economy and Industry and of Supplies and Trade were dismissed by Salih and the two Ministries were united into one, under a new Minister.[13] However, Salih's continuing public emphasis on the need to eliminate deficiencies and low productivity in the economy attested to the problems the YAR was still facing. The stream of returning migrant workers from the Gulf states,[14] on whose remittances the YAR was heavily dependent, further underlined North Yemen's problems.

FOREIGN AFFAIRS

PURSUANCE OF NEUTRALIST POLICIES

During 1986 the YAR sought to continue its policy of regional and international non-alignment. Deriving from the YAR's inherent strategic need to balance the diverse influences of its Marxist South Yemeni and conservative pro-Western Saudi Arabian neighbors against each other, neutralism developed into the YAR's survival strategy. Hence, by pursuing a non-aligned stance, San'a was able to maintain good relations with all Arab parties while obtaining assistance from both superpowers (see all previous volumes of *MECS*). However, given the deep-rooted disputes in the Arab world, and the fear of a new revolutionary and aggressive Government in the PDRY (see essay on inter-Arab relations and chapter on the PDRY in this volume), the YAR found it difficult to devise a comprehensive policy to cover all aspects of its foreign relations. San'a rather developed several tactics which reflected its inclination to non-alignment: avoiding involvement by taking blunt steps in the PDRY dispute; supporting topics which were normally undisputed in the Arab world; and developing good relations with both superpowers.

ATTITUDE TOWARD THE PEOPLE'S DEMOCRATIC REPUBLIC OF YEMEN

The internal PDRY dispute of January 1986 presented major threats to the YAR: the reversal of 'Ali Nasir Muhammad's cooperative policies toward the YAR could lead to renewed acts of PDRY-initiated subversion in North Yemen (on PDRY-YAR relations, see this and all previous volumes of *MECS*); and the historically close intertribal, family and ideological contacts between the populations of both States could easily transfer the PDRY feud to the YAR.

Hence, once fighting broke out in Aden and 'Ali Nasir fled, the YAR sought to reinstate him in order to reestablish friendly relations between the two States. On 18 January 1986, Salih even attempted to intervene in the PDRY by calling for a cease-fire, which would be supervised by members of the Palestine Liberation Organization (PLO).[15] However, either because of a Soviet warning to refrain from outside interference in the PDRY (see below) and/or the obvious victory of 'Ali Nasir's rival there, the YAR changed its attitude toward Aden. For the rest of 1986, the YAR leaders sought to improve their relations with the PDRY by portraying a friendly posture and by cooperating with the new Government in Aden. Hence, Salih, his Minister of Foreign Affairs 'Abd al-Karim al-Iryani and others reiterated San'a's commitment to strengthen unity between the Yemens and to work together toward this end.[16] Several meetings between PDRY and YAR Ministers took place in the capitals of both States. San'a was also careful not to side openly with 'Ali Nasir and legitimize his attempts to regain control in Aden, in spite of the latter's frequent visits to San'a and personal friendly relations with Salih.

In Aden's view one major obstacle in its relations with San'a was the continuous flow of pro-'Ali Nasir PDRY inhabitants into the YAR. Different reports put their numbers at between 10,000 and 40,000; some of them had been high-ranking officials and army officers. The refugees constituted a burden on the YAR's economy and transportation and communication facilities in the southern parts of the country, and were also a potential danger to the new PDRY Government. These considerations prompted the YAR leaders to seek a solution for the problem. Apparently, a meeting between Salih and the PDRY's new President, Haydar al-'Attas, in July 1986 in Tripoli produced no results.[17] (For further details, see chapter on the PDRY in this volume.) However, in November 1986 a Sudanese source close to both Presidents reported that a formula to allow PDRY citizens to return to their country, and to improve inter-Yemeni relations, was in the offing.[18] Hence, despite the turbulent conditions, the YAR's policies helped to keep outstanding problems between the two Yemens under control.

SUPPORT OF ARAB INTERESTS

In the light of continuing inter-Arab disputes during the period under review, the YAR went on record as a supporter of several relatively undisputed Arab interests, thus generating for San'a a favorable and non-partisan image. First and foremost was the YAR's support for Iraq in the Gulf war. A Yemeni infantry brigade fighting alongside the Iraqi forces was mentioned again, as a mobile unit which moved among different fronts.[19] The YAR media were also adamant in praising Iraq's efforts for peace, and denouncing Iran's aggression, as manifested in the latter's attack on Faw in February 1986 (see the essay on the Iraqi-Iranian war in this volume).[20] YAR relations with Iraq seemed particularly close in 1986, with numerous state visits and the signing in August of a protocol for economic and technical cooperation between the two States.[21]

The YAR was also open in its support for the Palestinian cause and in reiterating its readiness to maintain PLO bases on its soil. The YAR's support came to the fore in early 1986, when Israel accused PLO elements in the Republic of attacking Yemeni Jews and raised the issue at the United Nations. According to Arab media sources, the US then promised the YAR $400m in return for San'a allowing Yemenite Jews to emigrate.[22] However, San'a spokesmen not only dismissed the accusations as an Israeli pretext for aggression against the YAR but reiterated their welcome to the PLO. They also stressed their readiness to defend themselves against any Israeli attack on their territory.[23] Frequent visits by Yasir 'Arafat and other PLO leaders to San'a were evidence of the close relationship between the YAR and the PLO during the year.

YAR leaders were particularly emphatic in displaying their basic loyalty to Arab interests by stressing their support for inter-Arab cooperation and conflict resolution. Hence, they supported the settling of disputes between Syria and Iraq, and among Syria, Jordan and the PLO[24] (see also essay on inter-Arab relations in this volume). When asked about his country's interest in joining the Organization of Arab Petroleum Exporting Countries, Salih stressed his intention to establish useful cooperation with all of them, rather than formally join the organization.[25] YAR leaders similarly supported Arab parties whenever one of them engaged in a dispute with a foreign power. Hence, they denounced Britain for severing diplomatic relations with Syria (in retaliation for Syria's support of terrorism), and depicted the British move as "psychological terrorism."[26] The US was also criticized for "aggression" against Libya[27] (see also below).

These moves did not result in participation in any tangible inter-Arab mediating initiative, but made it possible for San'a to maintain friendly relations with most Arab states.

RELATIONS WITH THE SUPERPOWERS

Exercising a policy of non-alignment between the superpowers was not only an extension of the YAR's neutralist policies in inter-Arab relations but an important means of obtaining economic and technical aid, notably the diversification of arms for the YAR (see also previous volumes of *MECS*). San'a had already stressed its inclination for non-alignment in December 1985, when Salih reportedly attempted to call a conference of all the states along the Red Sea and the Horn of Africa to discuss the removal of the Red Sea from international disputes.[28] The plan did not materialize but San'a's interests were placed on record.

In addition, the YAR attempted to maintain cordial relations with both superpowers. San'a's relations with the USSR, which had improved in previous years, continued mostly in the same fashion in 1986. The only exception to this trend occurred several days after fighting broke out in the PDRY, when the Soviets publicly warned the YAR and other Arab parties not to intervene in South Yemen's turmoil (see above and chapter on the PDRY in this volume). The situation was discussed in a meeting between the Soviet First Deputy Minister of Foreign Affairs, Viktor Maltsev, and Salih in San'a in late January 1986.[29] The timing of the visit led observers to surmise that Maltsev was attempting to allay San'a's fears of unwarranted developments in the PDRY and Soviet policies over this issue. Hence, the PDRY war apparently did not adversely affect relations with Moscow.

In June, a protocol for cooperation in water and cement projects was signed between the YAR and the Soviet Union, indicating Moscow's further assistance to the YAR.

A visit by US Vice President George Bush to the YAR in April 1986 marked an improvement in relations between San'a and Washington. Statements by both the YAR media and the Vice President of the Republic, 'Abd al-Karim al-'Arshi, stressed the American heritage of liberty and stressed Washington's major role in Middle East politics. Past accusations of "US Imperialism" were not mentioned during the visit, while criticism of Washington's insufficient efforts over the Palestinian question was muted in statements urging the US to take definite steps toward realization of Palestinian rights.[30] Moreover, statements made by Bush and Yemeni officials stressed the improvement of bilateral relations between the two States. They stressed that it was an American company — Hunt Oil — which had struck oil in the Ma'rib region. The issue of the YAR's oil exports was raised in discussions with Bush in light of the US wish to prevent problems between Saudi Arabia and the YAR over oil searches near the undemarcated frontier separating the two States (see chapter on Saudi Arabia in this volume). However, the results of these discussions remain unknown.[31]

NOTES

For the place and frequency of publications cited here, and for the full name of the publication, news agency, radio station or monitoring service where an abbreviation is used, please see "List of Sources." Only in the case of more than one publication bearing the same name is the place of publication noted here.

1. *Al-Sharq al-Awsat*, 8 September 1986.
2. *Al-Majalla*, 26 February 1986.
3. R. San'a, 25 August — DR, 4 September 1986.
4. Salih's interview with *al-Majalla*, 7 October 1986.
5. *Al-Hurriyya*, 18 May; *Nidal al-Sha'b*, 2 June 1986.
6. *Al-Tadamun*, 28 December 1986.
7. Ibid.
8. R. San'a, 14 December — DR, 19 December 1985.
9. *MM*, 31 March 1986.
10. *Middle East Times*, 5 October 1986.
11. R. San'a, 18 March — DR, 10 March 1986.
12. *Al-Thawra*, San'a, 4 February 1986.
13. R. San'a, 16 July — DR, 17 July 1986.
14. *CR*: North Yemen, September 1986, pp 26–45.
15. R. San'a, 18 January 1986.
16. Cf Salih's interview with *al-Majalla*, 7 October; or 'Abd al-'Aziz al-Ghani, the YAR Prime Minister's interview with *al-Sharq al-Awsat*, 27 February 1986.
17. *Al-Ittihad*, Abu Dhabi, 3 July 1986.
18. Ibid, 20 November 1986.
19. IRNA, 25 May — SWB, 31 May 1986.
20. Cf R. San'a, 9 August — DR, 12 August 1986.
21. R. San'a, 25 August — DR, 26 August 1986.
22. *Al-Watan al-'Arabi*, 27 December 1985; *al-Ra'y al-'Amm*, 21 January 1986.
23. Iryani's interview with *al-Majalla*, 22 January 1986.
24. Cf Salih's interview with *al-Ra'y al-'Amm*, 7 June 1986.

25. R. San'a, 16 October — DR, 20 October 1986.
26. *Al-Thawra*, San'a, 30 October 1986.
27. Cf Salih's interview with *al-Ra'y al-'Amm*, 7 June 1986.
28. *Al-Watan al-'Arabi*, 27 December 1985.
29. SWB's announcement, 3 February 1986.
30. R. San'a, 10, 11 April — DR, 11 April 1986.
31. Ibid, and Salih's interview with *al-Ra'y al-'Amm*, 7 June 1986.

INDEX

NOTE

Most political parties, organizations, public bodies and institutions have been indexed by name rather than by country, and where it is not otherwise obvious the name of the country is shown in parentheses at the end of the entry. Page numbers in **bold** type indicate principal references. Alphabetical order is word-by-word.